D1522774

CORNERSTONE
BIBLICAL
COMMENTARY

General Editor
Philip W. Comfort
D. Litt. et Phil., University of South Africa;
Tyndale House Publishers;
Coastal Carolina University.

Consulting Editor, Old Testament
Tremper Longman III
PhD, Yale University;
Robert H. Gundry Professor of Biblical Studies, Westmont College.

Consulting Editor, New Testament
Grant Osborne
PhD, University of Aberdeen;
Professor of New Testament, Trinity Evangelical Divinity School.

Associate Editors
Jason Driesbach
MA, Biblical Exegesis and Linguistics, Dallas Theological Seminary;
Tyndale House Publishers.

Mark R. Norton
MA, Theological Studies, Wheaton Graduate School;
Tyndale House Publishers.

James A. Swanson
MSM, Multnomah Biblical Seminary;
MTh, University of South Africa;
Tyndale House Publishers.

CORNERSTONE
BIBLICAL
COMMENTARY

MINOR PROPHETS
Hosea–Malachi

Richard D. Patterson
Andrew E. Hill

GENERAL EDITOR
Philip W. Comfort

with the entire text of the
NEW LIVING TRANSLATION

TYNDALE HOUSE PUBLISHERS, INC. CAROL STREAM, ILLINOIS

Cornerstone Biblical Commentary, Volume 10

Visit Tyndale's exciting Web site at www.tyndale.com

Hosea, Joel, Obadiah, Jonah, Nahum, Habakkuk, & Zephaniah copyright © 2008 by Richard Patterson. All rights reserved.

Amos, Micah, Haggai, Zechariah, & Malachi copyright © 2008 by Andrew Hill. All rights reserved.

Designed by Luke Daab and Timothy R. Botts.

Unless otherwise indicated, all Scripture quotations are taken from the *Holy Bible, New Living Translation,* copyright © 1996, 2004. Used by permission of Tyndale House Publishers. Inc., Carol Stream, Illinois 60188. All rights reserved.

TYNDALE, New Living Translation, NLT, Tyndale's quill logo, and the New Living Translation logo are registered trademarks of Tyndale House Publishers, Inc.

Library of Congress Cataloging-in-Publication Data

Cornerstone biblical commentary.
    p. cm.
  Includes bibliographical references and index.
  ISBN-13: 978-0-8423-3436-5 (hc : alk. paper)
  ISBN-10: 0-8423-3436-X (hc : alk. paper)
  1. Bible—Commentaries. I. Hill, Andrew E.   II. Patterson, Richard D.
BS491.3.C67 2006
220.7´7—dc22   2005026928

Printed in the United States of America

14   13   12   11   10   09   08
7   6   5   4   3   2   1

CONTENTS

CONTRIBUTORS TO VOLUME 10

Hosea, Joel, Obadiah, Jonah, Nahum, Habakkuk, Zephaniah: Richard D. Patterson
MDiv, Northwest Baptist Seminary
ThM, Talbot Theological Seminary
PhD, University of California, Los Angeles
Retired Chair of the Department of Biblical Studies and Retired Professor
  of Old Testament and Hebrew, Liberty University

Amos, Micah, Haggai, Zechariah, Malachi: Andrew E. Hill
MDiv, Grand Rapids Baptist Seminary
MA, University of Michigan
PhD, University of Michigan
Professor of Old Testament Studies, Wheaton College

GENERAL EDITOR'S PREFACE

The *Cornerstone Biblical Commentary* is based on the second edition of the New Living Translation (2004). Nearly 100 scholars from various church backgrounds and from several countries (United States, Canada, England, and Australia) participated in the creation of the NLT. Many of these same scholars are contributors to this commentary series. All the commentators, whether participants in the NLT or not, believe that the Bible is God's inspired word and have a desire to make God's word clear and accessible to his people.

This Bible commentary is the natural extension of our vision for the New Living Translation, which we believe is both exegetically accurate and idiomatically powerful. The NLT attempts to communicate God's inspired word in a lucid English translation of the original languages so that English readers can understand and appreciate the thought of the original writers. In the same way, the *Cornerstone Biblical Commentary* aims at helping teachers, pastors, students, and laypeople understand every thought contained in the Bible. As such, the commentary focuses first on the words of Scripture, then on the theological truths of Scripture—inasmuch as the words express the truths.

The commentary itself has been structured in such a way as to help readers get at the meaning of Scripture, passage by passage, through the entire Bible. Each Bible book is prefaced by a substantial book introduction that gives general historical background important for understanding. Then the reader is taken through the Bible text, passage by passage, starting with the New Living Translation text printed in full. This is followed by a section called "Notes," wherein the commentator helps the reader understand the Hebrew or Greek behind the English of the NLT, interacts with other scholars on important interpretive issues, and points the reader to significant textual and contextual matters. The "Notes" are followed by the "Commentary," wherein each scholar presents a lucid interpretation of the passage, giving special attention to context and major theological themes.

The commentators represent a wide spectrum of theological positions within the evangelical community. We believe this is good because it reflects the rich variety in Christ's church. All the commentators uphold the authority of God's word and believe it is essential to heed the old adage: "Wholly apply yourself to the Scriptures and apply them wholly to you." May this commentary help you know the truths of Scripture, and may this knowledge help you "grow in your knowledge of God and Jesus our Lord" (2 Pet 1:2, NLT).

PHILIP W. COMFORT
GENERAL EDITOR

ABBREVIATIONS

GENERAL ABBREVIATIONS

b.	Babylonian Gemara	Heb.	Hebrew	NT	New Testament
bar.	baraita	ibid.	*ibidem,* in the same place	OL	Old Latin
c.	*circa,* around, approximately	i.e.	*id est,* the same	OS	Old Syriac
cf.	*confer,* compare	in loc.	*in loco,* in the place cited	OT	Old Testament
ch, chs	chapter, chapters	lit.	literally	p., pp.	page, pages
contra	in contrast to	LXX	Septuagint	pl.	plural
DSS	Dead Sea Scrolls	𝔐	Majority Text	Q	Quelle ("Sayings" as Gospel source)
ed.	edition, editor	*m.*	Mishnah	rev.	revision
e.g.	*exempli gratia,* for example	masc.	masculine	sg.	singular
et al.	*et alli,* and others	mg	margin	*t.*	Tosefta
fem.	feminine	ms	manuscript	TR	Textus Receptus
ff	following (verses, pages)	mss	manuscripts	v., vv.	verse, verses
fl.	flourished	MT	Masoretic Text	vid.	*videur,* it seems
Gr.	Greek	n.d.	no date	viz.	*videlicet,* namely
		neut.	neuter	vol.	volume
		no.	number	*y.*	Jerusalem Gemara

ABBREVIATIONS FOR BIBLE TRANSLATIONS

ASV	American Standard Version	NCV	New Century Version	NKJV	New King James Version
CEV	Contemporary English Version	NEB	New English Bible	NRSV	New Revised Standard Version
ESV	English Standard Version	NET	The NET Bible	NLT	New Living Translation
GW	God's Word	NIV	New International Version	REB	Revised English Bible
HCSB	Holman Christian Standard Bible	NIrV	New International Reader's Version	RSV	Revised Standard Version
JB	Jerusalem Bible	NJB	New Jerusalem Bible	TEV	Today's English Version
KJV	King James Version	NJPS	The New Jewish Publication Society Translation (*Tanakh*)	TLB	The Living Bible
NAB	New American Bible				
NASB	New American Standard Bible				

ABBREVIATIONS FOR DICTIONARIES, LEXICONS, COLLECTIONS OF TEXTS, ORIGINAL LANGUAGE EDITIONS

ABD *Anchor Bible Dictionary* (6 vols., Freedman) [1992]

ANEP *The Ancient Near East in Pictures* (Pritchard) [1965]

ANET *Ancient Near Eastern Texts Relating to the Old Testament* (Pritchard) [1969]

BAGD *Greek-English Lexicon of the New Testament and Other Early Christian Literature,* 2nd ed. (Bauer, Arndt, Gingrich, Danker) [1979]

BDAG *Greek-English Lexicon of the New Testament and Other Early Christian Literature,* 3rd ed. (Bauer, Danker, Arndt, Gingrich) [2000]

BDB *A Hebrew and English Lexicon of the Old Testament* (Brown, Driver, Briggs) [1907]

BDF *A Greek Grammar of the New Testament and Other Early Christian Literature* (Blass, Debrunner, Funk) [1961]

BHS *Biblia Hebraica Stuttgartensia* (Elliger and Rudolph) [1983]

CAD *Assyrian Dictionary of the Oriental Institute of the University of Chicago* [1956]

COS *The Context of Scripture* (3 vols., Hallo and Younger) [1997–2002]

DBI *Dictionary of Biblical Imagery* (Ryken, Wilhoit, Longman) [1998]

DBT *Dictionary of Biblical Theology* (2nd ed., Leon-Dufour) [1972]

DCH *Dictionary of Classical Hebrew* (5 vols., D. Clines) [2000]

DJD *Discoveries in the Judean Desert* [1955–]

DJG *Dictionary of Jesus and the Gospels* (Green, McKnight, Marshall) [1992]

DOTP *Dictionary of the Old Testament: Pentateuch.* (T. Alexander, D.W. Baker) [2003]

DPL *Dictionary of Paul and His Letters* (Hawthorne, Martin, Reid) [1993]

EDNT *Exegetical Dictionary of the New Testament* (3 vols., H. Balz, G. Schneider. ET) [1990–1993]

HALOT *The Hebrew and Aramaic Lexicon of the Old Testament* (L. Koehler, W. Baumgartner, J. Stamm; trans. M. Richardson) [1994–1999]

IBD *Illustrated Bible Dictionary* (3 vols., Douglas, Wiseman) [1980]

IDB *The Interpreter's Dictionary of the Bible* (4 vols., Buttrick) [1962]

ISBE *International Standard Bible Encyclopedia* (4 vols., Bromiley) [1979–1988]

KBL *Lexicon in Veteris Testamenti libros* (Koehler, Baumgartner) [1958]

LCL Loeb Classical Library

L&N *Greek-English Lexicon of the New Testament: Based on Semantic Domains* (Louw and Nida) [1989]

LSJ *A Greek-English Lexicon* (9th ed., Liddell, Scott, Jones) [1996]

MM *The Vocabulary of the Greek New Testament* (Moulton and Milligan) [1930; 1997]

NA^{26} *Novum Testamentum Graece* (26th ed., Nestle-Aland) [1979]

NA^{27} *Novum Testamentum Graece* (27th ed., Nestle-Aland) [1993]

NBD *New Bible Dictionary* (2nd ed., Douglas, Hillyer) [1982]

NIDB *New International Dictionary of the Bible* (Douglas, Tenney) [1987]

NIDBA *New International Dictionary of Biblical Archaeology* (Blaiklock and Harrison) [1983]

NIDNTT *New International Dictionary of New Testament Theology* (4 vols., C. Brown) [1975–1985]

NIDOTTE *New International Dictionary of Old Testament Theology and Exegesis* (5 vols., W. A. VanGemeren) [1997]

PGM *Papyri graecae magicae: Die griechischen Zauberpapyri.* (Preisendanz) [1928]

PG *Patrologia Graecae* (J. P. Migne) [1857–1886]

TBD *Tyndale Bible Dictionary* (Elwell, Comfort) [2001]

TDNT *Theological Dictionary of the New Testament* (10 vols., Kittel, Friedrich; trans. Bromiley) [1964–1976]

TDOT *Theological Dictionary of the Old Testament* (8 vols., Botterweck, Ringgren; trans. Willis, Bromiley, Green) [1974–]

TLNT *Theological Lexicon of the New Testament* (3 vols., C. Spicq) [1994]

TLOT *Theological Lexicon of the Old Testament* (3 vols., E. Jenni) [1997]

TWOT *Theological Wordbook of the Old Testament* (2 vols., Harris, Archer) [1980]

UBS^3 *United Bible Societies' Greek New Testament* (3rd ed., Metzger et al.) [1975]

UBS^4 *United Bible Societies' Greek New Testament* (4th corrected ed., Metzger et al.) [1993]

WH *The New Testament in the Original Greek* (Westcott and Hort) [1882]

ABBREVIATIONS FOR BOOKS OF THE BIBLE

Old Testament

Gen	Genesis	1 Sam	1 Samuel	Esth	Esther
Exod	Exodus	2 Sam	2 Samuel	Ps, Pss	Psalm, Psalms
Lev	Leviticus	1 Kgs	1 Kings	Prov	Proverbs
Num	Numbers	2 Kgs	2 Kings	Eccl	Ecclesiastes
Deut	Deuteronomy	1 Chr	1 Chronicles	Song	Song of Songs
Josh	Joshua	2 Chr	2 Chronicles	Isa	Isaiah
Judg	Judges	Ezra	Ezra	Jer	Jeremiah
Ruth	Ruth	Neh	Nehemiah	Lam	Lamentations

Ezek	Ezekiel	Obad	Obadiah	Zeph	Zephaniah
Dan	Daniel	Jonah	Jonah	Hag	Haggai
Hos	Hosea	Mic	Micah	Zech	Zechariah
Joel	Joel	Nah	Nahum	Mal	Malachi
Amos	Amos	Hab	Habakkuk		

New Testament

Matt	Matthew	Eph	Ephesians	Heb	Hebrews
Mark	Mark	Phil	Philippians	Jas	James
Luke	Luke	Col	Colossians	1 Pet	1 Peter
John	John	1 Thess	1 Thessalonians	2 Pet	2 Peter
Acts	Acts	2 Thess	2 Thessalonians	1 John	1 John
Rom	Romans	1 Tim	1 Timothy	2 John	2 John
1 Cor	1 Corinthians	2 Tim	2 Timothy	3 John	3 John
2 Cor	2 Corinthians	Titus	Titus	Jude	Jude
Gal	Galatians	Phlm	Philemon	Rev	Revelation

Deuterocanonical

Bar	Baruch	1–2 Esdr	1–2 Esdras	Pr Man	Prayer of Manasseh
Add Dan	Additions to Daniel	Add Esth	Additions to Esther	Ps 151	Psalm 151
Pr Azar	Prayer of Azariah	Ep Jer	Epistle of Jeremiah	Sir	Sirach
Bel	Bel and the Dragon	Jdt	Judith	Tob	Tobit
Sg Three	Song of the Three	1–2 Macc	1–2 Maccabees	Wis	Wisdom of Solomon
	Children	3–4 Macc	3–4 Maccabees		
Sus	Susanna				

MANUSCRIPTS AND LITERATURE FROM QUMRAN

Initial numerals followed by "Q" indicate particular caves at Qumran. For example, the notation 4Q267 indicates text 267 from cave 4 at Qumran. Further, 1QS 4:9-10 indicates column 4, lines 9-10 of the *Rule of the Community*; and 4Q166 1 ii 2 indicates fragment 1, column ii, line 2 of text 166 from cave 4. More examples of common abbreviations are listed below.

CD	Cairo Geniza copy of the *Damascus Document*	1QIsa[b]	Isaiah copy [b]	4QLam[a]	Lamentations
		1QM	*War Scroll*	11QPs[a]	Psalms
1QH	*Thanksgiving Hymns*	1QpHab	*Pesher Habakkuk*	11QTemple[a,b]	*Temple Scroll*
1QIsa[a]	Isaiah copy [a]	1QS	*Rule of the Community*	11QtgJob	*Targum of Job*

IMPORTANT NEW TESTAMENT MANUSCRIPTS

(all dates given are AD; ordinal numbers refer to centuries)

Significant Papyri ($\mathfrak{P}$ = Papyrus)

$\mathfrak{P}$1 Matt 1; early 3rd
$\mathfrak{P}$4+$\mathfrak{P}$64+$\mathfrak{P}$67 Matt 3, 5, 26; Luke 1-6; late 2nd
$\mathfrak{P}$5 John 1, 16, 20; early 3rd
$\mathfrak{P}$13 Heb 2-5, 10-12; early 3rd
$\mathfrak{P}$15+$\mathfrak{P}$16 (probably part of same codex) 1 Cor 7-8, Phil 3-4; late 3rd

$\mathfrak{P}$20 James 2-3; 3rd
$\mathfrak{P}$22 John 15-16; mid 3rd
$\mathfrak{P}$23 James 1; c. 200
$\mathfrak{P}$27 Rom 8-9; 3rd
$\mathfrak{P}$30 1 Thess 4-5; 2 Thess 1; early 3rd
$\mathfrak{P}$32 Titus 1-2; late 2nd
$\mathfrak{P}$37 Matt 26; late 3rd

$\mathfrak{P}$39 John 8; first half of 3rd
$\mathfrak{P}$40 Rom 1-4, 6, 9; 3rd
$\mathfrak{P}$45 Gospels and Acts; early 3rd
$\mathfrak{P}$46 Paul's Major Epistles (less Pastorals); late 2nd
$\mathfrak{P}$47 Rev 9-17; 3rd

𝔓49+𝔓65 Eph 4-5; 1 Thess
  1-2; 3rd
𝔓52 John 18; c. 125
𝔓53 Matt 26, Acts 9-10;
  middle 3rd
𝔓66 John; late 2nd
𝔓70 Matt 2-3, 11-12, 24; 3rd
𝔓72 1-2 Peter, Jude; c. 300

𝔓74 Acts, General Epistles; 7th
𝔓75 Luke and John; c. 200
𝔓77+𝔓103 (probably part of
  same codex) Matt 13-14, 23;
  late 2nd
𝔓87 Phlm; late 2nd
𝔓90 John 18-19; late 2nd
𝔓91 Acts 2-3; 3rd

𝔓92 Eph 1, 2 Thess 1; c. 300
𝔓98 Rev 1:13-20; late 2nd
𝔓100 James 3-5; c. 300
𝔓101 Matt 3-4; 3rd
𝔓104 Matt 21; 2nd
𝔓106 John 1; 3rd
𝔓115 Rev 2-3, 5-6, 8-15; 3rd

Significant Uncials

א (Sinaiticus) most of NT; 4th
A (Alexandrinus) most of NT;
  5th
B (Vaticanus) most of NT; 4th
C (Ephraemi Rescriptus) most
  of NT with many lacunae;
  5th
D (Bezae) Gospels, Acts; 5th
D (Claromontanus), Paul's
  Epistles; 6th (different MS
  than Bezae)
E (Laudianus 35) Acts; 6th
F (Augensis) Paul's Epistles; 9th
G (Boernerianus) Paul's
  Epistles; 9th

H (Coislinianus) Paul's
  Epistles; 6th
I (Freerianus or Washington)
  Paul's Epistles; 5th
L (Regius) Gospels; 8th
Q (Guelferbytanus B) Luke,
  John; 5th
P (Porphyrianus) Acts—
  Revelation; 9th
T (Borgianus) Luke, John; 5th
W (Washingtonianus or the
  Freer Gospels) Gospels; 5th
Z (Dublinensis) Matthew; 6th
037 (Δ; Sangallensis) Gospels;
  9th

038 (Θ; Koridethi) Gospels;
  9th
040 (Ξ; Zacynthius) Luke; 6th
043 (Φ; Beratinus) Matt,
  Mark; 6th
044 (Ψ; Athous Laurae)
  Gospels, Acts, Paul's
  Epistles; 9th
048 Acts, Paul's Epistles,
  General Epistles; 5th
0171 Matt 10, Luke 22;
  c. 300
0189 Acts 5; c. 200

Significant Minuscules

1 Gospels, Acts, Paul's Epistles;
  12th
33 All NT except Rev; 9th
81 Acts, Paul's Epistles,
  General Epistles; 1044
565 Gospels; 9th
700 Gospels; 11th

1424 (or Family 1424—a
  group of 29 manuscripts
  sharing nearly the same
  text) most of NT; 9th-10th
1739 Acts, Paul's Epistles; 10th
2053 Rev; 13th
2344 Rev; 11th

f¹ (a family of manuscripts
  including 1, 118, 131, 209)
  Gospels; 12th-14th
f¹³ (a family of manuscripts
  including 13, 69, 124, 174,
  230, 346, 543, 788, 826,
  828, 983, 1689, 1709—
  known as the Ferrar group)
  Gospels; 11th-15th

Significant Ancient Versions

SYRIAC (SYR)
syr^c (Syriac Curetonian)
  Gospels; 5th
syr^s (Syriac Sinaiticus)
  Gospels; 4th
syr^h (Syriac Harklensis) Entire
  NT; 616

OLD LATIN (IT)
it^a (Vercellenis) Gospels; 4th
it^b (Veronensis) Gospels; 5th
it^d (Cantabrigiensis—the Latin
  text of Bezae) Gospels, Acts,
  3 John; 5th
it^e (Palantinus) Gospels; 5th
it^k (Bobiensis) Matthew, Mark;
  c. 400

COPTIC (COP)
cop^bo (Boharic—north Egypt)
cop^fay (Fayyumic—central Egypt)
cop^sa (Sahidic—southern Egypt)

OTHER VERSIONS
arm (Armenian)
eth (Ethiopic)
geo (Georgian)

TRANSLITERATION AND NUMBERING SYSTEM

Note: For words and roots from non-biblical languages (e.g., Arabic, Ugaritic), only approximate transliterations are given.

HEBREW/ARAMAIC

Consonants

א	aleph	= '	מ, ם	mem	= m
ב, בּ	beth	= b	נ, ן	nun	= n
ג, גּ	gimel	= g	ס	samekh	= s
ד, דּ	daleth	= d	ע	ayin	= '
ה	he	= h	פ, פּ, ף	pe	= p
ו	waw	= w	צ, ץ	tsadhe	= ts
ז	zayin	= z	ק	qoph	= q
ח	heth	= kh	ר	resh	= r
ט	teth	= t	שׁ	shin	= sh
י	yodh	= y	שׂ	sin	= s
כ, כּ, ך	kaph	= k	ת, תּ	taw	= t, th
ל	lamedh	= l			(spirant)

Vowels

ַ	patakh	= a	ָ	qamets khatuf	= o
ַח	furtive patakh	= a	ֹ	holem	= o
ָ	qamets	= a	וֹ	full holem	= o
ָה	final qamets he	= ah	ֻ	short qibbuts	= u
ֶ	segol	= e	ֻ	long qibbuts	= u
ֵ	tsere	= e	וּ	shureq	= u
ֵי	tsere yod	= e	ֲ	khatef patakh	= a
ִ	short hireq	= i	ֳ	khatef qamets	= o
ִ	long hireq	= i	ְ	vocalic shewa	= e
ִי	hireq yod	= i	ַי	patakh yodh	= a

Greek

α	alpha	= a	ε	epsilon	= e
β	beta	= b	ζ	zeta	= z
γ	gamma	= g, n (before γ, κ, ξ, χ)	η	eta	= ē
			θ	theta	= th
δ	delta	= d	ι	iota	= i

κ	kappa	= k		τ	tau	= t
λ	lamda	= l		υ	upsilon	= u
μ	mu	= m		φ	phi	= ph
ν	nu	= n		χ	chi	= ch
ξ	ksi	= x		ψ	psi	= ps
ο	omicron	= o		ω	omega	= ō
π	pi	= p		ʽ	rough	= h (with
ρ	rho	= r (ῥ = rh)			breathing	vowel or
σ, ς	sigma	= s			mark	diphthong)

THE TYNDALE-STRONG'S NUMBERING SYSTEM

The Cornerstone Biblical Commentary series uses a word-study numbering system to give both newer and more advanced Bible students alike quicker, more convenient access to helpful original-language tools (e.g., concordances, lexicons, and theological dictionaries). Those who are unfamiliar with the ancient Hebrew, Aramaic, and Greek alphabets can quickly find information on a given word by looking up the appropriate index number. Advanced students will find the system helpful because it allows them to quickly find the lexical form of obscure conjugations and inflections.

There are two main numbering systems used for biblical words today. The one familiar to most people is the Strong's numbering system (made popular by the *Strong's Exhaustive Concordance to the Bible*). Although the original Strong's system is still quite useful, the most up-to-date research has shed new light on the biblical languages and allows for more precision than is found in the original Strong's system. The Cornerstone Biblical Commentary series, therefore, features a newly revised version of the Strong's system, the Tyndale-Strong's numbering system. The Tyndale-Strong's system brings together the familiarity of the Strong's system and the best of modern scholarship. In most cases, the original Strong's numbers are preserved. In places where new research dictates, new or related numbers have been added.[1]

The second major numbering system today is the Goodrick-Kohlenberger system used in a number of study tools published by Zondervan. In order to give students broad access to a number of helpful tools, the Commentary provides index numbers for the Zondervan system as well.

The different index systems are designated as follows:

TG Tyndale-Strong's Greek number   ZH Zondervan Hebrew number
ZG Zondervan Greek number   TA Tyndale-Strong's Aramaic number
TH Tyndale-Strong's Hebrew number   ZA Zondervan Aramaic number

So in the example, "love" *agapē* [TG26, ZG27], the first number is the one to use with Greek tools keyed to the Tyndale-Strong's system, and the second applies to tools that use the Zondervan system.

---

1. Generally, one may simply use the original four-digit Strong's number to identify words in tools using Strong's system. If a Tyndale-Strong's number is followed by a capital letter (e.g., TG1692A), it generally indicates an added subdivision of meaning for the given term. Whenever a Tyndale-Strong's number has a number following a decimal point (e.g., TG2013.1), it reflects an instance where new research has yielded a separate, new classification of use for a biblical word. Forthcoming tools from Tyndale House Publishers will include these entries, which were not part of the original Strong's system.

Hosea

RICHARD D. PATTERSON

INTRODUCTION TO
Hosea

HOSEA PRESENTS A STUDY in God's love for his own. Despite the fact that God's people had become self-reliant, God maintained his love and concern for them. Although Hosea warned that God's judgment on Israel must come, sending them into exile, he assured the people that one day a redeemed and faithful remnant would know God's forgiveness, restoration, and blessings. Israel's spiritual journey provides a lesson for believers of all ages: God reserves his best for his faithful servants.

AUTHOR

Hosea prophesied during part of the reigns of several eighth-century BC kings of Judah (Uzziah, Jotham, Ahaz, and Hezekiah) and Israel (Jeroboam II). The son of a man named Beeri (1:1), he ministered to the people of the northern kingdom (see "Audience" below). Laetsch (1956:9-10) points out that early Jewish tradition identified his father with the tribe of Reuben, which was carried away into exile by Tiglath-pileser III (cf. 1 Chr 5:6, 26), and that another Jewish legend reports that Hosea died in Babylon but was buried at Safed, northwest of the Sea of Galilee. Laetsch also calls attention to an early Christian tradition which suggests that he came from the tribe of Issachar. All of this, of course, is mere speculation.

Hosea, God's prophet, was ordered to marry a harlot, a situation that would spiritually symbolize God's own relation with apostate Israel (Hos 1–3). From this union at least three children were born (Hos 1). Hosea was motivated by a genuine concern for God's person and will, and concern for Israel's besetting sinfulness. Thus, Wood remarks, "Hosea should be thought of as a hard-working prophet, fully dedicated to the will of God, ministering faithfully to the sinful people of his day in spite of the great sadness of his own marriage" (1985:281). A man of deep spiritual convictions, "Hosea was concerned primarily with moral, religious, and political abominations in the nation" (Harrison 1969:871).

While in the past critics have suggested that not all of the book was authored by Hosea, current scholarship tends to acknowledge that a great preponderance of the material stems from Hosea's messages. Many suggest, however, that the actual writing may have come from Hosea's disciples or that some of the messages may contain redactional interpolations, such as references to Judah (Emmerson 1984) and hopeful oracles of salvation (1:10–2:1; 2:14-23; 3:5; 11:8-11; 14:4, 7). Nevertheless, all such suggestions are basically *a priori* assumptions that reflect theological predisposition rather than demonstrable proof. Dillard and Longman (1994:355) aptly observe, "It must be said that such critical conclusions restrict the future vision of the prophet (judgment and hope) as well as his concern for the whole people of God (north and south)." I concur with Garrett (1997:3), who said, "There is no reason to doubt that [all] the messages of Hosea came from the prophet himself."

DATE AND OCCASION OF WRITING

Given the historical notices of the kings who reigned during his ministry (1:1), Hosea must have delivered his messages across a great deal of the eighth century BC. While it is difficult to pinpoint the various occasions of his messages with certainty, some of the prophecies appear to reflect particular historical circumstances in that era (see the Introduction to Joel). For example, the prediction of judgment concerning the house of Jehu (1:4) must have taken place in the reign of Jeroboam II (792–752 BC), for Jeroboam's son was assassinated a scant six months into his reign (2 Kgs 15:8-12). The rapid change of royalty in the following 30 years, which saw five kings elevated in accordance with changing political fortunes, appears to be considered in 8:4.

Moreover, one can sense the prophet's condemnation of the spiritual indolence and moral complacency of life in the northern kingdom in the early chapters (e.g., ch 2), giving way to growing crises in relations with the Neo-Assyrian empire (e.g., 5:8-13; 8:7-9; 12:1; 14:3; cf. 2 Kgs 15:19-31) and Egypt (7:11; 12:1; cf. 2 Kgs 17:3-4) and in relation to internal affairs (7:1-7; 10:1-4; 12:7; 13:10-11). Indeed, in his closing prophecies, the end of the northern kingdom seems assured (13:9-16; 14:1). Accordingly, Stuart (1987:9) appears to be correct in suggesting that Hosea's prophecies "proceed more or less chronologically," even though some portions of the latter part of the book appear to prove an exception to this rule of thumb (e.g., 12:7-8).

Since Hosea does not specifically mention the fall of Samaria, an event that would provide a natural setting for expanding on the sins that occasioned the fall of the northern kingdom (cf. 2 Kgs 17:7-18, 20-23), it would seem that the book was completed before 722 BC. Therefore, since the prophecies reflect the greater portion of the eighth century BC, a date of 760–725 BC for the oral delivery and collection of the messages would seem to be reasonable.[1]

AUDIENCE

Hosea delivered his oracles primarily to the northern kingdom, although a few remarks for Judah are scattered throughout the book (e.g., 5:10-14; 6:4, 11; 8:14). At times, he addressed particular groups such as the priests (4:4-9; 5:1) and the royal house (5:1), all Israel/Ephraim (5:1; 9:1; 11:8) or Judah (6:4, 11), and even particular cities (8:5; 10:15). Whether or not Hosea delivered his oracles personally to these audiences, his words were obviously intended for them and no doubt ultimately reached them.

Hosea spoke to a people in need of a word from God. In the early years of his ministry, he addressed a society that had experienced outward success and renewed prosperity under the long reign (792-752 BC) of Jeroboam II (2 Kgs 14:23-29). Politically, the relative weakness of their traditional Assyrian enemies allowed the northern kingdom to extend its borders to nearly the same size as that enjoyed in the Solomonic era. Economically, it was a time of renewed commerce, building activities, and the amassing of personal wealth (8:14; 12:7-8). But unfortunately, such wealth was often accrued at the expense of common folk (12:7; cf. Amos 4:1-2; 8:4-6) and was a reflection of an immoral and unjust society that had been loosed from its spiritual moorings. Such conditions only worsened as political disintegration set in, first with the assassinations of Zechariah and Shallum in 752 BC and the bloody contests that followed in the days of Menahem, Pekahiah, and Pekah (2 Kgs 15:16-31).

The long history of prevailing sin that characterized Israel's history finally reached its climax during the reign of its last king, Hoshea (732-722 BC). When the spiritual degeneration of the northern kingdom had reached intolerable limits (2 Kgs 17:7-17, 20-23), God brought judgment upon his unfaithful people in the form of the defeat and deportation of its populace at the hands of the Assyrians (2 Kgs 17:1-6). Conditions at this time were not much better in the southern kingdom (2 Kgs 17:18-19); only the rising prominence of Hezekiah stemmed the tide of God's eventual judgment on Judah.

To such an era and such a people, God's prophet was sent with the message of God's undying love for them, as well as a declaration of his unwavering standards and conditions for spiritual success. No doubt it was too often a discouraging ministry. Yet through it all, Hosea, like God himself (11:1), loved his people and held out the consoling prospect of God's ultimate blessing to his repentant and restored people (14:4-7).

CANONICITY AND TEXTUAL HISTORY

The canonicity of Hosea has never been in doubt. It appears as the first of the Minor Prophets in the listing of 2 Esdras 1:39-40 (c. second century AD). It was also accepted as Scripture earlier by the Qumran community, where Hosea was read and a commentary (or *pesher*) was written about it. Hosea was fully accepted by Jesus himself (Matt 9:13; 12:7) and is cited or alluded to by several of the New Testament writers (e.g., Matt 2:15; Luke 23:30; Rom 9:25-28; 1 Cor 15:55; 1 Pet 2:10; Rev 6:16). Its canonicity was also traditionally received by the Jewish and early Christian communities, being cited in Philo, Josephus, the Talmud (*b. Bava Batra* 14b), and such early Christian Fathers as Melito of Sardis, Origen, Jerome, and Athanasius.

The text of Hosea is another matter. Even so conservative a scholar as Stuart (1987:13) has said, "With the possible exception of the book of Job, no other OT book contains as high a proportion of textual problems as does Hosea." While Andersen and Freedman (1980:66-67) emphasize the many difficulties of the Masoretic Text versions of Hosea, they also note that the early versions are seldom of much help in establishing the text. They go on to point out that "the knowledge of ancient Hebrew gained through epigraphic studies and related disciplines has provided new ways of explaining the text without changing it. . . . As a result, there is less need to alter the text to remove a supposed difficulty." Moreover, R. K. Harrison (1969:872) demonstrates that "many of the alterations appear to be accidental," often consisting of such matters as confusion of one consonant for another, or the transposing of consonants, and differing word divisions. Recognizing the long history of the transmission of the Masoretic Text and armed with the cautions and observations of Andersen and Freedman, one can move with cautious optimism in suggesting reconstructions in those places in the text that prove troublesome.[2]

LITERARY STYLE

Hosea used both literary modes, prose and poetry, to deliver his messages. His style in either case, however, is so high that even his prose has been termed elevated (Wolff 1974:xxiv). Scholars have often disagreed as to whether the prophet was writing in prose or poetry. Andersen and Freedman (1980:60-66) concluded from evidence based upon syntactic devices typical of poetry that chapters 4–14 are poetic, while the first three chapters are largely prose narrative (especially 1:2–2:3 and 3:1-5). Although one may not concur in every detail with this estimate, it does nicely demonstrate the soundness of the reader's natural impression that chapters 1–3 and 4–14 form distinct units in the book. The oracles embedded in the prose narrative of the first three chapters are clustered around the chiastically constructed marriage theme. The oracles of judgment and warning that comprise chapters 4–14 are presented in a collage of divine speeches intertwined with prophetic pronouncements.[3]

It is generally conceded that the most distinctive feature of Hosea's work is his use of simile and metaphor.[4] Dillard and Longman (1994:359) observe that these two literary devices can be viewed with reference to God or Israel, and also as to "whether God's attitude toward Israel is positive or negative." Thus, for example, God can be viewed as a jealous (2:2-13) or forgiving husband (3:1-5). On the one hand, he is a dispenser of judgment who comes against his people like a hungry moth or advancing rot (5:12), like a lion (5:14), or a trapper with his net (7:12). On the other hand, he proceeds as a father forgiving his wayward son (11:1-3) or a redeemer who tenderly cares for his liberated people (11:4; 12:9; 13:4).[5]

Israel, for its part, is portrayed spiritually as an unfaithful wife (chs 1–3) whose love is like a morning cloud or early dew that quickly disappears (6:4). Blithely unaware of their mortal danger, God's people are likened to a man with gradually graying hair or an unturned pancake over a fire (7:7-9). These figures and images, and others, make the book colorfully picturesque and its messages distinctively poignant—hence Hosea is of high aesthetic as well as theological value.

MAJOR THEMES

Hosea's imagery is incorporated into several important literary themes. Especially significant are those dealing with family relations, such as God being portrayed as a loving father longing for his wayward son (11:1-3). The best known of these images is, of course, that of marriage, centered in Hosea's relation to Gomer (chs 1–3). While several interpretations (discussed later in the commentary) have been put forward as to that relationship, the whole marriage scenario is obviously intended to dramatize the relationship between God and Israel. Much as adulterous Gomer was unfaithful to Hosea, so Israel had proven to be unfaithful to God.

Closely related to the theme of infidelity is that of prostitution. It is used not only in the case of Gomer but to describe Israel's own spiritual condition (4:14-15, 18; 5:3-4; 6:10; 7:4; 8:9; 9:1; 11:7; 14:4). Spiritually speaking, Israel was a harlot; God's people had been untrue to their heavenly husband and gone into pagan idolatry (4:10-17; 8:4-6; 9:10, 15; 10:5; 11:2; 12:11).

All of this underscores yet another theme—that of the covenant. Despite the fact that God had redeemed his children by bringing them out of Egyptian bondage (11:4; 12:9; 13:4), they had broken the covenant with their God and become unfaithful to him, no longer meeting his conditions for blessing (6:7; 10:1-3). The people of the northern kingdom persisted in covenant violations (8:1-14; 13:16). Israel's hope lay solely in God's redeeming love (3:1-5), through which they could, as a restored people, enter into the blessings of a new covenant born in righteousness, justice, love, and compassion (2:18-23).

Several of the themes in the book have their origin in the agrarian and animal worlds.[6] Hosea spoke of sowing and reaping (2:23; 8:7; 10:12-13), of vine, vineyard, and wine (2:9, 12, 15; 9:2, 4, 10; 10:1; 14:7), and of threshing and harvest (2:6, 8-9, 11, 22; 6:11; 9:2). Although Israel was once a trained heifer that continually fed as she threshed the grain (10:11), she had become stubborn and unruly and was therefore in danger of God's correction (4:16). In her lust to chase after other nations and their gods, she had become like a wild donkey in heat (8:9-10) or a senseless dove, flitting back and forth to this nation or that (7:11). Accordingly, God would be required by the covenant to bring severe judgment on his people. He would come like a great lion that tears its prey (5:14-15; cf. 13:7-8 where God is compared to a stalking leopard or an angry bear robbed of its cubs). Yet, in a future day the lion would roar and his young would then hear his voice and come trembling homeward (cf. 11:10-11 where the exilic returnees are likened to trembling birds—doves seeking their nest).

These themes, often woven into the fabric of Hosea's messages under a variety of figures (see "Literary Style"), provide a vividness that portrays the desperate condition of God's people. The careful reader will be impressed with the need to apply the truths of Hosea's prophecies to our own contemporary world. Grammatical, historical, and literary information thus combine with theological data to guide the reader in the interpretative process.

THEOLOGICAL CONCERNS
Theologically, Hosea reminds his hearers that God is a God of faithfulness, love, and mercy (2:18-23; 11:1, 3, 8; 14:1-4). He is also a God of redemption (11:4; 12:9;

13:4) who cares for (13:5) and blesses (2:8) his own. Nevertheless, where sin and injustice abound, he is also a God of justice who moves in judgment against sin, even against his own people (8:14; 9:7). For Israel, such could mean desolation of land (4:3), destruction of city and countryside (5:8-9), and exile (9:3, 6; 10:6).

Through all of God's dealings with Israel, his people were challenged to regard the high standards expected of a covenant people (4:1-9; see "Major Themes" above). As such, they were reminded both of the primacy and sufficiency of God's word and of the binding nature of its precepts. Stuart (1987:6-7) puts it well: "Understanding the message of the book of Hosea depends upon understanding the Sinai covenant. The book contains a series of blessings and curses announced for Israel by God through Hosea. Each blessing or curse is based upon a corresponding type in the Mosaic law."

So serious was Israel's spiritual condition that Hosea used 15 different words for sin in cataloging its crimes. Through Hosea, God called upon his people to repent and pursue genuine righteousness and godliness (10:12; 12:6). He alone can and will restore such a people (6:1-3) and once again pour out his blessings upon them (2:21-23; 14:4-7). In announcing these hoped-for blessings of the end times, Hosea may well have been including a veiled hint of the means of their achievement: One would come who alone is the redeemer and founder of a new and better covenant for all humanity (1:10-11; 2:18-20; 3:5).

OUTLINE

A perusal of the many special studies and commentaries on Hosea yields little agreement as to the basic structure and individual segments of the book. The difficulties of language and imagery, as well as the author's often elliptical writing style, make consensus nearly impossible. Accordingly, the outline provided is merely provisional and proceeds simply on the basis of perceived textual clues and emphases, as the following data illustrate.

The generally agreed-upon division between chapters 1-3 and 4-14 is followed here. The first portion of the book, dealing with Hosea's marriage to Gomer and its symbolic relevance to God's relationship to Israel, is understood to be presented by means of a thematic chiasm. After the superscription, the opening section (1:2-9) recounting Hosea's marriage to Gomer is balanced by the couple's renewed relationship (3:1-5). Covenantal considerations dominate 1:10-2:1 and 2:14-23 with the rebuke of Israel's unfaithfulness occupying the center of the chiasm (2:2-13).

Chapters 4-14 contain an interplay between divine and prophetic oracles. This section can be subdivided into three segments, each marked by the prophet's advice to his people (6:1-3; 10:12-15; 14:1-3) coming just before the recording of a divine rhetorical question: "O Israel and Judah, what should I do with you?" (6:4); "Oh, how can I give you up, Israel? How can I let you go?" (11:8); and "O Israel, stay away from idols!" (14:8; lit., "What have I [the Lord] to do with idols?"). The first two major subsections begin with an imperative heading to the oracle: "Hear the word of the LORD, O people of Israel!" (4:1); "Sound the alarm!" (8:1). The final major subsection features an initial consideration of Ephraim (11:12–13:16) before ending with an exhortation to repentance (14:1-3) and God's concluding oracle, which in the Hebrew text contains a penetrating rhetorical question (14:4-8). Although no claim to finality can be made for this arrangement, verbal and thematic stitching links the individual segments, including the smaller units, and does at least suggest its workability.

Superscription (1:1)
    I. A Prophetic Portrayal of Unfaithful Israel (1:2–3:5)
        A. Israel's Rejection—Symbolized by Hosea's Marriage (1:2-9)
        B. Israel's Restoration on the Basis of the Covenant (1:10–2:1)
        C. God's Rebuke of Unfaithful Israel (2:2-13)
        D. Israel's Renewal on the Basis of the Covenant (2:14-23)
        E. Israel's Reconciliation—Symbolized by Hosea's Marriage (3:1-5)
   II. Divine and Prophetic Perspectives on Unfaithful Israel (4:1–14:8)
        A. Opening Complaints against Israel (4:1–7:16)
           1. The threefold indictment (4:1-14)
           2. Hosea's condemnation of prostitute Israel (4:15-19)
           3. The three guilty parties (5:1-3)
           4. Hosea's charge: God's people are unfaithful (5:4-7)
           5. The threefold alarm (5:8-15)
           6. Hosea's advice: return to the Lord (6:1-3)
           7. God's concern for disloyal Israel (6:4–7:16)
        B. Further Charges against Israel (8:1–11:11)
           1. Israel is a covenant-breaker (8:1-14)
           2. Hosea's reaction: Israel is doomed (9:1-9)
           3. Israel is an unprofitable plant (9:10-17)
           4. Hosea's reaction: Israel is a wayward vine (10:1-8)
           5. Israel is a perennial sinner (10:9-11)
           6. Hosea's warning: seek God or perish (10:12-15)
           7. God's compassion for disobedient Israel (11:1-11)
        C. Concluding Considerations concerning Israel (11:12–14:8)
           1. The folly of deceitful politics (11:12–12:1)
           2. Hosea's observation: Israel has a history of deceit (12:2-6)
           3. The folly of deceitful practices (12:7-11)
           4. Hosea's observation: God will repay Israel's deceit (12:12-14)
           5. The folly of deceitful pride (13:1-16)
           6. Hosea's admonition: repent and confess all sins (14:1-3)
           7. God's consolation for repentant Israel (14:4-8)
Subscription (14:9)

ENDNOTES

1. The mention of Hosea's activity during the reign of Hezekiah has caused many to push the date of the book to 715 BC. Because Hezekiah served as co-regent with his father, Ahaz, from about 729/728 BC, however, and because no context in the book can be positively linked with Samaria's fall, it is not necessary to postulate so late a date. For details as to the chronology and events of Hezekiah's reign, see my remarks in Patterson and Austel 1988:253-277.

2. It is refreshing to see commentaries that defend the MT as the best available text (e.g., Garrett, McComiskey), while examining seriously its specific problems.

3. Garrett (1997:177) suggests that this feature is distinctive to chapters 8–11, where "Yahweh and Hosea antiphonally speak in lamentation over Israel's sin," while the accounts of Hosea's three children given in chs 1–2 provide shaping for 4:1–7:16, which is dominated by a pattern of repeated threes. Damaging to this thesis, however, is the obvious weaving together of divine speeches and prophetic oracles throughout the whole book and the attested series of threes, which often appear in chapters 8–14 (e.g., 9:16; 10:11, 12).

4. See, for example, R. Johnson, "Hosea 4–10: Pictures at an Exhibition," *Southwestern Journal of Theology* 36 (1993):20-26; P. Kruger, "Prophetic Imagery: On Metaphor and Similes in the Book of Hosea," *Journal of Northwest Semitic Languages* 14 (1988):143-151.

5. Garrett (1997:63-69) finds in this evidence for Hosea's unresolved tension between divine judgment and covenant faithfulness the necessity for the proper recognition of an element of paradox both hermeneutically and theologically.

6. For examples of Hosea's use of the agrarian and animal worlds, see Patterson 1998.

Hosea

◆ Superscription (1:1)

The LORD gave this message to Hosea son of Beeri during the years when Uzziah, Jotham, Ahaz, and Hezekiah were kings of Judah, and Jeroboam son of Jehoash* was king of Israel.

1:1 Hebrew *Joash*, a variant spelling of Jehoash.

NOTES

1:1 *The LORD gave this message.* In a manner similar to that of several of the OT prophets, Hosea opened his prophecy with a declaration of the divine source of the words that will follow.

kings of Judah . . . king of Israel. Hosea indicated that his prophetic service was during the time of the kings whose reigns spanned the greater part of the eighth century BC (see Introduction). The failure to mention any of Jeroboam II's successors may indicate something of the conflicting claims for legitimacy of rule in the turbulent closing years of the northern kingdom.

COMMENTARY

Hosea made it clear at the onset of his prophecy that what he had to say and record was not of human origin. The opening narrative and succeeding oracles that make up the prophetic collection and lead to the closing piece of prophetic wisdom were not born of mere human experience and observation but came from God. All that Hosea experienced and the messages he received were the Lord's appointment for him and communication through him (cf. 2 Pet 1:20-21).

Hosea's opening words remind all believers that God is a God of revelation; his person and work are made known in the Scriptures (cf. 2 Tim 3:16). There believers may find strength and direction for life in its divinely inspired words (Ps 119:105; Prov 1:1-7). Accordingly, believers should turn to the Bible and follow its precepts so as to find direction and the true joy of living (Ps 119:111).

◆ I. A Prophetic Portrayal of Unfaithful Israel (1:2–3:5)
A. Israel's Rejection—Symbolized by Hosea's Marriage (1:2-9)

²When the LORD first began speaking to Israel through Hosea, he said to him, "Go and marry a prostitute,* so that some of her children will be conceived in prostitution.

This will illustrate how Israel has acted like a prostitute by turning against the LORD and worshiping other gods."

³So Hosea married Gomer, the daughter of Diblaim, and she became pregnant and gave Hosea a son. ⁴And the LORD said, "Name the child Jezreel, for I am about to punish King Jehu's dynasty to avenge the murders he committed at Jezreel. In fact, I will bring an end to Israel's independence. ⁵I will break its military power in the Jezreel Valley."

⁶Soon Gomer became pregnant again and gave birth to a daughter. And the LORD said to Hosea, "Name your daughter Lo-ruhamah—'Not loved'—for I will no longer show love to the people of Israel or forgive them. ⁷But I will show love to the people of Judah. I will free them from their enemies—not with weapons and armies or horses and charioteers, but by my power as the LORD their God."

⁸After Gomer had weaned Lo-ruhamah, she again became pregnant and gave birth to a second son. ⁹And the LORD said, "Name him Lo-ammi—'Not my people'—for Israel is not my people, and I am not their God.

1:2 Or *a promiscuous woman.*

NOTES

1:2 *Go and marry a prostitute.* Lit., "a wife of harlotry." Several positions are held as to whether God actually told his prophet to marry an unholy woman: (1) The marriage was merely hypothetical, the account itself being a literary parable or allegory (Calvin). (2) The account is a dream or vision (Ibn Ezra, Maimonides). (3) The whole narrative is simply a stage play (Kaufman). (4) Hosea married a woman with promiscuous tendencies who later committed adultery (Hubbard, Wood), perhaps as a cult prostitute (Andersen and Freedman, Craigie, Mays). (5) Hosea's wife was only guilty of spiritual adultery (i.e., of idol worship—Stuart). (6) Hosea married an already adulterous woman (Garrett, McComiskey). Although the NLT text most naturally supports the last view, the accompanying textual note leaves open the possibility that Hosea is to marry a woman with promiscuous tendencies. In keeping with the full context, this appears to be the better choice. Such an understanding provides a clear parallel with God's own relation to his covenant people as demonstrated throughout Hosea's prophecies (cf. Jer 2:24-35). This position preserves both the integrity of God's character and the standards of his word, while allowing Hosea's life situation to serve as a visible spiritual lesson for the people to whom he was called to minister.

Several other variations have also been proposed; see Garrett 1997:43-50 and Laetsch 1956:21. Complicating the matter is the problem of whether ch 3 speaks of relations between Hosea and Gomer (whether supplying new details or being a duplicate account of ch 1) or of Hosea's dealings with a different woman (cf. Stuart 1987:64-65).

has acted like a prostitute by . . . worshiping other gods. God's primary charge against apostate Israel was its failure to worship him alone (cf. Exod 20:3-5; Deut 5:7-9; 6:4, 14-15; Matt 4:10). This theme surfaces repeatedly among the various oracles and undergirds God's final rhetorical question (represented as an exclamation in the NLT) to his wayward people in 14:8.

1:4 *Name the child Jezreel.* Jezreel means "may God sow/scatter." While the meaning inherent in the name will be brought up later, here it calls attention to that place where "Jehu was swept to power over all Israel on a mighty tide of bloodshed" (Hubbard 1989:61).

avenge the murders he committed at Jezreel. Details of Jehu's bloody deeds at Jezreel are found in 2 Kgs 9:17-37; 10:7-8. It was a bloodbath that carried over into Samaria (2 Kgs 10:17-27).

bring an end to Israel's independence. The NLT rendering combines the wording of vv. 4 and 5 in the MT. The end of the northern kingdom was to come nearly 100 years after the death of Jehu in 814 BC. His dynasty, however, came to an end in 752 BC, some 30 years before the fall of Samaria. The punishment of Jehu's dynasty and the end of the northern kingdom are thus telescoped into a single prediction. Such telescoped prophecies are attested elsewhere in the Scriptures (e.g., Isa 61:1-3; cf. Luke 4:16-21).

1:6 *Lo-ruhamah.* The Hebrew root underlying the name of the second child is located in the noun *rekhem* [TH7358, ZH8167] (womb), from which come the denominative verb *rakham* [TH7355, ZH8163] (have compassion/pity) and the related nominal derivatives, which carry the thought of compassion or mercy. A deep emotional concept is thus associated with the second child's name (cf. NIDOTTE 3.1096-1097).

or forgive them. Scholars are divided as to the meaning of the MT. As Garrett (1997:60) observes, "The most obvious meaning of the line is, 'But I will certainly forgive them.'" This rendering makes a stark contrast between the final phrase and the previous part of the verse, which speaks of God's lack of compassion for Israel. The interpretation of this phrase will also affect one's treatment of v. 7. Garrett decides on a positive reading of both, suggesting that God intends the reader to hold both Israel's judgment and its hope of forgiveness in dynamic paradoxical tension. In contrast, Andersen and Freedman (1980:188-194) take a negative approach, holding that the earlier negative of v. 6 ("I will no longer," NLT) controls all that follows, so that both Israel and Judah may expect God's judgment, not his deliverance. Steering a middle course between these two positions, most commentators (e.g., Keil, Laetsch, McComiskey, Stuart, Wood) and translations (e.g., LXX, Vulgate, and all the standard English versions) opt in some fashion for Israel's condemnation and God's assurance of continued support for Judah.

Although some scholars (e.g., G. A. Smith, Wolff) have argued that v. 7 is a later interpolation, this conjecture is without textual support. Even Emmerson (1984:88-95), who finds several Judean passages in Hosea to be intrusive secondary redactions, hesitates to exclude 1:7 from the primary Hosean corpus. For a critique of Emmerson's work, see my remarks in *Hebrew Studies* 29:112-114.

1:9 *Lo-ammi.* Some have suggested that neither the second nor the third child born to Gomer after her marriage to Hosea was Hosea's. Nothing in the text makes this certain, however. "Not my people" would remind Israel of the sanctions inherent in the Sinaitic covenant (Exod 6:7; Lev 26:12; Deut 27:9).

As indicated in the outline (see Introduction) Hosea's relationship with Gomer bookends the first section of the book, Hosea's marriage to Gomer (1:2-9) being balanced by God's instructions to take back his estranged wife (3:1-5). Woven into the chiastic structure of the first three chapters is an orderly presentation of narrative features. Each chapter is dominated by God's command, after which further comment or narrative details occur. In chapters 1 and 3 the prophet's compliance follows God's command.

COMMENTARY

God instructed Hosea to take a wife whose promiscuity would not only cause him heartaches but also bring a separation between them (1:2-3). Having done what God asked him to do (1:4), the subsequent events of the narrative provide divine comment upon Hosea's tenuous situation with Gomer (1:5-9). The names of the three children born to Gomer reflect the fragile nature of their marriage due to her promiscuity.

It is evident that Hosea's relationship with Gomer and the names of the three children are symbolic. Thus, Gomer depicts God's relation to the nation, often represented metaphorically as his wife (e.g., Isa 54; Jer 2:2-3; 3:1-9). Just as Gomer was to prove unfaithful, so Israel had worshiped other gods and done horrendous deeds. Likewise, the details relative to the three children carry a prophetic significance, much as Isaiah and his family did (Isa 8:18). The names of the three children represent the people of Israel and warn of God's judgment upon the nation and its citizenry.

God stated through the name Jezreel that he would bring to justice the standing crimes of Jehu and his dynasty. Not only would Israel's fourth dynasty be brought to an end but the irreversible tide of sin set in motion by Jehu's bloody deeds would eventuate in the demise of the northern kingdom. Critics have often accused God of inconsistency in first commanding Jehu to extirpate the dynasty of Ahab and then, as here, condemning him for it. Such criticism, however, deals amiss with the facts. For while Jehu did fulfill his divine commission, he exceeded it by exterminating even his remotest rivals. Further, his halfhearted devotion to God and his law became evident in his embracing the apostate state religion instituted by Jeroboam I (2 Kgs 10:31). His manipulation of events to suit his own selfish ends is illustrated in the Black Obelisk of Shalmaneser III of Assyria, where his submission, accompanied by heavy tribute to the Assyrian king, is recorded.

Nor were his successors any better. Jehu and his dynasty were thus duly condemned. When people use the name of God as a pretext for their own desires and plans, like Jehu and his dynastic successors, they stand in danger of divine punishment. H. Hailey (1971:137) observes, "One may do the command of the Lord and yet be in rebellion against Him, doing the thing commanded because it is what the individual desires and not because it is what God desires."

The names of the second and third children are also instructive. God's tender compassion for his nation and people would be exchanged for "no pity/no mercy." The time of divine judgment was fast approaching. The nation and people that he had taken into covenant with himself had violated the conditions of the covenant by disobedience and would suffer the consequences. No longer "my people," they would suffer many disasters, including defeat and deportation at the hands of their enemies (Deut 28:25-29; cf. 2 Kgs 17:1-23). As Sweeney (2000:21-22) comments, the name of the third child is a virtual reversal of God's statement at the founding of the nation (cf. Exod 6:6-7; Lev 26:12) and signals "the disruption of the relationship between YHWH and Israel."

Oh, that Israel would follow the example of Judah, which (though it would later come in for its share of criticism) was the repository of God's covenantal future blessings (1:6-7)! As heirs of the promises in the Abrahamic, Sinaitic, and Davidic covenants, Judah could look forward to that era when God's new covenant would be realized in David's heir (Ezek 34:20-31; 36:21-28). In Judah was centered the promise that they would be God's people (Jer 31:33). In that day they would know God and obediently live out God's precepts as written in their hearts (Jer 31:34).

This passage is instructive for the Christian believer. Most significantly it lays stress on the crucial importance of obedience and faithfulness. Hosea was obedient to God in taking a wife that he would not have chosen for himself. His nation and people, however, were not obedient, for they had fallen into a dead orthodoxy mixed with the worship of Baal; these evils had infected Israel's total life situation. In this they had failed to keep covenant with God (Exod 19:5) and his commandments (Deut 27:10; Jer 32:23); hence, they became liable to the penalties for disobedience (Deut 11:27-28; 28:15-28).

The situation of ancient Israel must not be that of today's believer. Indeed, by the very act of believing, believers have come to enjoy right standing before God. Such has been accomplished through the obedience of Christ who, though he is God's son (Heb 3:6), "learned obedience from the things he suffered. . . . and he became the source of eternal salvation for all those who obey him" (Heb 5:8-9; cf. Phil 2:8). As those who "belong to his dear Son" (Eph 1:6; 1 Pet 1:2), Christians too must walk in obedience even as he did (1 John 2:6). May we be obedient to God's claim upon our lives (cf. Acts 26:19ff), serving him not in merely routine, outward service or for our own selfish ends, but out of a pure heart. May we be ever mindful not only of whom we serve (1 Thess 1:9; 2 Tim 1:3), but of Christ's own example and the price of his provision for us (1 Pet 1:14-15).

Although believers may not be God's symbols to an entire community as were Hosea and his family, they are nonetheless his witnesses (Acts 1:8) and ambassadors (2 Cor 5:20). Therefore, they are so to live as not to be detriments to the cause of Christ (Matt 16:19; 1 Cor 8:9; 2 Cor 6:3; Phil 1:27). Rather, they should be those whose consistency and faithfulness are attractive to others so that they too might come into the joy of the obedience of Christ (1 Cor 9:19; Phil 4:5; 1 Pet 2:11-17).

◆ B. Israel's Restoration on the Basis of the Covenant (1:10–2:1)

10*"Yet the time will come when Israel's people will be like the sands of the seashore—too many to count! Then, at the place where they were told, 'You are not my people,' it will be said, 'You are children of the living God.' 11Then the people of Judah and Israel will unite together. They will choose one leader for themselves, and they will return from exile together. What a day that will be—the day of Jezreel*—when God will again plant his people in his land.

2:1*"In that day you will call your brothers Ammi—'My people.' And you will call your sisters Ruhamah—'The ones I love.'

1:10 Verses 1:10-11 are numbered 2:1-2 in Hebrew text.   1:11 *Jezreel* means "God plants."   2:1 Verses 2:1-23 are numbered 2:3-25 in Hebrew text.

NOTES

1:10 [2:1] *like the sands of the seashore.* This image often appears as an indication of large numbers (e.g., Josh 11:4; 1 Sam 13:5; Rom 9:27). As here, the simile is applied at times to Israel's future hope, especially in connection with the Abrahamic covenant as culminating in the new covenant (Gen 22:17-18; Jer 33:22).

children of the living God. Those who had been called "not my people" will become God's acknowledged family. In contrast to Baal and the dead idols, Israel's God is the true and living God. In him alone are life (Pss 42:2; 84:2) and the hope for success (Josh 3:10).

1:11 [2:2] *the day of Jezreel.* This speaks of a day when God's scattered people will be freshly planted (see note on 1:4 on the meaning of "Jezreel") in the land. The double sense (cf. 1:4-5; 2:22-23) indicated by the name Jezreel here indicates a future reversal of Israel's imminent scattering among the nations. As plants sown in the soil come up from earth, so a reinstituted Israelite state will emerge in its land.

2:1 [3] *Ammi . . . Ruhamah.* Jezreel's brother(s) and sister(s) will likewise experience a life-transforming name change: "Not my people" (1:9) will become "My people," and "Not loved" (1:6) will become "The ones I love." The NLT follows the MT in reading plural nouns here. Although the LXX has smoothed out the problem by reading singular nouns, the difficulty of the MT argues for the retention of the plurals.

McComiskey (1992:32) insists that the plural nouns "brothers and sisters" (especially the latter) must refer to children born to Gomer before her marriage to Hosea. However, the plurals may be explained as referring both to the children mentioned previously and what they represent—all the people of restored Judah and Israel now united under one leader. Just as Jezreel represents the nation, so "the brothers to whom the new name 'Ammi' is given in v. 3 and the sisters who are now called 'Ruhama' equally represent the whole nation" (Andersen and Freedman 1980:213).

COMMENTARY

Tempering the gloomy prediction of 1:2-9, God indicated that Israel's historical judgment and exile would be but a first step in the eventual restoration to the Land of Promise. In accordance with the standing promises to Abraham (Gen 12:1-3; 13:14-17; 17:1-8; 22:15-18) and David (2 Sam 7:11-16; 1 Chr 17:10-14; Ps 89:1-4, 27-37), God will once again restore his people to "his land," and the place of their inheritance. All of this will be realized in a new relationship between Israel and God. Once judged, they will again be called his children. As faithful members of his family, they will enjoy all the blessings that only a heavenly Father can bestow.

Israel had been called to be God's children, his special treasure (Exod 4:22; 19:5-6; Deut 14:1-2; Jer 2:3). Although he had tenderly cared for them all along, they had repeatedly taken him for granted, even being disobedient and at times unfaithful children (Deut 1:31; 32:5-20; Isa 1:2-4; Jer 3:4). Therefore, despite his great desire to bless his children (Jer 3:19-20), God frequently had to chastise them (Deut 8:1-5). Nevertheless, God's love for his people remained (11:1, 8-9), as he often pleaded with them to repent and come back to him (e.g., 14:1; Jer 3:22). Then they would know his forgiveness as he purified them and restored them to the land. In that future day, he will make a new covenant with David's heir on the throne and pour out the blessings he had always intended for them (Jer 31:31-34; 32:40-44; 33:6-8; Ezek 34:13-16, 23-31; 36:22-27; Zeph 3:9-20). Hosea's message of hope, then, is in harmony with standard Old Testament teaching.

Hosea's prophecy (1:10; cf. 2:23) was cited by Paul (Rom 9:22-29) to illustrate God's further intentions. The judgment upon Israel's obdurately unfaithful people will fulfill the latent blessings inherent in God's promissory covenants. Not only faithful Israelites but Gentiles, too, will make up those who are called God's people (cf. 1 Pet 2:10). Then a redeemed people, Jew and Gentile alike, will stand together united under one head, David's heir, the Lord Jesus Christ.

Indeed, God's covenant with Abraham envisioned that Gentiles would eventually be included within the family of God (Gen 12:3; 22:18; 26:4; 28:14; Gal 3:8). The terms of the Abrahamic covenant, channeled through the Davidic covenant, passed into the new covenant (Jer 31:31-34; 33:15-26; Ezek 34:20-31; 37:15-27). The New Testament makes it clear that this line of promises has already been put into effect through the atoning death and resurrection of Jesus Christ (cf. Acts 2:29-39). Christ himself affirmed that he was effecting the terms of the new covenant (Matt 26:27-29; cf. 1 Cor 11:25). Paul points out that God had made him a minister to represent the new covenant (2 Cor 3:6), a covenant which the author of Hebrews demonstrates is both in effect and superior to the old Mosaic covenant (Heb 8–10).

Whatever eschatological implications there may be in the age-old promise to Abraham, it is also true that such blessings have already been initiated in Christ (Rom 4:13-17; 8:14-17; 11:13-32). For he has rendered obsolete those external matters that separated Jew and Gentile, and created "in himself one new people from the two groups" (Eph 2:14-15; cf. Gal 3:26-29). Through his death on the cross, the body of Christ (the believing church) is united by its living head. As God's dear children (Gal 3:26), all believers have been brought into the very presence of Christ (Col 1:18-22). Taken into union with Christ (Gal 2:20), believers now enjoy a vital oneness with him.

The New Testament represents this union under a number of metaphors and phrases; many emphasize the "togetherness" of the believer with Christ. Some are positional: Thus although believers were crucified (Gal 2:20), died (Col 3:3), and were buried together with Christ (Rom 6:4), they have been made alive, raised, and seated together with him in the heavenly realms (Eph 2:6). Others are experiential: Although believers may suffer with Christ, they shall be glorified together with Christ (Rom 8:17) and eventually reign together with him (2 Tim 2:12).

Accordingly, believers may live victorious lives, free from sin's domination, and they can reflect the characteristics of the one who has taken up his residence in them (Col 3:1-17). What potential there is, then, for Christian believers! As members of the family of the living God and energized by their union with Christ and the power of the indwelling Holy Spirit (1 Cor 3:16; Eph 5:18), believers should lead meaningful and productive lives. Like Israel of old, Christians also look forward to a future day, a time when Christ himself will reign in the midst of a purified people coming from every nation, tribe, people, and language (Rev 7:9; cf. Dan 7:13-14; Rev 11:15).

◆ ## C. God's Rebuke of Unfaithful Israel (2:2-13)

2 "But now bring charges against Israel—
   your mother—
for she is no longer my wife,
and I am no longer her husband.
Tell her to remove the prostitute's
   makeup from her face
and the clothing that exposes
   her breasts.

3 Otherwise, I will strip her as naked
   as she was on the day she was
   born.
I will leave her to die of thirst,
   as in a dry and barren wilderness.
4 And I will not love her children,
   for they were conceived in
   prostitution.

⁵Their mother is a shameless prostitute
    and became pregnant in a
        shameful way.
She said, 'I'll run after other lovers
    and sell myself to them for food
        and water,
for clothing of wool and linen,
    and for olive oil and drinks.'

⁶"For this reason I will fence her in
    with thornbushes.
I will block her path with a wall
    to make her lose her way.
⁷When she runs after her lovers,
    she won't be able to catch them.
She will search for them
    but not find them.
Then she will think,
'I might as well return to my husband,
    for I was better off with him than
        I am now.'
⁸She doesn't realize it was I who gave
    her everything she has—
the grain, the new wine, the olive oil;
I even gave her silver and gold.
    But she gave all my gifts to Baal.

⁹"But now I will take back the ripened
    grain and new wine

I generously provided each harvest
    season.
I will take away the wool and linen
    clothing
I gave her to cover her nakedness.
¹⁰I will strip her naked in public,
    while all her lovers look on.
No one will be able
    to rescue her from my hands.
¹¹I will put an end to her annual festivals,
    her new moon celebrations, and her
        Sabbath days—
all her appointed festivals.
¹²I will destroy her grapevines and fig
    trees,
    things she claims her lovers gave her.
I will let them grow into tangled
    thickets,
    where only wild animals will eat the
        fruit.
¹³I will punish her for all those times
    when she burned incense to her
        images of Baal,
when she put on her earrings and
    jewels
    and went out to look for her lovers
but forgot all about me,"
    says the LORD.

NOTES

2:2 [4] *bring charges against Israel.* In addition to its place in the chiastic scheme of
chs 1–3, the second chapter, like the first, has an order of presentation that begins with a
command (and assumed compliance) and is followed by comment (2:3-23). The text literally reads "your mother" rather than "Israel." The NLT rendering calls attention to the fact
that it is the nation that is in primary focus in this denunciation.

The Hebrew root *rib* [TH7378, ZH8189], which underlies the NLT's "bring charges against,"
connotes striving or quarreling with someone. Because the verb appears in several OT texts
involving a hearing for adjudication before a council or religious authority (e.g., Deut
19:17; 21:5; 2 Sam 15:1-6), some (e.g., Stuart; cf. NJB) have suggested that in prophetic
texts where Yahweh calls Israel to account, *rib* envisions a lawsuit (e.g., Mic 6:1-8). This
appears unlikely here, however, for the context deals more with correction and threatened
punishment than with a case of legal jurisprudence. Moreover, Andersen and Freedman
(1980:219) rightly point out that the passage omits several features of a typical lawsuit
and conclude: "A legal note is certainly present but the juridical framework is neither rigid
nor realistic."

no longer my wife. Citing an Akkadian document from Nuzi, Gordon (1936:277-280)
suggests that the language here is reflective of common ancient Near Eastern divorce formulae. For the later Jewish formula attested at Elephantine (in Aramaic), see Friedman
1980:199-204. Despite similarities of language, the full context makes such unlikely. The

issue is that of separation due to adultery (cf. McComiskey 1992:32). Hubbard (1989:72) proposes that the language indicates "the divorce is contemplated but not yet decided."

2:6 [8] *I will fence her in . . . block her path.* The divine announcement begins with the particle *hinneh* [TH2009, ZH2180] and a participle, indicating a solemn pronouncement. Although many commentators see a hint of Israel's vacillating foreign policy and its eventual captivity, the contextual emphasis appears to be on frustrating Israel's fascination with idolatry.

2:8 [10] *the grain, the new wine, the olive oil.* These important agricultural products were also utilized in Israel's worship ceremonies. Their availability was tied to Israel's faithfulness to God's covenant in their use (cf. Deut 28:51; see commentary on Joel 1:10).

2:10 [12] *strip her naked in public.* Nakedness was a sign of deprivation and shame (2 Sam 10:4; Job 24:7, 10; Mic 1:11). The denuded land is symptomatic of a deeper shame. Gordon (1936:277-280) suggests, on the basis of ancient practice found particularly in Mesopotamia, that the denuding of the wife was a common part of divorce procedures. While such is a possibility in ancient Israelite society, it does not appear to have been routinely practiced (cf. Deut 24:1-4). Nakedness is mentioned as one of the curses that God would impose upon Israel for violating the terms of the covenant (Deut 28:48). Therefore, the prophets at times seize upon the term as a metaphor for the Lord's judgment (Jer 13:26-27; Ezek 16:39; 23:29; see note on Nah 3:5).

No one will be able to rescue her. The threat of Israel's captivity is added to the physical and material loss the nation would suffer. Nothing can stay God's course of judgment.

2:11 [13] *all her appointed festivals.* Israel's ability to observe the sacred festivals to God would be ended in the severe judgment upon the land and nation. Whether the observance was annual (Deut 16:16-17), monthly (Amos 8:5), or weekly (Exod 20:10; 23:12), it will be terminated. God will no longer support a debased worship ritual that has been compromised by syncretistic practices associated with the worship of Baal.

The verb translated "put an end to" comes from the same Hebrew root as the noun translated "Sabbath." The precise placement of verb and noun accomplishes two things: (1) It reinforces the truth that the Sabbath lies at the heart of all the other festivals, and (2) it provides a clear play on ideas. The force of the latter is to suggest that even the day of rest will be put to rest. Because the Levitical system was built around the observance of the Sabbath, cutting off the Sabbath was tantamount to causing the whole ritual system to collapse.

2:12 [14] *grapevines and fig trees.* The vine and the fig tree were often used as symbols of God's blessing (cf. 2:12; Amos 4:9; Mic 4:4 with 1 Kgs 4:25; 2 Kgs 18:31; see also Pss 80:8-15; 105:33; Isa 5:2-6; 36:16; Jer 2:21; 5:17; 8:13; Hag 2:19; Zech 3:10).

2:13 [15] *all those times . . . of Baal.* Lit., "the days of the Baals." The reference is uncertain. Hosea used the phrase "days of" in several ways (cf. the Heb. of 2:15 [17]; 9:7; 10:9; 12:9 [10]). Thus, "the days of the Baals" could refer to (1) Israel's long flirtation with this Canaanite god, (2) those festival days of syncretistic worship mentioned in 2:11, or (3) the many occasions of Baal worship at various cult shrines throughout the land, or even to all three. The plural term "Baals" probably relates to the many cultic shrines to Baal, where he was worshiped under various local manifestations and practices.

COMMENTARY

Hosea's prophecy now reaches the centerpiece of the opening section of the book: God will brook the infidelity of wayward Israel no longer. In condemning Israel and announcing its punishment, Hosea's separation from Gomer served as a visible symbol of God's estrangement from Israel. Just as Gomer was sent from her house and husband, so Israel would be judged by God and sent into captivity. Just as Gomer would be bereft of economic and material resources, so God would afflict the land and crops with devastating losses.

God's purpose in this was twofold. First, Israel must pay the price for its infidelity. Israelite society, leaders and people alike, stood condemned. In ancient Israel guilt could be considered both corporate and individual; this was the case primarily on the basis of Israel's covenant with the Lord, which also became the cultural norm. Indeed, there was corporate solidarity between nation and people (cf. Josh 7:22-26). Israel's specific adultery was the worship of Baal. The nation's infectious flirtation with this Canaanite god had spread to every locality. All Israel and its people were covered with shame. Therefore, the nation must suffer the consequences of its disobedience (cf. Deut 28:15-68). Although Israel had not been faithful, God would faithfully keep his word. The penalty for covenant violation must be imposed.

Second, God intended more than punishment. The stringent measures laid upon his people were meant to make them see the folly of their false affection for Baal. Israel had a long history of being attracted to Baal (e.g., Num 25:2-3; Judg 2:11-13; 1 Kgs 16:31-33; 18:19-40). Baal was a storm-god whose legendary battles against other nature gods such as Yamm (the god of the sea) and Mot (the god of death) were told in the great myths of ancient Ugarit. As a storm-god, he was considered responsible for the fertility and productivity of the ground. This and his sexual exploits with the goddess Anat (his wife or sister, depending on the tale) appear to lie behind the cultic ritual practices.

God's prophets repeatedly condemned the people's involvement with the heinous practices associated with Baal, and they pronounced God's judgment against them for it (e.g., Jer 11:11-17; 32:26-35; Zeph 1:4).[1] And so it is here. Because the people had come to regard their material gain and agricultural productivity as the fruits of Baal worship, Israel's real benefactor, God, would take these things away. With their fields devastated, resulting in a severe economic reversal, it could be hoped that Israel would realize that all it possessed came ultimately from God, not Baal. Cut off from either human help or that of any false god, perhaps God's people might consider their condition and return to their only true source of help— God himself.

The Hebrew root ba'al [TH1166, ZH1249] is used in ways other than to refer to the Canaanite god Baal. The verb can indicate possessing or ruling, hence the nouns "master" and "lord." Particularly important was its use in the marriage relationship. In such contexts, the Hebrew root appears as a verb to indicate a man's marrying a wife (Deut 24:1) or of the state of marriage (Prov 30:23). As a noun it can designate the husband (Deut 24:4). Here the concepts of master and husband become intertwined in accordance with ancient Israelite culture.

Metaphorically, God's relation to Israel is also described by the figure of marriage. God is Israel's husband and redeemer (Isa 54:1, 5). Tragically, Israel had become unfaithful (Jer 31:32). The motif of God's marriage to Israel is also prominent in Jeremiah. It was a marriage which Judah, as a wicked wife, had broken (Jer 2:1–3:10). Jeremiah pleaded with Judah to repent (Jer 3:12-14) in order that she may receive God's full blessing (Jer 3:15-18). In doing so, the prophet made a clever play on words: "'Return home, you wayward children,' says the LORD, 'for I am your master'" (*ba'al*; Jer 3:14). Did Judah chase after Baal? Her real "baal" was Yahweh, her husband. Why should she seek a false master?

Hosea's message is much the same. Unfaithful Israel had left her true husband to debase herself with Baal. Thinking to gain all that she ever desired, she would learn that she had lost it all. Her only recourse was to return to God, her faithful husband (2:7) so as to again enjoy the blessings of marriage (cf. 2:14-23; 3:4-5; Isa 62:4-5). In that day, however, Israel will no longer refer to God as her *ba'al*. So odiously will that word be viewed that the noun *'ish* [TH376, ZH408] (man, husband) will be employed instead (2:16-17).

The warnings of this passage to those of the old covenant serve as a lesson for today's believers who are participants in the new covenant (Matt 26:28; 1 Cor 11:25; 2 Cor 3:6; cf. Heb 8:8-13). Much as God was Israel's redeemer and husband, so Christ, the Redeemer, is the bridegroom of his bride, the church (Eph 5:22-27). As such, the believing church must be a faithful and spotless bride, remembering the price that Christ paid for her redemption (1 Cor 6:20). May the apostle John's admonition to keep ourselves from idols be ever before us (1 John 5:21).

ENDNOTES

1. Because of the loathsome nature of Baal and his religious rites, the faithful scribes who copied the OT often deliberately changed the royal name Baal-zebul ("Prince Baal") to Baal-zebel ("lord of dung") and Baal-zebub ("lord of flies"; e.g., 2 Kgs 1:2; cf. Beelzebub, Matt 10:25; 12:24, 27). For the problem of Zebub, see my note in *The Expositor's Bible Commentary* (Grand Rapids: Zondervan, 1988), 4.172. For helpful information on Baal, see P. Craigie, *Ugarit and the Old Testament* (Grand Rapids: Eerdmans, 1983), 61-66. For a succinct summary of the origin and growth of the Baals, see Hubbard (1989:81-82). For discussion and translation of the myths concerning Baal, see M. Coogan, *Stories from Ancient Canaan* (Philadelphia: Westminster, 1978), 75-115.

◆   **D. Israel's Renewal on the Basis of the Covenant (2:14-23)**

¹⁴ "But then I will win her back once
   again.
   I will lead her into the desert
   and speak tenderly to her there.
¹⁵ I will return her vineyards to her
   and transform the Valley of
   Trouble* into a gateway
   of hope.
She will give herself to me there,

as she did long ago when she
   was young,
when I freed her from her captivity
   in Egypt.
¹⁶ When that day comes," says the LORD,
   "you will call me 'my husband'
   instead of 'my master.'*
¹⁷ O Israel, I will wipe the many names
   of Baal from your lips,

and you will never mention them
again.
18 On that day I will make a covenant
with all the wild animals and the
birds of the sky
and the animals that scurry along
the ground
so they will not harm you.
I will remove all weapons of war
from the land,
all swords and bows,
so you can live unafraid
in peace and safety.
19 I will make you my wife forever,
showing you righteousness and
justice,
unfailing love and compassion.
20 I will be faithful to you and make
you mine,
and you will finally know me
as the LORD.

21 "In that day, I will answer,"
says the LORD.
"I will answer the sky as it pleads
for clouds.
And the sky will answer the earth
with rain.
22 Then the earth will answer the thirsty
cries
of the grain, the grapevines, and
the olive trees.
And they in turn will answer,
'Jezreel'—'God plants!'
23 At that time I will plant a crop
of Israelites
and raise them for myself.
I will show love
to those I called 'Not loved.'*
And to those I called 'Not my
people,'*
I will say, 'Now you are my people.'
And they will reply, 'You are our God!'"

2:15 Hebrew *valley of Achor.*   2:16 Hebrew *'my baal.'*   2:23a Hebrew *Lo-ruhamah;* see 1:6.   2:23b Hebrew
Lo-ammi; see 1:9.

NOTES

2:14 [16] *I will win her back once again.* In the midst of Israel's hopeless condition
(as a result of the divine punishment), her merciful God alone will come to her aid.

the desert. This noun denotes a wilderness area—hence, desert or steppe land. The harsh-
ness of such areas "forces the individual to rely upon God, and the Bible often attributes
survival in the wilderness to his grace" (Garrett 1997:89). While the term could be used
in many ways, in the prophetic literature it was used to remind a disobedient Israel of the
time in its history when God's people had come to trust their redeemer. There, because of
their faithfulness, they enjoyed an intimate relation with the Lord. Accordingly, in some
contexts the desert or wilderness came to symbolize renewed hope (Jer 31:2). The pristine
purity of Israel's relationship with God could be realized again. For a thorough study of the
desert motif, see Talmon 1966:31-64.

2:15 [17] *the Valley of Trouble.* Lit., "Valley of Achor." The Valley of Achor reminded
Hosea's hearers of Israel's failure due to Achan's sin in keeping forbidden spoils of war
(Josh 7). The tragedy of Achor will be erased in renewed opportunity to do the will of God.
"Both Jezreel and Achor carry a double meaning—death under Yahweh's judgment, new
life under his mercy" (Andersen and Freedman 1980:275).

2:16 [18] *my husband . . . my master.* Because Baalism had brought an idolatrous connotation to the noun *ba'al* [TH1167, ZH1251], which can mean master or husband, Israel would
use the noun *'ish* [TH376, ZH408] (man, husband) in the future. See commentary on 2:2-13.

Although many biblical names were compounded with *ba'al* in the early days, so loathsome was the worship of this deity that his very name became identified with shame.
Hosea 9:10 speaks of Israel's shame in being lured into the sacred prostitution involved
with Baal during their stay in Shittim (Num 25:1-4; cf. Num 31:16; Rev 2:14). Therefore,
Jewish scribes would often substitute the element "shame" for Baal in names compounded

with the noun associated with that deity. Thus Esh-baal (1 Chr 8:33; 9:39), Saul's son, is rendered Ishbosheth in Samuel (e.g., 2 Sam 2:8-11), while Jonathan's son Merib-baal (1 Chr 8:34; 9:40) becomes Mephibosheth (2 Sam 4:4), and Jerub-baal (Judg 6:32; 8:35) becomes Jerub-besheth (2 Sam 11:21, NLT mg). Still later Satan became identified as Beel-zebub (Matt 10:25; 12:24).

2:19 [21] *righteousness and justice.* This pair of divine attributes often occurs together. They were to be the pillar of Solomon's reign (1 Kgs 10:9; 2 Chr 9:8), for they reflected the essence of God's own rule (Deut 32:4; Pss 33:5; 89:14; 97:2; 103:6; cf. Isa 28:17). The former lays stress on God's consistency in acting in accordance with the standards of his own holy and just nature. The latter emphasizes his absolute integrity and evenhanded fairness in dealing with people and nations. He can do no less for his covenant nation, Israel.

unfailing love and compassion. These two divine qualities appear elsewhere together to describe both God's past (Ps 103:4) and future (Isa 54:8) redemption of Israel. The former speaks of God's great loving-kindness in taking people into a living relationship with himself, particularly his covenant nation, Israel (Deut 7:9, 12; 1 Kgs 8:23). The latter adds a touch of tenderness to God's dealings (Deut 4:31; Ps 78:38).

2:20 [22] *faithful.* This fifth characteristic of God emphasizes his trustworthiness and consistency in acting according to his being and word. Groups of five characteristics of God occur elsewhere in the OT (e.g., Deut 32:4; see commentary on Jonah 4:2 and Hab 2:4).

you will finally know me as the LORD. What Israel had forgotten (2:13) would be reversed when they fully acknowledged their Lord (cf. Joel 2:27). God's faithfulness and Israel's response provide the climax to God's intention to establish a new covenant with his people. Like v. 18, this verse looks forward to Jeremiah's proclamation of God's new covenant (Jer 31:31-34).

2:21 [23] *I will answer.* The Lord's promise stands as a reward for covenant faithfulness (cf. comments on Joel 2:23). God is the real provider, not Baal.

2:23 [25] *I will plant.* This verb (*zara'* [TH2232, ZH2445]) forms a wordplay with "Jezreel" in v. 22, for it makes up part of the name. God will not only reverse the devastation to nature because of Israel's judgment (2:22), but he will "plant" a people for himself. The long-standing shame of Jezreel would, at last, be remedied (cf. 1:3-5; 2 Kgs 9:21-28, 30-37; 10:1-10).

COMMENTARY

God had not given up on his people. He intended to seek them out. After their due judgment, he would enter into a fresh relationship with them, and it would be as though those early days (when the nation first entered into the desert in loving dependence upon God) were reborn. Thus, the judgment Hosea announced upon Israel would accomplish its intended purpose. In that grand future day, God would establish a new covenant with his people, brought about not only in accordance with the constraints of his righteousness and justice but by his unfailing love and compassion, demonstrating that God is faithful to his person and nature, as well as to his word and promises to his people. And at last, God's people would fully surrender to him. God and people would live in intimate communion, each acknowledging the other in loving harmony. Moreover, Israel would be restored to the Land of Promise and live there in absolute peace and safety. Even nature would be transformed, the refreshing rains causing the ground to yield its fruit again with abundant fertility.

Hosea's words are in agreement with the Old Testament prophets who proclaimed that God would not abandon his people. Although God must judge them for their waywardness, he would establish a new relationship with them that would ensure their everlasting peace and well-being (see commentary on Joel 3; on Obad 1:15-16, 17-21; and on Zeph 3:9-13, 14-20).

God's judgment of old-covenant Israel and renewed communion with a repentant and faithful people looks forward to Paul's admonition to the Corinthians to be faithful to the Lord so that they may dwell together with him in fellowship (2 Cor 6:14–7:21). There he reports God's promise: "I will be their God, and they will be my people" (2 Cor 6:16; cf. Lev 26:1-12; Jer 32:38-41; Ezek 37:20-28). As heirs of God's new covenant, gentile believers who were formerly "far away from God" are now "brought near" through the blood of Christ; Jew and Gentile alike are "one people" (Eph 2:13-14). Christian believers also look forward to that day when it shall be proclaimed: "Look, God's home is now among his people! He will live with them, and they will be his people," and Christ himself shall say, "Look, I am making everything new" (Rev 21:3, 5).

What comfort, then, for today's believers. Even though the believer may drift into sin, God's love never fails. He longs to meet with his own so as to bring them to himself. The God of redemption is also the God of restoration. Where there is repentance and confession of sin, God "is faithful and just to forgive us our sins and to cleanse us from all wickedness" (1 John 1:9).

Christians are also challenged by this passage. The divine qualities of righteousness and justice, steadfast love and compassion, and absolute faithfulness ought to be reproduced in every believer's conduct. As those created anew in Christ (Eph 4:23), who is the full image of God (Col 1:15; Heb 1:3), believers are to be "renewed as [they] learn to know [their] Creator and become like him" (Col 3:10). The believer's life should reflect those same qualities that God extends towards those to whom he promised a new covenantal relationship. In sum, believers ought to live so as to be persons whose lives are characterized by the active pursuit of the righteousness that God has given them (Rom 1:17), a concern for fairness in all their dealings, a heartfelt devotion to God their heavenly Father, a genuine compassion for the spiritual and temporal needs of all people, and a life of total faithfulness to God and the standards of his Word.

◆   ## E. Israel's Reconciliation—Symbolized by Hosea's Marriage (3:1-5)

Then the LORD said to me, "Go and love your wife again, even though she* commits adultery with another lover. This will illustrate that the LORD still loves Israel, even though the people have turned to other gods and love to worship them.*"

²So I bought her back for fifteen pieces of silver* and five bushels of barley and a measure of wine.* ³Then I said to her, "You must live in my house for many days and stop your prostitution. During this time, you will not have sexual relations with anyone, not even with me.*"

⁴This shows that Israel will go a long time without a king or prince, and without sacrifices, sacred pillars, priests,* or

even idols! [5]But afterward the people will return and devote themselves to the LORD their God and to David's descendant, their king.* In the last days, they will tremble in awe of the LORD and of his goodness.

3:1a Or *Go and love a woman who.*   3:1b Hebrew *love their raisin cakes.*   3:2a Hebrew *15 shekels of silver,* about 6 ounces or 171 grams in weight.   3:2b As in Greek version, which reads *a homer of barley and a measure of wine;* Hebrew reads *a homer* [5 bushels or 182 liters] *of barley and a lethech* [2.5 bushels or 91 liters] *of barley.*   3:3 Or *and I will live with you.*   3:4 Hebrew *ephod,* the vest worn by the priest.   3:5 Hebrew *to David their king.*

NOTES

3:1 *Go and love your wife again.* The third chapter again follows the format of command (3:1), compliance (3:2-3), and comment (3:4-5). The NLT rendering assumes the most likely position, that the woman mentioned here is Gomer, Hosea's wife, though as the NLT mg indicates, the Hebrew is more ambiguous. Thus the focus returns to the symbolism of Hosea and Gomer. It was time for Hosea to bring back his adulterous wife.

she commits adultery. The NLT rendering combines two thoughts in the MT: (1) Gomer is loved by another, and (2) she is an adulteress.

love to worship them. Lit., "love their raisin cakes" (NLT mg). Raisin cakes were a delicacy that could be enjoyed on special occasions (2 Sam 6:19). Here, they apparently formed part of the religious experience connected with Baal worship. Scholars are divided on the question as to whether it was the idolatrous Israelites who loved the raisin cakes or the idols (i.e., they were offerings made to Baal). The NLT favors the former.

3:2 *I bought her back.* Scholars have reached varying conclusions regarding who received Hosea's payment. Wolff (1974:61) theorizes that Gomer had been someone's slave or had become a temple prostitute. Wood (1985:18) suggests that the payment was made to Gomer as a sort of marriage present (cf. Stuart 1987:66, who views this woman as Hosea's second wife).

fifteen pieces of silver and five bushels of barley and a measure of wine. Hosea paid for Gomer both in money and produce. Thirty shekels of silver was the value of a slave (Exod 21:32; Lev 27:4) and became a standard way in the ancient Near East to refer to something of little value. Although many scholars suggest that the combined payment in silver and produce brought the total value up to 30 shekels, and hence that Gomer had gone into some kind of slavery, the exact value of the other commodities is uncertain. Stuart (1987:66) is probably correct in remarking, "Neither the barley, an inexpensive grain, nor the jug of wine were expensive. . . . Thus the total price was not excessive."

3:3 *you will not have sexual relations.* Garrett (1997:102) is probably correct in holding that "Hosea means that she should live with him in total abstinence of sexual relations for 'many days' until the two of them could resume the normal life of husband and wife." The NLT rendering of the verse also agrees with this idea.

3:5 *David's descendant, their king.* Lit., "David, their king." The rendering of the NLT is *ad sensum;* it is not the historical David who is in view but the heir of the Davidic covenant (cf. Ps 89:3-4).

last days. The reference is to the eschatological future. From a NT point of view, the future begins with the present age and stretches on to the eschaton (the end of the world). Both periods are at times designated by similar terminology: the last days, the latter days, the last times (1 Tim 4:1, 11; 2 Tim 3:1-8; Heb 1:1-2; Jas 5:3; 1 Pet 1:5, 20; 4:7; 2 Pet 3:1-9; 1 John 2:18; Jude 1:18; see also commentary on Joel 2:28-32).

COMMENTARY

Hosea was instructed to go, get, and bring back his wife. Despite her infidelity, he was to love her even as the Lord loved unfaithful Israel. Hosea faithfully obeyed, obtaining her for a small redemption price. Although she was returned to the family, she had to undergo a disciplinary period when normal conjugal relations with her husband were suspended. For Gomer personally, this would serve as punishment for her promiscuity as well as being a test of her renewed purity and faithfulness to her husband. When the prescribed period was completed, she would be able to enter into the full blessings of family life.

All of this was to once again symbolize God's relation to his people Israel. Like Gomer, Israel would be alienated from the Lord, be without political and religious leadership, and be unable to carry on the normal temple worship. Idolatry would be a thing of the past. For at the end of days, in accordance with God's program, his repentant people will present themselves in reverential awe before the Lord. Then they will experience the fullness of God's great goodness.

This passage stands in witness to the integrity of the inspired Scriptures. To some extent Israel still lives within the "many days" of the prophecy. With the fall of the northern kingdom in 722 BC and the southern kingdom in 586 BC, Israel entered into a long period when it would be "without a king or prince, and without sacrifices" (3:4). Although Israel has been restored to its land for over half a century, it is still without a king or temple or sacrificial system. Further, idolatry has not become the besetting sin to Israel that it was in Hosea's day.

This section also supports other portions of Old Testament eschatology in predicting the return of the Davidic kingship (e.g., Jer 33:15-26). Ezekiel prophesied a coming time when David's heir will protect a restored Israel as a shepherd protects his sheep (Ezek 34:11-24). It will be a united Israel over which he will rule in an era of great peace permeated by the presence of God himself (Jer 23:6; Ezek 37:15-28). He will appear as the righteous Branch of David's line and will execute justice and righteousness in the land (Jer 23:5; 33:15). As Israel's promised Messiah (Ps 18:50 [51]; cf. Ps 2:2), he will be known as "The LORD [is] Our Righteousness" (Jer 23:6).

The New Testament declares Christ as that promised heir (Acts 2:34-35; 13:22-23, 32-34), a fact attested by the risen Christ himself (Rev 22:16). Hailey (1971:146) observes with regard to Hosea 3:5 that "the 'David' of the passage is David's illustrious descendant, Jesus the Christ." In the last book of the New Testament it is declared that Christ, David's heir, will ultimately triumph (Rev 5:5; 11:17).

Several comparisons and contrasts may be drawn between the Old Testament and the New Testament teachings. Thus, as national Israel was for so long absent from its land, so the Anointed One is absent bodily from the earthly scene. Although national Israel was exiled due to its sinful disobedience, the Lord Jesus came to die on behalf of the sins of the world (John 3:16-18; 2 Cor 5:21) and went away so that the fullness of God's promises may be realized in all people, Jew and Gentile alike (John 14:2; 16:7; Acts 2:33-36; Rom 11:25-27; Eph 1:20-23; Phil 2:9-11). As the Old Testament prophets declare that national Israel would come again to its land in realization of the Abrahamic, Davidic, and new covenants (e.g., Ezek 37:21-28), so Christ will come again at the end of the latter days (Matt 24:29-31; 26:64; John 14:3; Acts 1:11; 1 Thess 4:13–5:11) to put down sin and establish his everlasting Kingdom (Rev 11:15; 19:11-21; 22:3).

Underlying all of Hosea's dealings with Gomer and God's relation to Israel is the theme of love. At the outset of the passage the word *love* occurs four times in the Hebrew text, twice of misplaced love (Gomer's adulterous love and Israel's love of raisin cakes) and twice of proper love (Hosea's love for Gomer and God's love of Israel). It is the last that is the key to it all. Hosea was not only to bring his wayward wife home but to love her genuinely. In a far greater way, God loves his errant people. God's love thus triumphs over the initial demands of punishment.

As Hosea pursued Gomer, so God seeks to bring back his own people to himself despite their callous disregard for him (Deut 10:14-16; Jer 7:25; 11:7-8; 25:3-7; 26:5-6; 29:19; 31:3; 32:33; cf. 11:2; 12:13-14). Indeed, it is God's love that will ultimately result in his people's restoration so that they can enjoy the blessings that God has reserved for them (11:8-11; 14:4; cf. NIDOTTE 1.277-299). Further, God's love seeks out all people (Luke 19:10; Rom 10:20; Eph 2:4; cf. 2 Pet 3:9). By his great love he provided for the world's salvation (John 3:16-18; Rom 5:8) through the atonement of his own son, Jesus Christ (John 1:29; 6:51; 10:17-18; 12:47; 1 John 2:2; 4:9-10). Because of his love, believers look forward to a blessed future with the Savior (John 14:1-4; 1 Cor 2:9; 2 Pet 3:13; Rev 21:1-4).

Unlike the example of a disobedient people under the old covenant, new covenant believers are to love God supremely (Matt 22:37-38), live out his word in their lives (John 14:15; 15:10), and serve him faithfully (1 Cor 4:2; 1 Pet 4:10). Moreover, because God has loved the believers, they are to live in love (Eph 5:1-2), loving one another (1 John 4:7-10) and their neighbors as themselves (Matt 22:39; cf. Luke 10:29-37). Because believers are the recipients of God's great love for all people, they are constrained to share that love with an unbelieving world (2 Cor 5:16-21) so that nonbelievers may come to experience the love of Christ and be filled with the fullness of life and power that comes from God (Eph 3:19).

The section ends on a high note—a restored Israel experiencing the Lord's blessings. Not only has Israel known God's goodness in the past (Josh 23:15; Neh 9:25), but she will do so again in a great future day (Jer 32:36-41). Hosea's readers are reminded that all the good they enjoy comes from God (Ps 16:2; Jas 1:17), who alone is ultimately good (Pss 84:11; 86:5; 100:5; Matt 19:17). It is because of God's gracious goodness and abundant kindness that people repent and come to know God (Rom 2:4; 2 Cor 7:10; cf. 2 Pet 3:9). So also today's believers may confidently call upon God in time of need (Pss 69:16; 109:21) and worship him with thankful hearts (Deut 12:5-28; Ps 116:12-14).

Believers should let God's goodness be reproduced in lives of willing service toward God and people alike (Mic 6:8; Gal 6:9-10; Eph 2:10; Col 1:10; Titus 2:14). In so doing, regardless of what may come into their lives, believers can understand that all that happens to them is what God intends for their good (Gen 50:20;

cf. Gen 45:4-8; see commentary on Hab 3:16-19). So it is that they may sense God's continuing goodness toward them both now and forever (Pss 23:6; 27:13; 34:10). Well does the psalmist exclaim: "How good it is to be near God!" (Ps 73:28). Looked at another way, the Hebrew may be understood as "the nearness of God is my good."[1] Because God, who is good (indeed, the ultimate good; see commentary on Nah 1:7), is ever near (Ps 119:151), believers not only have a source of refuge and strength but can rest secure in the knowledge that they have the very best that life can offer.

ENDNOTES

1. This noun is feminine in gender; the Hebrew feminine gender often marks abstract nouns. See Waltke and O'Connor 1990:104-105, 6.4.2b. Note the translation by M. Dahood, *Psalms* in The Anchor Bible (Garden City: Doubleday, 1968), 187, 196 (who, however, wrongly relegates the words to the future state): "The nearness of God will be my happiness." Note also the rendering "Being united with God is my highest good" (Ps 73:28, GW). Thus understood, the emphasis falls on God's continuous nearness to the psalmist rather than the psalmist's drawing near to God.

◆ II. Divine and Prophetic Perspectives on Unfaithful Israel (4:1–14:8)
   A. Opening Complaints against Israel (4:1–7:16)
      1. The threefold indictment (4:1–14)

[1] Hear the word of the LORD, O people of Israel!
The LORD has brought charges against you, saying:
"There is no faithfulness, no kindness, no knowledge of God in your land.
[2] You make vows and break them; you kill and steal and commit adultery.
There is violence everywhere— one murder after another.
[3] That is why your land is in mourning, and everyone is wasting away.
Even the wild animals, the birds of the sky, and the fish of the sea are disappearing.

[4] "Don't point your finger at someone else
and try to pass the blame!
My complaint, you priests, is with you.*
[5] So you will stumble in broad daylight,
and your false prophets will fall with you in the night.
And I will destroy Israel, your mother.
[6] My people are being destroyed because they don't know me.
Since you priests refuse to know me, I refuse to recognize you as my priests.
Since you have forgotten the laws of your God,
I will forget to bless your children.
[7] The more priests there are, the more they sin against me.
They have exchanged the glory of God for the shame of idols.*

[8] "When the people bring their sin offerings, the priests get fed.
So the priests are glad when the people sin!
[9] 'And what the priests do, the people also do.'
So now I will punish both priests and people
for their wicked deeds.

¹⁰They will eat and still be hungry.
 They will play the prostitute and
  gain nothing from it,
 for they have deserted the LORD
¹¹ to worship other gods.

 "Wine has robbed my people
  of their understanding.
¹²They ask a piece of wood for advice!
 They think a stick can tell them the
  future!
 Longing after idols
  has made them foolish.
 They have played the prostitute,
  serving other gods and deserting
  their God.
¹³They offer sacrifices to idols on the
  mountaintops.

They go up into the hills to burn
 incense
in the pleasant shade of oaks,
 poplars, and terebinth trees.

"That is why your daughters turn to
 prostitution,
and your daughters-in-law commit
 adultery.
¹⁴But why should I punish them
 for their prostitution and adultery?
For your men are doing the same
 thing,
sinning with whores and shrine
 prostitutes.
O foolish people! You refuse to
 understand,
so you will be destroyed.

4:4 Hebrew *Your people are like those with a complaint against the priests.* 4:7 As in Syriac version and an ancient Hebrew tradition; Masoretic Text reads *I will turn their glory into shame.*

NOTES

4:1 *Hear the word of the LORD.* The Lord's oracle begins with an imperative; the same occurs in several units in chs 4–14 (e.g., 5:1, 8; 8:1; 9:1; 10:12; 14:1). Here commences the portion of the book where Hosea first records God's oracle and then, under divine direction (cf. 1:1), comments on it.

brought charges against you. The NLT rendering is in harmony with those suggestions that God's presentation came in the form of a lawsuit against the offending people (e.g., Wolff 1974:66; Stuart 1987:72-87). For contrary views, see Garrett 1997:108-109; Hubbard 1989:96; Andersen and Freedman 1980:331-333. As Sweeney (2000:42) points out, although there is legal language here, "The existence of a clearly defined covenant lawsuit speech is increasingly questioned by scholars, however, in that no standard literary structure or terminology is apparent throughout all of the various examples of the form that have been put forward, and there are great difficulties in portraying YHWH as both plaintiff and judge in a legal proceeding."

no faithfulness, no kindness, no knowledge of God. The word rendered "faithfulness" is commonly translated "truth." The charge is a basic lack of integrity that displays itself in word and deed. For the issue concerning the translation of "faithfulness" or "faith," see the commentary on Hab 2:4. For kindness, see the note and commentary on Jonah 2:8. The Lord's loving-kindness has not been reproduced in the people's lives. Israel's knowledge of God was also flawed both in theory and in practice.

4:2 *commit adultery.* Israel's shameful behavior is in clear violation of the Mosaic law. "All these wrongs relate directly or indirectly to the Decalogue, the normative expression of Yahweh's will for the nation" (McComiskey 1992:57). In addition, such conduct is condemned frequently in various places in the OT, especially in the legal pronouncements of Exodus, Leviticus, and Deuteronomy.

violence . . . murder. These two crimes are linked together in Ezek 18:10-13 in the case of a son whose violent and sinful ways led to murder. Stuart (1987:76) proposes that the noun translated "murder" (lit., "bloodshed") should be read as "idols," and the passage is therefore a condemnation of the rampant idolatry in the northern kingdom.

4:3 *your land is in mourning.* Lit., "the land mourns." Joel similarly reported desperate conditions in the land (Joel 1:10-12, 17). Isaiah predicted that such will mark God's judgment of the earth in future days (Isa 24:1-5).

the wild animals, the birds . . . the fish. Several commentators find an allusion to the creation and flood accounts here. God's creative work is reversed and "the animal kingdom is pictured in language that outstrips the flood story" (Hubbard 1989:98). Similar imagery is known elsewhere in the prophets (e.g., Jer 4:23-28; see also comments on Zeph 1:2-3). For fuller details, see Patterson 1991:298-302.

4:4-5 *priests . . . prophets . . . Israel.* All segments of Israel's social fabric stand guilty before the Lord. The sins of the spiritual leadership have contaminated all areas of society. Therefore, the nation (doubtless including Israel's civil leadership) was doomed to destruction.

4:6 *they don't know me.* Knowledge is an important theme in the book. Here God's previous charge is restated. Israel's basic problem was its failure to know God as God. God, however, had full knowledge of Israel and its sin (5:3). All Israel should at least know that its sin would lead to the day of reckoning (9:7). Therefore, God's people must repent and come to a living knowledge of the Lord so that they may again experience his healing and restoration (6:1-3).

4:7 *They have exchanged the glory of God.* The NLT follows the lead of the traditional Masoretic emendation (the *Tiqqune Sopherim*), a reading attested in the Peshitta and the Targum and followed by some English versions (e.g., NIV, NJB, NRSV). The MT, however, reads: "I will exchange their glory," a reading followed by the LXX, Vulgate, and several English versions (e.g., KJV, NKJV, NASB, REB, GW). The latter rendering understands the verb as predicting a judgment against the priests. Their present honored position will be exposed for the disgrace that it is and will be dealt with accordingly.

4:10 *prostitute.* Israel's involvement in the ritual prostitution of the Canaanite fertility rites reflected its spiritual adultery (cf. 4:12). Because this spoke so grievously of Israel's violation of the covenant, prostitution is a key theme in the book. See the helpful study of Stuart (1987:19-23).

4:13 *They go up into the hills . . . in the pleasant shade of oaks, poplars, and terebinth trees.* Similar language describing Israel's participation in Canaanite fertility rites occurs elsewhere in the OT (e.g., Deut 12:2; 1 Kgs 14:23; 2 Kgs 17:10; Jer 2:20; 3:6; Ezek 6:13). Ritual prostitution supposedly insured the fertility of birth and the produce of the land. Moreover, because the sacrifices would be eaten by the participants and because of the sensual pleasure involved in the practice, the rites associated with Baal worship were extremely attractive. Stuart (1987:82) suggests that "many of the sacrifices offered at these 'high places' were probably dedicated syncretistically to Yahweh, whatever other Baal-Asherah overtones may have attended the worship." Certainly religious syncretism is hinted at strongly in Hosea and condemned elsewhere in the OT (e.g., Zeph 1:5). For Baalism and religious syncretism, see Patterson 1991:303-304.

4:14 *why should I punish them.* God's punishing Israel's cult prostitutes alone would be unfair, for Israel's men were as guilty as they. All Israel must suffer God's judgment.

COMMENTARY

Hosea called his hearers to pay attention, for he would declare the Lord's very words. God's oracle clearly points out the toxic condition of Israel's religious experience. The Lord told the people plainly that there was neither a sense of integrity nor any demonstration of the loving-kindness that comes from a vital, living relationship with its covenant Lord. Nor was there any real commitment to God. The order is climactic: God's people really did not know him, nor had they grasped God's covenantal standards. The sins abounding throughout the land violated the Decalogue and the tenets of Hebrew law. All Israel stood guilty before the Lord, beginning with the leadership.

Worse still, Israel's priests and many of the prophets had abandoned their duty of leading God's people into a deeper, consistent walk with God. Rather, they had led them into the shame and disgrace of idolatry and its associated evils. For their part, the priests had encouraged Israel to worship Baal. It was all for selfish reasons. Indeed, they sold themselves to the people as indispensable to their religious experience. Thereby they hoped to enjoy not only prestige but personal gain. The three basic areas of sin—the lust of the flesh, the lust of the eyes, and the pride of life (1 John 2:16)—thus surfaced in those who should have been leading the people in renouncing them.

How foolish of God's people! They had given themselves over to a religious system that cannot achieve what it promises to do. For it is Yahweh alone who ensured the fertility of the land and the resultant prosperity, not Baal or any false god. Indeed, God attempted to make this clear by sending natural calamities upon the land, but with no results in the hearts of the people. Therefore, they could expect even worse calamity.

Hosea's Israel stands as an example to every believer of the disastrous results of failing to submit to God and his standards. Where God and his will are not acknowledged or are even spurned for selfish ends, the marks of judgment will eventually be found. Where no fidelity to God exists, there can be no acts of godly loving-kindness. As in the case of Israel, Christians who claim the name of God can fall into a similar danger of divine chastisement. For it is one thing to confess God in dogma but another to let him truly be Lord of one's life. How easy it is to be carried away with self and to live for personal gain—such can only lead to spiritual ruin.

Christian leaders are especially to be warned, for they know they are accountable to God (Heb 13:17). God will condemn those ministers who fail to preach the whole counsel of God, who instead tell people whatever they want to hear (2 Tim 4:3). Christian leadership is a sacred trust that requires total fidelity to the Lord and the Word of God (cf. Acts 20:26; 1 Cor 4:2).

Not only believers and Christian leaders are to be warned; where sins such as those detailed in this passage are rampant in a nation, its spiritual and moral fiber are weakened and its collapse will inevitably occur. The parade of the passing of great nations is a grim reminder of this fact. The declaration of Scripture remains true: "Godliness makes a nation great, but sin is a disgrace to any people" (Prov 14:34).

◆   2. Hosea's condemnation of prostitute Israel (4:15-19)

15 "Though you, Israel, are a prostitute,
   may Judah avoid such guilt.
Do not join the false worship at Gilgal
   or Beth-aven,*
even though they take oaths there
   in the LORD's name.
16 Israel is stubborn,
   like a stubborn heifer.

So should the LORD feed her
  like a lamb in a lush pasture?
17 Leave Israel* alone,
  because she is married to idolatry.
18 When the rulers of Israel finish their
  drinking,

off they go to find some prostitutes.
  They love shame more than honor.*
19 So a mighty wind will sweep them
  away.
  Their sacrifices to idols will bring
  them shame.

4:15 Beth-aven means "house of wickedness"; it is being used as another name for Bethel, which means "house of God." 4:17 Hebrew *Ephraim*, referring to the northern kingdom of Israel. 4:18 As in Greek version; the meaning of the Hebrew is uncertain.

NOTES

4:15 you, Israel, are a prostitute. Prostitution forms the thematic thread that stitches these verses to the preceding 14 verses.

Beth-aven. The name contains a pun. By its apostate worship, Bethel (house of God) has become Beth-aven (house of iniquity). Both Bethel and Gilgal are denounced by Hosea's contemporary, Amos (Amos 5:4-5).

4:16 like a stubborn heifer . . . like a lamb in a lush pasture? Hosea, fond of similes, often used them to draw comparisons from the animal and agrarian worlds (see "Literary Style" and "Major Themes" in the Introduction).

4:18 finish their drinking. The verb *sar* [TH5493, ZH6073] (finish) forms a nice play on sounds with the verb for "stubborn" (*sarar* [TH5637, ZH6253]) in v. 16. Not content with the drinking at supposed religious sites, when the liquor is gone, the men turn to the cult prostitutes (cf. Ezek 23:42).

They love shame more than honor. This last part of v. 18 in the MT is notoriously difficult. Because of the constraints of the flow and the sense in the context, the NLT follows the LXX, which apparently read a slightly variant form of the Hebrew. As a result, the LXX reads literally "they loved dishonor on the basis of [or because of] their snorting." The Greek term "snorting" was likewise used metaphorically for insolence, loose or unrestrained— even promiscuous—behavior. Therefore, it has been translated *ad sensum* with such rendering as "shameful behavior" (NET) or "lewdness" (RSV).

COMMENTARY

Hosea's reaction to the Lord's pronouncement was one of concern—concern for Judah first of all. Hosea's fondest wish was that Judah not be caught up in spiritual adultery. The citizens of the northern kingdom had compromised the worship of God by combining it with the debased rites of Canaan. Feigning loyalty to Yahweh, they ardently pursued Baal. Consequently, proud, stubborn Israel would find itself helpless in the fast-approaching day of judgment. No Baal would help them then. Rather, Israel would die a shameful death.

The dangers of spiritual compromise and disloyalty are evident here. Israel was to have no other god but Yahweh (Exod 20:2-4). To fail to give single-hearted allegiance to him alone was to invite disaster (Deut 8:19-20). Adulterous Israel was also guilty of taking oaths in the Lord's name by pretending to worship him—a clear violation of the spirit of the third commandment (Exod 20:7). They had not heeded Moses's words that "the LORD will not let you go unpunished if you misuse his name" (Deut 5:11).

Christians, too, are to remember that their hope of eternal salvation lies in God alone as revealed in Jesus Christ (John 10:27-30; Acts 4:12). Accordingly, they are to keep themselves from false worship practices and any worldly pursuit that would compromise either the person of Christ or the testimony of his name (2 Cor 6:14–7:1; 1 John 5:21). God's sentence of judgment upon Israel stands as a reminder that Christians will also stand before Christ to be judged (2 Cor 5:10; cf. Rom 14:10). There is, however, another promise. If believers will seek to live according to God's will for their lives (Col 1:9-10) and pursue it faithfully—come what may—theirs is the crown of life (Rev 2:10).

◆   3. The three guilty parties (5:1-3)

1 "Hear this, you priests.
    Pay attention, you leaders of Israel.
Listen, you members of the royal
    family.
Judgment has been handed down
    against you.
For you have led the people into
    a snare
by worshiping the idols at Mizpah
    and Tabor.

2 You have dug a deep pit to trap them
    at Acacia Grove.*
But I will settle with you for what
    you have done.
3 I know what you are like, O Ephraim.
    You cannot hide yourself from me,
    O Israel.
You have left me as a prostitute leaves
    her husband;
    you are utterly defiled.

5:2 Hebrew *at Shittim*. The meaning of the Hebrew for this sentence is uncertain.

NOTES

5:1 *leaders of Israel*. Lit., "house of Israel."

royal family. Lit., "house of the king." Three classes of leadership covering both the civil and religious segments of society are grouped together in 5:1 for condemnation: priests, leaders, and the royal family.

Mizpah and Tabor. The Mizpah intended here is probably a city in Benjamin about 10 kilometers north of Jerusalem; Mount Tabor is situated southwest of the Sea of Galilee. Apparently both had become cult centers by Hosea's time.

5:2 *You have dug a deep pit . . . at Acacia Grove*. This line is notoriously difficult to translate. The ancient versions struggled with it and provide little help. The NLT rendering (cf. NRSV, REB) depends on two minor emendations to the MT but has the advantage of providing a third location, "Acacia," to match the three areas of leadership listed in 5:1. Those who attempt to make sense of the MT as it stands most commonly view the text as indicating the depth of Israel's sin (e.g., "you are deeply involved in sin," GW; cf. NIV, NASB, NKJV), perhaps even hinting at the heinous crime of child sacrifice (Andersen and Freedman 1980:380; Hubbard 1989:114).

5:3 *I know what you are like, O Ephraim*. Israel is identified here with its most prominent region, Ephraim. The whole nation, however, is culpable. While many commentators assume that 5:1-3 constitutes Hosea's words, 5:6 suggests that they are the Lord's, as recorded by Hosea.

as a prostitute leaves her husband. The theme of adultery as illustrative of the relation between God and his people surfaces again (cf. 3:1-5). The symbolic experience of Hosea provides a background for the pronouncement.

COMMENTARY

This short oracle of judgment was aimed at Israel's leadership. Those who were held responsible for the people's well-being had failed to provide it. This was particularly true in the area of Israel's religious experience, for its leaders had left the true worship of God and sponsored the idolatrous and adulterous rites associated with Baal. They were to be warned: God had seen it all and would soon punish them for their actions. Little chance of avoiding God's judgment exists. Because all Israel followed its corrupt leaders, its flagrant sins rendered the northern kingdom utterly defiled (5:3).

Here again the importance of godly and dedicated leadership is stressed. It is difficult for people to rise above the level of their leadership spiritually or ethically. This is true whether in the church or in the home. Good leaders must be responsible people, for they are held accountable for their decisions, actions, and the example they provide (1 Tim 4:12; Heb 13:17). They are to be those who are faithful and trustworthy (Neh 7:2), who have a genuine concern for those in their trust, and who always try to do the right thing (Mic 3:2; 1 Tim 6:11-12). They are to be those who do not misuse their position for selfish gain (Amos 5:4-12; 1 Pet 5:1-4). Leadership is a privilege, a responsibility, and an opportunity to do special service for God (1 Tim 3:1-13; Titus 1:6-9).

May God's church have dedicated leaders who are faithful servants of the Lord (2 Chr 19:9; 1 Cor 4:1-2; Eph 6:21; 1 Tim 1:12; Heb 3:2). May they be those who live out and teach the principles of his Word (Phil 4:9; Col 3:16; 2 Tim 2:15; 4:2) so that, in turn, there may be a legacy of trustworthy people who are able to pass them on to others (2 Tim 2:2).

◆   ## 4. Hosea's charge: God's people are unfaithful (5:4-7)

⁴Your deeds won't let you return
   to your God.
You are a prostitute through and
   through,
and you do not know the LORD.

⁵"The arrogance of Israel testifies
   against her;
Israel and Ephraim will stumble
   under their load of guilt.
Judah, too, will fall with them.
⁶When they come with their flocks
   and herds

to offer sacrifices to the LORD,
   they will not find him,
because he has withdrawn from
   them.
⁷They have betrayed the honor of
   the LORD,
   bearing children that are
   not his.
Now their false religion will devour
   them
   along with their wealth.*

5:7 The meaning of the Hebrew is uncertain.

NOTES

5:4 *You are a prostitute.* Hosea seized upon the Lord's simile comparing Israel's desertion of God to a prostitute's abandonment of her husband. Although the NLT renders the verbs in the second person, thus seemingly continuing the Lord's words from 5:1-3, the verbs are third person in the MT and favor the view that Hosea is now giving his own reaction to the Lord's pronouncement.

5:5 arrogance. Lit., "pride." Israel's vaunted prosperity is that which will bear witness to its wayward course of action. When the good times come to an end, Israel's source of pride will prove to be misguided. Later, God will point out that already their ground of boasting is shaky at best (7:8-10).

stumble under their load of guilt. The northern kingdom will fall due to its sin. Ultimately, Judah will fare no better.

5:7 bearing children that are not his. Israel's devotion to Baal produced a generation of people who had not only been immersed in spiritual adultery but had passed it on to the next. The image of prostitution is thus carried forward. Like a wayward wife who has borne children out of wedlock, so apostate Israel has given birth to a society that does not know Israel's true God.

C O M M E N T A R Y

Hosea pointed out the seriousness of Israel's spiritual desertion. So entrenched had Israel become in its devotion to Baal that, humanly speaking, Baal's ubiquitous presence kept the people from knowing God. Because of the great prosperity during the eighth century BC, Israel was all the more attracted to Baal. As the weather and fertility god, he was considered to be the provider of all that they enjoyed. When God's judgment came against the northern kingdom, the people would see that they had put their trust in a false religious system. They would make frantic attempts to resume their worship of the Lord and its associated sacrifices. By then, however, the tide of doom would be irreversible. Rather than finding God, they would find that their abandonment of him had severed their relationship with him. Indeed, they would face the coming invader alone and without help. The price of betrayal would take its toll. Neither their prosperity nor their Canaanite god would be able to save them in that crucial hour.

How foolish it is to trust in worldly wealth! For it can all disappear so easily (Prov 11:28; 23:4-5; 27:24; Rev 18:14). Riches can do nothing to secure the salvation of one's soul or make one's eternal destiny sure (Ps 49:12, 16-20; Luke 12:13-21; 16:19-31). In fact, they may serve to hinder one's quest for immortality (Matt 19:23-24; Luke 8:14). The wise person will be concerned to receive the eternal riches of God's Kingdom rather than being preoccupied with the transitory needs of this world (Matt 6:25-33).

It is far better to possess the riches of God's grace in Christ Jesus, through whom there is the forgiveness of sins (Eph 1:7) and the availability of eternal life (Acts 4:12; Eph 2:7; 3:8; Col 1:27). With eternal riches secured, the believer can come to understand the nature of true wealth and experience God's provision of those spiritual blessings that accompany genuine godly living (Phil 4:19; Col 3:16; 1 Tim 6:17-19).

◆   5. The threefold alarm (5:8-15)

8 "Sound the alarm in Gibeah!
   Blow the trumpet in Ramah!
   Raise the battle cry in Beth-aven*!
   Lead on into battle, O warriors
      of Benjamin!

9 One thing is certain, Israel*:
   On your day of punishment,
      you will become a heap of rubble.

10 "The leaders of Judah have become
      like thieves.*

So I will pour my anger on them like
a waterfall.
¹¹ The people of Israel will be crushed
and broken by my judgment
because they are determined to
worship idols.*
¹² I will destroy Israel as a moth
consumes wool.
I will make Judah as weak as rotten
wood.

¹³ "When Israel and Judah saw how sick
they were,
Israel turned to Assyria—

to the great king there—
but he could neither help nor
cure them.
¹⁴ I will be like a lion to Israel,
like a strong young lion to Judah.
I will tear them to pieces!
I will carry them off,
and no one will be left to rescue
them.
¹⁵ Then I will return to my place
until they admit their guilt and
turn to me.
For as soon as trouble comes,
they will earnestly search for me."

5:8 *Beth-aven* means "house of wickedness"; it is being used as another name for Bethel, which means "house of God." **5:9** Hebrew *Ephraim*, referring to the northern kingdom of Israel; also in 5:11, 12, 13, 14. **5:10** Hebrew *like those who move a boundary marker.* **5:11** Or *determined to follow human commands.* The meaning of the Hebrew is uncertain.

NOTES

5:8 *Sound the alarm . . . Blow the trumpet . . . Raise the battle cry.* Another group of three dominates this section. The NLT rendering assumes that war is both imminent and in progress.

Lead on into battle, O warriors of Benjamin! The sudden mention of Benjamin is perplexing and has been variously understood. Its inherent difficulty has occasioned several emendations (e.g., LXX; Stuart 1987:97-98; Wolff 1974:104). The rendering of the NLT suggests a battle shout. Several other translations take a similar approach: "Look behind you!" (NRSV, NKJV); "We are with you!" (REB); and "We are behind you!" (NJB).

The matter is far from certain. The phrase could be a simple declaration giving the reason for the alarm: "[The enemy is] after you, Benjamin." Following a still different course Stuart (1987:97-98, 103) takes the Hebrew preposition used here as a construct noun and reads, "descendants of Benjamin." Thus translated, the phrase refers to the citizens of the previously mentioned towns.

It is noteworthy that similar phraseology occurs in Judg 5:14 where the difficult text is best understood as Ephraim's following behind Benjamin in the marching order (cf. Patterson 1981:128, 135-136). Doubtless, Hosea was readapting the Judges passage. Here, however, the order of presentation is reversed: The dangers to Benjamin are mentioned before the fate of Ephraim is described.

5:9 *Israel.* Lit., "Ephraim." In declaring the judgment on Israel, the MT singles out Ephraim for special mention.

day of punishment. Stuart (1987:103) proposes that "'day of punishment' may be a metonymy for the 'day of the Lord.'"

5:10 *like thieves.* Lit., "like those who move boundary stones." The moving of boundary stones (a common means of stealing property from a neighbor) was prohibited in the Mosaic law (Deut 19:14; 27:17).

5:11 *idols.* The NLT follows the lead of several translations in translating this difficult word as "idols." The Hebrew word occurs elsewhere only in Isa 28:10, 13 where it either forms part of some drunkards' mimicking of childish prattle (McComiskey 1992:81-83) or a human precept (Keil 1954:92; Laetsch 1956:49). The latter understanding views the Hebrew *tsaw* [TH6673, ZH7417] as being derived from the root *tsawah* [TH6680, ZH7422] (command). Several commentators take this approach here and regard Hosea's concerns as being about human rules, whether Israel's own state policies (Laetsch 1956:53) or those imposed on Israel by Assyria (Garrett 1997:152-153). Those who relate *tsaw* to idols (so LXX, Peshitta, NIV) perceive it to be a shortened form of *shaw'* [TH7723, ZH8736] (vanity, worthlessness), a familiar prophetic charge in the denunciation of idolatry (cf. HALOT 3:1009).

5:13 sick. The NLT combines the sickness of Ephraim and the sons of Judah into one word. The illness of the two kingdoms refers to the loss of internal strength and prosperity that came as a result of national decay and the rising external force of Assyria.

great king. Heb. *melek yareb* [TH4428/3377, ZH4889/3714]. In earlier days in the ancient Near East only the king of a "super power" could be called a great king. However, the later Neo-Assyrian kings appropriated the title for themselves. See my note on 2 Kgs 18:19 in Patterson and Austel 1988:260.

5:14 like a lion. Lion imagery was a prominent feature in ancient Assyria (see commentary on Nah 2:11; cf. Machinist 1983:719-737). The figure of a tearing lion to symbolize violent defeat is a familiar one in the prophets (e.g., Isa 31:4; Jer 25:38). The threat provides an interesting twist. God's people turned to Assyria for help, yet it was the Assyrians who would one day bring an end to the northern kingdom (2 Kgs 17:1-6; 18:9-12) and periodically prove to be a menace to Judah, especially in the days of Hezekiah (2 Kgs 18:13–19:36).

5:15 turn to me . . . search for me. Two different Hebrew verbs are used here. While the first (*baqash* [TH1245, ZH1335]) is a more general, though emotive, term, the latter (*shakhar* [TH7836, ZH8838]) contains a more intense desire for earnest seeking. Both verbs are used of approaching God in prayer.

C O M M E N T A R Y

The correct understanding of this passage depends a great deal on whether the historical background can be ascertained. Since the pioneering study of Albrecht Alt, modern scholarship has largely held to the position that this section and at least the first eight verses of chapter 6 refer to the Syro-Ephraimite War (2 Kgs 15:29-30; 16:5-9; 2 Chr 28:5-21; cf. Isa 7:1-16).[1] According to this theory, during the campaign of the Aramean Rezin and Pekah of the northern kingdom to take Jerusalem, Ahaz appealed for help from the Assyrian king, Tiglath-pileser III (c. 735 BC). The Assyrian king then launched a series of campaigns in which Ashkelon, Gaza, and Gezer were captured (734 BC). Two years later, Damascus fell and Israel capitulated, maintaining its fragile existence by submitting to Assyria and placing a new king on the throne (i.e., Hoshea, 732–722 BC).[2] According to the best scenario of this view, in the defeat of the Syro-Ephraimite coalition Judah saw an opportunity to extend its borders northward (Hubbard 1989:120). A few dissenting voices have been raised against so facile an explanation.[3] Particularly troublesome to the Syro-Ephraimite theory are the verification of Judah's aggression (5:10) and the fact that in that war it was Judah who turned to Assyria for help, not Ephraim nor Israel (5:13; Garrett 1997:149).

Therefore, it seems best to view the details of this section as reflecting the unsettled conditions of the middle to latter part of the eighth century BC that presaged the northern kingdom's coming demise. So understood, verse 10 need not refer to any unknown border aggression against Benjamin but may liken Judah's growing welcome of pagan religious practices to those who move boundary stones. Likewise, the order of cities mentioned in verse 8 may not necessarily refer to a military incursion by Judah but may indicate the perspective of those in southern Benjamin. Looking northward they note the alarms that have been sounded from southern Benjamin to the northern border. The order would be climactic—Bethel, the vilest of all, being mentioned last even though it would be the first to feel Assyria's might.

Due to Israel's settled spiritual adultery (5:1-7, 11), God warned of the coming invasion. All Israel could expect to feel the invader's heel from the north clear to Benjamin's southern border. Israel's vaunted prosperity would be reduced to a pile of rubble, crushed and broken in accordance with God's sentence of judgment. Nor should Judah think that it would escape divine wrath. Indeed, God was angry with both kingdoms, for both had gone over to Baal and the false gods. Baal had long held the fascination of the Israelites; Judah had also fallen under his spell. In a series of graphic similes, God compared his anger to a flowing waterfall and his disastrous judgment of Israel to a consuming moth and dry rot in wood.

In the end, no human help could reverse the situation. Although Israel had repeatedly courted the Assyrians' favor (e.g., 2 Kgs 15:19-20; for Judah cf. 2 Kgs 16:7-18), ultimately it would do no good. To the contrary, the Assyrians would crush the northern kingdom. In a further simile, God likened his judicial punishment of his people to a tearing lion, which none can oppose (5:14-15). Like a lion returning to his lair, God would then withdraw and await the time when his people would realize their guilt and turn in repentance to God.

This passage is instructive for unbelievers and believers alike. For people to escape God's judicial wrath, they must come to the end of themselves and turn in repentance and faith to accept God's appointed means of salvation (John 1:12; 3:16-18; 5:24; Acts 4:12). Likewise, for believers who have fallen into sin there is yet hope of forgiveness and the possibility of a renewed life in Christ (1 John 1:8-10).

A proper prayer life is impossible until such is done (cf. Ps 66:18; Jer 26:4-6). Indeed, where there is godless living (Isa 56:11-12), lack of concern for others in their need (Isa 58:6-9), and carelessness with regard to the clear instructions of the Word of God (Jer 35:17), God cannot honor the one who prays. Rather, such a one stands in danger of divine judgment (Zech 7:8-14). May God keep us from such habits of life. May this passage "teach us all by His Spirit to seek Him early, that so we may find Him" (Fausset 1948:478).

ENDNOTES

1. See A. Alt, "Hosea 5:8-6:6. Ein Krieg und Seine Folgen in Prophetischer Beleuchtung," in *Kleine Schriften zur Geschichte des Volkes Israel* (München: Beck, 1953), 2.163-187. For the Syro-Ephraimite War see my remarks in Patterson and Austel 1988; see also E. Merrill, *Kingdom of Priests* (Grand Rapids: Baker, 1987), 393-395, 405-407.

2. Tiglath-pileser claims to have installed Hoshea as his client king (cf. Luckenbill 1927:1.293). The Bible indicates that Hoshea seized the throne in a *coup d'etat* (2 Kgs 15:29-30). According to 2 Kgs 17:4-6, Hoshea was later involved in an anti-Assyrian plot which brought the northern kingdom to an end.

3. See, for example, H. G. Reventlow, "Zeitgeschichtliche Exegese prophetischer Texte? Uber die Grenzen eines methodischen Zuganges zum Alten Testament (am Beispiel

von Hos 5,8-14)," in *Prophetie und geschichtliche Wirklichkeit im alten Israel: Festschrift fur Siegfried Herrmann zum 65 Geburststag* (Stuttgart: Kohlhammer, 1991), 155-164. Note also Garrett 1997:148-149 and McComiskey 1992:81.

◆   ## 6. Hosea's advice: return to the Lord (6:1-3)

[1] "Come, let us return to the LORD.   so that we may live in his presence.
He has torn us to pieces;   [3] Oh, that we might know the LORD!
   now he will heal us.   Let us press on to know him.
He has injured us;   He will respond to us as surely as the
   now he will bandage our wounds.   arrival of dawn
[2] In just a short time he will   or the coming of rains in early
   restore us,   spring."

NOTES

6:1 *Come, let us return.* The LXX (cf. NRSV) inserts the word "saying" (Gr. *legontes* [TG3004, ZG3306]) before this exhortation, thereby making the prayer to be that of the people. Such a position, however, is without textual support. Rather, it is Hosea who prays on behalf of his people. The prayer assumes an attitude of true repentance. As Garrett (1997:158) notes, "Returning to Yahweh is a major theme of the book."

6:2 *In just a short time he will restore us.* Lit., "after two days he will revive us, on the third day he will raise us up." The NLT properly renders according to the sense but obscures an important biblical motif regarding three-day time periods (see commentary below).

6:3 *Oh, that we might know the LORD!* Failure to know God was "one of the primary failings of the people (4:1)" (Garrett 1997:159). Isaiah (Isa 54:13) looked forward to the day when Israel would be taught by the Lord.

as surely as the arrival of dawn or the coming of rains. Once again, Hosea's love of picturesque similes is seen. God's response to his people's repentance can be counted on as surely as the regularity of dawn and the arrival of the seasonal rains.

COMMENTARY

Building on the Lord's statement that it is only when God's people realize their hopeless position that they will search for God, Hosea prays vicariously on behalf of all Israel. He urged them to join him in heartfelt repentance and recognition that their present troubles are divinely sent. Because it is God who ordered them, only he can alleviate the situation. This he will do if only his people turn once again to him. Once this is done, in his set time he will restore his people to his favor and they will live in his blessed presence (Isa 54:1-8).

Hosea's presentation of his assurance of God's forgiveness and restoration of Israel is accompanied by the motif of the third day. From the beginning of Israel's redemption, the third day plays an important part. God appeared to Israel on Mount Sinai on the third day (Exod 19:10-16). The third day was a day of crucial decision (1 Kgs 12:12; Esth 4:16; 5:1). It was also a day of healing and sacrifice (Lev 7:17-18; 19:6-7; Num 19:12, 19-20). Accordingly, it was a day fit for Hezekiah's recovery (2 Kgs 20:8).

The third day, of course, is also significant for the capstone of Jesus' saving work. Jesus often told his disciples of a coming third day when, after his death, he would rise again (Matt 16:21; 17:23; 20:19; Luke 9:22). And so it came to pass, for Christ was gloriously raised on the third day (Luke 24:21; 1 Cor 15:4). All along the way, it would seem, God was preparing people for the great climactic event: the granting of new life and the institution of a new covenant with believers through the death and resurrection of his Son and our Redeemer, Jesus Christ.

The emphasis in this passage on the crucial importance of knowing God intimately reminds believers that such a quest is continuously theirs. Paul declared that, by faith in the resurrected Christ, the believer can really know Christ and experience the mighty power that raised him from the dead (Phil 3:10). He went on to point out, however, that this task consumes a lifetime. Accordingly, he remarked that his focus was on forgetting the past and looking forward to what lies ahead— the prize for which God, through Christ Jesus, is calling us up to heaven (Phil 3:13b-14).

May we therefore be "third-day Christians"—those who have put implicit faith in the one who was crucified for our sins and raised on the third day (1 Cor 15:4) to make us right with God (Rom 4:25). All Christians may join in Paul's journey to know God with ever increasing intimacy. For such is the opportunity available to them through the power of the resurrected Christ. In union with him they may live out the new life he has granted in all its fullness (Rom 6:4, 10-11; 1 Pet 2:24).

◆   7. God's concern for disloyal Israel (6:4–7:16)

4 "O Israel* and Judah,
    what should I do with you?" asks
    the LORD.
"For your love vanishes like the
    morning mist
    and disappears like dew in the
    sunlight.
5 I sent my prophets to cut you to
    pieces—
    to slaughter you with my words,
    with judgments as inescapable
    as light.
6 I want you to show love,*
    not offer sacrifices.
I want you to know me*
    more than I want burnt offerings.
7 But like Adam,* you broke my
    covenant
    and betrayed my trust.

8 "Gilead is a city of sinners,
    tracked with footprints of blood.

9 Priests form bands of robbers,
    waiting in ambush for their victims.
They murder travelers along the road
    to Shechem
    and practice every kind of sin.
10 Yes, I have seen something horrible
    in Ephraim and Israel:
My people are defiled by
    prostituting themselves with
    other gods!

11 "O Judah, a harvest of punishment
    is also waiting for you,
    though I wanted to restore the
    fortunes of my people.

CHAPTER 7

1 "I want to heal Israel,* but its sins
    are too great.
Samaria is filled with liars.
Thieves are on the inside
    and bandits on the outside!

² Its people don't realize
  that I am watching them.
Their sinful deeds are all around them,
  and I see them all.
³ "The people entertain the king with
    their wickedness,
  and the princes laugh at their lies.
⁴ They are all adulterers,
  always aflame with lust.
They are like an oven that is kept hot
  while the baker is kneading the
    dough.
⁵ On royal holidays, the princes get
    drunk with wine,
  carousing with those who mock
    them.
⁶ Their hearts are like an oven
  blazing with intrigue.
Their plot smolders* through the night,
  and in the morning it breaks out like
    a raging fire.
⁷ Burning like an oven,
  they consume their leaders.
They kill their kings one after another,
  and no one cries to me for help.

⁸ "The people of Israel mingle with
    godless foreigners,
  making themselves as worthless as
    a half-baked cake!
⁹ Worshiping foreign gods has sapped
    their strength,
  but they don't even know it.
Their hair is gray,
  but they don't realize they're old
    and weak.
¹⁰ Their arrogance testifies against them,

yet they don't return to the LORD
    their God
  or even try to find him.
¹¹ "The people of Israel have become like
    silly, witless doves,
  first calling to Egypt, then flying
    to Assyria for help.
¹² But as they fly about,
  I will throw my net over them
and bring them down like a bird from
    the sky.
I will punish them for all the evil
  they do.*
¹³ "What sorrow awaits those who have
    deserted me!
Let them die, for they have rebelled
  against me.
I wanted to redeem them,
  but they have told lies about me.
¹⁴ They do not cry out to me with sincere
    hearts.
Instead, they sit on their couches
  and wail.
They cut themselves,* begging foreign
  gods for grain and new wine,
  and they turn away from me.
¹⁵ I trained them and made them strong,
  yet now they plot evil against me.
¹⁶ They look everywhere except to the
    Most High.
They are as useless as a crooked bow.
Their leaders will be killed by their
    enemies
  because of their insolence toward me.
Then the people of Egypt
  will laugh at them.

6:4 Hebrew *Ephraim*, referring to the northern kingdom of Israel. **6:6a** Greek version reads *to show mercy.* Compare Matt 9:13; 12:7. **6:6b** Hebrew *to know God.* **6:7** Or *But at Adam.* **7:1** Hebrew *Ephraim*, referring to the northern kingdom of Israel; also in 7:8, 11. **7:6** Hebrew *Their baker sleeps.* **7:12** Hebrew *I will punish them because of what was reported against them in the assembly.* **7:14** As in Greek version; Hebrew reads *They gather together.*

NOTES

6:4 *what should I do with you?* The first series of divine oracles and prophetic responses reaches it climax with the record of God's poignant question here (see "Outline" in the Introduction).

6:6 *I want you to show love, not offer sacrifices.* Sacrificial observance without heartfelt devotion was unacceptable to God (1 Sam 15:22-23; Ps 40:6-8; Isa 1:11-20; Jer 7:21-23; Amos 5:21-27; Mic 6:6-8). Israel's syncretistic religion and its dead orthodoxy were not pleasing to God. For an interesting discussion of the dimensions of the Hebrew word translated "love" here, see Edin 1998:355-363.

6:7 like Adam. Several different positions have been held as to the understanding of these words. (1) Some modern translations (e.g., NRSV, NJB) and many commentators (e.g., Garrett 1997:164-165; Andersen and Freedman 1980:435-436; Chisholm 1990:35; Hubbard 1989:128-129) understand Adam to be a place name, either Adam near the Jordan River (Josh 3:16) or Admah (REB), the city that was overthrown in the judgment against the cities of the plain (Gen 10:19; 14:2, 8; Deut 29:23; cf. Gen 19:29). (2) Others translate the Hebrew noun as "men" (KJV, NRSV), hence the thought being "as mankind commonly does." (Note also the LXX: *hōs anthrōpos* [TG5613/444, ZG6055/476], "like/as a man"; and the French *La Sainte Bible: comme le vulgaire.*) (3) Still others understand Adam to be the well-known biblical person (e.g., Keil 1954:100; Hailey 1971:157; von Orelli 1977:38-39; McComiskey 1992:95; so GW). In accordance with this reading, 6:7 became a proof text for the covenant of works in some earlier systems of reformed theology (see, e.g., Berkhof 1959:213-218).

6:8 Gilead is a city. Other than a few vague references (e.g., Judg 10:17; 12:7), Gilead is not known as a city but only as a district beyond the Jordan River. McComiskey (1992:95) suggests that Hosea may have used Gilead to designate all of Israelite Transjordan much as he employs Ephraim in referring to the northern kingdom (cf. NIDOTTE 4.682-683). Hosea probably used the term "city" (*qiryat*) as a metaphor. The whole district was one big "city" of iniquity and bloody deeds. What a contrast with the integrity of Gilead's earlier settlers (Num 32:16-32)! Hosea would speak of Gilead in another connection later (12:11).

sinners. Lit., "doers of evil." The same noun for "evil" ('*awen* [TH205, ZH224]) was used earlier to depict Bethel: Due to its housing of the cult shrine, Hosea called it Beth-aven ("house of wickedness") in 4:15.

footprints of blood. The word for "footprints" denotes particularly the heel ('*aqubbah* [TH6121, ZH6814]), but is used here as a synecdoche for the foot (hence, "bloody footprints" rather than "bloody heels"). The noun's root is the same as that underlying Jacob's name (*ya'aqob* [TH3290, ZH3620]). Because of the juxtaposition of the noun for wickedness (see prior note on "sinners") and a noun from the same root as Jacob's name, it may be that the point Hosea makes in 12:2-6 is hinted at here. Thus Garrett (1997:163) remarks, "The point here appears to be that the Israelites . . . instead of being transformed into Israel, into people of God, remained Jacob, a name that Hosea has transformed into the grim phrase, 'stained with footprints of blood.'"

6:10 horrible. A similar form of this rare word (*sha'arur* [TH8186, ZH9136]) occurs in Jeremiah to designate the deceit and wickedness of Israel's spiritual leadership (Jer 5:30; 23:14) and the almost unbelievable fact that Israel had forgotten God and gone after idols (Jer 18:13-15).

6:11 I wanted to restore the fortunes of my people. This sentence is often understood to form an introductory clause to the sentence in 7:1, "When I restore the fortunes of my people, when I heal Israel, the guilt of Ephraim will be revealed" (cf. NIV, NRSV, REB). The NLT rendering agrees with many commentators and translations (KJV, NKJV, NJB, GW) that, following the MT, take the clause with 6:11 and consider it a reminder that Judah, too, will not escape judgment during the process of God's restoring his people's fortunes (e.g., Keil 1954:103; Hailey 1971:157; Laetsch 1956:61; cf. 10:13; Isa 63:3). For the phrase "restore the fortunes," see the note on Joel 3:1.

7:1 liars . . . Thieves . . . bandits. Hosea's penchant for grouping items in three is seen once more (cf. 5:1). Three classes of people are singled out: deceivers, thieves who break into buildings, and robbers who wait outside to do their mischief. Another group of three (king, princes, and people) is clustered in 7:3. Thus, all Israel is condemned.

7:4 *like an oven.* The simile of the heated oven dominates these verses (7:4-7). The MT is difficult in its reading and interpretation. Therefore, these verses have occasioned many suggested emendations and varied interpretations. The NLT rendering envisions a setting that likens Israel's adulterous passion to an oven kept hot while the bread dough is left to rise. In a slight twist, the people's political intrigues are compared to an oven whose fire is banked, smolders all night and grows to a red-hot blaze by the morning. So it is that the heat of the people's deception, at last, comes forth in violent behavior.

7:6 *Their plot smolders.* The MT reads, "their baker sleeps." The difficulty in understanding who the baker is and why he slept while the fire grew hotter has led to a repointing of the Hebrew. The NLT seemingly draws the idea of plotting from "intrigue" in the previous line and follows the lead of the Syriac and the Targum by reading *'appehem* [TH639, ZH678] ("nose"; figurative of anger; cf. NASB, RSV, NIV, ESV) rather than the MT's *'opehem* [TH644A, ZH685] ("baker"; cf. NASB mg; NLT mg). This involves no change in the consonantal text of the MT.

7:8 *half-baked cake!* Lit., "a cake not turned." If the imagery here builds on the previous simile, the flat cakes are those pressed upon the oven wall. Left unturned, the bread would be burned on the one side and doughy on the other. The imagery, however, may envision cakes laid on hot stones (1 Kgs 19:6). Thus, A. Ross explains, "The stones would be well-heated, the cinders knocked off, and then the cakes laid on the stones and covered with ashes. Later the ashes would be removed and the cake turned over (7:8) to obtain a balanced baking" (NIDOTTE 4.434).

7:9 *hair is gray.* As hair gradually turns gray (almost imperceptibly) with age, so Israel seems unaware of its ever-increasing inner wickedness.

7:11 *like silly, witless doves.* Israel's foreign policy was likened to a dove that flutters about erratically.

7:12 *like a bird from the sky.* As a fowler brings down a bird from the sky, so God would bring Israel down; God's people are doomed.

for all the evil they do. Lit., "according to the report to their assembly." The NLT emends the MT (within the constraints of the context) by reading the consonants as *'al-ra'atam* [TH5921/7451B, ZH6584/8288] instead of the MT's *la'adatam* [TH3807.1/5712, ZH4200/6337] (cf. Wolff 1974:107). This change involves the transposition of the letters resh and ayin and the replacement of a resh (ר) in the MT with a daleth (ד) (resh and daleth were often confused; see the note on 7:14). Several other suggested emendations have been put forward (cf. Stuart 1987:115-116; Andersen and Freedman 1980:471).

If the MT is to be retained, God's punishment of Israel will proceed on the basis of "a report that will come to the community" (McComiskey 1992:112). Keil (1954:109), however, suggests that the report is one already known to the congregation, being written in the law (Lev 26:14-35; Deut 28:15-68) and proclaimed often by God's prophets.

7:13 *What sorrow awaits those who have deserted me!* The NLT catches well the force of the MT, which casts these final verses in the form of a woe oracle: "Woe to them, for they have strayed from me."

told lies. The charge repeats the notice that Samaria is filled with liars (7:1).

7:14 *They cut themselves.* The NLT (like the RSV, ESV) follows the reading of the LXX (Gr., *katetemnonto*) and numerous Hebrew mss that read the root *gadad* [TH1413, ZH1517] here rather than *garar* [TH1481, ZH1591] (drag away) found in the MT (cf. HALOT 1.204), which is usually rendered as "assemble themselves" (or similarly, cf. NASB; NIV) and creates an unintelligible reading. Similar cultic lacerations are recorded of the prophets of Baal and Asherah on Mount Carmel (1 Kgs 18:28).

grain and new wine. For the significance of grain and wine, see comments on Joel 1:10. God here repeats his earlier charge against his people (cf. 2:8).

7:16 *They look everywhere except to the Most High.* The opening line is terse and notoriously difficult. It has occasioned various emendations. The NLT follows the common suggestion of understanding the *'al* after *lo'* [TH3808, ZH4202] (except) to be the substantive *'al* [TH5920, ZH6583], meaning "that which is alone on high" (cf. 11:7; 2 Sam 23:1; Laetsch 1956:65). The normal noun for "Most High" is *'elyon* [TH5945B, ZH6610], although the Canaanite *'ly* has often been suggested for some OT texts (cf. Dahood 1953:452-457). Andersen and Freedman (1980:477) propose that the MT's *lo' 'al* means "no god" (cf. LXX, "nothing"), a derogatory epithet referring to Baal. Idolatry is often condemned in the OT as a worthless worshiping of that which is not a god (e.g., Deut 32:21; Isa 37:19; 44:9-20; Jer 16:20).

as a crooked bow. Lit., "as a loose bow." This simile compares the policies of Israel's leadership to a bow that has lost its tension and hence cannot hit its mark. The NLT envisions a crooked bow, which yields the same result.

the people of Egypt will laugh at them. S. M. Paul (1995:707-712) makes the interesting suggestion that the Israelite ambassadors who were carrying on negotiations with Egyptian officials will be mocked because of their crude attempts to speak in Egyptian. Their efforts would likewise amount to little more than meaningless gibberish.

COMMENTARY

Hosea recorded God's great disappointment and frustration with his people. Despite all that he had done for them and despite the constant warnings that the Lord's prophets had delivered, God's people remained spiritually unmoved. Like Adam, they were covenant-breakers. In an extended series of graphic similes, the sinful nature and deeds of God's people are presented. Israel's love for God was as ephemeral and fleeting as the morning mist and early dew, which disappear with the rising sun (6:4). Feigning continued devotion to God, the citizenry, leaders and people alike, had gone after other gods (6:10; cf. 7:9, 10, 14). God wanted their heartfelt affection, and he wanted them to know him experientially. Mere ritual sacrifice would not do (6:6).

Indeed, lackluster love had caused Israel to perpetuate all manner of wickedness. Their society abounded with thievery and robbery. Even the priests behaved like marauding brigands waylaying devotees on the highway to Shechem. Thereby they reproduced the same evil associated with that city (6:9; cf. Gen 34). All of this took place despite God's longing to restore and bless his people (6:11b).

In another simile, God warned his people that judgment was coming, as surely as day follows night (6:5). Adopting an agricultural metaphor, God called that judgment a harvest—a harvest of punishment for Israel (6:11a).

God's charges against Israel continue in chapter 7, this portion again being laced with a string of powerful similes. Having termed Samaria (capital of the northern kingdom and representative of the whole) a bunch of liars, thieves, and bandits (7:1), God told them that he had seen all of it (7:2). Therefore, he would punish them for their wickedness. Indeed, debauchery haunted the highest places of state; the whole royal household was infected. Not content with crimes of deceit and thievery, God's people were filled with adulterous passion. Their lustful hearts were likened to an oven that is kept aflame, even though it should have been banked while the dough was rising (7:4).

Moreover, the kingdom was ablaze with intrigue like a fiery furnace. Such plotting was like a fire which, having smoldered all night, burns with raging fire by morning. Certainly such political deceit, together with plots and counterplots, marked the closing years of the northern kingdom. After the death of Jeroboam II in 752 BC, six kings occupied the throne in the space of 30 years. Only Menahem escaped a violent end, and he himself was an assassin (2 Kgs 15:13-14, 16-22). Some of the intrigue was occasioned by Israel's vacillating foreign policy. Kings were often deposed and killed in accordance with the prevailing pro- or anti-Assyrian sentiment (2 Kgs 15:19-20, 29-30; 17:3-6; cf. my remarks in Patterson and Austel 1988:236-237, 239-240).

Israel's uneven attempts at dealing with the rising power of Assyria (see commentary on 5:8-13) not only weakened its spiritual and moral fiber (7:8) but would ultimately destroy the nation (7:16). Israel's moral condition was likened to baking bread in an ancient oven without turning it, leaving it burnt on one side and doughy on the other. Like the worthless half-baked bread, so Israel's conduct had no redeeming value. Spiritually, the dangers that they had forged for themselves by worshiping foreign gods had weakened the soul and strength of the nation. Like an aging man who ignores the graying of his hair, blissfully unaware of his diminishing strength, so Israel's spiritual prostitution had robbed it of the vitality to sustain itself.

How foolish Israel's foreign policy had been! Flitting back and forth like directionless doves, they turned to the powers of the day, Egypt and Assyria (cf. 2 Kgs 17:2-4). But like a flying bird, which the fowler traps with his net, so God would bring his people down because of all their evil (7:11-12).

The chapter closes with the only woe oracle in the book (7:13-16). God assured his wicked and apostate people that they would be horribly punished. Despite his longing for them and desire to bring them back to himself, they had been insincere toward him. For they had lacerated themselves in meaningless rituals aimed at securing the fertility of the land. How foolish! It was Yahweh, not Baal or the other so-called gods, who had sustained them all along the way. Rather than calling on him in trouble (cf. Ps 69:17-18), they turned everywhere but to the true God. Accordingly, like a bow that had lost its proper tension so that the archer cannot hit his mark, their deceitful policies would fall back upon them. Those in whom they had placed their trust would prove to be their executioners (cf. 2 Kgs 17:5-6). This would be the reward of their unfaithfulness, for they had treated their Redeemer and Helper most insolently. Moreover, the very ones to whom they turned for sustenance would laugh at them. How tragic are the fruits of disloyalty and disobedience! Unrealistically thinking to define God for themselves, they had thrown away the one who alone is ultimately real. Thus Pusey (1953:78) observes, "All God's creatures are made for His glory, and on earth, chiefly man; and among men, chiefly those whom He had chosen as His people. In that, then, they set themselves to diminish that glory, giving to idols, they, as far as in them lay, *devised evil against Him. Man would dethrone God, if he could."*

This section details many of the dangers inherent in turning away from a wise and holy God. Covenant-breaking Israel cast off its proper allegiance to the Lord in favor of what was at best a dead orthodoxy mingled with pagan ritual. The results would prove to be disastrous. From top to bottom, Israelite society became plagued with all manner of crimes. Corporately and individually, the abandonment of God's standards of righteousness for the pursuit of pagan beliefs brought morality to a new low. Deceit, intrigues, adultery, prostitution, and drunken revelry were rampant. By bringing Yahweh down to the level of Baal, God's people were deceiving themselves in the pursuit of sensual pleasures.

Such is the fate of any nation or society that abandons the true revelation of God so as to recreate him in its own selfish image and exchange pleasure for God's guidance (Prov 11:14; 14:34; 29:18; Isa 2:1-6). Paul predicted that such an egoistic hedonism would be a distinguishing mark of earth's final era before the return of Christ (2 Tim 3:1-5).

Indeed, when people abandon God and his standards for their own self-gratification, the pursuit of pleasure too often becomes a dominating purpose. Not only unbelievers but Christians can be thus afflicted. For it is all too easy for people to fall into a daily routine that takes God for granted and superimposes personal desires upon a professed orthodoxy. Paul reminded the believers that such unchristian behavior ought not to mark those who have come to faith in Christ (Titus 3:1-8).

The Scriptures warn that the pursuit of pleasure can choke out the effectiveness of prayer (Jas 4:3) and God's Word (Luke 8:14) in one's personal life. Even Christian gatherings can be corrupted by the indulgence of worldly pleasures (2 Pet 2:13). How much better for the believer to live a life of faith that chooses (as did Moses) to live for God and be identified with those who love him, rather than follow the temporary pleasures of sin (Heb 11:25). Believers do well to remember that the pursuit of aimless, self-indulgent, sinful pleasure is a mark of the fool (Prov 10:23; Eccl 7:4) and can easily lead to poverty (Prov 21:17). The verdict of the wise author of Ecclesiastes was that pleasure as an end in itself "was all so meaningless—like chasing the wind" (Eccl 2:11). How much better, then, for nations, societies, and individuals to desire the true and eternal pleasures that God gives to his faithful followers (Ps 33:12).

◆ ## B. Further Charges against Israel (8:1–11:11)
1. Israel is a covenant-breaker (8:1–14)

[1] "Sound the alarm!
The enemy descends like an eagle on
the people of the LORD,
for they have broken my covenant
and revolted against my law.
[2] Now Israel pleads with me,

'Help us, for you are our God!'
[3] But it is too late.
The people of Israel have rejected
what is good,
and now their enemies will chase
after them.

⁴The people have appointed kings
     without my consent,
     and princes without my knowledge.
 By making idols for themselves from
     their silver and gold,
     they have brought about their own
     destruction.

⁵"O Samaria, I reject this calf—
     this idol you have made.
 My fury burns against you.
     How long will you be incapable
     of innocence?
⁶This calf you worship, O Israel,
     was crafted by your own hands!
 It is not God!
     Therefore, it must be smashed
     to bits.

⁷"They have planted the wind
     and will harvest the whirlwind.
 The stalks of grain wither
     and produce nothing to eat.
 And even if there is any grain,
     foreigners will eat it.
⁸The people of Israel have been
     swallowed up;
     they lie among the nations like an
     old discarded pot.
⁹Like a wild donkey looking for a mate,
     they have gone up to Assyria.

The people of Israel* have sold
     themselves—
     sold themselves to many lovers.
¹⁰But though they have sold themselves
     to many allies,
 I will now gather them together for
     judgment.
 Then they will writhe
     under the burden of the great king.

¹¹"Israel has built many altars to take
     away sin,
     but these very altars became places
     for sinning!
¹²Even though I gave them all my laws,
     they act as if those laws don't apply
     to them.
¹³The people of Israel love their rituals
     of sacrifice,
     but to me their sacrifices are all
     meaningless.
 I will hold my people accountable for
     their sins,
     and I will punish them.
 They will return to Egypt.
¹⁴Israel has forgotten its Maker and
     built great palaces,
     and Judah has fortified its cities.
 Therefore, I will send down fire on
     their cities
     and will burn up their fortresses."

8:9 Hebrew *Ephraim*, referring to the northern kingdom of Israel; also in 8:11.

NOTES

8:1 *Sound the alarm!* Lit., "A horn to your palate!" The NLT renders according to the sense of the image. The trumpeter is instructed to put the horn to his mouth/lips to sound the alarm in the face of imminent danger. "Palate" is a metonymy for mouth/lips and occurs in parallel with the lip in Prov 5:3 and 8:7. This first subunit (8:1-3) closes with a further note concerning the invader.

The enemy descends like an eagle on the people of the LORD. Lit., "like an eagle/vulture on the house of the LORD." The sentence is elliptical and beset with difficulties. Since the second half of the verse charges the people with covenant violation, "house" must be viewed as a metaphor for those who inhabit the land, which is threatened with danger. Thus, the land where God and his covenant people dwell is also metaphorically called a "house." Jeremiah (Jer 2:7) similarly charges Judah with defiling "my land."

8:3 *what is good.* The people's preoccupation with Baal had made them lose intimate contact with the ultimate good, God himself, and his goodness to them. See commentary on 3:1-5.

8:5 *O Samaria . . . this calf.* Lit., "your calf, O Samaria." Since no calf is known to have been erected in the city of Samaria, it is best to understand that by saying "Samaria," Hosea was pointing to the whole northern kingdom (cf. 1 Kgs 13:32). The calves were set up in Dan and Bethel (1 Kgs 12:25-33).

8:6 *This calf . . . crafted by your own hands!* Lit., "for [it is] from Israel and it a craftsman makes." The NLT rendering captures the sense. The pronoun "it" stands at the head of its clause in anticipatory emphasis—the objective pronoun with the verb being viewed as resumptive. For such constructions, see Waltke and O'Connor 1990:75-76, 529. I owe the term "anticipatory emphasis" to Gardiner (1957:114-116), who cites numerous examples from ancient Egyptian as well as modern languages. See also the note on v. 8.

8:7 *planted the wind . . . harvest the whirlwind.* The imagery suggests that what Israel has done will come back on them with overwhelming force (McComiskey 1992:128).

stalks of grain wither . . . even if there is any grain. Such a construction is termed a pseudo-sorites, "in which the speaker says that event A will not happen but even if it did, it would be undone by event B" (Garrett 1997:184).

8:8 *like an old discarded pot.* Lit., "like a vessel, there is no pleasure in it." The NLT has rendered the force of the sentence well.

8:9 *Like a wild donkey looking for a mate.* Similarly, God charged Israel with being unable to keep itself from seeking foreign alliances.

8:10 *the great king.* Lit., "the king of princes." Isaiah (Isa 10:8) represents the Assyrian king as boasting that his commanders were all kings in their own right. Assyrian local officials often styled themselves as kings.

8:13 *their sacrifices are all meaningless.* Because Israel's sinful observances had become mere rituals and were laced with the syncretistic worship of Baal, the sacrifices made to God were contrary to Mosaic law in spirit and form and hence unacceptable to him (cf. Isa 1:11-14).

will return to Egypt. Garrett (1997:188) properly observes, "Reference to 'Egypt' here does not mean that all the people would literally return to Egypt (although some did). It is a reversal of the Exodus and implies removal from the land and nullification of covenant promises." See Deut 28:68.

COMMENTARY

God first warned his people through Hosea that judgment was imminent—he was already preparing the enemy for invasion. The people deserved judgment because they were proven covenant-breakers. They had failed to uphold the divine standards both in form and in spirit. In their syncretism, they deceived themselves, for they rejected him who is the ultimate good. In so doing, they rejected all the blessings that come from allowing his Spirit to regulate their lives (cf. 4:6-7).

The Lord then went on to note a further area of Israel's culpability. In their internal political proceedings, they had chosen godless leaders for themselves, neither seeking God's advice nor gaining his approval. Furthermore, they persisted in the abominable worship of the golden calves at Dan and Bethel. Even Jehu's purging of Baalism did nothing to eradicate Jeroboam I's established state religion (2 Kgs 10:28-29). Moreover, after Jehu, devotion to Baal quickly returned in full vigor—if indeed it ever lost its fascination to the bulk of the population. Their worship of a god of their own making, who was no god at all, was both foolish and condemnable (8:4-6).

In a third divine oracle (8:7-10) Israel's tragic course of conduct is picturesquely presented by means of several figures. Israel's external political policies are condemned as sheer folly. Its constant maneuvering so as to woo various foreign powers, particularly Assyria, is portrayed as sowing a wind that becomes a tempest of trouble. Those nations whose favor Israel curried will turn out to be its invaders. So complete will the despoiling of the country be that all the produce of their land will be eaten by foreigners. The fate of the nation is also likened to an old discarded pot.

How stupid the Lord's people had been! Like a lusting wild donkey, Israel had sought the affections of other nations, particularly Assyria (cf. 2 Kgs 17:3-4). The heavy cost to the citizens of the northern kingdom incurred by Menahem's submission to Tiglath-pileser III during the Assyrian king's first campaign may be intended here.[1] God informed his people that he was about to gather them for judgment at the hands of the very Assyrians with whom they had cast their lot.

In a final movement (8:11-14), God returned to the matter of Israel's spiritual infidelity. Whatever worship they engaged in was done at altars polluted with the syncretistic worship of Baal and the immoral practices carried out there. Even the multiplication of altars was expressly forbidden in the law (Deut 12:4-7). Once again (cf. 8:1) Israel was shown to be a covenant-breaker. It is no wonder, then, that God would no longer condone their sacrifices or worship rites (6:4-10; cf. Isa 1:5-15). Nothing short of actual captivity would bring his people to their senses. Nothing could forestall their fate even though they might falsely take pride in their fortified cities and citadels. Rather, the invader's fire would destroy them all.

This final judgment oracle emphasizes the consequences of disloyalty to God and his word. Where the Lord and the Scriptures are cast aside in the life of the believer or the church, there is a heavy penalty to pay. Halfhearted allegiance to Christ is insufficient, for Jesus himself declared, "All who love me will do what I say" (John 14:23). Where God and the Bible are made the center of one's life, there can be no other course but that of submission to the Lord both in faith and practice, come what may (see commentary on Hab 3:16-19). All of life becomes permeated by the presence of the indwelling Christ and the high ethical and moral standards of the Word of God. All of one's life takes on proper perspective so that the believer truly experiences life as God intends.

This chapter also reminds the believer of the folly of making common cause with the purveyors of the unrighteousness so rampant in the secular world. Believers do not solve problems by abandoning God and his standards in order to seek counsel and help from those who would lead them away from God and his word. Individuals and churches must also be cautious in their use of secular methodologies. The apostle Paul declared that he did not use worldly wisdom in his planning and activities (2 Cor 1:12, 17-18; 5:16). How easy it is to compromise a little here and a little there and then pursue a path that, although it seems to lead to instant success and gratification, ends in the fire of God's judgment.

What is true of individuals and churches is also true of nations (see commentary on 6:4-7:16). For a nation to abandon God and his standards is to court disaster and join the long list of those prosperous and seemingly invincible nations that have risen to fame, held power for a time, and then succumbed. Rather, it remains true that godliness exalts a nation, but sin is a disgrace to any people (Prov 14:34; cf. Ps 33:12).[2]

ENDNOTES

1. J. B. Payne (*Encyclopedia of Biblical Prophecy* [New York: Harper & Row, 1973], 404), however, suggests Tiglath-pileser's second western campaign. The NLT rendering illustrates Garrett's proposal (1997:186) that Israel is behaving like a man "who tries to gain love by giving money to prostitutes, only to discover that he has both squandered his money and gained no love in return." Israel's flirtation with Assyria is well documented not only in the OT but in the Assyrian Annals. See, for example, Jehu's tribute to Shalmaneser III: "Tribute of Iawa [Jehu], son of Omri" (Luckenbill 1927:211).

2. Fausset (1948:488) remarks, "Whenever professing believers, instead of making God their confidence, have recourse to the godless world and its unhallowed powers, at the cost of religious principle, to save them from anticipated evils, God, in just retribution, makes those very world powers the instruments of executing His judgments on them."

◆   ## 2. Hosea's reaction: Israel is doomed (9:1-9)

¹O people of Israel,
  do not rejoice as other nations do.
For you have been unfaithful to
    your God,
    hiring yourselves out like prostitutes,
    worshiping other gods on every
      threshing floor.
²So now your harvests will be too small
    to feed you.
  There will be no grapes for making
    new wine.
³You may no longer stay here in the
    LORD's land.
  Instead, you will return to Egypt,
  and in Assyria you will eat food
    that is ceremonially unclean.
⁴There you will make no offerings of
    wine to the LORD.
  None of your sacrifices there will
    please him.
  They will be unclean, like food touched
    by a person in mourning.
  All who present such sacrifices will
    be defiled.
  They may eat this food themselves,
    but they may not offer it to the LORD.
⁵What then will you do on festival days?
  How will you observe the LORD's
    festivals?

⁶Even if you escape destruction from
    Assyria,
  Egypt will conquer you, and
    Memphis* will bury you.
  Nettles will take over your treasures
    of silver;
    thistles will invade your ruined
      homes.

⁷The time of Israel's punishment has
    come;
  the day of payment is here.
  Soon Israel will know this all too
    well.
  Because of your great sin and hostility,
    you say, "The prophets are crazy
    and the inspired men are fools!"
⁸The prophet is a watchman over Israel*
    for my God,
  yet traps are laid for him wherever
    he goes.
  He faces hostility even in the house
    of God.
⁹The things my people do are as
    depraved
    as what they did in Gibeah long ago.
  God will not forget.
  He will surely punish them for
    their sins.

9:6 Memphis was the capital of northern Egypt.   9:8 Hebrew *Ephraim*, referring to the northern kingdom of Israel; also in 9:11, 13, 16.

NOTES

9:1 rejoice as other nations do. Lit., "Do not rejoice, O Israel, unto exultation as the peoples [do]." The NLT combines "rejoice" and "exultation" of the Hebrew text into one thought. The MT's *'el gil ka'ammim* [TH1524A/5971A, ZH1637/6639] (unto exultation as the nations) is altered by some scholars (e.g., Stuart 1987:14) who redivide the consonantal text so as to read *'al gileka 'ammim* (do not shout for joy, my people) or emend *'el gil* to read *'al tagel* [TH408/1524A, ZH440/1637] ("do not exult"; Wolff 1974:149; cf. LXX, Vulgate, NRSV). The MT is defensible, however, and should be understood as continuing the negation of the previous clause: "do not rejoice" (*'al tismah*). McComiskey (1992:136) points to similar phraseology in Job 3:22: *hassemekhim 'ele-gil*, "those who exceedingly rejoice."

hiring yourselves out like prostitutes. Hosea's remarks serve as a connection to the previous oracle (cf. 8:9, 13), as do the mention of harvests in 9:2 (cf. 8:7) and the exile of the people in 9:3 (cf. 8:13).

9:2 harvests . . . grapes. Lit., "threshing floor and wine vat . . . new wine." The NLT catches the intention of the prophet's words. The products of the field and vineyard were the gracious bestowal of God upon a loyal people. Their withholding was a sign of divine chastisement (see notes and commentary on Joel 1:7, 9, 10) and warned of possible invasion and captivity (cf. Deut 28:38-41, 49-51).

9:4 They will be unclean, like food touched by a person in mourning. The law with regard to eating the bread of affliction had to do especially with bread eaten at funeral meals (Deut 26:14). It was regarded as unclean because all who came in contact with the house were defiled by the presence of the corpse. The captivity will be like a condition of mourning. Laetsch (1956:73) suggests, however, a different legal precedent: "All food which was not sanctified to the Lord by the presentation of the firstfruits was unclean food to Israel (Exod 22:29; 23:19; 34:22, 26; Lev 23:10-12, 15-17). In the heathen lands Levitically clean food could hardly be obtained."

9:6 Even if you escape destruction from Assyria. Lit., "for behold they have gone from destruction." The NLT follows the lead of many translations and expositors in rendering this as a conditional clause detailing an unlikely occurrence ("Even if"). The syntax of the MT, however, suggests that this clause should be read as a prophetic perfect, a future event that is viewed as having already taken place. The prophet's words were predictive: Covenant-breaking Israel would go into exile amidst the destruction of their land.

Memphis. The word *mop* [TH4644, ZH5132] is used here rather than the usual *nop* [TH5297, ZH5862] (cf. Isa 19:13; Jer 2:16; 44:1; Ezek 30:13, 16). The Egyptian name for Memphis (*mn nfr*) owes its origin to the pyramid and city of the sixth-dynasty pharaoh Pepi I, who reigned in Memphis in the third millennium BC. The name may have meant "[Pepi is] established [and] beautiful" (Gardiner 1957:183). Always a major city in Egypt and traditionally an administrative capital, it fell to the Assyrian king Esarhaddon (681–668 BC) in 671 BC.

Although some (e.g., McComiskey 1992:141, 188) understand the reference to Egypt and Memphis as mere metaphors for the future captivity in Assyria, it is instructive that Jewish refugees from the Babylonian conquest of Jerusalem did seek asylum in Memphis (Jer 44:1).

Nettles . . . thistles. The NLT renders the syntactical force of the anticipatory emphasis in the MT: "As for their silver and valuables, briers/nettles will possess them [and] thorns/brambles [will be] in their tents." The point is that God's people will be despoiled and left desolate (cf. Keil 1954:122).

9:7 prophets are crazy . . . inspired men are fools! "Inspired men" is lit., "men of the spirit." God's prophets were often condemned as madmen and fools (e.g., 2 Kgs 9:11;

Jer 29:26). Covenant-breaking Israel's taunts against God's prophets were "rooted in the magnitude of their sins' guiltiness and their 'hostility'" (Stuart 1987:146).

9:8 *The prophet is a watchman.* The OT prophets were often likened to watchmen (e.g., Jer 6:17; Ezek 3:17; 33:2, 6-7; see note on Hab 2:1).

9:9 *Gibeah.* The reference is to the horrors surrounding the rape and murder of the Levite's concubine in the days of the judges (Judg 19-21). See commentary on 10:9-11.

COMMENTARY

Hosea's response to God's message in 8:1-14 was in full agreement with the Lord's condemnation of Israel. As God had charged, Israel had been disloyal to its Lord. Spiritually and politically, Israel was a transgressor. In a forceful simile, the conduct of the people was likened to that of a prostitute. Israel appeared to be ready to receive and submit to any god other than the true God. Therefore, in keeping with his covenant with them the Lord would bring decreased productivity to the land. The reduction of grain and wine should stand as a warning to Israel of God's displeasure with their disobedience (9:1-2).

Not only that, but continued disloyalty would lead to Israel's captivity. There they would not be able even to offer the sacrifices that they now take so lightly. God's people faced the imminent threat of exile to Assyria and the likelihood that many of them would die. Some would perish in a vain attempt to avoid capture by fleeing to Egypt. Again and again, God had sent his prophets to his people, commissioning them to serve as watchmen warning of approaching danger—all to no avail. For in callous disdain, even sheer hatred, the citizenry had branded them as madmen and sought to do them harm. There was no safety for God's servants even in the house of the Lord.

Yet what God's messengers reported would come to pass. For in God's sight, Israel's spiritual and moral condition was as vile as that of all those responsible for what occurred in Gibeah so long ago when the Levite's concubine was raped, murdered, and dismembered (Judg 19). God could not overlook the guilt of Hosea's Israel either. He would deal severely with them because of their sins (9:3-9; cf. 7:2).

The issues presented here have come up before. Thus, Hosea's condemnation of Israel's covenant unfaithfulness (e.g., 2:18-23; 4:1, 12; 5:4-7; 6:7; 8:1-6) and idolatrous worship practices (e.g., 4:14-19; 5:1; 8:4-6) is a familiar theme. The former has too easily led to the latter; both are labeled "prostitution," a term that implies spiritual unfaithfulness, religious egocentrism, and moral perversion (see, e.g., 4:10-19; 5:3-4; 6:10). Hosea brought them together here to point out that Israel's sin stemmed basically from its low view of God. In this, Israel had followed the shameful practices of non-revealed religion and reproduced sin in its basic form: the rejection of God's rightful place as sovereign over people's lives, whether individually or corporately (cf. Exod 20:3; Deut 6:4-6; Mark 12:28-30; Luke 10:25-28; 1 John 5:21).[1]

Likewise, Hosea repeatedly recorded God's denunciation of Israel's flirtation with the surrounding nations (e.g., 5:13-15; 7:8-16; 8:8-10). Then he pointed out the end result of such foolish preoccupation. They would go into captivity and, tragically, they would not be able to offer proper sacrifices to the Lord. This would violate Mosaic regulations in several ways. First, they would eat food that would be regarded as unclean, thereby rendering themselves unclean (Lev 11; 14:1-21).[2] Second, because there would not be a properly sanctioned site to worship the Lord where sacrifices could be presented to him (cf. Lev 1:3; 3:1-2; 4:4, 13-14; 5:5-6; 6:14, 25; 7:1-2), the sacrifices would be unacceptable. This being the case, contact with the slain sacrificial animals would also render the offerers impure and their sacrifice unacceptable. Third, many of them would die in exile. Mosaic law specified that contact with the dead, whether animals or humans, rendered the person ritually unclean (Lev 11:24, 28, 35-40; Num 19:11-22). Because the specified purification procedures could not be observed, the uncleanness would remain.

Hosea spoke of the bread of mourning (9:4). Periods of mourning could be observed for various reasons such as sorrow in response to an announcement of judgment (Ezek 7:27; Joel 2:12-14) or contrition for sinning against God (Ezra 10:6). Wicked Haman grieved over his humiliation at the hands of Mordecai, whom he hated (Esth 6:12). David mourned his separation from his fleeing son Absalom (2 Sam 13:37). Even nature is said to mourn due to God's judgment (4:3; Joel 1:10). The greatest sorrow came from the death of a loved one (2 Sam 1:17-27; 19:1-4). In connection with the Mosaic law regarding the triennial tithe, the offerer was to declare concerning it, "I have not eaten any of it while in mourning; I have not handled it while I was ceremonially unclean; and I have not offered any of it to the dead" (Deut 26:14). Hosea's mentioning of "food touched by a person in mourning" may well have some allusion to this Deuteronomic legislation (McComiskey 1992:140).

Hosea's words are instructive. No mere carrying out of sacrificial ritual is pleasing to the Lord. Those who would truly worship God must come to him in purity and sincerity of heart (Ps 24:3-6; John 4:24). Where sin clutters the life, it must be confessed and God's forgiveness sought (Ps 51:1-12; Matt 6:12; Jas 4:7-10; 1 John 1:8-9). Thank God that One has come and offered the perfect sacrifice by which the believer may have full access to God's presence (Heb 10:19-22). Indeed, in him alone can the mourner find true comfort (Isa 61:1-2) and a life of full productivity and satisfaction both for one's self and, more importantly, for God.

ENDNOTES

1. Thus M. Erickson (*Christian Theology* [Grand Rapids: Baker, 1987], 580) rightly points out, "Anyone who truly believes God to be what he says he is will accord to him his rightful status. Failure to do so is sin. Setting one's own ideas above God's revealed Word entails refusal to believe it to be true. Seeking one's own will involves believing that one's own values are actually higher than those of God. In short, it is failing to acknowledge God as God."
2. The need to retain dietary purity figures prominently in the biblical account of Daniel and his three friends (Dan 1:8-16) and in the intertestamental story of Judith (Jdt 11:11-15; 12:1-4).

◆   3. Israel is an unprofitable plant (9:10-17)

¹⁰The LORD says, "O Israel, when I first
        found you,
    it was like finding fresh grapes in
        the desert.
When I saw your ancestors,
    it was like seeing the first ripe
        figs of the season.
But then they deserted me for
        Baal-peor,
    giving themselves to that shameful
        idol.
Soon they became vile,
    as vile as the god they worshiped.
¹¹The glory of Israel will fly away like
        a bird,
    for your children will not be born
or grow in the womb
    or even be conceived.
¹²Even if you do have children who
        grow up,
    I will take them from you.
It will be a terrible day when I turn
        away
    and leave you alone.
¹³I have watched Israel become as
        beautiful as Tyre.

But now Israel will bring out her
        children for slaughter."

¹⁴O LORD, what should I request for
        your people?
    I will ask for wombs that don't
        give birth
    and breasts that give no milk.

¹⁵The LORD says, "All their wickedness
        began at Gilgal;
    there I began to hate them.
I will drive them from my land
    because of their evil actions.
I will love them no more
    because all their leaders are rebels.
¹⁶The people of Israel are struck down.
    Their roots are dried up,
    and they will bear no more fruit.
And if they give birth,
    I will slaughter their beloved
        children."

¹⁷My God will reject the people of Israel
    because they will not listen or obey.
They will be wanderers,
    homeless among the nations.

NOTES

9:10 *fresh grapes . . . first ripe figs.* Grapes and figs figure prominently in expressions concerning the covenantal relation between God and his people, especially under the image of the vine and the fig tree (see note and commentary on Joel 1:7). God's early contact with his people was one of fresh vitality and joy.

Baal-peor. Israel's flirtation with the fertility god Baal came about as a result of Balaam's failed attempts to pronounce the doom of Israel (Num 22–24). When the hireling prophet was unable to curse Israel, "[He] showed Balak how to trip up the people of Israel. He taught them to sin by eating food offered to idols and by committing sexual sin" (Rev 2:14; cf. Num 25:1-3; 31:16). Israel's sin brought about the death of thousands of people (Num 25:4-9).

vile as the god they worshiped. Lit., "detestable as their love." Israel's fascination with the Baal rites and the resultant lust in their lives made their capacity to love and their expressions of love debased. "The Hebrew language is hard-pressed to come up with a more degrading term to describe the depths to which Israel's initial and continued contact with Baal had lowered them" (Hubbard 1989:165).

9:12 *Even if you do have children who grow up.* Hosea again employed the pseudo-sorites (see note on 8:7). Whatever children managed to survive death in the womb or at birth would die prematurely.

9:13 *I have watched Israel become . . . as Tyre.* The rendering of the first half of v. 13 is uncertain. Nearly every word in the line has been contested. The problem is as old as the

LXX, which envisions Ephraim giving its children over to be like hunted beasts. The Vulgate treats the line in similar fashion to the NLT: "As I saw [it] was founded in beauty." Great variation exists among the modern translations and commentators, with many proposed emendations. Particularly troublesome is the Hebrew *tsor* [TH6865A, ZH7450] which has been understood as either the Phoenician city Tyre or as a palm tree (from Arabic *tsawr*), or has been emended to read *tsayid* [TH6718, ZH7473] (a hunt) or *tsur* [TH6697, ZH7446] (rock). Because the line must make tolerable sense for that which follows, the NLT is not without merit, although it too depends on some emendation.

Retaining the consonants of the MT while reading *tsur* [TH6696, ZH7443] ("to lay siege"; see HALOT 3.1015) rather than *tsor* (Tyre), and recognizing the parallelism between this word and the *lehotsi'* [TH3318, ZH3655] (to lead out) of the next line, it is possible that the intended meaning of the whole verse is something like: "Even as I chose Ephraim [= Israel] *to lay siege* to that which was planted in pasture land [= the land of Canaan], so I have chosen Ephraim to bring out its sons to the slayer." So understood, the verse reminds the Israelites that it was God who gave them the land of Canaan and who will also take it from them in bloody warfare.

9:14 *what should I request for your people?* Hosea responded to the Lord's oracle with a rhetorical question. He would answer it himself, for he knew what he would do if it were up to him.

wombs that don't give birth . . . breasts that give no milk. Hosea's comments amount to a reversal of the ancient blessing for fertility given in Gen 49:25. See the excellent discussion by Krause (1992:191-202). Essentially, God's prophet came to agree with the divine sentiment. "There had been a hundred last chances but none had done any good; finally the line had to be drawn. And so Hosea changes his prayer: he concurs with the divine words and asks that they be fulfilled" (Craigie 1985:62).

9:15 *All their wickedness began at Gilgal.* After God's people clamored for an earthly king rather than having just a God in heaven (1 Sam 8:4-22), Saul was eventually confirmed as king at Gilgal (1 Sam 11:14-15). It was also there that God rejected Saul as king due to his disobedience (1 Sam 15:10-29). The city later became a cult center (cf. 4:15; 12:11). Gilgal thus epitomizes God's condemnation of Israel: Israel's political and religious leadership had led the people down a path of irreversible doom.

9:16 *The people of Israel.* Lit., "Ephraim."

will bear no more fruit. Stuart (1987:154) suggests a possible literary pun here that plays on the name "Ephraim" and the word for "fruit" (*peri* [TH6529, ZH7262]): "Ephraim the 'doubly fruitful' (cf. Gen 41:52) is now Ephraim the completely fruitless."

if they give birth. In yet another pseudo-sorites, Hosea reemphasized the terrible pronouncement of 9:11-13.

9:17 *My God will reject the people of Israel.* Here again Hosea interacted with God's reiteration of the awful loss of an Israelite generation. Israel's disobedience would lead them to be dislodged from their homeland so as to live as displaced wanderers in many foreign lands (cf. Gen 4:13-14).

COMMENTARY

This section contains a dialogue between the Lord and his prophet. The Lord spoke first. He began by resuming his denunciation of the northern kingdom. He reminded them of those earliest days when he and his people lived together in pristine purity. There was a freshness and vitality to their relationship that could be likened to finding grapes in the wilderness unexpectedly or discovering the season's first ripe figs. How refreshing was their fellowship then!

Yet they soon turned their backs on him for another. At Peor they became fascinated with Baal. When Balaam failed, in four oracles, to curse Israel (Num 23–24), he suggested to Balak, the Moabite king, a way to corrupt the Israelites (Num 31:16). Surely they would respond to the licentious fertility rites associated with Baal. Further, by indulging themselves with Moabite women they would separate themselves even more from the high ethical standards and spiritual purity expected of God's covenant people. The New Testament writers called this Balaam's teaching (Rev 2:14); they condemned Balaam's willingness to earn money by doing wrong (2 Pet 2:15; cf. Jude 1:11).

The people's embrace of Baal in the northern kingdom had rendered them as corrupt as the misguided souls of that earlier day. Accordingly, God pronounced a terrible sentence: He would condemn the next generation of babies to death, either at the time of birth or within the womb. Some women would not be able to conceive. What few infants did survive would quickly face death in one way or another, with the result that their parents would be left without the joy of their children in their homes. How sad! The people whom God had brought into a land of fruitfulness and then blessed must now face invasion, exile, and the bereavement of their precious little ones.

Israel's own wickedness had made any other resolution impossible. Hosea could only concur with God's evaluation. He could pray in no other way than to ask the Lord that the women be unable to bear or nurse their children. Far better would it be not to have children at all than to experience the tragedy of miscarriage, still birth, or the death of a child.

So gravely real was the prospect of the awful sentence upon Israel and its children that God repeated it in the form of a condemnation of Israel's leadership (9:15-16). Not only at Baal-peor but also at Gilgal, Israel demonstrated its abandonment of God. For there, their demand for a king and their abnegation of the theocracy became realized. There they confirmed their choice of a king who would prove to be inept both as a political leader and spiritual example. After the split between the northern and southern kingdoms, the religious and civil leadership of the northern kingdom proved no better. Although God had blessed the people with a prosperous and fruitful land, all of that would change. The famine that he would bring to the land symbolized the greater dearth of the loss of Israel's most precious commodity: the children.

Hosea replied in kind (9:17). Because Israel rejected God, refusing to listen to him and obey his laws, God must reject them. In the foreseeable future they would be uprooted and live in exile—outcasts doomed to wander among the nations. Once again (cf. 4:18; 5:8-15; 7:15; 8:1-3, 13-14; 9:5-7) God and his prophet reminded the people that due to their sin, judgment must inevitably come. As Hubbard (1989:168) remarked, "As blood-chilling as this passage is, it serves, perhaps as forcefully as any in Scripture, to remind us of the zeal with which the Lord hates sin and the length to which he will go to purge his people of it."

Such is the sentence for any nation if, despite God's forbearance (2 Pet 3:15) and a multitude of opportunities to turn to him and establish righteousness, it fails to honor God and his laws. Such conduct only courts disaster. A message so often given ought not to be taken lightly or ignored. "If, then, God so punished the apostasy of His own elect nation, what guarantee of impunity can any Christian nation, or any individual professors, have, that they shall escape the wrath of God, if they fail to bring forth fruits consonant to their high calling? (Rom. xi, 10, 21)" (Fausset 1948:492).

◆   ## 4. Hosea's reaction: Israel is a wayward vine (10:1-8)

¹How prosperous Israel is—
a luxuriant vine loaded with fruit.
But the richer the people get,
the more pagan altars they build.
The more bountiful their harvests,
the more beautiful their sacred
pillars.
²The hearts of the people are fickle;
they are guilty and must be
punished.
The LORD will break down their altars
and smash their sacred pillars.
³Then they will say, "We have no king
because we didn't fear the LORD.
But even if we had a king,
what could he do for us anyway?"
⁴They spout empty words
and make covenants they don't
intend to keep.
So injustice springs up among them
like poisonous weeds in a farmer's
field.

⁵The people of Samaria tremble in fear
for what might happen to their calf
idol at Beth-aven.*
The people mourn and the priests wail,
because its glory will be stripped
away.*
⁶This idol will be carted away to
Assyria,
a gift to the great king there.
Ephraim will be ridiculed and Israel
will be shamed,
because its people have trusted in
this idol.
⁷Samaria and its king will be cut off;
they will float away like driftwood
on an ocean wave.
⁸And the pagan shrines of Aven,* the
place of Israel's sin, will crumble.
Thorns and thistles will grow up
around their altars.
They will beg the mountains, "Bury us!"
and plead with the hills, "Fall on us!"

10:5a *Beth-aven* means "house of wickedness"; it is being used as another name for Bethel, which means "house of God."   10:5b Or *because it will be taken away into exile.*   10:8 *Aven* is a reference to Beth-aven; see 10:5a and the note there.

NOTES

10:1 *luxuriant vine.* Hosea's metaphor is a reminder of the covenant relationship that Israel enjoyed with Yahweh (cf. Isa 5:1-7; see note on Nah 2:2 and the commentary on Joel 1:7). The NLT follows the lead of many translations that render the Hebrew participle *boqeq* [TH1238A, ZH1328] as "luxuriant" (cf. *bqq* II, HALOT 1.150). Although this meaning is unique in the OT, support among the Semitic languages may be found in the Arabic *baqqa* (be abundant). Most of the English versions, as well as the German, French, Italian and Spanish versions, the LXX, and Vulgate, handle the problem similarly. Andersen and Freedman (1980:549-550) treat the form as an active verb and take God as its subject: "He made Israel, the vine, luxuriant." Another approach has been to relate *boqeq* to the root *bqq* I [TH1238, ZH1327] (destroy), a verb that is found eight times elsewhere with negative or destructive force (cf. note on Nah 2:2). English versions that have followed this meaning include the KJV and NKJV, which lay stress on the concept of emptiness or being barren.

Commentators are divided as to the emphasis here. Many focus on the fruitfulness of the vine as pointing to Israel's prosperity (e.g., Keil 1954:128; Hubbard 1989:171). Garrett (1997:206) provides the novel suggestion that Israel is just all vine and devoid of fruit. Stuart (1987:159) proposes a double entendre here: Although "Yahweh had abundantly prospered Israel, . . . this 'vine' has not fulfilled its purpose, which was to serve its role as Yahweh's faithful people." Whatever one decides concerning the etymology and meaning of the Hebrew form, in harmony with the succeeding lines it must indicate that Israel has misspent its God-given prosperity on the idolatrous worship of foreign gods.

loaded with fruit. The form of the Hebrew verb (*shawah* [TH7737/7737A, ZH8750/8751]) has two possible meanings: "smooth/make level" or "place/set." The latter meaning is in keeping with its four occurrences in the Psalms (Pss 16:8; 21:5 [6]; 89:19 [20]; 119:30). Stuart (1987:157) favors an understanding not unlike the former alternative, proposing that this form of the verb "means basically to make something come up to par, to a level or standard it ought to meet." The NLT's rendering according to the sense of the context is most closely related to this idea. In any case, the emphasis of the metaphor is that despite the fact that conditions were favorable to good growth and good fruit (Garrett 1997:207), Israel has stored up its fruit for itself, not for God. The point of the first two lines is therefore contrastive: Israel is indeed a fruitful vine, but it lays up its treasures solely for its own ends, not God's.

10:2 hearts . . . are fickle. The verb *khalaq* [TH2505, ZH2744] (to be smooth or slippery) is frequently used of deceptive speech. Thus, it portrays the seductive words of the wayward woman (Prov 2:16; 7:5). The NLT's "fickle" captures the force of the context, which emphasizes Israel's vacillating loyalties. As Sweeney (2000:103) remarks, the Hebrew verb "conveys a sense of duplicity and divided allegiance."

break down their altars. This verb (*'arap* [TH6202, ZH6904]) occurs elsewhere of breaking the neck of an animal (Exod 13:13; 34:20).

10:4 They spout empty words and make covenants. The syntax of the MT is debated. Perhaps the best solution (and that followed by the NLT here) is that proposed long ago by Keil (1954:129; cf. HALOT 1.51 *'lh* I, qal) to take *'aloth* as an infinitive absolute from *'alah* [TH422, ZH457] (take an oath)—its unusual form to be accounted for by its assonance with the following *karoth* [TH3772, ZH4162] (cf. Andersen and Freedman 1980:554). Syntactically, the two infinitive absolutes qualify the preceding verb (speak) by describing "the manner or the attendant circumstances of that situation" (Waltke and O'Connor 1990:588). Thus, by making oaths and promises they don't intend to keep, Hosea's people just speak words.

10:5 tremble. This is a notoriously difficult verse. Among the problems is the precise understanding of the verb *gur* [TH1481/A/B, ZH1591/1592/1593], which can be understood as coming from any of three possible roots in the OT: (1) seek refuge, (2) attack, and (3) dread. It may well be that Hosea intended a double entendre playing upon the first of the three possible meanings listed above: The people who tremble in worshipful fear before the idol will become refugees in a strange land.

priests wail. The word "priests" is a special term used exclusively for those who officiate in idol worship (see note on Zeph 1:4). The verb translated "wail" normally means "rejoice/exult." In these cases it often describes the worshiper's praise of God for who he is or what he has done (Pss 9:14; 13:5; Isa 29:19; Hab 3:18). Here it also is to be understood in a context of worship—the celebrations associated with the calf idol. Thus, the people and priests who rejoice over the glory of the calf idol of Bethel will mourn over the loss of the glory that they have heaped upon it.

be stripped away. Hosea intended another double entendre (cf. note on "tremble" above); the verb that means "uncover" or "reveal" is also used of going into exile/captivity.

10:6 *the great king.* See note on 5:13.

10:7 *Samaria and its king will be cut off.* The NLT renders the sense. Only one verb occurs in the verse in the MT. The verb *nidmeh* [TH1819/1820/A, ZH1948/1949/1950] permits a few possible meanings: "be silent," "be cut off/destroyed/ruined." The Lord has already used it to warn of the destruction of the nation and its people (4:5-6). Hosea's observation focuses on the capital city of the northern kingdom and its king. Hosea will later call special attention to the king's demise (10:15). The precise meaning intended depends on the imagery that follows (see next note).

like driftwood on an ocean wave. The Latin Vulgate reads *quasi spumam super faciem aquae* ("like foam upon the face of the waters"; cf. KJV). The imagery in this case depends on foam being viewed as the result of the churning of the angry waters (Laetsch 1956:79). The homograph *qetsep* [TH7110/7110A, ZH7912/7913] occurs elsewhere in the OT predominantly with the meaning "wrath," especially of the Lord's anger (e.g., Deut 29:27; Jer 21:5; cf. NIDOTTE 3.962-963). The NLT follows the LXX, Theodotion, and Peshitta here in taking *qtsp* to be a "twig" (driftwood when on the water), a meaning that occurs only here in the OT but is followed by several English versions (e.g., NIV, NRSV). The underlying verb behind this word may be related to a form of the Hebrew verb *qatsats* (cut off/cut down). Sweeney (2000:106) acknowledges both the meanings "wrath" and "chip of wood" and suggests that the idea of a chip "probably refers to a cut-off branch from a tree or bush, and the image of the severed fragment floating helplessly on the water as it is carried off aptly conveys the prophet's views. In most of its occurrences, *qetsep* means 'wrath,' and thereby provides another double entendre in reference to YHWH's wrath and the result for the king."

10:8 *Aven.* Lit., "wickedness" (*'awen* [TH205, ZH224]). This noun has been applied to Bethel previously (i.e., Beth-aven; 4:15; 5:8; 10:5). Although it occurs here without the compound element "Beth-" (house of), it "still recalls the derogatory name given to the city" (McComiskey 1992:169). Here it is the city's pagan shrines that are dubbed evil or wicked: *bamoth 'awen* [TH1116/205, ZH1195/224] (high places of wickedness).

Thorns and thistles. The image of wild plants overgrowing former places of civilization is familiar prophetic language describing destruction brought about as a result of the Lord's judgment at the hands of an enemy (e.g., 9:6; Isa 5:6; 7:23-25; 32:13; 34:13).

COMMENTARY

Hosea's reactions toward the people's apostasy must mirror God's own feelings. Despite the God-given prosperity of his people, they had forgotten God (cf. Deut 8:11-14) and abused his grace by spending their wealth on the construction of pagan altars. Increased riches were used to build statues and idols in order to facilitate the worship of foreign gods. Never satisfied with all that God had done for them, they gave him lip service and went off to worship other deities.

The portrayal of Israel as a luxuriant vine should have reminded the people that they were the cultivation of Yahweh, the divine husbandman. Theirs was a unique relationship, for God and his people were bound together as a covenant community. Blessed by God they could be expected to be a faithful and productive nation (Lev 26:1-13; Deut 11:15; 28:1-14). To be unfaithful, however, courted the Lord's justifiable anger and judgment (Lev 26:14-29; Deut 28:15-68). The very conditions that existed in Hosea's day were those that Israel was warned about from the beginning (cf. Deut 11:16-17) so the threat of foreign invasion and captivity were still valid (cf. Lev 26:17; Deut 28:36-37, 45-57, 64-68).

Hosea reported that the great irony in all of this was that the one whom they rejected was their real benefactor. Hosea predicted that those whom they had chosen, Baal and their human king, would be of no benefit to them in the coming struggle. For the pagan altars, together with their idols, would be smashed to bits, and the great calf idol of Bethel (cf. 1 Kgs 12:25-30) would be carried off to Assyria. That idol before which they once stood in reverential fear, gazing upon its glorious countenance, would have its grandeur stripped away, leaving the people to fear for their safety, grieving over their loss.

Nor would their reliance on human kingship serve them well. That for which they clamored (1 Sam 8:4-5, 19-20; cf. 1 Kgs 12:16) would collapse and become an admitted failure. The capital city of Samaria would be captured and its king carried off. What little remained would be overrun by thorns and thistles, the whole place becoming a desolation. Those who manage to survive the invasion will wish for a speedy death to end their misery. Even then, Israel would still refuse to submit to Yahweh, their rightful king.

Alas, so it came to pass (2 Kgs 17:5-6). When the inspired historian of 2 Kings looked back on the disaster, his judgment of the situation, like Hosea's, was in accordance with the Lord's pronouncement. Israel's entrenched fascination with idolatry and its attendant evils in general and its commitment to the state religion instituted by Jeroboam I had taken their toll. When the Lord's patience had reached full limit, his righteous judicial wrath came upon them (2 Kgs 17:7-23).

Several literary figures embellish the message. Israel was pictured metaphorically as a luxuriant vine—and the lesson that is based upon it describes its performance and fate (10:1-2). The ethical practices of Israelite society, now divorced from the standards of divine law, were termed perverted justice, which had sprung up like poisonous weeds in a farmer's field. Israel's reliance on kingship was exposed for its foolishness in a colorful simile that predicted that the king himself would be carried away like a chip of wood floating on an ocean's wave. The climax to the message of divine condemnation and judgment comes in verse 8, where the utter hopelessness that ensues upon the invasion of the northern kingdom is portrayed in dramatic fashion. Thorns and thistles will mask the former pomp and magnificence of Samaria. The few survivors in the land will long only for death to end their unrelieved misery, even calling upon the mountains and hills to fall on them and bury them.

What a disobedient Israel could expect to receive from God is that which lies in store for an obdurately sinful world. For the text here is utilized later to depict a far greater conflict than that which Israel faced. The Scriptures make it clear that a world system in rebellion against God is on a crash course with God and the forces of heaven. That eschatological event will take place in a period known most frequently as "a time of trouble for my people Israel" (lit., "Jacob's trouble"; Jer 30:7; cf. Dan 12:1), "the great tribulation" (Rev 7:14; cf. Matt 24:21; Mark 13:19), or "the day of the Lord" (2 Pet 3:10; cf. Joel 2:1-11, 28-32).

The affliction, horror, and carnage of those days are graphically presented in many places in Scripture (e.g., Isa 66:14-16; Rev 15–16). Perhaps none is so striking as John's description of those who experience the terrors of that time of God's judicial wrath (Rev 6:12-17). Not only is the bloodshed of worldwide war described, but a cataclysm in the physical world so enormous that those who dwell on earth will hide themselves in caves and among the rocks of collapsing mountains and cry out, "Fall on us and hide us from the face of the one who sits on the throne and from the wrath of the Lamb" (Rev 6:16). What an awesome picture! The gentle Lamb of God who takes away the sin of the world will come as the Divine Warrior (Rev 19:11-21), who comes to pour out his anger against sin, to sit in judgment over the world (Rev 20:11-15), and to establish his eternal, righteous Kingdom (Rev 11:15; 21–22; cf. Dan 7:13-14). Peter's challenge stands before us all: "Since everything around us is going to be destroyed like this, what holy and godly lives you should live" (2 Pet 3:11-12).

◆   5. Israel is a perennial sinner (10:9-11)

9 The LORD says, "O Israel, ever since Gibeah,
there has been only sin and more sin!
You have made no progress whatsoever.
Was it not right that the wicked men of Gibeah were attacked?
10 Now whenever it fits my plan, I will attack you, too.
I will call out the armies of the nations to punish you for your multiplied sins.

11 "Israel* is like a trained heifer treading out the grain—
an easy job she loves.
But I will put a heavy yoke on her tender neck.
I will force Judah to pull the plow and Israel* to break up the hard ground.

10:11a Hebrew *Ephraim*, referring to the northern kingdom of Israel.   10:11b Hebrew *Jacob*. The names "Jacob" and "Israel" are often interchanged throughout the Old Testament, referring sometimes to the individual patriarch and sometimes to the nation.

NOTES

10:9 *there has been only sin . . . You have made no progress.* Lit., "you have sinned, O Israel, there they stood." Mixture of subjects is not uncommon in Hosea. The MT may be explained as first a condemnation of Israel's sin at Gibeah (you have sinned) and second, a reference to the perpetuity of Israel's sins since that time (i.e., the people and their sins have remained there). The spirit of rapacity and violence at Gibeah infected Israel ever since that time. See note on 9:9.

Was it not right that the wicked men of Gibeah were attacked? The NLT rendering assumes a reference to a past event (cf. NIV, KJV, NKJV) such as that of Judg 19–21 (see note on 9:9). The MT, however, suggests a future tense either (1) as a question (even though the usual interrogative marker is missing): "Will not war overtake them in Gibeah?"; or (2) as a statement of fact (reading the negative particle *lo'* [TH3808, ZH4202] as the asseverative particle *lu'* [TH3863, ZH4273], "certainly, indeed"): "War will [indeed] overtake the wicked people in Gibeah" (GW).

10:10 *to punish you.* The NLT follows the lead of the LXX in translating the Hebrew *be'aseram* as derived from the verb *yasar* [TH3256, ZH3579] (punish); cf. RSV; NRSV; GW. The verbal form is better understood, however, as coming from *'asar* [TH631, ZH673] (bind): "at their binding" (Keil 1954:132)—hence a reference to the time when God has them bound for their double iniquity (cf. NASB, NKJV). Both views recognize that the Hebrew consonants *b'srm* were deliberately chosen so as to serve as alliteration with the previous *w'srm* (I will chastise them).

10:11 *Israel is like a trained heifer.* Lit., "Ephraim is a trained heifer." The NLT has rendered the Hebrew metaphor as a simile. The verse returns to the imagery of farming (see "Major Themes" in the Introduction).

I will force Judah to pull the plow. Several scholars attribute the reference to Judah as a redactional addition to Hosea's original text (e.g., Emmerson 1984:83-86; Mays 1969:145). The many references to Judah woven throughout divine oracles and Hosea's speeches, however, argue for their authenticity. In fact, "the names of *Judah* and *Israel* are intertwined in other pericopes in Hosea in which the inclusion of Judah is essential to the integrity of the passage" (McComiskey 1992:177). Indeed, as G. A. Smith (1929:233) observes, it would be strange if Judah were not included within the purview of the prophet. This is especially true since Hosea takes great pains to date his prophecy in accordance with the reigns of a broad range of Judean kings (1:1).

The inclusion of Judah provides yet another cluster of threes, so common in the book: Ephraim, Judah, and Jacob (NLT, "Israel"). "Ephraim, the northern kingdom, will be made to carry a rider; Judah, the southern kingdom, will have to draw the plow; Jacob, the twelve tribes . . . will, like sinful, fugitive Jacob, be driven out of their homeland exile, into hard labor of slavery" (Laetsch 1956:84). The mention of Jacob here anticipates the application of the patriarch's actions and character to the nation in 12:2-4.

COMMENTARY

The Lord's short oracle (10:9-11) continues the lesson of Gibeah (cf. Judg 19–21). The city was mentioned previously in God's oracle of warning in 5:8 and in Hosea's condemnation of current Israelite society in 9:9. Here the Lord notes the perpetuity of Israel's sin since that bloody night. Unfortunately, Israel made little spiritual progress. Its capacity for violence and injustice had remained the same throughout the intervening years. In accordance with the sins of Gibeah, God's people would be judged and punished; God would send other nations to chastise the northern kingdom, binding its citizens and carrying them away captive. So it was that Israel would pay for its double sins, from the crimes of Gibeah to those of its society in Hosea's day.

In characterizing that coming captivity, God called Israel a trained heifer that was admirably suited for its task of treading out the grain. The work of the unyoked and unmuzzled ox (Deut 25:4) was not particularly laborious and was rewarding. Israel had been accustomed to living like that animal, working freely and happily without restraint and free from bondage. Now it must suffer the consequences of its unbridled self-will. Like an animal put to the yoke to plow the soil, so God's people would know the yoke of captivity and be forced to do hard service. This would include not only the northern kingdom but ultimately Judah, for the sins of Israel were also those of the southern kingdom.

The lesson is clear. God's people must neither misuse the Lord's gift of freedom nor mistake his seeming inattention to their self-will as indicating that no day of reckoning will come. Believers must take care not to abuse the Lord's many blessings in order to consume them on their own lusts. Desiring to be "free" by abandoning the constraints of the Scriptures, people can all too readily sow the seeds of wickedness that can lead to their own destruction (Prov 22:8; Gal 6:7-8; 1 Pet 2:11, 16; 1 John 5:16b). True freedom comes by taking Christ's yoke and experiencing the strength and fullness of life that he alone can provide (Matt 11:28-30; John 8:34-35; Rev 1:5). May the love of God, along with devotion to him and his Word, so grip our hearts that in all that we do we may be approved by God (Eph 3:16-19; 2 Tim 2:15).

◆　　6. Hosea's warning: seek God or perish (10:12-15)

¹²I said, 'Plant the good seeds of
　　righteousness,
　　and you will harvest a crop of love.
Plow up the hard ground of your
　　hearts,
　　for now is the time to seek the LORD,
that he may come
　　and shower righteousness upon you.'

¹³"But you have cultivated wickedness
　　and harvested a thriving crop
　　　of sins.
You have eaten the fruit of lies—
　　trusting in your military might,

believing that great armies
　　could make your nation safe.
¹⁴Now the terrors of war
　　will rise among your people.
All your fortifications will fall,
　　just as when Shalman destroyed
　　　Beth-arbel.
Even mothers and children
　　were dashed to death there.
¹⁵You will share that fate, Bethel,
　　because of your great wickedness.
When the day of judgment dawns,
　　the king of Israel will be completely
　　　destroyed.

NOTES

10:12 I said. The NLT follows the general consensus in taking 10:9-15 as a single unit. Against this, however, is the fact that the MT does not contain a reference to God in the first person in 10:12. Rather, 10:12-15 looks very much like another of Hosea's observations on Israel's condition, together with advice and warnings of what lies ahead if Israel doesn't change its ways (cf. 4:15-19; 6:1-3; 9:1-9). If such is the case, Hosea's admonition is given in terminology that provides thematic connection with the imagery of farming in the previous divine oracle.

Plant . . . harvest . . . Plow. All three verbs are imperatives in the MT. Once again Hosea's habit of expressing things in groups of three is evident (cf. 5:8; 9:11).

righteousness . . . love . . . righteousness. For love or "loving-kindness" (*khesed* [TH2617A, ZH2876]), see the note on Jonah 2:8. The term has appeared several times (e.g., 2:19; 4:2; 6:4, 6) and will be seen again in 12:6. Two different words for righteousness occur here. Considerable overlap can be seen in the use of these two terms so that their precise nuance depends on matters of context. McComiskey (1992:177-178) proposes that Hosea moves from the more general term for righteousness (*tsedaqah* [TH6666, ZH7407]) to one that emphasizes righteousness that flows from God's covenantal standards (*tsedeq* [TH6664, ZH7406]).

to seek the LORD. The verbal root *darash* [TH1875, ZH2011] (seek) often stresses personal concern on the part of the plaintiff who wants to know and do God's will (cf. 2 Kgs 22:13; Amos 5:4). It can also be used of inquiring of God or consulting an oracle.

10:13 *you have cultivated wickedness.* The verb translated "cultivate" also appears in 10:11 where it is used of Israel and Judah's need to break up hard ground.

harvested a thriving crop of sins. Although Hosea urged the people to harvest a crop of love (10:12), their sowing and reaping yielded only sins.

eaten the fruit of lies. This forms a third negative trait answering to the three positive qualities that Hosea urged upon his readers in 10:12 (see commentary below).

10:14 *Shalman . . . Beth-arbel.* Neither Shalman nor Beth-arbel is known elsewhere. Some have suggested that the name Shalman was a shortened form of the Assyrian king Shalmaneser (2 Kgs 17:3; cf. Astour 1971:383-389). Due to the horrendous nature of the atrocity and given the past record of the Moabites (e.g., 2 Kgs 3:27), others have championed Shalmanu, the king of Moab mentioned in an inscription of Tiglath-pileser III (Wolff 1974:188).

While most scholars identify Beth-arbel with a town in Transjordan southeast of the Sea of Galilee (modern Irbid), 1 Macc 9:2 records an Arbela in Galilee, where the forces of Demetrius II camped on their way to Jerusalem. Strengthening the identification of Shalman as a Moabite king and Beth-arbel as a Transjordanian location in Gilead is the boast of the Moabite king Mesha that in taking the Reubenite town of Nebo (Num 32:3), he "took it and slew all: seven thousand men, boys, women and [girls] and female slaves," which he had consecrated to his god Ashtar-chemosh (the Moabite Inscription, lines 15-17 [Thomas 1961:195-199]; cf. ANET 320; Arnold and Beyer 2002:160-162). The incident mentioned here, while known to Hosea's readers, is not attested elsewhere in the OT or extrabiblical texts of the ancient Near East.

mothers and children. The atrocities of war in the ancient world are well documented (e.g., 2 Kgs 8:12; see the note on Nah 3:10).

10:15 *completely destroyed.* Lit., "utterly cut off." The fate of Israel's last king Hoshea is uncertain. It may be assumed that he died in captivity (2 Kgs 17:4). The fall of Samaria brought an end to the northern kingdom and its monarchy (see note on 10:7).

COMMENTARY

In this section, Hosea gives some positive advice for his contemporaries in the northern kingdom. Building on the earlier admonition to return to the Lord and really come to know him (6:1), he now urges his readers to put into their lives those qualities that come from God's own nature and are available to them: righteousness and loving-kindness. Indeed, these are fundamental to their covenant relationship with Yahweh. If they will but cultivate these characteristics and let them flow from their hearts, God will respond in righteousness and bless them accordingly (10:12).

Having urged the people to adopt a new lifestyle, Hosea then warned them of the dire consequences of continued apostasy and its attendant wickedness. For they had chosen to proceed in a way permeated by personal iniquity, social injustice, and the buildup of military capabilities. They would soon learn the folly of their self-deception. Neither their armed forces nor their fortifications would deliver them in the coming day of battle. Rather, they would experience a devastating defeat and bloody slaughter that would bring the northern kingdom and its monarchy to an end (10:13-15).

The imagery Hosea used was both picturesque and meaningful to an agrarian society. Much as a farmer prepares the soil, sows the seed, and cares for his field in order to gain a bountiful harvest, so God's people were instructed to plow up the unbroken soil of their hearts and yield to God. They must sow in righteousness with a view to reaping in their lives those qualities that come from a close walk with the Lord. In order to facilitate the growth of such qualities of character, God would rain down his righteousness. Thus they could harvest the blessings that come with covenant fidelity.

Hosea pursued the agrarian image further. Having delivered three positive admonitions necessary for Israel's recovery, he pointed out three negative qualities that were prohibiting them from being "good farmers." In doing so, he completed his argument. In place of the wickedness they had cultivated, they were to plant the good seeds of righteousness; where they had raised a crop of sins, they were to harvest God's love; instead of eating the fruits of lies, they were to break up the hard ground of their hearts and seek the Lord. This they must do, or their fascination with idolatry and its attendant evils, which had taken their toll upon them, would eventually lead to their destruction at the hands of invaders.

Hosea's readers of all ages can be admonished by the imagery here. Thus Jeremiah urged his readers, "Plow up the hard ground of your hearts! Do not waste your good seed among thorns" (Jer 4:3). Jeremiah likewise emphasized that the road to spiritual vitality begins with heartfelt repentance before God (Jer 4:4) and proceeds with a conscious adoption of a righteous regimen of life. Genuine commitment to God must be nourished by the Word of God, which is to be received not in a cavalier fashion or extinguished by worldly concerns, but with gladness and resolve to let "the message about Christ, in all its richness, fill your lives. Teach and counsel each other with all the wisdom he gives" (Col 3:16).

A conscious seeking after God and a consistent attention to his Word are imperative for our spiritual well-being. The old-fashioned disciplines of prayer (see commentary on Jonah 2:2-4) and the study of the Scriptures are still the key to godly living. Believers often despair of knowing God's will for their lives; yet these time-honored spiritual graces are their basic resource.

Christians also have another avenue of help. In addition to prayer (Ps 139:23-24) and the Word of God (2 Tim 2:15), they have the availability of the indwelling Holy Spirit (1 Cor 3:16) as their guide "into all truth" (John 16:13). It is he who helps and intercedes for the praying believers so that they may have perfect communion with the mind of God and know his will (Rom 8:26-27).

What a privilege is ours! We can learn of God's general purposes for people and his standards for us by reading God's precious Word daily. What power is ours! We can learn of God's special will for each of us by spending time with him in prayer each day. Would we know the will of God for our lives? It is ours to have fully through his Word, prayer, and the guidance of the Holy Spirit.

◆   ## 7. God's compassion for disobedient Israel (11:1-11)

1 "When Israel was a child, I loved him,
    and I called my son out of Egypt.
2 But the more I* called to him,
    the farther he moved from me,

offering sacrifices to the images
    of Baal
    and burning incense to idols.
3 I myself taught Israel* how to walk,

leading him along by the hand.
But he doesn't know or even care
    that it was I who took care of him.
⁴I led Israel along
    with my ropes of kindness and love.
I lifted the yoke from his neck,
    and I myself stooped to feed him.

⁵"But since my people refuse to return
        to me,
    they will return to Egypt
    and will be forced to serve Assyria.
⁶War will swirl through their cities;
    their enemies will crash through
        their gates.
They will destroy them,
    trapping them in their own evil
        plans.
⁷For my people are determined to
    desert me.
They call me the Most High,
    but they don't truly honor me.

⁸"Oh, how can I give you up, Israel?
    How can I let you go?
How can I destroy you like Admah
    or demolish you like Zeboiim?
My heart is torn within me,
    and my compassion overflows.
⁹No, I will not unleash my fierce anger.
    I will not completely destroy Israel,
for I am God and not a mere mortal.
    I am the Holy One living among you,
    and I will not come to destroy.
¹⁰For someday the people will follow me.
    I, the LORD, will roar like a lion.
And when I roar,
    my people will return trembling
        from the west.
¹¹Like a flock of birds, they will come
        from Egypt.
    Trembling like doves, they will
        return from Assyria.
And I will bring them home again,"
    says the LORD.

11:2 As in Greek version; Hebrew reads *they.*   11:3 Hebrew *Ephraim,* referring to the northern kingdom of Israel; also in 11:8, 9, 12.

NOTES

11:1 When Israel was a child. The metaphor of God being a father to Israel is a familiar one in the OT (e.g., Deut 14:1-2; Isa 1:2; Jer 3:19; 4:22). Two different nouns are used to describe Israel in this verse. The first, translated "child" (*na'ar* [TH5288, ZH5853]), can be used of any age group from infancy (1 Sam 4:21) to early adulthood (Gen 41:12). At times, it also carries the meaning "servant" (Gen 18:7; 2 Kgs 4:12; 5:20). Its wide range of applicability makes it an appropriate term for the nation's formative years in Egypt.

I called my son out of Egypt. The second noun, "son," points to God's paternal care of his people. The Exodus motif is widely drawn upon by the authors of both the OT and NT.

11:2 the more I called to him. The NLT follows the lead of the LXX in reading a first-person verb here, as do many contemporary versions (e.g., NIV, NJB, NRSV, REB, GW). The MT, however, reads, "they called to them." The NLT's rendering of "them" as "him" stems from its continuation of the image that views Israel as a child.

Those who favor the tradition represented by the LXX hold that the issue deals with Israel's stubborn refusal to respond to Yahweh's call (e.g., Stuart 1987:178; Craigie 1985:78). Those who support the MT identify those who were calling as various groups. Some suggest the OT prophets (e.g., Keil 1954:137; McComiskey 1992:184-185). Others propose the Israelites calling to the Egyptians during the time of the Exodus (e.g., Garrett 1997:222), or the people (especially women) of Moab calling to them and leading them astray (e.g., Hubbard 1989:187; Andersen and Freedman 1980:577-578). Laetsch (1956:87, 89) proposes taking the verb as a passive (= indefinite plural): "As often as they (i.e., pious Israelites) were called."

the farther he moved from me. The LXX similarly translates the clause, "Even so they went from my face/presence (= me)," but as it stands, the MT reads "he moved from them."

Whether to read "them" or "me" follows from the choice made in reading the first clause of the verse (but note the Peshitta's "from me"; so also Laetsch 1956:87). Andersen and Freedman (1980:578; cf. Hubbard 1989:87) support the latter translation by noting the widely followed redivision of the Hebrew consonants *mpnyhm* into *mpny hm*. Thus, after repointing the Hebrew, *mippenehem* (from them) becomes *mippanay hem* (from me, even they). They also point out that the second construction appears "typical of Hosea." On the whole, this approach appears to be the most workable. Although God had called Israel out of Egypt (11:1), when the purveyors of idolatry beckoned to them, they departed from the Lord to go to them (11:2).

11:3 *I myself taught Israel how to walk, leading him along by the hand.* The NLT trans-lates the sense of the passage, using the singular consistently, where the Hebrew uses both singular and plural forms. The metaphor is that of a father teaching his child to walk. Two unusual forms occur here: (1) *tirgalti* [TH7270, ZH8078], "I taught to walk," is generally taken as a *tiphil* (= *hiphil*) denominative verb from *regel* [TH7272, ZH8079] (foot). (2) Also, the Hebrew word *qakham* (leading them) may be viewed as a dialectical form of *leqakham* [TH3947, ZH4374] (he took them, he led them) or as a unique infinitive. The plural object may stress God's concern for individual Israelites as well as the whole nation (Laetsch 1956:90).

it was I who took care of him. Lit., "I healed them." The reference may be to the healing of the bitter water at Marah (Exod 15:22-26), where Yahweh declared, "I am the LORD who heals you."

11:4 *with my ropes of kindness and love.* Lit., "with the cords of a man, with the ropes of love." Rather than the ropes used on animals or on servants, God's tie to Israel was one of love. The rope could be a symbol of submission as it is in 1 Kgs 20:31-32.

the yoke from his neck. Lit., "a yoke upon their cheeks." Some have suggested the figure of lifting an infant to the cheek (e.g., Wolff 1974:191; cf. NJB, NRSV, REB) by reading *'ul* [TH5764, ZH6403] (infant) rather than the MT's *'ol* [TH5923, ZH6585] (yoke). But the near context here is freedom from servitude rather than fatherly affection. The image is that of a farmer easing or adjusting "some kind of bit or harness device that either went into an animal's mouth or around its face" (Garrett 1997:225).

11:5 *Egypt . . . Assyria.* The NLT follows the lead of some recent translations in postulating a return of God's people to Egypt where Assyria will rule over them (see note and commen-tary on 9:6). Such a procedure necessitates taking the negative particle *lo'* [TH3808, ZH4202] either (1) as the asseverative *lu'* [TH3863, ZH4273] and translating as a positive statement: "They shall return to the land of Egypt" (NRSV, REB) or (2) treating the sentence as a rhe-torical question: "Will they not return to Egypt?" (NIV). The Hebrew particle can also be taken as a simple negative statement: "He [Israel] will not return to Egypt, but Assyria will be his king" (cf. NASB, NJB, KJV, NKJV).

11:6 *gates.* The enigmatic noun *bad* [TH905B, ZH964] (cf. HALOT 1.108-109) has been vari-ously understood by commentators as "boasting" (Garrett 1997:226), "false prophets" (Stuart 1987:180), "strongman" (i.e., a member of an influential class, Andersen and Freedman 1980:586), "oracle priests" (Mays 1969:150), or "gate bolt" (Keil 1954:140; cf. NIV, NASB, ESV). On the whole, the last sense is to be preferred, the "crossbars" or "gate bolt" on the gates serving as a metonymy for the gates themselves (cf. Job 17:16).

11:8 *Oh, how can I give you up, Israel?* For the structural significance of this rhetorical question, see the "Outline" in the Introduction.

Admah . . . Zeboiim. These two cities of the plain were destroyed along with Sodom and Gomorrah (cf. Gen 10:19; 19:23-25). Their destruction, like that of the better-known pair, became symbolic of total devastation and God's hand of judgment (e.g., Deut 29:23; Isa 13:19; Amos 4:11).

11:9 *I will not completely destroy.* Lit., "I will not destroy." This seeming contradiction (present in the MT in light of the historical fact of the fall of the northern kingdom) is nicely avoided by the NLT. The force of the context argues for the Lord's punishment but not a permanent obliteration of his nation. Such an understanding eliminates the unlikely proposal that the promise not to punish Israel is simply for the "future day of restoration" (Wood 1985:214).

I will not come to destroy. Lit., "I will not come into a[ny] city." In no case will God enter an Israelite city to destroy it as he did to destroy the cities of the plain. The NLT (cf. NIV; NRSV) renders according to the sense of the context. This understanding is also favored by some commentators (e.g., Keil 1954:142) who relate the Hebrew noun *'ir* II [TH5892B, ZH6552] to a noun meaning "agitation," hence "wrath/fury" (cf. HALOT 2.822).

11:10 *I, the LORD, will roar like a lion.* The figure of the roaring lion is a familiar one (e.g., Gen 49:9; Num 24:9; Ps 22:13). The prophets apply the figure to God's judicial wrath against the ungodly (Jer 25:30; Amos 1:2; see note on Joel 3:16).

11:10b-11a *my people will return . . . Like a flock of birds.* This image depicts the homeward return of God's people from exile among the nations of the world (see notes and commentary on Zeph 3:9-20).

COMMENTARY

By means of a rhetorical question, God reminded his people of his prior claim upon them. It was he who delivered them from Egyptian bondage. Nevertheless, they quickly were lured away by the worship of Baal. Although he guided them, provided for their needs, and healed their wounds, they went on in their own way. They seemingly neither noticed nor were concerned about the Lord's constant beneficences to them (11:1-4).

Therefore, God warned them that he would judge them with another time of bondage—this time at the hands of the Assyrians. Moreover, their cities would experience the invader's heel and the accompanying devastation. God had no other recourse, for his people were abandoning their covenant God. They gave him lip service, but there was no spiritual reality (11:5-7).

In a poignant query, God poured out his heartfelt agony to them: How could he give them up to captivity and their land to destruction? The Lord was torn between two emotions. On the one hand, as a holy God, his justice compelled him to punish his people for their entrenched rebelliousness. On the other hand, because he is not like mortal men, he would not seek vengeance. Rather, his holiness constrained him to impart that holiness to others, and his compassion overflowed with a desire for his people to come to him. Therefore, he would not destroy Israel's towns as he did the cities of the plain so long ago (11:8-9). His long-range plans for Israel included bringing his people home again from foreign captivity. A repentant people would come to him with adoration, for they would revere him as their defender and deliverer from their enemies (11:10-11).

A holy and just God is also a God of love. While his plans called for the temporary rigors of chastisement as a means to the final resolution of Israel's ungodliness, he genuinely cared for them. Indeed, he was deeply moved by the severity of what he must necessarily do to bring them to himself.

If God's heart is thus moved for the unrepentant, surely those who claim his name should be similarly concerned for the condition of sinful mankind. Herein is a great missionary and evangelistic challenge. The obvious need of a lost world to know the Lord, as well as God's great love in providing for mankind's redemption, should be motivation enough for believers to share the gospel of Christ (John 3:16-18; 2 Cor 5:14). The clear command of Christ makes it a categorical imperative (Matt 28:18-20; John 20:21).

Particularly significant in this passage is the opening verse concerning God calling his people out of Egypt. Matthew saw an analogy between this event and the Lord's instructions to Joseph to take the boy Jesus to Egypt and remain there until he should tell him to return (Matt 2:13-15, 19-23). While many have attempted to distort Hosea's words so as to suggest that Hosea actually foresaw the later coming out of Egypt, Matthew's use of the Old Testament rather reflects his appreciation of the reproduction of Israel's history in the events surrounding the birth and infancy of Jesus.

Matthew's use of analogy to relate Old Testament events to the early years of Christ here is instructive. Building on Hosea's prophecy, Matthew pointed out that like Israel of old, Jesus was called out of Egypt. Like Israel, Jesus came to the homeland of the Hebrews. Similarly, Matthew saw an analogy between Jeremiah's depiction of Rachel weeping over those who were killed at the fall of Samaria or would be killed during the siege and captivity of Jerusalem (Jer 31:15) and the community's mourning over Herod's slaying the infants in a vain attempt to kill the Christ child (Matt 2:18). Again, Matthew perceived in Jesus' parents' return to Nazareth a connection with Isaiah's prediction that the Messiah would be "a new Branch (*netser* [TH5342, ZH5916]) bearing fruit from the old root" (Isa 11:1).

Although Matthew called all of these fulfillments, they should not be misconstrued as events which the Old Testament prophets actually predicted, as when Jesus cited Isaiah 61:1-2a in the synagogue in Nazareth (Luke 4:18-19). Rather, in such cases (cf. Matthew's use of Isa 6:9-10 in Matt 13:14-15) the original passage takes on canonical significance but one that in no way alters the meaning of the original text. Thus in reading such Old Testament passages one has an appreciation of the wider use of the text. In this sense the New Testament makes the context of the Old Testament fuller (i.e., fulfills the passage).

The appearance of the exodus motif here is in harmony with its employment elsewhere. Citations and allusions to the Exodus appear throughout the Old Testament (e.g., Josh 3:5; 4:14, 18-24; 5:10-15; 1 Sam 12:6; Pss 105:26-45; 106:7-12; Jer 11:7; Hab 3:3-15). Often the Old Testament prophets recast the account and applied it to God's future intervention on behalf of his people. At that time he will defeat Israel's enemies, return them to their land, and pour out his blessings upon them (cf. Isa 11:11-16; 51:9-11; Jer 16:14-15; 23:7-8; Mic 7:14-15). The story of the Exodus continued to be drawn upon by the intertestamental writers (e.g., 3 Macc 2:6-8; 6:4; *1 Enoch* 89:10-27; *Jubilees* 49) and those of the New Testament, especially the Apocalypse of John (Rev 15:3-4).

The retelling of the Exodus story provided a conscious reminder of God's gracious redemption of his people. What had happened in the original Exodus was a precursor to liberation from Babylonian exile and the eventual gathering of God's people from the nations of the world in eschatological times. All of this finds spiritual application in the ministry of Christ whose coming to ransom the lost out of the bondage of this world "is like a third exodus because he has come to lead sinners—Jews and Gentiles—into the full experience of salvation."[1]

ENDNOTES
1. W. A. VanGemeren, *Interpreting the Prophetic Word* (Grand Rapids: Zondervan, 1990), 276. See further E. Merrill, "Pilgrimage and Procession: Motifs of Israel's Return," in *Israel's Apostasy and Restoration*, ed. A. Gileadi (Grand Rapids: Baker, 1988), 61-72. F. F. Bruce (*The New Testament Development of Old Testament Themes* [Grand Rapids: Eerdmans, 1968], 49) points out that "The presentation of the redemptive work of Christ in terms of the Exodus motif in so many strands of New Testament teaching shows how primitive was the Christian use of this motif—going back, quite probably, to the period of Jesus' ministry. Jesus' contemporaries freely identified Him as a second Moses—the expectation of a second Moses played an important part in popular eschatology at the time—and with the expectation of a second Moses went very naturally the expectation of a second Exodus." Although VanGemeren and Bruce use different terminology, their basic point is the same.

◆   **C. Concluding Considerations concerning Israel (11:12-14:8)**
    1. The folly of deceitful politics (11:12-12:1)

[12]*Israel surrounds me with lies and deceit,
but Judah still obeys God
and is faithful to the Holy One.*

CHAPTER 12
[1]*The people of Israel* feed on the wind;

they chase after the east wind all day long.
They pile up lies and violence;
they are making an alliance with Assyria
while sending olive oil to buy support from Egypt.

11:12a Verse 11:12 is numbered 12:1 in Hebrew text.   11:12b Or *and Judah is unruly against God, the faithful Holy One.* The meaning of the Hebrew is uncertain.   12:1a Verses 12:1-14 are numbered 12:2-15 in Hebrew text.   12:1b Hebrew *Ephraim*, referring to the northern kingdom of Israel; also in 12:8, 14.

NOTES
11:12 [12:1] *Israel surrounds me with lies and deceit.* Lit., "Ephraim has surrounded me with lies and the house of Israel with deceit." The NLT combines the two proper nouns into one subject: Israel. The full verse of the MT once again displays Hosea's fondness for groups of three: Ephraim, house of Israel, and Judah.

Judah still obeys God and is faithful to the Holy One. Verse 12b is somewhat ambiguous and has met with varying treatment. Two alternatives are most prominent: (1) The NLT follows the lead of those who understand it as a cautious endorsement of Judah's spiritual pilgrimage (cf. NRSV, KJV, NKJV; see McComiskey 1992:197-198; Emmerson 1984:13-16). (2) Many suggest that these words parallel the condemnation of Israel in the first half of the verse. Thus the NIV (cf. NLT mg) reads, "And Judah is unruly against God, even against the faithful Holy One" (cf. NASB, REB, GW; see Laetsch 1956:95; Andersen and Freedman 1980:600-603). On the whole, this negative reading regarding Judah appears more appropriate (cf. Jer 2:31).

Key to the choice between the two is the understanding of the verb *rad* [TH7300, ZH8113] ("roam, move about freely"; NLT: "obeys") and the noun *qedoshim* [TH6918A, ZH7705] ("holy ones," whether deities or saints; or as a plural of majesty in reference to God, the "Holy One"). If the verb and noun are viewed positively ("moves with God," alternative 1), the text takes its place beside others in Hosea where Judah receives a favorable evaluation (e.g., 1:7, 11; 3:5). If both are taken negatively ("moves against God," alternative 2), Judah is charged with roaming about against God, the Holy One. The condemnation would then anticipate the boast of Judah to be free of God's constraint that Jeremiah later reports (Jer 2:31). Judah's misconduct could also be understood as its wandering about with *'el* [TH410A, ZH446] ("deity," especially the Canaanite god by that name), the *qedoshim* referring to the Canaanite pantheon. Garrett's conjecture (1997:230-231) that *'el* and *qedoshim* were deliberately chosen because the terms had an orthodox ring but covered the real worship of pagan deities, while imaginative, is forced at best. Israel's longstanding fascination had been with Baal (cf. Num 25:3; Judg 2:13). This was especially true in the post-Solomonic era (see 13:1; 1 Kgs 16:31; 2 Kgs 17:16; cf. the commentary on 2:8).

Among those who take a negative approach, Keil's solution (1954:144-145) is perhaps the simplest. Judah rambled about in unruly fashion towards God, even towards the faithful Holy One. Such an interpretation allows the preposition *'im* [TH5973, ZH6640] (with, toward) the same force in both clauses, preserves the distinctive meaning of God's attribute of holiness, and provides a stitching link both with the previous section (11:9) and the negative tone of Hosea's comments in the passage that follows (12:2-6).

12:1 [2] *The people of Israel.* Lit., "Ephraim" (see note on 5:3).

feed on the wind; they chase after the east wind. The metaphor is graphic and provides yet another image taken from farming (cf. 10:4, 11-13). Rather than grazing on good provision, Israel feeds on the wind—a hot east wind at that. In this it is foolish, for that wind (symbolic of Assyria) will one day scorch them.

while sending olive oil to buy support from Egypt. Lit., "oil is carried to Egypt." The NLT rendering emphasizes Israel's attempt to curry Egypt's favor (2 Kgs 17:4). The MT underscores the foolishness of the northern kingdom by depicting Israel's folly. Although Canaan was noted for its plentiful supply of olive oil, various types of vegetable oils were certainly readily available in Egypt. Andersen and Freedman (1980:605) may be correct in holding the view that because oil was used in covenant-making, treaties were probably consummated with both Assyria and Egypt.[1] If oil is viewed as being shipped both to Egypt and Assyria, it should be noted that oil was also not in scarce supply in Mesopotamia.[2]

COMMENTARY

God announced his displeasure with both the northern and southern kingdoms (see note on 11:12). Israel had flaunted its worship before God with lying and deceitful practices. Judah's performance was little better, for it went merrily on its own way doing as it pleased in the face of God—who was known for his holiness and fidelity.

The northern kingdom, however, was especially culpable. Rather than being faithful to Yahweh the covenant God, Israel feigned allegiance and dependence upon him while serving other gods (especially Baal) and while making alliances and arrangements with the surrounding powerful nations. Such deceit spawned a spiritually and morally defunct society that was filled with lies and violence. This was true both internally and internationally. Israel's deception often took the form of playing one nation against the other (cf. 2 Kgs 17:3-4). All such conduct could lead only to Israel's ultimate defeat and demise (2 Kgs 17:5-6).

When nations, organizations, or individuals abandon God in order to be "free" to pursue their own ways and plans, they embark on a perilous, if not self-destructive, path. True freedom comes with knowing and following the one who is the truth (John 8:32, 36; 14:6). Divorced from God and the constraints of the Scriptures, people are confronted with the lure of selfish decisions. Being in Christ, however, allows one to be free from the slavery of sin in order to enjoy true freedom (cf. Ps 119:30-32; Rom 6:22-23). Believers ought to heed the bad example of God's people of old and use caution in their walk before God so that their freedom is neither exercised to indulge their sinful old nature (Gal 5:13) nor pursued in such a way as to cause another to stumble (1 Cor 8:9). Peter's advice is most apropos: "For you are free, yet you are God's slaves, so don't use your freedom as an excuse to do evil. Respect everyone" (1 Pet 2:16-17).

ENDNOTES
1. See J. White, *Everyday Life in Ancient Egypt* (New York: Capricorn, 1967), 104; D. B. Sandy, *The Production and Use of Vegetable Oils in Ptolemaic Egypt,* Bulletin of the American Society of Papyrologists: Supplements (Atlanta: Scholars Press, 1989).
2. See H. W. F. Saggs, *Everyday Life in Babylonia and Assyria* (New York: G. P. Putnam's Sons, 1965), 35, 68; "Samnu," in *The Assyrian Dictionary,* "S," Part I, ed. E. Reiner, et al. (Chicago: University of Chicago Press, 1989), 321-330.

◆   ## 2. Hosea's observation: Israel has a history of deceit (12:2-6)

²Now the LORD is bringing charges
   against Judah.
He is about to punish Jacob* for all
   his deceitful ways,
and pay him back for all he has done.
³Even in the womb,
   Jacob struggled with his brother;
when he became a man,
   he even fought with God.
⁴Yes, he wrestled with the angel
   and won.

He wept and pleaded for a blessing
   from him.
There at Bethel he met God face
   to face,
   and God spoke to him*—
⁵the LORD God of Heaven's
   Armies,
   the LORD is his name!
⁶So now, come back to your God.
Act with love and justice,
   and always depend on him.

12:2 *Jacob* sounds like the Hebrew word for "deceiver."   12:4 As in Greek and Syriac versions; Hebrew reads *to us.*

NOTES
12:2 [3] *charges against Judah.* See note on 4:1.

Jacob . . . his deceitful ways. God's people have begun to display the same sort of deceit as the patriarch Jacob.

12:3 [4] *Jacob struggled with his brother.* The verb translated "struggle" (*'aqab* [TH6117, ZH6810]) forms a play on the name Jacob (*ya'aqob* [TH3290, ZH3620]). Etymologically "struggle" is associated with a noun having to do with the heel of the foot. The verb itself connotes the idea of supplanting or seizing. Jacob came into life grasping his brother's heel (Gen 25:26), and so his name forms a wordplay with the word "heel" in that context. Two nominal derivatives from this verb reflect the thought of deception or trickery: *'aqob* [TH6121A, ZH6815] (deceitful) and *'oqbah* [TH6122, ZH6817] (trickery). These two form a wordplay with Jacob's name in the context of his deceitful actions later in life (Gen 27:36). But a second verbal root, the homograph *'qb* II, which carries the meanings "watch" or "protect," probably lies behind the ancient name "Jacob." Names compounded with the root *'qb* are frequently attested in the extrabiblical literature of the ancient Near East. Thus, at Tell Mari may be noted *ya-ah-qu-ub-el*: "may God protect" (cf. Huffmon 1965:303-304).

when he became a man. The consonants of the noun for manhood (*'on* [TH202, ZH226]) form a play on the noun for deception or iniquity (*'awen* [TH205, ZH224]), which Hosea used previously in discussing the calf at Bethel, calling that city Beth-aven (4:15; 5:8; 10:5).

he even fought with God. The verb connotes the notion of struggling. Its consonants are associated with Jacob's change of name to Israel (*yisra'el* [TH3478, ZH3776], Gen 32:28; 35:9; see note on 12:4). A second verb which might be the root of *yisra'el* is *sarar* I [TH8323, ZH8606], with the meaning "rule," stemming from the noun *sar* [TH8269, ZH8569] (prince, ruler).

12:4 [5] *he wrestled with the angel.* The verbal form here (*wayyasar*) is unique. Most expositors think the verb is the same as that in 12:3 (*sarah* [TH8280, ZH8575]). As such, they understand that Jacob's struggle with God was culminated by his striving with the angel.

at Bethel he met God face to face. God met with Jacob twice at Bethel, first in his flight from Esau (Gen 28:10-22) and second on his return there (Gen 35:9-14).

God spoke to him. Lit., "God spoke with us" (*'immanu* [TH5973/5105.2, ZH6640/5647]). The suffix on the preposition here is commonly understood to be an alternate third masculine singular (cf. LXX; Stuart 1987:187). For attestation of such a third-person form, see the discussion in Andersen and Freedman (1980:615). The more usual third-person form, however, would be *'immo* [TH5973/2050.2, ZH6640/2257]. If the strict MT parsing ("with us") is maintained, it could indicate Hosea's intention to identify contemporary society with its patriarchal progenitor (Andersen and Freedman 1980:640). Thus, when God twice spoke to Jacob at Bethel, his heirs were seminally present there. Kaiser remarks, "It was not only Jacob the individual but also the total nation that was intended. The shift from 'him' to 'us,' from the patriarch to the nation, is at the heart of the prophet's design" (1985:41-42).

12:6 [7] *love and justice.* For this pair of ethical qualities, see the notes on 2:19.

always depend on him. The NLT renders the verb *qawweh* [TH6960, ZH7747] (wait) in accordance with the constraints of the context. The piel stem attested here connotes the idea of an expectant waiting. For example, Jeremiah used the derived noun *tiqwah* [TH8615A, ZH9536] to speak of future hope for the exiles (Jer 29:11; 31:17). Hosea also used this noun in declaring that the Valley of Achor would be made a door of hope (2:15). Judah's future hope lay in renouncing its deceitful ways and (like Jacob, who became Israel) living in full dependence upon the Lord.

COMMENTARY

Hosea understood the Lord's words to mean that God had a controversy with Judah, in addition to Israel. All of God's people had been behaving like Jacob, the trickster of old. "Jacob's trickery became legendary. Accordingly, it served as a ready symbol for the prophets to seize upon in condemning the grasping, greedy ways of contemporary society" (Patterson 1999:390). The patriarch was a deceiver even while he was still in Rebekah's womb. He displayed his eventual penchant for trickery by seizing his brother's heel. Such would surface in tricking Esau out of his birthright in exchange for a bowl of stew (Gen 25:27-34) and by tricking Isaac into giving him the fatherly blessing that rightfully belonged to Esau.

All his life Jacob struggled with God until he wrestled with God's angel at Peniel. There he pleaded for a blessing, and as a result his name was changed to Israel (Gen 32:22-30). The change of name was subsequently confirmed at Bethel (Gen 35:9-14). Indeed, both in an earlier encounter at Bethel (Gen 28:10-22) and in this second meeting, Jacob was confronted with the supremacy and lordship of Yahweh. On both occasions, God blessed him. In that later meeting, he not only confirmed Jacob's name change but reiterated to him the provisions of the Abrahamic covenant (cf. Gen 28:13-18; 35:10-12). Jacob the trickster at last became a man who could live a princely life by letting God rule over him.

Unfortunately, God's people in Hosea's day still practiced the deceit of their patriarchal heritage. At Bethel, the very place where Jacob the trickster finally came to the end of himself, Hosea's contemporaries deceived themselves by feigning allegiance to God in their syncretistic worship (a charge Hosea frequently brought against Israel), while being devotees of Baal at heart.

The worship of Baal (who is no god at all) at Bethel was foolish. Was not Bethel the traditional site where the Lord God Almighty twice revealed himself to their forefather? Like Jacob of old, they needed to meet with God, submit to him, and reflect his standards in their lives. Not to do so was to follow the old Jacob, the trickster. Indeed, in following their own ways they only deceived themselves and were tricked by their own deceptive practices (cf. Prov 28:10; 1 Cor 3:19).

Like Israel of old, believers can be tricked by their own desires. The mind and heart are all too cunning (Ps 64:6). Jeremiah cautioned that the heart is deceitful (Jer 17:9) and Isaiah (Isa 5:21) denounced those who are wise in their own eyes and clever in their own sight. In another matter—that is, our efforts to evangelize and minister to others—we do well to remind ourselves that Paul reported that his labors in the gospel were from neither impure motives nor trickery (1 Thess 2:3). May Paul's standard be that of contemporary Christianity as well.

◆   ## 3. The folly of deceitful practices (12:7-11)

7 But no, the people are like crafty
     merchants
   selling from dishonest scales—
   they love to cheat.
8 Israel boasts, "I am rich!
   I've made a fortune all by myself!
   No one has caught me cheating!
   My record is spotless!"

9 "But I am the LORD your God,
   who rescued you from slavery
     in Egypt.
   And I will make you live in tents again,
   as you do each year at the Festival
     of Shelters.*
10 I sent my prophets to warn you
   with many visions and parables."

¹¹ But the people of Gilead are worthless
  because of their idol worship.
And in Gilgal, too, they sacrifice bulls;

their altars are lined up like the
  heaps of stone
along the edges of a plowed field.

12:9 Hebrew *as in the days of your appointed feast.*

NOTES

12:7 [8] *crafty merchants.* God accused the citizens of the northern kingdom of being no better than those whom he had dispelled from the land—the Canaanites. The noun translated "merchants" is *kena'an* [TH3667B, ZH4047] (cf. "Canaan" [TH3667, ZH4046]; see the note on Zeph 1:11).

12:9 [10] *tents . . . Festival of Shelters.* The Festival of Shelters (or Tabernacles) commemorated the time of God's protection of Israel after their deliverance from Egypt. God warned that he would bring his people back to the wilderness where he could again teach them to trust in him (see note on 2:14).

12:10 [11] *parables.* The word here (*damah*) implies similarity or likeness. Hosea often used similes in conveying God's messages to the people.

12:11 [12] *the people of Gilead are worthless.* Despite the people's boasting of great accomplishments done without wrongdoing, God had given them warning through the visions and words of his prophets, who often delivered their messages in parabolic speeches or proverbs that were largely ignored. Nevertheless, Hosea added yet another.

Gilgal. Like Bethel, Gilgal was condemned for its worship of Baal. By combining Gilead and Gilgal, Hosea achieved assonance and simultaneously used two places to represent all of the northern kingdom. Both socially (Gilead) and religiously (Gilgal), Israel was corrupt.

heaps of stone. Another literary play is intended here. The noun *gallim* [TH1530, ZH1643] (heaps) comes from the same root as the name Gilgal. The worthless pagan altars are as plentiful as stones cast away from carefully plowed fields. Their great number testifies to the widespread observance of idolatry in the northern kingdom.

COMMENTARY

God condemned Hosea's contemporaries for their unholy ways. Whether in their commercial dealings, their social contacts, or their religious observances, the Israelites were guilty of all kinds of deceit and falsehood. In calling them worthless (*'awen* [TH205, ZH224]; 12:11), God employed a term that was used not only for all sorts of evil, but one that dredged up bad memories from the life of Jacob.

God had described his people in this way before (6:8; see note). The noun had often been used in a compound term for Bethel: Beth-aven (4:15; 5:8; 10:5, 8). Here God used it as a reminder of that equation (Beth-aven = Bethel) and as a way of reminding them of the significance of Bethel in the life of Jacob. The notice of the wickedness of Gilead also reached back to the story of Jacob. For there was a time when Jacob's fleeing entourage deceived a pursuing Laban and his company there (Gen 31:19-55). Gilead was still filled with deception and evil. Like Bethel/Beth-aven, the northern kingdom was filled with the false worship of Baal. Like bloody Gilead (6:8), it perpetuated Jacob's deceitful ways economically and socially.

All of this had come about because of Israel's deceptive bent. Pretending to be true to God, they were committed to Baal. Despite God's repeated pleadings and warnings of the past and those still being declared through his prophets, they continued in their own willful and stubborn way. So calloused had their con-sciences become that they pronounced themselves innocent of any wrongdoing, even in the face of their well-known dishonest practices.

Conditions in Hosea's Israel provide a grim reminder of the folly of abandoning fellowship with God and ignoring his word. Where there is no divine revelation, society all too easily runs amok. Where people refuse to live by God's clear revela-tion, matters fare no better: "When people do not accept divine guidance, they run wild" (Prov 29:18).

Believers must heed the same truth. Though the word of God will last forever (Ps 119:89; Isa 40:8), believers must allow it to work in their lives (Ps 119:16-17) if they are to keep themselves from sin (Ps 119:9, 11) and experience the fullness of God's guidance (Ps 119:133, 169; cf. Col 3:16; 2 Tim 3:16-17).

◆   4. Hosea's observation: God will repay Israel's deceit (12:12-14)

¹²Jacob fled to the land of Aram,
    and there he* earned a wife by
    tending sheep.
¹³Then by a prophet
    the LORD brought Jacob's
    descendants* out of Egypt;
    and by that prophet

they were protected.
¹⁴But the people of Israel
    have bitterly provoked the
    LORD,
so their Lord will now sentence
    them to death
in payment for their sins.

12:12 Hebrew *Israel.* See note on 10:11b.   12:13 Hebrew *brought Israel.* See note on 10:11b.

NOTES

12:13 [14] *by a prophet.* This is a reference to Moses, the prophet of the Exodus period (Deut 18:15-19).

they were protected. The NLT reflects some of the connotations in the verb *shamar* [TH8104, ZH9068] (guard). Hosea used the term here and in 12:12 (where it is translated "tending") to form a continuity between the two.

12:14 [15] *their Lord.* The MT reads *'adonayw* [TH136/2050.2, ZH151/2257] (his master). Yahweh reminded Israel that he is its real master, not Baal. Baal can also mean "master" (see commentary on 2:12-13).

sins. Lit., "blood guiltiness." The northern kingdom was condemned previously for its bloody deeds (1:4; 4:2; 6:8). Hosea now warned his people that their many crimes would soon come back upon their heads.

COMMENTARY

Hosea grasped the deeper implication of the Lord's closing words concerning Gile-ad and therefore returned to the case of Jacob. Jacob, the refugee in Aram, worked many long years for his wife, having been tricked by Laban into serving extra time to attain the woman he loved (Gen 29:14–30:43). Building on that experience, Hosea went on to discuss Jacob's descendants. In later life, Jacob went to live in Egypt after Joseph rose to a high position in government (Gen 46:1-7). Those who descended from Jacob spent many years in Egypt. When a change of Pharaohs came, there was a change of attitude toward the Hebrews and they were forced into bondage. Theirs was a greater bondage than that which Jacob endured under Laban (Exod 1:8-14).

In the course of time, God raised up a prophet named Moses who led the people out of Egypt (Exod 12:1-36; Deut 26:5-8). Although God's prophet cared for them in every way, the people soon showed disrespect for God and his leader and accordingly were forced to spend 40 years in the wilderness before entering Canaan (cf. Exod 32:1-10; Deut 1:26-36).

Hosea's generation had proven to be no better. Although Hosea attempted to give counsel to these later descendants of Jacob, they disdained him—much as Jacob's heirs did to Moses in the wilderness. Even worse, they turned their backs on him who had appointed Hosea—God himself—by choosing to follow Baal. Therefore, the time had come for Israel to pay for its long history of sinning.

While the certainty of death for sin faces everyone, a just but loving God has graciously provided for the forgiveness of sins and the potential for everlasting life (Acts 10:43; Rom 3:23; 6:23; Eph 2:4-9). He did this by sending the Prophet promised of old (Deut 18:15-19). Jesus acknowledged that he was a prophet when he said to his fellow citizens that "a prophet is honored everywhere except in his own hometown and among his own family" (Matt 13:57; cf. Mark 6:4; John 4:44). Likewise, the people acknowledged his prophetic status (Luke 24:19; John 4:19), especially as he entered Jerusalem during what would prove to be the last week before his crucifixion (Matt 21:11).

The early church also proclaimed that Jesus was indeed the promised great Prophet (Acts 3:22-23; 7:37). As that Prophet, Jesus is the climax of the chain of prophets inaugurated by Moses. Even more so, Jesus is greater than Moses (Heb 3:1-6). For although Moses was the mediator of the old covenant, Jesus is the mediator of the prophesied new covenant (Jer 31:31-34; Matt 26:28; 1 Cor 11:25; 2 Cor 3:6; Heb 8–9), which grants to its adherents eternal life (John 3:36; 6:54).

Like the Old Testament prophets, Jesus delivered God's message, but his was the culmination that their prophecies anticipated. The Old Testament prophets were often called to pronounce God's judgment upon their fellow countrymen, yet they delivered messages of hope for the future. Their kingdom oracles spoke not only of universal judgment but gave a promise of ultimate blessing for a repentant and restored people of God. Jesus also proclaimed the certainty of the coming of the Kingdom of God (Matt 24–25). Although he affirmed that his Kingdom did not have its origin or derive its character from this world (John 18:36), he did acknowledge that it would assuredly come with cataclysmic force (Matt 24:27-31; Luke 21:10-28).

Believers have already become citizens of that Kingdom via the new birth (John 3:3-7; Col 1:12-14; 2 Pet 1:11) and enjoy the reality of the risen Christ enthroned in their hearts (John 14:23-24; Gal 2:20; Col 1:27). Nevertheless, they look forward to that day when personally, physically, and visibly, Christ will return to earth (Matt 24:30; Acts 1:11; Rev 1:7; 22:7, 12, 20) and this world will become "the Kingdom of our Lord and of his Christ, and he will reign forever and ever" (Rev 11:15). Knowing this truth, the believer can cry "Amen! Come, Lord Jesus!" (Rev 22:20).

◆   ## 5. The folly of deceitful pride (13:1-16)

¹When the tribe of Ephraim spoke,
   the people shook with fear,
   for that tribe was important in
      Israel.
But the people of Ephraim sinned
      by worshiping Baal
   and thus sealed their destruction.
²Now they continue to sin by making
      silver idols,
   images shaped skillfully with
      human hands.
"Sacrifice to these," they cry,
   "and kiss the calf idols!"
³Therefore, they will disappear like the
      morning mist,
   like dew in the morning sun,
like chaff blown by the wind,
   like smoke from a chimney.

⁴"I have been the LORD your God
   ever since I brought you out of Egypt.
You must acknowledge no God but me,
   for there is no other savior.
⁵I took care of you in the wilderness,
   in that dry and thirsty land.
⁶But when you had eaten and were
      satisfied,
   you became proud and forgot me.
⁷So now I will attack you like a lion,
   like a leopard that lurks along
      the road.
⁸Like a bear whose cubs have been
      taken away,
   I will tear out your heart.
I will devour you like a hungry lioness
   and mangle you like a wild animal.

⁹"You are about to be destroyed,
      O Israel—
   yes, by me, your only helper.
¹⁰Now where is* your king?
   Let him save you!

Where are all the leaders of the land,
   the king and the officials you
      demanded of me?
¹¹In my anger I gave you kings,
   and in my fury I took them away.

¹²"Ephraim's guilt has been collected,
   and his sin has been stored up for
      punishment.
¹³Pain has come to the people
   like the pain of childbirth,
but they are like a child
   who resists being born.
The moment of birth has arrived,
   but they stay in the womb!

¹⁴"Should I ransom them from the
      grave*?
   Should I redeem them from death?
O death, bring on your terrors!
   O grave, bring on your plagues!*
   For I will not take pity on them.
¹⁵Ephraim was the most fruitful of all
      his brothers,
   but the east wind—a blast from
      the LORD—
   will arise in the desert.
All their flowing springs will run dry,
   and all their wells will disappear.
Every precious thing they own
   will be plundered and carried away.
¹⁶The people of Samaria
   must bear the consequences of
      their guilt
   because they rebelled against
      their God.
They will be killed by an invading
      army,
   their little ones dashed to death
      against the ground,
   their pregnant women ripped open
      by swords."

13:10 As in Greek and Syriac versions and Latin Vulgate; Hebrew reads *I will be.*   **13:14a** Hebrew *Sheol;* also in 13:14b.   **13:14b** Greek version reads *O death, where is your punishment? / O grave* [Hades], *where is your sting?* Compare 1 Cor 15:55.

N O T E S

13:2 *idols, images.* The former word was sometimes reserved for the worship of specific foreign gods (e.g., Isa 46:1; Jer 50:2). Hosea, however, used it as a general term for idols.

As in 8:4-5, it is employed here to delineate idols cast from precious metals. It appears also in 4:17 and 14:8. Although the latter term denotes images cast from metal, one cannot always discern a distinction in this term among the many Hebrew words for idols (see note on Hab 2:18).

"Sacrifice to these," they cry. The NLT follows the lead of many in reading a plural imperative (*zibekhu* [TH2076, ZH2284]) for the MT's substantival participle *zobekhe* (the sacrificers of men). Once again, the syntax is so abnormal that it is an almost insoluble crux. Therefore, it has occasioned several suggestions and emendations.

The problem revolves around the question of whether *zobekhe 'adam* (1) stands in apposition to "they say" (NLT "they cry") so as to read "to them they say, that is, those who sacrifice men" or (2) the word for "sacrifice" is to be viewed as an imperative: "to them they say, 'Sacrifice!'" The following *'adam* [TH120, ZH132] (man) would then be the subject of the subsequent plural verb (i.e., "men are kissing calves" or "let men kiss [the] calves"; cf. NJB, NRSV).

Scholars are commonly divided along lines compatible with one of these positions. The first alternative above takes the passage to refer to the practice of human sacrifice in the northern kingdom (cf. LXX, Vulgate, NIV, REB, GW). That human sacrifice of children was practiced in connection with Baal can scarcely be doubted (cf. 2 Kgs 23:10; Jer 7:31; 19:5-6; 32:35; see further my note on 2 Kgs 16:3 in Patterson and Austel 1988:245-246). The NLT follows the second alternative but ties *lahem* [TH3807.1/1992.1, ZH4200/2157] (to them) to the imperative: "Sacrifice to them."

Among many other proposals, one that may be noted in a few translations is to take the debated *zobekhe 'adam* to be the subject of the following verb: "Let the men who sacrifice kiss the calves" (cf. NASB, KJV, NKJV). This would appear to rest in part on an interesting suggestion made long ago by the medieval Jewish scholar David Kimchi (AD 1160-1235, as cited by Keil 1954:154), but often overlooked by expositors: to understand *zobekhe 'adam* as a type of subjective genitive, that is, "sacrificers of men" = "men who sacrifice." Such a construction, though uncommon, is not unknown in Hebrew. Thus Isa 29:19 reads *'ebyone 'adam* [TH34/120, ZH36/132] ("poor of men" = "men who are poor"); Gen 16:12 has *pere' 'adam* [TH6501/120, ZH7230/132] ("a wild ass of a man" = "a man who is a wild ass"); and Prov 15:20 speaks of *kesil 'adam* [TH3684/0120, ZH4067/132] ("a fool of a man" = "a foolish man"). Such is the verdict of Cohen (1985:49) and of Keil (1954:154-155) and G. A. Smith (1929:332), although with differing results. Following this approach and taking *zobekhe 'adam* in apposition to *hem* (they), the MT can be understood in yet another way: "To them [the craftsmen] those who sacrifice are saying that they will kiss the calves [= idols]." Whatever the proper solution, God is condemning the apostate and foolish people for their wanton idolatry.

13:4 You must acknowledge no God but me. God's declaration reinforces the first commandment (Exod 20:3; Deut 5:7). As here, both expressions of the Decalogue tie the commandment to God's deliverance of his people from Egypt. The word translated "have" is literally "know" in the MT. As such, it reminds the people of both their guilt in following other gods and their failure to really know and honor God (see note on 4:6).

13:5 I took care of you. Lit., "I knew you." Once again (see the commentary below), the importance of knowledge is emphasized. Knowing/knowledge is a key theme in the book, being woven into the fabric of several oracles. The book will end with a reminder of the importance of exercising proper knowledge (14:9).

in that dry and thirsty land. The NLT rendering of the hapax legomenon occurring in the MT is in harmony with those who relate the *tal'uboth* [TH8514, ZH9429] to Semitic cognates signifying drought or arid conditions.

13:9 *You are about to be destroyed . . . by me, your only helper.* The abrupt style of the Hebrew has occasioned varying interpretations. Many expositors have devised elaborate schemes to bring a specific rule of syntax to bear on this sentence, often referring to obscure grammatical possibilities. The relevant difficulties are best understood as follows: (1) *shikhetheka* [TH7843, ZH8845] is a third singular verb, prophetic perfect—"it (i.e., the beast of 13:8) will destroy you" or "it will bring you into ruin" (i.e., Israel's pride, cf. 13:6); (2) *ki* [TH3588, ZH3954] is an adversative particle—"yet/but"; (3) *bi* [TH871.2/2967.1, ZH928/3276] is a preposition with a first common singular suffix—"in me"—and *be'ezreka* [TH5828, ZH6469] (your help) stands in apposition to *bi*. For a penetrating study of the syntactical force of the preposition *be-*, see Futato 1978:69-83.

Nevertheless, the main point seems clear: Israel's low esteem, if not outright disdain, for God will bring its destruction. This will happen despite the availability of God, its only true helper. Thus understood, the verse serves as a literary hinge between the threats based on the historical lesson and the condemnations that follow in vv. 10-11. The NLT has rendered in accordance with the flow and sense of the context.

13:10 *Now where is your king?* The turmoil occasioned by the rise of competing kings who rapidly succeeded one another only intensified the reality of Israel's hopeless situation. In the face of the Assyrian threat, no human king could save them.

13:11 *I gave you kings.* Lit., "I gave you a king." Most translations and scholars render this Hebrew prefix conjugation verb as past tense (= the older preterite; cf. Num 23:7). So understood, it refers to Israel's first request for a king so as to be "like all the other nations" (1 Sam 8:5). Some take the verb to be present tense: "I keep giving" (e.g., Laetsch 1956:101; McComiskey 1992:221; G. A. Smith 1929:333; cf. *La Sacra Biblia*). The Vulgate renders it as a future: "I will give," referring to the coming invasion by the king of Assyria (cf. Garrett 1997:261).

13:12 *collected . . . stored up.* The metaphor is that of wrapping up some item and putting it in storage for future use. Andersen and Freedman cite the contribution of Vuilleumier-Bessard who "has suggested that the imagery is derived from the practice of wrapping up precious manuscripts and putting them in storage. The manuscripts found at Qumran afford the best-known example" (1980:637). They themselves propose that "what is described here is the removal of idols to safe storage, with the intention of retrieving them again in the future" (Andersen and Freedman 1980:638). Perhaps the simplest solution is to view the text as an application of Deut 32:28-35. There God points out his patience with the sinning people but warns, "Am I not storing up these things, sealing them away in my treasury?" (cf. Cohen 1985:51; Keil 1954:159; Wood 1985:221).

13:13 *a child who resists being born.* The metaphor is that of an "overdue" baby. The image points to Israel's failure to recognize an opportunity—even at this late hour—to avert certain doom. Its downward slide to destruction could yet be reversed by submitting to Yahweh, its true king. By so doing, it would be born anew to renewed spiritual and moral vitality, and extended national existence. Their situation was like a baby resisting its birth.

Since babies obviously do not choose to delay their birth, some (e.g., Garrett 1997:263-264; Stuart 1987:206) suggest that the reference is to a baby that is mispositioned in the womb. While this may be the actual cause of the tardiness in delivering, the point here is the urgency of the time. It was the final hour for Israel. Not to submit to its only helper was sheer and stubborn stupidity. In a slightly different twist in imagery, Hezekiah likened Judah's extreme danger during the Assyrian king Sennacherib's siege of Jerusalem to a mother who, though the hour of her delivery had come, did not have the strength to bear the child. Only God's intervention could deliver them (2 Kgs 19:3-5).

13:14 *the grave?* Lit., "Sheol." In the OT, Sheol refers to the state of death or the grave, the place of the dead body (e.g., Gen 37:35; 44:31; Num 16:30-33; Ps 88:3), but most commonly the term is reserved for the abode of the wicked dead (Ps 49:13-14; Isa 14:11). The NLT textual note points out a variant understanding in the LXX, which contains a rhetorical question implying a positive outlook. Paul appears to be drawing upon the LXX in 1 Cor 15:55 although he replaces the word "hades" (which he "never uses"; Robertson and Plummer 1911:378) with "death," thus reading death in both parallel lines. (Note that Ellicott n.d.:327, however, suggests that Paul's words are "a free use on the Apostle's part of the prophet as they appropriately rise in his memory.") In context, "Hosea 13:14 will become a reality for God's people. With powerful effect, Paul quotes Hosea's striking rhetorical questions" (Mare 1976:291).

O death, bring on your terrors! O grave, bring on your plagues! The NLT renders according to the sense. If the previous two sentences are rhetorical questions expecting a negative answer, then these two invite the agents of terminal judgment to begin their horror. The invitations to death and Sheol are given in inverse order to their appearance in the previous two lines, thus forming a neat chiasmus.

13:15 *Ephraim was the most fruitful of all his brothers.* Lit., "for he—a son of/among brothers—shall be fruitful." The MT has been variously emended. Most commonly, *ben 'akhim* [TH1121/251, ZH1201/278] (son of brothers) has been changed to read something like *ben 'akhu* [TH996/260, ZH1068/286] ("among reeds"; NASB, NRSV; cf. Cohen 1985:51; Mays 1969:179; Wolff 1974:22). Although the text is admittedly difficult, the reading "son among brothers" (cf. KJV, NIV, ASV, NLT) may be defended as both fitting the imagery and artistry of Hosea and as corresponding to other OT passages about Ephraim.

Genesis 48 shows that Joseph's sons Ephraim and Manasseh were reckoned among Jacob's sons in the blessing/inheritance (Gen 48:5). In that blessing (Gen 48:16), Jacob prayed for their increase and said of their father "Joseph is a fruitful tree, a fruitful tree beside a spring" (Gen 49:22 mg). In Hosea itself, the life of Jacob (cf. 12:3-5, 12) and the imagery of fruitfulness (10:1) and the east wind (= Assyria; 12:1) have already appeared. Their use here, though somewhat obscure, is not as perplexing as it might seem at first glance; further, an extended pun on the consonant pairing *pr* (pe, resh) is clearly intended. To start with, the words used of fruit (*peri* [TH6529, ZH7262]) and fruitfulness (*para', porath*) contain this pair. The reference to the "east wind" as a symbol for Assyria also provides a tie to 8:9, where the noun "wild donkey" is used in describing Israel's courting of Assyria—another instance of the *pr* pairing, as the noun has the same consonants as the verbal stem behind "was . . . most fruitful" (*para'* [TH6500, ZH7229]; see note and commentary on 8:9). Finally, the name Ephraim also contains the consonant cluster *pr*. In sum, Ephraim, who has become fruitful in accordance with the ancient promise of Gen 48, will nonetheless be devastated. The nation after which Ephraim chased like a wild donkey in heat would come against it like a hot east wind (cf. 12:1).

13:16 [14:1] *their little ones dashed to death . . . their pregnant women ripped open.* See 10:14; 2 Kgs 8:12-15; Isa 13:16; Amos 1:13. Cf. note on Nah 3:10.

COMMENTARY

God's final judgment oracle begins with a reminder to Ephraim that as the representative tribe of the northern kingdom, it bore a noble heritage. Despite being a leader among the other tribes, however, they had gone over to the worship of Baal. This, along with the perpetuation of the state religion of the calves established by Jeroboam I, had led the northern kingdom into gross idolatry. They would soon bring about their own destruction—such was imminent. In a series of colorful similes, the Lord warned them that like morning mist before the rising sun, like chaff borne along by the wind, or like smoke rising from a chimney into the air, theirs would be a rapid and complete end (13:1-3).

The Lord went on to remind Ephraim that it was he (the Lord) who redeemed them from Egyptian bondage long ago. It was he who lovingly cared and provided for them in the wilderness. They simply had no other true savior and guide. Yet, when God had richly blessed them, rather than being grateful or even taking note of him, they became self-satisfied and proud. Rather than remembering God, they forgot him.

Here again, the crucial importance of true knowledge is underscored. It was their refusal to acknowledge God for who he truly is and their neglect of their covenant relationship with him that lay at the heart of Israel's problem (cf. 2:8, 20; 4:6; 5:3-4; 11:3; 13:4). Unfortunately, they failed to realize that "the meaning of human life cannot be determined apart from God, the giver of life" (Craigie 1985:81).

Failing to know God experientially, the people fell into all manner of grievous sin. Becoming spiritually and morally apostate, they nonetheless feigned acknowledgment of God. But it was too late. The enemy was already on the move (cf. 8:1-4) and Israel's punishment was certain (cf. 9:7). God himself would turn from defender to attacker. Using another graphic simile, he likened himself in his judicial wrath to a series of vicious animals that would rip them apart and devour them. The northern kingdom was doomed (13:4-8). "How sad the change, when He who had been Israel's Creator and Preserver became her Destroyer!" (Fausset 1948:506).

Accordingly, Israel must take urgent notice. The death of the northern kingdom was at hand. To whom could they turn? Surely not to their leadership, for they were all degenerate. Moreover, the kings Israel had chosen were not God's choice from the beginning. To be sure, God had made provision for a human king to reign over them, but this one was to be a man of the Lord's choosing, a man of godly character (Gen 49:10; Num 24:17; Deut 17:14-20). They, however, had chosen a king and a path that were displeasing to God (cf. 8:4; 10:2; 1 Sam 8:4-22). Moreover, when Israel split off from Judah, its first king set a precedent for turning away from God by instituting the state religion of calves at Dan and Bethel (1 Kgs 12:25-33). This became a besetting sin in Israel and was a precipitating cause of Israel's slide into further idolatry and eventual demise (2 Kgs 17:7-23). God warned his people that although he allowed them to elect to have a king and to select their own leader (1 Sam 8:22), he would now bring the whole system of royalty down, together with the kingdom itself (13:9-11).

God had no other choice. Israel had accumulated a record of gross sins for far too long. Their judgment was long overdue and had to come quickly. Hosea used a metaphor that, though illogical, is so striking that it would instantly catch his hearers' attention. Israel's stubborn refusal to repent and return in submission to God in order to avert disaster and acquire renewed vitality is likened to a baby in the birth canal who refuses to be born. As that baby resists coming into life, so Israel refused to be born anew into the full fellowship and blessings of God. How foolish! As that baby endangered his own life and that of the mother, so God's sinning people were facing not only their own death but that of the nation (13:12-14).

The chapter closes with another reminder of Israel's folly. The Lord returned to the subject of Ephraim's privileged position and prosperity. Blessed beyond measure, Israel had added to their idolatry, immorality, and self-will by selecting apostate kings who carried on foolish foreign policies. Not only had this been sapping the nation's vitality and moral fiber, but the very ones in whom Israel put its trust would turn on them and destroy them. Israel would fall, and many of its people would be savagely put to death. Their precious possessions would be carried off as booty, while the land itself would suffer great devastation. Such would be the costly price of their spiritual rebellion against God.

All of the emphases of this chapter have been introduced earlier in the book. Their reiteration here underscores their vital importance to God. At least four should be noted. First, Israel's problems began with a lack of gratitude that led them to serve self rather than God. In addition, Israel went off into the worship of other gods and the work of their own hands (13:1-3). Believers of all ages need to heed Israel's bad example and determine to be faithful to God and his claim upon their lives (Rev 2:10). It is so easy to slip almost imperceptibly into putting something other than God as the focus of one's life. To do so is idolatry. John's warning is still well taken (1 John 5:21). Likewise, believers should be "thankful and please God by worshiping him with holy fear and awe" (Heb 12:28).

Second, Israel had also forgotten their redeeming God, as well as his care and concern for them (13:4-6). God certainly has ordered it otherwise. God himself ordained the rainbow to be a symbolic memorial of his pledge that there would never again be "a flood [to] destroy the earth" (Gen 9:11). He also established the Passover for Israel, as a memorial of his mighty deliverance of his people out of Egypt (Exod 12:1-10; 13:3, 8-10). All of the set feasts of Israel were designed to be more than mere rituals. They were given to make God's people enter into an active, conscious fellowship with God, their Redeemer and Lord (see, e.g., Deut 16). The children of Israel were charged with remembering. They were to recall that God had ransomed his oppressed people (Deut 5:15) and so to act with special kindness toward the oppressed of society (Deut 24:17-22).

Paul encouraged gentile believers to remember, with gratitude, their salvation through Christ (Eph 2:11-19). John affirmed that godly remembrance can stimulate the church to repentance and renewed faithfulness (Rev 2:5; 3:3). In the familiar Pauline instructions concerning the Lord's Supper, the apostle rehearsed our Lord's admonition concerning regular remembrance of this ordinance (cf. Luke 22:19 with 1 Cor 11:24-25). As Christ's body was broken, so the believer's will is to be yielded in total dedication and obedience to God. As Christ's blood was poured out, so the believer's life is to be poured out unreservedly in grateful, joyous, and willing service to him. As those who are redeemed, may believers remember the Lord's full provision by giving their lives in faithful service to him.

Third, Israel had renounced God's kingship in favor of choices made to suit themselves. God's people therefore brought on themselves certain judgment (13:9-11). The lesson is clear: Godless leadership can ruin any nation (Prov 14:34; see the commentary on 4:1-14; 6:4-7:16; and 8:1-14). Contrariwise, when any nation or individual has God as leader, they can ask for help and he will graciously supply it (Ps 118:5-7; Isa 30:19).

Fourth, Israel established a long record of guilt that would be dealt with severely (13:12-16). Believers, too, should remember that God will judge unconfessed sin when we each "stand before the judgment seat of God" (Rom 14:10). There "we will each receive whatever we deserve for the good or evil we have done in this earthly body" (2 Cor 5:10). Nevertheless, God does not desire to keep a permanent record of our sins (Ps 130:3) but has so arranged matters that confessed sin is freely forgiven (1 John 1:8-9). May each believer keep short accounts with the Lord!

The messages of personal and national death given in 13:14 "become words of victory in 1 Corinthians 15:54-55."[1] Because the first half of 13:14 is cast in an interrogative sentence, a certain ambiguity exists. Accordingly, many have opted for a note of hope here rather than that of strict judgment. The apostle Paul seized upon that possibility and sounds a note of triumph for the believer. Because of Christ's resurrection "the ransom and redemption that God intended for Israel (13:14a) have been fulfilled. The backs of Sheol and death have been broken" (Hubbard 1989:223).[2] Believers now have the assurance of their own bodily resurrection on that day when Christ will return to take them unto himself. Moreover, as those united to the resurrected Christ, the victor, Christians have the potential and power to live victorious lives.

ENDNOTES

1. R. Nicole, "The New Testament Use of the Old Testament," in *The Right Doctrine from the Wrong Texts*, ed. G. K. Beale (Grand Rapids: Baker, 1994), 36. For a discussion of the textual relations between Hos 13:14 and 1 Cor 15:55, see G. Archer & G. Chirichigno, *Old Testament Quotations in the New Testament* (Chicago: Moody, 1983), 146-147. For the suggestion that Paul's citation of Hos 13:14 stands as "a free use on the Apostle's part of the words of the prophet, as they appropriately rise in his memory" rather than being a direct citation, see J. Ellicott, *St. Paul's First Epistle to the Corinthians* (Minneapolis: James Family, reprint edition [n.d.]), 327.
2. That Sheol is not, as commonly taught, the common receptacle of all disembodied spirits or that there is a double compartment in Hades with a gulf standing between good and evil spirits, can be demonstrated by the many OT texts which assert that the OT believer expected to go to be with God at death (e.g., Pss 49:15; 73:23-26). See the incisive studies of A. Heidel, *The Gilgamesh Epic and Old Testament Parallels* (Chicago: University of Chicago Press, 1963), 173-223; W. G. T. Shedd, *Dogmatic Theology*, 3 vols. (Grand Rapids: Zondervan, [n.d.]), 2.591-640; J. Lightfoot, *A Commentary on the New Testament from the Talmud and Hebraica*, 4 vols. (Grand Rapids: Baker, reprint 1979), 3.167-172; contra C. von Orelli, *The Old Testament Prophecy of the Consummation of God's Kingdom*, trans. J. S. Banks (Edinburgh: T & T Clark, 1889), 240-241.

◆   **6. Hosea's admonition: repent and confess all sins (14:1-3)**

[1] Return, O Israel, to the LORD your God,
for your sins have brought you
down.
[2] Bring your confessions, and return
to the LORD.
Say to him,

"Forgive all our sins and graciously
receive us,
so that we may offer you our
praises.
[3] Assyria cannot save us,
nor can our warhorses.

Never again will we say to the idols we
   have made,
     'You are our gods.'

No, in you alone
   do the orphans find
     mercy."

NOTES

14:1 [2] *Return, O Israel.* Hosea's admonition remains the same as that given previously
(6:1-3): Repent and submit once more to the Lord. Hosea will repeat his charge in 14:2.
God used the same verb (*shub* [TH7725, ZH8740]) to promise Israel that upon their repentance
his anger "will be gone forever" (14:4). Then his people "will again live under my shade"
(14:7). Similar language was used to announce Israel's turning to the Lord "and to David's
descendant, their king" (i.e., the Messiah; 3:5).

the LORD your God. Hosea reminded Israel that Yahweh is their covenant God. There is no
other—particularly not Baal.

your sins have brought you down. Lit., "you have stumbled in your iniquity." Israel's guilt
has been emphasized previously by the same verb (*kashal* [TH3782, ZH4173]). All Israel had
stumbled in their blatant sinful behavior (4:5).

14:2 [3] *Forgive all our sins.* Scholars have treated the somewhat abnormal Hebrew syntax
of this verse in various ways. Although most English translations take a similar approach to
that of the NLT (e.g., "take away all our guilt," NRSV), the REB reads, "You will surely take
away iniquity."

graciously receive us. This line expresses a positive side of Hosea's petition: "Receive that
which is good." Hosea's prayer is for God's acceptance of whatever good his people may
offer. In context, this refers to their words of confession expressed from a contrite heart.

so that we may offer you our praises. The MT's "we shall offer our lips as bulls" is difficult
to understand, unless Keil is correct in suggesting it means "the offering of our lips as bull-
ocks . . . i.e., present the prayers of our lips as thank-offerings" (1954:163-164; cf. Cohen
1985:53; Laetsch 1956:108). Many follow the reading of the LXX, *karpon cheileōn hēmōn*
[TH2590/5491, ZH2843/5927] (the fruit of our lips), repointing the MT (*parim*) to *perim* [TH6529,
ZH7262] (fruits) to be understood either as a double accusative or with "our lips" in apposition to "fruits." The consonants *prym* could also be viewed as *peri* [TH6529, ZH7262] with an
enclitic mem (cf. Wolff 1974:231). This final mem could also be taken with the following
noun, as the preformative preposition *min* [TH4480, ZH4946] (fruit *from* our lips), although
such a construction would be an unusual one. All such attempts to justify the LXX are
cumbersome at best. The NLT catches the spirit of the context and anticipates the sentiment
of Heb 13:15.

14:3 [4] *the orphans.* Since the son (11:1) has become Lo-ammi, meaning "not my people" (1:9), covenant-breaking Israel was cut off from the family of God—that is, orphaned.
Hosea called upon the Lord to show compassion to this orphan (cf. Deut 10:17-18; Pss
10:14; 68:5).

COMMENTARY

Once again Hosea pleaded with his fellow countrymen to renounce their idolatrous
and sinful ways and to return to their covenant God. Yahweh—and he alone—was
their God. Their sins caused them to stumble grievously and burdened them with
the weight of guilt. It was now more imperative than ever for Israel to repent and
pray for God's forgiveness.

    The elements of such a prayer are carefully detailed here. (1) Israel was to come
into God's presence with a heartfelt confession on their lips. (2) Having repented and

come to God with good and proper intentions, they were to petition God for forgiveness of their sins and guilt. (3) They were to praise God with wholehearted devotion. What the whole burnt offering symbolized in consecration of life (Lev 1; 6:8-13)—a life fully dedicated to God—was to be the genuine expression of their lips.

Further, their prayer was to contain a personal resolve to renounce their most persistent sins: (1) the reliance on other means of deliverance, whether their own military preparedness or their powerful neighbors such as Assyria, and (2) their fascination with other gods. The latter had been the more often rehearsed, being denounced in every previous chapter. The former had been called to their attention in several oracles (e.g., 5:13; 7:8, 11-12, 15; 8:9-10; 12:1).

Hosea's prayer reached its climax with a declaration of adoration of God's revealed character in his great compassion. It is in him that even the orphan finds mercy. The reference to God's concern for the orphan takes up the prominent theme of God's caring for the downtrodden of society: the widow, the orphan, and the poor, as well as the foreigner. Mosaic law declared that God was the protector of these groups (Exod 22:21-24; 23:6; cf. Deut 10:18-19; 27:19). The psalmist praised God as Father and defender of such people (Pss 68:5; 82:3-4). The prophets condemned Israel for its failure to care for them as God would (see Isa 1:16-18, 23; Jer 7:4-16; Ezek 22:6-7). In the New Testament their cause is likewise singled out (Acts 6:1; 9:39-41; 1 Tim 5:3-16). Thus, James reminded his hearers that "pure and genuine religion in the sight of God the Father means caring for orphans and widows in their distress" (Jas 1:27).

Spiritually, Paul assured the believing church that she is no widow but ever Christ's bride (Eph 5:25-32). Nor did Jesus leave those who followed him as orphans (John 14:18). Rather, he gave the Comforter, the Holy Spirit, as that other "Advocate, who will never leave you" but provide guidance "into all truth" (John 14:16-17). The Christian is also delivered from spiritual poverty for "though he [Jesus] was rich, yet for your sakes he became poor, so that by his poverty he could make you rich" (2 Cor 8:9). What an abundant and richly fulfilling life awaits the believer! Indeed, those who claim Christ's name can also exclaim with the psalmist, "You brought us to a place of great abundance" (Ps 66:12).

◆   ## 7. God's consolation for repentant Israel (14:4-8)

4 The LORD says,
"Then I will heal you of your
   faithlessness;
my love will know no bounds,
for my anger will be gone forever.
5 I will be to Israel
like a refreshing dew from heaven.
Israel will blossom like the lily;
it will send roots deep into the soil
like the cedars in Lebanon.

6 Its branches will spread out like
   beautiful olive trees,
as fragrant as the cedars of
   Lebanon.
7 My people will again live under
   my shade.
They will flourish like grain and
   blossom like grapevines.
They will be as fragrant as the wines
   of Lebanon.

8 "O Israel,* stay away from idols!   I am like a tree that is always
    I am the one who answers your   green;
        prayers and cares for you.   all your fruit comes from me."

14:8 Hebrew *Ephraim*, referring to the northern kingdom of Israel.

NOTES

14:4 [5] *I will heal you.* The verb for healing (*rapa'* [TH7495, ZH8324]) appeared several times before. God reminded Israel that turning to the king of Assyria could provide no healing for its problems (5:13). God himself desired to heal the people of their sins, but their entrenched apostasy prohibited him from doing this (7:1). Nevertheless, Hosea pleaded with his countrymen to return to the Lord, who alone could heal them from their sins (6:1).

faithlessness. The noun in the MT here is *meshubah* [TH4878, ZH5412] (waywardness). Derived from the same root as the verb translated "return" (*shub* [TH7725, ZH8740]), the root provides thematic stitching for both main sections of the chapter. It is Israel's apostasy that remains the basic flaw that has occasioned all its sin and guilt.

14:5 [6] *like a refreshing dew.* Previously God condemned Israel's love for him as being no more lasting than the dew that disappears quickly with the rising sun (6:4). Israel's fascination with idolatry would soon be so thoroughly judged that they themselves would disappear "like dew in the morning sun" (13:3). The imagery here emphasizes the refreshing nature of the dew, which nourishes the land and its vegetation (cf. Isa 26:19). Micah predicted that one day a restored Israel would be "like dew sent by the LORD" (Mic 5:7).

like the lily. It is unclear which of the many flowers called "lily" (*shushan* [TH7799, ZH8808]) is intended here. Keil (1954:165) declares that it is a white lily, while Stuart (1987:210) calls it a crocus. Walker (1957:114, 118) identifies *shushan* both as an iris that "is very delicate in color, of soft lemon and slight orchid-blue shade" and as the red chalcedonicum lily, which is "known as the Scarlet Martagon because of its brilliant scarlet petals and sepals."

like the cedars in Lebanon. "Cedars" does not occur in the MT here or in 14:6, but probably both are intended—Hosea often wrote elliptically. Garrett (1997:278) suggests that the sudden threefold reference to Lebanon here at the end of the book contains an underlying implication that "all of the good things that Israel thought to get from Baal will finally come from Yahweh."

14:6 [7] *branches.* Lit., "shoots." The NLT extends the tree imagery to include shoots that grow to maturity as blossoming branches.

like beautiful olive trees. Lit., "its splendor will be like the olive tree." The olive was a staple in Israel. Walker (1957:154) reports that "one tree could supply a whole family with fats, for olive oil was used instead of butter" and that "a full-sized tree yields a half ton of oil yearly."

14:7 [8] *My people will again live under my shade.* Lit., "they who dwell in its shadow will return." The fact of a return meant that captivity and exile had to precede the return. The predicted return was also an assurance of God's continuing love for his people.

grain . . . grapevines. Together with the olive tree, the mention of grain and wine is an indication of Israel's renewed covenant status (see notes on 2:8; commentary on Joel 1:10).

14:8 [9] *O Israel, stay away from idols!* Lit., "O Ephraim, what more have I to do with idols?" The NLT has used "Israel" in place of "Ephraim" in this verse for simplicity and clarity. The NLT has also formulated the rhetorical question found in the Hebrew as an exclamation, capturing its general force.

a tree that is always green. This tree has been identified as a juniper (LXX), a cypress (NRSV), or a pine (NIV; cf. Isa 60:13). Stuart (1987:211) renders it simply "fir." Because the yielding of fruit is mentioned in connection with the tree that is ever green, it may intend the stone pine, which produces edible seed.

fruit. The noun here is also used to depict Israel as a plant that bears no fruit because its roots are dried up and withered (9:16). In another context, Israel was charged with misusing God's fruitful blessing by pursuing pagan worship practices (10:1) and by trusting in military buildup rather than God (10:13). Fruitful Israel (Ephraim) has also courted other nations, one of which will ultimately come against them and destroy them (13:15).

COMMENTARY

God's last oracle through Hosea is a reminder to Israel of who he is and how he will respond to them should they follow Hosea's admonition to repent. Only he can heal their apostate condition. Their long history of unfaithfulness and idolatry can yet find forgiveness and cleansing. Their return and submission to him will allow them to experience the fullness of his undying love for them. True repentance and acknowledgment of the Lord would mean the relenting of his judicial anger toward them—forever.

What blessing could be theirs! In yet another series of sparkling similes, God likened his renewed relation to his people to the morning dew, which brings fresh vitality to the landscape. In a series of agricultural images, God promised that with his renewed provision Israel would again blossom like the lily. Its natural beauty would mirror the abundance of its prosperity. Like the fabled cedars of Lebanon, a restored people in a newly established state would have deep roots in the soil of the land.

Continuing the tree imagery, the Lord pointed out that Israel's splendor would be like that of an olive tree, a gift from the Lord of the covenant (cf. Josh 24:13). Israel would no longer be a stench in the nostrils of the nations but would be held in such esteem that they would resemble the fragrance of Lebanon's cedar forests and finest wine. (Although the wine of Lebanon is not celebrated in the OT, it was apparently well-known in the ancient world; cf. Pliny *Natural History* 14.7.) Further, a productive Israel will be sought after for its agricultural and viticultural prominence.

Completing the imagery, God assured his people that one day Israel would return to dwell in safety in the land. God's love and concern for his people is always as fresh and available as an evergreen tree that remains fruitful throughout the year. God's power and availability is not seasonal but continuous.

Therefore, God can ask the penetrating question (see note on 14:8 [9]) that succinctly summarizes his whole case against Israel: "What have I (ever had and even now have) to do with idols?" Idols and Yahweh have nothing in common. Not only is idolatry expressly forbidden in the second commandment, but in the final analysis, no comparison exists between God and the gods represented by the idols (cf. Deut 6:4, 13). Indeed, Hosea's rhetorical question (see the note on 14:8 [9]) invites the people to consider the impossibility of comparing Yahweh with the idols of mankind. Hosea's contemporary Isaiah also castigates the settled idolatry of the people, condemning as utter folly those who first manufacture the idols

(Isa 2:8; 40:19-20) and then bow down and worship the work of their own hands (Isa 44:12-20). Rather, Israel must realize that the Lord is the incomparable one (Isa 40:18) who alone is the almighty creator and sustainer of mankind (Isa 40:25-31) and the only God who is the source of man's righteousness and strength (Isa 45:22-25). Therefore, those who confess to being believers should "stay away from idols" (14:8)—not only those manufactured by man but "anything that might take God's place in your hearts" (1 John 5:21).

Could Israel not see this? All their long history of fascination and preoccupation with Baal had brought them nothing but guilt before God—hence, his rapidly approaching judgment (cf. Isa 42:15). Only a sincere return to him could ever give them the things they thought they had gained by going over to Baal and the other false gods. It was a time of decision. Would they choose their present path (leading to death; cf. Deut 8:19) or all the abundant blessings available in the one who alone could heal them?

Unfortunately, the Israel (and Judah) of past history made the wrong choice. They persisted in apostasy and political intrigues right up to the end. Although they missed the opportunity for the blessings God wanted to pour out upon them, the prophets predicted that one day Israel would be restored to the land that God promised to Abraham and his descendants (Gen 13:14-15; cf. Isa 10:21-22; 35:8-10; 49:9-13; Jer 31:7-14; Ezek 34:13-16; 36:24-28; 37:21-27; Amos 9:14-15).

There they would know the great blessings assured to them in the new covenant (Isa 54:1-10; Jer 31:31-34; Ezek 37:21-28). For David's descendant, the Messiah, will dwell among them, reigning in holiness, righteousness, and justice. He will provide safety, peace, and everlasting felicity for all (cf. Isa 11:1-9; 61:1-3; Jer 33:15-18; Ezek 34:25-31; Dan 7:13-14, 26-27; see the commentary on Joel 3:17-21 and on Zeph 3:9-20).

New Testament believers also look forward to that blessed time. As Old Testament believers hoped for that era when they would be regathered to the land, so Christians look to that day when Christ shall come and gather them unto himself (John 14:3; 1 Thess 4:16-17). As Old Testament believers cast their eye toward that age when God's enemies would be defeated and the Messiah would extend his just and glorious reign over a new and refreshed earth (cf. Isa 2:3-5; 60:1-22; 62:1-5; 65:17-25; Zech 14:1-9), so New Testament believers long for the coming of Christ to subdue all evil and to reign over a new and revitalized world where sin and death cannot exist and believers can live in fellowship with their King and Lord forever (Rev 11:15-18; 19:11–22:20).

◆ Subscription (14:9)

9 Let those who are wise understand these things.
Let those with discernment listen carefully.
The paths of the LORD are true and right,
and righteous people live by walking in them.
But in those paths sinners stumble and fall.

NOTES

14:9 [10] *Let those who are wise understand these things. Let those with discernment listen carefully.* The skillful and discerning use of wisdom will bring true knowledge. The grouping of these three words often associated with knowledge (*khakam* [TH2450, ZH2682], "wise"; *bin* [TH995, ZH1067], "understand"; *yada'* [TH3045, ZH3359], "know") points to Hosea's acquaintance with the wisdom genre (cf. Macintosh 1995:124-132).

true and right. The NLT rendering provides two of the qualities of character that the Hebrew root *yashar* [TH3474/3477, ZH3837/3838] (straight, upright) connotes. The declaration is based on Deut 32:4.

righteous people live by walking in them. But in those paths sinners stumble. Uprightness (i.e., integrity) and righteousness are natural corollaries of each other (see note and commentary on Hab 2:4). Hosea had spoken of Israel's stumbling previously (4:5; 5:5; see the note on 14:1). Here stumbling characterizes any person who chooses to violate God's revealed standards rather than live by them.

COMMENTARY

Hosea brings his prophetic collection to a close by adding a personal note. He intended to encourage those hearers who had been attentive listeners. Having been given a great deal of information, they were to be those who perceived the issues involved so as to draw proper conclusions. They were to employ them skillfully in their spiritual lives. Above all, Hosea had repeatedly confronted them with the clear distinction between proper and improper courses of action. Accordingly, people are wise if they make the right decision to follow God's straight path to righteous living (Ps 1:1-3). In so doing, they will experience God's blessings and protection, while the rebellious will fall by the way and perish (cf. Ps 1:6).

The theme of the two ways is a familiar one in the Old Testament. Moses warned the Israelites about departing from the right way after his death (Deut 30:19-20; 31:29). Joshua admonished his people not to stray from the Lord to serve other gods (Josh 24:14-15). One psalmist pronounced his blessing upon the one who disdained the paths of the wicked so as to walk according to the way of the law of the Lord (Ps 1), while another prayed that he might be delivered from deceitful ways, for he resolved to follow the way prescribed in God's law (Ps 119:29-32). The author of Proverbs urged his children to heed his wise instructions in order that they might choose the straight path he laid out before them and so avoid the evil way (Prov 4:10-19). Choosing one's own way rather than God's can only lead to death (Prov 16:25). The need to follow the way of the righteous and shun the way of evil also became a frequent theme in the prophets (e.g., Isa 26:7-11; Jer 5:4-5; Ezek 18:5-9, 21-32; 33:12-20; Hab 2:4; Mal 2:7-9).

The theme of the two ways is also attested in the intertestamental apocryphal and pseudepigraphical books (e.g., 2 Esdr 7:6-14; Sir 21:11-14; *The Testament of Asher* 1:3, 5), as well as the Dead Sea Scrolls (e.g., 1QS 3:18–4:26). Jesus later spoke of the two ways (Matt 7:13-14) in delineating the way of true discipleship. Although it is a narrow road, the true way leads to life, unlike the broad way, which leads to destruction. Those who take the former will enter God's final Kingdom; those who choose the latter will perish.

To forsake God and his revealed standards is to invite disaster. Those who arrogantly make their own way apart from God will ultimately miss the rich blessings that God has for those who love him and obey his Word. The truly wise person, unlike the wicked hearer (Isa 42:18-25; Jer 5:21; Ezek 12:2), will have an ear attuned to God's truth (Matt 13:9; Luke 14:25-35; cf. Rev 2:7, 11, 17, 29; 3:6, 13, 22) and will be sensitive to walk in his ways (Ps 119:1-5). Fausset (1948:510) wisely observes, "'The ways of the Lord are right,' not because we see the *reason* of them all, but simply because they are *the Lord's* ways."

If we have listened well to Hosea's prophecies, we perceive that what he wished for his fellow countrymen can be for us and for believers of all ages. We do wisely (1) to let God be God of our lives and (2) to abandon whatever idols we may have erected that cloud the sense of his love for us. Indeed, we demonstrate our love for Christ by walking in the way he commanded (John 14:15). As those who are truly wise, may we let the message of Hosea direct us on our way. For "the paths of the LORD are true and right, and righteous people live by walking in them" (14:9).

BIBLIOGRAPHY

Anderlini, G.
1988 Eset Z(e)nunim (Os 1,2). *Bibbia e Oriente* 30:169-182.
1989 GMR BT DBLYM (Os 1,3). *Rivista Biblica* 37:305-311.

Andersen, F. L. and D. N. Freedman
1980 *Hosea.* The Anchor Bible. Garden City: Doubleday.

Arnold, B. T. and B. E. Beyer
2002 *Readings from the Ancient Near East.* Grand Rapids: Baker.

Astour, M.
1971 841 BC: The First Assyrian Invasion of Israel. *Journal of the American Oriental Society* 91:383-389.

Ausin, S.
1994 La Tradición de la Alianza en Oseas. Pp. 127-146 in *Biblia Exégesis y Cultura: Estudios en Honor del Jose Maria Casciaro.* Pamplona: EUNSA.

Bergen, R. D.
1993 Calling Forth Yahweh's Curses: Hosea's Judgment of Israel in 8:1–10:15. *Criswell Theological Review* 7:39-50.

Berkhof, L.
1959 *Systematic Theology.* Grand Rapids: Eerdmans.

Bons, E.
1995 Zwei Überlegungen zum Verständnis von Hosea xi. *Vetus Testamentum* 45:285-293.

Cassuto, U.
1973 The Prophet Hosea and the Books of the Pentateuch. Pp. 79-100 in *Biblical and Oriental Studies,* vol. 1. Jerusalem: Magnes.

Chapman, K.
1993 Hosea 11:1-4—Images of a Loving Parent. *Review and Expositor* 90:263-268.

Chisholm, R. B., Jr.
1990 *Interpreting the Minor Prophets.* Grand Rapids: Zondervan.

Cohen, A.
1985 *The Twelve Prophets.* Soncino Books of the Bible, 12th ed. New York: Soncino.

Craigie, P. C.
1985 *Twelve Prophets.* Philadelphia: Westminster.

Dahood, M.
1953 The Divine Name ^{c}*Eli* in the Psalms. *Theological Studies* 14:452-457.

Davies, G. I.
1992 *Hosea.* New Century Bible. London: Pickering.

Dillard, R. B. and T. Longman III
1994 *An Introduction to the Old Testament.* Grand Rapids: Zondervan.

Donner, H. and W. Röllig
1966 *Kanaanäische und Aramäische Inschriften.* Wiesbaden: Otto Harrassowitz.

Dyrness, W. A.
1992 Environmental Ethics and the Covenant of Hosea 2. Pp. 263-278 in *Studies in Old Testament Theology.* Dallas: Word.

Edin, M. H.
1998 Learning What Righteousness Means: Hosea 6:6 and the Ethic of Mercy in Matthew's Gospel. *Word and World* 18:355-363.

Ellicott, C.
n.d. *St. Paul's First Epistle to the Corinthians.* Minneapolis: The James Family.

Emmerson, G. I.
1984 *Hosea.* Journal for the Study of the Old Testament, Supplement Series 28. Sheffield: Journal for the Study of the Old Testament Press.

Fausset, A. R.
1948 Hosea. Pp. 458-510 in *A Commentary Critical, Experimental and Practical on the Old and New Testaments*, vol. 4. Grand Rapids: Eerdmans.

Feinberg, C. L.
1976 *The Minor Prophets.* Chicago: Moody.

Friedman, M. A.
1980 Israel's Response in Hos 2:17b, "You Are My Husband." *Journal of Biblical Literature* 99:199-204.

Futato, M.
1978 The Preposition "Beth" in the Hebrew Psalter. *The Westminster Theological Journal* 41:69-83.

Gardiner, A.
1957 *Egyptian Grammar.* Oxford: Oxford University Press.

Garrett, D. A.
1997 *Hosea, Joel.* New American Commentary. Nashville: Broadman & Holman.

Gesenius, W. and E. Kautzsch
1910 *Gesenius' Hebrew Grammar.* Translator, A. E. Cowley. Oxford: Clarendon.

Gordon, C.
1936 Hosea 2:4-5 in the Light of New Semitic Inscriptions. *Zeitschrift für die Alttestamentliche Wissenschaft* 54:277-280.

Hailey, H.
1971 *A Commentary on the Minor Prophets.* Grand Rapids: Baker.

Harper, W. R.
1936 *Amos and Hosea.* The International Critical Commentary. Edinburgh: T & T Clark.

Harrison, R. K.
1969 *Introduction to the Old Testament.* Grand Rapids: Eerdmans.

Hubbard, D. A.
1989 *Hosea.* Tyndale Old Testament Commentaries. Downers Grove: InterVarsity.

Huffmon, H.
1965 *Amorite Personal Names in the Mari Texts.* Baltimore: Johns Hopkins.

Irvine, S. A.
1995 The Threat of Jezreel (Hosea 1:4-5). *Catholic Biblical Quarterly* 57:494-503.

Kaiser, W. C.
1985 Inner Biblical Exegesis as a Model for Bridging the "Then" and "Now" Gap: Hos 12:1-6. *Journal of the Evangelical Theological Society* 28:33-46.

Kaufmann, Y.
1960 *The Religion of Israel.* New York: Schocken.

Keil, C. F.
1954 *The Twelve Minor Prophets.* Biblical Commentary on the Old Testament. Translator, J. Martin. Grand Rapids: Eerdmans. (Orig. pub. 1873)

Krause, D.
1992 A Blessing Cursed: The Prophet's Prayer for Barren Womb and Dry Breasts in Hosea 9. Pp. 191-202 in *Reading Between the Texts: Intertextuality and the Hebrew Bible.* Editor, D. Fewell. Louisville: Westminster/John Knox.

Laetsch, T.
1956 *The Minor Prophets.* St. Louis: Concordia.

Landy, F.
1995 In the Wilderness of Speech: Problems of Metaphor in Hosea. *Biblical Interpretation* 3:35-59.

van Leeuwen, C.
2003 Meaning and Structure of Hosea x 1-8. *Vetus Testamentum.* 53:367-378.

Light, G. W.
1993 The New Covenant in the Book of Hosea. *Review and Expositor* 90:219-238.

Livingston, G. H.
1989 Hosea. Pp. 602-617 in *Evangelical Commentary on the Bible.* Editor, W. A. Elwell. Grand Rapids: Baker.

Luckenbill, D. D.
1927 *Ancient Records of Assyria and Babylonia.* Chicago: University of Chicago Press.

Machinist, P.
1983 Assyria and Its Image in First Isaiah. *Journal of the American Oriental Society.* 103:719-737.

Macintosh, A.
1995 Hosea and the Wisdom Tradition: Dependence and Independence. Pp. 124-132 in *Wisdom in Ancient Israel: Essays in Honor of J. A. Emerton.* Editor, J. Day. Cambridge: Cambridge University Press.

Mare, H.
1976 1 Corinthians. Pp. 173-298 in *Romans–Galatians.* The Expositor's Bible Commentary, vol. 10. Editor F. E. Gaebelein. Grand Rapids: Zondervan.

Mays, J. L.
1969 *Hosea: A Commentary.* Philadelphia: Westminster.

McComiskey, T. E.
1992 Hosea. Pp. 1-238 in *The Minor Prophets,* vol. 1. Grand Rapids: Baker.

Mulzer, M.
1992 Zur Funktion der GML-Aussage in Hosea 1,8a. *Biblische Notizen* 65:35-39.

Oestreich, B.
2000 Absurd Similes in the Book of Hosea. Pp. 101-126 in *Creation, Life, and Hope.* Editor, J. Moskalal Berrien Springs, MI: Andrews University.

von Orelli, C.
1977 *The Twelve Minor Prophets,* Reprint ed. Translator, J. S. Banks. Minneapolis: Klock & Klock Christian Pub.

Patterson, R. D.
1981 The Song of Deborah. Pp. 128-136 in *Tradition and Testament: Essays in Honor of Charles Lee Feinberg.* Editors, J. Feinberg and P. Feinberg. Chicago: Moody.

1988 Review of *Hosea: An Israelite Prophet in Judean Perspective,* by Grace I. Emmerson. *Hebrew Studies* 29:112-114.

1991 *Nahum, Habakkuk, Zephaniah.* Chicago: Moody.

1993 Old Testament Prophecy. Pp. 296-309 in *A Complete Literary Guide to the Bible.* Editors, L. Ryken and T. Longman III. Grand Rapids: Zondervan.

1998 Hosea, Book of. Pp. 401-402 in *Dictionary of Biblical Imagery.* Editors, L. Ryken and T. Longman III. Downers Grove: InterVarsity.

1999 The Old Testament Use of an Archetype: The Trickster. *Journal of the Evangelical Theological Society.* 42:385-394.

Patterson, R. D. and H. J. Austel
1988 1, 2 Kings. Pp. 243-444 in *1 Kings–Job.* The Expositor's Bible Commentary, vol. 4. Editor, F. E. Gaebelein. Grand Rapids: Zondervan.

Paul, S. M.
1995 Hosea 7:16: Gibberish Jabber. Pp. 707-712 in *Pomegranates and Golden Bells: Studies in Biblical, Jewish, and Near Eastern Ritual, Law, and Literature in Honor of Jacob Milgrom.* Winona Lake, IN: Eisenbrauns.

Priebe, D.
1996 A Holy God, an Idolatrous People, and Religious Pluralism: Hosea 1–3. *Currents in Theology and Mission* 23:165-172.

Pusey, E. B.
1953 *The Minor Prophets,* vol. 1. Grand Rapids: Baker.

Rallis, I. K.
1990 Nuptial Imagery in the Book of Hosea: Israel as the Bride of Yahweh. *St Vladimir's Theological Quarterly* 34:197-219.

Robertson, A. and A. Plummer
1911 *I Corinthians.* International Critical Commentary. Edinburgh: T & T Clark.

Rooker, M. F.
1993 The Use of the Old Testament in the Book of Hosea. *Criswell Theological Review* 7:51-66.

van Rooy, H. F.
1993 The Names Israel, Ephraim and Jacob in the Book of Hosea. *Old Testament Essays* 5:135-149.

Smith, D. A.
1994 Kinship and Covenant in Hosea 11:1-4. *Horizons in Biblical Theology* 16:41-53.

Smith, G. A.
1929 *The Book of the Twelve Prophets*, vol. 1. New York: Doubleday.

Smothers, T. G.
1993 Preaching and Praying Repentance in Hosea. *Review and Expositor* 90:239-246.

Stuart, D.
1987 *Hosea—Jonah*. Word Biblical Commentary. Waco, Texas: Word.

Swaim, G. G.
1978 Hosea the Statesman. Pp. 177-183 in *Biblical and Near Eastern Studies*. Editor, G. Tuttle. Grand Rapids: Eerdmans.

Sweeney, M. A.
2000 *The Twelve Prophets*. Berit Olam. Collegeville, MN: Liturgical.

Talmon, S.
1966 The "Desert Motif" in the Bible and in the Qumran Literature. Pp. 31-64 in *Biblical Motifs*. Editor, A. Altmann. Cambridge: Harvard.

Thomas, D. W.
1961 *Documents from Old Testament Times*. New York: Harper & Row.

Walker, W.
1957 *All the Plants of the Bible*. New York: Harper and Row.

Waltke, B. K. and M. O'Connor
1990 *An Introduction to Biblical Hebrew Syntax*. Winona Lake, IN: Eisenbrauns.

Wolff, H. W.
1974 *Hosea*. Hermeneia. Translator, G. Stansell. Philadelphia: Fortress.

Wood, L.
1985 Hosea. Pp. 159-226 in *Daniel, Minor Prophets*. The Expositor's Bible Commentary, vol. 7. Editor, F. E. Gaebelein. Grand Rapids: Zondervan.

Joel

RICHARD D. PATTERSON

INTRODUCTION TO
Joel

JOEL WARNED HIS PEOPLE of the coming Day of the Lord. Unless repentance was forthcoming, God's judgment would come against them. The Scriptures indicate that the Day of the Lord that Joel's contemporaries faced was just a foretaste of a final, universal judgment: In the future, God will deal with all sinful nations and people. He will then establish for himself a redeemed, purified people upon whom he will pour out his blessings. Peter's use of Joel's prophecy (cf. Acts 2:17-21 with Joel 2:28-32) gives assurance that all believers in Christ can experience the blessings of spiritual life prior to the great judgment of God.

AUTHOR

Modern scholarship largely accepts the unity of the book of Joel and has agreed that Joel was its author. Beyond his name (meaning "Yahweh is God") and patrilineage (the son of Pethuel [Bathouel in the LXX]), little is known of his personal circumstances. Although some have suggested the possibility that Joel might have been a priest, due to his strong interest in ritual fasting and prayer (Finley 1990:2), all that can be said with certainty is that the prophet was a man of vitality and maturity who understood the spiritual significance of contemporary issues.

DATE AND OCCASION OF WRITING

When an unprecedented locust infestation blanketed the land, Joel understood it as nothing less than the Day of the Lord's judgment, a foretaste of an even greater judgment if the people did not mend their ways. Accordingly, Joel wrote to call the people to repentance and restoration to God's favor so as to avoid that coming divine punishment. The issues concerning the Day of the Lord would afford the prophet the opportunity to reveal God's intentions for the great Day of the Lord in the eschatological future.

The date of the book's composition must coincide with the time of a terrible locust plague. But this is a matter of heated scholarly debate. Conjectures have ranged from the ninth century BC to the time of the Maccabees in the second century BC. Some (e.g., Keil) have found evidence for the time of the boy-king Joash (835–796 BC) in the fact that Joel does not mention any king and because prominence is given to the Temple and priesthood. Some (e.g., Pusey) have opted for an early eighth-century date, citing correspondences between Joel's material and that of Amos, as well as the locust plague itself (cf. Amos 1:2; 4:9; 7:1-3 with Zech 14:5). Others opt for a late preexilic time, stressing either Joel's supposed receptivity to Jeremiah's influence (e.g., Kapelrud) or the actions in 3:2b as being best explained as reflecting a time between the Babylonian invasions of Jerusalem in 597 and 586 BC (e.g., Rudolph). Still others favor an exilic setting (e.g., Reicke) or an early (e.g., Allen) or later (e.g., Wolff) postexilic date (400 BC and later).

In addition to these data, scholars have noted that Joel often speaks in terms that are paralleled in other prophets. The question, of course, is whether Joel has drawn upon others for his text, or whether they have utilized his prophecy, or whether all have drawn upon a common prophetic repertoire. Wolff (1977:10-11) avers that Joel is a debtor to other prophets, some as late as Malachi (cf. 2:11b; 3:4 with Mal 3:2; 4:5). Because of this, Joel must have been written "in the century between 445 and 343 BC" (Wolff 1977:15). But, as Chisholm (1990:53) notes, "Arguments based on verbal parallels are notoriously subjective and inconclusive." Indeed, one could just as easily point to a rather strong case for Zephaniah's use of Joel (cf. 2:1-2, 11 with Zeph 1:14-18), as well as dozens of lexical and theological correspondences that Joel has in common with the other eighth-century prophets, making Joel a spokesman of that era.

The complexities of the data and arguments preclude any dogmatic decision, but there is much to commend the traditional conservative preference for a preexilic date. Perhaps most telling is the plague itself. While such incursions are common enough in the ancient Near East, the late eighth-century Assyrian hymn to Nanaya, which bears specific literary and linguistic parallels to Joel,[1] and the utilization of the plague motif by Amos (Amos 4:9; 7:1-3), who also has phraseology (Amos 1:2; 9:13; cf. 3:17-18) and subject matter (Amos 1:6, 9; cf. 3:2-4) in common with Joel, make the theory of an eighth-century date at least an attractive possibility.

In the first half of that century, Israel and Judah enjoyed a time of great prosperity. Together the two kingdoms managed to acquire nearly the same territorial dimensions that Solomon held. Both Jeroboam II in the north and Uzziah in the south were strong monarchs who expanded and strengthened their kingdoms (2 Kgs 14:25; 2 Chr 26:6-15).

The kings who followed in the latter half of the eighth century were not of the same caliber as these two, however. Moreover, they found themselves caught up in the rising power of the Neo-Assyrian Empire, beginning with Tiglath-pileser III (745-727 BC), who fought two western campaigns (744-743 BC; 734-732 BC), the second of which saw the capture of age-old Damascus, to Israel's north. Around that time, the northern kingdom was being led by a series of weak kings and finally fell to the Assyrians in 722 BC. Although Judah managed to survive, it did so at the cost of vassalage in the days of the wicked Ahaz (735-720 BC). Some degree of independence was achieved with the withdrawal of Sennacherib's forces from Jerusalem in the face of divine intervention during the reign of the godly Hezekiah (Sennacherib's third campaign—701 BC; cf. 2 Kgs 18:13-19:37).

Thus, accepting a date for Joel sometime during the eighth century BC, we may say that Joel prophesied in exciting and pivotal times. Whatever the exact period in this century of change, Joel would have ministered to a southern kingdom beset by great spiritual problems. The first half of the century saw an empty formalism grip the people, while outright apostasy set in with the reign of Ahaz, a condition that remained rampant until the reforming efforts of Hezekiah (2 Kgs 18:3-6; 2 Chr 29-31). Despite the best efforts of that king, however, a spiritual vacuum that already existed in Judah (2 Kgs 17:18-20) would resurface even more vehemently in the days of the evil Manasseh (698/697–642 BC). To such a people, Joel's message of imminent judgment and the need of immediate repentance was both timely and necessary. The danger was real. How would the people respond to the divine message given through his faithful prophet?

AUDIENCE

Whatever the time period involved, it is clear that Joel wrote to the citizens of Judah. He often refers to Judah and Jerusalem (2:32; 3:1, 17-18, 20) and their leaders (1:9, 13-14; 2:17) and citizens (3:6, 8, 19), or to Zion (2:1, 15, 23; 3:17, 21) and its people (2:15-17, 23). He was familiar with their history and geography (1:2; 3:2-8, 12, 14, 18) and was fully aware of the Temple and its services (1:9, 13-16; 2:14, 17; 3:18).

CANONICITY AND TEXTUAL HISTORY

The canonicity of Joel seems never to have been in question. Allen (1976:32-33) suggests that it enjoyed authoritative acceptance from the start. Certainly by the onset of the second century BC, such was the case for all of the Minor Prophets, as attested by Ben Sirach (Sir 49:10). Although Joel stands in a different order in the Septuagint (between Micah and Obadiah), the Septuagint's textual variations from the Masoretic Text are few and of questionable value (1:5, 8, 18; 2:12; 3:1). The second-century AD manuscript of portions of 2:20–3:21 found at Wadi Murabba'at, which reflects a proto-Masoretic tradition, underscores the fact that the text of the book has been well preserved.[2] The necessity for proposed emendations is minimal at best.

LITERARY STYLE

Thematically, Joel builds his prophecy around the Day of the Lord, every chapter being marked by that theme. In proclaiming that message, Joel employs strategically placed oracles of judgment (e.g., 2:1-11), interspersed with lament oracles featuring a call to mourning together, followed by a reason for doing so (1:5-7, 8-10, 11-12, 13-18, 19-20; 2:12-14, 15-17)—all aimed at bringing the populace to repentance. All of this culminates in what may be termed "kingdom oracles" (Patterson 1993:302-303), messages designed for the eschatological future, which blend together pronouncements of universal judgment and salvation oracles promising hope for God's long-beleaguered people (e.g., 2:28-32; 3:9-17, 18-21).

Scholars have inquired as to whether Joel's prophecies are at times apocalyptic in nature. He speaks of wonders in the sky accompanied by upheaval on earth (e.g., 2:2-3, 10, 30-31; 3:14-16). And he speaks of the intervention of the Divine Warrior himself into the affairs of men so as to bring earth's history to its final resolution (2:11, 28-32; 3:1-21). Like Zephaniah, however, Joel's prophecy appears to make use of themes and terms that would only later emerge as markers of full-blown apocalyptic literature in the intertestamental period. As with the other Old Testament prophets, Joel's vision of the future is one that arises out of the present, whereas the apocalyptists foretold that the future would make a dramatic intrusion into the present, which was at times viewed as the culmination of episodic happenings (Morris 1972:62; Sandy and Abegg 1995:178-181).[3]

Joel adds vividness to a basic theme by drawing upon familiar scenes from the natural and agrarian worlds around him. He speaks freely of vine and fig tree (1:7, 12), ruined harvests (1:2-4, 10-12, 16-17; 2:25) and the resultant suffering of men (1:11-12) and animals (1:18-20) alike. He reinforces it all by several striking literary devices, including simile and metaphor. For example, the devastating locusts are compared to a nation (1:6, NLT mg) and an invading army (2:3-11, 20, 25), while the coming universal judgment is called a ripe harvest and a full winepress (3:13). In brilliant apostrophes, Joel pictures God addressing the citizens of Tyre and Sidon (3:4) and calls on him to bring down his celestial warriors (3:11). In such a vivid and impassioned book, the careful reader will encounter several examples of metaphor and simile (e.g., 1:6, 19, 20; 2:2-11, 20, 25; 3:16), metonymy (1:11), allegory (2:1-11), hyperbole (3:12), personification (2:21-23), merism (2:16, 23), rhetorical questions (1:2, 16; 2:11, 14; 3:4, cf. NASB), hendiadys (1:16; cf. NASB), and numerous instances of verbal and thematic repetition and recapitulation (cf. 1:4 with 2:25; 1:5 with 3:18; 1:6 with 2:2, 5; 3:9). Joel's "whole composition has been constructed as an intricate literary mosaic with remarkable skill and care" (Allen 1976:42).[4]

MAJOR THEMES

As noted above, the dominant theme of Joel is the Day of the Lord, about which "no other Old Testament witness gives . . . as detailed and systematic a treatment" (Wolff 1977:12). Building on the well-known Divine Warrior theme,[5] the present judgment of Israel (ch 1) is viewed as a precursor to one impending in the near future (1:15; 2:1-11), both being preparatory to God's later intention to judge all the nations in the eschatological future (ch 3). Whatever the time, that dreadful day (2:11) is described as one of darkness and gloom, clouds and blackness (2:2), darkened luminaries (2:10; 3:15), and upheaval of nature (2:10, 30; 3:16). It is sent by the Almighty himself (1:15) whose forces (2:2, 11; 3:11b) effect widespread destruction (1:15) upon the countryside (1:19-20; 2:3-5), cities (2:6-9), and nations (3:2-8, 12-14, 19), leaving all terrified in its wake (2:6, 11). Because the nations have sinned against God and his people, judgment must inevitably come (3:1-8, 19, 21).

Moreover, Israel itself had been brought to shame for its treatment of God (2:27). Accordingly, a second theme emerges in Joel's prophecies—that of repentance. Israel must turn to God in unswerving faithfulness if it hopes to ameliorate or avoid the impending catastrophe it faces (1:14; 2:12-17). These two themes provide the basis for yet a third: God's judgment and his people's faithfulness will ultimately result in Israel's full deliverance and everlasting felicity (2:27, 32; 3:16-20).

Several other themes are also present: (1) Judgment takes the form of an invasion in all three chapters. (2) The people are warned of danger by the sound of the shofar (2:1, 15). (3) The valley is the scene of the nations' defeat (3:2, 12, 14). (4) Mount Zion is the place of salvation and final blessing (2:32; 3:17, 21). It may be noted, as well, that the person (2:13-14) and works (e.g., 2:18-32) of Yahweh, Israel's covenant God, undergird the whole of Joel's prophecy.

THEOLOGICAL CONCERNS

Joel participates in the Zion theology so prevalent in the book of Psalms.[6] Zion theology has its focus on the only true God (2:27), who is Israel's God (2:17), the eternal Divine Warrior (1:15; 2:11; 3:11-16) who punishes his foes (3:1-8, 12, 19, 21), while protecting (3:16) and caring for (2:18-27) his own. A patient, gracious, and merciful God (2:13, 17), he deals with all people justly (2:23; 3:1-8) and receives all who call upon him in faith (2:28). A sovereign God, he expects his followers to submit willingly to him and worship him (1:13-14; 2:15-17) from the heart (2:12-13) in order that they may live in his righteousness and goodness (2:23-27), while looking forward to his blessed presence forever (3:17-21).

OUTLINE

  I. Joel's Present Instructions (1:1–2:27)
    A. Lessons from the Locust Plague (1:1-20)
      1. The prospect: the locust invasion (1:1-4)
      2. A plea for personal penitence (1:5-13)
      3. A call for worship (1:14-15)
      4. The resultant scene (1:16-20)
    B. Warnings Based on the Locust Plague (2:1-27)
      1. The prospect: the coming invasion (2:1-11)
      2. A plea for communal repentance (2:12-14)
      3. A call for worship (2:15-17)
      4. The resultant scene (2:18-27)
  II. God's Future Intentions (2:28–3:21)
    A. The Prospect: The Outpoured Spirit (2:28-32)
    B. The Coming Judgment (3:1-8)
    C. The Climactic Battle (3:9-17)
    D. The Resultant Scene (3:18-21)

ENDNOTES

1. For details, see V. A. Hurowitz, "Joel's Locust Plague in Light of Sargon II's Hymn to Nanaya," *Journal of Biblical Literature* 112 (1993):597-603. Although Hurowitz rightly makes no decision as to the relationship between the two texts, he demonstrates that in the Nanaya Hymn (rev. II 24:1–28:1), "nearly every detail . . . has either general or quite specific parallels in Joel's description of the locusts afflicting Judah" (599). Hurowitz also mentions that three letters from the archives of Sargon II (721–705 BC) referring to locust infestations are also known, although one cannot be sure that they refer to the same event. Whether the presence of pestilence in Syria from the time of Ashur-dan III (771–754 BC), which forced his troops to abandon their campaign, is to be linked to Joel's locust plague is at best problematic.

2. Crenshaw (1986:53) calls attention to an unpublished manuscript from Qumran, Cave four (4QXIIg = 4Q82), which contains portions of Joel and several other Minor Prophets. Likewise, he cites 4QXIIc [4Q78], which "has tiny segments of 1:11–2:1; 2:8-23; and 4:6-21[3:6-21]."

3. On the subject of apocalyptic, see P. D. Hanson, *The Dawn of Apocalyptic* (Philadelphia: Fortress, 1975); John J. Collins, *The Apocalyptic Imagination* (New York: Crossroad, 1984); D. S. Russell, *The Method and Message of Jewish Apocalyptic* (Philadelphia: Westminster, 1964); Sandy and Abegg 1995:177-196. For OT prophecy, see Patterson 1993:296-309.

4. See further, Patterson 1985:233-234.

5. For the motif of the Divine Warrior, see F. M. Cross Jr., "The Divine Warrior in Israel's Early Cult," in *Biblical Motifs*, ed. Alexander Altman, (Cambridge: Harvard University Press, 1966), 11-30; Tremper Longman III, "Psalm 98: A Divine Warrior Victory Song," *Journal of the Evangelical Theological Society* 27 (1984):267-274; Tremper Longman III, "The Divine Warrior: The New Testament Use of an Old Testament Motif," *The Westminster Theological Journal* 44 (1982): 297-302; Tremper Longman III and Daniel G. Reid, *God Is a Warrior* (Grand Rapids: Zondervan, 1995).

6. For a fine discussion of Zion theology, see W. A. VanGemeren, "Psalms," in *The Expositors Bible Commentary* (Grand Rapids: Zondervan, 1991), 5.354-357.

COMMENTARY ON
Joel

◆ I. Joel's Present Instructions (1:1–2:27)
    A. Lessons from the Locust Plague (1:1–20)
        1. The prospect: the locust invasion (1:1–4)

The LORD gave this message to Joel son of Pethuel.

² Hear this, you leaders of the people.
    Listen, all who live in the land.
In all your history,
    has anything like this happened
      before?
³ Tell your children about it in the years
    to come,
and let your children tell their
    children.
Pass the story down from generation
    to generation.
⁴ After the cutting locusts finished
    eating the crops,
the swarming locusts took what
    was left!
After them came the hopping locusts,
    and then the stripping locusts,* too!

1:4 The precise identification of the four kinds of locusts mentioned here is uncertain.

NOTES

1:1 *The* LORD *gave this message.* Joel announces at the outset that what he has to say was given to him by the Lord. Joel has been commissioned to deliver a divine message to his countrymen.

Joel son of Pethuel. Like Hosea, Micah, and Zephaniah, Joel identifies his family lineage. The LXX renders Pethuel as Bathouel, a reading followed by the Syriac and Old Latin. This was the name of Rebekah's father ("Bethuel," Gen 22:23) and others (cf. Josh 19:4; 1 Chr 4:30). Joel's name (meaning "Yahweh is God") attests to a family commitment to Israel's covenant God.

1:2 *Hear this.* Joel's message begins with an imperative. The subgenre of this opening prophecy is often debated. Thus, for example, Crenshaw (1995:82, 84) opts for an invitation to pay attention to Joel's summons to lament and return to Yahweh; Stuart (1987:239) decides for a call to communal lament; and Allen (1976:46-48) thinks it is a summons to national lament. All of these bear an element of truth and fall loosely under the rubric of instructional prophecy, containing warnings and exhortations (Patterson 1993:303-304). Such prophecies typically begin with an imperative and are followed by the reason for the warning, which is frequently introduced by the Hebrew particle *ki* [TH3588, ZH3954] ("for" or "because").

leaders. This word (*zeqenim* [TH2205, ZH2418]) can refer either to those of old age (Crenshaw 1995:86, "old timers") or those civil leaders who enjoyed an official role in communal life. The NLT follows the latter. Allen (1976:48) remarks, "The elders were ever a force in Israelite government, whether in the context of the local, tribal, or national community."

Listen. Joel turns from the elders to the general populace (lit., "all who dwell in the land").

has anything like this happened before? This rhetorical question is to be answered with a firm "No!" The calamity Joel is about to describe is unparalleled in anyone's memory. Crenshaw (1995:86) points out Sumerian literary parallels, citing unprecedented events or activities, so the motif itself is not without parallel.

1:3 Tell your children. So extraordinary and significant are current events that the account of them is to be passed on to subsequent generations. The preservation of significant events was a normal Hebrew tradition (see Exod 12:24-27; Deut 4:9; 6:6-8, 20-23; 32:7; Esth 9:20-28).

1:4 locusts. The nature of the locust plague is often debated. Some (e.g., Kapelrud, Sellers, Thompson) think that the four words for locusts here represent successive stages in the development of the locusts. Most scholars point out that the four nouns do not exhaust either the stages of the locusts or the various names assigned to locusts in the Scriptures (the OT has several others) or elsewhere in Hebrew literature. Therefore, the four words here are taken to reflect successive waves of attack, thus pointing to the intensity of the infestation and the total devastation of the land. Keil (1954:181-182) observes, "The thought is rather this: one swarm of locusts after another had invaded the land, and completely devoured its fruit."

There is disagreement also as to whether the locusts are to be understood literally or figuratively. While most take the text at face value as referring to actual locusts, some (Stuart 1987:232-234) follow a different approach, viewing the locusts as depicting an enemy invasion. Andinach (1992:441) treats the locusts as "a metaphor that clarifies and enforces the characteristics of a human army in its action against the people and the land." Amos also refers to locust plagues, pointing out that God's people had failed to respond to divinely sent locusts by returning to the Lord (Amos 4:9), and that on occasion his intercession had staved off God's renewed sending of the locusts (Amos 7:1-3).

Helpful discussions as to the nature of locusts together with examples of locust invasions can be found in J. D. Whiting, "Jerusalem's Locust Plague," *National Geographic* 28 (1951):511-550; Driver 1915:84-92; Pusey 1953:161-162.

COMMENTARY

Joel begins his prophecy by pointing out that what he had to say was not born of his own wisdom but had come from God himself. As with the other prophets, Joel clearly believed in divine revelation. The eternal God and covenant Lord of Israel had chosen to communicate himself to his people through his prophet. Thus, the basic nature of prophecy as being the proclamation of God's message is underscored.[1]

Joel then begins his instructions to the populace. He invites all the people to hear his words. Could anyone recall such a locust devastation? It was the kind of event that should and would be retold by the succeeding generations. A series of locust infestations had swept across the land destroying all the crops. The mention of four types of locusts may indicate that the locusts had appeared in a series of four waves. If so, Joel's notice coincides with other prophets who spoke of God's judgment in terms of four types of punishment (cf. Jer 15:3; Ezek 14:21). If, as has been argued in the Introduction, Joel prophesied in the eighth century BC, it is of interest that Amos, Joel's contemporary, also mentioned a severe locust plague (Amos 4:9).

These opening verses are a reminder, not only to God's people in Joel's day but also to believers of succeeding generations, that God takes note of sinful behavior and will take serious measures to chastise his people so as to bring them back to himself.

Therefore, all who read Joel's words ought to bring themselves to self-examination and so live as to reflect the standards of a holy God in their lives. To be sure, not all disasters in the natural world can be viewed as cases of divine judgment. Yet the fact that God does use such methods (cf. Lev 26:15-16; Deut 28:20-24; Amos 4:9; 7:1-3) to bring correction to people should cause them to examine their spiritual condition when they do occur. Such instances may be opportunities for sinners to repent and seek God's face and for saints to renew their spiritual commitment.[2]

ENDNOTES
1. On the genre and types of Old Testament prophecy, see Patterson 1993:296-309.
2. Fausset (1948:514) remarks, "The judgments of God are mutually united as the links of a chain, each link drawing on the other; and yet so arranged that at each successive stage time and space are allowed for the averting of the succeeding judgment by repentance."

◆   2. A plea for personal penitence (1:5-13)

[5] Wake up, you drunkards, and weep!
     Wail, all you wine-drinkers!
All the grapes are ruined,
     and all your sweet wine is gone.
[6] A vast army of locusts* has invaded
     my land,
     a terrible army too numerous to
     count.
Its teeth are like lions' teeth,
     its fangs like those of a lioness.
[7] It has destroyed my grapevines
     and ruined my fig trees,
stripping their bark and destroying it,
     leaving the branches white and bare.

[8] Weep like a bride dressed in black,
     mourning the death of her husband.
[9] For there is no grain or wine
     to offer at the Temple of the LORD.
So the priests are in mourning.
     The ministers of the LORD are
     weeping.
[10] The fields are ruined,
     the land is stripped bare.

The grain is destroyed,
     the grapes have shriveled,
     and the olive oil is gone.
[11] Despair, all you farmers!
     Wail, all you vine growers!
Weep, because the wheat and barley—
     all the crops of the field—are
     ruined.
[12] The grapevines have dried up,
     and the fig trees have withered.
The pomegranate trees, palm trees,
     and apple trees—
     all the fruit trees—have dried up.
And the people's joy has dried up
     with them.
[13] Dress yourselves in burlap and weep,
     you priests!
Wail, you who serve before the
     altar!
Come, spend the night in burlap,
     you ministers of my God.
For there is no grain or wine
     to offer at the Temple of your God.

1:6 Hebrew A nation.

NOTES
1:5 *Wake up . . . weep . . . Wail.* Those singled out for special warning are given a three-fold challenge: wake, weep, and wail. Typically, Joel forms his instructional/lament oracles (which make up the bulk of the first two chapters and 3:9-17) with imperatives, followed by motive clauses introduced by the particle *ki* [TH3588, ZH3954] ("for" or "because").

drunkards. Crenshaw (1986:94) views these *shikkorim* [TH7910A, ZH8893] in a positive or, at least, neutral sense, pointing to positive statements in the OT as to the benefits of wine. The root, however, is overwhelmingly used in a negative sense so that the vast majority of interpreters take the word here (as does the NLT) in a condemnatory sense. From the root *shakar* [TH7937, ZH8910] come the derived nouns *shikkor* [TH7910, ZH8893] (drunkard), *shikkaron* [TH7943, ZH8913] (drunkenness), and *shekar* [TH7941, ZH8911] (strong drink). Wine and strong drink are often paired in warnings against intoxication (Lev 10:9; Prov 20:1). The ready availability of wine in the northern kingdom during the eighth century is illustrated in the Samaria Ostraca, many of which deal with receipts for wine. It is likely Judah was no different. Whatever the precise emphasis on wine here, God's people are pictured as pursuing their own pleasure, oblivious to the great danger to which their spiritual lethargy had exposed them.

grapes . . . sweet wine. The NLT renders according to the sense. With the grape harvest ruined, there would be no wine. Therefore, wine drinkers would lament the loss of the new wine. The Hebrew text indicates that such "sweet wine" ('*asis* [TH6071, ZH6747], wine fermented "only five to seven days instead of the usual nine" [Crenshaw 1995:95]) was "cut off from your mouth" (cf. NRSV). While wine itself was considered a sign of God's blessing (cf. 2:23-24) and was used in the drink offering (Lev 23:12-13), the use of the common words for wine indicates the possibility of excess to the point of intoxication. For *yayin* [TH3196, ZH3516] (wine), see Prov 20:1; for *tirosh* [TH8492, ZH9408] (new wine), see Hos 4:11; and for '*asis* (sweet wine), see Isa 49:26.

1:6 *A vast army of locusts.* Lit., "a nation of locusts." The NLT has rendered the Hebrew metaphor according to its sense. The locusts are likened to a nation whose invading army is not only powerful but too vast to number. The comparison of armies and locusts is often attested not only in the literature of the ancient Near East (Thompson 1955:52-55) but also in the OT (Judg 6:5; 7:12; Jer 51:14; see commentary on Nah 3:15-17; cf. also Job 39:19-20; Rev 9:7).

terrible army. The adjective '*atsum* [TH6099, ZH6786] (strong, powerful) is also used by Daniel to describe the mighty army of the king of the south (Dan 11:25), but the locusts in the Exodus plague, for example, are described by the psalmist (Ps 105:34) as innumerable rather than powerful. Hubbard (1989:45) records a modern-day invasion that "was described in the newspapers in terms reminiscent of Joel. In one county 200,000 acres were covered with insects over every inch and in some places stacked on top of each other." See also Wolff (1977:27-28).

like lions' teeth. The cutting strength of locusts was often reported in ancient times. Pliny the Elder (*Natural History* 1:212) noted that the various locusts could even gnaw through doors. Two terms for "lion" ('*aryeh* [TH738A, ZH793] and *labi* [TH3833, ZH4233]) appear here, rendered as "lion" and "lioness" in the NLT.

1:7 *grapevines . . . fig trees.* The vine and the fig tree were often used as symbols of God's blessing (cf. Hos 2:12; Amos 4:9; Mic 4:4; Hag 2:19; Zech 3:10; see also 1 Kgs 4:25; 2 Kgs 18:31; Ps 105:33; Isa 36:16; Jer 5:17; 8:13). The vine also functioned as a symbol of the nation (Ps 80:8-15; Isa 5:2-6; Jer 2:21).

bark . . . branches. The denuding of trees, leaving them without bark and whitened, as well as the thorough devastation left by invading locusts, is well documented (Smith 1929:394-395; Pusey 1953:163).

1:8 *Weep.* The verb '*alah* [TH421, ZH458] is found only here in the OT. It is cognate with the Syriac '*ela* (lament) and Arabic '*alla* (mourn). Unlike the more general term for weeping found in 1:5 (*bakah* [TH1058, ZH1134]), it specifically denotes crying born of deep sorrow. The Hebrew root *bkh* can designate weeping for various reasons, such as joy (Gen 33:4), pouting (Judg 14:16-17), grief (2 Sam 19:1-2), repentance (Neh 1:4), or personal (2 Sam 12:15-23) or public (Zech 7:3) distress. The imperative '*eli* [TH421, ZH458] is feminine singular, either suggesting the personification of Jerusalem as a woman (cf. Jer 31:15; Lam 1) or reflecting the image of the bereaved virgin that follows.

like a bride dressed in black. Lit., "like a virgin clothed in sackcloth." For the wearing of sackcloth as a symbol of sorrow or remorse, see the note on Jonah 3:5.

mourning the death of her husband. Although the Hebrew text does not mention the death of a husband, such is the natural assumption of the virgin's putting on sackcloth. The NLT's "husband" should not be taken to indicate that the marriage had been consummated—the young woman may yet have been in her father's household. Wolff (1977:30) points out that the young woman had been acquired as the prospective bridegroom's wife "by the binding legal act of paying the bridal price."

1:9 *there is no grain or wine to offer.* The absence of grain and wine seriously impaired the daily burnt offerings. Both products were an integral part of the sacrificial ritual (Lev 2; 6:14-18; 9:16-17; 23:18, 37).

the priests are in mourning. Because the priests were allowed to eat a portion of the grain offering (Lev 2:3, 10), they would feel the loss of grain and wine. Although it can be used figuratively (e.g., "the earth mourns," Isa 24:4) and in parallelism with verbs of weeping (2 Sam 19:2), the verb *'abal* [TH56, ZH61] is often used of mourning for the dead (2 Sam 13:31-37) or in connection with an announcement of coming judgment (Neh 1:4; Esth 4:3).

ministers of the LORD. The Hebrew root of the word translated "ministers" (*sharath* [TH8334, ZH9250]) was often employed to depict the religious duties of the Levites and priests who served in the Tabernacle and Temple (cf. Exod 28:35, 43; 1 Chr 16:4, 37). It also became a technical term for one who does special or responsible service. Joseph was a minister to Potiphar (Gen 39:4), Joshua was Moses's minister (Exod 24:13; 33:11; Josh 1:1), and Elisha performed a similar function for Elijah (1 Kgs 19:21). The Greek word *leitourgia* [TG3009, ZG3311] (service) in the NT is similar in that it conveys the notion of priestly service.

1:10 *fields are ruined, the land is stripped bare.* The devastation of the fields is highlighted with alliteration featuring a play on harsh sibilants: *shuddad sadeh* [TH7703/7704, ZH8720/8441], "ruined fields." Likewise, the phrase "the land is stripped bare" is composed with alliteration: *'ablah 'adamah* [TH56A/127, ZH62/141]. The verb translated "stripped" (*'abal* [TH56A, ZH62]) is the same verb used previously to describe the priests' mourning, hence literally: "the ground mourns."

grain . . . grapes . . . olive oil. The loss of these crops, customarily harvested in the fall, points to God's fulfilling the threatened judgment upon his nation for covenant unfaithfulness and transgressions (cf. Deut 28:51). All three were important agricultural products and deemed to be the result of God's blessing upon his people—blessings that could be withdrawn as punishment for sin (Num 18:12; Deut 7:13; 11:14; 28:51; Jer 31:12).

1:11 *Despair . . . Wail.* The imperatives directed at those who tend the crops reflect a sense of shame and intense disappointment, which is reflected in a terrified look and bitter cry (cf. Amos 5:16-17). The word translated "despair" is *hobishu* (from the verb *bosh* [TH954, ZH1017], "be ashamed/dismayed") and represents a play on sounds with the verbal phrase of the previous verse: "the [new] wine is dried up" (*hobish* from the verb *yabesh* [TH3001, ZH3312]; NLT, "grapes have shriveled").

all the crops of the field. The NLT rendering gives the intended sense of the MT. "Wheat and barley" function as a metonymy representing the total loss of the agricultural harvest.

1:12 *pomegranate . . . palm . . . and apple trees.* The representative nature of these products of the orchard follows in the next phrase: "all the fruit trees." The noun translated "apple" (*tappuakh* [TH8598, ZH9515]) has been taken by some (Allen 1976:54) to mean apricot. Support for the meaning "apple" comes not only from postbiblical Hebrew but also from Gordon (1965:499), who sees a relationship between the Minoan pictograph for apple, with phonetic value *tu*, Hebrew *tappuakh*, Ugaritic *tuppuh*, and Arabic *tuffah*.

COMMENTARY

Joel begins his instructions with a triple imperative calling for lamentation: Wake up, weep, and wail! He first turns to the general populace, calling them a group of drunkards. The lives of God's people had become obsessed with the pursuit of pleasure. Although the first half of the eighth century BC had seen some spiritual awakening in Judah (2 Chr 26:4-5), King Uzziah was not always the spiritual leader he should have been (2 Kgs 15:4). Ultimately, his sinful pride led to his downfall (2 Chr 26:2, 6-21). Nor were things better in the north. Indeed, the eighth-century prophets indicate that the spiritual level of the populace had not risen above that of the kings of the northern and southern kingdoms (cf. Hos 4:11-19; 7:5, 13-14; Amos 2:4-8; 6:6). No doubt, the very prosperity of the eighth century contributed to the desperate spiritual condition of God's people. How tragic it is that times of ease and prosperity too often lead to spiritual and moral lethargy, and to compromise and defeat. The great military and economic gains of the era for both north and south are detailed in the Scriptures and validated by the archaeologist's spade. Excavations at various biblical sites illustrate the condition of the times. At Samaria a cache of ostraca was found which proved to be receipts for wine, oil, and barley. The names of those involved in the transaction often included the name of the pagan deity Baal, attesting to the growing loss of true religion.

Joel's designation of the populace as "wine drinkers" was thus appropriate. They had turned what God intended as a blessing into a wanton consumption that all too often led to drunkenness and debauchery. Israel's religious experience was seriously affected, degenerating into an empty formalism devoid of spiritual vitality. The eighth-century prophets denounced the wine-drinking habits of the people, complaining that such had permeated all levels of society (from the king downward) and had infected every area of the peoples' lives (cf. Isa 5:11-12, 22; 22:13; 28:1; Hos 4:11-19; 7:5, 13-14; Amos 2:4-8; 6:6; Mic 2:11).

Accordingly, Joel chides the people as those who would mourn the loss of vineyards, for that meant the loss of wine for drinking. In so doing, however, he calls attention not only to the vine but also to the fig tree. Both were well-known symbols of God's blessing for his covenant people (cf. Hos 2:12; Amos 4:9; Mic 4:4; see also 1 Kgs 4:25; 2 Kgs 18:31). In this, Joel recognized that the unprecedented locust plague was nothing less than the judgment of God upon his wayward people.

Joel's evaluation of his society stands as a warning to ours. That which so easily brings intoxication and personal degradation (Gen 9:21; 19:32; Prov 20:1; Isa 28:7) can easily corrupt one's thinking, even that of God's people (Hos 4:11). Far better is it to be free of its influence (Deut 29:6; Jer 35:6) and to be filled with the power of the Holy Spirit (Eph 5:18).

While excessive drinking can lead to a degenerate lifestyle, it is not the only besetting sin. Whatever exerts so dominating and controlling an influence on a person's life that it takes away spiritual vitality and productivity is sin; it needs to be abandoned (Rom 6:1-14; 14:23b; 1 John 5:21). May God help us to be preoccupied with Christ, not with selfish indulgence (Phil 3:7-11).

Joel goes on to point out that great spiritual issues were at stake in the destructive locust plague (1:8-10). He mentions the loss of grain and wine, key ingredients not only to Israel's economy but to its worship experience. Desperate as conditions were for the people's source of food and drink, there were greater issues to be considered. The worship of God had been placed in jeopardy. Rather than grieving over what their loss of grain and wine meant to their daily consumption, they ought to have mourned the loss of their opportunities to perform the daily sacrifices.

Without these products, the meal and drink offerings could not be offered. Both were crucial products in the sacrificial system. The drink offering is particularly significant to the full scriptural record. It was employed chiefly to accompany and culminate the offerings that are spoken of as having a pleasing aroma before God and that symbolize full dedication (the burnt offering, together with its grain offering, signifying active service) and loving communion (the peace offering) with God (Exod 29:38-42; Lev 2; 6:14-18; Num 15:1-10; 28:3-8; 29:30).

It is this image that Paul drew upon expressly in Philippians 2:17-18, as he emphasized both the Philippians' consecration and his own commitment to Christ's will for his life. Were Paul to die in the Roman prison from which he was writing, his death would be merely a joyous drink offering to the dedicated sacrifice (= the burnt offering) and priestly service (= the grain offering), which the Philippians' faith had evidenced. Accordingly, he could rejoice and urged them to rejoice as well. Theirs had been a sacrificial faith and loving service. What would be more appropriate than for Paul to crown that consecration with the drink offering of his life?

May we learn a lesson from this symbol of strong devotion. May our churches, like that of Philippi, have those kinds of people that a Paul (or our pastor) would gladly die for. May our lives be characterized by a faith that produces such a total dedication that it issues forth in fruitful service for Christ. May we live lives that are consciously poured out in joyous surrender to him who "bore the sins of many and interceded for rebels" (Isa 53:12).

Such godly devotion was lacking in the populace of Joel's day, and with the judgment on the crops, even the outward forms of such devotion would be beyond their reach to attain (cf. 2:14). In light of the real significance of the losses of grain and wine, it is no wonder that Joel tells them that their sorrow should be akin to that of a young lady whose husband has died. It is only natural that the priests should realize what the loss of those crops meant not only to their inability to perform the sacrificial offerings but to Israel's spiritual condition. The loss of the opportunity even to offer the sacrifices should have caused the citizenry as a whole to realize that their spiritual service had degenerated into a meaningless formalism (cf. Isa 1:2-20). Further, their unfaithfulness and syncretistic practices (Hos 2:5; Amos 2:8) had established them as those who had broken the covenant bond between themselves and the Lord (cf. Deut 8:19-20; 30:15-18). Israel's condition was serious. Far more disastrous than what the locusts had done was what it symbolized! God would no longer tolerate their duplicity. Rather, he had taken away the ability and high privilege of offering those sacrifices that were intended to symbolize his people's devotion to him (cf. Hos 2:9-13; 9:1-4).

The lesson is obvious. True religion is an active one that comes from the heart (Deut 6:4-5; Jas 1:22-27). Mere ritual and routine, without the genuine spiritual reality that is evidenced by a demonstrated allegiance to a sovereign God, is unacceptable to him (1 Sam 15:22-23; Ps 40:6-8; Isa 1:10-20; Mic 6:8). May we be those who put our faith into action in true devotion, both in worship and service, while attending to our daily pursuits (Deut 10:12-13; Josh 22:5; 1 Sam 12:24; 1 Kgs 9:4; Ps 101:1-3; Matt 22:37-40).

Joel's words to those who tend the crops (1:11-12) are also instructive. Although they would weep over the economic loss and the cutoff of their food supply, the commodities mentioned also had spiritual significance. Especially noteworthy are the vine and fig tree. These appear at times in the Scriptures to symbolize the basic relation of God to his people, as well as the blessings he bestows on them for their obedience (Ps 80:8-15; Isa 5:2-6; Jer 2:21; cf. Matt 21:18-21, 28-46). Indeed, the divine promise to a faithful remnant spoke of a future peace, prosperity, and felicity, symbolized by sitting under one's own vine and fig tree (Mic 4:4; Zech 3:10). Likewise, the pomegranate, palm, and apple trees were not only important to the economy but often symbolized spiritual nourishment, refreshment, joy, and fruitfulness of life (Deut 8:6-10; Ps 92:12; Song 2:3).

The Scriptures picture the believer's basic spiritual relationship with the Lord using the motifs of the vine and the fig tree. As God saw in Israel the prospect of faithful service as an obedient people (Hos 9:10), so the Lord expects believers (the branches) to abide in Christ (the vine) in order that they may live fruitful and productive lives (John 15:4). Failure to maintain a close walk with the Lord, however, can only spell spiritual disaster (Matt 21:19-21; Luke 13:6-9; John 15:5-6). Further, a display or pretense of spirituality without real fruit-bearing invites the Lord's judgment, much as Jesus cursed the fig tree for showing a promise of fruit without actually bearing any (Matt 21:18-19). Believers are thus reminded that the Lord expects his followers to be active, genuine, and faithful Christians who serve the Lord out of a pure heart, regardless of the exigencies of life (cf. Hab 3:17-19).

A final lesson comes from Joel's admonition to the priests. Having noted their lamenting (1:9), he calls upon them to spend the night in heartfelt contrition and penitence (1:13). The situation was severe, as they should be the first to recognize. For theirs was the exalted task of ministering before the Lord. Surely they were to set the example for all as to the proper course of spiritual action (cf. Luke 12:48). But the other eighth-century prophets indicate that the priests had scarcely done so previously. Given to drink (Isa 28:7-10), yet teaching for a price (Mic 3:11; cf. 2 Cor 2:17), they personally ignored God's law. Such conduct could only cause God's people to perish for lack of spiritual knowledge (Hos 4:4-9).

Joel's challenge to the false spiritual leadership thus stands in distinct contrast to the work of the one who is the promised Prophet and Great High Priest (Deut 18:15-18; Heb 8:6; 9:21-28). So also it should be with believers. For as a kingdom of priests (Exod 19:6; 1 Pet 2:9), they are said to do spiritual service for God. This is not only true for those specially called to minister before God but for all believers. Theirs is to be a wholesome, balanced, and spiritually maturing walk and witness before the Lord (cf. Ps 101:6 with Matt 5:48; 2 Cor 13:11). All of the believer's life should be seen as spiritual service for Christ (Rom 12:1-2; 15:26-27; 2 Cor 9:12-13; Phil 2:17).

◆   ## 3. A call for worship (1:14-15)

14 Announce a time of fasting;
  call the people together for a
    solemn meeting.
  Bring the leaders
    and all the people of the land
    into the Temple of the LORD your God,

and cry out to him there.
15 The day of the LORD is near,
  the day when destruction comes
    from the Almighty.
  How terrible that day will be!

NOTES
1:14 *Announce a time of fasting; call the people together for a solemn meeting.* Such fasts customarily lasted for a day (1 Sam 14:24) and were called in order to seek God's favor (Judg 20:26; 1 Sam 7:6). National fasts were extraordinary (Neh 9:1-3; Jer 36:9), but this was an unprecedented emergency.

Bring the leaders . . . and cry out. The elders were to take the lead as the whole congregation came together and poured out their heartfelt cries to the Lord (cf. Ezek 30:2-3).

1:15 *when destruction comes from the Almighty.* The assonance in the Hebrew is striking here: *ukeshod mishadday* (cf. Isa 13:6). One might colorfully render it: "Like a shattering from Shaddai." The etymology and origin of the Hebrew noun *shadday* [TH7706, ZH8724] ("Almighty" in the NLT) is disputed. The NLT follows the older view that derives it from the root *shadad* [TH7703, ZH8720] (devastate). The meaning "almighty" for this word is also at times attested in the LXX (*pantokratōr* [TG3841, ZG4120]) as in Job (e.g., Job 5:17) and in the Vulgate (*omnipotens*; e.g., Gen. 17:1).

How terrible that day will be! The LXX and the Vulgate read the cry three times in contrast to the one phrase in the MT, thus emphasizing the need for sorrow and dread at the judgment still to come. The locust plague pointed ominously to the imminence of the day of the Lord's judgment.

COMMENTARY
Joel continued his instructions to the priests by telling them to call the people together for a time of fasting. This was to be no ordinary fast but rather one that involved the entire populace. The religious and civic leaders were to set the pace by coming to the Temple and making their pleas to the Lord. Deeply moved, Joel wanted the leadership to experience his same spiritual concern. They were to lead the people in genuine repentance, calling on God for his forgiveness in order to avoid a still greater calamity (cf. 2:15-20). Like the citizens of Nineveh (Jonah 3:5), those of Jerusalem were to confess their sins publicly.

Fasting ought not to be simply routine or a matter of ritual (Matt 6:16-18). Rather, it should reflect the kind of anguish of heart that results from acknowledging sins committed (1 Sam 7:6) or recognizing a dire threat (2 Chr 20:1-3; Esth 4:1-3) or experiencing deep concern for another (e.g., Ps 35:13; Dan 6:18 [6:19]). Trying to achieve spiritual insight or make a spiritual decision can also be an occasion for fasting (Dan 9:1-19; 10:1-3; Acts 13:2; 14:23). Above all, it should be accompanied by a consistent lifestyle of righteous conduct (Isa 58:5-12; cf. Matt 6:16-18).[1]

Joel warned his hearers that the locust plague was but a precursor to the imminent, terrible Day of the Lord. Due to Israel's sin (cf. Amos 3:1–5:13), that day was surely to occasion its demise (cf. Amos 5:16-20). The almighty God would send such destruction that life as God's people knew it would be completely shattered.

The Day of the Lord can refer to a judgment in the near future (Jer 46:10; Amos 5:18-20) or to a more distant, comprehensive judgment (3:14-15; Zech 14:1-21; 2 Pet 3:10-13). Often the two blend into one future scene (Obad 1:15; Zeph 1:7, 14-18). The Scriptures teach that the Day of the Lord is one of judgment, whether for God's people (Isa 2:12-22; 13:5) or for their enemies (Isa 13:6, 9; Jer 46:10; Mal 4:5-6 [3:23-24]). Prophecies describe it as a day of unprecedented warfare and cosmological events set in a scene of dark clouds. It will be accompanied by a mood of despair and pervading gloom (Zeph 1:14-15; cf. Rev 6:12-17). These same oracles are often accompanied by promises of deliverance for God's faithful people (e.g., Isa 59:15b-21; Zeph 3:8-20). All of these features, already attested from the eighth century BC onward, provide elements for the emerging apocalyptic corpus both of the Scriptures and the extrabiblical writings of Judeo-Christian literature.[2] The Day of the Lord thus stands as a vivid reminder to all that God does judge sin, and he will ultimately bring earth's history to its proper and just culmination.

ENDNOTES

1. A. Richardson (*A Theological Word Book of the Bible* [New York: MacMillan, 1962], 80) rightly remarks, "Fasting, like all personal discipline, is but a means to an end; if it loses sight of the end, 'for the Gospel's sake', it becomes merely a 'work of law', an attempt to earn merit, and then it ceases to have any Christian value or sanction." Fausset (1948:515) adds, "'Fasting' . . . must be a sanctified fast, in which we seek not to glory in self-mortification, but to cultivate a humble, chastened, and loving spirit."
2. See further, Patterson 1985:256-257.

◆   4. The resultant scene (1:16–20)

16 Our food disappears before our very eyes.
No joyful celebrations are held in the house of our God.
17 The seeds die in the parched ground, and the grain crops fail.
The barns stand empty, and granaries are abandoned.
18 How the animals moan with hunger!
The herds of cattle wander about confused,
because they have no pasture.
The flocks of sheep and goats bleat in misery.

19 LORD, help us!
The fire has consumed the wilderness pastures,
and flames have burned up all the trees.
20 Even the wild animals cry out to you because the streams have dried up,
and fire has consumed the wilderness pastures.

NOTES

1:16 *Our food disappears.* Joel envisions chiefly the food offerings necessary for the sacrificial system, as the parallel line indicates.

joyful celebrations. Lit., "joy and gladness." The NLT properly renders the two Hebrew nouns as a hendiadys (two words expressing one thought).

1:17 *seeds.* The Hebrew noun is unusual, occurring only here in the OT. It appears to be related to the Syriac *perda'* (grain) (cf. Egyptian *prt,* "fruit").

die. The NLT renders the sense of this difficult hapax legomenon (*'abash* [TH5685, ZH6308]). The word should probably be related to the Arabic *'abisa* (shrivel up). For a discussion of this verb and other difficulties in this verse, see Allen 1976:61-62, 83-84.

in the parched ground. The NLT renders this difficult Hebrew phrase according to the sense. It is frequently translated "under their clods" (cf. NIV, NRSV, NJB, REB, KJV, NKJV). The Anchor Bible reads "under their shovels," while GW has "in their shells."

grain crops fail. The Hebrew verbal form comes from the root *yabesh* [TH3001, ZH3312] (be dry).

granaries. This noun (*mammegurah* [TH4460, ZH4923]) is usually considered to be a third hapax legomenon in the verse. However, Hummel has suggested that the form may simply reflect the noun *megurah* [TH4035, ZH4476] ("barn"; cf. Hag 2:19), the first mem being considered an enclitic, so as to be read with the preceding verbal form.

1:18 *animals . . . cattle . . . sheep.* The NLT reflects three Hebrew terms: *behemah* [TH929, ZH989] ("domesticated cattle" in general), *baqar* [TH1241, ZH1330] (large cattle, herds), and *tso'n* [TH6629, ZH7366] (sheep, small cattle, flocks). Large and small cattle were often mentioned in ancient Semitic inscriptions. For example, on Sennacherib's well-known third campaign (against Syro-Palestine) he boasted of taking 46 of Hezekiah's cities together with "horses, mules, asses, camels, cattle and sheep without number." See Luckenbill 1927:120; note also the Karatepe Inscription, which mentions (in Phoenician) that the city will be a place for raising bulls (*'lpm*) and flocks (*s'n*). See also Donner and Röllig 1966:26A III 9.

moan . . . wander . . . bleat. The three verbs describe the misery of the animal kingdom. The first, *'anakh* [TH584, ZH634], is related to the Akkadian *anahu,* which in a derived stem signifies a moaning sound (*The Assyrian Dictionary* "A" Part II, A. Oppenheim [Chicago: The Institute, 1968], 105-106); a relationship with Akkadian *anahu* (be exhausted from toil) is also not that inappropriate. The second, *buk* [TH943, ZH1003], connotes the thought of the herds' listless wandering to and fro. The MT form, *buk,* is not likely to be from the verb *bakah* [TH1058, ZH1134] (weep) as read in *The Anchor Bible,* even though the LXX reads *eklausan* [cf. TG2799, ZG3081] (wept). The third, *'asham* [TH816, ZH870] (suffer punishment), signifies the agony of the sheep. Taken together, the three verbs depict an animal kingdom in deep misery and suffering from lack of food—hence, creatures crying out as they wander about searching for good pasturage.

1:19 *wilderness pastures.* The reference is to uncultivated land where small animals would graze. As Crenshaw (1995:111) remarks, "The emphasis of the verse falls on the region beyond normal cultivation, thus suggesting that the usual area to which one might go to supplement a bad harvest can offer no relief on this occasion."

flames have burned up all the trees. Although a literal wildfire could be intended, more than likely fire is a metaphor associated with the locust invasions. What a consuming wildfire would do to the countryside, the voracious locusts have done. The disastrous effects of large-scale locust infestations have often been documented (e.g., Driver 1915:84-93; Smith 1929:390-395). Thus, Smith (1929:394) cites the following testimony: "Bamboo groves have been stripped of their leaves and left standing like saplings after a rapid brush fire, and grass has been devoured so that the bare ground appeared as if burned." For the appearance of fields blackened by the destructive locusts, Finley (1990:38) points out that the OT uses of fire in connection with divine judgment "highlight the judgmental nature of the locusts and drought."

1:20 cry out. The verb *'arag* [TH6165, ZH6864] occurs elsewhere in the OT only in Psalm 42:1[2]. Accordingly, its scarcity has occasioned several suggestions: "pant loudly" (NIV, NJB); "cry out" (KJV, NKJV, NRSV); "look up" (LXX, Vulgate, REB). A relationship between the Hebrew root and the Ethiopic verb *'araga* (ascend) is possible both here and in the psalm. In any case, the emphasis is upon suffering animals that look, with longing desire, to God as their only resource.

streams. The force of the Hebrew term is debated, but likely refers to those small streams that dry up under a summer's heat or during a drought. If so, such watercourses had dried up thoroughly—clear to their center channel. For the verb "dried up," see the note on "despair" in v. 11 (cf. vv. 10, 12, 17).

COMMENTARY

Having called for a community-wide fast and sacred assembly at the Temple (1:14) and having warned his hearers of the dire calamity that could lie ahead (1:15), Joel turned to a consideration of the current conditions, all of which were before the people's very eyes. The implications should have been obvious to any sober-minded person. Not only was their food source cut off, but far worse, this meant that the meal offerings that accompanied key sacrifices could no longer be made. The very worship system of God's people was thus imperiled. There could be no sounds of joy in the courts of the Lord's house.

Joel goes on to describe the dismal scene. With the ground stripped bare and blackened by the voracious locusts, the heat of summer only added to the misery of all concerned. Because the ground lay parched and dried, there could be neither seed nor crop. Therefore, the storehouses lay empty and deserted. Rather than grazing, the nearby livestock milled about in hopeless confusion.

Accordingly, Joel cried out to God for help. Only the Lord could help his beleaguered people.[1] Only God could forgive them and deliver them from disaster. Joel reminded the Lord of the conditions that pressed down upon his people. Any trace of vegetation was gone, for field and trees were completely denuded (cf. Deut 28:38-40). Would any survive to worship God once again? Could not God hear the moans of the animal kingdom? Even suffering wild animals joined in crying out to God for relief. They did not have even water to drink, for all the water sources had dried up.

Joel's words were doubtless intended not only for the populace's information but for their instruction. As he had done, so should they. They needed to follow his instructions to fast and to come together to implore the God of all mercy and grace for help. There could be deliverance from no other—even the animals seemed to sense this![2]

Did the people not understand what all of this meant? The dryness and barrenness of the land reflected the spiritual dearth of their hearts (cf. Jer 23:10). Worship and service had given way to a mere routine that left their lives devoid of spiritual vitality. Surely they needed to realize that the present devastation was but a portent of a still greater catastrophe should they not repent and return to the Lord.

Today's societies and whole nations can also so conduct themselves that, like the Israel of Joel's time, they stand in danger of divine judgment. God cannot continue to bless any nation that ignores his person and standards and consequently reproduces sins of which Sodom and Gomorrah would be ashamed. National calamities, however, can be occasions for collective personal examination (Prov 14:34; Acts 17:31).[3] Oh that believers everywhere would lift up holy hands in prayer (1 Tim 2:8) and call upon God so that their land might be cleansed of wickedness and injustice (2 Chr 7:14). Perhaps God's goodness and gracious bounty might be enjoyed in everlasting peace and felicity, in accordance with the promises in his Word (Deut 28:1-14; Isa 45:22; 51:4-6).

How tragic it is when God must bring into the lives of his children conditions that mirror the spiritual callousness of their hearts.[4] What is true of individuals is true of churches. Where there is merely a cold, empty formalism devoid of spiritual reality, God cannot be pleased. Yet herein the loving concern of a gracious God can be seen. For when God is taken for granted and his rightful sovereign place in a person's life (or a congregation's worship) degenerates into a meaningless, formal routine, then he must do that which is necessary to restore such a one to spiritual health and vitality. Hope for renewal lies with God. God's chastisement may lead to genuine repentance and a turning away from sin.

The words that close Joel's first chapter are those of instruction and warning to us all. They remind us that God is sovereign. He is in control of the forces of nature (Job 37:5, 10; Ps 104:14, 21, 28) and over the affairs of nations (Ps 66:7) and individuals (Pss 75:6-7; 139:3, 16; Prov 16:33; Acts 17:26-28). He is also a righteous judge who both punishes sinners and rewards those who willingly observe his standards (Pss 7:11; 96:13; Ezek 7:3, 8; Acts 17:31; 2 Tim 4:8; 1 Pet 1:17).

Therefore, God should be given his rightful place in the believer's life. It is one thing to confess one's faith in God; it is another to surrender to him as God in everyday life. May our worship not be one of empty formality but that which is experienced in truth (1 Chr 16:29; John 4:24). May our lives not be merely routine; rather, let us give God his rightful place as Lord so that what we think and do is to the glory of God and thus for our own good (Ps 84:11; Rom 8:28-30; 15:17; Phil 2:13; Heb 13:20-21; Jas 1:5).

The passage also is a reminder that believers have a real need for constant prayer (Luke 18:1; cf. Acts 1:14; 1 Thess 5:17). While this is particularly true in times of need, danger, and difficulty (cf. Ps 32:6), such as the case was in Joel's day, believers always need to have a consistent prayer life. Believing prayer, together with confession of sin, can bring cleansing to the soul (1 John 1:9). Moreover, prayer is important for daily guidance and direction in every aspect of life (Phil 4:6; Jas 5:13-16; see the commentary on Jonah 2:1-10 and Zeph 2:1-3). Such a habit of life will pay eternal dividends and assure the believer of a continuing fellowship with God, free from sin's dominance (Pss 66:17-20; 73:23-26; 1 Pet 3:12).

ENDNOTES

1. Pusey (1953:161) points out the impossibility of remedying their situation without divine help: "All sin stupefies the sinner. All intoxicate the mind, bribe and pervert the judgment, dull the conscience, blind the soul and make it insensible to its own ills."

2. Allen (1976:64) remarks, "Joel yearns for the people to take their cue from the rest of animate creation, and to engage themselves in earnest prayer to God in the sanctuary."

3. Thus Craigie (1985:94-95) comments, "It is appropriate for a nation to pause and take stock when disaster has overtaken it, or looms on the horizon. But it is important, when engaging in national contrition, to see things correctly."

4. Feinberg (1976:74) cautions that God "does not willingly afflict the children of men, but by chastisements, often severe but always purposeful, He would bring them back from their evil ways and from the pit of destruction."

◆   B. Warnings Based on the Locust Plague (2:1-27)
      1. The prospect: the coming invasion (2:1-11)

¹Sound the alarm in Jerusalem*!
  Raise the battle cry on my holy
    mountain!
  Let everyone tremble in fear
  because the day of the LORD is
    upon us.
²It is a day of darkness and gloom,
  a day of thick clouds and deep
    blackness.
  Suddenly, like dawn spreading across
    the mountains,
  a great and mighty army appears.
  Nothing like it has been seen before
  or will ever be seen again.
³Fire burns in front of them,
  and flames follow after them.
  Ahead of them the land lies
    as beautiful as the Garden of Eden.
  Behind them is nothing but
    desolation;
  not one thing escapes.
⁴They look like horses;
  they charge forward like
    warhorses.*
⁵Look at them as they leap along the
    mountaintops.
  Listen to the noise they make—like
    the rumbling of chariots,
  like the roar of fire sweeping across
    a field of stubble,

or like a mighty army moving into
    battle.
⁶Fear grips all the people;
  every face grows pale with terror.
⁷The attackers march like warriors
  and scale city walls like soldiers.
  Straight forward they march,
  never breaking rank.
⁸They never jostle each other;
  each moves in exactly the right
    position.
  They break through defenses
  without missing a step.
⁹They swarm over the city
  and run along its walls.
  They enter all the houses,
  climbing like thieves through
    the windows.
¹⁰The earth quakes as they advance,
  and the heavens tremble.
  The sun and moon grow dark,
  and the stars no longer shine.
¹¹The LORD is at the head of the column.
  He leads them with a shout.
  This is his mighty army,
  and they follow his orders.
  The day of the LORD is an awesome,
    terrible thing.
  Who can possibly survive?

2:1 Hebrew *Zion;* also in 2:15, 23.   2:4 Or *like charioteers.*

NOTES

2:1 *Sound the alarm . . . Raise the battle cry . . . Let everyone tremble.* Once again (cf. 1:5), Joel begins his message with a series of imperatives followed by the particle *ki* [TH3588, ZH3954] (because). The "trumpet" (*shopar* [TH7782, ZH8795]) was made of a ram's horn. It was blown not only on ceremonial occasions (e.g., Lev 25:9) and to call people to religious assemblies (2:15) but also to summon men to battle (Judg 6:34) or for sounding an alarm in times of imminent danger (Hos 5:8; Amos 3:6). The people were to tremble because of the coming Day of the Lord.

my holy mountain! The mention of Jerusalem (lit., "Zion") and the holy hill, where Yahweh dwelt in the Temple, points to the spiritual nature of the coming events. (For a discussion of Zion theology, see the commentary on Obad 1:17-21.) The reference to Zion emphasized that the Lord was Israel's king who had chosen Jerusalem as his dwelling place (Ps 132:13) and who would ultimately establish his Kingdom on earth among those who love him and submit to his rule (Ps 87:2-6). The Zion theology here prepares Joel's hearers for the motif of the Divine Warrior to follow.

the day of the LORD. Some identify the events of ch 2 with ch 1, deciding that both deal with either a local locust plague (Finley, von Orelli) or a human army (Andinach, Stuart). A variation of this view suggests that 2:1-11 is "a more dramatic, semi-apocalyptical account of the locust invasion which itself is a harbinger of the Day" (Hubbard 1989:53). Some suggest that this passage, as well as the entire book, is made up of symbolic descriptions of military attacks (Freeman 1968:150-154). Others think that the locust plague of ch 1 is a precursor to the coming military invasion of eschatological times described in apocalyptic terms in ch 2.

The position taken here is a variation of the latter view, taking ch 1 as a literal locust invasion, which Joel sees as a harbinger of the Day of the Lord. Joel 2:1-11 describes that day in the form of a tightly structured judgment oracle containing quasi-apocalyptical terminology, the whole to be understood as an allegory. That day is not exclusively eschatological (contra Feinberg, Wolff), but the whole, unfolding process culminates at distant times. (In favor of this view is the fact that Joel's imagery goes beyond the activities of locusts and that he uses a clearly observable story line in developing his metaphor of locusts = armies.) Joel's primary concern, however, was the near future—seeing, in the westward push of the Neo-Assyrian kings, an imminent danger for God's disobedient people.

2:2 *darkness and gloom . . . thick clouds and deep blackness.* The terminology used by Joel is highly expressive. All four terms became standard vocabulary with regard to the dreadful Day of the Lord (e.g., Isa 13:10; Ezek 34:12; 38:9; Amos 5:18-20; Zeph 1:15). The NT likewise speaks of Christ's coming in association with clouds (Matt 24:30; 26:64; Acts 1:9-11; 1 Thess 4:17; Rev 1:7).

like dawn spreading across the mountains. Keil (1954:190) fancies here a reflection of the sun's rays from the locusts' wings. However, the simile probably envisions a comparison between the sudden appearance and gradual spreading of the light of dawn with the first sight and growing spectacle of the locusts.

great and mighty. Joel had described the earlier locusts as powerful and innumerable. The emphasis here is upon the sheer might of the great army that will invade the land.

Nothing like it has been seen before. Joel's description echoes that of 1:2.

2:3 *Fire burns in front of them, and flames follow after them.* The MT speaks of fire before and flame behind the invaders. Joel has already used the image to describe the devastation of the locusts (1:19). Fire is often employed to depict the divine presence (e.g., Exod 19:18; Dan 7:9). "In front of" serves to stitch the various portions of this section together (see commentary). Finley (1990:44-45) notes the use of the "before and after" motif throughout Joel's prophecy.

as the Garden of Eden. Ezekiel used the Garden of Eden in a figure portraying the lavish splendor of Tyre (Ezek 28:13) and Assyria (Ezek 31:8-9, 16, 18). The motif is used elsewhere in connection with the contrast between plenty and desolation (Isa 51:3; Ezek 36:35).

2:4 *like horses.* A comparison between locusts and horses occurs in Job 39:19-26 and Rev 9:7. The resemblance of locusts' heads to horses' heads is reflected in the Italian *cavalletta* (little horse) and German *Heupferd* (hay horse)—both words for locust.

they charge forward. The verb here (*yerutsun* [TH7323, ZH8132]) is the first of seven with the archaic ending *-un*. Whether a syntactical distinction exists in such forms in the OT is debated. Their relative rarity, however, may suggest that Joel employs them to give his poem more vividness and to create a certain dramatic flair and emphasis (cf. Wolff 1977:46) for his readers. Prinsloo (1985:42) opts for a certain weightiness to the description drawn from the idea of movement.

2:5 *leap along the mountaintops.* Sennacherib boasted of scaling mountain heights to capture loftily situated cities: ". . . on the peak of Mount Nipur, a steep mountain, like the nests of the eagle (vulture), king of birds, . . . Gullies, mountain torrents and waterfalls, dangerous cliffs, I surmounted in my sedan chair. Where it was too steep for my chair, I advanced on foot. Like a young gazelle I mounted the high(est) peaks in pursuit of them" (Luckenbill 1927:2.122).

like the rumbling of chariots. The advance of the locusts, with wings whirring ceaselessly, is likened to the thunderous rumbling of chariots. The simile is an apt one, for soon literal chariots would appear signaling Israel's day of reckoning. The Assyrian chariotry was greatly feared. Sennacherib called his war chariot "the vanquisher of the wicked and evil" and "the vanquisher of the enemy."

like the roar of fire. The crackling sound made by locusts chewing up the landscape is likened to a raging prairie fire.

like a mighty army. In a third simile the orderly advance of the locusts is compared to that of an army on the march, a figure that would become all too meaningful to God's people in the near future.

2:6 *Fear grips all the people.* Lit., "before his face peoples are in anguish." The word translated "fear," which is used of the anguish of a woman in travail (Isa 13:8), is often employed colorfully to describe the fear of those who face an enemy invasion (Deut 2:25; Jer 51:29; Ezek 30:16). The introductory *mippanayw* [TH4480/6440/2050.2, ZH4946/7156/2257] (before his face) harkens back to *lepanayw* in v. 3 and provides lexical stitching between vv. 3-5 and 6-9.

every face grows pale. Several suggestions have been made for the derivation of the term "grows pale," which occurs only here and in Nah 2:10[11]. The LXX translates it as "like a cooking pot," perhaps envisioning a pot made bright by heat. The NLT translates according to the sense of the passage: The faces of all are devoid of color due to fear.

2:7 *march like warriors . . . scale . . . like soldiers.* The double simile continues the comparison of locusts with armies. Chariotry is joined by infantry. On the basis of Ps 18:29, Crenshaw (1995:123) observes that the verb for "march" should probably be understood as "attack." The fear of the populace at the sight of the locusts thus becomes intensified due to their actual arrival. God's people would soon know the full force of Joel's words!

never breaking rank. Because the Hebrew verb used here is usually translated "take a pledge" (cf. Deut 24:10), other etymologies have been sought for the verb here. Of the several suggestions, two are most likely. (1) Guillaume (1965:2.27) relates the Hebrew root *'abat* [TH5670A, ZH6293] to Arabic *hbt* (deviate), the force being "none leaves his path" (cf. LXX, "do not turn aside"). (2) The Hebrew verb may be related to the Akkadian *ebetu* ("be tied"; see *The Assyrian Dictionary* "E", Oppenheim [Chicago: The Oriental Institute,

1958], 13-14), with the negative particle *lo'* [TH3808, ZH4202] (not) repointed and read as the asseverative *lu'* [TH3863, ZH4273] (yea), thus giving the phrase a sense like "they hold to their own paths" (see Waltke and O'Connor 1990:211-212). In this regard, Driver (1915:90-91) cites an eyewitness report of the orderly advance of locusts during an invasion (cf. Prov 30:27). The NLT has caught the sense of the context and accords with traditional understandings (cf. KJV, RSV, NASB, NIV).

2:8 They break through defenses without missing a step. The second part of this could also be rendered, "and no weapon can stop them" (NIDOTTE 2.198-199). This meaning is followed by several translations (LXX, NRSV, REB) and expositors (Keil, Stuart, Wolff). Others prefer to understand it as a defensive watercourse (Allen, Crenshaw, Hubbard) or defenses in general (NIV, Finley). In that light, a relation to the Akkadian *salhu* (outer wall) is not impossible. (See *The Assyrian Dictionary,* "S" Part I, Reiner [Chicago: The Oriental Institute, 1989], 243-244; see also Patterson 1985:250.)

2:9 city . . . walls . . . houses . . . windows. The invaders have breached the defenses and penetrated into the inner recesses of the city. Driver (1915:91) cites an eyewitness report about a locust plague. The eyewitness said that the locusts "entered the inmost recesses of the houses, were found in every corner, stuck to our clothes, and infested our food." The closing simile, "like thieves through the windows," points to the unexpected means of entry used by the invaders. Stuart (1987:251) points out the scriptural parallel of the plague of locusts that filled the Egyptian houses (Exod 10:6) and then adds, "On the military level, however, capture and destruction of houses brings to completion the conquest of a city (cf. Deut 28:30; 32:25; 2 Kgs 25:9; Neh 7:4)."

2:10 earth quakes . . . heavens tremble. Once again (cf. 2:1-2) the reader hears of terrifying events in nature—the incalculable numbers of the invaders and the declaration that it is the Day of the Lord. The cataclysmic upheaval of heaven and earth depicted here and in the description of the sun, moon, and stars that follows, owes its origin to the portrayal of the Divine Warrior in the Exodus epic literature. For the motif of the Divine Warrior, see notes and commentary on Hab 3:8-15.

2:11 He leads them with a shout. The Lord's shout before his army contrasts with the trumpet blast of 2:1. Paul reports that Christ will "come down from heaven with a commanding shout" when he returns for his own (1 Thess 4:16).

Who can possibly survive? The rhetorical question assumes a negative answer: "No one!" Malachi (Mal 3:2) similarly asks of the day when the messenger of the covenant arrives, "Who will be able to endure it?"

COMMENTARY

The opening verses of chapter 2 repeat several vocabulary items and themes already found in chapter 1—especially the presence of a powerful army (cf. 1:6 with 2:2, 4-5, 11); the unprecedented locust attack (cf. 1:2-4 with 2:2); the nearness of the Day of the Lord (cf. 1:15 with 2:1-2, 10-11); and the image of consuming fire (cf. 1:19-20 with 2:3). This section also has clear ties with what follows. Indeed, the oracle of 2:1-11 only reaches full closure in the subsequent verses. It prepares the reader for Joel's teaching concerning the Day of the Lord (2:12-17) and the Lord's projected response, should the people repent (2:18-27). There, the locusts of this unit are pictured as repulsed, while the land that was overrun and devastated by locusts (cf. 1:4-13) is to be restored to its former beauty (2:25-26a).

Though this section shares many similar features with chapter 1, the passage has its own distinctive form and message. First, it may be noted that verses 1-2 and 10-11 form an inclusio encompassing the entire section. The alarm warning of the imminent Day of the Lord, with its awesome portents and the appearance of an unprecedented and powerful army (2:1-2), is balanced by further notices of cosmic phenomena and the vastness of that army on the Day of the Lord (2:10-11). Second, the middle portion (2:3-9) also has its unique features. Here, the army whose near arrival was announced has now arrived, and its impact is being felt (2:3). The appearance of the forces drawn up for battle is then detailed (2:4-5), together with the effect of that sight upon the defending populace (2:6). All of this is capped by a description of the orderly attack and penetration of the invaders into the city.

Structurally, verses 3-9 fall into two strophes, each of which is similarly introduced; we find the lexically related words *lepanayw* (in 2:3) and *mippanayw* (in 2:6), both of which may be translated "before them" (cf. NRSV). It should be noted, as well, that verse 10 also begins with *lepanayw* and verse 11 contains the phrase *lipene khelo* [TH2428, ZH2657] (before his army). There is, therefore, unity to the entire passage: a warning concerning that awful day and the appearance of the invaders (2:1-2), their success (2:3-9), and the display in nature (2:2, 10) that accompanies the vast army moving against the helpless populace (2:11).

From a literary perspective, it seems that Joel intended his carefully crafted poetry to be understood allegorically. It is important to note that a plot line is clearly discernable in the imagery (metaphor and simile) that abounds throughout the section. Building on the metaphor of locusts as armies, Joel painted a scene that would be all too vivid for a people who had just witnessed several waves of locust invasions. He wanted to convey to his hearers and readers that these events were but a precursor to a still greater catastrophe.

In quasi-apocalyptic terms, Joel portrayed the arrival of a new wave of "locusts"— an army of unprecedented magnitude and power that could descend from the north (2:20) at any time, should the warnings inherent in the recent locust plague not be heeded. The Lord had sent the locusts to bring his people to a realization of their empty formalism and sinful practices. He would yet send a greater striking force should there be no repentance (cf. 2:12-17). But he would remit the penalty if they would repent (2:18-27). Only if such were forthcoming could the threatened disaster be averted.

That Joel presented a scene of coming human armies by using the figure of locusts is understandable both from a literary standpoint and from ancient precedent. As for the former, it has been noted that much of Joel's message is presented in the form of similes. Similes may express an equivalent identification or a looser point of relationship. Thus, if a son carries on the precise ideals of his father, he can be said to be "like his father" in the full sense of the comparison. If, however, a father likes classical music and the son enjoys American jazz, while the son could be said to be "like his father," a lover of music, the comparison would not be equivalent. Joel had already used a simile of equivalence: The Lord's day would come as it will come (2:1)—and it will be a shattering from Shaddai (2:2).[1] Now he employs another simile. The coming army is like the coming of a horde of locusts (2:11; cf. 1:6). The comparison is an apt one because both the army and the locusts are the Lord's.

The comparison of locusts and armies is well documented in the ancient literature of Egypt, Ugarit, Sumer, and Assyria, as well as in the Old Testament (Judg 6:3-5; 7:12; Jer 46:23).[2] The Old Testament prophets were fond of comparing human nations and cities to insects and animals. Thus, Egypt is compared to flies and Assyria to bees (Isa 7:18), Babylon's Nebuchadnezzar is likened to an eagle or vulture (Ezek 17), Pharaoh is compared to a fish (Ezek 29:3-5), and God's people to a lioness (Ezek 19). Nahum compares Assyria to a lion (Nah 2:11-12) and the people of Nineveh to locusts (Nah 3:15b). The fact that the prophesied attack comes from the north, whereas locust invasions customarily arrived from the east or southeast, gives further weight to the suggestion that armies are intended here, though presented under the figure of locusts.

Joel's allegory combines the imagery of locusts as armies with the theme of the Day of the Lord. The apocalyptic-like imagery of the passage (2:1-2a, 10-11) makes it certain that Joel understood that the process that would eventuate in the eschatological Day of the Lord (see the commentary on 1:14-15 and the note on 2:1) was about to begin. God's people stood in imminent danger.

Theologically, this passage centers on the awesomeness of the coming Day of the Lord. It informs its hearers and readers that the day is one of darkness. Light will be withdrawn from the celestial luminaries, while the earth itself is thrown into convulsions. It will be a time of warfare, as the Lord himself stands at the head of the armies of earth in order to bring judgment to God's people. Much of this is reflective of other prophetic passages dealing with the Day of the Lord, so there may be a certain standard prophetic stylization here.[3] Nevertheless, the descriptions indicate that ultimately, when God brings the Day of the Lord to its culmination, catastrophic happenings will occur. Moreover, there is danger for those who live in ungodliness all along the way.

Joel, like the other prophets, views the Day of the Lord as a process that repeats itself over historical time.[4] He understood that danger was very near (1:15; 2:1) and would soon be realized in the succeeding decades. Indeed, it would come in the form of several invading nations: Assyria, the Neo-Babylonians, and the Romans.

What was true in Joel's time remains true today. The time of the Lord's judgment is ever near. The culmination of the whole process of the Day of the Lord, though known only to God, will come quickly and with frightful force (Luke 21:24b-26; 1 Thess 5:1-2; 2 Pet 3:8-10; Rev 6–19).[5] Accordingly, people ought not to live so as to become the objects of God's wrath but rather in accordance with the holy standards of God (1 Thess 5:9-24; Heb 12:14-29; Jas 5:8-9; 1 Pet 4:7-11; 2 Pet 3:11-16).

The justice of God is clearly presented in this passage. God, the righteous judge (cf. 2 Tim 4:8), does and will judge sin, whether among the unrighteous or among his own people (Ps 9:7-8; Ezek 18:30-32; Acts 17:31; Heb 10:26-31). Believers often take refuge in the truth that, whereas the unrepentant face eternal judgment (Rom 3:23; 6:23), they stand forgiven in God's sight through the atoning work of Christ

(2 Cor 5:21; 1 Pet 2:24). Nevertheless, it is also true that believers will stand before God to give an account of their lives (Rom 14:10-12; 2 Cor 5:7-10). Further, where unconfessed sin arises in a believer's life, God will bring his chastising judgment to bear, as evidenced in the lives of God's saints throughout the ages (Heb 12:6). Well should the body of Christ be warned that where such things as empty religiosity, greed, pride, and self-centeredness mark the lives of the church and society, Joel's Day of the Lord remains near at hand (Jas 5:9; 2 Pet 3:8-10; 1 John 2:18a; 5:20; Rev 3:11-14).

ENDNOTES

1. For an example of another simile of equivalence, see Ezek 26:10 (MT). Note also the scorpion-like locusts, which symbolized Satan's demonic hosts in Rev 9:1-11, whose appearance and description are reminiscent of Joel. As is typical of poetry, Joel mixes his figures, the description at times being more applicable to locusts and at other times to a human army.
2. For details, see Thompson 1955:52-55 and Andinach 1992:438-439; cf. *The Chicago Assyrian Dictionary* "E", Oppenheim, (Chicago: The Oriental Institute, 1958), 257-258.
3. See 2:30-31; 3:14-16; Isa 2:12-22; 13:9-13; Jer 4:23-31; 46:10; Ezek 30:2-3; Amos 5:18-20; 8:8-10; Obad 1:15-16; Zeph 1:14-18; Zech 14:1-7; Mal 4:1-3; cf. Matt 24:29-31; Rev 6:12-17. And see texts containing the Divine Warrior theme: Judg 5:4-5; Pss 18:7-15; 68:7-8; 77:16-18; 114:1-7; 144:5-6; Nah 1:3-6; Hab 3:3-15; Zeph 1:14-18; 3:8; cf. Rev 19:11-21.
4. Pusey (1953:180) points out that "the Prophet is speaking of the whole aggregate of God's judgments unto the Day of Judgment." So also Fausset (1948:521) remarks, "Each successive day of visitation for sin has had its own distinctive character, so that no former visitation has been altogether like it . . . And all this shall be the introduction to 'the great and very terrible day of the Lord.'"
5. Craigie (1985:100) observes, "The point of the prophet was not so much to predict some future event, as it was to see the possibility of such a future in the present."

◆   ## 2. A plea for communal repentance (2:12-14)

12 That is why the LORD says,
    "Turn to me now, while there is time.
Give me your hearts.
    Come with fasting, weeping, and
    mourning.
13 Don't tear your clothing in your grief,
    but tear your hearts instead."
Return to the LORD your God,
    for he is merciful and
    compassionate,

slow to get angry and filled with
    unfailing love.
He is eager to relent and not punish.
14 Who knows? Perhaps he will give you
    a reprieve,
sending you a blessing instead of
    this curse.
Perhaps you will be able to offer grain
    and wine
    to the LORD your God as before.

NOTES

2:12 *Turn . . . Give me your hearts.* In accordance with the age-old prediction (Deut 4:30), Joel pleads with the populace to recognize their sinfulness and self-centeredness and to turn to God with all their hearts (cf. Deut 30:2). Joel's contemporaries Hosea and Amos similarly recognized the coldness of the people's hearts and urged them to repent (Hos 6:1; 14:1-2; Amos 4:6-11). For a discussion of the verb translated "turn" (*shub*), see NIDOTTE 4.55-59.

fasting, weeping, and mourning. True repentance was to be accompanied by outward practice. Each was to complement, not take the place of, the other.

2:13 *tear your hearts.* Far beyond the customary tearing of clothing as a sign of grief over some calamity or misfortune, God wanted broken hearts. Crenshaw (1995:135) rightly observes, "Joel recognized the danger of empty ritual, its deadening capacity to lull the worshipper into a false sense of security, and consequently sought to combat external religion that did not penetrate into the depths of one's being."

merciful and compassionate, slow to get angry and filled with unfailing love. These attributes of God are often mentioned in the OT, occurring in various combinations. Especially to be noted is the parallel in Jonah 4:2 (see the relevant notes there).

2:14 *Who knows? Perhaps.* This is another rhetorical question. Joel did not dare to presume upon the divine prerogative. The prophet's encouraging words that follow are based on the known character of God described in 2:13 (cf. Jonah 3:9; Zeph 2:3). Wolff (1977:50) remarks, "The 'perhaps' of hope is appropriate to the humility of one who prays."

give you a reprieve. Lit., "turn and relent." The verb *shub* [TH7725, ZH8740] reappears here (cf. 2:12), thus enveloping the material of vv. 12-14.

COMMENTARY

Joel now supplies the application for his allegory. The dangers of the great Day of the Lord could yet be averted or at least alleviated. This would call for a total recommitment on the part of the whole populace. Beyond the former plea for penitent sorrow (1:5-13), demonstrated in such outward signs as tearing garments or wearing sackcloth, there needed to be a deep-seated, heartfelt return to God. It would involve a complete reorientation of the lives of everyone concerned. Only then could they hope for the gracious mercy of God to be applied to their situation. If that were to happen, what blessings could ensue! Not only would they have renewed plenty for their needs, but more importantly, they could again offer the grain and drink offerings that had ceased because of the devastation caused by the locusts.

Here again is an emphasis on the high moral attributes of God and his absolute sovereignty. Humans should not presume upon God's person and works (Amos 5:15; Zeph 2:3), for he always acts in the freedom of his sovereign will (Ps 115:3; Rom 9:14-21). Nevertheless, it is reassuring for the believer to understand something of God's character so as to be able to rely on his perfect response to any situation. God is consistent in his character: He is gracious and merciful, not easily angered, and full of kindness.

All of these attributes are vital to the believer's spiritual pilgrimage. In God's grace he extends his compassion for all his people in their times of need (Deut 4:31). Moreover, in accordance with his great loving-kindness, God is slow to take offense and many times has even relented from sending the punishment that sinners deserve (Ps 78:38; Jer 4:1-2; 2 Pet 3:9). Not only is he the only true God (Deut 6:4; Ps 115:4-8), he is a God of truth so his acts are perfect, just, reliable, and consistent (Deut 32:4; see commentary on Hab 2:4). Accordingly, the believer may count on him in times of trouble (Ps 46:1) and be assured that where there is true repentance and confession of sin (Ps 32:1-5), God will see the heart's condition (Ps 139:23), grant forgiveness (1 John 1:9), and bring healing (Ps 51:12-17; Isa 57:15). Nevertheless, Joel's admonition is a reminder of the need for consistency in one's spiritual experience. How much better it is to keep short accounts with God, so as to avoid the need for chastisement to bring us to confession and repentance.

◆   3. A call for worship (2:15-17)

¹⁵Blow the ram's horn in Jerusalem!
   Announce a time of fasting;
   call the people together
      for a solemn meeting.
¹⁶Gather all the people—
      the elders, the children, and even
         the babies.
   Call the bridegroom from his quarters
      and the bride from her private room.
¹⁷Let the priests, who minister in the
      LORD's presence,

stand and weep between the
   entry room to the Temple and
   the altar.
Let them pray, "Spare your people,
   LORD!
Don't let your special possession
   become an object of mockery.
Don't let them become a joke for
   unbelieving foreigners
   who say,
   'Has the God of Israel left them?'"

NOTES

2:15 *Announce a time of fasting*. Lit., "sanctify a fast." The time of fasting was to be observed out of genuine holiness (2:12-14), not merely empty ritual. Once again, Joel piled up the imperatives in these verses to emphasize the urgency of the situation.

2:16 *Gather all the people*. Lit., "sanctify an assembly." Like the fast, the people assembled in solemn meeting were to have come as a holy and repentant people.

***elders . . . children . . . babies*.** The total population was to come; none was exempted from the call. Crenshaw (1995:141) calls attention to just such an assembly in the late second-century BC book of Judith (Jdt 4:9-13).

***bridegroom . . . bride*.** Even newlyweds, who would not ordinarily be expected to participate in the ceremonies or would be exempted from such observances (Deut 20:7; 24:5), were summoned to this solemn occasion. A case of total mobilization for war that brought the bridegroom from his chamber is recorded in the tale of Keret in the ancient Ugaritic literature: "Even the new husband came out" (see Coogan 1978:60, 62-63; for the text itself, see Gordon 1965:250-251).

2:17 *stand and weep between the entry room to the Temple and the altar*. The priests were to take their place between the entrance hall to the Temple (1 Kgs 6:3) and the brazen altar of burnt offering situated within the inner (or priests') court (1 Kgs 8:64). The people were to stand in the outer court, which lay beyond that of the priests (2 Chr 4:9). Later in Israel's history, 25 priests would blasphemously turn their backs on the vestibule and the Temple and worship the sun (Ezek 8:16).

***your people . . . your special possession*.** A basic premise of OT theology was that Israel was God's particular possession (Deut 9:26, 29; 14:2; 32:9; 2 Sam 14:16; Pss 74:2; 135:4; Isa 40:1; Hos 2:23; Joel 3; etc.). Though all the earth was his, Israel would have a unique place among the nations.

Don't let them become a joke. The psalmists express a similar concern with emphasis on God's own reputation (Pss 74:10; 79:9-10; cf. Ps 44:9-16).

Has the God of Israel left them? Joel is fond of using interrogative sentences to express his point (cf. 1:2; 2:11, 14; 3:4). The spirit of Joel's question, which had been asked by Moses earlier (Exod 32:11-12; Deut 9:26-29), is reechoed by the psalmist (Ps 115:2).

COMMENTARY

Once again, the trumpet blast is to be heard (cf. 2:1). This time it is to convene a solemn assembly (cf. 1:14). Joel bids all to come—from the eldest to the youngest. Not even newlyweds would be exempt. Priests and people were to stand facing the vestibule of the Temple and pour out their pleas to God from hearts moved by real repentance. They were to ask God to spare his people, not just for their benefit, but for the sake of God's sacred name and reputation (cf. 2:17 and 2:26). His name ought not to be ridiculed and brought into disrepute because of Israel's sin.

The name of God is often referred to in the Scriptures to signify his character, attributes, and activities (e.g., Exod 34:5-7; Ps 7:17; Isa 29:23; 42:8; Hos 12:5). The name of the Lord came to represent God in all his revealed nature and reputation (Isa 63:14; Ezek 36:22-23; Dan 9:18-19; Zeph 3:12). So much did "the name" become identified with the Lord that "the name" (*hashem* [TH1886.1/8034, ZH2021/9005]) became an accepted pronunciation for the tetragrammaton (*yhwh* [TH3068, ZH3378]).

God's saints went forth in the assurance of the power and authority of God's name (Deut 18:20; 1 Sam 17:45; Ps 118:26; Jer 15:16). It was prophesied that God's servant the Messiah would both go in the name of the Lord (Mic 5:4) and would himself be given the name depicting his essential nature (Isa 9:6-7; Jer 23:5-6). So it was that the Lord Jesus went about in the name of the Lord (Matt 21:9; Luke 4:18; Acts 10:38), having been endowed with a special name designating his task of saving people from their sins (Matt 1:21-23; Luke 1:31-33). Indeed, like God in the Old Testament (Lev 24:11) Jesus could be referred to as "The Name" (3 John 1:7). Because of his redeeming work, his is the only name to be called on for salvation (John 3:16-18; Acts 4:12) in order that people may become members of God's family (John 1:12). At his name every knee shall one day bow and every tongue confess that he is Lord (Phil 2:9-11).

Jesus' name, like that of God the Father (Ps 119:55), may be called on in prayer (John 14:13-14). Believers should be pleased to bear Christ's name, whatever the cost (Acts 5:41), and live so as not to bring disrepute upon him (Col 3:17; 2 Thess 1:11-12; 1 Tim 6:1). Indeed, as believers we need to remind ourselves that whatever we do reflects upon the name of the Lord. Likewise, parents would do well to instruct their children to exercise caution in their lives. For whatever they do reflects not only upon their own reputation and that of the family, but their church and, above all, the Lord himself.

Keeping God's name and reputation in mind may be facilitated by remembering that as believers under the old covenant were enjoined to practice God's holy standards in every area of their lives (Deut 7:6-11; 14:1-2; 26:16-19), so also believers under the new covenant have been made God's particular possession (1 Pet 2:9-10) and, as such, are to live so as to be a credit to him who loved them and gave himself for them (Gal 2:20; cf. Eph 2:4-10; Titus 2:14).

Joel's concern was genuine. More than Israel's existence was at stake. Where sinful attitudes and practices mar the testimony of God's people, God will adopt firm measures. Joshua understood that (Josh 7:6-26), as did the New Testament church (Acts 5:1-11). Although such drastic actions as those of biblical times are not practiced in today's churches, it is certainly true that the good name of Christ's church and his holy reputation still ought to be guarded carefully (1 Cor 5:1-13; Gal 6:1-10; Eph 4:17-32; Phil 4:8-9). Likewise, nations (and communities) would do well to remember that "sin is a disgrace to any people" (Prov 14:34).

◆ ## 4. The resultant scene (2:18-27)

¹⁸Then the LORD will pity his people
and jealously guard the honor of
his land.
¹⁹The LORD will reply,
"Look! I am sending you grain and
new wine and olive oil,
enough to satisfy your needs.
You will no longer be an object of
mockery
among the surrounding nations.
²⁰I will drive away these armies from
the north.
I will send them into the parched
wastelands.
Those in the front will be driven into
the Dead Sea,
and those at the rear into the
Mediterranean.*
The stench of their rotting bodies will
rise over the land."

Surely the LORD has done great things!
²¹ Don't be afraid, my people.
Be glad now and rejoice,
for the LORD has done great things.
²²Don't be afraid, you animals of the field,
for the wilderness pastures will soon
be green.
The trees will again be filled with fruit;
fig trees and grapevines will be
loaded down once more.
²³Rejoice, you people of Jerusalem!

Rejoice in the LORD your God!
For the rain he sends demonstrates his
faithfulness.
Once more the autumn rains will
come,
as well as the rains of spring.
²⁴The threshing floors will again be piled
high with grain,
and the presses will overflow with
new wine and olive oil.

²⁵The LORD says, "I will give you back
what you lost
to the swarming locusts, the
hopping locusts,
the stripping locusts, and the cutting
locusts.*
It was I who sent this great
destroying army against you.
²⁶Once again you will have all the food
you want,
and you will praise the LORD your
God,
who does these miracles for you.
Never again will my people be
disgraced.
²⁷Then you will know that I am among
my people Israel,
that I am the LORD your God, and
there is no other.
Never again will my people be
disgraced.

2:20 Hebrew *into the eastern sea, . . . into the western sea.*   2:25 The precise identification of the four kinds of locusts mentioned here is uncertain.

NOTES

2:18 Then the LORD will pity . . . and jealously guard. The vowel pointing of the MT indicates that the two verbs ("pity" and "be jealous") have already taken place: "and the Lord was jealous for his land and took pity upon his people" (cf. LXX, Vulgate, Peshitta, NRSV, NJB, REB). The reading of the NLT rests on a repointing of the Hebrew forms to indicate a future promise, an understanding favored by Luther and followed by some English translations (NIV, KJV, NKJV, NASB). That the unpointed form could be understood as other than past time is indicated in Theodotion's Greek version of the OT, where volitive future forms are read. Justification for this position comes from the notion that the Hebrew form could also be read as a jussive ("may the Lord be jealous and take pity") and thereby be seen as a continuance of the prayer in 2:17.

Because Joel does not report such repentance and restoration of blessing and because of the future promises that are given in the verses that follow, the rendering of the NLT appears to be justified. Chisholm (1990:61-62) proposes a compromise position, preserving the MT and viewing God's compassion in Joel's day and the following prophecy (vv. 19-27) as conditional: "Because of its repentant spirit Joel's generation would not experience humiliation at the hands of the Gentiles. Each successive generation would also be kept from such shame if it sustained the same kind of loyalty."

pity. The Hebrew verb has the double nuance of showing compassion and sparing from disaster.

2:19 will reply. Whether one views this verb as future or past is contingent upon the decision made as to the verbs in v. 18. The NLT takes the former alternative.

Look! I am sending. This Hebrew construction (*hinneh* + present participle) indicates that God already is putting his promise into motion.

2:20 armies from the north. The point of reference is variously understood, some thinking that locusts are intended, others that human armies are in view. Since locusts do not normally invade Israel from the north, what is described would be an extraordinary event. The locust infestation had indeed been unprecedented (1:2-4) so that some unusual significance must be attributed to it. It would seem best, then, to consider that the locusts' approach from the north symbolized the gathering threat of invading armies from the north, the most usual direction of foreign invasion (cf. Jer 1:13-15; 4:6; 6:1-5, 22-23; Ezek 38:6, 15; 39:2).

front . . . rear. The mention of front and rear columns echoes the before and after motif connected with the earlier locust invasion (see note on 2:3). Likewise, as Finley (1990:63) observes, "The similarities between locusts and an invading army form the basis for the military terms used in the passage . . . 'its vanguard,' . . . and 'its rear guard.'"

The stench of their rotting bodies. The figure is doubly apropos. Like the smell of rotting locusts over wasteland as well as those driven ashore by the waves of the two seas involved (the Mediterranean and the Dead), so the stench of the rotting bodies of enemy soldiers will leave a foul odor over the area. One such case of mass death in Israel is recounted in Sennacherib's aborted attempt to take Jerusalem in the days of Hezekiah. Struck dead by God's angel, 185,000 Assyrian corpses were revealed with the morning light (2 Kgs 19:35).

2:21 my people. Lit., "O land." The NLT reading understands the Hebrew noun to refer to the land of Israel (cf. 1 Kgs 8:40; 2 Chr 6:31), so that Joel's admonition is to the people in the land. Because the ground was pictured as being in mourning over the loss of the same products mentioned as being restored here (cf. 1:10 with 2:24), Joel may be personifying the ground. Here the ground's mourning has been turned to confidence.

2:22 animals . . . pastures . . . fig trees and grapevines. The Lord's blessings would affect the whole environment. It would mean productivity and resources for all, people and animals alike.

2:23 the rain he sends demonstrates his faithfulness. The underlying Hebrew phrase has been variously understood. Most have followed the traditional understanding of *moreh* [TH4175A, ZH4620] as "rain." Nevertheless, the usual word for early rain is *yoreh* [TH3138, ZH3453; cf. TH3384C, ZH3722], a reading found in some Hebrew mss in the second occurrence of the word in the verse (NLT, "autumn rains"). The variant may be the proper reading there. This word *moreh* [TH4175A, ZH4620] occurs elsewhere only in Ps 84:6[7], where it is also traditionally rendered "early rain," although this meaning is far from certain.

Already the ancient versions had difficulty in understanding Joel's use of *moreh*, the LXX and Peshitta relating it to words dealing with food, while the Vulgate reads "teacher [of righteousness]," a conclusion also reached in one edition of the LXX (*ton hupodeiknuonta* [TG5263, ZG5683], "him who gives instruction") and followed by some contemporary authors (e.g., Nowell). Interestingly, the Greek verb used in the latter case lays stress on that which is taught indirectly or by induction. Such a meaning is well suited to the context in Joel, for it would allow the Hebrew participial form its natural force. Thus rendered, the full phrase may be translated "that which gives instruction in righteousness." The arrival of the seasonal rains would assure the populace of God's renewed blessings upon his repentant people (cf. Ps 85:10-13). See the rendering of W. Rudolph (1967:249), who repoints the accusative marker *eth-* attached to the first *hammoreh* [TH4175A, ZH4620] as a separate noun, *'oth* [TH226, ZH253], and translates: "The sign that points to salvation." See also Patterson 1985:253-255.

autumn rains . . . rains of spring. Although the NLT gives the sense of the passage, the previous line of the MT indicates that such rains will come in abundance. The early or autumn rains generally came in October–November, the late or spring rains in March–April. The three terms for rain—*geshem* [TH1653, ZH1773] (rain), *yoreh* [TH3138, ZH3453] (early rain), and *malqosh* [TH4456, ZH4919] (latter rain)—appear together in Jer 5:24.

2:25 I will give you back. Crenshaw (1995:157) points out that the verb translated "give back" is derived "from a legal context and designates payment for losses incurred." The retention, albeit not in the same order, of the names for locusts (cf. 1:4) assures the people of equal compensation. The great disaster will be reversed; loss will be swallowed up in superabundant blessings.

2:26 you will have all the food you want. The NLT captures well the force of the MT, which stresses the promise of continued feasting to full satisfaction. God will give even better than equal compensation: it will be a bountiful blessing (cf. Ps 66:8-12).

you will praise the LORD your God. The MT reads "the name of the Lord your God." God's name had been damaged due to the people's judgment in the locust plague. Now his name would be vindicated.

2:27 you will know that I am among my people. Hosea 11:9 records God's continuing love for his people despite their sins: "I am God . . . the Holy One living among you." Isaiah 52:5-10 tells of a day when a dispersed Israel will again know God's name, for he will provide their salvation in the sight of all. Zephaniah 3:15-20 prophesies of a time when God will rejoice over them in their midst. Joel will return to the theme of God's presence among his people in 3:17, 21.

COMMENTARY

The familiar prophetic theme of reversal (e.g., Hos 1–2; Zeph 1, 3) comes into prominence here. The agricultural products of the land, which were destroyed in the locust plague, will flourish with even greater fertility (cf. 1:9-12 with 2:19, 22b-26). The invader will be permanently expelled (cf. 1:6; 2:2-11 with 2:20, 25), the animal kingdom will enjoy the plenty of the land (cf. 1:18-20 with 2:22a), and the people's callous disregard for God will be transformed into a living relationship with him (cf. 1:5-13; 2:12-13 with 2:27). Based on the populace's proper response to Joel's instructions with respect to confession of sin and repentance, God promises that he will restore all that was lost in the locust plague and more.

What a time that will be! The ground will experience full revitalization. The whole natural world will bask in its exceedingly great fertility. God's people will rejoice in the timely arrival of the life-giving rains that will so nourish the productivity of cultivated lands, orchards, and vineyards that the storehouses will be stocked to overflowing. The Lord is truly the God of all grace (Exod 34:6; Neh 9:17; Isa 30:18; Rom 5:17-21; Rev 21:22-26). Moreover, the surrounding nations' mocking of Israel will be silenced, for Israel's enemies will be repulsed with staggering losses. The ridicule that Israel had known (cf. 2:17) would never be heard again (cf. Isa 29:22-24; 54:4-8, 11-14; Zeph 3:11).

Above all, the Lord wanted his people to understand the lesson of the locust plague. The locusts had been his destroying army and had been sent in response to his people's wayward behavior (cf. Jer 17:13; Hos 4:17-19; 10:6). However, the people were still God's people and God was still their God (cf. Hos 2:23). With full repentance would come full forgiveness and deliverance from the disgrace of divine chastisement.

Several important theological truths are evident in this section. Immediately, one is impressed with the high value of genuine repentance and prayer. Although these do not compel God to be moved to remit deserved punishment, God is a God of great compassion, who does hear and respond to genuine prayer (1 Kgs 8:18-30, 33-40; Ps 4:1-3; Isa 65:24-25; 1 John 1:8-9). Accordingly, the psalmist brings his prayer of contrition to the Lord with full confidence that God will hear and forgive him (Pss 6:9; 32:1-11; 51:1-17). Further, Paul reports that God is a God of all grace so that "as people sinned more and more, God's wonderful grace became more abundant" (Rom 5:20).

Believers, therefore, are encouraged to be in constant prayer, both confessing their sins and spending time in communion with the Lord (1 Thess 3:10; 5:17; 1 Tim 2:8; see commentary on Jonah 1:17–2:10). In so doing, they discover that God's faithfulness and compassion are ever present and that he longs to fellowship with his own in order to pour out blessings upon his obedient and faithful followers (Deut 28:1-2, 12; Neh 9:30, 33; Lam 3:22-23). Indeed, Jeremiah often reports that God "rose early" (KJV), hoping to meet with his people (cf. Jer 7:13; 25:3; etc.). How sad it is when believers "get up early" not to commune with God but only to pursue their corrupt ways (Zeph 3:7).

While the time of day for meeting with God is not the crucial thing, the Lord's own example (Mark 1:35) does at least encourage believers to set aside that part of the day when they are "at their best." As believers, we need to come into his presence to praise and thank him for his grace and goodness (Eph 2:7; Phil 4:19) and thereby gain strength and direction for daily living (Ps 5:3; Matt 6:9-15).

God's compassion and his justice are clearly seen in this passage. God not only promised his people forgiveness and deliverance, but the restoration of all that had been lost. God does indeed deal firmly with all, meting out punishment and reward commensurate with the occasion and needs (3:4-8; Deut 32:4; cf. Isa 9:7; 24:14-23; 2 Thess 1:6-8). Although this may not always seem to be the case, over the long term it is perfectly true—God's judgment is just.

Greater still, God's abundant mercy and goodness often move him to treat people in a far better way than they deserve, graciously withholding the deserved punishment and generously bestowing his blessings upon them far beyond their expectations (Job 42:12-17; Matt 20:1-15; Eph 2:4-9; 1 Tim 1:15-16; 2 Pet 3:9). Since this is true, those who claim God's name ought also to be just and fair in all their dealings with others (Lev 19:15; Deut 16:18-20; Prov 24:23; Mic 6:8; Hab 2:4). This is especially true within the Christian community (Phil 4:8-9; 1 Tim 5:21; Jas 2:1-13; 1 Pet 5:1-4). May our lives reflect the gracious demeanor of our Savior.

◆ II. God's Future Intentions (2:28–3:21)
A. The Prospect: The Outpoured Spirit (2:28-32)

28*"Then, after doing all those things,
I will pour out my Spirit upon all people.
Your sons and daughters will prophesy.
Your old men will dream dreams,
and your young men will see visions.
29 In those days I will pour out my Spirit
even on servants—men and women alike.
30 And I will cause wonders in the heavens and on the earth—
blood and fire and columns of smoke.

31 The sun will become dark,
and the moon will turn blood red
before that great and terrible* day of the LORD arrives.
32 But everyone who calls on the name of the LORD
will be saved,
for some on Mount Zion in Jerusalem will escape,
just as the LORD has said.
These will be among the survivors whom the LORD has called.

2:28 Verses 2:28-32 are numbered 3:1-5 in Hebrew text.   2:31 Greek version reads *glorious.*

NOTES
2:28 [3:1] *Then, after doing all those things.* The NLT links the familiar Hebrew introductory formula (*wehayah 'akhare-ken*) with "those things"—i.e., the preceding divine pronouncement concerning the renewed rain that will be instrumental in the land's restored fertility (2:23). The formula itself is often used to initiate fresh prophetic oracles and speaks of an undetermined future. Context alone must be sought in order to determine whether the predicted events will occur in the near future (Exod 11:1) or as late as the eschatological era (Isa 1:26). Peter applies this passage to the inaugurated eschaton in his sermon on Pentecost (Acts 2:16-21).

all people. Lit., "all flesh." Although this phrase could mean all people everywhere, the qualifications that follow show that Joel intended believing members of the covenant community.

sons and daughters . . . old men . . . young men. The various spiritual gifts are illustrative and not restricted to individual groups. Interestingly, the outpoured Spirit is rendered in the Targum, "my Holy Spirit."

2:29 [3:2] *I will pour out my Spirit.* In the MT, Joel completes his all-embracing statement by repeating this phrase, with which he had begun his remarks in 2:28, at the end of this verse, thus forming a nice inclusio.

servants. Not only will age and sex not be a barrier to reception of the Spirit's outpouring, but social status will not be a deterrent. Thus Allen (1976:99) remarks, "Distinctions of age, sex, and social class would be swept away in this common spiritual endowment."

2:30 [3:3] *wonders.* The noun here (*mopeth* [TH4159, ZH4603]) is one of three common words employed to mark some extraordinary supernatural event. The other two are *'oth* [TH226, ZH253] (sign) and *pele'* [TH6382, ZH7099] (wonder). While these three nouns are used somewhat interchangeably to depict the miraculous, on occasion *'oth* conveys the *distinctive purpose* of the miracle (Deut 4:34-35; Isa 7:11-16), *pele'* the *effect* upon those who behold it (Exod 15:11; Ps 119:129), and *mopeth* the *awesome* happening (at times itself a portent of something dreadful yet to occur—Exod 4:21-23; Deut 28:43-46). Thus, what was to take place was designed to assure God's covenant people of the Lord's presence among them. Their wonderment would lead them to single-hearted faith in Yahweh as the only God with whom they had to deal.

heavens . . . earth. Crenshaw (1995:167) takes these two nouns to be a figure of speech (specifically, merism) for "everywhere."

blood . . . fire . . . smoke. All three are imagery associated with warfare (Num 21:28; Josh 8:20-21; Ezek 38:21-22).

2:31 [3:4] *sun . . . moon.* Sun and moon are often linked together in a display of God's supernatural activity (e.g., 3:15; Josh 10:12-13; Isa 13:10; Hab 3:11; Matt 24:29).

dark . . . blood red. Because the scene describes extraordinary activities, Joel may intend a full eclipse of the sun (cf. Amos 8:9).

great and terrible day of the LORD. The Day of the Lord theme grows in progressive intensity in Joel's presentations. Announced as coming in 1:15 and present in 2:1, it is described as an awesome and terrible thing in 2:11 and as great and terrible here, with full details relating to events of that time to follow in 3:9-16.

2:32 [3:5] *calls on the name of the LORD.* Calling on the name of the Lord is used for approaching him with a heart full of faith and a mouth full of praise and worship (Gen 4:26; 12:8; Pss 99:6; 116:17; 145:18; Zeph 3:9; Rom 10:13).

will be saved. The verb *yimmalet* [TH4422, ZH4880] is used to denote "escape from danger" (1 Sam 19:10, 12, 17-18), especially from the divine judgment that awaits the wicked (Prov 11:21). This pronouncement anticipates the succeeding phrases: "some . . . will escape" and "among the survivors." Joel's prophecy of deliverance depends on calling on the Lord in faith and on the Lord's calling of his people.

on Mount Zion in Jerusalem. Joel's perspective clearly embraces believing Israelites because Jerusalem is the site of God's presence. This verse forms part of the OT teaching on Zion theology (see commentary on Obad 1:17-21).

just as the LORD has said. Joel may be referring to God's promise given in 2:27 (cf. Obad 1:17).

survivors whom the LORD has called. Although the primary reference is to Israelite believers, the rendering of the NLT allows for a wider group of refugees, the escapees in Jerusalem forming part of a larger remnant called by the Lord. Therefore, this text could be called upon by the authors of the NT. "Christians became known as those who called on the Lord. Peter leaves no doubt that 'calling on the name of the Lord' meant call on the name of Jesus, the only name by which we must be saved (Acts 4:12; cf. Acts 4:9-12; 9:14, 21; 22:16; 1 Cor 1:2; 2 Tim 2:22). Paul argues that there is no difference between Jew and

Gentile, and that all who call on the name of the Lord will be saved (Rom 10:12)" (Dillard 1992:298). The verse ends as it began—with a call. We, with all Joel's hearers and readers, are called to call upon the Lord.

COMMENTARY

Looking beyond the promised restoration and blessing of a repentant people (2:18-27), Joel points out the reason why Israel could look forward to a day when it would never again be disgraced (2:27): The renewed pouring down of rain was to be a harbinger of the day when God would pour out his Holy Spirit upon all people. While in earlier times the Spirit came upon selected individuals in order to accomplish divinely sanctioned tasks (e.g., Gen 41:38; Num 11:25-26; 27:18; Deut 34:9; Judg 3:10; 11:29; etc.), now the Spirit would be given in full measure to all, regardless of age, sex, or social standing.

Despite the extensive spiritual activity, that future era will be marked by dreadful times. God will set extraordinary phenomena in the heavens and on the earth. It will be a time of great upheaval, with turmoil and unprecedented warfare among the human populace (cf. 3:15; Ezek 38–39; Zeph 1:14-18; Zech 14:1-5) and cataclysmic events (e.g., a solar eclipse, volcanic eruptions, and earthquakes) in nature (cf. Rev 6:12-17). It will be a time of God's outpoured wrath, inasmuch as blood (Exod 7:17; Rev 6:12-17; 14:14-20), fire (Exod 3:2-3), and smoke (Exod 19:16-18; Rev 15:8; 18:16-18) often speak of the superintending power of a holy God. That day is justly called the "great and terrible day of the Lord." Unless God himself intervenes, none will survive.

The result of all this heightened activity will be the safe deliverance of all who call, in faith, upon God's name. In that era God will be especially active. Both in Jerusalem, the dwelling place of his earthly presence, and among his dispersed people, God will call a godly remnant to himself.

The full section speaks not only of deliverance from the dangers of that time but of God's soteriological working. The passage, which begins with an emphasis on the outpouring of the Spirit so as to transform the spiritual experience of all classes of people, ends on a high note with God's particular work in calling a people for himself. Here, blended together in perfect balance, we see God's mysterious election, the response in faith of his chosen people, and the working of the Spirit in the lives of individual believers.

It is no wonder, then, that the apostle Peter would be led to this text in his address on Pentecost (Acts 2), the occasion of the historical outworking of the promise of the outpoured Holy Spirit. Peter and the apostles saw in this event, which initiated the New Testament church, the beginning of those last days that would witness God's Holy Spirit at work, not only among the Jewish remnant but among all who would believe. It would be a time of increased missionary activity. For whoever calls upon the Lord in believing faith will be saved (Rom 10:13). That age will be closed by tumultuous happenings in the natural and political realms and be closed by the return of Christ in glory (Luke 21:25-27; Acts 2:19-20; Phil 3:20-21; 1 Thess 5:1-10; 2 Pet 3:10; Rev 6:12-17; 16:11-20; 19:11-21; see also the commentary on 2:12-14).

Pentecost thus stands as a fulfillment of Joel's prophecy but does not exhaust it. The coming of the Holy Spirit at Pentecost fulfills Joel's prophecy with regard to the outpouring of the Holy Spirit and the resultant Good News of salvation for all. It sets in motion the age of the Spirit (the last days), an era climaxed by a renewed and heightened spiritual activity (cf. Isa 42:1; 44:3-5; 59:21; Ezek 36:27) and the miraculous signs heralding the Day of the Lord and Messiah's return. While some details of Joel's prophecy may reach their culmination only in the time of Christ's second coming, Pentecost guarantees that the full prophecy will indeed come to pass.[1]

Schematically the relationship of Joel's prophecy to Pentecost and to the future can be outlined as follows:

Pentecost	renewed prophecy and the coming of the Holy Spirit
Present Age	the ministry of the Holy Spirit with the message of salvation
End of the Age	heightened spiritual activity, signs and wonders, closed by the Messiah's return in judgment and the Day of the Lord
Second Advent	the consummation of all of Joel's prophecy

Granted, then, that Peter used Joel's prophecy in the way that it was intended and that it was fulfilled at Pentecost, yet without consummation, the further question remains as to the *raison d'etre* of Pentecost. Why Pentecost at all? What is the divine intention of Pentecost?

The answer to this question may lie in Pentecost's relation to its Jewish prototype, the Feast of Weeks (or Festival of Harvest; Exod 34:22), which in time became known as Pentecost (2 Macc 12:32). This feast, falling on the fiftieth day (Lev 23:16) after the barley offering during the Passover celebration, commemorated the beginning of the celebration of firstfruits (cf. Num 28:26).

Without going into the rites and history of the feast itself, the theological significance may be noted as twofold: (1) the thanksgiving of a grateful people for the ingathering of the firstfruits of the grain harvest to God—to whom the harvest properly belonged, and from whom their daily provision came; and (2) a committal of heart that caused the thankful people to share God's bounty with the poor and stranger in the land.

Pentecost was one of three major annual feasts for the Jewish nation, the other two being Passover (which was attached to the Festival of Unleavened Bread) and the Festival of Shelters (Deut 16:16). Each of these feasts held a special theological significance. Passover reminded the people of their divinely provided redemption. Pentecost symbolized the thankfulness of a people who were not only grateful for the firstfruits of the grain harvest but who looked forward with joy and anticipation to the culmination of the harvest season in the fall. The Festival of Shelters marked the climax of the religious year, when a thankful people entered fully into the anticipated promises, resting fully in the God who had supplied their needs.

Each of these feasts was designedly prophetic of the completed redemption that the Messiah would accomplish. Passover looked forward to the Messiah's accomplished redemption, which was realized in Christ's death and resurrection (1 Cor 5:7b; 15:3-4). The Festival of Shelters looks on to the final rest in that age when Messiah shall raise the fallen "shelter" of David (Amos 9:11; "house," NLT) and reign as king among his people in a period of blessed peace and unsurpassed gladness (cf. Rom 11:25-32 with Rev 19:15-17). Pentecost marks the inception of the Christian church (Acts 2:11-17) and the inauguration of an era during which the souls of all people will be gathered in with great fullness through the gospel proclamation (cf. Rom 11:13-24; 1 Cor 15:20-23).

Like the Old Testament Pentecost, the New Testament Pentecost stands as a distinctive event and yet an earnest harbinger of that day when Messiah shall gather in the completed harvest from all the nations of earth and rule in power and glory among a regathered and grateful people. It is of singular interest, as well, that the promised Holy Spirit, who himself serves as the earnest of the believer's full redemption (2 Cor 1:20-22; 5:5; Eph 1:13-14), should have come on the day that serves as the pledge of the full ingathering of God's prophetic purposes!

ENDNOTES
1. Allen (1976:105) appropriately observes, "The Church's birthday marked the coming of age of God's people. The Lord who is the object of faith is also the hope of the Church, the guarantee of a full and final salvation." For a careful discussion of the relation of Joel's prophecy to Pentecost, see Garrett 1997:370-374.

◆ B. The Coming Judgment (3:1-8)

¹"At the time of those events," says the LORD,
"when I restore the prosperity of Judah and Jerusalem,
²I will gather the armies of the world into the valley of Jehoshaphat.*
There I will judge them
for harming my people, my special possession,
for scattering my people among the nations,
and for dividing up my land.
³They threw dice* to decide which of my people
would be their slaves.
They traded boys to obtain prostitutes and sold girls for enough wine to get drunk.

⁴"What do you have against me, Tyre and Sidon and you cities of Philistia? Are you trying to take revenge on me? If you are, then watch out! I will strike swiftly and pay you back for everything you have done. ⁵You have taken my silver and gold and all my precious treasures, and have carried them off to your pagan temples. ⁶You have sold the people of Judah and Jerusalem to the Greeks,* so they could take them far from their homeland.

⁷"But I will bring them back from all the places to which you sold them, and I will pay you back for everything you have done. ⁸I will sell your sons and daughters to the people of Judah, and they will sell them to the people of Arabia,* a nation far away. I, the LORD, have spoken!"

3:1 Verses 3:1-21 are numbered 4:1-21 in Hebrew text.   3:2 Jehoshaphat means "the LORD judges."
3:3 Hebrew They cast lots.   3:6 Hebrew to the peoples of Javan.   3:8 Hebrew to the Sabeans.

NOTES

3:1 [4:1] At the time of those events. Lit., "indeed in those days and at that time." The introductory formula affirms the temporal setting of the prophecy by linking it to the projected future promises that immediately precede it. "In those days and at that time" occurs elsewhere only in Jeremiah (Jer 33:15; 50:4).

when I restore the prosperity. The NLT rendering is reflected in many modern translations (e.g., "when I restore the fortunes," NIV; cf. NASB, NRSV, NJB). Alternatively, many follow the lead of the ancient versions (LXX, Vulgate, Syriac) and KJV in reading something like "when I bring back the captivity/captives" (e.g., NKJV; cf. GW, *La Sacra Biblia, La Sainte Bible, Die Heilige Schrift*).

3:2 [4:2] armies of the world. The NLT reflects the sense of the MT, which reads "all nations." The Lord's decision to bring all nations to judgment is mentioned in Zeph 3:8 (see commentary; cf. Isa 66:18; Mic 4:12).

valley of Jehoshaphat. Because no such valley is mentioned elsewhere in the OT, the locality involved must derive its name (meaning "Yahweh has judged") from the Lord's determination to judge the forces of this world there. The name is thus a play on words symbolizing the divine activity in that place (cf. 3:12). Subsequently (3:14), it is called the valley of decision. Kapelrud (1948:144-148) speaks of a valley tradition involving judgment. To be noted are the valley of Ben-Hinnom (Jer 7:30-34; 19:1-7), the Valley of Vision (Isa 22:1-13), and the Valley of the Travelers, which becomes the Valley of Gog's Hordes (Ezek 39:11).

harming . . . scattering . . . dividing. The syntax of the MT demands that the harming of God's people Israel be understood as twofold: (1) scattering them among the nations and (2) dividing up their land. God reminds the guilty parties that both people and land were his ("my people," "my land").

3:3 [4:3] threw dice. Lit., "They cast lots" (cf. NLT mg). Obad 1:11 mentions Edom's consent to foreigners casting lots over Jerusalem. Similarly, Nah 3:10 (see note) records the casting of lots for coveted slaves when Thebes was conquered.

my people would be their slaves. The Jewish people were to learn the reality of this prediction (cf. 1 Macc 3:41; 2 Macc 8:11, 25; Josephus *Antiquities* 12.298-299; *War* 6.414–419). The practice was commonplace in ancient times. See also Thucydides *Peloponnesian War* 3:50. Regrettably, already in OT times God's covenant people themselves were not above engaging in such practices (1 Kgs 9:21; Amos 2:6; cf. Deut 24:7).

traded boys to obtain prostitutes and sold girls for . . . wine. Children were sold for the price of debauchery. Such deals, while reprehensible, were apparently commonplace in ancient times. In an ancient Phoenician inscription, King Kilamuwa speaks of a deal that he had made with an Assyrian king by citing a traditional proverb: "A maid for a lamb, a man for a garment" (for text and commentary, see Donner and Röllig 1966:I:5, line 8; II:31, line 33).

3:4 [4:4] Tyre and Sidon. The Phoenicians were well known as slave traders in the ancient world. In the early eighth century BC, the Phoenicians again rose to prominence as successful merchants. They were condemned by Israel's prophets (Isa 23:1-18; Amos 1:9-10).

cities of Philistia? Joel correctly points out that the Philistines were noted for their independent cities, particularly the five cities of the Philistine Pentapolis, each of which was ruled by its own overlord: Ashdod, Ashkelon, Ekron, Gaza, and Gath. The Philistines were perennial adversaries of the Israelites, a situation that necessitated Uzziah's campaigning against them in the eighth century BC (2 Chr 26:6-7). Amos (Amos 1:6) condemned the Philistines for their crime of enslavement.

3:5 [4:5] silver and gold . . . to your pagan temples. The charge is that of plundering Israel's valuables, particularly their religious items. The word translated "temples" could also be rendered "palaces." Perhaps both are intended.

3:6 [4:6] *to the Greeks.* The Greeks were known to be active in international trade from the middle of the eighth century onward. Their commercial enterprises covered a wide swath from the Black Sea to Italy. The Hebrew word here may indicate the Ionian Greeks who lived on both sides of the Aegean Sea, including what is now mainland Turkey. There the Greeks monopolized the major trade routes of the area. The Ionian Greeks were already known from Assyrian sources in the eighth century BC. According to Ezek 27:13, 19, the Ionian Greeks were involved with the Phoenicians in the despicable slave trade.

3:7 [4:7] *I will bring them back . . . and I will pay you back.* Once again, the promise of restoration from exile is heard (cf. Deut 30:3-5; Isa 11:11-12; 43:5-7; cf. commentary on Zeph 3:9-13). God repeats his intention to apply the principle of *lex talionis* to his enemies: As they have done, so it will be done to them.

3:8 [4:8] *people of Arabia.* Lit., "the Sabeans." The land of Sheba, in southern Arabia, is mentioned in the OT in the days of Solomon (1 Kgs 10:1-13). Sabean trading enterprises are known to have taken place even earlier (Job 6:19; cf. Job 1:14-15; Ezek 27:22-24). Hubbard (1989:76-77) notes that "their penchant for caravan trading meant that slaves sold to them could ultimately be dispersed almost anywhere from the Indian Ocean to the East Coast of Africa."

C O M M E N T A R Y

Building on the twin themes of hope and judgment in the preceding verses, Joel records in 3:1-8 God's intention to bring the nations of this world to judgment. Gathering them together (cf. Zeph 3:8) in the valley of Jehoshaphat, God will bring charges against them for their treatment of his people and misappropriation of his land. Not content with these activities, some had sold Israelite children into slavery merely for the sake of satisfying their own lusts and appetites. God acts here both as prosecuting attorney, who brings his charges against the violators of his people, and as righteous judge, who warns of their stiff penalty.

God singled out particular antagonists: Tyre and Sidon, as well as the Philistines, are charged with plundering the treasures of God's people. Moreover, they had dealt with Greek traders in selling Israel's people to lands far from their homeland. For all of this (and probably more) these people will receive judgment proportionate to their crimes. Further, God will bring back his scattered people, while seeing to it that the guilty parties will lose their children to captivity and slavery in far-off lands.

While each of the nations singled out for divine judgment is doubtless representative of any nation who will ultimately reap the consequences of its ill treatment of God's people, it is also true that each of these peoples mentioned did suffer defeat at the hands of invaders. The Philistines, who experienced Judah's wrath in the campaigning of Uzziah (2 Chr 26:6), were repeatedly subdued in the eighth century BC by the Assyrian kings (Tiglath-pileser III in 734; Sargon II in 720 and 713/712; and Sennacherib in 701). They remained under Assyrian control until the Chaldean king Nebuchadnezzar II brought them into the orbit of the Neo-Babylonian Empire in 604 BC. Sidon was sacked and its citizens resettled in various localities. Rebellious Tyre survived by repeatedly doling out heavy tribute both to Esarhaddon and to Ashurbanipal (668–626 BC). With the decline of Assyria, Tyre regained its independence, although its influence was curtailed throughout the Neo-Babylonian and Persian periods.

Esarhaddon (681–668 BC) subsequently rebuilt Sidon and it remained under foreign domination throughout the Neo-Assyrian, Neo-Babylonian, and Persian eras. On one occasion, however, after Artaxerxes III suffered a setback in Egypt, Sidon played a leading role in a Phoenician revolt against Persia. In response, the Persian king gathered a huge army in Babylon, marched against Sidon, and overwhelmed it (345 BC). Later, Alexander the Great overran the area, even capturing the island city of Tyre in 331 BC. Both Tyre and Sidon recovered, however, and experienced renewed prosperity in Hellenistic and Roman times. Both are mentioned in the New Testament. Nevertheless, their several defeats in ancient times stand as a grim example and reminder that God ultimately will deal with all oppressors, particularly those who have wronged his people.

Joel has already pointed out that God's settling of accounts will take place in the era he outlined in 2:28-32, which was for him a time in the distant future. Therefore, the historical notices mentioned above are also harbingers of the judgment that must occur near the end of the present age. Elsewhere, the Scriptures warn of a great sociopolitical system that will oppose God's people (Dan 11:36-45; 2 Thess 2:3-4; Rev 17–18) but be defeated by the coming of the Son of Man to execute judgment (Ezek 38–39; Dan 7:9-14; Zech 14:1-5; Matt 24:3-31; Rev 19:11-21).

This passage reemphasizes the twin truths of God's sovereign and perfect justice. The Scriptures make it clear that the God who sovereignly rules over the universe (Ps 103:19) likewise has dominion over the affairs of nations (Ps 22:28[29]; Isa 40:21-26; Acts 17:26) and all people (1 Sam 2:6-8; Dan 4:34-35). Moreover, divine providence is not merely a matter of administrative power and operation, but has direction and purpose (Isa 46:8-10). For he has set a day when all earth's history will be consummated through his Son, Jesus Christ (Phil 2:9-11; Col 1:19-20; Rev 11:15). His providential control also assures his people of his concern for their well-being (Pss 4:6-8[7-9]; 84:11-12[12-13]) and eternal destiny (Ps 73:22-23; John 10:27-29). Such knowledge should spur the believer's trust (Prov 3:5-6) and dynamically activate his or her prayer life (Ps 32:6-7; Phil 4:4-7; Col 4:2).

Joel's words are also a reminder that God is just and rules justly over the affairs of nations and people (Ps 67:4[5]; Dan 4:37; see commentary on 2:18-27). Indeed, because he is a God of justice he will deal with all people fairly, whether that means reward (2:18-27) or punishment (Isa 51:6). Such knowledge is comforting to believers. For not only has God's justice been satisfied in Jesus Christ, giving believers right standing before God (Rom 3:21-26; 1 John 2:2), but God's people may be certain that God will ultimately rectify the seeming inequities and unrequited evil that permeates society (Ps 49:5-14).

Individuals and nations have experienced unjust treatment repeatedly through the ages. Likewise, it is true that injustice continues to haunt the contemporary scene—and, sadly, it seems that the perpetrators of wickedness are not forced to account for their deeds. Nevertheless, it is also certain that the Day of the Lord is coming, however slowly it may seem (2 Pet 3:8-9). Then, each person will stand before the bar of God's justice (Pss 50:3-4; 96:13; 98:9; 110:6; Acts 10:42; 17:31; Rev 11:16-18). In that day, the Lord, the righteous judge, will take his seat on his throne (Dan 7:13-14; Matt 19:28) and rule in perfect righteousness and justice (Isa 2:4; 9:7), receiving the adulation of all nations (Phil 2:9-11; Rev 15:3-4).

Such assurance should inspire believers to unswerving trust in the Lord (Ps 52:8-9; Isa 26:3-4) and enable each one to be committed to him who "always judges fairly" (1 Pet 2:23), regardless of life's circumstances (Ps 31:10-14[11-15]; Isa 56:1; Hab 3:17-18; 1 Pet 4:17-19). May all of God's people respond in faith to Paul's admonition: "Let the message about Christ, in all its richness, fill your lives. Teach and counsel each other with all the wisdom he gives" (Col 3:16) so that we might do "what is right, just, and fair" (Prov 1:3; cf. Mic 6:8; Zech 7:9). In so doing, perhaps some of the evils of society will be mitigated (Prov 29:7; Isa 1:17) and others encouraged to seek the Lord of all justice (Isa 1:27).

◆ C. The Climactic Battle (3:9-17)

⁹Say to the nations far and wide:
  "Get ready for war!
Call out your best warriors.
  Let all your fighting men advance
  for the attack.
¹⁰Hammer your plowshares into swords
  and your pruning hooks into spears.
  Train even your weaklings to be
  warriors.
¹¹Come quickly, all you nations
  everywhere.
Gather together in the valley."

And now, O LORD, call out your warriors!

¹²"Let the nations be called to arms.
  Let them march to the valley of
  Jehoshaphat.
There I, the LORD, will sit
  to pronounce judgment on them all.
¹³Swing the sickle,
  for the harvest is ripe.*
Come, tread the grapes,
  for the winepress is full.

The storage vats are overflowing
  with the wickedness of these people."

¹⁴Thousands upon thousands are waiting
  in the valley of decision.
There the day of the LORD will soon
  arrive.
¹⁵The sun and moon will grow dark,
  and the stars will no longer shine.
¹⁶The LORD's voice will roar from Zion
  and thunder from Jerusalem,
  and the heavens and the earth
  will shake.
But the LORD will be a refuge for
  his people,
  a strong fortress for the people
  of Israel.

¹⁷"Then you will know that I, the LORD
  your God,
  live in Zion, my holy mountain.
Jerusalem will be holy forever,
  and foreign armies will never
  conquer her again.

3:13 Greek version reads *for the harvest time has come.* Compare Mark 4:29.

NOTES
3:9 [4:9] *Say to the nations.* Some disagreement persists as to the speaker here. Is it God in the presence of the holy angels (Allen, Crenshaw, Hubbard) or Joel himself (Craigie, Finley)? Perhaps the question is academic, for the message ultimately is the Lord's, whether given directly or through his prophet (cf. Amos 3:6-8).

Get ready for war! The nations are charged to prepare themselves for fighting a war they cannot win, as the following verses declare. Allen (1976:115) finds a touch of irony in this. Several OT passages contain a summons to enemies to come to a battle they will lose (e.g., Jer 46:3-6, 9-10). The proclamation reads literally "sanctify a war" (echoing the earlier commands to "sanctify a fast" and "sanctify an assembly," 2:15-16). All the men were to observe the proper religious rites preceding battle that were customary in ancient warfare.

Call out your best warriors. The word translated "warriors" (cf. 2:7) often connotes a sense of valiant action, hence "heroes" (Keil 1954:226).

advance for the attack. The rendering of the NLT properly combines the force of two asyndetically juxtaposed jussive verbs: "Draw near [so as to] go up." The purpose of the advance is to prepare for the final assault. The Hebrew verbs in the verse provide an air of urgency and excitement. One can imagine the commander's orders being shouted in quick succession and the hurried response of those summoned to the fray: "Get ready, men!" "Move out!" "Charge!"

3:10 [4:10] *plowshares into swords . . . pruning hooks into spears.* The eschatological promise of peace (Isa 2:4; Mic 4:3) is reversed in a context that speaks of preparation for all-out warfare.

Train even your weaklings to be warriors. Lit., "let the weakling say, 'I am a warrior.'" The challenge in this total mobilization stands in contrast to normal protocol (cf. Deut 20:8; Judg 7:3). Much as in the case of Moab (Jer 48:14), however, such boasting and any measures taken (cf. NLT) will prove to be misguided. The mustering of a whole population for war is detailed in the Keret Epic of ancient Ugarit (Coogan 1978:60-63; Gordon 1965:250-251).

3:11 [4:11] *Come quickly . . . Gather together.* These imperatives underscore the need for hurrying the summons to earth's great conflict. The meaning of the Hebrew verb treated adverbially by the NLT ("quickly") is uncertain, but the NLT reading corresponds to the Vulgate's *erumpite* (rush forth), possibly assuming an equivalence of the Heb. *'ush* [TH5789, ZH6429] ("to hurry" or "to help") with *khush* [TH2363, ZH2590] (hurry). In postbiblical Hebrew the verb *'ush* came to mean "come to help" or "take care," and in modern Hebrew it means "hurry, make haste."

Gather together in the valley. Lit., "gather yourselves together there." The NLT renders the contextual sense. The reference is to the valley of Jehoshaphat mentioned in v. 2 and again in v. 12.

And now, O LORD. In a poignant apostrophe, Joel interrupted the narrative with a call for the Lord's intervention.

your warriors! Joel used the term "warriors" in several places in his prophecy. The description of the warrior-like locusts of 2:7 and the summoning of the warriors of the nations (3:9), including even the hoped-for result in the weakest of men (3:10), is now capped by the call for God's mighty warriors (i.e., his angelic host; cf. Deut 33:2-3; Ps 103:19-20).

3:12 [4:12] *called to arms . . . march.* Previously the nations had been told to rouse (*ha'iru* [TH5782, ZH6424]) their warriors so that they might come together and move out (*ya'alu* [TH5927, ZH6590]) to battle (3:9); now they are instructed to call their forces to arms (*ye'oru* [TH5782, ZH6424]) so as to march (*ya'alu* [TH5927, ZH6590]) into the predetermined valley where a righteous judge awaits them. The play on words and sounds is striking.

Jehoshaphat . . . pronounce judgment. The force of the previously mentioned valley of Jehoshaphat (3:2) is here explained. Wherever its location, it is the scene of God's judicial sentencing. Whereas God appears earlier as a prosecuting attorney (see commentary on 3:1-8), he now takes his seat as sentencing judge. The repeated theme serves both to stitch those two sections together and to tie the first strophe (3:12-13) of vv. 12-17 to the second (3:14-17).

3:13 [4:13] *sickle . . . harvest.* God's judgment is symbolized by the metaphor of the harvest. As the harvester cuts ripened grain, so the time for the nations' judgment has come (cf. Isa 17:5).

winepress is full . . . vats are overflowing. Joel shifted to viticultural imagery. Like a winepress full to overflowing and a field ready for harvesting, so the wickedness of the nations is too great for their judgment to be delayed any longer (cf. Isa 63:1-3). Allen (1976:118) remarks, "Such a mass of grapes was piled in the press that its own weight was forcing the liquid down the channels into the nearby vats, which were spilling over and clamoring for attention. What a harvest! How ripe for judgment were the assembled nations who overflowed the boundaries of the broad valley!" Both these images of the harvest metaphor are found in Rev 14:14-20.

3:14 [4:14] *Thousands upon thousands.* The Hebrew noun not only designates the presence of untold multitudes brought to the great battle but carries with it the idea of the uproar caused by the total confusion of the massed throngs at that terrible scene (cf. Isa 13:4; 17:12; see also Pusey 1953:210).

valley of decision. The valley of judgment is now termed the valley of decision—the place where the verdict of God, the righteous Judge, is given. The root underlying the noun translated "decision" suggests the image of cutting. God cuts/issues a decree with regard to the determination of man's life expectancy (Job 14:5) and announces the details relative to the culmination of earth's history (cf. Dan 9:26-27).

3:15 [4:15] *sun . . . moon . . . stars.* Once again, we learn of darkened celestial bodies. The language is quasi-apocalyptic. That which was applied to the frightening time of the locusts, itself a symbol of coming warfare (2:10), and then to the extraordinary day of the outpouring of the Spirit (2:31), is now linked to the awesome eschatological scene. The imagery anticipates the exceedingly intense conditions of the great and terrible Day of the Lord.

3:16 [4:16] *The LORD's voice will roar from Zion.* The NLT renders the force of the text. The metaphor is that of the lion roaring over its prey. The same image appears in Amos 1:2 and may help account for the placement of Joel beside Amos in the canonical order of the Minor Prophets. Joel's placement is further facilitated by noting the similar vocabulary used in Hosea's closing chapter and in Joel 1. Hosea 14 emphasizes God's blessings upon future Israel, whose flourishing is likened to abundant grain, vines, and wine (Hos 14:7). The same terminology appears in 1:10-12.

thunder from Jerusalem. The same phraseology occurs in Amos 1:2. Earlier, Joel had pictured God as thundering before his mighty army in the Day of the Lord (2:11). The image of God's thunderous voice is often portrayed in the Scriptures both in connection with the natural world (e.g., Job 36:29; 37:4; Pss 29:3; 68:33; Jer 51:16) and with divine judgment (Jer 25:30). Revelation 10:3-4 pictures the future coming of a mighty angel who gives a shout like a lion's roar, accompanied by the voices of seven thunders.

the heavens and the earth . . . shake. Joel has used this imagery previously (2:10). The Lord is often portrayed in connection with seismic activity (e.g., Nah 1:5), especially with regard to the protection and deliverance of his own people (Pss 18:7[8]; 77:18[19]; 114:3-7; Hab 3:6, 10). In Rev 16:18, the divine judgment of wicked Babylon is described in terms of an unparalleled earthquake, as well as lightning and thunder.

the LORD will be a refuge . . . fortress. God's protection of his own is often described in terms of being a refuge or fortress (e.g., Pss 46:1[2]; 62:7[8]; 91:2; Jer 17:17; Nah 1:7). The particular words used here may have been chosen for their sound: *makhaseh le'ammo uma'oz.* The Hebrew writers often played on sounds in order to convey their message (Watson 1986:242-243). The sound play could be employed for emphasis, effect, or ease of memory. The effect here is to emphasize that God not only was his people's refuge, but even more—their "strong fortress."

3:17 [4:17] *Then you will know.* As in 2:27 the section ends with a statement of God's presence and protection. Both texts emphasize the fact that Israel will never know the disgrace of facing conquerors. Joel's final prophetic word will reemphasize God's dwelling among his people.

Zion, my holy mountain. God's dwelling on Mount Zion is affirmed in Isa 8:18. God's presence sanctified the Temple mount (Ezek 43:12) and all Jerusalem (Isa 52:1; Zech 14:20-21). This text takes its place among many others in developing the scriptural teaching relative to Zion theology (see commentary on Obad 1:17-21).

COMMENTARY

Building on the previous prophecy of divine judgment, Joel records the Lord's proclamation. The nations are to prepare for the war of all wars (3:9-11). There is to be a total mobilization of the godless forces of the nations. Whether courageous or cowardly, all are to be summoned from their homes. Every means shall be utilized and every implement used, for ordinary labor is to be retooled into a weapon of war.

In the light of such staggering details, Joel cried out for God to call out his warriors (3:11b). The enemy is coming—will God not respond? The Lord's answer is swift in coming. As he had already said, the nations must be brought to that valley where God, the righteous judge and sovereign overseer of all, will sit in judgment on them (3:12). No, the Lord was not unaware of the evil designs of the wicked (cf. Ps 2:1-3). Rather, all of this was part of his purposes in dealing with the kingdoms of this world (3:12; cf. Ps 110:1-3, 5-6; Matt 25:31-46; Rev 19:11-21).

In what follows, Joel takes his hearers to the scene of that climactic battle in earth's history (3:13-16). God commands his hosts to defeat the enemy, for the time of divine judgment against wickedness has come. Untold multitudes are seen and heard amidst the din of the immense struggle that is taking place. Not only is there clamor and confusion everywhere, but there is also an awesome spectacle that occurs in the physical world. The earth heaves and sways, undulating beneath the deafening thunder that booms and rolls across the darkened sky. Such things signal the presence of the Divine Warrior himself (cf. Isa 24:17-23).

Suddenly, as though hesitant to describe the dreadful carnage, the description is discontinued. A deathly silence seems to permeate the whole. For the outcome has been certain and doubtless has been quick in coming. Indeed, this is not only the valley of God's judgment but his determination to put an end to all wicked opposition against his people (cf. Isa 17:12-14).

God's people need not fear this day, for the Lord himself will be their refuge and strength. Moreover, the tables will be turned on their enemies, as the forces of evil fall before the Lord's mighty warriors, angelic and human (cf. Mic 4:11-13). With victory complete, God's people will again dwell in the Holy City in the presence of a holy God, free forever from the invader's boot (3:17; cf. Ezek 34:27-28; 36:24-30; Obad 1:20; Zeph 3:19-20).

Theologically, these verses form a central part of Old Testament eschatology. They take their place beside several passages that predict the assembling of the nations for a great final battle near Jerusalem. Thus, Ezekiel tells of the coming of powerful forces that will invade the Holy Land, determined to despoil God's people (Ezek 38:1-13; cf. Zech 12:2-3). Isaiah (Isa 24:17-23) foretells the terror and death that awaits the nations of earth in a vivid description that parallels that of Joel. Zephaniah describes the horrors of that day, both in the natural world and in the conflict itself (Zeph 1:14-18). Micah (Mic 4:11-13) warns the assembled nations that God has gathered them for judgment as a harvester bringing his sheaves to the threshing floor.

Ezekiel echoed Joel's prophecy that God's people would learn much concerning the sovereignty of God through the coming events. God would be manifest before the nations as the true and only God, and to his people as a sovereign and holy God (Ezek 38:14-23; 39:21-24). Moreover, he would bring back his scattered people to their land and pour out his Spirit upon them (Ezek 39:25-29). Like Joel, other prophets predicted that God himself would live among his restored people (e.g., Isa 49:22-25; Jer 24:6-7; Ezek 39:25-29; 48:35; Zeph 3:14-17). Further details are added, of course, in the other prophets and in the New Testament, including the rise of antichrist, the growing world apostate government, and the return of Jesus Christ. Nevertheless, Joel's prophecy is crucial to a full understanding of biblical eschatology.

Likewise, this portion of Joel is important to the unfolding revelation of the Divine Warrior and to the development of Zion theology. In harmony with other Scriptures, Joel reveals God as the one who intervenes on behalf of his people, both to subdue the enemy and to deliver and provide for his chosen people. It is he who redeemed Israel out of Egypt and placed them in the Land of Promise (Exod 15:1-18) and who fought on their behalf on various occasions (e.g., Judg 5:19-23; 2 Kgs 19:21-36; Ps 78:65-66). He will yet again go out to put an end to wickedness (Zeph 1:14-18; 3:8, 15-17; Rev 19:11-21), deliver his people (Isa 61:1-2; Zeph 3:14-15, 17), and establish everlasting righteousness for a believing humankind (Isa 1:26-27; Zeph 3:14-20). Joel partakes of both aspects of this theological motif. The Divine Warrior will crush his and his people's enemies, and his resident holiness will permeate his land and the city of Zion—forever free from the fear of foreign invasion (cf. Zech 14:3-5, 20-21).

This portion of Joel also adds to the development of Zion theology: In earlier days, David had captured the fortress of Zion (2 Sam 5:7). Subsequently, he oversaw the relocation of the Ark of the Covenant to the city (2 Sam 6:12-19). Later, after the Ark was placed in the Holy of Holies in Solomon's Temple (1 Kgs 8:1-9), "the glorious presence of the Lord filled the Temple" (1 Kgs 8:11). God's dwelling in and connection with Zion are often mentioned in the Psalms (e.g., Pss 9:11; 50:2; 65:1; 74:2; 84:7; 87:1-2; 99:2; 132:13). The presence of the Holy One in the Temple made all Jerusalem holy and sacred to all who followed him.

As this passage demonstrates, Zion theology is interwoven with the motif of the Divine Warrior. Because he is the deliverer of his people, who has established the throne of his Kingdom in Jerusalem, the people need not fear (Pss 27:1-6; 48:12-14). As those who are the Lord's special possession (Ps 135:3-4), believers are to trust the Lord (Ps 125:1-2) and live in accordance with the standards of holiness and righteousness that will reflect the character of the one who inhabits Zion (Isa 1:16-27).

Being a citizen of Zion means living in anticipation of that day when the Lord will return his exiles to their homeland and usher in worldwide peace and felicity (cf. Isa 12:4-6; 51:3; 52:7-10; 62:11-12; Jer 31:10-14; Mic 4:3-4; Zeph 3:14-20). Then, the anointed King will rule in holiness and righteousness (Pss 2:6-9; 110:1-3; Isa 1:27; 33:5-6; 35:8-10; Mic 4:3) over a redeemed people (Zeph 3:9-13). Zion will be desired as the place of worship for all people (Jer 31:3-6; Mic 4:1-2; Zech 14:9-11, 16-18).

Zion theology is not only integral to the Old Testament but also to the eschatology of the New Testament. The hope of that future universal salvation, well-being, and joy is assured because the Lord's promised Anointed One (the Christ) has come (cf. Zech 9:9-10 with Matt 21:4-5; John 12:12-15). With him lies the hope of being a member of that redeemed multitude that will enjoy the presence of the Lord and his blessings forever (Rom 8:30-34; 1 Pet 2:4-10). Therefore, New Testament believers are to conduct themselves with all godliness in eager anticipation of that blessed time (Titus 2:11-14; 3:4-8).

It is not enough, however, to await the coming of the Day of the Lord when wickedness will be punished and everlasting righteousness established. The present world will be better served if, while confident of their future hope, believers live both so as to attract others to desire to be partakers of the coming blessings of Zion and so as to make the present world more like the future Zion (Heb 12:22–13:21). Craigie (1985:119) remarks, "We should be more true to Joel's purpose if we sought not simply to discern the future, but rather to change the future by present action."

◆   ## D. The Resultant Scene (3:18-21)

18 In that day the mountains will drip
      with sweet wine,
   and the hills will flow with milk.
   Water will fill the streambeds of Judah,
      and a fountain will burst forth from
      the LORD's Temple,
      watering the arid valley of acacias.*
19 But Egypt will become a wasteland
      and Edom will become a wilderness,
   because they attacked the people of
      Judah

and killed innocent people in
      their land.
20 "But Judah will be filled with people
      forever,
   and Jerusalem will endure through
      all generations.
21 I will pardon my people's crimes,
      which I have not yet pardoned;
   and I, the LORD, will make my home
      in Jerusalem* with my people."

3:18 Hebrew *valley of Shittim*.   3:21 Hebrew *Zion*.

NOTES

3:18 [4:18] *In that day.* This is a familiar prophetic formula used to introduce details relative to the eschatological future (e.g., Isa 24:21; 26:1; 27:1; Jer 30:8; Amos 9:11; Mic 4:6; Zeph 3:16; Zech 14:4).

sweet wine. Cf. the note on 1:5, where the same Hebrew word is used. The availability of wine had been cut off due to the locust plague. Its restoration was promised based on full repentance and a turning to the Lord (2:13-14, 24). Now it is prophesied to be in ready supply in that day when the Lord again dwells in Zion (cf. Amos 9:13).

milk. As the Lord had promised (Deut 27:3), God gave Israel a land "flowing with milk and honey" (Jer 32:22). Like the wine, in that future time milk will again be plentiful.

Water. The dry wadis and streambeds (1:20) will again gush with water. The presence of wine, milk, and water in great abundance was symbolic of God's blessings.

a fountain . . . from the LORD's temple. Joel's eschatological perspective is in harmony with that of Ezekiel, who reports that the streams so initiated will terminate in the Dead Sea, changing that salty and lifeless body to one of fresh water (Ezek 47:7-12). Zechariah (Zech 14:8) prophesies of water flowing both eastward and westward from Jerusalem, with the former emptying into the Mediterranean Sea and the latter into the Dead Sea. The psalmist (Ps 46:4[5]) likewise speaks of a stream that "brings joy to the city of our God, the sacred home of the Most High." In connection with the restored paradise of the new earth, John sees "a river with the water of life, clear as crystal, flowing from the throne of God and the Lamb. It flowed down the center of the main street. On each side of the river grew a tree of life" (Rev 22:1-2a). All of this clearly testifies to the abundant fertility of the land in which the Messiah will make his habitation (3:17, 21).

arid valley of acacias. The acacia tree was used extensively for construction of the Tabernacle. Like the valley of Jehoshaphat and the valley of decision, this name may be purely symbolic. In this case it may simply imply that the narrowest, deepest gorge (*nakhal* [TH5158, ZH5707]), now dry (1:20), will experience renewed fertility. If a literal valley is to be sought, it may be best to identify it with Wadi en-Nar, which goes out from the Kidron Valley to the Dead Sea. Acacia trees are known to grow there.

3:19 [4:19] *Egypt . . . Edom.* Rather than having an abundance of water, the land of these two perennial enemies of Israel will be made desolate and laid waste. The eighth-century prophets Isaiah (Isa 19; 30:1-5; 31:1-3) and Hosea (Hos 7:11; 12:1) condemn Israel's ill-advised reliance upon Egypt. Joel's prediction would be particularly troublesome for Egypt, which had relied on the Nile for its very existence and livelihood from time immemorial. The eighth-century king Amaziah campaigned against Edom (2 Kgs 14:7). Proud and rich from its trading enterprises (Obad 1:3, 6), Edom would be particularly hard hit if it became a wasteland.

because they attacked the people of Judah and killed innocent people. No specific occasion may be in view here. Both nations were repeatedly guilty of crimes against the Holy Land. Earlier pharaohs made frequent forays into Israel. Especially to be noted is the tenth-century BC pharaoh Sheshonq I (Shishak), who swept through much of Israel and Judah carrying away much plunder (1 Kgs 14:25-26). Edom likewise was known for its continued enmity against Israel. Already in the ninth century BC, when hostilities broke out between Israel and Edom, a coalition of Arabs and Philistines invaded Judah, taking away many members of the royal family together with many goods (2 Chr 21:8-17; 22:1). Still further hostilities erupted in the eighth century during the days of Amaziah and Uzziah (2 Kgs 14:7-14) and Ahaz (2 Chr 28:16-21). Obadiah (Obad 1:11-14) apparently speaks of yet another later occasion when Edom transgressed against Judah and Jerusalem (see commentary below).

Whether or not Joel had specific occasions in mind, Egypt and Edom were often guilty of crimes against God's people. The tables would be turned. Israel's neighbors would have their fertility and wealth taken away, while Israel would experience the Lord's bountiful provision.

3:20 [4:20] *through all generations.* Joel varies the temporal construction he used with *dor* [TH1755A, ZH1887] (generation) in 2:2. There he employed the term in a general way to call attention to that which had never been seen and never would be in the future. Here the temporal clause stresses the continuous occupation of Judah throughout the succeeding ages.

3:21 [4:21] *I will pardon my people's crimes, which I have not yet pardoned.* This sentence is notoriously difficult. The LXX (cf. Peshitta) suggests the meaning "I will avenge their blood and will not acquit (it/them)." Such a reading requires some emendation and envisions the pronouncement to be a continuance of the denunciation of Egypt and Edom. Stuart (1987:264-265) views it similarly but treats the sentence as a question and answer: "Will I leave their bloodshed unpunished? I will not leave it unpunished!" Both understandings take the word *dam* [TH1818, ZH1947] ("blood[shed]"; NLT, "crimes") to be referring to the same event. Keil (1954:232) also takes the bloodshed as referring to Egypt and Edom, remarking, "The eternal desolation of the world-kingdoms mentioned here will wipe out all the wrong which they have done to the people of God, and which has hitherto remained unpunished." The NLT follows the MT but takes the reference to be to Judah and Jerusalem, mentioned in the previous verse. The waw on the suffix conjugation construction with which the verse begins favors this understanding. This understanding of the verse strengthens the indication that God's people who inhabit Judah and Jerusalem will be a repentant and purified people (cf. Zeph 3:9-13). Indeed, because God does not acquit the guilty (Exod 34:7; Num 14:18), his forgiveness would be on the basis of repentance and confessed sin (1 John 1:9). The former blood guiltiness of Judah and Jerusalem thus stands in contrast to the innocent blood shed by Egypt and Edom.

I, the LORD, will make my home in Jerusalem. Lit., "the LORD dwells in Zion." The verb here (*shakan* [TH7931, ZH8905]) is the same translated "live" in v. 17. Both concluding sections (3:9-17, 18-21) thus end with the same theme: God's permanent dwelling in the city of Zion (i.e., Jerusalem; cf. Ezek 48:35). From the root for the verb "dwell" came the later Hebrew word *Shekinah*, which became a technical term for God's visible presence among his people.

COMMENTARY

Joel ends his prophecy on a high note. He predicts that the environment where God's future people will live will be marked by superabundant fertility. All that had been lost in the locust plague will, as God promised (2:18-27), be restored in effusive quantity. The landscape will flourish again; the streams and even the dry wadis will flow freely, bringing life and health to the land and all its inhabitants. Jerusalem's underground water sources will also gush forth, bringing refreshing vitality to ground that has long been parched with aridity. Even the Dead Sea will come alive and be rejuvenated by the fresh waters of Jerusalem's Temple Mount (see note on 3:18).

The fortunes of Israel's long-standing enemies, typified by Egypt and Edom, however, will be reversed. God's judgment will rest upon them, leaving them barren. By way of contrast, God's land and city will be inhabited forever by a repentant and redeemed people. With their sins forgiven, a purified people will thus be made ready for life with the Holy One who will reside in their midst (3:19-21).

Several truths stand out in this closing section. The mention of the ready availability of wine and water give testimony to the fact that God is a promise-keeping

God. He had given assurance that there would be restoration from the effects of the locust plague if genuine repentance and change of life should occur. Joel now declares that God will keep that promise. God is like that. What he promises, he does (Josh 23:5, 10, 14-15; Pss 119:140; 145:13). Therefore, believers ought to have confidence in God (Ps 119:148) and live so as to realize God's promises to those who keep his commandments. This should be the case regardless of what may happen in their lives (1 Kgs 9:4-5; Isa 43:12).

Just as God fulfilled his promise to bring Israel into a land flowing with milk and honey (Deut 6:1-3; Jer 32:22), so Joel sees that God will not only put his purified people in a land of fruitfulness (wine) and vitality (water), but he will give added benefits. The goats and cattle, fattened by the extreme fertility of the land, will yield their milk in full measure. How good God is! Truly, "The LORD will withhold no good thing from those who do what is right" (Ps 84:11). All of this is a reminder of the riches of God's grace, which is bestowed freely on his own (Eph 2:7). May today's believers, even as those in the day which Joel predicts, claim God's promises and live faithful and godly lives in the knowledge of the coming of the One in whom all of God's promises shall be realized (Heb 10:32-38; 2 Pet 1:3-11).

The final divine promise that Joel records is that God will reside permanently among his redeemed people, even as he had promised so long ago (Lev 26:3-12). This truth is the culmination of frequent scriptural indications of God's active presence among his people—yet in great power and splendor (the Shekinah glory). Joel's prophecy looks on to John's revelation of the glorious, everlasting reign of Christ over a refreshed and glorified earth, when he will dwell among a believing humankind (Rev 21:3).

John, however, declares that before that great era to come, there was a prior dwelling of God among people, which was no less glorious (John 1:14). When Christ "became human," it was no less than a visitation of the Shekinah glory. He was the promised Immanuel—God with us! Nor was he less glorious when he hung on the cross for our salvation and rose triumphantly from the grave (John 12:23-28; 17:1-4).

Paul reminds us that with Christ's incarnate mission, accomplished at Calvary and in the resurrection, the ascended Lord has taken the believer into union with himself (Eph 2:19-22). Accordingly, the Christian has not only a sure hope of that glorious future (Col 1:27) that Joel and John foretold but an ever-present source of strength in his spiritual service (2 Cor 12:9) to reveal that one to others (Gal 1:16). Herein the future can be realized in the present.

May Joel's great prophecy be an encouragement to believers everywhere. May the assurance of life lived throughout the future ages with the Lord himself be increasingly confirmed in a life lived in the conscious reality of Christ's ever-abiding presence even now—"Christ in you, the hope of glory" (Col 1:27, NIV).

BIBLIOGRAPHY

Ahlstrom, G. W.
1969 *Hammoreh Lisdaqah in Joel II 23.* Vetus Testamentum Supplement 19:25-36. Leiden: Brill.

Allen, L. C.
1976 *The Books of Joel, Obadiah, Jonah and Micah.* New International Commentary on the Old Testament. Grand Rapids: Eerdmans.

Andinach, P. R.
1992 The Locusts in the Message of Joel. *Vetus Testamentum* 42:433-441.

Bewer, J. A.
1911 *Commentary on Obadiah and Joel.* International Critical Commentary. Edinburgh: T & T Clark.

Brodsky, H.
1990 An Enormous Horde Arrayed for Battle—Locusts in the Book of Joel. *Bible Review* 6/4:32-39.

Chisholm, R. B. Jr.
1990 *Interpreting the Minor Prophets.* Grand Rapids: Zondervan.

Coogan, M. D.
1978 *Stories from Ancient Canaan.* Philadelphia: Westminster.

Craigie, P. C.
1985 *Twelve Prophets,* vol. 1. Philadelphia: Westminster.

Crenshaw, J. L.
1986 The Expression *mi yodea'* in the Hebrew Bible. *Vetus Testamentum* 36:274-288.

1994 Who Knows What Yahweh Will Do? The Character of God in the Book of Joel. Pp. 197-209 in *Fortunate the Eyes That See.* Editors, A. H. Bartlett, et al. Grand Rapids: Eerdmans.

1995 *Joel.* The Anchor Bible. New York: Doubleday.

Dillard, R.
1992 Joel. Pp. 239-314 in *The Minor Prophets,* vol. 1. Editor, T. E. McComiskey. Grand Rapids: Baker.

Donner, H. and W. Röllig
1966 *Kanaanäische und Aramäische Inschriften.* Wiesbaden: Otto Harrassowitz.

Driver, S. R.
1915 *The Books of Joel and Amos.* Cambridge: Cambridge University Press.

Driver, G. R.
1972 Linguistic and Textual Problems: Minor Prophets, III. Joel. *Journal of Theological Studies* 15:400-402.

Eiselen, F. C.
1907 *The Minor Prophets.* New York: Eaton & Mains.

Fausset, A. R.
1948 Joel in *A Commentary Critical, Experimental and Practical on the Old and New Testaments,* vol. 4: Jeremiah—Malachi. Grand Rapids: Eerdmans.

Feinberg, C. L.
1976 *The Minor Prophets.* Chicago: Moody.

Finley, J. T.
1990 *Joel, Amos, Obadiah.* Chicago: Moody.

Freeman, H.
1968 *An Introduction to the Old Testament Prophets.* Chicago: Moody.

Garrett, D. A.
1985 The Structure of Joel. *Journal of the Evangelical Theological Society* 28:289-297.

1997 *Hosea, Joel.* New American Commentary. Nashville: Broadman & Holman.

Gordon, C.
1965 *Ugaritic Textbook.* Rome: Pontificium Institutum Biblicum.

Guillaume, A.
1965 *Hebrew and Arabic Lexicography.* Leiden: Brill.

Hosch, H.
1972 The Concept of Prophetic Time in the Book of Joel. *Journal of the Evangelical Theological Society* 15:31-38.

Hubbard, D. A.
1989 *Joel and Amos.* The Tyndale Old Testament Commentary. Downers Grove: InterVarsity.

Hummel, H.
1979 *The Word Becoming Flesh.* St. Louis: Concordia.

Kapelrud, A. S.
1948 *Joel Studies.* Uppsala: Almquist & Wiksells.

Keil, C. F.
1954 *The Twelve Minor Prophets.* Biblical Commentary on the Old Testament, vol. 1. Translator, J. Martin. Grand Rapids: Eerdmans.

Laetsch, Theo
1956 *The Minor Prophets.* St. Louis: Concordia.

Launderville, D.
1989 Joel: Prophet and Visionary. *The Bible Today* 27:81-86.

Luckenbill, D. D.
1927 *Ancient Records of Assyria and Babylonia.* Chicago: University of Chicago Press.

Morris, Leon
1972 *Apocalyptic.* Grand Rapids: Eerdmans.

Nash, K. S.
1989 The Cycle of Seasons in Joel. *The Bible Today* 27:74-80.

Nowell, I.
1989 The Coming of the Spirit in the Book of Joel. *The Bible Today* 27:87-92.

Ogden, G. S.
1983 Joel 4 and Prophetic Responses to National Laments. *Journal for the Study of the Old Testament* 26:97-106.

von Orelli, C.
1977 *The Twelve Minor Prophets.* Reprint ed. Translator, J. S. Banks. Minneapolis: Klock & Klock Christian Pub.

Patterson, R. D.
1985 Joel. Pp. 227-266 in *Daniel, Minor Prophets.* The Expositor's Bible Commentary, vol. 7. Editor, F. E. Gaebelein. Grand Rapids: Zondervan.

1993 Old Testament Prophecy. Pp. 296-309 in *A Complete Literary Guide to the Bible.* Editors, L. Ryken and T. Longman III. Grand Rapids: Zondervan.

Prinsloo, W. S.
1985 *The Theology of the Book of Joel.* Beihefte zur Zeitschrift für die alttestamentliche Wissenschaft. Berlin: Walter de Gruyter.

1992 The Unity of the Book of Joel. *Zeitschrift für die alttestamentliche Wissenschaft* 104:66-81.

Pusey, E. B.
1953 *The Minor Prophets,* vol. 1. Grand Rapids: Baker.

Reicke, B.
1970 Joel und seine Zeit. Pp. 133-141 in *Wort-Gebot-Glaube: Beitrage zur Theologie des Alten Testaments.* Editor, H. Stoebe. Abhandlungen zur Theologie des Alten und Neuen Testaments 59. Zurich: Zwingli.

Rudolph, W.
1967 Ein Beitrag zum hebräischen Lexikon aus dem Joelbuch. Pp. 244-250 in *Hebräische Wortforschung.* Editors, G. W. Anderson, et al. Leiden: Brill.

Sandy, D. B. and M. C. Abegg Jr.
1995 Apocalyptic. Pp. 177-196 in *Cracking Old Testament Codes.* Editors, D. B. Sandy and R. L. Giese, Jr. Nashville: Broadman & Holman.

Sellers, O. R.
1936 Stages of Locust in Joel. *American Journal of Semitic Languages and Literatures* 52:81-85.

Simkins, R. A.
1993 God, History, and the Natural World in the Book of Joel. *Catholic Biblical Quarterly* 55:435-452.
1995 The Day of the Locusts. *The Bible Today* 33:23-27.

Smith, G. A.
1929 *The Book of the Twelve Prophets*, vol. 2. New York: Doubleday.

Stuart, D.
1987 *Hosea—Jonah*. Word Biblical Commentary. Waco: Word.

Sweeney, M. A.
2000 *The Twelve Prophets*. Berit Olam. Collegeville, MN: Liturgical.

Thompson, J. A.
1955 Joel's Locusts in the Light of Near Eastern Parallels. *Journal of Near Eastern Studies* 14:52-55.

Waltke, B. K. and M. O'Connor
1990 *An Introduction to Biblical Hebrew Syntax*. Winona Lake: Eisenbrauns.

Watson, W. G. E.
1986 *Classical Hebrew Poetry*. Sheffield: Journal for the Study of the Old Testament Press.

Wolff, H. W.
1977 *Joel and Amos*. Philadelphia: Fortress.

Amos

ANDREW E. HILL

INTRODUCTION TO
Amos

AMOS WAS A SHEPHERD and a sycamore-fig farmer from Tekoa, a village about ten miles south of Jerusalem. His denial of any association with the religious establishment emphasized his detachment from the formal institutions of the royal court and Temple (7:14-15). Given his platform as an independent layman, Amos had the freedom to proclaim God's message unfettered by vested interests or public opinion. Religious apostasy, moral decay, social injustice, and political corruption in the northern kingdom prompted God to send Amos across the border of Judah to preach in Bethel of Israel. Amos condemned Israel because they had "forgotten how to do right" (3:10). Since the preaching of Amos is dated to the early or mid-eighth century BC, he is the first Old Testament prophet to address the theme of the "day of the LORD" (5:18; chs 7–8). His understanding of the ethical implications of Israel's covenant relationship with God for individual and corporate behavior made him a champion of social justice (5:7, 15, 24; 6:12).

AUTHOR

The book is silent on the specifics of authorship, although it is generally assumed that the prophetic word formula ("This message was given to Amos," 1:1) signifies that Amos was responsible in some fashion for writing down his own message. The exact details concerning how the oracles that Amos delivered to Israel at Bethel came to be recorded remain unknown. He may have dictated his revelations to a scribe or composed them himself. The latter seems more likely given the first-person accounts of his messages and visions. He may have committed his revelations to writing shortly after his return to Tekoa from his brief "preaching campaign" in the northern kingdom of Israel. His ministry covers a period of less than two years (1:1), and in fact was likely only a few months (G. Smith 2001:209-210) or even a few days long (cf. Hayes 1988:46-47, who connects Amos's preaching with the Marheshvan festival instituted by Jeroboam as an alternative to the fall pilgrimage Festival of Shelters; 1 Kgs 12:32-33).

Apart from the facts that the name Amos means "burden-bearer" and that he was from Tekoa (1:1), all we know of Amos comes from his own confession that he was not a professional prophet but a shepherd and sycamore-fig farmer (cf. 7:14-15). This disclaimer about not being a member of the "religious establishment" is significant because it implies his freedom to proclaim God's message without any political motivations. As an "independent layman" and a "blue-collar" worker without formal academic and religious training, Amos reminds us that God shows no partiality in calling people to serve his cause. This is a timely admonition in our age of "professionalism."

DATE AND OCCASION OF WRITING

The message of Amos is dated to the reigns of Uzziah, king of Judah (c. 791/783–742/740 BC) and Jeroboam II, king of Israel (793/786–753/746 BC). Since the reigns of both of these kings extended over a period of more than four decades, and further, the exact dates for the rule of each king vary by some two to seven years depending upon the source consulted,[1] this leaves some ambiguity as to the exact date. Traditionally, the date of the book of Amos has been assigned to the middle years of the reign of Jeroboam II, sometime in the 760s BC (Niehaus 1992:316; Smith 2001:206). More recent historical analysis and chronological calculations have pushed the date for the message of Amos nearer the end of the reign of Jeroboam II, perhaps around 750–748 BC (cf. Hayes 1988:26-27).

The reference to the "two years before the earthquake" in the superscription (1:1) provides little help in determining the precise date of Amos's prophecy. Archaeological findings at sites like Samaria and Hazor have been interpreted by some to attest to such destruction by an earthquake around this general time (see the discussions in Hayes 1988:46-47; Anderson and Freedman 1989:198-199), and Zechariah's reference to the natural disaster indicates that this tremor was long remembered in Israel (Zech 14:5), but attempts to pinpoint the year in which the earthquake occurred are speculative. As a consequence, it seems best to assign the time of Amos's prophetic activity to a general period ranging from 760–750 BC.

The general occasion prompting Amos's message to Jeroboam II and Israel was the religious apostasy and moral and social decay of the northern kingdom (cf. 2:6-16). More specifically, the Lord God of Heaven's Armies had become weary of Israel's sins of idolatry and oppressive greed (3:13–4:2). God's patience had expired, and his decree of judgment and exile signaled the "sudden end" of Israel (7:9). The earthquake itself may have been the event prompting the prophet to publish his experience. The citation of the devastating natural disaster in the superscription suggests that Amos viewed the event as a partial fulfillment of his oracles to Israel and as confirmation of his divine commission (cf. 9:1).

The biblical records of the reigns of Uzziah and Jeroboam II are found in 2 Kings 14:17–15:7 and 2 Chronicles 26. Both kings brought political stability and economic prosperity to their respective kingdoms. Both kings expanded their territorial borders by means of successful military campaigns. For instance, Uzziah fortified the walls and towers of the city of Jerusalem and built other defense outposts throughout Judah (2 Chr 26:9). His policies also increased agricultural productivity (2 Chr 26:10). In addition, he assembled a well-equipped army that enabled Judah to subdue the Philistines, Arabs, and Ammonites (2 Chr 26:6-8, 11-15). Although regarded a righteous king by the biblical historians, Uzziah was stricken with a skin disease as divine punishment for usurping priestly duties (2 Kgs 15:3-5; 2 Chr 26:16-20). The malady was God's judgment against the king's pride, and it plagued him until his death, making him a social outcast in his own kingdom (2 Chr 26:21).

Jeroboam II similarly expanded the political control of Israel into the Aramean regions of Damascus and Hamath by means of military achievements (2 Kgs 14:28). We learn (indirectly) from the prophets Amos and Hosea that under the policies of Jeroboam II the northern kingdom enjoyed greater economic prosperity than anytime in its history since the united monarchy of David and Solomon (3:15; 4:1-2; Hos 5:7; 8:14). Unlike Uzziah, however, Jeroboam II was assessed as an evil king by the biblical historians because he perpetuated the idolatry of his predecessors (2 Kgs 14:24).

Despite the facade of material wealth during what has been called the "Silver Age" of Israelite history (Paul 1991:1), Amos looked past external appearances and charged that the nation was guilty before God of sinning again and again (2:6) and forgetting how to do right (3:10). Thus, Israel was "ripe" for divine judgment (8:1-2). Underneath the veneer of political stability and economic prosperity, the cancer of social and moral decay metastasized. The success of Jeroboam II had come at the expense of the poor (who were oppressed by social injustice; 2:6; 4:1; 5:11) and of true worship (which was corrupted by religious apostasy; 3:14; 4:4-5). A just and holy God had no choice but to punish the people who had violated the intimacy of their covenant relationship with him (3:1; 5:25-27).

AUDIENCE

Broadly understood, the people of the kingdoms of Judah and Israel were the intended audience of Amos's message (2:4-16; 3:1, 13; 5:1; 6:1; 7:15). Specific groups or classes of people within the northern kingdom were targeted, including the "wealthy" (3:15; cf. 4:1; 6:4) and the "famous and popular" (6:1). Likewise, certain individuals, including Jeroboam II, king of Israel, and Amaziah, the priest of Bethel, were also recipients of the prophet's oracles (cf. 7:10-17).

CANONICITY AND TEXTUAL HISTORY

Amos is the third book in the collection known as the Minor Prophets (or the "Book of the Twelve" in the Hebrew Bible). The Twelve Prophets are usually grouped with the other Latter Prophets (Isaiah, Jeremiah, and Ezekiel) and, without exception, are found in the earliest delineations of the Old Testament canon. These twelve books were always copied on one scroll in the ancient Hebrew manuscript tradition. The order of the Twelve Prophets is uniform in the Masoretic tradition of the Hebrew Bible (Hosea, Joel, Amos, Obadiah, Jonah, Micah, Nahum, Habakkuk, Zephaniah, Haggai, Zechariah, Malachi). The order of the Twelve Prophets does vary, however, in some canon traditions. For example, Amos and Micah immediately follow Hosea in the Septuagint (LXX).[2] According to Hubbard (1989:88-89), the position of Amos as third among the Twelve Prophets is warranted because of the book's length, antiquity, and comprehensiveness. More important, the movement from "disaster to rescue" in the prophet's message distills the themes of the collection as a whole.

Overall, the Hebrew text (MT) of Amos is well preserved. Only portions of Amos are extant in fragments in the Dead Sea Scrolls (cf. DJD 15.246-249, 294-309). Generally the ancient versions provide a faithful witness to the MT, although on occasion the general tendencies for interpretive expansion and loose paraphrasing in the ancient versions are evident in the Septuagint and the Aramaic Targum (e.g., 4:13; 5:2, 8, 26; 6:9; 7:5). The book contains several passages where the MT proves difficult to understand, thereby prompting emendations based upon the ancient versions or conjecture at times (e.g., 1:3; 2:7; 3:12; 5:6, 26; 7:2; 8:1).

One example of such interpretive expansion is the grizzly (and somewhat sensationalist) translation of Amos 1:3b based on the ancient versions (LXX, Latin Vulgate): "because they threshed the pregnant women of Gilead with iron threshing sledges" (so Stuart 1987:304). Yet Andersen and Freedman (1989:238-239) view this as an illustration of the ancient trend to interpret obscure passages in light of other sources. They regard the gloss to "pregnant women" as a clear contamination of the Masoretic Text from Amos 1:13 (perhaps due to a connection with 2 Kgs 8:12 and Elisha's prediction that Hazael would rip open the pregnant women of Israel). The NLT inserts "my people" in Amos 1:3 ("they beat down my people in Gilead," following the Aramaic Targum, which reads, "they threshed the inhabitants of the land of Gilead"; cf. Cathcart and Gordon 1989:77).

LITERARY STYLE

Earlier form-critical analysis of the book of Amos questioned the authenticity of numerous isolated verses and pericopes in the book on the basis of historical, literary, or theological grounds.[3] More recent scholarship has asserted the overall unity of Amos based on the demonstration of the "literary coherence" of the diverse ingredients comprising the book (Andersen and Freedman 1989:144). In fact, there is a growing appreciation for the prophet's literary skills. The bold and arresting style of the book indicates that Amos was a man of integrity and conviction. The fact that the prophet was "shown the words" that God revealed to him in the form of visions explains the vivid language of the book (cf. 7:1). The pastoral imagery of the illustrations, metaphors, and rhetorical questions of Amos's sermons reveals his rural root as a shepherd and orchard keeper. Finally, the hymnic portions of the book (e.g., 5:1-2) and the doxologies (e.g., 4:13; 5:8-9; 9:5-6) indicate Amos had some poetic and musical ability (or, at the least, that he borrowed from existing popular songs).

Andersen and Freedman (1989:xxv-xliii) identify three books in the larger structure of Amos: the Book of Doom (1:1-4:13), the Book of Woes (5:1-6:14), and the Book of Visions (7:1-9:15). The Book of Doom and the Book of Woes are composed of eight oracles against the nations (1:3-2:16) and five prophetic "messages" or sermons against the kingdom of Israel (chs 3-6). These five prophetic sermons are counterbalanced by five prophetic visions (7:1–9:10). The book concludes with an epilogue promising blessing and renewal for Israel (9:11-15).[4]

Like other prophetic books of the Old Testament, Amos is a literary hybrid—a blend of prose and poetry sometimes labeled "oracular prose" (Andersen and Freedman 1989:145-149). Amos accents his message by utilizing a variety of prophetic speech forms, repeated words and phrases, and stock literary constructions. For example, the book contains the proclamation formula ("Listen to me," 4:1), revelation formula ("the Sovereign LORD showed me," 7:1), and oath formula ("the Sovereign LORD has sworn," 4:2). Several types of prophetic oracles may be found in Amos's messages, including judgment (2:6-8), instruction or admonition (i.e., "do" or "do not," 5:4-5), repentance ("come back," 5:6), and woe or indictment oracles (5:18). In keeping with typical prophetic speech patterns, rhetorical questions are sprinkled throughout every sermon of the book (e.g., 3:3-8; 6:11-14).

MAJOR THEMES

The opening proclamation of the prophet's message serves as the theme verse for the entire book: "The LORD's voice will roar from Zion" (1:2). Beyond this, the oracles against the nations (1:3–2:16) set the tone for the message of the book in that they all emphasize destruction and in some cases exile. The book's message springs logically from the general outline of its content and is closely connected to Amos's prediction of judgment and exile for Israel. The prophet's first message promises divine judgment against the sins of the nations (1:3–2:3). The second message forecasts the destruction of Judah's cities (2:4-5) and destruction and exile of the northern kingdom of Israel (2:6-16). The third message condemns specific acts of social injustice and religious apostasy (3:1–6:14). This portion of the message of Amos also called the people to repentance, encouraging a return to covenant obedience, and repudiated the popular notion that "the day of the LORD" was a time of national blessing only. The fourth message reinforces the themes of divine judgment and exile for Israel by means of a series of visions in which the prophet introduces the theme of a "remnant of Israel" (7:1–9:4). The prophet's final message is a promise of messianic restoration and blessing—a word of hope reminding the people that God's judgment is not final.

Niehaus (1992:327) has aptly observed that "if much of biblical theology is the story of salvation, much of biblical anthropology is the story of sin." Amos accuses both Israel and Judah of lapsing into two basic categories of sin: social injustice (e.g., 2:6-8) and idolatry (e.g., 5:26). The essential themes of the message of Amos emerge from the prophetic indictment of these sins of idolatry and religious hypocrisy and the inability to "do right" by practicing social justice (3:10). Interestingly, as noted by Andersen and Freedman (1989:91), "the crimes of the other nations are international in character, while the crimes charged against Judah and Israel are internal matters, involving their behavior to God and fellow citizens."

THEOLOGICAL CONCERNS

The prophet Amos espouses a simple, but not a simplistic, theology. By "theology" I mean the understanding of who God is and how he works in the world as portrayed in the sermons and visions of Amos. The statement that reports what the prophet "saw and heard" serves as a theme verse for the entire book: The message of Amos is all about the Lord who "roars" against sin from his Temple on Mount Zion in Jerusalem (1:2). In fact, according to Gowan (1996:346), "God's primary role in this book is to be the judge and executioner of those persons [and nations] who have refused to obey divine standards of justice." We must remember, however, that although God is presented as the severe judge of the nations, he is also "just and impartial" (Andersen and Freedman 1989:91).

First and foremost, God is the creator of heaven and earth—the cosmic or universal deity of all that exists (4:13; 5:8-9; 9:5-6). These declarations about God as creator are not so much a theological treatise about creation "as practical statements of God's power" (Smith 2001:214). There are only two categories of reality: "God and everything else. Everything else is subordinate and dependent upon the deity for its existence and whatever else it has or is" (Andersen and Freedman 1989:90).

This means Yahweh of Israel is sovereign over all the nations by virtue of the majesty, power, and authority he inherently possesses as the universal God of heaven and earth. As ruler of the universe and the nations, God is also the Lord of history (cf. Andersen and Freedman 1989:90-91). Although the prophet Amos differs from his Old Testament counterparts by first addressing sins of the nations before indicting the Hebrew kingdoms of Judah and Israel, he clearly sides with them in acknowledging Yahweh as the Lord of human history. Yet, the prophet offers no explanation as to why the nations should be held accountable to the God of Israel. This may be understood as an expression of the "practical monotheism" of the book, since Amos assumed the oneness and superiority of Yahweh and that he "has the power to judge all who violate basic principles of justice" (Gowan 1996:347). Hubbard (1989:111) concludes that "this all-embracing picture of sovereignty serves one basic purpose in the text: to bring Israel's fantasies of invulnerability down to size."

Amos never applies the word "judge" to God, but it is clear that Yahweh fills this role as the deity who both indicts and punishes the nations (1:3-2:16). The teaching associated with the "day of the LORD" further supports the idea of God as the divine judge (5:20). God's judgment of the nations is his divine right by virtue of his work as creator of heaven and earth (5:8). This office of "cosmic" judge suggests some standard by which divine judgment is meted out. Explicitly, this punishment of sin among the nations is rooted in God's character, his holiness (4:2) and righteousness (5:7, 24; 6:12). Implicitly, the measuring rod of divine justice for Israel and Judah is "the instruction of the LORD" (2:4), as seen in the prophet's use of words like honesty, truth, and justice as applied to the poor and oppressed of society (2:6; 5:7, 10). God is vindicated in judging the sin of Israel and Judah because they have violated the sacred trust of his covenant relationship with them as his elect nation (3:1-2).

Finally, Amos understands God as the divine healer and restorer (9:11-15). Like Ezekiel, the prophet knows that God does not delight in the death of the wicked— but rather that they should "come back to the LORD and live!" (5:4, 6; cf. Ezek 18:23, 32). Even in judgment God will not destroy Israel completely (9:8) because he is also a God of mercy (5:15). God desires to be Israel's "helper," but he can only help those who decide to "hate evil and love what is good" (5:15).

OUTLINE
  I. Introduction (1:1-2)
  II. God's Judgment on Israel's Neighbors: Damascus, Gaza, Tyre, Edom, Ammon, and Moab (1:3-2:3)
  III. God's Judgment on Judah and Israel (2:4-16)
     A. Judgment against Judah (2:4-5)
     B. Judgment against Israel (2:6-16)
  IV. Further Oracles against Israel (3:1-6:14)
     A. Listen, People of Israel (3:1-15)
     B. Listen, Cows of Bashan (4:1-13)
     C. Listen, People of Israel (5:1-17)
     D. How Terrible for Those Anxious for the Day of the Lord (5:18-27)
     E. How Terrible for Those Who Lounge in Jerusalem and Samaria (6:1-14)
  V. Visions of Judgment (7:1-9:10)
     A. Three Visions: The Plague of Locusts, Devouring Fire, and the Lord's Plumb Line (7:1-9)
     B. Interlude: Amaziah Challenges Amos (7:10-17)
     C. Fourth Vision: A Vision of Ripe Fruit (8:1-14)
     D. Fifth Vision: A Vision of God at the Altar (9:1-10)
  VI. Epilogue: The Restoration of Israel (9:11-15)

ENDNOTES
  1. See the comparative chronological chart in Hill and Walton 2000:480.
  2. According to Jones (1995:3-5, 54-55), the overlapping chronological information in the superscriptions, the size of the books, and the literary parallels between the three books may be seen as evidence that Hosea–Amos–Micah formed a unified literary corpus.
  3. Sellin and Fohrer (1968:436-437) are representative of such scholarship, as they confidently list passages that "surely do not derive from Amos" (e.g., 4:13; 5:8-9; 8:8; 9:5-6, 8-15). On the redaction of Amos, see further the discussions in Hayes 1988:37-38 and Hubbard 1989:98-102.
  4. See Dorsey 1999:277-286 for more on the literary structure of Amos, including a discussion of Limburg's "sevenfold" organization of Amos.

COMMENTARY ON
Amos

◆ I. Introduction (1:1-2)

This message was given to Amos, a shepherd from the town of Tekoa in Judah. He received this message in visions two years before the earthquake, when Uzziah was king of Judah and Jeroboam II, the son of Jehoash,* was king of Israel.
²This is what he saw and heard:

"The LORD's voice will roar from
   Zion
and thunder from Jerusalem!
The lush pastures of the shepherds
   will dry up;
   the grass on Mount Carmel will
   wither and die."

1:1 Hebrew *Joash*, a variant spelling of Jehoash.

NOTES

1:1 *This message.* Lit., "the words of Amos." The term (*dabar* [TH1697, ZH1821], "word") is used here as a technical term for divine revelation, in this case, oracles of Yahweh delivered by Amos. As a title, the expression may be understood as "the story of Amos" or "the record of Amos" (i.e., materials connected with the name of Amos; cf. Andersen and Freedman 1989:184-185).

shepherd. The word for "shepherd" (*noqed* [TH5349, ZH5924]) is rare, used in the OT only here and in 2 Kgs 3:4. It is unclear whether Amos was a tender of flocks or an owner of sheep (cf. Stuart 1987:299, "sheep breeder"). His autobiographical statements to Amaziah concerning his profession suggest the prophet was "just a shepherd" (i.e., a hired hand, not a wealthy owner and breeder of flocks; see 7:14).

Tekoa. A hill-country village allotted to the tribe of Judah located 10 miles southwest of Jerusalem (Josh 15:59, LXX). Tekoa was home to one of David's mighty warriors (2 Sam 23:26) and the unnamed wise woman who brokered Absalom's return to Jerusalem after his slaying of Amnon (2 Sam 14:1-24).

visions. The word "vision" (*khazah* [TH2372, ZH2600]) is a technical expression for one form of divine revelation. Amaziah identified Amos as a "seer" (*khozeh* [TH2374, ZH2602]; 7:12, NLT reads "prophet"), a title Amos accepted for himself, unlike the title "prophet" (*nabi'* [TH5030, ZH5566]), which he rejected (7:14). According to Andersen and Freedman (1989:189), the vision is the experience in which the divine revelation is received and both "auditory and visionary components were integral to the prophet's close encounter with God." It is also noted that the term "seer" (*khozeh* [TH2374, ZH2602]) is applied to Judean prophets alone, perhaps because of their emphasis on the divine council motif (cf. Hubbard 1989:125).

Uzziah . . . and Jeroboam II. Cf. 2 Kgs 14:17–15:7. The incomplete date formula sets the ministry of Amos during the period of the divided Hebrew kingdoms sometime in the mid-eighth century BC. The precise dating of the oracles of Amos to "two years before the earthquake" is of little help in establishing the chronology of the prophet's ministry (see "Date and Occasion of Writing" in the Introduction).

1:2 LORD. The divine name (Yahweh) associated with Israel's covenant experience at Mount Sinai is the prophet's favorite title for God and is found 60 times in Amos.

roar. The verb "roar" (*sha'ag* [TH7580, ZH8613]) is often connected with the roaring of a lion (e.g., Judg 14:5; Isa 5:29). Amos made the direct association between Yahweh and a roaring lion later in his message to Israel (3:8). This roaring of Yahweh serves as a call to repentance in Hosea 11:10, while Joel used the same word to threaten judgment against the nations (Joel 3:16). Yahweh's roar is a metaphor for divine judgment in Amos, indicated by the effect of his thunderous outburst—the death of living things! Later Jeremiah uses the same expression to describe God's judgment against the whole earth (Jer 25:30).

Zion . . . Jerusalem. The geographical movement from the specific site of the Temple to the city of Jerusalem emphasizes the location of true worship for the Hebrew people—the place where Yahweh set his name. The association of the divine presence of Yahweh with Jerusalem and Judah implicitly indicted the false worship centers of Dan and Bethel in the northern kingdom of Israel (cf. 7:13). The NLT "thunders from Jerusalem" (*qol* + *natan*; lit., "gives" or "utters his voice," NRSV) is interpretive based on the parallelism of the preceding line describing Yahweh's voice like that of a roaring lion.

Mount Carmel. The peak is part of a mountainous area in northern Israel dividing the plain of Acco to the north from the plain of Sharon to the south. The lush tree cover of Mount Carmel made it a symbol of beauty and fertility (Isa 35:2). The larger context of Amos's message suggests that Carmel is also a symbol for the kingdom of Israel itself that will soon experience the "withering" judgment of God (cf. 9:3). No doubt the reference to Carmel is also an allusion to the earlier triumph of Yahweh over Baal during the days of Elijah the prophet (1 Kgs 18:20-40).

dry up . . . wither. The verbs *'abal* [TH56A, ZH62] (dry up) and *yabesh* [TH3001, ZH3312] (wither) are often found in contexts describing divine judgment (e.g., Isa 24:4, 7; Ezek 17:9, 24) and at times are paired together to indicate the extent of the devastation (e.g., Joel 1:10). The word *yabesh* especially connotes the power of God, as it is used to describe the drying up of the Sea of Reeds and the Jordan River (Josh 4:23; Ps 74:15).

COMMENTARY

The superscription (1:1) is a formal statement that corresponds to the title of a document. It serves to classify literature by genre or literary type (in this case as an oracular or prophetic text) and to identify the author, audience, date, and sometimes the occasion prompting the divine message. This superscription identifies the author of the book as Amos and includes a brief biographical sketch noting him as "a shepherd from the town of Tekoa in Judah." It also classifies the genre as prophetic revelation given in the form of a vision, and broadly dates the book to the reigns of rival kings of the divided Hebrew monarchies. The theological purpose of the superscription is to emphasize that God himself is the source and authority behind the message of Amos (cf. 2 Pet 1:20-21).

The book of Amos is unusual among the Minor Prophets in that an introduction to the prophet's message (1:2) is coupled with the superscription (1:1; note the prelude to Zechariah's visions [Zech 1:2-6] that accompanies the superscription to the book [Zech 1:1]). The introduction sets both the tone and the theme of the message of Amos. The mood of the book is ominous and threatening, evidenced in the "roaring" and "thundering" of the voice of Yahweh. The theme of the book is the destruction and death associated with divine judgment, seen in the descriptions of pasture lands "drying up" and grass "withering and dying" (1:2). Theologically, the introduction legitimizes God as the divine Judge because the name "LORD" (yhwh [TH3068, ZH3378]) signifies his position as the suzerain or king in his covenant relationship with the vassal Israel. Later, the prophet Jeremiah would illustrate this master–servant relationship with his message about the potter and the clay (Jer 18:1-17).

◆ II. God's Judgment on Israel's Neighbors: Damascus, Gaza, Tyre, Edom, Ammon, and Moab (1:3–2:3)

³This is what the LORD says:

"The people of Damascus have sinned
    again and again,*
and I will not let them go
    unpunished!
They beat down my people in Gilead
    as grain is threshed with iron
    sledges.
⁴So I will send down fire on King
    Hazael's palace,
and the fortresses of King Ben-
    hadad will be destroyed.
⁵I will break down the gates of
    Damascus
and slaughter the people in the
    valley of Aven.
I will destroy the ruler in Beth-eden,
    and the people of Aram will go as
    captives to Kir,"
says the LORD.

⁶This is what the LORD says:

"The people of Gaza have sinned again
    and again,
and I will not let them go
    unpunished!
They sent whole villages into exile,
    selling them as slaves to Edom.
⁷So I will send down fire on the walls
    of Gaza,
and all its fortresses will be
    destroyed.
⁸I will slaughter the people of Ashdod

and destroy the king of Ashkelon.
Then I will turn to attack Ekron,
    and the few Philistines still left will
    be killed,"
says the Sovereign LORD.

⁹This is what the LORD says:

"The people of Tyre have sinned again
    and again,
and I will not let them go
    unpunished!
They broke their treaty of brotherhood
    with Israel,
selling whole villages as slaves
    to Edom.
¹⁰So I will send down fire on the walls
    of Tyre,
and all its fortresses will be
    destroyed."

¹¹This is what the LORD says:

"The people of Edom have sinned
    again and again,
and I will not let them go
    unpunished!
They chased down their relatives,
    the Israelites, with swords,
showing them no mercy.
In their rage, they slashed them
    continually
and were unrelenting in their anger.
¹²So I will send down fire on Teman,
    and the fortresses of Bozrah will
    be destroyed."

¹³This is what the LORD says:

"The people of Ammon have sinned
  again and again,
  and I will not let them go
  unpunished!
When they attacked Gilead to extend
  their borders,
  they ripped open pregnant women
  with their swords.
¹⁴So I will send down fire on the walls
  of Rabbah,
  and all its fortresses will be
  destroyed.
The battle will come upon them with
  shouts,
  like a whirlwind in a mighty
  storm.
¹⁵And their king* and his princes will
  go into exile together,"
  says the LORD.

CHAPTER 2

This is what the LORD says:

"The people of Moab have sinned
  again and again,*
  and I will not let them go
  unpunished!
They desecrated the bones of Edom's
  king,
  burning them to ashes.
²So I will send down fire on the land
  of Moab,
  and all the fortresses in Kerioth
  will be destroyed.
The people will fall in the noise of
  battle,
  as the warriors shout and the ram's
  horn sounds.
³And I will destroy their king
  and slaughter all their princes,"
  says the LORD.

1:3 Hebrew *have committed three sins, even four;* also in 1:6, 9, 11, 13.   1:15 Hebrew *malcam,* possibly referring to their god Molech.   2:1 Hebrew *have committed three sins, even four;* also in 2:4, 6.

NOTES

1:3 Damascus. The capital of modern Syria and one of the oldest continuously occupied cities in the world. The city is situated some 50 miles inland from the Mediterranean Sea in an oasis at the base of Mount Qasyun. Damascus was the capital city of the kingdom of Aram in OT times. The Arameans were historically one of the enemy nations on Israel's northern border. The Hebrews controlled the region of Aram briefly during the reigns of David and Solomon (2 Sam 8:5-6) and again during the divided Hebrew monarchies at the time of Jeroboam II (2 Kgs 14:28). By extension, Damascus can also refer to the whole kingdom of Aram (cf. 1:5).

sinned again and again. The expression (lit., "for three sins, even four"; cf. NLT mg) indicates that the city or nation indicted is guilty of "crime after crime" or repeated sin (Andersen and Freedman 1989:217). The number "four" is emphatic or climactic since Amos mentions only the last or worst crime committed, what Hubbard (1989:129) terms the "back-breaking transgression that triggered the divine judgment."

Gilead. This is a region of the Transjordan situated between the Yarmuk and Arnon Rivers (Deut 3:8-10). The Hebrew tribes of Reuben, Gad, and (East) Manasseh settled in Gilead (Josh 22:9).

sledges. This term (*kharuts* [TH2742B, ZH3023]) refers to threshing equipment, either a wooden sled with iron prongs or a low-slung wagon on wheels with iron spikes or teeth mounted on the underside (cf. Andersen and Freedman 1989:237). The threshing sledge was dragged over harvested grain to separate the chaff from the kernels of grain. The expression is a metaphor for the cruelty and violence of warfare (and may be an allusion to decimation of Jehoahaz's army by the Arameans (2 Kgs 13:7).

1:4 Hazael. Probably a reference to the Aramean king Hazael who ruled from c. 843–796 BC and "caused mayhem for Israel's [kings] Jerhoram . . . Jehu . . . and Jehoahaz" (Hubbard 1989:131; cf. 2 Kgs 8:7-15, 28-29; 9:14-15; 10:32-33; 13:3, 22-23).

fortresses. The term *'armon* [TH759, ZH810] may refer to fortified palaces or citadels on the acropolis of walled cities (see the discussion in Andersen and Freedman 1989:242, especially concerning the chiasmus formed by the repetition of the word in 1:4, 7, 10, 12, 14; 2:2, 5).

Ben-hadad. Probably a reference to the Aramean king Ben-hadad III, Hazael's son (c. 796–770 BC). King Jehoahaz of Israel defeated King Ben-Hadad of Aram and recaptured Israelite towns previously taken by his father King Hazael (2 Kgs 13:24-25; see Hubbard 1989:131).

1:5 *valley of Aven.* An unknown valley in Lebanon, perhaps the region around Baalbek northwest of Damascus (so Hubbard 1989:132).

Beth-eden. An Aramean city-state identified with Bit-Adini on the Euphrates River south of Carchemish (cf. 2 Kgs 19:12).

Kir. A city or region of Mesopotamia, perhaps the city of Der located on the main route between Elam and Babylon east of the Tigris River. The Assyrian king Tiglath-pileser III deported the populace of Damascus to Kir after conquering the Aramean capital in 733 BC (cf. 2 Kgs 16:9).

1:6 *Gaza.* The most important of the Philistine city-states and the southernmost of the five principal Philistine cities. It was located about four miles inland from the Mediterranean Sea. The city marked the southern limits of the territory of Judah during the Hebrew united monarchy and divided kingdoms. Zephaniah and Zechariah also condemn Gaza for its role in international slave trade (Zeph 2:4; Zech 9:5).

1:8 *Ashdod . . . Ashkelon . . . Ekron.* These Philistine cities were located on the coastal plain of Israel south of the port city of Joppa; along with Gaza and Gath they made up the five principal cities of the Philistines (cf. 1 Sam 6:17). The prophets Zephaniah (Zeph 2:4) and Zechariah (Zech 9:5-7) pronounce similar judgments against the same four Philistine cities Amos mentions.

1:9 *Tyre.* One of the twin Phoenician port cities, along with Sidon, located on the Mediterranean coast north of Israel (modern-day Lebanon). The cities were independent city-states and legendary for their wealth as a result of maritime trade. The OT prophets condemned the pride and social injustice practiced by the two cities and predicted their eventual destruction (cf. Isa 23; Ezek 26:3-14; Zech 9:2).

1:11 *Edom.* The name Edom is another name for Esau which means "ruddy" or "red," and the nation of Edom was located in the highlands and red sandstone cliffs on the southeastern edge of the Dead Sea. The territory of Edom extended from the Brook Zered in the north to the Gulf of Aqaba in the south. The Edomites and the Israelites were kin according to the ancestral traditions of Genesis, as Edom traced its origins to Esau and Israel traced its origins to Jacob—both sons of Isaac (Gen 33–36). God had purposed to totally destroy the nation of Edom for their treacherous treatment of their relatives, the Israelites (Isa 34:5-6; Jer 49:7-22; Ezek 25:12-14; Obad 1:10-14; Mal 1:3-4). Despite their kinship, the Bible records a long history of animosity between the two nations of Israel and Edom (cf. Num 20:14-21; 2 Sam 8:13-14; 1 Kgs 11:14-15). Andersen and Freedman (1989:265) comment that there is no specific event recorded in the history of the eighth century BC that best accounts for Amos's reference to Edomite atrocities against Judah, although both Amaziah (2 Kgs 14:7; 2 Chr 25:11-15) and Uzziah (2 Kgs 14:22) waged successful campaigns against the Edomites.

1:12 *Teman.* The chief southern stronghold of the Edomites, and like Bozrah, an important commercial center due to its location on the trade route.

Bozrah. The chief northern stronghold of the Edomites and the capital city of Edom. The city was an important commercial center since it was strategically located along the King's

Highway, the easternmost trade route connecting Egypt with Mesopotamia. The OT prophets condemned Bozrah's pride in its invincibility and predicted its doom (Isa 34:6-10; Jer 49:13-16).

1:13 *Ammon.* The name Ammon means "son of my people." Historically, the Ammonites traced their lineage to Ammon, the son Lot had by his younger daughter after their flight from Sodom (Gen 19:38). The territory of the Ammonite kingdom extended northeast of the Dead Sea between the Arnon and Jabbok Rivers (Num 21:24). Along with Moabites, the Ammonites were excluded from the assembly of the Lord because they conspired to oppose Israel after the Exodus by hiring Balaam to curse the Hebrews (Deut 23:3-6).

ripped open pregnant women. Amos asserts that "all is not fair in war." Atrocities committed against the civilian population during warfare are an affront to any basic understanding of decency and the common dignity of humanity. Smith (1989:60) has noted the senselessness of the crime in that "a helpless and defenseless pregnant woman was of no military significance, and the heartless murder of unborn children had no purpose."

1:14 *Rabbah.* The capital city of the Ammonite kingdom, located in the Transjordan near one of the major sources of the Jabbok River. Rabbah was renamed Philadelphia by the Ptolemy Philadelphus (285–246 BC) and became one of the important cities of the Decapolis during the Roman era. The ruins of Rabbah are in close proximity to Amman, the modern capital of Jordan. The city was conquered by David and Joab, but the Ammonites regained autonomy during the era of the Hebrew divided kingdoms (2 Sam 12:26-29; 1 Chr 20:1-3). The OT prophets targeted the city for divine judgment because of the Ammonite oppression of the Israelites living in the Transjordan (Jer 49:1-3; Ezek 25:1-7).

2:1 *Moab.* The name Moab means "from my father." Historically, the Moabites traced their lineage to Moab, the son Lot had by his older daughter after their flight from Sodom (Gen 19:37). The territory of Moab was located in the Transjordan highlands along the southeastern coast of the Dead Sea ranging from the Arnon River in the north to the Brook Zered in the south. Along with the Ammonites, the Moabites were excluded from the assembly of the Lord because they conspired to oppose Israel after the Exodus by hiring Balaam to curse the Hebrews (Deut 23:3-6).

desecrated the bones. The crime of the Moabites was showing utter disrespect for the rights of the dead by burning the bones of a dead Edomite king. According to Smith (1989:62), "the desecration of a tomb or a dead body was a means by which a nation could show its total disrespect for its enemies (2 Kgs 23:16) or for criminals (Lev 20:14; 21:9)."

2:2 *Kerioth.* A fortress city in Moab (cf. Jer 48:24). The exact location of the city remains uncertain. The Moabite Stone (cf. ANET) indicates that the city was home to a temple for the god Chemosh, and in the OT the Moabites were known as the "people of Chemosh" (Num 21:29; Jer 48:46). The prophet Jeremiah condemned the Moabites for trusting in their wealth, and he predicted exile for the god Chemosh and the people of Moab (Jer 48:7).

COMMENTARY

The oracles of doom against the nations are cleverly arranged in such a way that the messages crisscross the borders of the Hebrew kingdoms and effectively climax with the prophet's "target" audience—the nation of Israel (see the map below). Chisholm (2002:378-386) has likened this to placing a noose around Israel's neck and slowly tightening it, as divine judgment against each of the surrounding nations is sounded off one by one.

It is widely noted that each of the seven oracles of doom is scripted in a stereotyped literary pattern that includes, with slight variations:

1. The opening messenger formula: "This is what the LORD says"
2. A numerical formula: "The people of _____ have sinned again and again" (lit., "sinned three, even four times")
3. The indictment of specific sins committed by the nations
4. The announcement of judgment (introduced by the formula "I will send down fire" in every case except the oracle against Israel)
5. An elaboration of the announcement of judgment extending to the people and the rulers (only in 1:5, 8, 15; 2:3)
6. A closing formula that includes the name of Yahweh (only in 1:5, 8, 15; 2:3)

This standardized literary form of the oracles of doom serves as one indicator of God's fairness or consistency in the application of divine justice to human affairs.

Andersen and Freedman (1989:208-209) have recognized that the 3 + 4 pattern of the numerical formula has implications for both the general structure and the internal organization of the oracles of doom. For instance, the first three oracles specify judgment against cities, while the latter four are directed against nations. The former are situated along the main routes of travel and would be the first to bear the brunt by an attack from an invading army, while the latter lay along a secondary line of march. Andersen and Freedman conclude, however, that even if Amos was envisioning an invasion from the north by Assyria, the list of nations indicted by the prophet is arranged according to literary and theological considerations—not military ones.

The oracles against the nations neighboring Judah and Israel may be understood as a unit for the sake of commentary (1:3–2:3). The indictments against Damascus, Gaza, Tyre, Edom, Ammon, and Moab are similar in that all involve crimes against humanity (Hubbard 1989:128). The word rendered "sinned" (*pesha'* [TH6588, ZH7322]; 1:3, 6, 9, 11, 13; 2:1; 3:14; 5:12) means to commit a legal offense and signifies an act of rebellion in the form of social transgression. Such treacherous "conduct constituted rebellion against Yahweh himself" (NIDOTTE 3.708).

The repetition of the messenger formula ("This is what the LORD says" [1:3], also found in the opening verse of each oracle) serves the dual purpose of emphasizing God as the source of the prophet's message and legitimizing his sovereign rule over the nations.

The repetition of the phrase "I will not let them go unpunished!" after the messenger formula is a sober reminder that God is holy and he will bring just punishment against sinners. The expression calls to mind the words of the prophet Nahum, who warned that "the LORD is slow to get angry, but his power is great, and he never lets the guilty go unpunished" (Nah 1:3). The reality and certainty of God's judgment emerges out of his character. First, he is holy. This means God is utterly perfect and absolutely pure in his character as a transcendent and unapproachable being (cf. Eichrodt 1961:272-280). Second, he is righteous. This means God responds to human behavior (whether individual or national) with right or just conduct and impartial judgment in all situations as divine judge (cf. Eichrodt 1961:239-241). So God's "deeds are perfect. Everything he does is just and fair" (Deut 32:4).

Implicit in each of the oracles against the neighbors of Judah and Israel is the truth that God sometimes uses other nations to bring judgment against renegade kingdoms and to accomplish his purposes of divine retribution on a cosmic scale. The vantage of historical perspective shows this to be the case with the oracles of Amos, as the ancient superpowers of Assyria and Babylonia did overthrow the peoples the prophet targeted for divine wrath. This reality proved a hard teaching for the prophet Habakkuk to accept when he learned that God had decreed the judgment of Judah at the hands of the Babylonians—a nation more wicked than the people of God (Hab 1:12-13). Yet the curses pronounced by Moses against Israel—should they fail to obey the stipulations of Yahweh's covenant—indicated that God would bring other nations against his people to judge their sin (cf. Deut 28:25-26, 36, 49-53).

◆ III. God's Judgment on Judah and Israel (2:4-16)
A. Judgment against Judah (2:4-5)

[4]This is what the LORD says:

"The people of Judah have sinned
again and again,
and I will not let them go
unpunished!
They have rejected the instruction of
the LORD,

refusing to obey his decrees.
They have been led astray by the
same lies
that deceived their ancestors.
[5]So I will send down fire on Judah,
and all the fortresses of Jerusalem
will be destroyed."

NOTES

2:4 *Judah.* This became the name of the southern kingdom after the split of the Hebrew united monarchy upon the death of Solomon (c. 930 BC). The kingdom of Judah was comprised of those Hebrew tribes that settled south of Jerusalem (essentially Judah, Benjamin, and Simeon, although the remnants of the Danites who chose not to migrate to the north still occupied territory to the west of Judah, cf. Josh 19:47; Judg 1:34; 13:1). God preserved the kingdom of Judah for the sake of his servant David and for the sake of Jerusalem, where his Temple resided (1 Kgs 11:34-39). The kingdom of Judah endured as a geopolitical entity from c. 930–587 BC, when the Babylonians conquered the nation and annexed the territory into their empire (cf. 2 Kgs 25:1-21).

the instruction of the LORD. The word "instruction" (*torah* [TH8451, ZH9368]) refers to the covenant instruction Moses received from Yahweh at Mount Sinai (cf. Exod 19–24). The name "LORD" (*yhwh* [TH3068, ZH3378]) is the covenant name for God, and his laws are "the embodiment of justice and righteousness and may be equated with the knowledge of God" (Smith and Page 1995:89).

2:5 Jerusalem. This was the capital city of Judah and the location of Yahweh's Temple, the place where God established his name (Deut 12:11; 14:23). God loves Jerusalem because his presence resides there symbolically, as associated with the Ark of the Covenant housed in the Temple (Pss 9:11; 74:2; 76:2; 87:2). But his love for the city would not stay his judgment of the people of Judah for their rebellion against him.

COMMENTARY

The prophet's indictment of Judah moves beyond crimes committed against humanity to open rebellion against God by rejecting the "instruction of the LORD" (2:4). Spurning the law of God is a breach of covenant and a rejection of his authority (NIDOTTE 3.708-709). Refusal to listen to the Lord and obey his commands provided grounds to invoke the covenant curses against Israel as Yahweh's treacherous vassal (Deut 28:15, 45). By contrast, God is faithful to his covenant with Israel, so much so that "faithfulness" is one of the defining attributes of the Godhead (Deut 7:9; 32:4; Pss 111:5; 145:13; Isa 30:18). The reference to the "same lies that deceived their ancestors" (2:4) is an oblique reference to idolatry according to Hubbard (1989:138). Alternately, Andersen and Freedman, based on the parallels with Isaiah 30:9-12, identify Judah's crime as a rejection of the prophetic message itself by "the contrary acceptance of false prophecies" (1989:299). Thus, to silence God's prophets "is to reject Yahweh himself" (Andersen and Freedman 1989:300; cf. 2:12; 7:12-13). In either case, Judah's rejection of the laws of the Lord was comparable to the atrocities committed by the nations, and the consequences would be equally similar—divine judgment (2:5; cf. Smith and Page 1995:59).

◆   B. Judgment against Israel (2:6-16)

⁶This is what the LORD says:

"The people of Israel have sinned
    again and again,
and I will not let them go
    unpunished!
They sell honorable people for silver
    and poor people for a pair of
    sandals.
⁷They trample helpless people in the
    dust

and shove the oppressed out
    of the way.
Both father and son sleep with the
    same woman,
corrupting my holy name.
⁸At their religious festivals,
    they lounge in clothing their
    debtors put up as security.
In the house of their god,
    they drink wine bought with
    unjust fines.

⁹"But as my people watched,
    I destroyed the Amorites,
though they were as tall as cedars
    and as strong as oaks.
I destroyed the fruit on their branches
    and dug out their roots.
¹⁰It was I who rescued you from Egypt
    and led you through the desert for
        forty years,
    so you could possess the land of the
        Amorites.
¹¹I chose some of your sons to be
        prophets
    and others to be Nazirites.
Can you deny this, my people of Israel?"
    asks the LORD.
¹²"But you caused the Nazirites to sin by
        making them drink wine,
    and you commanded the prophets,
        'Shut up!'

¹³"So I will make you groan
    like a wagon loaded down with
        sheaves of grain.
¹⁴Your fastest runners will not
    get away.
The strongest among you will
    become weak.
Even mighty warriors will be unable
    to save themselves.
¹⁵   The archers will not stand their
        ground.
The swiftest runners won't be fast
    enough to escape.
Even those riding horses won't be
    able to save themselves.
¹⁶On that day the most courageous
    of your fighting men
will drop their weapons and run
    for their lives,"
says the LORD.

NOTES

2:6 Israel. This became the name of the northern kingdom after the split of the Hebrew united monarchy upon the death of Solomon (c. 930 BC). The kingdom of Israel was comprised of the 10 Hebrew tribes that settled north of Jerusalem and east of the Jordan River. The total number of tribes comprising the northern kingdom of Israel varies depending upon how the half-tribes of Manasseh and Ephraim and the northern Danites are enumerated. The rival kingdom of Israel was established by God through the prophet Ahijah as a punishment for Solomon's sin of idolatry (1 Kgs 11:29-39). The kingdom of Israel endured as a geopolitical entity from c. 930-722, when the Assyrians conquered the nation and annexed the territory into their empire (cf. 2 Kgs 17:7-23).

2:8 clothing their debtors put up as security. Amos refers here to the abuse of Mosaic laws that permitted Hebrews to take clothing from their neighbors as a security deposit for a loan (Exod 22:25-27; Deut 24:10-12).

unjust fines. Amos refers here to the abuse of Mosaic laws that permitted fines intended as compensation for misconduct (Exod 21:22; Deut 22:19).

2:9 Amorites. Broadly understood, the Amorites were various West Semitic people groups inhabiting Syria–Palestine since before the time of Abraham (Gen 15:16). More specifically, the name refers to the indigenous peoples of the hill country of Canaan and surrounding regions that the Israelites encountered after their Exodus from Egypt (Deut 1:7). The post-Exodus victories of the Hebrews over the Transjordan city-states of the Amorite kings Sihon and Og were a significant first step in the Israelite conquest of Canaan (Num 21:21-31; Deut 3:1-11).

2:11 Nazirites. The word *nazir* [TH5139, ZH5687] signifies a "consecrated one" or a "devoted one." The Nazirite is one who has taken a vow to be separated unto the Lord. Such a vow may be taken by a Hebrew man, woman, or even a slave—but not a Gentile (Num 6:1-21). A parent could make such a vow for a child (cf. Judg 13:5; 1 Sam 1:11). The vow consisted of three important abstentions: refraining from all products associated with the grapevine, never cutting one's hair, and avoiding any contact with the dead. The Nazirite vow might be taken for a specific time period (e.g., a month or a year), or it may be made as a lifetime vow (Judg 13:7).

COMMENTARY

The repetition of the pronoun "you" in 2:10 identifies the true "target" audience of the prophet's message—the nation of Israel (i.e., the northern Hebrew kingdom). Smith and Page (1995:61) rightly observe that Amos's oracles against the nations were intended to bring a theological message to the political and religious leaders of the kingdom of Israel, namely: God is sovereign over the nations and all kingdoms are accountable to him; God is equally patient with those nations in rebellion against him (implied in the formulaic expression "sinned again and again" prefacing each of the oracles); and God's judgment of the nations is certain and impartial (i.e., divine punishment will match the crime whether meted out against the Hebrews or the Gentiles).

The more comprehensive indictment of the sin of the kingdom of Israel also indicates Amos has this nation in his "prophetic sights." The catalog of crimes charged against Israel included: selling people into slavery (2:6b), oppressing the poor (2:7a), engaging in illicit sex (2:7b), perverting justice (2:8a), drunkenness (2:8b), and irreverent treatment of Nazirites (2:12). All of these offenses are dealt with in more detail in the subsequent messages proclaimed by the prophet.

The primary sin of Israel is the abuse and oppression of the poor, prompting Andersen and Freedman to note that "it is in the domestic scene, not the international stage, that Israel's crimes are exposed" (1989:308). The nation of Israel was guilty of the same breach of covenant as her sister nation Judah, rejecting the laws of the Lord (cf. 2:4). Specifically, Amos accused Israel of flagrantly violating covenant stipulations designed to protect the socially disadvantaged (see notes on 2:8). Like the neighboring nations, Judah and Israel are reminded that God is holy and he will bring righteous judgment against sinners—"he never lets the guilty go unpunished" (Nah 1:3).

The link between the kingdoms of Judah and Israel as the one people of God is further established in Amos's reference to the two great acts of divine deliverance experienced by the ancestors of Judah and Israel when they were a single people emerging from Egyptian captivity (2:9-10). The references to the destruction of the Amorites (2:9) and to the Exodus from Egypt (2:10) hearken back to the ratification of the covenant charter that established the Hebrews as the singular people of God—a unified "kingdom of priests" unto the Lord (Exod 19:4-6). The message of Amos foreshadows the work of God in restoring the unity of Judah and Israel as one nation in the eschaton (Jer 50:4; Ezek 36:15ff). This restored unity of the nation of Israel anticipates the New Testament teaching on the church as the one body of Jesus Christ (Eph 4:4-6; cf. John 17:21).

The prophet's reference to "the house of their god" (2:8) hints at the sin of idolatry that plagued the northern kingdom of Israel. Amos addresses the issue more explicitly in a later message (5:5, 26). Like his counterparts in prophetic ministry, Amos knew that God is the only true God and that he is a jealous god—he will not give his glory to another (Deut 5:9; Isa 42:8; 45:18, 21; Ezek 39:25).

This initial message against Israel does not end with the judgment formula

"I will send down fire" like the other oracles against the nations (1:4, 7, 10, 12, 14; 2:2, 5), but it does end with a declaration of judgment (2:13-16). (A similar judgment formula does, however, close Amos's second oracle against Israel; cf. 3:13-15.) According to Smith and Page (1995:61), this change is deliberate in order to heighten the impact of the announcement of divine punishment: "By changing the conclusion from the expected to the unexpected, Amos's words were heard more clearly than otherwise." The ominous tone of the message also signifies that God's judgment is imminent; the threat of Assyrian exile was only one generation removed from Israel when Amos preached in Bethel. God warns his people of impending doom out of his great compassion—he does not delight in the death of anyone (Ezek 18:23, 32).

◆ IV. Further Oracles against Israel (3:1–6:14)
A. Listen, People of Israel (3:1-15)

Listen to this message that the LORD has spoken against you, O people of Israel and Judah—against the entire family I rescued from Egypt:

2 "From among all the families on the earth,
I have been intimate with you alone.
That is why I must punish you
for all your sins."

3 Can two people walk together
without agreeing on the direction?
4 Does a lion ever roar in a thicket
without first finding a victim?
Does a young lion growl in its den
without first catching its prey?
5 Does a bird ever get caught in a trap
that has no bait?
Does a trap spring shut
when there's nothing to catch?
6 When the ram's horn blows a warning,
shouldn't the people be alarmed?
Does disaster come to a city
unless the LORD has planned it?

7 Indeed, the Sovereign LORD never does anything
until he reveals his plans to his
servants the prophets.

8 The lion has roared—
so who isn't frightened?
The Sovereign LORD has spoken—

so who can refuse to proclaim his message?
9 Announce this to the leaders of Philistia*
and to the great ones of Egypt:
"Take your seats now on the hills around Samaria,
and witness the chaos and oppression in Israel."

10 "My people have forgotten how to do right,"
says the LORD.
Their fortresses are filled with wealth
taken by theft and violence.
11 Therefore," says the Sovereign LORD,
"an enemy is coming!
He will surround them and shatter their defenses.
Then he will plunder all their fortresses."

12 This is what the LORD says:

"A shepherd who tries to rescue a sheep from a lion's mouth
will recover only two legs or a piece of an ear.
So it will be for the Israelites in Samaria lying on luxurious beds,
and for the people of Damascus reclining on couches.*

¹³"Now listen to this, and announce it throughout all Israel,*" says the Lord, the LORD God of Heaven's Armies.

¹⁴"On the very day I punish Israel for
its sins,
I will destroy the pagan altars
at Bethel.

The horns of the altar will be cut off
and fall to the ground.
¹⁵And I will destroy the beautiful homes
of the wealthy—
their winter mansions and their
summer houses, too—
all their palaces filled with ivory,"
says the LORD.

3:9 Hebrew *Ashdod.* **3:12** Or *So it will be when the Israelites in Samaria are rescued / with only a broken bed and a tattered pillow.* **3:13** Hebrew *the house of Jacob.* The names "Jacob" and "Israel" are often interchanged throughout the Old Testament, referring sometimes to the individual patriarch and sometimes to the nation.

NOTES

3:1 *Listen.* This imperative verb (*shama'* [TH8085, ZH9048]) introduces a formulaic summons to listen (cf. Deut 4:1; 6:4; Hos 4:1; Mic 6:1). In prophetic contexts the word typically denotes "listen to; heed by acting upon or putting into practice what has been said" (NIDOTTE 5.178). The formula signals that "an important message is coming. A principle, an issue, a teaching, or a truth is about to be revealed" (Stuart 1987:321). Amos used the imperative, "listen," to open three of his messages in this central section of the book (3:1; 4:1; 5:1).

family. The term *mishpakhah* [TH4940, ZH5476] denotes the largest sub-tribal unit between the tribe and the family and may be called a "clan." Amos 3:1 is the only reference to Israel as a "family" in the OT. According to Andersen and Freedman (1989:380-381), the prophet used the designation to "downgrade" Israel by placing them beside all other nations ("families on the earth," 3:2) as members of a larger unit, a single tribe of humanity. This leveling of the two "houses" (Israel and Judah) in the family of the Hebrew people with the six other people groups surrounding Israel (chs 1–2) places all equally under the jurisdiction of the one God.

3:2 *intimate.* The word *yada'* [TH3045, ZH3359] usually means "to know." In this context the term refers to an experiential or relational knowledge and indicates a special intimacy that God enjoys with Israel. No doubt Amos has in mind God's election of Israel by means of the covenant relationship established with Abram and later with the nation of Israel at Mount Sinai (Gen 12:3; 28:14; Exod 19:4-6). Andersen and Freedman (1989:381) note that equally pertinent is the use of the word "know" (*yada'*) in marital relations (e.g., Gen 4:1, 25). The representation of Yahweh as husband and Israel as wife is common in prophetic literature (especially Hosea, Jeremiah, and Ezekiel), so the similar reference in Amos is entirely appropriate.

punish. This verb (*paqad* [TH6485, ZH7212]) means "to visit" (with the purpose of inspection) in a neutral sense (cf. 3:14; NIDOTTE 3.659). When coupled with the word "sins," the expression is an idiom for divine judgment (i.e., punishment results if God's inspection reveals a flaw, a fault, some disobedience or sin).

3:7 *reveals.* The term *galah* [TH1540, ZH1655] means "to uncover"; in the context of prophetic speech the word indicates the disclosing of a secret. Thus, the expression became a "theologically filled concept" capable of conveying the essential features of the Hebrew understanding of divine revelation (cf. TDOT 2.487). God's knowledge of the future and his ability to declare this information to his prophets separates him from all would-be gods (cf. Isa 41:22-23; 42:8-9; 44:25-26; 45:21-22).

3:8 *lion.* Smith and Page (1995:76) connect the clause "the lion has roared" with God on the basis of parallelism with the following line: "the Sovereign LORD has spoken." Andersen and Freedman (1989:400) associate the "lion" with the nation of Assyria and the "tramp of the Assyrian army" on the move (since they were known as the "lion-people" and were often symbolized by the lion in their iconography). Stuart (1987:325) is probably correct in recognizing this as an instance of double entendre.

proclaim. This verb (*naba'* [TH5012, ZH5547]) means "to speak as a prophet (*nabi'* [TH5030, ZH5566])." The prophet was one who delivered a message on behalf of another (in this case the Sovereign Lord). Typically, the prophet's message was one of warning and instruction based on the blessings and curses attached to Israel's obedience to the law of Moses (e.g., Lev 26; Deut 28).

3:9 Announce. The prophet rhetorically sets up a scenario where heralds are "sent to two pagan nations with an invitation to come as witnesses to the violence and oppression in Samaria" (Smith and Page 1995:77).

Philistia. The MT reads "Ashdod," one of the five principal cities of the Philistines.

Egypt. The summons to the leaders of Ashdod and Egypt bring unlikely witnesses to the "courtroom drama"—historically, both nations were brutal oppressors of the Hebrews. Ironically, the rich and powerful of Philistia and Egypt are brought to witness Yahweh's indictment of the rich and powerful of Samaria who had stored up ill-gotten treasures at the expense of the poor. According to Hubbard (1989:151), this startling device has a two-fold purpose: First, it served to spotlight the depth of corruption in Israel by having nations that were the epitome of evil judge their misconduct. Second, it showed that covenant law was not the only criterion that would condemn Israel's behavior; by any standards of human decency they stood guilty as charged.

Samaria. The city was located seven miles northwest of Shechem and was established as the capital of the northern kingdom of Israel by King Omri (1 Kgs 16:24). In Amos, God turns the environs of Samaria into a great outdoor courtroom where he will make his case against his people (so Hubbard 1989:151).

witness. The Mosaic law required at least two witnesses in legal cases where the death penalty was imposed (Deut 17:6).

chaos and oppression. The combination of plural nouns (*mehumoth* [TH4103, ZH4539], "tumult, panic, unrest" and *'ashuqim* [TH6217, ZH6935], "oppression") depict "a scene of unchecked social chaos" (Smith and Page 1995:78). Andersen and Freedman (1989:406) suggest that there was a relationship between the oppression of the poor and the social upheaval Israel experienced. This should not be surprising given the cause-and-effect character of the retribution principle in God's economy of divine punishment—people "harvest what [they] plant" (Gal 6:7).

3:10 theft and violence. The terms (*khamas* [TH2555, ZH2805] and *shod* [TH7701, ZH8719]) are hendiadys for the "rewards of lawless behavior" (Andersen and Freedman 1989:407). There is a certain irony in the pattern of God's judgment. Those material goods garnered by theft and violence will be removed from Israelite storerooms in like manner—theft and violence on the part of the Assyrians (cf. Hosea's punishment for those Israelites seduced by fertility cult worship, "wombs that don't give birth and breasts that give no milk"; Hos 9:14).

3:12 luxurious beds . . . reclining on couches. These are symbols of wealth and ease for the prophet Amos (6:4; cf. Ezek 23:41). Such wealth and ease for these few had come at a high price—namely, the exploitation and oppression of the poor and needy (2:6-7; 4:1; 5:12).

3:14 Bethel. A town 12 miles north of Jerusalem on the Benjamin–Ephraim tribal border. The sites of Dan and Bethel were the locations where King Jeroboam established rival shrines housing golden calves so that the citizens of the northern kingdom would not make pilgrimages to worship at the Jerusalem Temple (1 Kgs 12:25-30). Amos delivered his message in Bethel and condemned the idolatrous worship conducted there (4:4; 5:5-6; 7:10-13).

horns of the altar. The altars for burning sacrifices had projections, or "horns," at the corners. They served the practical function of holding the wood and the sacrificial victim in place on top of the altar. The priest dabbed the blood of sacrificial offerings on the horns of the altar as a symbol of atonement or the covering of sin (Lev 4:30; 16:18). The horns of the altar were also a place of sanctuary for those appealing to the king for mercy in legal cases that were capital offenses (cf. 1 Kgs 1:50; 2:28). The destruction of the horns of the altar "means the loss of the last refuge; the destroyer will be undeterred by the holiest taboos" (Andersen and Freedman 1989:411).

3:15 *winter mansions . . . summer houses.* Given the extremes of the climate in Palestine, having a separate residence for each season marked the height of luxury.

ivory. The use of ivory inlay in furniture was a decorative feature restricted to the wealthy in the ancient world. The word symbolizes the extravagant lifestyle of royalty and the very rich (6:4; cf. 1 Kgs 10:18, 22; 22:39).

COMMENTARY

The middle portion of the book of Amos is comprised of five prophetic "messages" or sermons delivered by the prophet against the kingdom of Israel (chs 3–6). Dorsey (1999:278) has observed a partial chiastic structure in the arrangement of the themes of the five messages:

A. Destruction of Bethel's cult center (3:1-15)
  B. Condemnation of wealthy Israelite women (4:1-13)
    C. Call to repentance and lament (5:1-17)
  B'. Condemnation of wealthy Israelite men (5:18–6:14)
A'. Destruction of Bethel's cult center (7:1–8:3)

The chiasm is actually completed with the early portions of the prophetic visions section of the book (7:1–8:3). The call to repentance (5:1-17) functions as the centerpiece of the book, both literarily and theologically.

Gitay (1980:293-309) has analyzed the rhetorical structure of chapter 3 and outlines the message of the sermon in this fashion: summons to listen (3:1); thesis statement concerning God's "visitation" (3:2); refutation of opponents' denial of divine punishment by means of a series of rhetorical questions asserting the certainty of God's judgment (3:3-6); statement of the prophet's divine authority (3:7-8); indictment and declaration of punishment (3:9-12); epilogue (3:13-15).

The message of Amos to the people of Israel and Judah (ch 3) underscores several theological truths concerning the nature and character of God. First, God is a deliverer, as attested by the prophet's reference to the Exodus from Egypt (3:1). The Old Testament prophets knew only one God, the Lord, who is mighty to save or deliver—there is no other deliverer (Isa 43:3, 11; Jer 14:8; Zeph 3:17). This suggests that deliverance is still possible; Israel had the opportunity to heed the prophet's warning and "come back to [God] and live" (5:4).

Second, implicit in the citation of God's special relationship with the Hebrews (3:2) is the idea that, by means of the covenant with Abraham, God chose one nation to bless all nations (Gen 12:1-3). This quite naturally calls attention to the fact that, elsewhere in the Old Testament, God is understood to be the creator or father of all nations (Isa 42:5; 45:12; Mal 2:10). In fact, an important theme in the Old Testament portrayal of God is his supremacy over the "local deities" of the nations as the "universal deity" who rules all creation (Jer 10:16). For instance, God demonstrated his supremacy over the gods of the Egyptians in the Hebrew Exodus (Exod 12:12) and the gods of Canaan through Elijah in the contest at Mount Carmel (1 Kgs 18:21, 38-39). Even his title, El-Elyon ("the Most High God") signifies his preeminence over all that is considered "god" by the nations (cf. Gen 14:18-20).

Third, the courtroom setting of the message (with heralds announcing a legal proceeding and the summoning of witnesses; see note on 3:9) reminds us that God is the just judge—the God of justice (Mal 3; see Van Gemeren 1990:219-220). He is a God who shows no partiality (Deut 10:17) and demonstrates great concern and care for the poor by maintaining their rights (Ps 140:12; cf. 1 Sam 2:8; Ps 82:3).

Finally, God not only knows the future but he declares it through his prophets (3:7; cf. Mic 3:8; 2 Pet 1:20-21). This foreknowledge makes him unique as God and marks him as the true God in contrast to all false gods (Isa 44:26; 45:21-22). For God's prophets, the expression "the day of the LORD" (5:18) meant cosmic judgment for both the nations and disobedient Israel—a day of human accountability before God. The goal of the Day of the Lord is the total transformation of all creation, prompting the godly to prepare themselves for the day of deliverance (see VanGemeren 1990:214-225). In one sense, God's foreknowledge concerning this cosmic judgment becomes a motivation for repentance (cf. Joel 2:12-14; 2 Pet 3:11-13).

None of these theological ideas is peculiar to the Old Testament, since it is the same triune God who speaks and acts in the New Testament as well. Thus, it is the living God who is the Savior or deliverer of all people (1 Tim 4:10). He remains supreme as the God who made the universe and everything in it and sustains it by his power (Heb 1:2-3). Peter understood that God shows no partiality, as evidenced by his acceptance of Gentiles who respond in faith to the good news of Jesus Christ (Acts 10:34-35). Like Amos and the Old Testament prophets, the apostles of the New Testament also knew God as the one who knew the future and declared it through his servants (John 16:13; Rev 22:6).

◆ B. Listen, Cows of Bashan (4:1-13)

¹Listen to me, you fat cows*
living in Samaria,
you women who oppress the poor
and crush the needy,
and who are always calling to your
husbands,
"Bring us another drink!"
²The Sovereign LORD has sworn this
by his holiness:
"The time will come when you will be
led away

with hooks in your noses.
Every last one of you will be dragged
away
like a fish on a hook!
³You will be led out through the ruins
of the wall;
you will be thrown from your
fortresses,*"
says the LORD.

⁴"Go ahead and offer sacrifices to the
idols at Bethel.

Keep on disobeying at Gilgal.
Offer sacrifices each morning,
     and bring your tithes every three
     days.
5 Present your bread made with yeast
     as an offering of thanksgiving.
Then give your extra voluntary
     offerings
     so you can brag about it
     everywhere!
This is the kind of thing you Israelites
     love to do,"
     says the Sovereign LORD.

6 "I brought hunger to every city
     and famine to every town.
But still you would not return to me,"
     says the LORD.

7 "I kept the rain from falling
     when your crops needed it the most.
I sent rain on one town
     but withheld it from another.
Rain fell on one field,
     while another field withered away.
8 People staggered from town to town
     looking for water,
     but there was never enough.
But still you would not return to me,"
     says the LORD.

9 "I struck your farms and vineyards
     with blight and mildew.
Locusts devoured all your fig and
     olive trees.

But still you would not return to me,"
     says the LORD.

10 "I sent plagues on you
     like the plagues I sent on Egypt
     long ago.
I killed your young men in war
     and led all your horses away.*
The stench of death filled the air!
But still you would not return to me,"
     says the LORD.

11 "I destroyed some of your cities,
     as I destroyed* Sodom and
     Gomorrah.
Those of you who survived
     were like charred sticks pulled from
     a fire.
But still you would not return to me,"
     says the LORD.

12 "Therefore, I will bring upon you all
     the disasters I have announced.
Prepare to meet your God in
     judgment, you people of Israel!"

13 For the LORD is the one who shaped
     the mountains,
     stirs up the winds, and reveals his
     thoughts to mankind.
He turns the light of dawn into
     darkness
     and treads on the heights of the
     earth.
The LORD God of Heaven's Armies
     is his name!

4:1 Hebrew *you cows of Bashan.*   4:3 Or *thrown out toward Harmon,* possibly a reference to Mount Hermon.
4:10 Or *and slaughtered your captured horses.*   4:11 Hebrew *as when God destroyed.*

NOTES
4:1 **Listen.** See the note on 3:1 concerning the "summons to listen" formula in prophetic
literature.

fat cows. Most commentators understand the expression as a satirical reference to self-
indulgent women of the ruling class in Israel ("pampered darlings," cf. Smith and Page
1995:85). The MT reads "cows of Bashan"; Bashan was the most fertile part of Gilead
along the Yarmuk River in the Transjordan, celebrated for its rich pasture lands. This
made Bashan a "byword for prosperity in agriculture and animal husbandry" (Hubbard
1989:155). Amos apparently makes reference to women of the royal court who enjoyed
luxurious lifestyles by exploiting the poor. By contrast, Andersen and Freedman (1989:421-
422) interpret "cows" as a parody of the warriors of Israel, comparing the prophet's taunt
or insult to other texts where soldiers behave like women (e.g., Isa 19:16; Nah 3:13). Koch

(1982:46) finds allusions to fertility cult worship by women who imagined themselves consorts of the bull-god of Samaria (cf. Hos 8:5). Note the ambiguity of the word "husbands" in Amos 4:1 (lit., "lords"; *'adon*). The prophet's charge of exploitation of the poor (in this case by the wealthy women of Samaria) best fits the context, since prophetic satire against warriors is often more obvious (cf. Nah 3:13).

oppress . . . crush. The word "oppress" (*'ashaq* [TH6231, ZH6943]) generally describes the intimidation and exploitation (with overtones of extortion and violence) of weaker members of the community by those who are stronger (NIDOTTE 3.557). The word "crush" (*ratsats* [TH7533, ZH8368]) means "to pulverize" or "abuse, mistreat" (NIDOTTE 3.1192). Ironically, the same two root words are used to describe the divine judgment of Israel for disobedience to the Mosaic covenant (Deut 28:33).

drink. Then as now, the idleness of the wealthy class led to binges of drunkenness and debauchery. The prophet Hosea decried the abuse of alcohol because it robbed God's people of their brains (Hos 4:11). God's judgment against the nations includes an indictment of those who trade little girls as slaves for more imported wine (Joel 3:3; cf. Walton 2000:763).

4:2 *sworn.* The verb (*shaba'* [TH7650, ZH8678]) introduces an oath formula that carries the force of a curse. The certain destruction of Samaria is sealed by Yahweh's swearing an oath by his own holiness, "an expression known from the context of Ps 89:35 to represent divine determination to enforce a covenant" (Stuart 1987:332).

hooks in your noses. The Hebrew text proves difficult to translate at this juncture (cf. Andersen and Freedman 1989:419, "they will take you away with grappling hooks, and your rear guard with fishhooks"). S. M. Paul (1971:128) translates it as, "you shall be transported in baskets, and the very last one of you, in fisherman's pots." Regardless of the exact meaning of the verse, the undignified departure of the wealthy oppressors will be as cruel as their treatment of their poor and needy fellow citizens.

4:4 *offer sacrifices.* The prophet's mocking command to engage in worship at the shrines of Bethel and Gilgal suggests a parody or caricature of priestly instruction as part of a call to worship for pilgrims gathered at the sanctuary (cf. Hubbard 1989:157; Smith and Page 1995:87). Paradoxically, in their false worship, the people only multiply their sins.

Gilgal. The site is mentioned in association with Bethel in 5:5 also. The location of Gilgal is uncertain (somewhere on the plain west of Jericho). The town was a worship site and administrative center during the days of Samuel and King Saul (1 Sam 7:15-17; 15:21). This may also have been the case earlier during the days of the Hebrew judges (cf. Judg 2:1; 3:19). The shrine at Gilgal apparently remained an important worship center into the time of Amos—perhaps even becoming a symbol of wickedness and false worship.

tithes every three days. Perhaps a reference to the special tithe collected for the benefit of the Levites every three years (Deut 14:28-29) or another local custom of voluntary tithes for crops given on the third day of a religious pilgrimage to one of the sacred sites.

4:5 *bread made with yeast.* Both leavened bread and unleavened bread were part of the thank offering (Lev 7:12-15). Though Israelite worship was idolatrous (NLT adds the word "idols" in 4:4), the issue Amos focused on was not wrong practice or the violation of ritual regulations. Rather, he "needles them for doing right acts" (Hubbard 1989:157). The people were doing the right things for the wrong reasons. The motivation for their worship was that they might "brag" about their religiosity—not to proclaim the glory of God. Amos's indictment of self-serving religion calls to mind Jesus' rebuke of the Pharisees who engaged in pious acts of worship for show (Matt 23:5).

offering of thanksgiving. Thank offerings were one type of fellowship offering (Lev 7:12-15; 22:29-30). The offering was presented in response to an unexpected blessing and included an animal sacrifice and was to be accompanied by various kinds of bread. Apparently the priests of Bethel replicated the Mosaic sacrificial system of the Jerusalem Temple (cf. 1 Kgs 12:31).

voluntary offerings. Free-will offerings were sacrifices of general thankfulness made in response to the goodness of God (Lev 7:16-17; 22:18-23).

thing you . . . love to do. The people loved the form and ritual of their worship but had no heart for what God loves—justice, righteousness, kindness, and mercy (5:24; Mic 6:8; cf. Matt 23:23).

4:6 *return.* In contexts expressing a covenant relationship between God and his people Israel, the word "return" (*shub* [TH7725, ZH8740]) signifies a change of loyalty by one of the covenant parties. Typically the term is understood as the act of "repentance," a complete change of direction back to God or a total reorientation toward Yahweh. The hard-heartedness of Amos's audience is underscored in the five-fold repetition of recalcitrant Israel's refusal to "return" to God (4:6, 8, 9, 10, 11).

4:10 *plagues.* Amos catalogs seven plagues (*deber* [TH1698, ZH1822]) in 4:6-11. The natural disasters and calamities cited by the prophet are past acts of Yahweh that were designed to prompt Israel to return to God in covenant obedience. Each of the plagues is mentioned in the curses for treaty violation attached to the stipulations of the Mosaic covenant: famine (4:6; cf. Lev 26:26), drought (4:7-8; cf. Lev 26:19; Deut 28:22-24), blight and mildew (4:9a; cf. Deut 28:22), locusts (4:9b; cf. Deut 28:38, 42), plagues (4:10a; cf. Lev 26:25; Deut 28:21-22, 27), war (4:10b; cf. Lev 26:25, 33), and destruction (4:11; cf. Deut 29:23). Despite the series of catastrophes used by God to warn and discipline his people, they refused to turn back to him.

4:11 *Sodom and Gomorrah.* The destruction of these two ancient cities (Gen 19) typified the suddenness and thoroughness of divine judgment in later biblical tradition (so Hubbard 1989:160; cf. Deut 29:23; Isa 1:9; Zeph 2:9; Matt 10:15).

charred sticks pulled from a fire. Later, Amos reveals that God will not completely destroy the nation of Israel (9:8). The "charred sticks" are symbolic of a remnant of Israelites spared destruction by the grace of God (cf. 3:12).

4:12 *Prepare to meet your God.* The prophet's declaration "was neither a call to repentance nor an invitation to covenant renewal; rather, it was a summons to judgment" (Smith and Page 1995:93). The outcome of the divine "visitation" or "inspection" forecast earlier (3:2, 14) would result in God's punishment of Israel's sins of idolatry and social injustice.

4:13 Lord *God of Heaven's Armies.* This compound name for God (with variations) is prominent in OT prophetic literature (used nine times in Amos: 3:13; 4:13; 5:14, 15, 16, 27; 6:8, 14; 9:5). The term "armies" (*tseba'oth* [TH6635, ZH7372]) has military connotations and refers to the angelic armies at God's disposal. The epithet emphasizes the invincible power that stands behind the commands of God.

COMMENTARY

Amos served a God who demands to be heard in all ages and places, whether pre-exilic Israel or postmodern North America. Three times in this section (chs 3–6), the prophet calls the people to attention to "listen" to what God has to say (3:1; 4:1; 5:1). "What they hear is that they have neglected the privileges inherent in being God's chosen people. By rejecting revelation they forget how to do right and are thereby turned over to the same sort of devastation all sinful groups receive (3:1-15)" (House 1998:360). Listening to God (with a view toward obeying his voice) is still the watchword according to the teaching of the New Testament: Those who listen to the voice of the Son of God will live (John 5:24-25; cf. Rom 10:17; Heb 2:1; Jas 1:19).

Amos's message to the nation of Israel anticipates the later teaching of Jesus— "When someone has been given much, much will be required in return" (Luke 12:48). The prophet's audience had assumed they were somehow exempt from divine judgment for their sin because they were God's elect—his chosen people (3:2). In fact, Amos chided those who wished for the arrival of the day of Lord because they had no idea that they were asking for judgment—not deliverance (5:18). They failed to realize that the privilege of covenant relationship with Yahweh also carried heavy responsibilities, including the imitation of the holiness of God, so that the Hebrews might be his light to the nations (Exod 19:6; Lev 11:44; Isa 42:6; 49:6). For this reason, when divine judgment comes "it must begin with God's household" (1 Pet 4:17).

The proper worship of God is an important theme in the message of Amos. The prophet boldly announced divine judgment against those engaged in the false worship of idolatry (e.g., 5:26; 8:14). The reference to "idols" (4:4), however, is an interpretive addition by the NLT (also "your gods" in 5:6). That idolatry was associated with the shrines at Bethel and Gilgal is not in question (1 Kgs 12:28-30; 14:9). But Amos's sarcastic call to sacrificial worship (4:4) is not so much about the false worship of idolatry as it is about the insincere worship of right acts of ritual offered with improper motivation (4:5). The Old Testament repeatedly rebukes those who perform the prescribed rituals of worship with the wrong motives—God rejects such worship (5:21-23; cf. Isa 1:10-14; Jer 6:20; Mal 1:10). Likewise, the Old Testament offers much instruction on the motives informing the appropriate worship of God, including obedience to the commands of God (1 Sam 15:21-22), a broken spirit and a contrite heart (Ps 51:16-17), blameless living (Pss 19:7, 11-14; 20:3, 7), and a lifestyle of social justice and merciful service to humanity (Mic 6:6-8). Again, the message of Amos serves as a forerunner to the instruction of Jesus who taught that acceptable worship of God must be done in spirit and in truth (John 4:24). This may be what David had in mind when he said that those who worship God must do so with a "pure heart" and "pure hands" (Ps 24:3-4). That means the spirit of the worshiper is in union with the Holy Spirit, and the worship exhibits a behavior pattern of conformity to God's directions for righteous living (cf. Ps 15; Isa 56:1-2; Rom 12:1-2; Jas 1:27).

The prophet Amos knew God as the shaper of mountains, the creator of winds, the revealer of thoughts, the maker of the dawn, and the one who treads the heights of the earth (4:13). The series of participles identifies this verse as a hymn fragment extolling God's sovereignty, perhaps from a catechetical poem or temple hymn (on the doxologies of Amos, see Paul 1971:152-156). Since God has made the world and everything in it, he wields all power in heaven and on earth. A God of such majesty and might easily executes the punishment he has decreed for those in rebellion against him. For this reason, "Israel should be shaken to their senses" by the summons to judgment announced in the previous verse—"prepare to meet your God" (4:12; Smith and Page 1995:93). Our God is still a "devouring fire" (Heb 12:29; cf. Amos 5:6).

◆ C. Listen, People of Israel (5:1-17)

Listen, you people of Israel! Listen to this funeral song I am singing:

2 "The virgin Israel has fallen,
    never to rise again!
She lies abandoned on the ground,
    with no one to help her up."

3 The Sovereign LORD says:

"When a city sends a thousand men
    to battle,
only a hundred will return.
When a town sends a hundred,
    only ten will come back alive."

4 Now this is what the LORD says to the family of Israel:

"Come back to me and live!
5 Don't worship at the pagan altars at
    Bethel;
    don't go to the shrines at Gilgal or
    Beersheba.
For the people of Gilgal will be
    dragged off into exile,
and the people of Bethel will be
    reduced to nothing."
6 Come back to the LORD and live!
Otherwise, he will roar through Israel*
    like a fire,
    devouring you completely.
Your gods in Bethel
    won't be able to quench the flames.
7 You twist justice, making it a bitter pill
    for the oppressed.
You treat the righteous like dirt.

8 It is the LORD who created the stars,
    the Pleiades and Orion.
He turns darkness into morning
    and day into night.
He draws up water from the oceans
    and pours it down as rain on the
    land.

The LORD is his name!
9 With blinding speed and power he
    destroys the strong,
    crushing all their defenses.

10 How you hate honest judges!
    How you despise people who tell
    the truth!
11 You trample the poor,
    stealing their grain through taxes
    and unfair rent.
Therefore, though you build beautiful
    stone houses,
    you will never live in them.
Though you plant lush vineyards,
    you will never drink wine from
    them.
12 For I know the vast number of your
    sins
    and the depth of your rebellions.
You oppress good people by taking
    bribes
    and deprive the poor of justice
    in the courts.
13 So those who are smart keep their
    mouths shut,
    for it is an evil time.

14 Do what is good and run from evil
    so that you may live!
Then the LORD God of Heaven's Armies
    will be your helper,
    just as you have claimed.
15 Hate evil and love what is good;
    turn your courts into true halls
    of justice.
Perhaps even yet the LORD God of
    Heaven's Armies
    will have mercy on the remnant
    of his people.*

16 Therefore, this is what the Lord, the LORD God of Heaven's Armies, says:

"There will be crying in all the public
squares
and mourning in every street.
Call for the farmers to weep
with you,

and summon professional mourners
to wail.
¹⁷There will be wailing in every vineyard,
for I will destroy them all,"
says the LORD.

5:6 Hebrew *the house of Joseph.*   **5:15** Hebrew *the remnant of Joseph.*

NOTES
5:1 *listen.* See note on 3:1.

funeral song. The term *qinah* [ᵀᴴ7015, ᶻᴴ7806] describes a lament or dirge for the dead; such funeral songs have a distinct meter or cadence. Typically, the dirge or funeral song consists of four discernible movements, including a description of the tragedy (5:2-3), a summons to respond (5:4-6, 14-15), a direct address to the fallen (5:7-13), and a call to mourning (5:16-17; cf. Stuart 1987:344).

5:2 *virgin Israel.* Amos addressed the kingdom of Israel as a virgin (*bethulah* [ᵀᴴ1330, ᶻᴴ1435]), perhaps a reflection of the nation's status as the bride of Yahweh (so Niehaus 1992:411). The image is that of a "youthful maiden" tragically and violently cut off in the prime of her life (Stuart 1987:345). Later, the prophet Jeremiah would apply the same expression to the kingdom of Judah (Jer 18:13; cf. Lam 1:15 [NLT mg], of where the city of Jerusalem is portrayed as a "trampled virgin").

has fallen. According to Niehaus (1992:411), the so-called prophetic perfect aspect of this verb views Israel as already fallen—her fate is sealed. The verb "fallen" (*napal* [ᵀᴴ5307, ᶻᴴ5877]) "evokes pictures of defeat in battle" (Andersen and Freedman 1989:474).

abandoned. Divine abandonment by Yahweh is a curse threatened against Israel for violation of covenant stipulations (cf. Deut 32:15, 20). God will "abandon" (*natash* [ᵀᴴ5203, ᶻᴴ5759]) those who abandon him by their worship of other gods. Jeremiah uses this word to describe Yahweh's forsaking of the kingdom of Judah as a result of idolatry (Jer 12:7).

5:4 *Come back to me.* The appeal to "come back" to God is the summons to respond to the prophet's funeral song (see note on 5:1). The repetition of the summons (5:6) and the use of the imperative form of the verb indicate the desperate situation Israel faced and the urgency of the hour for making a decision. The word translated "come back" (*darash* [ᵀᴴ1875, ᶻᴴ2011], "seek"; cf. NIDOTTE 1.993) may be translated "worship" in some contexts; here it connotes "one's whole duty to God" (Smith and Page 1995:99). For Amos, seeking God required the tangible demonstration of imitating his holiness through a lifestyle committed to social justice. Simply stated, this meant both doing good and running from evil (5:14). The chiastic restatement of this truth addresses the relationship between motive and action, as the people need to hate evil and love what is good (5:15). Andersen and Freedman (1989:482) summarize: "The key is in finding not the right place to go, but the right thing to do and the right way to do it. The true search for God, like the search for the true God, begins in the heart."

live. Life is connected with the worship of the true God (also 5:14) because the fear of the Lord is a life-giving fountain (Prov 14:27). The Lord God is the source of Israel's life (Ps 68:26). Only destruction and death follow in the wake of idol worship (5:5-6; cf. Prov 11:19; 14:12). Later, the prophets Jeremiah and Ezekiel will call the kingdom of Judah to heed God's word and thus live (Jer 17:21; Ezek 18:32). It is possible that Amos had more in mind than physical life, more than simply escaping the violence and death of impending war, in his summons to Israel to seek God and live. The word "live" implies a basic restoration of covenant blessing (Stuart 1987:346). The prophet may also have had inklings of spiritual life and even life after death, since already the psalmist understood something about the "Book of Life" (Ps 69:28; cf. Exod 32:33).

5:5 Bethel. See note on 3:14.

Gilgal. See note on 4:4.

Beersheba. Apparently Beersheba had become a place of pilgrimage and idolatry for the Hebrews, perhaps both for the people of Judah and Israel (cf. 8:14). The reference to Beersheba, located 25 miles southwest of Hebron, shows that the prophet included Judah in this threat of divine judgment (cf. 2:4-5).

exile. The scattering of Israel into foreign lands as punishment for the sin of idolatry is one of the curses threatened by Yahweh for violation of his covenant (Deut 28:36-37, 64; cf. Lev 18:24-30, where the land of covenant promise "vomits out" those who defile it).

5:6 fire. Fire is a symbol of both judgment (e.g., Deut 9:3) and purification (e.g., Mal 3:2) in the OT. Destruction by fire is a curse invoked by Yahweh and is associated with covenant violation, especially idolatry (cf. Deut 32:22). God himself is described as "a devouring fire. . . a jealous God" (Deut 4:24; cf. Heb 12:29).

5:7 twist justice . . . righteous like dirt. The prophet pairs "justice" (*mishpat* [TH4941, ZH5477]) and "righteousness" (*tsedaqah* [TH6666, ZH7407]) three times in this section (5:7, 24; 6:12). Hubbard (1989:167) observes that is "the best summary available to define the covenant responsibilities of God's people. Just because justice (cf. Isa 30:18) and righteousness (Mic 7:9) are essential activities of Yahweh, they must become prime duties of his people." See note on 5:24.

5:8 Pleiades and Orion. This reference to the constellations is part of a hymn fragment containing three creation doxologies (see the discussion in Andersen and Freedman 1989:486-488). Pleiades is a star cluster in the constellation of Taurus ("the Bull"), and Orion is the constellation known as "the Hunter." The pair is also mentioned in Job as testimony to God's wisdom and power (Job 9:9; 38:31). In addition to God's power and wisdom, Amos emphasized the order and rhythm of God's creation (with the cycle of constellations crossing the heavens [5:8a], the temporal patterns of day and night [5:8b], and the seasonal rainfalls [5:8c]).

5:10 honest judges. The office of judge was established by Moses after the Exodus as a practical solution to the burden he shouldered in arbitrating legal cases (Exod 18:17-22, 24-26). The judges were to be capable and honest individuals who feared God and hated bribes (Exod 18:21). Those appointed judges were charged to make fair decisions for Hebrews and foreigners alike (Deut 1:16-17). Since they were serving as judges for God himself, who is a perfectly fair judge, they must render similar justice (Ps 7:11; see also commentary on 3:1-15). The Mosaic law enacted prohibitions against bribing judges because the practice blinded the eyes of the wise and corrupted the decisions of the godly (Exod 23:8; Deut 10:17; 16:19). Sadly, the testimony of the OT prophets indicates this law often went unheeded (cf. 5:12; Isa 1:23; 5:23; Mic 7:3; Hab 1:4). Both the OT and the NT foster expectations for an ideal judge, the righteous judge who will never judge by appearance, false evidence, or hearsay (Isa 11:3; cf. 2 Tim 4:8).

5:11 The punishments cited here are listed among the curses that will be inflicted upon Israel for disobedience to Yahweh's covenant stipulations (Deut 28:30).

5:12 sins. Amos employed the same word (*pesha'* [TH6588, ZH7322]) in his indictment of Israel's neighboring nations (see commentary on 2:6-16).

5:13 evil time. Amos had summed up the evil of his day as a lack of justice (5:7, 12, 15) and here says that the prudent should remain quiet during such times, perhaps in keeping with the advice of Hebrew wisdom tradition ("a time to be quiet," Eccl 3:7).

5:14 helper. Lit., "the LORD God of Heaven's Armies will be with you." The expression alludes to the language of the covenant "adoption formula"—"I will be your God and you will be my people" (cf. Jer 31:33). The reference to God's presence with his people may be an allusion to the refrain, "the LORD of Heaven's Armies is here among us," part of the poetic affirmation that God is Israel's helper (Ps 46:7, 11).

5:15 *hate evil . . . love what is good.* See note on 5:4.

mercy. This is the only time Amos used the word *khanan* [TH2603, ZH2858] (mercy). This verb means "show favor, be gracious" and usually occurs with God as the subject (cf. NIDOTTE 2.203-206). The prophet had hope that perhaps God would show mercy to the people who remained because that is an aspect of his character—he has the capacity to show mercy to anyone he chooses (Exod 33:19).

5:16 *professional mourners.* Lit., "the ones who know lamenting" (*yod'e nehi* [TH3045/5092, ZH3359/5631]). Jeremiah mentions "the women who mourn" (Jer 9:17), professionals paid by families to mourn at funerals and other catastrophic events like plagues and wars. See S. M. Paul 1971:179-180 on the guilds of professional mourners in the biblical world.

5:17 *wailing.* The noun *misped* [TH4553, ZH5027] (wailing) is repeated three times in 5:16-17. The emphasis on mourning is an ominous foreboding of the impending destruction of the Hebrew northern kingdom. S. M. Paul (1971:178) has noted that this message from Amos (5:1-17) begins as it ends—with "the tones and sounds of lamentation."

COMMENTARY

The oracle addressed to the people of Israel (5:1-17) is the third of five messages delivered by Amos that comprise the middle section of the book (chs 3-6). Andersen and Freedman analyze chapters 5-6 as a distinct "book" of prophecy— the "Book of Woes." They summarize that the theme of the middle section of the book of Amos is one of woe rather than doom, warning rather than certain judg- ment—"the prophet still has hope that repentance might avert the final catastro- phe" (1989:461). Others recognize the woe oracles as an indication that God has firmly determined to destroy the nation of Israel since the prediction of future judg- ment "is treated as a judgment already executed" (Mays 1969:84; cf. Van Gemeren 1990:132). According to this view, Amos invites the people of Israel to their own funeral because they are already as good as dead as far as God's judgment is con- cerned (cf. Jeremias 1998:85). One may mediate the two poles of understanding by recognizing that the woe oracles or laments serve both to announce the certain doom of the nation as a whole and to warn individuals to heed the call to seek God in repentance. As G. Smith (2001:312) appropriately observes: "The prophet's pur- pose is to convince the nation that things are so bad that God will soon bury its memory, but in the process he persuades a few responsive people to seek God and live."

Wendland is among those scholars who understand a major break in the literary structure of chapters 5 and 6 with the interjection "woe" (*hoy* [TH1945, ZH2098]) and the introduction of the woe oracles proper (5:18; 6:1). In fact, Wendland (1988:14) identifies chiastic features in this rhetorical unit and analyzes the message of 5:1-17 as "the structural-thematic center of Amos." He then proceeds to isolate the hymn fragment (5:8-9) as the centerpiece of the section, flanked by the speech-acts of lam- entation, exhortation, and accusation arranged in an inverted pattern. Of special interest to our study is the hymn fragment (5:8-9), "which sets forth the nature of the God of Israel" (Smith and Page 1995:96).

First, Amos's hymn fragment celebrates God as creator by acknowledging the stars as his handiwork (5:8a). Implicit in this testimony is God's majesty and power. Oden (1998:66-67) views those attributes of God that display his way of being present to, knowing, and influencing the world of creation as intrinsic qualities of the divine majesty. These intrinsic qualities include God's omnipresence, omniscience, and omnipotence. Amos recognized that God is everywhere in all the heavens and earth (Jer 23:24; cf. Acts 17:28); that God knows the end from the beginning (Isa 46:9-10; cf. Rom 11:33-34); and that God is all-powerful—nothing is too hard for him (Jer 32:17; cf. Matt 28:18).

Second, Amos understood that it is God who brings order to creation and to life (5:8b and c). The biblical Creation account depicts a God who brings order out of chaos by his very word (Gen 1-2; cf. Ps 33:6). The unfathomable wisdom behind the design and order of creation is personified as a master architect (Prov 8:30), and his handiwork in the natural world is obvious (Ps 19:1-4). Much like the story of Job, in which the challenge to divine justice is met by God's appeal to his own activity in ordering the universe (Job 38-41), so Amos appeals to God as creator in his preaching about divine justice.

Third, no human achievement is beyond God's destructive power (5:9). The story of the tower of Babel illustrates this truth in a literary fashion, with God intervening to topple the monument built to exalt "human greatness" (Gen 11:4). The history of the nation of Edom is another example of God bringing low the proud, rooting them out of their seemingly impenetrable rock fortresses (Jer 49:15-16; cf. Obad 1:3). Hubbard (1989:171) comments, "once again (cf. 1:4; 3:9, 11; 4:3), Amos acknowledges God's special enmity against the human arrogance that thinks itself impregnable to divine judgment." This is why the psalmist admonishes us not to trust in puny human strength or flawed human ingenuity (Ps 147:10; cf. Ps 33:16-17), but rather to affirm God as our strength and fortress (Pss 18:1; 46:1; cf. Jer 16:19).

In summarizing the theology of the hymn fragments in Amos (4:13; 5:8-9; 9:5-6), Andersen and Freedman (1989:490) state, "they celebrate his limitless, terrifying power, his control of the elements and forces in his creation, and his continued supervision and deployment of these agencies and forces. The most ominous threat of all is that every aspect of creation can be canceled, the work reversed and undone."

We must take note of one final theological tenet that encases the hymn fragment (5:8-9) in this portion of Amos's message to the people of Israel (5:1-17). Three times the prophet exhorts his audience to "come back to the LORD and live" (5:4, 6, 14). We have already established the relationship the Bible develops between "life" and "God" (see notes on 5:4). But this relationship between life and God naturally prompts a follow-up question: What does it mean for God to be "a living God"?

The title "living God" is applied to the Godhead in both the Old Testament and the New Testament (Josh 3:10; 1 Sam 17:36; Jer 10:10; Heb 12:22; Rev 7:2). Likewise the people of God in both testaments are known as those who belong to the "living God" (Dan 6:20; Hos 1:10; 2 Cor 6:16; 1 Tim 3:15). According to Oden (1998:65), the divine tetragrammaton (*yhwh* [TH3068, ZH3378], "I am") "points awesomely to God's incomparable aliveness." The reality of this dynamic, eternal, underived life-energy of God's being means the Godhead cannot be represented by static images, idols of gold, silver, stone, and wood (Ps 115:2-8). In fact, "idols do not live, except in the imagination of death-bound mortals" (cf. Jer 10:10-11; Oden 1998:64). For this reason, the Old Testament prophets mock the gods who cannot see, hear, or act, as well as those who worship and seek help from the inert images they themselves have fashioned (cf. Isa 44:6-20; 46:5-7; Hab 2:18-20).

◆   D. How Terrible for Those Anxious for the Day of the Lord (5:18-27)

18 What sorrow awaits you who say,
   "If only the day of the LORD were
      here!"
You have no idea what you are
      wishing for.
That day will bring darkness,
   not light.
19 In that day you will be like a man
      who runs from a lion—
   only to meet a bear.
Escaping from the bear, he leans his
      hand against a wall in his house—
   and he's bitten by a snake.
20 Yes, the day of the LORD will be dark
      and hopeless,
   without a ray of joy or hope.

21 "I hate all your show and pretense—
   the hypocrisy of your religious
      festivals and solemn assemblies.

22 I will not accept your burnt offerings
      and grain offerings.
   I won't even notice all your choice
      peace offerings.
23 Away with your noisy hymns of praise!
   I will not listen to the music of your
      harps.
24 Instead, I want to see a mighty flood
      of justice,
   an endless river of righteous living.

25 "Was it to me you were bringing sacrifices and offerings during the forty years in the wilderness, Israel? 26 No, you served your pagan gods—Sakkuth your king god and Kaiwan your star god—the images you made for yourselves. 27 So I will send you into exile, to a land east of Damascus,*" says the LORD, whose name is the God of Heaven's Armies.

5:26-27 Greek version reads *No, you carried your pagan gods—the shrine of Molech, the star of your god Rephan, and the images you made for yourselves. So I will send you into exile, to a land east of Damascus.* Compare Acts 7:43.

NOTES

5:18 *What sorrow.* The repetition of the Hebrew interjection *hoy* [TH1945, ZH2098] (woe) in 5:18 and 6:1 marks 5:18-27 as a distinct rhetorical unit. Three different sources have been suggested as the background for the literary form of the woe oracle: the curse of the prophetic judgment speech, the funeral lament, and the instruction of the Hebrew wisdom tradition (perhaps as a foil to the term "blessed"). The most likely source for the woe oracle is the funeral lament, suggesting that the recipients of the woe oracle(s) are dead already (cf. G. Smith 2001:323). Often the woe oracle signifies a divine curse that precludes any further opportunity for repentance, so it seems best to understand the literary form as a variation of the prophetic judgment-speech (cf. Westermann 1991:189-194). Amos seems to blend the message of doom characterized by the woe oracle with the warning of the judgment-speech calling for repentance by both announcing the certainty of Israel's destruction (3:12-15; 4:12; 5:16-17) and offering some glimmer of hope for any remnant of Israel who repent and renew covenant relationship with Yahweh in the aftermath of divine judgment (5:4, 6, 15). Jesus used the woe oracle as a form of prophetic judgment-speech against the Pharisees (Matt 23).

day of the LORD. The phrase refers to the "eschatological day" of divine intervention in history that brings both judgment of the wicked and deliverance and restoration of the righteous. It is a day of cosmic upheaval and reversal, a day of theophany (an appearance of the Lord) and holy war against the pagan nations. The "day of the LORD" is an indefinite period of time of divine activity, but always an impending event. Amos is the earliest prophet that the OT records using the expression "day of the LORD" (*yom yhwh* [TH3117/3068, ZH3427/3378]); see the discussion in S. M. Paul 1971:182-184. He cursed those Hebrews who longed for the day of Yahweh because they assumed it was a day of deliverance and blessing for the people of God (5:18-20). It is clear from the teaching of later Hebrew prophets that the day of the Lord was also one of testing and purification for the righteous as well (cf. Joel 2:1-11; Zech 14:1-3; Mal 3:1-5).

darkness . . . light. The day of the Lord will be the exact opposite of what the people of Israel were wishing would happen. Hubbard (1989:179) notes that here the contrast of light and darkness is not one of righteousness versus wickedness but of safety versus disaster.

5:19 *lion . . . bear . . . snake.* The prophet's nightmarish parable conveys the certain fact that coming disaster is inescapable.

5:21 *hate.* The word *sane'* [TH8130, ZH8533] (hate) has the sense of "despise" or "reject" in covenantal contexts such as this. The word is the antonym of the verb "to love" (*'ahab* [TH157, ZH170]). The two terms are used as a polar word-pair in OT legal and prophetic texts (e.g., 5:15; Deut 7:9-10). The expression "hate" describes the "formal renunciation or severance of a relationship" (Andersen and Freedman 1989:525).

5:22 *burnt offerings.* This type of sacrifice (*'olah* [TH5930, ZH6592]) was a sin offering in which the entire animal was consumed by fire upon the altar (Lev 1). It symbolized total homage to God and was intended to effect atonement for personal sin (Lev 1:3-4).

grain offerings. This type of sacrifice (*minkhah* [TH4503, ZH4966], "gift") was a gift of cereal or meal presented as a general thank-offering for the firstfruits of the soil (Lev 2).

peace offerings. This type of sacrifice (*shelem* [TH8002, ZH8968]) required the offering of an animal, portions of which were shared in a fellowship meal by the priest and the family of the worshiper as a symbol of their devotion to God and communion with one another (Lev 3).

5:23 *hymns of praise.* Singing was essential to Hebrew worship (see Stuart 1987:354-355). Songs of praise to God sung by worshipers who engaged in various acts of social injustice were only so much "noise" (*hamon* [TH1995, ZH2162], "acoustic din, dissonance") to God.

harps. The "harp" (*nebel* [TH5035A, ZH5575]) was commonly associated with the music that accompanied Hebrew worship (cf. 1 Chr 13:8; 15:16; 25:1). According to Hubbard (1989:182), "the precise size and structure of the harp we cannot tell. It may have had a curved yoke with a bulging, jar-like sound-chamber."

5:24 *justice . . . righteous living.* According to Hubbard (1989:168), the terms "justice" (*mishpat* [TH4941, ZH5477]) and "righteousness" (*tsedaqah* [TH6666, ZH7407]) "have to do with covenantal responsibilities, and are close to being synonymous . . . justice puts some slight emphasis on establishing and preserving order in society by righting wrongs and punishing wrong-doers, while *righteousness* emphasizes the relationships that covenantal society entails and insists that each partner in the covenant do all that is necessary to keep the covenant working right." See notes on 5:7.

5:25 *forty years in the wilderness.* This is the second reference to the desert experience of the Hebrews following the Exodus (cf. 2:10). The period of Israelite wilderness wanderings after their deliverance from slavery in Egypt is sometimes portrayed as the ideal expression of covenant relationship between Yahweh and Israel (cf. Jer 2:1-3). Smith and Page (1995:114-116) suggest, however, that the idolatry rebuked by Amos was a problem for the Hebrews in the wilderness as well; this is the view the NLT rendering of 5:25-26 indicates.

5:26 *Sakkuth . . . Kaiwan.* According to Andersen and Freedman (1989:533-534), both names are astral deities and both represent the same celestial body—the planet Saturn. Moses had warned the Israelites against the seductive appeal of such astral worship, prevalent among the people groups of the ancient Near East (Deut 4:19). The passage demonstrates that the idolatry of Mesopotamia had infiltrated the religious life of Israel (cf. Hubbard 1989:185-186).

5:27 *exile.* See note on 5:5.

Damascus. The Assyrian empire (responsible for the exile of the Hebrew northern kingdom of Israel; cf. 2 Kgs 17:5-23) was located east of Damascus.

COMMENTARY

The apostle John wrote that "God is love" (1 John 4:16). That God is love implies that he consistently acts with benevolence, goodwill, and compassion in response to his creation. God's love is supremely demonstrated in the Christ-event: "This is real love—not that we loved God, but that he loved us and sent his Son as a sacrifice to take away our sins" (1 John 4:10). "Consequently love is of all terms the one most directly attributable to God as essential to God's being" (Oden 1998:118).

The word "hate" (5:21) is a harsh term, especially when used of God's response to the human beings he created. The fact that "God is holy" (Ps 99:9; Isa 6:3), however, means that divine "hate" is the necessary corollary of divine love (cf. TDOT 1.102). E. Jacob (1958:90) discerns that as a result of the unity of the Godhead, both Yahweh's love and hate issue from his holiness—so much so that "the entire history of Israel is the work of [God's] holiness." Both are absolute and unconditional, in the sense that God does not love or hate by degrees—it is a matter of love or no love, hate or no hate. For this reason God hates evil and evildoers (Pss 5:5; 31:6). He has also vowed to punish all who oppose him in their wickedness, whether the nations (Pss 7:8; 94:10; Jer 25:15-16) or his own people Israel (5:15; Zech 7:13-14).

The covenant context of Amos's message indicates that God's "hatred" of Israel's worship (5:21) is to be understood as divine rejection. The word "hate" depicts "the hostility of a broken covenant relationship" (Andersen and Freedman 1989:545). By virtue of their idolatry (5:5-6), Israel's worship lacked the character and integrity worthy of the Lord who created the stars (5:8). God had no choice but to reject their insincere and duplicitous worship as "hypocrisy" (5:21). The lesson in all this, now as then, is that God is faithful to the relationships he establishes and he expects the same from those bound to him in covenant trust. God hates betrayal of any kind, whether in human relationships like marriage (God hates divorce, Mal 2:16) or in the spiritual relationship of redeemed creatures responding in worship to their Redeemer (5:21-23). The faithlessness of such betrayal is antithetical to the nature and character of God, who is ever faithful to his covenant word (Exod 34:6; Pss 25:10; 40:11).

Yahweh's rejection of hypocritical worship is not peculiar to the message of Amos. For example, the prophet Isaiah decried the worship of Judah as "meaningless" and "false" (Isa 1:11-17), and Malachi wished that the Temple doors might be boarded up rather than have the people offer their contemptible sacrifices to God (Mal 1:10). Nor is the message of hypocritical worship restricted to the old covenant, given Paul's stern warning that the Christian "cannot drink from the cup of the Lord and from the cup of demons" (1 Cor 10:21). In light of Amos's message, then, John's admonition is all the more germane: "dear children, keep away from anything that might take God's place in your hearts" (1 John 5:21; cf. TNIV, "Dear children, keep yourselves from idols"). M. J. Dawn (1995:41-56) aptly reminds us that idolatry need not be restricted to carved images of metal or stone or wood, but includes "contemporary idolatries" such as the god of efficiency, the god of choice, the idolatry of money, the idolatry of complacency, the idolatry of famous people, the god of competition, the idolatry of success, and the idolatry of power.

◆   ## E. How Terrible for Those Who Lounge in Jerusalem and Samaria (6:1-14)

¹What sorrow awaits you who lounge
  in luxury in Jerusalem,*
and you who feel secure in Samaria!
You are famous and popular in Israel,
  and people go to you for help.
²But go over to Calneh
  and see what happened there.
Then go to the great city of Hamath
  and down to the Philistine city of
    Gath.
You are no better than they were,
  and look at how they were
    destroyed.
³You push away every thought of
    coming disaster,
  but your actions only bring the day
    of judgment closer.
⁴How terrible for you who sprawl on
    ivory beds
  and lounge on your couches,
eating the meat of tender lambs from
    the flock
  and of choice calves fattened in
    the stall.

⁵You sing trivial songs to the sound
    of the harp
  and fancy yourselves to be great
    musicians like David.
⁶You drink wine by the bowlful
  and perfume yourselves with
    fragrant lotions.
You care nothing about the ruin
  of your nation.*
⁷Therefore, you will be the first to be
    led away as captives.
  Suddenly, all your parties will end.

⁸The Sovereign LORD has sworn by his own name, and this is what he, the LORD God of Heaven's Armies, says:

"I despise the arrogance of Israel,*
  and I hate their fortresses.
I will give this city
  and everything in it to their
    enemies."

(⁹If there are ten men left in one house, they will all die. ¹⁰And when a relative

who is responsible to dispose of the dead*
goes into the house to carry out the bodies, he will ask the last survivor, "Is anyone
else with you?" When the person begins
to swear, "No, by . . . ," he will interrupt
and say, "Stop! Don't even mention the
name of the LORD.")

¹¹ When the LORD gives the command,
   homes both great and small will be
      smashed to pieces.

¹² Can horses gallop over boulders?
   Can oxen be used to plow them?
   But that's how foolish you are when
      you turn justice into poison

and the sweet fruit of righteousness
   into bitterness.
¹³ And you brag about your conquest of
   Lo-debar.*
   You boast, "Didn't we take Karnaim*
      by our own strength?"

¹⁴ "O people of Israel, I am about to bring
   an enemy nation against you,"
   says the LORD God of Heaven's
      Armies.
"They will oppress you throughout
   your land—
   from Lebo-hamath in the north
   to the Arabah Valley in the south."

6:1 Hebrew *in Zion.*   6:6 Hebrew *of Joseph.*   6:8 Hebrew *Jacob.* See note on 3:13.   6:10 Or *to burn the dead.*
The meaning of the Hebrew is uncertain.   6:13a *Lo-debar* means "nothing."   6:13b *Karnaim* means "horns,"
a term that symbolizes strength.

NOTES

6:1 *What sorrow.* The interjection (*hoy* [TH1945, ZH2098]) continues the woe oracles begun
in 5:18. (See note on 5:18.)

Jerusalem . . . Samaria. The capital cities of the Hebrew kingdoms of Judah and Israel
respectively. (See notes on 2:5 and 3:9.)

6:2 *Calneh.* An Aramean city-state, probably the Kullani of Assyrian records, located some
eight miles northwest of Aleppo in Syria (cf. Calno, Isa 10:9; Canneh, Ezek 27:23).

Hamath. A fortress city on the Orontes River located on one of the southern trade routes
from Asia Minor (modern-day Hama in Syria). Hamath was considered the northern
boundary of Israel (according to Num 13:21; Josh 13:5). Calneh and Hamath were Aramean city-states under Israelite control, perhaps as a result of Jeroboam II's northern
campaign (2 Kgs 14:28). The two cities are sometimes mentioned together since they
were the major cities of eastern Aram or Syria (cf. Isa 10:9).

Gath. One of the five principal city-states of the Philistines, located nine miles east of
Ashdod and six miles south of Ekron.

6:5 *trivial songs.* The prophet condemned vain entertainment and the lavish use of wine
and perfumes (6:6) as symptomatic of self-interest that compromised national interests.

6:8 *sworn by his own name.* This divine oath is an unusually strong introduction to a
judgment oracle. The expression may be rendered "by his own life" (*nepesh* [TH5315, ZH5883])
and signifies the certainty of Yahweh's judgment—he "will stake his very life on the fulfillment of this deadly promise" (Hubbard 1989:195).

6:10 *dispose of the dead.* Or, "to burn the dead" (so NLT mg). The expression proves difficult because the ancient Israelites did not practice cremation, an act Amos condemned
earlier (cf. 2:1). Burning was reserved for notorious criminals or cases of plague (e.g., Lev
20:14; 21:9; 1 Sam 31:12). On a more pragmatic note, however, the burning of corpses in
the aftermath of military campaigns may have been practiced both to simply deal with
the number of dead and to effectively address the potential threat of disease and plague
after such a catastrophic event. The LXX emends the text and translates "and they will
strenuously exert themselves to carry their bones from the house." English versions have
attempted to solve the problem with suggested readings like "the one who anoints him for

burial" (ESV); "embalmer" (NEB); "undertaker" (NASB); or omitting the phrase altogether (so NJB). Hubbard's (1989:197) solution to read the word in question (*mesarepo*; from *sarap* [TH5635, ZH6251]) as a synonym of "close relative" (*dod* [TH1730, ZH1856]) is a reasonable alternative: "And when a person's near relative, whether on his father's side or his mother's side, shall carry him to bring his corpse out of the house." The NLT interprets the clause "to burn the dead" to refer more broadly to the task of "disposing" of the large number of corpses left in the wake of the enemy invasion.

the bodies. Lit., "bones" (*'atsamim* [TH6106, ZH6795]), here understood as corpses.

6:11 *homes both great and small.* Perhaps a reference to the "winter mansions" and "summer houses" mentioned previously by the prophet (cf. 3:15).

6:12 *Can horses gallop over boulders? Can oxen be used to plow them?* The rhetorical questions serve as an analogy for Israel on the principle of reductio ad absurdum, because their "actions are completely the opposite of what is proper" (Stuart 1987:364).

6:13 *Lo-debar.* A border town in Gilead (between the tribes of Gad and East Manasseh) located east of the Jordan River and south of the Sea of Galilee (although the site has not been identified with certainty).

Karnaim. A Transjordan city and regional center for the Arameans that was located about halfway between Samaria and Damascus. Along with Lo-debar the city was probably reclaimed from the Arameans by Jeroboam II (2 Kgs 14:28). Amos mocked Israel's pride in its military accomplishments by punning, choosing the sites of Lo-debar (meaning "nothing") and Karnaim (meaning "double-horned" or "doubly strong"). These supposed "trophies" were really of "no consequence at all" (Hubbard 1989:199).

6:14 *enemy nation.* Though unnamed, there is little doubt that Amos had the nation of Assyria in mind (cf. 5:27).

Lebo-hamath. Lit., "the entrance to Hamath." Probably the southern boundary of the territory controlled by the city-state of Hamath (recognized as the northern boundary of Canaan in Num 13:21; 34:8).

Arabah Valley. Possibly a reference to the Wadi Arabah or the Wadi Qelt. The Arabah Valley generally is the Jordan River valley between the Sea of Galilee in the north to the Dead Sea, and on to the Gulf of Aqaba in the south. Taken together the two sites, Lebo-Hamath and the southern Arabah, represented the northern and southern boundaries of the kingdom of Israel (cf. 2 Kgs 14:25), thus emphasizing the total defeat of the nation (Stuart 1987:365).

COMMENTARY

The interjection "What sorrow" or "Woe" (*hoy* [TH1945, ZH2098]) marks the beginning of three rhetorical units (5:18-27; 6:1-3; 6:4-14). The two so-called "woe oracles" against Israel (5:18-27 and 6:1-14) complete the five messages of Amos that comprise the middle portion of the book (chs 3–6). The characteristic features of the woe-cry are found in Amos, including the interjection of woe (e.g., 6:1), verbs in participle form describing God's grievances (e.g., 6:3-4), and the word of divine judgment (e.g., 6:7). The woe-cry is a harsh form of prophetic speech and indicates that while individuals may yet respond to the threat of divine punishment by turning to God in repentance, Yahweh's judgment against the nation is irrevocable.

The oracle addressed to the people of Israel (5:1-17) is the third of five messages delivered by Amos that comprise the middle section of the book (chs 3–6). Whether one understands this middle section of the book as one of woe and warning rather than doom and judgment (see commentary on 5:1-17), the situation for the northern kingdom of Israel is dire. The prophet's sense of urgency arises from his awareness that the critically ill "patient" is about to have the life-support system "removed."

Amos's denouncement of the "arrogant" (6:8) suggests that he was familiar with Hebrew wisdom tradition. His theological understanding was informed by precepts that taught that God despises and punishes the proud (Prov 15:25; 16:5). The psalmist lamented the seeming injustice of the proud boasting of their oppression of the poor and God's apparent unresponsiveness to the plight of the helpless (Ps 10:2-4). Yet in the end, the psalmist also knew that God would rescue the humble and humiliate the proud (Ps 18:27). The other Old Testament prophets echo this same theme of divine judgment against the proud (e.g., Isa 2:12; Jer 13:9, 17; Ezek 7:11).

But not only does God resist and destroy the proud, he shows favor to the humble (Prov 3:34). This is a word of great hope for the righteous in the Old Testament because the humble will see their God at work and be glad (Ps 69:32), and he will crown the humble with salvation (Ps 149:4). The New Testament affirms that these same truths are to inform our relationships with God and each other in the church of Jesus Christ (1 Pet 5:6). All of this is in keeping with the instruction of Jesus, who came with the humility of a servant (Matt 11:29) and taught that "those who exalt themselves will be humbled, and those who humble themselves will be exalted" (Luke 14:11).

◆ V. Visions of Judgment (7:1–9:10)
A. Three Visions: The Plague of Locusts, Devouring Fire, and the Lord's Plumb Line (7:1–9)

The Sovereign LORD showed me a vision. I saw him preparing to send a vast swarm of locusts over the land. This was after the king's share had been harvested from the fields and as the main crop was coming up. ²In my vision the locusts ate every green plant in sight. Then I said, "O Sovereign LORD, please forgive us or we will not survive, for Israel* is so small."

³So the LORD relented from this plan. "I will not do it," he said.

⁴Then the Sovereign LORD showed me another vision. I saw him preparing to punish his people with a great fire. The fire had burned up the depths of the sea and was devouring the entire land. ⁵Then I said, "O Sovereign LORD, please stop or we will not survive, for Israel is so small."

⁶Then the LORD relented from this plan, too. "I will not do that either," said the Sovereign LORD.

⁷Then he showed me another vision. I saw the Lord standing beside a wall that had been built using a plumb line. He was using a plumb line to see if it was still straight. ⁸And the LORD said to me, "Amos, what do you see?"

I answered, "A plumb line."

And the Lord replied, "I will test my people with this plumb line. I will no longer ignore all their sins. ⁹The pagan shrines of your ancestors* will be ruined, and the temples of Israel will be destroyed; I will bring the dynasty of King Jeroboam to a sudden end."

7:2 Hebrew *Jacob;* also in 7:5. See note on 3:13.   7:9 Hebrew *of Isaac.*

NOTES

7:1 *showed me a vision.* This form (a hiphil perfect) of the verb (*ra'ah* [TH7200, ZH8011]) means, lit., "cause to see" or "reveal." In prophetic literature it is a technical word signifying a vision or revelation from God. Hubbard (1989:201) reminds us that the prophetic vision was both a visual and auditory experience; thus the report of the prophet's dialogue with Yahweh is also part of the visionary encounter; (see note on 1:1). The emphasis is not on Amos or his message (since no direction is given to the prophet). Rather, the emphasis is on the Lord and his prerogative to initiate divine punishment because it is he who forms the locust swarm and reveals the future to his servants the prophets (Ps 105:34; Isa 42:8-9). Though not translated in the NLT, the exclamatory adverb "Look!" or "Behold" (*hinneh* [TH2009, ZH2180]) introduces four of the five visions in this section of the book (7:1, 4, 7; 8:1). This, the presentative exclamation, "is intended to attract attention, to interrupt the line of dialogue, and to alert the reader that something important is about to be communicated" (Andersen and Freedman 1989:613).

locusts. This specific word for "locust" (*gobay* [TH1462A, ZH1479]) occurs only in Amos 7:1 and Nah 3:17.

king's share. Probably a reference to the first "mowing" of the pasture grasses. Apparently the monarchy had the right to tax the lands of farmers for fodder to feed the royal livestock (so Hubbard 1989:206; cf. 1 Kgs 18:5).

main crop. Lit., "latter growth" or "second crop" (*leqesh* [TH3954, ZH4381]). The word occurs only here in the OT and serves to pinpoint the time of the locust plague at the end of the spring rainy season (cf. Smith and Page 1995:128). The long drought of summer would prevent any further growth of pasture grasses or crops, thereby creating an agricultural disaster for farmers and their livestock.

7:2 *please forgive.* The word (*salakh* [TH5545, ZH6142]) "is used exclusively of God's pardon" (Hubbard 1989:206; cf. Num 14:20; 1 Kgs 8:30; Isa 55:7). Like the psalmist, Amos knew that God is good and is "ready to forgive" (Ps 86:5). The prophet's terse interjection (employing the polite imperative) is not an uncommon address to God in situations of extreme distress (e.g., Pss 3:7; 4:1).

7:3 *relented.* The word (*nakham* [TH5162, ZH5714]) means to have a change of heart or a change of mind (cf. TDOT 9.343-347; see the thorough discussion in Andersen and Freedman 1989:638-679; see also the commentary below).

7:4 *fire.* At times in prophetic literature, fire is a metaphor for God's anger and symbolic of his divine judgment (e.g., Isa 66:15; Jer 4:4; Ezek 36:5). Contrary to typical use, the prophet Zechariah had a vision of God protecting a restored Jerusalem like a wall of fire (Zech 2:5).

7:7 *plumb line.* Lit., "tin lump" (*'anak* [TH594, ZH643]). The plumb line (a cord with a tin or lead weight attached to one end) was used to establish right-angle verticality in construction (cf. Zech 4:10). Stuart (1987:372-373) considers the repetition of the word *'anak* ("plumb line") in 7:8a as an example of paronomasia or wordplay with *'anak* in 7:8b since he associates the term with the Hebrew root *'nkh* [TH584, ZH634] or *'nq* [TH5008, ZH5543], meaning "to moan, groan." Thus he translates 7:8 as "Yahweh said to me, 'What do you see, Amos?' I said, 'Tin.' [Yahweh] said, 'I am going to put tin [moaning] with my people Israel. I will no longer pass by him.'"

7:9 *pagan shrines.* This expression (*bamoth* [TH1116, ZH1195], "high places") denotes sites used for religious purposes, often located on a hill or some sort of raised, earthen or stone platform. Typically these sites were devoted to local Canaanite deities or to syncretistic worship and "they were subject to the severest censure by the prophets" (NIDOTTE 1.670; cf. Jer 17:3; 19:5; Hos 10:8). The destruction of these religious shrines is listed among the curses invoked against Israel for covenant disobedience (Lev 26:30).

ruined. The word (*shamem* [TH8074, ZH9037]) means "to suffer destruction, with the implication of being deserted and abandoned" (NIDOTTE 4.168). The term is used by the prophets to depict God's judgment of Israel (cf. Jer 12:11; Ezek 6:4; Mic 6:13). Such destruction of Israel's places of worship is invoked in the curses of the Mosaic covenant (Lev 26:31).

temples. The term (*miqdash* [TH4720, ZH5219]) describes a sanctuary or holy place (see further NIDOTTE 2.1078-1087). Amos most likely referred to the rival sanctuaries built at Dan and Bethel by Jeroboam I (1 Kgs 12:25-33).

destroyed. The word (*khareb* [TH2717, ZH2990]) is frequently used by the prophets to describe the devastation of the people, towns, and shrines of Israel and Judah (see Jer 25:9; Ezek 6:6; cf. TDOT 5.152-154).

COMMENTARY

The time at which Amos received the five visions contained in the last section of the book is imprecise. As Craigie (1985:174) has noted, it is uncertain whether the visions provided a portion of the content for the prophet's brief public ministry (it lasted only one day; see "Author" in the Introduction) or if "they were simply a part of his own spiritual development." The accounts of the visions contain references to Amos in the first person, suggesting he recorded them in a diary or perhaps dictated them to a disciple or amanuensis.

The first vision (7:1-3) was a vast swarm of locusts. A locust swarm is a metaphor for divine judgment in prophetic literature (Isa 33:4; Rev 9:7; cf. Exod 10:4). The locust swarm may be understood in the literal sense of a blight of flying or hopping insects that ravage vegetation or in the figurative sense as a symbol for a rapidly growing group or class of people (e.g., Assyrian merchants, Nah 3:17) or as an invading army (e.g., Jer 51:14; Joel 1:4, 6). Since locust plagues were one of the curses God threatened to bring against Israel for covenant disobedience, this may be what Yahweh showed Amos (Deut 28:38).

The second vision (7:4-6) was a great devouring fire. The fire described by Amos may be understood literally, perhaps as ravaging brush fires as a result of extreme drought, or as a symbol for the severe drought (so Smith and Page 1995:131). The locust swarms and wild fire were the two worst enemies of the agricultural societies in the ancient world. The prophet Amos, himself a farmer, "recoiled at the sight" of such devastation (Hubbard 1989:202).

The third vision (7:7-9) was a wall that had been built using a plumb line. Amos saw God symbolically testing or measuring his people against the standard or "plumb" in his second vision. The "wall" (Israel) had been built to plumb (i.e., implicit in the standard of God's righteous law framing his covenant relationship with them, cf. Isa 28:17), but the nation was out of plumb when tested due to their violation of God's covenant stipulations, justifying God's verdict of judgment. Amos no longer interceded for Israel; he could only bear witness to the outcome of the measurement of the plumb line—"Israel's life is too crooked to warrant either pardon or relief" (Hubbard 1989:209).

Hubbard (1989:204) identifies a single dominant theme in the three visions: the sovereignty of Yahweh. God's rule of creation and the nations is symbolized in the divine name that is prominent in the larger literary unit (7:1-2, 4-6; 8:1, 3, 11; 9:8). The epithet "Sovereign LORD" (NLT) could be more literally rendered "My Master Yahweh," thus expressing the intimate connection between Yahweh and the acts of judgment threatened in the visions.

The themes of God's sovereignty and divine judgment have already been introduced in the earlier messages of the prophet (in chs 3–6). The significant theological feature of the visions section of the prophet's message is the revelation that God's sovereignty is "seasoned with compassion" (Hubbard 1989:204). We especially see this in 7:3 and 7:6, where it says "the Lord relented from this plan." As noted before (see note on 7:3), the Hebrew word for "relented" (*nakham* [TH5162, ZH5714]) means to have a change of heart or a change of mind. It also means "to groan inwardly," usually in contexts addressing remorse about something (Niehaus 1992:452). The expression is used several times to describe the idea of the Lord changing his mind about intended punishment (Exod 32:12-14; Jer 18:8; Joel 2:13-14; Jonah 3:10). Achtemeier emphatically affirms that even the threat of divine judgment is an act of love because "it is only when God leaves us alone that he no longer loves us" (1986:180). Rabbi Heschel (1962:194) concurs, noting God's judgment is conditional, not absolute: "a change in man's conduct brings about a change in God's judgment."

Based upon this understanding of God's character, Amos believed God would relent of planned judgment in response to repentance or intercessory prayer. The prophets had a special duty to intercede on behalf of the people they served, and they stood in a long biblical tradition of intercessory prayer (e.g., Abraham, Gen 18:16ff; Moses, Num 11:2; 21:7; Deut 9:20, 26). Israel's history had demonstrated that God is not so static or rigid or uncaring that he cannot respond to "human factors" in any given situation with gracious compassion (Exod 34:6-7; cf. NIDOTTE 3.82). As a result of Amos's pleading, God relented of the judgment he had planned to unleash on Israel in the first two visions (7:3, 6).

The precedent for such an appeal to God's compassion is found in Abraham's intercession for Sodom (Gen 18:22-32) and Moses's pleading for the people of Israel after the golden calf episode (Exod 32:11-14). Andersen and Freedman conclude that Yahweh's capacity to relent is rooted in the personal nature of his being and is never capricious or arbitrary. Rather, "repentance" on God's part may occur in reaction to certain events or developments in the human scene, in response to intercession on the part of a prophetic figure, or in response to genuine repentance on the part of people (cf. Andersen and Freedman 1989:638-679). The lesson in all this is constant across the testaments: The prayer of the righteous is indeed effective (cf. Joel 2:13-14; Jas 5:16).

◆ **B. Interlude: Amaziah Challenges Amos (7:10-17)**

¹⁰Then Amaziah, the priest of Bethel, sent a message to Jeroboam, king of Israel: "Amos is hatching a plot against you right here on your very doorstep! What he is saying is intolerable. ¹¹He is saying, 'Jeroboam will soon be killed, and the people of Israel will be sent away into exile.'"

¹²Then Amaziah sent orders to Amos:

"Get out of here, you prophet! Go on back to the land of Judah, and earn your living by prophesying there! ¹³Don't bother us with your prophecies here in Bethel. This is the king's sanctuary and the national place of worship!"

¹⁴But Amos replied, "I'm not a professional prophet, and I was never trained to be one.* I'm just a shepherd, and I take care of sycamore-fig trees. ¹⁵But the LORD called me away from my flock and told me, 'Go and prophesy to my people in Israel.' ¹⁶Now then, listen to this message from the LORD:

"You say,
'Don't prophesy against Israel.
    Stop preaching against my people.*'
¹⁷But this is what the LORD says:
'Your wife will become a prostitute
    in this city,
and your sons and daughters will
    be killed.
Your land will be divided up,
    and you yourself will die in a foreign
    land.
And the people of Israel will certainly
    become captives in exile,
    far from their homeland.'"

7:14 Or *I'm not a prophet nor the son of a prophet.*   7:16 Hebrew *against the house of Isaac.*

NOTES

7:10 *Amaziah, the priest of Bethel.* The title is unique and indicates Amaziah was the ruling priest among the priests assigned to the shrine in Bethel. His role as the head or chief priest at Bethel is further supported by his action to send a message (presumably an official letter) to King Jeroboam. It is unclear whether Amaziah was a Levite or a descendant from among the non-levitical priests Jeroboam I appointed to serve the shrines of the northern kingdom (cf. 1 Kgs 12:31). Other than his position as priest and his loyalty to Jeroboam, nothing else is known of Amaziah.

Jeroboam. Jeroboam II ruled Israel from c. 793–753 BC. He brought economic prosperity and political stability to the northern Hebrew kingdom and expanded Israel's borders by means of several successful military campaigns.

7:11 *Jeroboam.* The king's name in this context represents his dynasty or "house," as in 7:9.

7:12 *prophet.* Amaziah literally called Amos a "seer" (*khozeh* [TH2374, ZH2602]), perhaps in conjunction with the visions of judgment he saw and explained to his audience.

7:13 *king's sanctuary and the national place of worship.* Amaziah employed hendiadys to describe the shrine at Bethel as a "state temple." Amaziah's self-interest is obviously reflected in his description of Bethel as an official religious site. According to Stuart (1987:376), "the high priest of a sanctuary was its administrator; Amaziah thus in effect claimed governmental authority to dismiss Amos."

COMMENTARY

The prose interlude of 7:10-17 is unique in the book and provides us with the only clear details of the historical setting and personal encounters of Amos's ministry. The exchange between Amos and Amaziah was triggered by the prophet's judgment against the dynasty of Jeroboam II (7:9). Amaziah, the chief priest of the Bethel shrine, accused Amos of conspiracy and banished him from Bethel. Amos countered by pronouncing a curse on Amaziah and his family (7:17).

Theologically, the narrative serves to confirm the accuracy of the impending divine judgment seen in Amos's third vision (the plumb line, 7:7-9). The report both explains the circumstance prompting the oracle against Amaziah (7:16-17) and anticipates the tone and theme of the fourth vision (the destruction and exile of

Israel, 8:1-14). In a way, the curse against Amaziah foreshadows the divine judgment in store for the nation of Israel.

The report of the confrontation between Amos and Amaziah reminds us that "there is no service of God without opposition, persecution, and trial" (Motyer 1974:170). Inevitably, the call of God to the office of prophet was a commission involving testing and suffering. Elijah was labeled a "troublemaker" for preaching against idolatry and calling Israel to repentance (1 Kgs 18:17). Isaiah's words of judgment were like a sharp sword and his message like an arrow (Isa 49:2). Amos's words against the kingdom of Israel had a similar impact on Amaziah the priest.

Amaziah chided Amos as being a prophet for hire (or a bribed messenger) and thus one who could easily be dismissed as a false prophet (cf. Mic 3:5, 11). But Amos responded, "I am not a prophet nor am I the son of a prophet" (a literal translation of 7:14). Amos refuted Amaziah's charge that he belonged to a prophetic guild by denying any connection with formal prophetic tradition whether by birth or education (cf. 2 Kgs 2:3, 5; 4:38; 6:1 on the groups or "schools" of prophets located at Bethel, Gilgal, and Jericho during the days of Elijah and Elisha). The biblical record suggests that both the kings of Judah and Israel included "prophets" on the royal payroll to ensure oracles favorable to the dynasty's family and political policies (cf. 1 Kgs 22:6-8; Jer 14:14-15, 18; Ezek 13:10, 16; Mic 3:5, 11). Amos was not one of these prophets; rather, he was a true prophet of God sent to proclaim the truth he received from God, no matter the consequences.

Motyer (1974:174-175) rightly observes that the word of God is "the divider"—either a word accepted or a word rejected. Jesus came into the world bringing this same sharp sword, one that forces the hearer to declare one's loyalties either for or against Jesus Christ (Matt 10:34-39). Since the message declared by the prophets exposes human sin and rebellion against God, the world hates those who proclaim the word of God's truth—even Jesus himself (John 15:18-25; cf. Heb 4:12-13). Although as Christians we will similarly be hated, we are to rejoice in such treatment because these trials make us partners in Christ's suffering and entitle us to share in his glory (1 Pet 4:12-19).

◆   ## C. Fourth Vision: A Vision of Ripe Fruit (8:1-14)

Then the Sovereign LORD showed me another vision. In it I saw a basket filled with ripe fruit. ²"What do you see, Amos?" he asked.

I replied, "A basket full of ripe fruit."

Then the LORD said, "Like this fruit, Israel is ripe for punishment! I will not delay their punishment again. ³In that day the singing in the Temple will turn to wailing. Dead bodies will be scattered everywhere. They will be carried out of the city in silence. I, the Sovereign LORD, have spoken!"

⁴Listen to this, you who rob the poor
     and trample down the needy!
⁵You can't wait for the Sabbath day
     to be over
     and the religious festivals to end
so you can get back to cheating the
     helpless.
You measure out grain with dishonest
     measures

and cheat the buyer with dishonest
scales.*
6 And you mix the grain you sell
with chaff swept from the floor.
Then you enslave poor people
for one piece of silver or a pair of
sandals.

7 Now the LORD has sworn this oath
by his own name, the Pride of
Israel*:
"I will never forget
the wicked things you have done!
8 The earth will tremble for your deeds,
and everyone will mourn.
The ground will rise like the Nile River
at floodtime;
it will heave up, then sink again.

9 "In that day," says the Sovereign LORD,
"I will make the sun go down at noon
and darken the earth while it is still
day.
10 I will turn your celebrations into times
of mourning
and your singing into weeping.
You will wear funeral clothes
and shave your heads to show your
sorrow—
as if your only son had died.
How very bitter that day will be!
11 "The time is surely coming," says the
Sovereign LORD,
"when I will send a famine on the
land—
not a famine of bread or water
but of hearing the words of the
LORD.
12 People will stagger from sea to sea
and wander from border to border*
searching for the word of the LORD,
but they will not find it.
13 Beautiful girls and strong young men
will grow faint in that day,
thirsting for the LORD's word.
14 And those who swear by the shameful
idols of Samaria—
who take oaths in the name of the
god of Dan
and make vows in the name of the
god of Beersheba*—
they will all fall down,
never to rise again."

8:5 Hebrew *You make the ephah* [a unit for measuring grain] *small and the shekel* [a unit of weight] *great, and you deal falsely by using deceitful balances.* 8:7 Hebrew *the pride of Jacob.* See note on 3:13. 8:12 Hebrew *from north to east.* 8:14 Hebrew *the way of Beersheba.*

NOTES

8:1 *showed me another vision.* See note on 7:1.

basket. This was a bushel-shaped harvesting basket most likely made of woven wicker (*kelub* [TH3619, ZH3990]; cf. Jer 5:27 where the rare word refers to a birdcage).

ripe fruit. This word (*qayits* [TH7019, ZH7811]) refers to summer fruit like figs, grapes, and olives that are harvested in early fall.

8:2 *Israel is ripe.* Lit., "the end is coming for my people Israel." Because of the similarities in their sounds and their related etymologies, the word "end" (*qets* [TH7093, ZH7891]) forms a wordplay with the expression "ripe fruit" (*qayits*) in 8:1-2.

8:3 *that day.* See note on "the day of the LORD" in 5:18. The songs of the harvest festival have been replaced by wailing and silence in response to the "harvest" of corpses left behind by the "grim reaping" of the foreign invaders (cf. Lev 23:39-41).

8:5 *Sabbath . . . religious festivals.* Commercial activity was prohibited on the Sabbath and New Moon festivals according to Mosaic law (Exod 35:1-3; Deut 5:13-14).

cheating the helpless . . . dishonest measures . . . dishonest scales. All these corrupt business practices were forbidden by Mosaic law because they perverted justice and fairness, aspects of God's very nature (Lev 19:35-36; Deut 25:13-16; Prov 11:1).

8:6 *enslave poor people.* The prophet condemns the merchants who are buying poor people as slaves by means of their dishonest business practices (v. 5). As a result of mounting debts, the poor were forced to sell themselves or their children to the wealthy merchants to cover their debts (G. Smith 2001:384). Earlier, Amos condemned selling the poor into slavery (cf. 2:6). As Stuart (1987:384) notes, "the poor have a determined protector in Yahweh" (cf. Deut 24:14-15; Ps 82; Isa 11:4).

8:7 *Pride of Israel.* Lit., "the pride of Jacob" (so NLT mg). Here the eponymous ancestor "Jacob" represents the people of Israel. This unusual epithet for God is rooted in the mutual pride shared by Yahweh and the nation of Israel as a result of the relationship created by the Abrahamic and Mosaic covenants (cf. Ps 47:4).

8:8 *rise like the Nile.* The heavy seasonal rains and melting snows at the headwaters of the Nile caused annual flooding of the river in Egypt, as much as 25 feet above its normal level during flood-stage. The point of the prophet's illustration is that, like the rising flood of the Nile River, Israel will be helpless under the "flood" of God's judgment.

8:9 *In that day.* The OT describes the day of the Lord as a time of cosmic upheaval, with ominous celestial signs and the disruption of the natural cycles of light and darkness (cf. Isa 24:23; 34:4; Ezek 32:7-8; Joel 2:10, 31). See note on "the day of the LORD" in 5:18.

8:10 *funeral clothes.* Lit., "every waist will wear sackcloth" (*saq* [TH8242, ZH8566]). The sackcloth garment was a rough cape or loincloth made of dark goat hair and was worn as a symbol of mourning and grief (cf. NIDOTTE 3.1270).

shave your heads. According to Stuart (1987:385), this was "a practice intended to symbolically disfigure and thus show empathy with those in the sad situation of having lost loved ones" (cf. Job 1:20; Jer 41:5).

8:11 *famine . . . of hearing the words of the LORD.* Even more essential than the staples of food and water, which are necessary for physical life, "no one could live without the power and guidance of the divine words" (Hubbard 1989:223-224). Jesus indicated as much when he quoted Deut 8:3 in response to the tempter: "People do not live by bread alone, but by every word that comes from the mouth of God" (Matt 4:4). The "famine of the word of the Lord" calls to mind the bleak days of the Israelite judges when "messages from the LORD were very rare" (1 Sam 3:1). God's judgment by the withdrawal of revelation is a form of "divine abandonment" associated with covenant trespass (cf. Deut 31:17-18; on the motif of divine abandonment, see Block 2001). Even though God's abandonment is "momentary," figuratively speaking (cf. Isa 54:7-8), it is still a frightening prospect to experience this divine rejection—like the one who runs away from a lion only to meet a bear (5:19).

8:12 *sea to sea . . . from border to border.* The expression signifies the totality of the vacuum of God's word in Israel.

8:14 *idols of Samaria.* Lit., "Samaria's shame" (*'ashmath* [TH819, ZH873]), an obvious foil with the "Pride of Israel" in 8:7 and probably refers to the Baal-Asherah idols of the shrines in Samaria.

god of Dan. This is a reference to the golden bull-god worshiped at the shrine in the city of Dan (cf. 1 Kgs 12:25-30; see note on 3:14).

god of Beersheba. Lit., the "way" (*derek* [TH1870, ZH2006]) or the "power" (cf. HALOT 1:232 §7) of Beersheba. It is possible the expression refers to some rite of pilgrimage to a pagan shrine in Beersheba. Hubbard's (1989:225) comment that the epithet "'Beersheba's way' could well be a succinct expression for all that the pilgrimage stood for" is cogent. Dan was the northernmost city in the territory of Israel and Beersheba was the southernmost city of Judah, so Amos makes reference to "the whole circle of gods worshiped everywhere in Israel (and Judah), from Dan to Beer-sheba" (Andersen and Freedman 1989:830).

COMMENTARY

The fourth vision (8:1-3) shown to Amos by the Lord needs no interpretation. The "fruit" is ripe for picking: The fate of Israel is now sealed. The death sentence has been announced and nothing can avert it. Previously, Amos had pleaded with the people to "come back to the LORD and live" (5:6). "Now all he could say was, 'It's too late; you must die.' " (Craigie 1985:182). The cluster of judgment oracles (8:4-14; described as anywhere from three to five distinct speeches depending on the source consulted) following the fourth vision rehearse the earlier indictments levied against Israel and further vindicate Yahweh's decision to punish his people (8:2). God's judgment is as terrifying as it is decisive (cf. 5:18; 6:1, 4). A series of four catastrophes associated with phenomena from the natural world will overtake Israel including earthquake (8:4-8), solar eclipse (8:9-10), famine (8:11-12) and drought (8:13-14). Whether these events are actual natural disasters or symbolize the devastation of the Assyrian onslaught is unclear. The most crushing news in Amos's report is the death of the young (8:13). "They carried the hope for a coming generation, so their deaths would reinforce all the more the death of future hope" (Craigie 1985:187). Andersen and Freedman (1989:802) note that the judgment speeches address social injustice (8:4-6) and religious hypocrisy (8:7-14) and "together they combine the ethical and theological aspects of covenant violation." God is true to his word; he remembers his covenant (Ps 111:5), whether for blessing or for cursing (Deut 30:19).

The several judgment oracles (8:4-14) appended to the fourth vision recall aspects of God's character highlighted in Amos's call to repentance (ch 5). God loves justice (5:24) and hates the callous greed that spawns social injustice and economic oppression (5:10-11, 15). This brings us to an interesting theological observation. According to Motyer (1974:183), there is one thing God cannot do (among others): "he cannot bestow mercy on those who do not show mercy." The prayer Jesus taught his disciples instructs the Christian to forgive those who have sinned against us because God has forgiven our sin in Christ (Matt 6:12). Jesus also told the parable of the servant who forfeited mercy because he failed to show mercy to a fellow servant indebted to him (Matt 18:28-35). God is the source of every mercy (2 Cor 1:3), and Jude's exhortation to show mercy to others is no doubt based on the example of God's mercy to the world in the person of our Lord Jesus Christ (Jude 1:21-23). This can be done only by means of the wisdom that comes from heaven—"full of mercy and good deeds" (Jas 3:17).

The prophetic ministry of Amos to the kingdom of Israel was the culmination of a series of warnings sent by God to the divided monarchies by his prophets and seers (2 Kgs 17:13). As Craigie (1985:182) sadly observes, the destruction of Israel had been determined and fixed by a long history of sin—namely the sin of idolatry (cf. 2 Kgs 17:9-12). God's covenant with Israel at Mount Sinai gave the Hebrew people the choice of life or death, based upon their love for God and obedience to his laws and decrees (Deut 30:19). Failure to choose life by walking in God's ways would result in certain destruction (Deut 30:15, 17-18). Hebrew wisdom tradition applies this general principle broadly to all of life: "There is a path before each person that seems right, but it ends in death" (Prov 14:12).

The New Testament confirms this basic theological understanding of fallen human behavior—evil desires lead to evil actions and evil actions lead to death (Jas 1:15). The Bible only knows two paths: the way of the godly and the way of the wicked (Ps 1:6; or the broad highway to hell and the narrow road to life as taught by Jesus, Matt 7:13-14). The path that leads to life leads to God himself, the source of Israel's life (Ps 68:26). As a result of the Incarnation, the path that leads to life leads to Jesus the Messiah and the triune God of the new covenant (John 1:4; 6:35). What a glorious message of hope for our world, which perpetuates a culture of death!

◆ D. Fifth Vision: A Vision of God at the Altar (9:1-10)

Then I saw a vision of the Lord standing beside the altar. He said,

"Strike the tops of the Temple
  columns,
  so that the foundation will shake.
Bring down the roof
  on the heads of the people below.
I will kill with the sword those who
  survive.
  No one will escape!

2 "Even if they dig down to the place
  of the dead,*
  I will reach down and pull them up.
Even if they climb up into the heavens,
  I will bring them down.
3 Even if they hide at the very top of
  Mount Carmel,
  I will search them out and capture
  them.
Even if they hide at the bottom of the
  ocean,
  I will send the sea serpent after
  them to bite them.
4 Even if their enemies drive them into
  exile,
  I will command the sword to kill
  them there.
I am determined to bring disaster
  upon them
  and not to help them."

5 The Lord, the LORD of Heaven's Armies,
  touches the land and it melts,
  and all its people mourn.

The ground rises like the Nile River
  at floodtime,
  and then it sinks again.
6 The LORD's home reaches up to the
  heavens,
  while its foundation is on the earth.
He draws up water from the oceans
  and pours it down as rain on the
  land.
  The LORD is his name!

7 "Are you Israelites more important
  to me
  than the Ethiopians?*" asks the LORD.
"I brought Israel out of Egypt,
  but I also brought the Philistines
  from Crete*
  and led the Arameans out of Kir.

8 "I, the Sovereign LORD,
  am watching this sinful nation
  of Israel.
I will destroy it
  from the face of the earth.
But I will never completely destroy
  the family of Israel,*"
  says the LORD.
9 "For I will give the command
  and will shake Israel along with
  the other nations
as grain is shaken in a sieve,
  yet not one true kernel will be lost.
10 But all the sinners will die by the
  sword—
  all those who say, 'Nothing bad will
  happen to us.'"

9:2 Hebrew to Sheol. 9:7a Hebrew the Cushites? 9:7b Hebrew Caphtor. 9:8 Hebrew the house of Jacob.
See note on 3:13.

NOTES

9:1 *altar.* Presumably a reference to a sacrificial altar adjoined to the shrine at Bethel. The appearance of the Lord (lit., "master"; *'adonay* [TH136, ZH151]) standing beside the altar signifies that the time for God's visitation in judgment has arrived. "The place where God had desired to meet his people in grace was now the site of his fierce and final judgment" (Hubbard 1989:229).

tops of the Temple columns. The pillar cap or top (*kaptor* [TH3730, ZH4117]) was the capital of a supporting column. The smashing of the support-column tops would cause the entire structure to collapse. The NLT rendering "Temple columns" is interpretive of the Hebrew "strike the pillar top." The context suggests Amos refers to the Bethel sanctuary, but archaeology has uncovered no columned or pillared shrine at the site.

9:2 *place of the dead.* The subterranean realm of the dead or netherworld (*she'ol* [TH7585, ZH8619]), and popularly thought to be outside the sway of God's sovereignty according to Hubbard (1989:230; cf. Job 10:20-22; 14:13). Like the psalmist, Amos knew that God's presence in and control of his creation extended to the domains of both the living and the dead (Ps 139:8).

heavens. The merism of "heaven and hell" speaks to the totality of God's influence and control, "there being no place his sovereignty does not extend" (Stuart 1987:392).

9:3 *Mount Carmel.* A prominent mountain that splits the coastal plain of northern Israel south of Acco. The height, dense forests, and numerous caves made the summit of Mount Carmel a natural hiding place. Yet even the most remote and inaccessible locations will not prevent God from apprehending fugitives from his justice.

sea serpent. The mythical dragon of chaos in ancient Near Eastern cosmology, known by the names of Rahab (Isa 30:7; 51:9) and Leviathan (Ps 74:14; Isa 27:1) in the OT. Escape from Yahweh's judgment is impossible, since even in the remote domain of the ocean bed, the sea monster does his bidding to execute divine judgment (cf. Paul 1971:279).

9:5-6 These two verses are considered a "hymnic doxology of judgment" that glorifies God's majesty and celebrates his absolute power to carry out his threats of judgment against Israel (cf. Paul 1971:279-280; see the notes on the hymn fragments for 4:13 and 5:8-9 above).

9:7 *Ethiopians.* The Nubians or Cushites (*kushiyim* [TH3569, ZH3934]) were black African tribes living south of the second cataract of the Nile, "a distant, relatively obscure people" (Stuart 1987:393).

Philistines from Crete. The reference recalls the migrations of the "sea-peoples" from the Aegean–Mediterranean regions to the coast of Palestine. The name Palestine is a legacy of this Philistine "exodus" from the island of Crete (*kaptor* [TH3731, ZH4116]; cf. Hubbard 1989:233-234).

Arameans out of Kir. The location of Kir is uncertain (on the Arameans or Syrians and the site of Kir see notes on 1:3-5). As Stuart (1987:393) notes, Israel "is merely on par with its hated neighbors" as people groups who had an "exodus" experience caused by God.

9:8 *I will never completely destroy.* God's promise to preserve a segment of his people introduces the remnant theme, prominent in OT prophetic literature. The remnant motif implies both judgment and deliverance, and the very existence of a remnant of Hebrews is based on the mercy of God. Amos applied the remnant motif to three types of groups: the historical remnant composed of survivors of the catastrophe of God's judgment (1:8); the faithful remnant of Hebrews who maintain a true faith relationship with Yahweh (5:15); and an eschatological remnant of Hebrews and Gentiles who will participate in the blessing of the restored Davidic kingdom (9:11-12; cf. NIDOTTE 4.14-15).

9:9 *sieve.* This word (*kebarah* [TH3531, ZH3895]) is unique in the OT and may refer to a screening device of some sort made of a mesh that facilitated the separation of the kernels of grain from the pebbles and soil of threshed wheat and barley. The LXX interprets the term as a "winnowing fan" (cf. Andersen and Freedman 1989:870).

COMMENTARY

Amos's fifth and final vision is dominated by Yahweh's lengthy first-person mono-logue (9:1b-4). The vision report (9:1) contains no formula introducing the visionary experience, no dialogue between God and the prophet, and no symbolic component as a key to interpreting the vision. The themes of God's sovereignty and divine judgment persist in this climactic vision. But "gone is the time for object lessons, pleas, repentance, and dialogue. Come is the time for the fullness of the judgment" (Hubbard 1989:227). Amos can only listen in silence. The means of divine punishment include earthquake and exile, threats that have loomed large throughout Amos's message (e.g., 1:1; 2:15; 3:14-15; 6:11; 8:8). Tragically, the unrelieved theme of the prophet's last vision is that there is no escape from divine retribution.

The series of five conditional clauses in Yahweh's monologue declare unalterably "that all possible escape routes are blocked off" (Paul 1971:277). The connections between Amos 9:1-4 and Psalm 139 (esp. Ps 139:7-12) in the description of Yahweh's inescapable presence are widely recognized (e.g., Stuart 1987:392; Hubbard 1989:230; Smith and Page 1995:155). Amos reminds us of one of the essential attributes of God—his omnipresence. Although the divine presence may not always be benign (as Amos's audience learned), it is important for us to remember that the Lord is a God nearby and not a God far away (Jer 23:24; Acts 17:28). "The Christian teaching of God's ever-present companionship is . . . an intimate comfort to know of and experience the divine availability" (Oden 1998:68). The psalmist knew that God is always ready to help in times of trouble (Ps 46:1), and Paul tells us that nothing can ever separate the Christian from the love of God in Christ Jesus (Rom 8:39). The prophet Amos helps us bridge the Old and New Testament understandings of God's omnipresence.

Amos's final vision touches on two additional theological truths. First, God cannot be contained; his "home" stretches from the earth to the heavens (9:6). The hymn fragment calls to mind Solomon's prayer of dedication for the Temple and his acknowledgment that neither earth nor the highest heavens can contain God—much less any conceivable building (1 Kgs 8:27; cf. Acts 7:49). This means God is immense or boundless with respect to spatial measures.

Finally, God is a promise keeper. Despite his necessary judgment for their covenant trespass of idolatry, Yahweh will not "completely destroy the family of Israel" (9:8). God remembers his everlasting covenant with Abraham forever (Pss 105:8-11; 111:5). Implicit in this declaration is the "remnant" theme, prominent in the Old Testament prophetic literature (e.g., Isa 11:11; Jer 23:3). God will always preserve a remnant of his people (Joel 2:32), and they will ultimately prevail and live in righteousness (Mic 5:7-8; Zeph 3:13). This, too, serves as a reminder that as God's people we are not to despise "small beginnings" (Zech 4:10) because they are his way to grow "mustard seeds" into "trees" (Matt 13:31-32).

◆VI. Epilogue: The Restoration of Israel (9:11-15)

¹¹"In that day I will restore the fallen house* of David.
I will repair its damaged walls.
From the ruins I will rebuild it
and restore its former glory.
¹²And Israel will possess what is left of Edom
and all the nations I have called to be mine.*"
The LORD has spoken,
and he will do these things.

¹³"The time will come," says the LORD,
"when the grain and grapes will grow faster
than they can be harvested.

Then the terraced vineyards on the hills of Israel
will drip with sweet wine!
¹⁴I will bring my exiled people of Israel back from distant lands,
and they will rebuild their ruined cities
and live in them again.
They will plant vineyards and gardens;
they will eat their crops and drink their wine.
¹⁵I will firmly plant them there in their own land.
They will never again be uprooted from the land I have given them,"
says the LORD your God.

9:11a Or *kingdom;* Hebrew reads *tent.* 9:11b-12 Greek version reads *and restore its former glory, / so that the rest of humanity, including the Gentiles— / all those I have called to be mine—might seek me.* Compare Acts 15:16-17.

NOTES

9:11 *In that day.* The expression is prophetic shorthand for "the day of the LORD," an indeterminate period of divine activity that includes the judgment of Israel and the nations, as well as the ultimate restoration of Israel (cf. Hos 12–14; Zech 12–14; see note on 5:18).

I will restore. The repetition of the verb *qum* [TH6965, ZH7756] in 9:11 calls attention to Yahweh's role as the agent of Israel's restoration. The word can mean "establish" in the sense of following through on a promise in contexts containing oath formulas or covenant language. This is the connotation Amos had in mind.

house of David. Lit., the word translated "house" (*sukkah* [TH5521, ZH6109]) denotes a "tent" or a "hut," a temporary shelter made of vines and branches associated with the Festival of Shelters, or Sukkot. In context, the reference is to a restored Davidic empire with emphasis on both the reunification of the northern and southern kingdoms into one nation and on the shepherd-king figure like David who will rule the people in righteousness (Jer 23:5-6; Ezek 34:22-23).

9:12 *Edom and all the nations.* "Edom is a synecdoche for the phrase 'all the nations' which parallels it" (Stuart 1987:398). Amos anticipates the global sovereignty of the Davidic ruler during the messianic age (cf. Mal 1:11).

he will do these things. The statement of divine intention appended to the oracle formula ("the LORD has spoken") is a unique construction in the OT. Hubbard (1989:242) suggests the line may be a hymn fragment taken from another source (cf. Mal 4:3).

9:14 *I will bring my exiled people.* The Hebrew expression *shabti eth-shebuth* [TH7622, ZH8654] is ambiguous (cf. NJB, NRSV, "I will restore the fortunes of my people"). How one understands the noun *shebuth* (either "exiles" or "fortunes"; cf. HALOT 4:1386) in this context determines the meaning of the expression. In either case, Yahweh is responsible for the reversal of circumstances depicted in 5:11. Implicit in the references to the security of rebuilt homes and cities and the prosperity of agricultural endeavors is the renewal of covenant relationship with Yahweh (cf. Ezek 28:25-26; Mic 4:4).

9:15 *I will firmly plant.* Amos unequivocally acknowledged Yahweh as the one who
restores, rebuilds, and replants his people as their covenant-making and covenant-keeping
God. "Yahweh is the hero, the prime mover of the events" (Stuart 1987:399).

land. This is the land of Canaan, the land granted to Abraham and his descendants as part
of God's covenant agreement with Abraham as Israel's patriarch (Gen 12:1-3). The NT
understands the "land" as a symbol of the "rest" that results from right relationship with
God through Christ Jesus (Heb 4:5-11).

never again be uprooted. God's forgiveness is complete and his restoration permanent.
The future Israel in view has paid the price for covenant trespasses and is assured continual
occupation of the land of covenant promise. Yet the subsequent history of Israel shows that
the people were displaced from the land again and again by foreign invaders. Some commentators identify the ultimate fulfillment of Amos's promises of God's restoration of
Israel with the promises fulfilled in the church as the "Israel of God" (so Smith and Page
1995:170). Others view Amos's salvation oracles as a later stage of development in an
eschatology that culminates in the kingdom of the Messiah (distinct from the church or
church age; cf. Matt 24; Rev 20; cf. Smith 1989:283-284).

COMMENTARY

The stark contrast between the judgment pronounced in the sermons and visions of
Amos and the two salvation oracles (9:11-12, 13-15) promising deliverance and restoration in the epilogue have prompted many scholars to question the authenticity
of the book's conclusion and assign these salvation oracles to a later writer or editor
(e.g., Mays 1969:166). This need not be the case, however, as the oracle structure of
Amos's message fits the basic speech pattern found in prophetic literature in the
Old Testament. This speech pattern commonly includes the following:

Indictment (a statement of the offense, typically covenant violations related
to idolatry and social justice)

Judgment (a statement of the punishment to be meted out, often including
the threat of exile)

Instruction (the expected response to the prophet's message, usually including
a call to repentance)

Aftermath (a promise of future deliverance and restoration offering hope to
those who persevere during the intervening period of divine judgment)

Hubbard (1989:236) aptly notes that the timing of the events is another key to
understanding how a book dominated by doom could end with such brilliant
hope. The eschatological phrase "in that day" (9:11) indicates an interval of time
during which both divine judgment and divine restoration will take place. Finally,
the genuineness of the concluding salvation oracles is supported by the continued
thread of God's covenant commitment to sustain his people Israel not because of
their justice and righteousness but on the basis of his love (Deut 4:37; Hubbard
1989:236; cf. Stuart 1987:397).

The reference to the "house of David" (9:11) is usually understood as some variation on the theme of prophecy about the messianic age. Typically the rebuilding of

the "house of David" is interpreted as the restoration of the Davidic monarchy as a result of God's reinstatement of the covenant he made with David (2 Sam 7). The installation of Zerubbabel, a Davidic descendant, as governor of post-exilic Judah is often cited as the fulfillment of this prediction (so McKeating 1971:70).

Hubbard (1989:239-240) is enamored with the idea that the restored "hut of David" prefigures a return to the pre-monarchic days of Hebrew history when David championed the cause of the peasantry of Israel prior to his kingship. The passage thus describes a future era of simple lifestyle, egalitarian relationship, and dependence upon God similar to the days when Israel trusted God and lived in "huts" during the days of desert wandering after the Exodus (cf. Isa 11).

Others have a different view of what this revitalized "tabernacle of David" will be. They equate it with the tent David erected to temporarily house the Ark of the Covenant until a suitable Temple could be constructed (1 Chr 15:1). And they see the daily worship of the Hebrew priests before the ark with offerings and songs of praise as foreshadowing an anointing of God's Holy Spirit that would revitalize worship and worship music in the "last days"—days the church is now beginning to experience (see Conner 1986).

Stuart (1987:398) more correctly identifies the restoration of David's dynasty with the great King David to come—the shepherd of God's people Israel (Isa 9:7; Jer 33:17; Ezek 37:24): The messianic age would witness the rise of a "new" David who would shepherd the people of Israel and restore their former glory—the glory of God's people rightly reunited in covenant relationship with him (cf. Jer 23:5-6).

According to the New Testament, Jesus the Messiah is the fulfillment of Amos's promise of a restored house of David (cf. Acts 2:29-36). Beyond this, James quotes Amos 9:11-12 in his arguments to the Jewish leaders assembled in Jerusalem at the first church council (Acts 15). James considered Israel's possession of the remnant of Edom and the nations as forecasted by Amos (9:12) as being fulfilled in the preaching of the gospel of Jesus Christ to the Gentiles and their inclusion as the people of God in the church of Jesus Christ (Acts 15:13-18).

The title "Son of David" was one of the epithets ascribed to Jesus by the crowds who followed his ministry (cf. Matt 9:27; 15:22; 20:30-31). The pattern of type and antitype that is characteristic of biblical typology demonstrates numerous parallels between King David and Jesus as the Son of David:

Jesus traced his lineage to the tribe of Judah and the family of David; in fact he is called the Lion of the tribe of Judah (Rev 5:5; cf. Matt 1:1; 2:1, 4-6; Rom 1:3)

Jesus was identified as "king of the Jews" at both his birth and death (Matt 2:2; 27:37; cf. John 18:37; Rev 17:14; 19:16)

Jesus assumed the role of priest, even as David took on priestly duties as God's "anointed" one (Matt 22:41-46; Heb 4:14–8:13; cf. 1 Chr 15:27; 16:2)

Jesus assumed the role of prophet, even as David was acknowledged as a prophet of God (Matt 21:11; John 4:19; 6:14; cf. Deut 18:15, 18; Acts 2:30)

Jesus fulfilled the role of shepherd of Israel (John 10:14; Heb 13:20; 1 Pet 5:4; Rev 7:17; cf. 2 Sam 5:2; Ezek 34:23-24)

For this reason, like Israel of old, the church still shouts,

Praise God for the Son of David!
Blessings on the one who comes in the name of the LORD!
Praise God in highest heaven! (Matt 21:9//Pss 118:25-26; 148:1)

BIBLIOGRAPHY

Achtemeier, E.
1986 *Nahum—Malachi.* Interpretation Series. Atlanta: John Knox.

Andersen, F. I., and D. N. Freedman
1989 *Amos.* Anchor Bible. New York: Doubleday.

Barton, J.
1980 *Amos' Oracles Against the Nations.* Cambridge: Cambridge University Press.

Block, D. I.
2001 *The Gods of the Nations: Studies in Ancient Near Eastern National Theology.* 2nd ed. Grand Rapids: Baker.

Carroll, R., and M. Daniel
2002 *Amos, the Prophet and His Oracles.* Louisville: Westminster John Knox.

Cathcart, K. J., and R. P. Gordon
1989 *The Bible in Aramaic: The Targum of the Minor Prophets,* vol. 14. Wilmington, DE: Michael Glazier.

Chisholm, R. B.
2002 *Handbook on the Prophets.* Grand Rapids: Baker.

Clements, R.
1988 *When God's Patience Runs Out: The Truth of Amos for Today.* Downers Grove: InterVarsity.

Coggins, R. J.
2000 *Joel and Amos.* New Century Bible. Sheffield: Sheffield Academic Press.

Conner, K. J.
1986 *The Tabernacle of David.* 2nd ed. Portland, OR: City Bible.

Coote, R.
1981 *Amos Among the Prophets: Composition and Theology.* Philadelphia: Fortress.

Craigie, P. C.
1985 *Twelve Prophets.* Philadelphia: Westminster.

Crenshaw, J. L.
1975 *Hymnic Affirmations of Divine Justice: The Doxologies of Amos and Related Texts in the Old Testament.* Missoula: Scholars Press.

Dawn, M. J.
1995 *Reaching Out Without Dumbing Down.* Grand Rapids: Eerdmans.

Dorsey, D. A.
1999 *The Literary Structure of the Old Testament.* Grand Rapids: Baker.

Eichrodt, W.
1961 *Theology of the Old Testament.* Translator, J. A. Baker. London: SCM Press.

Finley, T. J.
1990 *Joel, Amos, Obadiah.* Chicago: Moody.

Gitay, Y.
1980 A Study of Amos's Art of Speech: A Rhetorical Analysis of Amos 3:1-15. *Catholic Biblical Quarterly* 42:293-309.

Gowan, D. E.
1996 The Book of Amos. Pp. 339-431 in *The New Interpreter's Bible,* vol. 7. Editor, D. L. Peterson. Nashville: Abingdon.

Hammershaimb, E.
1970 *The Book of Amos: A Commentary.* Oxford: Blackwell.

Harper, W. R.
1955 *A Critical and Exegetical Study on Amos and Hosea.* International Critical Commentary. Edinburgh: T & T Clark.

Hasel, G. F.
1991 *Understanding the Book of Amos: Basic Issues in Current Interpretations.* Grand Rapids: Baker.

Hayes, J. H.
1988 *Amos: His Times and His Preaching.* Nashville: Abingdon.

Heschel, A.
1962 *The Prophets.* New York: Harper & Row.

Hill, A. E., and J. H. Walton
2000 *A Survey of the Old Testament.* 2nd ed. Grand Rapids: Zondervan.

House, P.
1998 *Old Testament Theology.* Downers Grove: InterVarsity.

Howie, C. G.
1959 Expressly for Our Times: The Theology of Amos. *Interpretation* 13:273-285.

Hubbard, D. A.
1989 *Joel and Amos.* Tyndale Old Testament Commentaries. Downers Grove: InterVarsity.

Jacob, E.
1958 *Theology of the Old Testament.* Translators, A. W. Heathcote and P. J. Allcock. New York: Harper & Row.

Jeremias, J.
1998 *The Book of Amos.* Old Testament Library. Translator, D. W. Stott. Louisville: Westminster John Knox.

Jones, B. A.
1995 *The Formation of the Book of the Twelve: A Study in Text and Canon.* SBL Dissertation Series 149. Atlanta: Scholars Press.

King, P. J.
1988 *Amos, Hosea, Micah—An Archaeological Commentary.* Philadelphia: Westminster.

Koch, K.
1982 *The Prophets: The Assyrian Period,* vol 1. Translator, M. Kohl. Philadelphia: Fortress.

McKeating, H.
1971 *Amos, Hosea, Micah.* Cambridge Bible Commentary. Cambridge: Cambridge University Press.

Martin-Achard, R.
1984 *The End of the People of God: A Commentary on the Book of Amos.* Grand Rapids: Eerdmans.

Mays, J. L.
1969 *Amos.* Philadelphia: Westminster.

Möller, K.
2003 *A Prophet in Debate: The Rhetoric and Persuasion in the Book of Amos.* Sheffield: Sheffield Academic Press.

Mowvley, H.
1991 *The Books of Amos and Hosea.* London: Epworth.

Motyer, J. A.
1974 *The Day of the Lion: The Message of Amos.* Downers Grove: InterVarsity.

Niehaus, J.
1992 Amos. Pp. 315-494 in *An Exegetical and Expository Commentary on the Minor Prophets.* Editor, T. E. McComiskey. Grand Rapids: Baker.

Oden, T. C.
1998 *The Living God.* Peabody, MA: Prince.

Paul, S. M.
1971 Amos 1:2-2:3: A Concatenous Literary Pattern. *Journal of Biblical Literature* 90:397-403.

1991 *Amos.* Hermeneia. Minneapolis: Augsburg Fortress.

Polley, M.
1989 *Amos and the Davidic Empire.* New York: Oxford University Press.

Sellin, E., and G. Fohrer
1968 *Introduction to the Old Testament.* Nashville: Abingdon.

Smith, B. K., and F. S. Page
1995 *Amos, Obadiah, Jonah.* New American Commentary. Nashville: Broadman & Holman.

Smith, G. V.
1989 *Amos: A Commentary.* Grand Rapids: Zondervan.

1997 Amos, Theology of. Pp. 373–377 in *New International Dictionary of Old Testament Theology & Exegesis.* Editor, W. A. VanGemeren. Grand Rapids: Zondervan.

2001 *Hosea, Amos, Micah.* NIV Application Commentary. Grand Rapids: Zondervan.

Stuart, D.
1987 *Hosea–Jonah.* Word Biblical Commentary. Waco: Word.

VanGemeren, W.
1990 *Interpreting the Prophetic Word.* Grand Rapids: Academie Books.

Vawter, B.
1981 *Amos, Hosea, Micah: With an Introduction to Classical Prophecy.* Wilmington, DE: Michael Glazier.

de Waard, J., and W. A. Smalley
1979 *A Translator's Handbook on the Book of Amos.* New York: United Bible Societies.

Walton, J. H., V. H. Matthews, and M. W. Chavalas
2000 *The IVP Bible Backgrounds Commentary: Old Testament.* Downers Grove: InterVarsity.

Watts, J. D. W.
1958 *Vision and Prophecy in Amos.* Grand Rapids: Eerdmans.

Wendland, E. R.
1988 The Word of the Lord and the Organization of Amos. *Occasional Papers in Translation and Textlinguistics* 2.4.

Westermann, C.
1991 *Basic Forms of Prophetic Speech.* Translator, H. C. White. Louisville: Westminster/John Knox.

Wolff, H. W.
1977 *Joel and Amos.* Hermeneia. Translators, W. Janzen, S. D. McBride, and C. A. Muenchow. Philadelphia: Fortress.

Wood, L. J.
1979 *The Prophets of Israel.* Grand Rapids: Baker.

Obadiah

RICHARD D. PATTERSON

Obadiah

OBADIAH WAS CALLED ON to experience the perils of life in a time of disaster. Not only was the kingdom of Judah in the process of collapse from its internal problems, but neighboring enemies were taking advantage of the kingdom's difficulties to despoil it. Nevertheless, God had a message for his people. One day their enemies would experience God's judgment. Then a purified Israel would inherit the Land of Promise, and God would dwell in their midst.

AUTHOR
The name Obadiah is a common one in the Scriptures, occurring 18 times in various forms. Jewish and Christian traditions have held that the prophet was the same Obadiah who was King Ahab's palace administrator (1 Kgs 18:3-16). Contemporary scholarship, however, has hesitated in settling upon any specific biblical person, so that Finley (1990:339) says, "Nothing is known about the author beyond his name and that he received a prophetic revelation." Although some have contended that Obadiah was a prophet who functioned as part of the Temple staff in Jerusalem, in the final analysis such remains unprovable. Allen (1976:137) remarks, "It is safer to conclude that Obadiah borrowed cultic and traditional themes in developing his prophecy."

DATE AND OCCASION OF WRITING
Suggested dates for the book range from the ninth century to the late fourth century BC. Conservative scholars have adopted a wide span of dates, including both preexilic and exilic eras (i.e., from the ninth century to the sixth century BC). Final determination has largely been based on the interpretation of the denunciation of Edom in 1:10-14. Some commentators (e.g., Keil, Niehaus) have followed the traditional ninth-century BC date, citing general association with the description of events during the reign of King Jehoram of Judah. Others have defended an eighth-century BC date, either in the time of Amaziah and Uzziah (e.g., Pusey) or Ahaz (e.g., Raven), or the time of Jeremiah (e.g., Young). Most scholars (e.g., Stuart, Raabe) have opted for a sixth-century BC date because they view these crucial verses (1:10-14) as referring to events concerned with the fall of Jerusalem in 586 BC. Thus Smith opts for a date somewhere between 587 and 500 BC.

A more precise date could be affixed if the relation of Obadiah 1:1-9 to Jeremiah 49:7-16 could be determined. Here again, scholars are divided as to whether Jeremiah borrowed from Obadiah (e.g., Keil, Pusey), Obadiah was dependent upon Jeremiah (e.g., Armerding, Bewer), or both drew upon common prophetic material (e.g., Finley). While Obadiah's penchant for drawing upon traditional Hebrew phraseology makes the second option most likely (Raabe 1996:22-33), the data are capable of such diverse evaluation that a final decision as to literary dependency seems unlikely.

The occasion of Obadiah's prophecy, then, would be variously understood. If a ninth-century BC date is decided upon, the denunciation of Edom would be tied in with the Edomite campaigning in Jehoram's day (2 Kgs 8:16-24) and the subsequent Arabian-Philistine invasion of Judah and Jerusalem (2 Chr 21:16-17). If the time period is that of Amaziah/Uzziah, Obadiah's prophecy would parallel the sentiment of Amos, whose general condemnation of Edom's perennial hostility merited a prophetic judgment oracle (Amos 1:11-12). If Obadiah is seen as prophesying during the reign of Ahaz, the prophet referred to the defeats by the Edomites and Philistines (2 Chr 28:17-18). Taking the setting of the book as exilic most naturally views Edom's vile behavior in connection with the fall of Jerusalem in 586 BC.

Like the date, then, the occasion of Obadiah's prophecy is difficult to determine. Yet the message of Edom's sure judgment for its traditional position of animosity toward God's people remains the same and is in harmony with the words of several other prophets (Isa 11:14; 21:11-12; 34:1-17; 63:1-6; Jer 25:21; 49:7-22; Lam 4:21; Ezek 25:12-14; 35:1-15; 36:1-38; Joel 3:19; Amos 1:11-12; 9:12; Mal 1:2-5). In that regard, Edom becomes representative of all of God's foes, who will ultimately be defeated in the great Day of the Lord (see especially Isa 34:1-17; 63:1-6; Ezek 35:1-15; 36:1-38).

AUDIENCE
Whatever the time period represented by the book, Obadiah wrote to citizens of Judah and Jerusalem. He was thoroughly familiar with events that had taken place in the holy city (1:11-14) and concerned about its sacred reputation and destiny (1:16-17, 21).

CANONICITY AND TEXTUAL HISTORY
In contrast to the debate over the date and occasion of the book, its canonicity is not in question. Like the rest of the Minor Prophets, its acceptance is attested at least by the second century BC by Ben Sirach (Sir 1:39).

Likewise, the text was largely well preserved, as attested by the second-century AD scroll of the Minor Prophets found at Wadi Murabba'at, reflecting the tradition of the Masoretic Text. One may safely say with Watts (1969:30) that "the text of Obadiah is generally in very good shape."

LITERARY STYLE

Despite its brevity, the prophecy displays a carefully structured format of prophetic poetry. Niehaus (1993:505) observes that Obadiah was "a master of various poetical techniques." The prophecy is also freely sprinkled with striking images. For example, Edom's stronghold is likened to an eagle's nest (1:4) and its eventual defeat is compared to a hot fire quickly burning stubble (1:18). Obadiah also employed irony to great effect: Although Edom's defeat will be a more thorough destruction than that of looters or robbers who at least leave something behind (1:5-6), it is a just reward for what Edom has done to others (1:15-16). The prophecy is also noteworthy for its elliptical style (1:19-20) and its effective use of repetition (1:11-14) and wordplay, such as the pun in 1:11-12 where "foreigners" (*nakrim* [TH5237A, ZH5799]) will effect "his [Edom's] misfortune" (*nakro* [cf. TH5235, ZH5798]).

MAJOR THEMES

The basic theme of the book is the judgment of Edom, a theme held in common with Joel and Amos. This major emphasis is developed around the motif of brotherhood, which links the two halves (1:1-14, 15-21) of the book together. Indeed, the conduct of Edom (called Esau in 1:6, 8-9, 18, 21) was particularly loathsome, for it had oppressed Judah and Jerusalem, its brother (called Jacob, 1:10; cf. 12, 17-18). Yet, just as Esau was to find his blessing in Jacob (Gen 25:23; 27:27-40), so the land of Edom would find its only deliverance through those who come from Jacob's descendants on Mount Zion (1:21).

Mountains form a significant motif in the book. Thus, the failure of the heights of Edom (1:2-4) stands in sharp contrast with the success of Mount Zion (1:17, 21). The subject of deliverance forms a subtheme, cast in a salvation oracle, that underscores the restoration of a remnant of God's people so they can participate in the Lord's final universal reign.

THEOLOGICAL CONCERNS

Obadiah's theological emphases reflect the major message of the book. The Day of the Lord is seen as a corollary to the Lord's universal sovereignty (1:15). This "day" is a time when his justice will be vindicated, as rebels are punished and God's people delivered and rewarded in accordance with the principles of God's retributive justice (1:15-21). Israel may be certain that God has not rejected his people but will reverse their present plight (Raabe 1996:60). In keeping with this latter emphasis, the theological themes of the Abrahamic covenant for the Lord's remnant can be seen (1:17-21). The teleological purposes of God's divine grant to his people find expression here. God is neither blind to present circumstances nor incapable of dealing with them. Ultimately, the God of history "is also the Lord of the future" (Allen 1976:139), for he will reign over all nations from Mount Zion, where his restored people will enjoy the age-old promises resident in the covenant granted by the God of Abraham, Isaac, and Jacob.

OUTLINE

Many outlines have been suggested for Obadiah, one of the most thorough being that of Raabe (1996:18-22). Although he makes a strong case for viewing the structure of Obadiah as built around (1) the divine speech formulae (1:1, 4, 8, 18), (2) perceived stitching devices between the resultant units (1:1-4, 5-7, 8-18, 19-21), and (3) the distinction between poetry and prose sections suggested in certain editions of the Hebrew text, one must proceed with caution in applying these data too stringently. This is because (1) divine speech formulae are often given for emphasis rather than as structural indicators; (2) a different set of thematic and stitching devices may be seen as readily as those suggested by Raabe; and (3) even granted the distinction between prose and poetry (although this is often difficult to ascertain in Hebrew prophecy), a change in literary medium need not be viewed as a thematic structural indicator.

Accordingly, the following outline is a simple thematic one that allows due weight to the progressive nature of Obadiah's message: the impending doom of Edom (1:1b-9), the causes for its demise (1:10-14), and a consideration of the Day of the Lord (1:15-21).

Superscription (1:1a)
  I. The Day of Edom's Destruction (1:1b-14)
    A. The Call to Battle against Edom (1:1b)
    B. The Course of Edom's Defeat (1:2-9)
    C. The Cause for Edom's Defeat (1:10-14)
  II. Edom and the Day of the Lord (1:15-21)
    A. The Judgment of the Nations (1:15-16)
    B. The Restoration of Israel (1:17-21)

Obadiah

◆ Superscription (1:1a)

This is the vision that the Sovereign LORD revealed to Obadiah concerning the land of Edom.

NOTES

1:1a *vision.* About this term of divine revelation, see note on Nah 1:1. Laetsch (1956:193) appropriately remarks, "What Obadiah wrote was not the product of his own reflection, of his keen insight into the political and religious conditions of his day; nor was it merely the application of God's Word to a given situation. It was a vision, a divine revelation of God's purpose."

Obadiah. Obadiah (whose name means "servant of Yahweh") is appropriately named, for as God's prophet he was also the Lord's servant (cf. 1 Kgs 14:18, NIV; see also 2 Kgs 9:7; Jer 7:25; Ezek 38:17, NIV; Zech 1:6).

concerning the land of Edom. While the phrase *le'edom* may be translated either "unto Edom" or "about/concerning Edom," the latter probably is to be understood here (cf. Jer 49:7), but without discounting the fact that God's message was also intended for Edom (see Wehrle 1987:34-42).

COMMENTARY

Obadiah's short prophecy deals with the perennial problem of Edom's hostility toward God's people, Israel. The first 14 verses speak of Edom's destruction: the call to battle against Edom (1:1b), the course of Edom's defeat (1:2-9), and the causes that precipitate its demise (1:10-14). The final verses (1:15-21) present the theme of the Day of the Lord, including the judgment of Edom and the nations (1:15-16), and the restoration of God's people to their land (1:17-21). Edom has had its "day" with God's people; now in the Day of the Lord, it would receive the just reward for its actions.

Edom owes its name to Esau, also called Edom (Gen 25:25, 30), who established his dwelling in the area formerly known as Mount Seir (Gen 36:8-9) after he drove out the Horites (Gen 14:6; cf. Deut 12:2). Edom was also known as Teman (1:9; Hab 3:3, NIV) after Esau's grandson (Gen 36:15). Edom was often the object of prophetic denunciation (Isa 34:1-15; Jer 49:7-22; Ezek 35:1-15; Joel 3:19; Amos 1:11-12; 9:12; Mal 1:2-5) due to its longstanding enmity toward God's people (cf. Num 20:14-21; Judg 11:16-17; 1 Sam 14:47-48; 2 Sam 8:14; 1 Kgs 11:14-25; 2 Chr 20:1-30).

The term "Sovereign LORD" (lit., "The Lord Yahweh") emphasizes the key theological perspective and theme of the book: God's sovereignty over the nations. The message Obadiah received was from the One who rules the universe and controls the destiny of nations. While that message was designed for Obadiah's audience, it also was of concern for Edom.

◆ **I. The Day of Edom's Destruction (1:1b-14)**
   A. The Call to Battle against Edom (1:1b)

We have heard a message from
   the LORD
that an ambassador was sent to
   the nations to say,

"Get ready, everyone!
   Let's assemble our armies and
   attack Edom!"

NOTES

1:1b We have heard. The parallel in Jer 49:14 reads, "I have heard." The plural here may indicate Obadiah's reception of the same message Jeremiah received (hence the plural *we*), or the plural *we* could include his audience in the implications of the divine message. Niehaus (1993:513) renders the compound preposition *me'eth* [TH4480/854, ZH4946/907] (lit., "from" + "with") as "straight from" and adds that this "suggests that the immediate source of the verb's action is Yahweh himself." The message is introduced in standard formula: "Thus says the Lord" (a phrase that occurs 133 times in the Latter Prophets), attesting to the fact that the prophet is God's messenger (Raabe 1996:99-105).

that an ambassador was sent. The NLT takes the Hebrew coordinate clause as subordinate to the hearing (indirect discourse); so also Luther's translation ("We have heard from the Lord that an emissary was sent among the heathen"). NIV and GW take the sending of the ambassador as direct discourse—the clause is a statement of the import of the news, that is, that a messenger had been sent. As the text stands, the particle more naturally introduces a statement of the steps that God had already taken for carrying out the message that was heard. "The Lord who is author of the oracle was already taking steps to carry out its message in clear demonstration to the faithful that he was Lord of history" (Allen 1976:145).

Get ready. . . . let's . . . attack. The two verbs reflect a typical Hebrew sequence in which the imperative with a cohortative yields virtual subordination to express intended purpose: "Arise in order to attack" (Waltke and O'Connor 1990:574-575). Although the Hebrew prepositional phrase reads "against *her*" (cf. Jer 49:14, NASB) rather than the expected masculine singular suffix used elsewhere in Obadiah when referring to Edom, the prophets are known to alternate between genders when referring to Edom (Jer 49:14, 17, NASB). Such variation may be accounted for on the basis of an implied head construct noun *'erets* [TH776, ZH824] (land) before Edom. Thus, in some cases authors retain the sense of the natural head; in others they make agreement with the resultant surface structure. In any case, we need not emend the text on the basis of Jer 49:14 or LXX; nor do we need to view the preceding *shullakh* [TH7971, ZH8938] (was sent) as a defectively written pual participle (Allen 1976:144), for the form is fully explicable as a pual suffix conjugation as it stands. If a participle is deemed necessary, one might suggest that the preceding mem of *baggoyim* [TH1471, ZH1580] (to the nations) serves as a double-duty consonant to be read also with *shullakh*. (For the principle of double-duty elements, see Lehman 1967:93-101.)

COMMENTARY

The summoning of the nations to battle demonstrates that human history moves at two levels. Behind the actions of nations stands the person of God himself, the controller of history. Thus, while people act out their plans, they are nonetheless circumscribed by the all-encompassing purposes of God, neither compromising human accountability nor God's standards of justice. Here the sovereignty of God is wedded to the theme of the Divine Warrior who enters the arena of human political affairs to bring judgment to the wicked and deliverance to his own. The blending of these two themes gives assurance to the weary believer that however dark the circumstances, the battle is the Lord's (1 Sam 17:47; 2 Chr 20:15). The scriptural perspective that the prophet's words are the special revelation of God is reinforced here. Obadiah reports that what he will say stems both from God's revelation to his prophet in a visionary experience and via a divine message. The truth that God can and does reveal himself to mankind thus finds specific confirmation here, a fact repeatedly reported by the other prophets.

◆   B. The Course of Edom's Defeat (1:2-9)

2 The LORD says to Edom,
"I will cut you down to size among
    the nations;
you will be greatly despised.
3 You have been deceived by your
    own pride
because you live in a rock fortress
and make your home high in the
    mountains.
'Who can ever reach us way up here?'
you ask boastfully.
4 But even if you soar as high as
    eagles
and build your nest among
    the stars,
I will bring you crashing down,"
says the LORD.

5 "If thieves came at night and robbed
    you
(what a disaster awaits you!),
they would not take everything.
Those who harvest grapes
always leave a few for the poor.
But your enemies will wipe you out
    completely!
6 Every nook and cranny of Edom*
will be searched and looted.
Every treasure will be found
    and taken.

7 "All your allies will turn against you.
They will help to chase you from
    your land.
They will promise you peace
while plotting to deceive and
    destroy you.
Your trusted friends will set traps
    for you,
and you won't even know
    about it.
8 At that time not a single wise
    person
will be left in the whole land
    of Edom,"
says the LORD.
"For on the mountains of Edom
I will destroy everyone who has
    understanding.
9 The mightiest warriors of Teman
will be terrified,
and everyone on the mountains
    of Edom
will be cut down in the slaughter.

6 Hebrew *Esau;* also in 8b, 9, 18, 19, 21.

NOTES

1:2 *I will cut you down to size.* Lit., "I have made you small." NLT translates according to the sense of the context. Proud, lofty Edom will be brought down from its height and high-mindedness. The Hebrew verb is a prophetic perfect, a prediction being viewed as already accomplished.

1:3 *rock fortress.* The noun *sela'* [TH5553, ZH6152] carries with it the nuance of a crevice of a rock, though it may also indicate a rock or cliff. It thus differs from such near synonyms as *tsur* [TH6697, ZH7446] (large rock) and *'eben* [TH68, ZH74] (stone). (See my remarks in TWOT 2.627.) Here a play on the name of Edom's capital city, Sela, is intended.

1:4 *eagles.* The metaphorical use of the eagle is quite common both in the OT (e.g., Deut 28:49 [NLT, "vulture"]; 2 Sam 1:23; Ezek 17:3, 7; Hos 8:1) and in the ancient Near East. Tiglath-pileser III (1114–1076 BC) reports that his ancestor Ninurta-apil-Ekur spread his wings over the land like an eagle (Grayson 1976:17), much like the Lord is said to have carried Israel (Exod 19:4). Sargon II (722–705 BC) reports that he caused his forces to fly over the mountains like valiant eagles (see *The Assyrian Dictionary* 325), and Sennacherib (705–681 BC) asserts that on his fifth campaign his enemies' abodes were located "on the peak of Mount Nippur, a steep mountain, like the nests of the eagle (vulture), king of birds" (Luckenbill 1927:122). (For a fine discussion of these and other parallels, see Niehaus 1993:517-518.) Likewise, the metaphorical use of the eagle is known from ancient Ugaritic literature. Thus, Baal is given two clubs which, in his hands, swirl like an eagle to strike down his enemy. (See Gordon 1965:3.68, lines 13-24. An English translation may be found in Coogan 1978:88-89.) It is not extraordinary, then, that Jer 49:22 predicts an enemy of Edom that "swoops down like an eagle, spreading his wings over Bozrah."

1:5 *thieves . . . Those who harvest grapes.* Obadiah continues his use of imagery here, employing irony and repetition. Like 1:4, which contains a double condition, 1:5 similarly has two conditional contexts: When thieves and robbers or grape gatherers do their work, they at least leave something behind. In both cases, the conditional clauses are introduced by the Hebrew particle *'im* [TH518, ZH561] (if), while in both, the contrast with Edom is preceded by the rhetorical *halo'* [TH1886.2/3808, ZH2022/4202] (Would it not . . . ?) and the exclamatory particle *'ek* [TH349, ZH375] (how) to emphasize the thoroughness of Edom's ransacking.

1:6 *Edom.* The MT reads *Esau* here and in verses 8b, 9, 18, 19, and 21. The reference to Edom as Esau is deliberate, emphasizing the heinous nature of Edom's crime. It violated the very nature of brotherhood (see Introduction, "Major Themes"). The verb that follows (NLT, "searched and looted"; Heb., *nekhpesu* [TH2664, ZH2924]) is plural, the controlling noun being viewed as a collective subject. Its form anticipates the following plural verb (NLT, "found and taken"; Heb., *nib'u* [TH1158, ZH1239]).

treasure. This word for treasure occurs only here in the OT but is related to a well-attested Semitic root meaning "hide," "store up," or "treasure" (*tsapan* [TH6845, ZH7621]). Thus, Moses was hidden three months due to Pharaoh's decree to put Hebrew male babies to death (Exod 2:2). Job complained that God stores up a man's punishment for his sins (Job 21:19), while the writer of Proverbs observed that God "grants a treasure of common sense to the honest" (Prov 2:7). The Hebrew root *tspn* finds its way into the Akkadian of Tell el-Amarna (*tsapanu*; El-Amarna 147:10). The noun can also refer to "secret (hiding) places" so that Raabe (1996:146) can say, "Neither the descendants of Esau nor their riches will go undetected by the enemies in spite of their hiding-places. Ordinary thieves and plunderers might not have the time necessary to discover such secret places (v. 5), but Edom's enemies will painstakingly and extensively seek after them and find them."

1:7 *They will help to chase you from your land.* The meaning of the passage depends on the understanding of the root *shalakh* [TH7971, ZH8938] (send) and the noun *gebul* [TH1366,

ZH1473] (border). If the verb is understood as "send away," the sense may be that of escort-ing or sending back to their border the Edomite envoys who have come to Edom's allies for help. If a wider range of the verb is maintained, it could be understood that the Edom-ites' former allies assist Edom's enemies in driving the Edomites from their land. The NLT (along with the majority of translations) favors the latter understanding; Keil and Niehaus, the former. Still a third solution favors the thought of sending Edomite refugees to their allies' borders, where they are still vulnerable to their enemies.

They will promise you peace while plotting to deceive and destroy you. This sentence forms the second of three parallel clauses in the Hebrew text. Those at peace with the Edomites are the very ones who will act deceitfully against them in their hour of greatest need. Significantly, each of the major clauses in the Hebrew text ends with a second mascu-line singular pronoun.

Your trusted friends will set traps for you. This sentence constitutes the third of the parallel clauses in the Hebrew text. Two problems stand out here. (1) Is the precise meaning of the Hebrew *lakhmeka* [TH3899, ZH4312] "[the men of] your bread," or by reading a substantive par-ticiple (*lokhameyka*), is it "those who eat your bread" (cf. Symmachus, Vulgate, Targum)? The NLT may be compatible with either solution. In any case, the mention of peace and the sharing of bread are well-known treaty terms. Together, they reinforce the idea that Edom's *trusted* allies could not be trusted. As Edom had deceived its kin Israel countless times, so it would be betrayed by its friends. (2) The second difficulty concerns the Hebrew noun *mazor* [TH4204, ZH4650]. Elsewhere it means "sore" or "wound" (e.g., Jer 30:13; Hos 5:13, NASB). Such a meaning, however, seems difficult in collocation with the following *takhteyka* [TH8478, ZH9393] (beneath you). Therefore, many have opted for a relation with a verbal root known in postbiblical Hebrew, "twist," "cover with a web," and in Syriac, "stretch out"; hence, NLT "set traps for you." Raabe (1996:154-155) thinks that "after the allies expel Edomites from their dwellings, non-Edomites will settle in their place" (cf. Zech 9:6). If the term refers to strangers, it ironically anticipates the theme of v. 11.

you won't even know about it. Nearly the same Hebrew construction is found in Deut 32:28, which the NLT translates "without understanding." Besides the NLT's rendering (cf. point 2 below), the words have been taken in several other ways: (1) If Edom had any sense, they would "know the awful end to which their covenant-breaking behavior must lead (Deut 32:29-30)" (Niehaus 1993:522); (2) Edom is so undiscerning that they will not be able to anticipate their allies' treachery (Allen); (3) the Edomites are simply bewildered, not knowing what to do or how to help themselves (Keil); and (4) with non-Edomites occupying the land, Edom's traditional wisdom will be absent (Raabe).

1:8 *At that time.* This phrase is often used in the prophets when speaking of the Lord's intervention, whether in judgment or deliverance (Armerding 1985:346). It appears frequently in an eschatological setting. In the Hebrew text, v. 8 begins with a rhetorical question expecting an affirmative answer: "Will I not . . . destroy the wise men from Edom?" The NLT translates according to the sense, giving the expected answer as a direct divine assertion (cf. NRSV)—the whole matter being emphasized by the following "says the LORD," a phrase that concluded a unit in v. 4 but introduces one here (Raabe 1996:163).

not a single wise person will be left. The force of the context and the parallel with Jer 49:7 demand not a complete annihilation of the wise men but a total abrogation of their wis-dom. Depressed and devoid of wise counsel, Edom's military situation stood in dire peril. Forms of the traditional terms "wisdom" (*khokmah* [TH2451, ZH2683]) and "understanding" (*tebunah* [TH8394, ZH9312]) underscore the seriousness of Edom's condition. The motif of God abrogating human wisdom is common not only to the wisdom literature but to the prophetic oracles as well.

mountains of Edom. The term (cf. 1:9, 19, 21) reflects Edom's pride in its mountain location (1:2-4) and forms a distinct thematic contrast with Mount Zion (1:17, 21; see the Introduction's "Major Themes").

1:9 *mightiest warriors.* Although it had sociological implications (see Allen 1976:153), the Hebrew term *gibbor* often carries with it a nuance of heroism (cf. 2 Sam 23:8-39; 1 Chr 11:15-19), particularly for designating soldiers. At times, such a one could be called a "mighty man of valor" (*gibbor khayil* [TH1368A/2428, ZH1475/2657]; e.g., 2 Chr 13:3b; 17:16). Thus Kosmala (TDOT 2.374) observes, "By far the most frequent use of the word *gibbor* occurs in connection with military activities, especially as a designation for a warrior, either a man who is eligible for military service or is able to bear arms, or one who has actually fought in combat, who has already distinguished himself by performing heroic deeds." Here, however, there is a touch of irony: The warriors are anything but heroic. Rather, being demoralized, they become terrified (cf. Isa 31:9). The verb here (root, *khatath*) is at times applied to defeated nations (2 Kgs 19:26; Isa 37:27). Edom is about to share the same fate as its neighbor Moab (Jer 48:20, 34).

Teman. This was one of Edom's chief cities (Amos 1:12), located in the northern part of the country. The term could thus stand for a region in the northern sector or for the entire country (Jer 49:7; Hab 3:3). Job's counselor Eliphaz came from Teman (Job 2:11).

slaughter. This noun was linked with v. 10 rather than v. 9 in the ancient versions. However, not only is the Masoretic punctuation against doing so, but as Finley (1990:363) points out, "The text of Obadiah in the Hebrew scroll of the Minor Prophets [from Wadi Murabba'at] supports the lack of a conjunction as in MT." The cutting down and slaughtering of the enemy is a feature commonly reported in the annals of the ancient Near Eastern kings.

COMMENTARY

In this opening section, the Lord himself reports that he will deal with Edom's pride. The word "behold," with which this judgment oracle begins, puts the Edomite nation on notice that God is active in the affairs of people, particularly proud nations and individuals who flaunt themselves defiantly in the face of God and mistreat his people. Such was Edom.

In the course of announcing Edom's destruction, Obadiah cites two basic sins that marked its condition: He indirectly notes its pride (1:2-9) and directly marks its overt crimes against God's people (1:10-14). He begins by condemning Edom's pride in its geographical location that provided it with a spectacular defensive system. Set on a high plateau, its capital city of Sela was surrounded by steep cliffs. Access could be gained only on its southeast side, which was well defended. So elevated, it could boast, "Who can ever reach us way up here?" Their pride, however, was both presumptuous (Raabe 1996:123) and ill-advised, for it foundered on two points: (1) Judah's former king Amaziah had already successfully campaigned there (2 Kgs 14:7); and (2) the forces that would attack it were sponsored by none other than the God of the universe. The hyperbolic imagery here is stirring. Was Edom located on the heights? It must reckon with him who rides on the clouds of heaven (cf. Deut 33:26; Ps 68:33; Isa 19:1; see Patterson 1985:37). Stuart (1987:417) observes, "Since Yahweh's power is unlimited, it does not matter how high set and well defended Edom might be. It will fall." Though it had the strength to soar like an eagle (cf. Isa 40:31) or put itself above the stars, these would not avail against the God who in his care for his own is likened to a great eagle (Exod 19:4; Deut 32:11) and is the one who created the stars (Gen 1:1, 14; Ps 8:3-4).

The implied condemnation contained in the announcement of Edom's judgment (given in 1:5-6) centers on Edom's wealth. Set high and seemingly secure from invasion, Edom had been able to amass considerable wealth, not only from its agriculture and mining, but from its vast trading enterprises and raiding forays. Nevertheless, unlike burglars who take only the most opportune and valuable items and grape gatherers who leave some gleanings behind, Edom's conquerors will thoroughly ravish its land and carry away every last hidden treasure.

How fleeting material wealth can be! How foolish to build one's life upon personal treasures (Luke 12:16-21), which can never satisfy (Eccl 4:8). So often it is squandered by those who have made it or by those to whom it is left (Pss 39:6; 49:6, 10). Moreover, for some, wealth can lead to conceit (1 Tim 6:17) and selfishness (Luke 12:17).

The sin that polluted Edom can also infect today's believers. It is far better to honor God with one's wealth (Prov 3:9) and seek the spiritual riches that only he can supply (Matt 6:33; Eph 1:7; 3:8; Phil 4:19; Col 2:2-3). Indeed, the believer's whole life is a treasure that God has freely given (Matt 13:11-16) and hence should be stewarded (1 Pet 4:10) with fruitful productivity (Matt 13:22-23). In so doing, the believer will come to know the glorious riches of Christ in him, the hope of glory (Col 1:27).

Israel was God's own special treasure (Ps 135:4) whom he had chosen and loved. Moreover, because he had solemnly promised its ancestors long ago that he would watch over Abraham's descendants, Israel on its part was to reflect God's holy standards in its walk before him (Deut 7:6-11; 14:1-2). God's people were to remember their covenant with him so as to serve him faithfully (Exod 19:5-6) and thus experience God-given success (Deut 26:16-19).

New Testament believers are likewise reminded that in God's great lovingkindness (Eph 2:4-7) they have become God's special possession (1 Pet 2:9-10) through the redeeming work of God's Son, Jesus Christ. Therefore, like Israel of old, they are to be a holy people, eager to do what is good (Eph 2:8-10; Titus 2:14). As such, today's believers are challenged to love each other with genuine affection (Rom 12:10). Rather than devouring one another like modern-day Esaus, Christians should treat each other with genuine brotherly affection, as Christ commanded (John 15:12; cf. 1 John 3:15-16). Not only would churches fare better, but nonbelievers might just be more likely to receive the message of Christ's sacrificial love for a lost world (John 3:16) if Christians were to follow Christ's command to love one another and live in harmony with each other.

Verse 7 focuses on treachery, its background coming from the situation between Jacob and Esau (see Introduction). Just as Edom has betrayed his brother Israel, so it will be treated by its allies in its hour of need. Not only will Edom's friends desert them, but they will turn against them, even laying traps for them, much as Edom had done to Israel (1:11, 14). Brotherhood and treaty obligations were held in high esteem in the ancient Near East, and the violation of either was considered a loathsome deed (cf. Prov 27:10; Isa 33:1; Jer 38:22; Amos 1:9).[1]

The Scriptures remind the believer that "a friend is always loyal" (Prov 17:17; cf. 18:24). The New Testament often speaks of brotherhood and friendship, the most significant comment being Jesus' own observation that "there is no greater love than to lay down one's life for one's friends" (John 15:13). In laying down his life for sinners, Christ makes them his friends who are therefore expected to return his love and to love others as Christ has loved them (John 15:9-17; Jas 2:23-24).

Verses 8 and 9 zero in on Edom's vaunted reputation for wisdom. Edom was noted as a center of wisdom (1 Kgs 4:30; Job 2:11), doubtless due to its advantageous position in the trading enterprises of the ancient Near East. Yet, even Edom's wisdom would prove to be of no avail before the omniscient Lord, who would commission Edom's attackers. Human wisdom scarcely challenges that of the omniscient one, nor is it fully formed apart from him (Prov 1:7; 14:16; 15:33; 22:4).

Not only would Edom's wisdom fail, but its warriors would prove ineffective (cf. Nah 3:13). Overcome by dismay and totally demoralized, their courage would turn into sheer terror.[2] Inevitable consequences would soon follow, proud Edom facing not only defeat but widespread slaughter.

In summary, this section (1:2-9) concerns Edom's certain defeat. Neither its natural defensive position (1:2-4), nor its vast wealth (1:5-6), nor its many business associates and supposed allies (1:7), nor its wisdom or warriors (1:8-9) could prevent its demise. While this section repeatedly emphasizes the sovereignty of God and his active intervention in the affairs of earth's history, the great need for God to do so is likewise made evident. Indeed, all of Edom's hopes rested on conceit and pride.

Edom was to learn what the prophets uniformly proclaim: No matter how strong or arrogant a nation, it may be assured that "the pride of her power will end" (Ezek 30:6). Pride brought down Sodom (Ezek 16:49-50) and Gomorrah; it caused Tyre to self-destruct (Ezek 28:17) and was the besetting sin for which Moab was to suffer the Lord's judgment (Jer 48:29-30). Whether in nations (Isa 2:11) or individuals, God is "able to humble the proud" (Dan 4:37). For "pride goes before destruction, and haughtiness before a fall" (Prov 16:18).

The Scriptures reveal that nothing so deceives the heart like pride (Jer 49:16) so that people are all too easily subject to the pride of life (1 John 2:16). God hates pride and arrogance (Prov 8:13; 16:5), so much so that he punishes the proud (Ps 31:23). Indeed, there is a day coming when the Lord "will punish the proud and mighty and bring down everything that is exalted" (Isa 2:12).

Although believers may take comfort in knowing that those who so arrogantly oppose God (cf. Rev 13:6) will ultimately fail and fall (cf. 2 Thess 2:4-10), they must realize that God is no less displeased with pride in those who claim his name (2 Chr 26:16; Jer 13:8-11; Zeph 3:11-12). Accordingly, they should remind themselves that God opposes the proud but gives grace to the humble (Prov 3:34; Jas 4:6). They must renounce pride and seek the humility that was demonstrated so clearly in Christ, their great example (Matt 11:29; 2 Cor 8:9; Phil 2:5-8). May God help us to forsake pride and selfish ambition and be clothed with genuine humility (Col 3:2; 1 Pet 5:5) so that individually and collectively we may be people dependent on God. May we be like Paul, who exclaimed, "God forbid that I should boast except in the cross of our Lord Jesus Christ" (Gal 6:14, NKJV).

ENDNOTES
1. Ancient Near Eastern tradition characteristically had clauses stipulating the conditions and importance of treaty obligations. The Assyrian Annals often mention the punishment of treaty violators. Niehaus (1993:522) gives several examples.
2. Thus Fausset (1948:570) remarks, "Pride goes before a fall; and the proud often pass suddenly from the height of self-confidence to the depth of despair. Overweening self-reliance passes into unreasoning and unreasonable fear. No human sagacity for which Edom was famed can be relied on in an exigency, if men ignore God."

◆   ## C. The Cause for Edom's Defeat (1:10-14)

10 "Because of the violence you did
   to your close relatives in Israel,*
you will be filled with shame
   and destroyed forever.
11 When they were invaded,
   you stood aloof, refusing to help
   them.
Foreign invaders carried off their wealth
   and cast lots to divide up Jerusalem,
   but you acted like one of Israel's
   enemies.

12 "You should not have gloated
   when they exiled your relatives
   to distant lands.
You should not have rejoiced
   when the people of Judah suffered
   such misfortune.
You should not have spoken arrogantly
   in that terrible time of trouble.

13 You should not have plundered the
   land of Israel
   when they were suffering such
   calamity.
You should not have gloated over
   their destruction
   when they were suffering such
   calamity.
You should not have seized their
   wealth
   when they were suffering such
   calamity.
14 You should not have stood at the
   crossroads,
   killing those who tried to escape.
You should not have captured the
   survivors
   and handed them over in their
   terrible time of trouble.

10 Hebrew *your brother Jacob*. The names "Jacob" and "Israel" are often interchanged throughout the Old Testament, referring sometimes to the individual patriarch and sometimes to the nation.

NOTES
1:10 *close relatives in Israel*. Lit., "your brother Jacob." The charge of violence against kin comes to the fore. The reference to Jacob builds on the story of Jacob and Esau in Gen 25:19-26. As the descendant of Esau, Edom had a long history of enmity against Israel (cf. Joel 3:19).

1:11 *When they were invaded*. The construction points to a specific occasion (lit., "In the day that . . ."). During the time of greatest need, these near relatives deserted their Israelite kinsmen. The Hebrew noun *yom* [TH3117, ZH3427] (day) occurs 10 times in vv. 11-14. The repetition hammers home the seriousness of Edom's crimes against its brother. For Jacob, it was a day when foreign invaders entered Jerusalem, a day of misfortune, destruction, and distress, a day of disaster, and a day of trouble. The concentration on Edom's crimes in the day of their relative's need forms a thematic connection with the final verses, which tell of the Day of the Lord (1:15-21).

Foreign invaders. Jerusalem's attackers are called both *zarim* [TH2114B, ZH2424] (strangers) and *nakerim* [TH5237A, ZH5799] (foreigners). The former term lays stress on those who are distant, whereas the latter indicates ethnic differentiation. The NLT simply combines the two ideas into one concrete idea.

wealth. While the Hebrew noun could mean "strength," "power," or "army," contextually the sense of strength must lay in the city's wealth, since it is that which is carried off as booty (cf. 1:13).

1:12 *You should not have.* The same Hebrew construction occurs eight times in vv. 12-14. The repetition emphasizes the seriousness of Edom's unethical behavior. The construction itself may be construed differently depending upon one's understanding as to whether the occasion with which these verses are concerned has occurred, is taking place, or is yet to happen. If the time is past, this phrase may be understood as "do not," with the prophet vividly reliving the tragic events he is describing (Allen) or as "you should not have" (KJV, NRSV, NLT). If the time is present and the prophet is an eyewitness of what is taking place, it can be translated "do not," expressing urgent emotive prohibition (Laetsch). If the time is future, the words could be understood either as "do not" (Fausset, Pusey) or "you should not." Interestingly, Keil (1954:363) suggests that the time issue may be viewed as all-inclusive: "The warning in 1:12-14 is only intelligible on the supposition, that Obadiah . . . regards this as an event that not only has already taken place, but will take place again."

The construction *'al* [TH408, ZH440] + prefix conjugation normally means "oh please, do not"; hence translations embracing the idea of "you should not" have been often maligned. Yet Finley (1990:366) observes that although this translation has drawn severe criticism, "In the final analysis very little difference may exist between the two interpretations." The NLT is best understood as indicating that the prophet imagines himself observing the debacle that overtook Judah and Jerusalem in the Babylonian crisis.

gloated. The force of the verb *ra'ah* [TH7200, ZH8011] (see) varies with the context. The sense here demands either "disdain" (NIV) or a reference to the act of looking with satisfaction at someone's misfortune, hence "gloat." The Edomites' feelings, as their forces joined in on the triumph over the covenant people, are reminiscent of the sentiment in several psalms (e.g., Pss 54:7; 112:8; 118:7; cf. Isa 52:8; Mic 7:10). A similar reaction may be noted in the Moabite Stone (line 4): "(Chemosh) caused me to look in triumph over my enemies." (For text and translation see H. Donner and W. Röllig 1966:1.33; 2.168.)

when they exiled your relatives to distant lands. Lit., "In the day of your brother, the day of his misfortune." The force of the continual reiteration of the phrase "the day of" is cumulative. "His misfortune" (*nakro* [cf. TH5235, ZH5798]) provides a wordplay on "foreigners" (*nakerim* [TH5237A, ZH5799]) in v. 11. The NLT translates the sense of the passage accurately.

rejoiced. The Hebrew verb carries with it the nuance of gleeful joy or merriment, hence, "to proclaim one's joy without reserve" (Keil 1954:364). As Waltke observes, "The root *samakh* [TH8055, ZH8523] denotes being glad or joyful with the whole disposition" (TWOT 2.879). Here it involves a totally malicious glee over Judah's misfortune (Raabe 1996:179).

should not have spoken arrogantly. Edom's reprehensible conduct, previously called gloating and rejoicing, is shown to be even more flagrant. The Hebrew phrase says that they enlarged their mouths, hence the translation "jeered at," or "crowed over." Such conduct is indeed loathsome but is also in keeping with Edom's character. Thus, Allen (1976:157) remarks, "The attitude of arrogant superiority revealed in this gloating and taunting sounds like a deliberate reminiscence of the description of Edom's mentality in 1:3; Edom's pride was there used as a contrast to emphasize their coming fall."

1:13 *calamity.* Three more aspects of the day of Jerusalem's and Judah's distress are singled out: Edom entered Jerusalem's gate and added to the plundering of the city, gloated over the disaster that was overtaking it (cf. 1:12), and carried off its remaining wealth as booty (cf. 1:11). The thrice-repeated term "disaster" (*'ed* [TH343, ZH369]) lies behind the word translated *calamity* in NLT.

should not have seized their wealth. The enigmatic Hebrew verbal form here should be read as the energic *tishlakhannah* (2nd masc. sg.) rather than the MT *tishlakhnah* [TH7971, ZH8938] (3rd fem. pl.). There is no need to emend the consonantal text as several have suggested (see further Allen 1976:157).

1:14 *stood at the crossroads.* Lit., "stood at the break"—i.e., the place where the roads divide. Although Rudolph (1971:305) makes a case for this as a reference to the narrow entrances into Edomite territory, given the known fact of Jerusalem's fleeing refugees (2 Kgs 25:4-5), it seems easier to understand that Edom stationed itself at the major crossroads to cut off fleeing Judeans.

killing. The verb here (lit., "cut off") gives the reason for the prophecy that Edom itself will be cut off (cf. 1:9-10). In choosing this wording, Obadiah once again displays his literary ability in playing on ideas and repetition.

those who tried to escape. The noun here (*palit* [TH6412, ZH7127], "escaped one") anticipates Zion's deliverance mentioned in v. 17 (*peletah* [TH6413, ZH7129], "escape"). A similar play on the concept of escape and deliverance occurs in Joel (cf. Joel 2:3 with Joel 2:32). Likewise, the term "survivors" (*sarid* [TH8300, ZH8586]) designates that which remains—hence, a survivor or escapee (cf. Josh 10:20). Obadiah will build upon this idea to emphasize the total annihilation of Edom; there will be no survivors (*sarid* 1:18; cf. 2 Kgs 10:11). The noun is used theologically of Israel's remnant, preserved by God and restored to the land of promise (cf. Isa 1:9 with Joel 2:32). Obadiah's use of these two nouns that also occur in Joel may be deliberate.

terrible time of trouble. Obadiah repeats the idea emphasized in v. 12 (*beyom tsarah* [TH6869, ZH7650]) to express Judah's disastrous situation.

COMMENTARY

Obadiah now catalogs the precipitating causes for Edom's punishment. Edom's overt sins against God's people included (1) failing to aid them at the time of the invasion and gloating over their misfortune (1:11-12), (2) participating in the looting of Jerusalem (1:13), and (3) the ambush and delivery of Jerusalem's refugees into captivity.

The question arises as to the precise time of these despicable activities (see Introduction). Many suggest the time of Jehoram (ninth century BC), when a coalition of Arabs and Philistines invaded Judah and took away both the royal family and goods (2 Chr 21:8-17; 22:1). Scholars who defend this date find supporting scriptural data in passages such as Pss 79; 83; Joel 3:19; and Amos 1:6-8, 11-12, in the canonical position of Obadiah among the preexilic Minor Prophets, and in the failure of Jeremiah to include verses 10-14 in his prophecy against Edom (Jer 49:7-22). While the scriptural references may point to a long-standing preexilic hostility between Edom and Israel, they by no means prove that Obadiah is therefore a preexilic prophet. The canonical position of Obadiah is more likely due to associated themes, stitch phrases, and words. (See the insightful discussion in Cassuto 1973:1-6.) Jeremiah's "failure" to mention Obadiah 1:10-14 rests upon the assumption that Jeremiah depended upon Obadiah, a view that has failed to gain widespread acceptance (see the discussion in Watts 1969:29-33). The question remains as to whether the events of Jehoram's day really fit Obadiah's prophecy, and even if they do, would they mean that Obadiah is reporting matters as an eyewitness or merely as a commentator on past events?

Others opt for the time of Ahaz (735–715 BC), when Edom joined a coalition of nations in their concerted hostility against Judah (2 Chr 28:16-21; cf. 2 Chr 29:8-9). But while Joel's prophecy can be harmonized neatly with these events, the data in Obadiah are not so easily identified with them, particularly since there is no clear indication of the capture of Jerusalem at this time.

The views that link Obadiah with events during the invasion of Judah (2 Chr 24:23-24) in the reign of Joash (835–796 BC) or that relate Obadiah to the capture of Jerusalem by Jeroboam II in the time of Amaziah (796–767 BC), together with open hostilities between Judah and Edom (2 Kgs 14:7-14), are unconvincing. Edom's role in the time of Joash is uncertain at best, and the invaders in Amaziah's day were fellow Israelites, not foreigners.

Accordingly, most commentators decide for a date for these events around the time of the fall of Jerusalem, with Obadiah as an eyewitness. The Babylonian invasions of 597 BC and 586 BC clearly resulted in the plundering of Jerusalem, the deportation of its population, the slaughter of its citizens, the flight of its refugees, and the razing of the city (2 Kgs 24:13-16; 25:1-21; 2 Chr 36:15-21; Jer 39:1-10; 52:4-30).

Of particular significance are the accounts of Edom's conduct at this time. There is evidence of its participation as an ally in a coalition of states in ancient Palestine against Nebuchadnezzar (Jer 27:3; 40:11); yet it was later accused of taking vengeance on Judah (Ezek 25:12) and of delivering the Israelites "over to the sword at the time of their calamity, the time their punishment reached its climax" (Ezek 35:5, NIV; cf. Lam 1:17). Edom was equally guilty at this time of rejoicing in Jerusalem's destruction (Ps 137:7; Lam 2:15-17; 4:21; Ezek 35:11-15; 36:2-6); and it is therefore at this time that the prophetic announcements of Edom's annihilation reached a climax (Jer 9:26; 25:21; Lam 4:21-22; Ezek 25:13; 32:29; 35:3-4, 7-9, 11, 14-15; 36:7).

All of this is in harmony with a series of recent finds that indicate that Edom had increased its presence in the eastern Negev as early as the seventh century BC. Indeed, a whole line of fortifications was constructed to guard against such incursions and the continual Edomite menace (see Beit-Arieh 1996:28-36).

Although final certainty as to the connection of Obadiah to any particular historical occasion is lacking, the most likely event would be the Babylonian invasions of

Judah and the capture of Jerusalem in the early sixth century BC, sometime before Nabonidus's capture of Edom in 553 BC. If, as seems likely, Obadiah was an eyewitness to these events, he doubtless viewed all of this as the culmination of a long series of hostile activities for which kinsman Edom could expect the severe judgment of God.

Whatever the date of Edom's hostility, all such activities described here are termed *khamas* [TH2555, ZH2805] (violence) against God's people. The word speaks of a relentless cruelty born of hatred. People filled with hate are said to breathe out violence (Ps 27:12). The Scriptures warn against harboring hatred in one's heart (Lev 19:17; cf. 1 John 2:9, 11, 15; 4:20). It is simply the case that believers who nourish hatred in their soul can neither fulfill the righteous standards of Christian morality nor experience the full love of Christ in their lives. Rather, they will find that deep-seated hatred will only eat at the soul like a cancer until their Christian joy and usefulness for Christ are diminished.

Believers are to love that which is good (Amos 5:15; Rom 12:9) and to hate evil and every wrong course of action and attitude (Pss 97:10; 119:104, 128) and thus to fear the Lord (Prov 8:13). Even though they may expect to be hated because of their stand for Christ (Matt 10:22; Mark 13:13), they may take assurance in the knowledge of greater blessing for it (Luke 6:22). Indeed, they are enjoined to love their enemies and pray for their persecutors (Matt 5:43-45) and so fulfill the injunction of Christ to "love your enemies! Do good to those who hate you. Bless those who curse you. Pray for those who hurt you" (Luke 6:27-28).

◆ II. Edom and the Day of the Lord (1:15-21)
A. The Judgment of the Nations (1:15-16)

15 "The day is near when I, the LORD,
   will judge all godless nations!
As you have done to Israel,
   so it will be done to you.
All your evil deeds
   will fall back on your own heads.
16 Just as you swallowed up my people

on my holy mountain,
so you and the surrounding nations
   will swallow the punishment I pour
   out on you.
Yes, all you nations will drink and
   stagger
and disappear from history.

NOTES

1:15 *The day is near.* Verses 15 and 16 both begin with the particle *ki* [TH3588, ZH3954] (because). Verse 15 gives the reasons for the denunciation of Edom in the preceding verses; verse 16 introduces the reasons why Edom's conduct will fall back on itself. Both verses have a similar structure: causal clause/particle + comparative clause introduced by *ka'asher* [TH3509.1/834, ZH3869/889] (just as).

The Day of the Lord is a familiar OT theological term. The usual conception that it always speaks of judgment is erroneous, for it also often contains the accompanying hope of deliverance, restoration, and end-time felicity (see commentary on Zeph 3:9-13). Keil (1954:1.365) rightly observes, "The primary meaning is not the day of judgment, but the day on which Jehovah reveals His majesty and omnipotence in a glorious manner, to overthrow all ungodly powers, and to complete His kingdom."

As you have done to Israel, so it will be done to you. The law of equal justice will be applied (cf. Lev 24:20; Deut 19:21). Similar judgment is prophesied of others: Babylon (Jer 50:15, 29); and the Phoenicians and Philistines (Joel 3:4, 7).

1:16 *as you swallowed . . . the surrounding nations will swallow.* The singular verb of v.15 gives way here to a plural, perhaps to point out the culpability of individual Edomites. It may also convey a veiled hint of applying to any subsequent invaders (of whom Edom is a representative example), for the Day of the Lord concerns all nations (Laetsch 1956:205). The flow of the context makes it unlikely that the shift in number signifies a shift to a condemnation of the Judeans themselves (Fausset 1948:567; Raabe 1996:203-204).

will drink and stagger. The verb (*la'a'* [TH3886, ZH4363]) translated "stagger" here basically means "swallow" (cf. the derived noun *loa'* [TH3930, ZH4350], "gullet"). The two verbs are perhaps intended to be understood as a hendiadys, "gulp down" (Niehaus 1993:536). The imagery of the NLT envisions the result of drinking: Having drunk fully the cup of judgment, the invader will stagger and fall in a drunken stupor (cf. Isa 51:21-22; Hab 2:15-17). For drinking the cup as a metaphor of judgment, see Ps 75:7-8; Isa 51:17-23; Jer 25:15-27; 49:12-13; Ezek 23:31-34. Here the metaphor is a mixed one: The cup of enjoyment of the fruits of conquest will become one of the bitterness of divine wrath. A similar picture with regard to Edom is described in Lam 4:21-22.

disappear from history. Lit., "be as though they have never been." Edom will disappear from history and be forgotten so thoroughly that it will be as though they never existed at all. What Job (Job 3:3-7) wished for in his misery will happen to Jerusalem's persecutors.

COMMENTARY

The latter portion of Obadiah's prophecy provides details of Edom's future judgment while revealing Judah's restoration. The theological terminology involved is the "Day of the Lord." It describes the time of divine intervention to judge Edom and all the godless nations in just measure for their conduct, especially with regard to God's people (1:15-16). Although Edom will be ravaged, Jerusalem will become a refuge permeated by the presence of the Holy One of Israel (1:17-18). Moreover, a repentant, regathered, and restored Israel will enjoy a Promised Land with expanded boundaries in a kingdom that will belong to him to whom it rightfully belongs (1:19-21).

Obadiah's prediction concerning the Day of the Lord reflects familiar prophetic truths: God is sovereign and active in the affairs of human history; God will often employ earthly nations to effect his will; and God is just in his judgment, for all nations will be judged in a way commensurate with their deeds.[1] Prophecies concerning the Day of the Lord include events that are fulfilled in history and events that will not be fulfilled until the eschaton. Both near and distant details are often telescoped into a single context.[2] Such seems to the be case here. Whatever historical fulfillments of the prophecy concerning Edom are involved (see commentary on 1:18), it must be remembered that Edom is also a representative of the Gentile nations in opposition to God.

In connection with the Day of the Lord, Obadiah once more mentions the motif of the mountain (see Introduction): The invader has trampled on God's holy mountain (1:16). Zion was holy because the Holy God of the universe had his residence there (cf. Exod 15:13, 17; Ps 74:2; Isa 8:18). Accordingly, those who intruded on Jerusalem transgressed against God himself. They defiled his holy city and must therefore face the penalty of God's offended holiness. Edom (Mount Seir) was especially guilty and would face complete desolation (Ezek 35).

In contrast, Mount Zion will once again be holy (cf. 1:17), for a holy God will take up his residence there (1:21; Ezek 43:1-12; 48:35; Joel 3:17, 21). A purified Israel will be restored to its land (Zeph 3:8-20) to enjoy the age-old promises to the patriarchs (Ezek 20:39-44; 37:21-28). Then Jerusalem will become the center of worship for all peoples (Isa 2:2-5; 66:22-23; Mic 4:1-5; Zech 8:3; 14:16-21).

The Day of the Lord, then, involves both judgment and hope: judgment for Israel because its idolatrous and immoral behavior has violated the holy standards of God; and judgment for the nations, for they have trampled on God's holy city, presuming upon his holy person. Nevertheless, there is hope—hope for Israel because God's punishment is intended for their purification (Isa 54:11-17), and hope for the nations because the charter of God's covenant nation included provision for their eventual salvation (cf. 1:21; Gen 12:1-3; Isa 49:22). Obadiah's use of the metaphor of drinking the cup is taken up in the New Testament. Jesus drank the cup of divine wrath to the full (John 18:11); therefore, the cup of the new covenant may be drunk by all who have experienced his saving grace (Luke 22:20; 1 Cor 11:25-28).

These verses remind today's believers that, as ones united to Christ, they should be conformed to the image of God's Son. Because God is holy, they too should live holy lives (cf. Lev 11:44-45; 19:2 with Matt 5:48; 1 Pet 1:15-16), separated from sin's defilement (2 Cor 6:16–7:1; 1 Thess 4:7). Niehaus (1993:535) points out the consistent application of God's standards of justice and cautions, "Knowing this, let us not live as Edomites—as those hostile to God and as those who have no hope (1 Thess 4:13). But let God's people live out Christ Jesus—who is in us, the hope of glory."

ENDNOTES
1. For helpful observations on the principle of *lex talionis*, see Hill 1989:642. Hill goes on to point out that "even Paul acknowledges that a man reaps what he sows."
2. Laetsch (1956:204) declares, "This term comprises not only this one day, but also all its manifold heralds and forerunners and the eternities following upon the Last Day. . . . Therefore every judgment of God upon the wicked world is in a certain sense and to a certain extent a Day of the Lord."

◆   **B. The Restoration of Israel (1:17-21)**

¹⁷ "But Jerusalem* will become a refuge
      for those who escape;
    it will be a holy place.
    And the people of Israel* will come back
      to reclaim their inheritance.

¹⁸ The people of Israel will be a
      raging fire,
    and Edom a field of dry stubble.
    The descendants of Joseph will be
      a flame

roaring across the field, devouring
everything.
There will be no survivors in Edom.
I, the LORD, have spoken!

¹⁹ "Then my people living in the Negev
will occupy the mountains of Edom.
Those living in the foothills of Judah*
will possess the Philistine plains
and take over the fields of Ephraim
and Samaria.
And the people of Benjamin
will occupy the land of Gilead.

²⁰ The exiles of Israel will return to their
land
and occupy the Phoenician coast as
far north as Zarephath.
The captives from Jerusalem exiled in
the north*
will return home and resettle the
towns of the Negev.
²¹ Those who have been rescued* will go
up to* Mount Zion in Jerusalem
to rule over the mountains of Edom.
And the LORD himself will be king!"

17a Hebrew *Mount Zion.*   17b Hebrew *house of Jacob;* also in 18. See note on 10.   19 Hebrew *the Shephelah.*
20 Hebrew *in Sepharad.*   21a As in Greek and Syriac versions; Hebrew reads *Rescuers.*   21b Or *from.*

NOTES

1:17 Jerusalem. Lit., "Mount Zion." The term refers particularly to the Temple Mount, the abode of Israel's God (Pss 2:6; 74:2; 132:13). The term "Zion" became identified with Jerusalem, the city where it was located (Isa 40:9; Lam 1:6, KJV; Mic 3:12) and still later was used to indicate the whole land (Ps 126:1, KJV) and its populace (Zech 9:13, KJV).

holy place. The Hebrew root carries with it the implication of separation from all that is defiling or impure, hence, that which is sacred. This noun (*qodesh* [TH6944, ZH7731]), usually translated "holiness," may have been chosen to signify that the Holy God who dwells on Mount Zion and who has brought back a redeemed and purified remnant has rendered the city, people, and environs a total sacred continuum (cf. Isa 4:5-6; Joel 3:17; Zech 14:20-21). It may also imply the rebuilding of the Temple (Raabe 1996:243).

inheritance. Lit., "possessions"; the noun *morashehem* [TH4180, ZH4625]. The ancient versions translate "their possessors," reading the participle *morishehem* [TH3423, ZH3769] and giving the sense that the people of Israel will lay claim to those who once possessed them. This alternate reading may envision the Edomites or all of Israel's enemies (Amos 9:12). The MT may point to Israel's despoiling its enemies' possessions (Zech 14:14) or, as the NLT indicates, the claiming of the age-old promise of a land in perpetuity (Gen 12:7; 15:18-21; Exod 3:16-17; 6:8; Deut 6:3, 23; Ezek 11:15). The theme of possessing provides a common thread stitching the whole fabric of vv. 17-21.

1:18 Israel . . . Edom. The NLT's "Israel" comprises two terms in the Hebrew text: the house of Jacob and the house of Joseph. By the former, Obadiah may intend Judah or all Israel in contrast to Edom (= the house of Esau); by the latter, the northern ten tribes, either in distinction from Judah (Keil) or as added emphasis that the prophet does not restrict his prophecy to the southern kingdom (Finley, Raabe). The latter suggestion has the advantage of preserving the Jacob/Esau motif more clearly while the former serves to preserve the north/south distinction mentioned elsewhere (e.g., Zech 10:6).

fire . . . stubble. The image of fire consuming stubble represents defeat in battle (Isa 47:14; cf. Joel 2:5), at times comprising judgment at the hands of the Divine Warrior (Exod 15:7; Nah 1:6, 10; Mal 4:1).

no survivors. See the note on v. 14. The repetition of the term here provides further stitching with the previous section (1:10-14; cf. Num 24:18-19).

1:19 my people living in the Negev. The NLT renders properly the metonymy resident in the Hebrew "the Negev." This southern section of Judah was part of the original commission given to Moses and Israel (Deut 1:7) but had become inhabited by Edomites (Ezek

35:10, 12; 36:2-5) and in intertestamental times would become an Edomite territory known as Idumea. Repossession of the Promised Land was also part of the Deuteronomic covenant code (Deut 30:3-5). Here the returnees are portrayed as moving eastward into Edomite territory (lit., "Mount Esau").

the foothills of Judah. Heb. *the Shephelah.* This area, which is amid the western lowlands and the Judean hill country, was the locale of much border conflict with the Philistines. It had fallen into Assyrian hands in the late-kingdom period. The verb "possess" does not occur in the Hebrew text but is properly supplied from the previous line.

take over . . . Ephraim and Samaria. The Hebrew text does not specify which of the returnees will occupy Ephraim and Samaria. The NLT ties the retaking of these territories to the inhabitants of the Shephelah. However, the verb *yarash* [TH3423, ZH3769] (possess, take away, occupy) occurs twice in the verse, the first with the taking of the Negev and Shephelah, and the second here. Thus, it is perhaps better to discern two groups of movements: (1) Some Judeans move into the Negev and eastward while those of the Shephelah move westward into former Philistine territory, and (2) other Judeans go northward into Ephraim and Samaria while those of Benjamin move eastward into Gilead. Others (e.g., Allen, Finley) suggest that the more northerly tribes would take over these latter territories and then move eastward across the Jordan. Ephraim doubtless is metonymy for the whole of the northern kingdom, with its capital in Samaria spelled out here. Thus Laetsch (1956:210) remarks, "Obadiah regarded it necessary to name both 'the fields of Ephraim' and 'the fields of Samaria,' in order to make it clear that he was speaking of the entire kingdom, not only of either the tribe of Ephraim or the city of Samaria."

Gilead. Gilead lay generally east of the Jordan River and south of the Sea of Galilee and Yarmuk River. It fell into Assyrian hands during the era of the divided kingdoms. Several scholars have had difficulty with the prediction that Benjaminites would move into this territory. Some have viewed the text as corrupt (Stuart) or have suggested that perhaps Gilead is the name of an Israelite city (cf. Judg 10:17; Hos 6:8). Obadiah, however, may once again be employing metonymy—"Gilead" standing for all of Israel that formerly lived east of the Jordan (cf. Judg 20:1; 2 Kgs 10:33; Jer 50:19; Zech 10:10). In this case the citizens of Judah are pictured as moving southward, westward, northward, and eastward to reclaim the Promised Land.

1:20 *exiles.* The collective noun translated "exiles" refers to those deported in the various captivities of God's people. As an abstract noun, it can also refer to the exile itself (Amos 1:15).

exiles of Israel. The underlying Hebrew phrase is difficult to understand. Lit., "exiles of this fortress for the sons of Israel." The noun *khel* [TH2426, ZH2658] (rampart, fortress) is normally used of fortresses, a meaning that clearly does not fit here. Therefore, most scholars prefer the reading *khayil* [TH2428, ZH2657] (company, host, army), which supplies a better contextual meaning. Some scholars, however, have suggested reading *khalakh* [TH2477, ZH2712] (Halah), an area of Israel's exile in northern Mesopotamia (NRSV; cf. 2 Kgs 17:6). The NLT is compatible with the former alternative. Obadiah's defective spelling of the noun *khel* may have been to distinguish it from the homograph he used in vv. 11 and 13, which means "wealth" or "substance," a meaning not impossible here.

The sentence is complicated still further by the following *libene yisra'el 'asher kena'anim* [TH3669, ZH4050] (to me/my[?] sons of Israel who are Canaanites). Many suggestions have been made as to the reading of these words. Most consider the preposition *li* [TH3807.1, ZH4200] to be a corruption and omit it from consideration. It is also strange to call the Israelites "Canaanites." But Isa 19:18 calls Hebrew the language of Canaan, and Zeph 1:11 appears to describe selfish Hebrew merchants as moneygrubbing "Canaanites." (For the term "Canaan," see TDOT 7.211-228.) Nevertheless, the phrase "who are Canaanites" has been emended to yield such readings as "who are in Canaan" (NIV), "who are among the

Canaanites" (NASB), "[shall possess] that of the Canaanites" (KJV), and "[will have] the Canaanite land" (JB; cf. LXX, "to the sons of Israel shall belong the land of the Canaanites"; Latin Vulgate, "all the places of the Canaanites"). Many, like the NLT, translate the sense of the passage. For example, REB has "Exiles from Israel will possess Canaan"; GW has "Exiles from Israel will take possession of Canaan." Problems such as this validate the observation of Finley (1990:376) that "from the standpoint of the Hebrew text, 1:20 is the most difficult in the entire book of Obadiah to interpret."

On the whole, it seems best to retain the difficult MT and, in the same way that *yarash* [TH3423, ZH3769] did double duty in each line of v. 19, understand the preposition *be* [TH871.2, ZH928] (in/among) and the verb "possess" (from the second line of 1:20) to be syntactically operative in the first line of 1:20. Thus, the verse should read "The exiles of this company, of the sons of Israel who are [among] the Canaanites, [shall take possession] as far as Zarephath and the exiles of Jerusalem who are in Sepharad shall possess the cities of the Negev." So construed, v. 20 adds to v. 19 the understanding that in addition to the expansion in all directions of those left behind during the captivity, those who were exiled will return and be resettled to the full limits of the Promised Land, from north to south.

Zarephath. Zarephath was a Phoenician town south of Sidon famed for Elijah's miracle in the preservation of the widow's oil (1 Kgs 17:9-10; cf. Luke 4:26). The city fell to King Sennacherib of Assyria in 701 BC (ANET 287) and was later put under the control of Phoenician Tyre by Esarhaddon (681–668 BC).

the north. Lit., "in Sepharad." The identification of Sepharad is uncertain. At least six sites have been suggested: (1) Sparta (Keil), (2) the district of Shaparda in Media (Niehaus, Stuart), (3) Spain (Peshitta, Targum), (4) the Hesperides, islands off the coast of Libya (Gray 1953:53-59), (5) the Bosphorus (Latin Vulgate), and (6) Sardis in Asia Minor. (Allen [1976:171] documents two fifth-century BC Aramaic inscriptions pointing to the presence of Jews in the general area, one of which refers to the Lydian capital as *sprd*.) On the whole, the last suggestion appears to be most favorable and is compatible with the NLT.

1:21 Those who have been rescued. In agreement with the ancient versions, the NLT has translated this active participle ("those who deliver") as a passive participle ("those who have been delivered"). Verse 17 indicates that there will be deliverance on Mount Zion (NLT, "refuge for those who escape"). Taken as active, these deliverers have regained Jerusalem by conquest (Armerding, Keil). Laetsch (1956:212-213) relates the participle to its verbal root in a spiritual sense of "save"; thus they are saviors.

to rule. The Hebrew verb is used of judging but carries with it an administrative sense. Niehaus (1993:540) points out that Othniel and Ehud were called deliverers (Judg 2:16; 3:9, 15; cf. 2 Kgs 13:5).

Edom. The Hebrew term is Mount Esau. The mountain motif once again comes forward forcefully. The Jacob/Esau motif that is threaded throughout the prophecy reaches its climax here: Quite properly, Jacob (Israel) and Mount Zion win out over Esau (Edom) and Mount Seir (or Mount Esau).

the LORD himself will be king! The Hebrew reads, "The kingdom will be the LORD's." The noun "kingdom," as Niehaus (1993:541) notes, often connotes the sense of royal authority or dominion. Whatever judges may be given to the kingdom, royal authority belongs to the Lord himself (cf. Ps 22:28).

COMMENTARY

Obadiah's prophecy of the Day of the Lord reaches its climax in verses 19-21. The account of the victory over Edom (and the nations) that regains Jerusalem as a refuge for the godly remnant (1:17-18) is filled out to give details concerning the renewed kingdom of that day. The revivification of Judah is considered first (1:19): As Judeans living in the Negev and Shephelah (see note) spread out to the east and west to occupy the lands of two protracted enemies (Edom and Philistia), others join them from neighboring Benjamin to repopulate the old contours of the northern kingdom and the Transjordanian territories. Those carried away into captivity and exiled to various northern districts will return and join in the resettlement of the Promised Land to its full limits and even beyond (1:20). Obadiah's final glimpse of the day shows a newly appointed leadership ruling in Jerusalem under the authority of the true king on Mount Zion. Jerusalem will be blessed with the presence of a holy God dwelling in the midst of a purified people. Indeed, the whole city will be rendered a holy habitation.[1] In that day the long-standing hostility between Jacob and Esau will be resolved, with Israel safely in the land and occupying former Edomite territory.

Obadiah's closing words thus contain important theological information for the future. Here again, the contrast between Israel and her persecutors is underscored. The oppressors will be judged and God's people delivered. Thus, Obadiah's teaching (drawn from God's own declaration, 1:18b) concerning the Day of the Lord provides a note of hope for God's people. The holy city, trampled down and looted by its captors, will once again be a refuge for the restored remnant of Jerusalem.

Moreover, Israel—all Israel, north and south alike, will enjoy living in the land promised to their forefathers (Gen 13:15-17; Deut 30:1-5). Israel's enemies will have the tables turned on them as they suffer irreversible defeat at the hands of God's people. Like stubble ignited by flaming fire, Israel will rage through former Edomite territory in a victory so complete that Edom will never rise again as a political power.

Whatever future application these verses may have, such literally came to pass in historical times. The Edomites were driven from their ancestral home beginning in the sixth century BC, and by the fourth century BC, the former Edomite territory was controlled by the Arabian Nabateans. The surviving Edomites gradually settled in the Negev with the result that by the fourth century BC this territory was known as "Edom's land" or "Idumea." During the period of Judah's resurgence under the Maccabees, the Idumeans were defeated and several of their cities were taken (1 Macc 4:61; 5:3, 65; 2 Macc 10:15-23). Final subjugation of the area was accomplished by John Hyrcanus I (135–104 BC), Edomite national identity thus coming to an end (Josephus *Antiquities* 13.9.1; 13.15.4).[2]

These last verses also rehearse several key Old Testament theological truths. Here, as throughout the book, Obadiah is concerned with emphasizing that the Lord God is sovereign and therefore the rulership of all nations belongs to him (Ps 113:4). Israel's sovereign God is also active in the affairs of nations, whether internally or in their relations with one another.

Central to God's dealings in history is the fact that his role as history's regulator is mediated through his chosen people, Israel (Deut 32:8-9). Further, in preserving and delivering a remnant of his people, God demonstrated that the promises contained in the Abrahamic and Davidic covenants will find their complete fulfillment. Crucial to their accomplishment was the promise that Israel would possess its land. Indeed, Israel's land was always viewed as a gift from the Lord (Deut 1:8; 5:16). They would find rest there (Deut 12:9-11; Josh 1:13; 21:44; cf. Ps 95:11), and God himself would dwell there (Ezek 48:35) and establish his name there (Deut 12:5, NASB).

Obadiah has given news of an expanded kingdom that will be given to God's people. Yet, in an ultimate sense, the kingdom is the Lord's (Ps 47:7). It is a universal kingdom (Mic 4:1-5; Hab 2:14) in which the benefits of godly rule will be enjoyed by those who are his (Isa 65:17-25; Joel 3:17-21).

The notice that deliverance would come upon Mount Zion provides a link with the Davidic covenant and Old Testament Zion theology. Together with its emphasis on the successes of the Divine Warrior and the expectation of the coming kingdom in an era of everlasting peace and felicity, it also demands of its citizens a concern for righteousness, justice, love, humility, and adoration of the King. Concomitant with all of this is the messianic hope of the coming of a greater David who will establish righteousness and justice and will bring to full fruition all the provisions contained in the Abrahamic and new covenants (cf. Gen 17:1-8; 2 Sam 7:12-16; Jer 31:31-34; Ezek 37:21-28; Gal 3:26-29). Thus, the Old Testament promises find their culmination in the work of Christ himself (Acts 3:19-26; Rom 4:18-25).[3]

The choice of the term "rescuers" (1:21; cf. NLT mg) may contain a veiled spiritual hint. If so, Obadiah anticipates the day when every knee shall bow and every tongue confess the lordship of Christ (Phil 2:10-11), the deliverer who came to Zion and "will reign forever and ever" (cf. Gen 49:10; Pss 2:7-9; 22:28; Isa 11:1–12:6; Dan 7:13-14; Rev 11:15; 12:10; 19:15).

Obadiah's condemnation of Edom leaves a sobering challenge. Remembering that Edom stands prophetically as a type of the nations (cf. Isa 34:1-17; 63:1-6; Ezek 35:1-15; 36:1-38), these verses remind the believer that there is a day coming in which the nations of this world will feel the weight of God's judgment (Joel 3:12; 2 Pet 3:7-15). Ultimately, the Son of Man will come to defeat the nations (Rev 19:11-21), bring them before him to judgment (Matt 25:31-46; Acts 17:31), and rule over the earth in great power and everlasting peace (Isa 11–12; Dan 7:13-14; Rev 11:15). Knowing the destiny of all nations, the believer may not only take encouragement from the assurance that right will ultimately triumph but should also be challenged both to purity of living and to greater missionary endeavor (Acts 1:6-8; 1 Thess 5:1-11).

ENDNOTES
1. Thus D. Stuart (1987:420) remarks, "In effect all of Jerusalem, not just the temple area, will become a holy place where only righteous people, by reason of God's regulations of purity, are entitled to dwell (cf. Lev 21:11-23; Num 19:20)."
2. See the helpful summary in Armerding 1985:354-355. See also J. R. Bartlett, "The Moabites and Edomites," *People of Old Testament Times*, ed. D. J. Wiseman (Oxford: Clarendon, 1973), 229-258.
3. W. A. VanGemeren ("Psalms," in *The Expositor's Bible Commentary*, ed. F. E. Gaebelein [Grand Rapids: Zondervan, 1991], 356) points out that "the Zion theology correlates in a magnificent vision of what God has done, does, and will do . . . The glory of Zion is nothing less than the adoration of God-with-us (Immanuel)."

BIBLIOGRAPHY

Allen, L. C.
1976 *The Books of Joel, Obadiah, Jonah and Micah.* The New International Commentary on the Old Testament. Grand Rapids: Eerdmans.

Armerding, C.
1985 Obadiah. Pp. 333-358 in *Daniel, Minor Prophets.* The Expositor's Bible Commentary, vol. 7. Editor, F. E. Gaebelein. Grand Rapids: Zondervan.

Baker, D. W.
1988 Obadiah. Pp. 17-44 in *Obadiah, Jonah, Micah.* Tyndale Old Testament Commentaries. Downers Grove: InterVarsity.

Beit-Arieh, I.
1996 Edomite Advance into Judah. *Biblical Archaeology Review* 22:28-36.

Bewer, J. A.
1911 *A Critical and Exegetical Commentary on Obadiah and Joel.* International Critical Commentary. Edinburgh: T & T Clark.

Cassuto, U.
1973 *Biblical and Oriental Studies.* Jerusalem: Magnes.

Chisholm, R. B., Jr.
1990 *Interpreting the Minor Prophets.* Grand Rapids: Zondervan.

Coogan, M. D.
1978 *Stories from Ancient Canaan.* Philadelphia: Westminster.

Craigie, P. C.
1984 *Twelve Prophets,* vol. 1. Philadelphia: Westminster.

Donner, H. and W. Röllig
1966 *Kanaanaische und Aramaische Inschriften.* Wiesbaden: Otto Harrassowitz.

Fausset, A. R.
1948 *Obadiah* in *Jeremiah–Malachi.* A Commentary Critical, Experimental and Practical on the Old and New Testaments, vol. 4. Grand Rapids: Eerdmans.

Feinberg, C. L.
1976 *The Minor Prophets.* Chicago: Moody.

Finley, J. T.
1990 *Joel, Amos, Obadiah.* Chicago: Moody.

Gasque, W.
1986 Obadiah in *The International Bible Commentary,* 2nd ed. Editor, F. F. Bruce. Grand Rapids: Zondervan.

Gordon, C.
1965 *Ugaritic Textbook.* Rome: Pontifical Biblical Institute.

Gray, J.
1953 The Diaspora of Israel and Judah in Obadiah 1:20. *Zeitschrift für die alttestamentliche Wissenschaft* 65:53-59.

Grayson, A. K.
1972–1976 *Assyrian Royal Inscriptions* in *Records of the Ancient Near East* 1-2 (2 vols). Wiesbaden: Harrassowitz.

Hailey, H.
1972 *A Commentary on the Minor Prophets.* Grand Rapids: Baker.

Hill, Andrew
1989 Obadiah. Pp. 638-643 in *Evangelical Commentary on the Bible.* Editor, W. A. Elwell. Grand Rapids: Baker.

Keil, C. F.
1954 *The Twelve Minor Prophets,* vol. 1. Translator, J. Martin. Grand Rapids: Eerdmans. (Orig. pub. 1873.)

Laetsch, T.
1956 *The Minor Prophets.* St. Louis: Concordia.

Lehman, I. O.
1967 A Forgotten Principle of Biblical Textual Tradition Rediscovered. *Journal of Near Eastern Studies* 26:93-101.

Luckenbill, D. D.
1927 *Ancient Records of Assyria and Babylonia.* Chicago: University of Chicago Press.

Nash, K.
1987 Obadiah: Past Promises, Future Hope. *The Bible Today* 25:278-282.

Niehaus, J.
1993 Obadiah in *The Minor Prophets,* vol. 1. Editor, T. E. McComiskey. Grand Rapids: Baker.

von Orelli, C.
1897 *The Twelve Minor Prophets.* Edinburgh: T & T Clark.

Patterson, R. D.
1985 A Multiplex Approach to Psalm 45. *Grace Theological Journal* 6:37.

Pusey, E. B.
1953 *The Minor Prophets,* vol. 1. Grand Rapids: Baker.

Raabe, P. R.
1996 *Obadiah.* The Anchor Bible. Garden City: Doubleday.

Raven, J. H.
1910 *Old Testament Introduction.* New York: Revell.

Rudolph, W.
1971 *Joel-Amos-Obadja-Jona.* Kommentar zum Alten Testament. Gutersloh: Gerd Mohn.

Smith, B. K.
2001 Obadiah. The New American Commentary, vol. 19b. Nashville: Broadman & Holman.

Snyman, S. D.
1988 Obadja (on)preekbaar? [Obadiah, (un)preachable?]. *Nederduits Gereformeerde Teologiese Tydskrif* 29:216-223.

1989 Cohesion in the Book of Obadiah. *Zeitschrift für die alttestamentliche Wissenschaft* 101:59-71.

Stuart, D.
1987 *Hosea-Jonah.* Word Biblical Commentary. Waco: Word.

Sweeney, M. A.
2000 *The Twelve Prophets.* Berit Olam. Collegeville, MN: Liturgical.

Waltke, B. K. and M. O'Connor
1990 *An Introduction to Biblical Hebrew Syntax.* Winona Lake, IN: Eisenbrauns.

Watts, J. D. W.
1969 *Obadiah.* Grand Rapids: Eerdmans.

Wehrle, J.
1987 *Prophetie und Textanalyse: Die Komposition Obadja 1-21 interpretiest auf der Basis Textlinguistischer und semiotischer Konzeption.* St. Ottilen: Eos.

Young, E. J.
1953 *An Introduction to the Old Testament.* Grand Rapids: Eerdmans.

Jonah

RICHARD D. PATTERSON

INTRODUCTION TO
Jonah

JONAH WAS A COMPLEX CHARACTER. He was called by God to announce to Assyria (the world power of his day) that it must repent or face the judgment of God. But Jonah believed that Nineveh (the capital of Assyria) deserved the judgment of God. So he ran away. Dramatically rebuked and recalled by God, his message to Nineveh was well received with the result that a period of national repentance occurred, which in turn prompted God's mercy on the city. Jonah was disappointed that God had spared the mighty city, but God reminded him that he cares for the souls of all people—a good lesson for us all.

AUTHOR

Some modern scholars maintain the traditional Jewish and Christian position that the chief character of the book, Jonah son of Amittai, is also its author (e.g., Schrader 1989:644). Since most of the book does not claim to be Jonah's words and proceeds in third-person narrative, most contemporary scholars prefer to think of it as being authored by a single narrator who, though he possibly could be Jonah, is not likely to have been that well-known person (Stuart 1987:431-432). If Jonah is viewed as the author, he is doubtless to be identified with the prophet from Gath-hepher, who ministered in the days of Jeroboam II (792–752 BC; 2 Kgs 14:25).

DATE AND OCCASION OF WRITING

Critical scholars have largely decided against both the traditional date and author-ship of this book. The critical view proceeds along several lines of argument. Histor-ical blunders are said to be evident. For example, the statement that Nineveh *was* an illustrious city of *three days' journey* (3:3) is doubly faulted. (1) Since Nineveh no longer existed after 612 BC, it indicates that the narrative could only take place after that date. (2) Because Nineveh was less than three miles across in the eighth cen-tury BC, Jonah would scarcely need three days to cross it. But both arguments are faulty. The former suggestion flounders on the obvious use of "was" as simply being part of the narrative perspective of the book. The latter fails to reckon that because the term "great city" is used elsewhere in the Old Testament of a large, cosmopolitan area (Gen 10:11-12), it may refer here to "greater Nineveh," an area including Calah and Khorsabad.[1] The terms "great" and "three days" as applied to Nineveh may also simply be ancient Near Eastern protocol for describing the relative importance of the city.

Likewise, the reference to the king of Nineveh (3:6), rather than to the king of Assyria, is said to be both unprecedented and inaccurate because Nineveh was not the capital in the early eighth century BC. Yet, in the Old Testament, kings are at times designated by a chief city, such as in the case of "Ahab king of Samaria" (1 Kgs 21:1, NASB) and the Aramean king who was known as the "king of Damascus" (2 Chr 24:23, NASB). Although Nineveh did not become the official capital of Assyria until the time of Sennacherib (705–681 BC), "Assyrian kings had their seats in Nineveh as early as the tenth century BC and at least two kings before the eighth century had their palaces built there."[2]

Other texts that have appeared to strain historical credulity include (1) the supposed figure of 600,000 people in Nineveh (an estimate based upon the 120,000 "children" in 4:11)[3]; (2) the issuing of the decree by king and nobles together in 3:7; and (3) the clothing of animals in sackcloth in 3:8. However, (1) the 120,000 figure may intend the total population of greater Nineveh or be symbolic of Nineveh's greatness; (2) granted the weak political position of the kings in the mid-eighth century BC, a decree may well have been issued together with the name of a strong provincial governor;[4] and (3) one cannot be certain of specific Assyrian customs.[5] Attempts to date the composition of the book to the fifth century BC due to its supposed purpose as an allegory designed to promote a more universalistic spirit in the face of the narrow nationalistic spirit of the age are scarcely convincing. As Archer (1974:309) points out, not only do numerous points in the Jonah narrative fail to fit the criteria of allegory, but "there is not the slightest historical evidence to show the existence of any such universalistic sentiment among the fifth-century Jews, as this theory predicates." Archer suggests further that this supposed zeal demonstrates circular reasoning: Jonah must have been written in a later period because of the supposed character of Jewish thought in that age—as attested only by the book of Jonah! The failure of the critical view to prove its case categorically, therefore, makes it clear that there is no certain historical reason to abandon the traditional eighth-century date for the setting of the book, regardless of whether one holds the view that Jonah authored the book (D. Alexander 1988:61).

Critics have also doubted the preexilic date on the basis of linguistic perceptions. Thus, Jonah is said to be typically late Hebrew, highly influenced by "Aramaisms," a sure indicator of the postexilic period. A closer analysis of the data, however, indicates that the critical conclusion is vastly overdrawn and that Jonah may even reflect a more northerly Hebrew dialect.[6] In any case, the presence of Aramaisms found as early as the second millennium BC in Ugaritic makes any supposed dating argument based on Aramaic somewhat tenuous. As Baldwin (1993:546) concludes, "On linguistic evidence there is no reason why the book should not be pre-exilic, even eighth-century, in origin."

The trustworthiness of Jonah is also questioned on the basis of the fish episode (a whale of a tale!) and the impossibility of a heathen city repenting at the preaching of an Israelite prophet. Both suggestions, of course, discount supernatural intervention. Moreover, the political weakness of the crown, as well as the presence of plagues in 765 and 759 BC (or through the whole period?), as well as the occurrence of a solar eclipse in 763 BC,[7] may have provided a ready environment for the reception of the message of this prophet of Yahweh.

In light of the above discussion, the setting of the book can be and is probably best dated to the reign of Jeroboam II, probably during the reign of the Assyrian ruler Ashur-dan III (771–754 BC). It was a time of Assyrian weakness, a time when royal political power had to be exercised cautiously through strong provincial governors who may have reduced the king to little more than king in name only—and that to little more than his city of residence (Grayson 1982:273-275; see also Olmstead 1951:172-174; Saggs 1984:82-84). Wilson (1985:186) points out that "Though Nineveh did not become the permanent capital of Assyria until Sennacherib ruled (705–682 BC), Assyrian kings had their seats in Nineveh as early as the thirteenth century BC. As a royal residence, Nineveh alternated with Ashur and Calah (Nimrud) throughout the Early, Middle, and Late Assyrian periods." Another view of the king living in Nineveh comes from Lemanski (1992:46) who suggests the possibility that Nineveh was, at this time of political weakness, "an independent or semi-independent city state with its own ruler."[8] Some evidence suggests that the era was also a time of economic difficulty for Assyria, a condition that was only worsened by the great plagues of 763 and 759 BC. This, together with the solar eclipse mentioned above and some military defeats, could make a superstitious and worried people quite ready to receive God's prophet and his words.

If, then, the traditional date for the ministry of Jonah can be adopted, there is little reason to suggest a much later time for the composition of the book. In light of Assyria's known past atrocities and the actual hostility of Shalmaneser III in the ninth century BC against Ahab and Jehu, neither Jonah nor his contemporaries would be able to understand why God would send him to Nineveh to warn that traditional enemy and impious city. Accordingly, following a return from Nineveh, Jonah may have recorded his own mistaken concept of God's concern for a lost mankind as a means of justifying the ways of God to his countrymen. The book, then, while containing prophetic and didactic historical narrative, is also a type of theodicy (see "Literary Style"). However tragic this incident in the prophet's life had proven to be, God would use it as a didactic tool to inform Israel that "God cares about all the people of the earth" (Limburg 1993:34).

AUDIENCE

D. Alexander (1988:62) cautions that "experience shows that any attempt to identify the audience of the book is likely to be too subjective to be of lasting value in determining its date of composition." However, if the previous argumentation as to the dating of Jonah's ministry is valid, it could be that Jonah's audience was his contemporaries in the northern kingdom. Despite the territorial gains during the years of Jeroboam II's reign, the old enmity with Assyria and the important city of Nineveh remained. Perhaps like Jonah, who was grateful enough for temporary shade from the heat of the day but unmoved concerning the people to whom he had been sent to minister, his peers were grateful enough for the God-given successes of Jeroboam but had little concern for others, particularly hated traditional enemies. In this regard, Jonah became a symbol to Israel of their "disobedience to God and indifference to the religious plight of other nations" (Hannah 1985:1462). They, like Jonah (and like all of us),[9] needed to learn something of the divine intention for people and nations, and "of the all-embracing love of that God we serve" (Baldwin 1993:548).

CANONICITY AND TEXTUAL HISTORY

The canonicity of Jonah has never been seriously doubted. It was accepted with the rest of the Minor Prophets by Ben Sirach (Sir 49:10) and is mentioned by several writers in a way that assumes its early canonical acceptance (cf. 3 Macc 6:8 of the first century BC). The book was apparently viewed as such in the first century AD by Jesus (Matt 12:40-41) and Josephus (*Antiquities* 9.208-214), as well as in the second century in 2 Esdras (1:38-40) and the *Sibylline Oracles* (2:241-248[307]).[10]

Scholars of all persuasions acknowledge that the text of Jonah is "exceedingly well preserved" (Allen 1976:191). Early standardization of the text is confirmed by its inclusion in the scroll of the Minor Prophets found at Wadi Murabba'at. D. Alexander (1988:94-95) remarks, "This scroll, copied shortly prior to AD 135, confirms that the Hebrew text of Jonah was carefully preserved by the Masoretes. But for a few minor differences in orthography, this text is identical to that of the best medieval manuscripts."

LITERARY STYLE

Scholars debate about the book's literary genre. Several proposals have been made. Among the many, T. D. Alexander (1985:36-37) lists "history; allegory; midrash; parable; prophetic parable; legend; prophetic legend; novelle; satire; didactic fiction; satirical, didactic, short story." To these could be added still others, such as prophetic tract (Ratner), didactic history (T. D. Alexander) or tale (Gese), tragedy (Woodward), comedy (McCann, Howell), and political cartoon (Trudinger). Essentially, however, the list can be viewed as to whether a given author considers Jonah to be fiction or fact.

Despite the amount of modern critical scrutiny, it is true that "the vast majority of early Jewish and Christian writers adopted the view that the events recorded in Jonah actually occurred" (T. D. Alexander 1985:57). The lack of unanimity among critics as to the nature of the genre, together with the opening statement of the book reflecting standard historical notices found in other narrative portions of prophetic material (Collins 1995:30-32) remind us that a good case can be made for taking Jonah as both factual and prophetic. While (as has been pointed out above) the book does display strong didactic purposes, these need not obviate its historicity. Historical fact can be narrated for didactic purposes, as well as for historical record.

Despite critical concerns, then, the book is best taken as it purports to be, a factual record in connection with Jonah's prophetic ministry in Nineveh. Thus, it is prophecy that is intended to be read as a didactic historical narrative, which justifies the ways of God to the citizens of the northern kingdom (thus it is also a theodicy).

The nature of its factual value in no way mitigates its high literary artistry. Particularly striking is the book's careful design, being developed in a structure by which chapters 1-2 are balanced with chapters 3-4 (Collins 1995:32-33). Many scholars have pointed to the fact that the book's well-developed plot structure is artfully crafted around the use of a specialized vocabulary.

In this regard, Jonah repeated certain words throughout his presentation, often with contextual distinction. For example, the concept of perishing ('abad [TH6, ZH6]) is used in the context of the sailors' fears (1:6, 14), the king of Nineveh's concern for the safety of his populace (3:9), and the plant that perished (4:10), while the idea of death (maweth [TH4194, ZH4638]) and dying (muth [TH4191, ZH4637]) is clustered in the fourth chapter (4:3, 8-9). Likewise, the concept of evil or calamity (ra'ah [TH7451B, ZH8288]) describes Nineveh's wickedness (1:2) and its citizens' evil practices (3:8, 10), the troublesome danger that Jonah's disobedience had brought upon the sailors (1:7-8), Jonah's displeasure with God's choice not to punish Nineveh (4:1), God's unrealized punishment itself (4:2), and Jonah's discomfort (4:6). The verb qara' [TH7121, ZH7924] is used of Jonah's commission to proclaim God's message (1:2; 3:2) and his eventual carrying out of the task (3:4), of people's calling on God (1:6, 14; 2:2[3]; 3:8), and of royal proclamations (3:5). The most frequently found word is the adjective gadol [TH1419, ZH1524] (great), being used of the city of Nineveh (1:2; 3:2-3; 4:11) and its nobles (3:7); of the great storm (1:4, 12) and the sailors' fear (1:10, 16); of the fish that swallowed Jonah (1:17[2:1]); and of Jonah's contrasting displeasure (4:1) and happiness (4:6).

Also to be noted is the use of sound play at various levels (see Halpern and Friedman 1980; Wilt 1992), as well as a section of psalmic material (2:1-9[2-10]). Noteworthy, as well, is the author's use of irony and satire (Ryken 1987:337-340). The conclusion of Dillard and Longman (1994:392) is apropos: "The book is a literary *tour de force*. It is brilliant in its use of structure, irony, and rhetorical ornamentation."

MAJOR THEMES

In keeping with the book's purposes and literary approach, several key themes may be discerned. Foremost among these is God's dealing with his runaway prophet. In this connection one may note the theme of "going" (i.e., up or down; e.g., 1:3, 6; 2:6[7]; 4:6-7). Because Nineveh's wickedness has come up before God, Jonah is to go to Nineveh (1:2). Instead, he fled and went down to Joppa and into a ship's hold (1:3, 6). Later, he went down to the depths in the fish's belly (2:6[7]), where he responded to God and followed the original command to go up to Nineveh (3:2). When, however, the Lord blessed his ministry with Nineveh's repentance, Jonah got angry. Accordingly, God provided a plant to go up over his sullen prophet, which dried up at the "going up" of the dawn (4:6-7). The motif thus expresses well Jonah's rising and falling fortunes in his spiritual struggle before and with God.

Other themes of note include that of calling (1:2, 6, 14; 2:2[3]; 3:2, 4, 6, 8), wickedness (1:2, 7-8; 3:8, 10; 4:1-2), and repentance and prayer (1:14; 2:7-9[8-10]; 3:5-10; 4:2). Underlying the whole, of course, are the theological themes of divine sovereignty, love, and forgiveness.

THEOLOGICAL CONCERNS

As noted above, the book of Jonah (like Daniel) reminds its readers of God's sovereignty (Schrader 1989:644). He is in control, not only of the elements of the natural world (e.g., the sea, the fish, the plant), but the destinies of people (the Ninevites, the sailors, and God's prophet). He is the only true God (1:9), the God whose wise direction and intervention into the flow of earth's history are intended for people's good (2:10[11]; 3:9-10; 4:6-8).

God is also shown to be one who genuinely loves and cares for all the people of the earth, Jew and Gentile alike, faithful believer, and even runaway prophet. The book emphasizes throughout that where there is true repentance, God may relent the threatened punishment. Both Jonah and the Ninevites experienced the full force of God's love and forgiveness. As Stuart (1987:98) appropriately observes, "People, no matter how wicked, are still valuable to God. They are intrinsically objects of his love." The book also reminds all people of the need for prayer (1:14; 2:1-9[2-10]) and the need to respond to God's goodness in genuine worship (1:16; 2:4[5], 8-9[9-10]; 3:5-9).

OUTLINE

I. The Prophet at Sea (1:1–2:10)
   A. Jonah's Commission and Response (1:1-3)
   B. Jonah and the Sailors (1:4-16)
   C. Jonah and God (1:17–2:10)
II. The Prophet at Nineveh (3:1–4:11)
   A. Jonah's Recommissioning and Response (3:1-3a)
   B. Jonah and the Ninevites (3:3b-10)
   C. Jonah and God (4:1-11)

ENDNOTES

1. See A. Parrot, *Nineveh and the Old Testament* (New York: Philosophical Library, 1955), 85-88. Other scholars have suggested that Jonah simply spent three days preaching from corner to corner (e.g., Archer 1974:310-311), or that ancient Near Eastern customs of hospitality would have dictated a three-day period with specific practical arrangements (Wiseman 1979:38), or that three days may be symbolic of a large, illustrious city (Wolff 1976:148).
2. See M. R. Wilson, "Nineveh," in *Major Cities of the Biblical World* (Nashville: Nelson, 1985), 186.
3. The NLT takes the Hebrew "who do not know their right from their left" as indicative of "spiritual darkness." It can also be taken as indicative of physical/mental immaturity, hence the understanding of some that these 120,000 are children.

4. See P. J. N. Lawrence, "Assyrian Nobles and the Book of Jonah," *Tyndale Bulletin* 37 (1986):121-132. J. Lemanski (1992:46) proposes that "it is quite possible that Nineveh at the time of Jonah's ministry was an independent or semi-independent city-state with its own ruler." Although he makes his case for the preceding two reigns of Adad-nirari III and Shalmaneser IV, there is little to suggest that conditions changed with Ashur-dan III and Ashur-nirari IV. It was the decisive role of Tiglath-pileser III (745–727 BC) that brought about change in the royal prestige.

5. See, for example, the clothing of animals in sackcloth recorded in Jdt 4:9-10.

6. See G. Loretz, "Herkunft und Sinn der Jonaerzahlung," *Biblische Zeitschrift* 5 (1961): 19-22; G. M. Landes, "Linguistic Criteria and the Date of the Book of Jonah," *Eretz Israel* 16 (1982):147-170.

7. Cf. comments on Jonah 3:5 and Joel 2:31. As for further arguments that Jonah is dependent on Jeremiah or Joel (cf. Jonah 3:9-10 with Jer 18:7-8; 26:3; Jonah 3:9 with Joel 2:14; Jonah 4:2 with Joel 2:13)—hence a late book—Stuart (1987:433) aptly remarks, "There simply is not enough evidence either to prove or to disprove such speculations."

8. Such a free city is known to have existed in the reigns of kings preceding the accession of Tiglath-pileser III in 747 BC. See D. Luckenbill, *Ancient Records of Assyria and Babylonia* (Chicago: University Press, 1926), 1.295-296.

9. C. J. Collins (1995:37) reminds us that God's final question (4:11) "still hangs in front of each new reader: 'You are Jonah—what is your answer?'"

10. See Limburg (1993:99-123) for Jonah's lively reception through the ages. Jonah is still read annually in the Jewish community on Yom Kippur as a solemn reminder that Israel's God is concerned to receive repentant Gentiles.

COMMENTARY ON
Jonah

♦ I. The Prophet at Sea (1:1–2:10)
   A. Jonah's Commission and Response (1:1-3)

The LORD gave this message to Jonah son of Amittai: ²"Get up and go to the great city of Nineveh. Announce my judgment against it because I have seen how wicked its people are."

³But Jonah got up and went in the opposite direction to get away from the LORD. He went down to the port of Joppa, where he found a ship leaving for Tarshish. He bought a ticket and went on board, hoping to escape from the LORD by sailing to Tarshish.

NOTES

1:1 *The LORD gave this message.* Lit., "and the word of the Lord came." Similar opening formulae occur in the OT over 100 times, each used to express divine communication to a prophet. The reception of the word of the Lord authenticated one as God's prophet. The exact Hebrew idiom *wayehi* [TH2050.1/1961, ZH2256/2118] (and it came to pass), however, appears as an opening phrase in a prophetic book only here and in Ezekiel.

Jonah. Jonah's name means "dove." Although various fanciful attempts have been made to relate the prophet's name symbolically to such matters as the plot of the narrative or to conditions in the northern kingdom, the common use of animal names for human beings in Hebrew makes such reconstructions precarious at best.

son of Amittai. Jonah's full designation identifies him with the prophet from Gath-hepher, who prophesied during the reign of Jeroboam II (2 Kgs 14:25). Taken at face value, this phrase indicates that the following narrative tells of events that took place in the first half of the eighth century BC (see Introduction). If it could be determined whether this episode in Jonah's life took place before or after that which is recorded in 2 Kings, it would have a distinct bearing on one's understanding of the prophet's spiritual odyssey.

1:2 *Get up and go.* Lit., "Arise! Go!" The double imperatives carry with them a sense of urgency. Since Hebrew syntax dictates that the major stress in such cases is on "the going" (*Gesenius' Hebrew Grammar*, §120g [286-287]), Jonah is to respond immediately to the Lord's command. Similar injunctions were given to Elijah (1 Kgs 17:9) and Jeremiah (Jer 13:6).

the great city of Nineveh. Like the Hebrews' own Jerusalem (Jer 22:8), Nineveh was termed a "great city" (cf. also Babylon, Dan 4:30; Gibeon, Josh 10:2). While the adjective could indicate size here, it may also have to do with the city's status or prominence (Wiseman 1979:35-36)—perhaps both are intended. By ancient Near Eastern standards, Nineveh was a sizeable and illustrious city. Nineveh's greatness serves as an important thematic thread woven throughout the fabric of the book (cf. 3:2-3; 4:11). Nineveh was a city with a long and important history stretching back to the third millennium BC, and God was concerned for the people in this city.

Announce my judgment against it. The root *qara'* [TH7121, ZH7924] is used with great frequency in the book (see Introduction). Here it is used with the preposition *'al* [TH5921, ZH6584], thus "preach against." Although some commentators equate the force of this phrase with *qara' 'el* [TH413, ZH448] (preach unto), Keil (1954:389) may be correct in insisting on their differentiation. The NLT has preserved the distinction (cf. 3:2).

I have seen how wicked its people are. Lit., "their wickedness has come up before me." The cause for the Lord's judgment against Nineveh is spelled out (cf. 3:8, 10). The noun translated "wicked" here (*ra'ah* [TH7451B, ZH8288]) is used elsewhere in Jonah in various senses and provides a thematic thread in three of the four chapters of the book (see Introduction). Sadly, Nineveh's extreme wickedness and cruelty would only intensify in the following century, as attested by Nahum and Zephaniah.

1:3 *Jonah got up.* God instructed Jonah to get up, and so he did; but he arose to follow a course opposite to that which the Lord had commanded him.

to get away from the LORD. The Hebrew text indicates that Jonah was attempting to flee from the presence of the Lord. Unlike Jeremiah (Jer 17:16), Jonah was a runaway prophet. Although Nineveh's case had come up before God, Jonah would go "in the opposite direction"—away from the Lord's presence. The play on words and ideas is instructive. As Limburg (1993:43) points out, "Only Cain, the murderer, is described in the Bible as making a similar attempt to run 'away from the presence of the LORD' (Gen 4:16)." Since Jonah himself acknowledged that God is the maker of heaven and earth (1:9) and since he was probably acquainted with the older story of Job (cf. Job 23:10; 38:4-14), he presumably would have been aware that no one could be out of the view of the omnipotent Creator and sustainer of the earth (cf. Ps 139:7-10). Thus, the motivation for Jonah's flight must be sought in something other than his physical removal from God. While Stuart (1987:450) suggests that "Jonah, the ardent nationalist, therefore, attempted to flee to a place where no fellow believers would be found, hoping that this would help insure that God's word would not come to him again," Calvin and others (cf. Allen 1976:205; D. Alexander 1988:101) are probably correct in affirming that the phrase simply indicates that Jonah is announcing his unwillingness to serve God in this capacity. Thus Laetsch (1956:222) observes, "To flee from His presence = to refuse to serve Him in this office."

He went down. This is the first of several instances of Jonah's "going down." Although Stuart (1987:437-438, 451-452) points to the simplicity of vocabulary in the Jonah narrative and the natural use of "going down" in the various occasions where the term is used in the book, the literary plays in the use of this and other items of vocabulary seem far too well-placed to be so easily dismissed.

Joppa. This port city (modern Jaffa) is known to have existed at least from the seventeenth century BC (Kaplan and Kaplan 1976:2.532-541). Known as Yapu in the fourteenth-century BC Egyptian Amarna Letters and Yappu in the neo-Assyrian inscriptions, it was likely controlled by the Philistines in the early centuries of the first millennium BC. Because it was the only natural harbor on the south Palestinian coast, it was important as a seaport for the area (2 Chr 2:16; Ezra 3:7). In New Testament times, the apostle Peter visited there, staying at the home of Simon, a tanner (Acts 9:43). Joppa was the location of Peter's well-known vision regarding ritual purity and his meeting with the Roman centurion Cornelius (Acts 10:1-11:18).

he found a ship. Sasson (1990:81) points out that "the verb *matsa'* [TH4672, ZH5162] . . . often involves an unexpected discovery or good fortune. From Jonah's perspective, as contrasted to the reader's or the author's, the fact that he found a ship going to the earth's other extremity must have promised a successful flight from God."

Tarshish. The location of Tarshish is uncertain. (For details, see my remarks in *The Expositor's Bible Commentary* 4.103, 4.169.) Although several sites have been suggested, Allen (1976:205) is probably correct in following Albright's dictum: "There were doubtless at

least as many Phoenician settlements which bore the name *Tarshish* as there were 'New
Towns' [= Carthage]." Wherever its location, the point is that Jonah was attempting to go
as far west from Nineveh (which lay to the east) as he possibly could. Tarshish was grouped
with other lands beyond the sea that had not heard of God nor seen his glory (Isa 66:19).

bought a ticket. Several expositors have suggested that Jonah paid the total expenses for
the whole ship. While the Hebrew phrase can be understood to mean "paid its (the ship's)
hire," the matter is far from certain. The jettisoning of the cargo (1:5), as well as the ship's
indicated destination, would tend to suggest that the ship had already been loaded for its
intended voyage and that Jonah had stumbled fortuitously upon it as it was about to set
sail. If so, it may be best to retain the traditional understanding as reflected in the NLT
(cf. LXX, Vulgate, NIV, NRSV).

the LORD. This is Yahweh (*yhwh* [TH3068, ZH3378]), the name of the covenant God of Israel;
it is found ten times in ch 1, five times in chs 2 and 4, and two times in ch 3. The generic
term for God, *'elohim* [TH430, ZH466], occurs some twelve times, while the compound designation *yhwh 'elohim* is found four times. The term *'el* [TH410A, ZH446] occurs but once (4:2).
Several expositors have commented on the careful deployment of the names. Thus Limburg
(1993:45-47) thinks *yhwh* is used to refer to the God a Hebrew would know, but *'elohim*
is employed when speaking of a god known to non-Israelites. He suggests further that the
compound *yhwh 'elohim* is a transitional name, while the single occurrence of *'el* is due to
traditional creedal formulations.

COMMENTARY

The opening words of the book remind all who read them that God is a God of revelation. His will and his standards have been communicated to mankind, and the
Scriptures are that revelation. Therefore, even when reading a good story in the
Bible, such as that of Jonah, the believer is to remember that the account has a
divine purpose, both for those involved in the various episodes and for those who
read them. Paul puts it well, "All Scripture is inspired by God and is useful to teach
us what is true and to make us realize what is wrong in our lives. It corrects us when
we are wrong and teaches us to do what is right. God uses it to prepare and equip his
people to do every good work" (2 Tim 3:16-17).

    This opening passage of Jonah also indicates that God does indeed call and com-
mission some to be his special ambassadors. Whether a Jeremiah of Old Testament
times (Jer 1:4-10) or a Paul of New Testament days (Acts 9:1-19; Gal 1:10-17), those
who would serve as pastors or missionaries should be conscious of God's claim
upon them (Eph 4:11).[1]

    These verses also testify to the nature and character of God. An omniscient God,
he knew not only the state of affairs in Nineveh and with his prophet, but was and is
cognizant of all that takes place on earth (Prov 15:3; Isa 46:10; Jer 23:23-25; Heb
4:13). The Scriptures also reveal that in addition to knowing the hearts of all people,
God cares about their well-being. The great city of Nineveh was in a desperate state.
The word translated "wicked" (*ra'ah* [TH7451B, ZH8288]) can also be used of personal or
corporate troubles or calamities. As such, it is admirably suited to depict not only
Nineveh's recent calamitous events (see Introduction), but its moral perversity that
may have occasioned such troubles.[2] If God has such concern for the welfare of a
people that merited only his judgment (cf. 4:11; 2 Pet 3:9), how much more should

believers understand that God knows their every need and longs to lead them into increasingly productive and satisfying lives.

This passage also teaches us about disobedience. God's disobedient prophet had willfully turned away from a sovereign God who wanted him to be an instrument of his will. One might think, "How shocking!" Yet how easy it is for all of us to do the same.[3] Like Jonah, each one of us must come to realize that because God is not only sovereign but truly omnipotent, disobedience is both useless and foolish (cf. 1 Sam 15:23). As Jonah was to pay a heavy price for his sinful behavior, so sin always pays heavy wages to those in its employ (Prov 14:11; Rom 6:23). May God help each of us to be obedient, faithful, and profitable servants so that we may experience the Lord's good favor not only throughout this life but also in that to come (Ps 31:23; Matt 25:23; 2 Tim 1:12).

ENDNOTES

1. R. Baxter (*The Reformed Pastor* [London: Epworth Press, 1950], 119-120) said of the pastoral office, "God hath determined by His word that there shall be such an office . . . and what sort of men, as to their qualifications shall receive it. . . . God also giveth men the qualifications which he requireth." C U. Wagner (*The Pastor* [Schaumburg: Regular Baptist Press, 1976], 1) remarks, "One of the most vital areas of pastoral theology is that of the call to the ministry; the awareness of such a call is imperative."
2. Thus Stuart (1987:449) observes, "God's compassion had been aroused by the misfortune. Instead of simply destroying the city for its evil, he would give it a chance to repent so as to remove the misfortune. Jonah would announce the chance."
3. Ellison (1985:369) astutely notes that "the Christian worker anxious to avoid the full impact of modern problems should have no difficulty in understanding Jonah's action."

◆   ## B. Jonah and the Sailors (1:4-16)

[4]But the LORD hurled a powerful wind over the sea, causing a violent storm that threatened to break the ship apart. [5]Fearing for their lives, the desperate sailors shouted to their gods for help and threw the cargo overboard to lighten the ship.

But all this time Jonah was sound asleep down in the hold. [6]So the captain went down after him. "How can you sleep at a time like this?" he shouted. "Get up and pray to your god! Maybe he will pay attention to us and spare our lives."

[7]Then the crew cast lots to see which of them had offended the gods and caused the terrible storm. When they did this, the lots identified Jonah as the culprit. [8]"Why has this awful storm come down on us?" they demanded. "Who are you? What is your line of work? What country are you from? What is your nationality?"

[9]Jonah answered, "I am a Hebrew, and I worship the LORD, the God of heaven, who made the sea and the land."

[10]The sailors were terrified when they heard this, for he had already told them he was running away from the LORD. "Oh, why did you do it?" they groaned. [11]And since the storm was getting worse all the time, they asked him, "What should we do to you to stop this storm?"

[12]"Throw me into the sea," Jonah said, "and it will become calm again. I know that this terrible storm is all my fault."

[13]Instead, the sailors rowed even harder to get the ship to the land. But the stormy sea was too violent for them, and they

couldn't make it. ¹⁴Then they cried out to the LORD, Jonah's God. "O LORD," they pleaded, "don't make us die for this man's sin. And don't hold us responsible for his death. O LORD, you have sent this storm upon him for your own good reasons."

¹⁵Then the sailors picked Jonah up and threw him into the raging sea, and the storm stopped at once! ¹⁶The sailors were awestruck by the LORD's great power, and they offered him a sacrifice and vowed to serve him.

NOTES

1:4 the LORD. The Hebrew construction here emphasizes the person ("the LORD") rather than the activities of the narrative. Like the availability of the Tarshish-bound ship, the sudden storm was an event of God's superintending providence. Several scholars have suggested a concentric (or chiastic) structure for vv. 4-16, but the pattern of these verses is more likely determined by the necessary constraints of the progress of the narrative. Stuart (1987:457) is probably correct in terming all such attempts "elaborate" and "forced."

hurled a powerful wind over the sea. The verb *tul* [TH2904, ZH3214] (hurled)occurs in three other verses in this chapter (1:5, 12, 15), always depicting energetic action. Much as a man may hurl an object (cf. 1 Sam 20:33), so God, like a mighty warrior, hurls the storm at the sea. The word "powerful" translates the oft-recurring adjective *gadol* [TH1419, ZH1524] (see Introduction) and is used of the violent storm that follows.

threatened to break the ship apart. Lit., "the ship thought to be breaking up." The NLT gives the sense of the personification here. While the Hebrew verbal phrase is not normally used of inanimate objects, here it provides not only vividness to the narrative but picturesque sound play: *khishebah lehishaber* [TH2803/7665, ZH3108/8689].

1:5 *Fearing for their lives.* "Fear" (*yare'* [TH3373, ZH3707]; see Introduction), has many shades of meaning—from outright deathly fear to anxiety, awe, respect, and reverence. The first alternative is indicated here. Though they were experienced sailors, they feared for their very lives.

sailors. Limburg (1993:49) points out, "The word translated 'sailors' occurs only here and in Ezek 27, where 'the good ship Tyre' is described (Ezek 27:9, 27, 29). That text gives some idea of the sort of vessel that was sailing the Mediterranean in the sixth century BC, with cypress planks, a mast of cedar, pine deck (27:5-6), and powered both by oars made of oak (27:6) and by linen sails (27:7)."

shouted to their gods for help and threw the cargo overboard. The frightened sailors take two actions: Religiously, each cries out to his god, and practically, all begin to jettison the ship's cargo so as to help it to ride out the storm. Ezekiel 27:25 indicates that the ships of Tarshish were filled with heavy cargo. Accordingly, there would be considerable activity and effort expended in the lightening of the ship. The word translated "threw" is the same verb rendered "hurl" in v. 4.

Jonah was . . . down in the hold. Jonah went down below deck, lay down, and fell into a deep sleep. The noun translated "hold" is literally "the far recesses" of the ship (*yarkethe hassepinah* [TH3411/5600, ZH3752/6208]). The word for "ship" (*sepinah*) is different from the usual *'aniyah* [TH591, ZH641] found elsewhere in this chapter (1:3-5), possibly due either to the full phrase's assonance with the following *wayyishkab* [TH7901, ZH8886] (and he lay down), or more probably, for stylistic variation. If an etymology for *sepinah* can be demonstrated to lie in the root *sapan* [TH5603, ZH6211] (cover, conceal, hide), a pun may be intended: Jonah's descent to the far region of the ship was as much for concealment as for rest.

sound asleep. The LXX humorously reports that an exhausted Jonah immediately began to snore!

1:6 *the captain went down after him.* The verb translated "went down" is not the same as the one in vv. 3 and 5. Rather, it carries the idea of approaching or drawing near to someone or something. While the NLT properly translates according to the constraints of the context, the implication of the Hebrew is that while going down to fetch further cargo or equipment, the captain discovers Jonah and comes up to him. "Captain" reflects the reading of some Greek versions (*kubernētēs* [TG2942, ZG3237]; cf. the Vulgate *gubernator*), while the LXX's *prōreus* understands the term as the first mate. The Hebrew noun seems to intend "chief of those who pull the ropes." As the chief officer on board, captain is probably a good English equivalent.

Get up and pray to your god! The captain's words would doubtless strike a familiar chord with Jonah. D. Alexander (1988:103) observes, "By repeating the imperatives *qum* [TH6965, ZH7756] (arise), and *qera'* [TH7121, ZH7924] (call), the captain parodies closely Jonah's initial summons from God (1:2). Each word mocks him." Jonah had been told to arise, go to Nineveh, and call down judgment *against* it (*qera' 'al* [TH5921, ZH6584]); here the captain tells him to arise and call *to* his God (*qera' 'el* [TH413, ZH448]).

Maybe he will pay attention to us. The captain does not presume upon Jonah's God. The sentiment is that expressed in Zeph 2:3. The verb "pay attention" occurs only here in the MT and appears to have the nuance "have favorable thought toward."

spare our lives. Lit., "and we will not perish." This clause is dependent upon the preceding one: "Perhaps God will think favorably toward us so that we will not perish."

1:7 *Then the crew cast lots.* The NLT turns the direct speech of the Hebrew text into descriptive narrative. Lit., the text reads: "And they said to one another, 'Come, let us cast lots so that we may know on whose account that we have this evil (calamity).'" Limburg (1993:52) points out that the casting of lots was practiced in biblical times for many reasons, one of which was the detection of a person guilty of committing an offense (Josh 7:14-26). Jonah is singled out much like Jonathan, who had unknowingly violated his father's vow (1 Sam 14:27, 40-42). As for the procedure in the casting of lots, Limburg (1993:51) says that "The process involved putting stones into the lap of one's garment or into a container and shaking it until a stone came out." Stuart (1987:459-460), however, suggests that the casting of the lots probably involved dice with alternatively light or dark colored sides. "Two dark sides up meant 'No.' Two light sides up meant 'Yes.' A light and a dark meant 'Throw again.'" Probably various systems were in use in the ancient Near East (see Laetsch 1956:223-224).

1:8 *Why has this awful storm come down on us?* Lit., "Because of whom do we have this evil/calamity (*ra'ah* [TH7451B, ZH8288])?" Just who was the God against whom Jonah had sinned?

What is your nationality? While this question may seem at first to duplicate the preceding query regarding Jonah's homeland, because many ethnic groups could make up the population of a given country, the question is quite apropos. Allen (1976:209) remarks, "Nationality and religion went together in the ancient Near East."

1:9 *I am a Hebrew.* "Hebrew" (*'ibri* [TH5680, ZH6303]) is derived from the root *'abar* [TH5674, ZH6296] (cross [over]). The origin of its application has been traced to the early Hebrew migrations from across the Euphrates River or to the eponymous ancestor Eber, the seventh descendant from Enoch. Others have linked it with the Hapiru, foreigners who at times made up a lower stratum of society or foreign personnel in military contingents. Whatever its origin, by Jonah's time the term had long since been established as a designation for the Hebrews, especially by foreigners (Egyptians—Gen 39:14; 40:15; Exod 1:15; Philistines—1 Sam 4:6, 9; 13:19), and Israel's traditional territory was known as the "land of the Hebrews."

I worship. Lit., "I fear." Here, *yare'* [TH3372, ZH3707] (fear) indicates Jonah's confirmation of faith in the Lord. It is the same verb translated "fearing" in v. 5 (see note on 1:10).

the God of heaven. Heb., *'elohe hashamayim* [TH430/8064, ZH466/9028]. By declaring that Yahweh ("the LORD") was the God of heaven, Jonah affirms that Yahweh is the true and supreme deity. The phrase would be particularly meaningful to pagan sailors, especially if, as seems likely, the sailors were Phoenicians who worshiped Baal Shamem ("Baal [is] heaven"). This deity, a storm god, was well known for his victory over Yamm, the sea god, as recorded in the earlier Ugaritic texts. As a controller of both the storm and the seas, he could be responsible for causing shipwrecks. This god was known to the Egyptians from the fourteenth century BC onward as a Semitic god of the heavens, mountaintops, and thunder. Thus Pharaoh's "battle cry is like (that of) Baal in the heaven" (see ANET 249). This deity was known also to the Assyrians. For example, a curse in a treaty between the seventh-century BC Assyrian King Esarhaddon and the king of Tyre reads: "May Baal-Semame . . . raise an evil wind against your ships" (see ANET 534).

who made the sea and the land. Using the merism (a figure of speech in which two opposites stand as a symbol of totality) of sea (*yam*) and dry land (*yabbashah* [TH3004, ZH3317]), Jonah indicated that the LORD is the Creator and controller of *all* the forces of nature. Not only was Yahweh the true master of the waves but also of the terra firma the sailors would have liked to see just then. Stuart (1987:461) affirms that Jonah's testimony "has the ring of an Israelite credal confession, and indeed a credal formula of this kind might have its basis or reflection in such hymnody as Ps 95:5 . . . (cf. Ps 135:7; Exod 10:13-19; 14–15; Num 11:31; Isa 50:2; Jer 49:32-36; Amos 4:13; Job 26:12)."

1:10 *The sailors were terrified.* Lit., "feared a great fear." The key terms "fear" and "great" appear together here to express the sailors' emotions. The Hebrew construction "is known in English as a cognate accusative and in Hebrew grammar as an internal object, which serves to strengthen the verbal idea" (Baldwin 1993:560). See notes on 1:16.

running away from the LORD. Ratner (1990:299-300) suggests that the sailors understood ancient Near Eastern protocol with regard to runaway servants. Although they were harboring a runaway servant, by returning him they might expect leniency from a human master. Since Jonah was fleeing from his God, however, they had been placed in great peril.

Oh, why did you do it? Lit., "What is this you have done?" Because the sailors knew that he had confessed to running away from the Lord, the NLT follows the lead of most commentators in treating these words as an expression of shock and terrified incredulity: "Oh no, how could you do such a thing!"

1:11 *the storm was getting worse.* The increasing severity of the storm only heightens the sailors' anxiety. The Hebrew construction forcefully expresses the gradually increasing ferocity of the stormy sea.

What should we do to you . . . ? Ellison (1985:372) remarks, "In a culture in which correct procedure in the service of the gods was essential, they had not merely to do the will of Yahweh but also to do it correctly. Only Jonah could guide them."

to stop this storm? Lit., "to make the sea calm around us." Although the sailors hoped for a calming trend, the storm that descended upon them so suddenly had worsened and would only intensify.

1:12 *Throw me into the sea.* Lit., "Pick me up and hurl me into the sea." The verb translated "throw" has appeared previously in vv. 4-5.

all my fault. Jonah was aware that the dangerous situation they all faced was due to his disobedience. He realized his guilt before God and resigned himself to its consequences— death in the sea. Jonah wished for death two other times later in the story (4:3, 8). His confession of sin may well be an occasion for God's mercy that follows (cf. Prov 28:13).

1:13 *rowed even harder to get the ship to the land.* The verb translated "rowed" basically means "hollow out," "dig"—the picture here being that of breaking through the waves

(Keil 1954:396). "To the land" translates the noun "dry land," which appeared in Jonah's confession of God's creative acts (1:9). The noun indicates that the boat itself was probably following a coastal route within sight of land.

stormy sea was too violent. The Hebrew syntax indicates that all the while the storm kept growing in intensity. Boats customarily put out or stayed out to sea so as to ride out the storm. It was a dangerous thing to make for shore.

1:14 *they cried out to the LORD.* Once again the verb *qara'* [TH7121, ZH7924] is employed (cf. 1:2, 6). This time it is the sailors who call on Yahweh. The short prayer is given in typical fashion: (1) opening address ("O LORD"), (2) petition proper—for absolution from guilt in committing Jonah to the sea, and (3) motivation for the request—it was simply not their fault, for God himself had sent the storm in accordance with his good purposes.

"O LORD," they pleaded. The sailors addressed Jonah's God by his covenant name. As Sasson (1990:131) points out, "This verse is the heart of Jonah's first chapter, for it catches the moment in which illumination finally strikes the sailors. The sailors utter the name of the Hebrew God for the first time, recognizing—as they did not in v 11—that mercy must be obtained not from the sea, but from that very God."

don't make us die. The sailors' double request asks first that their lives be spared through the great storm. It was Jonah's sin that necessitated the storm so that there was no reason that they should die for his transgression.

And don't hold us responsible for his death. The second request asks that because Jonah himself had given instructions to throw him into the sea to calm the storm, they should be absolved from any criminal charges in this situation. The force of the Hebrew text is that they not be charged with shedding innocent blood (*dam naqi'* [TH1818/5355, ZH1947/5929]; cf. Joel 3:19). The killing of an innocent person was considered a heinous crime (Deut 19:10, 13; 27:25; Prov 6:17; Jer 26:15).

for your own good reasons. The motivation for the sailors' request stresses the fact that the Lord can do as he pleases but acknowledges that he has good and sufficient reasons for doing so. The sentiment recalls that of Pss 115:3 and 135:6. Limburg (1993:56) records Rabbi Eliezer's version of the casting of Jonah into the sea, which emphasizes the sailors' reluctance in throwing Jonah overboard. "They put him in the water up to his knees and the storm stops; but when they take him out, it starts up again. Next, they put him in the water up to his navel and then to his neck; each time the storm stops but starts up again when they pull him up out of the water."

1:15 *threw him into the raging sea.* Once again, the root *tul* [TH2904, ZH3214] is used. Earlier, God had "hurled" a powerful wind over the sea (1:4) and the sailors had reacted by throwing the cargo overboard (1:5). Jonah subsequently instructed them, "Throw me into the sea" (1:12) in order to calm the waters. Now that instruction is carried out.

the storm stopped at once! Lit., "the sea ceased from its raging." Jonah's prediction came to pass. The verb "stopped" is not the same one as that in vv. 11 ("stop") and 12 ("become calm"). Rather, it is customarily used of humans and refers to ceasing from something (e.g., Gen 29:35). Likewise, the word for "raging," used of the stormy sea, normally appears with the actions of personal beings (e.g., Prov 19:12; Isa 30:30). The narrator used personification for vividness of effect.

1:16 *The sailors were awestruck by the LORD's great power.* Lit., "And the men feared the LORD with a great fear." The verb *yare'* [TH3372, ZH3707] occurs once again (cf. 1:5, 9-10). While it describes physical or emotional fear in 1:5 and 10, it is used of Jonah's reverence for God in v. 9. The latter meaning is felt here. The sailors were awestruck by God's might and majesty in stilling the storm. But their fear moves on to reverential worship as they make a sacrifice to Jonah's God.

they offered him a sacrifice. The question of how the sailors could make a sacrifice on shipboard has perplexed scholars through the ages. The Targum suggests that they promised to make sacrifices later (cf. Allen 1976:212). Jerome proposed that it was a sacrifice of the spirit. Sasson (1990:139-140) points out ancient testimony of sacrifices actually made on shipboard and indicates that such could indeed have taken place. Stuart (1987:464-465) observes that such would have been impossible, granted the jettisoning of the cargo and the fact that sacrifices customarily were made at shrines or temples. Therefore, the sacrifice probably took place later on shore at some Yahwistic shrine. The narrator simply does not elaborate on how and when the sacrifices took place, so the precise scenario is speculative at best.

vowed to serve him. Likewise, the sailors made a vow (i.e., a solemn promise; cf. Deut 23:21-23) to the Lord. Jonah would later promise to make sacrifices and pay his vow to the Lord (2:9). The sailors' full acknowledgment of the Lord is stressed in the syntax of the verse, which uses three cognate accusatives to indicate their newly found reverence: "They feared a great fear," "They sacrificed a sacrifice to the Lord," and "They vowed their vows." True acknowledgment of the person and power of the Lord is followed by genuine sacrifice and solemn promises to him. Hailey (1971:65) points out that, "God is able to use all incidents in the life of His servants for their good and His glory. Some good can come even from mistakes such as Jonah's. In his flight from God and in the storm that arose, a tremendous impression was made on the seamen. They were caused to fear Jehovah, offer sacrifices, and make vows to Him."

COMMENTARY

The narrative moves along smoothly and climactically in accordance with the notices of the storm. In the first section (1:4-6) of Jonah's adventurous voyage, God suddenly hurls a ferocious storm against the boat in which Jonah has booked passage in an attempt to escape God. Like a mighty warrior hurling his heavy spear, God sent a storm so fierce that the experienced sailors feared the worst. Even the ship was pictured as expecting to break up and sink to the bottom. In the face of seemingly certain disaster, each of the sailors called upon his god for deliverance, and as a practical measure, they began jettisoning the cargo.

As the ship's captain went below to search for additional items for disposal, he discovered Jonah fast asleep. How could Jonah sleep at so critical a time? Shouting at him at the top of his voice, both to overcome the noise of the fearsome gale and to rouse this passenger who was deep in sleep, he urged Jonah to get up and to pray to his God just as all of them had. At this point, the captain's sense of religion was greater than Jonah's.

This opening section contains several theological truths. From the onset, it is clear that if Jonah thought he could escape God's call to service, he was mistaken. God's claim upon his life was neither conditional nor to be fulfilled in an option of Jonah's choosing. Further, as Jonah would later confess (1:9), God is the creator and controller of the sea and the dry land. Therefore, any thought of really escaping God's presence by running away to another heathen land was surely doomed to failure. In any case, he knew better than that. He was doubtless familiar with such Scriptures as Job 23:10: "But he knows where I am going." Yet a person in willful sin does not usually behave rationally and seldom calls upon biblical knowledge. Accordingly, God's sovereignty and prior claim upon individual lives are strongly emphasized in this section.

God's omnipotence is also underscored. He had the power not only to bring the storm but to destroy any who were in his way. Likewise, the inadequacy of the foreign gods is also seen. None of them could still the storm or deliver either the crew or the ship. Once again, the impotence of the so-called "gods" is exposed (cf. Isa 40:18-26; 41:21-29; 42:8-9, 17; 44:9-20; 46:5-7; 48:3-8).

The captain's charge to Jonah is instructive. As can be seen in the exhortation of Zephaniah 2:1-3, one should not presume upon divine grace. Although it is true that God is gracious and merciful, and longs to deliver his people in time of trouble (Pss 41:1; 46:1; Isa 43:2), one must not assume that God will choose to do so in every instance, particularly if a person's sinful behavior has occasioned his plight. It is better to petition God to intervene in one's case and to desire that God's will be accomplished.

In a second movement (1:7-12), Jonah is identified as the cause of the storm. The lot falls upon Jonah in no uncertain fashion. Therefore, the sailors pepper him with a barrage of questions. What has Jonah done to cause such an awful storm? Just who was Jonah, and what was his business? From what country did he hail, and to what nation did he belong? All of this would be important to determine what god had been offended and why their fortunes had been cast with Jonah. His offended God could claim their lives as well.

Jonah's confession only confirmed their worst fear. Jonah was a Hebrew, a worshiper of Yahweh. Was it not this God who had led his people into Canaan and had established such powerful kings as David and the famed Solomon? If it was this God, the creator of all things, including the very sea that was even now tossing them about, and if Jonah was running away from such a one, what hope did they have? Absolute terror gripped them. How could he have done this to himself and to them?

As the storm grew even more intense, they asked Jonah how they could appease this God. Jonah's reply was direct: If he were thrown into the sea, it would become calm, for he was the cause of it all. Was Jonah penitent, generous, even noble? One wonders whether Jonah was simply resigned to death. At least in that way he would not have to go to Nineveh. He would have a Pyrrhic victory.[1]

Theologically, this section further emphasizes God's absolute supremacy over the world that he created. The Lord is the creator of land and sea (Ps 95:5). Jonah's admission displays the folly of attempting to run away from God. No one can hide from an omnipotent and omnipresent God; there is no way to evade his authority. The sailors' reply recognizes humanity's finitude. The Lord is the God with whom all have to deal (cf. 2 Chr 6:28-31; Acts 17:24-31). What a pity that their practical perception was superior to Jonah's own dogmatic knowledge. For throughout this episode one never reads of Jonah praying to the Lord.

One is reminded of another story in the Bible in which a believer was cast together with a group of men sailing on the Mediterranean Sea (Acts 27). The apostle Paul was among a group of prisoners that had been entrusted to a Roman centurion. Their destination was Rome. Despite Paul's warning, the ship set sail only to be overtaken by a tempestuous northeaster. The sailors on this occasion likewise threw the cargo overboard, but to no avail. All aboard gave up hope of survival—all, that is, except Paul. Although we are not specifically told that Paul had prayed, it is obvious that he did, for he kept close to the Lord through it all and moreover was visited by an angel who assured him that none would perish, despite the impending shipwreck (cf. 2 Cor 11:25-26).

Instructive comparisons can be drawn between the two incidents. Both Paul and Jonah were aboard pagan ships on the Mediterranean Sea. Both were involved in a tumultuous storm that resulted in the sailors' efforts to save the ship by jettisoning the cargo. By way of contrast, however, one may note that although the crew on Jonah's ship addressed their gods, such was not the case on Paul's ship. While Paul obviously trusted the Lord through the terrible storm and even received an angelic visitation, Jonah could only resign himself to being cast into the sea. Thus, whereas Paul's presence could be a source of encouragement to his companions, Jonah could merely cause them trouble—trouble that could only be alleviated by his expulsion.

There was a basic difference in the two occasions. Despite the unhappy circumstances, Paul went in the assurance that God wanted him to minister in Rome (Acts 23:11). Because Jonah was abandoning his commission to preach in Nineveh, however, he caused the disastrous circumstances. How important, then, it is for us to be responsive to the call of God in our lives and to serve him faithfully. In doing so, we will accomplish his wise and holy purposes and be a source of blessing to others (Pss 1:1-3; 118:26; Prov 3:5-7; 31:10-12, 28-31; Jer 17:7-8).

The third portion of this section (1:13-16) indicates that, although the sailors attempted to avoid so disastrous a solution as throwing a man overboard, the worsening storm forced them to comply with Jonah's advice. Therefore, they picked him up and threw him into the sea. When this was done, the storm instantly abated and the sea became calm. This miracle caused the sailors to acknowledge the power of Yahweh and to worship him. Whether the sailors merely added Jonah's God to the other deities they worshiped or became exclusive worshipers of the Lord cannot be determined with certainty. Their response in both sacrifice and vows, however, indicates at least that they genuinely believed in God's might so greatly that they would henceforth acknowledge and serve him.

One cannot but admire the humanity and magnanimity of the crew.[2] When disaster struck, they prayed. They even challenged God's prophet to do likewise. After they learned that Jonah was the reason for the storm, they nonetheless further endangered their lives despite the increasing severity of the storm by trying to put Jonah safely ashore. Because they were conscious of the high ethical standard of not shedding innocent blood, they did not want to have a charge of murder added to their already impossible predicament. At last, when all human effort to right the circumstances failed and their casting Jonah overboard resulted in the miraculous calming of the sea, they worshiped the Lord.[3] They were convinced by the sufficiency of the evidence. Oh, that all people everywhere would respond to the established facts of the gospel message (e.g., 1 Cor 15:20, 56-57).

As noted before, the whole passage repeatedly emphasizes the sovereignty of the

Lord. He is the creator and master of all nature, including the sea (cf. Pss 89:9; 95:5; Ezek 28:2; Nah 1:4; Hab 3:8; Acts 27:13-44). Not only does he rule over all things he created (Gen 1:1; Ps 103:11; John 1:3; Col 1:16), but he is also sovereign in the affairs of nations (Ps 66:7; Acts 17:26) and people (Pss 75:6-7; 139:16; Prov 16:33). Both Jonah and the sailors came to realize the force of these truths. Indeed, the Lord was not absent from the sea but directing its events.

The drama on the Tarshish-bound ship, where God's prophet lay fast asleep, is reminiscent of another such occasion. The Gospel accounts (Matt 8:23-27; Mark 4:35-41; Luke 8:22-25) tell of a day when the Prophet lay fast asleep on board a boat crossing the Sea of Galilee. Here, too, a strong storm suddenly burst upon the craft. Here, too, the sailors feared for their very lives and awakened the man of God. Here, too, the storm was stilled through the instrumentality of God's Prophet.

As in the case of Paul in Acts 27, however, the contrast with Jesus is also significant. Whereas Jonah tried to hide from God, Jesus was doing the Lord's work. Although a sinful Jonah needed to be cast overboard so that God would still the winds and calm the waves, the sinless Lord Jesus accomplished the same with a simple, "Silence! Be still!"

The conclusions to both episodes record the viewers' wonder at the spectacular miracles. The sailors in the Jonah account worshiped the Lord with sacrifice and vows, while the awestruck disciples marveled at Jesus' great power and authority (Matt 8:27; Luke 8:25) and feared him (Mark 4:41). How paradoxical! Jesus' disciples had hoped that *somehow* he could do something to help. Yet they were amazed when he did! With the Prince of Peace on board, they, too, as he, should have known peace, despite the fiercest tempest.

Yet, how many times we, his modern disciples, need to be reminded of his presence when the "winds of adversity" and the "storms of life" seem too great for us. How often, too, we need to remind ourselves that as believers who have been taken into union with Christ (Gal 2:20), we have all the potential for perfect peace. Since that is true, the captain (Heb 2:10) of peace (John 14:27; 16:33) is "on board" (Col 1:27) for all of life's situations, giving peace however dark the "seas of circumstance" may appear. Such peace is based on the presence of God, however, and those running away from God, like Jonah, shouldn't expect it!

Jonah's instructions to the sailors to cast him into the sea provide a further comparison with the Lord Jesus. Jonah went into the water seemingly to perish and by that act brought safety and knowledge of God to the crew. So also Christ willingly offered himself on Calvary's cross and entered the shades of death for the redemption of mankind (Isa 53:4, 12; Rom 5:6-8; Titus 2:14; 1 Pet 2:21-24) in order that all may have the knowledge of "the glory of God that is seen in the face of Jesus Christ" (2 Cor 4:6).

Unlike Jonah, however, Jesus was not a victim of circumstances. Neither was he simply resigning himself to death, either as an offender or someone finding yet another way to avoid God's will. Christ was no runaway. Rather, he came to do the will of God the Father (John 6:38) and he always did that which pleased him (John

8:29). Further, he was conscious of his determined end as the Savior of the world (John 12:23-27).

Unlike Jonah, who although he did not pray, was graciously rescued by God and did not die, Jesus did pray (John 17:1-26), died a real death, and rose bodily from the dead (1 Cor 15:3-4). Now as believers' great High Priest, he "lives forever to intercede with God on their behalf" (Heb 7:25). Accordingly, unlike Jonah, who apparently chose not to pray when he sinned and fell into difficult circumstances, believers have an Advocate with the Father (1 John 2:1-2). They, therefore, have the assurance of both sins forgiven (1 John 1:8-9) and God's guidance through life's most trying experiences (Ps 23:4; Isa 43:2; 1 Pet 4:19).

We who have received Christ and have the full light of the gospel can respond to God's working in our lives in a far deeper way than the sailors of Jonah's day. May ours be a daily worship of the Lord and a consistent walk before him. May we live with such trust in the Lord that we will acknowledge his hand in whatever occurs in our lives, so that we may grow in appreciating God's grace (Prov 3:5-6; 2 Pet 3:18). Above all, may we not be "runaways" but those who respond positively to the challenge of God's gracious call to let Christ be seen in all that we do (cf. Gal 1:15-16).

ENDNOTES

1. Pyrrhus (318–272 bc) was a Greek ruler of Epirus who was caught up in the internecine conflicts of the wars of Alexander the Great's successors. Desirous of conquests to the west, he invaded Italy. Although he won some battles, his losses were so heavy (especially at Heraclea) that victories involving staggering losses have come to be called "Pyrrhic."

2. Yet, lest we overly sympathize with the sailors, Craigie's sober caution (1985:224) needs to be heeded: "But for all their decency and positive human qualities, they were on the verge of drowning in the depths; they needed to be rescued. And again we perceive the way in which the sailors portray the pathos of the human condition."

3. Craigie (1985:224) observes: "Those simple sailors, no doubt having their share of human decency, simply needed one to save them from their plight. They found that deliverance in God, and such is the path of all true conversion."

◆   C. Jonah and God (1:17–2:10)

17*Now the LORD had arranged for a great fish to swallow Jonah. And Jonah was inside the fish for three days and three nights.

CHAPTER 2

1*Then Jonah prayed to the LORD his God from inside the fish. 2He said,

"I cried out to the LORD in my great
      trouble,
   and he answered me.

I called to you from the land
      of the dead,*
   and LORD, you heard me!
3You threw me into the ocean
      depths,
   and I sank down to the heart
      of the sea.
The mighty waters engulfed me;
   I was buried beneath your wild
      and stormy waves.
4Then I said, 'O LORD, you have driven
   me from your presence.

Yet I will look once more toward
your holy Temple!'

⁵"I sank beneath the waves,
and the waters closed over me.
Seaweed wrapped itself around
my head.
⁶I sank down to the very roots of the
mountains.
I was imprisoned in the earth,
whose gates lock shut forever.
But you, O LORD my God,
snatched me from the jaws of
death!
⁷As my life was slipping away,

I remembered the LORD.
And my earnest prayer went out to
you
in your holy Temple.
⁸Those who worship false gods
turn their backs on all God's
mercies.
⁹But I will offer sacrifices to you with
songs of praise,
and I will fulfill all my vows.
For my salvation comes from the
LORD alone."

¹⁰Then the LORD ordered the fish to spit
Jonah out onto the beach.

1:17 Verse 1:17 is numbered 2:1 in Hebrew text.   **2:1** Verses 2:1-10 are numbered 2:2-11 in Hebrew text.
2:2 Hebrew *from Sheol.*

NOTES

1:17 [2:1] *the LORD had arranged.* The Hebrew verb used here occurs three times elsewhere in the narrative (4:6-8). God would later arrange for a leafy plant for Jonah's benefit
(4:6). He would also prepare a worm to eat the plant (4:7) and send a scorching east wind
to buffet his prophet (4:8). The divine name *Yahweh* is chosen here to stress the graciousness of Jonah's covenant God. It was with this God that Jonah must do spiritual business,
and he would subsequently do so.

a great fish. The adjective "great" is used once more, this time to depict the sea creature.
The nature of the great fish has often been debated. The Greek text renders it as a (great)
sea monster (*kētos* [TG2785, ZG3063]; cf. Matt 12:40), while the Latin Vulgate simply reproduces the Hebrew as *piscem grandem* (big fish). Limburg (1993:61) notes that Jonah's creature has artistically "been depicted in forms ranging from the serpent-like monster found
on a fourth-century AD Christian sarcophagus in Rome and the pig-like animal depicted
in ivory sculptures from Asia Minor to ferocious or friendly-looking whales in painting,
sketches, sculpture, or stained glass."

The great sea creature has also been the subject of many literary allusions, discussions,
and stories of sensational deliverances from animals in the sea. (Such was the supposed
rescue of one James Bartley from a sperm whale, where he had resided for some 36 hours.
The tale proved to be merely the spinning of a great sea yarn—see Allen 1976:176.) The
possible availability of a sea creature that could have swallowed Jonah has often been
demonstrated, especially in the case of sharks. Note, for example, the photo of six
men standing erect in the jaws of a *charcharodon megalodon* on the cover of *Science* 174
(Oct 1971).

If, as it is often understood, Jesus (Matt 12:40) is authenticating Jonah's actual stay in the
great fish rather than just drawing a comparison between details in a well-known story and
his own coming period of entombment, then the case is settled by divine pronouncement.
That the sovereign creator and controller of the sea and dry land (1:9) could prepare such
a fish is in harmony with the tenets of Judeo-Christian theology.

three days and three nights. The motif of three days and three nights appears elsewhere
both in the extrabiblical literature of the ancient Near East (e.g., the Sumerian Myth of
Inanna) and the Scriptures (1 Sam 30:12; Matt 12:40). As Carson (1984:296) points out,

"According to Jewish tradition, 'three days and three nights' need mean no more than 'three days' or the combination of any part of three separate days." If so, both Jonah's stay in the fish and the Lord's period in the tomb may not require a literal 72-hour period.

2:1 [2] *Then Jonah prayed.* At last, Jonah prays, and his prayer is in the form of a psalm. A great deal of controversy has arisen due to the nature of this psalm as one of thanksgiving for deliverance. Because deliverance is expressed as past and because the psalm can be deleted without apparent loss of continuity in the narrative, many have suggested that it is a late interpolation. However, it should be understood that Jonah, finding himself delivered from the waves and safe inside a great sea creature, prayed thankfully, taking his present condition as a pledge of further deliverance from the fish (Keil 1954:399). After his expulsion from the fish, he would have put his words into final form.

Several other features are to be noted. (1) Schrader (1989:646) points out some points of comparison between the first two chapters of Jonah. "Just as in chapter 1 the sailors have a crisis on the sea, pray to Yahweh, are delivered from the storm, and then sacrifice and make vows to Yahweh, so in chapter 2 the prophet has a crisis in the sea, prays to Yahweh, is delivered from drowning, and then promises to sacrifice and make good his vows to the Lord." (2) Jonah's experience in the sea and the fish becomes the pivotal point thus far in his spiritual odyssey. His repentance and rekindled faith were to lead to his recommissioning. Craigie (1985:227) suggests that Jonah had a change of heart before his descent into the waters.

the LORD his God. Jonah's prayer was directed to Yahweh, the covenant God of Israel. The one whom Jonah confessed before the sailors on the raging sea is now the object of his praise.

from inside the fish. Unlike the use of the masculine form in 1:17 and 2:10, "fish" here is feminine. No convincing reason has been suggested for the alteration of gender. Sasson (1990:156) may be correct in postulating that "a storyteller could simply use either gender for an animal—or both at once—when the sex of the animal was of no importance to the tale."

2:2 [3] *I cried out . . . I called to you.* Jonah began his prayer with a verb that can refer to prayer (*qara'* [TH7121, ZH7924]), which has appeared earlier in the narrative (see Introduction). As Baldwin (1993:569) observes, the parallel verb *shawa'* [TH7768, ZH8775] ("called" cf. Ps 30:2) is one of several verbs in the OT for addressing a deity (cf. *za'aq* [TH2199, ZH2410], "shouted," 1:5).

Jonah's prayer contains several elements typical of thanksgiving psalms and may be conveniently outlined as follows:

   I. The psalmist is cast into the sea (2:2-4)
      A. Statement of thanksgiving (2:2)
      B. Note of personal crisis (2:3)
      C. The psalmist's response (2:4)
   II. The psalmist is delivered from the sea (2:5-9)
      A. The psalmist's desperate situation, with testimony to his God-given rescue (2:5-6)
      B. Closing note of commitment to God (2:7-9)

It may be noted that each stanza is closed by a strophe containing the phrase *wa'ani* [TH2050.1/589, ZH2256/638] (but as for me) and a reference to the Lord and his holy Temple and that Jonah's prayer is filled with phraseology drawn from the biblical psalms. For Jonah's psalm as a psalm of thanksgiving, together with biblical parallels, see the excellent discussion in Limburg 1993:63-66.

land of the dead. Lit., "the belly of Sheol." Jonah's situation was seemingly hopeless—
he was as good as dead. "Sheol" is used at times as a synonym for death (cf. Pss 6:5; 18:5).
(For a thorough discussion of ancient Near Eastern concepts of death and the afterlife,
see Heidel 1963:137-223.)

answered . . . heard. The call–answer motif here is reminiscent of Pss 31:22; 120:1. See
commentary on Hab 1:2-4.

2:3 [4] *You threw me into the ocean depths . . . to the heart of the sea.* For the sentiment
itself, see Pss 18:4-5; 88:6. The NLT supplies the verbal phrase "I sank down" *ad sensum* to
accommodate the Hebrew text's missing preposition before "ocean depths." In addition to
its literal meaning (cf. Exod 15:5), the noun translated "ocean depths" can often refer figuratively to personal distress (Pss 69:2, 15; 88:6). Micah (Mic 7:19) reports that God will
throw the sins of his people "into the depths of the ocean."

I was buried beneath your wild and stormy waves. Lit., "the current engulfed me; all your
breakers and waves passed over me." The imagery is akin to that of Ps 42:7. The noun "current" (*nahar* [TH5104, ZH5643]) is usually translated "river" or "torrent/flood." As a plural it
can also be used of the sea (Ps 24:2). The NLT has rendered the sense of the MT forcefully.

2:4 [5] *Then I said.* Although *'amar* [TH559, ZH606] (said) can be used with many contextual
nuances so that in cases like this one the meaning "thought" might be deemed appropriate
(cf. Stuart 1987:468-469), Jonah may well have expressed his thoughts audibly to God. In
any case, the full phrase is emphatic, expressing Jonah's strong feelings with regard to the
implications of his plight.

from your presence. Lit., "from in front of your eyes" (cf. Ps 31:22). As Sasson (1990:178)
points out, "The phrase 'eye(s) of the Lord/God' is very frequent in Scripture. It refers to
God's constant vigil over mankind or it is found embedded in the idiom, 'good/bad in the
sight (i.e., opinion) of God.'"

Yet I will look once more toward your holy Temple. This suggests that even in the sea
God's prophet expected to be rescued and to worship again in Jerusalem. Others translate
the sentence as a question, "Will I ever . . ?" (GW), or as a wish, "May I yet continue to gaze
toward your holy sanctuary?" or as Jonah's musings, "I thought I was banished from your
sight and should never again look toward your holy temple" (REV). Pusey (1953:409)
declares that Jonah's looking was a spiritual one made from the bosom of the fish: "Yet
what he could not do in the body, he would do in his soul."

2:5 [6] *I sank beneath the waves.* Lit., "Water encompassed me up to the neck." The NLT
renders the implications of the MT. The Hebrew noun *nepesh* [TH5315, ZH5883] bears many
meanings including "soul," "throat/neck" (as here), "desire," and "life" (Wolff 1981:10-25).
For the image of water up to the neck, see Ps 69:1.

the waters closed over me. Lit., "the deep engulfed me." Like the earlier account of Jonah's
encounter with the sea (2:3), v. 5 proceeds in three movements.

Seaweed. "Seaweed" is a contextual meaning; the noun *sup* [TH5488, ZH6068] more commonly refers to reeds along the shore (Exod 2:3, 5; Isa 19:6). The noun also occurs in the
compound *yam-sup* [TH3220, ZH3542] ("sea of reeds," "Red Sea"; Exod 15:4). (For discussion
of the Re[e]d Sea, see Patterson 1995:453-461.) The LXX reads the Hebrew noun as *sop*
[TH5490, ZH6067] (end) and translates, "The farthest abyss encompassed me," but this necessitates taking the word "head," which occurs at the end of this verse, with the opening words
of v. 6 [7]: "My head sank to the depths of the mountains."

2:6 [7] *I sank down.* Jonah's downward movement reaches its lowest point.

the very roots of the mountains. Jonah's language refers to the mountain bases at the bottom of the sea (note the phrase as referring to the continental foundations in Sir 16:19).

I was imprisoned in the earth, whose gates lock shut forever. The NLT gives the sense of the difficult appositional phrase in the Hebrew. The noun *'erets* [TH776, ZH824] is taken here as referring to the realm of the dead (cf. Ps 22:29; Isa 26:19; cf. TDOT 1.399-400). The Hebrew text speaks of the "land whose bars [closed] behind me forever" (cf. Baldwin 1993:568). Stuart (1987:477) observes that the "bases of the mountains" and the "bars of the Underworld" are "expressions which have a background in ancient Near Eastern and OT imagery relating to death." Allen (1976:217) remarks, "He had reached the land of no return: what awaited him but inescapable death?"

But you, O Lord my God. Contrary to Jonah's expectations, the Lord had snatched him from the yawning jaws of death (*shakhath* [TH7845, ZH8846], "pit"; cf. Job 33:28; Ps 103:4; Ezek 28:8). Death is pictured here as a voracious monster, seeking a victim. Jonah's God, however, had performed a miracle, bringing him up alive from the pit (cf. Ps 49:7-9 [8-10]).

2:7 [8] *As my life was slipping away.* The Hebrew text reads, "When my life was slipping away" (cf. Ps 142:3). The word "life" is the same as "neck" in v. 5 (*nepesh* [TH5315, ZH5883]; see notes on 2:5). Once again, the NLT has rendered the resultant sense of the passage: With his life almost gone, so also was Jonah's hope.

I remembered the Lord . . . in your holy Temple. Jonah reported that he remembered the Lord. Like the psalmist (Pss 42–43; 63), Jonah was far from the Lord in his Temple. His soul, therefore, went out in fond remembrance of the Lord and the times of worship in the Temple.

my earnest prayer. The verbal root of *tepillah* [TH8605, ZH9525] (prayer) has occurred in 2:1 [2] (*palal* [TH6419, ZH7137]) and will appear again in 4:2. It is the most common root among the many words for "prayer" in the OT. The verb commonly is used of intercessory prayer (cf. 1 Kgs 8:28). If that is the emphasis here, Jonah's prayer is both a longing for the Lord and the fond wish that God would return him safely to the Temple and the communal worship. The theme of the Lord and his holy Temple recaptures the sentiment of v. 4.

2:8 [9] *Those who worship false gods.* The participial form "those who worship" (*meshammerim* [TH8104, ZH9068]) occurs only here in the OT. The verbal root normally means "keep/guard" but must mean here "pay regard to," hence, "worship." Jonah's strong warning is that all other forms of worship are nothing but clinging to worthless idols. The word for "idols" here is normally reserved for the concept of vanity/emptiness (e.g., Eccl 1:2). It is applied to idol worship in such "false gods" contexts as Ps 31:6 and Jer 8:19. The Hebrew expression *hable shaw'* [TH1892/7723, ZH2039/8736] (false gods) has been taken by some as a superlative, "totally worthless vanities." Jonah adds his condemnation of idolatry to that of the other prophets (see commentary on Hab 2:18-20).

turn their backs on. Lit., "abandon/forsake." The Hebrew verb here is used elsewhere in the OT of Israel's forsaking the true God for the worship of false deities (Deut 31:16; Judg 10:10; Jer 1:16). To do so branded Israel as a covenant-breaker (Deut 29:24-26), who was guilty of spiritual adultery (Hos 4:10).

God's mercies. The noun translated "mercies" (*khesed* [TH2617, ZH2876]) has many nuances but basically denotes someone's gracious treatment of another, especially a superior's treatment of one of lower status. It is used of God's loving-kindness toward human beings (Pss 118:1-2; 136), particularly of his covenant nation Israel (Deut 7:9, 12; 1 Kgs 8:23). The NLT renders the form *khasdam* (their mercy/loving-kindness) as a noun with an objective suffix: God's love toward them. Thus, those who have abandoned God to worship false gods have cut themselves off from the sphere of God's grace (cf. Gal 5:4).

2:9 [10] *sacrifices . . . vows.* Jonah's words pick up the actions of the sailors in 1:16 with the result that, like the narrative of ch 1, so the poem of ch 2 ends on a high note of sacrifice and a pledge to fulfill one's religious vows (cf. Ps 66:13-15).

songs of praise. The noun *todah* [TH8426, ZH9343] characteristically represents the thank offering. Limburg (1993:70) points out that the noun "is often used in parallel with song (Ps 69:30) or singing (Ps 95:2) and since it occurs with verbs denoting singing (Neh 12:27; Ps 147:7; Isa 51:3), the sense here appears to be songs accompanying the making of a sacrifice." The once runaway prophet, now a grateful servant, thus promises to come to God with songs of praise via the designated sacrifices and with the fulfilling of his vows (cf. Pss 22:25; 50:14; 116:14, 17-19).

salvation comes from the LORD. Lit., "Salvation belongs to the Lord." The noun *yeshu'athah* [TH3444A, ZH3802] (salvation, deliverance) has an extended ending beyond the usual *yeshu'ah*, a phenomenon particularly associated with poetry (see *Gesenius' Hebrew Grammar*, §251). Jonah's psalm of thanksgiving appropriately ends on a note of praise that features "LORD" (Yahweh) as its last word. The Hebrew accents, together with the insertion of a paragraph marker (the *setumah*, which indicates a new beginning of thought, while often suggesting reflection on what has been said before) at the end of the verse, calls attention to a climactic end to Jonah's psalm that marks a definite pause in the book. The Wadi Murabba'at Scroll recognizes this tradition by leaving an empty line after this verse before resuming with the story line. Sasson (1990:201) follows Perowne (1905:73) in declaring that "such a sharply chiseled ending is 'at once a confession and praise, a Creed and a *Te Deum!*'"

2:10 [11] ***Then the LORD ordered the fish.*** The appearance of the words "LORD" and "fish" form an *inclusio* with 1:17, framing the entire pericope.

spit Jonah out onto the beach. Jonah, who had been swallowed by the fish (1:17), is now vomited onto the beach. The word translated "beach" is literally "dry land." Jonah's God is master both of the sea and the dry land, and all things in them (Gen 1:6-13, 20-27; Ps 95:5). He has thus demonstrated himself to be all that the prophet had confessed (1:9). For a consideration of the record of Jonah being swallowed by, staying in, and being vomited from the great fish, see Davis 1989:38-41. Kahn (1994:87-100) views Jonah 2:10 as the pivotal verse in the book, encapsulating its major themes.

COMMENTARY

The opening verse of this section reports God's intervention in the life of his prophet. God's sovereignty over creation and the destinies of individuals is clearly indicated. What Jonah perceived to be the end of his life would prove to be but a turning point. It is a reminder that life's disappointments, suffering, and trials often serve as opportunities for divine grace.

The first verse of this section (1:17), tells us that Jonah spent three days and nights in the belly of a giant sea creature. A three-day period is often used in the Scriptures to depict some new, especially spiritual, beginning or opportunity (e.g., Hos 6:2, NASB). On the third day of Israel's encampment at Sinai, God descended upon the mountain in visible power (Exod 19:11). A three-day period was crucial for deciding important political matters (1 Kgs 12:5, 12). Hezekiah was assured that he would recover from his illness and worship on the third day (2 Kgs 20:5, 8). The Lord Jesus repeatedly predicted that his own ministry would culminate in his death and then his resurrection on the third day (e.g., Matt 16:21; Luke 9:22; cf. Luke 24:7), and Jesus explained the significance of all of this to his disciples shortly after his resurrection (Luke 24:46-48). Afterward, Peter (Acts 10:39-40) and Paul (1 Cor 15:4) gave testimony to the fact that Jesus did rise from the dead on the third day (see further discussion below). The third-day motif stands not only as an attestation to the accuracy of prophecy and its fulfillment relative to the Resurrection, but also as a reminder to the believer to exercise thoughtful preparation in anticipation of renewed opportunities for spiritual service.

The first portion of Jonah's psalm (2:2-4) rehearses his plea for God's help. Thrown into the sea, he called to the Lord of the seas (Ps 29:3, 10) and all creation, and God answered him. Overwhelmed by the raging waters and sinking down to the point of death, he cried out to him alone who could deliver him (Pss 46:1; 107:6, 13, 19, 28). In the stormy waves Jonah must have instantly realized the magnitude of his sin. Yet by faith he reached out to the God of all mercy (Pss 6:9; 28:2, 6; Jas 5:11). Once inside the fish's belly and beneath the troublesome waves that God had sent to reclaim his wayward prophet, he realized God's delivering hand. Then a wave of confidence broke over him: He would look toward God in his holy Temple.

Theologically, several truths emerge from Jonah's frightful experience. First and foremost is the realization of God's sovereignty over creation and the lives of all individuals (Pss 22:28; 103:19; Prov 16:33; Acts 17:24-28). It was God who had sent the great fish. It was God who had caused the storm and brought the "wild and stormy waves" that engulfed Jonah. And it was he who, true to his character, answered the cry of his fleeing prophet (cf. Ps 102:1-2 with Isa 65:24). How important it is that people let God truly be God in their lives, for he brings all things to pass, not only for his glory but for their good (Pss 36:9; 145:9, 15, 16).[1]

To be noted also is God's mercy and patience with his prophet. He is a God who is rich in mercy (Eph 2:4; cf. Ps 145:8-9; Mic 7:18; Rom 9:15-18; Jas 5:11), especially to those who fear him (Pss 31:22; 123:1-3). He is also long-suffering toward all (1 Pet 3:20; 2 Pet 3:15). Accordingly, believers also ought to show mercy just as God does (Luke 6:36) and patience toward all (Prov 19:11; Eph 4:2; Col 3:12; 1 Thess 5:14).

The high value of personal faith is also underscored. Troublesome times test the mettle of resident faith (Ps 138:7). True faith will ultimately prove to be a claimed resource in times of great peril. Genuine faith will be manifest not only in the believer's steadfastness under trial (1 Pet 1:7) but also in the one to whom the believer appeals for help. Jonah immediately called upon God; true believers will do the same (Pss 4:1; 73:23-28).

True faith perseveres (Heb 11:1). Not only will such faith cause the believer to trust God for every situation in life (Jas 1:3), but it will give the believer that God-given inner resource, which enables one to endure all that life presents (1 Pet 1:8). Prayer is particularly important to the believer (cf. Acts 4:23-31). The instant reaction of Jonah was to pray, first when he was in the waves and then from within the sea creature. (Would that he had prayed while he was on the storm-tossed boat or, better, even before he decided to run away!) Jonah's experience in prayer is instructive: He prayed in the language of Scripture, calling upon many scriptural truths.

Jonah's case reminds believers that they ought always to pray (1 Thess 3:10; 5:17; 1 Tim 2:8). Even in times of disobedience, when the believer's fellowship with God is most strained, the believer not only has a scriptural resource that may be claimed, but a God of mercy, love, and concern who stands ready to receive and revitalize his wayward servant (1 John 1:9). Then, too, the believer should remember that current difficulties, like Jonah's, may be God's way of bringing his own back to himself.

In verses 5-6, Jonah again recounts his close brush with death. Cast into the sea, he had plunged through the angry surface waves seemingly to its very depths. Apparently entombed in his watery crypt, he had experienced a miracle. The LORD, Yahweh, Israel's covenant God and his, was not yet through with his seaweed-draped prophet. Jonah's repentance and faith would be revealed as the Lord plucked him out of the very "jaws of death."[2] Jonah was not unmindful of all that God had done for him. He understood his situation—he had gotten what he deserved. The God of all grace and mercy, however, had intervened on his behalf.

How important faith and prayer are. When those times of great peril arise, believers have a resource to see them through. But how much more important it is to remain faithful to God in vital fellowship so as to know the joy of victorious faith on a daily basis (John 15:1-11; 1 John 5:4). Surrendered and obedient believers may be assured that God "continues to lead us along in Christ's triumphal procession" (2 Cor 2:14).

Jonah's rescue from death is a reminder of a still greater victory over death. For the Scriptures reveal that Christ entered the realm of death but arose victorious over death and the grave. Therefore, death has been swallowed up in his victory. Hosea's words (Hos 13:14) have taken on an even greater significance: "O death, where is your victory? O death, where is your sting?" (1 Cor 15:55). As a result, those who know God through faith in Christ Jesus have the assurance of victory over death (John 11:25; 1 Cor 15:56-57) and the prospect of eternal life with their victorious Redeemer (John 3:16; 10:27-29).

In the final portion of the poem (2:7-9), Jonah told of his experiences in the sea yet a third time (cf. 2:3-4, 5-6). Each of the accounts adds a distinctive dimension to his adventure. While exact narrative sequences are not always absolutely discernible in poetry, something like the following must have occurred.

Thrown into the raging waters, Jonah sank downward so rapidly that the strong waves might well have become his watery tomb (2:3). Initially, however, he had hope. He could not believe that this was to be the end. Surely he would yet worship God in his Temple (2:4). But with seaweed wrapped around his head like a slimy burial cap, he sank even further—it seemed to the deepest point, where sea and mountain base meet. Death now appeared to be his certain fate. Then, just as suddenly, God sent a great sea creature to rescue him. But had he gone from one graveyard to another (2:5-6)?

With no possibility of escape, humanly speaking—with all hope gone, his faith directed him to think of the Lord (2:7). It may be that he came to realize at this point that the marine rescue was evidence of God's intention to deliver him fully. Rising in faith, he prayed to the one who inhabits the Holy of Holies in the Temple in Jerusalem. How awesome was this one who is gracious to all who call upon him in repentance and faith (1 Kgs 8:46-50).

Therefore, unlike those who consort with false gods and thereby find themselves alienated from the operation of God's grace, Jonah would yet offer the proper sacrifice and fulfill his vows to God. So willingly and gratefully would he do so that the air would be filled with his songs of praise. For no human effort, no pagan deity, could have accomplished such a rescue as had happened and as yet would happen to Jonah. Only the covenant God of Israel could accomplish such miracles. Truly, salvation belongs to the Lord (2:8-9)!

Once again, the importance of prayer and faith is emphasized in this portion. Jonah's faith had given him hope of once again seeing the worship services in the Temple. His faith had recognized the hand of God in the rescue from the sea while he was in the great fish. At the point of death, he could think only of the Lord and then pray.

How important it is that believers be people of genuine, practicing faith. From beginning to end ours is to be a pilgrimage of faith (see commentary on Hab 2:4). In times of trial and peril, faith will sustain the believer through it all (2 Chr 20:20; Isa 26:2-4; 1 Pet 1:3-7; 1 John 5:4). Even at the last hour, at the moment of passing from this life, like Jonah, believers may in faith entrust their souls to their Heavenly Shepherd (Ps 23:4; John 14:1-3; 2 Cor 5:1-8).

Several truths about God are also brought out in this section. Above all, God is seen to be a gracious, loving, and merciful God. This is in keeping with his own revealed character elsewhere in the Old Testament (Exod 34:6-7; Pss 86:15; 103:8; 145:18). Not only was he gracious and faithful to his covenant people Israel (Deut 7:7-9), but he has always been concerned for the welfare of all people everywhere, desiring that his goodness will bring all to repentance and faith (Rom 2:4). This he has made fully known through the saving work of Christ (Titus 3:4-7) who has taken the believer into union with himself (Eph 2:4-6), thereby demonstrating for all time the incomparable riches of God's grace and loving-kindness.[3]

Accordingly, if God's loving-kindness reaches out to a needy world, believers ought to exercise this fruit of the Spirit (Gal 5:22) in all situations (cf. 2 Cor 6:6) and toward all. Thus Paul admonishes, "Since God chose you to be the holy people he loves, you must clothe yourselves with . . . kindness" (Col 3:12). The uniqueness of God is also emphasized here. Israel's ancient confession (Deut 6:4) is true: He alone is God—all other supposed gods are false and therefore to be rejected (Exod 20:3, 23; Ps 81:9-10). God's uniqueness and power are seen especially in that in him alone is salvation. Moreover, the God who delivered Israel (Exod 15:2; Isa 12:2; Ps 118:8-9, 14, 21, 28) has sent his Son to be the Savior of the world (John 1:10-12; 3:16, 36) so that with his completed work "there is salvation in no one else! God has given no other name under heaven by which we must be saved" (Acts 4:12). Therefore, believers are to worship the Lord only and love and serve him with all their strength (Deut 6:13-15; Matt 4:10; Mark 12:29-30).

Significantly, Jesus drew upon the account of Jonah's three-day adventure with the great sea creature and his subsequent reception by the people of Nineveh to illustrate his own ministry and its reception by the scribes and Pharisees

(Matt 12:38-42; Luke 11:29-32). Finding an analogy between the experiences of Jonah and himself, Jesus pointed out that both he and Jonah were signs to those to whom they were sent to minister. Like Jonah, who spent three days in the belly of the sea monster, Christ would be entombed for three days. Like Jonah, who was delivered from the creature within a three-day period (see note on 1:17), so Christ would arise on the third day. The Ninevites apparently recognized God's hand in Jonah's deliverance from the sea creature and therefore repented at his proclamation of God's impending judgment. But the Jewish leadership of Jesus' day rejected the one who was greater than Jonah and whose message was infinitely more significant. Accordingly, their judgment would be greater than those who were born outside of the family of Abraham!

Ironically, the very ones who rejected Christ would be those through whom the sign of Jonah would be effected, for it was they who condemned Jesus to death and the three-day period in the tomb. Henceforth, the sign of Jonah would stand in full significance. Lamentably, the New Testament indicates no great turning to Christ on the part of those who heard his teaching on that day. Nor does the New Testament record any great response in subsequent days. The Jewish leaders simply missed the import of Jesus' words—teachings at which even Gentiles may well have repented, as did the Ninevites.

While Jesus referred to well-known Old Testament personages in his discourses, it was not often that he mentioned Gentiles. When he did, he customarily intended the reference as an example of God's love for all people (e.g., a widow who lived in gentile territory [Luke 4:26] and Naaman the Aramean [Luke 4:27]), or as an example of those who would be more likely to repent than those Jews who had opportunities to respond to God's word (Luke 10:8-12) or Christ's miracles (Luke 10:13-15).

Thus, the Ninevites and the Queen of Sheba were mentioned by Jesus as those who responded to their opportunities to embrace spiritual things. The Queen of Sheba came from a great distance to hear wisdom from Solomon's lips; yet Jesus' contemporaries shunned the teaching of him who was the personification of true wisdom. The Ninevites repented at the preaching of God's prophet; yet the scribes and Pharisees found only negative criticism for the prophet par excellence.

With the passing of years one would suppose that the evidence of Jesus' resurrection would encourage people of all persuasions to repent and turn to Christ as their Savior, much as the Ninevites found deliverance in the message of Jonah. Indeed, the scriptural data demand a real, bodily resurrection. How else are we to explain the displacement of the massive tombstone guarded by the Roman soldiers (Matt 27:62-66; 28:2) or the empty tomb in which lay Christ's undisturbed graveclothes (Mark 16:6; John 20:6-7)? How else can one explain the transformation of timid, doubting disciples into those who proclaimed the message of the risen Christ with a conviction for which they were prepared to die (cf. Mark 14:50; Luke 24:11; Acts 2:29-36)? Indeed, the truth of the Resurrection became the defining theme of the early messages of the church (e.g., Acts 2:22-24, 32; 3:15; 4:10; 10:39-40; 13:29-33).

It is the resurrection of Christ alone that can adequately explain the origin of the

Christian church and its worship on Sunday, "the Lord's Day" (e.g., Acts 20:7; 1 Cor 16:2; Rev 1:10). Moreover, the New Testament Scriptures themselves owe their existence in large measure to the Lord's resurrection (e.g., 1 Cor 15; Rev 1:18-19). These very Scriptures attest several post-Resurrection appearances by the risen Christ. Five distinct instances are documented on the day of the Resurrection itself.[4] He also appeared on at least five other occasions before his ascension.[5]

Further testimony to belief in the message of the Resurrection may be found in the secular writings of the first century AD and in the experience of Christian believers who have testified to the reality of the risen Christ, alive and resident in their lives. Yet despite the weight of evidence of this fulfilled "sign of Jonah," the person of Christ and the record of his messages, atoning death, and resurrection have fared little better with the critics of our day than they did with the scribes and Pharisees. Paul's admonition to the Corinthian Christians to serve as ambassadors to a Christ-rejecting world is therefore still relevant today (2 Cor 5:14-15, 18-19).

Further, the Resurrection message challenges the believer to live in the conscious appropriation of Christ's resurrection power, which stands available to him. Not only is Christ's resurrection a guarantee of the believer's personal salvation but also the assured hope of his own future resurrection (Acts 3:26; 1 Cor 15:22-23, 55-57; 1 Pet 1:3). The resurrected Christ has taken up his abode in the Christian in vital, spiritual, organic union with him (Gal 2:20). Imagine it! The risen Christ lives in us (John 1:14; Col 1:18-19, 27). What reality, what genuine godliness and holy living that should bring to our lives (Col 3:1-4)!

ENDNOTES

1. L. Berkhof (*Systematic Theology* [Grand Rapids: Eerdmans, 1959], 71) remarks, "This benevolent interest of God is revealed in His care for the creature's welfare, and is suited to the nature and the circumstances of the creature.... And while it is not restricted to believers, they only manifest a proper appreciation of its blessings, desire to use them in the service of their God, and thus enjoy them in a richer and fuller measure."

2. Stuart (1987:477) points out that "the deep-sea drowning metaphor is expanded to depict the physical sensation of being trapped, down in the ocean, unable to breathe, water everywhere. This is a vivid, powerful metaphor for the sensation of dying, and it happens also to be the sort of thing that literally did happen to Jonah."

3. "Loving-kindness," though archaic, seems to be the best understanding of the Hebrew noun *khesed* [TH2617, ZH2876], and also seems most appropriate in several NT passages which speak about God's *chrēstotēs* [TG5544, ZG5983] (kindness). This is true despite the fact that the LXX does not translate *khesed* by *chrēstotēs*. Interestingly, in his Hebrew translation of the New Testament, Franz Delitzsch appreciates the theological significance of the Ephesians and Titus passages cited here, translating *chrēstotēs* by *khesed* (cf. 2 Cor 6:6; Gal 5:22).

4. The five appearances are recorded as follows: (1) Matt 28:1-10; (2) Mark 16:1-9; cf. John 20:11-18; (3) Luke 24:34; cf. 1 Cor 15:5; (4) Luke 24:13-35; cf. Mark 16:12-13; and (5) John 20:19-23; cf. Mark 16:14-18; Luke 24:36-43; 1 Cor 15:5.

5. These five occasions are recorded as follows: (1) John 20:26-28; (2) John 21:1-23; (3) Matt 28:16-20; cf. 1 Cor 15:6; (4) 1 Cor 15:7; and (5) Acts 1:3-8; cf. Mark 16:19; Luke 24:50-52.

◆ II. The Prophet at Nineveh (3:1–4:11)
A. Jonah's Recommissioning and Response (3:1-3a)

Then the LORD spoke to Jonah a second time: ²"Get up and go to the great city of Nineveh, and deliver the message I have given you."

³This time Jonah obeyed the LORD's command and went to Nineveh,

NOTES

3:1 *second time.* Jonah's recommissioning is stated in words identical to his initial commissioning (1:1), except for the addition of "a second time." Like Jeremiah (Jer 1:13; 13:3), Jonah experienced a "second word" from the Lord. Although the formula is absent, Ezekiel was also commissioned and recommissioned as a prophetic watchman for his people (Ezek 3:16-17; 33:7).

3:2 *Get up and go to the great city of Nineveh.* The charge to Jonah repeats the phraseology of 1:2. God did not condemn Jonah; he simply repeated the charge.

deliver the message I have given you. Lit., "proclaim the proclamation." Jonah was commanded to preach against (*qara' 'al*) Nineveh on the first occasion (1:2); here he is told simply to proclaim (*qera' 'el* [TH7121/413, ZH7924/448]) God's message to the city. The change of prepositions allows more latitude in God's purposes and gives Nineveh an opportunity to react to God's message. (See Sasson 1990:72-75; see also Sasson 1984:23-79, where he carefully distinguishes between the implications in the difference of prepositions in 1:2 and 3:2.)

3:3a *This time Jonah obeyed . . . and went to Nineveh.* Lit., "And Jonah got up and went to Nineveh." Rather than fleeing from the Lord's presence (1:3), Jonah carried out the divine command. The NLT's "obeyed" connotes the force of the added Hebrew phrase "according to the word of the LORD." Stuart (1987:482) observes that Jonah "had learned his lesson about trying to avoid the call of Yahweh."

COMMENTARY

Jonah obeyed God's renewed command to go to Nineveh with the previously assigned divine pronouncement. God's patience with Jonah illustrates that the heavenly Father often gives his children an undeserved second chance (cf. 1 Kgs 19:1-19). Here was a runaway prophet; yet God reinstated him and gave him the awesome opportunity and privilege of being the bearer of God's message. While human patience may have dictated the discharge of such a messenger, God saw something in Jonah worth reclaiming (cf. Acts 9:1-20; Gal 1:11-24).

As believers, we too must remember that our opportunities to share God's Word are likewise a gracious privilege. Moreover, those who proclaim God's Word must be careful to give it accurately and with less attention to their own opinions.

God's continued concern for the great city of Nineveh is a reminder of his loving concern for all the world (John 3:16). Jonah's renewed commission thus stands as a strong missionary charge. There are many "great cities" around the world where God's message needs to be proclaimed so that people everywhere may hear the word, repent, believe, and be saved (Isa 45:22-23; Acts 1:7-8). May we believers be responsive to God's commission to take the gospel message to all the world (Matt 28:18-20).

◆   ## B. Jonah and the Ninevites (3:3b-10)

a city so large that it took three days to see it all.* ⁴On the day Jonah entered the city, he shouted to the crowds: "Forty days from now Nineveh will be destroyed!" ⁵The people of Nineveh believed God's message, and from the greatest to the least, they declared a fast and put on burlap to show their sorrow.

⁶When the king of Nineveh heard what Jonah was saying, he stepped down from his throne and took off his royal robes. He dressed himself in burlap and sat on a heap of ashes. ⁷Then the king and his nobles sent this decree throughout the city:

"No one, not even the animals from your herds and flocks, may eat or drink anything at all. ⁸People and animals alike must wear garments of mourning, and everyone must pray earnestly to God. They must turn from their evil ways and stop all their violence. ⁹Who can tell? Perhaps even yet God will change his mind and hold back his fierce anger from destroying us."

¹⁰When God saw what they had done and how they had put a stop to their evil ways, he changed his mind and did not carry out the destruction he had threatened.

3:3 Hebrew *a great city to God, of three days' journey.*

NOTES

3:3b *a city so large.* Lit., "a great city to God." While some view the Hebrew phrase as indicating the city's superlative size (Stuart 1987:268), it probably points to the importance of the city in God's sight. The NLT translates according to the first sense and relates it to what follows, viewing the whole description in terms of Nineveh's size.

three days. The connection of the three days with Nineveh is debated. The NLT follows the lead of those who believe that the term has to do with Nineveh's size (e.g., Feinberg 1976:143). The city, however, was probably no more than three miles across and less than eight miles in circumference. It could be that the size here refers to the entire administrative district, including not only Nineveh but Calah (Nimrud) and Khorsabad. Nothing in the narrative, however, indicates that anything other than Nineveh proper was visited.

Some think that, in accordance with ancient Near Eastern protocol, three days were required for Jonah to accomplish his business. Thus, Wiseman (1979:38) suggests that "the 'three day' journey could refer to the day of arrival in the city, followed by the customary day of visiting, business and rest, then the day of departure." This suggestion would accord with the ancient Near Eastern practice of hospitality whereby the first day is for arrival, the second for the primary purpose of the visit, and the third for return. While this is possible, such protocol in the court was likely extended only to official guests. Jonah might not qualify in this regard. Perhaps it is simplest to view the phrase as indicating Nineveh's relative importance and Jonah's need to visit various quarters of the city in order to deliver God's message.

3:4 *he shouted.* Lit., "he proclaimed and said." Once again, the verb *qara'* [TH7121, ZH7924] (proclaim) is employed (see Introduction). No indication is given as to whether Jonah spoke in Assyrian, Aramaic (the language of international diplomacy), or Hebrew. The emphasis here is on the content, not the vehicle, of the message.

Forty days. The forty-day period is reminiscent of other time periods mentioned in the Scriptures: the Flood (Gen 7:4, 12, 17), Moses on Mount Sinai (Exod 24:18), the mission of the Hebrew spies (Num 13:25), Goliath's taunting of Israel's armies (1 Sam 17:16), Elijah's trip to Horeb (1 Kgs 19:8), Jesus' fasting (Matt 4:2), and the period in which Jesus appeared between his resurrection and ascension (Acts 1:3). The Greek translation reads "three days," a figure probably influenced by the number in v. 3.

destroyed! The form of the verb here (*nehpaketh* [TH2015, ZH2200], "overturned") may serve as a double entendre, indicating the potential for Nineveh's destruction or the reversal of its spiritual fortunes.

3:5 The people . . . believed God's message. The verb translated "believed" comes from a root meaning "be firm/secure." In this construction it denotes "trust" or "believe." (See the extended treatment of this Hebrew root by Barr 1983:161-205.) This construction normally expresses the idea of trusting a person. Hence, the Hebrew here literally reads "believed [in] God." To be noted is the fact that the text does not say "believed in Yahweh," the covenant God of Israel. The NLT rendering emphasizes the Ninevites' response to the divine message. Probably both ideas are latent: Believing in the power of Israel's God came through Jonah's warning.

from the greatest to the least. This expression emphasizes the total citizenry of Nineveh.

declared a fast. Communal fasts and times of mourning were called in cases of dire or ominous circumstances such as invasion, a total solar eclipse, earthquake, flood, famine, plague, or epidemic (Stuart 1987:490-492). Even animals could be included in the event. Limburg (1993:81) remarks, "Those fasting wore sackcloth, put dirt on their heads, and sat in ashes (3:6-9; Jer 4:8; Neh 9:1). Since fasts were occasioned by national emergencies, fast days were proclaimed as needed." Sasson (1990:245) records a Neo-Assyrian royal edict dealing with prayer and public weeping before Adad, as well as the making of burnt sacrifices. Such proclamations illustrate the activities of the king.

burlap. Usually made of goat hair, burlap (sackcloth) symbolized the repudiation of earthly comforts in exchange for humility, sorrow, or penitence. As Herr observes (ISBE 4.256), "Sackcloth was frequently worn at times of repentance (Neh 9:1; Jonah 3:5f., 8; etc.)."

3:6 When the king of Nineveh heard. Lit., "And the word reached the king of Nineveh." The word of the Lord had come twice to Jonah (1:1; 3:1), and now, news of the divine message through Jonah came to the king of Nineveh. Although critics have faulted the historicity of this account that there was a king of Nineveh at this time, such objections are not substantive (see Introduction).

He dressed himself in burlap and sat on a heap of ashes. The king traded his royal robes for coarse burlap and his throne for ashes (cf. Job 1:20; 2:8, 12-13). He provided an example of penitence and mourning for his people. David similarly told Joab and his companions to "tear your clothes and put on burlap" as they mourned the death of Abner (2 Sam 3:30-37). Interestingly, the people of Joel's day were instructed to fast, weep, and mourn, but with broken hearts, not torn garments (Joel 2:12-13).

3:7 the king and his nobles sent this decree. Critics have doubted both (1) the issuing of a royal decree in the name of the king and his nobles and (2) the accuracy of the word used here for "decree." The former may indicate the relative weakness of the crown or that Nineveh had its own ruler (see Introduction). The word for "decree" (*ta'am* [TH2940, ZH3248]) is usually understood as "taste," with the derived sense of discrimination (Ps 119:66; Prov 26:16). Here it reflects the meaning of the Aramaic *te'em* [TA10302, ZA10302] ("decree"; see Ezra 4:21; Dan 3:10, 29). Some lexicons also suggest the meaning "edict," possibly reflecting the Akkadian *temu* (see Koehler and Baumgartner 1974:2.361). Such a meaning for *temu*, however, is discounted by Sasson (1990:253-254).

No one . . . may eat or drink anything at all. Lit., "may [they] not taste anything; let them not eat or drink water." The word for "taste" (*yit'amu* [TH2938, ZH3247]) echoes the word translated "decree" (*ta'am* [TH2940, ZH3248])—both being derived from the root *ta'am*. Also the word "eat" (*ra'ah* [TH7462, ZH8286]) forms an intended play on the word for "evil" (*ra'ah* [TH7451, ZH8273]), which appears in v. 8. The fast is both total in its participation and extreme in its implementation. Serious times call for strong measures.

not even the animals. The mourning is total. In a move demonstrating living solidarity, food and drink are withheld even from the animals. Appropriately, the book of Jonah ends on a note of God's concern for both humans and animals (4:11). Joel reported that the animals, like their human counterparts (Joel 1:8-12), felt the effects of the locust plague and cried out to the Lord (Joel 1:18, 20). Both were assured of God's acting on their behalf (Joel 2:21-24). The intertestamental book of Judith (Jdt 4:9-10) similarly reports of humans and animals wearing sackcloth in the face of an Assyrian threat.

3:8 *wear garments of mourning . . . pray earnestly.* "Pray" repeats the verb *qara'* [TH7121, ZH7924], attested already in 1:2, 6, 14; 2:2; 3:2, 4-5. Hezekiah likewise donned garments of mourning and prayed in the face of Sennacherib's attack on Jerusalem (2 Kgs 19:1-2). "Earnestly" translates the Hebrew "with strength." The king's edict contains a note of urgency.

turn from their evil ways. Once again, the word *ra'ah* [TH7451, ZH8273] (evil) appears (cf. 3:7; see Introduction). The king's plea sounds a note that is familiar to the Hebrew prophets (e.g., Jer 18:11; Ezek 20:44; Zech 1:4) and wisdom literature (Prov 28:10). Unfortunately, Israel failed to heed that which the Lord communicated to Solomon upon the completion of the Temple (2 Chr 7:14); for this disobedience, Israel paid the price of deportation and exile (2 Kgs 17:13-20).

stop all their violence. Even as Obadiah (Obad 1:10) condemned the violence that Edom did to God's people, Habakkuk decried the violence that he saw in society all around him (see notes on Obad 1:10 and Hab 1:2). Here, in contrast to what seems to have been a lack of response to their messages, the gentile Ninevites turn from their violence.

3:9 *Who can tell? Perhaps even yet God will change his mind.* The Hebrew expresses the thought here as "who knows whether . . . ?" A similar sentiment is expressed by David regarding the death of his son (2 Sam 12:22) and by the citizens of Jerusalem in praying for God's mercy during the great locust plague (Joel 2:13-14; cf. commentary on Zeph 2:1-3). The verb translated "have pity" is rendered by others as "repent" (KJV) or "relent" (NKJV, NRSV, NIV). Limburg (1993:87) suggests "change his mind." It appears again in 3:10 and in 4:2.

fierce anger. As Sasson (1990:262) observes, "The expression *kharon 'ap* [TH2740/639, ZH3019/ 678] 'heating up of the nose/nostrils/face' is a metaphor for 'anger,' and this expression . . . is always about God's anger."

COMMENTARY

On the very first day, as Jonah fulfilled his commission to warn the people of imminent judgment, the populace of Nineveh responded positively to the divine message. Donning sackcloth, they began to fast in attestation of their sorrow. Even the king of Nineveh was moved to repentance, going so far as to leave his throne, exchange his royal attire for sackcloth, and sit down in ashes. He issued a proclamation that required the people and animals of Nineveh to wear sackcloth. Further, each person was to pray urgently and turn from wickedness in the hope that Jonah's God might relent from the threatened judgment. God saw their genuine penitence and had compassion on them. The prophesied destruction was averted.

The instantaneous, mass repentance of Nineveh's citizens has, of course, met with great skepticism. That animals would be involved in such measures has also been doubted. Such things are deemed impossible. From a human perspective this skepticism is justified. But one must remember that (1) Jonah went with the message of the Lord and in his power[1] and (2) "with God everything is possible"

(Matt 19:26). Moreover, if Jonah's message came at a time of Assyrian royal weakness and significant natural and political calamities (see Introduction), the possibility of Nineveh's about-face becomes all the more credible.[2]

The case of Nineveh also throws light on the issue of God's seeming change of mind in certain circumstances. At first glance, this passage appears to be at variance with texts that declare that God is not a mere mortal who changes his mind (Num 23:19; 1 Sam 15:29). God is also represented elsewhere in Scripture as being immutable (Mal 3:6; Jas 1:17). Even Jonah, however, was aware that God is compassionate and loving, always desirous of reclaiming the sinner (4:1-2). Therefore, God's immutability is to be understood as pertaining to his consistency of character and actions. It was right to announce the certain doom of Nineveh because this was intended to produce the desired effect. Further, Nineveh would be "overturned" one way or another, either in destruction or in change of lifestyle. For God to act in accordance with Nineveh's response to the prophecy was consistent with his pronouncements elsewhere (Jer 18:7-10; Ezek 18:21-24). Accordingly, God had not changed his mind but had taken into consideration the changed circumstances and character of people.[3]

Above all, this section illustrates the wedding of God's justice and loving patience. Although justice demanded Nineveh's severe judgment, a patient God was willing to wait forty days before exacting the penalty. Throughout this section God shows himself to be a God of love who has concern for all people (cf. 4:2, 11). The message of judgment contained a veiled prophecy: "Forty days from now Nineveh will be [overturned]" (3:4). "Overturned" it was, but not with destruction. Rather, its unrighteous lifestyle was changed so greatly that God was moved to relent from bringing punishment upon them (3:10).

Such oracles of judgment are often conditioned upon human interaction. God himself announced that when any nation destined for divine judgment repents of its evil ways after hearing his message, he will relent from inflicting the threatened disaster (Jer 18:7-9; 26:3, 13, 19). This had been the case in Moses's day (Exod 32:12-14) and through the intercession of Amos (Amos 7:1-6). Hezekiah was also delivered from the sentence of death (2 Kgs 20:1-11). (Thus also, Nebuchadnezzar's opportunity to capture Tyre was left to Alexander the Great to fulfill; Ezek 26:7-21.)

Peter's pronouncement is true (2 Pet 3:9). Rather than wishing for people to perish, God patiently deals with them, desiring that they should come to repentance. As Jesus pointed out (Matt 12:41), the example of the Ninevites stands as an illustration of the possibilities of repentance when people respond to the preaching of the Word of God.

God's desire to reclaim the great city of Nineveh provides an example for contemporary society. Although it is true that punishment ought to fit the crime (Exod 21:12-36), it is also certain that society is best served when a violator is reclaimed and becomes a responsible and productive member of the community (cf. Gal 6:1). Therefore, while upholding the proper demands of justice, it may also be helpful for society (and churches) to make sure that lawbreakers take conscious responsibility for their actions and to make every attempt to redeem offenders. In so doing, society will improve its own situation and that of the individuals concerned. In an ultimate sense, of course, such restoration can best be accomplished when offenders recognize themselves as sinners, repent, and receive the pardon that comes through faith in Christ.[4]

ENDNOTES

1. Laetsch (1956:239) observes that "at Nineveh the speaker was not a sensationalistic broadcaster. He was a prophet of Jehovah!"
2. That no record of Jonah's visit to Nineveh or change of lifestyle by the Ninevites in this period has been preserved in the Assyrian literature is understandable since Assyrian Royal Annals reported the king's victories and accomplishments. It would be unlikely for an Assyrian king to describe humbling himself in response to the words of a foreign prophet. Regarding the animals, Ellison (1985:383) points out from several examples of public mourning in which animals were involved, so there is nothing alien to the ancient Near Eastern mind in the practices that Jonah mentions.
3. Fausset (1948:582) correctly observes: "When God repents of the evil (3:10) that He said He would do unto men, the change is not really in Him, but in them. Were He not to change His mode of dealing with them, when they have changed their dealings towards Him, He would be really changing from His own immutable righteousness. His threats are expressed absolutely, without the condition being expressed, in order to mark the absolute inviolability of His principle that sin unpardoned brings inevitable punishment, and that the sinner may be the more roused to flee from the wrath to come."
4. P. Hughes (*Christian Ethics in Secular Society* [Grand Rapids: Baker, 1983], 118) suggests that "the return to God starts with man's recognition of himself as a guilty sinner under divine condemnation and with his thankful and trusting reception of the grace of God freely offered him in and through Christ Jesus, who made full atonement for the sinner by His substitutionary death, Man for man."

◆ C. Jonah and God (4:1-11)

This change of plans greatly upset Jonah, and he became very angry. [2]So he complained to the LORD about it: "Didn't I say before I left home that you would do this, LORD? That is why I ran away to Tarshish! I knew that you are a merciful and compassionate God, slow to get angry and filled with unfailing love. You are eager to turn back from destroying people. [3]Just kill me now, LORD! I'd rather be dead than alive if what I predicted will not happen."

[4]The LORD replied, "Is it right for you to be angry about this?"

[5]Then Jonah went out to the east side of the city and made a shelter to sit under as he waited to see what would happen to the city. [6]And the LORD God arranged for a leafy plant to grow there, and soon it spread its broad leaves over Jonah's head, shading him from the sun. This eased his discomfort, and Jonah was very grateful for the plant.

[7]But God also arranged for a worm! The next morning at dawn the worm ate through the stem of the plant so that it withered away. [8]And as the sun grew hot, God arranged for a scorching east wind to blow on Jonah. The sun beat down on his

head until he grew faint and wished to die. "Death is certainly better than living like this!" he exclaimed.

⁹Then God said to Jonah, "Is it right for you to be angry because the plant died?"

"Yes," Jonah retorted, "even angry enough to die!"

¹⁰Then the LORD said, "You feel sorry about the plant, though you did nothing to put it there. It came quickly and died quickly. ¹¹But Nineveh has more than 120,000 people living in spiritual darkness,* not to mention all the animals. Shouldn't I feel sorry for such a great city?"

4:11 Hebrew *people who don't know their right hand from their left.*

NOTES

4:1 *This change of plans greatly upset Jonah.* Lit., "It was displeasing to Jonah with great displeasure." The Hebrew cognate adverbial construction indicates that Jonah was deeply offended by God's compassion for Nineveh. The words translated "upset" are *ra'a' . . . ra'ah* [TH7489/7451B, ZH8317/8288]; the second Hebrew word is rendered "evil/calamity" elsewhere (cf. 1:2; see Introduction).

he became very angry. Jonah was so upset that his emotions gave way to burning anger. He was simply furious.

4:2 *So he complained to the LORD.* The Hebrew verb is the same as that translated "prayed" in 2:1. The NLT renders the sense of the passage. Jonah's prayer was to Yahweh, the covenant God of Israel.

Didn't I say? Lit., "Was this not my word?" The phraseology parallels that of Exod 14:12. Jonah asks, "Isn't this what I said would happen?"

before I left home. Lit., "while I was still in my [own] country." The noun translated "home/country" is most commonly rendered "ground/land." Baldwin (1993:583) notes the relation of this noun (*'adamah* [TH127, ZH141]) to *'adam* [TH120/121, ZH132/134] (Adam, human) and remarks that it "is a reminder of Genesis 2:7 and humanity's origin from dust of the earth and destiny to return to it (Gen 3:19)."

LORD! Jonah's address to God is the same as the sailors in 1:14. In the Hebrew text it appears at the opening of Jonah's prayer, thus standing in the polite and honorific position.

I ran away to Tarshish! Although he has been previously represented as fleeing from the presence of the Lord (1:3, 10), Jonah did not admit to this. He only confessed to going to Tarshish because he knew about God's gracious character. His reason simply is that "he wanted nothing to do with bringing benefit to the Assyrians. Jonah thus argued with God, complaining at God's goodness!" (Stuart 1987:502). In Jonah's thinking, for God to act compassionately in this case would bring about injustice, not justice, for surely the Assyrians were worthy of judgment.

I knew that you are . . . merciful . . . compassionate . . . slow to get angry . . . filled with unfailing love . . . eager to turn back from destroying people. Jonah listed five attributes of God as his reason for knowing that God would change his plans: God is gracious, compassionate, patient/long-suffering, abounding in love, and willing to relent punishment given certain conditions. Jonah's confession contains the same five essential components as found in Joel 2:13. Both passages ultimately derive from Exod 34:6-7.

merciful and compassionate. These two qualities were affirmed by God himself to Moses, although in reverse order (Exod 34:6), and are often mentioned in the OT (e.g., 2 Chr 30:9; Neh 9:17, 31; Pss 111:4; 145:8; Joel 2:13). God alone is known by the combined adjectives *khannun* [TH2587, ZH2843] (merciful/gracious) and *rakhum* [TH7349, ZH8157] (compassionate). In addition to the above texts, "compassionate" is used of God in Deut 4:31 and Ps 78:38. Its relationship to the noun *rekhem* [TH7358, ZH8167] (womb) gives it a tender quality like unto a mother's love.

slow to get angry and filled with unfailing love. Both characteristics of God are found in Exod 34:6. The former lays stress on God's infinite patience. Limburg (1993:91) observes that "it is the opposite of having a hasty temper (Prov 14:29) or a hot temper (Prov 15:18) and is better than might (Prov 16:32) or pride (Eccl 7:8)." For the latter quality, see the note on 2:8 and the commentary on 2:7-10.

eager to turn back from destroying people. Jonah understood God's forgiving nature from the very start. What God had done for Nineveh (3:10) was in accord with what Jonah originally feared would happen.

4:3 *Just kill me now, LORD!* Lit., "And now, O LORD, please take my life from me." The prophet Jeremiah likewise fell into despondency and wished for death—in fact, that he might never have been born (Jer 20:14-18). Moses (Num 11:1-15) and Job (Job 6:8-9; 17:1, 10-16) expressed similar feelings of depression. For the word translated "life" (*nepesh* [TH5315, ZH5883]), see the note on 2:5. Like Elijah of old (1 Kgs 19:4), Jonah asked the Lord to take his life. Elijah had been disappointed with the lack of spiritual change after his preaching (1 Kgs 19:9-14). Jonah lamented the triumph of God's compassion. Ironically, Jonah resented God's compassion toward the Ninevites while forgetting God's earlier compassion toward him.

if what I predicted will not happen. Jonah's understanding of the outcome of his prophesying did not take into account his own knowledge of God's compassion and capacity to forgive. So striking are Jonah's words that the Masoretes insert a *setumah* (cf. note on 2:9) here so that the reader might pause to consider the implications of what Jonah said.

4:4 *Is it right for you to be angry?* God did not grant Jonah's wish, but he went to the heart of Jonah's problem: Jonah was angry over the seeming injustice of God's sparing wicked Nineveh after Jonah had announced its destruction. God will ask the question of his prophet again in v. 9.

4:5 *Jonah went out to the east side of the city.* Some expositors understand the verb here as "had gone out," so that the reader is given a sort of flashback (cf. Stuart 1987:504). Yet as Keil (1954:412) points out, it is difficult to see how Jonah could be so angry with God before the allotted 40 days had been completed. Whether through direct revelation or by observing that the city remained after the appointed time had passed, Jonah was aware that God had changed his mind.

a shelter. The Hebrew noun envisions a temporary shelter, whether for humans (1 Kgs 20:12, 16; Isa 1:8) or animals (Gen 33:17). Jonah's makeshift shelter must have been something like the "booths" made of intertwined leafy branches used in the Festival of Shelters (Lev 23:40-43).

4:6 *And the LORD God arranged.* The narrator plays on the verb *manah* [TH4487, ZH4948] (arranged, appointed) three times in these verses (cf. 1:17). Not only did God provide the leafy plant (4:6), but the plant-eating worm (4:7), and the scorching east wind (4:8). Sasson (1990:291) calls attention to the fact that the name for God changes with each occurrence of this verb: at 1:17 "it is *yhwh* [TH3068, ZH3378]; at 4:6, *yhwh-'elohim* [TH430, ZH466]; at 4:7, *ha'elohim* [TH1886.1/430, ZH2021/466]; and at 4:8, *'elohim* [TH430, ZH466]. It may be accidental that the narrator reaches this particular progression or scheme; but we can nevertheless observe a move from the most (*yhwh*) to the least (*'elohim*) personal of God's names."

a leafy plant. Since Jonah's shelter would have had at best only a few leafy branches, his protection from the sun would be partial at best. A growing plant would provide better comfort. The nature of the plant (*qiqayon* [TH7021, ZH7813]) is greatly debated (Robinson 1985:390-403), but is most often identified as some sort of gourd or castor bean plant (*ricinus communis*). If it was a gourd, it may have grown over Jonah's shelter and given double protection. Those who favor the castor bean plant (e.g., Baldwin 1993:586) point to a possible linguistic identification with the Egyptian *kiki* and Assyrian *kukkanitu* (see Walker 1957:94).

This eased his discomfort. Lit., "to deliver him from his evil [situation]." The verb for deliver (*lehatsil* [TH3807.1/5337, ZH4200/5911]; NLT "eased") forms a sound play with the previous noun for shade (*tsel* [TH6738, ZH7498]). The LXX was seemingly affected by this paronomasia and translated "to shelter him," apparently reading *tsalal* [TH6751, ZH7511] (grow dark) rather than the Hebrew text's *natsal* [TH5337, ZH5911] (deliver). The noun *evil* (*ra'ah* [TH7451B, ZH8288]; NLT "discomfort"), which describes Jonah's situation, is a key term in the book (see Introduction). The NLT renders the sense of the narrative.

Jonah was very grateful. Lit., "Jonah rejoiced . . . with a great joy." Once again, the author employed a cognate accusative to express Jonah's great happiness (see the note on 1:16).

4:7 But God also arranged for a worm! First, God supplied a plant; then, he sent a worm to destroy the plant. The exact nature of the "worm" is unclear; "larva," "maggot," "weevil," "beetle," and "centipede" have all been suggested (Sasson 1990:301). Usually cited unfavorably (e.g., Deut 28:39; Job 25:6), the noun is used to describe the suffering psalmist in Ps 22:6 and the lowly state of exiled Israel (Isa 41:14). The text does not use the name "Yahweh" or "Lord God" (4:6) to designate the one who sent the worm; it uses "God" (*ha'elohim* [TH1886.1/430, ZH2021/466]), the omnipotent sovereign and creator of all things who was disciplining Jonah.

The next morning. The worm began its work at the crack of dawn, when the first rays of the sun streaked across the sky. Accordingly, the heat of the day could take its effect upon a pouting Jonah.

the worm ate through the stem. Although the Hebrew simply reports that the insect attacked the plant, the NLT gives the required sense of the worm's voracious activity.

withered away. Once again the narrator draws upon the root *yabesh* [TH3001, ZH3312; cf. TH3004, ZH3317]. Jonah had acknowledged God as the creator of the sea and dry land (*yabbashah* [TH3004, ZH3317]; 1:9). The sailors had attempted to row to land (1:14), and Jonah was vomited by the great fish onto dry land (2:10). Here it describes the smitten plant which is drying up and withering away (cf. Joel 1:12).

4:8 as the sun grew hot. Lit., "when the sun rose." By the time the sun had risen in the sky, the worm had done its work. As it rose, God (*'elohim* [TH430, ZH466]) sent a scorching wind to buffet Jonah.

scorching. The exact force of this adjective is uncertain. Most suggest something to do with oppressive heat: "heat" (GW, also *Dios Habla Hoy*); "burning" (LXX, *La Sainte Bible*); "sweltering" (NRSV, cf. Keil; *La Sacra Biblia*, "oppressive"); and "withering" (Luther, cf. Stuart). The NLT's "scorching" is reflected in several English versions (NASB, NIV, NJB, REB). The suggestion of "vehement" (NKJV; cf. Sasson, "fierce") is taken up in 1QH 7:5. The nature of the context favors the idea of a strong, hot, and stifling wind. Since it is the effect of the heat that is stressed in the verse, the NLT's rendering is as good as any.

east wind. Because in Nineveh southwesterly winds off of the Arabian Desert often brought extreme heat, the mention of an east wind is significant. Jonah had gone to the east side of the city (4:5). God met him there with the heat of an east wind. If the plant and the worm were not sufficient to convince Jonah that God was dealing with him, the location of these events and the direction of the scorching wind ought to do so.

The sun beat down on his head until he grew faint. The verb translated "beat down" is the same as that rendered "ate through" in v. 7. As the worm vigorously attacked the plant, the sun beat down on Jonah viciously. Wind and sun combined to make Jonah faint. Sasson (1990:304) suggests that the major purpose of the wind was to sweep away the shelter that

Jonah had erected previous to the appearing of the plant. With no protection available, Jonah would easily suffer sunstroke.

wished to die. Lit., "asked his soul to die." Like Elijah (1 Kgs 19:4), Jonah wished only for death. The image of a person talking with the soul is exemplified in an Egyptian tale of a man's dispute over the merits of suicide with his soul (Lichtheim 1973:1.163-169). So eloquent is his reasoning that his soul (*ba'*) agrees to remain with him rather than desert him at death and cause his annihilation. One of the famous verses reads: "Death is before me today like the fragrance of myrrh, like sitting under sail on breeze day" (Lichtheim 1973:1.168).

4:9 *Then God said to Jonah.* Jonah was questioned a second time (cf. 4:4) about his anger. This time the divine name *'elohim* [TH430, ZH466] (God) rather than *yhwh* [TH3068, ZH3378] (the LORD) appears. Perhaps this is the narrator's touch to remind the reader that the omnipotent God of all men is now posing the question to the man Jonah.

because the plant died? God wanted Jonah to understand the object lesson he had provided in the plant that appeared and disappeared so suddenly. As Stuart (1987:506) remarks, "By reducing the question to the particular issue of the gourd, God focused the question in a way that would cause Jonah to condemn himself by his own words. Jonah did just that."

angry enough to die! Jonah's anger was such that he would have preferred death to life. In the previous inquiry (4:4), Jonah had answered God by walking away from him. Here he actually gave God an answer, one that would allow God to make his point.

4:10 *the LORD.* The covenant name "Yahweh" reappears here as the Lord now deals tenderly with his prophet in an attempt to enlighten him.

You feel sorry about the plant. The verb translated "sorry" connotes a deep feeling of compassion, mercy, and genuine sympathy, especially "the shared sufferings due to the misfortune or disaster that befalls another" (TDOT 4.272).

you did nothing to put it there. Lit., "you did not toil over it or make it grow." Jonah's sorrow could not be personal for he himself had not labored over or cared for the plant.

It came quickly and died quickly. The Hebrew text points out that the plant came up in a night and perished in a night. Allen (1976:234) represents God as saying, "Your attachment to it could not be very deep, for it was here one day and *gone the next.* Your concern was dictated by self-interest, not by a genuine love."

4:11 *120,000 people.* Sasson (1990:311-312) cites studies that estimate that in the days when Nineveh flourished, the population was about 300,000 people. Whether the population was that high in Jonah's day is unknown. Scholars have often debated the meaning of the figure 120,000 here, some (e.g., Keil 1954:416-417; Feinberg 1976:151; Pusey 1953:426) suggesting that this reflected the number of children, so that the total population would be something like 600,000. If 120,000 represents the men available for military service (cf. e.g., Num 1; 2 Sam 24:2-9), then a total population of Nineveh could come close to 300,000. It is possible, of course, that 120,000 is simply a round figure, perhaps reflecting the symbolism of the numbers 10 and 12. Sasson (1990:311-312) speaks for many (e.g., Allen 1976:234), however, who think that 120,000 is "not at all implausible for Nineveh even before its heyday." God would have spared Sodom and Gomorrah for 10 people (Gen 18:32); why should he not be moved for 120,000?

people living in spiritual darkness. Lit., "who do not know their right hand from their left." Some commentators (Keil 1954:416-417; Laetsch 1956:242-243; Feinberg 1976:151) take the phrase to refer to children below the age of accountability. The NLT has applied the emphasis of the right hand/left hand motif: The Ninevites are totally blind spiritually. Applying this motif in a slightly different manner, one may say that whereas Israel was to

deviate neither to the right hand nor the left but to follow the Lord and his commandments (Deut 17:11, 20 [NASB]; Josh 1:7; Prov 4:23-27), the Ninevites had no knowledge
of spiritual truth—hence, they didn't know what lay to either side of it.

people . . . animals. Both humans and animals had been involved in the public display of
penitence. The Scriptures indicate that Israel's God was concerned about people and animals (Neh 9:6; Pss 36:6; 145:16; Joel 1:16-20; 2:21-27; Matt 10:29-31). Limburg (1993:98)
observes that Jonah's story "has a special concern to show God's love for the outsiders, the
people of the world—and even for their cattle!"

Shouldn't I feel sorry for such a great city? God's argument is from the lesser to the
greater (*a fortiori*), a familiar method known both in the Scriptures (Gen 44:8; Exod 6:12;
Deut 31:27; 2 Kgs 5:13; Jer 12:5; Ezek 14:12-23; 15:1-6; Matt 6:30; 10:25; 12:11-12; Luke
11:13; 12:24, 28) and the rabbinic literature. (For a concise discussion of the principles
of rabbinic exegesis, see Kaiser 1981:52-55.) If Jonah could feel sorrow for the dead plant
over which he had not toiled, should not God be concerned for Nineveh? Allen (1976:
234) depicts God's feelings as meaning, "All those people, all those animals—I made
them, I have cherished them all these years. Nineveh has cost me no end of effort, and
they mean the world to me. Your pain is nothing to mine when I contemplate their
destruction."

COMMENTARY

The concluding chapter of the book presents the reader with an unexpected conclusion. Rather than rejoicing over the effectiveness of his preaching, Jonah was greatly
displeased. His displeasure gives way to absolute fury. He blurted out his anger by
telling the Lord that he was afraid of this outcome all along. Because he knew that
God was gracious and compassionate (Exod 34:6-7), Jonah had feared that if the
Ninevites responded with repentance at his announcement of God's judgment,
God might forgive them and remit the threatened penalty. Since God himself had
said that Nineveh was a wicked city (1:1), why should they not perish? Would not
his preaching be in vain? Rather than facing that possibility, Jonah had fled to
Tarshish—at least, he had attempted to do so.

Despite the bitterness of his prophet, God gently chided him: "Is it right for you
to be angry about this?" Because God is a gracious and merciful God, as Jonah knew
him to be, Jonah should rather have considered his mission to have been highly
successful since the result was in keeping with who Jonah knew God to be.

Jonah, however, would hear none of it. Once again walking away from God (cf.
1:3), he went out to the east side of the city and sat down. Perhaps God would see
Jonah's righteous cause and give the Ninevites their justly deserved destruction. But
outside the city, Jonah found no shelter from the oppressive heat of the day. Therefore, he built a rude hut for himself and there he sat, a disgusted prophet waiting for
God to change his mind and destroy the city.

However, God was not through with his prophet. He would attempt to teach him
a spiritual lesson. Because Jonah's hastily built hut was inadequate to spare him
completely from the scorching sun, God miraculously intervened on behalf of his
pouting prophet. He caused a plant to grow above him so as to shade him from the
piercing rays of the sun. How grateful Jonah was! Yet God had more purposes in
mind than temporarily shading him. When Jonah greeted the rising sun on the next

day, he found that God had commissioned a worm to destroy his newly acquired shelter. Moreover, an unusual east wind served only to add scorching heat to the weight of the sun beating down upon his head. Jonah was beside himself in anguish and pain. Faint and near exhaustion, he wished only to die.

Once again, God came to his prophet with a question: "Is it right for you to be angry because the plant died?" Jonah averred that it was—he was furious to the point of death itself. Again the Lord reasoned with Jonah. Did he not see that his sorrow over the plant was self-serving? He had lost something that he had not labored for. By contrast, God reclaimed an entire population of a great city over which he had sorrowed. The Lord is not only Israel's God but the God of the whole world which he created and nourishes. Jonah should have rejoiced that these members of the human race had repented of their wickedness. Didn't Jonah see this? Rather than being a failure, his preaching had helped to overturn (cf. 3:4 and note) the wicked lifestyle of an entire populace, not to mention the fate of many animals.

Did Jonah learn the lesson of the plant?[1] Did he respond positively to God's patient dealing with him? One would like to think that he did and, like a recommissioned Elijah (1 Kgs 19:9-21), was available to deliver other messages for God.[2] If Jonah's preaching in the days of Jeroboam II (2 Kgs 14:25) took place after his mission to Nineveh, then Jeroboam's great military exploits would have taken place toward the end of his long reign (792–752 BC). The most likely historical scenario would put Jeroboam's campaigning after the death of Adad-nirari III of Assyria in 783/782 BC and during a period of both Assyrian (782–746 BC) and Aramean (773–750 BC) weakness.[3] Because Jonah's ministry in Nineveh is most likely to be dated around 758–755 BC (see Introduction), this would leave little time for Jeroboam's foreign wars before his death in 752 BC. Moreover, signs of the Israelite weakness that appeared after his passing could be seen in the immediately preceding years.

Accordingly, one can, at best, only hope that Jonah wrote the story of his activities to remind his fellow countrymen both of God's love for all people, Jew and Gentile alike, and of the need for all prophets to respond positively to God's claim upon their lives.[4] If Jonah is indeed the author of the book that bears his name, perhaps he intended for his readers to learn the lesson of obedience from his failure. If so, Jonah may have repented and reported for subsequent duty.

Theologically, this chapter reveals a great deal about God's activities and character. Because he is a God of grace, compassion, and loving-kindness, he reaches down to people in their need (cf. Joel 2:13). This, together with his infinite patience, makes his forgiveness of repentant sinners a rather natural feature of his dealing with them (cf. Exod 34:6-7; Neh 9:17; 2 Pet 3:15; 1 John 1:8-9). The ultimate expression of these features reached a climax in the life and atoning death of Jesus Christ. God's Son gave himself for a sinful world so as to bring to himself a people who are eager to reproduce these qualities in their lives (Rom 3:22-25; 2 Cor 8:9; Eph 1:3-8; Titus 2:11-14; 3:4-8).

This chapter adds to the picture of God's patience with Jonah that is presented throughout the book. Thus, rather than punish Jonah when he disobeyed God's summons and fled to Joppa, God let Jonah play out his role. Once Jonah was on the sea, God sent a storm to get Jonah's attention and then rescued him from the waters by means of a "great fish" (1:17). By this, God demonstrated that he is not only the God of the land of Israel but the sea as well. Then, as the fish vomited Jonah on land (2:10), Jonah's own confession was seen to be true: "The LORD, the God of heaven, who made the sea and the land" (1:9). God had patiently but surely brought his prophet back to a position of trust and obedience (2:4, 7-9).

When Jonah obeyed a second commission and preached (apparently with not-altogether-pure motives) the coming judgment, God blessed his message so that the people of Nineveh turned from their wicked ways. God then relented from the threatened judgment (3:1-10). Rather than being grateful and happy over the results of his ministry, Jonah became angry with God. Therefore, God again dealt patiently with his prophet. He provided a plant to shade him from the heat of the day in the very spot where Jonah had positioned himself. By the next day, however, a "worm" of some sort had destroyed Jonah's means of shelter (4:5-7). When Jonah faced the renewed heat of the sizzling sun and scorching wind, he again became angry (4:8). And once again God asked whether it was right to be angry, now over the plant that died (4:9). When Jonah said that it was and that he was angry enough to die, God patiently and tenderly explained the lesson of the plant to him. If Jonah could feel sorry for the plant that had been provided for him, should not God feel compassion for so many human beings, not to mention animals, who are the objects of his sustaining power (4:9-11)? Apparently, Jonah had forgotten how God had provided a sea creature to bring him to repentance. Yet Jonah was not willing to grant God the prerogative of accepting the penitence of the Ninevites. Jonah grieved over a plant that God had provided but was unwilling to grant God the privilege of compassion for needy human beings. Once again God did not punish Jonah but, in patience, reasoned with him theologically.

All along the way, then, God's infinite patience can be seen. What Jonah experienced is in keeping with what the Scriptures reveal concerning God: He is infinitely patient (Exod 34:6; Num 14:18; Pss 86:15; 103:8; Joel 2:13; Nah 1:3). Because he is patient, he bore with the total spiritual bankruptcy of the world in Noah's day (1 Pet 3:20). Similarly, he still delays the great day of judgment in order to prolong the day of salvation (2 Pet 3:15). Accordingly, God's patience should lead people to repentance (Rom 2:4; 9:22-29) so that ultimately, through faith and patience, they become those "who are going to inherit God's promises" (Heb 6:12). God's patience with Jonah and compassion for wicked Nineveh stand as a challenge for today's believing church. How easy it is to give up on those who "just won't listen" or seem irretrievably reprobate. How tempting it is to write off those individuals, communities, or nations that "are just asking for God to strike them down." Yet if God had compassion on wicked Nineveh, should not believers have a godly concern for those individuals and nations who appear to violate the ethical and moral standards of civilized society? If God dealt patiently with wayward Jonah, should we not be slow to take offense and quick to forgive backsliding Christians (Prov 19:11; Gal 6:1-5)?

Jonah's experiences also warn us that believers can be out of fellowship with God—even while seeking to serve him. It would be easy to assume that having received Christ as Savior we would thereafter make steady spiritual progress in our Christian lives. Such is frequently not the case, however. The truth is that believers often struggle with the will and standards of God as much as Jonah did. How grateful we should be that God is gracious and compassionate, ever willing to forgive and receive repentant sinners back to a place of intimate fellowship and profitable service (Exod 34:6-7; 2 Pet 3:17-18; 1 John 1:5-9).

Jonah's own struggle with God's relenting from judging Nineveh revealed his conception of God's gracious character. His understanding of Israel's elect place in God's economy left little or no room for outsiders. How easy it is to find fault with Jonah. Nevertheless, Jonah's problem has plagued segments of the believing church throughout the ages and still permeates many a congregation.[5] It is all too easy to confine God's love to those of one's own fellowship or denomination. May God help believers to have a vision of God's grace, compassion, loving-kindness, and concern for all people everywhere.

The lesson of Jonah and Nineveh reinforces the gospel call. In what many have termed a post-Christian generation, Jonah's message takes on even greater force. A world of lost "Ninevites" still faces God's certain judgment (Acts 17:30-31). There remains, however, the possibility that unbelieving lives may be "overturned" (3:4). Like Saul on the road to Damascus (Acts 9:1-16; 22:6-21; 26:12-23; Gal 1:11-17), many may be waiting to be told the message of saving grace in Christ Jesus in order that their lives may be turned to faithful service for him (Acts 20:24; 2 Tim 4:7-8). Jonah's story thus reminds us of the need for sharing the Word of God with an unbelieving world and for praying for all people everywhere (cf. 1 Tim 2:1-6). The desperate condition of the lost and the urgency of the times demand that an unrepentant generation be confronted with the lesson of Nineveh: "Someone greater than Jonah is here" (Matt 12:41).[6]

ENDNOTES

1. What exactly was the lesson of the plant? D. N. Freedman ("Did God Play a Dirty Trick on Jonah at the End?" *Bible Review* 6/4 1990:26-31) suggests that Jonah's readers were to understand that whereas in earlier days, Hebrew doctrine held that wrongdoers were punished, now repentance was to be held as equivalent to retributive punishment. In Nineveh's case, however, "God is telling Jonah that that is what's behind the whole—pity, compassion for his children. This whole repentance business was just a charade. . . . God is now saying that regardless of the repentance, he would have saved them" (31).

Freedman's proposed "new view" is, of course, not new. For the ideas of confession and forgiveness were already propounded by David (Ps 32:1-2) and Solomon (1 Kgs 8:46-53) and were implicit in the earlier regulations of the Levitical offerings (e.g., Lev 5:5-6). As Freedman admits, confession and forgiveness were part of the classic code concerning God's attributes and activities, and, in any case, Jonah was not tricked, for before he ever left home (4:2), he understood that with repentance and sincere change of lifestyle, God could relent the intended punishment (cf. Joel 2:12-14).

2. One might hope for a similar recommissioning in the case of Elisha's servant Gehazi (2 Kgs 8:4-6).

3. For details, see R. D. Patterson and H. J. Austel, "1, 2 Kings," *Expositor's Bible Commentary* 4:223-224; E. Merrill, *Kingdom of Priests* (Grand Rapids: Baker, 1987), 374-375.

4. B. Woodward (1993) treats the book of Jonah as tragedy. Under such a scenario, Jonah is likely to have forfeited any further opportunity to serve God as a prophet. Laetsch (1956:243) remarks, adding the words of Huxtable, "Jonah would not have written so sincerely repentant . . . 'By the very act of penning it [his confession], Jonah at once emerges out of his former character and appears in our view not merely as a prophet, but as a remarkable humble and noble-spirited saint.'"

5. Allen (1976:235) warns Jonah's modern-day readers that "a Jonah lurks in every Christian heart, whimpering his insidious message of smug prejudice, empty tradition-alism, and exclusive solidarity."

6. A. J. Brown (*The Foreign Missionary* [New York: Revell, 1950], 27-28) remarks, "No changes that have taken place or that can possibly take place can set aside the great central facts that Jesus Christ means the temporal and eternal salvation of men; that it is the duty of those who know Him; that no matter how distant the ignorant may be, no matter how different in race, we must get to them."

BIBLIOGRAPHY

Alexander, D.
1988 *Obadiah, Jonah, Micah.* Tyndale Old Testament Commentaries. Downers Grove: InterVarsity.

Alexander, T. D.
1985 Jonah and Genre. *Tyndale Bulletin* 36:35-59.

Allen, L. C.
1976 *The Books of Joel, Obadiah, Jonah and Micah.* The New International Commentary on the Old Testament. Grand Rapids: Eerdmans.

Archer, G. L. Jr.
1974 *A Survey of Old Testament Introduction.* Rev. ed. Chicago: Moody.

Baldwin, J.
1993 Jonah in *The Minor Prophets,* vol. 2. Editor, T. E. McComiskey. Grand Rapids: Baker.

Barr, J.
1983 *The Semantics of Biblical Language.* London: SCM.

Carson, D.
1984 Matthew. Pp. 1-600 in *Matthew, Mark, Luke.* The Expositor's Bible Commentary, vol. 8. Editor, F. E. Gaebelein. Grand Rapids: Zondervan.

Collins, C. J.
1995 From Literary Analysis to Theological Exposition: The Book of Jonah. *Journal of Translation and Textlinguistics* 7:28-44.

Couffignal, R.
1990 Le Psaume de Jonas (Jonas 2,2-10). Une catabase biblique, sa structure et sa fonction. *Biblica* 71:542-552.

Craigie, P. C.
1985 *Twelve Prophets,* vol. 1. Philadelphia: Westminster.

Davis, M. S.
1989 Jonah in History and Legend. *Biblical Illustrator* 16:38-41.

Dillard, R. B. and T. Longman III
1994 *An Introduction to the Old Testament.* Grand Rapids: Zondervan.

Elata-Alster, G. and R. Salmon
1984 Eastward and Westward: The Movement of Prophecy and History in the Book of Jonah. *Dor le Dor* 13:16-27.

Ellison, H.
1985 Jonah. Pp. 359-392 in *Daniel, Minor Prophets.* The Expositor's Bible Commentary, vol. 7. Editor, F. E. Gaebelein. Grand Rapids: Zondervan.

Fausset, A. R.
1948 Jonah in *A Commentary Critical, Experimental and Practical on the Old and New Testaments,* vol. 4: Jeremiah—Malachi. Grand Rapids: Eerdmans.

Feinberg, C.
1976 *The Minor Prophets.* Chicago: Moody.

Gese, H.
1985 Jona ben Amittai und das Jonabuch. *Theologische Beiträge* 16:256-262.

Gesenius, W., E. Kautzsch, and A. E. Cowley
1910 *Gesenius' Hebrew Grammar.* Oxford: Clarendon.

Grayson, A. K.
1982 Assyria: Ashur-dan II to Ashur-nirari V (934–745 BC). Pp. 238-281 in *The Cambridge Ancient History,* vol. 3.1. 2nd ed. Editors, J. Boardman, I. E. S. Edwards, N. G. L. Hammond, and E. Sollberger. Cambridge: Cambridge University Press.

Guilmin, S.
1986 Jona. *Etudes Théologiques et Religieuses* 61:189-193.

Hailey, H.
1971 *A Commentary on the Minor Prophets*. Grand Rapids: Baker.

Halpern, B. and R. E. Friedman
1980 Composition and Paronomasia in the Book of Jonah. *Hebrew Annual Review* 4:79-92.

Hannah, J. D.
1985 Jonah. Pp. 1461-1473 in *The Bible Knowledge Commentary*. Editors, J. F. Walvoord and R. B. Zuck. Wheaton: Victor.

Heidel, A.
1963 *The Gilgamesh Epic and Old Testament Parallels*. Chicago: University of Chicago Press.

Howell, M.
1995 A Prophet Who Pouts. *The Bible Today* 33:75-78.

Kahn, P.
1994 An Analysis of the Book of Jonah. *Judaica* 43:87-100.

Kaiser, W.
1981 *Toward an Exegetical Theology*. Grand Rapids: Baker.

Kaplan, J. and H. Kaplan
1976 Jaffa. *Encyclopedia of Archaeological Excavations in the Holy Land*. London: Oxford University Press.

Keil, C. F.
1954 *The Twelve Minor Prophets*. Biblical Commentary on the Old Testament. Translator, J. Martin. Grand Rapids: Eerdmans. (Orig. pub. 1873)

Koehler, L. and W. Baumgartner
1974 *Hebräisches und Aramäisches Lexikon zum Alten Testament*, 3rd ed. Leiden: Brill.

Laetsch, T.
1956 *The Minor Prophets*. St. Louis: Concordia.

Lehman, M. R.
1989-1990 The Background to the Prophet Jonah's Behavior According to Biblical Sources. *Beth Mikra* 35:348-350.

Lemanski, J.
1992 Jonah's Nineveh. *Concordia Journal* 40-48.

Lescow, T.
1992 Die Komposition des Buches Jona. *Biblische Notizen* 65:29-34.

Lichtheim, M.
1973 *Ancient Egyptian Literature*. Los Angeles: University of California Press.

Limburg, J.
1993 *Jonah*. The Old Testament Library. Louisville: Westminster/John Knox.

Lubeck, R. J.
1988 Prophetic Sabotage: A Look at Jonah 3:2-4. *Trinity Journal* 9:37-46.

McCann, J. F.
1988 Jonah: Doctor Strangelove. *The Bible Today* 26:298-303.

Mulrooney, J.
1991 The Spiritual Pilgrimage of Jonah: God Does Not Give Up on Us. *The Bible Today* 29:163-168.

Olmstead, A. T.
1951 *History of Assyria*. Chicago: University of Chicago Press.

von Orelli, C.
1897 *The Twelve Minor Prophets*. Edinburgh: T & T Clark.

Patterson, R. D.
1995 The Song of Redemption. *Westminster Theological Journal* 57:453-461.

Payne, R.
1989 The Prophet Jonah: Reluctant Messenger and Intercessor. *Expository Times* 100:131-134.

Perowne, T. T.
1905 *Obadiah and Jonah*. The Cambridge Bible for Schools and Colleges. Cambridge: Cambridge University Press.

Person, R. F.
1996 *In Conversation with Jonah: Conversation Analysis, Literary Criticism, and the Book of Jonah.* Journal for the Study of the Old Testament Supplemental Series 220. Sheffield: Sheffield Academic Press.

Pusey, E. B.
1953 *The Minor Prophets,* vol. 2. Grand Rapids: Baker.

Ratner, R. J.
1990 Jonah, the Runaway Servant. *Maarav* 5 & 6:281-305.

Robinson, B. P.
1985 Jonah's Qiqayon Plant. *Zeitschrift für die alttestamentliche Wissenschaft* 97:390-403.

Rover, L.
1995 The God Who Surprises. *The Bible Today* 33:298-302.

Ryken, L.
1987 *Words of Delight.* Grand Rapids: Baker.

Saggs, H. W. F.
1984 *The Might That Was Assyria.* London: Sidgwick & Jackson.

Sasson, J. M.
1984 On Jonah's 2 Missions. *Henoch* 6:23-79.
1990 *Jonah.* The Anchor Bible. New York: Doubleday.

Schrader, S.
1989 Jonah. Pp. 644-650 in *Evangelical Commentary on the Bible.* Editor, W. A. Elwell. Grand Rapids: Baker.

Smith, B. K.
2001 *Jonah.* The New American Commentary, vol. 19b. Nashville: Broadman & Holman.

Smith, G. A.
1929 *The Book of the Twelve Prophets,* vol. 1. Rev. ed. Garden City: Doubleday.

Stuart, D.
1987 *Hosea—Jonah.* Word Biblical Commentary. Waco: Word.

Sweeney, M. A.
2000 *The Twelve Prophets.* Berit Olam. Collegeville, MN: Liturgical.

Trudinger, P.
1989 Jonah: A Post-Exilic Verbal Cartoon? *Downside Review* 107:142-143.

Walker, W.
1957 *All the Plants of the Bible.* New York: Harper & Row.

Wilson, M. R.
1985 Nineveh. *Major Cities of the Biblical World.* Editor, R. K. Harrison. Nashville: Thomas Nelson.

Wilt, T. L.
1992 Lexical Repetition in Jonah. *Journal of Translation and Textlinguistics* 5:252-264.

Wiseman, D. J.
1979 Jonah's Nineveh. *Tyndale Bulletin* 30:29-51.

Wolff, H.
1976 *Obadiah and Jonah.* Minneapolis: Augsburg.
1981 *Anthropology of the Old Testament.* Philadelphia: Fortress.

Woodward, B.
1993 Jonah. Pp. 348-357 in *A Complete Literary Guide to the Bible.* Grand Rapids: Zondervan.

Micah

ANDREW E. HILL

Micah

MICAH WAS A PREEXILIC PROPHET who ministered to both the kingdoms of Judah and Israel. He was a contemporary of the prophet Isaiah, who also prophesied during the eighth century BC (1:1; cf. Isa 1:1). The name Micah means "Who is like Yahweh?" and his message to God's people was a play on his name—he presents the LORD as incomparable and supreme. For instance, Micah recognized his God, Yahweh, as "the LORD of all the earth" (4:13), who would one day settle international disputes and bring all wars to an end (4:3). This meant Micah's God was worthy of the worship of the peoples of the world (4:1). He also knew God as a jealous champion of his covenant relationship with his people Israel—he would tolerate no rivals (4:4-5; 5:12-14; 6:16). Micah acknowledged God as a righteous God who hated injustice and who sided with the poor and oppressed (2:1-2, 8-9; 3:1-2). Micah's God was one to be feared because he could both destroy the wicked and deliver the righteous (2:3; 3:12; 4:11-12; 5:15). Micah's God delights to show his compassion and mercy to the repentant (7:18-20). Because of all this and more, Micah knew God as a unique God and could therefore ask, "Where is another God like you?" (7:18).

AUTHOR

The book is silent on the specifics of authorship, although it is generally assumed that the prophetic word formula ("The Lord gave this message to Micah," 1:1) signifies that Micah was responsible, in some fashion, for writing down his own message. The so-called first-person "editorial suture" in 3:1 ("I said") also suggests "that Micah had a hand in editing the book traditionally assigned to him" (Alexander, Baker, and Waltke 1988:149). The exact details of how the visions God showed Micah came to be recorded remain unknown.

As mentioned, the name Micah means "Who is like Yah[weh]?" and it is presumed that the title "Micah of Moresheth" (1:1) means he was from the village of Moresheth-Gath some 20 miles southwest of Jerusalem. Craigie's (1985:2) observation that Micah resided as an "outsider" in Jerusalem and suggestion that the title "Micah of Moresheth" was intended to distinguish Micah the prophet from the other Micahs living in Jerusalem at the time has merit.

Little else is known about Micah since the sermons of his book contain no autobiographical information. It appears he was among the professional prophets centered in Jerusalem. As with all true prophets of God, the source of his message was the Spirit of the Lord (3:8). Micah must have been a man of some courage, as well, since he boldly challenged the false prophets of his day (cf. 2:6-11). A century later, Micah was remembered by Jeremiah as the prophet who brought revival to King Hezekiah and the people of Judah, averting (for the time) the terrible disaster of divine judgment (Jer 26:17-19). He is not to be confused with Micaiah, son of Imlah, a prophet of the northern kingdom during the reign of King Ahab (874–852 BC; cf. 1 Kgs 22:8-28).

DATE AND OCCASION OF WRITING

The message of Micah is dated generally to the reigns of three kings of Judah: Jotham, Ahaz, and Hezekiah. The reigns of these kings extended over a period of more than six decades; they ruled in Jerusalem from approximately 750 to 687 BC. The exact dates for the rule of each king vary by some eight to ten years depending upon the source consulted (see the comparative chart in Andersen and Freedman 2000:xviiii; cf. Thiele 1983:131-134, 174-176). The alternative dating schemes for the reigns of the three Judahite kings are compared below:

KING	HIGHER OT CHRONOLOGY	LOWER OT CHRONOLOGY
Jotham	759–744 BC	750–732 BC
Ahaz	743–727 BC	735–716 BC
Hezekiah	727–699 BC	716–687 BC

The biblical records of the reigns of Jotham, Ahaz, and Hezekiah are found in 2 Kings 15:32–16:20; 18–20; and 2 Chronicles 27–32. Only kings Jotham and Hezekiah receive a favorable theological review from the biblical historian (cf. 2 Kgs 15:34; 18:5-6). The exact date (or dates, assuming the book came together during the stages of Micah's ministry) for the writing of the messages is impossible to determine.

Form-critical scholarship of the Old Testament has disputed the authenticity of several oracles in the book of Micah, especially 2:12-13; 4:1–5:9; and 7:8-20 (see the discussion in Alexander, Baker, and Waltke 1988:145-149). Dates for the contested speeches are assigned variously to the exilic or postexilic period of Hebrew history, depending upon the source. Recent study addressing the literary integrity of Micah assesses the book more favorably as showing "signs of overall integration" (Andersen and Freedman 2000:27). Hillers (1984:4) ends up rejecting the redaction-criticism of Micah due to its highly speculative character and prefers a synchronic approach that reads "the book as arising for the most part out of one situation."

According to Waltke (Alexander, Baker, and Waltke 1988:149), if one rejects the posture of skepticism towards the superscription (1:1), then there is nothing to rule out an eighth-century provenance for the book. Andersen and Freedman

(2000:112-113) concur, suggesting that the editorial headings of the four eighth-century prophets (Amos, Hosea, Isaiah, Micah) have a terminus *ad quem* in the reign of King Hezekiah of Judah (Hezekiah's reign took place anywhere from 727 to 687 BC, depending upon the source cited). This being the case, it may indicate that the writings of the four prophets were assembled and published as a single corpus in the latter years of Hezekiah's reign.

Typically, the impetus for Micah's oracles is connected historically to the Assyrian threat that arose in the aftermath of the Syro-Ephraimite War (734 BC). For instance, Micah begins his message (1:3-7) by forecasting the fall of Samaria (this event occurred in 722 BC after a three-year siege of the city; cf. Allen 1976:241). Some have interpreted the judgment pronounced against Judah in 1:9-16 as a reference to the siege of Jerusalem in 701 BC by King Sennacherib of Assyria (2 Kgs 18:17-37). R. L. Smith (1984:5) interprets the pericope of 1:10-16 as a description of the march of Sennacherib from Lachish to Jerusalem. Yet none of the individual oracles of the book is dated (directly or indirectly). Beyond this, Micah betrays no awareness of the dramatic events associated with Sennacherib's siege of Jerusalem in 701 BC. In fact, Andersen and Freedman (2000:113) suggest that Micah 1:10-16 refers to an earlier period when Samaria and Jerusalem were under similar threats from enemies (perhaps during the reigns of Jotham or Ahaz). It seems best to simply recognize that Micah's oracles were prompted generally by the impending threat of the Assyrian empire to the welfare of both Samaria and Jerusalem.

In short, then, Micah prophesied sometime between 750 and 690 BC. He directed his sermons of judgment and hope to the divided Hebrew kingdoms of Israel and Judah. Micah was a contemporary of the prophets Isaiah (cf. Isa 1:1) and Hosea (cf. Hos 1:1). Micah observed what Amos had documented a generation earlier: two nations ripe for the judgment of God because of widespread corruption in the civil leadership (3:9-11), rampant social injustice (6:10-12), shameless religious apostasy (5:12-15), misplaced confidence in their own military might (5:10-11), and twisted theological thinking about God and the day of his visitation (2:6-11). (See "Theological Concerns" below.)

Micah ministered during the period of the great Assyrian crisis in Hebrew history. The nation of Assyria began to reemerge as an international "superpower" during the reign of Ashurnasirpal II (883–859 BC), who extended Assyrian influence along the upper Euphrates River and is credited as the founder of the Neo-Assyrian empire. His successor, Shalmaneser III (858–824 BC) expanded Assyrian rule westward in a series of military campaigns (during which time King Jehu was forced to pay tribute to Assyria and Israel was reduced to vassal status).

After half a century of decline, Assyrian imperialism once again threatened the west under the arrogant and ruthless leadership of Tiglath-pileser III (744–727 BC). King Menahem of Israel was forced to pay tribute to Assyria as a vassal-state (2 Kgs 15:19-20), and later during the reign of Pekah, Tiglath-pileser invaded Israel and annexed the northern portion of the Israelite kingdom (2 Kgs 15:29-30). King Ahaz of Judah also paid tribute to Tiglath-pileser as payment for Assyrian intervention in the invasion of Judah by the armies of Israel and Aram (in retaliation for Judah's refusal to join the coalition against Assyria, 2 Kgs 16:5-9). Tiglath-pileser's son, Shalmaneser V (727–722 BC) laid siege to Samaria in a western campaign (2 Kgs 17:3-4). The capital city of Israel actually fell to Shalmaneser's successor, Sargon II (722–704 BC), after a three-year siege (2 Kgs 17:5-6).

Sargon's son and successor, Sennacherib (704–681 BC), continued the policy of westward expansion in a campaign that included the invasion of Judah (2 Kgs 18–19). According to the Old Testament record, the city of Jerusalem was spared when the Assyrians withdrew from Judah after the angel of the Lord mysteriously killed a large portion of the Assyrian army (2 Kgs 19:35-36). (For more on the historical background to the book of Micah, see Hillers 1984:4-8; Alexander, Baker, and Waltke 1988:138-143; and G. V. Smith 2001:421-426.)

Micah witnessed three major historical events associated with Assyrian aggression against the Hebrew kingdoms of Israel and Judah, including (1) the defeat of the Israelite and Aramean coalition by Tiglath-pileser III in the Syro-Ephraimite war (734–732 BC; cf. 2 Kgs 15:29); (2) the fall of Samaria to Sargon II and the Assyrians in 722–721 BC (2 Kgs 17:5-6); and (3) the invasion of Judah by Sennacherib in 701 BC. Out of this experience, Micah could speak firsthand both about the horrific destruction left behind in the wake of Assyrian imperialism (5:5-6) and the stunning deliverance that God was able to provide for his people if they would only trust in him (4:10; 7:15-16; cf. Jeremiah's commentary on Hezekiah's response to Micah's preaching, Jer 26:18-19).

AUDIENCE
Broadly understood, Micah addresses "all the people of the world" (1:2). This represents the theological perspective of a prophet who understands God as sovereign over all the nations (4:2-3). More specifically, Micah preached to the people and the leaders of the divided kingdoms of Judah and Israel (e.g., 1:16; 3:1; although Allen [1976:272] notes that at times Micah uses the names "Jacob" and "Israel" ambiguously because he speaks to the whole nation since both kingdoms are equally guilty before God). The prophet also targeted specific groups of people for indictment, including the wealthy (e.g., 2:1-2) and the political and religious establishment (e.g., 3:11). According to Jeremiah, Micah had some success in his ministry because his oracles prompted King Hezekiah and the people of Judah to turn from their sins and worship the Lord (Jer 26:17-19).

CANONICITY AND TEXTUAL HISTORY
Micah is the sixth book in the collection known as the Minor Prophets (or "Book of the Twelve" in the Hebrew Bible). The Twelve Prophets are usually grouped with the other Latter Prophets (Isaiah, Jeremiah, and Ezekiel) and without exception are found in the earliest delineations of the Old Testament canon. These twelve books were always copied on one scroll in the ancient Hebrew manuscript tradition. The order of the Twelve Prophets is uniform in the Masoretic tradition of the Hebrew

Bible (Hosea, Joel, Amos, Obadiah, Jonah, Micah, Nahum, Habakkuk, Zephaniah, Haggai, Zechariah, Malachi). The order of the Twelve Prophets does vary, however, in some canon traditions. For example, Amos and Micah follow Hosea in the Septuagint (see further discussion in Andersen and Freedman 2000:6-7).

Overall, the Hebrew Masoretic Text (MT) of Micah (along with Hosea) is one of the more poorly preserved books of the Minor Prophets (so Smith, Ward, and Bewer 1911:5-6; Hillers 1984:10). A few passages pose difficulty in translation (due to the obscurity of the Hebrew preserved in the MT or the corruption of the MT in transmission), such as: 1:10-16; 2:7-10; 6:9-12; and 7:11-12 (so Simundson 1996:536). R. L. Smith (1984:9) has identified a handful of textual corruptions, including improper word divisions (2:12; 6:9), incorrect vowel pointing (1:8; 2:12; 3:10), and copying errors of various sorts (1:7; 2:6; 6:9-10; 7:12; cf. the list of MT transmission errors in Smith, Ward, and Bewer 1911:5). According to Allen (1976:253) the Greek Septuagint (LXX) is valuable in attesting the original Hebrew text in places where the Masoretic Text has suffered in transmission (e.g., 1:5; 2:9-10; 3:3). The fragments related to Micah found among the Qumran documents are important witnesses to the integrity of the Hebrew text but are of limited value for improving the Masoretic Text. The Syriac Peshitta and Latin Vulgate offer relatively little help in informing the Masoretic Text since they are largely dependent upon the Septuagint.

LITERARY STYLE

Waltke (Alexander, Baker, and Waltke 1988:144) states that "one could think of [the book of Micah] almost as a preacher's file of sermons delivered on different occasions in the life of the [city of Jerusalem]." Micah's drawer of sermon files contains independent oracles of judgment and salvation, lawsuit speeches, disputations, instructions, laments, prayers, and hymns. The abrupt transitions between form and theme in the book reflect the manner in which the prophet or his disciples edited the separate oracles into a prophetic corpus. Commentators, however, have identified numerous verbal links, lexical hinges, and catchwords that bind the work into a unified literary composition (cf. Allen 1976:259-260; Andersen and Freedman 2000:22-24, 27-28; and Dorsey 1999:296-298 for specific examples of this "verbal artistry").

In addition to the variety of literary genres employed in Micah, the style of the book is considered highly poetic. Like Amos and Hosea, Micah is a blend of prose sentences and poetic elements characteristic of the eighth-century Hebrew prophets (Hillers 1984:10). For a detailed discussion of the poetic features of Micah, see Andersen and Freedman (2000), who comment on the poetry of each literary unit of the book. They meticulously note the usual features of classical Hebrew poetry, especially the parallelism between adjacent pairs of colons or lines of poetic text (cf. Andersen and Freedman 2000:133-134 on the poetry of 1:2-7 for an example).

Allen (1976:257-261) has convincingly demonstrated that the book of Micah is a structurally coherent literary composition. Based on the earlier analysis of Willis (1966), he has identified three distinct sections (or "books," as understood by

Andersen and Freedman 2000:23-24, 28) arranged in an overall A–B–A pattern. Each unit contains oracles of both doom and hope and may be outlined as follows (Allen 1976:260):

Unit One: 1:2–2:13
1:2–2:11 doom (long section)
2:12-13 hope (short section)

Unit Two: 3:1–5:15
3:1-12 doom (long section)
4:1-5 hope (short section)
4:6-8 hope with distress allusions (for remnant)
4:9–5:6 distress and hope
5:7-9 hope with distress allusions (for remnant)
5:10-14 doom (long section)
5:15 hope (short section)

Unit Three: 6:1–7:20
6:1–7:7 doom (long section)
7:8-20 hope (short section)

The structure of the book is thus a concentric arrangement, counterbalancing speeches of doom and hope in a "kaleidoscopic picture of the judgment and salvation of God's city and God's people" (Allen 1976:260). The focal point of Unit Two and the center of the whole book is the section 5:1-6, which announces the establishment of a secure and peaceful theocracy ruled by a Shepherd-Messiah. Like the prophet Amos, Micah's hope for Israel rests in the Messianic rejuvenation of the Davidic dynasty (cf. Amos 9:11).

MAJOR THEMES
Allen's (1976:257-261) analysis of the literary structure of Micah reveals that the book is essentially a foil or contrast of two theological themes: doom (or divine judgment) and hope (or divine restoration). The prophet's oracles of doom threaten judgment, punishment, and distress leading to purification. The prophet's oracles of hope promise deliverance, renewal, and restoration (cf. Waltke 2007:14-15). In either case, whether judgment or salvation oracle, God is the main character of Micah's message. Andersen and Freedman (2000:28-29) summarize: "Both themes of judgment and redemption occur and recur from beginning to end. . . . God's mercy does not arrest his justice—it operates beyond judgment. His wrath does not quench his love; his compassion does not cancel his anger. . . . It is possible to restore relationships because God himself takes up the task of salvation."

THEOLOGICAL CONCERNS
Like Amos, Micah (and virtually all of the OT prophetic books) offers "variations" on similar theological themes. Since the prophet Micah knew God as "the LORD of

all the earth" (4:13), he envisioned a day when people from all over the world would stream to Jerusalem to worship "Jacob's God" (4:2). This same God will settle international disputes and bring peace to the nations because his word will go out from Zion and he will teach people "his ways" (4:2-4). This stands in stark contrast to the twisting of justice and "all that is right" (3:9) by corrupt rulers, priests, and prophets (3:11).

The God Micah served was the covenant God, addressed by his covenant name "Yahweh" more than 35 times in the prophet's sermons. His use of expressions like "the LORD's people" (2:5), "family of Israel" (2:7), "my people" (2:8; 6:3) are modifications of the adoption formula ("I will be your God and you will be my people," cf. Jer 31:1). They are intended to recall the Exodus event and Sinai experience when God made Israel his "special possession" (7:14; cf. Exod 19:5-6).

As the covenant God, Yahweh jealously guards his relationship with his people Israel. For this reason, Yahweh will tolerate no sin or rebellion on the part of his covenant partner. Of particular concern for Micah was the infidelity of false worship—Yahweh's people paying homage to idols ("the works of [their] own hands"; 5:12-13). A second burden for God's prophet was the perversion of social justice— the "skinning alive" of God's people by cheating, extortion, and violence (3:2-3; 6:10-12). The Sinai covenant created a "community of Yahweh" (2:5, NJB) that was to be characterized by love of neighbor and respect of persons (Lev 19:18; Deut 6:4-9). Micah's response to Israel's disloyalty has become the signature verse of the prophet's message: "The LORD has told you what is good, and this is what he requires of you: to do what is right, to love mercy, and to walk humbly with your God" (6:8).

We also learn from Micah's lawsuit oracles that God is a just judge and he punishes covenant violators (2:1-5; 3:8-12; 6:1-3, 13-15). Simundson (1996:537) reminds us that "the anger of God is an issue too often avoided . . . the book of Micah gives one an occasion to reflect upon God's wrath." As Lord of all the earth, God is free to use other nations as an instrument of his justice to accomplish his purposes of judgment and purification (5:5-6; cf. 4:11-12). "But the God who destroys is also the God who delivers" (Allen 1976:256; cf. 2:12-13; 4:6-7; 7:14-15). The agent of God's deliverance of Israel is their royal shepherd (2:12-13)—a ruler from Bethlehem who leads with the Lord's strength and is the source of peace (5:1-5a). Here Micah builds a "theological bridge" across seven centuries of Hebrew history, as we learn from the New Testament that on the basis of Micah 5:2, the Jews believed the Messiah would be born in Bethlehem—and "Jesus was born in Bethlehem" (Matt 2:1).

Finally, Micah knew God as a unique God—"Where is another God like you?" (7:18). Two specific actions made God unique among the gods of the ancient world for Micah: first, God's ability to pardon the sin and guilt of his people (7:18a), and second, God's capacity for showing his people his unfailing love (7:18b). Such actions are rooted in Yahweh's character as a compassionate and faithful God (7:19-20). The reference to the Israelite patriarchs, Abraham and Jacob, demonstrates the continuity of God's activity with earlier Hebrew history (7:20). As House observes, "it is significant that the book closes with a statement on the removal of sin as part of Yahweh's promises to Abraham. Defeating sin both fulfills the purpose for which the Lord called Abraham in the first place and demonstrates God's specific love for Abraham's descendants" (1998:371).

OUTLINE

Superscription (1:1)
 I. The Book of Doom (1:2–3:12)
    A. Grief over Samaria and Jerusalem (1:2-16)
    B. Judgment against Wealthy Oppressors (2:1-5)
    C. True and False Prophets (2:6-11)
    D. Hope for Restoration (2:12-13)
    E. Judgment against Israel's Leaders (3:1-12)
 II. The Book of Visions (4:1–5:15)
    A. The Lord's Future Reign (4:1-5)
    B. Israel's Return from Exile (4:6–5:1)
    C. A Ruler from Bethlehem (5:2-6)
    D. The Remnant Purified (5:7-15)
 III. The Book of Judgment and Pardon (6:1–7:20)
    A. The Lord's Case against Israel (6:1-8)
    B. Israel's Guilt and Punishment (6:9-16)
    C. Misery Turned to Hope (7:1-20)

COMMENTARY ON
Micah

◆ Superscription (1:1)

The LORD gave this message to Micah of Moresheth during the years when Jotham, Ahaz, and Hezekiah were kings of Judah.

The visions he saw concerned both Samaria and Jerusalem.

NOTES

1:1 *The LORD gave this message*. Lit., "the word of the LORD came." The combination of the verb "to be" (*hayah* [TH1961, ZH2118]) with the phrase "the word of the Lord" (*debar-yhwh* [TH1697/3068, ZH1821/3378]) constitutes the prophetic word formula. The formula commonly introduces a report of prophetic revelation in the oracular speech of the OT.

***Moresheth*.** This was the prophet's hometown, a village located in the Shephelah region of Judah some 20 miles southwest of Jerusalem.

***Jotham, Ahaz, and Hezekiah*.** The mention of these kings sets the ministry of Micah during the period of the Hebrew divided kingdoms sometime toward the end of the eighth century BC (see "Date and Occasion of Writing" in the Introduction).

***visions*.** The title of the book recognizes "vision" (*khazah* [TH2372, ZH2600]) as both the occasion and the medium of the message of Yahweh. "The verb describes extraordinary kinds of seeing and particularly those connected with the reception of messages from a deity" (Andersen and Freedman 2000:119). This technical term for prophecy may also refer to the wider perception of divine revelation and in "Micah's case it was evidently of an auditory nature" (Allen 1976:265).

***Samaria*.** The city was located seven miles northwest of Shechem and was established as the capital of the northern kingdom of Israel by King Omri (1 Kgs 16:24). According to Andersen and Freedman (2000:126), the naming of kingdoms after their capital cities was not normative practice for the Hebrews. It does reflect contemporary usage, however, as other states during this time period were named after their capital.

***Jerusalem*.** The capital city of Judah and the location of Yahweh's temple, the place where God established his name (Deut 12:11; 14:23). God loved Jerusalem because his presence resided there symbolically, as associated with the Ark of the Covenant housed in the Temple (Pss 9:11; 74:2; 76:2; 87:2). But his love for the city would not keep him from judging the people of Judah for their rebellion against him.

COMMENTARY

The superscription (1:1) is a formal statement that corresponds to the title of a document. It serves to classify literature by genre or literary type (in this case as an oracular or prophetic text) and to identify the author, audience, date, and sometimes the occasion prompting the divine message. This superscription identifies the author of the book as Micah and notes his "hometown" as Moresheth. It also classifies the genre as prophetic revelation given in the form of a vision, and broadly dates the book to the reigns of three kings of the Hebrew divided monarchy of Judah.

The theological purpose of the superscription is to emphasize that God himself is the source and authority behind the message of Micah (cf. 2 Pet 1:20-21). The use of the covenant name "Yahweh" (or "LORD," 1:1) for God is appropriate and antici-pates the summons to trial issued to Samaria and Jerusalem for "sins and rebellion" in violation of the Mosaic covenant (1:5). The reference to the "kings of Judah" (1:1) may foreshadow Micah's vision of the "king" who would ultimately restore the Hebrews as a unified nation (cf. 2:13; 5:2).

◆ I. The Book of Doom (1:2–3:12)
  A. Grief over Samaria and Jerusalem (1:2-16)

2 Attention! Let all the people of the
  world listen!
Let the earth and everything in
  it hear.
The Sovereign LORD is making
  accusations against you;
  the LORD speaks from his holy Temple.
3 Look! The LORD is coming!
He leaves his throne in heaven
and tramples the heights of the
  earth.
4 The mountains melt beneath his feet
  and flow into the valleys
like wax in a fire,
  like water pouring down a hill.
5 And why is this happening?
Because of the rebellion of Israel*—
  yes, the sins of the whole nation.
Who is to blame for Israel's rebellion?
  Samaria, its capital city!
Where is the center of idolatry
  in Judah?
  In Jerusalem, its capital!

6 "So I, the LORD, will make the city
  of Samaria
  a heap of ruins.
Her streets will be plowed up
  for planting vineyards.
I will roll the stones of her walls into
  the valley below,
  exposing her foundations.
7 All her carved images will be smashed.

All her sacred treasures will
  be burned.
These things were bought with
  the money
  earned by her prostitution,
and they will now be carried away
  to pay prostitutes elsewhere."

8 Therefore, I will mourn and lament.
  I will walk around barefoot and
  naked.
I will howl like a jackal
  and moan like an owl.
9 For my people's wound
  is too deep to heal.
It has reached into Judah,
  even to the gates of Jerusalem.

10 Don't tell our enemies in Gath*;
  don't weep at all.
You people in Beth-leaphrah,*
  roll in the dust to show your despair.
11 You people in Shaphir,*
  go as captives into exile—naked and
  ashamed.
The people of Zaanan*
  dare not come outside their walls.
The people of Beth-ezel* mourn,
  for their house has no support.
12 The people of Maroth* anxiously wait
  for relief,
but only bitterness awaits them
as the LORD's judgment reaches
  even to the gates of Jerusalem.

¹³Harness your chariot horses and flee,
  you people of Lachish.*
You were the first city in Judah
  to follow Israel in her rebellion,
  and you led Jerusalem* into sin.
¹⁴Send farewell gifts to Moresheth-
    gath*;
  there is no hope of saving it.
The town of Aczib*
  has deceived the kings of Israel.
¹⁵O people of Mareshah,*

I will bring a conqueror to capture
  your town.
And the leaders* of Israel
  will go to Adullam.

¹⁶Oh, people of Judah, shave your
  heads in sorrow,
  for the children you love will be
  snatched away.
Make yourselves as bald as a vulture,
  for your little ones will be exiled
  to distant lands.

1:5 Hebrew *Jacob;* also in 1:5b. The names "Jacob" and "Israel" are often interchanged throughout the Old Testament, referring sometimes to the individual patriarch and sometimes to the nation. 1:10a *Gath* sounds like the Hebrew term for "tell." 1:10b *Beth-leaphrah* means "house of dust." 1:11a *Shaphir* means "pleasant." 1:11b *Zaanan* sounds like the Hebrew term for "come out." 1:11c *Beth-ezel* means "adjoining house." 1:12 *Maroth* sounds like the Hebrew term for "bitter." 1:13a *Lachish* sounds like the Hebrew term for "team of horses." 1:13b Hebrew *the daughter of Zion.* 1:14a *Moresheth* sounds like the Hebrew term for "gift" or "dowry." 1:14b *Aczib* means "deception." 1:15a *Mareshah* sounds like the Hebrew term for "conqueror." 1:15b Hebrew *the glory.*

NOTES

1:2 Attention! Lit., "Listen!" (*shama'* [TH8085, ZH9048]). This imperative verb introduces a summons-to-listen formula (cf. Deut 4:1; 6:4; Hos 4:1; Amos 3:1). In prophetic contexts the word typically means "listen to, heed by acting upon, or putting into practice what has been said" (NIDOTTE 5.178). The formula signals that an important message is forthcoming or a divine truth is about to be revealed. Micah uses the imperative "listen!" elsewhere in 3:1, 9; 6:1, 2, 9.

Sovereign LORD. This epithet literally means "my Master Yahweh"; the title expresses the intimate connection between Yahweh and the acts of judgment threatened in the prophet's sermons. God's rule of creation and the nations is embodied in this compound divine name.

accusations. Lit., "witness" (*'ed* [TH5707, ZH6332]). The word connotes a courtroom setting. God will serve as both the witness who brings testimony against Israel and the court that carries out the sentence (see the discussion in Andersen and Freedman 2000:155-156).

holy Temple. "The earthly shrine [i.e., the Jerusalem Temple] was but an outpost, a replica of the real headquarters [of God] in heaven" (Andersen and Freedman 2000:157).

1:3 throne. The NLT thus renders "place" (*maqom* [TH4725, ZH5226]) interpretively due to its parallel construction with "holy Temple" (1:2). Allen (1976:270) notes that the description of God's leaving his Temple to "[trample] the heights of the earth" (1:3) "is a mode of expression that denies any suggestion that Yahweh is limited to his terrestrial sanctuary" (cf. Judg 5:4-5; Ps 11:4; Hab 2:20).

1:5 rebellion. This word (*pesha'* [TH6588, ZH7322]; 1:5, 13; 3:8; 6:7; 7:18) means to commit a legal offense and signifies an act of rebellion in the form of social transgression. Such treacherous "conduct constituted rebellion against Yahweh himself" (NIDOTTE 3.708). Andersen and Freedman (2000:170) further note, "in a political setting it means 'treason,' in religion 'apostasy.' Both ideas merge in idolatry as Israel's worst violation of covenant obligations to Yahweh."

Israel. This is the name of the northern kingdom after the split of the Hebrew united monarchy upon the death of Solomon (c. 930 BC). The kingdom of Israel was comprised of those 10 Hebrew tribes that settled north of Jerusalem and east of the Jordan River. This rival kingdom to Judah was established by God through the prophet Ahijah as a punishment for Solomon's sin of idolatry (1 Kgs 11:29-39). The kingdom of Israel endured as a geo-political entity c. 930-722 BC, when the Assyrians conquered the nation and annexed the territory into their empire (cf. 2 Kgs 17:7-23).

sins. The word *khatta'th* [TH2403A, ZH2633] is often used by the OT prophets of covenant violations (especially idolatry; cf. Lev 26:18, 21; Deut 9:21; Jer 17:3). The term refers not only to the evil action or deed committed but also to the associated consequences (cf. TDOT 4.312).

Judah. This is the name of the southern kingdom after the split of the Hebrew united monarchy upon the death of Solomon (c. 930 BC). The kingdom of Judah was comprised of those Hebrew tribes that settled south of Jerusalem (essentially Judah, Dan, and Simeon). God preserved the kingdom of Judah for the sake of his servant David and for the sake of Jerusalem, where his Temple resided (1 Kgs 11:34-39). The kingdom of Judah endured as a geo-political entity from c. 930-587 BC, when the Babylonians conquered the nation and annexed the territory into their empire (cf. 2 Kgs 25:1-21).

1:7 *carved images.* The word *pasil* [TH6456, ZH7178] refers to statues of gods (or goddesses) carved from wood or stone (and sometimes overlaid with silver or gold; cf. NIDOTTE 3.644-646). Such carved images were prohibited for the Hebrews by Mosaic law (Exod 20:4; Deut 5:8). The Hebrew prophets consistently condemned the worship of these carved images, often with scathing satire (e.g., Isa 44:9ff; Hab 2:18).

sacred treasures. The term *'ethnan* [TH868, ZH924] means "gift" generally, often in the context of a harlot's pay (e.g., Deut 23:18; Hos 9:1). Micah associated the carved images with the earnings of prostitutes. It is unclear whether the idea is that these idols were donated to the prostitute or purchased with her wages (cf. Andersen and Freedman 2000:181). The NLT opts for the latter ("bought with the money earned"; 1:7).

prostitution. This is probably a reference to the ritual prostitution characteristic of Canaanite fertility cult worship incorporated into Hebrew worship by means of religious syncretism. According to Allen (1976:273-274), the Israelites had degraded Yahweh into a fertility cult god and "the destruction of its material representations is Yahweh's vindication of himself and his true character."

1:8 *mourn and lament.* The impending destruction of Samaria and Jerusalem prompted Micah to break into lamentation over the two cities. The prophet's pastoral heart for his people caused him to weep for his audience (cf. Alexander, Baker, and Waltke 1988:154).

barefoot and naked. This was one of several rituals for mourning the dead in the biblical world. The stripping away of clothing and footwear signified the laying aside of one's former status and was a symbolic admission of defeat (Walton, Matthews, and Chavalas 2000:781; cf. the enacted prophecy of Isaiah, Isa 20:2).

jackal . . . owl. The habitations of these animals are typically associated with desert wastelands (cf. Isa 34:13; Jer 50:39).

1:10 *Gath.* One of the five principal city-states of the Philistines, located nine miles east of Ashdod and six miles south of Ekron. Gath was a border town and the nearest of the Philistine city-states to the east of Judah. The words introduce a funeral lamentation (see 1:8-9). Micah did not want the pagan Philistines, who were the archrivals of the Hebrews, to gloat over their downfall (cf. 2 Sam 1:20).

Beth-leaphrah. A village or town of unknown location (probably in the Shephelah region), mentioned in the OT only by Micah.

1:11 *Shaphir.* A village or town of unknown location (probably in the Shephelah region), mentioned in the OT only by Micah.

Zaanan. A village of unknown location, possibly the Zenan (Josh 15:37) of the Shephelah near Lachish (cf. Andersen and Freedman 2000:209).

Beth-ezel. A village of unknown location (probably in the Shephelah region), mentioned in the OT only by Micah.

1:12 *Maroth.* A village of unknown location (probably in the Shephelah region), mentioned in the OT only by Micah. Andersen and Freedman (2000:209) discount the identification with Maarath (Josh 15:59) because of its southern location in the hill country of Judah.

1:13 *Lachish.* A former Canaanite city-state prominent in Joshua's conquest (Josh 10:31). The city was a chariot city from the time of Solomon and a strategic fortress in Judah due to its location on a main route from the coastal plain to the Hebron hills. The city was fortified by Rehoboam after the split of the Hebrew united monarchy (2 Chr 11:9), and it was captured by the Assyrian King Sennacherib in his assault on Jerusalem in 701 BC (2 Kgs 18:14, 17; 19:8). Later, the city was conquered by king Nebuchadnezzar and the Babylonians (Jer 34:7), and Hebrews resettled there after the Babylonian exile (Neh 11:30).

1:14 *Moresheth-gath.* This was most likely the hometown of Micah the prophet. The hyphenated name suggests that the Hebrew village was close enough to Gath to be considered a satellite of that Philistine city (cf. McKeating 1971:160). (See also the discussion of Moresheth in the note on 1:1.)

Aczib. Probably the Aczib near Mareshah on the border of the Shephelah with Judah (cf. Josh 15:44). The better-known Aczib located in Asher is not a candidate for this reference (cf. Andersen and Freedman 2000:211).

1:15 *Mareshah.* A village allotted to the tribe of Judah (Josh 15:44) located in the Shephelah some 13 miles northwest of Hebron. Rehoboam fortified the town after the split of the Hebrew united monarchy (2 Chr 11:5-12). The prophet Eliezer, son of Dodavahu was from Mareshah (2 Chr 20:37).

Adullam. A fortress city like Lachish, fortified by Rehoboam after the split of the Hebrew united monarchy (2 Chr 11:7). The site has a long history of occupation and had associations with the patriarch Judah (cf. Gen 38:12) and David (one of his hideouts, 1 Sam 22:1).

1:16 *shave your heads.* This was a custom associated with mourning the dead. The symbolic disfigurement was intended to show empathy with those in the throes of grieving over deceased family members (see Walton, Matthews, and Chavalas 2000:782).

COMMENTARY

The lament over Samaria and Jerusalem (1:2-16) is the first installment of a series of judgment oracles against the divided kingdoms of Israel and Judah in the prophet's "book of doom" (1:2–3:12). Micah's first sermon may be outlined in two sections: the judgment oracle against Samaria (1:2-7) and the introduction to the song of lament (1:8-16). The song of lament over the fallen cities of Judah may be divided into three sections: the introductory call declaring the prophet's intention to mourn (1:8-9), the lament song commemorating the fall of the Judean cities (1:10-15), and the epilogue addressed to a personified Jerusalem (1:16). The unity of the passage is derived from "the actuality of the vision that created the report of the theophany (1:3-4), the threat (1:5-7), and the agonized response (1:8-16)" (Andersen and Freedman 2000:203). The tone of this literary unity is "panic," even "hysteria," brought about by Yahweh's visitation. The purpose of the section is to declare Yahweh's intent to destroy his own people on account of their breach of covenant relationship with him.

There is general agreement among the commentators that there is a certain amount of wordplay in the itinerary of the lament song (1:10-15). A look through the various text notes to 1:10-15 in the NLT margin gives a glimpse of what's going on here: Many of the villages and towns listed in the itinerary feature wordplays between the name of the site and its predicted doom (see the chart in Andersen and Freedman 2000:213, which identifies seven examples of potential wordplay in the list of 13 villages and cities; cf. Isa 10:24-32 for an example of similar wordplay). Andersen and Freedman (2000:214) conclude that the wordplay in the lament is not systematic but rather an improvisation by free association for the purpose of making negative statements about each site (on wordplay more generally in Micah see Petrotta, 1991). Peterson (2000:508) captures the prophet's punning in contemporary language:

> [10]Don't gossip about this in Telltown.
>   Don't waste your tears.
> In Dustville,
>   roll in the dust.
> In Alarmtown,
>   the alarm is sounded.
> [11]The citizens of Exitburgh
>   will never get out alive.
> Lament, Last-Stand City:
>   There's nothing in you left standing.
> [12]The villagers of Bittertown
>   wait in vain for sweet peace.
> Harsh judgment has come from God
>   and entered Peace City.
> [13]All you who live in Chariotville,
>   get in your chariots for flight.
> You led the daughter of Zion
>   into trusting not God but chariots.
> Similar sins in Israel
>   also got their start in you.
> Go ahead and give your good-bye gifts
>   to Good-byeville.
> [14]Miragetown beckoned
>   but disappointed Israel's kings.
> [15]Inheritance City
>   has lost its inheritance.
> Glorytown
>   has seen its last of glory.
> [16]Shave your heads in mourning
>   over the loss of your precious towns.
> Go bald as a goose egg—they've gone
>   into exile and aren't coming back.

There is some disagreement, however, on whether or not the list of villages and cities in the itinerary represents a historical and topographical catalog or a literary and theological one. Waltke contends the itinerary is a literary one, designed primarily to give the lament "a dynamic and dramatic effect" (Alexander, Baker, and Waltke 1988:153). By contrast, others consider the list of doomed sites a plausible itinerary for the military invasion of the Shephelah, the western hill region of Judah (Walton, Matthews, and Chavalas 2000:781-782). All of the villages and towns mentioned are within a ten-mile radius of Moresheth-Gath (Micah's hometown), and only Mareshah is out of order, assuming a campaign moving from Gath to Lachish and on to Jerusalem. Beyond this, there remains the question as to whether Micah's lament reflects events associated with the invasion of Judah by the Israelite and Aramean coalition of the Syro-Ephraimite War (c. 735 BC) more generally or the Assyrian campaign against Judah led by King Sennacherib in 701 BC more specifically. The latter seems more likely given that the 12 cities mentioned in vv. 10-15 lay on the path of Sennacherib's march to Jerusalem (cf. 2 Kgs. 18:13-16). Although Micah's account is not a topographical order of the march of Sennacherib, the literary arrangement of the materials complements the Assyrian report of the invasion.

Micah's opening oracle describes a theophany, a visible or audible manifestation of God in the created order. We learn in the Old Testament that such visitations by God may be for good or ill, for blessing or curse (e.g., Judg 13:23; 1 Sam 3:11-14). God does not act in a capricious or arbitrary way when he leaves his throne to encounter creation and humanity in some direct fashion. God always behaves in accordance with his word—specifically the stated threats and promises related to his covenant with Israel, or more generally with the nations in the constancy of his holy and righteous character. Reports or visions of theophanies in the Old Testament are significant theologically because they remind us that "God is active in the world . . . God is involved in all that happens . . . God is a participant and not merely an observer who set up the system but no longer gets in the way" (Simundson 1996:545). The truth brings comfort to those in distress. It may also incite fear and confusion when we experience terrible events and ponder whether or not God caused the catastrophe (or ask why he did not prevent it). But the point is not for us to determine guilt or innocence on the basis of the retribution principle (i.e., the righteous are blessed and the wicked are cursed). Nor is it incumbent upon us to try to determine the timing of God's next theophany on the basis of some interpretive formula derived from analysis of biblical prophecy. The point is our recognition of God's person and character, his power and glory, his sovereignty and freedom (Exod 6:6-8).

The prophet's vision of theophany (1:2-4) led McKeating (1971:157) to raise the question: "What has prompted this terrifying visitation?" The answer is both simple and disturbing. Micah's God is a God who denounces sin, the sin of the nations and his people Israel (as he speaks from his holy Temple, 1:2). Not only does God testify against sin, he visits the earth and punishes sin and rebellion (1:3-5). G. V. Smith (2001:444-445) has rightly observed that certain principles are manifest in the pattern of divine behavior exhibited in Micah's theophany (and all biblical theophanies), namely:

God is a universal God; he rules all nations and peoples; no person or thing stands outside God's control (1:2).

God is holy, so his rule is characterized by the administration of true justice (1:2).

God is witness to the deeds of all people and all nations; nothing escapes his notice (1:2).

God is so overpowering that even the solid and permanent aspects of the created order dissolve before him (1:3-4).

Humanity is helpless to avert the enforcement of divine judgment (1:3-4).

God's judgment is the complete destruction of all that sinful humanity holds dear and trusts in (1:5-7).

For this reason G.V. Smith (2001:445) concludes, "It is essential that every person understands the nature of God and his ways, so that the mistakes and misunderstandings that existed in Micah's audience do not persist."

◆ ## B. Judgment against Wealthy Oppressors (2:1-5)

What sorrow awaits you who lie awake
   at night,
   thinking up evil plans.
You rise at dawn and hurry to carry
   them out,
   simply because you have the power
   to do so.
² When you want a piece of land,
   you find a way to seize it.
When you want someone's house,
   you take it by fraud and violence.
You cheat a man of his property,
   stealing his family's inheritance.

³ But this is what the LORD says:
"I will reward your evil with evil;
   you won't be able to pull your neck
   out of the noose.

You will no longer walk around
   proudly,
   for it will be a terrible time."

⁴ In that day your enemies will make
   fun of you
   by singing this song of despair
   about you:
"We are finished,
   completely ruined!
God has confiscated our land,
   taking it from us.
He has given our fields
   to those who betrayed us.*"
⁵ Others will set your boundaries then,
   and the LORD's people will have
   no say
   in how the land is divided.

2:4 Or *to those who took us captive.*

NOTES

2:1 *What sorrow.* The interjection is literally rendered "woe" (*hoy* [TH1945, ZH2098]) and "to pronounce a 'woe' on someone meant to announce their funeral" (Limburg 1988:169). Three different sources have been suggested as the background for the literary form of the woe oracle: the curse of the prophetic judgment speech, the funeral lament, and the instruction of the Hebrew wisdom tradition (perhaps as a foil to the word "blessed").

Since the woe oracle signifies a divine curse that precludes any further opportunity for repentance, it seems best to understand the literary form as a variation of the prophetic judgment-speech (cf. Westermann 1991:189-194). Jesus used the woe oracle as a form of prophetic judgment-speech against the Pharisees (Matt 23).

2:2 seize. The verb (*gazal* [TH1497, ZH1608]) means to take by force (NIDOTTE 1.844-845). Hebrew wisdom tradition warned against robbing the poor because God is their protector (Prov 22:22; cf. Ps 35:10). This kind of robbery is one of the curses God would inflict upon the Israelites as punishment for their covenant disobedience (Deut 28:29).

violence. The word "violence" (or "oppression," *'ashaq* [TH6231, ZH6943]) describes the intimidation and exploitation (with overtones of extortion and violence) of weaker members of the community by those who are stronger (NIDOTTE 3.557). This kind of oppression is one of the curses God would inflict upon the Israelites as punishment for their covenant disobedience (Deut 28:29).

family's inheritance. The term (*nakhalah* [TH5159, ZH5709]) refers to the land allotted to the families of each Hebrew tribe when priests parceled territory during the days of Joshua's conquest of Canaan (Josh 11:23). "At the forefront of Israelite economic theory stood the principle that the land was Yahweh's and that the people received it from him as a sacred trust which was handed down from generation to generation, from heir to heir" (Allen 1976:288-289). The family inheritance of land was inalienable (Lev 25:23). Robbing people of their family property struck at the very core of the covenant relationship with Yahweh because the land was a family's social security—loss of the family inheritance usually meant poverty for families so affected.

2:3 reward. Earlier the prophet condemned those who "planned" (*khashab* [TH2803, ZH3108]) evil while lying awake at night (2:1). Now with a twist of irony, Micah declares that Yahweh is "planning" (*khashab*) evil against the robbers and extortionists. Their "reward" will be inescapable punishment, like the hangman's noose already tightening around the neck.

2:4 make fun of you . . . song of despair. The combination of words underlying the translation here, "proverb" (*mashal* [TH4912, ZH5442]), "lament" (*nahah* [TH5091, ZH5629], found elsewhere in the OT only in Ezek 32:18), "lamentation" (*nehi* [TH5092, ZH5631]), and "mournful" (*nihyah* [TH5093, ZH5632]), conveys the idea of a "taunt-song" embodying an example or object lesson. "The fallen are made to serve as an example to be shunned, a lesson to others not to travel the path that leads to this disastrous end" (Allen 1976:290).

2:5 set your boundaries. Lit., "casting (the) rope by lot" (*mashlik khebel begoral* [TH1486, ZH1598]; see further the discussion in Andersen and Freedman 2000:289-290). The expression hearkens back to the division of the land of Canaan under Joshua (Josh 18:8) and ultimately to the Song of Moses, in which God is identified as the one who establishes the boundaries of the peoples (Deut 32:8).

COMMENTARY

The first chapter of Micah's book is a warning of divine judgment and destruction (1:2-16). The second chapter of the book is an indictment listing prominent violations of Yahweh's covenant by his people. It contains three oracles in the prophet's larger book of doom addressed to the divided kingdoms of Israel and Judah (1:2–3:12). The first message pronounces divine judgment against the wealthy oppressors of the middle class and poor (2:1-5). The second message is a dispute between the false prophets (perhaps representing wealthy land-grabbers trying to silence Micah) and Micah, God's true prophet (2:6-11). The third message shifts abruptly from the theme of judgment to a word of hope promising God's deliverance and future restoration for a remnant of Israel (2:12-13). This is in keeping with the kaleidoscopic pattern of the oracle structure in the book.

Micah used a word in his oracle against those who "grab" and "do violence" in accumulating their possessions (2:2) that occurs in the Decalogue and is usually rendered "covet" (*khamad* [TH2530, ZH2773], 2:2; "want," NLT). The tenth command-ment explicitly prohibits coveting a neighbor's house, spouse, or property of any kind (Exod 20:17; Deut 5:21). Like Isaiah, Micah confronted greedy "land-grabbers" who "buy up house after house and field after field, until everyone is evicted and you live alone in the land" (Isa 5:8). Coveting is a theme that runs through the Bible. Limburg (1988:172) has defined it as "self-centered greed which longs for that which belongs to another."

A certain destructive pattern may be observed in coveting, whether David's lust for Uriah's wife (2 Sam 11) or Ahab's obsession with Naboth's vineyard (1 Kgs 21). Typically, greedy desires lead to scheming, scheming results in the implementation of devious plans, and devious plans enacted leave human wreckage in their wake (cf. Jas 4:1-2).

God hates coveting, and his prophets decry this sin because it denies God's own-ership of all creation (Job 41:11). It subverts the principle of human stewardship of all of God's resources, which were created good (Gen 1:28; 2:15), and it injures (or even kills) innocent people (e.g., Josh 7:20-21, 25; 1 Kgs 21:11-14). In fact, the New Testament equates coveting with idolatry (Col 3:5-6; cf. Eph 5:5)—bringing the first and the tenth commandments full circle. The sin of coveting, like idolatry, is not restricted to the biblical world. Numerous contemporary idolatries associated with coveting may be identified, including the idolatry of choice, the idolatry of success, and the idolatry of money. (On contemporary idolatries, see Dawn 1995:41-56.) How much more do we need contemporary prophets reminding us of Jesus' teach-ing about our attempts to serve both God and money (Matt 6:24) or Paul's exhorta-tion to practice true religion with contentment, since we carry nothing with us when we die (1 Tim 6:6-7)? When is the last time you saw a hearse en route to the cemetery with a U-Haul trailer in tow?

◆   C. True and False Prophets (2:6-11)

6 "Don't say such things,"
  the people respond.*
"Don't prophesy like that.
  Such disasters will never come our
  way!"

7 Should you talk that way, O family of
  Israel?*
  Will the LORD's Spirit have patience
  with such behavior?
If you would do what is right,

you would find my words
  comforting.
8 Yet to this very hour
  my people rise against me like an
  enemy!
You steal the shirts right off the backs
  of those who trusted you,
making them as ragged as men
  returning from battle.
9 You have evicted women from their
  pleasant homes

and forever stripped their children
of all that God would give them.
¹⁰ Up! Begone!
This is no longer your land and home,
for you have filled it with sin
and ruined it completely.

¹¹ Suppose a prophet full of lies would
say to you,
"I'll preach to you the joys of wine
and alcohol!"
That's just the kind of prophet you
would like!

2:6 Or *the prophets respond*; Hebrew reads *they prophesy*. 2:7 Hebrew *O house of Jacob?* See note on 1:5a.

NOTES

2:7 patience. The Hebrew idiom here (referring to Yahweh) is "has the spirit (*ruakh* [ᵀᴴ7307, ᶻᴴ8120]) been shortened (*qatsar* [ᵀᴴ7114B, ᶻᴴ7918])?" That is, "the spirit of Yahweh has not been exhausted; he has filled Micah with power to declare Israel's sin (3:8)" (Andersen and Freedman 2000:311). God is indeed patient and slow to anger, but he will eventually confront the guilty and punish sin (cf. Exod 34:6-7; Nah 1:2-3).

do what is right. Lit., "the one who walks with the just" (*yashar* [ᵀᴴ3477A, ᶻᴴ3838] + *halak* [ᵀᴴ1980, ᶻᴴ2143]). Since Yahweh is upright, he expects his people to behave in like manner (cf. Ps 25:8). The word "just" or "upright" (*yashar*) is prominent in Hebrew wisdom tradition, where we learn that the upright will be rescued (Prov 11:6) and will live in the land (Prov 2:21).

2:8 steal. Lit., "strip off" (*pashat* [ᵀᴴ6584, ᶻᴴ7320]). It is unclear whether Micah was condemning those who were actually robbing people of their outer garments by stripping them of their cloaks and stealing them or whether he condemned the wealthy creditors seizing the cloaks of debtors as pledges without warning. Given the economic context of this oracle and the one preceding it, Allen (1976:296-297) favors the latter. If this is the case, then the wealthy creditors were in violation of an ancient covenant stipulation that prohibited the retention of garments taken in pledge overnight (Exod 22:26-27).

2:9 evicted. The verb (*garash* [ᵀᴴ1644, ᶻᴴ1763]) "describes forcible expulsion" and continues Yahweh's indictment of the wealthy oppressors begun in 2:8 (Andersen and Freedman 2000:321).

stripped . . . of all. Lit., the wealthy oppressors have "taken away" (*laqakh* [ᵀᴴ3947, ᶻᴴ4374]) "my glory" (*hadar* [ᵀᴴ1926, ᶻᴴ2077]) from the children. "Micah draws a pathetic picture of the eviction of a peasant family; the women driven *from their pleasant homes*, the children robbed of their expectations, of their title to share in God's own land, his *glory*" (McKeating 1971:165).

2:10 Up! Begone! Taken together, the two imperative verbs (*qum* [ᵀᴴ6965, ᶻᴴ7756], "arise"; and *halak* [ᵀᴴ1980, ᶻᴴ2143], "go") signal Israel's exile from the land of covenant promise in anticipation of the later promise of restoration (2:13; cf. Lev 18:24-30).

land and home. Lit., "the rest area is not this place" (cf. "for this is not your resting place," NIV). Theologically, the land of covenant promise, Canaan, was understood as the place of "rest" (*menukhah* [ᵀᴴ4496, ᶻᴴ4957]) with respect to peace, security, and spiritual well-being because of right relationship with God (Deut 12:9; Ps 95:11; cf. Heb 3:18–4:3).

sin. Lit., "uncleanness" (*tam'ah* [ᵀᴴ2931.1, ᶻᴴ3239]). The word often connotes defilement and ritual impurity that compromises worship and a right relationship with God (Lev 5:3; 7:20). Hosea described a similar situation where the land had been defiled by the sin of idolatry and the Israelites would be expelled from their land and exiled to Assyria (Hos 5:3; 6:10; 9:3-4). This is in keeping with the warnings threatening exile from the land of covenant promise if the Hebrews defiled themselves with the pagan practices of the surrounding Canaanites (Lev 18:24-30).

2:11 *prophet full of lies.* The words "falsehood/deception" (*sheqer* [TH8267, ZH9214]) and "to lie/deceive" (*kazab* [TH3576, ZH3941]) are consistently associated with false prophets in the OT (cf. Isa 9:15; Jer 5:31; Ezek 13:22). Micah used the same terms to describe those who would preach a false message to the people. The authentic prophet of God both speaks the truth (Jer 26:15) and lives an upright life (Ezek 2:5-8; cf. Isa 28:7; Zeph 3:4).

COMMENTARY

God's prophetic messengers often faced stiff opposition from both civil and religious leaders (cf. 3:11). False prophets were one such group of organized opponents. They dogged the true prophets of Yahweh and challenged their right to speak (2:6). They countered their call to repentance and covenant renewal with self-indulgent teaching pleasing to their audience (2:11; cf. Jer 5:31). They denied that God would bring disaster upon his people for their sin (cf. Jer 5:12-13); in fact, their preaching and teaching was often a denial of reality (cf. Ezek 13:10). Later, Micah indicates that these false prophets promise peace to those who can feed them well (3:5-11). As Waltke (1997:938) notes, the false prophets addressed but one dimension of Yahweh's covenant with Israel since they "preached only God's promises, not his threatened judgment." Jeremiah summed up the ministry of the false prophets in a similar fashion, since "they offer superficial treatments for my people's mortal wound" (Jer 8:11).

Micah's message to the false prophets prompted Kaiser (1992:43) to warn of the "evil of placebo preaching." The true prophet of God must "tell the rest of the story" as it were; or as Waltke frames it, like Micah, the true prophet of Yahweh must "not flinch from delivering the ever unpopular message that the wages of sin is death" (1997:938). False teaching and preaching springs from bad theology, as evidenced by Micah's antagonists who assumed that God's presence among his people as symbolized by the Jerusalem Temple meant only peace and security for Israel (3:9-12; cf. Jer 7:4-11). Micah's experience serves as a reminder to the Christian church that not only must we preach the "whole purpose" of God (Acts 20:27, NRSV; "I didn't shrink from declaring all that God wants you to know," NLT), but also we must be committed to teach and live out "wholesome teaching" (Titus 1:9, 13; 2:1). The Lord sent his prophets to Israel in Old Testament times to cut them to pieces and slaughter them with his words (Hos 6:5). The same should be no less true today, as M. J. Dawn would challenge us: "In a society doing all it can to make people cozy, somehow we must convey the truth that God's Word, rightly read and heard, will shake us up. It will kill us, for God cannot bear our sin and wants to put to death our self-centeredness" (1995:206).

◆ **D. Hope for Restoration (2:12-13)**

¹² "Someday, O Israel, I will gather you;
  I will gather the remnant who are
  left.

I will bring you together again like
  sheep in a pen,
  like a flock in its pasture.

Yes, your land will again
     be filled with noisy crowds!
¹³ Your leader will break out
     and lead you out of exile,

out through the gates of the
     enemy cities,
     back to your own land.
Your king will lead you;
     the LORD himself will guide you."

NOTES

2:12 gather. The gathering (*qabats* [TH6908, ZH7695]) of the Hebrews scattered in exile due to covenant disobedience is an eschatological motif in the OT prophetic books (e.g., Isa 11:12; Jer 31:8; Ezek 34:13). The theme is consistent theologically with the teaching of Moses's prophetic sermon that God would one day gather his people from exile among the nations and restore their fortunes in their ancestral homeland (Deut 30:3-5).

remnant who are left. The "remnant" (*she'erith* [TH7611, ZH8642]) motif implies both doom and salvation and is directly related to Yahweh's covenant faithfulness. The remnant motif is rooted in the saving work of a merciful God and serves to bridge the threat of punishment with the promise of restoration (see further the discussion in NIDOTTE 4.14-17 and the commentary below).

sheep . . . flock. The pastoral imagery portraying Israel as God's flock is common in the Psalms and the OT prophetic books (e.g., Pss 77:20; 79:13; Ezek 34:15, 22). Micah's prophecy overturns the vision of Israel—scattered on the mountain like sheep without a shepherd—seen by Micaiah the prophet (1 Kgs 22:17).

2:13 leader will break out. Lit., "the one who breaks through" (*happorets* [TH6555, ZH7287]). Kaiser (1992:45) understands "the Breaker" as a title for God and sees the role of "Breaker" fulfilled ultimately in the ministry of Jesus the Messiah.

king. The parallelism "LORD" (*yhwh* [TH3068, ZH3378]) in the following line suggests that the prophet understands God as the king who will lead the Hebrew people out of exile and back to their homeland. The pastoral imagery gives way to a military one, since Yahweh is both shepherd and king of his people (cf. Ps 100:3). The passage may anticipate the Messianic shepherd introduced in 5:4.

the LORD himself will guide you. Lit., "Yahweh is at their head" (*yhwh bero'sham* [TH7218, ZH8031]). Yahweh himself "leads the column of march, like a general or a shepherd" (Andersen and Freedman 2000:341). The passage recalls the Exodus from Egypt when Yahweh led his people in the fire and the cloud (Exod 13:21).

COMMENTARY

God's promise to preserve a segment of his people through the punishment of his divine judgment for covenant trespass introduces the remnant theme (2:12), prominent in Old Testament prophetic literature (e.g., Isaiah, who popularized the idea by naming his son Shear-jashub, or "a remnant will return," Isa 7:3). The remnant motif implies both judgment and deliverance. The very existence of a remnant of Hebrews is based on the mercy of God. The Old Testament prophets apply the remnant motif to three types of groups: (1) the historical remnant composed of survivors of the catastrophe of God's judgment (Jer 23:3); (2) the faithful remnant of Hebrews who maintain a true faith relationship with Yahweh (Amos 5:15); and (3) an eschatological remnant of Hebrews and Gentiles who will participate in the blessing of the restored Davidic kingdom (Amos 9:12; cf. NIDOTTE 4.14-15).

Micah refers to a "remnant" (*she'erith* [TH7611, ZH8642]) five times (2:12; 4:7; 5:7, 8; 7:18), and each is connected with oracles of hope (see Waltke's discussion in

NIDOTTE 4.938-939). The remnant purified, who go out strong as a lion (5:7-8), represent the eschatological remnant who will share in the blessing of the restored Davidic kingdom (cf. 5:2-5). The remaining four references to the Hebrew remnant appear to combine type one (a historical remnant of those who survive the Assyrian and Babylonian exiles) and type three (an eschatological remnant who will be purified and experience the restoration of the Davidic kingdom). Such telescoping of near historical fulfillment and distant eschatological fulfillment is not uncommon in biblical prophecy.

Theologically, the remnant theme is important because it mediates the tension of the Abrahamic and Mosaic covenants. The first "guaranteed Israel an everlasting status in God's program of redemption," while the second "threatened a sinful nation with death" (NIDOTTE 4.938). God's true prophets resolved the theological tension by espousing the doctrine that he would preserve a godly remnant of Israelites through the judgment associated with the curses of the Mosaic covenant (Deut 28; cf. Deut 30:1-5).

The remnant theme testifies to God's faithfulness in keeping his covenant promises (Ps 145:13; Dan 9:4), and it displays his great mercy because he does not remain angry with rebellious Israel forever (Isa 57:16; Jer 3:12). In the New Testament, the remnant of Israel (i.e., the Jews) is not displaced or eliminated, but stands united with those Gentiles (or wild olive branches grafted into Abraham's tree, Rom 11:17) called to be one people of God (cf. Rom 9-11; see further DPL 796-805). There is a sense in which Jesus the Messiah is himself the ultimate "remnant of Israel" because he fulfilled the Law of Moses as the lone righteous Hebrew (Matt 5:17-18; Heb 7:26), and as the firstborn from the dead he is "head" of the church (Col 1:18).

◆   E. Judgment against Israel's Leaders (3:1-12)

1 I said, "Listen, you leaders of Israel!
  You are supposed to know right
    from wrong,
2 but you are the very ones
    who hate good and love evil.
  You skin my people alive
    and tear the flesh from their bones.
3 Yes, you eat my people's flesh,
    strip off their skin,
    and break their bones.
  You chop them up
    like meat for the cooking pot.
4 Then you beg the LORD for help in
    times of trouble!
  Do you really expect him to answer?
  After all the evil you have done,
    he won't even look at you!"

5 This is what the LORD says:
  "You false prophets are leading
    my people astray!
  You promise peace for those who give
    you food,
    but you declare war on those who
    refuse to feed you.
6 Now the night will close around you,
    cutting off all your visions.
  Darkness will cover you,
    putting an end to your predictions.
  The sun will set for you prophets,
    and your day will come to an end.
7 Then you seers will be put to shame,
    and you fortune-tellers will be
    disgraced.
  And you will cover your faces

because there is no answer from
God."

8 But as for me, I am filled with power—
with the Spirit of the LORD.
I am filled with justice and strength
to boldly declare Israel's sin and
rebellion.
9 Listen to me, you leaders of Israel!
You hate justice and twist all that
is right.
10 You are building Jerusalem
on a foundation of murder and
corruption.
11 You rulers make decisions based
on bribes;

you priests teach God's laws only
for a price;
you prophets won't prophesy unless
you are paid.
Yet all of you claim to depend
on the LORD.
"No harm can come to us,"
you say,
"for the LORD is here among us."
12 Because of you, Mount Zion will be
plowed like an open field;
Jerusalem will be reduced to
ruins!
A thicket will grow on the heights
where the Temple now stands.

NOTES

3:1 *Listen.* See the discussion on "attention!" in the note on 1:2.

leaders. The term (*ro'sh* [TH7218, ZH8031], "head") refers to judges and other judicial officials in the national court system. According to Allen (1976:306), the "heads" of families and clans formed a type of "people's court" that dated back to the time of Moses (cf. Exod 18:17-26). The court was apparently under the control of the monarchy with regard to appointment and policy.

know right from wrong. Lit., "to know the judgment" (*mishpat* [TH4941, ZH5477]). According to Andersen and Freedman (2000:351), the term "judgment" refers to the entire process of the administration of justice, including hearing the case, rendering a decision, pronouncing a verdict, and implementing the sentence.

3:2-3 *hate good and love evil.* The leaders had inverted the basic principles established by covenant relationship with Yahweh that were foundational for social justice in Hebrew society. The covenant community was called to love good and hate evil in their imitation of Yahweh's holiness (Ps 97:10; Isa 1:17; Amos 5:14-15).

skin my people alive . . . chop them up. This series of brutal metaphors calls attention to both the callousness and the degree of social oppression the legal system had inflicted upon the people.

you eat my people's flesh. This was a common figure of speech for oppression and injustice (Allen 1976:307). The repetition of the verb *gazal* [TH1497, ZH1608] ("skin my people alive," 3:2) connects the section to the earlier indictment of the wealthy land-grabbers, who seized land by fraud and violence (2:2).

3:4 *beg . . . for help.* The verb (*za'aq* [TH2199, ZH2410]) means to "cry out in distress, call for help." Ironically, the prophet saw a certain poetic justice in the judges who had brought distress on others now crying out in distress for help from God.

he won't even look. The idiom is "to hide the face," and it "symbolizes covenant violation and breach of fellowship between God and Israel. The expression signifies the wrath of God, the rejection of his people (temporarily), and the initiation of covenant curses against Israel for their sin" (NIDOTTE 3.301).

3:5 *This is what the LORD says.* The construction *koh 'amar yhwh* [TH3541/559/3068, ZH3907/606/3378] constitutes the messenger formula in OT prophetic speech and signifies the oral transmission of a message by a third party. The expression suggests the divine assembly or council of the gods in ancient Near Eastern thought. The messenger of the council stands as an observer in council sessions and then, as an envoy of the council, reports what he has heard to others (ABD 2.214-217). The formula emphasizes the divine source of the message.

false prophets. The prophets (*nabi'* [TH5030, ZH5566]) were considered "false" because they led God's people astray (*ta'ah* [TH8582, ZH9494]) with bogus visions (cf. Jer 23:32, where Jeremiah condemns the false prophets who lead people astray with concocted dreams).

promise peace . . . declare war. The prophetic message was either favorable or unfavorable, depending upon whether or not the people could meet the prophet's demand for payment (cf. Andersen and Freedman 2000:364, who suggest the "prophecy for pay" scam was some type of "protection racket" for the wealthy in that the bribes they paid to the false prophets caused the prophets to ignore the injustices perpetrated by the wealthy against the poor).

3:6 the night will close around you. Ironically, God would cut off the revelations to the false prophets in the darkness of the night—a time when seers would typically receive their dreams and visions.

visions. Micah did not deny that the false prophets were endowed with God-given abilities, but "his stress is that those psychic gifts will be taken away because they have been used improperly" (Allen 1976:312).

Darkness. This is a metaphor for divine judgment, even death (e.g., Job 10:21; Prov 20:20; cf. NIDOTTE 2.313-314). The false prophets will fade into obscurity in the darkness of the night of God's judgment, even as "their crystal balls will become black" (Alexander, Baker, and Waltke 1988:163).

3:7 seers. This word is derived from *khazah* [TH2372, ZH2600] and describes those who see visions. According to Andersen and Freedman (2000:374) the terms "visionary" (*khozeh* [TH2374, ZH2602]) and "prophet" (*nabi'* [TH5030, ZH5566]) are interchangeable in eighth-century usage.

shame. The false prophets will be shamed (*bosh* [TH954, ZH1017]) for two reasons: First, they will have to admit their messages and visions were fraudulent; and second, they will have nothing to say—God will not answer them.

fortune-tellers. The fortune-tellers (*qosemim* [TH7080A, ZH7876]) are a class of prophets who resorted to mantic or mechanical means of prognostication (e.g., casting lots, examining animal livers, spilling arrows onto the ground, etc.; cf. NIDOTTE 3.945-946). Mosaic law condemned fortune-tellers and prohibited most forms of divination among the Hebrews (cf. Lev 19:31; Deut 18:10-14). Allen (1976:313) comments that "it speaks well for Micah's objectivity and fair-mindedness that he concentrates his attack not on methods but on motives."

disgraced. The verb *khapar* [TH2659, ZH2917] describes dismay when something unexpected happens and is usually found in parallel with *bosh* [TH954, ZH1017] (Andersen and Freedman 2000:374).

cover your faces. The Hebrew idiom implies shame and means "to cover up to the lips" or "to wrap oneself in a robe right up to the mustache, leaving only nose and eyes visible" (Andersen and Freedman 2000:375). A harlot (Gen 38:14), a mourner (Ezek 24:17), or a leper (Lev 13:45) might wrap themselves up in this fashion.

3:8 filled with . . . the Spirit of the LORD. Micah's autobiographical comment stresses "that the source of Micah's authority . . . lies not in himself but in God" (Alexander, Baker, and Waltke 1988:163). The OT prophets were Spirit-filled messengers sent from God (Isa 48:16). The NT teaches that "no prophecy in Scripture ever came from the prophet's own understanding . . . those prophets were moved by the Holy Spirit, and they spoke from God" (2 Pet 1:20-21).

justice. "The sign of being filled with the Spirit is speaking of justice" (Alexander, Baker, and Waltke 1988:164). The touchstone of Micah's message is "doing what is right" or practicing justice (*mishpat* [TH4941, ZH5477]), 6:8; see further the note on 3:1.

strength. "The strength conveyed by the word (*geburah* [TH1369, ZH1476]) is a gift from God" (NIDOTTE 1.812). Such divine enablement was necessary given the demands of the prophetic call.

sin and rebellion. See the notes on "sins" and "rebellion" in 1:5 above.

3:11 *rulers.* See the note on 3:1.

bribes. The OT condemns bribery (*shokhad* [TH7810, ZH8816]) because it perverts justice in the judicial sphere and equity in the social sphere of the Hebrew covenant community (cf. Exod 23:8; Deut 16:19; Prov 17:23).

priests teach God's laws. The religious leaders of the Hebrew people were charged with overseeing the sacrificial worship of the sanctuary and commissioned to teach and guide the community in the Law of Moses (Deut 33:8-11; Jer 18:18; Ezek 7:26; Mal 2:5-9).

price. The word *mekhir* [TH4242, ZH4697] indicates money that was exchanged for priestly rulings on the Torah or law of Moses. Andersen and Freedman (2000:384) note that "the torah [TH8451, ZH9368] that is sold will be made to please the buyer."

prophets. The prophets (*nabi'* [TH5030, ZH5566]) were supposed to be the "watchmen" (Jer 6:17; Ezek 3:17) and "conscience" of Israel (cf. 1 Kgs 18:17). Their task was to warn the people of divine judgment for covenant trespasses and call the people to repentance and covenant renewal with Yahweh (Ezek 33).

paid. Like the leaders and the priests, the office and ministry of the prophet was corrupted by greed—by prophecy for pay (*kesep* [TH3701, ZH4084]).

all of you claim to depend on the LORD. This claim was based on the idea of the divine presence symbolized by the Ark of the Covenant housed in Solomon's Temple. The corrupt leadership of Jerusalem "justified their lives of lies with the half-truth that the Lord's presence guaranteed the nation's security, forgetting that God made his presence contingent on ethical behavior" (Alexander, Baker, and Waltke 1988:165; cf. Exod 17:7; 33:3, 5, 14-16; 34:9).

3:12 *Mount Zion.* This was the easternmost ridge of Jerusalem, adjacent to the Kidron Valley and the Gihon Spring. The "stronghold of Zion" was the name applied to the Jebusite city conquered by David (2 Sam 5:7). Zion was the site of Solomon's Temple and became a synonym for the greater city of Jerusalem.

Jerusalem. God's commitment to justice is such that he is willing to lay waste to his "hometown." Jerusalem was sacked and Solomon's Temple destroyed by Nebuchadnezzar and the Babylonians in 587 BC (cf. 2 Kgs 25).

COMMENTARY

The ministry of the Old Testament prophets was essentially one of revealing the nature and character of God, making him known to Israel and the nations (7:18; cf. Hos 6:3). Like Amos and Zechariah, Micah was concerned that the Israelites of his day know God both as creator and redeemer (cf. 1:2; 7:7, 15, 18). To that end, "Micah, along with other inspired men, puts aside his chaste veil of modesty in controversy" and boldly claims that he is empowered by the Spirit of Yahweh (3:8; Alexander, Baker, and Waltke 1988:164). Both Amos and Zechariah testified to the same work of the Spirit of God in their respective prophetic ministries (cf. Amos 3:8; Zech 4:6). In fact, the Spirit of God and the Old Testament prophetic ministry were vitally linked because "it is through the Spirit prophets are called, inspired, transported, motivated . . . to accomplish their difficult tasks within the nations" (Hildebrandt 1995:27). The work of the Spirit in the lives and ministries of the Old Testament prophets speaks to the very nature of God's person as a "plurality" of being.

The Christian church has struggled with the mystery of the triune nature of the Godhead for twenty centuries. Yet, as Augustine knew, we must speak of the Trinity not because we are able to fathom it with overwhelming confidence, but because we cannot keep silence on a matter so crucial to biblical faith (Augustine *Trinity* 3.1.3.5). Although there is no explicit reference to the Trinity in the Old Testament, God is constant and consistent in who he is and how he reveals himself to humanity. The references to the Holy Spirit in the Old Testament speak to the plurality of the Godhead and point to the triune God revealed more explicitly in the New Testament (e.g., at the baptism of Jesus, Matt 3:13-17; in the benedictions of the Epistles, 2 Cor 13:14). According to Oden, nearly all classical Christian exegetes have argued that broadly scattered throughout the Old Testament are prophetic anticipations of triune teaching (1998:88-94). The recognition of the work of the Holy Spirit by Micah and other of the Minor Prophets reminds us that Yahweh is the triune God of the Old Testament, too, and that "the Holy Spirit has been eternally present throughout the whole historical process" (Oden 1998:183). The renewed interest in biblical theology with its increasing emphasis on the theological continuity between the old and new covenants has spawned a new appreciation for the work of the Holy Spirit in the Old Testament. A summary of his work includes:

1. Presiding with God over the act of creation (Gen 1:2)
2. Authoring and interpreting Scripture (3:8; Amos 3:8; Zech 7:12; cf. Acts 4:25)
3. Convicting and illuminating people's hearts (Neh 9:30-32; Ps 51)
4. Regenerating God's people (Ezek 36:26-27; John 3:5-8)
5. Indwelling and giving spiritual renewal to God's people (Ps 139:11-12; Isa 63:10-11; Hag 2:5; Zech 4:6)
6. Sealing the relationship of the faithful with God (as perhaps in the oath of adoption; cf. Josh 4–5; Jer 31:33)
7. Filling people for ministry, enabling them, gifting them for service (Exod 28:3; 31:3; Num 11:25; Judg 13:25; 1 Sam 16:13)

In light of the Holy Spirit's activity in the Old Testament, the promise of Jesus to send another Advocate (John 14:16) to his disciples may be understood not so much as "another" Advocate but as an expanded role for the ministry of the Advocate (or Holy Spirit) already present in God's "salvation history" (cf. Wood 1976; Hildebrandt 1995).

Oden says, "the triune understanding of God gives us a way of looking at the meaning of the whole of history, which, as the arena of God's revelation, is the subject of theology. Trinity rehearses and embraces the entire story of salvation, attesting to the church's attempt to view history synoptically, to try to grasp a unified picture of God in creation, redemption, and consummation" (1998:182). If Oden is correct in his assessment of the importance of the doctrine of the Trinity, it seems the Christian church needs to reintroduce the tenet in its theological catechism for two reasons. First, in a world awash in religious pluralism, the doctrine of the Trinity makes Christianity unique among the world's religions. In a postmodern world given to the "experience of mystery," what better distinctive to promote as one of the defining doctrines of Christianity? Second, like it or not, we find ourselves living in a society that craves a future without a past. Increasingly, North American culture is characterized by a "centripetal individualism" that scorns any communal record framed in the "past tense" because of its preoccupation with self-gratification in the "present tense." A vibrant doctrine of the Trinity gives the church the only metanarrative that meaningfully addresses the human condition and its solution—the message of "Good News" the church must take to the world.

◆ II. The Book of Visions (4:1–5:15)
   A. The Lord's Future Reign (4:1–5)

¹In the last days, the mountain of the
    LORD's house
will be the highest of all—
the most important place on earth.
It will be raised above the other hills,
    and people from all over the world
    will stream there to worship.
²People from many nations will come
    and say,
"Come, let us go up to the mountain
    of the LORD,
to the house of Jacob's God.
There he will teach us his ways,
    and we will walk in his paths."
For the LORD's teaching will go out
    from Zion;
his word will go out from Jerusalem.
³The LORD will mediate between
    peoples

and will settle disputes between
    strong nations far away.
They will hammer their swords into
    plowshares
    and their spears into pruning hooks.
Nation will no longer fight against
    nation,
    nor train for war anymore.
⁴Everyone will live in peace and
    prosperity,
    enjoying their own grapevines and
    fig trees,
    for there will be nothing to fear.
The LORD of Heaven's Armies
    has made this promise!
⁵Though the nations around us follow
    their idols,
    we will follow the LORD our God
    forever and ever.

NOTES

4:1 *last days.* This expression is prophetic shorthand for "the day of the LORD," the eschatological day of divine intervention in history that brings both the judgment of the wicked and the deliverance of the righteous. It is a day of cosmic upheaval and reversal, a day of theophany (an appearance of the Lord) and holy war against the pagan nations. The "day of the LORD" is an indefinite period of time, but always an impending event for the OT prophets.

mountain of the LORD's house. A reference to Mount Zion and the Temple of Yahweh (see note on Mount Zion in 3:12). The Temple that was laid waste as a result of God's judgment of Judah's sin will be restored (cf. 3:12), presumably after the heavenly prototype (cf. Ps 11:4; Heb 9:23). Mountains (*harim* [TH2022, ZH2215]) were the gateways to the abode of the gods in the minds of the ancients—"the psychic and spiritual entrance into the heavens" (Alexander, Baker, and Waltke 1988:168).

4:2 People from many nations will come. Jerusalem and the Temple of Yahweh as the cosmic center of God's universal kingdom is a repeated motif in the eschatological visions of the OT prophets (e.g., Isa 56:6-7; Hag 2:7; Zech 14:16-19). The Day of the Lord culminates in the universal worship of Yahweh, and Micah's vision anticipates John's Apocalypse where the nations are gathered around the throne of the Lamb (Rev 7:9-10; cf. Rev 21:10-27).

teach. The verb (*yarah* [TH3384E, ZH3723]) means to "teach, instruct" (NIDOTTE 2.537-539), but is related to another root sharing the same spelling "to shoot an arrow" (NIDOTTE 2.535-536). The word "teaching, instruction" (*torah* [TH8451, ZH9368]) is derived from this same verb cluster. The instruction of Yahweh may be compared to archery in the sense that the "arrow" of God's teaching (i.e., the laws, commandments, and statutes of the Mosaic covenant) was aimed at a "target"—God's holiness. This is what the Hebrews were called to imitate as God's people, his holiness (Lev 11:45).

walk in his paths. This is the Hebrew idiom for covenant fidelity with Yahweh, a lifestyle that confesses, loves, obeys, and relies upon the God of Abraham, Isaac, and Jacob (cf. Ps 1:2).

LORD's teaching . . . his word. Lit., "instruction" (*torah* [TH8451, ZH9368]; cf. NIDOTTE 4.893-900), the very word of Yahweh (*debar-yhwh* [TH1697/3068, ZH1821/3378]). As Yahweh proclaimed his Torah from Mount Sinai to Israel, so the Lord's instruction will be "broad-cast" from Mount Zion to all nations. "This Torah is not simply head knowledge, a body of dogma or doctrine. It is instruction, a word from the Lord which calls for a response resulting in a new way of living for those who hear it" (Limburg 1988:181).

4:3 mediate. Yahweh will mediate (*shapat* [TH8199, ZH9149], "judge") between the nations and "Jerusalem will become the international court whose findings [will] be accepted with-out quibble. Disputes would be settled amicably, for such would be Yahweh's prestige that even great nations in far-flung corners of the world would acknowledge his equity" (Allen 1976:325).

nations . . . will hammer . . . plowshares. The nations will "retool" instruments of war and death into implements of peace and agricultural production as part of the cosmic reversal of the day of the Lord (cf. Isa 2:4; Joel 3:10). Mays (1976:98) notes that "people will use the scarce and valuable materials of earth to cultivate life instead of crafting death."

4:4 enjoying their own grapevines and fig trees. The reference to vines and fig trees is an idiom for living in peace and security (cf. Zech 3:10) and recalled life during the "golden age" of King Solomon (1 Kgs 4:25).

LORD of Heaven's Armies. This compound name for God is prominent in OT prophetic literature and is variously translated "LORD of Hosts" (NRSV) or "LORD Almighty" (NIV). The Hebrew expression (*yhwh tseba'oth* [TH3068/6635, ZH3378/7372]) is often understood as a construct-genitive, as is the case here. More precisely, the construction is one of absolute nouns in apposition, perhaps conveying a verbal force ("Yahweh creates armies"; cf. TDOT 5.515). The term translated "heaven's armies" (*tseba'oth*) has military overtones and, in this case, refers to the angelic armies at God's disposal. The epithet emphasizes the effective power behind the Lord's commands, and the use of the name of God assures the prophet's audience that the fulfillment of the divine promises concerning Judah's deliverance and restoration is certain.

4:5 we will follow the LORD. The cosmic reversal of the day of the Lord will finally see a rebellious and unfaithful Israel cured of idolatry and fully restored to a relationship with Yahweh characterized by covenant obedience and loyalty (cf. Jer 31:31-34; Ezek 36:25-27).

COMMENTARY

This salvation oracle begins the Book of Visions (4:1–5:15) and marks a shift in the tone of Micah's message from judgment to restoration. According to Andersen and Freedman (2000:397), the Book of Visions "is an apocalypse, a vision of the end and consummation of history." R. L. Smith (1984:36) observes further that this passage "is freighted with eschatological overtones . . . Jerusalem and the Temple may be destroyed but they will be restored in a grander style than before." Most striking is the transformation of the Jerusalem Temple from a local shrine for the Hebrew tribes to a universal worship center for people from all over the world (4:1). The prophecy is a highly stylized poem, "rhapsodical" in its presentation, in the assessment of Andersen and Freedman (2000:399; see further their discussion of the poetry of 4:1-5 [2000:398-399]).The first portion of the oracle (4:1-3) is very similar in form and content to Isaiah 2:2-4, but scholars disagree as to the relationship between the two pericopes (cf. the discussion in Hillers 1984:51-53). Allen (1976:323) is probably correct in his analysis that Micah took over and adapted an existing composition. A segment of the latter portion of the oracle (4:4) has affinities with Zechariah 3:10. The peace and security of Israel amid the nations portrayed in the salvation oracle stands in stark contrast to the preceding picture (in the oracle of judgment) of Jerusalem as a plowed field and a heap of rubble (3:12).

Micah described the day of the Lord as a day of reversal. He envisioned a day in which Jerusalem is the "navel" of the earth (4:1), a day when weapons of war are retooled as instruments of peace (4:3), a day when peace prevails over war (4:4), and a day when the worship of Yahweh is the "gold standard" among competing religious traditions (4:5). The idea of reversal is a common motif in the prophetic literature addressing the topic of the day of the Lord. This theme of reversal is sometimes called a "world upside down" (van Leeuwen 1986:599-610). God is a God of a "world upside down" in the sense that he is a God of surprises, a God of the unexpected. The Old Testament stories of Joseph, Gideon, Ruth, Hannah, David (among many others) reveal to us that God is such a God. Zechariah depicts God as a God of "small beginnings" (Zech 4:10). Jesus confirmed this in his teaching that compared the Kingdom of God to a mustard seed—the smallest of all seeds that eventually grows into a large tree (Matt 13:31-32). Paul explained to the Corinthian Christians that God deliberately chose to work through the foolish and weak things of this world so that humanity cannot boast in its achievement—rather, God receives all the glory (1 Cor 1:26-29). How much more does the New Testament story of the incarnation of Jesus the Messiah reveal God as a God of the unexpected, a God of surprises!

What might we learn from our discovery that God is the God of a "world upside down"? First, God has not changed. His thoughts are completely different than ours, and his ways are beyond anything we can imagine (Isa 55:8-9). Second, God is still in the business of doing "new things"—reversals like creating highways and rivers in the desert (Isa 43:19). Third, many in the religious communities of the Old and New Testaments missed seeing the hand of God in these surprises and failed to comprehend his work in the turnabout of unexpected events. This should sober us and make us ever alert and vigilant as a people of faith so that we do not find ourselves among those who are rebuked for having eyes but failing to see and ears but failing to hear (Mark 8:17-18). Finally, we must take the examples of Elisha (and his prayer that his servant's eyes might be opened to the spiritual reality around him, 2 Kgs 6:17) and Paul (who constantly prayed that the eyes of the hearts of the Christians in Ephesus might be enlightened, [Eph 1:18, NIV]) as models of prayer. We need to ask God that our own "hearts will be flooded with light" so that we can begin to "understand the incredible greatness of God's power for us who believe him" (Eph 1:18-19, NLT).

◆   B. Israel's Return from Exile (4:6–5:1)

6"In that coming day," says the LORD,
"I will gather together those who
    are lame,
    those who have been exiles,
    and those whom I have filled
        with grief.
7Those who are weak will survive
        as a remnant;
    those who were exiles will become
        a strong nation.
Then I, the LORD, will rule from
        Jerusalem*
    as their king forever."
8As for you, Jerusalem,
    the citadel of God's people,*
your royal might and power
    will come back to you again.
The kingship will be restored
    to my precious Jerusalem.

9But why are you now screaming
        in terror?
Have you no king to lead you?
Have your wise people all died?
    Pain has gripped you like a woman
        in childbirth.
10Writhe and groan like a woman in
        labor,
    you people of Jerusalem,*
for now you must leave this city
    to live in the open country.

You will soon be sent in exile
    to distant Babylon.
But the LORD will rescue you there;
    he will redeem you from the grip
        of your enemies.

11Now many nations have gathered
        against you.
    "Let her be desecrated," they say.
    "Let us see the destruction of
        Jerusalem.*"
12But they do not know the LORD's
        thoughts
    or understand his plan.
These nations don't know
    that he is gathering them
        together
to be beaten and trampled
    like sheaves of grain on
        a threshing floor.
13"Rise up and crush the nations,
        O Jerusalem!"*
    says the LORD.
"For I will give you iron horns and
        bronze hooves,
    so you can trample many nations
        to pieces.
You will present their stolen riches
        to the LORD,
    their wealth to the LORD of all
        the earth."

CHAPTER 5

¹*Mobilize! Marshal your troops!
   The enemy is laying siege
      to Jerusalem.

They will strike Israel's leader
   in the face with a rod.

4:7 Hebrew *Mount Zion.* 4:8 Hebrew *As for you, Migdal-eder, / the Ophel of the daughter of Zion.*
4:10 Hebrew *O daughter of Zion.* 4:11 Hebrew *of Zion.* 4:13 Hebrew *"Rise up and thresh, O daughter
of Zion."* 5:1 Verse 5:1 is numbered 4:14 in Hebrew text.

NOTES

4:6 *that coming day.* The phrase is repeated in 2:4; 4:6; 7:11 and is "shorthand" in the
OT prophets for "the day of LORD" (cf. "last days" in 4:1).

says the LORD. The divine utterance formula (*ne'um yhwh* [TH5002/3068, ZH5536/3378]) is a
nominal exclamation in the OT prophets and affirms the divine source and authority of
the prophet's message.

gather. The two verbs (*'asap* [TH622, ZH665] + *qabats* [TH6908, ZH7695], "I will assemble" and
"I will gather") are rendered in the NLT by the single expression, "I will gather together."
The same two verbs are paired in 2:12 (see note).

exiles. These were the Hebrews banished or scattered (*nadakh* [TH5080, ZH5615]) into foreign
lands as punishment for the sin of idolatry. Such exile is one of the curses threatened by
Yahweh for violation of his covenant (Deut 28:36-37, 64; cf. Lev 18:24-30, where the land
of covenant promise "vomits out" those who defile it).

4:7 *strong nation.* The expression *goy 'atsum* [TH1471/6099, ZH1580/6786] is used to describe
the growth of the nation of Israel during their Egyptian sojourn, which threatened Pharaoh
and the people of Egypt (Deut 26:5); it echoes the promise made to Abraham to make a
mighty nation from his descendants (Gen 18:18).

I, the LORD, will rule. The kingship of God is a central theme in OT theology. The Lord
reigns over heaven and earth by virtue of his work as creator and sustainer of all that exists
in the universe (Pss 93:1; 97:1; 99:1; Col 1:15-17; cf. NIDOTTE 2.960-961). (See further
the discussion about "king" in the note on 2:13.)

4:8 *The kingship.* This is a reference to the promises associated with the Davidic covenant
for perpetual kingship in Israel (2 Sam 7:16). The day of the Lord will witness the emer-
gence of a shepherd-king like David who will rule in righteousness over Israel (5:2; Jer
33:15-18; Ezek 34:23-24).

4:9 *wise people.* The counselor or adviser (*yo'ets* [TH3289A, ZH3446]) was usually a member
of the royal cabinet or part of the council of elders who advised the king (cf. NIDOTTE
2.490-491). The counselor or sage was one of the three major leadership offices in Hebrew
society responsible for instructing the people (along with prophet and priest, cf. Jer 18:18;
Ezek 7:26).

4:10 *exile . . . Babylon.* The reference to Babylon is a metaphor for a dark and distant
pagan land (cf. Alexander, Baker, and Waltke 1988:179; see note on 4:6 above).

rescue. The verb *natsal* [TH5337, ZH5911] means "to save, deliver" and is ascribed to Yahweh
"as the deliverer par excellence" by the OT prophets (cf. NIDOTTE 3.144-145). The word
recalls the deliverance Israel experienced by the mighty hand of Yahweh at the time of the
Exodus from Egypt (Exod 3:8; 18:9-10; Deut 32:39).

redeem. The verb *ga'al* [TH1350, ZH1457] can mean "to deliver, redeem, ransom." Theologically, the word attests God's faithfulness to his election of Israel and his identity as a compassionate husband who takes back his erring wife (see further the excellent theological
discussion of this rich term in NIDOTTE 1.789-794).

4:12 *the LORD's thoughts.* The Lord's thoughts or purposes (*makhashabah* [TH4284, ZH4742]) are different than and far beyond human thoughts (Ps 92:5; Isa 55:8-9). His thoughts for Israel were ultimately for good, for a future and a hope (Jer 29:11).

plan. The plans (or "counsel"; *'etsah* [TH6098, ZH6783]) of the Lord cannot be thwarted and stand forever (Ps 33:11; Isa 46:10). The Spirit of this counsel rests upon the Messiah (Isa 11:2) as a part of God's plan for "the whole earth" that will be accomplished (Isa 14:26).

gathering. The day of the Lord is not only a day of "gathering" and restoration for scattered Israel (see note on 2:12), but also a day of "gathering" (*qabats* [TH6908, ZH7695]) the nations for judgment (cf. Isa 66:16-18; Joel 3:2).

threshing floor. The crushing of grain and sifting of chaff associated with the threshing floor (*goren* [TH1637, ZH1755]) is symbolic of divine judgment (Isa 21:10; Jer 51:33; Amos 1:3; cf. NIDOTTE 1.893).

4:13 *riches . . . wealth to the LORD.* The day of the Lord is characterized by reversal. God will turn the tables and do to the nations as they have done to the people of Israel. The flow of the wealth of the nations into Jerusalem overturns the looting of the city that was implied in the destruction of Mount Zion announced earlier by the prophet (3:12). Zechariah's reference to the great quantities of gold and silver coming to Jerusalem (Zech 14:14) recalls Haggai's prediction that one day the "treasures of all the nations" would come to Yahweh's Temple (Hag 2:7-8).

5:1 [4:14] *Israel's leader.* Lit., "the judge of Israel" (*shopet yisra'el* [TH8199, ZH9149]), a reference to the Hebrew king as the supreme judge of the land.

strike . . . the face with a rod. The act signifies humiliation because "the victim is so defenseless he cannot even defend his face" (Alexander, Baker, and Waltke 1988:182; cf. Job 16:10; Ps 3:7; Isa 50:6. See further the discussion of the ritual abasement of the king from Mesopotamian sources in McKeating 1971:177). Isaiah likened the Assyrian army to a rod (*shebet* [TH7626, ZH8657]; Isa 10:5, 15). Kaiser (1992:63-64) sees the passage fulfilled in Nebuchadnezzar's treatment of King Zedekiah of Judah, but the Assyrian siege of Jerusalem during the reign of King Hezekiah seems a more likely reference (cf. Allen 1976:341).

COMMENTARY

This section of Micah's message (4:6–5:1) continues the salvation oracle begun in 4:1-5. The three speeches of the passage (4:6-8, 9-10; 4:11–5:1) are connected by references to Jerusalem as "daughter of Zion" in the Hebrew text (4:8, 10, 13, NRSV), and each begins with the present distress before contrasting the prospects for the future (cf. Allen 1976:332, 335). The first speech is a message of hope promising a restored Jerusalem (4:6-8), the second speech emphasizes the present suffering (with pastoral empathy, 4:9-10), and the third speech is a message of reversal for Jerusalem from siege to victory (4:11–5:1). The entire unit "is a summons to faith in the God who is able to transform the powerlessness of his people into power and glory" (Allen 1976:329).

This lengthy salvation oracle provides considerable grist for theological reflection. First, the phrase "last days" (4:1) introduces the theme of "the day of the LORD" (or "the day of Yahweh"). This expression "was used by the prophets to indicate the time when the current state of affairs will be replaced by the Lord's intended order of things. Most of the oracles in the prophetic literature represent movement toward this ideal condition" (Walton and Hill 2000:523). The day of the Lord is a day of justice, where the God of justice will intervene in history for the purposes of vindicating the righteous and judging the wicked (Mal 3:18). The day of the Lord is a process, a sequence of events over indefinite periods of time—not a single cataclysmic event. The day of the Lord is also a time of great upheaval and reversal of fortune in the cosmic, spiritual, social, and political realms.

Beyond all this, it is Yahweh's day! God is the lead actor on the stage of history and all the "press" rightly belongs to him (Zeph 1:14; 3:8). The prophetic understanding of the day of the Lord also reminds us that history is linear, that it continues to move to a climax or denouement. The day of Yahweh culminates in a new creation, a new heaven and a new earth (Isa 65:17; 2 Pet 3:13; Rev 21:1). This is an important lesson for our times, given the influence of enlightenment ideas such as "Hegelian synthesis" and Eastern ideas of reincarnation on the contemporary understanding of history in North America. (On "the day of the LORD," see further the commentary on Amos 5:18-27; 9:11-15; Zech 9:9-17; 12:1-14; 13:1-6; Mal 3:13–4:3.)

Second, Simundson (1996:569) calls attention to the theological tensions emerging from the complicated relationship between human freedom and God's sovereignty. For example, the nations gathered to gloat over Israel's destruction (4:11), unaware that God was gathering them for their own judgment and destruction (4:12-13). One thing is certain: God habitually turns what people intend for evil into something good for the faithful of God and to accomplish his redemptive purposes for history (cf. Gen 50:20; see further the discussion of human freedom and divine sovereignty in the commentary on Zech 13:7-9).

Third, Micah introduces us to the "mind" of God (4:12). Elsewhere we learn that God's thoughts are categorically different than those of mortals (Isa 55:8-9), deep and innumerable (Pss 40:5; 92:5; 139:17). "Who can know the LORD's thoughts? Who knows enough to teach him?" (1 Cor 2:16; cf. Isa 40:13). This portion of Micah's sermon should give us pause and instill a deep sense of humility in us, much like the psalmist who determined not to concern himself with matters too great for consideration (Ps 131:1). Job learned this lesson the hard way, challenging and critiquing the thoughts and plans of God from his fallen and finite perspective (cf. Job 40:2; 42:2-6). The apostle Paul wrote "no one can know God's thoughts" (1 Cor 2:11). Yet, the marvel and the mystery is that as Christians "we have the mind of Christ . . . and we have received God's Spirit . . . so we can know the wonderful things God has freely given us" (1 Cor 2:16, 12). In light of this truth, how much more should we walk humbly with our God? (6:8).

◆   C. A Ruler from Bethlehem (5:2-6)

2*But you, O Bethlehem Ephrathah,
     are only a small village among all
        the people of Judah.
Yet a ruler of Israel will come from
     you,

one whose origins are from the
     distant past.
3 The people of Israel will be abandoned
     to their enemies
until the woman in labor gives birth.

Then at last his fellow countrymen
will return from exile to their
own land.
⁴And he will stand to lead his flock
with the LORD's strength,
in the majesty of the name of the
LORD his God.
Then his people will live there
undisturbed,
for he will be highly honored around
the world.
⁵ And he will be the source of peace.

When the Assyrians invade our land
and break through our defenses,
we will appoint seven rulers to watch
over us,
eight princes to lead us.
⁶They will rule Assyria with drawn
swords
and enter the gates of the land
of Nimrod.
He will rescue us from the Assyrians
when they pour over the borders
to invade our land.

5:2 Verses 5:2-15 are numbered 5:1-14 in Hebrew text.

NOTES

5:2 [1] *Bethlehem* A Judean village located five miles southwest of Jerusalem, notable for its association with King David (1 Sam 16:1). The name Bethlehem means "house of bread" or "house of food" in the sense of storehouse or granary, perhaps explaining, in part, the need for the specification of Bethlehem's district as that of Ephrathah (since there was a Bethlehem of Zebulun, cf. Josh 19:14-15). The town was home to Naomi, Boaz, and Ruth (Ruth 1:2; 2:1). When King Herod inquired of the Jewish leaders where the Messiah would be born, they indicated Bethlehem, citing 5:2 (cf. Matt 2:3-6).

Ephrathah. The name of the district in which the village of Bethlehem was located (cf. Ps 132:6). The name means "fruitful." Jesse, the father of David, is described as "an Ephrathite from Bethlehem in the land of Judah" (1 Sam 17:12).

ruler. The word *moshel* [TH4910A, ZH5440] is a general term for ruler or even tyrant in a negative sense (e.g., Isa 14:5). Theologically, the use of the root *mashal* in the OT suggests that "God is the beginning and end of all 'dominion' in the universe and among human beings" (TDOT 9.71). The use of the word *mashal* instead of *malak* [TH4427, ZH4887] may indicate the rule of the Messiah is more than simply the continuation of Hebrew kingship or a copy of pagan kingship (cf. Kaiser 1992:64). Rather, it may signify a kingship "in which a qualitatively different dominion is realized" (TDOT 9.70).

5:4 [3] *lead his flock.* God tends Israel like a flock (*ra'ah* [TH7462, ZH8286]) and his Messiah will do likewise as a shepherd-king (Isa 40:11; Jer 31:10; Ezek 37:24).

majesty of the name of the LORD his God. According to Allen (1976:346), God's name (Yahweh) stood for authority accepted in 4:5, and here "it stands for authority delegated." The authority vested in the name Yahweh recalls the revelation of the divine name and the commissioning of Moses as the deliverer of Israel (Exod 3:14-15).

5:5 [4] *source of peace.* One of the titles for Messiah is "Prince of Peace" (Isa 9:6). Peace will characterize the rule of Messiah (cf. Isa 55:12; 66:12; Jer 33:6; Ezek 34:25; 37:26). Andersen and Freedman (2000:476) take this phrase (*zeh shalom* [TH2088/7965, ZH2296/8934]) as a title and see an allusion to King Solomon as "the One of Peace." The word "peace" (*shalom*) connotes both well-being and prosperity in a physical and material sense, and spiritually in relationship to God and his righteousness (see the discussion in NIDOTTE 4.131-132).

Assyrians. The impending threat of Assyrian imperialism is the historical backdrop for Micah's preaching (see the Introduction).

seven rulers . . . eight princes. The expression is a literary device indicating that "an indefinite yet adequate number of leaders will arise to overthrow the Assyrians (Prov 30:15, 18,

21, 29; Eccl 11:2)" (R. L. Smith 1984:45). The eventual defeat of Assyria and the ensuing peace "are representative of the Messiah's yet wider triumph" (Alexander, Baker, and Waltke 1988:185).

princes. The term is an archaic tribal title (*nasik* [TH5257A, ZH5817]) and is found in two contexts: the heroic age of the judges (cf. Josh 13:21) and the end time (e.g., Ps 2:6; Ezek 32:29; cf. Andersen and Freedman 2000:479).

5:6 [5] Nimrod. A general reference to the land of Babylonia (Gen 10:8-12). The sequence of the names Assyria and Nimrod may indicate that Assyria had conquered Babylonia, thus confirming the eighth-century BC date for Micah's oracles (cf. Alexander, Baker, and Waltke 1988:185).

rescue. See note on 4:10.

COMMENTARY

This unit of Micah's message (5:2-6) is a salvation oracle promising deliverance from the Assyrians and a return from exile. The extent of the pericope is variously understood by commentators (e.g., 5:1-4, so R. L. Smith 1984:42; 5:2-5a, so Simundson 1996:570; 5:1-6, so Limburg 1988:185). The prophet's promise comes at the end of a series of sharp contrasts between present defeat (e.g., 2:1-11; 3:1-12) and a glorious future (e.g., 2:12-13; 4:1-5), what Simundson (1996:570) calls the "movement from 'now' to 'then.'" The humiliation of Israel's king (see note on 5:1 for possible identifications of the Hebrew king) will be overturned completely in the cosmic reversal of the day of Yahweh. For Micah, "the present remains a time of suffering, and it may get worse before relief comes, but the people should not lose heart. Again, the movement is from suffering to salvation, from defeat to victory" (Simundson 1996:570).

The prophet Isaiah, a contemporary of Micah, declared that there is "no peace for the wicked" (Isa 57:21). Rather, they are like "the restless sea, which is never still but continually churns up mud and dirt" (Isa 57:20). Like Isaiah, Micah understood that ultimately "peace" was a person, not a virtue, concept, or idea (5:5; cf. Isa 9:7). Although the prophet Micah does not use the term "Messiah" (*mashiakh* [TH4899, ZH5431], "anointed one"), this passage (5:2-6) is usually identified as a "messianic text" by biblical interpreters (especially since later Jewish tradition identified 5:2 with the Messiah, cf. Matt 2:4-6). The Messiah in the Old Testament came to be understood as an eschatological figure "anointed" to a royal office and divinely commissioned for the task of "delivering" the people of Israel from their enemies and establishing a kingdom characterized by righteousness (Limburg 1988:187-188). Thus, "the word 'messianic' has come to be used to describe hope for a new leader who will come from the family of David to guide the people from present oppression and suffering to glorious victory" (Simundson 1996:571).

Micah confirmed that the "Messiah" is a person, connected genealogically to the family of David and associated historically with the town of Bethlehem (5:2; cf. Isa 7:14; 9:6-7; 11:1). This person will also be a "ruler" who will deliver Israel from its enemies (5:5-6) and establish a government that promotes peace (5:4-5). Kaiser (1992:64) notes that this one called Ruler is a ruler "to me" (i.e., "to God," untranslated in the NLT) because first and foremost the Messiah was for the benefit of the Lord's plans, and only secondarily a response to Israel's predicament. The origins of this Ruler are rooted in the "distant past" (5:2b), or "from eternity on" (connecting Messiah to the eternal God; cf. Pss 2:7; 110:1). This Ruler will earn a global reputation for his leadership of Israel (5:4b). Finally, his rule will result in peace (5:4-5; cf. Isa 11:6-9). Indeed, peace, or "shalom," is not only the work of this Ruler, but also the very character of the Messiah—"the source of peace" (5:5a, lit., "this one is peace").

The New Testament identifies the fulfillment of Micah's prophecy about the ruler who will come from Bethlehem Ephrathah (5:2) with Jesus' birth to Mary and Joseph in Bethlehem (Luke 2). Jesus is the self-proclaimed shepherd who stands with his sheep (John 10:11; cf. Mic 5:4), and he is identified as the shepherd struck down by God (Matt 26:31). As the source of peace (5:5), Jesus granted "peace" to his disciples (John 14:27). Beyond this, the church is commissioned to preach the gospel of the Kingdom to the world—the Good News of peace through Jesus Christ (Acts 10:36). The ultimate realization of this divine peace will be accomplished when Jesus the Messiah returns a second time to rule the earth and restore the created order—the nations living in the light of God's glory (Rev 21:4-5, 22-27; cf. Mic 5:4).

The biblical vision of "peace" (*shalom* [TH7965, ZH8934]) is "the outgrowth of a covenant of *shalom* (cf. Ezek 34:25), in which persons are bound not only to God but to one another in a caring, sharing, rejoicing community with none to make them afraid" (Brueggemann 1982:17). An entire cluster of words is required to express the multiple dimensions of biblical shalom—words like love, loyalty, truth, grace, salvation, justice, blessing, righteousness, and wisdom (Brueggemann 1982:15-16). This *shalom* is rooted in God (Zech 8:12; Mal 2:5); he dispenses peace to his people, especially those who love and obey his law (Ps 29:11; 119:165; Isa 26:3). This *shalom* is also connected to the Messiah, the Davidic shepherd-king who brokers the covenant of shalom with the people of God (Ezek 37:24-28; on the Messiah in Micah, see Kaiser 1995:148-154). Limburg (1988:188) aptly announces that "the unanimous testimony of the New Testament is that this Messiah . . . has come in the person of Jesus of Nazareth." Peace, shalom, is truly a person—the person of Jesus. He is our peace (Eph 2:14); he gives the gift of peace to his disciples—peace of mind and heart (John 14:27; cf. 16:33).

The God of peace (Rom 15:33; 1 Thess 5:23; Heb 13:20) expects his people to be people of peace—even peacemakers: "God blesses those who work for peace, for they will be called the children of God" (Matt 5:9). The teaching of Jesus in the Beatitudes is based upon similar Old Testament injunctions to "search for peace, and work to maintain it" (Ps 34:14; "seek peace, and pursue it," NRSV). The gospel of Jesus the Messiah is the Good News of peace with God through this same Jesus who is Lord of all (Acts 10:36). The Good News of peace not only addresses an individual's relationship with God (i.e., sinful people reconciled to God, 2 Cor 5:18), but also one's relationships with family, neighbors (broadly understood), and nations (cf. Matt 5:9; 1 Pet 3:11). Limburg (1988:184) reminds us that the Christian church ought to be concerned with both evangelism and peacemaking because the

Kingdom of God is all about "living a life of goodness and peace and joy in the Holy Spirit" (Rom 14:17). This means working for peace at the interpersonal level, as well as pursuing peace at the international level.

◆   ## D. The Remnant Purified (5:7-15)

7 Then the remnant left in Israel*
    will take their place among the
    nations.
They will be like dew sent by the LORD
    or like rain falling on the grass,
which no one can hold back
    and no one can restrain.
8 The remnant left in Israel
    will take their place among the
    nations.
They will be like a lion among the
    animals of the forest,
like a strong young lion among
    flocks of sheep and goats,
pouncing and tearing as they go
    with no rescuer in sight.
9 The people of Israel will stand up
    to their foes,
and all their enemies will be
    wiped out.

10 "In that day," says the LORD,
    "I will slaughter your horses
    and destroy your chariots.
11 I will tear down your walls
    and demolish your defenses.
12 I will put an end to all witchcraft,
    and there will be no more fortune-
    tellers.
13 I will destroy all your idols and
    sacred pillars,
so you will never again worship
    the work of your own
    hands.
14 I will abolish your idol shrines with
    their Asherah poles
    and destroy your pagan cities.
15 I will pour out my vengeance
    on all the nations that refuse
    to obey me."

5:7 Hebrew in Jacob; also in 5:8. See note on 1:5a.

NOTES

5:7 [6] *the remnant.* See note on 2:12.

dew. The dew (*tal* [TH2919, ZH3228]) is sometimes used figuratively as a symbol of divine blessing (e.g., Ps 133:3; Hos 14:5; Zech 8:12; cf. Alexander, Baker, and Waltke 1988:187). Andersen and Freedman (2000:485) equate the situation of the Hebrew remnant with the parched grass awaiting the moisture of the dew and rain. For them the figure of speech is an exhortation to the remnant to wait upon the Lord (cf. Isa 40:31). The more natural reading of the word-picture is that restoration of the place of Israel among the nations is sure, even irrepressible—just like the dew and the rain, which no one can hold back.

5:8 [7] *like a lion.* Reversal characterizes the day of the Lord. The picture of Israel as a flock of sheep, scattered, lame, and weak (4:6-7), gives way to a portrait depicting the Hebrew people as a raging bull and a roaring lion among the nations (4:13).

5:9 [8] *Israel will stand up.* The reversal of "that coming day" continues as Israel, once trampled by the nations (3:12), will trample their enemies with God's help (4:13; 5:8).

5:12 [11] *witchcraft.* The word (*keshep* [TH3785, ZH4176]; "sorcery, magic arts") involved the use of spells, incantations, charms, and amulets, and special rituals for the purpose of manipulating both natural and spiritual powers so as to influence circumstances, people, and the gods (NIDOTTE 2.735-736). Such practices were forbidden to the Hebrews by Mosaic law (Lev 19:26; Deut 18:9-14).

fortune-tellers. The word (*'anan* [TH6049A, ZH6726]; "interpret signs, tell fortunes, conjure up spirits") refers broadly to the practice of occultic arts (cf. Isa 57:3; Jer 27:9). Such practices were forbidden to the Hebrews by Mosaic law (Lev 19:26; Deut 18:9-14).

5:13 [12] *idols.* See the note for "carved images" in 1:7 above.

sacred pillars. The sacred pillars (*matsebah* [TH4676, ZH5167]) were freestanding stones associated with Canaanite fertility cult worship (NIDOTTE 3.135). The stones were stylized representations of the male deity (e.g., Baal, 2 Kgs 3:2) and libations or drink-offerings were poured over the stone as an act of worship (Alexander, Baker, and Waltke 1988:190). According to Mosaic law, the Hebrews were to destroy the sacred pillars they found in the land of Canaan when they entered (Exod 23:24; 34:13; Deut 7:5; 12:3), and they were prohibited from erecting such standing stones (Deut 16:22). Setting up of stone pillars as memorials to Yahweh (Gen 28:18; 35:14) or as witnesses to Yahweh's acts in Israel's history (Josh 4:20; 1 Sam 7:12), however, was sanctioned in the OT.

5:14 [13] *Asherah poles.* As the wife of El, Asherah was the "mother of the gods" in Canaanite mythology. Her symbol was the tree, represented by a wooden pole erected in the Canaanite fertility cult worship centers. Mosaic law commanded that the Hebrews destroy the sacred poles of the Canaanites (Deut 7:5; 12:3), and it prohibited them from fashioning and worshiping such objects (Deut 16:21). Failure to obey these injunctions led to the destruction and exile of the divided kingdoms of Israel (2 Kgs 17:16) and Judah (2 Kgs 21:7).

5:15 [14] *vengeance.* God's vengeance (*naqam* [TH5359, ZH5934]) "is a consequence of his holiness (Jer 50:28-29); zeal (Isa 59:18), coupled with his wrath (Mic 5:14), is subordinate to his justice (Isa 63:1, 4)" (NIDOTTE 3.155). Vengeance is the punitive retribution of God usually set in the context of war or breach of covenant. The notion of vengeance is the prerogative of God because he is Creator, King, and Judge (cf. Deut 32:35; Rom 12:19; Heb 10:30). One of Yahweh's titles is "the God of Vengeance" (*el-neqamoth* [TH410A/5360, ZH446/5935], Ps 94:1). God avenges his covenant (Lev 26:25), his enemies (Deut 32:41), the sins of the nations (Ps 149:7), his people (Isa 63:4), and his Temple (Jer 50:28).

COMMENTARY

The final section of Micah's "Book of Visions" (4:1–5:15) comprises a salvation oracle (5:7-8), a prayer (5:9), and a concluding oracle of judgment (5:10-15). The oracle of salvation foretells the purification of the remnant of Israel and the expansion of Messiah's kingdom among the nations. The oracle of judgment warns that God intends to destroy all the false hopes of Israel and the nations. The Book of Visions ends much like the preceding Book of Doom (1:2–3:12), with a pronouncement of God's sentence of judgment against the accused (i.e., the Hebrew divided kingdoms of Israel and Judah; cf. 3:1-12; 5:10-15). The destructive power of God's vengeance is extended to "all the nations that refuse to obey" him (5:15).

The prophet introduces a difficult and disturbing theological truth in his concluding oracle of judgment, namely the "vengeance" of Yahweh. When used of God, the word "vengeance" (*naqam* [TH5359, ZH5934], "avenge, take vengeance, revenge") refers to divine retribution, or the demonstration of "God's righteousness in compensating the wrong with right" (Elwell 1996:795). Divine vengeance relates to God's sense of justice in restoring what is right and good. In fact, one of God's titles is the "God of Vengeance," and his vengeance is equated with his "glorious justice" (Ps 94:1). The "day of the LORD" is called "the day of vengeance" (NIV); it will be a day of both judgment and redemption for Israel and the nations (Isa 61:2; 63:4). God's vengeance is

directed against the nations for their sins against humanity, wanton militaristic imperialism, oppression, social injustice, and the rejection of what God has established as
right and good according to his revealed word (Isa 47:3; Nah 1:2; cf. Amos 1:3–2:3).
God's vengeance is directed against his people Israel for breaking his covenant (Lev
26:15). This divine retribution against Israel "is usually disciplinary in nature and
aims at the restoration of lawfulness and the covenant in order that Zion will turn
into a 'city of righteousness' again (Isa 1:24-26)" (NIDOTTE 3.155).

The psalms of imprecation, by definition, are those psalms containing passages
that seek the hurt of someone else by invoking curses or vengeful punishments
against them as enemies (e.g., Pss 5, 12, 55, 137). True imprecation recognizes that
vengeance belongs to God alone (Deut 32:35; Rom 12:19; Heb 10:30) and understands the theological principle of retribution that acknowledges God as the judge of
sin in this life and the next (Pss 109:13; 137:9). "The imprecation, in its deepest intention, is a cry for the breakthrough of God's kingdom in liberation and vengeance.
Without God's vengeance there is no justice (Ps 58:11) and no future (Deut 32:43; Ps
149:7-9)" (NIDOTTE 3.155; note the implications of this for the "disciple's prayer"
[Matt 6:10] that God's "Kingdom come" and his "will be done on earth").

God's vengeance is related to his "jealousy" (*qana'* or *qanna'* [TH7065/7067, ZH7861/
7862], "be jealous, envious, zealous"; cf. NIDOTTE 3.937-440), his zeal for his own
reputation (Ezek 39:25) and his own glory (Isa 42:8). In a positive sense, God is
"jealous" or passionate about his relationship with his people (Exod 34:14), and
his love is so great for his chosen people that his jealousy is also their defense and
hope of restoration (Ezek 36:5; Zech 1:14). In a negative sense, God's "jealousy"
means the fire of his anger will break out against those who break covenant relationship with him (Deut 4:23-24; 5:9). Most often God's jealousy is related to the
practice of idolatry because God is a jealous God who will not share the affection of
his people with any other god (Exod 20:5; cf. 34:14). God reveals himself as a jealous God because he is the one true and living God, and as Creator and Redeemer, he
has the exclusive right to the worship of his creatures (see further the discussion of
God's jealousy in the commentary for Zech 1:7-17).

Micah addressed a series of false securities from which the Hebrews needed to be
purified, including military armaments and strategic defenses, occultic practices,
and all forms of false religion (5:10-15). These false securities represent a lack of
dependence upon God, and as potential idols, they are a threat to provoke God's
jealousy and unleash the fire of his judgment (Deut 29:20; 32:21; cf. Craigie
1985:43-44; G. V. Smith 2001:535-537). Simundson reminds us that Micah's list of
the false securities that God will purge from Israel has a very familiar and contemporary ring to it: "Idolatry is not simply a matter of setting up statues or using symbols
borrowed from very different and incompatible religious traditions. To place one's
hope and ultimate security in any thing or person or idea that is less than God is to
be guilty of idolatry" (Simundson 1996:576). John's admonition to the Christian to
"keep away from anything that might take God's place in your hearts" (1 John 5:21)
takes on new significance in light of Micah's preaching.

◆ III. The Book of Judgment and Pardon (6:1–7:20)
A. The Lord's Case against Israel (6:1–8)

Listen to what the LORD is saying:

"Stand up and state your case
   against me.
Let the mountains and hills be
   called to witness your complaints.
² And now, O mountains,
   listen to the LORD's complaint!
He has a case against his people.
   He will bring charges against Israel.

³ "O my people, what have I done to you?
   What have I done to make you tired
      of me?
   Answer me!
⁴ For I brought you out of Egypt
   and redeemed you from slavery.
   I sent Moses, Aaron, and Miriam
      to help you.
⁵ Don't you remember, my people,
   how King Balak of Moab tried to
      have you cursed
   and how Balaam son of Beor blessed
      you instead?

And remember your journey from
   Acacia Grove* to Gilgal,
when I, the LORD, did everything
   I could
to teach you about my faithfulness."

⁶ What can we bring to the LORD?
   What kind of offerings should we
      give him?
Should we bow before God
   with offerings of yearling calves?
⁷ Should we offer him thousands of
      rams
   and ten thousand rivers of
      olive oil?
Should we sacrifice our firstborn
      children
   to pay for our sins?

⁸ No, O people, the LORD has told you
      what is good,
   and this is what he requires of you:
to do what is right, to love mercy,
   and to walk humbly with your God.

6:5 Hebrew *Shittim.*

NOTES

6:1 Listen. The imperative verb (*shama'* [TH8085, ZH9048]) introduces a covenant lawsuit in 6:1-5 (although McKeating [1971:181] and Alexander, Baker, and Waltke [1988:191] regard all of 6:1-8 as a lawsuit oracle). The prophet serves as "a kind of officer of the court" as he summons the disputants and witnesses to the trial (Andersen and Freedman 2000:513).

Stand up. The imperative verb (*qum* [TH6965, ZH7756]) is a call to action, an official "call to order" opening the court session. It is possible that in the legal proceedings of the biblical world the plaintiff and defendant were literally called to stand and state their case (so Mays [1976:131], "Israel is commanded to 'stand up' in preparation for speaking and listening as a participant"; cf. Deut 29:10, 15; Job 23:4-5).

case. The word *rib* [TH7378, ZH8189] is a term signifying a type of formal legal case known as a covenant lawsuit (see the discussion of the covenant-lawsuit oracle in Alexander, Baker, and Waltke 1988:191-196; Allen 1976:363-369; Mays 1976:128-36; G. V. Smith 2001:547-558) According to Westermann (1991:199-200), the lawsuit oracle is a variation of the prophetic judgment-speech and incorporates standard elements, including a call on witnesses, the case itself, a statement of Yahweh's loyalty, the indictment, and the sentence (VanGemeren 1990:400-402).

6:2 O mountains. Yahweh calls the mountains to witness the trial because they have "stood" over humanity from the beginning of creation and have "seen" the history of Israel and all humanity unfold. The cosmic witnesses serve to validate the legal proceedings and testify (since heaven and earth are invoked) as witnesses in Moses's song of witness sealing the covenant at Sinai (Deut 31:19; 32:1; cf. Hillers 1984:77).

complaint. Yahweh has a case (*rib* [TH7379, ZH8190]) against Israel, making him both defendant and plaintiff in the lawsuit. Later God will act as prosecuting attorney (6:6-8, 9-12) and pass sentence as judge (6:13-16).

6:4 redeemed. The verb *padah* [TH6299, ZH7009] (redeem, ransom) means "to free someone who is bound by legal or cultic obligation by the payment of a price" (Mays 1976:134). In Deuteronomy the term "designates a legal act of redemption from slavery" (NIDOTTE 3.579). Yahweh paid the ransom for freeing Israel from slavery in Egypt and making the nation his "firstborn" child (cf. NIDOTTE 3.578). Israel's debt to Yahweh as a ransomed people was covenant obedience, not extravagant ritual sacrifices (6:6-7).

Moses, Aaron, and Miriam. Not only did God ransom Israel from slavery in Egypt, he gave them a plurality of leadership for organization and oversight in the process of transforming the Hebrew slaves into the people of Yahweh. The OT idiom "I sent . . . to help you" (*shalakh* [TH7971, ZH8938] + *paneh* [TH6440, ZH7156], lit., "I sent before you") emphasizes the divine appointment of the three siblings (cf. Andersen and Freedman 2000:518-519). Moses, Aaron, and Miriam were the children of Amram and Jochebed, descendants of Levi (Exod 6:20; 1 Chr 6:3). Moses was called and commissioned by God to be Israel's deliverer and lawgiver, and he embodies the Sinai experience for Israel (Exod 3:10; cf. Mal 4:4). Moses's epitaph is that of a unique prophet of God, one who knew the Lord "face to face" (Deut 34:10). Aaron was the older brother of Moses and the first high priest of Israel (Exod 4:14-16; 29:29-30). He was appointed as a spokesman for Moses and is best known for his role in the golden calf episode after the Exodus from Egypt (Exod 32). Micah is the only OT prophet to mention Aaron. Andersen and Freedman (2000:521) note that Aaron is an OT character without a story of his own, that is, "there are no Aaron stories without Moses." Miriam was the sister of Aaron and Moses, and she is mentioned only twice outside the Pentateuch (6:4; 1 Chr 6:3). She was a prophetess and a singer, and her association with the victory hymn commemorating the Exodus may account for her presence in Micah's list (Exod 15:20-21).

6:5 King Balak of Moab. He conspired with the leaders of Midian to hire Balaam to destroy the Hebrews by a prophetic curse as they traveled from Sinai to Canaan after the Exodus. His plan was to thus preserve the autonomy of the Moabite kingdom (Num 22:1-8). Due to God's intervention, however, Balaam could only bless the Hebrews, much to Balak's consternation (Num 23:11, 25; 24:10).

Moab. See note on Amos 2:1.

Balaam son of Beor. A prophet and diviner from Pethor on the Euphrates River in Mesopotamia (perhaps an Aramean or Syrian) hired by King Balak of Moab to pronounce a curse upon Israel and halt their advance through the Transjordan into the land of Canaan (Num 22:4-11). The NT condemns Balaam for his greed as a prophet seeking to profit from his oracles of divine revelation (2 Pet 2:15-16; Jude 1:11).

Acacia Grove to Gilgal. Micah telescopes the post-Exodus experience in the Sinai desert with Yahweh in his reference to Acacia and Gilgal. Acacia (or Shittim, NIV) "was the last staging post in the wilderness and Gilgal the first encampment in the promised land" (McKeating 1971:184). Sandwiched between the two is the tragic episode of Israel's unfaithfulness to Yahweh at Baal-Peor (Num 25; cf. Josh 3:1; 4:19).

faithfulness. Lit., the "righteous acts of Yahweh" (*tsidqoth* [TH6666, ZH7407]). On Micah's use of the Hebrew word *tsadaq* in recalling "a mighty act of deliverance," see NIDOTTE 3.763; cf. Allen's (1976:362) translation of 6:5b: "try to appreciate Yahweh's saving acts."

6:6 bow. Bowing the head or bowing low before God is a common worship posture in the OT (cf. Ps 95:6), although the word used in this context is quite uncommon (*kapap* [TH3721, ZH4104]; cf. NIDOTTE 2.689).

offerings. The reference here is to burnt offerings (*'olah* [TH5930, ZH6592]). This type of sacrifice was a sin offering in which the entire animal was consumed by fire upon the altar (Lev 1). It symbolized total homage to God and was intended to effect atonement for personal sin (Lev 1:3-4).

yearling calves. Calves could be sacrificed once they were a week old (cf. Lev 9:3; 22:27). Yearling calves were considered the best, "obviously, the older the beast, the more had been spent on its upkeep and the greater the economic loss to the worshiper" (Allen 1976:370).

6:7 *thousands of rams.* The ram (*'ayil* [TH352, ZH380]) was an animal used for sin offerings (Lev 5:15; 6:6; 16:3). The large numbers may be an allusion to the thousands of animals offered in sacrifice by King Solomon at the dedication of the Temple (1 Kgs 8:63).

ten thousand rivers of olive oil. According to Allen (1976:370), "oil was the ceremonial accompaniment of a number of offerings . . . here its amount is rhetorically exaggerated."

6:8 *requires.* Lit., "seeking" (*darash* [TH1875, ZH2011]). The participial form of the verb suggests this is an ongoing expectation on God's part. Micah may have Deut 10:12-13 in mind where Moses indicates that God asks his followers to fear and obey him, and to love and worship him wholeheartedly (cf. 2 Chr 16:9).

do what is right. Lit., "do justice" (*mishpat* [TH4941, ZH5477]). See the note for "justice" in 3:8.

love mercy. The word *khesed* [TH2617, ZH2876] (mercy) describes the loyal love of Yahweh for his people. "It is a word of relationship, expressing an attitude of covenant obligation. . . . As a word of partnership it betokens mutual loyalty, not only the faithfulness of God to man but man's faithfulness to God" (Allen 1976:373).

walk humbly. The verb "walk" (*halak* [TH1980, ZH2143]) connotes one's basic pattern of behavior or lifestyle (cf. Mays 1976:142, "a way of life that is humble . . . as by considered attention to another"). The word for "humble" (*tsana'* [TH6800, ZH7570]) is a rare term, found in the OT only in 6:8 and Prov 11:2 (cf. Andersen and Freedman 2000:529, "the traditional meaning is 'humbly,' but it is possible that the meaning inclines more to 'circumspectly' or even 'scrupulously'"). God lives with those whose spirits are "contrite and humble" (Isa 57:15), and Jesus taught that the humble will inherit the earth (Matt 5:5; on humility, see the commentary on Amos 6:1-14). The three expressions ("to do what is right, to love mercy, and to walk humbly with your God") are related to each other as representative of both the communal and the personal obligations of covenant relationship with Yahweh. For Micah they also define the "good" that God seeks from his people (6:8).

COMMENTARY

This unit of Micah's message (6:1-8) begins the Book of Judgment and Pardon (6:1–7:20). The oracle is a combination of two kinds of literary material: the covenant lawsuit (6:1-5) and a Torah liturgy in a question and answer format (6:6-8; see the discussion of literary form in R. L. Smith 1984:50). Limburg (1988:189-190) connects the catechetical structure to the questions posed in the entrance Psalms about who may enter the Temple for worship. The covenant lawsuit summoned Israel to appear in court and hear God's case against his people (6:1-3). The recitation of God's mighty deeds of deliverance associated with the Exodus from Egypt served to remind Israel of their obligation to Yahweh as the one who "redeemed" the nation (6:4-5). The Torah liturgy (6:6-8) is essentially a call to covenant obedience. The text is one of the great passages of the Old Testament because it epitomizes the message of the eighth-century Hebrew prophets. As Mays comments (1976:136), the passage is justly famous "because it raises and answers the fundamental question of faith: What does the sinner do to restore his (or her) relation to God?" Micah's answer to the question is formulated in two parts: The first addresses the priority of Israel's covenant faithfulness; the second pertains to the appropriate responses to God's covenant faithfulness, namely proper worship and the practice of social justice. Allen (1976:363) regards this passage as a notable example of messages of accusation in Old Testament prophetic literature that "end by issuing a warning and providing an explicit opportunity for the miscreants to mend their ways."

Biblical commentators have showered accolades on Micah 6:8 as one of the classic texts of the entire Bible. Barker and Bailey (1988:113-114) have aptly summarized the litany of praise for this motto of "practical religion" (cf. Smith, Ward, and Bewer 1911:123). Jewish commentary on the passage has been no less laudatory, as Boadt has observed, "the rabbis who commented on this verse in the early centuries of the Christian era called it a one-line summary of the whole Law" (1984:336). Micah's charge to pre-exilic Israel "to do what is right, to love mercy, and to walk humbly with your God" (6:8) anticipated the teaching of Jesus (some eight centuries later), who offered a digest of the requirements of the Mosaic covenant in his "double-love" command: " 'You must love the LORD your God with all your heart, all your soul, and all your mind.' This is the first and greatest commandment. A second is equally important: 'Love your neighbor as yourself.' The entire law and all the demands of the prophets are based on these two commandments" (Matt 22:37-38; cf. Deut 6:5; Lev 19:18).

Micah's hypothetical exchange with his audience begins with a question about worship, specifically, "What can we bring [to make up for what we've done]?" (6:6). As Mays (1976:136) notes, "the question is formulated and the answer delivered as though the saying were intended to settle the problem in a comprehensive and final way." The series of possible responses to the query escalates from a modest offering of yearling calves to the absurd extreme of the sacrifice of a firstborn child (6:6b-7). Micah's audience learns that God is not after things, but people—"it's you, not something, God wants" (Mays 1976:136). Limburg's (1988:192) analysis is pertinent: "The worshiper's question had been based on the false assumption that God wanted some *thing*." Micah's message has relevance for the contemporary Christian church because this is still an operating premise of many Christians—the false assumption that God wants my money, my time, my talents and abilities. Somehow we forget that God is still in the business of seeking people "whose hearts are fully committed to him" (2 Chr 16:9). This is the mission of Jesus, the Son of Man, and his church—to seek and to save those who are lost (Luke 19:10).

What does it mean "to do what is right, to love mercy, and to walk humbly with your God"? (6:8) Simundson (1996:580) notes that Micah's threefold statement of what God expects from people is intentionally "a general summary, leaving the details to further explication." Biblical commentators have adequately provided that explication. For example, "to do what is right" means to practice social justice and "work for fairness and equality for all, particularly the weak and powerless" (Simundson 1996:580). To "love mercy" is to extend loving-kindness "where no giving is required, it acts when no action is deserved, and it penetrates both attitudes and activities" (Craigie 1985:46). The third requirement, "to walk humbly with your God," is an orientation to life or a lifestyle of conformity with God's will (Alexander, Baker, and Waltke 1988:196). But Craigie (1985:47) insightfully observes that "although we may learn deeply from each of the three parts of the prophet's message, it is the collective whole which is most vital." That "collective whole" is nothing less than our obedience to God. The false worshiper thinks "God's favor, like theirs, can be bought" so they "offer the Lord everything but what he asks for: their loving and obedient hearts" (Elwell 1996:527).

God's demands have not changed since Micah's day. He still seeks obedience from his people. In fact, this is the purpose of Jesus' gospel "that [all] . . . might believe and obey [Christ]" (Rom 16:26). As followers of Jesus, Christians are called to "live as God's obedient children" (1 Pet 1:14); and it is by being "obedient to the Good News of Christ" that God is glorified (2 Cor 9:13). As Waltke has recognized, "only those who comprehend his grace can and will offer him that (obedience)" (in Elwell 1996:527). God grant the realization of Paul's prayer for the church, that we may have "the power to understand, as all God's people should, how wide, how long, how high, and how deep his love is" (Eph 3:18).

◆ **B. Israel's Guilt and Punishment (6:9-16)**

⁹Fear the LORD if you are wise!
His voice calls to everyone in Jerusalem:
"The armies of destruction are coming; the LORD is sending them.*
¹⁰What shall I say about the homes of the wicked
filled with treasures gained by cheating?
What about the disgusting practice of measuring out grain with dishonest measures?*
¹¹How can I tolerate your merchants who use dishonest scales and weights?
¹²The rich among you have become wealthy
through extortion and violence.
Your citizens are so used to lying that their tongues can no longer tell the truth.

¹³"Therefore, I will wound you!
I will bring you to ruin for all your sins.

¹⁴You will eat but never have enough.
Your hunger pangs and emptiness will remain.
And though you try to save your money,
it will come to nothing in the end.
You will save a little,
but I will give it to those who conquer you.
¹⁵You will plant crops
but not harvest them.
You will press your olives
but not get enough oil to anoint yourselves.
You will trample the grapes
but get no juice to make your wine.
¹⁶You keep only the laws of evil King Omri;
you follow only the example of wicked King Ahab!
Therefore, I will make an example of you,
bringing you to complete ruin.
You will be treated with contempt, mocked by all who see you."

6:9 Hebrew *"Listen to the rod. / Who appointed it?"* 6:10 Hebrew *of using the short ephah?* The ephah was a unit for measuring grain.

NOTES

6:9 Fear the LORD. The MT actually reads "see your name" (*yir'eh* [TH7200, ZH8011]) rather than "fear your name." The same consonants may be read as "fear" (*yare'* [TH3372, ZH3707]), which is the reading the NLT has opted for, along with many other modern versions (NASB, NIV, RSV, ESV). The fear of Yahweh is the beginning of wisdom. The word may signify terror or dread, respect, reverence, and even worship. Here the prophet may have worship in mind, since "the fear of the Lord associated with worship is characterized by obedience to his decrees and commandments" (NIDOTTE 2.530).

wise. The word *tushiyah* [TH8454, ZH9370] "is associated with prudence and knowledge . . . it means the successful application of sound wisdom" (Andersen and Freedman 2000:546). Perhaps the expression is an example of Micah's sarcasm since the people had foolishly ignored the teaching of the Hebrew wisdom tradition (cf. Prov 2:12-15; 3:7). Commentators note that the text of 6:9 is badly damaged (cf. the preceding note), "too uncertain to comment upon" according to Alexander, Baker, and Waltke (1988:196-197).

6:10 cheating. Lit., "wickedness, evil" (*rasha'* [TH7563A, ZH8401]). The context of Micah's indictment suggests the treasures of the rich were secured by dishonest means.

dishonest measures. Lit., a "short ephah" (*'epath razon* [TH374/7332, ZH406/8137]). The ephah was a standardized unit of dry measure equivalent to approximately one-half bushel (cf. Walton, Matthews, and Chavalas 2000:786). Defrauding consumers with false measures was a violation of Mosaic law; such practices are detestable to God (Lev 19:35-36; Deut 25:13-16; cf. Amos 8:5).

6:11 dishonest scales and weights. The "scales of wickedness" (*mo'zene resha'* [TH3976/7562, ZH4404/8400]) refers to the vendor's trick of tampering with the balance bar and two scale pans in such a way that the consumer was shorted in the amount of product actually purchased. The "bag of false weights" (*kis 'abene mirmah* [TH3599/68/4820, ZH3967/74/5327]) refers to the deception of using stone weights heavier than the standard shekel weight utilized in commercial dealings. Defrauding consumers with false weights was a violation of Mosaic law (Lev 19:35-36; Deut 25:13-16).

6:12 violence. In the OT prophets the word (*khamas* [TH2555, ZH2805]) describes various forms of exploitation of the socially disadvantaged, accomplished by means of physical and psychological violence (cf. NIDOTTE 2.177-179).

lying. The word (*sheqer* [TH8267, ZH9214]) indicates pretentious behavior and deceptive words, "breaking faith with others by presenting deception/falsehood rather than truth" (NIDOTTE 4.248). The word is understood as false testimony in the ninth commandment of the Decalogue (Exod 20:16; see note on Mic 2:11).

6:13 ruin. The curses threatened against Israel for covenant disobedience include "ruin" or "desolation" (*shamem* [TH8074, ZH9037]; cf. Lev 26:31-32).

6:14 never have enough. The irony of the sins of selfishness like greed and covetousness is that those who fall prey to them are never satisfied (cf. Prov 27:20; Eccl 1:8; 5:10).

6:15 plant crops but not harvest them. The curses for covenant disobedience include being denied the opportunity to enjoy the fruit of one's labors, whether in the field, orchard, or vineyard (cf. Deut 28:30, 33, 38-40).

6:16 laws of evil King Omri. Although King Omri predated Micah by more than a century, "the text assumes that the sins of the infamous Omri and Ahab have become legendary and serve as a paradigm of apostasy, turpitude, cupidity, and injustice" (Alexander, Baker, and Waltke 1988:199). The OT record preserves no specific laws or rulings exemplifying the evil character of Omri's reign (cf. 1 Kgs 16:21-28).

example of wicked King Ahab. Micah referred, no doubt, to Ahab's marriage to the Tyrian princess Jezebel (1 Kgs 16:31), the subsequent importation of the Phoenician Baal cult into the northern kingdom of Israel (1 Kgs 16:32-33), and Ahab's murder of Naboth for the purpose of seizing his vineyard as "crown property" (1 Kgs 21).

COMMENTARY

The second message (6:9-16) in the Book of Judgment and Pardon (6:1-7:20) is a judgment oracle. The passage is a continuation of the lawsuit oracle of the preceding speech (6:1-5) and includes the indictments against Israel (6:9-12) and the sentence (6:13-16). "Micah now shuts the door that left open the possibility of restoration (6:1-8) and publicly proclaims the sentence condemning the city to destruction" (Alexander, Baker, and Waltke 1988:196).

Micah employed vocabulary connected especially with the book of Proverbs, indicating his familiarity with the Hebrew wisdom tradition (i.e., "Fear the LORD," and "wise"; see notes on 6:9). The Hebrews understood the way of wisdom as instruction that prompted the practical outworking of godliness in human behavior. Yet, they also recognized that wisdom was more than the mere teachings of the sages or the distillation of human experience garnered over the years and passed on to the next generation. The ultimate goal of Hebrew wisdom was a proper relationship to Yahweh, the very God of Wisdom (Job 12:13; Isa 31:1-2). This "Lord who is wise" has revealed his knowledge and understanding in creation, and he continues to display his wisdom in the providential oversight of human affairs and rule of the nations (e.g., Ps 104:24; Prov 3:19; Isa 10:13). As the God of wisdom, he also grants this gift to those searching for it like hidden treasure (1 Kgs 3:28; Prov 2:4; Dan 2:21). This implies an active search for wisdom on our parts, much like the miner who extracts precious gems from the rock-cut caves of the mountains (cf. Job 28). Thankfully, the New Testament also teaches us that the pursuit of divine wisdom is ultimately an exercise in prayer, since God liberally dispenses wisdom to those who ask him for it (Jas 1:5).

The Old Testament expression "the fear of the LORD" best conveys this relational dimension of Hebrew wisdom (Ps 111:10; Prov 1:7). The fear of the Lord was the foundation of Hebrew wisdom, and the tenet represents a theological matrix of interrelated ideas, attitudes, and actions, including the following:

1. The desire to gain understanding arising from a decision grounded in the human will (Prov 1:29; 2:5)
2. Awe and reverence for the God of creation and redemption that prompts genuine worship and willing obedience to his commands (Prov 24:21)
3. Dread at God's holiness and trepidation of his divine judgment (Eccl 12:13-14)
4. Faith and trust in God's plan for human life, and a rejection of self-reliance (Ps 115:1; Prov 3:5-6)
5. Hating and avoiding evil, and a refusal to envy the wicked (Prov 3:7; 9:13; 16:6; 23:17)

6. Generally the reward of prosperity (whether material or spiritual) and long life to the prudent (Prov 10:27; 14:27; 19:23)
7. Disciplined instruction that instills wisdom, humility, and honor (Prov 15:33; 22:4)

The personification of wisdom in the book of Proverbs also illustrates the relational aspects of the theological concept of the fear of the Lord. Wisdom is portrayed both as an itinerant female teacher seeking students at the city gates (Prov 8:1-12) and as a preexistent master architect involved in the design and implementation of God's creative works (Prov 8:22-31). In each case, special emphasis is placed on the experience of a relationship with the person of wisdom.

The New Testament further develops this concept of the person of wisdom by identifying Jesus the Messiah as the pre-existent One by whom God created all things and in whom all things hold together (Col 1:15-17). Elsewhere the apostle Paul indicates that the Christian's journey in the way of wisdom begins when he or she acknowledges that God made Christ to be wisdom itself for our benefit (1 Cor 1:30). Even the heavenly worshipers praise the Lamb as the only one worthy to receive power, riches, wisdom, strength, honor, and glory (Rev 5:12). Micah subtly reminds us that in our worship of God we worship the person in whom all wisdom dwells—Jesus the Messiah.

◆   C. Misery Turned to Hope (7:1-20)

¹How miserable I am!
I feel like the fruit picker after the harvest
who can find nothing to eat.
Not a cluster of grapes or a single early fig
can be found to satisfy my hunger.
²The godly people have all disappeared;
not one honest person is left on the earth.
They are all murderers,
setting traps even for their own brothers.
³Both their hands are equally skilled at doing evil!
Officials and judges alike demand bribes.
The people with influence get what they want,
and together they scheme to twist justice.
⁴Even the best of them is like a brier;

the most honest is as dangerous as a hedge of thorns.
But your judgment day is coming swiftly now.
Your time of punishment is here, a time of confusion.
⁵Don't trust anyone—
not your best friend or even your wife!
⁶For the son despises his father.
The daughter defies her mother.
The daughter-in-law defies her mother-in-law.
Your enemies are right in your own household!

⁷As for me, I look to the LORD for help.
I wait confidently for God to save me,
and my God will certainly hear me.
⁸Do not gloat over me, my enemies!
For though I fall, I will rise again.
Though I sit in darkness,
the LORD will be my light.

⁹I will be patient as the LORD
 punishes me,
 for I have sinned against him.
But after that, he will take up my case
 and give me justice for all I have
 suffered from my enemies.
The LORD will bring me into the light,
 and I will see his righteousness.
¹⁰Then my enemies will see that the
 LORD is on my side.
They will be ashamed that they
 taunted me, saying,
"So where is the LORD—
 that God of yours?"
With my own eyes I will see their
 downfall;
 they will be trampled like mud in
 the streets.

¹¹In that day, Israel, your cities will be
 rebuilt,
 and your borders will be extended.
¹²People from many lands will come and
 honor you—
 from Assyria all the way to the
 towns of Egypt,
from Egypt all the way to the
 Euphrates River,*
 and from distant seas and
 mountains.
¹³But the land* will become empty and
 desolate
 because of the wickedness of those
 who live there.

¹⁴O LORD, protect your people with your
 shepherd's staff;
 lead your flock, your special
 possession.
Though they live alone in a thicket
 on the heights of Mount Carmel,*

let them graze in the fertile pastures
 of Bashan and Gilead
 as they did long ago.

¹⁵"Yes," says the LORD,
 "I will do mighty miracles for you,
like those I did when I rescued you
 from slavery in Egypt."

¹⁶All the nations of the world will stand
 amazed
 at what the LORD will do for you.
They will be embarrassed
 at their feeble power.
They will cover their mouths in silent
 awe,
 deaf to everything around them.
¹⁷Like snakes crawling from their holes,
 they will come out to meet the LORD
 our God.
They will fear him greatly,
 trembling in terror at his presence.

¹⁸Where is another God like you,
 who pardons the guilt of the
 remnant,
 overlooking the sins of his special
 people?
You will not stay angry with your
 people forever,
 because you delight in showing
 unfailing love.
¹⁹Once again you will have compassion
 on us.
 You will trample our sins under your
 feet
 and throw them into the depths of
 the ocean!
²⁰You will show us your faithfulness and
 unfailing love
 as you promised to our ancestors
 Abraham and Jacob long ago.

7:12 Hebrew *the river.* 7:13 Or *earth.* 7:14 Or *surrounded by a fruitful land.*

NOTES

7:1 *How miserable I am!* Micah's use of a rare interjection of "woe" (*'alelay* [TH480, ZH518]; only in 7:1; Job 10:15) sets the tone of lament for the first message of the book's final oracle (cf. Mays 1976:151).

7:2 *godly people have all disappeared.* Lit., "perished" (*'abad* [TH6, ZH6]). This is a common complaint of the righteous in biblical lament literature, as people despaired over the seeming triumph of evil (cf. Ps 12:1; Isa 57:1). The psalmist assures us that in the end it is the unrighteous who will "disappear" (Ps 1:6).

traps. The word (*tsud* [TH6679, ZH7421]) refers to hunters trapping animals with nets (NIDOTTE 3.775). Jeremiah compares the wicked lying in wait for victims like hunters hiding behind a blind (Jer 5:26).

7:3 bribes. The prophet continues his use of unusual vocabulary (*shillum* [TH7966, ZH8936], "repayment, retribution, bribe"; only in 7:3; Isa 34:8; Hos 9:7). See notes on 3:11.

7:4 brier . . . hedge of thorns. The brier (*khedeq* [TH2312, ZH2537], only 7:4; Prov 15:19) and the thorn hedge (*mesukah* [TH4534, ZH5004], only 7:4) symbolize the godless (Ezek 2:6; cf. Allen 1976:387). Like worthless thorns, the wicked are burned in the fire of divine judgment (cf. 2 Sam 23:6; Isa 33:12).

judgment day. Lit., "the day of your watchmen" (*tsapah* [TH6822, ZH7595]). The NLT follows the proposal of the BHS to read *mishpat* ("judgment") for the MT *mitspeh* ("watchman") in view of the previous reference to *mishpat* in v. 3 (cf. Mays 1976:149, who omits *mitspeh* ["your watcher"] as a gloss). The watchman or sentinel was a lookout posted on the towers of city walls; it was their job to alert the city of any threat of danger. The expression "is a metaphor for the prophets who announced the approaching day of God's judgment" (Alexander, Baker, and Waltke 1988:201).

punishment. The word (*pequddatheka* [TH6486, ZH7213], "your visitation") is used by the prophets Isaiah, Hosea, and Jeremiah to refer to the time of God's judgment associated with the day of the Lord (Isa 10:3; Jer 8:2; 10:15; 11:23; 23:12; Hos 9:7).

time of confusion. Another rare word in Micah's vocabulary (*mebukah* [TH3998, ZH4428], "terror, alarm"; only 7:4; Isa 22:5). The uncertainty and chaos of "confusion" (*mehumah* [TH4103, ZH4539]) is listed among the curses threatened against the Hebrews for violation of Yahweh's covenant (Deut 28:20, 28). The day of the Lord is associated with divinely instigated confusion, tumult (Isa 22:5; Ezek 7:7), and panic (Zech 12:4; 14:13).

7:5-6 The prophet described a scene of social anarchy in which the most basic relationships between family and friends have disintegrated. Jeremiah described a similar situation that would surely bring divine punishment (Jer 9:4-5, 9). Jesus made reference to 7:5-6 to describe the terrible social conditions into which he sent his apostles (Matt 10:21, 35-36).

7:7 I wait confidently. This is one of the evidences of faith: waiting on the Lord to act on behalf of his people (cf. Job 13:15; Pss 33:22; 71:14; Lam 3:21, 24). The word *yakhal* [TH3176, ZH3498] "denotes an enduring, expectant hope" because God himself is the object of that waiting (NIDOTTE 2.436).

save. The word (*yesha'* [TH3468, ZH3829]) is prominent in the prophetic salvation oracles and refers in the more immediate sense to Yahweh's physical restoration of the nation of Israel after the people's exile (e.g., Zech 8:13). The term is also used in an eschatological sense to refer to the physical and spiritual restoration of Israel as the elect of God in the day of the Lord (e.g., Ezek 34:22). The same root word (*yasha'* [TH3467 (cf. 3444), ZH3828 (cf. 3802)], "to deliver, save") is applied to the Exodus from Egypt, the "salvation-event" of the OT (cf. Exod 14:13, 30; 15:2). Salvation, or "victory," belongs to the Lord (Ps 3:8), and only the God of Israel has "the power to save" (Isa 63:1).

my God will certainly hear me. The great hope and surety of the righteous is that God hears and responds to their prayers (cf. 1 Kgs 8:29-30; Pss 4:3; 6:9). The fact that God "hears" (*shama'* [TH8085, ZH9048]) prayers distinguishes him from the idols (Isa 46:7; Hab 2:19). (See further the discussion of the "Living God" in the commentary on Amos 5:1-17.)

7:8 darkness . . . light. The reversal of darkness into light is a repeated motif in Isaiah describing the transforming character of the day of the Lord (cf. Isa 9:2; 42:16; 58:8, 10).

Light ('or [TH216, ZH240]) is the symbol of the various aspects of Yahweh's covenant blessings, including his divine presence and all the attendant material and spiritual benefits that accompany being in right relationship with God (e.g., Deut 28:1-14; cf. NIDOTTE 1.327-328). Jesus the Messiah is the culmination of this dramatic movement from darkness to light. He is the Light of the World as the Son of God (John 8:12; 9:5), and his ministry of teaching, healing, and redemption through the cross rescued us from the kingdom of darkness and brought us into the kingdom of light (cf. Eph 5:8; Col 1:13; 1 Pet 2:9; see note on Mic 3:6).

7:9 punishes. The verb (za'ap [TH2197, ZH2408]) in this context means "storming rage" in the sense of "just anger" not "uncontrolled fury" (cf. NIDOTTE 1.1129-1130). "The knowledge of YHWH lets Zion accept her distress as the effect of his rage . . . she may appear to be in the power of the enemy, but she experiences his punishment of her" (Mays 1976:159).

I have sinned. The justification of God's judgment "is acknowledged with a simple and unqualified confession: 'I have sinned against him'" (Mays 1976:159; cf. Pss 41:4; 51:4; Lam 1:18; 3:26-27).

my case. Previously Yahweh's "lawsuit" or "case" (rib [TH7379, ZH8190]) was one of indictment and punishment as prosecutor (see note on 6:2). Now Yahweh takes up Israel's case as a defense attorney for the purpose of reparation and restoration.

justice. See note on 3:8.

7:11 In that day. This phrase (with variations) is prophetic shorthand for the eschatological day of the Lord. See the notes on 2:4; 4:1; 4:6.

7:14 shepherd's staff. The word (shebet [TH7626, ZH8657]) may refer to a "rod, staff, scepter, tribe" (cf. NIDOTTE 4.27-29). The shepherd's staff in this context is a symbol of God's protection and pastoral care for his people Israel (cf. Ps 23:4). The prophet mentions the rod or staff as an instrument of punishment or discipline in 5:1 (see note).

special possession. The nation of Israel is Yahweh's special possession or "inheritance" (nakhalah [TH5159, ZH5709]) by virtue of his election of the ancestors of the Hebrew people (Gen 17:7), his deliverance of the Hebrew people from slavery in Egypt (Deut 7:6; 14:2), and his covenant charter with them, ratified at Mount Sinai (Exod 19:5; cf. NIDOTTE 3.79-80). The special relationship God has with Israel is depicted variously in the OT as that between a parent and a child (Deut 32:6; Isa 66:13), a husband and a wife (Jer 2:2), or even a shepherd and a flock of sheep as in this passage (cf. Ezek 34:17, 22).

Carmel. A mountainous area dividing the plain of Acco to the north and the plain of Sharon to the south in northern Israel. The lush tree cover of Mount Carmel made it a symbol of beauty and fertility (cf. Isa 35:2).

Bashan and Gilead. The region of biblical Bashan was located east and northeast of the Sea of Galilee and, like Lebanon, its defining features were superb stands of timber and fertile pastureland (Josh 12:5; Isa 2:13; Jer 50:19). The region of biblical Gilead was located in the Transjordan between the Yarmuk and Arnon Rivers (cf. Deut 3:8-10). Gilead featured rugged wooded highlands and excellent pastureland (cf. Num 32:1).

7:15 miracles. The word pala' [TH6381, ZH7098] refers especially to the plagues God brought against the Egyptians as the means by which he secured Israel's deliverance from Pharaoh (Exod 3:20; Ps 106:21-22a).

I rescued you from slavery in Egypt. The Exodus is the defining redemptive event in the OT for Israel as the "delivered" or "rescued" people of God (Ps 80:8) and Yahweh as the "deliverer" or "savior" of Israel (Ps 106:21). "So fundamental to Israel's experience as a redeemed community was this act of deliverance that it became a central element of her confession" (cf. Deut 26:8; NIDOTTE 2.499). Beyond this, in the Exodus Yahweh executed judgment upon all the gods of the Egyptians (Exod 12:12) and publicly demonstrated his superiority over all the gods of the people (Exod 15:11). Elsewhere in the OT it is this ability of Yahweh to deliver his people from their enemies that marks him as the one truly omnipotent God among all gods (Deut 3:23-24; Isa 36:11-20; see note on Mic 6:4).

7:18 Where is another God like you? This rhetorical question (*mi-'el kamoka* [TH4310/3644, ZH4769/4017]) may be a pun on the prophet's name: "Micah" (*mikah* [TH4318, ZH4777]), "who is like Yah[weh]?"

pardons. The Hebrew idiom here (*nasa'* [TH5375, ZH5951] + *'awon* [TH5771, ZH6411], "to lift up sin, guilt") means to "remove guilt" or "forgive sin" (cf. NIDOTTE 3.162). The prophet Isaiah called upon Israel to seek the Lord because he will have mercy on sinners, "he will forgive generously" (*salakh* [TH5545, ZH6142]) (Isa 55:7; see note on Amos 7:2).

you delight in showing unfailing love. The word is a highly emotive term (*khapets* [TH2654, ZH2911]; cf. TDOT 5.92-93, 104-105), suggesting God is so eager to demonstrate his *khesed* [TH2617, ZH2876] to human beings that he trembles with delight at the thought (cf. Jer 9:24; Hos 6:6).

7:19 you will have compassion. God saves and restores his people because of his "compassion" (*rakham* [TH7355, ZH8163]). The word embodies female attributes of caring and nurturing, of maternal concern for one's children (see the discussion in Meyers and Meyers 1993:193). Compassion is an attribute of God (Ps 111:4), but it is also a divine prerogative, as he will show compassion to anyone he chooses (Exod 33:19). God's compassion extends to all those who fear him (Ps 103:13) and is bounded only by the greatness of his unfailing love (Lam 3:32).

trample our sins under your feet and throw them into the depths of the ocean! The nature of God's salvation is such that once he pardons sin, he blots them out "and will never think of them again" (Isa 43:25; cf. Ps 103:12; Isa 1:18; 44:22; Jer 31:34).

7:20 faithfulness. The word (*'emeth* [TH571, ZH622]) can mean "fidelity, truth, faithful(ness)." God is a faithful God (Ps 31:5). He keeps every promise (*'emeth*) forever (Ps 146:6).

unfailing love. The word (*khesed* [TH2617, ZH2876], "loyalty, faithfulness, kindness, favor") is a covenant term. It is rooted in the very character of God (Lam 3:22), and embedded in the treaty he established with Israel at Mt. Sinai through Moses (Deut 7:9; 30:16). In God, faithfulness and unfailing love meet together (Ps 85:10). The appropriate response to this God who embodies faithfulness and unfailing love as attributes of his divine being is worship and thanksgiving (Ps 138:2). (See the discussion of "Divine hesed" in NIDOTTE 2.213-217.)

promised . . . Abraham and Jacob. This a reference to the covenants Yahweh made with Abraham and Jacob that included promises to make a great nation out of their innumerable descendants (cf. Gen 17:5; 22:17; 28:14). God's promise (*shaba'* [TH7650, ZH8678]) "is tantamount to an oath . . . it was unthinkable that his word would not come to pass" (NIDOTTE 4.32-33). As Allen (1976:404) observes, "The Christian Church is no stranger to this assurance, for the same theme of laying claim to the heritage of promised grace reappears in Acts 3:25; Gal. 3:6-29."

COMMENTARY

The final speech (7:1-20) of Micah's Book of Judgment and Pardon (6:1–7:20) begins on a note of gloom and despair but ends with a word of hope. The concluding oracle is comprised of a song of lament (7:1-6) and a prophetic liturgy (7:7-20; so R. L. Smith 1984:56) or liturgical hymn (so Alexander, Baker, and Waltke 1988:202). All are agreed that the closing passage of the book is a "liturgy" because "it takes the form of a psalm in which more than one voice is heard" (Allen 1976:392-393). There is some disagreement, however, on the division of two pericopes (e.g., R. L. Smith 1984:54 and Mays 1976:149-150 break the lament at 7:6, while Alexander, Baker, and Waltke 1988:199 and Allen 1976:383 include 7:7 in the lament). Andersen and Freedman (2000:563) identify 7:1-6 as a literary unit (on the basis of the pronoun "I" in the opening and closing colons of the lament) but admit that "perhaps v. 7 should be included, especially as it picks up the root *tsapah* [TH6822, ZH7595] from v. 4." It is possible that the confession of trust in Yahweh in 7:7 serves double-duty as the transitional refrain between the lament and the liturgical hymn.

Micah resorts to the lament (7:1-6) to bewail the evil times in which he lives, to express what Mays (1976:150) describes as the "helpless hopelessness he feels." Like Elijah, he was convinced that he alone was left among the community of the righteous (cf. 1 Kgs 19:10). The prophet bore a heavy burden because he stood as mediator between Yahweh and the people of Israel. His task was "not only to pass [God's] word on to them but to pray concerning them. This lament fulfills both functions, relieving before God his feelings of despair and trust and also making plain to the people the divine view of their corruption" (Allen 1976:384). Micah's lament omits any address to God and moves directly to his sorrowful complaint over the moral failure of his audience (7:1-4a). He then offers a brief confession of trust in God's justice (4b), followed by a negative confession of trust directed to the people (i.e., all relationships sharing a bond of trust have disintegrated in society, 7:5-6).

Allen (1976:393) understands the hymn (7:7-20) as a comprehensive literary unit, a "liturgical symphony" made up of four movements: (1) a psalm of confidence spoken by Zion (7:7-10; although Allen begins the psalm with 7:8); (2) an oracle of salvation for Jerusalem and the people of Israel pronounced by the prophet (7:11-13); (3) a prayer of supplication (probably offered by the prophet, 7:14-17); and (4) a concluding doxology (sung [?] by the prophet, 7:18-20). It is possible Micah sang the liturgical hymn in the Temple, perhaps as part of some formal worship occasion.

The Hebrew lament tradition of the Old Testament has much to teach us today about the God of the Bible and our faith responses to him. First, it is necessary to distinguish "lament" from "lamentation" in the Old Testament. The "lamentation" is an expression of grief over a calamity that cannot be reversed (e.g., the death of an individual or the destruction of a city). The lamentation, then, is similar in tone and content to a funeral dirge. By contrast, the "lament" is an appeal to God's compassion for the purpose of intervening and changing a desperate situation for the better. The lament arises out of a circumstance or situation in which the final outcome has yet to be determined. The suppliant offers the prayer of lament as a vote of confidence in Yahweh as the faithful God who hears and answers the prayers of the needy. The lament may be an individual or community prayer, and each has a distinctive structure. The structure of the lament generally follows this form (Anderson 2000:60-65):

347

MICAH 7:1-20

1. Address to God (a formal appeal to God using one or several divine names or titles, often very brief)
2. Complaint (the airing of a specific crisis or distressing situation—e.g., war, famine, sickness, theodicy, etc.—sometimes the complaint includes a plea of forgiveness or the protestation of innocence)
3. Confession of trust (an expression of confidence in God despite present circumstances, often introduced by "but" or "nevertheless" and usually employing the word "trust")
4. Petition (a direct appeal for God to intervene and deliver the supplicant from the given trial)
5. Words of assurance (an expression of faith in God and the belief that the prayer will be heard and answered)
6. Vow of praise (a concluding exclamation of praise, often in the form of an oath testifying to the greatness of God)

Micah's use of the lament (7:1-6) in his concluding oracle reminds us that God is not too weak to save us, and he is not becoming deaf (Isa 59:1). Those who have placed their hope in God need the assurance that their hope is not misplaced. The lament tradition certifies that the hope of the righteous is not misplaced and that "the earnest prayer of a righteous person has great power and produces wonderful results" (Jas 5:16). Perhaps equally significant, however, the lament tradition offers the righteous a legitimate vehicle for expressing honest doubt in the form of complaint to God. As the "triumphalism" of modernist Christianity gives way to the transparency and brokenness of postmodern Christianity, believers in Christ increasingly recognize that God is receptive to hear even our honest doubt (cf. Ps 13:1). God knows how weak we are, he knows we are only dust (Ps 103:14). Why not come to God with our "masks" off? The lament tradition offers the Christian church a biblical pattern for dealing with honest doubt before it becomes bitterness and cynicism. The virtue and beauty of the lament is that it turns the complaint, our honest doubt, into a vow of praise. This nurtures biblical faith and glorifies God (cf. Brueggemann 1995:98-111). Like Micah, the lament tradition enables us to look to God for help and wait confidently for him to save (7:7).

Allen (1976:401) likens Micah's prophetic hymn to a liturgical symphony, wherein he identifies the fourth and last movement (7:18-20) as "a choral piece of devotion and doxology." But Micah's doxology is more than a "praise chorus" extolling the attributes of God. The relationship of his concluding doxology (7:18-20) to Yahweh's revelation of his name and confession of its meaning is widely recognized (e.g., Mays 1976:167; Simundson 1996:589). Waltke notes, "that ancient creed guarantees each generation of the faithful that God will keep his promise to the fathers and not terminate Israel's history in a cul-de-sac" (Alexander, Baker, and Waltke 1988:207). So then, Micah's doxology also has a creedal quality that documents God's redemptive response to Israel's egregious sin of forging and worshiping a calf of gold soon after their Exodus from Egypt (Exod 32). This divine response is rooted in the character of God, his benevolent attributes of faithfulness and unfailing love, compassion, and a forgiving spirit (7:18-20).

Micah's creedal doxology is important for several reasons. First, it has value in and of itself as a catechism on the essential nature of God. Second, it serves to remind us that divine revelation is vitally connected to Israel's history. Third, Micah's doxology anticipates the New Testament creedal hymns of Paul that laud the person and work of Jesus the Messiah (e.g., 1 Cor 15:3-4; 1 Tim 3:16). But beyond all this, Micah's creedal hymn is precious to the contemporary Christian church simply because it is a creed! The basic purpose of the creed "is to compress historical events into a summary statement" (Webber 1994:75). Such creedal statements not only recall historical events but they attest the special (covenant) relationship Yahweh had with his people. Thus, there is a sense in which "the recitation of these events in faith renews the relationship of the covenant they represent" (Webber 1994:75).

The same is no less true for the New Testament creedal doxologies (and to a lesser degree the Christological creeds of the early church). The recitation of the creedal statement is a confession of faith that renews and affirms loyalty to a God who is faithful and loving, and who in his compassion forgives sin and restores right relationship with repentant people—whether Israel's worshiping the golden calf episode or the struggling Corinthian church of Paul's day. The creedal recitation of God's capacities to show compassion and pardon sin not only provides historical and theological continuity with the past, but also offers hope for the present.

The creedal doxology we find in these last verses of Micah gives testimony to the fact that God is still in the habit of delighting in showing mercy to sinners in this historical era, as well. This is also the "good news" of the Christian gospel, the truth about God's great kindness to sinners in Jesus Christ (Col 1:6). What better message to take to a world doomed because of its many sins than the story of the God who is rich in mercy (Eph 2:1-5)?

BIBLIOGRAPHY

Alexander, D., D. W. Baker, and B. Waltke
1988 *Obadiah, Jonah, Micah.* Tyndale Old Testament Commentary. Downers Grove: InterVarsity.

Allen, L.
1976 *The Books of Joel, Obadiah, Jonah, and Micah.* New International Commentary on the Old Testament. Grand Rapids: Eerdmans.

Andersen, F. I., and D. N. Freedman
2000 *Micah.* Anchor Bible. New York: Doubleday.

Anderson, Bernhard W.
2000 *Out of the Depths: The Psalms Speak for Us Today.* 3rd ed. Louisville: Westminster.

Augustine
1956 On the Trinity in the *Nicene and Post-Nicene Fathers* (Series 1). Editor, P. Schaff. Grand Rapids: Eerdmans.

Barker, K. L., and D. W. Bailey
1988 *Micah—Zephaniah.* New American Commentary. Nashville: Broadman & Holman.

Boadt, L.
1984 *Reading the Old Testament.* New York: Paulist.

Brueggemann, W.
1982 *Living Toward a Vision: Biblical Reflections on Shalom.* New York: United Church Press.

1995 The Costly Loss of Lament. Pp. 98-111 in *The Psalms and the Life of Faith.* Editor, P. D. Miller. Minneapolis: Augsburg Fortress.

Bullock, C. H.
1986 *An Introduction to the Old Testament Prophetic Books.* Chicago: Moody.

Chisholm, R. B.
2002 *Handbook on the Prophets.* Grand Rapids: Baker.

Craigie, P. C.
1985 *Twelve Prophets.* Philadelphia: Westminster.

Dawn, Marva J.
1995 *Reaching Out without Dumbing Down.* Grand Rapids: Eerdmans.

Dorsey, D. A.
1999 *The Literary Structure of the Old Testament.* Grand Rapids: Baker.

Elwell, W.
1996 *Evangelical Dictionary of Biblical Theology.* Grand Rapids: Baker.

Hagstrom, D. G.
1988 *The Coherence of the Book of Micah: A Literary Analysis.* SBL Dissertation Series 89. Atlanta: Scholars Press.

Hildebrandt, Wilf
1995 *An Old Testament Theology of the Spirit of God.* Peabody, MA: Hendrickson.

Hillers, D. R.
1984 *Micah.* Hermeneia. Philadelphia: Fortress.

House, Paul R.
1998 *Old Testament Theology.* Downers Grove: InterVarsity.

Kaiser, W. C.
1992 *Micah—Malachi.* Communicator's Commentary. Waco: Word.

1995 *The Messiah in the Old Testament.* Grand Rapids: Zondervan.

King, P. J.
1988 *Amos, Hosea, Micah—An Archaeological Commentary.* Philadelphia: Westminster.

van Leeuwen, Ray
1986 Proverbs 30:21-23 and the Biblical World Upside Down. *Journal of Biblical Literature* 105:599-610.

Limburg, J.
1988 *Hosea–Micah*. Interpretation. Louisville: Westminster/John Knox.

McComiskey, T. E.
1985 Micah. Pp. 395-445 in *The Expositor's Bible Commentary*. Editor, F. E. Gaebelein. Grand Rapids: Zondervan.

McKane, W.
1998 *The Book of Micah*. International Critical Commentary. Edinburgh: T & T Clark.

McKeating, H.
1971 *Amos, Hosea, Micah*. Cambridge Bible Commentary. Cambridge: Cambridge University Press.

Mays, J. L.
1976 *Micah*. Philadelphia: Westminster.

Meyers, E., and C. Meyers
1993 *Zechariah 9–14*. Anchor Bible. New York: Doubleday.

Oden, T. C.
1998 *Systematic Theology: The Living God*. Peabody, MA: Prince.

Peterson, E., H.
2000 *The Message: The Prophets*. Colorado Springs: NavPress.

Petrotta, A. J.
1991 *Lexis Ludens: Wordplay and the Book of Micah*. American University Studies; Series VII, Theology and Religion 105. New York: Lang.

Prior, D.
1998 *The Message of Joel, Micah and Habakkuk*. Downers Grove: InterVarsity.

Shaw, C. S.
1993 *The Speeches of Micah: A Rhetorical–Historical Analysis*. Journal for the Study of the Old Testament Supplement 145. Sheffield: Journal of Study of the Old Testament.

Simundson, D. J.
1996 The Book of Micah. Pp. 553-589 in *The New Interpreter's Bible*. Editor, D. L. Petersen. Nashville: Abingdon.

Smith, G. V.
2001 *Hosea, Amos, Micah*. NIV Application Commentary. Grand Rapids: Zondervan.

Smith, J. M. P., W. H. Ward, and J. A. Bewer
1911 *A Critical and Exegetical Commentary on Micah, Zephaniah, Nahum, Habakkuk, Obadiah and Joel*. International Critical Commentary. Edinburgh: T & T Clark.

Smith, R. L
1984 *Micah–Malachi*. Word Biblical Commentary. Waco: Word.

Sweeney, M. A.
2001 *The Twelve Prophets: Micah, Nahum, Habakkuk, Zephaniah, Haggai, Zechariah, Malachi*. Collegeville, TX: Liturgical Press.

Thiele, Edwin R.
1983 *The Mysterious Numbers of the Hebrew Kings*. Grand Rapids: Zondervan.

VanGemeren, W. A.
1990 *Interpreting the Prophetic Word*. Grand Rapids: Zondervan.

Waltke, B. K.
1993 Micah. Pp. 591-764 in *An Exegetical and Expository Commentary on the Minor Prophets*. Editor, T. E. McComiskey. Grand Rapids: Baker.

1997 Micah: Theology of. Pp. 936-940 in *New International Dictionary of Old Testament Theology & Exegesis*. Editor, W. A. VanGemeren. Grand Rapids: Zondervan.

2007 *A Commentary on Micah*. Grand Rapids: Eerdmans.

Walton, H., V. H. Matthews, and M. W. Chavalas
2000 *Bible Background Commentary: Old Testament*. Downers Grove: InterVarsity.

Walton, John H., and Andrew Hill
2000 *A Survey of the Old Testament.* 2nd ed. Grand Rapids: Zondervan.

Webber, R. E.
1994 *Worship Old & New.* Rev. ed. Grand Rapids: Zondervan.

Westermann, C.
1991 *Basic Forms of Prophetic Speech.* Translator, H.C. White. Louisville: Westminster/John Knox.

Willis, J. T.
1966 *The Structure, Setting and Interrelationships of the Pericopes in the Book of Micah.* Ph.D. dissertation, Vanderbilt Divinity School.

Wolff, H. W.
1978 *Micah the Prophet.* Translator, R. D. Gehrke. Philadelphia: Fortress.

Wood, Leon J.
1976 *The Holy Spirit in the Old Testament.* Grand Rapids: Zondervan.

Nahum

RICHARD D. PATTERSON

INTRODUCTION TO
Nahum

NAHUM'S PROPHECY presents a graphic prophetic description of the fall of wicked Nineveh. Rather than continuing in the attitude of repentance displayed about a century earlier (see Jonah 3:6-10), the Ninevites resumed their godless oppression of others. Therefore, God's sure judgment would fall upon them. All nations, no matter how successful, will experience God's judgment if they are continually godless.

AUTHOR

Little is known of Nahum, the author of this short prophecy, beyond that which can be gleaned from his writings and the statement in the superscription that he was an "Elkoshite." This identifier has been understood to refer to a geographical location. A number of sites have been suggested, one on the left bank of the Tigris River, two in Galilee, and at least three in Judah. None of these views is conclusive, however. The author was acquainted with the people and places of Nineveh, but not in such a way that would necessitate more than good general knowledge. Thus the suggestion that Nahum's family may have been deported to Assyria after the fall of the northern kingdom, and that there Nahum gained firsthand knowledge of the area before returning to Judah, is speculative at best.

What is certain, however, is that the author had a high view of God and his word (1:2-10; cf. 1:12, 14; 2:2, 13; 3:5), preached against idolatry (1:14), immorality (3:4), injustice (2:11-12; 3:16, 19), and believed strongly in the eventual restoration of all God's people (1:12-13, 15; 2:2).[1]

DATE AND OCCASION OF WRITING

Because 3:8 mentions the fall of Thebes (663 BC) and predicts the fall of Nineveh (612 BC), the setting for Nahum's prophecy, if predictive, lies between these two events. The era largely parallels the reign of the Assyrian king Ashurbanipal (668–626 BC), a time when Assyrian imperialism was at its height and marked by a cultural flowering and a socio-political system that spanned the length and breadth of the Fertile Crescent (thus it has been termed the *Pax Assyriaca*). The book of Nahum is intimately bound up with this period. But to what portion of the period from the fall of Thebes to that of Nineveh does it belong? Those who place more weight on God's prophets as keen critics and observers of the times or who discount the plausibility of predictive prophecy tend to date the book late, either close to the time of Nineveh's fall or around the time of its capture (J. M. P. Smith 1911; Haupt [1907] places it as late as the Maccabbean era).

Conservative scholars usually assign a date to the book that antedates the fall of Nineveh but differ as to how long before 612 BC it was written. The position taken here assumes a time shortly after the fall of Thebes, whose collapse was a fresh lesson in the minds of Nahum's readers. Moreover, a civil war between the Assyrian ruler Ashurbanipal and his brother Shamash-shum-ukin was settled in 648 BC only after a bitter struggle and a gruesome massacre at the latter's power base in Babylon. From that time on, Nahum might well be expected to hold up the example of age-old Babylon, not Thebes, to the Assyrians. Further, the closer that one dates Nahum's prophecy to 612 BC, the more one would expect some mention of the forces that were to spell Assyria's doom, such as the Chaldeans, Medes, and Scythians. The failure to mention them could imply a time well before these peoples came to international prominence. All things considered, a date between 660 and 645 BC would appear to be most likely for the setting of the book.

AUDIENCE
Given the matters of authorship and the circumstances of writing mentioned above, I conclude that Nahum wrote to the people of Judah during the reign of Manasseh (698/697–642 BC). Judah's was a humbled and disillusioned populace, which had suffered not only the wickedness of its own king but also the reduction of the nation to Assyrian vassalage during the campaigning of Ashurbanipal (648 BC). Under such conditions, could Israel's God be viewed as still faithful to the promises to Abraham and David? Was he truly sovereign over the nations of this world?

Nahum's answer was a resounding yes! Despite all that had come to pass, God was in control of earth's history. All that had happened was but a prelude and a means to the judgment of both Judah and Nineveh and was, in turn, part of the process that would accomplish the restoration of God's people. Accordingly, Nahum wrote his short prophecy (1) to announce the doom of Nineveh and the demise of the mighty Assyrian empire and (2) to bring a message of consolation to a sin-weary and oppressed Judah.

CANONICITY AND TEXTUAL HISTORY
The canonicity of the book has never been seriously questioned. Its prevalence among biblical manuscripts from the intertestamental period, its use by the sectarians at Qumran as a source for application to certain events in their own day, and its employment in the New Testament (Rom 10:15 cf. 1:15; Isa 52:7) and by the early church Fathers (Tertullian, Lucian) give witness to its acceptance. The text is especially well preserved, with possible corruptions being noted in few places (e.g. 1:4b; 3:18). The discoveries of the text of Nahum at Qumran (mostly from 4QpNah, a commentary on Nahum), a Hebrew scroll of the Minor Prophets at Wadi Murabba'at, and fragments of a Greek text of the Minor Prophets at Nahal Hever demonstrate that the consonantal text of Nahum "has been handed down with incredible accuracy for nearly two thousand years at least" (Cathcart 1973a:13).

LITERARY STYLE

Nahum's message of God's judgment against Nineveh and protection for his own people finds corroboration in the bifid structure of the book, which breaks between chapter 1 and chapters 2–3 (see "Outline"). Moreover, the author has developed his work in accordance with principles of compilation and composition known to writers of the Old Testament and the Semitic world at large, such as bookending or *inclusio,* and the hooking or stitching of distinctive thought units at various levels.[2]

Nahum was a master literary craftsman (Patterson 1990). An abundance of literary features can be found, such as metaphor (Nineveh's troops are called women, 3:13), simile (Nineveh's guards are said to be like locusts, 3:17), hypocatastasis (implied comparison; e.g., Nineveh's leaders are called slumbering shepherds, 3:18), synecdoche (Nineveh's gates are represented by its door bars, 3:13, MT), rhetorical question ("Are you any better than the city of Thebes?" 3:8), irony (Nineveh is instructed to prepare for a siege but is told it will be to no avail, 2:1; 3:14-15), satire/taunt song (2:11-13; 3:8-13, 14-19), woe oracle (3:1-7), various types of parallelism (e.g., 3:15b), and numerous instances of alliteration and assonance (e.g., *buqah umebuqah umebullaqah,* 2:10 [11]).

Nahum was also a master of imagery.[3] His observations on life and the world around him were most colorful. Thus, he spoke of the fig tree and its fruit (3:12), the lion and its pride (or family, 2:11-12), locusts or grasshoppers (3:15-17), and also of shepherds (3:18), harlots (3:4-7), and building operations (3:14). In the social sphere, Nineveh's leadership and its merchants are likened to locusts that stripped the land of its foliage (3:16). Nineveh and its leadership could be compared to harlots who had willfully misled and misused mankind by their immoral behavior (3:4-6); they had filled the world with their constant cruelty.

Nahum is best remembered for his prophecies in the political realm. Thus, he speaks of political alliances (1:12; 3:9), vassalage (1:13), and military invasion (2:3-4). His depictions of warfare and the siege of a city are particularly graphic (2:1-10; 3:1-3, 7-8, 10-17) and are filled with descriptive details told with picturesque brevity (2:3-10; 3:1-3).

MAJOR THEMES

Nahum's basic theme is the judgment of Nineveh, which is first declared in the opening half of the book (1:2-15) and then described in the latter half of the book (2:1–3:19).[4] In keeping with his basic purpose, Nahum used several oracles of judgment (e.g., 2:1, 3-10), including a woe oracle (3:1-7). Nahum's warnings of judgment, however, were not his sole message. For not only was Nineveh's doom good news for all (3:19), but coupled with these declarations are some distinct salvation oracles bringing hope to God's beleaguered people (1:7, 12b, 15; 2:2). Contrary to the prevailing critical assumption that when "hopeful sayings" appear in collections of judgment oracles they are likely to be interpolations, the two quite commonly occur together as twin revelations of the Lord. Indeed, rejecting the genuineness of the "hopeful sayings" in Nahum would necessitate doing so in virtually every prophetic book, for the prophets uniformly combine condemnation and comfort in their messages.[5]

Nahum also employed several well-known motifs in his portrayal of Nineveh's sure demise, such as that of the shepherd and the sheep (Nineveh's leaders and populace, 3:18) and that of the message or messenger, with which each major unit or subunit concludes (1:15; 2:13; 3:19). Felt throughout the whole work is the motif of the Divine Warrior who subdues both the natural world and all his earthly enemies while protecting his own people (1:2-15; 2:2; 3:5-7).

THEOLOGICAL CONCERNS

Perhaps the most basic theological perspective of Nahum is that of God's sovereignty. God is seen as supreme over nature (1:4-6, 8), nations (1:15; 2:1, 3-7)—including Nineveh/Assyria (1:11-12a, 14; 2:8-13; 3:5-7, 11-19), Judah (1:12b-13; 2:2), Thebes/Egypt (3:8-10)—and all people (1:3, 6-10). As a sovereign God, he is also the controller of earth's history (1:12; 2:13; 3:5-7) who moves in just judgment against his foes (1:2-3a, 8-10, 14; 2:13; 3:5-7, 11-19) but with saving concern for those who put their trust in him (1:7-8a, 12b-13, 15; 2:2). God is shown also to be a God of revelation (1:1) who, although he is a jealous (1:2) and omnipotent God (1:3) who abhors sin (3:4-6, 19), is also long-suffering (1:3) and good (1:7) and has distinct purposes for his redeemed people.

Tremper Longman (1993:776) points out that a key element in Nahum's theological perspective is his employment of the Divine Warrior motif. He notes that already in the opening portion (1:2-8) the reader is presented with the "Divine Warrior whose appearance causes the cosmos to quake. This Warrior destroys his enemies and effects the salvation of his people." Concomitant with this presentation is the theme of God's wrath against his enemies who have provoked him to action (Becking 1995:277-296).[6]

Many have suggested that when Nahum adapted Isaiah's messianic promise (Isa 52:7) to his message concerning Nineveh's downfall (1:15), Nahum must have understood that God's dealings with Judah and Assyria were part of his purposes with respect to the coming of the Messiah.[7] In any case, it is certain that the messianic import of Nahum's words was utilized by the early church and has brought comfort to the saints throughout the succeeding ages, who look forward with confidence to the coming of that One who will reign in righteousness and execute perfect peace.

OUTLINE

Superscription (1:1)

II. The Doom of Nineveh Described (2:1–3:19)
  A. God, the Just Governor of the Nations (2:1-2)
  B. First Description of Nineveh's Demise (2:3-10)
  C. The Discredited City (2:11-13)
  D. Second Description of Nineveh's Demise (3:1-7)
  E. The Defenseless Citadel (3:8-19)
    1. A comparison of Nineveh and Thebes (3:8-13)
    2. A concluding condemnation of Nineveh (3:14-19)

ENDNOTES
1. All biblical references are to the English text unless otherwise noted. In such cases the reference to the Hebrew versification will be included in brackets (e.g., 1:15[2:1]).
2. Though differing in specific details of presentation, M. Sweeney's article, "Concerning the Structure and Generic Character of the Book of Nahum," *Zeitschrift für die alttestamentliche Wissenschaft* 104 (1992):364-377, also argues for the unity of Nahum, rightly observing that "the book of Nahum has a coherent structure." Nahum's literary artistry points to the removal of critical doubt as to the unity of the book. See further H. Peels, *Voed het old vertrouwen weder. De Godsopenvaring bij Nahum* (Kampen: Kok, 1993).

    Although I previously attempted to defend a partial or broken acrostic in verses 2-10 (see Patterson and Travers 1988:56-57), I have now largely abandoned the effort. The most that can be said for a proposed acrostic is that (1) three pairs of alphabetic sequence in directly following lines may be observed: beth–gimel (1:3b-4a), he–waw (1:5), and heth–teth (1:6b-7); (2) several other letters in the sequence of aleph–kaph (except daleth; 1:4) are present, though not always at the beginning of a line or in immediately following lines as in standard acrostics; and (3) a general pattern of progression may be seen in the Hebrew letters from aleph to kaph.

    The analysis of Floyd (1994:437) yields a similar result: "One can nevertheless conclude with regard to this unit itself that the hypothesis of an alphabetical acrostic here should now be laid to rest. This is partly because the evidence for the acrostic is itself so dubious, but also because the claim that the existence of an acrostic is supposed to support, namely that Nah 1:2-10 is basically a hymn, is also not viable."

    It is better, then, to conclude that the two-part poem detailing the Lord's revealed character and activities contains a high degree of repetition of letters, sounds, and ideas.
3. See Longman 1993:771-775; Patterson and Travers 1990:437-444.
4. See Patterson 1991:8-11; Patterson and Travers 1988:21-43.
5. See R. D. Patterson, "Old Testament Prophecy," in *A Complete Literary Guide to the Bible,* eds. Leland Ryken and Tremper Longman III (Grand Rapids: Zondervan, 1993), 302.
6. B. Becking (1995) relates the theme of divine wrath to covenantal theology, the Assyrian being viewed as a disobedient vassal to Yahweh. Becking also argues for the unity of Nahum, as well as a date in the seventh century BC. For the Divine Warrior theme, see the discussion of major themes in the introduction to Joel, the commentary on Habakkuk 3:8-15, and T. Longman III and D. G. Reid, *God Is a Warrior* (Grand Rapids: Zondervan, 1995).
7. In this regard Craigie (1976:67) remarks: "Nahum . . . here anticipates the Gospel. . . . In the same way, the message of the glad tidings of the Gospel comes to those who are oppressed and in despair. The message is one of peace, a peace from external oppression and a new kind of peace with the God who is the giver of all life."

COMMENTARY ON

Nahum

◆ **Superscription (1:1)**

This message concerning Nineveh came as
a vision to Nahum, who lived in Elkosh.

NOTES

1:1 *message*. Because the noun *massa'* (oracle, message) is derived from the verb *nasa'* (lift
up), two meanings have traditionally been assigned to it: (1) "burden" and (2) "oracle."
Those who favor the first translation call attention to the more natural reading of the root
in the idea of a burden that is carried, whether that of animals (2 Kgs 5:17) or people
(Jer 17:21-22; cf. Deut 1:12), and to the customary following of the terms by an objective
genitive ("the burden concerning X"). Those who take the noun to mean something like
"oracle," "utterance," or simply "prophecy" point out that the term is used often to introduce non-burdensome prophecies (e.g., Zech 12:1; Mal 1:1) and that the associated verb is
used of speaking in such cases as lifting up the voice (Isa 3:7; 42:11), of lifting up or taking
up a parable (Num 23:7), proverb (Isa 14:4), prayer (Isa 37:4), lamentation (Amos 5:1), or
the name of God (Exod 20:7; see Barker 1985:657). The strength of parallels in Ugaritic as
well as the many biblical examples of *nasa'* [TH5375, ZH5951] used in a context of "lifting up
the voice" appear to tip the weight in favor of the latter suggestion.

Nineveh. The mention of Nineveh in the superscription is significant in that without this
notation the direction of the message of the entire first chapter could be unclear. Indeed,
Nineveh is not specifically named until 2:8. The inclusion of the Assyrian capital in the
superscription, therefore, identifies the object of the announcement of God's judgment
with which the book begins.

vision. By calling his prophecy a vision, Nahum underscored the fact that what he said was
not of his own invention but was that which God had specially revealed to him (cf. Obad
1:1). At the outset, then, Nahum made it clear that his words were not his own insights
based on his observations of the events of his time. Rather, they were nothing less than the
message given to him by the sovereign God whose word he must deliver, however difficult
it might be.

Nahum. Hummel (1979:342) suggests that the meaning of Nahum's name ("comfort") is
quite apropos. God's justice means judgment on the enemy but "comfort" to the faithful.
Hummel goes on to say, "The point is not that God's people go scot-free, but precisely the
reverse: if God so judges those whom He employs temporarily as instruments of His judgment upon His unfaithful people, how much more fearful the judgment upon His own people if they finally miss the message." The Hebrew text calls Nahum's prophecy "The book of
the vision of Nahum." Accordingly, some (Keil 1954; Longman 1993) have suggested that
the original prophecy was written and not delivered orally. While this is possible, the use of
the phrase may simply suggest that Nahum's burdensome vision, whether delivered orally or
not, had, under divine inspiration, been committed to a permanent record that all may read.

COMMENTARY

Nahum begins his prophecy with the observation that what is recorded here is not of his own invention but is both a prophetic oracle and a vision. The latter term, while dealing primarily with the communication of received revelation, may imply that the prophet, or *khozeh* [TH2374, ZH2602] (seer), was one who, as God's chosen servant, saw things from God's point of view and attempted to get others to see them too. The word "seer" may also indicate that Nahum was allowed a visionary glimpse of Nineveh's actual siege and fall before the events occurred.

Nahum asserted that God is a God of revelation and one who is active in the course of earth's history. As a revealer, unlike the god of the deists, Israel's God can and does make his will known to mankind (Num 24:4, 16; 2 Chr 32:32; Isa 2:1; Dan 2:26; 4:10; Amos 1:1; Obad 1:1). In specifically addressing Nineveh, Nahum emphasized that God does truly intervene in the affairs of nations.

The address to Nineveh also reminds all readers that God is a God of justice. To be sure, he allowed the Assyrians to punish Israel for its unfaithfulness and immoral behavior, but he who serves God ought not to use such service for selfish ends. The Assyrians had gone beyond their commission in the brutal way they carried out their divine assignment. Therefore, they would eventually face the certain and severe judgment of God.

Although Nahum's name was a common one, it may give a clue as to an important purpose of the book, that of giving "comfort" to God's people: However fierce and foreboding the circumstance might seem, God is indeed still sovereign and is concerned for the welfare and ultimate good of his own. Whatever trial or chastisement they may be enduring, God intends it for their benefit so as to make them stronger and more productive believers (cf. Isa 40:1-2; 1 Pet 1:5-7).

◆ I. The Doom of Nineveh Declared (1:2-15)
    A. First Rhetorical Question (1:2-6)

2 The LORD is a jealous God,
    filled with vengeance and rage.
He takes revenge on all who oppose
    him
    and continues to rage against his
    enemies!
3 The LORD is slow to get angry, but his
    power is great,
    and he never lets the guilty go
    unpunished.
He displays his power in the whirlwind
    and the storm.
The billowing clouds are the dust
    beneath his feet.
4 At his command the oceans dry up,
    and the rivers disappear.

The lush pastures of Bashan and
    Carmel fade,
    and the green forests of Lebanon
    wither.
5 In his presence the mountains
    quake,
    and the hills melt away;
the earth trembles,
    and its people are destroyed.
6 Who can stand before his fierce
    anger?
Who can survive his burning
    fury?
His rage blazes forth like fire,
    and the mountains crumble to dust
    in his presence.

NOTES

1:2 *a jealous God, filled with . . . rage.* The English words translate two interesting Hebrew phrases: *'el qanno'* [TH410A/7072, ZH446/7868] and *ba'al khemah* [TH1167/2534, ZH1251/2779] (lit., "possessor of wrath"). The names of the Canaanite gods El and Baal are immediately apparent. Cathcart (1973a:38-39) follows the lead of Albright in suggesting that their use here, together with the common characteristic jealousy of the Canaanite deities, may indicate Nahum's adoption of Canaanite hymnody. As Roberts (1991:43) points out, however, *ba'al* [TH1167, ZH1251] is often compounded with other nouns without any necessary connection with deity. In any case, there is no need to see wholesale adoption of a Canaanite composition dedicated to Baal, as some suggest (cf. Gaster 1961:143). At most, Nahum may simply be displaying his literary skill in utilizing old poetic themes to give a veiled attack against the rampant Baalism initiated by King Manasseh (2 Kgs 21:3). Yahweh (not Baal) is the true Lord of the universe (cf. 1:3b-5) and will execute his righteous anger against sin and rebellion.

vengeance . . . revenge. In the Hebrew text "vengeance" occurs three times; twice sandwiched between the words for jealousy and rage and a third time with the thought of taking "revenge" (NLT) on the adversary. This is a key to unlocking the door of understanding to Nahum's prophecy. In reading of God's vengeance, however, one must not think of the familiar human vindictiveness condemned in the Scriptures (cf. Deut 32:35 and Prov 25:21-22 with Rom 12:19-20; Lev 19:18 with Matt 19:19). Although God may delegate the operation of vengeance to constituted authority (Num 31:1-2; Josh 10:13; Esth 8:13), it primarily belongs to him (Deut 32:35-43; Heb 10:30-31).

continues to rage. Like the Syriac *netar*, the underlying Heb. verb here (*natar* [TH5201A, ZH5757]) means basically to "keep," "guard," or "maintain," and hence has the same semantic range as *natsar* [TH5341, ZH5915] (cf. Old Aramaic *nesar* with classical Aramaic *netar* [TA10476, ZA10476]) and also *shamar* [TH8104, ZH9068] with which it occurs in parallel in Jer 3:5; (cf. Amos 1:11, Syriac). In addition, *natar* appears to more clearly employ the meaning "be angry" or "bear a grudge" in several contexts (e.g., Lev 19:18; Ps 103:9; Jer 3:5, 12). Thus, some scholars have suggested that both verbs have a second root signifying "rage" (cf. HALOT 2.695). The meaning, however, may be better understood as contextually derived and not as the result of another root.

all who oppose him . . . his enemies! The nouns here (*tsar* [TH6862A, ZH7640] and *'oyeb* [TH341, ZH367]) are recognized poetic parallels (Yoder 1971:475-476).

1:3 *The LORD is slow to get angry.* Some critical scholars (e.g., J. M. P. Smith) have suggested that v. 3a be treated as a gloss, possibly supplied from Numbers 14:18, so as to soften the force of God's wrath. However, as Cathcart (1973a:46-47) points out, the essential integrity of vv. 2-3a is supported by the heaping up of the consonants nun and qoph (six times each) and the combination of the ideas of strength/wrath and gentleness/mercy found in extrabiblical literary sources such as the Babylonian *Ludlul Bel Nemeqi*, in which Marduk is described as one whose "anger is irresistible, his rage is a hurricane, but his heart is merciful, his mind forgiving." (For the full text of *Ludlul Bel Nemeqi*, see Lambert 1960:30-62.)

his power. The thought might parallel that of Ps 147:5: "How great is our LORD! His power is absolute!"

whirlwind . . . storm. Both nouns occur in Isa 29:6 in a context of judgment. Watson (1986:196) may be correct in suggesting that the use of the two words for "storm" here is an example of hendiadys. He translates the line, "In the tempestuous whirlwind his road." Yahweh's power over the storm could be viewed as a veiled denunciation of both the Canaanite Baal (who was often worshiped in poetic lines of similar sentiment and whose worship was even then rampant in Judah) and Hadad, the Assyrian storm god.

billowing clouds. The image is reminiscent of such phrases as "him who rides the clouds" (e.g., Ps 68:4), "he rides across the heavens" (Deut 33:26), and "riding on a swift cloud" (Isa 19:1). Similarly, the storm god Hadad appears in the Ugaritic literature as "lord of the storm clouds" and in the Atrahasis Epic as the one who "rode on the four winds, (his) asses." (For the term "the Rider on the Clouds," see Patterson 1985:37.)

1:4 *oceans . . . rivers.* "Sea" and "river" are persistent players in the Canaanite mythological texts and appear as parallel pairs in both Ugaritic texts and the OT. (See the full discussion in Cooper 1981:369-383.)

Bashan . . . Carmel . . . Lebanon. The mention of Bashan, Carmel, and Lebanon is reminiscent of Isa 33:9. All three were noted for being places of special fertility. Bashan (south of Mount Hermon on the east side of the Jordan) was fabled for the productivity of its land and therefore its fine cattle (Mic 7:14); Carmel (the promontory along the Mediterranean Sea in central Canaan south of the Bay of Acre) was prized for its beauty and fruitfulness (Song 7:5; Jer 50:19); and Lebanon (home of the lofty mountains of coastal Syria) was famed for its great cedars (1 Kgs 5:14-18; Isa 2:13). The conquering Mesopotamian kings frequently boasted of traveling to the forests of Lebanon. (See Sennacherib's penetration of this area as recorded in Luckenbill 1926:161-162. Sennacherib's boast is also noted in 2 Kgs 19:23.) Robertson (1990:67) adds, "In the graciousness of God, Israel was promised that they would experience a return some day to the fruitfulness of Bashan, Carmel, and Lebanon (Isa 33:9-10; 35:2; Jer 50:18-19)."

fade . . . wither. For the unusual word *'umlal* [TH535, ZH581] (wither), which occurs twice in this verse, see Isa 24:4. Roberts (1991:44) suggests emending to some form of the verb *dalal* [TH1809, ZH1937] (become little) so as to restore the missing daleth of the acrostic (cf. Isa 19:6). Such an emendation could be justified for one of the occurrences since the ancient versions uniformly use two different words in translating the Hebrew text. However, the scroll of the Minor Prophets from Wadi Murabba'at supports the MT. Moreover, Joel uses *'umlal* together with *yabesh* [TH3001, ZH3312] ("dry up"; Joel 1:10, 12). Nahum may be adopting Joel's language here. If scholars argue for an acrostic in vv. 2-10 (see Introduction, endnote 2), they must settle for a broken one at best and one whose succeeding letter does not always occur in the initial position in its line. Such a broken alphabetic acrostic occurs in Pss 9-10, where the letter daleth is likewise missing.

1:5 *mountains quake . . . hills melt away.* For the NLT's "melt away," the NEB reads "swell," and the NJB "reel." Support for such renderings comes not only from the parallel with the quaking mountains but from the ancient versions: LXX *esaleuthēsan* [TG4531, ZG4888] (are shaken, sway) and Peshitta *'etparaq* (be rent, be broken). Possible etymological support may also be found in Arabic *maja* (surge). This thought is supported further by such thematic parallels as Ps 18:7; Jer 4:24; Hab 3:6. Conversely, the more usual translation of *mug* [TH4127, ZH4570] as "melt" is favored by a comparison with Ps 97:5; Mic 1:4.

its people are destroyed. The NLT thus renders the emphasis of the verbless second clause of the original text. The Hebrew for the full line reads, "The earth quakes before him, even the world and all who dwell in it" (my translation). The parallel nouns *'erets* [TH776, ZH824] (earth) and *tebel* [TH8398, ZH9315] (world) appear together elsewhere (cf. 1 Sam 2:8; Isa 18:3; 24:4; 26:9, 18; 34:1). Another proposal comes from Moran (1965:71, 83), who links the *we-* [TH2050.1, ZH2256] (and) of the form *wekol-* [TH3605, ZH3972] (and all) with *tebel* and repoints it as a verb *tebalu* (from *'abal* [TH56, ZH61]), thus viewing it as a remnant of an ancient *taqtulu[na]* form): "all its inhabitants *mourned.*" However, the MT is sufficiently clear as it stands.

1:6 *fury.* The figure of wrath is continued in this verse. It is a wrath that burns so intensely that even usually impenetrable rocks are broken up before it (cf. Deut 32:22; 1 Kgs 19:11; Jer 4:26; 23:29; 51:26; Mic 1:4). The Hebrew word *khemah* [TH2534, ZH2779] that occurs here forms an *inclusio* with 1:2, thus bracketing 1:2-6 together.

COMMENTARY

Nahum began his prophetic oracles with a poem featuring two themes. Verses 2-6 are formed largely from texts commemorating the Exodus, while verses 7-10 are built around declarations that the Lord is a sovereign and righteous God who deals justly with all people. After giving his opening thesis (1:2), each section begins with a statement concerning the Lord, cast as a verbless sentence: (1) "The LORD is slow to get angry" (1:3a) and (2) "The LORD is good" (1:7a), which is followed by several descriptive assertions (1:3b-5, 7b-8) and a rhetorical question and closing declaration (1:6, 9-10). The whole poem proceeds around a general description of the Lord's sovereign power toward both the faithful and those who oppose him. Nahum wanted to underscore two truths: (1) Although the Lord is long-suffering, he will assuredly judge the guilty with all the force that a sovereign God can muster (1:3-6); and (2) although the Lord is good and tenderly cares for the righteous (particularly in times of affliction), he will destroy those who plot against him (1:7-10). The full poem provides the basis for Nahum's subsequent oracles.

Nahum initially declares (1:2-3) that God is a God of justice who will not allow his person or power to be impugned. He will deal justly with the ungodly. The theme of judgment is balanced by the knowledge that God is "slow to get angry." His judicial wrath is not always immediate. At times, he holds back his wrath against his foes until the proper occasion. God's government, including his judicial processes, is on schedule, even though to a waiting humanity his timing may seem to lag.

Indeed, his justice may be "slow" in coming, for he is a God of infinite patience who has an overriding concern for the souls of people (cf. 2 Pet 3:9-15). Far from being an omnipotent sovereign who executes justice with rigid disinterest, God is a God of truth and love who, because he longs to bring people into a relationship with himself, abounds in forbearance toward those who deserve only judgment.

Despite his abundant patience, a God of truth and justice (Pss 9:9; 31:5) will not acquit the guilty but must ultimately confront unrepented sin so that justice triumphs in the punishment of the guilty (Exod 34:7; Num 14:17-18; Deut 28:58-68; Joel 3:4-8, 19). Moreover, as an omnipotent sovereign he has the inherent strength to effect his justice: He is "great in power." The theophany portrayed in the metaphor of verse 3b is a familiar one in the Old Testament: Yahweh is the God of the storm. The figure is often utilized for contexts dealing with judgment (e.g., Isa 29:6; 66:15; Zech 9:14). In contrast to the impotent pagan storm gods, the Lord is in control of the natural world, as well as the affairs of mankind (Job 37:1–42:6; Ps 104; Acts 17:24-28).

Nahum's description of God's omnipotence and sovereignty is in harmony with mainstream Hebrew orthodoxy and is phrased in familiar imagery: God is in the whirlwind and the storm (Ps 83:15 [16]; Isa 29:6); he treads the lofty clouds under his feet (cf. Exod 19:16-19; Pss 68:4 [5]; 97:2; 104:3; Matt 24:30; 26:64; 1 Thess 4:17; Rev 1:7); he controls the rivers and seas (cf. Exod 14:21-22; 15:8; Pss 66:6; 77:16; Hab 3:15); he can make desolate the most luxurious of lands (e.g., Bashan and Carmel); the mountains and earth quake and collapse at his presence (cf. Hab 3:6, 10) so that the world and its inhabitants are helpless before him—even the most impenetrable of rocks lies shattered before his fiery wrath.

Nahum thus gives a graphic picture of the limitless and invincible power of God. Accordingly, he can ask whether any could stand in the face of such an almighty one when he executes his wrath. The answer is "No one, no one at all!" By implication, this response anticipates the subject of his prophecy: Not even mighty Nineveh, home of the Assyrian world empire, would be able to withstand the sovereign God of all nature. The creator, controller, and consummator of this world and its history is the same one who will not leave the guilty unpunished.

◆ B. Second Rhetorical Question (1:7-10)

7 The LORD is good,
    a strong refuge when trouble comes.
    He is close to those who trust
      in him.
8 But he will sweep away his enemies
    in an overwhelming flood.
    He will pursue his foes
    into the darkness of night.

9 Why are you scheming against
    the LORD?
    He will destroy you with one blow;
    he won't need to strike twice!
10 His enemies, tangled like thornbushes
    and staggering like drunks,
    will be burned up like dry stubble
    in a field.

NOTES

1:7 refuge. Lit., "for a refuge." The unexpected preposition before the noun has been variously treated either as (1) a comparative particle, "better than" (NJB), (2) an asseverative particle, "yea," "indeed" (Christensen 1975:22), or (3) intended for an omitted noun, understood on the basis of the LXX so that the line reads, "The Lord is good to those who wait upon him, a place of refuge in the day of affliction" (Roberts 1991:42-45). Despite the difficulty, the MT is defensible—the preposition explained as one providing logical connection, meaning "with respect to" (Gen 17:20; 41:19). This explanation yields the rendering, "The Lord is good as a refuge." The NLT renders the sense adequately.

He is close. Several suggest an expanded use of *yada'* [TH3045, ZH3359] here, such as "care for" (NIV, NEB) or "recognize" (NJB). Because this verb has a wide semantic range when used of divine knowledge, however, it is perhaps better to translate "and he knows" and leave the precise nuance to the expositor.

1:8 his enemies. The Hebrew reads "its/her place" (cf. NASB; Keil 1954). The NLT follows the lead of the Septuagint and several scholars in repointing the consonants so as to read "those who rise up against him," hence, "his enemies." Roberts (1991:42, 45; following Rudolph) repoints the consonants as an abstract noun and translates, "He totally annihilates the opposition."

into the darkness of night. The NLT renders the phrase according to the sense. The word "night" does not occur in the Hebrew text, however, so other possibilities for understanding "darkness" include the land of death—the final end of the wicked (a thought found in such texts as Job 10:20-22; 17:13; 18:18; Ps 35:6, 8, 10-12), or simply as an idiom for God's relentless pursuit that brings the final extermination of his foes (Isa 8:22; Zeph 1:15). Robertson (1990:72) observes, "*Darkness* in Scripture symbolizes distress, terror, mourning, perplexity, and dread. A combination of all these experiences will be the final fruition of Nineveh for all the years that she oppressed and brutalized other nations."

1:9 Why are you scheming? The NLT views the text as a rhetorical question. It could also be taken as a statement: "whatever you plot against Yahweh" (cf. NIV, NASB). Either way, it corresponds to a similar development in the first section of the hymn (cf. 1:6) and "suggests the idea that any devices against Yahweh are futile" (Longman 1993:795).

He will destroy. Although the NLT renders the sense of this phrase and the rest of the verse adequately, it fails to bring out the many plays on words and sounds that occur between vv. 8 and 9 in the MT (see Longman 1993:795).

1:10 His enemies. Verse 10 is an often debated *crux interpretum*. Cathcart (1973a:60) affirms: "This must be one of the most difficult texts in the Old Testament. No satisfactory translation of the passage has been offered to date." Each line of the verse, as well as the sense of the whole, has been subjected to critical scrutiny. The first two images have been particularly troublesome. (1) "Tangled like thornbushes" (lit., "entangled thorns") has met with such despair of solution that many (e.g., J. M. P. Smith 1911) have dubbed it hopelessly corrupt. Various textual emendations and rearrangements have been attempted, none of which appears to be an improvement upon the basic figure given in the MT. (2) "Staggering like drunks" (lit., "like those drunken from their drink") is usually translated so as to yield a rendition that emphasizes becoming totally drunk. Although numerous conjectures have been put forward, none has met with scholarly consensus or proved to be entirely satisfactory.

Not only must the difficulty of establishing the precise meanings of the words involved in the two figures be solved, but once the meanings of the first two difficult figures are established, they must be related to the third image of the verse: "like dry stubble in a field." Some commonality must be found if one is to make good sense of the three parallel lines. The point of the comparison in all three seemingly unrelated cases is that of total consumption: the bush by its thorns, the drunkard by his drink, the stubble by fire. Doubtless each of the lines belongs to the proverbial literature. The three are brought together by Nahum as a fitting conclusion to the hymn to reemphasize the impossibility of God's enemies ever rising up again after he has judged them. The verse and the whole hymn look forward to God's judgment of Nineveh. He will make a complete end of the proud city.

burned. The reference to fire not only echoes the concluding lines of the first portion of the hymn (1:6) and adds dramatic pathos to the divine sentence of judgment in this section but is also distinctly accurate: The ruins of Nineveh show abundant evidence of the intense conflagration that consumed the fallen city.

COMMENTARY

Nahum began the latter portion of his poem with the second of his statements regarding God's nature. He pointed out that God's goodness and concern for his own do not diminish his power and determination to judge the wicked. Rather, God's goodness assures all people that he will execute his judgment equitably.

The careful balance in God's character is maintained here. Just as the Lord is slow to anger, yet great in power (1:3), so is he a stronghold in the day of distress (1:7; cf. Ps 37:37-40). This declaration stresses that in times of judgment and destruction, the believer may take refuge in the realization that God's goodness provides protection in the midst of it all. The Scriptures remind us that there is also a richness in God's goodness by which individuals may be led to repentance (Rom 2:3-4; cf. Ps 145:7-12). Although Nineveh had experienced God's patience and kindness in Jonah's day, there would be no repentance in this day and no remittance of God's judgment.

Nahum pointed out that the Divine Warrior will come against Nineveh like a victorious commander pursuing his foes to the farthest recesses of the earth. Indeed, God's enemies will come to understand that he will overturn their insolent plotting against him so thoroughly that, like men entangled in thorns or overcome with their own drunkenness, they will be easily overthrown. As dry stubble is devoured by fire, God's fiery wrath will consume them. They will not devise their devious plot a second time.

The contrast between the fortunes of believers and the wicked is often drawn in the Scriptures (e.g., Pss 1; 37; Prov 4:10-19; Matt 7:13-14, 24-27). Those who trust in God are the ones who know and believe in him (cf. Gen 15:6) and hence have the assurance (Isa 26:3) that God will take note of them in the adversities of life (Pss 17:7; 18:30; 31:19-20), when life's circumstances rush in upon them like an overwhelming flood (Pss 18:1-6; 32:6-7; 124). Indeed, God's goodness reaches out to all such believers; he becomes their fortress in distress (Exod 15:2; Pss 27:1-3; 28:8; 91:2; Isa 25:4; Jer 16:19).

Conversely, those who trust in self, who rise up against God, will find that he will, in turn, stand against them. Those who plot against him (Pss 1:1; 2:1-3; 21:11) can be assured that their plotting will self-destruct, leaving them in danger of judgment (cf. Pss 1:4-5; 2:12; Hos 7:15-16).

Taken together with the opening description of God's character (1:2-6), these verses demonstrate that the Lord is the God of both Israel and the nations. He exercises complete control over the forces and destinies of all creation. Accordingly, people ought to put their trust in him (Isa 26:3-4). Not only should they place their trust in God as their refuge, but theirs should be an absolute and total commitment of life to God. Such a trust entails the reproduction of God's own character in their lives. The psalmist puts it well:

> Trust in the LORD and do good.
> Then you will live safely in the land and prosper.
> Commit everything you do to the LORD.
> Trust him, and he will help you. (Ps 37:3, 5)

◆ C. The Consequences (1:11-15)

[11] Who is this wicked counselor of yours who plots evil against the LORD?

[12] This is what the LORD says:
"Though the Assyrians have many allies,
they will be destroyed and disappear.
O my people, I have punished you before,
but I will not punish you again.
[13] Now I will break the yoke of bondage from your neck

and tear off the chains of Assyrian oppression."

[14] And this is what the LORD says concerning the Assyrians in Nineveh:
"You will have no more children to carry on your name.
I will destroy all the idols in the temples of your gods.
I am preparing a grave for you because you are despicable!"

15*Look! A messenger is coming over the
mountains with good news!
He is bringing a message of peace.
Celebrate your festivals, O people of
Judah,

and fulfill all your vows,
for your wicked enemies will never
invade your land again.
They will be completely
destroyed!

1:15 Verse 1:15 is numbered 2:1 in Hebrew text.

NOTES

1:11 *wicked counselor.* The participial phrase from which this rendering is drawn contains the term *beliya'al* [TH1100, ZH1175], a word that always has unsavory associations in the OT. It is used of reprobates (Judg 19:22; 1 Sam 10:27) and serves as an appropriate designation for Jezebel's two false witnesses against Naboth (1 Kgs 21:10; see further discussion in Robertson 1990:74-77). As formulated here, it stands in stark contrast to the coming Messiah, who will be a "Wonderful Counselor" (Isa 9:6).

plots evil. The term rendered "plots" here (*khashab* [TH2803, ZH3108]) constitutes the literary hook between this section and the preceding poem (cf. "plot" with "scheming" in 1:9; both words are from the same root).

1:12 *This is what the LORD says.* While a prophet's words are often introduced by some such phrase as "thus says the LORD," this phrase occurs only here in Nahum. The singular use of so common a formula argues for a certain deliberate emphasis, perhaps expressing Nahum's sense of the awesomeness of the Lord's pronouncement he was about to deliver.

Though. The divine sentence is expressed in the form of a condition whose protasis is formed with the particle *'im* [TH518, ZH561] and a participle. Such constructions usually have a present or immediate future time reference and express a real contingency or possibility. Therefore, the likelihood of a strong and sizeable military force at the disposal of the Assyrians is in view.

allies. The NLT's rendering simplifies a difficult phrase that has been variously translated and emended. The translation "allies" for *shelemim* depends on a study by D. J. Wiseman (1982:311-326) and is perhaps the best solution to the time-honored crux. Together with the *weken rabbim* [TH2050.1/3651A/7227, ZH2256/4027/8041] ("many", NLT; cf. Exod 1:12), it suggests this thought: "even though they will have allies and so be all the more numerous." Thus construed, the following apodosis becomes an argument *a fortiori*: so much the more will they be cut off and their armies pass away. Roberts (1991:46-47) suggests that the *weken rabbim* here "refers back to the thicket of interwoven thorns mentioned in v. 10." Similarly he takes the second *weken* with which the next clause begins to refer "back to the destruction of the dry stubble mentioned in v. 10. Just as dry stubble is devoured, so the Assyrians will be cut off and pass away."

disappear. Scholars customarily read the masculine singular of the Hebrew text as a plural by redividing the words so that the waw beginning the next word (*we'innithik*) is read as finishing this word: *we'aberu* (plural from *'abar* [TH5674, ZH6296]). So construed, the verbs "be destroyed" and "disappear" are in agreement, both being plural. As the MT stands, however, the form could be considered a collective singular.

punished. The underlying Hebrew verb *'anah* [TH6031, ZH6700] is at times used in contexts of God's judicial punishment of his people (see Deut 8:2-3; Pss 90:15; 119:75). Joel reports that the Assyrians would be used as instruments of God's chastisement if no repentance was forthcoming in Judah and Jerusalem (Joel 2:1-27). Habakkuk similarly warns of God's use of the Babylonians (Hab 1:5-11). The LXX apparently confused this word with a homonymous verb meaning "to answer": "*Your report* will be heard no more."

1:13 Now. The rhetorical function of the Hebrew particle found here is to introduce the next point in consequence. Not only will conditions between Assyria and Judah be reversed, but God's people will also be set free from Assyrian vassalage.

chains. Although some feel compelled on the basis of the Greek text and Vulgate to emend the Hebrew text to read "his scepter" rather than "chains" (lit., "yoke") here, the Hebrew text makes perfectly good sense as it stands. Yokes are commonly mentioned in the ancient literature to depict the fate of those held in vassalage by treaty arrangement with their over-lord (cf. Jer 27:1-10). Thus Nabopolassar boasts: "As for the Assyrians who since distant days had ruled over all the people and with heavy yoke had brought misery to the people of the land, from the land of Akkad I banished their feet and cast off their yoke." For the inscription, see Langdon (1912:17ff). The Lord's promise of freedom from chains for those who follow him stands in bold contrast with the complaint of those who would refuse his rightful sovereignty over them (Ps 2:1-3).

1:14 *children to carry on your name.* The loss of descendants and family name would mean total annihilation for Nineveh. Armerding (1985:468) rightly remarks: "The 'name' of a population represented its living identity, perpetuated in its 'descendants'; to be desti-tute of descendants therefore represented obliteration of identity and of life itself." For a discussion of the textual problems connected with the *mishimeka* [TH4480/8034, ZH4946/9005] (of/from your name) in the MT, see Patterson 1991:50; Longman 1993:799.

all the idols. The NLT combines two Hebrew terms (the images and idols). The first is usu-ally taken to refer to carved images and the second, to those that are molten. As such, they constitute two of several words for idols and images in the OT. But the usual definitions do not always apply, and the original significance of the two terms is uncertain.

I am preparing. Some scholars relate the Hebrew verb to another root meaning "devas-tate," hence, God's intention to desecrate the Ninevites' tombs. The context, however, appears to focus on God's personal preparation of Nineveh's grave rather than on Nine-veh's dread of the destruction of her grave.

despicable. The charge here represents a moral extension of the root *qalal* [TH7043, ZH7837] ("be light"; in this case, lacking moral value or weight). The root is used of a person's slighted reputation (2 Sam 6:22) and also of actively treating someone contemptuously (2 Sam 19:43 [44]; Isa 23:9), hence of cursing (Gen 12:3; 1 Sam 17:43; 2 Sam 16:5). LXX "because you are swift" depends on a different derived sense of the verb. Other views to be rejected include (1) relating the verb to the Ugaritic *qll* (fall) and (2) emending the text into a noun such as *qiqaloth* [TH7022, ZH7814] (dung heap) or *qlyt* ("shame"; G. R. Driver). (See the discussion in Patterson 1991:51.)

1:15 [2:1] *Look!* Nahum uses this particle (*hinneh* [TH2009, ZH2180]) to call attention to key descriptive statements in his prophetic discourses. Here it introduces the close of the first portion of the book.

messenger. The theme of the messenger/message closes each major section of Nahum's prophecy (cf. 2:13; 3:7, 19). Nahum's words are drawn from Isa 52:7, one of several instances of his dependence upon Isaiah. Armerding (1985:455) suggests that the ubiquity of the interrelationship between Isaiah and Nahum may corroborate Isaiah's authorship of all the prophecy that bears his name.

good news! The Hebrew root *bsr* [TH1319, ZH1413] does not necessarily mean a message of good news but simply indicates the bearing of a message (cf. 1 Sam 4:17-18). Similarly, the Akkadian cognate *bussuru* means basically "bring a message." Nevertheless, it is most often used in the OT, as also in Ugaritic, of bearing glad tidings, hence is translated that way in most English versions. For the combination of good news and peace, see Isa 52:7; Luke 2:10, 14; Acts 10:36.

festivals . . . vows. The great yearly feasts centered on God's saving acts on behalf of his people (Deut 16:16). Votive offerings were a matter of the believer's free will; but once such vows were made, they were to be kept and the offerings were to be of high quality (Lev 22:18-25; 27:1-13; Num 15:2-16; Deut 12:6-7; 23:21-23).

your wicked enemies. Lit., "the wicked one" (*beliya'al* [TH1100, ZH1175]). See note on 1:11 and commentary.

completely destroyed! The promise of complete annihilation of the enemy such that it could never again invade Jerusalem/Judah, together with the promise of peace and prosperity for God's people, is repeated elsewhere in the writings of the prophets (e.g., Isa 52:1, 7; Joel 3:17). The prophecy of certain judgment and sure deliverance is basic to the scriptural teaching concerning the Day of the Lord. Roberts (1991:54) adds, "One should note how thoroughly this judgment was carried out in the collapse of the Assyrian empire, when Nineveh was permanently destroyed, the gods of Assyria desecrated, and the Assyrian monarchy brought to an end."

COMMENTARY

With the completion of the poem (1:2-10), Nahum turns to the two nations and their capitals that are the subject of his prophecies. The latter half of his poem had been directed against those who plot against God. Keying in on that term, Nahum turns to the supreme example of such activity: Assyria and its capital city of Nineveh. In four short verses, Nahum brings God's charges against Nineveh. God will judge the city (1:11) regardless of its seemingly limitless strength (1:12a, 14), a judgment that will result in a respite for Judah in its affliction (1:12b-13). The section is closed with a stirring message of good news: Because wicked Nineveh has been judged, a repentant Judah may once again worship God in peace (1:15).

In a dramatic structural shift from poetic to narrative style, Nahum pronounces judgment on Nineveh. Nineveh (as well as Assyria) is identified as a plotter, an identification that seems obvious in the light of the military exploits of its most prominent kings. The primary reference may well be to Sennacherib, who launched his infamous third campaign against the western countries of the Fertile Crescent in general and Judah in particular. According to his records, he subdued the northern lands and took control of Eltekeh, Timnah, and Ekron on the Philistine coast, as well as some 46 cities of Judah. Although he failed to subdue Jerusalem, the booty he carried away from the campaign was enormous. The scriptural record likewise indicates that the Judahite king paid a huge tribute to Sennacherib and that the Assyrian king spent considerable time in taking the key towns of Lachish and Libnah in the western Shephelah (2 Kgs 18:13-19:8). The writer of Kings also records something of Sennacherib's own secret plottings against the Lord at that time (2 Kgs 19:21-28). Because of the viciousness of the plotter's thoughts, he is aptly termed "one who counsels wickedness."

The initial phase of Nahum's messages against Nineveh appears in 1:12-14. The Lord had a personal word for each of the parties involved. For Judah, there was reassurance that its Assyrian vassalage would soon pass away, a condition that became a virtual reality during the latter days of Josiah's reign (2 Kgs 22-23; 2 Chr 35). In contrasting Judah's previous and future situations, Nahum compared

Judah's unjust treatment to a yoke and shackles, all of which would be broken (1:13). For Nineveh, there was the solemn affirmation that her long night of cruel domination was soon to end. This vile and ruthless nation would shortly pass from the scene of earth's history.

The pronouncement that Nineveh would lack descendants to bear her name reads literally in the Masoretic Text: "There will not be sown [any] of your name anymore." As a farmer sows his seed in anticipation of harvest, so a man's posterity is viewed as his seed (e.g., Gen 13:16). The metaphor is common in the Old Testament. Stress is laid here on the impossibility of Nineveh's recovery. Never again will it know its former fame, for it will have neither status nor descendants to perpetuate its name.

Along with the idea of sowing, Nahum's use of the word "name" is particularly appropriate. To "cut off the name" was to destroy a person or leave him without descendants (cf. 1 Sam 24:21; Job 18:17; Isa 14:22). Conversely, a man continued to exist in his posterity, for it was his name and seed (Isa 66:22; cf. Jer 13:11). Nineveh (and Assyria) would never again have its name sown![1]

The pathos of Assyria's demise is further deepened by the notice that none of its vaunted gods, so long venerated in Mesopotamia, would be able to deliver it from God's sentence of death. Rather, their limitations are clearly spelled out. These "gods" are what they appear to be—mere temple "images" and "idols" that could never be of help (cf. Isa 44:9-10) to a doomed Nineveh. Worse still, those same gods will be cut off. This reflects the usual custom in the ancient world whereby the victor desecrated the temples of the conquered foe and carried off the idols. The Assyrians themselves were past masters of such activities. Now it was their turn to suffer such indignities.

The divine sentence ends with a dreadful dictum. So hopeless was Nineveh's case and so devastating would be its demise that it would not even have a memorial left to its greatness (cf. Ps 49:16-17), nor would anyone erect a monument to its memory. Further reason for the necessity of the divine interment is given in the observation that none will want to preserve Nineveh's remembrance, for the city is utterly reprobate. Because of its debased activity, it has gained such contempt for itself that its demise will bring to the lips of the observers a sigh of relief and a song of rejoicing (1:15; cf. 3:19). These verses put all on notice that Israel's God is not only the sole true God of the universe but also the God of true justice with whom all have to deal. Robertson (1990:83) remarks, "Because of the broader redemptive-historical structures of Scripture, this deliverance from Assyria's oppression may be perceived as a microcosmic depiction of deliverance from all the oppression that comes as a consequence of sin, Satan, and death."

The closing proclamation of the messenger reminds the believer that there is still a place for good news. A believing mankind will yet enjoy the peace and felicity that come with the final defeat of evil. Israel would doubtless join in that exultation and take comfort in the good news (cf. 1:7, 12, 15; 2:2). Her dreaded enemy was gone, a reminder of God's promise concerning his judgment against all Israel's foes. In a sense, Nahum's prophecy is a near historical realization of Isaiah's prophecy relative to the eschatological scene. For Isaiah foresaw the day when an oppressed Israel would be freed at last from oppressors and invaders; its people would not only hear the message of the Lord's salvation but also experience the everlasting serenity that comes with his presence in royal power in their midst (Isa 52:1-10; cf. Joel 3:18-20). At that time, Jerusalem will be holy (cf. Jer 33:16) and in turn bear the good news of the tender care of its saving shepherd to the other cities of Judah (Isa 40:9-11). Under the direction of the Messiah (Isa 52:13–53:12), Zion will be rebuilt and its enemies subdued, and it will live in everlasting felicity with its God (Isa 61:1-7).

The emphasis of Isaiah and Nahum on God's good news becomes an important motif for the New Testament revelation. Jesus' birth was thus announced as an occasion of glad tidings (Luke 2:10), and Christ announced that his ministry fulfilled the message of salvation and joy that Isaiah prophesied (cf. Isa 61:1-2 with Luke 4:16-21). Peter made it clear to Jew and Gentile alike that Christ effected their full salvation, with the result that God's full peace can be enjoyed by all (Acts 10:34-43), a message of good news that Paul likewise affirms (Eph 2:14-18).

Nahum's prophecy, together with that of Isaiah 52:7, is thus related not only to Paul's missionary challenge but also to the theme of the good news of Christ's saving work. Because of the saving work of the Messiah, all can rejoice in the essence of Nahum's great prophecy. May the saints of all ages carry the completed message of good news to a needy mankind and live faithfully in the certain hope of that coming era of earth's completed redemption.

ENDNOTE

1. The term "name" also has important connotations for understanding God, for it calls attention to his revealed character and reputation. It eventually became a technical term for God (cf. Dan 9:18-19; Amos 2:7; 9:12) and hence was applied by the writers of the New Testament and the early church fathers to Christ (e.g., Acts 4:12; 5:41; 3 John 1:7; Ignatius *To the Ephesians* 3:1; 7:1; *To the Philippians* 10:1; *2 Clement* 13:1, 4; and often in the *Shepherd of Hermas*). It is still used to this day and may be frequently heard in the Hebrew equivalent of the phrase "God willing" (*'im yirtseh hashem*), literally, "if the Name is willing."

◆ II. The Doom of Nineveh Described (2:1–3:19)
   A. God, the Just Governor of the Nations (2:1-2)

1*Your enemy is coming to crush you,
   Nineveh.
Man the ramparts! Watch the
   roads!
Prepare your defenses! Call out
   your forces!

2Even though the destroyer has
   destroyed Judah,
   the LORD will restore its honor.
Israel's vine has been stripped of
   branches,
   but he will restore its splendor.

2:1 Verses 2:1-13 are numbered 2:2-14 in Hebrew text.

NOTES

2:1 [2] *enemy.* The Hebrew term is more literally "scatterer." The announcement of the advance of the "scatterer" provides a thought that is matched in 3:18-19 by the mention of the scattered refugees. The thought of destruction in 2:1-10 forms a literary link with 1:11-15 (esp. 1:14). Attempts to identify any one particular scatterer (e.g., Cyaxares the Mede, Nabopolassar, or Nebuchadnezzar) are pointless—the masculine singular participle being either the common collective singular or simply singular because the precise enemy was not further identified in Nahum's predictive perception. If Nahum had been written after Nineveh's destruction, as some critics affirm, more than likely the foe(s) would have been clearly designated. Conceivably, the "scatterer" could be the Lord himself (cf. Num 10:35; Ps 68:1; Jer 18:17).

Man the ramparts! Roberts (1991:57) suggests that the noun "ramparts" (*metsurah* [TH4694, ZH5193]) should be pointed *matsarah* [TH4712.1, ZH5211] (guard post), thus providing a cognate accusative with the verb *natsar* [TH5341, ZH5915]: "Man the guard post."

2:2 [3] *Israel's vine has been stripped of branches.* The NLT renders the resultant sense of the Hebrew text's "plunderers have plundered . . . their [vine] branches." The Hebrew verbal root connotes the thought of laying waste to something or some place. The vine was a well-known symbol of the covenant relation between God and Israel (Isa 5:1-7; Ezek 17; cf. Ps 80:8). Together with the fig tree, the vine was symbolic of God's blessing his people (Hos 2:12; Amos 4:9; Mic 4:4). The evidence of his presence and blessings consisted in the fruitfulness of the vine. When the vine lay devastated by plague (e.g., Joel 1:4) or the invader's heel (as here), it indicated God's chastisement of his people. God used such means and symbols to bring his people to repentance and spiritual growth. With repentance and restoration would come renewed splendor and fruitfulness. For *zemorah* [TH2156, ZH2367] (branch), Cathcart (1973a:85-86) suggests a connection with Ugaritic *dmr* (protect), hence "soldiers." Longman (1993:802) proposes the root *zamar* [TH2167, ZH2376] (sing), hence "songs." The thought probably is "branches," a synecdoche for the whole vine plant.

If Nahum prophesied during the reign of wicked Manasseh, the recent campaigns of Sennacherib and Esarhaddon would have been fresh in his memory as well as that of all Judah. Esarhaddon recorded that he summoned his vassal Manasseh to Nineveh: "And I summoned the kings of the Hittiteland [Syria] and [those] across the sea,—Ba'lu, king of Tyre, Manasseh, king of Judah. . . ." (see Luckenbill 1926:2.265). If Nahum's prophecy dates from as late as Ashurbanipal's later western campaigns (650-648 BC), his words would be all the more vivid.

restore its splendor. The noun *ga'on* [TH1347, ZH1454] is commonly translated "glory" or "splendor." A negative connotation, "pride," is sometimes attached to the noun (e.g., Prov 8:13; 16:18; Isa 16:6), but that seems unlikely here (contra Maier 1959:230-233). Rather, a repentant, redeemed Israel will be freed from exile and restored to its promised land to enjoy an era of peace and prosperity permeated by the glorious presence of her heavenly Redeemer. Attempts to emend the noun to *gepen* [TH1612, ZH1728] (vine) so as to form a parallel to "branches" (J. M. P. Smith 1911:305) are unnecessary.

COMMENTARY

The fate of plotting Nineveh (cf. 1:11-15) is carried forward in the announcement of the arrival of its attacker. In the light of this critical announcement, Nahum issues a fourfold command. Each of the imperatives is expressed asyndetically, thus producing a staccato effect and lending urgency and drama to the scene. Nahum's admonitions are probably to be understood as sarcastic. The defenders are urged to make full preparations to secure the city's defense. Because Nineveh's doom had already been announced (ch 1), all such efforts were obviously destined for failure. Mighty Nineveh would be powerless before its assailants, despite any and all efforts to defend it.

Nahum's announcement of the fall of Nineveh, despite its precautions, illustrates the old adage "Man proposes, God disposes." In God's time a "scatterer" would bring an end to this adversary of all nations. For Nineveh it would be the Chaldean Nebuchadnezzar II (605–562 BC), who would capture the Assyrian capital on behalf of his father, Nabopolassar, in 612 BC. Behind the movement of the Neo-Babylonian troops, however, stood an ultimate Scatterer, who as the Divine Warrior would use his human instruments to accomplish the purposes of his divine government. Such activities remind the believer of that climactic day when the last enemy will be subdued and the world will "become the Kingdom of our Lord and of his Christ, and he will reign forever and ever" (Rev 11:15).

In contrast to the Ninevites, God's people would know the restoration and splendor that only a sovereign and beneficent God can give. Indeed, the prophets frequently predicted that God would yet "restore the fortunes" of his people (cf. Hos 6:11; Joel 3:1; Amos 9:14) in an era of renewed refreshment, prosperity, and happiness. The promise harks back to God's people as heirs of the Abrahamic covenant (Gen 17:3-8; 22:17-18; 28:13-15). The realization of Israel's full covenant blessings will find fulfillment in a great future day when the Glorious One (Isa 24:14-16) will dwell in the midst of his people (Ezek 48:35; Joel 3:17, 21), thus giving glory to his nation and land (cf. Deut 33:27-29; Isa 4:2; 60:15).

◆   ## B. First Description of Nineveh's Demise (2:3-10)

3 Shields flash red in the sunlight!
   See the scarlet uniforms of the
      valiant troops!
Watch as their glittering chariots
   move into position,
   with a forest of spears waving above
      them.
4 The chariots race recklessly along the
      streets
   and rush wildly through the squares.
They flash like firelight
   and move as swiftly as lightning.
5 The king shouts to his officers;
   they stumble in their haste,
   rushing to the walls to set up their
      defenses.
6 The river gates have been torn open!
   The palace is about to collapse!
7 Nineveh's exile has been decreed,

and all the servant girls mourn
   its capture.
They moan like doves
   and beat their breasts in sorrow.
8 Nineveh is like a leaking water
   reservoir!
The people are slipping away.
"Stop, stop!" someone shouts,
   but no one even looks back.
9 Loot the silver!
   Plunder the gold!
There's no end to Nineveh's
      treasures—
   its vast, uncounted wealth.
10 Soon the city is plundered, empty,
   and ruined.
Hearts melt and knees shake.
The people stand aghast,
   their faces pale and trembling.

NOTES

2:3 [4] *Shields flash red.* The reddened shields refer perhaps to highly polished metal fittings that gleamed in the sunlight or to the dyeing of the shields with red color so as to strike terror into the hearts of the enemy. Some have suggested that it might be a veiled reference to the Assyrians' blood that would yet be spattered on them.

scarlet uniforms. Some evidence exists for the wearing of reddish or purple dress into combat, perhaps to intimidate the enemy (see Xenophon *Cyropaedia* 6.4.1; cf. Ezek 23:5-6) or to minimize the attackers' panic in the event of a wound, the blood creating a less noticeable effect on a scarlet uniform. It is possible, of course, that this term may have simply been selected as a suitable parallel for *me'addam* [TH119, ZH131], both words being used metonymically for the enemy's spattered blood on the warriors' shields and garments.

glittering chariots. The meaning of the word translated "glittering" is much in dispute. Among the ancient versions, the LXX and Vulgate take it to refer to the chariot reins, while the Syriac understands it in relation to the word "firelight" (or "torches") in the next verse. Several modern versions trace it to an Arabic or Syriac root designating a type of metal, while some commentators (e.g., Cathcart 1973a; Longman 1993; Roberts 1990) suggest some type of chariot covering or adornment. Thus construed, the thought is that the reflected gleam of the bedecked horses and chariots would further daunt the hearts of those who beheld the chariots moving into position for battle.

spears. The noun *habberoshim* [TH1265, ZH1360] indicates a type of tree such as the cypress or juniper. Since the spear shaft came from such wood, by metonymy it came to stand for the spear itself. Roberts (1991:58), however, calls attention to a suggestion by C.-L. Seow to take it as a reference to the wooden framework of the chariots. Thus understood, the lines would read, "The chariot attachments are like fire in the day of his preparation, and the chariot frames quiver." Still others follow a different approach by proposing that there was scribal confusion in the initial *bet* of the word with the letter *pe* (a well-attested interchange in the ancient Semitic languages). In that case, the noun would refer to the horses (NRSV, NEB) or horsemen (NJB, LXX).

2:4 [5] *streets . . . squares.* Interpreters have disagreed as to whether the nouns refer to streets and squares inside the city walls or outside. The latter noun is used most often for wide places within a city or village (cf. Deut 13:16; Ezra 10:9; Neh 8:1; Esth 4:6) but may possibly designate open places outside the city as well. One must decide whether the flow of thought best fits the point of view of the defenders or the attackers. The NLT takes the former alternative here and in the succeeding verses; Roberts (1991:65), the latter (see my remarks in Patterson 1991:66). The two words are used in parallel in such texts as Prov 5:16; 7:12; 22:13; Jer 5:1; 9:21 [20]; and Amos 5:16.

flash like firelight . . . swiftly as lightning. The description here depicts the swift movement of the chariots with their polished metal gleaming in the sunlight. If the reference is to the attackers, the whole effect is designed to produce further awe and fright in the defenders beholding the activity.

2:5 [6] *king shouts.* Lit., "he remembers" (cf. LXX, Vulgate, NASB, NKJV). The usual meaning of the verb *zakar* [TH2142, ZH2349] seems to make little sense in the context unless, as some suggest, Yahweh is the subject, not the attacking enemy. The difficulty has occasioned numerous alternative suggestions for understanding the verb, such as "summon" (NIV, RSV, cf. NJB) or "recount" (KJV) or "calls" (NRSV), as well as several conjectural emendations, none of which seems convincing (Maier 1959:92-93; J. M. P. Smith 1911:330). The NLT rendering suits the military operations of the context well and has the advantage of reflecting a nuance found in its Akkadian cognate *zakaru* (give orders to).

they stumble. The Hebrew verb here, when used in military contexts, customarily indicates weakness and lack of progress (Cathcart 1973a:94), a thought that does not suit this context well. The basic meaning of the root, "stumble," however, does fit nicely here—the sense being a stumbling caused by a sudden rapid movement of hastening to the wall.

their defenses. The hapax legomenon *hassokek* [TH1886.1/5526B, ZH2021/6116] must refer to some type of covering, as a glance at its cognates shows (see my comments in TWOT 2.623-624). The consistent attention directed to the activities of the scatterer suggests a mantelet, or large protective shield, used by the attackers to shield them from the arrows and missiles of the defenders on the wall. Roberts (1991:59) decides for "the various roofed and mobile siege towers that were used by besieging armies to protect their sappers and their troops manning the battering rams."

2:6 [7] *river gates.* With the Hebrew *she'arim* [TH8179, ZH9133] (sluice/dam gates) compare the Old South Arabic *t'rt* (sluices), and note the Akkadian *bab nari* (door of the river) to indicate sluice gates for controlling water flow.

2:7 [8] *decreed.* The form *wehutsab* [TH5324, ZH5893] has proven to be a time-honored *crux interpretum*. Maier (1959) provides a list of more than a dozen suggestions that have been put forward as a sample of the many ideas that have been proposed. The ancient versions are likewise in disagreement. Basically three positions have been taken. (1) The form is a noun (*hutsab*) meaning something like "beauty," "lady," or "mistress" and refers either to Nineveh itself or to the statue of Ishtar that was housed there (Cathcart 1973a; Longman 1993). (2) The form is a verb that is to be translated "it is decreed" (NIV, NKJV). (3) The form should be emended entirely. The problem is heightened by the two feminine verbs that follow. J. M. P. Smith (1911:320-321) declares the form "insoluble" and the meaning of the whole line "hopelessly obscured."

Perhaps the solution lies along literary lines in (1) understanding *hutsab* in the sense of "dissolved" (cf. Akkadian *nasabu* [suck out] and Arabic *dabba* [to hew to the ground]) and (2) placing the word in 2:6, a procedure that would yield a poetic 3/3 structure for this verse and a resultant double set of 2/2 in the following verse. This placement would also provide a second consecutive verse that is closed by a passive suffix-conjugation verb. Thus construed, the verse yields good sense: "The palace collapses and crumbles" (due to the rising waters that inundate the city; cf. Saggs 1969b:221-222).

its capture. This word, *gulletah* [TH1540, ZH1655] (she was stripped), is taken by some to refer to the Assyrian queen carried away into captivity. It could also refer to Nineveh, here personified as a captive warrior (Roberts 1991:66). Others have suggested the carrying away of the statue of Ishtar. By reading *galutah* [TH1546, ZH1661], one could also argue for "her exiles/captives," a meaning anticipating the same figure in 3:10. Still another possibility is to view the consonantal text as a passive or intransitive verb, a reading reflected in the NIV's "the city be exiled"—see the Vulgate's *captivus abductus est* ("is carried away captive") and the NEB's "the train of captives goes into exile."

beat their breasts in sorrow. A similar sentiment occurs in the *Curse of Agade* (cf. J. S. Cooper, *The Curse of Agade.* Baltimore: Johns Hopkins University Press [1983]). Such actions were typically carried out by women who were pleading for mercy in situations like these. The figure of the weeping woman is abundantly attested in the literature and artistry of the ancient Near East and the OT, as is the action of beating the breast in contrition (cf. Jer 31:15; Luke 18:13; 23:27). About women weeping and pleading for mercy and subsequently lamenting their captured state, see Layard 1849:286-287.

2:8 [9] *The people are slipping away.* The Hebrew line is notoriously difficult and has occasioned numerous comments. The NLT plays on the metaphor of the previous line to form an implied simile: Nineveh is like a leaky reservoir; just as its waters drain away, so the city's populace is slipping away from it.

no one even looks back. Lit., "no one turns around." The words are reminiscent of Jer 46:5, 21. Cathcart (1973a:101) calls attention to the heaping up of the letter mem in this verse (nine times), an assonance that enhances dramatic effect.

2:9 [10] *Loot . . . . Plunder.* The double imperatives answer the two calls to stop in the previous line.

silver. . . . gold! Silver and gold often appear as a set pair to indicate wealth or booty (Gen 24:35; Josh 6:19).

There's no end. This phrase occurs in the OT outside Nahum only in the remarkable parallel Isa 2:7.

2:10 [11] *plundered, empty, and ruined.* The Hebrew text is full of alliteration and assonance: *buqah umebuqah umebullaqah.* If one were to attempt a similar effect in English, one might render the phrase, "destroyed and despoiled and denuded." Cathcart (1973a:103) calls attention to a stylistic resemblance with Isa 22:5. Isa 24:1 employs the same two roots, *balaq* [TH1110, ZH1191] and *baqaq* [TH1238, ZH1327], followed by the use of *baqaq* with *bazaz* [TH962, ZH1024] two verses later. Although this type of paronomasia is common enough in the OT (e.g., Joel 2:2), the parallels with Isaiah are striking and may point to a further literary relationship between the writings of the two prophets.

Hearts melt. Cathcart (1973a:104) demonstrates the close connection of the last three lines of v. 10 with the thought of Isa 13:7-8: Both texts mention the melting of hearts. In Nahum, there is mention of the trembling of the knees; in the Isaiah text, weakness of the arms. Anguish in the loins and the change of the color of the face are found in both passages. Once again a connection between Isaiah and Nahum seems certain.

COMMENTARY

Nahum's description of the attack on Nineveh follows a clear pattern: the enemy's assembling of his forces (2:3), the initial advance (2:4), the all-out attack (2:5-6), and its aftermath (2:7-10). The attack is rendered in vivid detail. The invading army's attire and equipment are described first (2:3). They are clad in scarlet and carry reddened shields; these would not only give a distinctive color to the army in the hand-to-hand combat that was sure to come but would also provide a grim forecast of the shedding of the defenders' blood—soon to be mingled with the clothing and equipment of the striking force. Adding to the awesome appearance of this "scatterer" was the terrifying sight of its chariots. With horse and chariot bedecked with highly polished metal that gleamed like fire in the brilliant sunlight and with soldiers equipped with polished cypress spears (which would give a reddish appearance), the effect of the whole spectacle was designed to strike terror into the stoutest of hearts.

After the initial preparations, the enemy commander gives the order to charge the wall (2:5). The seasoned warriors respond instantly. Rushing forward, they reach Nineveh's massive city wall where they put in place the mantelet that will give them protection from Nineveh's defenders during the siege operations (2:5; cf. Jer 52:4; Ezek 4:2). Thus protected from the flying arrows, falling stones, and lighted torches that would come down from the city's protectors atop the wall, the process of breaching the city could begin. Typically, such an attack would include the use of siege mounds and towers, scaling ladders and tunneling operations, battering rams and axes, and the torching of the city gate. For Nineveh, the means of defeat, however, came from an unexpected source. Nineveh trusted not only in her massive walls, which Sennacherib had begun and named "The Wall That Terrifies the Enemy" (outer wall) and "The Wall Whose Splendor Overwhelms the Foe" (inner wall), but also in her surrounding moat and the proximity of the Tigris River. Yet ironically these defenses would work against the proud city. Diodorus reports that a series of torrential downpours swelled the "Euphrates" (i.e., the city's river systems: the Khosr, which flowed through the city, and the Tigris) and flooded Nineveh, thereby undermining its wall and causing the collapse of a significant part of it.

Sennacherib had also built a double dam for the Khosr River to form a reservoir for Nineveh's populace (cf. 2:6). This reservoir was augmented by a series of dam gates or sluices to regulate the supply of water to the city. The primary intent of Nahum's prediction is that the advancing enemy would shut the sluices, thereby cutting off the city's drinking supply. With the reservoir full, the gates would again be opened, causing the already flooded Khosr to destroy the surrounding walls where it entered the Ninlil Gate. Maier (1959:253) remarks, "The Quay Gate, at which the Khosr left the city, might also be devastated and in the intervening city much serious damage done. After the flow subsided, the entrance to Nineveh would have been made much easier for the besiegers."

Nahum next envisioned the subsequent collapse of Nineveh's magnificent palace. As the account unfolds, the attackers would gain entrance to the city, for the Assyrians are seen as being captured and led away into exile, while the women, pleading for mercy and bewailing their fate, are being led away moaning plaintively. The inevitable consequences that follow a city's capture are then given in detail. Conquered Nineveh is said to be "like a pool of water." The simile is both effective and apropos. Mighty Nineveh was situated in a favorable location that blessed her with an adequate water supply, one made more abundant by wise administrative leadership. But the blessing turned to a curse at the hands of the enemy, whose siege operations left Nineveh a veritable "pool of water."

From the floodwaters and the crumbling city the masses fled in sheer panic (2:8). In the midst of the clamor of the departing throng, an impassioned voice rings out: "Stop, stop!" No one turns around, much less halts, in his desperate flight. Another cry is heard (the entire scene is depicted with the author's characteristic picturesque brevity): "Loot the silver! Plunder the gold!" (2:9) Are they the words of the invaders, the prophet, or God himself? Regardless, it is ultimately the certain judgment of God. Nineveh, who had heaped up hordes of captured treasure, would face despoliation. The precious possessions of many nations that poured into the Neo-Assyrian capital as a result of trade, tribute, and booty were almost beyond counting. Now Nineveh would have her riches taken away.

All that wealth—gone in an instant! The graphic description of Nineveh's fall stands as a grim reminder of the fate of misspent greed, power, and opportunity. The proverbial dictum is ever true: "Godliness makes a nation great, but sin is a disgrace to any people" (Prov 14:34). Nineveh had played the rich fool (cf. Luke 12:16-20). Unlike rich fools who live only to aggrandize themselves, believers must learn the lessons of true wealth: "Beware! Guard against every kind of greed. Life is not measured by how much you own. . . . Yes, a person is a fool to store up earthly wealth but not have a rich relationship with God" (Luke 12:15, 21). Several further theological lessons emerge from this passage. (1) God is sovereign over the disposition of nations and uses them to do his bidding. (2) Behind the fall of Nineveh stands the heavenly specter of the Divine Warrior. (3) While wickedness may seem to bring victory, it ultimately reaps its just reward. The proud city, whose forces had so often treated others contemptuously and violently, would meet a similar end. The principle of equal justice is fully operative here: "As you have done . . . it will be done to you" (Obad 1:15).

◆   C. The Discredited City (2:11-13)

¹¹ Where now is that great Nineveh,
     that den filled with young lions?
 It was a place where people—like lions
     and their cubs—
 walked freely and without fear.
¹² The lion tore up meat for his cubs
     and strangled prey for his mate.
 He filled his den with prey,
     his caverns with his plunder.

¹³ "I am your enemy!"
     says the LORD of Heaven's Armies.
 "Your chariots will soon go up in smoke.
     Your young men* will be killed in
     battle.
 Never again will you plunder
     conquered nations.
 The voices of your proud messengers
     will be heard no more."

2:13 Hebrew *young lions.*

NOTES

2:11 [12] lions and their cubs. The several words for lion here seem intended to represent the whole family (or pride) of lions: *'ari* [TH738, ZH787] (lion), *kepir* [TH3715, ZH4097] (young lion), *labi'* [TH3833, ZH4233] (lioness), and *gur 'aryeh* [TH1482/743.2, ZH1594/793] (lion cub). The ancient versions, however, understand *labi'* as an infinitive construct, apparently reading *labo'* [TH3807.1/935, ZH4200/995] from *bo'* (enter). Accordingly, some (Maier 1959; Roberts 1991) take the MT reading as a Hiphil infinitive construct form shortened from *lehabi'* [TH3807.1/935, ZH4200/995] ("to bring"; cf. Jer 27:7).

a place where. This particle (*'asher* [TH834, ZH889]) has locative force. The relative pronoun here betrays its Akkadian origin as a noun *ashru*, meaning "place," from which a particle *ashar* developed as a locative relative particle (cf. Aramaic/Syriac *'atar* with secondary development into a locative relative "place where" with further development in Hebrew as a general relative particle).

2:12 [13] cubs. In the various mss, there are two readings: *gur* [TH1482, ZH1594] (whelp) and *gor* [TH1484, ZH1596] (lion cub); both are masculine nouns but occur with a feminine plural ending in this verse. Since masculine Hebrew nouns frequently take feminine plural endings, there is no need to emend the text to a masculine plural as some have done.

tore up . . . strangled. The two verbs in the Hebrew text are *tarap* [TH2963, ZH3271] (tear) and *khanaq* [TH2614, ZH2871] (strangle). As to the former, the root *tarap* occurs three times in this verse, strategically placed in poetic parallelism and in *chiasmus* so as to emphasize the viciousness of the lion with regard to its prey. The root reappears in 2:13 (NLT "plunder") and forms a literary link with the next section, where it appears again in 3:1 (NLT "victims"). As for the latter, although some charged that the idea of lions strangling their prey is unrealistic (with the result that some such translation as "tore up" [cf. NJB] has been substituted), the verb means "strangle" throughout the Semitic family of languages and is consistently so used in the OT. As Cathcart (1973a:107) observes, "Lions do strangle their prey and we have excellent representations from the Near East of lions strangling their prey."

2:13 [14] I am. Heb. *hineni* (behold me). Nahum uses the particle *hinneh* [TH2009, ZH2180] several times at strategic points as a transitional device (e.g., 1:15; 3:13). It is often used to introduce divine pronouncements and to authenticate a prophet's words. Here *hinneh* is reinforced by the noun *ne'um* [TH5002, ZH5536] (declaration), which is frequently used to confirm the divine source of a prophet's message (cf. Jer 9:22 [21]; 23:31; Ezek 20:3; Zech 12:1).

Your young men Lit., "your young lions" (so NLT mg). The literary practice of calling royalty, leaders, or warriors by animal names is common in both Ugaritic and Hebrew. The figure of devouring the prey is continued here, but with image transfer: The young lions are now the prey devoured by the enemy's sword.

COMMENTARY

Contemplating the demise of arrogant Nineveh, Nahum utilized a taunt song, a literary form that was common in the ancient Near East (cf. Patterson 2007). A taunt song is a subtype of satire. The first of three such satires was directed against Nineveh (cf. 3:8-13; 3:14-19). The tone is personal, invective, and morally indignant. Using an extended metaphor (or allegory), Nineveh is ironically compared to a lion's den—no longer the lair of an invincible predator or a den of refuge for its cubs, but reduced to ashes. The point of the satirical taunt song is clear: Nineveh will be judged for its selfishness, rapacity, and cruelty.

The lion motif is particularly appropriate. History attests that Sennacherib compared himself to a lion, decorating his palace freely with sphinx-like lion statues. Other Assyrian kings referred to themselves as lions and adorned their palaces with various artistic representations of the lion (Johnston 2001:287-307). Reliefs of the Assyrian kings on the lion hunt appear frequently on the palace walls. The mighty lion of the nations (Assyria) used to proceed at will from its impenetrable lair (Nineveh) to return with its prey to its pride (the citizens of Nineveh). At one time, Nineveh bulged with the bounteous booty that her kings had brought within its walls. But all that would soon change.

In the light of Assyrian rapacity, God's pronouncement again is heard: "Behold, I am against you." Such is the solemn utterance of the Lord of Heaven's Armies (Yahweh Sabaoth). This term (found about 260 times in the OT) declares God's sovereignty not only over creation (Amos 4:13) but also over all nations and over earth's history (Isa 37:16). Although God had used Assyria as his agent to punish an unrepentant Israel, he could and would still another army (which, in turn, would one day suffer God's chastisement for its own sin; Jer 50:18) to effect the just judgment of haughty Assyria (Zeph 2:13-15), the very nation for whom a merciful God had earlier been so concerned (Jonah 4:2, 11). Ultimately, Israel herself will triumph through her Lord of Heaven's Armies, who will rule eternally over all forces, heavenly and earthly alike (1 Sam 17:45; Isa 24:21-23; 34:1-10).

The satirical taunt with which the chapter closes underscores both the helplessness of arrogant Assyria and the sovereignty of Almighty God. The proud Assyrian in his royal city of Nineveh, whom all viewed as an unconquerable lion, has met his tamer. The One who is the sovereign and omnipotent ruler of the world is he who removes kings and sets others on their thrones (Dan 2:21), and who does as he pleases with those who live on earth (Dan 4:35). He is not unmindful of the cruelty of men and nations, as the parade of fallen dictators and evildoers testifies. For his "eyes watch the proud and humiliate them" (2 Sam 22:28).

In an interesting twist, a world alienated from God will be brought into subjection by the Lion of the tribe of Judah (Rev 5:5; 19:11-21). Accordingly, the believer may take heart and so live as to fulfill Micah's admonition: "The LORD has told you what is good, and this is what he requires of you: to do what is right, to love mercy, and to walk humbly with your God" (Mic 6:8; cf. Jas 4:16; 1 Pet 5:6-7).

◆   D. Second Description of Nineveh's Demise (3:1-7)

What sorrow awaits Nineveh,
   the city of murder and lies!
She is crammed with wealth
   and is never without victims.
² Hear the crack of whips,
   the rumble of wheels!
Horses' hooves pound,
   and chariots clatter wildly.
³ See the flashing swords and glittering
   spears
   as the charioteers charge past!
There are countless casualties,
   heaps of bodies—
so many bodies that
   people stumble over them.
⁴ All this because Nineveh,
   the beautiful and faithless city,
mistress of deadly charms,

enticed the nations with her beauty.
She taught them all her magic,
   enchanting people everywhere.
⁵ "I am your enemy!"
   says the LORD of Heaven's Armies.
"And now I will lift your skirts
   and show all the earth your
   nakedness and shame.
⁶ I will cover you with filth
   and show the world how vile you
   really are.
⁷ All who see you will shrink back
   and say,
'Nineveh lies in ruins.
   Where are the mourners?'
Does anyone regret your
   destruction?"

NOTES

3:1 *What sorrow.* The Hebrew text reads *hoy* [TH1945, ZH2098] (woe). As Longman (1993:812) points out, "Woe-oracles are quite common in prophetic literature (Isa 5:18-19; Amos 5:18-20; 6:1-7; Mic 2:1-4) to name only a few." Woe oracles typically contain the following elements: invective ("woe to"), threat, and criticism (the reason for the denunciation and threatened judgment).

city of murder. Lit., "city of blood." Maier (1959:292) notes the extreme cruelty of the Assyrians and remarks, "The atrocious practice of cutting off hands and feet, ears and noses, gouging out eyes, lopping off heads and then binding them to vines or heaping them up before city gates; the utter fiendishness by which captives could be impaled or flayed alive through a process in which their skin was gradually and completely removed—this planned frightfulness systematically enforced by the 'bloody city' was now to be avenged." For examples of

Assyrian cruelty and rapacity, see Luckenbill 1926:2.304, 309; see also Freeman 1985:36-38; Maier 1959:281-283.

lies! The Assyrian practice of using deception as a psychological tool to gain the submission of a besieged city can be illustrated from the archives of the Assyrian kings. Saggs (1969a:17) finds an interesting parallel to Sennacherib's siege of Jerusalem (2 Kgs 18:15-19:37) in the records of Tiglath-pileser III (745-727 BC).

3:2 The short phraseology that makes up vv. 2-3 yields a dramatic effect. The verses are characterized by a staccato style and filled with words that take on an almost onomatopoeic quality. It is a fine example of picturesque brevity. There is also progression in the individual lines that comprise the passage, providing a strong touch of realism.

crack . . . rumble. The word *qol* (twice in the verse) [TH6963, ZH7754] (noise, voice) is found in a similar martial context in Joel 2:4-5. Whereas Joel speaks of the horses running and of the chariots, Nahum focuses on the rumbling of the chariot wheels. Although *ra'ash* [TH7494, ZH8323] ("shake"; here, with *qol* = "rumble") is at times used for the din of battle (Isa 9:5 [4]; Jer 10:22), it is often used for the shaking of the earth (Amos 1:1; cf. the verbal root in Judg 5:4; 2 Sam 22:8; Ps 68:8; 77:18).

chariots clatter. This phrase exhibits both alliteration and assonance: *umerkabah meraqqedah*. The verb *raqad* [TH7540, ZH8376] (clatter) is related to Akkadian *raqadu* ("leap/ skip"; cf. also Ugaritic *rqdm*, "dancers"; Arabic *raqada*, "leap"). The Assyrian battle chariot was feared far and wide. Sennacherib called his private war chariot "The Vanquisher of the Wicked and Evil" and also "The Vanquisher of the Enemy." (For the text, see Borger 1963: table 49, V:70; table 50, VI:8; for English translation, see Luckenbill 1926:126-127.)

3:3 *flashing swords and glittering spears.* Both descriptions provide picturesque images of awesome battle weapons, reflecting the sunlight in their wielders' hands. Both adjectives are used frequently in military contexts under various figures (cf. 2:4; Deut 32:41; Job 39:23; Ezek 21:15; Hab 3:11).

casualties. The next four lines contain three terms for the bodies of those slain in battle: *khalal* [TH2491, ZH2728] (slain), *peger* [TH6297, ZH7007] (corpse), and *gewiyah* [TH1472, ZH1581] (dead body). One is reminded of the frequent Assyrian boast of leaving behind a host of dead bodies after the battle. Note, for example, Ashurnasirpal's boast at the siege of Damdamusa:

> With the masses of my troops and by my furious battle onset I stormed, I captured the city; 600 of their warriors I put to the sword; 3,000 captives I burned with fire; I did not leave a single one among them alive to serve as a hostage. Hulai, their governor, I captured alive. Their corpses I formed into pillars; their young men and maidens I burned in the fire. Hulai, their governor, I flayed; his skin I spread upon the wall of the city of Damdamusa; the city I destroyed, I devastated, I burned with fire. (Luckenbill 1926:146)

Roberts (1991:73) remarks, "There are so many dead bodies that the attackers stumble over them in their advance, and it seems clear from the larger context that these dead are the defenders and inhabitants of Nineveh. The city of bloody oppression is getting its own treatment in full measure."

3:4 *All this because.* Scholars and translators have disagreed as to whether, syntactically, v. 4 continues v. 3 (so NIV) or belongs with v. 5 (so NRSV). The NLT rightly takes the verse as an independent, transitional verse between vv. 1-3 and 5-7. As such, it forms a literary hinge between the two subunits. On literary hinging, see Parunak 1983:540-541.

deadly charms. Lit., "sorceries." Nineveh is the enchantress *par excellence.*

enticed. Lit., "sells." The Hebrew verb is related to the Akkadian *makaru* (use in business). Nineveh is thus described as "she who makes merchandise of the nations" by her numerous harlotries and sorceries.

people everywhere. Heb. *mishpakhah* [TH4940, ZH5476] (lit., "families"). This Hebrew noun is often used in a sense wider than the English term, meaning "clan," "kindred." In Josh 7:16-18 it designates one of the clans of the tribe of Judah. The noun can refer to familial relations at several levels or have a still wider use (cf. Gen 12:3; 28:14; Zech 14:17). For, at times, it forms a subunit of the terms *goyim* [TH1471, ZH1580] (nations) and *'ammim* [TH5971A, ZH6639] (peoples); or *mishpakhah* even appears as a parallel term to *goyim* (e.g., Gen 12:2-3). Nahum, then, may mean here both nations and the peoples who compose them.

3:5 lift your skirts. Such actions were often applied as punishment for prostitution (cf. Jer 13:22, 26-27; Ezek 16:37-39; 23:10, 29; Hos 2:3, 9-10). Several scholars have followed the lead of Hillers (1964:58-60) in seeing a relation between the biblical data cited here and the curse pronounced in an Aramaic inscription of Sefire: "[And just as] a [ha]r[lot is stripped naked], so may the wives of Mati'el be stripped naked, and the wives of his off-spring and the wives of [his] no[bles]" (COS 2.213).

3:6 show the world how vile you really are. The Hebrew verb here carries the significance "treat as a fool," hence "treat contemptuously." Nineveh will be treated as that which is detestable, as an utter disgrace and a public spectacle.

3:7 shrink back. Lit., "flee." The Greek tradition renders the Hebrew text by such verbs as *apopēdēsetai* (will leap away), *katabēsetai* [cf. TG2597A, ZG2849] (will descend), and *anachōrēsei* [TG402, ZG432] (will draw back), suggesting uncertainty in the exemplar or lack of under-standing of the root (cf. Maier 1959:313).

shrink back . . . Nineveh . . . ruins . . . the mourners. Nahum skillfully plays both on sounds and meaning of these words in the verse. He intentionally heaps up the letters daleth and nun, each occurring five times in this verse.

COMMENTARY

The woe oracle of these verses includes a catalog of the Assyrians' crimes. Nineveh itself was guilty of bloody atrocities and deceptive practices. The latter description depicts the Assyrians' use of treachery and alluring platitudes to gain others' loyalty. They also employed psychological warfare, couching their words in false promises and outright lies to gain the submission of enemy cities in times of siege (cf. 2 Kgs 18:28-32). Their idolatry, arrogant pride (cf. Zeph 2:15), and misrepresentation of God himself (2 Kgs 19:21-27) were particularly loathsome. Nineveh's ravenous appetite for robbery and plunder is also mentioned, a trait that harkens back to the preceding taunt song and the figure of Nineveh as a lion's den to which her ill-gotten prey was taken. In every way, then, Nineveh was known to all as a wicked city (cf. Jonah 1:2).

So many would lose their lives—and for what? It was because Nineveh housed an unalterably proud, selfish, and unholy people. The Assyrians had made Nineveh a splendid and sophisticated metropolis by making merchandise out of other nations and people, either through military might or economic exploitation. Nine-veh had played the harlot via such seductions. Accordingly, they who had so mali-ciously treated others would receive just recompense for their deeds, while the city itself would lie in ruins with none to mourn its demise.

This passage reminds all that God is a God of justice (Ps 9:7-8), who abhors sin and will reward men and nations equitably in accordance with their deeds (Ps 67:4; Isa 1:27; Jer 46:28; Joel 3:1-8; Acts 17:31). This truth is in harmony with the further scriptural revelation that the Messiah will bring justice to the nations (Isa 42:1-4;

Matt 12:18-21). His justice will include the judging of the great harlot of the future, the worldwide socio-religio-economic system known prophetically as Babylon (Rev 17). This world system will be brought to an end (Rev 18) by the returning Christ (Rev 19:1-3, 11-21), who "judges fairly" (Rev 19:11) and whose "judgments are true and just" (Rev 19:2). In addition, his just activity will culminate in the establishment of salvation and righteousness for all (Isa 51:4-6). Seeing, then, that they may look forward with confidence to that time when the earth will be administered in true and holy justice (Isa 32:1; Ezek 34:16; Rev 15:3-4), believers should be challenged to act justly here and now (Mic 6:8; cf. Isa 1:17; Jer 7:5) and entrust their lives to him "who always judges fairly" (1 Pet 2:23).

The passage also reminds believers that when the wicked have received just judgment for their sins, there will be none to comfort or mourn for them. How much better to have lived so that others will not only be touched with compassion in one's time of passing but be blessed by the remembrance of a gracious life and godly testimony (Prov 10:7; cf. Prov 22:1).

◆   E. The Defenseless Citadel (3:8-19)
       1. A comparison of Nineveh and Thebes (3:8-13)

⁸Are you any better than the city of Thebes,*
situated on the Nile River,
surrounded by water?
She was protected by the river on all sides,
walled in by water.
⁹Ethiopia* and the land of Egypt gave unlimited assistance.
The nations of Put and Libya were among her allies.
¹⁰Yet Thebes fell,
and her people were led away as captives.
Her babies were dashed to death against the stones of the streets.
Soldiers threw dice* to get Egyptian officers as servants.

All their leaders were bound in chains.

¹¹And you, Nineveh, will also stagger like a drunkard.
You will hide for fear of the attacking enemy.
¹²All your fortresses will fall.
They will be devoured like the ripe figs
that fall into the mouths of those who shake the trees.
¹³Your troops will be as weak and helpless as women.
The gates of your land will be opened wide to the enemy and set on fire and burned.

3:8 Hebrew No-amon; also in 3:10. 3:9 Hebrew Cush. 3:10 Hebrew They cast lots.

NOTES
3:8 *Thebes.* Heb. *no' 'amon* [TH4996A, ZH5531]. The Assyrians knew the city as *ni'u* (Amarna *ni*), and the Greeks called it *Dios Polis* (Divine City). In Egypt itself it was known as *n'iwt rst* (Southern City) or as simply *n'iwt* (the City). Accordingly, Ezekiel (Ezek 30:14-16) can also call it just *no'* [TH4996, ZH5530]. *'amon* is a reference to the god Amun, who rose to prominence in Egypt's twelfth dynasty and, after subsequently being assimilated with the sun-god Re, became the principal national deity Amun-Re, patron deity during the New Kingdom era (c. 1570–1085 BC).

protected by the river on all sides. Thebes counted heavily on its watery position for its defense—the waters serving virtually as the city's protective walls.

3:9 Put. The exact location of this land is uncertain (see the note on the fall of Thebes in 3:10), despite its close association with Ethiopia and Egypt elsewhere (Gen 10:6; in Ezek 27:10; 30:5; 38:5, NLT identifies Put with Libya). Jeremiah (Jer 46:9-10) likewise prophesied that Egypt's allies—Cush, Put, and Lydia—would be no deterrent to its defeat in the day of the Lord's judgment against Egypt.

were among her allies. Lit., "were your helpers." The Hebrew phrase is wide ranging and includes all sorts of supporting resources, not just military aid.

3:10 Thebes fell. The city fell to the Assyrians under King Ashurbanipal in 663 BC. Before Ashurbanipal's victory, Thebes had seemed unconquerable. Surrounded by a strong defensive wall and a water system that included lakes, moats, canals, and the Nile, Thebes had been able to boast of the help of not only all Egypt but also its seventh-century allies: Sudanese Cush, Put (perhaps the fabled land of Punt in coastal Somaliland), and Libya. None of these, however, was to prove effective in protecting Thebes.

dashed to death. The practice of exterminating infants is recorded elsewhere in the Scriptures (2 Kgs 8:12; Ps 137:9; Isa 13:16, 18; Hos 10:14; 13:16; cf. Matt 2:16-18). The perpetration of barbaric acts of cruelty against captive cities is abundantly attested in the Assyrian annals. Ashurbanipal reports that in the Elamite campaign against Bit-Imbi, "The people dwelling therein, who had not come forth and had not greeted my majesty, I slew. Their heads I cut off. [Of others] I pierced the lips [and] took them to Assyria as a spectacle for the people of my land" (Luckenbill 1926:306).

threw dice. This practice is noted elsewhere in the OT (cf. Joel 3:3; Obad 1:11). It is also documented in extrabiblical literature, as is the binding in chains of captured nobility (cf. 2 Kgs 25:7; Isa 45:14; Jer 40:1, 4).

3:11 And you . . . also. The flavoring connective particle *gam* [TH1571, ZH1685] is employed twice in this verse and twice in the previous verse. Its recurrence has the effect of the clarion peal of a bell dolefully sounding out the awful truth that Nineveh, too, must surely reenact the tragic experience of Thebes.

stagger like a drunkard. Several scholars suggest an emendation here so as to read "you will hire yourself out," that is, as a prostitute, echoing the familiar example of wartime conditions described in the KRT epic of Ugarit (lines 97-98; for the text, see Gordon 1965:250). Although the Ugaritic parallel is interesting, the pointing of the Hebrew verb makes sense as it stands and is appropriate to the desperate conditions described here. Moreover, Nahum has mentioned the image of drunkenness earlier in another connection (in 1:10).

3:12 fortresses. The underlying Hebrew noun is generally associated with a root meaning "restrain/cut off," hence "fortify." Cathcart (1973a:138-139) relates the Hebrew root to Cyrus Gordon's suggestion for the Ugaritic verb *bsr* (soar). The idea behind the word "fortress" would then be derived from the act of "raising defenses higher." Parrot (1955:279) understands the fortresses here to refer to Nineveh's supporting towns of Ashur and Tarbisu, which fell in 614 BC, two years before Nineveh itself was captured.

ripe figs. For the image of early ripe figs taken into the mouth of the eater, see Isa 28:4. Robertson (1990:119) calls attention to the use of this motif to depict the coming cataclysms in Rev 6:13-17.

3:13 Your troops. The particle with which this verse begins (*hinneh* [TH2009, ZH2180]; cf. 1:15; 2:13) once again is used toward the end of a literary unit. The word translated "troops" is normally rendered "people" (cf. KJV). The military situation involved here, however, has led several commentators (e.g., Cathcart, R. L. Smith) and modern versions (e.g., NIV,

NRSV) to abandon the traditional understanding of the word. Nahum's taunt concerning Nineveh's warriors being like women is illuminated by Hillers' reminder (1964:66-68) of Near Eastern treaty curses in which warriors are compared to women, especially in the treaty between Ashurnirari V of Assyria and Mati'ilu of Arpad, where the curse of warriors becoming women is juxtaposed with that of Mati'ilu's wives becoming prostitutes.

COMMENTARY

With his woeful description of Nineveh's destruction completed, Nahum once again uses a taunt song to depict Nineveh's dire plight. The section (3:8-19) flows in two movements. The first, opening with a rhetorical question, reminds Nineveh that she is no more secure than once-proud Thebes, which also fell. Rather, her allegedly impregnable defenses will fall as easily as ripe figs the eater shakes from the tree, and her most virile champions will prove to be little more than helpless women. In the second portion the prophet ironically ridicules Nineveh's defenders, urging them to make all necessary preparations. It will be to no avail, for her protectors will be shown to be inept at best, deserters at worst. In the end, the message of her fall will be rehearsed to a rejoicing mankind (3:14-19).

Both halves of the taunt, like the taunt song in 2:11-13, are splendid examples of satire: Both contain a specific object of satirical attack—Assyria/Nineveh; both provide a rhetorical vehicle for carrying forward the satire—portraiture, irony, simile, and metaphor; both have a satirical tone—Juvenalian attack and sarcasm; and both reveal a distinct trait that merits correction—Nineveh's pride as seen in her trust in her vaunted defenses and Nineveh's haughtiness as evidenced in her disdainful cruelty toward others.

Nahum first cites the example of Thebes, whose fate Assyria knew from firsthand experience. Thebes was the illustrious and time-honored capital of Egypt. Situated on both sides of the Nile in Upper Egypt, it achieved its greatest fame as the political, religious, and cultural center of Egypt's great New Kingdom dynasties. Thebes was still a thriving metropolis in the waning days of Egypt's Twenty-fifth (Nubian) Dynasty (c. 751–656 BC), even though the dynastic capital appears to have been situated farther north in Memphis. After Esarhaddon of Assyria defeated Pharaoh Taharqa (690–664 BC) at Memphis in 671 BC, the final king of the dynasty, Tanwetamani (664–656 BC), eventually abandoned Egypt in the face of the advance of Ashurbanipal. This Assyrian king conquered Thebes in 663 BC, taking vast plunder and leaving behind a client kingdom that would ultimately develop into Egypt's last great kingdom, the Twenty-sixth (Saite) Dynasty.

Verses 12-13 depict the hopelessness of Nineveh's defensive measures. Nahum blends simile and metaphor to point out that the city's massive fortifications would crumble as readily before the eager attackers as first ripe figs fall into the mouths of those who shake the trees. Further, its famed defenders would prove to be no more successful in protecting the city than would untrained and weak women. Neither defenses nor defenders would be effective in the face of the coming onslaught.

The reminder to Nineveh that it would prove to be no more invulnerable than the once impregnable Thebes emphasizes the fact that no human institution or fortification is invincible. When confronted by forces controlled by God, all human effort and preparations are useless. For God is head over all the nations (Pss 22:28; 47:7; 99:1-2). He sees to their successes and defeats (Ps 46:6). An omniscient and omnipotent God, he sovereignly deals with individuals in similar fashion (Job 34:21-27).

How blessed, then, is the nation whose God is the Lord, for he alone is their sure defense (Ps 33:12-22). Similarly, believers may take strength and solace that they belong to the sovereign God of the universe who is their sure defense (Ps 27:1-3) and shelter amid the vicissitudes of life (Pss 18:1-6; 31:19-20).

◆   ## 2. A concluding condemnation of Nineveh (3:14-19)

14 Get ready for the siege!
  Store up water!
  Strengthen the defenses!
  Go into the pits to trample clay,
    and pack it into molds,
    making bricks to repair the walls.

15 But the fire will devour you;
    the sword will cut you down.
  The enemy will consume you like
      locusts,
    devouring everything they see.
  There will be no escape,
    even if you multiply like swarming
      locusts.
16 Your merchants have multiplied
    until they outnumber the stars.
  But like a swarm of locusts,
    they strip the land and fly away.
17 Your guards* and officials are also like
    swarming locusts

that crowd together in the hedges
  on a cold day.
But like locusts that fly away when
  the sun comes up,
  all of them will fly away and
  disappear.

18 Your shepherds are asleep, O Assyrian
    king;
  your princes lie dead in the dust.
  Your people are scattered across
    the mountains
  with no one to gather them
    together.
19 There is no healing for your wound;
    your injury is fatal.
  All who hear of your destruction
    will clap their hands for joy.
  Where can anyone be found
    who has not suffered from your
    continual cruelty?

3:17 Or *princes.*

NOTES

3:14 *defenses!* This noun provides the literary hook with the previous section (3:8-13), the word being the same as that translated "fortresses" in 3:12.

molds. The Hebrew noun has been variously understood as "brick kiln" (KJV; Keil 1954), "brick mold" (NRSV; Cathcart 1979; Longman 1993; Maier 1959; Roberts 1991; Robertson 1990), or "brick work" (NIV; cf. Akkadian *libittu*). If this last alternative is chosen, it may refer to the 50-100 foot thick walls surrounding Nineveh. The NLT follows the second alternative.

3:15 *fire will devour . . . sword.* Again, the figure of consuming/eating is employed for dramatic emphasis. In addition, as Maier (1959:342-343) points out, the terms "fire" and "sword" often appear together as a pair in connection with catastrophes. The two are also often placed together in Ugaritic. (See Gordon 1965:168, text #49, 2.30-33; 197, text #137, line 32.)

3:16 *merchants*. The underlying noun comes from the root *rakal* [TH7402, ZH8217], which is known, for example, in Old South Arabian where it means "go about as a trader."

3:17 *guards*. Cf. NLT mg, "princes." The precise significance of the Hebrew noun (*minnezar* [TH4502, ZH4964]) is variously understood. Luther's *herren*, as well as the French (*princes*) and Italian (*principi*), translate it as "crowned ones" (cf. KJV). Roberts decides for "officials," preferring a derivation from Akkadian *manzazu* (courtier). (But note that the NLT's "officials" comes from *tapsar* in the second line of the verse and is not part of its rendering of *minnezar*.) The Latin Vulgate reads *custodes* ("guards"; cf. NIV, NRSV, NASB, NLT). If the reading "guards" is followed, the Hebrew noun may be related to the Akkadian verb *nasaru* (guard), which has undergone regressive contiguous phonemic dissimilation. Alternation between *z* and *s* is common enough in Akkadian. Certainly *nasaru* is attested with *z* written for *s* and with dissimilation via *n* (nasalization), particularly in Babylonian. For details, see *The Assyrian Dictionary* (Chicago: The Oriental Institute, 1977, 1980), vol. 10, part 1, 333-334; vol. 11, part 2, 34-47.

fly away and disappear. Lit., "and the place where they are is not known." The word *where* (*'ayyam* [TH335, ZH361]) is situated ambiguously between vv. 17 and 18 in some editions of the Hebrew Bible, allowing for two interpretations. Most translations take it with v. 17 (e.g., NIV, NRSV, NLT). If it is to be taken with v. 18, Nahum has once again closed a literary unit with a question: "Where are they [the princes/shepherds]?" (cf. 1:6; 2:11; 3:7).

3:18 *princes*. The Hebrew noun means "shepherds." As such, it anticipates the subsequent figure of the people as scattered sheep.

are asleep . . . lie dead. The verbs here are *namu* [TH5123, ZH5670] (slumber) and *shakan* [TH7931, ZH8905] (dwell, lie down). In the second line, Nahum uses *shakan* instead of the more familiar *yashen* [TH3462, ZH3822] (be asleep) as double entendre (i.e., the final sleep, death; cf. Ps 94:7; Isa 26:19). The semantic range represented in the words of the MT may contain a picturesque progression. The king of Assyria's trusted officials, far from being awake to the emergency, grow drowsy and take their rest—one that will prove to be final. As Bailey (1999:241) suggests, "'Sleep' may also be a metaphor for death, a poignant description of Assyria's certain destruction."

scattered. The picture is one of a totally dispersed populace, officials and citizens alike, scattered across the countryside like sheep on the mountains with no shepherd to gather them to safety (cf. 1 Kgs 22:17).

3:19 *healing*. The Hebrew word is a hapax legomenon. If it is taken from the root *kahah* [TH3543, ZH3908] (grow faint, grow dim), it may mean something like "relief."

COMMENTARY

At verse 14, Nahum approaches the end of his prophecy. The verses that follow form the second portion of an extended taunt song that again functions as satire. Although the closing verses constitute one literary unit, several movements are discernible. This short pericope contains two short, ironic commands (3:14-15a, 15b-17) and a final gibe that forms both a concluding denunciation and a doleful dirge (3:18-19).

The first movement emphasizes the futility of physical preparations in view of the coming siege. Nahum's sarcasm is evident throughout. He told the Ninevites first of all to lay in a good water supply (3:14). Similarly Nahum urged the citizens of Nineveh to strengthen the strategic points of the city's defenses. The force of the irony becomes immediately apparent. In those matters where the most extensive preparations were urged to be taken—water and walls—the city was to meet its demise.

Nahum prophesied that Nineveh would know the besieger's fiery torch and sword, as the enemy swept through the city like a horde of devouring locusts. The mention of the fearsome locusts occasions Nahum's shift in the use of irony. Nahum called upon Nineveh to be like locusts, multiplying their defensive forces to locust-like proportions (3:15). Should that not be easy for Nineveh? Indeed, it could be truly said of the city that she had acted before like a locust. As a result of her far-flung conquests, Nineveh had become filled with booty and with the famed Assyrian merchant who, plying his trade, had filled the city with every conceivable commodity. But with the coming of the threat of invasion, Nineveh's merchants would take their wares and flee, leaving the city deprived of its provisions, many of which would be desperately needed in the ensuing struggle. As locusts that come only to satisfy their insatiable appetites and then fly off, so her merchants would take their goods and go, leaving a needy populace behind.

Likewise, Nineveh's trusted officials could be likened to locusts that come out of the ground in great swarms, lodge during the cooler part of the day on walls, and then, with the rising of the sun, fly away. Ancient sources record the flight of the Assyrian nobility at the advance of the combined enemy force against Nineveh.[1]

As Nahum came to the end of his prophecy, he changed the figure one last time. He compared Nineveh's leaders to shepherds (cf. Jer 23:1-2) who had nodded off to sleep and allowed the sheep (the Ninevites) to be scattered (in flight or in exile) and subjected to harm. Even worse, no one came to regather them. The choice of this motif as the final one for the book may suggest, as many commentators have observed, that the "sleep" of the shepherds or officials is the sleep of death (cf. Jer 51:57). With its officials dead in battle, Nineveh's citizens fled or were captured. With all leadership lost, there was none left to gather them. The "scatterer" (2:1; see note) had come and done his work.

Nahum's last words once again underscore the hopelessness of human arrogance before the judging hand of God. Regardless of any and all preparations, defense is useless in the face of certain judgment. Moreover, Nineveh would learn what all tyrannical kingdoms have learned: When faced with the threat of extinction and death, even a vaunted leadership will desert the cause (Prov 25:19).

It was Nineveh's final hour. The once mighty city had fallen and would soon become a ghost town; it would become a ruins, haunted only by wild animals moving through the rubble (cf. Zeph 2:13-15). Nahum's final denunciation of the city tolls out like a bell for a state funeral: Gone! Gone! Both city and citizenry, gone! Nineveh's last wound had been the *coup mortel*. But there would be no lamentation over the deceased city, only universal relief and rejoicing. She who had so cruelly treated mankind would reap the reward of her evil deeds (cf. Prov 11:16-19; Hos 8:7).

The specter of Assyria's disappearance haunts every great empire. Nahum's opening words concerning divine justice are general, so that wherever a godless lifestyle so pervades a nation as to be characteristic of its people, it stands in danger of judgment. The words of warning by P. C. Craigie (1976:76) are apropos: "If we have grasped Nahum's message, we will not volunteer to join the ranks of Nineveh's attacker; rather, we shall seek to transform the evil within the nation to which we belong."

Nahum's closing motif of the slumbering shepherds (officials) and the scattered sheep (people) stands in stark contrast to the picture of Israel's hope. Unlike Assyria's shepherds, Israel's eternal Shepherd "slumbers not, nor sleeps" (Ps 121:4, Mendelssohn's *Elijah*); he will yet regather its lost sheep (Jer 23:3) so that Israel's redeemed cities can "be filled with flocks of people" (Ezek 36:38, NIV). Moreover, the divine Shepherd himself (Ps 23:1) will be with them: "I will be their God, and they will be my people" (Ezek 37:27). May Nahum's words, as well as those of all God's prophets, teach all God's people to trust him who is the Shepherd and Guardian of their souls (1 Pet 2:25).

ENDNOTES
1. See Diodorus Siculus, *Bibliotheca historica* 2.26.8; the text and its translation are given in the *Loeb Classical Library*, edited by E. H. Warmington, translated by G. H. Oldfather (Cambridge, MA: Harvard University Press, 1933), 1.439. See also D. J. Wiseman, *Chronicles of Chaldaean Kings* (London: Trustees of the British Museum, 1956), 61.

BIBLIOGRAPHY

Armerding, C. E.
1985 Nahum. Pp. 446–489 in *Daniel, Minor Prophets.* Expositor's Bible Commentary, vol. 7. Editor, F. E. Gaebelein. Grand Rapids: Zondervan.

Austel, H. J.
1989 Nahum. Pp. 659-665 in *Evangelical Commentary on the Bible.* Editor, W. A. Elwell. Grand Rapids: Baker.

Bailey, W.
1999 Nahum in *Micah, Nahum, Habakkuk, Zephaniah.* The New American Commentary, vol. 20. Editor, E. R. Clendenen. Nashville: Broadman & Holman.

Baker, D. W.
1988 *Nahum, Habakkuk and Zephaniah.* Tyndale Old Testament Commentaries. Downers Grove: InterVarsity.

Barker, K.
1985 Zechariah. Pp. 592-697 in *Daniel, Minor Prophets.* Expositor's Bible Commentary, vol. 7. Editor, F. E. Gaebelein. Grand Rapids: Zondervan.

Becking, B.
1995 Divine Wrath and the Conceptual Coherence of the Book of Nahum. *Scandinavian Journal of the Old Testament* 9:277-296.

Blaiklock, E. M.
1986 Nahum. Pp. 938-942 in *The International Bible Commentary.* Editors, F. F. Bruce, H. L. Ellison and G. C. D. Howley. Grand Rapids: Zondervan.

Borger, R.
1963 *Babylonisch-Assyrische Lesestucke.* Rome: Pontificium Institutum Biblicum.

Cathcart, K. J.
1973a *Nahum in the Light of Northwest Semitic.* Rome: Biblical Institute Press.

1973b Treaty Curses and the Book of Nahum. *Catholic Biblical Quarterly* 35:179-187.

1979 More Philological Studies in Nahum. *Journal of Northwest Semitic Languages* 7:1-12.

Charles, J. D.
1989 Plundering the Lion's Den—A Portrait of Divine Fury (Nahum 2:3-11). *Grace Theological Journal* 10:183-202.

Christensen, D. L.
1975 The Acrostic of Nahum Reconsidered. *Zeitschrift für die alttestamentliche Wissenschaft* 87:17-30.

1987 The Acrostic of Nahum Once Again. *Zeitschrift für die alttestamentliche Wissenschaft* 99:409-415.

1988 The Book of Nahum: The Question of Authorship within the Canonical Process. *Journal of the Evangelical Theological Society* 31:51-58.

Cooper, A.
1981 Divine Names and Epithets in the Ugaritic Texts. Pp. 333-469 in *Ras Shamra Parallels,* vol. 3. Editor, S. Rummel. Rome: Pontificium Institutum Biblicum.

Craigie, P. C.
1976 *The Minor Prophets.* Chicago: Moody.

Driver, G. R.
1935 Studies in the Vocabulary of the Old Testament III. *Journal of Theological Studies* 36:361-366.

Feinberg, C. L.
1973 *Nahum Zephaniah Habakkuk.* Chicago: Moody.

Floyd, M. H.
1994 The Chimerical Acrostic of Nahum 2:1-10. *Journal of Biblical Literature* 113:421-437.

Freeman, H. E.
1985 *Twelve Prophets,* vol. 2. Philadelphia: Westminster.

Gaster, T. H.
1961 *Thespis.* New York: Harper & Row.

Gordon, C. H.
1965 *Ugaritic Textbook.* Rome: Pontifical Biblical Institute.

Grayson, A. K.
1972–1976 *Assyrian Royal Inscriptions.* Records of the Ancient Near East (2 vols). Wiesbaden: Otto Harrassowitz.

Hailey, H.
1972 *A Commentary on the Minor Prophets.* Grand Rapids: Baker.

Haupt, P.
1907 *The Book of Nahum.* Baltimore: Johns Hopkins Press.

Hillers, D. R.
1964 *Treaty-Curses and the Old Testament Prophets.* Rome: Pontifical Biblical Institute.

Hummel, H.
1979 *The Word Becoming Flesh.* St. Louis: Concordia.

Johnson, E. E.
1985 Nahum. Pp. 1493-1504 in *The Bible Knowledge Commentary.* Editors, J. F. Walvoord and R. B. Zuck. Wheaton: Victor.

Johnston, G. H.
2001 Nahum's Rhetorical Allusions to the Neo-Assyrian Lion Motif. *Bibliotheca Sacra* 158:287-307.

Keil, C. F.
1954 *The Twelve Minor Prophets.* Biblical Commentary on the Old Testament. Translator, J. Martin. Grand Rapids: Eerdmans. (Orig. pub. 1873)

Laetsch, T.
1956 *The Minor Prophets.* St. Louis: Concordia.

Lambert, W. G.
1960 *Babylonian Wisdom Literature.* Oxford: Clarendon.

Langdon, S.
1912 *Die Neubabylonischen Königsinschriften.* Leipzig: Hinrichs.

Layard, A. H.
1849 *Nineveh and Its Remains.* New York: Putnam.

Longman, T., III
1993 *Nahum* in *The Minor Prophets,* vol. 2. Editor, T. E. McComiskey. Grand Rapids: Baker.

Luckenbill, D. D.
1926–1927 *Ancient Records of Assyria and Babylonia* (2 vols.). Chicago: University of Chicago Press.

Maier, W. A.
1959 *The Book of Nahum.* Grand Rapids: Baker.

Moran, W. L.
1965 The Hebrew Language in Its Northwest Semitic Background. Pp. 61-83 in *The Bible and the Ancient Near East.* Editor, G. Ernest Wright. Garden City: Doubleday.

von Orelli, C.
1977 *The Twelve Minor Prophets.* Translator, J. S. Banks. Minneapolis: Klock & Klock. Reprint.

Parrot, André
1955 *Nineveh and the Old Testament.* New York: Philosophical Library.

Parunak, H. VanDyke
1983 Transitional Techniques in the Bible. *Journal of Biblical Literature* 102:540-541.

Patterson, R. D.
1985 A Multiplex Approach to Psalm 45. *Grace Theological Journal* 6:29-48.

1990 A Literary Look at Nahum, Habakkuk, and Zephaniah. *Grace Theological Journal* 11:17-28.

1991 *Nahum, Habakkuk, Zephaniah.* Chicago: Moody.

2003 *Nahum, Habakkuk, Zephaniah.* Dallas: Biblical Studies.

2007 Prophetic Satire as a Vehicle for Ethical Instruction. *Journal of the Evangelical Theological Society* 50:47-69.

Patterson, R. D. and M. Travers
1988 Literary Analysis and the Unity of Nahum. *Grace Theological Journal* 9:45-58.

1990 Nahum: Poet Laureate of the Minor Prophets. *Journal of the Evangelical Theological Society* 33:437-444.

Pusey, E. B.
1953 *The Minor Prophets,* vol. 2. Grand Rapids: Baker.

Renaud, B.
1987 La Composition du Livre de Nahum. *Zeitschrift für die alttestamentliche Wissenschaft* 99:198-219.

Roberts, J. J. M.
1991 *Nahum, Habakkuk, and Zephaniah.* The Old Testament Library. Louisville: Westminster/John Knox.

Robertson, O. P.
1990 *The Books of Nahum, Habakkuk, and Zephaniah.* New International Commentary on the Old Testament. Grand Rapids: Eerdmans.

Rowley, H. H.
1956 Nahum and the Teacher of Righteousness. *Journal of Biblical Literature* 75:188-193.

Saggs, H. W. F.
1969a *Assyriology and the Study of the Old Testament.* Cardiff: University of Wales.

1969b Nahum and the Fall of Nineveh. *Journal of Theological Studies* 20:221-222.

1984 *The Might That Was Assyria.* London: Sidgwick & Jackson.

Schulz, H.
1973 *Das Buch Nahum.* Berlin: Walter de Gruyter.

Smith, J. M. P.
1911 *A Critical and Exegetical Commentary on Zephaniah and Nahum.* International Critical Commentary. Edinburgh: T & T Clark.

Smith, R. L.
1984 *Micah–Malachi.* Word Bible Commentary. Waco: Word.

Stonehouse, G. G. V.
1929 *The Books of the Prophets Zephaniah and Nahum.* Westminster Commentaries. London: Methuen.

Watson, W. G. E.
1986 *Classical Hebrew Poetry.* Sheffield: JSOT Press.

Weiss, R.
1963–1964 A Comparison Between the Masoretic and the Qumran Texts of Nahum III, 1-11. *Revue de Qumran* 4:433-439.

Wiseman, D. J.
1982 Is It Peace? Covenant and Diplomacy. *Vetus Testamentum* 32:311-326.

Yoder, P. B.
1971 A-B Pairs and Composition in Hebrew Poetry. *Vetus Testamentum* 21:475-476.

Habakkuk

RICHARD D. PATTERSON

INTRODUCTION TO
Habakkuk

HABAKKUK felt deeply the injustice of his society. He took his case to God, who explained his purposes to the prophet with the result that Habakkuk placed his faith solely in God (3:15-19). As today's believers struggle with the problems of evil and godless societies, they, like Habakkuk, can be assured that God is in control. And they, like Habakkuk, must place their faith in the Lord.

AUTHOR

The identity of the prophet Habakkuk remains a mystery. As for his name, some have seen etymological relationships to an Assyrian plant called the *hambaququ* (e.g., Roberts 1991, Rudolph 1975) or to the Hebrew verb *khabaq* [TH2263, ZH2485] ("embrace"; cf. Bailey 1999). The former would suggest, as in rabbinic tradition, that Habakkuk may have lived and been educated in Assyria (Nineveh), while the latter could be taken to indicate that he was the son of the Shunammite woman who received Elisha's promise that in the following year she would "be holding a son" (2 Kgs 4:16). The first suggestion is specious at best, and the second is historically impossible since Habakkuk would then have been born two centuries too early. The reading in one Septuagintal tradition of the first-century BC addition to Daniel titled *Bel and the Dragon* claims that Habakkuk was the "son of Jesus of the tribe of Levi" lacks historical validity. Indeed, other editions of this work fail to mention this relationship, and in the apocryphal *Lives of the Prophets* (ch 12), Habakkuk is linked with the tribe of Simeon. In any case, these books are late intertestamental works, and, as Craigie (1985:77) remarks, "There is little of historical value that can be drawn from this later reference." Equally improbable is the conjecture some make by relating Habakkuk 2:1 with Isaiah 21:6, that the "watchman" Habakkuk is Isaiah's prophetic successor.

DATE AND OCCASION OF WRITING

Habakkuk's prophecy has been variously assigned to dates between the ninth century BC and the Maccabean period. Although critical scholars are divided as to late preexilic or exilic dates, evangelical scholars traditionally have favored the preexilic era. Taken at face value, Habakkuk's short prophecy is set in a time of national upheaval characterized by gross social injustice (1:2-4) and by the imminent advent of the Babylonians (Chaldeans) as the foremost international power (1:5-11). These factors suggest a preexilic setting. A key factor in the discussion is the precise force of 1:5-6 (see commentary). There the Lord tells Habakkuk that he is going to raise up the Chaldeans as his agents of judgment. If this is to take place in the near future and to Habakkuk's amazement, this would seem to imply that Habakkuk's ministry is set in the early days of Josiah's reign or slightly earlier. If the Chaldeans were already a power to be reckoned with, Habakkuk's astonishment would not be as great.[1] Admittedly, Habakkuk could simply be amazed that God would use such a ferocious people.

Among evangelical scholars, three major positions have been articulated. (1) The majority date the prophecy to the time of Jehoiakim, whose godless disposition (2 Kgs 24:1-3; Jer 26:20-23) occasioned prophetic utterances of condemnation together with the threat of a Babylonian invasion (Jer 25). (2) Others (e.g., Pusey 1953) opt for a date in the reign of Josiah before the discovery of a copy of the law in 621 BC. Supporting this proposal as a time of social ills such as those Habakkuk describes is the apostasy that Josiah was called upon to correct from the earliest days of his reign (2 Chr 34:1-7), as well as the fact that the Temple's restoration called for the king's special attention. Indirect evidence comes from the widespread reforms and revival that followed upon finding the Book of the Law in 621 BC (2 Chr 34:23–35:19). (3) Still others (e.g., Keil 1954) defend a date in the time of Judah's most wicked king, Manasseh. They cite the degraded moral and spiritual level of that time (2 Kgs 21:1-26; 2 Chr 33:1-10), an era whose debauchery was so pronounced that it drew God's declaration that he would effect a total "disaster on Jerusalem and Judah" (2 Kgs 21:12). Supporting the third alternative is the clear scriptural indication of extreme wickedness during the reign of Manasseh. According to 2 Kings 21:1-18 and 2 Chronicles 33:1-9, that evil king not only reinstituted the loathsome Canaanite worship practices of Asherah and Baal (which Hezekiah, his father, had done away with) but also introduced a state astral cult. He built pagan altars in the outer courts and priests' courts and placed an Asherah pole within the Temple itself. He also indulged in sorcery, divination, and witchcraft, as well as the abominable rites of infant sacrifice. A date for Habakkuk during Manasseh's reign, which is supported by Jewish tradition, would be particularly attractive if it could be demonstrated that both Zephaniah and Jeremiah knew and utilized Habakkuk's prophecy (cf. Hab 1:8 with Jer 4:13; 5:6; Hab 2:12 with Jer 22:13-17; Hab 2:13 with Jer 51:58; Hab 2:20 with Zeph 1:7). According to this scenario—in which Manasseh was carried away into captivity in the later part of his reign and subsequently repented and initiated several religious reforms—a date for the book shortly before the western campaigns of King Ashurbanipal of Assyria (652 BC and thereafter) would be a good estimate.

Although final certainty as to the date of the book is elusive, Habakkuk's prophecies would seem to have had their greatest force either in the early period of Josiah's rule or in the time of Manasseh. The former would make Habakkuk and Zephaniah contemporaries; the latter would have the prophet contemporary with Nahum. Either view would date the prophecy in the time of the reign of King Ashurbanipal (668–626 BC), during the *Pax Assyriaca* of the Neo-Assyrian era (see Introduction to Nahum).

The book has its origin in recounting the prophet's intense personal experience with God. Specifically, it records Habakkuk's spiritual perplexities as to God's seeming indifference in an era of moral decay and spiritual apostasy and God's patient responses to his prophet. The book rehearses Habakkuk's experience with God, which came as a climax to his spiritual wrestling and relates the prophet's transformation from a person questioning God to one fully depending on him.

AUDIENCE

Whichever proposed preexilic date for the book is settled upon, Habakkuk obviously wrote for the people of Judahite society at large as well as the faithful remnant. He wanted them to understand both the coming judgment for the present sin and apostasy of their society and God's ultimate goal for his covenant nation. Both groups needed to be challenged: Would they remain faithful to God in the face of severe danger? Did they understand that this danger was imminently real? Had the lesson of the fall of the northern kingdom in the previous century been forgotten? When the enemy did arrive, would the people of Judah be cast on a sea of doubt as Habakkuk initially was?

CANONICITY AND TEXTUAL HISTORY

Habakkuk's canonicity is not an issue. As one of the twelve Minor Prophets, Habakkuk enjoyed full acceptance as part of the Old Testament canon. The declaration of Armerding (1985:496) is apropos: "Habakkuk was early grouped with the other so-called Minor Prophets in the Book of the Twelve (attested as such in Sir 49:10— c. 190 BC), the acceptance of which is never questioned, either in Jewish or Christian circles."[2]

The Masoretic Text of Habakkuk contains many difficulties. In addition to the obscurities in the third chapter (in which Albright proposed more than three dozen "corrections"),[3] several hapax legomena occur elsewhere (e.g., 1:4, 9; 2:11). There are also grammatical (2:4) and scribal (2:16) problems. It is no wonder, then, that the text of the Septuagint differs often from that of the Masoretic Text. In addition, significant differences from the Masoretic Text have been noted in 1QpHab. Thus Wurthwein remarks: "Some sixty examples of its deviations from M [the Hebrew text] which are more than purely orthographical (e.g., scriptio plena) are cited in the third apparatus of BHK."[4]

However, one must not overly dramatize the textual difficulties. In addition to Albright's pioneering efforts, many have labored successfully in bringing better understanding to the consonantal text of the third chapter. As for the variation between the Masoretic Text and 1QpHab, although the evidence points to some fluidity in the Hebrew textual tradition (a condition that was soon altered with the adoption of the MT), one must not set aside the traditional text in too cavalier a fashion. Thus, one may say with Robertson (1990:42), "Although some of the LXX readings may support the text of Qumran over against the MT, that fact alone does not automatically mean that the LXX reading is to be regarded as the preferred text. In general, the text . . . is well preserved in the Masoretic tradition."

LITERARY STYLE

Habakkuk could not understand the gross sin of Judah nor God's seeming indifference to the rampant corruption he saw all around him (1:2-4). This problem is developed in a dialogue format in the first two chapters as Habakkuk rehearses God's answers (1:5-11; 2:2-20) to his perplexities (1:2-4; 1:12-2:1). The dialogue comes to a climactic conclusion (3:16-19) after Habakkuk's contemplation and utilization of an ancient epic-like victory psalm recording God's deliverance of his people from Egypt, his preservation of them through the time of their wilderness wanderings, and his triumphal leadership in their conquest of the Promised Land (3:3-15).[5]

The first two chapters utilize common prophetic subgenres, the prophet's questions being cast in the form of a lament, while the second of God's answers is composed of a series of taunt songs. The overall structure of the third chapter may be viewed as a prayer psalm (*tepillah* [TH8605, ZH9525], 3:1; cf. Pss 17, 86, 90, 102, 143). Indeed, many of the features common to this type of poetry are present: an opening cry/statement of praise, an attestation of reverence/trust (3:2a), petition/problem (3:2b), praise and exaltation of God (3:3-15), statement of trust and confidence in God (3:16-18), and concluding note of praise (3:19).

Something of Habakkuk's literary ability may be seen in his use of simile and metaphor. The Babylonians' greed is likened to death (2:5). Babylon's cavalry is compared to the fierceness of evening wolves and vultures seeking their prey; their advance, to the swiftness of cheetahs (1:8). Their captives are portrayed as fish caught in a net (1:14-15). Several graphic images appear in the oracles of chapter 2, such as metonymy (2:5), allegory (2:15-16), personification (2:11), rhetorical question (2:13, 18), and several cases of alliteration and assonance (2:6, 7, 15, 18).[6]

MAJOR THEMES

Central to the message of Habakkuk is the theme of faith.[7] In the face of life's inequities and perplexities, will one's faith waver or remain steadfast? Today, as in Habakkuk's day, the injustices and immorality of corrupt, secular, and idolatrous societies make it seem as though life is less than fair, and therefore one could be tempted to wonder whether God really is sufficient for the vicissitudes of life (1:1-4). Hence, several themes in Habakkuk deal with divine justice, such as the problems of human sin and suffering in their relation to divine sovereignty, and the problems of morality and social justice in the face of the demand for holiness. These come through most forcefully in Habakkuk's second encounter with God (1:12-2:20). In that section Habakkuk decries God's use of a "less holy" instrument (the Babylonians) to chastise God's people for their unholy actions and is told plainly that a person needs to leave such cases to God. The Lord will, in turn, deal with that unholy instrument, but meanwhile the righteous person is to live a life of faith (2:4) and devotion (2:20), being mindful of God's ultimate purposes (2:14).

A theme woven in with Habakkuk's spiritual quest is the necessity of prayer. Indeed, as Thompson (1993:53) points out, "It is surely significant that so much of the book of Habakkuk is expressed in the terms and language of prayer. . . . It is as if for this prophet the prophetical and woe oracles serve a somewhat subservient function to those prayers that are employed to express what are the most significant parts of the prophet's burden."

Habakkuk's doubts had led him to come to God and share his thoughts and perplexities with him. A caring and patient God answered his prophet's perplexities and communicated to him something of his parameters of operation (2:4) and even allowed him to see something of the Lord's dynamic dealing with injustice and oppression—whether in fresh theophany, in contemplation of an earlier appearance of God handed down in epic tradition, or both. Here, once again, one finds the dynamic theme of the Divine Warrior (3:3-15), who, in triumphing over evil, gives victory to his followers so they may live secure and faithful lives (3:16-19).[8]

THEOLOGICAL CONCERNS

Habakkuk told his readers certain facts concerning God's person and work. He informed his readers that the everlasting (1:12; 3:3, 6) God of glory (2:14; 3:3-4) is sovereign over all individuals and nations (1:5, 14; 2:6-20; 3:3-15), guiding them according to his predetermined purpose to bring glory to himself (2:14). God is a God of holiness (1:12-13; 2:20; 3:3) and justice (1:12-13; 2:4) who, although he judges godlessness and injustice (1:2-11; 2:5-19; 3:12-15), mercifully tempers his righteous anger against sin (3:2, 8, 12).

A God of omnipotence (3:4-7, 8-15), he works for the deliverance and salvation of his people (3:13, 18). A God of revelation (1:1; 2:2-3), he hears the cries and prayers (1:2-4, 12-17; 2:1; 3:1-2) of his own and answers them (1:5-11; 2:4-20; 3:3-15). As a result of these dialogues, Habakkuk came to learn that the issues of life and death rest with God. Similarly, the righteous individual will, by faith (2:4-5), come to realize that God is sufficient for every situation (3:16-19).

OUTLINE

Superscription (1:1)

I. The Prophet's Perplexities and God's Explanations (1:2–2:20)

    A. First Perplexity: How Can God Disregard Judah's Sin? (1:2-4)

    B. First Explanation: God Will Judge Judah through the Babylonians (1:5-11)

    C. Second Perplexity: How Can God Employ the Wicked Babylonians? (1:12–2:1)

    D. Second Explanation: God Controls All Nations according to His Purposes (2:2-20)

    1. Preliminary instructions and guiding principles (2:2-4)

    2. The first taunt: the plundering Babylonians will be despoiled (2:5-8)

    3. The second taunt: the plotting Babylonians will be denounced (2:9-11)

    4. The third taunt: the pillaging Babylonians will be destroyed (2:12-14)

    5. The fourth taunt: the perverting Babylonians will be disgraced (2:15-17)

    6. The fifth taunt: the polytheistic Babylonians will be deserted by their idols (2:18-20)

II. The Prophet's Prayer and God's Exaltation (3:1-19)

    A. The Prophet's Prayer for the Redeemer's Pity (3:1-2)

    B. The Prophet's Praise of the Redeemer's Person (3:3-15)

        1. The Redeemer's coming (3:3-7)

        2. The Redeemer's conquest (3:8-15)

    C. The Prophet's Pledge to the Redeemer's Purposes (3:16-19)

Subscription

ENDNOTES

1. Thus Vasholz (1992:50-52), for example, opts for a date before the accession of Nabopolassar in 626 BC.

2. R. K. Harrison (1969:271) includes the words of the pronouncement of the second-century BC *baraita* contained in the Talmudic tractate *Bava Batra:* "The order of the prophets is Joshua, Judges, Samuel, Kings, Jeremiah, Ezekiel, Isaiah, the Twelve (Minor Prophets)." For full discussion of the early canonicity of all of the prophets, see Beckwith (1985:138-180).

3. See Albright 1950:1-18. Although the list of authors who have worked on this portion of Scripture is filled with the names of many prestigious scholars, a critical consensus as to its reading and interpretation is far from being reached. The difficulties of the text have challenged the efforts of exegetes of all theological persuasions.

4. See Wurthwein 1979:146. W. Brownlee (1959:146) lists 19 of these as major variants.

5. Sweeney (1991:80) points out that "it is clear that Hab. iii functions as a corroborating conclusion that responds to the issues raised in Hab. i-ii," and therefore concludes that "the book has a coherent structural unity." It may be added that distinct opening formulae and careful stitching can be seen in the first two chapters. For details, see Patterson 1990:18-20.

6. For a consideration of Habakkuk's literary features, see Patterson 1987:163-194; 1991:119-126; see further Thompson 1993:33-53.

7. Merling (1988:138-151) stresses that as a messenger of judgment, justice, and salvation, Habakkuk was unique in his role of communicating the message of the righteousness that comes by faith.

8. Regarding the Divine Warrior, see the commentary on Habakkuk 3:8-15. It may be added that in Habakkuk 3, Herman (1988:199-203) sees Yahweh portrayed not only as the Divine Warrior but also as the Lord of nature whose victories imply his coming as Divine King.

Habakkuk

◆ **Superscription (1:1)**

This is the message that the prophet Habakkuk received in a vision.

NOTES

1:1 message. See the note on Nah 1:1.

vision. Lit., "the message which Habakkuk the prophet saw." The prophet stressed his own participation in the revelatory process. Yet he would have his readers understand that his words contain the actual communication of God to his hearers. The particular verb employed (*khazah* [TH2372, ZH2600], "saw") is appropriate, not only denoting what the prophet received and was passing on but also allowing for personal seeing of certain details, such as the theophany of 3:3-15.

COMMENTARY

Habakkuk began his prophecy with a firm declaration that God is a God of revelation and that he, God's messenger, had received God's word. What he would transmit was the record of God's dealing with him and God's communication to others. Today's preacher would do well to be certain that his message, likewise, is that which *God* has laid upon his heart.

◆ **I. The Prophet's Perplexities and God's Explanations (1:2–2:20)**
   A. First Perplexity: How Can God Disregard Judah's Sin? (1:2-4)

²How long, O LORD, must I call for help?
   But you do not listen!
"Violence is everywhere!" I cry,
   but you do not come to save.
³Must I forever see these evil deeds?
   Why must I watch all this misery?
Wherever I look,
   I see destruction and violence.

I am surrounded by people
   who love to argue and fight.
⁴The law has become paralyzed,
   and there is no justice in the courts.
The wicked far outnumber the
   righteous,
so that justice has become
   perverted.

NOTES

1:2 How long, O LORD, must I call for help? The phrase "how long" indicates Habakkuk's repeated cries to God. The form is typical of lament (cf. Ps 13:1-2). Habakkuk's plea emphasizes his frustration and exasperation with the state of affairs at that time. The prophet's concern was a long-standing one, so that his doubts and questionings were not those of a fault-finding, negative critic or a skeptic but rather the honest searchings of a holy prophet of God. The Hebrew word for "call" carries with it the idea of a cry for help. Something of the prophet's literary artistry surfaces here at the beginning of his prophecy, for the word *shiwwa'ti* [TH7768, ZH8875] probably forms an intentional alliterative chiasmus with the verb "save" (*toshia'* [TH3467, ZH3828]) at the end of the verse.

Violence. Regarding this term (*khamas* [TH2555, ZH2805]), see the commentary on Obad 1:10. The cry and the need for divine help are reminiscent of Job's lament (Job 19:7; see also Job 9:17-20; 16:12-14; 30:11-15). Jeremiah (Jer 6:7; 20:8) also complained of the violence and destruction of Judahite society, a charge echoed by Ezekiel (Ezek 45:9).

1:3 misery. The noun translated "misery" also occurs with the following noun "destruction" in Prov 24:2 in describing the evil machinations and corrupt words of wicked men.

1:4 law. Habakkuk declared that society must be based on God's law if righteousness is to prevail. To neglect God's law was to invite "the ruination of God's land and people" (Laetsch 1956:318).

no justice. Social justice forms a key consideration in Habakkuk's oracles (Marks 1987:219). The themes of justice and righteousness are central in the book and will reach a climax in 2:4. Their placement in the middle two lines of the chiastic structure of the verse provides emphatic effect.

outnumber. The Hebrew word carries with it the sense of "encircle, surround"; here it is used with the connotation of hostile intent. Thus, Roberts (1991:90) remarks, "The use of the verb . . . suggests the imposition of severe limitations on the freedom of action of the encircled party, the frustration of the righteous man's plans and expectations."

perverted. This hapax legomenon is related to a root attested in Syriac ('*aqal*, "twist") and Arabic ('*aqqala*, "bend"); cf. Heb. '*aqalqal* [TH6128, ZH6824] (twisted); '*aqallathon* [TH6129, ZH6825] (crooked).

COMMENTARY

The nature of Habakkuk's complaint can be appreciated by the four words he used to describe Judah's social situation: violence, sin, misery, and destruction. All are strong words that contain moral and spiritual overtones. In order, they depict a society that is characterized by malicious wickedness (cf. Gen 6:11, 13; Ps 72:14), deceitful iniquity—both moral (cf. Job 34:36; Prov 17:4; Isa 29:20) and spiritual (cf. Isa 66:3)—oppressive behavior toward others (cf. Isa 10:1), and the general spiritual and ethical havoc that exists where such sin abounds (cf. Isa 59:7). It is little wonder that under such conditions, people love to "argue and fight" and the legal system becomes subverted.

In Habakkuk's eyes, then, Judahite society was spiritually bankrupt and morally corrupt. Because sin abounded, injustice was the norm. Habakkuk described the judicial situation in two ways: (1) Because of the basic spiritual condition, the operation of God's law was sapped of the vital force necessary for it to guide ethical and judicial decisions. Accordingly, righteousness did not characterize Judahite society, and justice was never meted out. (2) Because the society itself had become godless, wicked men could hem in the attempts and actions of the righteous so that whatever justice might exist became so twisted that the resultant decision was one of utter perversity.

These verses, then, underscore the prophet's consternation as to the seeming divine indifference to all the debauchery he saw around him. Habakkuk was disturbed also by God's silence with regard to his repeated cries for help and intervention. Additional understanding on this latter point may be gained by considering the relation of Habakkuk's words to the well-known "call-answer" motif. This theme is used often in the Scriptures to assure believers that they may call upon God for refuge and protection in times of trouble and distress (Pss 17:6-12; 20:6-9; 81:6-7; 102:1-2; 138:8). Further, the believer may find guidance from God (Ps 99:6-7; Jer 33:2-3) and experience intimate communion with him both in this life and in the next (Job 14:14-15; Ps 73:23-26). The motif also touches upon God's future plans for Israel, which include full restoration to divine fellowship (Isa 65:24; Zech 13:7-9).

Unfortunately, this motif has its negative side, as well. It teaches that when sin is present, God does not answer the one who calls on him (Ps 66:18). The believer must honor God (Ps 4:1-3) and call upon him in truth (Ps 145:17-20). Where there is godless living (Isa 56:11-12), unconcern for the needs of others (Isa 58:6-9), or indifference to the clear teachings of the Word of God (Jer 35:17), there is danger of divine judgment (Zech 7:8-14). Thus, the unanswered call becomes a sign of broken fellowship. The careful believer will call on the Lord with confidence and thus experience the satisfaction that comes from being in full fellowship with his sovereign God (Ps 91:14-16).

◆ B. First Explanation: God Will Judge Judah through the Babylonians (1:5-11)

⁵The LORD replied,

"Look around at the nations;
    look and be amazed!*
For I am doing something in your
    own day,
    something you wouldn't believe
    even if someone told you about it.
⁶I am raising up the Babylonians,*
    a cruel and violent people.
They will march across the world
    and conquer other lands.
⁷They are notorious for their cruelty
    and do whatever they like.
⁸Their horses are swifter than
    cheetahs*
    and fiercer than wolves at dusk.
Their charioteers charge from
    far away.

Like eagles, they swoop down
    to devour their prey.
⁹"On they come, all bent on
    violence.
Their hordes advance like a desert
    wind,
    sweeping captives ahead of them
    like sand.
¹⁰They scoff at kings and princes
    and scorn all their fortresses.
They simply pile ramps of earth
    against their walls and capture
    them!
¹¹They sweep past like the wind
    and are gone.
But they are deeply guilty,
    for their own strength is
    their god."

1:5 Greek version reads *Look you mockers; / look and be amazed and die.* Compare Acts 13:41. 1:6 Or *Chaldeans.* 1:8 Or *leopards.*

NOTES

1:5 look. The verb used here (*nabat* [TH5027, ZH5564]) had formed a critical part of Habakkuk's complaint (1:3), and God used the same word in his reply. It thus serves as a literary "hook" between the first two sections. It will figure in the next portion as well (1:13). Further hooks in this section can be seen in the words for justice (1:4, 7, though not reflected in the NLT) and violence (1:2, 9).

the nations. MT, *baggoyim* [TH1471, ZH1580]. The LXX reads "O despisers," perhaps reflecting *bogedim* [TH898, ZH953] (treacherous ones), a reading followed by Paul in his address at Pisidian Antioch (Acts 13:41).

I am doing. The personal pronoun is omitted in the Hebrew text, as is frequently done in cases where the subject has already been mentioned or is sufficiently clear from the context. The same construction occurs in 2:10 with the omission of the second pronoun.

in your own day. Robertson (1990:146) appropriately observes, "Swiftness in the execution of judgment is characteristic of the Lord's activity throughout the ages. Although extremely patient and forbearing with rebellious sinners, the Lord is not slow to act once he has determined that the iniquity of the people is full, and the time for judgment has arrived."

1:6 I am raising up. The construction found here is often used to refer to future events, the details of which God is about to set in process.

Babylonians. MT, *kasdim* [TH3778, ZH4169] (Chaldeans). This is also the reading of 1QpHab (2:11) among the DSS, although the term is then interpreted to refer to the Kittim (i.e., the Romans). By the time of the Neo-Assyrian era, the term "Chaldea" was used of those tribes that lived in southernmost Mesopotamia. Many of them were designated by the word *bit* (house of), such as Bit Yakin, which was situated on the Persian Gulf. One of the most famous Chaldean kings was Merodach-baladan, the perennial enemy of Assyria, who sent his emissaries to Hezekiah (2 Kgs 20:12-19). By 705 BC at the latest, Merodach-baladan took the title "King of Babylon," with the result that the terms "Chaldean" and "Babylonian" were used interchangeably in the OT (cf. Isa 13:19; 47:1, 5; 48:14, 20).

cruel and violent. The two adjectives are alliterated in the Hebrew text (*hammar wehannimhar* [cf. TH4751/4116, ZH5253/4554]) and reflect the ideas of ferocity/bitterness and speed. As it is the Babylonians' disposition that is being characterized here, the NLT rendering perfectly reflects their ruthless and violent nature.

march across the world. Robertson (1990:150-151) notes the worldwide brutality envisioned in this phrase and then remarks: "Interestingly, Rev 20:9 echoes precisely the LXX rendering of this phrase. Satan goes out to deceive the nations. His troops are like the sand of the seashore in number. . . . This awesome army 'marched across the breadth of the earth.'"

1:7 do whatever they like. The Babylonians know no other law, whether human or divine, than themselves and their own might (cf. 1:11). The word *mishpat* [TH4941, ZH5477] (justice) appears in this verse, forming a literary link with 1:2-4 and serving as a key stitchword through 2:1. As Robertson (1990:152) remarks, "This nation shall not look to God for a criterion for righteousness; it shall determine its own standard of truth."

1:8 swifter than cheetahs. Cf. NLT mg, "leopards." Roberts (1991:96-97) appropriately observes: "The various comparisons of the Babylonian horses to leopards, wolves, and a vulture rushing toward food all convey the idea of the speed with which the Babylonian cavalry reaches its objective, but the choice of these animals of prey as the terms of comparison already intimates the nature of that objective."

eagles. Many commentators suggest the translation "vultures" here. Although such a translation is admissible and serves the line well, if the image of "coming from afar" is carried through, the more traditional rendering here is perhaps better (cf. Deut 28:49). The far-reaching Babylonians are also compared to eagles in Jer 4:13; 48:40; 49:22.

1:9 *Their hordes advance.* Lit., "the totality of their faces is toward the east." The clause is a difficult one. Ward (1911:9) gives it up as "untranslatable" and adds: "It is a corrupt intrusion; or possibly represents the remnant of a member of a lost couplet." Textual uncertainty is already evident in the ancient versions, whose attempts to translate *ad sensum* produced widely varying results. Modern efforts have proved no more convincing (see, e.g., the discussions in Hulst 1960:248-249 and in Dominique Barthélemy, *Preliminary and Interim Report on the Hebrew Old Testament Text Project* [New York: United Bible Societies, 1980], 5:352-353). The chief difficulties center on the first and third words of the Hebrew phrase. The former is a hapax legomenon and is generally considered to be derived from the root *gamam* [TH4041, ZH4480] ("be abundant/filled"; cf. HALOT 1.545). The precise nuance of the word has, however, been variously understood, some opting for the idea of eagerness (NASB mg) on the part of the Babylonians or the endeavor etched on their faces; others for the thought of totality (NEB). Accordingly the first two words are rendered "hordes" (NIV) or "horde of faces" (NASB).

The final decision as to the translation of the first word is tied to that of the third word, which has been related to the idea of advancing, hence "moving forward" (NASB), or to the figure of the east wind (NJB), a suggestion found already in 1QpHab 3:9 (cf. Vulgate). The latter solution is favored by the following figure of the gathering of captives like sand. The NLT attempts to retain both meanings with the third word and translates according to the flow of the passage.

1:10 *ramps of earth.* The building of siege mounds as a battle tactic is widely attested both in the Scriptures (e.g., 2 Sam 20:15; 2 Kgs 19:32; Jer 32:24; Ezek 17:17) and in the extra-biblical literature of the ancient Near East. (Note, for example, Sennacherib's report of using "well-tempered (earth) ramps" for his third campaign; see Luckenbill 1927:2.120.)

1:11 *sweep past like the wind.* The underlying Hebrew of this verse is variously under-stood, with many proposed solutions and emendations. Some suggest that the word trans-lated "wind" should be rendered "spirit," whether of the personified Babylonians (KJV, "mind") or of God's revealing spirit. The NLT simply translates according to the sense of the context.

guilty. Roberts (1991:97) points out that nearly all exegetes regard the form of the word in question as corrupt, although he himself retains the Masoretic reading by viewing the word as a first-person verb from *shamem* ("be atonished"): "It [the spirit] departed, and I was astonished." Ward (1911:11) decides that the clause yields no reasonable sense and is cor-rupt. Keil (1954:59) takes *'ashem* [TH816, ZH870] as a verb and translates it "offends." Others take the form to mean "become guilty" (e.g., R. L. Smith). 1QpHab 4:9 reads *wysm*, which has been understood by some as a form derived from *sim* [TH7760, ZH8492] (to set) and by others as being from *shamem* [TH8074, ZH9037] ("be desolate"; Driver, Brownlee 1959). The NLT captures the force of the context—the whole sentence perhaps bearing the nuance, "But he whose strength is his god is/will be held guilty" (cf. NASB, NJB).

COMMENTARY

In his reply to Habakkuk, God seized upon the very words Habakkuk had used. The prophet had complained that he constantly had to behold evil all around him. And God himself had seen it all—apparently with unconcern, because he had done nothing to correct either the people or the condition. God now tells Habakkuk to look—to look at the nations, to take a good look. God was already at work in and behind the scenes of earth's history to set in motion events that would change the whole situation. And when Habakkuk learned what would happen, he would be utterly amazed. In fact, he probably would not be able to believe it.

The reason for Habakkuk's projected astonishment becomes apparent in verse 6: God would raise up the Babylonians (an empire that was to reach its height of power under Nebuchadnezzar II [605–562 BC] and last until it experienced a crushing defeat at the hands of the Persians in 539 BC). Since God's prophet would be surprised at his announcement about the Babylonians, God reinforced their identity with a brief resume of their character and potentially devastating power (1:6-11). They were fierce, cruel people who never tired in pursuit of their goal of conquest. Their successes struck fear into the hearts of all who stood in their path. A terror and dread to all, they arrogantly acknowledged no law but themselves.

Skilled military tacticians, their cavalry could cover vast distances quickly in their insatiable thirst for conquest and booty. Moreover, their well-trained and battle-seasoned army could move forward with such precision that the whole striking force would march as one to achieve its objectives, at the same time taking many captives. No wonder, then, that enemy rulers were merely a joke to them. With disdain they laughed at them and moved against their cities, however strongly fortified. Using siege techniques, they captured them. Although the language is hyperbolic throughout, in light of the ancient records, it is not inappropriate (see Wiseman 1956:61, 67). Long years of contact with the Assyrians must have served the Chaldeans well in terms of military knowledge. Delaporte (1970:73-74) is doubtless correct in saying that "the Babylonian army must have been organized much like the Assyrian army in the last days of the Sargonids' empire."

The picture of Babylonian armed might is thus complete. Its armies have been portrayed as the finest and fiercest in the world, being capable of moving swiftly across vast stretches of land to strike the enemy. Babylon was an arrogant bully who contemptuously mocked all its foes and knew no god but strength. Habakkuk was informed, however, that God's avenging host was not without accountability. When nations make themselves and their own strength their only god rather than acknowledging the true God, who is their sponsor, they will be held guilty for their actions.

God's answer to his prophet's first perplexity emphasizes three important truths. First, God is a righteous judge who is aware of all that takes place in the world. When sin occurs it will be punished, even if it is the sin of God's own people (cf. 1:9 with Deut 28:41; Prov 14:34). How crucial it is for all people and nations to remember Paul's pronouncement: "For he has set a day for judging the world with justice by the man he has appointed, and he proved to everyone who this is by raising him from the dead" (Acts 17:31).

Second, God is sovereignly active in the affairs of earth's history, even though that may not be evident to human observation. This point underscores the familiar scriptural truth that God is the sovereign governor of the world and its destiny (Pss 22:28; 47:8; 103:19; 113:4-9; Isa 40:21-24, 28; 65:17-19; 66:22; Dan 4:34-35; 1 Tim 1:17; 6:15; 2 Pet 3:5-7). Accordingly, believers who ignore the will of God actually deny God his rightful place in their lives, preferring rather to play God themselves. If they believe that God is, as he has revealed himself to be, the sovereign creator, controller, and consummator of the universe (1 Chr 29:11-12; Acts 17:24-26), then surely the believers' part is to trust God in full commitment to him and let God truly be God in all of life's activities (Prov 3:5-7).

Third, God does hear and answer prayer, even though his answer may be something other than what is expected. Too often, believers come to God with the answer they want. Because of our own finitude and our own set manner of dealing with things, it is all too easy at times either to be unable to see things from God's point of view or to presume to instruct God as to the way he should act (cf. Jas 4:3). While it is not wrong to share one's desires as to the outcome of a given petition, it must be done with the realization that God's ways are not necessarily ours (Isa 55:8-9). His way, however, is always the best.

◆   C. Second Perplexity: How Can God Employ the Wicked Babylonians? (1:12–2:1)

12 O LORD my God, my Holy One, you who are eternal—
surely you do not plan to wipe us out?
O LORD, our Rock, you have sent these Babylonians to correct us,
to punish us for our many sins.
13 But you are pure and cannot stand the sight of evil.
Will you wink at their treachery?
Should you be silent while the wicked swallow up people more righteous than they?

14 Are we only fish to be caught and killed?
Are we only sea creatures that have no leader?
15 Must we be strung up on their hooks and caught in their nets while they rejoice and celebrate?
16 Then they will worship their nets and burn incense in front of them.
"These nets are the gods who have made us rich!"
they will claim.
17 Will you let them get away with this forever?
Will they succeed forever in their heartless conquests?

CHAPTER 2

1 I will climb up to my watchtower and stand at my guardpost.
There I will wait to see what the LORD says
and how he* will answer my complaint.

2:1 As in Syriac version; Hebrew reads I.

NOTES

1:12 my Holy One. This phrase, with its inclusion of "my," occurs only here in the OT. Therefore, some editions of the Hebrew text suggest reading, "my Holy God." But the title "Holy One" here anticipates its use in the epic psalm of the third chapter (3:3). It is also appropriate as a basis for the ethical dimension of the present context. A similar title, "the Holy One of Israel," is used often in Isaiah.

eternal. The Hebrew form means lit., "from aforetime" but is usually employed in the sense of (1) "from of old" (Neh 12:46; Ps 77:11; Isa 45:21; 46:9), (2) "from most ancient times"

(Ps 74:12), or (3) "from everlasting" (Mic 5:2). Any of its common meanings is possible here, and each has its advocates. Thus R. L. Smith (1984) favors the first and the NJB the second. Most English versions (e.g., KJV, NASB, NIV, ESV) and conservative expositors have followed the third alternative because the focus of the passage is more on God's existence than on his past deeds (which come into view in ch 3). The NLT follows the third option.

wipe us out? The NLT rendering gives the sense of the Hebrew (*lo' namuth* [TH3808/4191, ZH4202/4637], "we shall not die"), turning it into a question for divine consideration. Interestingly, Roberts (1991:101) cites this as one of the "corrections of the scribes," restores the text as *lo' tamuth*, and views it as a rhetorical question, "You will not die, will you?" Yet, as Robertson (1990:157-158) points out, the text as it stands is a statement of prophetic faith: "Instead of serving as an instrument of annihilation, the enemy being raised up by God against Israel must function as the divine tool for justice and for rebuke."

our Rock. The term "rock" (*tsur*) is often used symbolically of God himself (cf. 1 Sam 2:2) as a place of refuge (Ps 18:2) for the trusting believer (Deut 32:15). Another word for "rock," *sela'* [TH5553, ZH6152], is similarly used. The image of God as a rock is applied to Christ in the NT (1 Cor 10:4; 1 Pet 2:6-8).

1:13 the wicked. The identity of the wicked has been the subject of some controversy and has played a role in the argument over the setting of the book. If 1:5-11 is excised as a late interpolation (e.g., Wellhausen 1963), one could conceivably view the wicked in 1:4 and 1:13 as being the same. In such a case, they could be identified not only with godless Judahites but also with Egyptians (G. A. Smith 1929), Assyrians (Weiser 1961), or Chaldeans (Wellhausen 1963). The case for identifying the wicked with the Babylonians here is defended by Johnson (1985:257-266), who theorizes that the Babylonian oppression of Judah occasioned a severe questioning of God by his prophet. Habakkuk had expected the blessing of God for the keeping of the Torah and justice in association with the Josianic reforms but instead saw only great evil and, rather than relief, the threat of increased Babylonian violence. One could also follow Duhm 1875 in assuming the wicked to be the Greeks on the basis of the identification of the *kasdim* [TH3778, ZH4169] with the *kittiyim* [TH3794, ZH4183] (cf. 1:6).

By following the MT in 1:6, however, the wicked must be the Babylonians who are dubbed the "fishermen" in 1:15-17. Thus, they are not identical with the wicked in Judah of 1:4. Habakkuk's argument is therefore *a fortiori:* As wicked as the Judahites were, they scarcely matched the Babylonians for wickedness.

swallow up people. Roberts (1991:103) suggests an allusion to the Ugaritic myth in which "Mot, the god of death swallows Baal" (Herdner 1963:5, i 5-8; ii 2-4). While this is possible, the remote time difference between Habakkuk and Ugaritic literature and the availability of this phrase as an image of defeat or the meting out of justice in Hebrew literature (e.g., Exod 15:12; Num 16:30-34) make the presumed allusion less than certain.

1:14 sea creatures. Although usually used of land creatures, the noun could refer also to gliding sea creatures (Ps 104:25).

1:15 nets. This plural noun translates two nouns in the Hebrew text: *kherem* [TH2764A, ZH3052] (dragnet) and *mikmereth* [TH4365, ZH4823] (fishnet). The latter word can also be used of a hunter's net (e.g., Mic 7:2), as can its cognates *mikmar* [TH4364, ZH4821] and *makmor* [TH4364A, ZH4821], both meaning "net" or "snare" (e.g., Ps 141:10; Isa 51:20). The Hebrew word *kherem* is perhaps related to the Arabic root *harama,* meaning "perforate," whereas *mikmereth* is cognate with Akkadian *kamaru* (trap with a snare). Though precise differentiation between the two words is difficult, Armerding (1985:507) seems to be correct in suggesting that "they appear to correspond to the two main types of net, the throw-net and the seine, used in New Testament times and up to the present in Palestine." Ezekiel 47:10

seems to relate *kherem* to nets that are cast by fishermen standing on the shore, while the *mikmereth* is mentioned by Isaiah (Isa 19:8) as being employed by fishermen on the water.

rejoice. The NLT verb renders the compound verbal expression for rejoicing in the original text: *yismakh weyagil* [TH8055/1523, ZH8523/1635] (he rejoices and is glad). While the former verb appears to emphasize the general feeling of joyfulness of disposition that a person "feels all over," the latter lays stress on the more emotional, enthusiastic, and, at times, spontaneous expression of joy. As in Ugaritic, so in Hebrew, they appear together as set parallel terms to express total gladness (e.g., Pss 14:7; 32:11).

1:16 worship . . . burn incense. Armerding (1985:508) points out that when these verbs occur together they always have connotations of illegitimate worship; hence the prophet was complaining that the Babylonians were cheating God of the honor due to him alone.

nets. This term may serve as a metaphor for the Babylonians' devotion to the military prowess that brought them such a high standard of living. "Adopting the imagery of fishing, Habakkuk portrays the scenario that God has set in motion as one of fishermen (Chaldeans), who use their sophisticated and powerful hooks and nets (Neo-Babylonian military might and methods) to catch helpless fish and creatures of the sea (the various conquered peoples)" (Patterson 1991:159).

1:17 Will you let them get away with this forever? The Hebrew text reads, "Shall he therefore keep on emptying his dragnet?" Various proposals for emending the text have been made, however. For the MT's *khermo* [TH2764A/2050.2, ZH3052/2257] (his net), Cathcart (1984:575-576) suggests *romekho* [TH7420/2050.2, ZH8242/2257] (his spear), while Roberts (1991:100-101) follows the lead of 1QpHab 6:8, which reads *kharbo* [TH2719/2050.2, ZH2995/2257] (his sword). Although "sword" makes good sense with the verb "empty" and the two words do occur together in the OT (e.g., Exod 15:9; Lev 26:33; Ezek 12:14), it is best to follow the MT, which preserves the imagery of fishing and the net found in the previous verses. For a discussion of further textual problems in the rest of the verse, see Patterson 1991:167.

2:1 I will climb up to my watchtower. Habakkuk reports his intention to assume the role of a watchman. As the city watchman manned his post atop the walls to look for any approaching danger (Ezek 33:2-6) or messenger (2 Sam 18:24-28; Isa 21:6-8; 52:7-10), or to keep watch over current events (1 Sam 14:16-17; 2 Kgs 9:17-20), so the OT prophet looked for the communication of God's will so as to deliver it to the waiting people (Jer 6:17; Ezek 3:16-21; 33:7-9; Hos 9:8).

watchtower. The Hebrew text carries with it the sense of standing watch (*mishmereth* [TH4931, ZH5466]) at the ramparts or at one's guard post (*matsor* [TH4692, ZH5189]). The noun *mishmereth*, although used at times with reference to a general post (Isa 21:8), stresses more the idea of *watching* as an activity (cf. Josh 22:3) or the object of such activity (cf. Deut 11:1). Accordingly, it is translated "watch" (KJV, NIV, RSV), whereas the place where such activity is carried on (i.e., a [guard] post; note NASB, NJB) is denoted by the cognate noun *mishmar* [TH4929, ZH5464] ("guard post," Neh 4:9 [3]). Thus, the emphasis here is probably more on the activity of standing watch, the place itself being supplied in the parallel line by *matsor*.

complaint. The NLT follows the lead of a great many commentators and translations in reading *tokakhath* [TH8433A, ZH9350] as "complaint." However, a number of commentators (e.g., Armerding 1985, Pusey 1953, Roberts 1991, Robertson 1990) and translations (e.g., KJV, NKJV, NASB) opt for "rebuke." Some think it is Habakkuk's rebuke of God, while others take it to mean God's rebuke of Habakkuk. Either way, "rebuke" is a better choice than "complaint" for two reasons: (1) The Hebrew noun is based on the verbal root found in 1:12 (*yakakh* [TH3198, ZH3519], "reprove," "correct") and thus is intentionally chosen both as a play on meanings and as a bookend to form an *inclusio* (1:12-2:1). (2) A confused, not criticizing, prophet awaited the Lord's response and rebuke. Habakkuk was not so much challenging God with a complaint as he was desiring to have his perplexities allevi-ated and his viewpoint corrected. His reaction to God's reproof would have a telling effect on his own spiritual condition and the effectiveness of his entire ministry. It was a crucial moment for God's prophet, and he was to prove worthy of the test. Thus, Armerding (1985:509) remarks, "He revealed a mature wisdom in his determination that this response be shaped by what God Himself would say. It is a wise man who takes his questions about God to God for the answers."

COMMENTARY

In reacting to God's first explanation, Habakkuk reminded himself of God's eternality and covenant relationship to Israel. By calling on Yahweh, Habakkuk revealed his awareness of the fact that God has seen it all. Despite any misgivings Habakkuk might have had, he put his confidence in the Lord who is eternal. As such, God alone was sufficient for his need. He not only is the eternally existent one but also has remained Israel's covenant God since the days of their forefathers (cf. Deut 7:6; Ps 89:1-37).

Habakkuk also addressed God with other familiar names and titles. He is *'elohim* [TH430, ZH466] (God), the sovereign and preeminent one. Habakkuk also called God "my Holy One." Because holiness is represented in the Scriptures as being the quin-tessential attribute of God (Exod 15:11; Ps 99:9; Isa 6:3), and is therefore the dynamic of the believer's ethic (Exod 19:6; Lev 11:44; 19:2; 1 Pet 1:16), God is often called "the Holy One" (e.g., Job 6:10; Isa 57:15) and especially the "Holy One of Israel" (Pss 71:22; 89:18; and 26 times in Isaiah!). Habakkuk also called God a rock. The word found here was often used symbolically of God himself (1 Sam 2:2) as a place of refuge (Ps 18:2) for the trusting believer (Deut 32:15). To whom else could Habakkuk turn?

Taken at face value, Habakkuk's words are a statement of the prophet's ultimate confidence in God. They reflect Habakkuk's firm grasp of covenant truth: Despite Israel's certain chastisement, God would remain faithful to his promise to the patri-archs (Gen 17:2-8; 26:3-5; 28:13-15), to Israel (Exod 3:3-15; Deut 7:6; 14:1-2; 26:16-18), and to the house of David (2 Sam 7:12-29).

While he rehearsed important scriptural truths relative to God's person, Habak-kuk also used them to challenge God's method of operation in the present circum-stances. Since God is a just God, how could he use an even more wicked nation as an agent to chastise his own people? The prophet had lost sight of several facts: (1) God's ways are not always in accordance with human thinking. (2) God truly was sovereign in this matter and therefore should be trusted. (3) God is a God of justice and will mete out the merited judgment for sin, even though the means of punishment may not be immediately understood. Habakkuk had momentarily lost track of the kind of God he served.

Lest we be too critical of God's prophet, we need to remember that Habakkuk was bringing his honest queries to God and laying them before him. Furthermore, there is every reason to think that he himself had second thoughts concerning his own line of argumentation (see note on 2:1, "complaint"). Where genuine doubt and perplexities exist, God patiently brings the needed reproof (cf. Jonah 4:10-11) and correction (cf. Ps 73:18-25). This would also be Habakkuk's experience (cf. 3:17-19). Habakkuk had noted that the Babylonians had been sent to reprove and correct the Judahites. Similarly, he expected and deserved God's correction concerning his doubts and his understanding of the full scope of God's plans for the future. Robertson (1990:167) observes, "Habakkuk braces himself for the rebuke of the Lord. He has presumed to breach the silence enshrouding the relation of his people to their God. Now having entered this dialogue, he must prepare to respond to the reproof that is sure to come."

This section reinforces the need of proper prayer and full honesty before God. Only thus can one's prayers be properly formed. The believer must desire God's will, not his own perception of it, to be done and to be willing to accept God's answer, even if it comes in a way totally foreign to his own thinking.

This portion of Scripture also stands as a firm reminder to evaluate life's priorities. The Babylonians, rather than thanking God for their success, worshiped that which brought them bounty: raw power. For each of us, this poses the question of how we handle our successes. How easy it is to make such a thing our god—whether it be prestige, power, position, wealth, or even home and family. John's warning is a timeless one: "Keep away from anything that might take God's place in your hearts" (1 John 5:21).

◆   D. Second Explanation: God Controls All Nations according
       to His Purposes (2:2-20)
       1. Preliminary instructions and guiding principles (2:2-4)

²Then the LORD said to me,

"Write my answer plainly on
tablets,
   so that a runner can carry
   the correct message to
   others.
³This vision is for a future time.
   It describes the end, and it will be
   fulfilled.

If it seems slow in coming, wait
patiently,
for it will surely take place.
It will not be delayed.

⁴"Look at the proud!
   They trust in themselves, and their
   lives are crooked.
But the righteous will live by their
   faithfulness to God.*

2:3b-4 Greek version reads *If the vision is delayed, wait patiently, / for it will surely come and not delay. / ⁴I will take no pleasure in anyone who turns away. / But the righteous person will live by my faith.* Compare Rom 1:17; Gal 3:11; Heb 10:37-38.

N O T E S
2:2 *tablets.* Ewald (1875) suggests that the tablet in question was customarily erected in marketplaces. Such tablets were set up so that public notices could be written on them. Since the Hebrew noun is plural, Laetsch (1956) proposes that these tablets might have been erected in any public place, including locations along highways or in temple courts. Keil (1954) thinks that the reference is general—the definite article referring to the particular tablets that Habakkuk was to inscribe. Though this observation is valid, Laetsch's

point concerning the erection of tablets has the advantage of historical parallel (cf. 1 Macc 14:25-49). For other scriptural examples of the motif of revelation inscribed on tablets, see Exod 31:18; Isa 8:1; 30:8; Jer 17:1. The NIV takes this to refer to a message that a herald would have taken and run with from one village to another.

a runner can carry the correct message to others. J. M. Holt proposes that this part of the command is to be taken metaphorically, the running being understood as living obediently (cf. Ps 119:32; 1 Cor 9:24-27; Phil 3:13-14). This suggestion raises the question of whether the command to write the revelation is to be understood literally or figuratively. The traditional interpretation takes the command to be literal and assumes that its main purpose is that of preserving (Armerding 1985) or disseminating (Laetsch 1956) the message. Keil (1954) opts for a figurative understanding, proposing that all of the passages dealing with prophetic activity and writing on tablets are also to be understood figuratively.

Whether literal or figurative, certainly all of the emphases that the commentators have suggested are true to the text. The message is to be clearly understood, assimilated, preserved, and propagated. The imagery of running suggests that even the most hurried passerby may see and quickly understand it (Driver 1950) and then herald its message to others. The idea of tablets brings to mind the lasting quality and applicability of a message that is geared for a "future time" (2:3).

2:3 *This vision is for a future time.* The emphasis is that the vision is a witness to the appointed time, for it testifies truly concerning that end (cf. Patterson 1991:174-175). Roberts (1991:110) remarks, "The vision is a witness to what God is going to do at a set time in the future. Because God's intervention is to take place in the future, the testimony about it is to be written down and preserved as a witness until the events of that day confirm it." By slightly modifying the Septuagintal reading here, the author of Hebrews (Heb 10:37-38) elucidates a messianic application in the text (Lunemann 1882:315).

it will surely take place. It will not be delayed. The force of the Hebrew in the first thought is caught nicely by the NLT. The appointed end is fixed! The verb "delayed" can also be understood as "be late," the point in either case being that the divine plan is unswervingly on schedule.

2:4 *proud!* The first line of 2:4 is notoriously difficult. Many suggestions have been made as to the understanding of both the syntax and words involved. (For the difficulties posed by 2:4, see Patterson 1991:211-223.) The NLT's rendering, "proud," captures well the arrogance connoted by the Hebrew word.

crooked. Lit., "not straight/upright" (*lo' yasherah* [TH3808/3474, ZH4202/3837]). Robertson (1990:174-175) remarks, "This position of pride and self-reliance also excludes from the proud the possibility of finding a righteousness outside himself. For he has presumed to define himself as the source of his own goodness."

the righteous will live by their faithfulness to God. Robertson (1990:175-176) points out, "The concept of righteousness . . . in the OT develops a distinctive flavor in that it is bound inseparably to the idea of judicial standing. . . . In Hab. 2:4b, the term for *the justified* or 'the righteous,'" (*tsaddiq* [TH6662, ZH7404]), "contrasts with the reference to the soul of the proud, which is not 'upright'," (*yasherah* [TH3474, ZH3837]), "in the immediately preceding phrase. The soul of the proud is not morally upright (*yasherah*) in him; but the one who is legally righteous (*tsaddiq*) shall live."

The word translated "faithfulness" has been treated variously by scholars, both as to etymology and as to whether the noun has an active (truthfulness) or passive (trustworthiness) meaning. More than likely both active and passive meanings are inherent in the word.

COMMENTARY

Once again, the Lord reminded Habakkuk that his ministry was God-inspired (2:2). The message that he was to record was nothing less than the revealed Word of God—he could be certain that it was a true word and a word that entailed responsive faith to wait for its fulfillment, for it speaks of a yet future time when all of God's predetermined plan will be consummated (2:3). God's instructions to Habakkuk reinforce the theological outlook of the whole Bible. The Scriptures are God's objectively verifiable revelation. They are inerrant in their original text, and their truths span the whole of earth's existence and human history (2 Tim 3:16; 2 Pet 3:5-10). Accordingly, God's word demands a proper response in faith on the part of those who claim his name. Further, these verses make it clear that the message should be passed on in order that all may read, heed, and react properly to it.

Habakkuk was also told the basic guiding principles upon which the operation of divine government unalterably proceeds until the coming of that final appointed time (2:3). God informs Habakkuk of the characteristic makeup of the wicked. Their basic problem is an underlying selfishness that shows itself in an arrogant and presumptuous attitude. Therefore, it can be said that what the wicked desire is not upright. Spiritually, morally, and ethically, the ungodly presumptuously ignore the path of God's righteousness to follow the way of selfish desires in the everyday decisions of life.

The upright are those who walk unwaveringly in accordance with God's standards. Fundamental to the use of the word translated "righteous" (2:4) is the concept of God's own righteousness, the truth that God's decisions and actions always conform to his holy and just nature.

The Hebrew noun translated "faithfulness" or "faith" (2:4; 'emunah [TH530, ZH575]) emphasizes firmness of belief and integrity of character, as well as the acts that flow from them. In reference to people of genuine faith, it denotes "a personal attribute of man, fidelity in word and deed . . . and, in his relation to God, firm attachment to God, an undisturbed confidence in the divine promises of grace" (Keil 1954:73). Taking both words together, Habakkuk 2:4 indicates that because the believer is one in whom God's righteous character has been reproduced, he can be expected to conduct himself in a manner consistent with his renewed being.

With regard to the terms "righteous(ness)" and "faith(fulness)," Keil (1954:73) tells us that it is impossible to mistake the reference to Genesis 15:6, which says that Abraham believed God, and God reckoned it to him as righteousness. Although the nature of Abraham's faith and his standing before God have been subjects of intense discussion among biblical scholars, the force of the words and the context makes clear that "Abram accepted the Word of the Lord as reliable and true and acted in accordance with it; consequently, the Lord declared Abram righteous and therefore acceptable" (Ross 1988:310).

The well-known statement concerning the patriarch's faith lies behind Habakkuk's words; consequently the idea of a genuinely righteous man with right standing before God would not be foreign to the prophet or his audience. Scriptural precedent thus reinforces the blending of active and passive meanings in 'emunah (faith[fulness]). The force of the words accordingly becomes all the stronger: A genuinely righteous person will live out the faith in faithful activity.

The crucial nature of Habakkuk 2:4b can be seen in its impact upon the believing community, Jew and Gentile alike. As Cranfield (1975:101) points out, "This is a great text. It could even be called *the* great text of the Bible. To understand it is to understand the Christian gospel and the Christian life. It is so important that it is picked up by the New Testament writers, twice by Paul (Rom 1:17; Gal 3:11) and once by the author of the Book of Hebrews (Heb 10:38)." C. L. Feinberg (1976:211) may not be too far wrong in dubbing this text the "watchword of Christianity," the key to Habakkuk, and "the central theme of all the Scriptures."

Luther's appreciation of Romans 1:17 originates in Paul's application of the text of Habakkuk 2:4b. Rather than stressing the faithfulness of the righteous believer, Paul understands the essential truth of the text to be "It is through faith that a righteous person has life"—that is, in an ultimate sense, such a believer really lives. The apostle emphasizes that the person's right standing before God is not based on works (Eph 2:8), not even those of the law (Gal 3:11), but only on genuine faith.

That the New Testament writers were aware of Habakkuk's intended meaning seems certain by the citation of his words in Hebrews 10:35-39, where, quoting the text of the Septuagint (and supplying to the Greek text the pronoun "my" after "righteous ones" and inverting the final two words of the verse, "My righteous ones will live by faith[fulness]"), the author of Hebrews applies the outworking of the believers' faith to their living in the certain hope of Christ's coming.

Thus the New Testament writers variously stressed two resident theological truths in Habakkuk 2:4b: (1) The righteous ones are deemed so because by faith they have right standing before God (Rom 1:17; 4:1-25; Gal 3:11; cf. Gen 15:6), and (2) the ones who have faith will be faithful (Heb 10:35-39). Faith and faithfulness, therefore, are twin aspects of a living reality. Genuine faith will be lived out in faithfulness to God and his precepts (cf. Jas 2:17-24). How crucial it is for all people everywhere to forsake arrogant self-preoccupation and to receive God's righteousness. Only then will they be those who are truly alive and so can live faithful and productive lives before their Creator. Craigie (1985:94) appropriately observes, "Habakkuk said it clearly: the meaning of our life and the possibility of righteousness flow from a commitment to God, in faith and in continuing faithfulness."

◆ ## 2. The first taunt: the plundering Babylonians will be despoiled (2:5-8)

5 Wealth* is treacherous,
and the arrogant are never at rest.
They open their mouths as wide as
the grave,*
and like death, they are never
satisfied.

In their greed they have gathered
up many nations
and swallowed many peoples.
6 "But soon their captives will taunt
them.
They will mock them, saying,

'What sorrow awaits you thieves!
Now you will get what you deserve!
You've become rich by extortion,
but how much longer can this
go on?'
7 Suddenly, your debtors will take
action.
They will turn on you and take
all you have,

while you stand trembling and
helpless.
8 Because you have plundered many
nations,
now all the survivors will plunder
you.
You committed murder throughout
the countryside
and filled the towns with violence.

2:5a As in Dead Sea Scroll 1QpHab; other Hebrew manuscripts read *Wine*.   2:5b Hebrew *as Sheol*.

NOTES

2:5 Wealth. The NLT follows 1QpHab 8:3 in reading "wealth" (*hon* [TH1952, ZH2104]) rather than the MT's "wine" (*hayyayin* [TH3196, ZH3516]). Although wine and wealth may be symptoms of an arrogant lifestyle, it is difficult to see how either of these was a precipitating cause of the Babylonians' demise. Another possibility is to follow the suggestion of M. T. Houtsma (1885:180-183) that the form should be read as *hawwan* or *hayyan* and understood as "proud/presumptuous one." Houtsma's idea is attractive in that (1) as a rare form it would explain the shift to the more familiar words "wine" and "wealth" and (2) its usage here after a form of the word *'apal* (proud) in 2:4 mirrors the usage of the two roots in parallel texts in the Torah: *'apal* [TH6075/6075A, ZH6752/6753] in Num 14:44 (cf. Hab 2:4); and *hun* [TH1951, ZH2103] in Deut 1:41 (cf. Hab 2:5). Indeed, the probability of the reflection of these two rare roots drawn from parallel Pentateuchal passages in one context is so unlikely that their appearance here is striking. Accordingly, while "wine" or "wealth" are translational possibilities here, a good case can also be made for "presumption": "Presumption betrays an arrogant man, and he is never at rest."

arrogant. This adjective (*yahir* [TH3093, ZH3400]) occurs elsewhere only in Prov 21:24, where it is parallel to *zed* [TH2086, ZH2294] (proud/insolent). It is rendered by the LXX as *kataphronētēs* [cf. TG2707, ZG2970] (contemptuous) and by the Peshitta as *maraha'* (willful, presumptuous, headstrong). Coupled with *geber* [TH1397, ZH1505] (man) and the following phrases, it yields a picture of a strong-willed man whose presumption knows no rest, so that in his greed he enslaves all who come in contact with him.

never at rest. This verbal hapax legomenon has been variously rendered. Thus the NASB (cf. KJV, NKJV) reads, "He does not stay at home"; the NJB reads, "He is forever on the move"; and Smith favors, "He shall not survive."

grave. Cf. NLT mg, "Sheol." The word has been variously translated as either "grave" (NIV), "death" (KJV), "hell" (NKJV), or "underworld" (LXX, Vulgate). The variations reflect the wide differences of opinion among scholars as to the concept of the afterlife in OT times and the semantic range of this word. At the very least, the meaning "grave" (cf. Gen 37:35; Ps 16:10; Hos 13:14) and "place of the (wicked) dead" (cf. Pss 49:14; 55:15) are established in the OT (see note on Hos 13:14).

2:6 their captives. The Hebrew text reads simply "these, all of them." The lack of an antecedent for these words has occasioned a great deal of disagreement among commentators as to the referent in these taunt songs. R. L. Smith (1984) appears to favor the thought that the woes are the expression of Habakkuk himself (so also Craigie 1985) or perhaps of everyone (reading *kulloh* [TH3605/1886.4, ZH3972/2024] for *kullam* [TH3605/3963.1, ZH3972/4392]). F. C. Eiselen opts for Habakkuk, who is putting his words into the mouths of the nations. Keil (1954) decides it is the true believers among the oppressed peoples, and many (e.g., Feinberg 1976, Hailey 1972, Laetsch 1956, von Orelli 1897) favor the nations as such.

Perhaps the whole matter is somewhat academic—the problem arising chiefly due to the literary demands of the section. Pronounced by God and communicated by his prophet, these words and those that follow will also be on the lips of the nations and the peoples who will suffer at the hands of the Babylonians. The NLT decides the reference is to the captive peoples.

taunt. The taunts of the captives begin with the words "what sorrow" (cf. 2:9, 12, 15, 19), an invective that customarily forms the first of three elements (invective, threat, criticism) in a woe oracle. The brevity of the individual "sorrows," however, has led most commentators to see instead a series of taunts here.

The word translated "taunt" (*mashal*) is usually translated "proverb." This noun is used in cases where the intended teaching is accomplished by drawing a comparison between matters that must be comprehended if their full implications are to be grasped. The presence of taunt songs in the literature of the ancient Near East, as well as in the OT (e.g., Isa 14:4-23, a taunt song against the Babylonian king), makes it clear that these verses are intended to be so understood. The original text goes on to say that the taunt songs will be accompanied by ridicule and riddles. The former designates a mocking poem or satire designed to heap scorn on its object by means of allusive discourse. The latter gives instructions through enigma (cf. Ezek 17:2-10; see Torczyner 1924:125-149). All three terms occur together in Prov 1:6 in a neutral setting.

extortion. The noun (*'abtit* [TH5671, ZH6294]) is a hapax legomenon from the root *'abat* [TH5670, ZH6292] (to give a pledge), itself usually considered to be denominative from *'abot* [TH5667, ZH6287] ("pledge"; cf. Akkadian *ebuttu*, "loan"). Roberts (1991:119) remarks, "The possessions [the nation] has obtained by conquest are thus seen, not as Babylon's own, but as simply on loan, as a burden of debt too heavy to pay back or to secure with pledges."

2:7 *your debtors.* Like the NIV, the NLT views the image as one of debtors who rise up against their creditors. Alternatively, these verses may reflect a turn in the thought, the trope being that of a debtor who, because he has been unjustly taken advantage of, has been accumulating an obligation from his creditor. Hence, he now becomes the creditor, one who will violently press his claims through his collectors, despoiling his former creditors.

For procedures relative to loans in the ancient Near East, see Roberts 1991:119. Roberts adds that the understanding of creditors here rather than debtors "also fits the context better, since the threat of creditors arising to collect what was owed them was a constant fear of debtors, and many debtors found themselves as an object of plunder to their creditors."

2:8 *plundered.* The verb *shalal* [TH7997A, ZH8964] (draw out, extort) is translated in accordance with the needs of the context: Since the emphasis of 2:7 is on despoiling the Babylonians, "plundering" makes an apt synonym. Robertson (1990:186-188) calls attention to the theme of retribution here as a deliberate literary device. He also notes the high literary quality of the whole taunt song, pointing out such devices as assonance and alliteration, double meaning in words, appeal to proverbial truth, and rhyming of phrases.

COMMENTARY

Utilizing the divine pronouncement and building on its principles, God's answer takes the form of an argument a fortiori: *If it is true that* the arrogant have ungodly desires and so, unlike the righteous, never come to enjoy the blessings of God, *how much more certain* is it that the qualities that accompany such an attitude will ultimately betray them!

In their sinful arrogance, the wicked are betrayed by presumption. In their impetuousness they are ever restless, so that their selfish ambitions foster an unholy desire toward everyone and everything. So insatiable is their greed that it can be compared to the uncontrollable appetite of death, here personified as a voracious monster. As death and the grave continue their never-ending quest to swallow up life, so the Babylonians would swallow up all that was before them. In their aggression and expansion, they would gather all nations and peoples under their control. Nevertheless, the underlying implication is clear: The Babylonians' selfishness and success will prove to be their undoing. The Scriptures reveal, however, that although death and the grave continue their never-ending quest to swallow up life, ultimately they will be conquered by the Life-giver (Hos 13:14; 1 Cor 15:55-57).

The first taunt song is a reminder of the principle of retributive justice. As the Babylonians have done to others, so it will be done to them (cf. Obad 1:15-16). Neither nation nor individual can go on taking advantage of others endlessly, for a day will come when the oppressed will say "Enough!" and turn on their oppressor. Further, God can send yet another, stronger oppressor to deal in kind with those who have so cruelly treated others.

This sudden calling-in of the debt came to pass as predicted. Although the Persian king Cyrus the Great spent the early days of his reign securing the subservience of neighboring peoples, he would one day be ready to move swiftly. His conquest of the Medes in 550 BC opened a claim to all the former Median territory, an area that composed the northern portion of the former Assyrian empire. After Lydia fell to Cyrus in 546 BC, Cyrus quickly subdued all of mainland Asia Minor and the adjacent Greek islands. Within a few short years, then, Cyrus found himself ruler of a territory that included all of the Iranian plateau westward across the northern Fertile Crescent and on to the Greek islands off the coast of Asia Minor. The next strike would take him against the Chaldeans, who capitulated rapidly after the loss of Babylon on October 13, 539 BC. (For details, see Olmstead 1948:34-58; Yamauchi 1990:72-74, 85-89.) So great was the relief felt by all in that day that Cyrus entered Babylon not as a conqueror but as a liberator. The temples were not profaned and the safety of the city was guaranteed. Cyrus took as his title "King of Babylon, Sumer and Akkad, and the four corners of the world." He went further and claimed to have been chosen by Marduk, as is shown in a Babylonian text: "Marduk gave thought to all the lands, he saw them and sought a righteous king, a king after his own heart whom he would lead by the hand. He called his name Cyrus, king of Anshan, and appointed him to be king over all things" (see Parrot 1956:121).

A further charge against the Babylonian conquerors was their reckless disregard of all that lay in their path, whether human life or country or city. This is an affront to the God who is concerned for the ecology of the whole world, human and nonhuman. It is a sober reminder to all that mankind is charged with the proper care, use, and development of all that makes up life on Planet Earth.

This taunt song reminds the believers that they must guard against the temptation to enhance themselves at the expense of others (cf. Gal 4:10-12; 5:13-15).

Greed too often accompanies selfishness and can also easily mar one's spiritual fiber. The Lord Jesus cautioned, "Beware! Guard against every kind of greed. Life is not measured by how much you own" (Luke 12:15), to which Paul added, "Let there be no sexual immorality, impurity, or greed among you. Such sins have no place among God's people" (Eph 5:3). How much better for Christian leaders (and worshipers) to not "lord it over the people assigned to [their] care, but lead them by [their] own good example" (1 Pet 5:3) and to heed James's warning against selfish ambition (Jas 3:16), while following his wise counsel: "For jealousy and selfishness are not God's kind of wisdom" (Jas 3:15). If, then, individuals commit to reproducing the principles of spiritual living laid down in the Scriptures, they lay for themselves a foundation for freedom from greed and selfish ambition (cf. Ps 119:36-37).

◆   ## 3. The second taunt: the plotting Babylonians will be denounced (2:9-11)

9 "What sorrow awaits you who build big houses
with money gained dishonestly!
You believe your wealth will buy security,
putting your family's nest beyond the reach of danger.

10 But by the murders you committed, you have shamed your name and forfeited your lives.

11 The very stones in the walls cry out against you,
and the beams in the ceilings echo the complaint.

NOTES

2:9 *beyond the reach of danger*. The imagery of the Hebrew text envisions setting one's nest on high so as to escape from the "grasp of disaster" (Laetsch 1956:335). The reference is doubtless to Nebuchadnezzar's many fortification efforts, particularly in Babylon. He enclosed his capital city with two massive walls, the outermost of which was entirely surrounded by a moat that stretched from its east side to the Euphrates on the city's west side. (For more details, see Patterson 1991:190-191; Laetsch 1956:335-336.)

2:10 *forfeited your lives*. Lit., "sinning against your soul." The NLT translates according to the sense of the passage, as do several other translations (e.g., NIV, NRSV).

2:11 *stones . . . beams*. The importance of wood in Mesopotamian buildings may be seen in Nebuchadnezzar's account of enlarging the palace built by his father, Nabopolassar:

> I built a structure of burned brick, and I built very high in its tower a large chamber with bitumen and burned brick for my royal dwelling-place, and joined it to my father's palace, and in a prosperous month, on a favourable day, I firmly laid its foundation in the bowels of the earth, and I raised high its turrets. . . . Mighty cedar trees from the snow-capped mountains, *ashuhu* trees with broad trunks, and cypress trees (with) costly stones, I laid in rows for its roofing. ("East India House Inscription of Nebuchadnezzar II" in *Assyrian and Babylonian Literature*, trans. C. D. Gray [New York: D. Appleton, 1901], 141-142)

COMMENTARY

The second taunt song underscores the Babylonians' capacity for cunning schemes against mankind. Building upon the imagery in the first woe, the Babylonians are portrayed as achieving wealth through violence and evil means. Used as a verb, the root *batsa'* [TH1214, ZH1298] (lit., "break off") means "gain one's end through violence," while as a noun (*betsa'* [TH1215, ZH1299]), it signifies "gain made by violence." Both occur here together for emphasis—the picture being further strengthened by the addition of the adjective "evil." A play on the root meaning may be intended: By violently accruing unjust gain for their "house," the Babylonians have "cut off" their own "house" with evil. By cutting off—degrading and destroying—many peoples, the Babylonians sin against themselves, sealing their own judgment before God. They too would be cut off forever.

The Babylonians were to have no lasting empire. The arrogant misuse of others along with selfish scheming against them for personal and national aggrandizement would one day backfire. Even the building materials in the proud city could not be silent. Though men may keep still, they who were mute witnesses to all of the Babylonians' greedy and grandiose plots could not. Fallen Babylon would one day be home to only the collapsed edifice of the Neo-Babylonian Empire. The proverbial dictum is ever true: "Godliness makes a nation great, but sin is a disgrace to any people" (Prov 14:34).

◆   ## 4. The third taunt: the pillaging Babylonians will be destroyed (2:12-14)

12 "What sorrow awaits you who build cities
with money gained through murder and corruption!
13 Has not the LORD of Heaven's Armies promised
that the wealth of nations will turn to ashes?

They work so hard,
but all in vain!
14 For as the waters fill the sea,
the earth will be filled with an awareness of the glory of the LORD.

NOTES

2:12 *build cities.* The Neo-Babylonian inscriptions often attest the Babylonians' preoccupation with building projects. So dedicated were they to such matters that Nabopolassar compelled his own son to do hard physical labor in the building of Etemenanki, the temple tower of Babylon. (See the "Inscription of Nabopolassar" in *Assyrian and Babylonian Literature*, trans. P. Bruce [New York: D. Appleton, 1901], 131-133.) Nebuchadnezzar inherited his father's passion for building, and his inscriptions recount many incidents of building projects. (See the several inscriptions of Nebuchadnezzar II in *Assyrian and Babylonian Literature*, 134-157.)

corruption! Lit., "injustice," "unrighteousness." The root of this feminine noun also appears as a masculine noun with little or no difference in meaning. Commenting on the masculine noun, Girdlestone (1956:79) remarks: "The word . . . is thought to designate the want of integrity and rectitude which is the accompaniment, if not the essential part, of wrong-doing." He goes on to point out that this noun is also translated "iniquity" in "about thirty passages [in the KJV]" where the stress is upon "a departure from that which is equal and right."

The Hebrew noun that occurs here is often used in parallel with terms of wickedness (e.g., "bloodshed," "ruthlessness," "treachery"). The word thus suggests wrongdoing and injustice of all sorts, often taking the form of oppressive, shameful, and sometimes violent acts (cf. 2 Sam 3:34; Mic 3:10). Such conduct is an affront to a holy and righteous God (Deut 32:4) and marks the Babylonians as those who, unlike the righteous who reflect God's standards, are arrogant and presumptuous.

2:13 Has not . . . ? The NLT has left the particle *hinneh* [TH2009, ZH2180] untranslated (cf. NIV, NRSV), viewing it as a simple flavoring particle. In his German translation of the OT (*Die Heilige Schrift*), Luther, however, is probably on the right track in translating it as an inferential particle: *"Wird's nicht also . . . geschehen?"* (Will it not therefore come to pass?). So viewed, the question introduces a solution drawn from the antecedent observations. Because of the Babylonians' violent acts, will not God see to it that they (or any such nation) will exhaust themselves in vain?

They work so hard, but all in vain! The synonyms *yaga'* [TH3021, ZH3333] and *ya'ep* [TH3286, ZH3615] ("toil" and "exhaust oneself") denote the effort and wearisome effects of hard work. The person so engaged is left with a fatigue that borders on being overcome with fainting.

2:14 glory. This glory (*kabod*) refers to God's self-manifestation in visible and active presence among people, as opposed to God's transcendence, for which *yashab* [TH3427, ZH3782] (to dwell) was used (e.g., 1 Sam 4:4). Both stand in distinction from *shekinah* [TH7931, ZH8905], the technical term for God's immanence (see the commentary on Joel 3:18-21).

COMMENTARY

The third taunt song proceeds on the basis of the previous one; the image of building found there is continued here. Now the chief materials used in constructing the Neo-Babylonian "house" are seen for what they are: murder and corruption. Despite the magnificence of the Babylonian edifice, God denounces all this splendor, for he sees the atrocities by which the Babylonians will aggrandize themselves in building lavishly endowed cities. All that effort will prove to be valueless, however, because it will be rewarded in the end by fire (cf. Jer 50:32; 51:58). Craigie (1985:98) observes, "The city that is built on a foundation of iniquity and constructed at the expense of bloodshed cannot flourish; all will be for nought."

Babylon must be judged—not only for its unbridled arrogance but also because God's purposes include a universal exhibit of his glory and judgment. The words of 2:14 are adapted from Isaiah 11:9 (cf. Num 14:21). Isaiah's prophecy looks ahead to the great messianic era in all its fullness and perfection; Habakkuk used Isaiah's prophecy to validate the pronouncement of the destruction of the Neo-Babylonian Empire. Because the Babylonians glorified only themselves and the gods of human manufacture (whose temples they would adorn and maintain), they scorned the living and true God and robbed him of his worship. If God is to be received fully on earth as in heaven, the earth must be filled "with an awareness of the glory of the LORD" (2:14). Isaiah's prophecy is thus personalized for the Babylonians. The prophetic words are a reminder that all other glory-seekers will be silenced so that God may have his rightful preeminence (cf. Isa 48:11).

By God's "glory" is meant his magnificence. The word is commonly used to depict his self-manifestation by which his inner excellence becomes visible. Further, glory lies behind all of his activities. The term is also used of the intrinsic honor that is due him (Pss 66:2; 79:9) and that is proper and essential for people to give (Ps 66:7-8; Jer 13:16). Thus the Babylonians' decision to honor self rather than the one God of the universe was equivalent to failure in achieving the primary purpose of being human (cf. Isa 42:8; 48:11); they were therefore culpable before God (cf. 1 Sam 8:7; 10:17-19; 12:19).

The glory of the Lord that filled the Tabernacle at its inauguration (Exod 40:34-35) and the Temple at its dedication (1 Kgs 8:10-12), that attended the announcement of Christ's birth (Luke 2:9-14) and is reflected in the lives of believers who are united to Christ (2 Cor 3:18), will one day be known and experienced by all (Isa 59:19) who confess that "Jesus Christ is Lord, to the glory of God the Father" (Phil 2:11).

◆   5. The fourth taunt: the perverting Babylonians will be disgraced
        (2:15-17)

15 "What sorrow awaits you who make
    your neighbors drunk!
You force your cup on them
so you can gloat over their shameful
    nakedness.
16 But soon it will be your turn to be
    disgraced.
Come, drink and be exposed!
Drink from the cup of the LORD's
    judgment,

and all your glory will be turned
    to shame.
17 You cut down the forests of
    Lebanon.
Now you will be cut down.
You destroyed the wild animals,
    so now their terror will be yours.
You committed murder throughout
    the countryside
and filled the towns with violence.

NOTES

2:15 *You force your cup on them.* This line is filled with difficulties in the original text and thus is rendered variously in the English translations. The basic idea is that of pouring out a cup (of wrath) until the guest is drunk. The NLT has reorganized the first two lines so as to yield the necessary image in simplicity.

2:16 *be exposed!* This graphic comparative literally means "show yourself as uncircumcised." Not even in the marks of his body could a Babylonian claim covenant relationship with Yahweh. Naked and without grounds for leniency, the Babylonians faced certain doom.

shame. The NLT combines two Hebrew nouns: *qalon* [TH7036, ZH7830], "shame" (from *qalah* [TH7034, ZH7829], "be light") and *qiqalon* [TH7022, ZH7814], "[utter] disgrace" (from *qalal* [TH7043, ZH7837], "be slight"); (cf. Akkadian *qalalu,* "be light"; *qullulu,* "despised"). Laetsch (1956:339) suggests that *qiqalon* is derived from the root *qi'* [TH6958, ZH7794] (spit, vomit), here used of shameful vomiting. Thus he remarks, "Dead drunk, the proud Chaldean shall lie naked on the floor in his own vomit, an object of horror and ridicule for all the world."

2:17 *Lebanon.* Habakkuk is probably referring to Nebuchadnezzar's exploitation of Lebanon's forests for his many building activities. As Roberts (1991:125) remarks, "Because Nebuchadnezzar had cut down these forests, Babylon would be covered, not by the shade of the cedars (Ps 80:11 [80:10 in English Bibles]) in their fine buildings, but by the same violence that had desecrated the sanctity of God's forests."

wild animals. The Hebrew noun *behemah* [TH929, ZH989] is used of cattle in general, here representing the whole animal kingdom much as Lebanon, with its cedars, represents the natural world. This word *behemah* was also doubtless employed because of its use in contexts that contrast animal and human behavior (cf. Ps 73:22) and because it is frequently paired with *'adam* [TH120, ZH132] ("human[kind]"; cf. Gen 2:18-20; Ps 49:12, 20), a combination that appears here.

their terror will be yours. Translators have debated whether the single verb of the original text has to do with the terror the Babylonians inflicted on the animal kingdom (NASB, KJV, NKJV) or the terror that will come upon the Babylonians. Since the latter idea assumes that the Babylonians' terror will be because of that which they perpetrated against the animal kingdom, the NLT has included both ideas in its translation. The verbal form *yekhithan* ("will terrify") is anomalous but probably is a remnant of an old energic form from the root *khathath* [TH2865, ZH3169]. For the existence of the energic verbal form in Northwest Semitic, see Gordon 1965:1.72-73. For the utilization of the energic in Hebrew, see Cross 1950:51 and Meyer 1969:2.100-101.

violence. God points out the Babylonians' wanton disregard of the value of the natural world, the animal kingdom, and civilized humanity. Once more, the subject of violence surfaces. Habakkuk had complained about the violence around him (1:2-3), and God had warned him that still greater violence lay ahead (1:9). God had already laid the charge of violence against the Babylonians (2:8); here he reiterates it with yet another instance of the Babylonians' ruthless activity. The natural and animal worlds are often made unwilling participants in man's sin and greed (cf. Joel 1:19-20; Rom 8:22). It is a crime that has increasingly plagued human society.

COMMENTARY

The fourth taunt song emphasizes the shame the Babylonians had brought upon others. Having sought their own honor and wealth at the expense of others, it would soon be their turn to feel that same shame. Once again the theme of equal retribution comes to bear upon the case (cf. 2:8). Woe to the Babylonians!

The song begins with an invective formed with a strong metaphor. The Babylonian is a man who gives his neighbor (strong) drink in seeming hospitality. The metaphor quickly gives way to allegory. The apparently innocent cup contains a draught of wrath, for it is designed to make the partaker drunk. Drunkenness is not the only misdeed of this untrustworthy friend: Having got his neighbor drunk, he denudes him.

As invective turns to threat, the allegory depicts the giver of the drink as one who is forced to imbibe his own drink and suffer the disgrace of exposure. Several familiar biblical motifs and expressions are contained in 2:15-16. The cup as a motif of judgment is well attested elsewhere (e.g., Pss 11:6 [MT]; 75:8; Isa 51:17, 22; Jer 25:15-28; 49:12; Ezek 23:31-34). Particularly enlightening is Jeremiah's use of the cup to portray God's relation to Babylon (Jer 51:6-8). For Jeremiah, Babylon is God's cup, a golden cup (cf. Daniel's interpretation of the head of gold, Dan 2:36-38), which had passed God's judgment to the nations. Those who drink of that cup lose all sense of perspective and become oblivious to the danger they are in. But Babylon will become a broken cup, for it will be smashed and never repaired.

Habakkuk makes the same point, although the image is slightly different. The

Babylonians will be God's cup of judgment (cf. 1:5-11), but rather than being conscious of their privileged responsibility, the Babylonians will use their position to take advantage of others and enslave them politically and economically.

The image of shame is heightened by the double figure of drunkenness and nakedness (cf. Gen 9:21-23). The first is condemned both by our Lord (Luke 21:34) and elsewhere in the Scriptures (e.g., Prov 23:29-35; Eph 5:18). Nakedness is likened to a shameful thing (cf. Gen 2:25 with Gen 3:7), and he who was stripped of clothing felt degraded (2 Sam 10:4; Ezek 16:39; 23:29). Both figures are used elsewhere to symbolize divine judgment (Nah 3:5, 11). All three symbols occur together in Lamentations 4:21, where Jeremiah portrays the Israelites' taunt of Edom. That nation, which had so often taken advantage of Israel's misfortune, would be given the cup of judgment, become drunk, and be stripped naked.

Habakkuk thus points out that the Babylonians will pour out a cup of wrath but in turn will drink it themselves. Indeed, they will drink it more deeply. The Neo-Babylonian Empire would come to know what every divinely employed agent must learn: When carrying out God's will is twisted to selfish advantage, the executor of divine justice must himself be judged (cf. 2 Kgs 10:28-31 with Hos 1:4). Modern day nations would do well to learn the lesson of the fourth song.

◆   ## 6. The fifth taunt: the polytheistic Babylonians will be deserted by their idols (2:18-20)

18 "What good is an idol carved by man, or a cast image that deceives you? How foolish to trust in your own creation— a god that can't even talk! 19 What sorrow awaits you who say to wooden idols, 'Wake up and save us!' To speechless stone images you say, 'Rise up and teach us!' Can an idol tell you what to do? They may be overlaid with gold and silver, but they are lifeless inside. 20 But the LORD is in his holy Temple. Let all the earth be silent before him."

NOTES

2:18 *What good is . . .* The question is a rhetorical one, expecting a negative answer. This song begins without the customary initial *hoy* [TH1945, ZH2098] (woe) with which the others begin, although *hoy* does occur in 2:19. Robertson (1990:207) is probably correct in suggesting that "Habakkuk alters the order of the oracle simply as a literary device to provide variety and climax in his expression."

idol carved by man . . . cast image . . . god. Three Hebrew words for idols lie behind the NLT rendering: *pesel* [TH6459, ZH7181] (carved image), *massekah* [TH4541, ZH5011] (cast image), and *'elilim* [TH457, ZH496] (idols). Although one may not always be able to press the distinctions in the first two words, they do at least serve as representative examples of idols in whatever way they are made (see the note on Nah 1:14). As for the third term, this word lays stress on the idols' lack of value, for it is denounced as an empty or worthless thing. It is compounded with the alliterated adjective *'illemim* [TH483, ZH522] (mute), perhaps to yield an effect something like "voiceless idols."

deceives. The Hebrew text calls such an idol as discussed here a "teacher of falsehood/lies." The word for teacher (*moreh* [TH3384E, ZH3723]) is read in 1QpHab 12:11 as *mry*, which Vermes (1995:346) understands to be a construct of *meri'* [TH4806, ZH5309] (fatling). It could also be understood as *meri* [TH4805, ZH5308] (rebellion).

2:19 Can an idol tell you what to do? Lit., "Shall it give you instruction?" The word *yoreh* [TH3384E, ZH3723] is properly a verb, although some have treated it as a nominal form (e.g., NASB, NJB). The accents of the MT demand that the phrase be treated as separate from what precedes (cf. KJV). Although some have regarded it as a statement (NJB, NKJV), it is usually understood as a question. Others have omitted it as a gloss (e.g., NEB). In any case, the wordplay with *moreh* [TH3384E, ZH3723] (in 2:18) is obvious.

2:20 Temple. "Temple" here probably refers not only to the Temple in Jerusalem (1 Kgs 8:10-11; 2 Chr 5:13-14; 7:1-3) but also to God's heavenly sanctuary (Ps 11:4; Isa 6:1-5; Mic 1:2; cf. Rev 4:2-11) from which, though it cannot contain him (1 Kgs 8:27), he hears and answers the prayers of those who know him and seek him (1 Kgs 8:28-30; Ps 73:17).

be silent. This word (*has* [TH2013A, ZH2187]) is an onomatopoeic interjection with the force much like the English "hush!"

C O M M E N T A R Y

The fifth taunt song, with which the series ends, examines the Babylonians' religious orientation. Their idolatrous polytheism is shown to be worthless. The condemnation of idolatry here is in harmony with that found in the other Old Testament prophets (cf. Isa 44:9-20; Jer 5:7; 44:1-8; Hos 8:4). The judgment of Babylon and its gods announced previously by Isaiah (Isa 21:9) is repeated by Jeremiah (Jer 50:2; 51:47-48, 52-53).

The oracle ends with a pronouncement that displays the vast difference between Israel's God and the gods of Babylon. Unlike those gods, who have neither life nor words of guidance for their followers (cf. Isa 44:9-11), Yahweh is a living God, the Lord of all the earth. He is in his holy Temple and available to all who fear him (cf. Deut 4:1-40; Ps 91:14-16). He is ever-present, superintending all that comes to pass (cf. Isa 44:6-8, 24-28).

It is no accident that John closes his first epistle with the admonition, "Little children, keep yourselves from idols" (1 John 5:21, NRSV). Not only should believers be reminded that religion and morality are inseparable, so that living a righteous life can only be done in the power of him who is life itself (1 John 5:20), but they should also realize that nothing should be allowed to take God's place as the center of their devotion.

Habakkuk 2:20 reminds us once again that God is sovereign over all individuals and nations, guiding them in accordance with his predetermined purpose to bring glory to himself (cf. 2:14 and the commentary on Nah 3:8-13). Further, he is a holy God (cf. 1:12) who expects not only the reverence and respect due him on the part of his followers but also that they reproduce that holiness in their lives.

The word to Habakkuk becomes doubly sobering for today's believers when they realize that their bodies are the temple of the Holy Spirit (1 Cor 6:19). As such, they belong to God and ought not to be profaned in thought or deed. Because the Holy Spirit indwells the believer (1 Cor 3:16), his or her life should reflect the One who alone is God (2 Cor 6:16-18), living in anticipation of that glorious day when the home of God will be permanently among his people (Rev 21:3).

◆ II. The Prophet's Prayer and God's Exaltation (3:1-19)
  A. The Prophet's Prayer for the Redeemer's Pity (3:1-2)

This prayer was sung by the prophet Habakkuk*:

²I have heard all about you, LORD.
  I am filled with awe by your
  amazing works.

In this time of our deep need,
  help us again as you did in years
  gone by.
And in your anger,
  remember your mercy.

3:1 Hebrew adds *according to shigionoth*, probably indicating the musical setting for the prayer.

NOTES

3:1 *was sung*. The NLT rendering takes the difficult term *shigyonoth* [TH7692, ZH8710] to be a musical term. Roberts (1991:130) raises and dismisses the possibility of a reflection of the Akkadian *segu*, a lament prayer here (cf. Watts 1975:144). Note that the *Chicago Assyrian Dictionary*, S, Part II (Chicago: The Oriental Institute, 1992), 413-414, treats the Babylonian lament prayer under *sigu*.

3:2 *heard . . . filled with awe*. Hiebert (1986:60-61) notes that these two terms "establish two motifs central to the poem: the hearing about the acts of God, and the response of great awe which this hearing evokes."

***help us again*.** Lit., "renew it." The verb can denote not only giving, calling, or creating life (Gen 7:3; Deut 32:39) but also reviving and renewing life (Pss 80:19; 85:6; 119:25) as well as preserving life (Gen 12:12 [NASB]; Deut 6:24; Ps 22:29 [NASB]). The reference here points to the redeeming work of God that is rehearsed in 3:3-15.

***as you did in years gone by*.** The NLT takes the phrase "in the midst of years" to be a reference to the past. Usually it is understood to refer to the future. Thus Robertson (1990:217) says, "Most likely *the midst of (the) years* refers to the time between the two acts of judgment revealed to Habakkuk in the process of his earlier dialogue. In the time between the purging judgment that must fall on the house of God itself and the consuming judgment that must avenge God's elect—in that crucial period before the destruction of God's enemies—may the Lord be sure to preserve life."

***anger . . . mercy*.** These two words are set in climactic parallelism and close the stanza. This final phrase is marked by alliteration and assonance, specifically the use of velars (e.g., gimel and kaph) and the letters zayin and resh.

COMMENTARY

The thought of God in his holy Temple, with which chapter 2 ends, provides a natural basis for Habakkuk's words in 3:1-2. He stood in awe before the God who sits enthroned in his holy Temple. In worshipful reverence, Habakkuk brought his prayer request before him. Not only had he heard the Lord's pronouncement, but he was reminded of all of God's miraculous deeds in bygone days. The choice of the word "LORD" (*yhwh* [TH3068, ZH3378]) rather than a more general term for God probably emphasizes the fact that Habakkuk addressed his words to Israel's covenant God.

In accordance with God's message of the coming chastisement of Judah, Habakkuk prayed for God's miraculous intervention. He asked that God would again make known his work of redemption. With aching heart, he urged God to be compassionate in the coming turmoil (cf. Exod 34:6-7; 1 Kgs 8:33-34, 46-53; 2 Chr 6:24-25, 36-39; Isa 54:8).

Habakkuk's prayer would be answered according to the terms of Israel's covenant with God (Deut 4:25-31) and also the prophecies of Jeremiah (Jer 25:1-11; 29:10-14; cf. 2 Chr 36:22; Ezra 1:1; Dan 9:2). His prayer and its realization stand as a harbinger of God's future gathering of his people in redemptive power (Deut 30:1-3; Ezek 36:24-38; 37:21-28; Amos 9:14-15; Mic 4:6; Zeph 3:20; Zech 10:5-12).

◆ **B. The Prophet's Praise of the Redeemer's Person (3:3-15)**
   1. The Redeemer's coming (3:3-7)

³ I see God moving across the deserts
   from Edom,*
the Holy One coming from Mount
   Paran.*
His brilliant splendor fills the heavens,
   and the earth is filled with his
   praise.
⁴ His coming is as brilliant as the
   sunrise.
Rays of light flash from his hands,
   where his awesome power is hidden.

⁵ Pestilence marches before him;
   plague follows close behind.
⁶ When he stops, the earth shakes.
   When he looks, the nations
   tremble.
He shatters the everlasting mountains
   and levels the eternal hills.
He is the Eternal One!
⁷ I see the people of Cushan in distress,
   and the nation of Midian trembling
   in terror.

3:3a Hebrew *Teman.*   3:3b Hebrew adds *selah;* also in 3:9, 13. The meaning of this Hebrew term is uncertain; it is probably a musical or literary term.

NOTES

3:3 *Edom*. Lit., "Teman" (see the note on Obad 1:9).

Mount Paran. Paran designates not only a mountain range west and south of Edom and northeast of Mount Sinai but also a broad desert area in the Sinai Peninsula. For the juxtaposition of Seir and Paran, see Gen 14:6. All three terms are used as parallel names for the southern area that stretched as far as the Sinai Peninsula (cf. Deut 33:1-2a; Judg 5:4-5). The text adds *selah* [TH5542, ZH6138], probably a musical term indicating an instrumental interlude (cf. the helpful excursus in Craigie 1983:76-77).

3:4 *Rays*. Hiebert (1986:17-19) prefers to retain the usual meaning for the noun *qarnayim* [TH7161, ZH7967] (horns) here, pointing out a possible association with the word "strength" at the end of the verse. Such literalness does not seem necessary in figurative poetry describing a theophany. Furthermore, it makes for too rough a transition from the previous expressions. The same applies to Albright's suggestion: "(Yahweh) attacked like a bull(?) provided with tossing horns" (1950:11-12). Moreover, the ancient versions all translate with a noun meaning "brightness." Roberts (1991:153) remarks, "The form Habakkuk sees has two prongs (*qarnayim*) extending from his hand. This is an apt description of the standard representation of the Syro-Palestinian storm god. He is usually portrayed standing, one hand grasping a lightning bolt as a weapon, and the end of the stylized lightning bolt that extends above the hand forks into two or more prongs that closely resemble horns. Here, of course, the description is of the Lord in all his radiant glory."

where his awesome power is hidden. Lit., "there is the hiding of his strength." The line may point to the unfathomable inner recesses of the divine power.

3:5 Pestilence . . . plague. The parallelism of the two terms involved here has often been noted, most viewing *deber* [TH1698, ZH1822] (pestilence) as an epithet or alternative name for Resheph (plague), the Canaanite god of pestilence and sterility (cf. Albright 1969:184; Day 1979:353-355). For the proposed Eblaite evidence, see the comments of M. Dahood in Pettinato 1981:296.

before him . . . close behind. The two phrases are set in chiastic arrangement in the Hebrew text.

3:6 shakes. The reading of the MT (*wayemoded* [TH4128, ZH4571]) has customarily been translated either "measured" (KJV, NKJV; cf. NASB, "surveyed") or "shook" (NIV, NRSV; cf. LXX, *esaleuthē* [TG4531, ZG4888]). The latter is more intelligible.

tremble. The MT's *wayyatter* [TH5425A, ZH6001] has occasioned several translations: *dietakē* ("melt," LXX), "drove asunder" (KJV), "startled" (NASB, NKJV), and "made to tremble" (NIV, NRSV). If the previous line is to be rendered "shakes," the NLT is most appropriate.

He is the Eternal One! Roberts (1991:136-137) suggests, "His are the primeval roots." The syntax of the line is reminiscent of Num 23:22b.

3:7 Cushan . . . Midian. The first line of 3:7 is extremely uncertain and is omitted by the NLT. For details concerning this crux, see Patterson (1991:237); see also Roberts (1991:137) and Robertson (1990:221). The land of the Midianites is identified primarily with the southern part of Transjordan (e.g., Gen 25:6; 36:35; Num 10:29), and evidence now exists that Cushan was also located there. An interesting parallel to the biblical account here, including the seismic activity, is in a fragmentary inscription found at Kuntillet 'Ajrud. As pointed out by Hiebert (1986:95; cf. McCarter's translation in COS 2.173), "The context is the battle of the divine warrior. His appearance is accompanied by light (cf. 3:4a) and the response to it is reflected in the convulsion of the cosmos: the mountains are melted and their peaks crushed." Such an inscription from the very area where the biblical account is set is particularly significant.

COMMENTARY

This first section of Habakkuk's psalm, like the entirety of Habakkuk, is replete with theological truth. In 3:3-4, God is shown to be not only Yahweh, Israel's covenant God, but also *'eloah* [TH433, ZH468], the Creator (Deut 32:15) and Lord of the earth (Pss 18:31[32]; 114:7). God is also declared to be the Holy One (Isa 6:3), the one who convicts of sin and judges the world (Lev 19:2; 20:7; Jer 50:29; 51:5), but who is Israel's Redeemer (Isa 41:14; 43:1-3). The one whom Habakkuk had addressed in his second perplexity (1:12–2:1) is the sovereign, holy God who had come long ago in all his glory.

The word for "glory" is often especially applicable to kingly authority (e.g., Num 27:20; 1 Chr 29:25; Ps 45:3[4]; Zech 6:13) and is associated with God's sovereignty over both the created world and the flow of earth's history (1 Chr 29:11-12; Job 40:10). God is thus seen here, in all his majesty, as the one whose splendor (cf. Job 37:22-23) permeates and transcends the heavens (Pss 8:1; 145:4).

Two of the common agents of judgment are spelled out: pestilence and plague (3:5; cf. Exod 9:15; Deut 28:21; 32:24; Amos 4:10). These form part of a standard listing of four kinds of judgment often instituted by God (cf. Jer 15:3; Ezek 14:21;

Rev 6:8). God's omnipotent control over the forces of nature is also emphasized. Here, as repeatedly emphasized in the Scriptures, nature itself is under the control of an omnipotent and sovereign God (cf. Pss 18:7-15; 29:3-10; 77:16-19).

The first poem thus closes with a consideration of God's initial strike against his enemy. It is a triumphant campaign. The tents (and tent curtains) of Cushan and Midian are described as "trembling in terror." The metonymy here suggests that a widespread area of the Jordan valley was thrown into upheaval. The Scriptures give evidence that seismic activity accompanied the Israelites at various stages of the Exodus, especially at the time of the conquest (Judg 5:4-5; Pss 18:7; 114:3-6). Under such conditions, it is little wonder that the inhabitants of the area were struck with terror (cf. Exod 15:14-16).

God is here portrayed as the Divine Warrior who intercedes on behalf of his own. This motif will reach its climax in 3:8-15 (see commentary). With such a defender available, the believing heart may rest secure (Ps 27:1). God's past victory is a harbinger of a yet future day when the Lord shall intervene once again on behalf of his own in awesome power (Rev 19:11-21). Robertson (1990:224) appropriately remarks, "These past manifestations on a limited scale may be regarded as anticipations of the great final epiphany of the glory of God, when the Son of Man shall come in the clouds, accompanied by lightning shining from the East to the West (Matt 24:27). Then every eye shall see him, and the vision of Habakkuk shall receive its finalized fulfillment."

◆   ## 2. The Redeemer's conquest (3:8-15)

⁸Was it in anger, LORD, that you struck
the rivers
and parted the sea?
Were you displeased with them?
No, you were sending your chariots
of salvation!
⁹You brandished your bow
and your quiver of arrows.
You split open the earth with
flowing rivers.
¹⁰The mountains watched and trembled.
Onward swept the raging waters.
The mighty deep cried out,
lifting its hands to the LORD.
¹¹The sun and moon stood still in the sky
as your brilliant arrows flew
and your glittering spear flashed.

¹²You marched across the land in
anger
and trampled the nations in
your fury.
¹³You went out to rescue your chosen
people,
to save your anointed ones.
You crushed the heads of the wicked
and stripped their bones from head
to toe.
¹⁴With his own weapons,
you destroyed the chief of those
who rushed out like a whirlwind,
thinking Israel would be easy prey.
¹⁵You trampled the sea with your
horses,
and the mighty waters piled high.

NOTES

3:8 *in anger.* The NLT translates the sense of the third masculine singular verb in the MT. The LXX reads *ōrgisthēs* [TG3710, ZG3974] (Were you angry?) so as to make this line agree with the following lines. But such an adjustment is not necessary (Pope 1977:303-304).

rivers . . . sea? Many have pointed out the Ugaritic parallelism of *ym* (cf. *yam* [TH3220, ZH3542]) and *nhr* (cf. *nahar* [TH5104, ZH5643]). Thus Roberts (1991:137) remarks, "The parallel pair River/Sea is a traditional pair, representing alternative names for a single cosmic enemy of Baal in the Ugaritic (and presumably Canaanite) mythology."

salvation! The translation of *yeshu'ah* [TH3444, ZH3802] as "salvation" is traditional. Despite Keil's (1954) objection, in a martial context, "victory" (NRSV) or "victorious" (NIV) is also appropriate. The metonymy here is effective—God's deliverance being represented by the "chariots of salvation."

3:9 You brandished. The NLT cuts through the problems of the difficult Hebrew line *shebu'oth mattoth 'omer.* Attempts to determine the precise reading and sense of the line are manifold. One such attempt is to follow the lead of some ancient versions (e.g., Peshitta) and many scholars in reading (with no consonantal change) *sibba'ta* [TH7646, ZH8425] (you were satisfied), an understanding attested elsewhere in contexts dealing with fighting and weaponry. In addition to Jer 46:10, one may note the case of Anat's fighting as recorded in the Baal cycle: "Anat fought hard and gazed (on her work), she battled . . . until she was sated, fighting in the palace" (Driver 1956:84-85). The NIV relates the Masoretic consonants to *sheba'* [TH7651, ZH8679] (seven) and translates "many arrows." Other versions trace the form to the verb *shaba'* [TH7650, ZH8678] ("swear"; NASB, KJV, NKJV), and some translate according to the sense: "You put (the arrow to) the string" (RSV; cf. NJB). Even though a final resolution for the line is not forthcoming, its association with the preceding lines and the literary motif of the Divine Warrior make the general sense of God's actions on behalf of his people clear enough.

The final two words of this line have likewise been hotly debated. It is possible to retain the consonants of the text and view the *mattoth* [TH4294, ZH4751] as a war club, the traditional weapon of Baal. If so, the final *'omer* [TH559/562, ZH606/608] (to say) might reflect a scribal pun on Baal's war weapon *aymur* (Expeller) known from the Ugaritic texts (see ANET 131). Still another possibility would be to take the final taw of *mattoth* as a double-duty consonant, read the final word as the imperfect *to'mar* [TH559, ZH606], and translate the whole line, "You were satisfied with the club *you commanded.*"

bow . . . arrows. The mention of a divinity having weapons of war is familiar from the literature of the ancient Near East. Thus Ward (1911:23) remarks: "Syrian and Hittite art frequently represents Adad-ramman, god of storm, as armed with the same weapons, while the Babylonian art gave this western god the forked thunderbolt."

3:10 Onward swept the raging waters. Hiebert (1986:29; cf. Roberts 1991:140) finds the influence of Ps 77:17 in this line, which he emends (with the support of a Heb. fragment from Wadi Murabba'at) to read *zoremu mayim 'aboth* [TH2229A/4325/5645, ZH2442/4784/6265] (clouds poured down water). Though the conjecture is attractive and has the advantage of some ancient manuscript support, as well as precedent in similar contexts (cf. Judg 5:4), the evidence is still too meager to set aside the MT, *zerem mayim 'abar* [TH2230/4325/5674, ZH2443/4784/6296], which is nicely rendered by the NLT.

3:11 sun and moon. The juxtaposition of sun and moon participating in earthly events is noted elsewhere (e.g., Josh 10:12-13; Isa 13:10; Joel 2:10; 2:31). The words are familiar set terms. For the participation of other celestial phenomena in earthly events, see Judg 5:20; Isa 60:19-20; and the remarks of Craigie (1977:33-49). For translational difficulties connected with the close of 3:10, see Patterson 1991:244-245.

brilliant arrows flew . . . spear flashed. Most modern translations take the subject of these prepositional phrases to be the sun and moon of the first line of the verse, an understanding found in some ancient versions (Vulgate, Peshitta) and followed by most commentators. The Masoretic accents, however, indicate that the subject of the two lines in question is to be understood differently, as reflected by Ward's (1911:21) translation:

"For light thine arrows go forth, for brightness the glittering of thy spear." So perceived, the two prepositional phrases are viewed as governed by subjects in their own lines. This arrangement is also reflected in the LXX, Old Latin, and Targum. The NLT properly indicates that the celestial luminaries are obscured by the brilliance of the electric storm.

3:12 You marched across. The verb here (*tsa'ad* [TH6805, ZH7575]) occurs with the verb *yatsa'* [TH3318, ZH3655] (3:13) elsewhere in the epic literature detailing God's actions on behalf of his people during the Exodus event (Judg 5:4; Ps 68:7). The reading of the LXX (*oligōseis*, "you will diminish") indicates that its translators probably read the verb *tsa'ar* [TH6819, ZH7592] (grow insignificant), doubtless due to the confusion between the similarly formed consonants daleth (ד) and resh (ר). The MT is supported by the Vulgate and Peshitta.

trampled. The term is a key one in Habakkuk's double psalm. Thus Armerding (1985:530) observes that 3:12 "recapitulates the imagery of earthquake from v. 10: in effect it resumes and integrates the content of both vv. 3-7 and vv. 8, 9-11 at the introduction to this concluding section (vv. 12-15) in which the goal of the Lord's 'wrath' and salvation becomes evident whether acting on the 'earth' or the 'nations.'"

anger . . . fury. This parallel pair appears elsewhere regarding God's indignation against his enemies (e.g., Isa 30:27). Especially instructive is Isa 10:5, where not only this pair is found but also *matteh* [TH4294, ZH4751] ("rod, club"; 3:9) appears: "What sorrow awaits Assyria, the rod of my anger. I use it as a club to express my anger."

3:13 to save. The Hebrew text contains a noun rather than an infinitive: "for the salvation of." The rendering of the NLT takes full note of the following particle *'eth* [TH853, ZH906], which normally marks a direct accusative after a verbal form. However, Pusey (1953:217) reads the particle as the preposition *'eth* [TH854, ZH907] (with) translating, "you went forth for victory *with* your people." Perhaps the simplest solution is to view the particle as an instance of its use with a noun carrying an implied causative verbal force, an employment expanded from its normal function of marking the definite direct object of a verb. Its force is thus emphatic here (Roberts 1991:142).

your anointed ones. This term (which is singular in the Hebrew text, "your anointed") has been taken as referring to the nation Israel (Ewald 1875), to Israel's Davidic king (Roberts 1991, R. L. Smith 1984), to Cyrus (Robertson 1990), or to the Messiah (Hailey 1972, Keil 1954, Laetsch 1956, von Orelli 1897). If the reference is primarily historical and has in view the era of the Exodus and wilderness wanderings, the term must at least initially refer to Moses.

stripped . . . head to toe. The Hebrew form of the verb "stripped" is an infinitive absolute detailing the activity of the main verb. The "stripping" could refer to severe wounding or loss of life (cf. Ps 141:8). If so, this act is then followed by the traditional blow to the head found in ancient Near Eastern literature. A victor first delivered a blow to the body of a foe and then crushingly to the head. By the phrase "head to toe" (more lit., "from foundation [thigh] to neck"), Habakkuk's poem maintains contact with the details of the two-stage fighting attested in the ancient literature, such as Marduk's slaying of Tiamat first by delivering an arrow down her throat and then by a crushing blow to her skull, the Egyptian Sinuhe's dispatching of his Amorite foe by an arrow to the neck followed by a deathblow with his battle-axe, and Baal's defeat of Yamm with a blow first to the body and then to the head.

3:14 easy prey. Verse 14 is extremely difficult. Thus Margulis (1970:427) declares, "This text seems to defy comprehension. It is at first sight the most seriously damaged portion of the poem." Despite Roberts's (1991:157) observations that "the extensive corruption in this verse makes any discussion of it somewhat problematic," the NLT has captured well the basic thrust of the verse.

3:15 *the sea.* For the figure of God treading upon the sea, see Ps 77:19.

piled high. The *tarassontas* [TG5015, ZG5429] (stirring up) in the LXX also represents a valid understanding of the Hebrew *khomer* [TH2563B, ZH2816]; cf. NIV. However, the idea of the heaping up of the waters (as in the NLT) is not inappropriate to the context, particularly as one that originates in the epic literature concerning the Exodus (cf. Exod 15:8; Josh 3:13, 16).

COMMENTARY

The second poem is a victory ode that sings of the mighty strength of Israel's Redeemer. His power is displayed at the waters of testing (3:8-9b), unleashed in the natural world (3:9c-11), and viewed by the enemy (3:12-15). Whereas the first two sections deal in a general way with the entire Exodus event (focusing particularly on the final movement into Canaan), the final section fixes its attention on the initial stage of the Exodus.

The rhetorical question with which the second poem begins is for emphasis and vividness. Using phraseology drawn from the epic literature familiar to the people of the Levant, particularly of Syro-Palestine, Yahweh is portrayed metaphorically as Israel's mighty warrior who appears in his battle chariot (3:8), armed with bow (3:9), club (3:9; see note), arrows (3:11), and spear (3:11). Though the literary allusion is probably to Baal's dispatching of his enemy Yamm (Sea) (Cassuto 1975:11-12), here Yahweh is shown to be the true master over the forces of nature.

This, however, is no cosmic battle between deities representing the forces of nature; Yahweh comes as Israel's champion against human opponents. In giving his people the victory, he uses his power over the elements to aid his people (cf. Judg 5:19-21). Not only at the Exodus from Egypt itself (cf. Exod 15:12-15), but also at the Jordan River, Yahweh showed himself to be sovereign over all forces and events.

The reference to waters here probably intends the activities of God in connection with the entire Exodus event. The theme of water is prominent not only in the triumph at the Red Sea (Exod 15) but also in passing through the Jordan (Josh 3–4). In accordance with his promise to defend his people (Deut 32:40-42), the God who is the Creator of the abyss and seas (Gen 1:6-8; Pss 24:2; 104:6; 2 Pet 3:5) and the controller of the flood (Gen 6–8; 2 Pet 3:6) and all watery domains (Job 38:8-11; Pss 24:2; 104:7-13; 2 Pet 3:5-7) moves the waters so that his people can make their escape.

In 3:10 the waters of the abyss (Gen 49:25; Deut 33:13) are said to cry out and lift up their hands, perhaps in terror or prayer. As a figure of battle, this doubtless refers to the force with which the waters roar from their subterranean prisons and the tossing waves that cap the surface of the waters. The imagery of a plaintiff crying to the God who alone rescues from danger may also be present. If nature is subject to the omnipotent one, surely the case is no different for mankind (cf. Pss 19:1-4[2-5]; 104:31-35; 148:1-4).

The drama of warfare continues in 3:11 with a hyperbolic description of the celestial scene. The Divine Warrior shoots his arrows and hurls his spears so that the sun and the moon appear to stand still in their courses. They are largely obscured by the darkness that attends the heavy clouds, seen only intermittently amid the flashing lightning.

The closing verses (3:12-15) describe both the defeat of Israel's enemies and the deliverance of God's people. The salvation of God's anointed is singled out for particular attention. Although historically the term here probably has reference to Moses, it can be applied also to the ruling member of the Davidic line, whose future coming was recorded by Moses (cf. Gen 49:10; Num 24:19). David understood his role as God's anointed (2 Sam 7:8-29; 23:1-7), and the Scriptures from his time forward proclaim the inviolability of the far-reaching provisions in the Davidic covenant (cf. Pss 2; 45:2-7; 89:3-4, 19-24, 27-37; 110:1-7; Jer 33:19-26; Ezek 34:20-31) that will find their ultimate realization in Israel's Messiah (Isa 42:1-7; 48:16-17; 49:1-7; 52:13–53:12; Jer 23:5-8; Ezek 37:24-28; Zech 9:9; cf. Isa 61:1-2 with Luke 4:18-19; see further Luke 1:68-79; Acts 2:29-36; 3:24-26; 15:16-17; Rev 11:15).

Because the primary orientation of these verses is the redemption in Exodus, probably the historical reference is to Pharaoh and the armies of Egypt over whom God, through Moses, his anointed, achieved the victory. The idea of a victorious Redeemer could be applied to the subsequent defeat of the enemy in the land (cf. Josh 6:10; Judg 5:19-23) and to all the victories that the Lord gave to Israel (e.g., 2 Kgs 19:32-36) and will yet accomplish in a future day (Ps 110:5-6; Isa 63:1-6; 66:14-16, 22-24; Ezek 38–39; Joel 3:9-17; Amos 9:11-12).

Verses 14b-15 provide a follow-up to the previous scene. The enemy's warriors storm out against the people of God like brigands coming upon the helpless. The event commemorated here may be the Egyptians' pursuit of the fleeing Hebrews (Exod 14:5-9). If so, the last verse of the poem is doubly apropos: It not only sings of the miraculous deliverance of the children of Israel through the "mighty waters" (cf. Exod 15:10) of the Red Sea (Exod 14:13-22, 29-31) but also bookends the theme of God's action against waters with which the poem began (3:8).

Thus this second poem deals with the great deliverance from Egypt, the entire psalm (3:3-15) being concluded on a note of redemption. Israel's God, who brought them through the waters of testing with a mighty power that left all nature in convulsion and who led his people in triumph, was the one who had been with them since the deliverance out of Egypt. A victorious Redeemer, he could be counted on to again save a repentant and submissive people. This truth should be a source of assurance for the troubled prophet.

Theologically, 3:8-15 continues to underscore the might of the Creator and Controller of earth's forces. River and sea, earth and sky, all are under his sovereign power. And not only that, they are but the arsenal of the Divine Warrior who acts on behalf of his own people. This motif of the Divine Warrior spans the literature of both Testaments.[1] The theme is particularly tied to Israel's Exodus, which commemorates Israel's deliverance from Egypt and the movement to Mount Sinai (Exod 15:1-18),[2] Israel's approach to the Promised Land from the south, and the triumphs of the early conquest period (cf. 3:3-15 with Judg 5:4-5; Pss 18:8-16; 68:8-9; 77:16-20; 144:5-6). The theme continues throughout the Hebrew Scriptures, the emphasis being on God's intervention on behalf of his people as their victorious Redeemer. As the spiritual basis for all of Israel's redemptive experience, nationally and individually, it is cited or alluded to repeatedly (e.g., Josh 3:5; 4:18-24; 5:10-15; 1 Sam 12:6; Pss 105:26-45; 106:7-12; Jer 11:7). The traditional account is then often recast by Israel's prophets to portray God's future intervention on behalf of his people so as to bring them once again to the land of blessing (e.g., Isa 11:11-16; 51:9-11; Jer 16:14-15; 23:7-8; Mic 7:14-15).

Attested in several intertestamental works (e.g., 3 Macc 2:6-8, 64; *1 Enoch* 89:10-27; *Jubilees* 49), the Exodus theme reaches into the New Testament where it is used to depict Christ's redemptive work. It culminates in our Lord's second coming as a Divine Warrior to liberate his followers from the realm of oppression in a new Exodus (e.g., Rev 15:3-4; 19:11-21). Strengthened by this knowledge, believers may take courage in the midst of spiritual warfare. Properly armed and equipped (Eph 6:10-18), they understand that their Redeemer and victorious Divine Warrior always leads his believers in triumph (2 Cor 2:14). Christians, therefore, can rest in that certain hope of final redemption in which Christ will triumph over death itself (Rom 8:18-25; 1 Cor 15:51-57).

ENDNOTES
1. Crucial among the many discussions of this motif are F. M. Cross, Jr., "The Divine Warrior in Israel's Early Cult," *Biblical Motifs*, A. Altmann, ed. (Cambridge: Cambridge University Press, 1966), 11-30; T. Longman III, "Psalm 98: A Divine Warrior Victory Song," *Journal of the Evangelical Theological Society* 27 (1984):267-274; "The Divine Warrior: The New Testament Use of an Old Testament Motif," *Westminster Theological Journal* 44 (1982):297-302.
2. For a discussion of Exodus 15:1-18 and the Exodus motif, see R. Patterson, "The Song of Redemption," *Westminster Theological Journal* 57 (1995):453-461.

◆   C. The Prophet's Pledge to the Redeemer's Purposes (3:16-19)

16 I trembled inside when I heard this;
     my lips quivered with fear.
My legs gave way beneath me,*
     and I shook in terror.
I will wait quietly for the coming day
     when disaster will strike the people
     who invade us.
17 Even though the fig trees have
     no blossoms,
     and there are no grapes on
     the vines;

even though the olive crop fails,
     and the fields lie empty and barren;
even though the flocks die in the fields,
     and the cattle barns are empty,
18 yet I will rejoice in the LORD!
     I will be joyful in the God of my
     salvation!
19 The Sovereign LORD is my strength!
     He makes me as surefooted as
     a deer,*
     able to tread upon the heights.

3:16 Hebrew *Decay entered my bones.*   3:19 Or *He gives me the speed of a deer.*

NOTES
3:16 *I trembled.* The root of this verb (*ragaz* [TH7264, ZH8074]) is a key one in ch 3, being found twice here and once in v. 7 in its verb form, and also in its noun form, *rogez* [TH7267, ZH8075], in v. 2.

inside. The noun *beten* [TH990, ZH1061] has several meanings, such as "belly" (KJV), "body" (NKJV, RSV), and "womb." In several places it refers to the personal inner recesses (cf. Job 15:35; 32:18; Prov 18:8; 20:27, 30; 22:18; 26:22) where a person's deepest desires lodge (Job 20:20, 23).

heard . . . lips. In the Hebrew text, this is an inverted parallelism. The verse makes a similar use of the verb *ragaz* [TH7264, ZH8074] (NLT, "tremble," "shook") to connect the first and second lines of v. 16; furthermore, the entire verse is arranged so that verbs enclose the whole verse: "I heard. . . . [they will] invade."

My legs gave way beneath me. Lit., "decay entered my bones." The NLT translates according to the constraints of the context, emphasizing the outward result of an inward condition in accord with the parallel line, "I shook in terror" (cf. "my steps tremble beneath me," NRSV).

I shook in terror. This line contains the underlying word *'asher* [TH834, ZH889], which as pointed by the Masoretes, is a relative particle. So construed, it must be related syntactically to the two lines that follow (cf. KJV, NKJV, NASB). But to read the text this way ruins the poetic balance, for it leaves the line with only two words and assigns four words to the next line. Accordingly, the consistent 3/3 meter of the verse is upset. To alleviate the imbalance of the line, many have suggested reading *'ashuray* [TH838/2967.1, ZH892/3276] ("my steps"; e.g., Roberts 1991:146). Others simply translate according to the sense of the passage, as does the NLT (cf. NJB). Retaining the consonants of the MT, one could translate the line, "And my steps tremble beneath me" (NRSV).

I will wait quietly . . . invade us. Hiebert (1986:52) follows Driver (1950:96-97), who declares that "this and the next line are most obscure and uncertain, the Hebrew being in parts ambiguous, and the text open to suspicion. . . . The case is one in which it is impossible to speak with confidence." Because of the emotional fervor of the moment, the opening "wait quietly" ("patiently"; NASB, NIV, NJB) has often been emended so as to read "I groaned/moaned" (Hiebert 1986; Ward 1911). Nevertheless, the point of the line is that in the midst of conflict and distress, the prophet rests securely in the knowledge of God's purposes. It is a rest of the spirit (cf. Isa 28:12) in full trust in the redeeming God. Thus, Habakkuk will be at rest with God as the day of affliction takes its course.

3:17 Even though. The NLT follows the lead of several other versions (KJV, NKJV, NASB, NIV, NRSV) in treating the opening particle concessively. The ancient versions (LXX, Vulgate, Peshitta), however, view it causally (because), and it could also be taken temporally (when).

grapes . . . olive crop. These products and resources were vital to Israel's economy. In addition, the fig tree and the vine had spiritual significance, for they symbolized the blessing of God upon an obedient people (cf. Hos 2:12; Amos 4:9 with 1 Kgs 4:25; 2 Kgs 18:31). Likewise, olive oil and the grain of the field (as well as the cattle) were objects of God's blessing (Deut 7:13; 11:14; 28:51; Joel 2:19).

fields. Roberts (1991:147) correctly points out that "the precise meaning of *shedemoth* [TH7709, ZH8727] is disputed; it may refer to cultivated terraces rather than fields in general." This plural form is twice used of terraced lands (2 Kgs 23:4; Jer 31:40) and is also employed of lands having grapevines (Deut 32:32; Isa 16:8).

flocks die in the fields. The difficult active force of the verb here (lit., "cut off") can be read also as a passive—i.e., "they are cut off/killed" (Hiebert 1986:55; Andersen 2001:347); whether by famine, disease, or invading forces is uncertain.

cattle barns. That this is the meaning of this hapax legomenon is assured both from the parallel lines of poetry and the ancient versions.

3:18 rejoice . . . be joyful. Robertson (1990:247) appropriately remarks, "The transition from the complaining prophet to the rejoicing prophet surely must be seen as a work of God's sovereign grace. Nothing else could explain how a person could be happy and contented in the face of the calamities Habakkuk had to undergo."

3:19 The Sovereign LORD is my strength! This statement reflects many terms drawn from the corpus of the Exodus epic (cf. Ps 18:32-33). The exultant praise found in 3:18 reflects Exod 15:3, and the use of *khayil* [TH2428, ZH2657] (strength) in this verse reflects Exod 15:4.

the heights. The usual sense of the noun seems to be demanded rather than seeing here the frequently suggested (e.g., Albright 1950:13, Hiebert 1986) association with the Ugaritic word *bmt* ("back"—i.e., of the vanquished foe). The sentiment of this line is found in two other pieces of ancient Hebrew poetry: Deut 32:13 and Deut 33:29.

COMMENTARY

Habakkuk ended his prophecy with affirmations of personal commitment and praise. Having been dramatically reminded of God's past exploits against the wicked and his saving intervention on behalf of his people, the prophet was overwhelmed. Once he understood who God is and the principles and methods of his activities, Habakkuk was satisfied. He would trust God through the coming hour of judgment and rejoice no matter what may happen. Borrowing phraseology from the repertoire of ancient Hebrew poetry, he closed the account of his spiritual odyssey on a high note of praise.

The prophet reported that he was so shaken by the awesome prospect of what he had understood that he convulsed to the depths of his being. His lips quivered, and it seemed as though his very bones were coming apart, perhaps decayed to the marrow. He reeled uncertainly on his feet, for the ground beneath him seemed to undulate incessantly. And yet Habakkuk was to experience what Paul later described in the statement: "When I am weak, then I am strong" (2 Cor 12:10). Quickly, he was flooded with the implications of all that had happened and what had been revealed to him. He could take comfort in knowing that although God would chastise his people, the vicious Babylonians would likewise undergo divine punishment. Further, he understood that what he had prayed for (3:2) was in keeping with God's own nature: He was a God of judgment as well as mercy (cf. Deut 32:34-43).

Therefore, when the day of distress came for Judah, Habakkuk could rest secure in the assurance that God is in charge of everything, working it all out in accordance with his perfect will. He could also be at peace, knowing that the God of justice would repay the Babylonian invaders for their crimes against Judah and all humanity. Habakkuk's new resolve and trust are immediately apparent. When the time of trouble comes for Judah, disrupting the productivity of the land and the security of the cattle, Habakkuk would not only remain at peace, resting in the sufficiency of God, but would rejoice through it in the Lord, who alone is his (and Israel's) Savior. Habakkuk was determined not merely to rest in the Lord's will through everything that would come to pass but to rejoice fully in his saving God. Israel's covenant Lord was still on the throne; that meant eventual blessedness for prophet and people alike (cf. Deut 30:1-10). Roberts (1991:158) observes, "The prophet . . . expressed a profound truth about eschatological existence. In the certainty of that coming salvation, Habakkuk appears to say, one is both able to stay on the path, as precarious as it may seem, and, what is more, to experience in the interim some foretaste of that coming victory over the powers of evil."

Habakkuk closed his prophecy by declaring that Yahweh was his Lord and strength (cf. Exod 15:2). The order is significant. Whatever strength he had he owed to the one who was his strength; but basic to everything is the fact that Yahweh was his Lord and his Master, the center of his life.

Habakkuk's use of divine titles reflects his spiritual journey. God's prophet had entertained several doubts. A number of matters concerning God's working and the life of faith had haunted him. Addressing God as the covenant Lord of Israel (*yhwh* [TH3068, ZH3378]), he expressed these problems with a heavy heart (1:2-4). When the Lord had answered his uncertainties in a way that left him somewhat more perplexed (1:5-11), Habakkuk reminded God (1:12) that he was not only Israel's covenant Lord (*yhwh*) but "my God" (*'elohay* [TH430/2967.1, ZH466/3276]), "my Holy One" (*qedoshi* [TH6918A/2967.1, ZH7705/3276]). These divine titles indicate that the God of all things is, above all, holy. Therefore, although God might have the power and authority to send a nation like the Babylonians to conquer Judah, Habakkuk questioned whether it would be just for a holy God to use so unholy an instrument to punish his people (1:12–2:1).

In reporting the Lord's answer to his second perplexity, Habakkuk again used the covenant designation "Yahweh" (2:2). The Lord's response made it clear to Habakkuk that the Lord truly is in control of all history. Nevertheless, he uses human agency and institutions to accomplish his purposes. In so doing, the distinction between the wicked on the one hand and the righteous who live by faith on the other becomes clear (2:4). Habakkuk learned that even the foremost power of the world is subject to God. Indeed, Israel's covenant Lord is the God of all people and even now is in his holy Temple to receive their acquiescence and adoration (2:20).

While the Lord's answer was satisfying to Habakkuk—so that he appreciated the statement relative to the principles of God's just operations in the world—Habakkuk was still concerned for his people. Would this chastisement be too severe for Judah to bear? Would an omnipotent God be too harsh in his punishment? Habakkuk pleaded with the Lord to show mercy amid the coming judgment. In so doing he once again employed the title "Yahweh" (3:2). Much like Job (Job 38–41), what Habakkuk needed was a clear perception of how God acts. This was supplied to him through his consideration of the epic material relative to the Exodus (3:3-15). There he saw God in all his might (*'eloah* [TH433, ZH468]) and yet in his holiness (*qadosh* [TH6918A, ZH7705], 3:3). It was he who delivered his people from the might of Egypt and led them to the land of promise (3:3-7). He is Yahweh, the covenant God of Israel (3:8), and as such, he is Israel's Redeemer and victor (3:8-15). Yahweh, Israel's Lord and the judge of all mankind, is in charge of earth's history. He also has a righteous concern for his covenant people. Accordingly, one can be assured that he will deal properly with Judah's case and fulfill his age-old promises to them.

Gone were Habakkuk's fears, doubts, and perplexities. He would trust in Yahweh and rejoice in his saving God (*'elohe yish'i* [TH430/3468/2967.1, ZH466/3829/3276], 3:18). Israel's Redeemer was his, the Master (*'adon* [TH113/136, ZH123/151]) from whom alone he gained his strength (3:19). So near to God did Habakkuk feel after this experience that in a bold simile he likened his spiritual climb to that of a deer swiftly ascending to the mountaintops and gracefully gliding over them.

Victory at last! Israel's Lord was truly Habakkuk's own, his leader and guide. God's prophet had walked a precarious path in questioning God. But lest we condemn Habakkuk too readily, we need to remember that the Lord did not do so; he merely corrected him. Ultimately Habakkuk's implanted faith bore spiritual fruit. The prophecy of Habakkuk thus not only reminds its readers of the importance of faith (2:4, 20) and of the final triumph of good through God's control of history (3:3-15), but it also provides important insight into a believer's personal relationship with his God. When times of doubt and discouragement come, as they inevitably do, believers need to come to God, as Habakkuk did, and share their concerns with him. Like Habakkuk, they need to come to God's Word and get a fresh glimpse of who and what God is and so come to a place of renewed trust in the one who alone is truly God and therefore sufficient for all of life. May Habakkuk's test of faith and triumphant joy in his saving Lord be an inspiration and example to all who must travel life's road!

◆ Subscription

(For the choir director: This prayer is to be accompanied by stringed instruments.)

NOTES

For the choir director. The closing subscription is one of several musical notations in ch 3 (3:1, 3, 9, 13) that give instructions for the possible use of Habakkuk's prayer psalm in public worship. While the term *shigyonoth* [TH7692, ZH8710] in the heading (3:1) appears to be an indication of the musical setting, and the repeated *selah* [TH5542, ZH6138] (3:3, 9, 13) a note relative to musical interlude, these final instructions are intended for the director of music (cf. 1 Chr 15:21-22; 2 Chr 34:12). All three terms could indicate that such pieces of music were part of the standard repertoire available for congregational worship (Waltke 1991:583-596).

BIBLIOGRAPHY

Abegg, M., Jr., P. Flint, and E. Ulrich
1999 *The Dead Sea Scrolls Bible.* San Francisco: Harper.

Ahuviah, A.
1985/1986 Why Do You Countenance Treachery? A Study in the Oracle Which Habakkuk the Prophet Saw (1:1–2:4). *Beth Mikra* 31:320-327.

Albright, W. F.
1950 The Psalm of Habakkuk. Pp. 1-18 in *Studies in Old Testament Prophecy Dedicated to T. H. Robinson.* Editor, H. H. Rowley. Edinburgh: T & T Clark.

1969 *Yahweh and the Gods of Canaan.* Garden City: Doubleday.

Andersen, F. I.
2001 *Habakkuk.* The Anchor Bible, vol. 25. New York: Doubleday.

Armerding, C. E.
1985 Habakkuk. Pp. 490-534 in *Daniel, Minor Prophets.* The Expositor's Bible Commentary, vol. 7. Editor, F. E. Gaebelein. Grand Rapids: Zondervan.

Bailey, W.
1999 *Habakkuk.* New American Commentary, vol. 20. Nashville: Broadman & Holman.

Baker, D. W.
1988 *Nahum, Habakkuk, Zephaniah.* Tyndale Old Testament Commentaries. Downers Grove: InterVarsity.

Beckwith, R.
1985 *The Old Testament Canon of the New Testament Church.* Grand Rapids: Eerdmans.

Brownlee, W. H.
1959 *The Text of Habakkuk in the Ancient Commentary from Qumran.* Journal of Biblical Literature Monograph XI. Philadelphia: Society of Biblical Literature.

1979 *The Midrash Pesher of Habakkuk.* Missoula: Scholars Press.

Bruce, F. F.
1993 *Habakkuk* in *The Minor Prophets,* vol. 2. Editor, T. E. McComiskey. Grand Rapids: Baker.

Cassuto, U.
1975 Chapter III of Habakkuk and the Ras Shamra Texts. Pp. 3-15 in *Biblical and Oriental Studies,* vol. 2. Translator, Israel Abrahams. Jerusalem: Magnes.

Cathcart, K. J.
1984 A New Proposal for Hab 1,17. *Biblica* 65:575-576.

1986 Legal Terminology in Habakkuk 2:1-4. *Proceedings of the Irish Biblical Association* 10:103-110.

Copeland, P. E.
1992 The Midst of the Years. Pp. 91-105 in *Text and Pretext: Essays in Honour of Robert Davidson.* Journal for the Study of the Old Testament Supplement 138. Sheffield: Journal for the Study of the Old Testament Press.

Craigie, P. C.
1966 *Kanaanaische und Aramaische Inschriften.* Wiesbaden: Otto Harrassowitz.

1977 Three Ugaritic Notes on the Song of Deborah. *Journal for the Study of the Old Testament* 2:33-49.

1983 *Psalms 1–50.* Word Biblical Commentary. Waco: Word.

1985 *Twelve Prophets.* Philadelphia: Westminster.

Cranfield, C. E. B.
1975 *The Epistle to the Romans.* The International Critical Commentary. Edinburgh: T & T Clark.

Cross, F. M., Jr.
1950 *Studies in Ancient Yahwistic Poetry.* Baltimore: Johns Hopkins.

Day, J.
1979 New Light on the Mythological Background of the Allusion to Resheph in Habakkuk iii 5. *Vetus Testamentum* 29:353-355.

Delaporte, L.
1970 *Mesopotamia.* Translator, V. Gordon Childe. New York: Barnes & Noble.

Driver, S. R.
1950 *An Introduction to the Literature of the Old Testament.* Rev. ed. New York: Scribners.
1956 *Canaanite Myths and Legends.* Edinburgh: T & T Clark.

Duhm, B.
1875 *Die Theologie der Propheten als Grundlage für die innere Entwicklungsgeschichte der Israelitischen Religion.* Bonn: Marcus.

Eaton, J. H.
1964 The Origin and Meaning of Habakkuk 3. *Zeitschrift für die Alttestamentliche Wissenschaft* 76:144-171.

Eiselen, F. C.
1907 *The Minor Prophets.* New York: Eaton & Mains.

Emerton, J. A.
1977 The Textual and Linguistic Problems of Habakkuk II.4-5. *Journal of Theological Studies* 28:2-17.

Ewald, G. H. A. von
1875-1881 *Commentary on the Prophets of the Old Testament.* Translator, J. F. Smith. London: Williams & Norgate.

Feinberg, C. L.
1976 *The Minor Prophets.* Chicago: Moody.

Floyd, M. H.
1993 Prophecy and Writing in Habakkuk 2,1-5. *Zeitschrift für die alttestamentliche Wissenschaft* 105:462-481.

Girdlestone, R.
1956 *Synonyms of the Old Testament.* Grand Rapids: Eerdmans.

Gordon, C.
1965 *Ugaritic Textbook.* Rome: Pontifical Biblical Institute.

Grayson, A. K.
1972-1976 *Assyrian Royal Inscriptions.* Records of the Ancient Near East. 2 vols. Wiesbaden: Otto Harrassowitz.

Gunneweg, A. H. J.
1986 Habakuk und das Problem des leidenen *sdyq. Zeitschrift für die Attestamentliche Wissenschaft* 98:400-415.

Hailey, H.
1972 *A Commentary on the Minor Prophets.* Grand Rapids: Baker.

Hallo, W. W. and K. L. Younger, Jr.
1997-2002 *The Context of Scripture.* 3 vols. Leiden: Brill.

Harrison, R. K.
1969 *Introduction to the Old Testament.* Grand Rapids: Eerdmans.

Herdner, A.
1963 *Corpus des tablettes en cunieformes alphabetiques.* Paris: Imprimerie Nationale.

Herman, W. R.
1973 The Laments of Habakkuk's Prophecy. *The Evangelical Quarterly* 45:21-29.
1988 The Kingship of Yahweh in the Hymnic Theophanies of the Old Testament. *Studia Biblica et Theologica* 16:169-211.

Hiebert, T.
1986 *God of My Victory.* Harvard Semitic Monographs 38. Atlanta: Scholars Press.

Holt, J. M.
1964 So He May Run Who Reads It. *Journal of Biblical Literature* 83:298-302.

Houtsma, M. T.
1885 Habakuk II, vs. 4 en 5 verbeterd. *Theologisch Tijdschrift* 19:180-183.

Hulst, A. R.
1960 *Old Testament Translation Problems.* Leiden: Brill.

Humbert, P.
1944 *Problemes du livre d'Habacuc.* Neuchatel: Secretariat de L'Universite.

Janzen, J. G.
1980 Habakkuk 2:2-4 in the Light of Recent Philological Advances. *Harvard Theological Review* 45:53-78.

Johnson, M. D.
1985 The Paralysis of Torah in Habakkuk I 4. *Vetus Testamentum* 35:257-266.

Keil, C. F.
1954 *The Twelve Minor Prophets.* Biblical Commentary on the Old Testament, vol. 2. Translator, J. Martin. Grand Rapids: Eerdmans. (Orig. pub. 1873)

Koch, D. A.
1985 Der Text von Hab 2,4b in der Septuaginta und im Neuen Testament. *Zeitschrift für die Neutestamentliche Wissenschaft* 76:68-85.

Laetsch, T.
1956 *The Minor Prophets.* St. Louis: Concordia.

Lehrman, S. M.
1985 *Habakkuk.* Soncino Books of the Bible. Editor, A. Cohen. London: Soncino.

Luckenbill, D. D.
1927 *Ancient Records of Assyria and Babylonia.* Chicago: University of Chicago Press.

Lunemann, G.
1882 *Critical and Exegetical Handbook to the Epistle to the Hebrews.* Edinburgh: T & T Clark.

Margulis, B.
1970 The Psalm of Habakkuk: A Reconstruction and Interpretation. *Zeitschrift für die Alttestamentliche Wissenschaft* 82:409-439.

Marks, H.
1987 The Twelve Prophets. *The Literary Guide to the Bible.* Editors, Robert Alter and Frank Kermode. Cambridge: Harvard University Press.

Merling, A. B.
1988 Habacuc, el profeta de la justificacion por la fe. *Theologika* 3:138-151.

Meyer, D. R.
1969 *Hebraische Grammatik.* Berlin: de Gruyter.

Olmstead, A. T.
1948 *History of the Persian Empire.* Chicago: University of Chicago Press.

von Orelli, C.
1897 *The Twelve Minor Prophets.* Edinburgh: T & T Clark.

Parrot, A.
1956 *Babylon and the Old Testament.* New York: Philosophical Library.

Patterson, R. D.
1987 The Psalm of Habakkuk. *Grace Theological Journal* 8:163-194.

1990 A Literary Look at Nahum, Habakkuk, and Zephaniah. *Grace Theological Journal* 11:17-27.

1991 *Nahum, Habakkuk, Zephaniah.* Chicago: Moody.

Pettinato, G.
1981 *The Archives of Ebla.* Garden City: Doubleday.

Pope, M. H.
1977 *Song of Songs.* The Anchor Bible. Garden City: Doubleday.

Pusey, E. B.
1953 *The Minor Prophets,* vol. 2. Grand Rapids: Baker.

Roberts, J. J. M.
1991 *Nahum, Habakkuk, and Zephaniah.* The Old Testament Library. Louisville: Westminster/John Knox Press.

Robertson, O. P.
1990 *The Books of Nahum, Habakkuk, and Zephaniah.* New International Commentary on the Old Testament. Grand Rapids: Eerdmans.

Ross, A. P.
1988 *Creation and Blessing.* Grand Rapids: Baker.

Rudolph, W.
1975 *Micha, Nahum, Habakuk, Zephanja.* Kommentar zum Alten Testament XIII 3. Gütersloh: Gütersloher.

Scott, J. M.
1985 A New Approach to Habakkuk ii 4–5a. *Vetus Testamentum* 35:330-340.

Smith, G. A.
1929 *The Book of the Twelve Prophets,* vol. 2. Rev. ed. Garden City: Doubleday.

Smith, R. L.
1984 *Micah–Malachi.* Word Bible Commentary. Waco: Word.

Sweeney, M. A.
1991 Structure, Genre, and Intent in the Book of Habakkuk. *Vetus Testamentum* 41:63-83.
2000 *The Twelve Prophets.* Berit Olam. Collegeville, MN: Liturgical.

Thompson, M. E. W.
1993 Prayer, Oracle and Theophany: The Book of Habakkuk. *Tyndale Bulletin* 44:33-53.

Torczyner, H.
1924 The Riddle in the Bible. *Hebrew Union College Annual* 1:125-149.

Tournay, R. J.
1994 A propos du verbe HUN/HIN. *Revue Biblique* 101:321-325.

Vasholz, R. I.
1992 Habakkuk: Complaints or Complaint? *Presbyterion* 18:50-52.

Vermes, G.
1995 *The Dead Sea Scrolls in English.* 4th ed. New York: Penguin Books.

van der Wal, A. J. O.
1988 *Lo' Namut* in Habakkuk I 12: A Suggestion. *Vetus Testamentum* 38:480-482.

Waltke, B. K.
1991 Superscripts, Postscripts, or Both. *Journal of Biblical Literature* 110:583-596.

Ward, W. H.
1911 *A Critical and Exegetical Commentary on Habakkuk.* The International Critical Commentary. Edinburgh: T & T Clark.

Watts, J. D. W.
1975 *The Books of Joel, Obadiah, Jonah, Nahum, Habakkuk, and Zephaniah.* Cambridge New English Bible Commentary. London: Cambridge University Press.

Weiser, A.
1961 *Introduction to the Old Testament.* London: Darton, Longman & Todd.

Wellhausen, J.
1963 *Die kleinen Propheten übersetzt und erklärt.* 4th ed. Berlin: de Gruyter.

Wiseman, D. J.
1956 *Chronicles of Chaldaean Kings.* London: British Museum.

Wurthwein, E.
1979 *The Text of the Old Testament.* 4th ed. Grand Rapids: Eerdmans.

Yamauchi, E. M.
1990 *Persia and the Bible.* Grand Rapids: Baker.

Zemek, G., Jr.
1980 Interpretive Challenges Relating to Habakkuk 2:4b. *Grace Theological Journal* 1:43-69.

Zephaniah

RICHARD D. PATTERSON

INTRODUCTION TO
Zephaniah

ZEPHANIAH FORESAW the ravages of the Day of the Lord. Zephaniah not only proclaimed the details of God's judgment, but he also conveyed that God's faithful people would one day live in a world of righteousness and experience the everlasting peace, prosperity, and joy that God has prepared for all who love him.

AUTHOR

The prophet Zephaniah traces his patrilineage four generations back to a certain Hezekiah. Jewish (e.g., Ibn Ezra, Kimchi) and Christian (e.g., Walker) commentators alike have commonly identified this Hezekiah with the king by that name. Although Laetsch (1956:254) is doubtless correct in stating that "Zephaniah's royal descent cannot be proven," the unusual notice concerning four generations of family lineage indicates, at the very least, that Zephaniah came from a distinguished family.

Zephaniah was a man for his times. Not only was he aware of the spiritual debauchery and materialistic greed of his people, as well as of world conditions, but God's prophet was a man of deep spiritual sensitivity who had a real concern for God's reputation (1:6; 3:7) and for the well-being of all who humbly trust in him (2:3; 3:9, 12-13).

DATE AND OCCASION OF WRITING

Although Zephaniah dates his ministry to the reign of Josiah (640–609 BC), a question remains as to the specific period within the Judean king's reign.[1] Some scholars (e.g., Feinberg, Keil) suggest that Zephaniah's denunciation of Judah's apostasy and immorality becomes more dramatic if delivered after the recovery of the Book of the Law (2 Kgs 22:8) in 621 BC and the subsequent Josianic reforms (2 Kgs 23:1-27; 2 Chr 34:29–35:19). Others (e.g., Pusey, Laetsch) decide for the earlier period, before the boy king was able to deal with the ruinous effects of Judah's two preceding wicked kings, Manasseh and Amon (2 Kgs 21).

Several conclusions drawn from Zephaniah's message seem to favor the earlier period in Josiah's reign: (1) Religious practices in Judah were still plagued with Canaanite syncretistic rites such as characterized the era of Manasseh (1:4-5, 9); (2) many failed to worship Yahweh at all (1:6); (3) the royalty were enamored with wearing the clothing of foreign merchants (1:8; see NASB, NIV) who had extensive business enterprises in Jerusalem (1:10-11); and (4) Judahite society was beset by socioeconomic ills (1:12-13, 18) and political and religious corruption (3:1-4, 7, 11). All this sounds like the same sort of wickedness that weighed heavily on the heart of Habakkuk. Moreover, several of the specific sins (e.g., 1:4-5, 9; 3:4) would have been corrected in Josiah's reforms.

Accepting such a date means that the historical setting has advanced little beyond that of Nahum and Habakkuk. Externally, the *Pax Assyriaca* held sway. Of that great era W. W. Hallo observes that, in addition to the Assyrian rulers' attention to administrative matters and details related to extensive building projects, literature and learning also came into their own, and the vast library assembled by Ashurbanipal at Nineveh is only the most dramatic expression of the new leisure. In spite of their protestations to the contrary, the later Sargonid kings were inclined to sit back and enjoy the fruits of empire.[2]

Ashurbanipal's preoccupation with the *belles lettres* inspired him to collect ancient texts, particularly those dealing with traditional wisdom and religious matters.[3] Ashurbanipal's more leisurely lifestyle is reflected not only in his literary interests but in various interests in matters other than the affairs of state. As a result of this attitude, the empire began to show signs of the decay that would hasten its demise a scant generation after his death in 626 BC.[4] Already by Zephaniah's day, an uneasy consciousness of impending disaster hung over the empire. The whole ancient Near East was in the grip of climactic change, as the balance of power in the Near Eastern world shifted radically from what it had been for nearly 300 years. Assyria's death throes were fast approaching.

Under such conditions, it is small wonder that Josiah was increasingly free to pursue his reform policies, extending them even to the former northern kingdom. In addition, Judah would know a political and economic resurgence that it had not experienced since the days of Hezekiah. When one considers that Josiah was only eight years old when he ascended the throne in 640 BC and that his reforms were not instituted until the twelfth year of his reign (628 BC), four years after his initial spiritual awakening (2 Chr 34:3), Zephaniah's prophetic activities may have had a salutary effect in the reformation of that era. Thus, a date of 635–630 BC is not unlikely.

Granted the conclusions reached above, the occasion for Zephaniah's prophecy lies in the deplorable spiritual and moral condition of Judahite society in the early days of Josiah's reign. Cognizant of the spiritual conditions that would surely spell the end of Judah itself, Zephaniah spoke out for God and against wickedness. He wrote to inform and warn his people of God's coming judgment, not only against all the world (1:2-3), especially the nations that had oppressed God's people (2:4-15), but also against Judah and Jerusalem (1:4-6; 3:1-7). In so doing, he exposed (1) the false worship practices that included the veneration of Baal and the astral deities and the syncretistic rites that emerged from attempting to blend their worship with that of Yahweh (1:4-6, 9; 3:2, 4) and (2) the corruption of Judahite society (3:1, 3, 5), especially its leaders and merchants (1:8, 10-13, 18; 3:5).[5]

Zephaniah also wrote to inform the people about God's future program. On the one hand, he tells of the fearsome events of the Day of the Lord (1:14-16) that must come because of man's sins (1:17-18) and, on the other, of the Lord's undying concern for his people (3:5, 7), especially those who are of a humble and contrite heart (2:3; 3:12). Zephaniah therefore wrote to exhort and admonish the people to surrender to God (1:7) and to repent and seek him (2:1-3), not only to avoid the force of the Lord's fiery blast but also in anticipation of that glorious time when a redeemed and purified people will rejoice in the salvation and delights of God's love (3:14-17).

AUDIENCE

Zephaniah's prophecies were delivered to a Judahite society beset by spiritual, socioeconomic, and moral corruption. Thoroughly at home in Jerusalem and aware of conditions there (1:10-13), this prophet of keen spiritual sensitivity and moral perception decried the apostate and immoral hearts of the people, especially those who were in positions of leadership (1:4-6, 9, 17; 3:1-4, 7, 11).[6] If, as suggested previously, Zephaniah was a man of social prominence and therefore had the ear of Judah's leadership, it reminds all of us who read his messages that God uses people of all social strata. Zephaniah's life and ministry are a testimony that one soul, yielded wholly to God, can effect great things.

CANONICITY AND TEXTUAL HISTORY

Although critical concern has been expressed as to the authenticity of Zephaniah, its canonicity has never been called into question. It was known to the author of *Apocalypse of Zephaniah* (as attested in line 7 of a Coptic Sahidic fragment [Frag. B]), accepted by Philo and Josephus, and included in the early-church canonical lists. Jesus appears to have drawn upon Zephaniah 1:3 in his parable concerning the end of the age (Matt 13:41), as did John (cf. Rev 6:17 with Zeph 1:14-18; Rev 14:5 with Zeph 3:13; Rev 16:1 with Zeph 3:8). In addition, the Talmud (*b. Sanhedrin* 98a) and early Christian Fathers (e.g., Clement of Alexandria, Cyprian, Augustine) cited Zephaniah as authoritative in their condemnations of pride and idolatry.

As for the text of Zephaniah, while it is true that the Masoretic Text is difficult to understand in places (e.g., 1:2, 14; 2:14), it may be safely affirmed that the Masoretic Text is the best form of the text available. Roberts (1991:163) appropriately remarks: "The text of Zephaniah is in relatively good condition. It has its text-critical problems, like many other prophetic books, but they are comparatively minor. . . . In general the book may be taken as a clear statement of the message of Zephaniah."

LITERARY STYLE

Zephaniah, like several other Old Testament books, is arranged as a bifid—that is, it has a two-part structure.[7] This conclusion is reinforced by considering its structural components. (1) The section 1:1–2:3 comprises an *inclusio* formed by the occurrence of the theme of God's dealing with the earth (1:2, 3; 2:2). A similar reference to the earth closes the second section and the book (3:20). (2) The two halves of Zephaniah are arranged in complementary fashion (see "Outline," below), each section being bound together by distinctive stitch words.

Although Zephaniah does not display the genius of an Isaiah or Nahum, his literary artistry is not lacking. In addition to making frequent use of the customary judgment oracles (e.g., 1:2-6, 14-18; 2:4-15), one of which is in the form of a woe oracle (3:1-7), and salvation oracles (e.g., 3:9-13, 14-20), he also utilizes the lament (1:10-11) and instructional exhortation (2:1-3). He also employs several literary figures, especially metaphor and simile (1:7; 2:2; 3:3), synecdoche (1:16), and metonymy (3:16).[8] Perhaps most distinctive of all is his frequent use of repetition and wordplay, at times displayed as puns (e.g., 2:4-7). In addition, Zephaniah is fond of literary allusions (1:2-3; 3:9-10).

Some (e.g., G. A. Smith) have suggested that Zephaniah made use of the apocalyptic genre in his teachings concerning the Day of the Lord. Although Zephaniah 1:14-18 contains material of a sort that would one day become prominent in apocalyptic literature, it is not an apocalypse as such. Rather, it displays themes that are found in prophetic eschatology. To the extent that Zephaniah utilizes cosmic themes and extreme language, he thereby anticipates later apocalyptic thought. With Zephaniah, however, we are removed from the fervor that is characteristic of later Jewish apocalyptic literature, such as 2 Enoch, 3 Baruch, and the fragmentary apocalyptic pseudepigrapha attributed to Zephaniah. Like Joel, Zephaniah is not so much concerned with a future that breaks into the present as he is with the unfolding of God's sovereign and ordered arrangement of history so as to bring it to its intended culmination.[9]

MAJOR THEMES

As in the book of Joel, Zephaniah's major theme is the Day of the Lord. That coming day is to be one that involves all nations (1:2-4; 3:8a; cf. 2:4-15) and a time when God will pour out his wrath in judgment (1:14-18; 3:8b) for mankind's sin and rebellion (1:2-6, 9-13; 2:1-3, 8-11; 3:2-4, 5-7). Accordingly, people are urged to humble themselves and repent (1:11; 2:1-3) in the hope that a loving and merciful God might ameliorate the penalty they deserve (2:3; 3:9-10).

Concomitant with the Day of the Lord theme is that of the remnant (cf. King 1994), which will be sheltered (2:3) and spared (1:12; 3:12) in that time of wrath. Therefore, believers are urged to wait for the Lord (3:8a) and his deliverance (3:14-17) in order that they may return to the land (3:18-20). There, they will become those who call upon the Lord and serve him (3:9, 13) so as to live in peace, purity, and everlasting felicity (3:13-14). The remnant theme thus contains within it both the realization of coming judgment and the expectation that God is a God who will hear the prayers of his repentant people, preserve them through danger, and deliver them to a joyful inheritance.

THEOLOGICAL CONCERNS

Zephaniah is best remembered for his presentation of God as the sovereign judge of all (1:2-3, 7, 14-18; 3:8), punishing the wickedness of people (1:8-9, 17; 3:7, 11) and nations (2:4-15; 3:6), particularly those who have opposed his people (2:8, 10).

Zephaniah also has much to say about the human condition. Zephaniah focuses on the basic problem of pride (2:15), which engenders a spirit of wickedness (1:3-6, 17; 3:1, 4). Such wickedness causes people to reason that God does not intervene in human affairs (1:12) and so to go on in their violence and deceit (1:9). Further, their greed occasions the oppression of those around them (1:10-11, 13, 18; 3:3). C. K. Lehman observes that "this book has gone to the greatest depths in its exposure of sin and man's sinfulness."[10]

These teachings are characteristically entwined in the Day of the Lord theme. As King (1995) shows, the day of the Lord's universal sovereignty and superiority is one both of judgment and salvation, at times invoked as a matter of covenant implementation. VanGemeren (1989:674-679) notes the highly developed theological features of the Day of the Lord. He points out that it is (1) the day of Yahweh's intrusion into human affairs, (2) the day of God's judgment on all creation, (3) a day that is both historical and eschatological, (4) a day in which all creation must submit to God's sovereignty (willingly or unwillingly), (5) a day which does not discriminate in favor of the rich and powerful but between the wicked and the humble, and (6) a day of deliverance, vindication, glorification, and full redemption of the godly.

Zephaniah holds out the hope that God will be receptive to everyone who repentantly surrenders to him (2:1-2). Such spiritual virtues as righteousness, humility, faith, and truth receive commendation and reward from Zephaniah (2:3; 3:12-13). The Lord has a plan for the humble and faithful remnant of his people (2:2-3, 9; 3:11-13).[11] He will purify them (3:9-10), gather and restore them to their land (3:20), and give them victory over their enemies (2:7, 9). Jerusalem will be a blissful place (3:11, 18) because Israel's saving God (3:17) will bless his people (3:14-17) and in turn make them a channel of blessing to all (3:19-20).

OUTLINE

Superscription (1:1)
I. The Announcement of the Day of the Lord (1:2–2:3)
    A. Pronouncements of Judgment (1:2-6)
    B. Warnings Based on Judgment (1:7-13)
    C. A Description of the Coming Judgment (1:14-18)
    D. An Exhortation in Light of the Judgment (2:1-3)
II. Additional Details concerning the Day of the Lord (2:4–3:20)
    A. Further Pronouncements of Judgment (2:4–3:7)
        1. Pronouncement on the nations (2:4-15)
        2. Pronouncement on Jerusalem (3:1-7)

B. Instructions Based on Judgment (3:8)
C. A Description of the Coming Deliverance (3:9-13)
D. Final Exhortation (3:14-20)

ENDNOTES

1. See the excellent discussion by M. A. Sweeney (1991). An occasional voice of protest has been heard regarding the Josianic setting of the book, however, from some authors (e.g., Smith and Lacheman 1950:137-142) who see Zephaniah as the work of an apocalyptist and opt for a date of c. 200 BC.

2. W. W. Hallo and W. K. Simpson, *The Ancient Near East* (New York: Harcourt Brace Jovanovich, 1971), 141.

3. One must not assume, however, that Ashurbanipal's interests were not much more diverse. Indeed, his famed library probably held texts representative of every type of Akkadian literature, as well as business and administrative documents and correspondence. Ashurbanipal also gave attention to great building projects and the *beaux arts*. See further A. T. Olmstead, *History of Assyria* (Chicago: University of Chicago, 1968), 489-503.

4. Some ancient sources indicate that Ashurbanipal himself grew increasingly degenerate; see W. Maier, *The Book of Nahum* (Grand Rapids: Baker, 1959), 129.

5. Many have seen in Zephaniah's condemnation of the rich a special concern for the poor. Not only are some materially poor, according to this theory, but also poor in spirit and hence shut up by faith to the provision of God, whereas the proud rich have cut themselves off from Israel's covenantal benefits. See, for example, S. M. Gozzo, "Il profeta Sofonia e la dottrina teologica del suo libro," *Antonianum* 52 (1977):3-37; C. Stuhlmueller 1986:385-390; J. Bewer, *The Literature of the Old Testament*, 3rd ed. (New York: Columbia University Press, 1962), 146.

6. Klaus-Dietrich Schunck ("Juda in der Verkundigung des Propheten Zefanja," *Alttestamentliche Glaube und Biblische Theologie: Festschrift für Horst Dietrich Preuss zum 65. Geburtstag*, eds. J. Hausmann and Hans-Jurgen Zobel [Stuttgart: Kohlhammer, 1992], 174-179) identifies several passages where Zephaniah addresses his message specifically to Judah, so that the prophet's ministry included not only Jerusalem but a wider Judean perspective.

7. For details, see Patterson 1990:20-22.

8. For details, see Patterson 1991:281-289.

9. See the Introduction to Joel.

10. C. K. Lehman, *Biblical Theology: Old Testament* (Scottdale, PA: Herald, 1971), 346.

11. Anderson (1977–1978:11-14) points out that the remnant motif can logically exist only in a context of judgment; thus, doom and hope are not incompatible prophetic elements. He stresses the fact that the idea of a remnant means more than mere existence; it is a "promise that those who, by the mercy of God, survive the judgment will by their very existence be a pledge of restoration and of God's continuing purpose of good for his people."

COMMENTARY ON
Zephaniah

◆ Superscription (1:1)

The LORD gave this message to Zephaniah when Josiah son of Amon was king of Judah. Zephaniah was the son of Cushi, son of Gedaliah, son of Amariah, son of Hezekiah.

NOTES

1:1 *The LORD gave this message.* Lit., "The word of the Lord that came." This common formula in the OT lays stress on the source and authority of Zephaniah's prophecy and authenticates him as God's spokesman.

Zephaniah. The meaning of the prophet's name has been traced to the root *tsapan* [TH6845, ZH7621] and most likely means either "Yahweh has hidden/protected" (Roberts 1991) or "Yahweh has treasured" (Opperwall-Galluch in ISBE 4.1189). The name "Zephaniah" is a common one both in the OT and the extrabiblical inscriptions (Patterson 1991:298). Despite Pusey's (1953:225) suggestion, there is no demonstrable designed correspondence between the prophet's name and the message of the book.

son of Hezekiah. See the discussion under "Author" in the Introduction. Some Hebrew mss and the Syriac Peshitta read "Hilkiah." A certain Hilkiah was overseer of King Hezekiah's household (2 Kgs 18:37). While this reading has its advocates, the plain reading of the long genealogy would seem to favor Zephaniah's royal ancestry.

COMMENTARY

Like several other prophets (e.g., Hosea, Joel, Micah), Zephaniah declares that what he is about to deliver is not the message of men but the word of the Lord. He can do this because God is a God of revelation, and Zephaniah is his authoritative messenger. The Christian doctrines of revelation and inspiration find direct support in the prophet's opening words.

◆ I. The Announcement of the Day of the Lord (1:2–2:3)
A. Pronouncements of Judgment (1:2-6)

2 "I will sweep away everything
  from the face of the earth," says
  the LORD.
3 "I will sweep away people and
  animals alike.

I will sweep away the birds
  of the sky and the fish in
  the sea.
I will reduce the wicked to heaps
  of rubble,*

and I will wipe humanity from the
face of the earth," says the
LORD.
4 "I will crush Judah and Jerusalem with
my fist
and destroy every last trace of their
Baal worship.
I will put an end to all the idolatrous
priests,
so that even the memory of them
will disappear.

5 For they go up to their roofs
and bow down to the sun, moon,
and stars.
They claim to follow the LORD,
but then they worship Molech,* too.
6 And I will destroy those who used
to worship me
but now no longer do.
They no longer ask for the LORD's
guidance
or seek my blessings."

1:3 The meaning of the Hebrew is uncertain. 1:5 Hebrew *Malcam*, a variant spelling of Molech; or it could possibly mean *their king*.

NOTES

1:2 I will sweep away. Here the Hebrew text puts together, in emphatic sequence, two verbs from two different roots: *'asap* [TH622, ZH665] (gather/remove) and *sup* [TH5486, ZH6066] (come to an end), hence "I will utterly/totally sweep away." Many suggestions for emending or reconstructing the text have been put forward because constructions such as these are more often built on a duplication of the same root in Hebrew.

Two arguments in defense of the MT are as follows: (1) The use of mixed roots is attested elsewhere (e.g., Isa 28:28; Jer 8:13); and (2) the skilled Masoretic scribes would hardly make such a "blunder" if it were unintelligible. Not only does the difficulty of the MT argue for its retention (Würthwein 1979:113-119), but the LXX already recognized the incongruity, rendering the phrase *ekleipsei eklipetō* [TG1587, ZG1722] (lit., "it will give out, let it fail"— hence, "let there be a complete failure"). Moreover, as Keil (1954:126-127) points out, the two verbs have a "kindred meaning," the compatibility of the ideas of "gathering up things" so as to "put an end to them."

from the face of the earth. The phrase is reminiscent of the warnings connected with the Flood (Gen 6:7; 7:4; 8:8, MT).

1:3 birds . . . humanity. Zephaniah's dependence on the creation account may be seen in his list of the objects of divine judgment in the reverse order of their creation (Gen 1:20-26). It seems unlikely, however, that either reversing the creative order to pre-creation conditions or canceling man's dominion over the lower creatures is being announced (De Roche 1980:104-109; Hannah 1978:1525). Indeed, the order of creation with man at its head is fixed by God and guaranteed in perpetuity (cf. Ps 8:5-9), a reality ultimately realized in Christ (Col 1:15-20; Heb 2:5-9).

reduce . . . to heaps of rubble. As Sabottka (1972:8) remarks, the latter phrase (only one word in Hebrew) has been "for translators a true stone of stumbling." The NLT reading is mirrored by that of the NIV. Alternatively, the word involved may be translated, "the things that cause the wicked to stumble" (cf. Roberts 1991:166) or "the stumbling blocks along with the wicked" (Berlin 1994:73).

1:4 last trace. Lit., "the remnant." The LXX reads, "the names of Baal," probably in anticipation of "the names of the pagan (idolatrous) priests" in the succeeding line.

all the idolatrous priests. The term "idolatrous priests" is rendered "temple guardians" by the Vulgate, but the Peshitta transliterates the word and the LXX omits it altogether. The English versions have handled it variously: "idolatrous priests" (NASB, NKJV, NRSV), "the pagan . . . priests" (NIV), "priests" (NJB), "Chemarims" (KJV). Despite its presence in the Semitic languages as a term for priest, it occurs only twice elsewhere in the OT:

(1) in Hos 10:5 of priests who officiated in the calf worship at Bethel, and (2) in 2 Kgs 23:5 of priests who led in rites associated with Baal and astral worship. In all three cases, then, the term refers to priests outside the established priesthood of Israel, each having a connection to Baalism.

1:5 *Molech*. Lit., "their king."At least three renderings have been given to the Hebrew consonants found here (*mlkm*): (1) Many understand the form to refer to Milcom (cf. 1 Kgs 11:5-7), the detested Ammonite deity (cf. Vulgate, Peshitta, NASB, NKJV, NJB, NRSV; so also Roberts 1991:168). (2) Some (e.g., Robertson, Sabottka, Sweeney) follow the pointing of the MT and understand "their king" (Hulst 1960:253), especially as an epithet of Baal, whose worship was a continued syncretistic fascination for Israel (2 Kgs 23:5-10). (3) Others take the form to be Molech (NIV), understanding the noun either as the name of a particular deity or as a divine epithet associated with the ritual passing of children through fire. The NLT has followed the last alternative. Sweeney (2000:502-503) proposes that the reference to Yahweh and their king reflects the fact of their close relationship in Jewish thinking (cf. Pss 2:2, 7-9, 12; 89:26-27; Isa 8:21).

1:6 *those who used to worship*. Lit., "those who turn back." Although the verbal root of this Hebrew word is used of natural movement (cf. Arabic *sa'ga*, "go and come"), the verb itself is commonly employed of vacillating or faithless behavior toward people (Jer 38:22) or God (Ps 53:3[4]). When it occurs in the Niphal stem (as here), it denotes a willful turning of oneself away or back from someone or something. When that someone is God (cf. Isa 59:12-13), it is a deadly condition.

ask . . . seek. The first verb lays stress on personal emotion in seeking or asking someone; the latter emphasizes the person's concern in the inquiry and hence is often used in prophetic encouragements to repentance (cf. Amos 5:4-6). The two verbs occur in parallel elsewhere in contexts dealing with seeking the Lord (e.g., Deut 4:29; 2 Chr 20:3-4; Ps 105:4).

COMMENTARY

Zephaniah begins his messages with God's doubly reinforced declaration: God will destroy everything upon the face of the earth, sweeping away all life before him whether on land, in the air, or in the water; and God will wipe away all humanity. The pronouncement is solemn—its phraseology reminiscent of the Noahic flood (cf. Gen 6:17; 7:21-23). The disaster envisioned here, however, is more cataclysmic, for although every living thing that lived on the land or inhabited the air died at that time, the fish remained.

Zephaniah's catalog of victims is arranged in inverse order to God's creative work: man, beast, the creatures of the air, those of the sea (cf. Gen 1:20-27). The order of creation found its climax in man, who was made in God's image and appointed as his representative. The coming destruction will begin with man, who has denied his Creator (1:6) and involved in his sin all that is under his domain. Man's sin is thus weighty, involving not only himself but his total environment (1:2-3).

The judgment that begins with man also concludes with man. All that alienates people from their Creator and Lord will be swept away, and each person will be left alone to face God. Last of all, people will be cut off from the land that has given them sustenance. Though the language is hyperbolic, it emphasizes the seriousness of sin and the universal extent of God's judgment.

God's announced purpose to sweep away everything in his just judgment is continued with an indication of his ultimate intentions (1:4-6). He will stretch out his hand of chastisement against Judah and Jerusalem. The motif of the outstretched hand of God emphasizes God's omnipotence (Jer 32:17) and is also used in connection with his creative power and sovereign disposition of history (Isa 14:26-27; Jer 27:5). It is especially used concerning God's relations with Israel, whether in deliverance (Exod 6:6; Deut 4:34; 5:15; 7:19; 9:29; 26:8; 2 Kgs 17:36; Jer 32:21; Ezek 20:33-34) or in judgment (Isa 5:25; 9:12, 17, 21; 10:4; Jer 21:5). It is the latter of these that is in view here. God's people needed to be reminded that the God of the universe and of all individuals and nations is Israel's God in particular. To him they owed their allegiance. When such was not forthcoming, when sin and apostasy set in, Israel could expect God's outstretched hand of judgment.

Both Judah's leadership and its people were guilty of gross sin in pursuing paganism, while feigning worship of the Lord. Sadly, Judah displayed little interest or concern for the Lord who redeemed his people (cf. Jer 2:13, 32-35; 3:6-10; 5:2-13; etc.). Outright apostasy is bad enough, but when hypocrisy and apathy hold sway, those involved are in grave spiritual danger. All too often it begins with a spirit of self-sufficiency and grows into indifference toward spiritual matters. As Zephaniah pointed out, such people will not commune with God. How vastly different the experience of the faithful believer who fellowships with God (see Pss 63:4-5; 73:23-28; 84:1-4).

◆   B. Warnings Based on Judgment (1:7-13)

7 Stand in silence in the presence of the Sovereign LORD,
for the awesome day of the LORD's judgment is near.
The LORD has prepared his people for a great slaughter
and has chosen their executioners.*
8 "On that day of judgment,"
says the LORD,
"I will punish the leaders and princes of Judah
and all those following pagan customs.
9 Yes, I will punish those who participate in pagan worship ceremonies,
and those who fill their masters' houses with violence and deceit.

10 "On that day," says the LORD,
"a cry of alarm will come from the Fish Gate
and echo throughout the New Quarter of the city.*
And a great crash will sound from the hills.
11 Wail in sorrow, all you who live in the market area,
for all the merchants and traders will be destroyed.

12 "I will search with lanterns in Jerusalem's darkest corners
to punish those who sit complacent in their sins.
They think the LORD will do nothing to them,
either good or bad.
13 So their property will be plundered, their homes will be ransacked.
They will build new homes but never live in them.
They will plant vineyards but never drink wine from them.

1:7 Hebrew *has prepared a sacrifice and sanctified his guests.*   1:10 Or *the Second Quarter,* a newer section of Jerusalem. Hebrew reads *the Mishneh.*

NOTES

1:7 Stand in silence. See note on Hab 2:20 regarding the word *has* [TH2013A, ZH2187].

day of the LORD's judgment. See commentary on 1:14-18 and Joel 2:28-31.

a great slaughter. Lit., "a sacrifice"; so also in 1:7b (cf. NLT mg). The sacrificial terminology used here of the Lord's slaughter of those enacting pagan rites is not otherwise developed and is probably built around a type of fellowship offering (cf. Lev 7:11-21). Several instances of such sacrificial banquets occur in the OT (e.g., 1 Sam 9:22-24; 2 Sam 15:11; 1 Kgs 1:9-10, 24-25; cf. TDOT 4.25-26). The invited guests have commonly been held to be "the pagan conquerors (mainly Babylon)" (Bailey 1999:427) but could also be God's people. (The NLT rendering "chosen their executioners" reflects the former understanding.) If the latter understanding is accepted, there could be an analogy here with the occasion when Jehu invited the ministers of Baal as his guests for a sacrifice to Baal (2 Kgs 10:18-29) and they became both the guests and the sacrificial victims. Likewise Zephaniah's prophecy, which is followed by a warning concerning the punishment of God's offending people (vv. 8-13) and subsequently by a prophecy relative to the Day of the Lord (vv. 14-18) may suggest that "those invited might also be the victims of the sacrifice" (Sweeney 2000:504), namely, God's own people (cf. NJB). The Day of the Lord is elsewhere associated with a sacrificial banquet (Isa 34:6; Jer 46:10; Ezek 39:17-20).

1:8 I will punish. Though the Hebrew verb *paqad* is often translated "visit," it must be contextually nuanced. In many cases, it is employed where a superior takes action for or against his subordinates. In contexts involving hostility, it connotes punishment (Jer 11:22; Hos 1:4; Amos 3:2, 14).

leaders. The Hebrew noun used here refers to officials at various levels, frequently coming from leading tribal families and forming powerful advisory groups throughout Israel's history (cf. Exod 18:13-26; 1 Kgs 4:2-6; 2 Kgs 24:12; 2 Chr 35:8). The term may designate the chieftains of Israel (Num 21:18), court officials (1 Chr 22:17), district supervisors (1 Kgs 20:14-15), city officials (Judg 8:6), military leaders (1 Kgs 2:5; 2 Kgs 1:9-14; 5:1; 25:23, 26), or even religious leaders (Ezra 8:24). The importance of such leaders in Zephaniah's day is underscored not only in their mention before the members of the royal family here, but also in their prominence in the enumeration of the levels of Judahite society during the reign of Josiah (Jer 1:18; 2:26; 4:9). Jeremiah emphasized their importance and responsibility, using the term more than three dozen times.

princes of Judah. Lit., "sons of the king." J. M. P. Smith (1911:196) rightly points out that "the reference here cannot be to the sons of Josiah, the eldest of whom was not born until six years after Josiah assumed the crown . . . and was not old enough to have wielded any influence until well toward the close of Josiah's long reign." If the date for Zephaniah adopted in the introduction is correct, the reference must be principally to the sons of the deceased King Amon.

those following pagan customs. Lit., "those clad in foreign clothes." As in the case of the following line in v. 9, the NLT brings out the implications of this phrase in a context of idolatrous practice. In this line, however, it may be only rich clothes supplied by merchants that are in view (cf. 1:11), an idea that would elaborate on the well-to-do status of the princes of Judah mentioned in the previous line.

1:9 those who participate in pagan worship ceremonies. Lit., "those who leap over the threshold." The citizens of Judah and Jerusalem perpetuated the custom of avoiding contact with the threshold of a temple by leaping over it. The practice had originated among the priests of Dagon during the incident of the collapse of his statue before the Ark of the Lord (1 Sam 5:1-5). The Targum renders the phrase, "all who walk in the laws of the Philistines." The NLT reading suggests that this practice may be representative of yet other pagan religious activities. Less likely are the views that suggest that this phrase has to do with those who force their way into houses to confiscate the property of the poor (an interpretation in medieval Jewry) or that the custom has to do with mounting the podium which held the god's statue (Sabottka 1972).

1:10 *New Quarter.* The Hebrew term used here is commonly translated "the second quarter" and was perhaps an addition to the upper Tyropoeon Valley.

1:11 *market area.* The term has been variously understood. Among the ancient versions, the Septuagintal tradition renders it three different ways, the Vulgate translates it "pillars," the Peshitta transliterates it as a proper noun, and the Targum identifies it as the Brook Kidron. Among modern versions, one may find "mortar" (NASB, NRSV, *La Sacra Biblia*), "hollow" (NJB), "market district" (NIV), "mill" (*Die Heilige Schrift*), or simple transliteration (KJV, *La Sainte Bible*, Cohen). Due to its derivation from *kathash* [TH3806, ZH4197] (to pound), it has been understood as a hollow or a place pounded out, and related to a commercial district, probably a functional rendering rather than an attempt at a geographical or etymological identification.

all you who live in the market area. Lit., "all the people of Canaan." The noun "Canaan," like the adjective "Canaanite," may often be translated "merchant" due to the Canaanites' (especially the Phoenicians') established reputation as traders (cf. Isa 23:8; Ezek 16:29; 17:4; Hos 12:7-8). This NLT rendering combines the thought of this line in the MT with that of the next (lit., "all who weigh out the silver will be cut off").

1:12 *I will search with lanterns.* J. M. P. Smith (1911:201) likens God's diligent searching of Jerusalem to that of Diogenes equipped with a lantern in his quest for truth. This is not a search for truth, however. Smith is on target when he goes on to observe that "the figure expresses the thought of the impossibility of escape from the avenging eye of Yahweh. . . . The figure is probably borrowed from the custom of the night-watchman carrying his lamp and may involve also the thought of the diligent search of Jerusalem that will be made by her conquerors in their quest for spoil."

those who sit complacent in their sins. Lit., "the men who are thickening on their lees." The image, drawn from wine left too long on its lees, portrays those who are indifferent to spiritual matters. The imagery envisions an indifference that goes beyond the smug self-satisfaction suggested by the word "complacency" to an attitude that has hardened into deliberate disregard for the Lord and his standards. Rose (1981:193-208) proposes that the affluent class had become so entrenched in its wealth that it assumed God must be supportive of its lifestyle. Thus wealth was interpreted as a sign of divine favor.

1:13 Willis (1987:74) calls attention to Zephaniah's use of parallelism here (in an A–B–A–B structure) to emphasize that "divine punishment is able to thwart the apparent prevalence of human achievements (cf. Ezek 27:33; 28:9; Amos 5:11)."

COMMENTARY

Having delivered God's pronouncement of judgment against all humanity and especially his covenant people, Zephaniah turns to exhortations. In view of the certainty and severity of coming judgment, God's prophet has some advice: "Be silent!" "Hush!" It is a call for submission, fear, and consecration.

While Yahweh is Judah's God, he is also the master of its destiny. Judah has perpetuated Israel's sin (2 Kgs 17:18-20) in following Baal and other pagan practices. In doing so, it has forsaken its rightful master to follow another master (Baal). The folly of such conduct would become apparent. Judah's true master was about to demonstrate the powerlessness of him who was no master at all. The last remnants of Baalism would be cut off.

Zephaniah also reminded his hearers that they stood in the presence of the living God whose all-seeing eye (Jer 32:19) had observed all their evil deeds and would reward them (Job 24:22-24; 34:21-22; Ps 66:7; Amos 9:8). Judah's idolatry was loathsome in his eyes (Jer 16:17). They had lost sight of the truth that God was the unseen observer in Israel, not only on occasions of religious ceremony, but also in every activity of life, and had strayed from the resulting mandate that their lives were to reflect his holy character in every facet (cf. Lev 19:2; 20:7, 22-24). Contrary to their foolish thoughts that either God had not seen their wickedness or did not care to intervene, their day of judgment was at hand.

Zephaniah's great concern for his people was underscored by his realization of the imminence of God's coming judgment. The Day of the Lord was near. As employed by the prophets, the "Day of the Lord" refers to that time when, for his glory and in accordance with his purposes, God intervenes in human affairs to execute judgment against sin and/or deliver his people (see King 1995:16-32). That time could be in the present (Joel 1:15), be in the near future (Isa 2:12-22; Jer 46:10; Ezek 13:5; Joel 2:1, 11; Amos 5:18-20), be future-eschatological (Isa 13:6, 9; Ezek 30:2-3; Mal 4:1-6), or be primarily eschatological (Joel 3:14-15; Zech 14:1-21; cf. 1 Thess 5:1-11; 2 Thess 2:2; 2 Pet 3:10-13). Zephaniah's urgent warning spoke of imminent judgment.

God's prophet went on to call that day the day of the Lord's sacrifice (see note on 1:7). The metaphor of the sacrificial banquet is a poignant one. The sacrifice itself is Judah and Jerusalem. But who are the guests? If one sees in the metaphor a second reason for the call for silence, the guests could be understood as the citizens of Judah and Jerusalem. Thus, the call for silence (= submission to the Lord) is issued (1) because of the awesome day of the Lord's judgment and (2) because that day can be survived only by genuine believers in Yahweh. The metaphor of the banquet (1:7) also strengthens the previous two lines while giving unity to the whole verse. The sacrifice was to be held in the presence of Yahweh, was imminent, was hosted by Yahweh himself, and was to be attended by his guests.

So construed, the metaphor of the sacrificial banquet reinforces the announcement of the Day of the Lord and provides a ray of hope in the clouds of doom. As guests called to a sacrificial feast were to come with their uncleanness removed, so the Judahites were urged to respond to the invitation of Yahweh their host. Although judgment was coming, there was still time. By acknowledging God as their master and responding in fear to the prospect of judgment, God's people could join a believing remnant and come to the feast as guests acceptable to him. There was yet hope.

The figure of the sacrificial banquet, however, also entailed a further word of caution because the alternative of being unfit for attendance carried with it an ironic twist: Guests who remained unrepentant, and hence unclean, would be disqualified and would, like those in Jehu's day (2 Kgs 10:18-28), discover that their invitation to the banquet also entailed their role as sacrificial victims. God had summoned others (the Babylonians) who would destroy both Judah and Jerusalem and the unrepentant people who inhabited them (1:8-13).

The call for the merchants to wail (1:11) was also especially dramatic. Their wealth would be taken away. Though one could hope for the lamenting that leads to repentance, such was unlikely. Rather, these people would lament their lost wealth. Ironically, Zephaniah told them to go ahead and wail, for such would suit their lot.

The money-loving merchants were also labeled for what they were: Canaanites and money-grubbers. The metaphor was an apt one, for like their Canaanite precursors they worshiped pagan gods and spent their lives trafficking in commercial pursuits. The merchants of Judah were no better than those of Israel (cf. Ezek 16:29; Hos 12:7), and both betrayed their Canaanite ancestry (Ezek 16:3). Jesus would also warn of the perils of the pursuit of wealth (Matt 6:24; Luke 16:19-31), and Paul would caution the church's leaders against being money-lovers (1 Tim 3:3). Lamentably, the temptation to make merchandise of the ministry must be mastered in every generation (cf. 2 Cor 2:17). Whereas money and wealth can be a useful resource for the advancement of the Lord's work and the rightful enjoyment of life, it must never become an end in itself (1 Tim 6:10; Heb 13:16).

No less revealing is the announced judgment on the citizens of Jerusalem (1:12-13). God will punish those whose greed and self-satisfaction has grown into a settled indifference toward God and his standards. Like wine left on its dregs so long that it has become sickeningly sweet and then spoiled, so also many of Jerusalem's citizens had remained in their apostate lifestyle so long that they had become satisfied with it and then grown indifferent to genuine piety.

If not in theory, then at least in practice, the people of Judah behaved like full-fledged pagans. They proclaimed that God does neither good nor harm to individuals or society (cf. Isa 41:23; Jer 10:5). To their surprise, God would demonstrate his intervention in human affairs. Not an absentee God, he would send an invading force that would search out and plunder Jerusalem. The implementation of the Lord's proclamation would come so quickly that all who had lived in pursuit of ill-gotten gain would not survive to enjoy their wealth. All that for which they had labored so hard and long would fall into the hands of others. In their preoccupation with self and riches, they would lose them both (cf. Luke 12:16-21). Thus, God's righteous standards would be upheld (Lev 26:27-33; Deut 28:30, 39). As they had been applied to Israel (cf. Amos 5:11; Mic 6:15), so they would be applied to Judah and Jerusalem.

Whereas today's believer may applaud Zephaniah's warnings to his fellow countrymen as necessary (due to the apostasy, immorality, and injustice of that time), it is another matter for one to apply them to oneself. But such conduct is no less culpable now than it was then. Indeed, a far more insidious danger lurks today. Apathy and inactivity abound, and these will ultimately take their toll. Where these attitudes form the dominant force in society, those who display them should not be surprised when they are caught up with evildoers in the very things that lead to the deterioration and destruction of that society. Craigie (1985:114) concludes, "Zephaniah's words on indifference touch the conscience of multitudes, those who are not guilty of unbelief, but are equally never overwhelmed by belief. . . . The way things are is partly because that is the way we have allowed them to become. We can sit back, smug and somnolent in a desperate world, but we cannot at the same time absolve ourselves from all responsibility, and we shall eventually be caught in the very chaos we permit."

◆   ## C. A Description of the Coming Judgment (1:14-18)

14 "That terrible day of the LORD is near.
  Swiftly it comes—
a day of bitter tears,
  a day when even strong men will
    cry out.
15 It will be a day when the LORD's anger
    is poured out—
a day of terrible distress and anguish,
a day of ruin and desolation,
  a day of darkness and gloom,
a day of clouds and blackness,
16   a day of trumpet calls and battle
    cries.
  Down go the walled cities
    and the strongest battlements!

17 "Because you have sinned against
    the LORD,
  I will make you grope around like
    the blind.
Your blood will be poured into the
    dust,
  and your bodies will lie rotting
    on the ground."

18 Your silver and gold will not save you
    on that day of the LORD's anger.
For the whole land will be devoured
    by the fire of his jealousy.
He will make a terrifying end
    of all the people on earth.*

1:18 Or the people living in the land.

NOTES

1:14 near. This is the first of more than a dozen terms found in vv. 14-18 that regularly occur in oracles dealing with the terrors of coming judgment (note especially Joel 2:1-11; see Patterson 1991:320-325).

Swiftly it comes. The adverbial flavor of the infinitive absolute here (from the root *mhr*) is little improved by attempts to relate the phrase to an Egypto-Semitic term for soldier. (For good discussions, see Sabottka 1972:50-52; R. L. Smith 1984:129. Sabottka calls attention to the Phoenician/Punic personal names *mhrb'l* and *b'lmhr*, which he understands as "[soldier] hero of Baal" and "Baal is the hero," respectively.) The repetition of the idea of nearness is not redundant; rather, the intentional emphasis underscores both the fact and the impending arrival of the Day of the Lord.

a day when even strong men will cry out. The word "cry" (*tsoreakh* [TH6873, ZH7658]) has been viewed as a verb (cf. Akkadian *sarahu*, "cry out, lament") as in Isa 42:13. A noun (*tserakh* [TH6873.1, ZH7659] "shriek, [battle] cry"; see NIDOTTE 3.844) has been conjectured for Jer 4:31; Ezek 21:27 but is uncertain at best. For translation problems relative to the last line of 1:14, see Roberts (1991:182).

1:15 anger. The term for "anger" here is suggestive of the overwhelming nature of the divine anger against sin.

distress and anguish. This picture of the terror that will come upon people who have defied God may have been drawn from Job 15:23-25, where terms and themes relative to the day of darkness and the sinner's defiance of God appear together. Instructive are the words "distress" and "anguish," which are common to both passages.

1:16 *strongest battlements!* The term probably refers to the corner towers, the key points in the defensive walls (so also in 3:6). Berlin (1994:90) notes, "Many royal fortresses in the eighth and seventh centuries [BC] were rectangular with a tower at each corner."

1:17 *poured.* Although Sabottka (1972:55) insists that the lack of examples of the verb *shapak* in the Piel stem necessitates viewing the form here as a Qal passive, the presence of a Hithpael elsewhere (Job 30:16; Lam 2:12; 4:1), attesting the use of the Piel stem in classical Hebrew, makes his pronouncement tenuous. See also the following note.

into the dust. The Hebrew text reads "like dust." As Berlin (1994:91) notes, "The imagery is unusual. The verb *shapak* [TH8210, ZH9161] is used of blood, and also of dust (Lev 14:41), but blood is usually poured out like water (Ps 79:3), not like dust. The combination of this particular tenor and vehicle, along with the accompanying 'fleshy parts like dung,' creates the vivid image of carnage strewn over a broad area."

your bodies. Lit., "their flesh." While "flesh" is the traditional reading of most ancient and modern translations, the NLT rendering has precedents in the Vulgate and the NJB ("their corpses"). The NLT's switch to second person ("your") provides added vividness, the force of the pronouncement becoming more personal.

1:18 *a terrifying end.* The syntax of this verse is like that of Isa 10:23, in each case the object noun being modified by affixing a Niphal participle. The common emphasis of the participle *nibhalah* [TH926, ZH987] is "to be disturbed by fear, to be terrified, to be frightened out of one's wits" (Gen 45:3; 2 Sam 4:1; Isa 13:8; 21:3; Ezek 26:18). As here, the word "end" (*kalah* [TH3617, ZH3986]) is customarily employed for divinely initiated destruction (cf. Neh 9:31; Jer 4:27).

COMMENTARY

Again Zephaniah declared that the Day of the Lord is near. He had previously used this event to encourage God's people to repentance. Here he supplies added details to amplify this reason for the citizens of Judah and Jerusalem to repent and submit to God. The day was near and coming quickly.

Zephaniah described conditions that will exist primarily in the final stages of the Day of the Lord. But the prophecy must be viewed as one vast event. Some matters that he mentions would soon take place at Jerusalem's fall in 586 BC; others would be repeated in various historical epochs (e.g., AD 70) until the whole prophecy found its ultimate fulfillment eschatologically. Such prophecies (cf. Joel 2:28-32 with Acts 2:17-26) are progressively fulfilled, and their individual segments can be termed "fulfillment without consummation."[1] Keeping this distinction in mind enables one to keep a clear perspective as to both the meaning of the text and the effect the prophecy must have had upon Zephaniah's hearers. However much the events detailed here may have full reference only to the final phase of the Day of the Lord, they were an integral part of the prophecy and could occur anywhere along the series. For the people of Zephaniah's time, the Day of the Lord was near—very near—and the catastrophic conditions had the potential to occur at any moment, with tragic consequences.

What a day the Day of the Lord will be! So horrifying will be the conditions (1:14-15) that the bravest hero will shriek bitterly. This is understandable, because it will be the time of God's great wrath. Because of his anger against sin, the earth will experience great distress and anguish. Other prophets report that the day will be so severe that it will be called the time of Jacob's trouble (Jer 30:7; cf. Dan 12:1).

Zephaniah goes on to describe conditions in the land and in nature (1:15). Destruction will dot the landscape; everything will be a desolate waste. Adding to the scene of misery are conditions in the natural world. All nature will be covered with clouds that form an impenetrable darkness. Although such darkness has not gripped the world of God's covenant people since early days, it will again fall heavily upon the objects of divine wrath in the great Day of the Lord (cf. Joel 2:2). It is a bleak picture.

From the physical world, Zephaniah turns again to the sociopolitical realm (1:16). That day will be a time of great warfare; out of the distance will come the sound of the trumpet and the battle cry (cf. Josh 6:5; Jer 4:5). This will be followed by the charge of the enemy army pushing into the towns of Judah (cf. Deut 28:49-52). Not even the most stoutly fortified city will be able to withstand the advance of these agents of the Lord's judgment. The synecdoche of citing towns and towers in reference to the devastation of all cities and lands is an effective one. If the strongest defenses will collapse, everything else will of course be laid waste. Zephaniah concludes by observing the tragic cost in human life and the experience that all of this will effect (1:17-18). In accordance with his judicial purposes, God will bring distress not only to Judah but also to all humanity. There is a play on words and ideas in 1:15. Because it is a day of distress and anguish, God will cause people distress. So intense will be the conditions that people will grope like the blind. How appropriate the punishment! Because they are blind ethically and spiritually (cf. Exod 23:8; Matt 15:14; Rom 2:19; 11:25; Eph 4:18; 1 John 2:11) and have sinned against God and his commandments, God's people will incur the just penalties of the covenant (Deut 28:28-29).[2]

The effect of these tragic conditions is further heightened in similes that liken the carnage of that day to blood poured out like worthless dust (cf. 1 Kgs 20:10; 2 Kgs 13:7; 23:12) and flesh treated like dung (cf. 1 Kgs 14:10; 2 Kgs 9:37; Jer 8:1-3; Lam 4:5). Human life (flesh and blood) is thus reduced to a thing of no value, with corpses being treated as despicable refuse (cf. Jer 9:20-22; 16:1-4; 25:32-33). The warfare connected with the Day of the Lord will thus be both extensive and bloody.

The chapter closes with a reiteration of two prominent themes: (1) the self-indulgent greed of the godless wealthy and (2) the certain judgment of all people and nations. As for the former, the wealthy have heaped up their riches at the expense of their fellow citizens in pursuit of material gain. However, it will all soon come to an end, and no amount of silver or gold will be able to pay off their despoilers. Their attempt to achieve deliverance will fail (cf. 2 Kgs 15:16-20; 16:17-19; 18:13-16). With regard to the latter theme, the judgment that always hangs over humanity will one day descend with sudden swiftness, and the world and all who dwell in it will experience the wrath of God.

Many years have passed since Zephaniah announced the coming of the awful Day of the Lord. While that day has come and gone repeatedly for Jerusalem, the consummation of Zephaniah's prophecy awaits its ultimate fulfillment. If God's people have not escaped judgment in the past, how should we who live in the present generation think we can escape the judgment of a holy God? If we ourselves fall into false-worship practices, or sit idly by as a sinful and lost world continues its plunge into the abyss of degradation, should we not expect the Lord's righteous anger? And if it is true that believers can and will experience chastisement, how much more will come upon those who reject God's rightful claim over their lives (Rom 2:1-4; Heb 2:3; 12:25; 1 Pet 4:17-18)?

ENDNOTES

1. See further R. T. France, *Jesus and the Old Testament* (London: Tyndale, 1971), 160-162. From a NT perspective, the Greek verb *plēroō* [TG4137, ZG4444] may at times refer to a literal, real, and necessary relationship between an OT context and the NT so that the NT text fulfills completely the OT meaning. More commonly, however, the NT writer cites an OT passage to establish an analogy or comparison between the OT and the NT contexts, thus filling out more fully the OT context. See commentary on Hosea 11:1.

2. For other examples of divine judicial blinding, see Gen 19:11; 2 Kgs 6:18. Robertson (1990:254-256) rightly points out Zephaniah's abundant use of phraseology drawn from Deuteronomy.

◆ D. An Exhortation in Light of the Judgment (2:1-3)

Gather together—yes, gather together,
    you shameless nation.
2 Gather before judgment begins,
    before your time to repent is blown
    away like chaff.
Act now, before the fierce fury of the
    LORD falls
    and the terrible day of the LORD's
    anger begins.

3 Seek the LORD, all who are
    humble,
    and follow his commands.
Seek to do what is right
    and to live humbly.
Perhaps even yet the LORD will
    protect you—
    protect you from his anger on
    that day of destruction.

NOTES

2:1 *Gather together—yes, gather together.* This is a double imperative in the Hebrew: "gather together and assemble yourselves." Zephaniah has utilized these denominative verbs to produce a play on ideas, their apparent derivation from *qash* [TH7179, ZH7990] (straw, stubble) accounting for their selection. They anticipate the reference to chaff blown away in 2:2 (as well as the figure of threshing) and provide an image that can be adapted to the sociopolitical and religious needs of the community. The metaphor is of judgment likened to winnowing. As one gathers the straw left from the threshing sledge and separates the grain from the chaff in the winnowing process, so the people of God will be divided into believers (straw) and unbelievers (chaff) by the winds of divine judgment. It was a time of spiritual harvest, and Zephaniah's countrymen needed to assemble and "gather straw." In genuine repentance they needed to entreat God to save them.

shameless. Hebrew *lo' niksap* [TH3808/3700, ZH4202/4083]. Two derivations have been suggested for the Hebrew participle: (1) Akkadian *kasapu* (break off) and (2) Arabic *kasafa* (cut out)—hence, in derived stems "disappoint," "put to shame" (cf. Aramaic *kesap*; "lose color, be ashamed"). The second etymology, however, has usually been assumed to lie behind the occurrences in Gen 31:30; Job 14:15; Pss 17:12; 84:2, where the meaning is "long for/desire," and is favored by many for 2:1 (e.g., Berlin, Roberts). The first etymology may well be more apt, however. Sweeney (2000:511) links the verb with a root used for silver and remarks that it "thereby provides an appropriate play of words on those who 'bear silver' (Zeph 1:11) and who are condemned by the prophet in the initial address of Zeph 1:2-18. In the present instance, the term for 'undesirable' becomes 'worthless' and further indicates that their wealth will not save them on the Day of YHWH (Zeph 1:18)." If the underlying agricultural image of the preceding imperatives is to be carried through, perhaps "not threshed," hence "wayward" is to be preferred. As grain must be broken off (threshed) into small pieces in preparation for winnowing, so a man must be broken spiritually in submission to God if he is to be delivered (cf. Pss 34:18; 51:17; 147:3).

2:2 *before judgment begins.* Lit., "before the birth of the decree." The metaphor here likens the time for the inception of divine judgment to that of pregnancy. Thus, O'Connor (1980:248) translates, "Before the womb comes to term" and explains: "The line refers to a natural term for the prophet's threat." The difficulty of the Hebrew line has occasioned many emendations (cf. Roberts 1991:187-188). But as Berlin (1994:97) remarks, "The more the suggestions and emendations multiply, the less certain any one of them appears."

the fierce fury of the LORD. Lit., "the burning anger of the LORD." This phrase occurs 33 times in the OT. Notable is the A–B–A–B parallelism in the closing lines to emphasize the imminence of divine punishment, which urgently called for repentance.

2:3 *Seek . . . to live humbly.* Lit., "seek humility." The noun "humility" occurs rarely: In 2 Sam 22:36 MT, it is used of God's condescension ("gentleness," KJV) on behalf of his people, and in Prov 15:33; 18:12; 22:4 it speaks of lowliness of spirit along with fear of the Lord as preconditions to greatness. Its derivation from *'anah* [TH6031, ZH6700] (be afflicted) and association with other words derived from this root reveal that inward affliction of soul and outward circumstances of affliction play a vital part in developing true humility (cf. Deut 8:2-3; Ps 34:6; Prov 16:19).

will protect. The traditional translation reflected here understands the Hebrew verb to be *satar* [TH5641, ZH6259] (hide). A case could also be made for the verb *sur* [TH5493, ZH6073] (turn aside) with infixed taw, hence "deliver oneself" or "escape" (see Dahood 1970:3.388-389).

COMMENTARY

In light of the horrifying spectacle of the judgment of the Day of the Lord, Zephaniah presses his fellow countrymen to gather together in repentance and humility before God. Utilizing images drawn from the process of separating straw from chaff, Zephaniah gives them a spiritual setting. He uses straw and its collection to symbolize the assembling of people for the purpose of collective repentance so as to escape the coming destruction (i.e., to be straw, not chaff; see notes on 2:1). He employed the concept of threshing to point to the necessity of being broken before God rather than going on in self-indulgent waywardness. He uses the idea of chaff in connection with the speed and ease with which it is blown away: Like chaff, the time before the day of judgment was rapidly disappearing; like chaff, wayward sinners would be destroyed in the Day of the Lord. They were not threshed; their hearts were unbroken and had no longing for God. Thus they could not survive the coming judgment, but like chaff they would soon be swept away in the winds of God's winnowing judgment. The threat of exile was before them.[1]

Gathering together meant coming together in genuine repentance and submission to the will of God. Zephaniah's plea was urgent, for God's decree was settled and would soon be put into effect. Moreover, as Zephaniah had already indicated (1:7-18), its implementation would bring with it the "fierce fury" (2:2) or burning anger of the Lord.

Yet even here, Zephaniah retains the hope that complete destruction (1:18) could be avoided. Although the judgment is even now descending, a proper response on the people's part could perhaps ameliorate or even avert the threatened disaster—and that before the full heat of the Lord's burning anger arrived.

Building on such a glimmer of hope, Zephaniah urged his hearers to seek the Lord. He called upon those most likely to respond—the poor who were victimized by the wealthy leaders and merchants of Judah and Jerusalem. In addition, if, as it sometimes does, "poor" refers to those who have kept God's commandments (Stuhlmueller 1986), this could have an additional emphasis. It should be noted, however, that Zephaniah's intended audience includes all who are poor in spirit and are seeking God.[2] He urged them to react to his pleas with the two qualities necessary for spiritual productivity: righteousness and humility. By the first is meant those spiritual and ethical standards that reflect the nature and will of God; by the second, submission to and dependence on God.

To all such, then, Zephaniah holds out a ray of hope. Although he would not presume on the divine prerogative, he hinted that deliverance might come. Probably this reflected his confidence that he who helped the needy would hear the prayer of the repentant and submissive (Ps 10:12-17). "Perhaps" God would graciously deliver them, as his wrath descended in judgment (2:3).

The charge to "seek humility" is a reminder of the soil where the seed of repentance may take root. Humility is a necessary ingredient for salvation (Rom 3:27). Further, just as humility marked Jesus' life (2 Cor 8:9; Phil 2:4-8), so it should mark the believer's life (Matt 11:29-30). It begins with humble submission to Christ and proceeds in selfless service (John 13:1-17), whether individually or collectively (Mic 6:8; Rom 12:9-14; Phil 2:1-3).

How sad it is when people cast aside the standards of God and forge their own rules of righteousness and ethical behavior. They will "gain" for themselves the "rewards" of the Day of the Lord. How tragic the situation, also, where the righteous allow their standards to slip into the morass of unrighteousness and therefore find themselves caught up in the judgment of the unrighteous.[3] Yet a God of mercy offers hope to the humble spirit and repentant heart. May we be aware both of God's fiery fury and his boundless mercy (Ps 145:17-20).

ENDNOTES

1. J. M. P. Smith (1911:213) correctly points out that wherever reference is made to chaff, it is employed as a simile of scattering, the lone possible exception being Isa 41:15.

2. For "poor" as a theological term for those dependent on God, see Stuhlmueller (1986:385-390). Stuhlmueller notes its primary socioeconomic reference here but sees a shift in perspective in Zeph 3:12. N. Lohfink ("Zefanja und das Israel der Armen," *Bibel und Kirche* 39 [1984]:100-108) separates Zephaniah's concern for the poor from any spiritual equation of them with the Lord's redeemed.

3. Craigie (1985:117) remarks, "But Zephaniah, like the other prophets, did not perceive the Day of the Lord to be merely a cosmic event, beyond human control. Its roots lay in human lives and human actions. In the last resort it is human beings who precipitate the dreadful Day of the Lord by working out in the world the corruption that festers within them."

◆ II. Additional Details concerning the Day of the Lord (2:4–3:20)

   A. Further Pronouncements of Judgment (2:4–3:7)

      1. Pronouncement on the nations (2:4-15)

⁴Gaza and Ashkelon will be abandoned,
   Ashdod and Ekron torn down.
⁵And what sorrow awaits you
   Philistines*
   who live along the coast and in the
      land of Canaan,
   for this judgment is against you,
      too!
The LORD will destroy you
   until not one of you is left.
⁶The Philistine coast will become
   a wilderness pasture,
   a place of shepherd camps
   and enclosures for sheep and goats.
⁷The remnant of the tribe of Judah will
      pasture there.
   They will rest at night in the
      abandoned houses in Ashkelon.
For the LORD their God will visit his
      people in kindness
   and restore their prosperity again.
⁸"I have heard the taunts of the
      Moabites
   and the insults of the Ammonites,
mocking my people
   and invading their borders.
⁹Now, as surely as I live,"
   says the LORD of Heaven's Armies,
   the God of Israel,

"Moab and Ammon will be destroyed—
   destroyed as completely as Sodom
      and Gomorrah.
Their land will become a place of
   stinging nettles,
   salt pits, and eternal desolation.
The remnant of my people will plunder
      them
   and take their land."
¹⁰They will receive the wages of their
      pride,
   for they have scoffed at the people
      of the LORD of Heaven's Armies.
¹¹The LORD will terrify them
   as he destroys all the gods in the
      land.
Then nations around the world will
      worship the LORD,
   each in their own land.
¹²"You Ethiopians* will also be
      slaughtered
   by my sword," says the LORD.
¹³And the LORD will strike the lands
   of the north with his fist,
   destroying the land of Assyria.
He will make its great capital, Nineveh,
   a desolate wasteland,
   parched like a desert.

¹⁴The proud city will become a pasture
    for flocks and herds,
  and all sorts of wild animals will
    settle there.
The desert owl and screech owl will
    roost on its ruined columns,
  their calls echoing through the
    gaping windows.
Rubble will block all the doorways,
  and the cedar paneling will be
    exposed to the weather.

¹⁵This is the boisterous city,
  once so secure.
"I am the greatest!" it boasted.
  "No other city can compare with
    me!"
But now, look how it has become
  an utter ruin,
  a haven for wild animals.
Everyone passing by will laugh
  in derision
  and shake a defiant fist.

2:5 Hebrew *Kerethites.* 2:12 Hebrew *Cushites.*

NOTES

2:4 *Gaza . . . Ashkelon . . . Ashdod . . . Ekron.* Some (e.g., Keil, Walker) have suggested that the mention of these four Philistine cities is representative of the judgment of all Philistia. The fact, however, that the prophets often proclaim judgment in groups of more than four cities or countries (e.g., Isa 13–23; Jer 46–51; Ezek 25–32; Amos 1:3–2:5), as well as the disappearance of Gath from both biblical and nonbiblical accounts by this historical period, may indicate its absence from the scene as the reason that Zephaniah does not denounce the traditional Philistine Pentapolis. Berlin (1994:98-99), however, notes the geographical orientation (south to north) of the listing and puts forward a suggestion of Freeman: "The choice of the cities may have been due more to poetic reasons than to geopolitical ones. Four is a symmetrical number that lends itself to poetic parallelism of two matching pairs. In fact, the pairing of these cities is always chiastic, based on their initial letters, Aleph (Ashkelon, Ashdod) and Ayin (Gaza ['*azzah*], Ekron). Gath, beginning with Gimel, has no sound pair."

This chiasm of sound produced by the order of listing has often been noted, as well as the paronomasia produced by the cities' names in connection with the pronouncement of their judgment. Thus, Gaza ('*azzah*) will be abandoned ('*azubah* [TH5800, ZH6440]) and Ekron ('*eqron* [TH6138, ZH6833]) will be uprooted (*te'aqer* [TH6131, ZH6827]).

Gordis (1987:487-490), building upon a suggestion of Lawrence Zalcman, detects the metaphor of a deserted woman. In addition, both scholars propose that the reason for the absence of paronomasia and the presence of, at best, weak assonance in the pronouncements against Ashkelon and Ashdod is because no verb could be found that was suitable for the needed assonance and paronomasia and that carried with it the double entendre of a woman and a city. Faced with a choice of proceeding with the metaphor or the constraints of assonance, Zephaniah chose the former. Thus, the verse contains four assertions that "present an ascending scale of suffering, thus heightening the pathos of the passage" and are to be understood as follows:

  Indeed, Gaza shall be deserted (like a betrothed woman),
  And Ashkelon will be desolate (like a deserted wife);
  Ashdod will be driven out in broad daylight (like a divorced woman),
  And Ekron will be uprooted (like a barren woman).

2:5 *Philistines.* Lit., "Kerethites." Apparently related to the name *Crete*, with which Philistine origins are partially linked, its precise significance is unclear. Kerethites were included among David's bodyguard (2 Sam 8:18; 15:18; 20:7; 1 Kgs 1:38, 44; 1 Chr 18:17). The Kerethites have been considered by some to be a tribe of the Philistines, by others as Cretans who first settled in Canaan during the Davidic era. In any case, their close association with the Philistines is assumed both here and in Ezek 25:16, where they are also linked with the seacoast.

the coast. Although the Hebrew phrase *khebel hayyam* [TH2256A/3220, ZH2475/3542] (the line of the sea) is unique to Zephaniah (the usual term for "seacoast" is *khop hayyam* [TH2348/ 3220, ZH2572/3542]; cf. Jer 47:7), the resultant term is clear.

the land of Canaan. The term "Canaan," which designates the land west of the Jordan River (including Philistia) northward through Syria to Lebo Hamath (modern Lebweh), is probably used with the further implication "that Philistia is to share the lot of Canaan, and lose its inhabitants by extermination" (Keil 1954:141). Canaan is thus not conterminous with Philistia, nor is Philistia identical to the modern term Palestine (except etymologically). Berlin (1994:120) plausibly argues that Zephaniah's entire listing of nations is dependent upon Gen 10, which "serves as the conceptual undergirding, and to a large extent the literary model, for Zephaniah 2:5-15."

2:6 *a wilderness pasture, a place of shepherd camps.* Robertson (1990:300) notes that these words have "been subjected to numerous emendations." The word translated "camps" is variously rendered in the versions as "Crete" (LXX), "Kerethites" (NIV), "Kereth" (NEB), "resting place" (Vulgate), "shelters" (NKJV), "cottages" (KJV), "meadows" (NRSV; cf. Cohen), and "caves" (NASB). If caves are in view, whether "natural, dug by nature, or artificial, man-made, . . . [they are] used by shepherds and their flocks as a shelter at night or in stormy weather" (Laetsch 1956:367). There is also a wordplay here involving the root *krth*: The land of the Kerethites (*kerethim* [TH3774, ZH4165]; 2:5) will become a place marked by "shepherd camps" (*keroth* [TH3741, ZH4129]).

2:7 *remnant.* Lit., "the remnant of the house of Judah." Zephaniah had spoken earlier of God's destroying "every last [remnant] of their Baal worship" (1:4), and Amos predicted that the "[remnant of] Philistines still left" would perish (Amos 1:8). Here God leaves a remnant of his people, which he, the Good Shepherd, will care for and restore to prosperity. Cf. note on 3:13.

restore their prosperity. Roberts (1991:192) observes, "All the [ancient] versions understand the expression *shab shebutham* [TH7725/7622, ZH8740/8654] to mean 'to restore the captivity,' but the expression has the more general meaning, 'to restore the fortunes.'" See note on Joel 3:1.

2:8 *taunts . . . insults.* The NLT rendering reflects two Hebrew nouns: *kherpah* [TH2781, ZH3075] (insult) and *giddupim* [TH1421, ZH1526] (revilings). The first is used of slanderous speech (Mic 6:16) that one person uses against another (2 Chr 32:17) or especially the disgrace that one party gives to another (Gen 30:23; Isa 4:1). It is often used of reproach placed upon a nation (e.g., 1 Sam 17:26; Isa 25:8; Jer 31:19; Lam 5:1; Ezek 36:30). The second denotes the act of throwing, hence idiomatically of hurling insults at one another. Taken together, these two word groups form a picture of slanderous taunting that has as its object a hurtful vilifying of another.

invading their borders. The verb here has been understood as the gloating (Roberts 1991) or boasting (Berlin 1994) of the Moabites and Ammonites over the violation of Israel's borders. It carries with it the idea of an arrogant boasting against others. The sense here probably also carries with it not only the repeated arrogant thrusts of the Transjordanian nations into Israelite territory but also their gloating over their successes (cf. Amos 1:13). Some suggest that the verb signifies the enlarging of Transjordanian borders at Israel's expense (e.g., R. L. Smith), while others (cf. NJB) propose that these nations boasted about their own territories.

2:9 *stinging nettles, salt pits.* Berlin (1994:109) points out that because the words involved are hapax legomena, "the exact meaning of these terms is uncertain. . . . The ancient versions struggled with this phrase, all producing different translations, showing that this is an age-old crux. The gist is that the area, which is near the Dead Sea, will be covered with weeds and salt deposits—that is, it will become permanently infertile." Salt sometimes symbolized ruinous waste (Deut 29:23; Job 39:6; Ps 107:34; Jer 17:6). Sowing the earth with salt was a mark of permanent judgment (cf. Judg 9:45), a practice that continued into Roman times, as witnessed in the Roman sack of Carthage (cf. Warmington 1964:255).

remnant. See note on 3:13.

2:11 *destroys.* Because the usual meaning of *razah* [TH7329, ZH8135] (make thin/lean) appears to be difficult in this context (cf. Robertson 1990:308), several other suggestions have been made. The NLT follows the lead of the LXX, Peshitta, Old Latin, NIV, Luther, *La Sainte Bible,* and *La Sacra Biblia* in translating the Hebrew verb as "destroy." Other ideas include "attend to" (Vulgate), "starve/famish" (NASB, RSV, KJV, Cohen), "shrivel" (NRSV), "reduce to nothing" (NKJV), and "scatter" (NJB). Sabottka (1972:90-91) postulates a relation with a Jewish (Palestinian) Aramaic root meaning "be strong/hard," hence "rule."

nations around the world. Lit., "the isles of the nations." Berlin (1994:111) notes a comparison with Gen 10:5 and understands the term to refer to the Japhethites: "Thus the picture is not one of universal acknowledgment of the Lord, but acknowledgment by the islands of the nations when they witness the Lord's judgment against Moab and Ammon."

each in their own land. Keil (1954:145) understands the phrase to mean the nations will go from their place to Jerusalem to worship (cf. Isa 2:3; Mic 4:1; Zech 14:16).

2:12 *Ethiopians.* Lit., "Cushites." Berlin (1994:111-113) notes four other identifications for this term in addition to Ethiopia: (1) Egypt, (2) Midian or tribes to the south of Judah, (3) tribes of the Arabian Peninsula, and (4) Mesopotamia, especially Assyria. Berlin prefers the last choice, thinking that Zephaniah is alluding to the order of nations in Gen 10:5-11, where "Cush" designates the forbearer of the later Assyrian Empire. Most commonly, those who favor the identification with Egypt suggest that by "Cushites" (NLT, "Ethiopians") Zephaniah is reminding Egypt's current leadership of their recent Cushitic conquerors' (25th dynasty) rise and fall—events that serve as a harbinger of the present dynasty's own fall.

The choice of "Cushites" here (as well as in 3:10) may also reflect a conscious literary touch, constituting wordplay on the name of Zephaniah's father (1:1). Whether "Cushite" reflects an African element in Zephaniah's patrilineage (note the similar problem in Jer 36:14), as several have suggested, remains uncertain.

will also be slaughtered. Rather than a future tense verb here, the Hebrew text has a third-person plural, independent personal pronoun: "they"; hence, "Also you, O Cushite—slain of my soul are they" (Robertson 1990:309). It may be simpler, however, to view the form as a copula, as is common in later Hebrew (cf. 2 Sam 7:28; Ps 44:4), and translate, "So also you Cushites are pierced through by my sword."

2:13 *desolate wasteland . . . desert.* Although considerable difference of opinion exists as to the meaning of the latter term, its use in the OT indicates a wide semantic range. "Wilderness," "wasteland," "desert," and "steppe land" can each describe the author's intent in a given context. E. S. Kalland proposes three basic understandings for the type of topography involved: "Pastureland (Josh 2:22; Ps 65:12; Jer 23:10), uninhabited land (Deut 32:10; Job 38:26; Prov 21:19; Jer 9:1), and large areas of land in which oases or cities and towns exist here and there" (TWOT 2.181).

2:14 *all sorts of wild animals.* The phrase has been greatly debated. While it can be literally rendered as "every creature of the nation," Zephaniah's point appears to be that in contrast to the mighty Assyrian nation that once lived in Nineveh, the nation that will inhabit the fallen city will be made up of every "sort" of creature. The word *goy* [TH1471, ZH1580] (nation) is used in Joel 1:6 of a great army of locusts.

desert owl and screech owl. The NLT follows the lead of Sabottka (1972:96-97) in terming both animals as different types of owls.

Rubble. For the word *khoreb* [TH2721A, ZH2997] (rubble), some (LXX, Vulgate, NRSV; cf. Berlin 1994; Roberts 1991) suggest reading *'oreb* [TH6158, ZH6854] (raven). Other suggestions include *khereb* [TH2719, ZH2995] (sword), as in Aquila, Symmachus, Peshitta. The NEB suggests that the sense of the passage demands something like "bustard."

cedar paneling . . . weather. The final line of the verse has been greatly debated. The MT, however, makes tolerable sense as it stands: The action of stripping bare the cedar work helps to account for the previously mentioned accumulation of debris.

2:15 *This is the boisterous city.* The NLT forms a declarative sentence announcing Nineveh's fate. Some (e.g., NRSV, Roberts) have suggested that the sentence is an unmarked interrogative (cf. 2 Sam 16:17), dripping with sarcasm: "Is this the joyful city (that said . . .)?"

No other city can compare with me! The NLT renders according to the sense dictated by the context. The Hebrew text reads Nineveh's boasts as "I am and there is no one else." The final yodh in *we'apsi* [TH657, ZH700] is probably not a first common singular suffix, hence, "besides me" (as has often been proposed; NASB, KJV, NKJV). While this is a meaning the form bears nowhere else, it provides an example of *hireq compaginis* or paragogic yodh (see *Gesenius' Hebrew Grammar* §90l; 152s).

laugh in derision and shake a defiant fist. Both gestures are those of scorn (cf. Jer 18:16; 50:13; Lam 2:15).

C O M M E N T A R Y

The second portion of Zephaniah's prophecies (2:4–3:20) likewise is made up of pronouncements (2:4–3:7), an exhortation (3:8), and teachings (3:9-20). After his preoccupation with the fate of his people in the first part of the book, Zephaniah turns his attention to the foreign nations (2:4-15). He began the first major portion of his prophecy by similarly considering all nations (1:2-3). Here he deals with specific nations that were mostly tied to Judah's situation geographically and politically as representatives of God's relations with the world.

Zephaniah begins his pronouncements against the nations by turning to the people on Judah's west, the Philistines (2:4-7), then going to those on the east, Moab and Ammon (2:8-11), and finally considering those on the south and north, singling out Cush (2:12) and Assyria (2:13-15).

His first words are for Judah's perennial enemy to the west—the Philistines. Though they had become vassals of Assyria in the eighth century BC, they nonetheless enjoyed a measure of independence so that they continued to be a source of danger and irritation to the people of God (cf. 2 Kgs 18:5-8; 2 Chr 26:6-8). Even as late as the closing days of the southern kingdom, the Philistines were being condemned by Judah's prophets (Jer 47; Ezek 25:15-17). Accordingly, Zephaniah's words of condemnation and judgment were neither unprecedented nor unexpected and doubtless would have been well received by the citizens of Judah and Jerusalem.

Each of the cities experienced the horrors of invasion. As for the main fact of Zephaniah's prophecy—the capture and destruction of the cities and territory of the Philistines—there can be little doubt, for the Babylonian Chronicles tell of their demise (cf. Wiseman 1956:69). Whatever future hope the region had lay in its relation to the Philistines' perennial enemies, the Israelites. The prosperous sea-coast district would become pastureland dotted with caves for Israelite shepherds and folds for their flocks.

Zephaniah's pronouncements of judgment then turned to Judah's eastern neighbors, the Transjordanian nations of Moab and Ammon. Like the Philistines, these nations were numbered among Israel's traditional foes. Zephaniah condemned both nations for their pride (cf. Isa 16:6; 25:10-11; Jer 48:29; 49:1-4), their blasphemous insults against God and his people (cf. Jer 48:26-27; 49:1), and their atrocities and incursions against Israelite territory (Amos 1:13–2:3).[1] Because of their vicious actions and their gloating over their seeming successes against the Israelites, Zephaniah predicted that both nations, which had often worked together, would be treated like another well-known pair: Sodom and Gomorrah. When God's judgment was accomplished, the whole area would be turned into a perpetual wasteland, overrun with weeds and pocked by salt pits, whereas its inhabitants would be taken into captivity.

Building on the concept of universal judgment, Zephaniah includes a notice that the judgment of Cush, too, is part of the punishment that will overtake all peoples. The Cushites probably denote the Egyptians (cf. Ezek 30:1-9). As the Cushite dynasty had passed, so also would Egypt (cf. Jer 46; Ezek 29–32), as will one day be the case with all earthly powers standing in opposition to the Lord (cf. Ezek 32:17-32).

Zephaniah's fourth message against the foreign powers swings around to the north. The order of his prophecies is doubtless climactic. He had delivered his messages against Judah's perennial enemies to the west and east; then he inserted a word against a traditional foe to the south. He then brought the series to a head by turning to the nation that had so long been the dominant power in the ancient Near East. Like Nahum before him, Zephaniah announced Assyria's fast-approaching demise. God would stretch out his hand and destroy it. Its capital city, Nineveh, would be rendered desolate. The proud royal city, once so busy and bustling with people, would be inhabited only by animals. Casting the eye upward, one would soon see on the tops of Nineveh's many pillars not stately structures but owls—owls of every sort screeching through the lonely nights. With the morning light one is confronted with the strangest of paradoxes: From the windows of razed and gutted buildings comes the song of birds, while below them lies only the rubble of collapsed walls, fallen timbers, broken bits of once-treasured possessions, and strips of cedar paneling. It is an eerie spectacle—the deceased metropolis populated only by creatures and ghosts of departed grandeur. Here is the once proud and festive city whose power and wealth were beyond measure, at one time approached with eager anticipation, respect, and fear. Now it is devoid of citizenry or visitors, and those who pass by and see the devastation give only a sneering hiss (cf. Jer 19:8; Mic 6:16) or scornful wave. Like Nahum, then, Zephaniah sees no future either for Assyria or its capital. Their doom is certain and irreversible (cf. Nah 1:14; 2:13; 3:19). *Sic transit gloria mundi!*

Several theological themes emerge in the condemnation of the nations of this world. Among these, one of the most prominent is that of the godly remnant.[2] Zephaniah's teaching is in harmony with the other prophets who predict that God will preserve a remnant of his people, which he will again gather to the land. These people will receive their Messiah and be blessed with everlasting felicity (e.g., Jer 23:1-8; Ezek 34:20-31; 37:15-28; Mic 4:1-8; cf. Zeph 3:9-20).

Thus judgment and hope become inextricably tied together.[3] Out of judgment comes hope and an assurance that God's justice is wedded to his loving concern and care for his own. Zephaniah's emphasis is even more inclusive, however, for it looks forward to that ultimate time when some from "every nation and tribe and people and language" will stand before the throne and before the Lamb and cry out, "Salvation comes from our God who sits on the throne and from the Lamb!" (Rev 7:9-10).

The flip side of the remnant theme is, of course, that of judgment. Beyond the condemnation of the historical nations lies the application of their punishment to all nations who similarly mistreat God's people and vaunt themselves against God (cf. Gen 12:1-3; 1 Sam 17:26, 36, 45; 2 Kgs 19:21-28; Ps 2; Jer 48:26-27; Joel 3:1-3; Matt 25:41). To such as oppose him will come a final time of reckoning, when the sovereign and omnipotent God (Deut 10:17; Ps 47:7-8), whose awesomeness (Ps 47:2) is beyond measure (Ps 89:7) and whose strength (Ps 89:8-13) makes him mighty in battle (Ps 24:8), will show himself fearsome (Ps 76:12) to all (Isa 66:14-16; Ezek 39:17-22; Joel 3:9-16). Then, people will learn that Israel's God alone is the one and only true God (Deut 6:4; Isa 42:8; 46:9). The false gods—who are not really gods (Isa 41:24)—like the nations, cities, and people with whom they are identified, will be subdued (cf. Isa 43:11-13; 44:17-20; 46:1-2; Jer 50:2-3; Zech 14:9), and God alone will be worshiped everywhere and by all (Ps 66:1-4; Isa 2:1-5; 66:19-21; Mic 4:1-5; Zech 14:16-21).

Concomitant with the threat of judgment is the seriousness of sin. Especially to be noted is the pride of nations that leads them to insult and mock God's people. For by taunting Israel, they cast reproach upon God as well. Some had gone so far in their arrogance as to mock God himself, for in claiming to be self-existent and self-sufficient (2:15), they had appropriated God's own claims (cf. Isa 43:10-11; 44:6; 45:5, 18, 21-22; 46:9; Rev 1:8, 17; 22:12-13) for themselves. Like others who made similar boasts, they will meet the fate of all those who presume upon the person and work of God (cf. Isa 14:12-23; Ezek 28:2-10, 17-19). God simply will not allow nations or individuals to keep on reproaching him or his people. Such is blatant sin and will meet the just judgment of God (cf. Exod 20:7; Deut 5:11; 8:19-20; Isa 52:5; Obad 1:10-15).

Underlying this whole passage is the familiar theme of God's sovereignty. For the disposition of all nations is in the hand of almighty God, who will both punish the evildoers and reward the righteous. He is not an absentee God. He knows fully the human character and condition and will deal with the situation in just measure so as to accomplish his ultimate purposes for all (1 Kgs 8:39; Ps 37:28-29; Isa 42:1; 46:10; Dan 4:34-35; Acts 17:31).

ENDNOTES
1. Moab's hostility toward Israel is illustrated in the well-known Mesha Stele (or Moabite Stone); see D. Winton Thomas, *Documents from Old Testament Times* (New York: Harper & Row, 1961), 195-199. For the text itself, see H. Donner and W. Röllig, *Kanaanaische und Aramaische Inschriften* (Wiesbaden: Harrassowitz, 1966), 1:33.
2. VanGemeren (1989:677) suggests that "the nations are symbolic of all kingdoms which oppose the rule of God. God's purpose is to establish out of the remnant of Judah and the nations a people who will submit themselves to him and worship him wherever they may be found." Baker (1988:105-106) adds, "The motif of the remnant is common in the prophets (cf. Jer 23:3; Amos 5:15; Mic 2:12; 5:7-8), exemplifying both the severity of God's punishment and also the graciousness of his mercy. Destruction will come, but not annihilation." For the remnant theme, see Hasel 1974; Anderson 1977-78:11-14; King 1994:414-427.
3. See King 1995:29-31; see further R. D. Patterson, "Old Testament Prophecy," *A Complete Literary Guide to the Bible,* eds., L. Ryken and T. Longman III (Grand Rapids: Zondervan, 1993), 302-303.

◆   ## 2. Pronouncement on Jerusalem (3:1-7)

¹What sorrow awaits rebellious,
  polluted Jerusalem,
  the city of violence and crime!
²No one can tell it anything;
  it refuses all correction.
It does not trust in the LORD
  or draw near to its God.
³Its leaders are like roaring lions
  hunting for their victims.
Its judges are like ravenous wolves
  at evening time,
  who by dawn have left no trace of
  their prey.
⁴Its prophets are arrogant liars seeking
  their own gain.
Its priests defile the Temple by
  disobeying God's instructions.
⁵But the LORD is still there in the city,
  and he does no wrong.

Day by day he hands down justice,
  and he does not fail.
But the wicked know no shame.

⁶"I have wiped out many nations,
  devastating their fortress walls
  and towers.
Their streets are now deserted;
  their cities lie in silent ruin.
There are no survivors—
  none at all.
⁷I thought, 'Surely they will have
  reverence for me now!
Surely they will listen to my
  warnings.
Then I won't need to strike again,
  destroying their homes.'
But no, they get up early
  to continue their evil deeds.

NOTES
3:1 What sorrow. Lit., "woe" (*hoy* [TH1945, ZH2098]). Woe oracles customarily contain such elements as invective, criticism, and threat. Not all oracles beginning with *hoy* bear the marks of woe oracles, however. See notes on Nah 3:1; Hab 2:6.

rebellious. The root of this word is debated. Some suggest the existence of a root *ro'i* II, meaning "excrement" (Jastrow, cf. HALOT 1.630). Some derive it here from *yare'* [TH3373, ZH3710] (fear, frightful), and others from *marah* [TH4784, ZH5286] (rebel). The NLT has followed the last alternative. This root is used overwhelmingly in the OT in contexts dealing with Israel's rebellion against God or his commandments, whether in word or deed.

polluted. Although the Hebrew root may be employed concerning discoloration in general (Isa 63:3), it is used often of religious defilement or disqualification (Ezra 2:62; Neh 7:64; Mal 1:7), particularly of the misdeeds of Israel's priesthood (Neh 13:29).

violence and crime! The NLT expresses the force of the Hebrew *yonah* [TH3238A, ZH3561] (oppression) by listing two characteristics of it. The Peshitta translates the word as "Jonah," assuming the city addressed here to be Nineveh (NLT's "Jerusalem" does not occur in the Hebrew text). However, this scarcely makes good sense in context (cf. 3:4, 11). The Hebrew term is utilized in a variety of ways but most frequently of intolerance toward or the suppression of the rights and privileges of others. It especially characterizes the rich and influential members of society who take advantage of the less fortunate (cf. Exod 22:21; Lev 19:33; Deut 23:16).

3:2 *correction.* By "correction" (or "chastisement") is meant the several instances of affliction and rebuke that God sends into the lives of his own to bring about their spiritual growth (Prov 1:7-8; 3:11-12). Like Zephaniah, Jeremiah lamented the people's failure to profit from God's chastening (Jer 5:3; 7:28).

3:3 *leaders . . . judges.* For the term "leaders," see note on 1:8. As for judges, this noun was used of those leaders of Israel to whom civic, as well as judicial, responsibilities were entrusted. In time, the latter sense became the dominant one, especially from Samuel onward (cf. 1 Sam 7:15-17; 8:1-2). These two terms, along with the mention of prophets and priests in v. 4, served as the focal point for Ezekiel's adaptation of 3:3-4 for his denunciation of God's people (Ezek 22:25-28). Fishbane (1985:463) singles out Ezekiel's use of Zephaniah as a classic case of intra-biblical exegesis.

ravenous wolves at evening time. The exact force of Zephaniah's simile has been greatly debated. The MT's "wolves of the evening" was followed by the Vulgate and the Peshitta, whereas the LXX translates, "wolves of Arabia." The dissatisfaction with the idea of evening wolves has led some to translate "wolves of the steppe/plain/wasteland" (e.g., NJB, REB). The NLT renders the graphic sense of the passage. (For a discussion of the term "wolves of the evening," see Elliger 1950:158-178; Sabottka 1972:104-105.)

3:4 *arrogant.* Von Orelli (1897:274) observes that the Hebrew root of the term rendered "arrogant" means "to overcook"; hence the prophets are those who boil over with personal desire. Jeremiah uses the root to describe the prophets' deceit. He charges them with falsehood of every kind (Jer 23:30-32).

3:5 *The LORD . . . does no wrong.* Lit., "the LORD is righteous." See commentary on Hab 2:4.

justice. Keil (1954:57) observes that the term involves more than rendering a righteous verdict; it includes "a righteous state of things." Robertson (1990:322) remarks, "As faithfully as the Lord provided daily manna for his people during their trial period in the wilderness, so in the chaotic last days of Jerusalem the Lord's righteousness was coming to light."

3:6 *walls and towers.* The NLT renders the force of the single Hebrew word here that designates the corner tower or key point in the defensive wall. See note on 1:16.

3:7 *Surely they.* The NLT reading provides a smoothing out of the enallage (grammatical interchange) in the Hebrew text that moves from the direct address of "surely you will fear me" to the indirect address of "therefore her dwelling will not be cut off." The resultant sense casts the whole sentence as a divine musing: God's concern was for Jerusalem's repentance so that in the coming judgment total destruction could be avoided. The LXX and Peshitta apparently read *me'eneha* [TH4480/5869/1886.3, ZH4946/6524/2023] (from her eyes/ sight) in place of *me'onah* [TH4583A/1886.3, ZH5061/2023] (her dwelling), a reading followed by G. A. Smith and J. M. P. Smith (cf. NJB, NRSV).

COMMENTARY

Having pronounced judgment on the surrounding nations, Zephaniah turned to his own nation and city. In cataloging Jerusalem's crimes (3:1-5), he noted that its people were totally rebellious against God. Jeremiah also charged that the people were stubborn and rebellious (Jer 4:17) and that their leaders had kept them from fearing God, thereby causing them to turn away from God so as to miss his good purpose for them (Jer 5:23-25). The nation had neither obeyed God nor responded to his correction (Jer 7:21-28; cf. 11:6-8; 22:21). Ezekiel reminded his hearers of Israel's penchant for impiety (Ezek 20:8, 13, 21). Because that sin was perpetuated in their day, it would bring God's wrath against them (Ezek 20:3-38). Zephaniah's point is much the same. He charged God's people with refusing to obey God's commandments and with an unwillingness to learn from chastisement.

Zephaniah went to the heart of the problem by noting the cause of Jerusalem's obstinacy. It had neither concern nor time for God and his standards. God's prophet called Jerusalem a defiled city. He pointed an accusing finger at Jerusalem's religious leadership, those most responsible for the spiritual and moral fiber of the populace. Its prophets, who should have been God's spokesmen, were non-prophets (cf. Jer 23:9-39). Their arrogance knew no bounds. Carried away by selfish conceit and personal ambition, they produced pompous pronouncements filled with idle boasting, platitudes, and lies.

The priests were no better (cf. Jer 2:8; 5:31; 6:13; 23:11). They who were charged with the purity of God's house and the sanctity of his law (Deut 31:9-13; 1 Chr 23:28) violated both. Ezekiel (Ezek 22:26) repeated the same charges, pointing out that conditions in his day had only worsened, for the priests willfully profaned all that was sacred.

Zephaniah exposed Jerusalem's leaders for what they were. The nobles who served as its officials and judges had betrayed their privileged positions. They who should have been fair and impartial became like ravenous beasts—roaring lions (cf. Prov 28:15; Ezek 22:25) preying on the possessions of the poor and the lives of the citizens, and wolves prowling about in the evening, gobbling up their unsuspecting prey and crushing them so thoroughly that none of their bones remained in the morning. Thus justice was perverted in the insatiable greed of Jerusalem's leadership.

Zephaniah condemned all Jerusalem for being eager (*shakam* [TH7925, ZH8899], "be eager," "rise early") to get going at their shameful acts. Jeremiah painted a similarly sad picture of Jerusalem's citizens. So apostate had they become in their desire to be about their own business that none had time to meet with God. Indeed, Jeremiah employed this same verb 11 times to picture God's eagerness to meet with his people. He rose, as it were, to be on hand at the beginning of each day, longing to meet with them—but to no avail. Zephaniah reported that the people were eager, "rose early," only to corrupt their ways further. It is little wonder then that Judah's end was not long in coming. Accordingly, those who claim God as king in our generation would be well advised to get up early and eagerly meet with him who "rises early" to meet with his people.[1]

God's evaluation of his people, delivered through his prophets, is timelessly instructive. Where people have abandoned the rightful sovereignty of God over their lives, preferring to play god themselves and departing from the standards of God's Word as a guide for their lives, they are in danger of personal failure and God's censure. People need to have their priorities in order, for misplaced trust in oneself is untrustworthy. Only God can serve as the central focus of a meaningful life (Deut 4:5-7; 6:4-6; Pss 84:12; 119:169; 125:1; Prov 3:5-6; Isa 26:3-4).

Likewise, leaders must be held accountable. Everything stands or falls on good Christian leadership. Woe to the church whose leaders, like those of Jerusalem, violate their high and holy calling and attempt to manipulate their sacred tasks for personal advancement.[2] In contrast to Judah's corrupt leaders, those who would serve as special ministers for Christ are reminded that theirs must be a wholesome, balanced, and spiritually maturing walk (cf. Ps 101:6 with Gen 17:1; Deut 18:13; Matt 5:48; 2 Cor 13:11). Indeed, all of their life ("sacred" and "secular") must be truly marked by humble, spiritual service for Christ (cf. Rom 15:26-27; 2 Cor 9:12-13), reflecting Christ's manner of service (Mark 10:45).

ENDNOTES
1. The morning hour is often commended as an ideal time for meeting with God to find direction and strength for the day (e.g., Pss 5:3; 88:13, NIV; 92:1-2; 143:8; cf. Mark 1:35).
2. As Craigie (1985:125) notes, "In Zephaniah's time, just as in our own, there were those persons engaged in the 'ministry of the Word' who had seen and exploited its possibilities for personal gain."

◆ B. Instructions Based on Judgment (3:8)

8 Therefore, be patient," says the LORD.
  "Soon I will stand and accuse these
     evil nations.
For I have decided to gather the
   kingdoms of the earth

and pour out my fiercest anger
   and fury on them.
All the earth will be devoured
   by the fire of my jealousy.

NOTES
3:8 *Therefore.* According to the Masorah, this is the only verse in the OT that contains all the letters of the Hebrew alphabet, including the final forms.

I will stand and accuse. The NLT follows the lead of the LXX, the Peshitta, and many scholars and versions in reading *le'ed* [TH3807.1/5707, ZH4200/6332] (as a witness) rather than the MT's *le'ad* [TH3807.1/5706, ZH4200/6331] ("for a prey"; cf. NASB, KJV). The NLT renders the sense of this idea with "stand . . . accuse." Some scholars (e.g., Berlin) follow the Vulgate in reading *la'ad* [TH3807.1/5703, ZH4200/6329] (forever), while Sabottka renders it *le'ad* (from my throne). In this he has followed Gordon (1965:453). This proposal necessitates understanding the preposition *le-* as "from," a meaning often found in Ugaritic.

I have decided. The noun *mishpat* [TH4941, ZH5477] (judgment) serves here as a stitch word connecting this verse with the previous section (cf. "justice," 3:5).

anger . . . fire. Berlin (1994:133) appropriately points out that "the imagery of wrath and fire echoes 1:15 and 2:2, and the same phraseology, 'the entire earth will be consumed by the fire of his/my passion,' occurs here and in 1:18."

COMMENTARY

In light of the waves of certain judgment that will flow over the nations and wash away Jerusalem in their wake, God exhorts his people: "Wait for me" (NLT, "be patient"). In a vivid metaphor, the prophet portrays a courtroom scene in which God rises first as witness (cf. Jer 29:23; Mal 3:5) on his own behalf before the assembly and then presides as judge (Job 9:15; Ps 50:6) to deliver his righteous sentence (Ps 72:2).

The motif of God as judge is a familiar one in the Old Testament. Indeed, God's coming to judge the earth is often announced (e.g., 1 Chr 16:33; Pss 96:13; 98:9). The language in Zephaniah is reminiscent of Psalms 82:8; 94:2. Here God confirms his decision to assemble all nations and peoples for judgment (Ezek 38:1–39:24; Joel 3:9-16).

God speaks of the fire of his jealousy, a phrase describing his righteous hatred of sin and his concern for his people (cf. Isa 66:13-16). And herein is a message of hope. Because God's judgment of the nations was so often linked with his concern for the salvation of his people, the righteous citizens of Jerusalem could take comfort. God's justice would avenge them. In light of God's great promises (cf. Isa 30:18-33; 33:22; 64:4), even the exhortation "wait for me" carried a note of hope. It was "only used for waiting in a believing attitude for the Lord and his help" (Keil 1954:153). It was just such a hope that Zephaniah would deliver in the sections that follow.

This verse thus underlines two familiar theological truths: (1) God does see the crimes of all nations and will bring them to justice—in his time (2 Pet 3:3-10); (2) God's mercy will prevail for those who trust him, however dark the circumstances may seem at the present (Hab 3:2, 16-18). Therefore, faithful believers are urged to wait for him, both as a daily practice and as an abiding expectation (Pss 5:3; 27:14; 33:20; 37:34; Prov 20:22). Such an attitude demands a commitment to trust in the Lord and wait patiently for his perfect will to be worked out in all circumstances and situations (Ps 37:3-7).

Perhaps Christians could better learn to wait patiently on the Lord if they considered that this same quality is resident in God himself. Because God is "long-suffering," he bore with a world of total spiritual bankruptcy in the days of Noah (1 Pet 3:20). Similarly, he yet delays the great day of judgment so as to prolong the opportunity for salvation (2 Pet 3:15). Indeed, God's patience ought to bring people to repentance (Rom 2:4; 9:22-24).

Because God is patient, believers ought also to be patient (cf. Matt 18:21-35), showing godly patience toward all people (1 Thess 5:14). Indeed, it is a fruit of the Spirit (Gal 5:22). By patiently waiting on God, believers can endure life's seeming inequities. They can stand fast in afflictions and trials (2 Cor 6:4; 2 Thess 1:4), being assured that tribulation works patience (Rom 5:3). This kind of patience tests faith (Jas 1:3) and produces hope (Rom 5:3-4), joy (Col 1:11), and God's commendation (1 Pet 2:19-20). If we would persevere in the Christian life, we need to be patient (Heb 10:32-39). If we would reign with Christ, we must also be patient (2 Tim 2:12).

◆   ## C. A Description of the Coming Deliverance (3:9-13)

9 "Then I will purify the speech of all people,
so that everyone can worship the LORD together.
10 My scattered people who live beyond the rivers of Ethiopia*
will come to present their offerings.
11 On that day you will no longer need to be ashamed,
for you will no longer be rebels against me.
I will remove all proud and arrogant people from among you.

There will be no more haughtiness on my holy mountain.
12 Those who are left will be the lowly and humble,
for it is they who trust in the name of the LORD.
13 The remnant of Israel will do no wrong;
they will never tell lies or deceive one another.
They will eat and sleep in safety, and no one will make them afraid."

3:10 Hebrew *Cush.*

NOTES

3:9 *I will purify.* Lit., "I will overturn." Known throughout the Semitic languages, this verbal root (*hpk*) is used in the OT transitively of turning someone or something (2 Kgs 21:13), overthrowing a city (Gen 19:21, 25, 29), or transforming/changing a thing/person (Ps 105:25). Intransitively, it is employed of turning back or into something (Lev 13:3-4; 2 Kgs 5:26-27). Here used transitively, it takes its place in a series of statements relative to God's transforming work with regard to people (1 Sam 10:6, 9; Jer 31:13; Hos 11:8). The sentence is elliptical, yet the point that the impure lips of the people will be changed to pure lips is clear.

together. Lit., "[with] one shoulder." The phrase is best taken as a figurative expression for unanimity of action or purpose (cf. NRSV, NKJV, KJV; "with one accord/consent"), hence the expression "shoulder to shoulder" (NASB, NIV, NJB).

3:10 *My scattered people.* The NLT combines the two designations of the MT ("my worshipers," "my scattered ones") into one. Both are omitted in the LXX and the Peshitta, and accordingly some suggest that they are a gloss here. However, their inclusion by the Vulgate and the difficulty in understanding them argue against their omission or the conjecture of a gloss. J. M. P. Smith (1911:249) declares the MT "quite . . . unintelligible." Nevertheless, the English versions have made tolerable sense of the text: "my suppliants, the daughter of my dispersed (ones)" (RSV, KJV); "my worshipers, my dispersed ones/scattered people" (NASB, NIV).

Although *'athar* [TH6282, ZH6985] (worshiper) is a hapax legomenon, the verb *'athar* [TH6279, ZH6983] (pray/supplicate) is attested. The form could also be pointed as a participle: "those who worship me." Adding to the difficulty is the fact that the phrase *bath-putsay* (NLT, "my scattered people") is without precedent. The usual sense of *bath* [TH1323, ZH1426] (daughter) in such cases is as a stereotyped title with a nationalistic emphasis such as "daughter of Jerusalem" or "daughter of Zion," while the passive participle of *puts* [TH6327, ZH7046] occurs nowhere else. Most probably the phrase is elliptical for *bath 'ammi happuts* (my scattered people), the sense being supplied from the *'ammim* [TH5971A, ZH6639] of 3:9.

the rivers of Ethiopia. Lit., "the rivers of Cush." Although Berlin (1994:134-135) once again argues vigorously for a Mesopotamian connection here (cf. Gen 2:13), most understand the distant headwaters of the Nile and their tributaries found in Sudan and Ethiopia. Thus J. M. P. Smith (1911:249) points out that "the rivers referred to are the branches of the Nile that traverse the most southern portion of the region; viz. the Atbara, the Astasobas, the Astapus or Blue Nile, and the Bahr-el-Abjadh or White Nile; cf. Is. 18:1-7." The phrase is a synecdoche, those of that distant region representing the farthest people of the earth.

present their offerings. Lit., "my offering." The noun *minkhah* [TH4503, ZH4966] can be used to indicate offerings of any kind, tribute (Judg 3:15; 1 Kgs 4:21), or presents. Among the ancient versions, the LXX and Vulgate decide for "sacrifices." Keil (1954:156-157) champions the meal offering, while Sabottka (1972:121) favors "tribute," a meaning that owes much to an Ugaritic cognate that is parallel to *argmn*, "tribute" (cf. *'argaman* [TH713, ZH763], "purple yarn"). Thus Zephaniah calls on earlier Canaanite literature, drawing from a context set in the contest between Yamm and Baal. In this instance, Baal was to be handed over to Yamm and sent to him as tribute:

> Thy slave is Baal, O Yamm,
> Thy slave is Baal forever,
> Dagon's Son is thy captive;
> He shall be brought as thy tribute [*argmn*].
> For thy gods bring thy gift [*mnkhy*],
> The holy ones are thy tributaries. (See Gordon 1965:197-198, text 137, lines 36-38)

The literary allusion here is rendered certain by the assembly of words apparently taken from that text: *'ebed* [TH5650, ZH6269] (slave, servant); *yabal* [TH2986, ZH3297] (bring); and *minkhah* [TH4503, ZH4966] (tribute). Thus, just as Baal was to be Yamm's servant and sent as tribute to him, so converted Gentiles who "call upon the name of the Lord" and "serve him shoulder to shoulder" will be "my worshipers" who will "bring my scattered ones" (the Jews) as "my tribute."

3:11 *On that day.* Lit., "in that day." Such temporal phrases can be used as formulae to introduce strophes or stanzas (cf. Joel 3:1; Amos 8:13; 9:11). The changed emphasis and subject matter, as well as the literary hook *ki 'az* [TH3588/227, ZH3954/255], render it certain that the phrase introduces a subunit in this section. It also forms a linking device with the following section (cf. 3:16).

be ashamed. Since the verb form is feminine singular, Jerusalem is probably being addressed. The verb can be taken in a subjective sense with the meaning "feel shame" (NASB) or in an objective sense meaning "be put to shame" (NIV, NKJV). The former emphasizes the forgetting of past shameful deeds against the Lord; the latter lays stress on the unlikely prospect of feeling shame ever again since its cause is removed. The latter course underscores the fact that in the future day the shameful acts perpetrated against God will no longer be practiced, for those who did such things will have been removed.

Berlin (1994:135-136) observes, "Most commentators understand this phrase to mean 'you will not be ashamed of your deeds,' but the issue is not whether Israel feels shame, but whether it is put to shame. God will remove Israel's guilt and shame by removing the cause of them—the prideful element of society."

proud and arrogant. Lit., "the exaltations of your pride," or "your exalters in pridefulness." Keil (1954:158) observes that the phrase "is taken from Isa 13:3, where it denotes the heroes called by Jehovah, who exult with pride caused by the intoxication of victory; whereas here the reference is to the haughty judges, priests, and prophets (vv. 3-4), who exult in their sinful ways."

3:12 *Those who are left will be the lowly and humble.* Lit., "and I will leave among you a humble and lowly people." Invaders customarily deported the leaders and skilled crafts-men of the lands they had conquered, leaving only the poor (2 Kgs 24:14; 25:12). So also God's invasion of Jerusalem leaves the humble and lowly (lit., "afflicted and poor"; cf. Job 34:28; Isa 26:6). Together, they made up the lower stratum of society who were plagued by physical difficulties and social and mental torment (cf. Prov 22:22). Here, however, these words are qualified by the statement that "they . . . trust in the name of the Lord." Accord-ingly, the arrogant of society will be replaced by those who humbly put their faith in God.

3:13 *The remnant of Israel.* Berlin (1994:136-137) follows Ben Zvi in suggesting that the "remnant of the house of Judah" is a geographical term, whereas "the remnant of Israel" is a religious one. The latter term "continues to be used in exilic and postexilic sources, where only the people of Judah can be meant, to signify members of the religious community (e.g., Ezra 2:70)."

will do no wrong. The ethical qualities predicated for the godly remnant of Israel were those that would characterize the Messiah himself (Isa 42:1-4; 53:3, 7-9; Zech 9:9; cf. Matt 11:28-30; 12:15-21; Phil 2:1-8; 1 Pet 2:22).

They will eat and sleep in safety . . . no one will make them afraid. The blessings prom-ised here are assured to those who faithfully keep God's commandments (Ps 1:1-3; Ezek 34:25-31; Mic 4:4-5; 7:14).

COMMENTARY

Two theological truths dominate this section: (1) The Day of the Lord involves both judgment and hope—beyond the coming judgment is the hope of restoration. (2) That hope centers in the familiar theme of the remnant. With regard to the first, it may be noted that judgment and hope are often twin themes. Certainly such is the case with the seventh-century BC minor prophets. All three have strong words of judgment (e.g., 1:14-18; Nah 3:8-19; Hab 2:6-20) along with those of hope and re-assurance (2:1-3; 3:9-20; Nah 1:7, 15; Hab 3:16-19). Even more significantly, all three prophets demonstrate that because judgment is an integral part of God's pro-gram for ending this age, it is designed ultimately to bless his people and his world. Judgment and hope, then, rather than being irreconcilable themes, are two aspects of one divine perspective. Both are designed and intertwined to accomplish God's purposes.

In these verses Zephaniah turns from judgment to its outcome—God's blessing of the people of the world. God's goal is to effect change in the hearts and lives of all. Such indeed will take place—and not just for Israel; rather, all people will be transformed so as to call on the Lord (cf. Isa 55:5) and serve him as one (cf. Isa 59:19-21). To "call on the name of the Lord" means to invoke his name in belief (cf. Gen 4:26; 12:8; 2 Kgs 5:11). God's worshipers will do this with "pure lips." Their desire will be to serve him in sincere devotion as one—"shoulder to shoulder." Thus, all people will know God (Hab 2:14) and enjoy his everlasting beneficence (Isa 2:1-4; 11:1-10; Mic 4:1-5).

In connection with the second theme, as proof of their new love for God, the

Gentiles will bring to him his covenant people (Isa 66:20). From the farthest reaches of the world, wherever they have been scattered in judgment (Deut 28:64-68), God's people will be returned to the land of promise (Deut 4:27-31; Isa 11:11-16) and enjoy God's richest blessings (Isa 66:7-14).

In that day, Jerusalem's past shameful acts against God will not be repeated. By then, those who have done such things will have been removed, and with their departure the spirit of haughtiness will disappear. In their place God will leave those who, in true humility, trust in him and will serve him faithfully. In addition, he will remove injustice and deception.[1] God will be well pleased with the godly remnant, for he, as their good shepherd, will give them sustenance, serenity, and security (3:11-13).

Christian believers would do well to emulate the faithfulness of Zephaniah's remnant.[2] Indeed, the terms used in this section take on a theological importance that recognizes that the saved of the world are those whose qualities of heart and mind enable them to submit to God. More than just being poor in this world's goods, they are poor in spirit (Isa 66:2; Mic 6:8; Matt 5:3). It is a godly remnant unencumbered by pride and committed to the Savior. May it be ever so with those who claim the Savior's name!

ENDNOTES

1. As King (1994:427) points out, all three emphases of the remnant theme are resident in Zephaniah's prophecy: historic (2:3, 7), faithful (3:12), and eschatological (3:15).
2. VanGemeren (1989:681) appropriately remarks, "Faithfulness is not only an attitude but also an expression of what one says and does. The essence of Old Testament piety is found here (cf. Pss 15:2-5; 24:3-6; Mic 6:8). The requirement is no different since the coming of Christ."

◆   D. Final Exhortation (3:14-20)

14 Sing, O daughter of Zion;
      shout aloud, O Israel!
   Be glad and rejoice with all your heart,
      O daughter of Jerusalem!
15 For the LORD will remove his hand
      of judgment
      and will disperse the armies of your
      enemy.
   And the LORD himself, the King of Israel,
      will live among you!
   At last your troubles will be over,
      and you will never again fear
      disaster.
16 On that day the announcement
      to Jerusalem will be,
   "Cheer up, Zion! Don't be afraid!

17 For the LORD your God is living
      among you.
   He is a mighty savior.
   He will take delight in you with
      gladness.
   With his love, he will calm all your
      fears.*
   He will rejoice over you with joyful
      songs."
18 "I will gather you who mourn for the
      appointed festivals;
   you will be disgraced no more.*
19 And I will deal severely with all who
      have oppressed you.
   I will save the weak and helpless
      ones;

I will bring together
    those who were chased away.
I will give glory and fame to my
    former exiles,
    wherever they have been mocked
    and shamed.
20 On that day I will gather you together

and bring you home again.
I will give you a good name, a name
    of distinction,
among all the nations of the earth,
as I restore your fortunes before their
    very eyes.
I, the LORD, have spoken!"

3:17 Or *He will be silent in his love.* Greek and Syriac versions read *He will renew you with his love.* 3:18 The meaning of the Hebrew for this verse is uncertain.

NOTES

3:14 *Sing . . . shout aloud . . . Be glad and rejoice.* Walker (1985:564) calls attention to the piling up of verbs of similar meaning here as an expression of strong emphasis. The future scene of God's blessing will be one of boundless joy. The use of personification, anthropopoeia, and metaphor in 3:14-16 is striking.

3:15 *remove . . . disperse.* The Hebrew verbs constitute a play on ideas: "turned aside . . . turned away." While the first verb (*sur* [TH5493, ZH6073]) indicates the removal of the source of stress, the second (*panah* [TH6437, ZH7155]) emphasizes their being sent away. Since the objects of the verbs are "judgment" and "enemy" respectively, the scene may be that of a courtroom where God the judge has overturned the sentence against his people and sent their enemies away. The second verb may have been chosen as a deliberate echo of the earlier use of *pinnah* [TH6438, ZH7157] (stronghold) in 1:16; 3:6.

hand of judgment. Zephaniah had previously brought up the themes of judgment and justice (2:3; 3:5, 8), so their presence here is not without precedent. God serves as witness against all the world and also as its judge (3:8). He is Jerusalem's righteous judge (3:5) who will deliver those who humbly practice his judgments and statutes (2:3). Now that there is a purified and humble remnant in the city, he may freely terminate its sentence and remove those he had sent to execute its punishment.

enemy. Roberts (1991:220) follows the lead of the LXX, Peshitta, and Targum in reading a plural here (enemies). The Hebrew noun is probably to be viewed as a collective plural and, as Berlin (1994:143) suggests, a noun designating a particular class.

you will never again fear disaster. For the Hebrew *lo'-thire'i* [TH3808/3372, ZH4202/3707], some mss (followed by the LXX and Peshitta; cf. KJV, NKJV) read *lo'-thir'i* [TH3808/7200, ZH4202/8011] (you will not see). But the weight of Hebrew mss favors the MT, a reading reflected in the Vulgate. Accordingly, most newer translations follow the MT (cf. NIV, NASB, NRSV, NJB). "Fear" also provides a play on the notion of Israel's failure to demonstrate proper fear in the midst of God's chastisement (cf. 3:7) and also anticipates the emphases of the next two verses. "Disaster" (*ra'* [TH7451A, ZH8273]) can designate any calamity, injury, or adverse circumstance, even God's judicial punishment.

3:16 *Cheer up . . . Don't be afraid!* The Hebrew text reads "fear not . . . let not your hands hang limp." The latter verb means basically "be slack."

3:17 *a mighty savior.* Lit., "a warrior who saves." In the OT, *gibbor* [TH1368A, ZH1475] is employed most frequently "in connection with military activities, especially as a designation for a warrior, either a man who is eligible for military service or is able to bear arms, or one who has actually fought in combat, who has already distinguished himself by performing heroic deeds" (TDOT 2.374). God is called El Gibbor, "The Mighty God" (Isa 10:21; cf. the Messianic title in Isa 9:6), and as Israel's hero and warrior par excellence, he gains the victory (Ps 24:8-10; Isa 42:13; Hab 3:8-15) and delivers his people (Exod 15:2; Ps 68:17-20). Although Israel was saved by the Lord (Deut 33:29), their physical deliverance was an outward sign of God's spiritual relation to them (Ezek 37:20-28).

he will calm all your fears. Lit., "he will quiet you with/in his love." The verb *kharesh* [TH2790A, ZH3087] has been explained variously as (1) keeping silent about or covering up people's sins (Rashi), (2) God's silence due to the overwhelming depths of his love (Keil 1954), (3) God's preoccupation with planning Israel's good (Nowack 1922), (4) God's resting in his love (Laetsch 1956), (5) a means for the believer to cultivate peace and silence in his heart (Luther), (6) God's singing out of the joy of his loving concern (O'Connor 1980), and (7) God's refraining from bringing accusation of wrongdoing against Jerusalem (Ben Zvi). In addition, a relation to the Akkadian *eresu* (to desire) might be suggested.

The uncertainty of meaning here and the force of the verbs in the succeeding parallel lines ("rejoice," "exult") have caused many scholars to suggest an emendation to the verb *khadash* [TH2318, ZH2542] ("renew"; e.g., G. A. Smith; cf. LXX, Peshitta, NRSV, NJB). Although the alternate reading simply involves a common confusion between the Hebrew consonants daleth (ד) and resh (ר), the Masoretic reading is not altogether inappropriate—the thought of quieting being perhaps related to Israel's fear in 3:16.

with joyful songs. The word *berinnah* [TH871.2/7440, ZH928/8262] (with singing) is positioned last in the clause and in the verse so as to form an *inclusio* with *ranni* [TH7442, ZH8264] in v. 14. Verses 14-17 thus compose a strophe within the final stanza.

3:18 *I will gather you who mourn . . . you will be disgraced no more.* This verse has defied the interpretive efforts of all ages. Each of the ancient versions reads differently, and the renderings of modern translations and commentators likewise show marked variation. While there is general agreement as to the first half of the verse, the latter half has proved to be an insoluble crux. The verb translated "mourn" (*yagah* [TH3013, ZH3324]) could also be understood as belonging to the root *nug* [TH3013A, ZH5652] ("depart"; cf. the Ugaritic Keret Epic text reading: *wng mlk lbty*, "depart, O king, from my house"; Gordon 1965:250, lines 11-12). So construed, the first half of the sentence may be understood as "I will gather those who were driven from your appointed feasts." The Hebrew appears to add a further note regarding the fact that Jerusalem's deportees were carried away as booty (or tribute) by the city's conquerors. (For a discussion of the difficulties of the Hebrew syntax here, see Patterson 1991:384-386.)

Because the latter half of the verse contains the prepositional phrase *'aleha* [TH5921/1886.3, ZH6584/2023] (upon her), it may suggest that driving out the festival worshipers was a disgrace upon Jerusalem. So taken, one may understand that God will regather those who, due to Jerusalem's sin, were carried away as booty for the Babylonian army—a fact that stands as a reproach upon the holy city. The NLT, however, has made tolerable sense of the whole verse by stressing the regathering of the disgraced exiles to the festivals for which they have mourned so long. Thus understood, it prepares the reader for the details of 3:19.

3:19 *And I will deal severely with.* The Hebrew construction opens with *hineni* ("behold"; cf. KJV, ESV), emphasizing the certainty and the immediacy of the action. The verb *'asah* [TH6213, ZH6913] (do/make) followed by the particle *'et* [TH853, ZH906] is often used in the sense of "deal with" (e.g., Jer 21:2; Ezek 22:14; 23:25, 29). Thus, God will deal vigorously and swiftly with those who afflict his people.

weak and helpless ones. Lit., "the lame and the outcast." Berlin (1994:147) calls attention to the similar sentiment in Mic 4:6 and remarks, "The image is of a shepherd rescuing his sheep from predators and keeping them from straying. The shepherd image is commonly used for kings in the ancient Near East and this metaphor continues the picture of God as king in v. 15."

I will give glory and fame to my former exiles, wherever they have been mocked and shamed. The Hebrew text reads, "I will set them for praise and honor in all the land, their shame." The syntax of the clause is awkward. Because the prepositional phrase "in all the land" contains a definite article, it would be grammatically anomalous for "their shame" to be part of that construction (i.e., "in all the land of their shame"). Among the many proposals for understanding this crux, the simplest solution seems to be to relate "their shame" to the controlling verb of the sentence and translate, "I will turn their shame to praise and honor in (throughout) all the earth" (cf. NRSV, NASB). The NLT gives the sense of the passage.

3:20 *restore your fortunes.* The KJV (cf. LXX, NKJV; so also Robertson 1990) reads, "I will turn back your captivity." Because the idea of the restoration of the captives would appear to be a first step in the total blessing of the restored remnant, however, the reading of the NLT is widely adopted by modern translations and scholars (e.g., NIV, NRSV, Roberts 1991).

their very eyes. Lit., "your eyes"; cf. LXX, Vulgate, Targum. The NLT follows the lead of the Peshitta and some Greek mss. Note also Roberts (1991:222), who observes, "The context, however, which speaks of Israel's fame among all the nations, suggests that this will happen when God restores Israel's fortunes before the eyes of these nations. They will see God's salvation of Israel and form a new opinion about these formerly oppressed people (cf. Isa 52:10-15)."

COMMENTARY

The consideration of the eschatological Day of the Lord, with which the prophecy closes, lays emphasis upon the felicity and serenity attendant to restored Israel's final state. Zephaniah's words of instruction will doubtless be carried out: Sing for joy, shout aloud, be glad and rejoice (3:14). The commands are happy ones, heaped up to underscore the great expectation of the joyous times that lie beyond the immediate punishment. In that coming day, there will be singing and shouting, together with joy and rejoicing such as has never been known. Although the command was aimed at the future Jerusalem, the message would certainly not be lost on the godly worshipers of Zephaniah's own day.

In connection with this happy scene, Israel was again reminded that the guarantee of its happiness lies in the person of God himself. He, the righteous judge would deem their punishment completed and Jerusalem's correction accomplished. Accordingly, the judicial sentence may be commuted and God could now deal with his agents of chastisement. He would turn them away from his city and people and judge them for their sins. Moreover, Yahweh, Israel's king (Isa 44:6), would again dwell in his royal city. Cleansed by long ages of corrective judgment, Jerusalem will now be made permanently holy by the presence of the Holy One of Israel (cf. Isa 54:4-8; 57:14-19; 62:10-12; Ezek 48:35; Joel 3:17, 21).

The promise of the release from fear is accompanied by words of encouragement to the people not to let fright or anxiety grip their hearts. Zion's citizens will at last be free of the all-too-common fear that had left their hands hanging limp in despondency, paralyzed from terror. Each will remind the other of God's abiding presence. He, the sovereign Lord of the universe and Israel's heavenly warrior, would deliver them from their enemies, effect their redemption, and live among them in glory.

Here the Divine Warrior motif reaches its culmination. He who can sweep away all creation (1:2-3) and who fights against all idolatry (1:4-6) and injustice, whether in the pagan nations (2:4-15) or in his own people (1:7-13; 3:1-7), has appointed a day in which he will go out to battle against entrenched sin (1:14-18; 3:8, 15-17). He will deliver his people (3:14-15, 17) and bring everlasting peace in all the fullness that *shalom* [TH7965, ZH8934] connotes (completeness, health, prosperity, safety, and well-being) for all believing people (3:9-10, 14-20). Thus, the Scriptures record that God is not simply the biggest and most powerful of the so-called gods of the earth, as is so often portrayed in typical treatments of the Divine Warrior motif. Rather, he is the God whose purpose in revealing himself according to human cultural forms is not only the suppression of evil, but the supplying of mankind's full felicity. That which is best for man shall be realized in the person of a sovereign and gracious God who himself is the *summum bonum*, the ultimate good.

The theme of restoration and final felicity centers in the motif and theological teaching of the divine shepherd. Zephaniah's metaphor of the good shepherd is a familiar one in the Old Testament. The figure of the shepherd was assumed by God himself. He had led Israel all along the way (Gen 48:15; Ps 80:1), taking care of their needs (Ps 23:1-2), protecting and guiding them in accordance with his good purposes for them (Isa 40:9-11; cf. Ezek 34:12; Zech 9:15-16).

God announced through his prophets that he would send his own true shepherd, the Messiah, who would save and care for his flock (Ezek 34:22-24). Jesus Christ affirmed that he was that good shepherd who would lay down his life for the sheep (John 10:11-18). The New Testament writers reveal that Christ is also that great shepherd who cares for the well-being of his believing flock (Heb 13:20-21; cf. 1 Pet 2:25), and he is the chief shepherd who has entrusted his work to other "under shepherds" until he himself will come again for his flock (1 Pet 5:1-4). May we of the present Christian community live as good sheep under the care of faithful shepherds, looking forward to that day when our divine shepherd will return and make us to "lie down" in the "green pastures" of his eternal and bountiful provision.

BIBLIOGRAPHY

Anderson, G. W.
1969-1970 Some Observations on the Old Testament Doctrine of the Remnant. *Transactions of the Glasgow University Oriental Society* 23:1-10.
1977-1978 The Idea of the Remnant in the Book of Zephaniah. *Annual of the Swedish Theological Institute* 11:11-14.

Bailey, W.
1999 *Zephaniah.* New American Commentary, vol. 20. Nashville: Broadman & Holman.

Baker, D. W.
1988 *Nahum, Habakkuk, Zephaniah.* Tyndale Old Testament Commentaries. Downers Grove: InterVarsity.

Berlin, A.
1994 *Zephaniah.* The Anchor Bible. Garden City: Doubleday.

Ben Zvi, E.
1991 *A Historical-critical Study of the Book of Zephaniah.* Beiheft zur Zeitschrift für die Alttestamentliche Wissenschaft 198. Berlin: W. de Gruyter.

Cohen, A.
1985 *The Twelve Prophets.* Soncino Books of the Bible. 12th ed. New York: Soncino.

Craigie, P. C.
1985 *Twelve Prophets,* vol. 2. Philadelphia: Westminster.

Dahood, M.
1964, 1970 *Psalms.* The Anchor Bible. Garden City: Doubleday.

Delcor, M.
1978 Les Kerethim et les Cretois. *Vetus Testamentum* 28:409-422.

De Roche, M.
1980 Zephaniah I 2-3: The "Sweeping" of Creation. *Vetus Testamentum* 30:104-109.

Elliger, K.
1950 Das Ende der "Abendwolfe" Zeph 3, 3, Hab 1, 8. Pp. 158-175 in *Festschrift A. Bertholet.* Editor, W. Baumgartner. Tübingen: J. C. B. Mohr.

Feinberg, C. L.
1976 *The Minor Prophets.* Chicago: Moody.

Fishbane, M.
1985 *Biblical Interpretation in Ancient Israel.* Oxford: Clarendon.

Freeman, H. E.
1973 *Nahum, Zephaniah, Habakkuk.* Everyman's Bible Commentary. Chicago: Moody.

Gordis, R.
1987 A Rising Tide of Misery. *Vetus Testamentum* 37:487-490.

Gordon, C.
1965 *Ugaritic Textbook.* Rome: Pontifical Biblical Institute.

Haak, R. D.
1995 "Cush" in Zephaniah. Pp. 238-251 in *The Pitcher Is Broken: Memorial Essays for Gosta W. Ahlstrom.* Journal for the Study of the Old Testament Supplement 190. Sheffield: Sheffield Academic Press.

Hailey, H.
1971 *A Commentary on the Minor Prophets.* Grand Rapids: Baker.

Hannah, J. D.
1978 Zephaniah. Pp. 1523-1536 in *The Bible Knowledge Commentary.* Editors, J. F. Walvoord and R. B. Zuck. Wheaton: Victor.

Hasel, G. F.
1974 *The Remnant.* Berrien Springs: Andrews University Press.

Hulst, A. R.
1960 *Old Testament Translation Problems.* Leiden: Brill.

Hyatt, J. P.
1948 The Date and Background of Zephaniah. *Journal of Near Eastern Studies* 7:25-29.

Ihromi
1983 Die Haufung der Verben des Jubelns in Zephanja iii 14f., 16-18: *rnn, rw', smh³, 'lz, sws* und *gîl. Vetus Testamentum* 33:106-110.

Jastrow, M.
1950 *A Dictionary of the Targumim, the Talmud Babli and Yerushalmi, and the Midrashic Literature.* New York: Pardes.

Kapelrud, A. S.
1975 *The Message of the Prophet Zephaniah.* Oslo-Bergen-Troms: Universitetsforlaget.

Keil, C. F.
1954 *The Twelve Minor Prophets.* Biblical Commentary on the Old Testament, vol. 2. Translator, J. Martin. Grand Rapids: Eerdmans. (Orig. pub. 1873)

King, G.
1994 The Remnant Theme in Zephaniah. *Bibliotheca Sacra* 151:414-427.
1995 The Day of the Lord in Zephaniah. *Bibliotheca Sacra* 152:16-32.

Laetsch, T.
1956 *The Minor Prophets.* St. Louis: Concordia.

Lemaire, A.
1979 Note sur le titre *bn hmlk* dans l'ancien Israël. *Semitica* 29:106-110.

Luckenbill, D. D.
1927 *Ancient Records of Assyria and Babylonia.* Chicago: University of Chicago Press.

Nowack, W.
1922 *Die kleinen Propheten.* Handkommentar zum Alten Testament. Göttingen: Vandenhoeck & Ruprecht.

O'Connor, M.
1980 *Hebrew Verse Structure.* Winona Lake, IN: Eisenbrauns.

von Orelli, C.
1897 *The Twelve Minor Prophets.* Edinburgh: T & T Clark.

Patterson, R. D.
1990 A Literary Look at Nahum, Habakkuk, and Zephaniah. *Grace Theological Journal* 11:17-27.
1991 *Nahum, Habakkuk, Zephaniah.* Chicago: Moody.

Pusey, E. B.
1953 *The Minor Prophets,* vol. 2. Grand Rapids: Baker.

von Rad, G.
1959 The Origin of the Concept of the Day of Yahweh. *Journal of Semitic Studies* 4:97-108.

Rice, G.
1979 The African Roots of the Prophet Zephaniah. *The Journal of Religious Thought* 36:21-31.

Roberts, J. J. M.
1991 *Nahum, Habakkuk, and Zephaniah.* The Old Testament Library. Louisville: Westminster/John Knox.

Robertson, O. P.
1990 *The Books of Nahum, Habakkuk, and Zephaniah.* New International Commentary on the Old Testament. Grand Rapids: Eerdmans.

Rose, M.
1981 "Atheismus" als Wohlstandserscheinung? [Zeph 1,12]. *Theologische Zeitschrift* 37:193-208.

Sabottka, L.
1972 *Zephanja.* Rome: Biblical Institute Press.

Smith, G. A.
1929 *The Book of the Twelve Prophets,* vol. 2. Rev. ed. Garden City: Doubleday.

Smith, J. M. P.
1911 *A Critical and Exegetical Commentary on Zephaniah and Nahum.* The International Critical Commentary. Edinburgh: T & T Clark.

Smith, L. P., and E. R. Lacheman
1950 The Authorship of the Book of Zephaniah. *Journal of Near Eastern Studies* 9:137-142.

Smith, R. L.
1984 *Micah–Malachi.* Word Bible Commentary. Waco: Word.

Stuhlmueller, C.
1986 Justice toward the Poor. *The Bible Today* 24:385-390.

Sweeney, M. A.
1991 A Form-Critical Reassessment of the Book of Zephaniah. *Catholic Biblical Quarterly* 53:388-408.
2000 *The Twelve Prophets.* Berit Olam. Collegeville, MN: Liturgical.

VanGemeren, W. A.
1989 Zephaniah. Pp. 674-682 in *Evangelical Commentary on the Bible.* Editor, W. A. Elwell. Grand Rapids: Baker.

Walker, L.
1985 Zephaniah. Pp. 535-565 in *Daniel, Minor Prophets.* The Expositor's Bible Commentary, vol. 7. Editor, F. Gaebelein. Grand Rapids: Zondervan.

Warmington, B. H.
1964 *Carthage.* Baltimore: Penguin Books.

Willis, J. T.
1987 Alternating (ABA'B') Parallelism in the Old Testament Psalms and Prophetic Literature. Pp. 49-76 in *Directions in Biblical Hebrew Poetry.* Journal for the Study of the Old Testament Supplement 40. Editor, Elaine R. Follis. Sheffield: JSOT Press.

Wiseman, D. J.
1956 *Chronicles of Chaldaean Kings.* London: Trustees of the British Museum.

Würthwein, E.
1979 *The Text of the Old Testament.* 4th ed. Grand Rapids: Eerdmans.

Zalcman, L.
1986 Ambiguity and Assonance at Zephaniah ii 4. *Vetus Testamentum* 36:365-371.

Haggai

ANDREW E. HILL

INTRODUCTION TO
Haggai

THE PROPHET HAGGAI was a champion for the "homeless"—in this case, the "homeless" God of the Hebrew people. The Jerusalem Temple had been sacked and plundered by the Babylonians nearly 70 years earlier. Sadly, it still lay in ruins nearly two decades after the Hebrews had returned to Judah from exile in Babylon. Haggai's task was that of a herald sounding a wake-up call to a community that was spiritually "asleep." Haggai was quick to point out the disparity between the desolation of the Temple precinct and the comfortable homes occupied by his audience. Surely God deserved better! His message was an exhortation to "get up and go to work"— that is, get to work rebuilding the Jerusalem Temple. The book of Haggai is a "success story"—a rarity among the Old Testament prophets. The people obeyed (1:12), worked (1:14), and eventually completed rebuilding the Lord's Temple in Jerusalem four years later, in 515 BC (cf. Ezra 6:15).

AUTHOR
The book is silent on the issue of authorship, although it is assumed that the prophet Haggai penned his own oracles on the basis of the prophetic word formula ("the LORD gave a message through the prophet Haggai"; 1:1). The Hebrew name Haggai means "festal" and is related to the Hebrew word *khag* [TH2282, ZH2504] (procession, festival). This is a fitting name for the prophet who called the Hebrews to rebuild the Temple of God (which had been destroyed by the Babylonians) and to reinstate the festal worship of Yahweh in Jerusalem. The Bible records no biographic information for Haggai, but his prophetic ministry in postexilic Jerusalem is attested by Ezra (Ezra 6:14). Two expressions identify Haggai as a "spokesperson" for God. He is called "the prophet" (1:1; 2:10-11; Ezra 6:14), and he is labeled "the LORD's messenger" (1:13). Both titles verify the prophet's divine commission.

DATE AND OCCASION OF WRITING
The date formula in 1:1 (cf. NLT mg) serves to root the speeches of Haggai in a specific historical context: the early years of the great Persian Empire (539–330 BC). The speeches of Haggai are dated precisely to the day, month, and year of the rule of Darius I, king of Persia. King Darius I (Hystaspes) ruled Persia from 522–486 BC. The equivalents for the date formulas are listed below:

SPEECH	DATE IN DARIUS'S REIGN	MODERN EQUIVALENT
Haggai 1:1	Year 2, month 6, day 1	August 29, 520 BC
Haggai 2:1	Year 2, month 7, day 21	October 17, 520 BC
Haggai 2:10	Year 2, month 9, day 24	December 18, 520 BC
Haggai 2:20	Year 2, month 9, day 24	December 18, 520 BC

It seems likely the book was written sometime between Haggai's challenge to rebuild the Temple (520 BC) and the completion of its reconstruction (516/515 BC), since the prophet does not mention that event. The immediate occasion prompting the speeches of Haggai was very likely a severe drought affecting the province of postexilic Judah (1:11). It is this event that prompted God's messenger to address the more important occasion for his oracles—the continued desolation of God's Temple despite the return of the Hebrews from Babylonian captivity (1:4). A second issue related to the prophet's concern for the rebuilding of the Temple is the public affirmation of the leadership of the Judean state in the blessing of Jeshua (2:4, or "Joshua," NLT mg) and Zerubbabel (2:23).

A decree issued in 538 BC by Cyrus the Great, the first of the Persian kings, permitted conquered people groups who had been deported to Mesopotamia by the Babylonians to return to their homelands. The royal edict was issued on a clay cylinder, the famous Cyrus Cylinder. This pronouncement naturally included the Jews, although they are not named on the cylinder. The first wave of emigrants to Jerusalem numbered 42,360, along with 7,337 servants (Ezra 2:64-65). They were led by Sheshbazzar, a prince of Judah and the first governor of the restoration community in postexilic Judah (Ezra 1:5-11). The foundation for a new Temple was laid during the early stages of his administration, sometime in 538 or 537 BC (Ezra 5:16). The meager project was soon abandoned, however, and the construction site lay neglected for nearly two decades. Not until the preaching of Haggai in 520 BC did the initiative to rebuild the Jerusalem Temple resume (1:14). The second Temple was completed in March of 515 BC (cf. Ezra 6:15) under the auspices of the Persian king, Darius I. The monies granted for the rebuilding probably took the form of "tax rebates" to Judah from the Persian royal treasury.

AUDIENCE
Haggai's first two oracles (1:1-15 and 2:1-9) are specifically addressed to Zerubbabel, the governor, and Jeshua, the high priest—the two leaders of postexilic Jerusalem. As a part of these pronouncements, the prophet also spoke a word of encouragement to the people of Judah (1:13; 2:5). Haggai's third speech is directed to the priests (2:10-19), while the fourth prophecy is spoken exclusively to Zerubbabel, the governor of Judah (2:20-23). We also learn that Zerubbabel, Jeshua, and the people obeyed the words of Haggai and applied themselves to rebuilding God's Temple (1:14).

CANONICITY AND TEXTUAL HISTORY
Haggai is the tenth book in the collection known as the Minor Prophets (or the "Book of the Twelve" in the Hebrew Bible). The Twelve Prophets are usually grouped with the Latter Prophets and without exception are found in the earliest delineations of the Old Testament canon. These twelve books were always copied on one scroll in the ancient Hebrew manuscript tradition. The order of the Twelve Prophets does vary in some renditions of the canon of the Hebrew Bible, but the sequence of books from Nahum through Malachi seems quite stable in the various canon lists.[1]

The books of Haggai, Zechariah, and Malachi form a distinct subcollection or literary corpus within the Book of the Twelve. All three prophets belong to the period of early postexilic Hebrew history and are unified by literary device (e.g., the rhetorical question) and theological theme (cf. Pierce 1984a). The Haggai–Zechariah–Malachi corpus is sometimes described as a narrative profile of postexilic Jerusalem, recounting the spiritual history of the Hebrew restoration community (e.g., Pierce 1984b). Pierce (1984b:411) understands the record of the postexilic prophets more negatively as one of covenant failure, since Malachi ends where Haggai begins—with a religious community in disarray. Others interpret the "spiritual history" of the restoration community as recorded in the Haggai–Zechariah–Malachi corpus from the more hopeful perspective of worship renewal prompting the return of the community to Yahweh.[2]

According to Meyers and Meyers (1987:lxvii), the Hebrew text (the Masoretic Text) of Haggai is in an excellent state of preservation. Portions of Haggai are attested by fragments from the Dead Sea caves of Wadi Murabba'at for 1:12–2:10; 2:12-23, dated to the second century AD. Verhoef (1987:18) cites only two minor variations in the extant Dead Sea manuscripts (which have 289 out of a total of 600 words in Haggai).

The Septuagint largely corresponds to the Masoretic Text, although it does rearrange several verses (e.g., 1:9 and 10 are spliced together; 1:15 becomes 2:1, affecting versification for all of ch 2). Generally speaking, the Septuagint is marked by both expansionist (e.g., 2:9, 14, 21, 22) and harmonizing tendencies (e.g., 2:17, 21). The Vulgate, Peshitta, and the Targum are essentially faithful witnesses to the Masoretic Text (granting some influence of the LXX on the Peshitta and the Targum). See further the discussions of the text of Haggai in Verhoef (1987:18-20) and Merrill (1994:17-18).

LITERARY STYLE
The speeches of Haggai are essentially prose summaries set in the third person. The messages are "oracular" in nature. That is, they represent authoritative prophetic speech motivated or inspired by God himself. This kind of prophetic speech is often characterized by formulaic language. Several of these stylized expressions occur in Haggai, including a date formula (month, day, etc., 1:1; 2:1, 10, 20), the prophetic word formula ("the Lord gave/sent a message," 1:1; 2:1, 10, 20), the messenger formula ("says the Lord" [or variations], e.g., 1:7, 13; 2:4), and the covenant relationship

formula ("for I am with you" [or variations], e.g., 2:4-5). Though not a literary masterpiece like Isaiah or Jeremiah, the book of Haggai does give evidence of considerable literary polish. This is especially the case in the use of a rhetorical question to emphasize a point in three of the four messages (e.g., 1:4; 2:3, 19 [cf. NASB]), the repetition of words or phrases to set a tone or mood (e.g., the repeated imperative "look at what's happening /think carefully" [or variations] in 1:5, 7; 2:15, 18), and even wordplay on occasion—for instance, the similar sounds of the words translated "ruins" (khareb [TH2720, ZH2992], 1:4) and "drought" (khoreb [TH2721, ZH2996], 1:11).

MAJOR THEMES

Haggai was a prophet with one mission—to stir the postexilic Jewish community to action in rebuilding the Jerusalem Temple, which had been sacked and plundered nearly 70 years earlier by the Babylonians. Beyond this, his four speeches were designed to awaken the residents of postexilic Jerusalem to the responsibilities, obligations, privileges, and promises of their covenant heritage.

The prophet's appeal for the reconstruction of the Temple building should not be construed as a contradiction of Jeremiah's warning about misplaced trust in a sacred building (Jer 7:4). Rather, Haggai underscored the importance of worship in the life of the Hebrew community and the need for a sanctuary so that the worship of Yahweh could take place properly, according to the law of Moses. He assumed that the appropriate attitudes of reverence, humility, and unfeigned behavior in obedience to the commandments of God would naturally accompany the worship conducted in the restored Temple (note the prophet's charge to the community to reflect upon their ways [1:5, 7; 2:15] and the response of obedience and worship on the part of the people [1:12]).

Haggai also emphasized the abiding presence of God's Spirit (1:13; 2:4-5), a theme shared with the book of Zechariah (cf. Zech 1:16; 4:6; 7:12). This pronouncement so sparked the enthusiasm of the leadership and the people that they began the work of rebuilding the Temple (1:14). It is possible Haggai intended his message concerning this restored presence of God in the postexilic community of Judah as a fulfillment of Ezekiel's earlier promise that God would again make his home among his people (Ezek 37:27-28).

The book presents two additional themes that are less developed: the divine blessing of prosperity bestowed upon the postexilic Hebrew community (2:7-9, 19), and the overthrow of the nations (2:20-22). Both connect the message of Haggai with the larger eschatological themes of Old Testament prophetic literature: God's promise of blessing to Israel and God's threat of judgment upon the nations. According to Ezra, postexilic Judah did realize a partial fulfillment of God's blessing as a result of the ministry of Haggai and Zechariah (Ezra 6:14).

THEOLOGICAL CONCERNS

Each of Haggai's four messages highlights a different theological concern that the prophet had for postexilic Judah. The first (1:1-15) is the call to the people of Jerusalem to reprioritize community life. Haggai directed the leadership of the Judean province to move out of their self-absorption by focusing on the restoration of proper worship of God (by means of the Temple liturgy) instead of focusing on the ease and security of their own "luxurious houses" (1:4).

The second message (2:1-9) assured the postexilic Hebrew community that God had not forgotten those previous promises of blessing and restoration made by earlier prophets like Isaiah, Jeremiah, and Ezekiel. It was important for community morale to understand that Haggai stood in the revered train of those prophetic predecessors. By his word of blessing and promise of restoration, he confirmed the continuity of his message with previous prophetic utterances concerning God's plan for the restoration of Israel after the Babylonian exile. These were not just more empty words of "hope deferred" to bolster a beleaguered remnant, these were the words of God's promise to his chosen people.

Ritual purity (both for the priests and the people) is the dominant theme of the third message (2:10-19). Haggai reminded his audience that the injunctions of the Law of Moses are still operative. God expected his people to be holy, even as he is holy (Lev 11:44-45).

Haggai's final, and perhaps most important message (2:20-23), reestablished the prominence of the Davidic line in the religious and political life of the nation of Israel. The Davidic dynasty was singled out as the key to the restoration of the Hebrew people after the Babylonian exile (cf. Jer 23:5; 33:15; Ezek 37:24). Tragically, God was forced to pronounce the curse of judgment upon King Jehoiachin (and the line of David) at the time of the Exile (Jer 22:24-30). Haggai's last speech overturns that curse of judgment upon the lineage of David and reinstates that ancient covenant of David as the vehicle by which God intended to make good on his promises of blessing and restoration to Israel (note especially the echo of the "signet ring" in Jer 22:24 and Hag 2:23; cf. Wolf 1976:54-55).

OUTLINE

ENDNOTES

1. See B. A. Jones, *The Formation of the Book of the Twelve: A Study in Text and Canon*, SBL Dissertation Series 149 (Atlanta: Scholars Press, 1995), 43-54.
2. For example, see D. A. Schneider, "The Unity of the Book of the Twelve." (Ph.D. diss., Yale University, 1979), 144-149.

COMMENTARY ON
Haggai

◆ I. First Message: Haggai's Challenge to Covenant Renewal (1:1–15)
   A. The Call to Reconsider Priorities (1:1–6)

On August 29* of the second year of King Darius's reign, the LORD gave a message through the prophet Haggai to Zerubbabel son of Shealtiel, governor of Judah, and to Jeshua* son of Jehozadak, the high priest.

²"This is what the LORD of Heaven's Armies says: The people are saying, 'The time has not yet come to rebuild the house of the LORD.'"

³Then the LORD sent this message through the prophet Haggai: ⁴"Why are you living in luxurious houses while my house lies in ruins? ⁵This is what the LORD of Heaven's Armies says: Look at what's happening to you! ⁶You have planted much but harvest little. You eat but are not satisfied. You drink but are still thirsty. You put on clothes but cannot keep warm. Your wages disappear as though you were putting them in pockets filled with holes!

1:1a Hebrew *On the first day of the sixth month,* of the ancient Hebrew lunar calendar. A number of dates in Haggai can be cross-checked with dates in surviving Persian records and related accurately to our modern calendar. This event occurred on August 29, 520 B.C. 1:1b Hebrew *Joshua,* a variant spelling of Jeshua; also in 1:12, 14.

NOTES

1:1 the LORD gave a message. Lit., "the word of the LORD came." The combination of the verb "to be" (*hayah* [TH1961, ZH2118]) and the phrase "the word of the LORD" (*debar-yhwh* [TH1697/3068, ZH1821/3378]) constitutes the prophetic word formula. The formula introduces a report of a prophetic revelation in the oracular speech of the OT.

through. This preposition translates *beyad* [TH871.2/3027, ZH928/3338] ("by the hand of") and denotes writing or speaking, a genitive of authorship (Waltke and O'Connor 1990:9.5.1c).

the prophet Haggai. The word *nabi'* [TH5030, ZH5566] (prophet) designates Haggai as an emissary, one who speaks with the authority of the commissioning agent.

Jeshua. The MT actually gives the name "Joshua" throughout Haggai, of which "Jeshua" is a variant (also in 1:12, 14; 2:1, 4). Both names are derived from the Hebrew root *yasha'* [TH3467, ZH3828], which means "to save, deliver." The NLT has opted to use the spelling "Jeshua" in Haggai (and elsewhere, e.g., Zech 3:3-9) to make a distinction between this high priest and the much earlier (and better known) leader of Israel by the same name, Joshua son of Nun (cf. Deut 31:1-8; Joshua).

1:2 This is what the LORD of Heaven's Armies says. This Hebrew construction (*koh 'amar* [TH3541/559, ZH3907/606] *yhwh tseba'oth*) constitutes the messenger formula in prophetic speech and signifies the oral transmission of a message by a third party. The term suggests the divine assembly or council of the gods in ancient Near Eastern thought. The messenger of the council stands as an observer in council sessions and then reports what he has heard as an envoy of the council to others (cf. ABD 2.214-217).

LORD *of Heaven's Armies.* This title for God is prominent in prophetic literature. It is Haggai's favorite designation for God (found 14 times, 1:2, 5, 7, 9, 14; 2:4, 6, 7, 8, 9[2], 11, 23[2]). The expression is often understood as a construct-genitive: "the LORD of Hosts." More precisely the construction is one of absolute nouns in apposition, perhaps conveying a verbal force: "Yahweh *creates* [angel] armies" (cf. TDOT 5.515). In either case, the epithet emphasizes "the invincible might behind the Lord's commands" (Baldwin 1972:39).

the time has not yet come. The NLT follows the LXX here, perhaps understanding the noun "time" (*'eth,* in the construction *eth-bo'* [TH6256/935, ZH6961/995]) as the adverb "yet" (*'attah* [TH6258, ZH6964], "now, yet"; cf. Baldwin 1972:39-40).

**1:3 Then the LORD *sent this message through.* The repetition of the prophetic word formula and the genitive of authorship (see v. 1 above) underscore the importance and divine source of the message and the urgency of the hour.

1:4 Why . . . ? The rhetorical question is an emphatic device in prophetic literature requiring agreement with the expected answer to the question rather than a formal reply (Waltke and O'Connor 1990:40.3.b; cf. 2:3, 19 in MT).

luxurious houses. This understanding of the word *sepunim* [TH5603, ZH6211] (often rendered "paneled") assumes that the contrast is between the elaborate homes of the people and the ruined Temple. Alternately, the contrast may be between the "finished" homes of the people and "the unfinished and thus unusable House of Yahweh" (Meyers and Meyers 1987:23).

ruins. The word *khareb* [TH2720, ZH2992] seems to be a deliberate echo of Jer 33:10-12, the promise of restoration for the "ruins" of Jerusalem.

**1:5 Look *at what's happening to you!* The repetition of this clause in the imperative mood (1:5, 7; 2:15) calls attention to the issue of volition or will—the people must choose to reflect and act upon the prophet's message. The positive imperative further stresses the urgency of the hour and demands an immediate and specific response on the part of the addressee(s) (Waltke and O'Connor 1990:34.4a).

**1:6 eat . . . drink . . . put on clothes.* The form of the Hebrew verb used in each case is the infinitive absolute conveying continuous action (cf. *The Message,* "you keep filling your plates . . . you keep drinking and drinking . . . you put on layer after layer of clothes.").

pockets filled with holes! Lit., "to a pierced bag," a purse with holes. The image emphasizes the instantaneous loss of a portion of wages earned (cf. Meyers and Meyers 1987:26). It is unlikely that a laborer's wages were paid in coinage at this early period. Baldwin (1972:41) suggests that the moneybag would have contained discs or wedges of copper, silver, or the like, approximately defined in value by weight.

COMMENTARY

Each of Haggai's four messages includes a date formula assigning the speech to the precise day and month in the second year of King Darius's rule over Persia. This practice has its precedent in the prophecies of Jeremiah and Ezekiel (cf. Jer 1:2-3; Ezek 1:1). Unlike their preexilic predecessors, exilic prophets such as Jeremiah and Ezekiel were unable to consistently date their revelations according to the reigns of the kings of Israel and Judah. Instead, they keyed their oracles to the year of Babylonian exile. The prophet Jeremiah had indicated that this banishment from the land of promise for punishment of covenant violations would last 70 years (Jer 25:11; 29:10). The exilic year-date formula thus served as a "covenant time clock" of sorts, marking the duration of the curse of captivity and counting down (with anticipation and hope) toward the promised blessing of release and restoration (cf. Jer 52:31; Ezek 20:1).

The postexilic prophets Haggai and Zechariah dated their prophecies to exact dates during the days of Persian rule because earlier Isaiah foresaw the importance of King Cyrus and the Persians to the fortunes of elect Israel (Isa 45:1-13). It seems likely that both Haggai and Zechariah were also influenced by Ezekiel's vision of the Temple (Ezek 40–48). The rebuilding of the Jerusalem Temple was understood as the cornerstone event of the long-awaited messianic age. The chronological precision attached to their oracles served as an important reminder of Yahweh's faithfulness to his covenant promises (Ps 111:9) and his good intentions to restore unified kingship in Israel under the prince of David (cf. Ezek 37:15-28).

Haggai's audience had assumed that the time had not yet come to rebuild the Lord's Temple (1:2). Apparently, the restoration community in Jerusalem was still struggling to establish itself politically and economically. The degree of self-sufficiency attained was understood to be sub-par, at least to the extent that the people calculated that it was unwise to siphon off already meager resources for the sake of investing in a high profile campaign like rebuilding Yahweh's Temple. Haggai's contemporary, Zechariah, also discerned that the real issue was one of self-interest when he proclaimed, "aren't you eating and drinking just to please yourselves?" (Zech 7:6). The episode calls to mind the words of Jesus in the New Testament: "Seek the Kingdom of God above all else, and live righteously, and he will give you everything you need" (Matt 6:33).

Those who argued for fiscal responsibility knew that the realities of an economic recession meant it was no time to take on the funding of "special projects" (cf. Zech 8:10, "Before the work on the Temple began, there were no jobs and no money to hire people. . . . No traveler was safe."). Yet Haggai knew, like Hosea, that "now is the time to seek the LORD" (Hos 10:12).

Implicit in Haggai's rhetorical question that compares the "living quarters" of the people of Judah with those of their God (1:4) is the issue of priority in the stewardship and distribution of resources. The people of Haggai's time consciously chose personal well-being over the well-being of God as manifest in the worship and service associated with his Temple. This pattern of attempting to satisfy religious obligations with half-hearted worship and second-rate offerings persisted into Malachi's time with the presentation of inferior animal sacrifices (Mal 1:8). Haggai inferred that the things of God should be our highest priority and that God is worthy of the very best that we might offer him in worship and service. This is true simply because he alone is God (Isa 45:5-6). This is also true because as Creator, God "owns" everything anyway (Pss 24:1; 50:11-12). And this was especially true for the Hebrews because of the mandate to present "choice" or "best" samples of the agricultural firstfruits to God (Exod 23:19; 34:26). Ultimately, even the biblical injunction to offer God our best is but an external symbol of an internal reality. God is far more interested in our hearts than he is in receiving our "choice offerings" or even a "palatial abode" as a result of our labors. King David understood this when he said,

"The sacrifice you desire is a broken spirit. You will not reject a broken and repentant heart, O God" (Ps 51:17). Likewise, the Apostle Paul urged the faithful to establish a similar spiritual platform for expressing devotion to God: "give your bodies to God because of all he has done for you. Let them be a living and holy sacrifice—the kind he will find acceptable" (Rom 12:1).

The Old Testament prophets often interpreted current events affecting the corporate life of the Israelites through the lens of covenant blessings and curses (cf. Deut 28). Haggai proves no exception, as he understood the calamity of drought (or perhaps blight, 1:6) as the hand of the Lord Almighty at work in the realm of nature (cf. Zech 10:1, "he makes the storm clouds"). The law of Moses forecasts just such a scenario for the people of Israel should they violate Yahweh's covenant. The catalog of divine punishments for disobedience includes drought, such that "all your work will be for nothing" (Lev 26:19-20).

God's intent in all of this was not capricious judgment for the purpose of destruction, since he affirmed he would not cancel his covenant with Israel (Lev 26:44-45). Instead, God would speak to his people through the economic circumstances of "supply and demand" in order to restore them to right relationship with himself. The poor standard of living experienced by the postexilic community (further eroded by inflation, cf. Mason 1977:16) was designed to instruct the people in the matter of priorities (cf. Verhoef 1987:57ff). Divine punishment may be disciplinary (sometimes severe but deserved), as Jeremiah recognized (Jer 30:11; 31:18). Haggai was also aware that on occasion God must discipline Israel like a father who must punish his wayward son, but always with love (cf. Jer 31:20; Heb 12:5-11).

Haggai's call to rebuild the Temple of Yahweh should not be construed as some kind of "magical incantation" holding the promise of a remedy for the many problems facing the postexilic Hebrew community. God cannot be manipulated into showering material blessings upon his people because of the works of their hands (1:5-6; cf. Achtemeier 1986:98-99). Nor should Haggai's message be viewed in contradiction to the words of warning pronounced by Jeremiah concerning misplaced trust in the physical structure of the Temple (Jer 7:4). Rather, Haggai summoned the people to the proper worship of God in contrast to blind faith in a "sacred building."

The appropriate attitudes of reverence and humility and a genuine posture of obedience to the law of God identified explicitly in Zechariah (e.g., Zech 7:4-10) are implicit in Haggai. The prophet knew the "Temple theology" of King Solomon's prayer of dedication—God does not dwell in houses made with human hands (1 Kgs 8:23ff). The prophet also knew the "worship theology" of his predecessors—God desires mercy, not sacrifice (Hos 6:6; Mic 6:8). Haggai understood that reviving the flow of God's covenantal blessings to Israel was contingent upon the people's careful and heartfelt obedience to the commandments of Yahweh's covenant—not merely the rebuilding of the Jerusalem sanctuary (cf. Deut 28:1-2, 9, 13).

◆   ## B. The Call to Rebuild the Temple (1:7-11)

⁷"This is what the LORD of Heaven's Armies says: Look at what's happening to you! ⁸Now go up into the hills, bring down timber, and rebuild my house. Then I will take pleasure in it and be honored, says the LORD. ⁹You hoped for rich harvests, but they were poor. And when you brought your harvest home, I blew it away. Why? Because my house lies in ruins, says the LORD of Heaven's Armies, while all of you are busy building your own fine houses. ¹⁰It's because of you that the heavens withhold the dew and the earth produces no crops. ¹¹I have called for a drought on your fields and hills—a drought to wither the grain and grapes and olive trees and all your other crops, a drought to starve you and your livestock and to ruin everything you have worked so hard to get."

NOTES

1:7 The Hebrew of this verse is an exact repetition of v. 5, minus the introductory adverb "now" (*'attah* [TH6258, ZH6964]).

Look at what's happening to you! The exhortation to reflect upon current conditions in Judah anticipates the prophet's cause-and-effect argument in 2:15-19.

1:8 *Now go up into the hills, bring down timber.* Meyers and Meyers (1987:28) suggest this verse refers to procuring lumber for construction equipment (like ramps, ladders, scaffolds, etc.), not the actual building materials. It is presumed that the local stands of trees around postexilic Jerusalem would have been insufficient to meet the demands of the Temple project, given the deforestation of the Jerusalem area during the Babylonian siege of the city and the timber required for the subsequent rebuilding of the city after the return from exile. See further the discussion in Taylor and Clendenen 2004:129, who suggest that the precedent of superior lumber from places like Lebanon for the construction of the first Temple may have been an issue as well.

be honored. See the discussion of this verb (*kabed* [TH3513, ZH3877]), which occurs here in its Niphal stem (possibly preserving a rare subjunctive ending—"that I may be glorified"), in Meyers and Meyers 1987:28.

1:9 *but they were poor.* The NLT agrees with the ancient versions (LXX, Syriac, Targum), understanding *hinneh* [TH2009, ZH2180] ("behold," cf. NASB) as the infinitive absolute *hayoh* [TH1961, ZH2118] ("they were," NLT). The meaning is roughly the same in either case.

And when you brought your harvest home. This may refer to the bulk of the grain harvest kept by the worshiper after the firstfruits sacrifices had been made at the altar (which had been rebuilt and put to use immediately by the restoration community during the reign of Cyrus; Ezra 3:2-3). Meyers and Meyers (1987:3, 29) translate this as "what you have brought to the House" and understand the expression as a reference to the firstfruits offerings themselves.

my house lies in ruins. The repetition of this clause completes an envelope construction, or *inclusio*, linking 1:4 and 1:9.

says the LORD of Heaven's Armies. The divine utterance formula (*ne'um yhwh tseba'oth* [TH5002, ZH5536]) is a nominal exclamation and is usually a closing formula in the prophets (Waltke and O'Connor 1990: 40.2.3a; cf. v. 13).

1:10 *the dew.* The NLT retains the MT's *mittal* ("from dew"), reading the noun *tal* [TH2919, ZH3228] (few), with a partitive *min* [TH4480, ZH4946] (from) prefixed to it (Waltke and O'Connor 1990:11.2.11e). Cf. BHS, which proposes "rain" (*matar* [TH4305, ZH4763], so NJB).

1:11 *drought.* Note the wordplay with "drought" (*khoreb* [TH2721, ZH2996]) and "ruin" (*khareb* [TH2720, ZH2992], 1:4).

COMMENTARY

The compound name "LORD of Heaven's Armies" is Haggai's favorite title for God. The exact meaning of the epithet is still the subject of much debate (see note on 1:2). Generally, commentators have understood the title to emphasize the absolute authority intrinsic to God's words and the sovereign power inherent in his command of the angelic hosts. Haggai, however, extended the idea of God's sovereignty to the realm of nature, specifically the agricultural productivity of the postexilic community ("harvests," 1:9 and "crops," 1:10-11). Seemingly, the people made no connection between their bleak situation and the rule of God in nature. Yet such associations should have been obvious from the terms of Yahweh's covenant with Israel (cf. Lev 26 and Deut 28). In fact, Haggai assumed his audience should have recognized divine activity in all spheres of life based upon their knowledge of previous Israelite experiences (e.g., the blight intended to bring people to repentance, as mentioned in Amos 4:6-10). We can only marvel at the profound subtlety of God in withholding something as mundane as dew (necessary to preserve ripening grain from the summer heat) to rebuke human pride and self-sufficiency (cf. Baldwin 1972:42).

Haggai summoned his audience to consider their circumstances four times in two brief chapters (1:5, 7; 2:15, 18). The Hebrew idiom (*sim* [TH7760, ZH8492] + *lebab* [TH3824, ZH4222]) rendered "look at what's happening" or "think about this" in the NLT is literally "to set one's heart" (or "ponder, consider, set one's mind," TDOT 7.409-410). The expression calls attention to the issue of human will or volition. The prophet exhorted the people to engage in careful reflection that would result in a change of heart or mind. They pursued a single policy, one of self-interest and personal well-being. Haggai urged the people to adopt a new agenda, one that elevated the glory of God and divine interests above the quest for the "good life." Craigie (1984:139-140) has aptly observed that the community "had adopted a policy of fending first for themselves." Though eminently practical, this policy was flawed because it skewed priorities. The fundamental priority in life for the righteous must always be God, not personal desires (cf. Craigie 1984:141).

The Covenant Code of Mount Sinai (Exod 21–23) gave the Hebrews ample warning that God must curse any human initiative motivated by an arrogant spirit and all achievement accomplished in hostility toward and rebellion against God (cf. Lev 26:19-20). The psalmist reflected on that covenant tradition poetically when he composed the familiar lines, "unless the LORD builds a house, the work of the builders is wasted" (Ps 127:1). Indeed, Haggai may have had this text in mind as he observed the futility of working "so hard" apart from cooperation with God in a spirit of faith and obedience (1:11; cf. Ps 127:2, "anxiously working"). It is apparent that the prophet also was acquainted with earlier wisdom sayings, especially in his agreement with the sage that plans will succeed only when one's work has been committed to the Lord (Prov 16:3; cf. 16:9; 19:21; 21:30). This theological principle transfers to the New Testament as evidenced in the teachings of both Jesus ("Seek the Kingdom of God above all else, and live righteously, and he will give you everything you need," Matt 6:33) and Paul ("Think about the things of heaven, not the things of earth," Col 3:2).

◆   C. The Response of the Remnant (1:12-15)

¹²Then Zerubbabel son of Shealtiel, and Jeshua son of Jehozadak, the high priest, and the whole remnant of God's people began to obey the message from the LORD their God. When they heard the words of the prophet Haggai, whom the LORD their God had sent, the people feared the LORD. ¹³Then Haggai, the LORD's messenger, gave the people this message from the LORD: "I am with you, says the LORD!"

¹⁴So the LORD sparked the enthusiasm of Zerubbabel son of Shealtiel, governor of Judah, and the enthusiasm of Jeshua son of Jehozadak, the high priest, and the enthusiasm of the whole remnant of God's people. They began to work on the house of their God, the LORD of Heaven's Armies, ¹⁵on September 21* of the second year of King Darius's reign.

1:15 Hebrew *on the twenty-fourth day of the sixth month,* of the ancient Hebrew lunar calendar. This event occurred on September 21, 520 B.C.; also see note on 1:1a.

NOTES

1:12 *the whole remnant.* The repetition of this phrase in 1:14 emphasizes the unity of purpose within the restoration community for the rebuilding project.

whom the LORD their God had sent. Some commentators read "whom Yahweh had sent to them" (emending the MT's *'elohehem* [TH430/1992.1, ZH466/2157] to *'alehem* [TH413/3963.15, ZH448/4392]) on the basis of the LXX (*pros autous* [TG4314/846, ZG4639/899], "to them"; see Petersen 1984:55). Other ancient versions (Syriac and Vulgate) read, "Yahweh their God sent him to them" (recognizing haplography and inserting *'alehem* [TH413/3963.15, ZH448/4392] after *'elohehem*; see Meyers and Meyers 1987:4). Verhoef (1987:82-83) rejects the emendation based upon scribal omission, arguing that the relative pronoun "whom" (*ka'asher* [TH3509.1/834, ZH3869/889]) refers not to the prophet but to his message ("which the LORD their God had sent him," cf. NJB).

1:13 *the LORD's messenger . . . this message from the LORD.* This unusual prophetic title may be explained by the presence of the wordplay of "messenger" (*mal'ak* [TH4397, ZH4855]) with the "message" in the following phrase (*bemal'akuth* [TH4400, ZH4857]). The title ascribes distinctive authority to Haggai as Yahweh's agent (cf. Petersen 1984:56).

I am with you. This is a covenant formula assuring the audience of God's personal presence and support in the building project (cf. Gen 26:3; Isa 41:10; 43:5; Jer 30:11).

1:14 *sparked the enthusiasm.* Lit., "stirred the spirit" (*ya'ar* [TH5782, ZH6424] + *ruakh* [TH7307, ZH8120]), frequently attributed to God's sovereign work in rousing people to accomplish his purposes (e.g., Ezra 1:1; Isa 13:17; 41:25; Jer 51:1, 11).

1:15 *the second year of King Darius's reign.* This concludes 1:15. The first verse of ch 2 reads, "On the twenty-first day of the seventh month . . ." and gives no regnal year. Most commentators assume that the reference to "the second year of King Darius's reign" in 2:1 has been lost in the MT due to haplography. Meyers and Meyers (1987:37) suggest the single reference to "the second year of King Darius's reign" at the end of 1:15 serves double duty in both date formulas (i.e., 1:15 and 2:1).

COMMENTARY

Haggai's use of the word "remnant" (*she'erith* [TH7611, ZH8642]) has triggered considerable debate among biblical commentators. No consensus has emerged as to the theological nuance the prophet intended when he addressed postexilic Judah as "the whole remnant of God's people" (1:12). Some have understood the term to refer to a core of righteous people embedded within the larger Hebrew community (Baldwin 1972:42; Mason 1977:17). Others doubt that the word "remnant" has any special theological connotations, noting that this expression is simply one of several the prophet utilizes (e.g., "the people," 1:2, 12; "all you people," 2:4; "this people," 2:14) to designate the people of the covenant (Verhoef 1987:81; cf. Meyers and Meyers 1987:34). In fact, the use here does seem to designate the entirety rather than only a portion of the people. The text is simply reporting the fact that the whole community responded to the prophet's message. This demonstration of unity of spirit and commonality of purpose was so striking it merited recording. More important, and often overlooked, is the following prepositional phrase "of God's people." The theological thrust of the verse is God's faithfulness in preserving an element of his elect nation and reestablishing them in the land of the promise. He is a God who "always remembers his covenant" (Ps 111:5).

The section reporting the response of the remnant to Haggai's message offers an interesting sequence of verbal action. First, the people obeyed (1:12). Next, we learn that the people "feared the LORD" (1:12). Finally, we are told that the people began their work on the house of the Lord (1:14). This ordering reinforces the biblical pattern of "worship" followed by "service." A similar model of response to God may be seen in the post-Exodus experience of Israel at Mount Sinai. There the obedience of the people to the directives of Moses included acts of preparation necessary for entering God's presence (Exod 19:14). The subsequent experience of formal worship (Exod 24:1) prompted acts of service in the form of giving to the construction of the Tabernacle (Exod 25:2-3).

The New Testament confirms this basic outline in the gospel account of the commissioning of the eleven disciples (Matt 28:16-20). The followers of Jesus obeyed by traveling to the mountain to which he had directed them, and there they worshiped (Matt 28:16). Only after acknowledging God in worship were the disciples instructed to go and serve in the name of Christ (Matt 28:19-20; cf. Heb 13:15-16 where the sacrifice of praise motivates sacrifices of doing good). All of this agrees in principle with Webber's second fundamental theme of worship: "God speaks and acts and the people respond . . . by remembering, anticipating, celebrating, and serving" (1994:27).

Interestingly, the Protestant "restoration" movement of the eighteenth century, founded by Thomas Campbell and others, appealed to texts like Haggai 1:12-14 (obey, worship, work) and 1 Thessalonians 1:9-10 (turn, serve, wait) in their attempts to recover the unity of the church by means of returning to biblical patterns of doctrine, worship, church discipline, and church government.

Haggai is described as "the LORD's messenger" only in 1:13. The title is unusual but not unique. In general, the Old Testament identifies the prophets and the priests as "messengers of God" (2 Chr 36:16; see also Mal 2:7). More specifically, the name of the prophet Malachi means "my messenger." Malachi announced the coming of another divine messenger as a forerunner of the Day of the Lord (Mal 3:1; usually identified as John the Baptist on the basis of Matt 11:14). This word, "messenger" (*mal'ak* [TH4397, ZH4855]), signifies an agent entrusted with a word of revelation from God. The term is sometimes associated with the divine council or assembly of the gods motif common to the earliest mythic literature of the ancient Near East (e.g., Meyers and Meyers 1987:7, 35; cf. ABD 2.214-217). By analogy, the Hebrew prophets are understood to act as couriers of the council of Yahweh. As a member of the council, the prophet hears the proclamation of Yahweh and is commissioned to report the exact word of revelation directly to the people. This helps account for the repetition of the numerous speech formulas in prophetic literature. Yahweh's prophets uttered the appropriate speech formulas to validate their role as divine messengers, clarify the source of the message, the fact of its transmission, and the authority of its contents (cf. Meyers and Meyers 1987; see notes on the prophetic word formula [1:1], the messenger formula [1:2], and the divine utterance formula [1:9]). The prophetic epithet, "the LORD's messenger," is important theologically for two reasons: First, it legitimizes the human messenger or agent as a true representative of the Godhead; second, it invests the message with divine authority and guarantees its authenticity as a true word from God. It is possible that Peter had this divine council imagery in mind when he wrote that "no prophecy . . . ever came from the prophet's own understanding . . . . No, those prophets were moved by the Holy Spirit, and they spoke from God" (2 Pet 1:20-21).

◆ II. Second Message: The Promise of Restoration (2:1-9)

Then on October 17 of that same year,* the LORD sent another message through the prophet Haggai. ²"Say this to Zerubbabel son of Shealtiel, governor of Judah, and to Jeshua* son of Jehozadak, the high priest, and to the remnant of God's people there in the land: ³'Does anyone remember this house—this Temple—in its former splendor? How, in comparison, does it look to you now? It must seem like nothing at all! ⁴But now the LORD says: Be strong, Zerubbabel. Be strong, Jeshua son of Jehozadak, the high priest. Be strong, all you people still left in the land. And now get to work, for I am with you, says the LORD of Heaven's Armies. ⁵My Spirit remains among you, just as I promised when you came out of Egypt. So do not be afraid.'

⁶"For this is what the LORD of Heaven's Armies says: In just a little while I will again shake the heavens and the earth, the oceans and the dry land. ⁷I will shake all the nations, and the treasures of all the nations will be brought to this Temple. I will fill this place with glory, says the LORD of Heaven's Armies. ⁸The silver is mine, and the gold is mine, says the LORD of Heaven's Armies. ⁹The future glory of this Temple will be greater than its past glory, says the LORD of Heaven's Armies. And in this place I will bring peace. I, the LORD of Heaven's Armies, have spoken!"

2:1 Hebrew *on the twenty-first day of the seventh month,* of the ancient Hebrew lunar calendar. This event (in the second year of Darius's reign) occurred on October 17, 520 B.C.; also see note on 1:1a.   2:2 Hebrew *Joshua,* a variant spelling of Jeshua; also in 2:4.

NOTES

2:1 *that same year.* Cf. NLT mg. See note on 1:15.

2:2 *and to the remnant.* Meyers and Meyers (1987:47) read "and to *all* the rest of the people" (inserting *kol* [TH3605, ZH3972] in the MT, following the LXX and Syriac).

2:3 The rhetorical question is one of the literary features unifying the Haggai–Zechariah–Malachi corpus (cf. Pierce 1984a). See note on 1:4.

2:4 *Be strong.* The threefold repetition of the imperative verb "be strong" (*khazaq* [TH2388, ZH2616]) marks the shift from rebuke and challenge to encouragement and affirmation in the prophet's message (cf. Achtemeier 1986:102).

2:5 *just as I promised.* Lit., "the word I cut with you." The verb *karath* [TH3772, ZH4162] and the noun *berith* [TH1285, ZH1382] form the Hebrew idiom for making a covenant (see Gen 15:9-10). This combination of the verb *karath* and the noun *dabar* [TH1697, ZH1821] (word) is exceptional, no doubt intended by the prophet to underscore the continuity of Yahweh's activity in delivering his people—first from Egypt and then from Babylonia. Petersen (1984:61) considers the clause a prosaic intrusion in the prophet's poetic discourse (esp. since the LXX omits these words; cf. NEB). Baldwin (1972:47) suggests the scribal marginal reference to Exod 29:45-46 was eventually incorporated into the text. Verhoef (1987:100) correctly argues for the originality of the line on the basis of the context of 2:4 (as an elaboration of God's promise to be with his people). Meyers and Meyers (1987:51-52) recognize that the initial position of "the word I cut with you" in the MT is a deliberate variation in the expected Hebrew syntax in order to heighten the authority of the prophet's command.

2:6 *In just a little while.* The MT is difficult—lit., "once again, in a little while" (*'od akhath* [TH5750/259, ZH6388/285] *me'at hi'*). The expression seems to connote both the sense of urgency or immediacy and the indefiniteness of the moment of divine judgment (cf. Meyers and Meyers 1987:52; Petersen 1984:61-62).

2:7 *treasures.* The word "treasures" is actually singular in the MT (*khemdath* [TH2532, ZH2775]). The LXX reads the plural in agreement with the plural verb. Verhoef (1987:92) simply understands the (construct) singular form of the MT as a collective (cf. Waltke and O'Connor 1990:7.2.1). The word refers to desirable, valuable, or coveted things (i.e., "magnificent treasures," TDOT 4.454). It is related to the root word for coveting in the tenth commandment (Exod 20:17; *khamad* [TH2530, ZH2773]). Ironically the treasures coveted by the nations will be given back to God, the maker and owner of all things. On the messianic understanding of "treasures," see Taylor and Clendenen 2004:160-161.

2:9 *in this place.* The preposition "in" is ambiguous, indicating either peace for those who come *into* the Temple or peace for all emanating *from* the Temple (cf. Baldwin 1972:49; Smith 1984:158). The LXX includes a scribal reflection on this promise of peace at the end of 2:9 ("and peace of soul as a possession for all who build, to erect this Temple"; Petersen 1984:61-62).

COMMENTARY

Haggai's reference to "Egypt" (2:5) sets the hortatory tone and establishes the covenant theme for this entire section. The citation is clearly a deliberate appeal to the historical traditions associated with the Exodus from slavery under the pharaoh (cf. Merrill 1994:37). The prophet probably alludes to Isaiah's oracles announcing the second exodus and the restoration of the Hebrews from captivity in Babylonia (e.g., Isa 40:3-5; 41:17-20; 42:14-16; cf. Motyer 1993:335-337, and Watts 1987:80-81 on Exodus typology in Isaiah). The clause "when you came out of Egypt" (2:5) looks at once both back to the past and forward in anticipation of the future in an effort to encourage those presently in despair. This flashback to the Exodus from Egypt was designed to demonstrate the continuity of Yahweh's activity in history for elect Israel. Haggai's audience could be assured that the presence and power of the God who delivered the Hebrews from Pharaoh would also deliver his people from Babylonia and restore them in the land of covenant promise.

The repetition of the clause "I am with you" (1:13; 2:4) calls to mind the new covenant promises made to the Hebrews prior to the Babylonian exile by the prophets Jeremiah (Jer 30:11) and Ezekiel (Ezek 34:30; 37:27). For some, this theme of God's presence with his people constitutes the theological center of the entire Bible. "Immanuel" or "God-with-us" theology has its origins in the intimate fellowship with God that humanity enjoyed before the Fall (Gen 3:8). (On the theme of the divine presence in the OT, see S. Terrien, *The Elusive Presence.* [New York: Harper & Row, 1978]; and C. Barth, *God with Us: A Theological Introduction to the Old Testament.* [Grand Rapids: Eerdmans, 1991.])

Later, the Tabernacle structure of the Exodus sojourn (Exod 25–40) was designed to symbolize the active presence of the Lord among the Hebrews (cf. Exod 25:8, "Have the people of Israel build me a holy sanctuary so I can live among them"). Haggai extended the biblical discourse on the divine presence by declaring the (partial) fulfillment of those earlier pronouncements of Jeremiah and Ezekiel concerning the realization of Yahweh's covenant promises. The prophet had every confidence in exhorting his audience to faithful obedience in completing the divine directive to rebuild the Temple solely on the strength of God's pronouncement, "I am with you" (see the discussion of postexilic use of the covenant formulas in Martens 1994:219-221). He understood that this simple covenant phrase expressed God's care and blessing for his people (Gen 26:24), assured them his divine protection (Jer 15:20), and promised them deliverance and restoration (Isa 41:10; 43:5; cf. Redditt 1995:22-23). The New Testament renews this theme of God's presence dwelling in the midst of humanity with the announcement found in John's Gospel ("The Word became human and made his home among us," John 1:14) and in the promise of God's abiding presence in the new creation ("God himself will be with them," Rev 21:3). During the interim, the church has the guarantee of this divine presence through the indwelling Holy Spirit (1 Cor 3:16; 6:19-20; cf. Eph 1:14).

The clause "my Spirit remains among you" (2:5) is a restatement of the reality that God is with his people (2:4). The reference to "my Spirit" should be understood as a personal manifestation of God's presence. According to Meyers and Meyers (1987:52), the associated verb *'amad* [TH5975, ZH6641] (remain) has the effect of personifying "Spirit" and makes this "a powerful expression of divine presence." Haggai seems to make reference to the function of God's Spirit after the manner of Isaiah's commentary on the Exodus—the Spirit of power works miracles in Israel's history (Isa 63:11; cf. Westermann 1969:389). This interpretation is supported by Haggai's contemporary Zechariah, who recognized that Israel's restoration would be accomplished by the power of God's Spirit—not human strength (Zech 4:6).

Echoes of covenant ideas and themes resound in the vocabulary of Haggai's second message (2:1-9). Specifically, the prophet alluded to Yahweh's covenant ties with Israel by mentioning the land (2:2, 4; cf. Gen 12:1, 7; Exod 3:8), the Temple

(2:3, 7, 9; an implicit reference to that place where Yahweh would establish his name, Deut 12:11; 14:23; 16:2), and the inauguration of peace (2:9; a key element of the new covenant promises of Jeremiah [30:10; 32:37] and Ezekiel [34:25; 37:26]). More striking are the assurance formulas ("be strong," 2:4; and "so do not be afraid," 2:5). Both are commonly found in covenantal contexts (e.g., Gen 15:1; 26:24; Exod 20:20; Isa 57:15). According to Petersen (1984:57-58), both serve to alleviate the apprehension and fear of the people by connecting Yahweh's current presence in the community with his future activity on behalf of his elect. Perhaps most significant is Haggai's wedding of the abiding presence of Yahweh (2:4) with the word of Yahweh's covenant promise (2:5). The prophet may have had Isaiah 59:20-21 in mind, where the combination of God's covenant word and the presence of his Spirit are tokens of Yahweh's unswerving commitment to the restoration of his people.

The prophet urged his audience not to despair over the diminished state of the second Temple in comparison with the memory of the grandeur of Israel's first Temple (2:3; cf. Ezra 3:12). Though Zerubbabel's Temple paled in comparison to the magnificence of Solomon's architectural wonder, Haggai predicted the "future glory" of the second Temple would outstrip the "past glory" of Solomon's majestic Temple (2:9). The prophet bolstered his claim by emphasizing that in the eschaton the tribute of the nations would flow into Jerusalem (2:7). The real glory of the Jerusalem Temple, however, will not be the revenues of silver and gold bursting its coffers. Rather, the glory of God's Temple will consist of his presence in it and among his people (2:4-5; cf. Merrill 1994:41). Perhaps Haggai's forecast of unrivaled future glory for the Lord's Temple anticipated the incarnation of Jesus Christ (Matt 1:23; John 1:14; cf. Isa 7:14). It may be that the return of the "divine presence" to Israel in the person of Jesus of Nazareth fulfilled this prophecy about the future glory of the Temple being far greater than its past glory (Luke 2:25-35, 49; cf. Wolf 1976:37-38).

Haggai's apparent fixation with the treasures of the nations deserves mention lest he be misrepresented as a vindictive nationalist and a crass materialist (2:7-8). Smith (1984:158) declares there is no hint of greed or covetousness on the part of the prophet here. Rather, as von Rad (1966:240) has correctly discerned, Haggai boldly predicted the complete recognition of God's sovereignty over the entire world. In the eschaton, the treasures of the world, once withheld from their true purpose as the property of Yahweh, will return to his exclusive control. This is only appropriate since he is the rightful owner of the wealth of the nations. Jones (1962:34-35) adds the element of universalism to Haggai's discussion of the wealth of the nations. He has noted that "racialism" is dead because in the Day of the Lord the nations come to Zion not only to bring tribute (2:7) and to receive instruction (Isa 2:2-4), but also to be incorporated into the people of God (Zech 2:11). All this is in keeping with Zechariah's vision of the eschaton—a time when the wealth and the worship of the nations will be centered in Jerusalem (Zech 14:14, 17).

◆ III. Third Message: The Call to Holiness (2:10–19)

¹⁰On December 18* of the second year of King Darius's reign, the LORD sent this message to the prophet Haggai: ¹¹"This is what the LORD of Heaven's Armies says. Ask the priests this question about the law: ¹²'If one of you is carrying some meat from a holy sacrifice in his robes and his robe happens to brush against some bread or stew, wine or olive oil, or any other kind of food, will it also become holy?'"

The priests replied, "No."

¹³Then Haggai asked, "If someone becomes ceremonially unclean by touching a dead person and then touches any of these foods, will the food be defiled?"

And the priests answered, "Yes."

¹⁴Then Haggai responded, "That is how it is with this people and this nation, says the LORD. Everything they do and everything they offer is defiled by their sin.

¹⁵Look at what was happening to you before you began to lay the foundation of the LORD's Temple. ¹⁶When you hoped for a twenty-bushel crop, you harvested only ten. When you expected to draw fifty gallons from the winepress, you found only twenty. ¹⁷I sent blight and mildew and hail to destroy everything you worked so hard to produce. Even so, you refused to return to me, says the LORD.

¹⁸"Think about this eighteenth day of December, the day* when the foundation of the LORD's Temple was laid. Think carefully. ¹⁹I am giving you a promise now while the seed is still in the barn.* You have not yet harvested your grain, and your grapevines, fig trees, pomegranates, and olive trees have not yet produced their crops. But from this day onward I will bless you."

2:10 Hebrew *On the twenty-fourth day of the ninth month,* of the ancient Hebrew lunar calendar (similarly in 2:18). This event occurred on December 18, 520 B.C.; also see note on 1:1a. 2:18 Or *On this eighteenth day of December, think about the day.* 2:19 Hebrew *Is the seed yet in the barn?*

NOTES

2:12 *stew.* The word *nazid* [TH5138, ZH5686] occurs elsewhere only in Gen 25:29, 34; and 2 Kgs 4:38-40, where context suggests a boiled dish—something akin to lentil soup or vegetable stew.

2:14 *Everything they do and everything they offer is defiled by their sin.* The LXX expands here: "Because of their early profits, they shall be pained because of their toil, and you have hated those who reprove in the gates" (Petersen 1984:71).

2:16 *winepress.* The MT distinguishes between the "wine vat" (*yeqeb* [TH3342, ZH3676], "collecting unit, reservoir" [i.e., the lower chamber of the wine press]) and the "wine press" (*purah* [TH6333, ZH7053], "pressing chamber" or "trough of the wine-press"); cf. JPS: "and if one came to the vat . . . the press would yield only twenty."

2:17 *blight and mildew and hail.* Two of the three natural disasters are listed in Deut 28:22 (*shiddapon* [TH7711A, ZH8730], "blight, scorching wind"; *yeraqon* [TH3420, ZH3766], "mildew"), further heightening the covenant implications of Haggai's message.

you refused to return to me. This follows the ancient versions instead of the MT: "but you are not *with* me" (*we'en-'ethekem 'elay;* cf. Amos 4:9).

2:18 *this eighteenth day of December, the day when the foundation of the LORD's Temple was laid.* The NLT understands "the day" (*hayyom* [TH3117, ZH3427]) as a reference back to the preceding date formula (the twenty-fourth day of the ninth month, or December 18; cf. 2:10) and equates that day with the laying of the foundation (*yussad* [TH3245, ZH3569]) for the second Temple (cf. Verhoef 1987:129). Merrill (1994:51) objects to this identification because the work on the Second Temple began on the twenty-fourth day of the sixth month (or September 21; cf. 1:15; Ezra 3:10-11). Baldwin (1972:52-53) discounts the issue of the timing of the laying of the Temple foundation stones by noting that the Hebrew verb *yussad* [TH3245, ZH3569] may be translated "build" or "rebuild" instead of "founded" (i.e., Zerubbabel and Jeshua only needed to raise a superstructure on the foundation that remained from Solomon's Temple). Petersen (1984:93) suggests that Haggai made reference to the formal dedication (or ritual purification) of the Temple foundation in 2:18 as a distinct event from the beginning of the restoration project (1:15). Wolf (1976:49) and Merrill (1994:51-52) prefer rendering the compound preposition (*lemin-* [TH3807.1/480, ZH4200/4946]) as "since" or "to the time from the day when the Temple of the LORD was founded" (so NRSV; cf. Kautzsch 1910:119c[n. 2]).

2:19 *I am giving you a promise now while the seed is still in the barn.* This is an expansion of the rhetorical question found in the MT: "Is there still seed in the barn?" (cf. NLT mg). Rather than implying that there is still seed in the barn, however, the rhetorical question suggests the answer "No!" because the seed has already been planted. The implied negative answer to the prophet's question is deduced from the crop failure mentioned in v. 18 and the timing of the third oracle. According to Meyers and Meyers 1987:64, the summer wheat harvest must provide enough grain both for consumption and fall planting. The prophet's message is dated to the month of December, after the first winter rains (Oct–Nov) but prior to early spring harvest. The blighted summer harvest threatens famine conditions in Judah (on the agricultural cycle in Palestine see further Meyers and Meyers 1987:64, who comment that household granaries must hold enough grain sufficient for sustenance and planting so "the question of 'seed in the storehouse' epitomizes the fragile dividing line in Palestine between need and plenty"). On the rhetorical question, see also the notes on 1:4 and 2:3.

COMMENTARY

Two months had elapsed since Haggai's second sermon (October 17; see 2:1), and the community was now three months into the Temple restoration project (September 21; see 1:15). The ninth month of the Hebrew calendar (Kislev, overlapping the Julian months of November and December) was the time for sowing the late season crops like wheat and barley (sesame, millet, lentils, and garden vegetables were planted from January until early March). The early rains of the winter season (falling from mid-October to early November) would have prepared the soil for planting. The latter rains of the winter season (arriving in early April) provided the necessary moisture for the maturation of the cereal crops (cf. ABD 5.612). Haggai hinted that the seed for the winter crops had been planted (see note on 2:19), so the farming community had to wait with patience for the latter rains to ripen the fields for harvest. It was during this time of uncertainty, especially given the fragile agricultural economy of Palestine, that God's messenger called his people to covenant faith by boldly predicting a bumper crop for the winter season harvest.

Theologically, the prophet's third message assumes God's sovereignty over the realm of nature as Creator (perhaps recalling Habakkuk's prayer in Hab 3:17-19). He also presumes the audience's knowledge of the agricultural blessings and curses associated with the "penalty clause" of the Mosaic treaty (cf. Deut 28:4-6, 11-12, 18, 22, 39-40).

Haggai's third speech consists of a warning oracle (2:10-14) and an oracle of blessing (2:15-19). The warning speech has a didactic thrust in that the priests are asked to answer two questions related to ritual purity. According to Craigie

(1984:148), by responding to the questions the priests "would learn from their answers something more than they knew." Such is often the case with dialogical speech, especially those discussions including rhetorical questions like those Haggai posed to the priests. These religious leaders would have had little difficulty in answering the hypothetical questions of the prophet given their professional knowledge. Yet the quizzing of the priests is typical of the prophetic method and important to Haggai's message because the exchange prepares the audience to receive divine instruction. This kind of dialogical speech belongs to the Hebrew wisdom tradition and is a form of "indirect communication." It also reveals one of the pedagogical techniques employed by God as "the master teacher" for delivering a new insight or further illumination (cf. Baldwin 1972:50). As Ellul (1990:118) has observed, sometimes "indirect communication is the only possibility, because it is the only accessible, bearable communication."

Applying the concepts of the holy, common, clean, and unclean to the physical, moral, and spiritual realms of life was basic to the ancient Hebrew worldview. These distinctions were grounded in the law of Moses and enabled the people to order their relationship to the natural world in such a way that they might indeed "be holy" as the Creator is holy (Lev 11:44). The distillation of Haggai's exchange with the priests on the question of ritual purity is the theological truth that holiness is not transferable, while impurity is transferable. The prophet then drew the logical and disturbing conclusion that the work and the worship of the people were defiled by virtue of impurity contaminating the community (2:14). Haggai's audience assumed that their service and sacrificial offerings were made pure and acceptable to God as a result of "contact" with the ordained priesthood and Yahweh's holy Temple. Here the prophet had to correct wrong thinking and bad theology!

The issue was not one of ritual pollution due to contact with "contaminated" people groups within the community (whether Samaritans or non-Yahwists among the Hebrews; see the discussions in Smith 1984:160-161; Verhoef 1987:112-120) or even an unconsecrated Temple site (cf. Petersen 1984:79-85). Rather, the real concern was the failure of the Hebrew community to fully "return" to Yahweh (2:17). In fact, the impurity compromising Hebrew worship, which Haggai decries here, was made public and denounced in a message delivered by Zechariah—the failure to be honest and just, the failure to show mercy and kindness, and the ongoing practice of oppression aimed at the socially disadvantaged (Zech 7:1, 8-11).

The prophet understood the value of reflection upon the past. Four times he instructed his audience to "think about" the past or assess the current situation (1:5, 7; 2:15, 18). Previously, Haggai called attention to the Exodus from Egypt (2:5). Then he exhorted the people to take another look back to their more immediate past: the two decades prior to the commencement of the Temple reconstruction project (2:15). This appeal to the past even included the citation of a portion of an earlier prophetic message addressing a similar situation (2:16-17, cf. Amos 4:8-9; see the discussion in Verhoef 1987:126-129).

Numerous theological insights may be extracted from Haggai's emphasis on the past, including the fact that history is the arena of God's redemptive activity (cf. Dan 2:20-23; Hab 3:16-19). For the Hebrews, the lessons learned from history were vital to the success of the next generation (Deut 4:9-14). Haggai also reminds us that there is great value in revisiting the word of God spoken to a bygone era. The psalmist recognized the importance of transmitting the records of the past for instilling faith in the next generation (Ps 78:1-8; cf. 1 Cor 10:11, "they [i.e., events of Israelite history] were written down to warn us"). We also benefit from observing the pattern of exhortation in Haggai. The prophet sustained the initiative to rebuild the Temple (1:14-15) by offering words of encouragement one month later (2:1-3) and again after three months had elapsed (2:10). The New Testament advocates this kind of exhortation on a daily basis (cf. 2 Cor 13:11; 1 Thess 5:11; Heb 3:13). Finally, any look back to the past must prompt a look ahead to the future. For Haggai the past was a springboard into God's plan for Israel's future—"but from this day onward I will bless you" (2:19).

The message of Haggai to rebuild the Temple and thus revive the flow of God's covenantal blessings to Israel should not be understood as a contradiction to the words of Jeremiah. By the time of Jeremiah (c. 627–582 BC), the Temple had become a talisman or a "lucky charm" of sorts. The people of Judah assumed that the mere association of Yahweh's Temple with Jerusalem and the people of God guaranteed divine protection and blessing. Jeremiah indignantly condemned such misplaced trust in a work of architecture and even predicted its eventual destruction (Jer 7-10, esp. 7:1-11).

Haggai called the people to rebuild the Temple for the purpose of the proper worship of God; he was not encouraging blind faith in a religious superstructure. The prophet also presupposed that the appropriate attitudes of reverence, humility, and unfeigned behavior demonstrating obedience to the law of God would naturally accompany the initiative to reconstruct the Jerusalem sanctuary. Only then would this second Temple again symbolize the covenant presence of Yahweh among his people and stamp the Hebrew repatriates as the elect of God among the nations.

The phrasing of the promise of blessing ("I will bless you," 2:19) echoes the language of the covenant God established with Abraham ("I will bless you," Gen 12:2) and the affirmation of that covenant with Isaac (combining divine blessing with the land of covenant promise, Gen 26:3). The construction emphasizes God as the source of this blessing and the reality that his grace is not subject to manipulation by human endeavor (cf. Mal 3:14). The only condition attached to divine favor is the "return" to God—repentance characterized by the fear of the Lord and obedience to his commands (2:17; cf. 1:12-13). The divine blessing of Haggai's promise is more than the crass materialism of a "prosperity theology." Granted, economic blessing in the form of agricultural bounty constitutes the tangible evidence of God's favor in context. The river of God's blessing, however, runs much wider and deeper than mere surplus of foodstuffs.

The parallels between Haggai 2:10-19 and Zechariah 8:9-23 are well documented (e.g., Smith 1984:159-160). The complementary message of Zechariah, Haggai's contemporary, outlines benefits of God's blessing far surpassing the anticipated agricultural prosperity, including peace (Zech 8:12), honor among the nations as a symbol and source of divine blessing (Zech 8:13), joyous worship (Zech 8:19), glory as the place where all peoples will worship the Lord Almighty (Zech 8:20-22), and the very presence of God in the midst of his people Israel (Zech 8:23; cf. Hag 2:4-5).

◆ IV. Fourth Message: Zerubbabel—Davidic Servant and "Signet Ring" (2:20-23)

²⁰On that same day, December 18,* the LORD sent this second message to Haggai: ²¹"Tell Zerubbabel, the governor of Judah, that I am about to shake the heavens and the earth. ²²I will overthrow royal thrones and destroy the power of foreign kingdoms. I will overturn their chariots and riders. The horses will fall, and their riders will kill each other.

²³"But when this happens, says the LORD of Heaven's Armies, I will honor you, Zerubbabel son of Shealtiel, my servant. I will make you like a signet ring on my finger, says the LORD, for I have chosen you. I, the LORD of Heaven's Armies, have spoken!"

2:20 Hebrew *On the twenty-fourth day of the [ninth] month;* see note on 2:10.

NOTES

2:21 *the heavens and the earth.* The LXX adds *kai tēn thalassan kai tēn xēran* [TG2281/3584A, ZG2498/3831] ("and the sea and the dry land"), an insertion based on the phrasing of 2:6.

2:22 *royal thrones.* The expression (*kisse' mamlakoth* [TH3678/4467, ZH4058/4930]) is a somewhat rare example of a plural genitival group in which only the second noun is plural (Joüon 1993:§136m; Kautzsch 1910:124.2c; cf. JPSV, NJB, "thrones of kingdoms").

2:23 *signet ring.* The "signet ring" was a symbol of kingship in the biblical world. The engraved stone set in the gold or silver finger ring was used to seal or endorse official documents. Haggai employed the image to emphasize the divine authority invested in Zerubbabel and to assure the people of God's continuing involvement in the restoration of Judah— even the political process. The designation of Zerubbabel as the "signet" of the Lord no doubt rekindled messianic expectations in the postexilic community since he was a descendant of King David.

I, the LORD *of Heaven's Armies, have spoken!* The threefold repetition of the divine utterance formula (*ne'um-yhwh* [TH5002/3068, ZH5536/3378]) in this verse emphasizes the certain fulfillment of Yahweh's promise.

COMMENTARY

The two key elements of Haggai's eschatology are the restored glory of the second Temple and "the shaking of the nations" in divine judgment (2:6-9, 20-22). The renewed association of God's glory with the Temple is a prophetic theme distinctive in Haggai, but in keeping with the idea of "the transformation of Zion" at the center of Old Testament eschatology (cf. Gowan 1986:4-20). Haggai's vision of God's shaking the heavens and the earth parallels Isaiah 13:13 and Joel 3:16. The image is one of divine wrath—God's fierce anger unleashed against the wicked for their rebellion against him and the oppression of his people Israel. Haggai used language traditionally associated with divine intervention in the Old Testament, especially Yahweh's "overthrow" of Egypt in the Exodus (Exod 15:1, 4, 7, 21; cf. Baldwin 1972:54, "he will act, and Judah will not need to fight"). Given the historical context, the graphic portrayal of God's power was a most appropriate way to dispel lingering doubt about God's sovereignty after the cataclysm of Babylonian exile (cf. Mal 2:17, "Where is the God of justice?"). In his prediction of the shaking of the nations, the prophet tried to convince the people that God was still sovereign and that he had not forsaken his justice. Haggai called his audience to what Baldwin (1972:55) has described as "zealous allegiance" to God and his covenant. The prophet was holding out the hope of "nothing less than a universal reordering of all things and the establishment of the Kingdom of God on earth" (Achtemeier 1986:101). God shook the earth once before at the Exodus (2:5; cf. Ps 114); for Haggai this was proof enough that God possessed sufficient power to do it again!

The identification of Zerubbabel with the "signet ring" (2:23), a symbol of kingship in the ancient world, marks an important episode in the historical development of postexilic Judah. Pragmatically speaking, the restoration community was in desperate need of stable political leadership in the aftermath of the Babylonian exile. The priests remained in place as authority figures by virtue of their role as ministers of Hebrew worship and teachers of the law of Moses (2:1-19; Mal 2:4-9). Haggai's endorsement of Zerubbabel assured the people of God's continuing involvement in the political process despite the failure of the Hebrew monarchies: Zerubbabel would complete the task God had assigned to him. Haggai's message recalls the cooperation between kingship and the priesthood under King David (cf. 1 Chr 23–26), and anticipates Zechariah's vision of shared leadership for the office of governor and the priesthood (cf. Zech 3–4).

The promises to Zerubbabel are significant theologically for at least two reasons. First, Haggai's word of affirmation overturns the divine curse of the Davidic line pronounced by Jeremiah upon King Jehoiachin of Judah (Jer 22:24-30). Haggai's fourth message both reinstates the family of Jehoiachin by reversing the earlier prophetic curse and reestablishes the provisions of the Davidic covenant for perpetuating the dynasty of King David (2 Sam 7:4-17; cf. Wolf 1976:54-55). Second, Haggai's prophecy over Zerubbabel rekindles the messianic hopes for the Israelites that had been dashed by the Babylonian exile. The language of Haggai's oracle echoes messianic terminology found in Isaiah, especially the designations "my servant" and "my chosen one" (cf. Isa 42:1; 52:13). His message is a pledge that God intends to fulfill the new covenant promises announced by Jeremiah and Ezekiel concerning the descendant of David (cf. Jer 33:17, 22, 26; Ezek 37:24-25).

BIBLIOGRAPHY

Achtemeier, E.
1986 *Nahum—Malachi.* Interpretation. Atlanta: John Knox.

Baldwin, J. G.
1972 *Haggai, Zechariah, Malachi.* Tyndale Old Testament Commentary. Downers Grove: InterVarsity.

Boda, M. J.
2004 *Haggai, Zechariah.* NIV Application Commentary. Grand Rapids: Zondervan.

Briant, P.
2002 *From Cyrus to Alexander: A History of the Persian Empire.* Translator, P. T. Daniels. Winona Lake: Eisenbrauns.

Christensen, D. L.
1992 Impulse and Design in the Book of Haggai. *Journal of the Evangelical Theological Society* 35:445-456.

Craigie, P. C.
1984 *The Twelve Prophets.* Philadelphia: Westminster.

Ellul, J.
1990 *The Reason for Being—A Meditation on Ecclesiastes.* Translator, J. M. Hanks. Grand Rapids: Eerdmans.

Gowan, D. E.
1986 *Eschatology in the Old Testament.* Philadelphia: Fortress.

Jones, D. R.
1962 *Haggai—Zechariah—Malachi.* Tyndale Bible Commentary. London: SCM Press.

Joüon, P.
1993 *A Grammar of Biblical Hebrew.* Translator, T. Muraoka. Subsidia Biblica 14/I, II. Rome: Pontifical Biblical Institute.

Kaiser, W. C.
1992 *Micah—Malachi.* Word Biblical Commentary. Waco: Word.

Kautzsch, E.
1910 *Gesenius' Hebrew Grammar.* 2nd ed. Revised by A. E. Cowley. Oxford: Clarendon.

Kessler, J. A.
1987 The Shaking of the Nations: An Eschatological View. *Journal of the Evangelical Theological Society* 30:159-166.

2002 *The Book of Haggai: Prophecy and Society in Early Persian Yehud.* Vetus Testamentum Supplement 91. Leiden: Brill.

March, W. E.
1996 The Book of Haggai. Pp. 707-732 in *The New Interpreter's Bible,* vol. 12. Editor, L. E. Keck. Nashville: Abingdon.

Martens, E. A.
1994 *God's Design: A Focus on Old Testament Theology.* 2nd ed. Grand Rapids: Baker.

Mason, R.
1977 *The Books of Haggai, Zechariah, and Malachi.* Cambridge: Cambridge University Press.

Merrill, E. H.
1994 *Haggai, Zechariah, Malachi: An Exegetical Commentary.* Chicago: Moody.

Meyers, C. L., and E. M. Meyers.
1987 *Haggai and Zechariah 1–8.* Anchor Bible. Garden City, NY: Doubleday.

Motyer, J. A.
1993 *The Prophecy of Isaiah: An Introduction and Commentary.* Downers Grove: InterVarsity.

Petersen, D. L.
1984 *Haggai and Zechariah 1–8.* Philadelphia: Westminster.

Peterson, Eugene H.
2002 *The Message.* Colorado Springs: NavPress.

Pierce, R. W.
1984a Literary Connectors and a Haggai–Zechariah–Malachi Corpus. *Journal of the Evangelical Theological Society* 27:277-289.
1984b A Thematic Development of the Haggai–Zechariah–Malachi Corpus. *Journal of the Evangelical Theological Society* 27:401-411.

von Rad, G.
1966 *The Problem of the Hexateuch and Other Essays.* Translator, E. W. T. Dicken. New York: McGraw-Hill.

Redditt, P. L.
1995 *Haggai, Zechariah, and Malachi.* New Century Bible Commentary. London: Marshall Pickering.

Rose, W. H.
2000 *Zemah and Zerubbabel: Messianic Expectations in the Early Postexilic Period.* Journal of the Study of the Old Testament Supplement 304. Sheffield: Sheffield Academic Press.

Smith, R. L.
1984 *Micah–Malachi.* Word Biblical Commentary. Waco: Word.

Sykes, Seth
2002 *Time and Space in Haggai–Zechariah 1–8.* New York: Peter Lang.

Taylor, R. A., and E. R. Clendenen
2004 *Haggai, Malachi.* New American Commentary 21A. Nashville: Broadman & Holman.

Verhoef, P. A.
1987 *The Books of Haggai and Malachi.* New International Commentary on the Old Testament. Grand Rapids: Eerdmans.

Waltke, B., and M. O'Connor
1990 *An Introduction to Biblical Hebrew Syntax.* Winona Lake: Eisenbrauns.

Watts, J. D. W.
1987 *Isaiah 34–66.* Word Biblical Commentary. Waco: Word.

Webber, R. E.
1994 *Worship Old & New.* 2nd ed. Grand Rapids: Zondervan.

Westermann, C.
1969 *Isaiah 40–66.* Translator, D. M. G. Stalker. Philadelphia: Westminster.

Wolf, H. M.
1976 *Haggai and Malachi.* Everyman's Bible Commentary. Chicago: Moody.

Wolff, H. W.
1988 *Haggai: A Commentary.* Translator, M. Kohl. Minneapolis: Augsburg.

Yamauchi, E. M.
1990 *Persia and the Bible.* Grand Rapids: Baker.

Zechariah

ANDREW E. HILL

INTRODUCTION TO
Zechariah

ZECHARIAH is classified as a type of prophetic writing, albeit a later iteration of that literary genre. The preaching of the postexilic prophets (Haggai, Zechariah, Malachi, and perhaps Joel) has affinities to the sermons of the earlier classical prophets (e.g., Amos, Hosea, Isaiah) in that they all tend to be narrated in third person, contain oracles alternating between first- and third-person speech, and call their audiences to repentance. Like their earlier counterparts, the postexilic prophets emphasize the ethical teaching of the Torah, but tend to appeal to the rhetorical device of applying earlier Scripture (especially prophetic literature) in an authoritative way to new situations (cf. 1:4). Finally, the postexilic prophets had a predilection to generalize the promises of the earlier prophets and cast them into a less specific, but not far distant, future (cf. Petersen 1977:13-16; Mason 1990:233-234). Mason (1990:234) summarizes the ministry of the postexilic prophets as one of preaching "the hopes of the [earlier] prophets to a people who could have easily become cynical about their lack of fulfillment, assuring them of both the present degree to which they had been and were being fulfilled and the certainty of their ultimate triumph."

The second half of the book (chs 9–14) is sometimes identified as apocalyptic literature, an offshoot of Old Testament prophetic literature given to the interpretation of current events and the prediction of future events by means of symbolic language, ciphers, and codes—usually accompanied by angelic mediation. The vivid imagery and the angelic mediation (e.g., 1:9) of the night visions (chs 1:7–6:15) give this portion of Zechariah a similar character. It seems best to characterize Zechariah as later Hebrew prophetic literature containing certain proto-apocalyptic features. In this sense, Zechariah may represent a stage of development in the literary shift from prophecy to apocalyptic literature in later Jewish writings of the intertestamental period. (See further "Literary Style" below.)

Three types of messages are usually associated with the visionary literature of the Bible. The first is a message of encouragement to the oppressed; the second, a warning to the oppressor; and the third, a call to faith for those wavering between God's truth and human wisdom. Zechariah's message to the oppressed people of God in postexilic Judah assured them of God's love for Jerusalem and his sure plans to once again live there with his people (1:14; 8:3). Zechariah's warnings include a word of admonition to his own people not to repeat the sins of the past that led to exile (1:6; 7:11-14). He also pronounced a word of judgment to the oppressing nations that God would repay them in full measure for their mistreatment of Israel (1:18-21; 12:9; 14:12). Finally, Zechariah's exhortation to those wavering between God's truth and human wisdom includes a call to repentance and a charge to practice justice in the land by obeying the commandments of Yahweh's covenant (1:3; 8:15-17).

AUTHOR

The book is silent on the issue of authorship, although it is assumed that the prophetic word formula ("the LORD gave this message to the prophet Zechariah," 1:1) signifies that Zechariah penned his own oracles. The name "Zechariah" means "Yah(weh) has remembered." This summarizes Zechariah's basic message to postexilic Judah: The Lord has remembered his covenant with Israel and plans to restore the fortunes of his people. The title "prophet" classifies Zechariah as a divinely commissioned spokesperson for God (1:1).

We learn from Ezra that Haggai and Zechariah were contemporary prophets of the early postexilic period (Ezra 5:1). The date formulas in the two books indicate that Zechariah began preaching in Jerusalem about two months after Haggai's brief, four-month ministry began (cf. 1:1; Hag 1:1; 2:20). Haggai and Zechariah were also complementary prophets in that Haggai exhorted the people to rebuild the Jerusalem Temple and Zechariah summoned the community to repentance and spiritual renewal. His task was to prepare the people for proper worship in the Temple once the building project was completed.

The book's superscription (1:1) identifies Zechariah as the son of Berekiah and the grandson of Iddo. The records of Ezra confirm Zechariah as a descendant of Iddo (Ezra 5:1; 6:14—the word "son" in this context simply designates "a descendant"). Nehemiah informs us that Zechariah's grandfather, Iddo, returned to Jerusalem from exile in Babylonia with Zerubbabel and Jeshua (Neh 12:4). Nehemiah also lists Zechariah as the head of the priestly family of Iddo (Neh 12:16). This suggests that Zechariah was a member of the tribe of Levi and that he served in Jerusalem as both a priest and a prophet.

DATE AND OCCASION OF WRITING

Three of Zechariah's speeches are dated to specific years and months (and sometimes days) of the reign of Darius I, king of Persia (cf. NLT mg at 1:1, 7; 7:1). The modern equivalents for the date formulas are listed below:

SPEECH	DATE IN DARIUS'S REIGN	MODERN EQUIVALENT
Zech 1:1-6	Year 2, month 8	Oct/Nov 520 BC
Zech 1:7-6:8	Year 2, month 11, day 24	15 February 519 BC
Zech 7-8	Year 4, month 9, day 4	7 December 518 BC

It seems likely that this first portion of the book (chs 1-8) was written sometime between 520 and 515 BC, since Zechariah makes no reference to the completion and dedication of the Jerusalem Temple in 515 BC (cf. Ezra 6:13-22). Zechariah's preaching was prompted by the prophet Haggai's message to begin reconstruction of the Lord's Temple delivered to Jerusalem on August 29, 520 BC (Hag 1:1).

Scholarly opinion is sharply divided over the authorship and date of the final two oracles in the book of Zechariah (chs 9-11, 12-14). Some biblical scholars assign chapters 9-11 to a "Second Zechariah" and chapters 12-14 to a "Third Zechariah." These alleged and anonymous writers were supposed to have lived and prophesied in Jerusalem sometime from the fourth to second centuries BC. It is often suggested that these two anonymous oracles, along with the book of Malachi, were added as an appendix to Zechariah 1-8 to complete the sacred number of the Twelve Prophets (i.e., the Minor Prophets; cf. "Canonicity and Textual History" below). According to this view, the final written form of Zechariah is assigned to the Maccabean period (c. 160 BC). The evidence typically offered in support of multiple authorship includes the perceived differences in style, tone, theology, and historical situation between the two parts of the book (chs 1-8 and chs 9-14). Notable among the arguments are the reference to Greece (9:13, which is considered an allusion to the Hellenistic period) and the distinctively apocalyptic character of chapters 12-14.

A remarkable literary continuity between chapters 1-8 and 9-14 exists, however; this can be seen via careful analysis of linguistic and grammatical features in Zechariah (cf. Hill 1982:105-134; Radday and Wickman 1975:30-55). An examination of the literary features in light of archaeological discoveries and socio-political considerations confirms an early Persian period date for Zechariah 9-14 (see Meyers and Meyers 1993:52-55). Finally, both Jewish and Christian tradition concerning the Hebrew Bible or Old Testament clearly associate Zechariah 9-14 with the prophet Zechariah and with chapters 1-8 of his book. The two undated oracles (chs 9-11 and 12-14) were most likely composed by the prophet Zechariah later in his life. Linguistic data retrieved from the Hebrew text of Zechariah suggest that the final draft of the book was probably completed sometime between 500 and 470 BC.

The setting for Zechariah's preaching, like that of Haggai's, was the reign of Darius I, king of Persia (522-486 BC). Although the Hebrews had returned to the land of Israel after the Babylonian captivity, the economic situation of the community was bleak; the people languished in apathy, despair, and hopelessness.

In response to this distress, God raised up two prophetic voices for the purpose of initiating programs for the physical rebuilding and the spiritual renewal of postexilic Jerusalem. The prophet Haggai was commissioned to exhort and challenge the Hebrew community to rebuild the Jerusalem Temple. He preached for only four months late in the year 520 BC. The people responded favorably to Haggai's message, and the reconstruction of the Lord's Temple began that year (Hag 1:12-15).

The prophet Zechariah complemented Haggai's message by calling for the spiritual renewal of God's people (1:3-6; 7:8-14). His ministry began just two months after Haggai's, and Zechariah's last dated message was delivered in 518 BC.

So Zechariah's ministry in postexilic Jerusalem lasted at least two years. The reference to Haggai and Zechariah in Ezra 5:1 suggests that they both continued to support and encourage the people until the Temple was completed and rededicated to the worship of Yahweh with the celebration of the Passover Feast in 515 BC (Ezra 6:13-22). The undated oracles of Zechariah (chs 9-14) may indicate that his prophetic ministry in postexilic Jerusalem continued well beyond the completion of the second Temple.

AUDIENCE

As in the case of Haggai's prophecy, the messages of Zechariah originated in Judah and were intended for the people living in postexilic Jerusalem and its environs (1:12). Embedded within Zechariah's sermons and visions are words specifically addressed to Zerubbabel, the governor, and to Jeshua, the high priest, along with the rest of the Levitical priesthood (e.g., 3:8-9; 4:6-7; 7:4-5)

CANONICITY AND TEXTUAL HISTORY

Zechariah is the eleventh book in the collection known as the Minor Prophets (or the Book of the Twelve in the Hebrew Bible). The Twelve Prophets are usually grouped with the Latter Prophets (Isaiah, Jeremiah, and Ezekiel) and, without exception, are found in the earliest delineations of the Old Testament canon. These twelve prophetic books were always copied on one scroll in the ancient Hebrew manuscript tradition. The order of the Twelve Prophets does vary in some canon traditions, but the sequence of books from Nahum through Malachi seems quite stable in the various canon lists (cf. Jones 1995:54). For example, Amos and Micah follow Hosea in the Septuagint (LXX), and one Qumran fragment places Jonah as the last book in the Twelve Prophets (4QXIIa). On the placement of Jonah at Qumran, see the discussion in Meyers and Meyers (1993:51). The books of Haggai, Zechariah, and Malachi form a distinct sub-collection or literary corpus within the Book of the Twelve. All three prophets belong to the early Persian period of postexilic Hebrew history and are unified by literary device (e.g., the rhetorical question) and theological theme (cf. Pierce 1984a).

The Hebrew text of Zechariah is remarkably well preserved and relatively free of textual problems (see the discussion in Meyers and Meyers 1993:50-51). In several instances in Zechariah 1-8, the NLT prefers the reading of the ancient versions (especially the LXX and the Syriac Peshitta) over the Masoretic Text (see the NLT text notes for 1:16; 5:6b; 6:11a, 14). The NLT appeals to the Septuagint in one instance against the Masoretic Text of Zechariah 9-14 (reading "him" for "you" in 14:5b), while the Syriac Peshitta is referenced as an alternative reading in Zechariah 11:13 (reading "treasury" for the "potter" as in the CEV, NRSV).

The Septuagint is generally a reliable (but at times an interpretive and expansive) witness to the Hebrew text of Zechariah (see further the discussion in McComiskey 1998:1009-1011). Portions of the book of Zechariah are attested by fragments of the Dead Sea Scrolls or Qumran manuscripts, including 1:4-6, 9-10, 13-14; 2:10-14;

3:2-10; 4:1-4; 5:8-11; 6:1-5; 8:2-4, 6-7; 10:11-12; 11:1-2; 12:1-3, 7-12; 14:18 (cf. Ulrich 1997:220-318). Meyers and Meyers (1993:50-51) note only three textual variations of significance between the Masoretic Text and the Qumran manuscripts; they conclude that the Qumran manuscripts support the Hebrew text underlying the Masoretic Text.

LITERARY STYLE

Zechariah's message was one of rebuke, exhortation, and encouragement—a tract for troubled times. The pastoral tone of Zechariah's messages is set in his exchange with the angel commissioned to relay the "kind and comforting words" from the Lord (1:13). The hortatory character of his sermons is seen in words of encouragement like "be strong" and "don't be afraid" (8:9, 13, 15). Zechariah's repeated appeals to the words of the "earlier prophets" authenticated his own ministry and assured his audience that they had not misinterpreted God's previous revelations (1:4; 7:7, 12).

The book of Zechariah neatly divides into two major units. The first includes the introductory verse (or superscription) with the call to repentance (1:1-6), the seven night visions (1:7–6:15), and two sermons addressing the topic of fasting (chs 7–8). The second part of the book consists of prophetic oracles, subdivided into two sections: the word of the Lord concerning the land of Hadrach (or Aram, chs 9–11), and the word of the Lord concerning Israel (chs 12–14). (On the literary history and structure of Zechariah, see further, Boda 2004:36-45).

Literary analysis of Zechariah's prophecy has identified an elaborate chiastic structure underlying the two parts of the book (Baldwin 1972:75-81, 85-86; Dorsey 1999:318-319). Although there is no overarching symmetric or parallel design connecting the two halves of the book, repeated themes serve to unify Zechariah's visions, sermons, and oracles. Prominent among these unifying themes are (1) the promise of divine presence in the midst of Israel, (2) the enabling work of the Holy Spirit, (3) God's judgment of the nations, (4) the call for social justice, (5) the establishment of divinely appointed leadership, and (6) the ultimate triumph of righteousness and the blessing of peace for Jerusalem (see "Major Themes" below).

Like Haggai and Malachi, the sermons of Zechariah are basically prose set in the third person. The speeches may be formally classified as belonging to the genre of "oracular prose." The messages are "oracular" in nature because they represent authoritative prophetic speech motivated or inspired by God himself. By "prose" I mean that the literary texture of Zechariah is a blend of prosaic and rhetorical features distinctive of prophetic style. This kind of prophetic speech is usually characterized by formulaic language. Examples of these stylized expressions in Zechariah include the date formula and prophetic word formulas (1:1), the messenger formula (1:3), and the divine validation formula (2:9, 11).

In addition, Zechariah contains a number of literary forms that are rhetorical in nature, including exhortation in the call to repentance (1:1-6), narrative in the form of a series of visions (1:7–6:8), prediction with revelation and interpretation formulas (5:1-4), inquiry with instructional response (6:1-8), symbolic actions (6:9-15), admonition with messenger and date formulas (7:1-7), and divine oracles of judgment and salvation (ch 10).

Portions of Zechariah (especially chs 12–14) are sometimes classified as "proto-apocalyptic" in contrast to the apocalyptic literature that appears in later Jewish writings of the intertestamental period (e.g., 1 Esdras and *1 Enoch*). It is true that the book exhibits certain features of apocalyptic writing like divine revelation cast in the form of visions, the presence of angelic messengers who both deliver and interpret the visions, the use of symbolism, and the themes of judgment for the nations and the deliverance of Israel. But other features of apocalyptic writing are notably absent, such as a rigid determinism (with regard to individual and national destinies), pervasive pessimism (with regard to the prospects for humanity in the future), the rewriting of earlier Hebrew history, and pseudonymity (or writing under a false name). In this respect, Zechariah (especially chs 9–14) is similar to a corpus of OT prophetic books that may be considered somewhat proto-apocalyptic in nature since they contain certain features of later apocalyptic literature, including Isa 24–27; Ezek 36–39; Dan 7–12; and Joel 2 (see Boda 2004:203).

Understanding Apocalyptic Literature. Biblical proto-apocalyptic literature and its later offshoot, intertestamental Jewish apocalyptic literature, are visionary genres given to interpretation of current events and prediction of future events in symbols, ciphers, and codes—usually by means of angelic mediation (e.g., 1:9). As such, they represent subcategories of the genre of prophecy in the larger scheme of hermeneutics, or biblical interpretation.

Apocalyptic (or visionary) literature is "crisis" literature, typically conveying specific messages to particular groups of people caught up in a dire situation. Several basic questions are helpful in the interpretation of visionary literature in the Bible: Who is addressed? By whom? When? In what setting? For what reason? What is the relationship of the passage to the rest of the Bible?

Apocalyptic literature announces an end to the way things are and opens up alternative possibilities to the audience as a result of God's impending intervention in human affairs. Three types of messages are usually associated with the visionary literature of the Bible. The first is a message of encouragement to the oppressed; the second, a warning to the oppressor; and the third, a call to faith for those wavering between God's truth and human wisdom.

Apocalyptic literature portrays settings, characters, and events in ways different from ordinary reality. While the visions depict literal events, the symbolic descriptions do not necessarily represent the events literally. Ryken (1984:165-174) offers helpful guidelines for reading and understanding visionary literature:

> Be ready for the reversal of the ordinary.
> Be prepared to use your imagination to picture a world that transcends
>   earthly reality.

Be prepared for a series of diverse, self-contained units that tend to be
kaleidoscopic in nature (instead of looking for a smooth flow of narrative).
Seek to identify the historical event or theological reality in salvation history
represented by the symbolism in the passage (observe the obvious, grasp the
total scene, do not press every detail of the vision for hidden meaning).
Read widely in visionary literature (both biblical visionary literature and
extra-biblical fantasy literature).
Recognize the element of mystery and the supernatural quality of the Bible
(and be willing to humbly admit that an exact understanding of a given
vision may be beyond us).

Finally, visionary literature in the Bible has given rise to four major interpretive
approaches to the understanding of the time orientation of the divine revelation.
The *preterist* approach views all the events described in the visions as past. By contrast, the *futurist* sees the events portrayed in the visions as yet to come. The *historicist*
appeals to the visions to trace the ideological or theological development of an age
or an era (e.g., the history of Israel or the church age). The *idealist* understands the
vision as a symbolic representation of the timeless conflict between good and evil
(cf. Klein, Blomberg, and Hubbard 1993:292-312; 369-374). The commentary that
follows will offer brief summaries of both the preterist and the futurist understandings of Zechariah's visions where appropriate. It should be understood,
however, that the visions of Zechariah cannot be reduced simply to an either–or
approach. The prophet's visions are complex and lend themselves to multiple interpretations, as evidenced in the biblical commentaries. The interpretive process is
further complicated by the fact that Zechariah only vaguely refers to historical
events occurring during the postexilic period of Hebrew history. Beyond this, our
knowledge of Persian oversight of the province of Yehud (or Judah) is sketchy,
making it more difficult to identify precise fulfillments of many of Zechariah's
prophecies.

MAJOR THEMES

The prophetic ministries of Haggai and Zechariah in postexilic Jerusalem over-
lapped chronologically and thematically. Haggai's primary message was a challenge
to rebuild the Temple of the Lord. Secondarily, he called for spiritual renewal
among the people of God so that they might offer appropriate worship in the new
sanctuary.

Zechariah's primary message, however, was an exhortation to repentance and
spiritual renewal—a return to right relationship with God (1:1-6). The central
theme of Zechariah's sermons is encouragement, and he often found his duty was
one of comforting (1:13) and strengthening the people (8:9, 13, 15). As a complementary voice to Haggai, Zechariah also reinforced the summons to the people to
rebuild the Jerusalem Temple (8:9, 13).

Zechariah's message of encouragement to a small and discouraged remnant of
God's people (8:6) is cast in the form of visions of the future. This series of visions

promised peace to Israel, divine judgment of the nations, the restoration of Jerusalem, responsible government as a result of divinely appointed leadership, and a covenant of righteousness in Zion (1:7–6:15). The theme of social justice is emphasized in lessons about fasting over the Babylonian exile and the destruction of Solomon's Temple (7:4-12; 8:14-19).

Zechariah's last two messages are also visions that were designed to instill hope in God by focusing on the future restoration of the people of Israel (chs 9–14). Specifically, the prophet forecasts the return of Yahweh to his Temple (9:8-10), the deliverance of Israel from her enemies (e.g., ch 12), and the establishment of God's kingdom in Jerusalem (14:9-11).

THEOLOGICAL CONCERNS

Behind Zechariah's call to repentance was the concern for right relationship with God, a renewal of the covenant established between Yahweh and Israel at Mount Sinai (Exod 19–24). This was a burden Zechariah shared with Haggai (Hag 1:12) and Malachi (Mal 3:7), and the Old Testament prophets generally (e.g., Isa 1:16-20; Hos 6:1-3). The prophet's interest in Israel's covenant relationship with Yahweh extended to issues of social justice. Obedience to the stipulations of God's covenant led to justice, honesty, fairness, mercy, and kindness (7:9-10; 8:16-17). Zechariah warned his audience not to repeat the sins of the past because such covenant violations had sent an earlier generation into exile (7:11-14).

Closely related to Zechariah's concern for maintaining covenant relationship with Yahweh is his assurance that God will once again live among his people and that the glory of the Lord will rest in Jerusalem (1:16; 2:5, 10-11; 8:3, 23). Zechariah shares this vision of the Lord's return with other Old Testament prophets (e.g., Isa 52:8; Joel 3:21). The restoration of the divine presence in Israel promised by the prophet seems to have both an immediate and an eschatological fulfillment. The immediate manifestation of the divine presence is associated with the reconstructed Temple, a spiritually restored Israel, and the resurgence of agricultural production (1:17; 4:8-9; 6:15; cf. Hag 2:19). The future manifestation of the divine presence is associated with the deliverance of Jerusalem and the people of Israel from enemy nations, the enthronement of the Lord as king over all the earth, and the universal worship of Yahweh (9:16; 10:6; 12:9; 14:9). In each case, the return of the Lord's presence to Jerusalem is connected with the enabling work of God's Spirit (4:6; 12:10; cf. Hag 2:5).

Finally, Zechariah addressed issues of theology proper—the knowledge of God. The emphasis on God's love for Jerusalem is evidence that he is a covenant-making and covenant-keeping God (1:14; 8:2, 15). The fact of God's sovereign rule over the nations and the reality of his compassion for Israel as his people mean that divine deliverance and divine judgment will be accomplished in the sphere of human history (12:6-12). The mystery of a Messiah presented by Zechariah as both a suffering shepherd (13:7) and a righteous king (9:9) will result in a redeemed people who testify of their loyalty to God (13:9). The awesome holiness of God will transform the created order, and the long-awaited kingdom of the Lord will be established over all the earth (14:9). As a result, all peoples will worship the King, the Lord Almighty (14:9, 16, 21).

Zechariah admonished the people that God must be given the freedom to accomplish his purposes for the good of Israel in his way and time. This is reflected in his exhortation to the prophet not to "despise . . . small beginnings" (4:10). Zechariah reminded his audience that God had acted in the past for the ultimate good of his people, even in the judgment of Babylonian exile (7:12-14; cf. 14:3). The people of Israel can take courage in the present and have hope for the future because God can be trusted to keep his word and fulfill the promises made through Zechariah the prophet (4:9). For this reason, all humanity is to be silent before the Lord, "for he is springing into action from his holy dwelling" (2:13).

OUTLINE

COMMENTARY ON
Zechariah

◆ **I. Prelude: A Call to Return to the Lord (1:1-6)**

In November* of the second year of King Darius's reign, the LORD gave this message to the prophet Zechariah son of Berekiah and grandson of Iddo:

²"I, the LORD, was very angry with your ancestors. ³Therefore, say to the people, 'This is what the LORD of Heaven's Armies says: Return to me, and I will return to you, says the LORD of Heaven's Armies.' ⁴Don't be like your ancestors who would not listen or pay attention when the earlier prophets said to them, 'This is what the LORD of Heaven's Armies says: Turn from your evil ways, and stop all your evil practices.'

⁵"Where are your ancestors now? They and the prophets are long dead. ⁶But everything I said through my servants the prophets happened to your ancestors, just as I said. As a result, they repented and said, 'We have received what we deserved from the LORD of Heaven's Armies. He has done what he said he would do.' "

1:1 Hebrew *In the eighth month.* A number of dates in Zechariah can be cross-checked with dates in surviving Persian records and related accurately to our modern calendar. This month of the ancient Hebrew lunar calendar occurred within the months of October and November 520 B.C.

NOTES

1:1 *November of the second year of King Darius's reign.* This date formula serves to root the message of Zechariah in a specific historical context: the early years of the great Persian Empire (539–330 BC). King Darius I (Hystaspes) ruled Persia from 522–486 BC.

the LORD gave this message. Lit., "the word of the LORD came." The combination of the verb "to be" (*hayah* [TH1961, ZH2118]) and the phrase "the word of the LORD" (*debar-yhwh* [TH1697/3068, ZH1821/3378]) constitutes the prophetic word formula. This formula commonly introduces a report of prophetic revelation in the oracular speech of the OT.

the prophet Zechariah. The word "prophet" (*nabi'* [TH5030, ZH5566]) designates Zechariah as an emissary, one who speaks with the authority of the commissioning agent—in this case, God himself.

1:3 *This is what the LORD of Heaven's Armies says.* This construction (*koh 'amar yhwh tseba'oth*) constitutes the messenger formula in prophetic speech and signifies the oral transmission of a message by a third party. The phrase suggests the divine assembly or council of the gods found in ancient Near Eastern thought. The picture is that the messenger of the council (i.e., the prophet) has stood as an observer in the council's session and is now reporting to others what he (as an envoy of the council) has heard (cf. ABD 2.214-217).

1:4 *earlier prophets.* This is a reference to the prophets of God who ministered during the preexilic period and were active in calling the kingdoms of Judah and Israel to repentance. The language of Zechariah seems to reflect especially the influence of the exilic prophets Jeremiah and Ezekiel (see Boda 2004:178-79).

Turn. In contexts expressing covenant relationship, the word *shub* [TH7725, ZH8740] (turn) expresses a change of loyalty on the part of Israel or God. Typically the term is understood as "repentance," a complete change of direction back to God, a total reorientation toward Yahweh. The imperative form of the verb conveys a sense of urgency and places a demand for immediate response on the audience. Baldwin (1972:90) notes that the preposition "from" indicates the prophet's admonition "is a call first of all to turn from evil ways" as a first step in their return to God.

evil ways . . . evil practices. The word pair "ways" (*derek* [TH1870, ZH2006]) and "practices" (*ma'alal* [TH4611, ZH5095]) often denotes a lifestyle in prophetic literature: The dispositions of the people's hearts and minds, as well as their actions, were bent toward evil (cf. Jer 4:18; 17:10; 32:19; Hos 4:9; 12:3; see the discussion in Boda 2004:179).

1:5 *ancestors.* This is a reference to the people of Israel (2 Kgs 17:13-14) and Judah (2 Chr 36:15-16) who were swept into exile because they were stubborn and refused to believe the word of the Lord. The same expression is found in King Hezekiah's "Passover Letter" calling the people of Israel and Judah to return to the Lord (2 Chr 30:7).

1:6 *servants the prophets.* The word "servant" (*'ebed* [TH5650, ZH6269]) was a title for Moses, the archetype of the OT prophet (Deut 34:5; cf. Deut 18:15; Mal 4:4). The true servant obeys the instructions of the overlord. A key trait of the OT prophets was their obedience to God's word (a fact that makes the story of Jonah all the more unusual; cf. Jonah 3:3). Jesus Christ, the ultimate Prophet, demonstrated this same obedient relationship to his Father (John 5:19-20; 12:49-50).

happened to your ancestors, just as I said. The term behind this expression (*hissigu* [TH5381, ZH5952], "overtake") alludes to the covenant curses of the Mosaic law pursuing and overtaking those who refuse to obey God's commands (Deut 28:15, 45).

COMMENTARY

The prelude to the book of Zechariah (1:1-6) includes the superscription (1:1) and a prologue (1:2-6). The superscription (1:1) is a formal statement that serves to classify biblical literature by genre (in this case as an oracular or prophetic text) and to identify the author, audience, date, and sometimes the occasion prompting the message from God. It is understood as distinct from an introduction in that the superscription stands outside the body of literature it prefaces.

The superscription to the book of Zechariah calls attention to two important theological truths. First, the date formula, rooting the prophet's message in time and space, affirms God as the sovereign ruler of history. He is the one who determines the course of world events and removes and establishes kings (Dan 2:21). Secondly, we learn that God willingly communicates with humanity by giving messages to particular individuals who "publish" this divine revelation through speeches and writings. God's ability to communicate with human beings sets him apart from the idols of false religions, which cannot hear or speak (cf. Isa 46:5-7). His omniscience makes him unique, alone as God and without rival (Isa 43:10-13).

The prologue (1:2-6) contains multiple layers of quoted material from earlier Old Testament prophets (1:4). Boda (2004:176) observes that "although difficult to follow, it [the prologue] reflects a rhetorical trend in later prophecy in which Yahweh is emphasized as the source of prophetic speech, even if that is at the expense of flow." The prelude to Zechariah (1:1-6) is widely recognized as an introduction to the first half of the book (chs 1-8), if not the book of Zechariah as a whole (cf. Baldwin 1972:87; Petersen 1984:110-111; Meyers and Meyers 1987:98; Boda 2004:181).

The Old Testament prophets were not averse to ascribing anger and wrath to God, as Zechariah does in 1:2 ("very angry"; *qatsap . . . qatsep* [TH7107/7110, ZH7911/7912]). God is a personal being, capable of love and anger. The emotion of God's anger is often described as an inward fire that erupts and burns with an unquenchable intensity (cf. Jer 4:4; 23:19). God's anger proceeds from his holiness, the essential attribute of his character (Ps 93:5; Isa 6:3; Rev 4:8). The objects of God's wrath are those who oppose him and those traveling the path of wickedness (Ps 1:4-6). Since God is also righteous, his anger is just (Ps 11:7; Isa 1:27; 5:16). Ultimately, God's wrath is divine retribution against sins committed by humanity. This means God's anger is not capricious or arbitrary, but rather it is a "legitimate reaction to the transgression of known stipulations" (Eichrodt 1967:260). The covenantal context of Zechariah's call to repentance alludes to the use of this word for anger in Deuteronomy 29:28 and Jeremiah 21:5, where God's anger burned against the Israelites because they broke faith with the Lord and worshiped other gods. The Lord is a jealous God: He will not give his glory to another (Deut 32:16, 21; Isa 42:8; 48:11). Thankfully, the Lord is also a merciful and gracious God, patient, and slow to anger (Exod 34:6; Nah 1:3). It is worth noting, according to Zechariah, that the people acknowledged that they had received what they "deserved" (1:6).

In contexts expressing covenant relationship, the word "return" (*shub* [TH7725, ZH8740], 1:3) is the Old Testament term for repentance. It signifies an "about-face" or a complete turnabout on the part of the person repenting. The expression connotes a change or shift in loyalty away from sin and self toward God, a reorientation to Yahweh and his covenant demands. The imperative form of the verb conveys a sense of urgency and places a demand for immediate and specific action on the part of those so addressed. The threefold repetition of the word "return" or "turn" (1:3-4) serves to heighten this sense of urgency. The liturgical formula in the prophetic summons to repentance ("return to me, and I will return to you") is repeated in Malachi 3:7 and has a precursor in Isaiah's plea to Jerusalem to "return to me [God], for I have paid the price to set you free" (Isa 44:22). The language of the liturgical formula may be rooted in the penitential prayers of the psalms (e.g., Pss 80:3, 7, 14, 19; 85:4-8; cf. Petersen 1984:131). (See the commentary on Mal 3:6-12 for more on the theology of repentance.)

On the human side of the ledger, returning to God and turning away from evil was essential for the forgiveness of sin. Naturally the "inward conversion of the heart in prayer and confession of sin" was assumed in this process of returning to God (Eichrodt 1967:472-473). On the divine side of the ledger, God promises to "return" to those who respond to the prophet's message by turning to him (1:3). This means that God, in his great love and compassion, accepts the repentant person by forgiving sin and restoring that individual to full covenant relationship with him (Jer 31:20; Hos 14:1-2). This reconciliation with God stays his anger, averts judgment, and brings healing to those who had broken covenant relationship with

Yahweh (Jer 4:1-2; Hos 14:4). The Hebrews returned to the land after the Babylonian exile, but they had not returned to God. As Baldwin (1972:92) has aptly observed, "on exactly the same terms as had been offered to their fathers, young and old alike are invited to return to God. If they do so, the covenant relationship will be renewed, and spiritual restoration will accompany the material restoration of the Temple." (See the discussion of the word "return" or "repent" in W. L. Holladay, *The Root Šûbh in the Old Testament*. [Leiden: Brill, 1958].)

Zechariah's rhetorical, even ironical questions (1:5) emphasize the eternal nature of God's word in contrast to the mortality of those who heard as well as those who delivered that divine revelation. The prophet reminded his audience that God's word was also a sure or true word since the things the prophets predicted happened just as the Lord had said (1:6). Petersen (1984:128) has identified those repenting and speaking in 1:6 as the audience of Zechariah, not their ancestors (as in the NLT). It seems quite clear in light of the context, however, that Zechariah refers to the ancestors of his audience in their admission of guilt, the justice of God, and their repentance after the destruction of Jerusalem (cf. Lam 1:18; 3:28-30, 37-40).

◆ II. Zechariah's Visions (1:7–6:15)
A. A Man among the Myrtle Trees (1:7-17)

[7]Three months later, on February 15,* the LORD sent another message to the prophet Zechariah son of Berekiah and grandson of Iddo.

[8]In a vision during the night, I saw a man sitting on a red horse that was standing among some myrtle trees in a small valley. Behind him were riders on red, brown, and white horses. [9]I asked the angel who was talking with me, "My lord, what do these horses mean?"

"I will show you," the angel replied.

[10]The rider standing among the myrtle trees then explained, "They are the ones the LORD has sent out to patrol the earth."

[11]Then the other riders reported to the angel of the LORD, who was standing among the myrtle trees, "We have been patrolling the earth, and the whole earth is at peace."

[12]Upon hearing this, the angel of the LORD prayed this prayer: "O LORD of Heaven's Armies, for seventy years now you have been angry with Jerusalem and the towns of Judah. How long until you again show mercy to them?" [13]And the LORD spoke kind and comforting words to the angel who talked with me.

[14]Then the angel said to me, "Shout this message for all to hear: 'This is what the LORD of Heaven's Armies says: My love for Jerusalem and Mount Zion is passionate and strong. [15]But I am very angry with the other nations that are now enjoying peace and security. I was only a little angry with my people, but the nations inflicted harm on them far beyond my intentions.

[16]"'Therefore, this is what the LORD says: I have returned to show mercy to Jerusalem. My Temple will be rebuilt, says the LORD of Heaven's Armies, and measurements will be taken for the reconstruction of Jerusalem.*'

[17]"Say this also: 'This is what the LORD of Heaven's Armies says: The towns of Israel will again overflow with prosperity, and the LORD will again comfort Zion and choose Jerusalem as his own.'"

1:7 Hebrew *On the twenty-fourth day of the eleventh month, the month of Shebat, in the second year of Darius.* This event occurred on February 15, 519 B.C.; also see note on 1:1. 1:16 Hebrew *and the measuring line will be stretched out over Jerusalem.*

NOTES

1:7 Three months later. This date formula governs all eight visions given to Zechariah (1:7–6:15); these were apparently a series of revelatory experiences during a single evening (cf. 4:1).

1:8 In a vision during the night, I saw. The technical expression (*ra'ithi hallaylah* [TH7200/3915A, ZH8011/4326]) means to receive revelation from God and implies more than mere human insight (cf. Isa 30:10). This experience is the result of divine inspiration and indicates that the prophet actually saw and heard the communication from God in some sort of "virtual reality."

myrtle trees. Mason (1977:36) connects the myrtle trees to the entrance of heaven, since myrtle trees represent the abode of the gods in ancient Near Eastern mythology. Baldwin (1972:95) is probably closer to a correct understanding in simply associating the myrtle trees with the Kidron Valley outside Jerusalem. The Lord had returned to the outskirts of the city, symbolically speaking, but had not yet entered Jerusalem because the second Temple was still under construction.

red, brown, and white horses. The specific colors of the horses are the subject of some debate. The colors, however, are insignificant to the meaning of this vision. These angelic riders' patrolling the earth simply indicates God was still concerned about Jerusalem (see the discussions in Baldwin 1972:95, 138-140; Petersen 1984:140-143; Redditt 1995:52-53). The NLT assumes the presence of "riders" on the other horses given the previous reference to a rider on the red horse (although lacking in the MT).

1:10 patrol. The (Hithpael) infinitive form of the verb *halak* [TH1980, ZH2143] (NLT, "patrol") simply denotes movement back and forth. The expression suggests a relentless crisscrossing and ongoing scrutiny of the earth by the angelic riders.

1:11 angel of the LORD. Lit., "messenger of the Lord." The title is given to the unnamed "man" (*'ish* [TH376, ZH408]) sitting on a red horse among the myrtle trees (1:8). This person has the ability to directly reveal information ordinarily hidden to human beings, so it seems the word "angel" or "messenger" signifies a heavenly being rather than a mortal. Often the appearance of the angel of the Lord in the OT is associated with action on behalf of the nation of Israel. At times, this angel may be a manifestation of God himself (e.g., Gen 16:13; Judg 13:21-22) but at other times appears to be a divine being distinguished from God the Father (perhaps Jesus Christ pre-incarnate, cf. Exod 23:23; 32:34; 1 Chr 21:27).

1:14 Jerusalem and Mount Zion. These are distinct and complementary entities according to Meyers and Meyers (1987:121), with Jerusalem as a broader term signifying the territories ruled by the Judean kings and Zion as the site of Yahweh's Temple.

1:16 measurements will be taken. The reference to the measuring line or builder's string (Qere is *qaw* [TH6957, ZH7742]; Kethiv is *qaweh* [TH6961, ZH7749]) symbolizes the first steps taken in the construction process. The stretching of the builder's string refers to general layout and design more than to taking actual, detailed measurements (cf. Job 38:5; Jer 31:39; see further Meyers and Meyers 1987:123).

1:17 again. The word *'od* [TH5750, ZH6388] is actually repeated four times in 1:17 (MT). The repetition speaks to the certainty of God's intention to restore Jerusalem.

overflow with prosperity. The term *puts* [TH6327A, ZH7046] usually means to scatter or disperse in defeat. The use of the word in this context suggests the image found in Prov 5:16 of water spilling out of a spring.

COMMENTARY

Zechariah's "book of visions" (1:7–6:15) contains eight revelations from God proclaiming a coming age of salvation for the Hebrew community in postexilic

Judah. The structure of the night visions follows a standard pattern for this form of visionary literature. The simple outline includes: (1) an introductory statement, (2) a description of the vision the prophet sees, (3) the prophet's request for an interpretation of the vision, and (4) an angelic explanation of the meaning of the vision. The date formula (1:7) indicates that Zechariah's series of eight visions occurred during a single night two months after Haggai's final two oracles, which promised a return of the divine presence and a great shaking of the cosmos (Hag 2:10-19, 20-23). The timing suggests that God was advancing the program of restoration announced by Haggai.

The first vision depicts God's concern for Jerusalem (1:7-15), and the supporting oracle of response (1:16-17) confirms God's intentions to rebuild his Temple and restore the prosperity of the city. The vision opens with a scene of troops of riders on horses of various colors patrolling the earth (1:8-11). There is some question as to the identity of the characters portrayed in the vision. The "man" on the red horse among the myrtle trees is later addressed as the "angel of the LORD" (1:11). The unnamed angel (1:9, 13-14) is a divine messenger who guides Zechariah through the vision and interprets the symbolic action the prophet witnesses. It is assumed that the troops of riders are also angelic beings of some unnamed sort or classification.

The horse was generally connected with warfare in the ancient world. The issue here seems to be the power, speed, and endurance represented by the horse. God's patrolling messengers crisscross the earth as his "eyes" and "ears," gathering data and reporting their findings. Interestingly, King Darius established a network of spies posing as "royal inspectors" that he called "the eyes and ears of the King" (cf. Briant 2002:343-344). The horses of various colors reappear in Zechariah's eighth vision pulling the chariots of the four spirits of heaven (6:2-3). We learn from visionary literature elsewhere in the Bible that the colors of the horses sometimes hold symbolic meaning (cf. Rev 6:1-8). Such does not seem to be the case here. Baldwin understands the angelic riders of Zechariah's vision as somewhat analogous to the messengers on horseback who functioned as a type of "pony express" system carrying messages across the empire to and from the Persian kings (1972:95).

The report delivered to the angel of the Lord is that "the whole earth is at peace" (1:11). This may mean that King Darius had quelled the revolts across the Persian Empire that greeted his succession to the throne. It may also signify that God had not yet, but soon would begin his campaign of "eschatological reversal" (so Redditt 1995:51). The essential message of the first night vision is that God still loves his people Israel and his city Jerusalem (1:14). Zechariah learned that God in his mercy planned to restore the city, its Temple, and once again bless the surrounding towns of Israel with agricultural bounty (1:16-17).

The "seventy years" of God's anger against Jerusalem and Judah is a reference to the duration of the Babylonian exile (1:12; cf. Jer 25:11-12; 29:10). If Daniel was taken captive during the first Babylonian invasion of Judah (c. 605 BC), then the exile lasted approximately 66 years and the number 70 is a round figure (placing the decree of Cyrus in 539 BC). God's anger was vented in reaction to the violation of his holiness. Israel was bound to God in covenant relationship, and they were charged to imitate God's holiness (Lev 11:44). Failure to do so brought the threat (and often the reality) of covenant curses against the Hebrews (cf. Lev 26; Deut 28). This divine judgment might be meted out in the form of natural calamity or as oppression by aggressor nations. The ultimate "curse" was the loss of the land of covenant promise, which involved the expulsion of the Hebrews from the land of Israel as a result of the "vomit theology" tied to the Mosaic covenant—that is, the threat that God would cause the land to "spew out" the Israelites should they adopt the idolatrous ways of the Canaanites (Lev 18:24-30). God was consistent in his application of this aspect of his divine judgment—the abominations of idolatry, gross immorality, child sacrifice, and occult practices meant expulsion from the land, whether for the Canaanite or the Hebrew (cf. 2 Kgs 21:2). The declaration that God intended to turn his anger against the nations (1:15) anticipates the message of divine judgment in the second vision (1:18-21).

God's passionate love for Jerusalem can be traced to the promises he made through Moses to choose a place for his name (Deut 12:11; 14:23). As a result of King David's conquest of Jerusalem and his vision for a Temple of Yahweh to be built there, that city became the place where God's name was honored (cf. 1 Kgs 8:29, 48). God's love for Jerusalem is tied to its designation as his residence (Ps 76:2); Mount Zion was home to the symbol of his divine presence on earth, the Ark of the Covenant, which was housed in the Temple (Ps 74:2). This means God maintained order in the cosmos and ruled over the nations of the earth from his holy city, Jerusalem—the city he loves more than any other city (Ps 87:2).

The expression "love . . . is passionate and strong" (1:14) renders a phrase that can be translated "I am jealous (qana' [TH7065, ZH7861]) . . . (with) great jealousy." This intense emotion is a single-minded devotion, which may produce hatred and envy when turned inward or zeal and selflessness when turned outward. God reveals himself as a jealous God because he is the one true and living God, and as Creator and Redeemer he has the exclusive right to the worship of his creatures. God's jealousy is first mentioned in conjunction with the Sinai covenant (Exod 20:5; 34:14). The special relationship created by this covenant means that Israel belongs to God and owes him the loyalty of a bride or adopted child (Jer 2:2). God will not share his glory with another, so any lapse on the part of Israel in maintaining the covenant relationship with Yahweh will result in experiencing his jealousy as a "devouring fire" (Deut 4:24). Yet God's love for his chosen people is so great that his jealousy is also their defense and hope of restoration (1:14; cf. Ezek 36:5; 38:19. See the discussion on "jealousy" in Baldwin 1972:101-103).

The preterist interpretation generally understands the first vision as fulfilled in the building of the second Temple by Zerubbabel and the physical and spiritual restoration of the people of Jerusalem as a result of the initiatives of Ezra and Nehemiah. Typically, the futurist interpretation identifies the rider on the red horse with Jesus Christ and associates the events of Zechariah's first vision with the Second Advent of Christ as depicted in Revelation 5–19.

◆   B. Four Horns and Four Blacksmiths (1:18-21)

¹⁸*Then I looked up and saw four animal horns. ¹⁹"What are these?" I asked the angel who was talking with me.

He replied, "These horns represent the nations that scattered Judah, Israel, and Jerusalem."

²⁰Then the LORD showed me four black-smiths. ²¹"What are these men coming to do?" I asked.

The angel replied, "These four horns—these nations—scattered and humbled Judah. Now these blacksmiths have come to terrify those nations and throw them down and destroy them."

1:18 Verses 1:18-21 are numbered 2:1-4 in Hebrew text.

NOTES

1:18 [2:1] *Then I looked up.* Baldwin (1972:103) suggests that the expression indicates that the prophet was "engrossed in thinking over all he had been hearing until another vision caught his attention" (note the repetition of the phrase in 2:1; 5:1; 6:1).

1:20 [2:3] *blacksmiths.* The word (*kharash* [TH2796, ZH3093]) is used generally of a craftsman of any sort (e.g., mason, carpenter, smith, etc.). If the horns representing the nations are made of metal (cf. 1 Kgs 22:11), then the blacksmith is the craftsman appropriate to the task of destroying the horns (cf. 2 Chr 24:12; Isa 44:12).

1:21 [2:4] *These . . . humbled Judah.* Lit., "those lifting up the horn against the land of Judah." Horns were generally symbolic of strength and authority.

throw them down. The word is a unique form of a rare word in the OT, a Piel infinitive of *yadah* [TH3034, ZH3343]. The word implies that the horns are cut off or cut down and then thrown to the ground—symbolizing an end to their authority and rule.

COMMENTARY

The meaning of the second vision is plainly stated: God plans to bring his judgment against the nations responsible for destroying Jerusalem and exiling Judah. This declaration of retribution makes explicit the threat of punishment earlier implied in God's anger with the nations enjoying peace and security at the expense of the Hebrews (1:15). In terms of sequence of events, the vision suggests that the restoration of Jerusalem will follow the overthrow of these aggressor nations.

The horn (*qeren* [TH7161, ZH7967]) was the symbol of power and authority in the biblical world and may represent an individual (e.g., 1 Sam 2:1 mg) or a nation (as in 1:19). In prophetic visions, the horn is commonly used in biblical prophecy to designate a king or a leader of a nation (often represented by a horn attached to an animal; e.g., Dan 7:8; 8:8). It would seem Zechariah has animal horns in mind in the retelling of his vision, although the context suggests metal horns of some kind (rather than ivory) since blacksmiths are summoned to beat the horns down and destroy them (1:20). It is possible that the horns of Zechariah's vision were horned crowns or even royal battle standards of some sort used as emblems for the nations (so Meyers and Meyers 1987:136).

The four horns of Zechariah's vision may represent four specific nations, or the number may be used symbolically to signify the totality or complete roster of nations guilty of oppressing Israel. Of the four beasts of Daniel's vision (which did not include a reference to Assyria), only the Babylonian Empire had come and gone at the time of Zechariah's preaching (cf. Dan 2:36-39; 7:17). Persia, Daniel's two-horned ram (Dan 8:20), was currently on the scene as the ruler of the ancient Near East (cf. Meyers and Meyers 1987:136-137, who argue against including Persia among those nations about to be overthrown). It seems likely, then, that Zechariah makes reference to those nations responsible for the destruction of the kingdoms of Israel and Judah and the deportation of the Hebrew citizens from those kingdoms.

Naturally, Assyria and Babylonia were among the "four horns" to be cut down since they conquered and exiled the Hebrew kingdoms of Israel and Judah respectively (cf. 2 Kgs 17:24-25; 25:1-2). Other nations oppressing the Hebrews included Egypt and Greece, both mentioned in Zechariah (9:13; 10:10-11). Babylonia overthrew Assyria and Persia overthrew Babylonia, which points to the conclusion that the divine judgment of the nations accused of scattering and humbling Israel was already well underway. One wonders if the prophet Malachi had Zechariah 1:18-21 in mind in his reference to the overthrow of Edom, one of the nations condemned for allying with the Babylonians against the Judean kingdom (Mal 1:4-5; cf. Ps 137:7-8).

God's use of the nations for the purpose of accomplishing both the punishment of the wicked and purification of the righteous is part of the mystery of his work as Sovereign Lord of history. God's rule of human history to accomplish his redemptive purposes is declared by Daniel (Dan 2:21) and acknowledged by the prophets (Isa 14:24-27). But this method of divine retribution troubled the prophet Habakkuk, who challenged God's use of nations more wicked than Israel to judge her sin (Hab 1:13). Likewise, God's willingness to extend mercy to the nations, like the brutal Assyrians, caused Jonah to refuse the call of God (Jonah 1:3; 4:3). God's judgment against these "horns" or nations is brought about, in part, because they overstepped their bounds as God's instrument of chastisement for his people ("the nations inflicted harm on them far beyond my intentions," 1:15; cf. Isa 47:6).

The preterist interpretation generally understands the "four horns" symbolically as those nations directly responsible for the overthrow of the Hebrew divided monarchies and the exile of Israelites (primarily Assyria and Babylonia and secondarily Egypt). The futurist understanding of the vision generally interprets the "four horns" literally as four specific nations (usually the four nations of the "times of the Gentiles" as identified in King Nebuchadnezzar's dream: Babylonia, Persia, Greece, and Rome; cf. Dan 2).

◆   C. Future Prosperity for Jerusalem (2:1-5)

*When I looked again, I saw a man with a measuring line in his hand. ²"Where are you going?" I asked.

He replied, "I am going to measure Jerusalem, to see how wide and how long it is."

³Then the angel who was with me went to meet a second angel who was coming toward him. ⁴The other angel said, "Hurry, and say to that young man, 'Jerusalem will someday be so full of people and livestock that there won't be room enough for everyone! Many will live outside the city walls. ⁵Then I, myself, will be a protective wall of fire around Jerusalem, says the LORD. And I will be the glory inside the city!' "

2:1 Verses 2:1-13 are numbered 2:5-17 in Hebrew text.

NOTES

2:1 [5] *I looked again.* See note on 1:18 above.

man. It is unclear whether this man with a measuring line in his hand is another angel or a human being, although the word "man" (*'ish* [TH376, ZH408]) suggests a human being.

measuring line. A different word is used for "measuring line" here than is found in 1:16mg. This is the only occurrence of the two-word phrase *khebel middah* [TH2256A/4060, ZH2475/4500] in the OT. The function of this measuring line appears to be that of a surveyor's line used to delineate an area rather than the builder's string (1:16) used in the construction process.

2:2 [6] *to measure Jerusalem, to see how wide and how long it is.* The infinitive verbal forms in this verse represented by "to measure" and "to see" are ambiguous regarding time and apply to either the then-present dimensions of Jerusalem (so NLT; "it is") or a future tense idea ("how long and wide it is to be," so NJPS).

2:4 [8] *that young man.* The comment is a reference to Zechariah who was in the company of the interpreting angel. The expression may be an indicator of the prophet's rather "youthful" age.

2:5 [9] *wall of fire.* This symbolic representation of divine protection calls to mind the horses and chariots of fire that surrounded Elisha when the king of Aram sent troops to capture God's prophet (2 Kgs 6:17).

I will be. The emphatic construction of the verb "to be" (*'ani* [TH589, ZH638] + *'ehyeh* [TH1961, ZH2118]) may be a direct reference to the revelation of the divine name Yahweh in Exod 3:14. The use of the words "fire" and "glory" (2:5) support the allusion to the Exodus from Egypt (cf. Exod 13:22, 14:20; 40:34).

COMMENTARY

The third vision injects two new developments in the sequence of Zechariah's visions. First, the scope of the vision narrows from the cosmos in vision one, to the nations in vision two, and finally to the city of Jerusalem. Second, the prophet moves from the place of an observer on the sidelines to that of a participant in the action of the world of the vision by addressing a question directly to the man with a measuring line (2:2). The vision is another salvation message and consists of two parts: the vision itself (2:1-3) and the oracle of response explaining the meaning of the vision (2:4-6). Baldwin (1972:105) has noted that taken together, the second and third visions portray God as working in appropriate ways to guarantee the protection of his people.

The vision describes a man with a measuring line plotting the length and width of Jerusalem (2:1-2). There is some question as to whether the man with the measuring line is an angel or a human being. Redditt's comment (1995:58) as to the purpose of the "measuring line" is cogent, since elsewhere the measuring line was a symbol of judgment (cf. the partitioning of Samaria by foreigners [Amos 7:17] and the destruction of Jerusalem [2 Kgs 21:13 mg]). But Zechariah and his accompanying interpreting angel are soon assured by a second angelic being that the measuring line symbolizes blessing, not judgment (2:3-6). Petersen (1984:169) connects "young man" (*na'ar* [TH5288, ZH5853]) of 2:4 with the man holding the measuring line (2:1). It seems more likely that the young man referred to is Zechariah the prophet, since the oracle of response would naturally be directed to the one asking the question (2:2).

The oracle of response (2:4-5) makes several important claims, including that Jerusalem will exist without walls, a large number of people and animals will populate the city, the Lord will be a wall of fire around Jerusalem, and the glory of God will reside in the city (cf. Petersen 1984:170-171). All this stood in stark contrast to the city as Zechariah knew it, with the Temple a rubble heap, the city walls in disrepair, and the people opting to live outside the confines of Jerusalem.

The preterist sees the fulfillment of the third vision in the Hebrew repatriation of the city of Jerusalem between the decree of Cyrus (538 BC) and the emigrations led by Ezra and Nehemiah (458–445 BC). The "glory" of God inside the city (2:5) is assumed to be a reference to the completed second Temple. The divine protection metaphorically depicted as a "wall of fire" (2:5) preserved the people of Jerusalem during the interim until the city walls were repaired under the leadership of Nehemiah. Generally, the futurist associates the prosperity and security Zechariah envisions for Jerusalem with the millennial glory of Christ's thousand-year reign on earth (Rev 20:1-6) or the new Jerusalem coming down from heaven at the recreation of heaven and earth (Rev 21:1-2).

◆   D. The Exiles Are Called Home (2:6-13)

⁶The LORD says, "Come away! Flee from Babylon in the land of the north, for I have scattered you to the four winds. ⁷Come away, people of Zion, you who are exiled in Babylon!"

⁸After a period of glory, the LORD of Heaven's Armies sent me* against the nations who plundered you. For he said, "Anyone who harms you harms my most precious possession.* ⁹I will raise my fist to crush them, and their own slaves will plunder them." Then you will know that the LORD of Heaven's Armies has sent me.

¹⁰The LORD says, "Shout and rejoice, O beautiful Jerusalem,* for I am coming to live among you. ¹¹Many nations will join themselves to the LORD on that day, and they, too, will be my people. I will live among you, and you will know that the LORD of Heaven's Armies sent me to you. ¹²The land of Judah will be the LORD's special possession in the holy land, and he will once again choose Jerusalem to be his own city. ¹³Be silent before the LORD, all humanity, for he is springing into action from his holy dwelling."

2:8a The meaning of the Hebrew is uncertain.   2:8b Hebrew *Anyone who touches you touches the pupil of his eye.*   2:10 Hebrew *O daughter of Zion.*

NOTES

2:6 [10] *Come away!* The repeated interjection (*hoy* [TH1945, ZH2098]) is translated variously as "Ho!" (KJV), "Up!" (NRSV), "Oh!" (NJB), "Listen!" (so Petersen 1984:172-173; cf. Isa 18:1; 55:1; Jer 48:6). The emphatic construction carries the force of a promise.

north. This is a metaphor for the "far reaches of the earth" as well as a literal statement since one needed to travel north (following the Tigris and Euphrates river valleys) when moving from east to west (or vice versa) in the biblical world (see the discussion in Peterson 1984:175). Military campaigns against Syro-Palestine typically came from the north, which is why Jeremiah refers to "armies of the kingdoms of the north" (Jer 1:13-16).

four winds. This is a figure of speech for the four major points of the compass (cf. Ezek 12:14; 37:9). The Hebrew exiles would return to Judah and Jerusalem from all directions.

2:7 [11] *in Babylon.* Lit., "dweller in the daughter of Babylon." See the discussion in Meyers and Meyers (1987:164) on the combination of the word "daughter" plus a toponym as a figure of speech for the collective inhabitants of a place. The immediate context suggests that the inhabitants addressed were the Hebrew exiles scattered throughout Babylonia.

2:8 [12] *After a period of glory, the Lord . . . sent me.* The line is especially difficult in the Hebrew text and the relation of the second half to the first is unclear (lit., "Thus says the Lord of hosts after [the] glory [he] sent me"). It is possible that the word "glory" refers to God (see 2:5), indicating that "the Glory" or God himself sent the prophet (NLT; so Petersen 1984:172-173; Meyers and Meyers 1987:162, 165).

precious possession. Lit., "the pupil of his eye." The idiom may refer to Israel as God's elect people and hence his precious possession. The expression may also mean that the one who harms Israel "touches the pupil of his (own) eye" and brings harm to himself in the form of divine judgment (i.e., harming God's elect is equivalent to poking yourself in the eye!).

2:9 [13] *you will know that the Lord of Heaven's Armies has sent me.* The pronoun "me" most likely refers to Zechariah as God's sent one (see commentary).

2:10 [14] *live.* The word is the same one used in reference to God's intention to "live" (*shakan* [TH7931, ZH8905]) in the Tabernacle (e.g., Exod 25:8).

2:12 [16] *special possession.* The phrase is unusual, consisting of the verb "take possession" (*nakhal* [TH5157, ZH5706]) and the noun "portion" (*kheleq* [TH2506, ZH2750]). The expression has covenant connotations, as Israel is the Lord's inheritance or "special possession" (Exod 34:9) and the people of Israel "belong to the Lord" (Deut 32:9-10).

holy land. The only time this designation for the land of Israel occurs in the OT. The land was made "holy" by virtue of the association of God's glory and presence with the Jerusalem Temple (cf. Pss 11:4; 15:1).

2:13 [17] *Be silent.* This word (*has* [TH2013A, ZH2187]) is an onomatopoetic word like our English word "hush" (cf. Hab 2:20; Zeph 1:7).

COMMENTARY

God's call for the return of the Hebrew exiles from Babylonia is one of two oracles accompanying the visions of Zechariah (see also 6:9-15). The prophetic exhortation divides neatly into two parts: The first promises a restoration of God's people to the land of Israel (2:6-9), and the second promises the restoration of God's presence with his people in Jerusalem (2:10-13).

The first message of the accompanying oracle continues the theme of divine protection emphasized in the third vision (2:8; cf. 2:5). The reference to slaves plundering their oppressors echoes events associated with the Exodus from Egypt when God predisposed the Egyptians to pay the Israelites to leave their land (2:9; cf. Exod 11:2-3; 12:35-36)! The second message anticipates the fourth vision—the cleansing of the High Priest as a necessary preparation for welcoming God's presence back to Jerusalem (3:1-10).

Taken together, the elements of Zechariah's message highlight several facets of God's character and redemptive work in history. First, God is just. He will not let the guilty go unpunished (Pss 7:17; 71:16; Nah 1:3). The hound of divine judgment will pursue and crush the nations who have plundered Israel (2:8). Second, God is a deliverer (Exod 12:42; 1 Sam 2:1; Pss 119:123; 144:2). Shouting and rejoicing typically mark Israel's celebration of God's deliverance (2:10; e.g., 9:9; Pss 20:5; 63:7; Isa 12:6; Zeph 3:14). The celebration of divine deliverance anticipates the festive joy of the enthronement of Yahweh as king in Jerusalem once again and may point to the shouting and rejoicing of the nations around the throne of the Lamb in the eschaton (cf. Pss 98:4-6; 132:8-9; Rev 7:9-10). Yet, in view of what God was about to do in reversing the fortunes of Israel and the nation who oppressed them, reverent silence is demanded (2:13). Third, despite his transcendent holiness, God desires to establish a home address among his people—to "move into the neighborhood," so to speak (2:10-11). The theme of the divine presence, showcasing the immanence of God, extends from the Tabernacle of Moses (Exod 25:8-9) to the restored creation (Rev 21:3). Finally, God's election of Israel as his "special possession" (2:11-12) results in blessing for the nations, as well, in fulfillment of the covenant made with Abraham (Gen 12:1-3).

The almost formulaic declaration "you will know that the LORD of Heaven's Armies has sent me" is repeated in each of the messages of the accompanying oracle (2:8, 9, 11). The same validation formula also appears in 4:9 and 6:15 in Zechariah's Visions (1:7–6:15). Among those former Hebrew captives recently arrived from Babylonia and other points to the east, a crisis of doubt had arisen concerning the prophetic word. God's people had been back in the land of covenant promise for two decades, but the predictions of Jeremiah and Ezekiel seemed to have failed. The people looked for much, like the new covenant promised by Jeremiah (Jer 31:31) and the peace and prosperity promised by Ezekiel (Ezek 36:11), but found little (cf. Hag 1:6). Zechariah stressed his divine commission to authenticate his ministry as God's prophet and to certify his message as the word of God. A series of impending events would indeed confirm the reliability of God's word to Israel through his prophet, beginning with the rebuilding of Yahweh's Temple in Jerusalem.

◆ E. Cleansing for the High Priest (3:1-10)

Then the angel showed me Jeshua* the high priest standing before the angel of the LORD. The Accuser, Satan,* was there at the angel's right hand, making accusations against Jeshua. ²And the LORD said to Satan, "I, the LORD, reject your accusations, Satan. Yes, the LORD, who has chosen Jerusalem, rebukes you. This man is like a burning stick that has been snatched from the fire."

³Jeshua's clothing was filthy as he stood there before the angel. ⁴So the angel said to the others standing there, "Take off his filthy clothes." And turning to Jeshua he said, "See, I have taken away your sins, and now I am giving you these fine new clothes."

⁵Then I said, "They should also place a clean turban on his head." So they put a clean priestly turban on his head and dressed him in new clothes while the angel of the LORD stood by.

⁶Then the angel of the LORD spoke very solemnly to Jeshua and said, ⁷"This is what the LORD of Heaven's Armies says: If you follow my ways and carefully serve me,

then you will be given authority over my Temple and its courtyards. I will let you walk among these others standing here.

8"Listen to me, O Jeshua the high priest, and all you other priests. You are symbols of things to come. Soon I am going to bring my servant, the Branch. 9Now look at the jewel I have set before Jeshua, a single stone with seven facets.* I will engrave an inscription on it, says the LORD of Heaven's Armies, and I will remove the sins of this land in a single day.

10"And on that day, says the LORD of Heaven's Armies, each of you will invite your neighbor to sit with you peacefully under your own grapevine and fig tree."

3:1a Hebrew *Joshua*, a variant spelling of Jeshua; also in 3:3, 4, 6, 8, 9.   3:1b Hebrew *The satan*; similarly in 3:2.   3:9 Hebrew *seven eyes.*

NOTES

3:1 *the angel of the LORD.* The prophet's vision depicts a heavenly courtroom with the "prosecuting attorney" (Satan) accusing the defendant (Jeshua the high priest) of being unfit for his priestly duties. The Lord is both "defense attorney" and "judge." He censured the arguments of the prosecution, dismissed the case, and declared Jeshua innocent by virtue of his divine election and cleansing. The "angel of the LORD" (3:1) and "the LORD" (3:2) seem to be one and the same divine being (see note on 1:11).

The Accuser, Satan. The construction of the word with the definite article, "the satan" (*hassatan* [TH1886.1/7854A, ZH2021/8477]), designates a functionary of the heavenly court whose role is to accuse human beings of wrongdoing.

right hand. This is a position of authority, marking "the Accuser" as "first officer" in the heavenly court (see the discussion of the Divine Council in Meyers and Meyers 1987:183-187).

accusations. The title "Satan" and the word "accusations" are based on the same root: *stn* [TH7853, ZH8476].

3:2 *reject . . . rebukes.* The emphatic repetition of the Lord's "rebuke" (*ga'ar* [TH1605, ZH1721]) of Satan's accusations serves as a reminder that even Satan is subject to the dictates of the Sovereign Lord. The Lord's example is also a model for the angelic hosts and the faithful people of God in withstanding the attacks of the evil one (and those in league with him) by rebuking the enemy in the name of the Lord Jesus Christ (cf. Eph 5:11; Jude 1:9).

3:5 *place a clean turban.* The turban of the high priest was set with a medallion of pure gold inscribed with the words "HOLY TO THE LORD" (Exod 28:36). The high priest was supposed to wear the turban at all times so that the Lord would accept the people of Israel (Exod 28:38). The placement of the turban on Jeshua's head was an act of ordination or dedication, reinstating him in the priestly office and as mediator for the people. The word for "turban" (*tsanip* [TH6797, ZH7565]) is rare in the OT (only found here and in Job 29:14 and Isa 62:3) and connotes an elaborate headdress associated with royalty (cf. Meyers and Meyers 1987:178; Petersen 1984:198). The use of such an unusual term here may anticipate the later "crowning" of Jeshua (6:9-15).

3:8 *my servant, the Branch.* The angel indicates that the high priest Jeshua and the other priests are "symbols" (*mopeth* [TH4159, ZH4603]) or types of greater realities. The terms "servant" and "Branch" are both titles for the Messiah. As servant, the Messiah obeys the will of God even to the point of becoming a sin offering so that many may be counted righteous (Isa 53:11; cf. Acts 3:13; 4:27). The Branch is a metaphor for kingship; this is first because the symbol identifies the Messiah as a descendant of David and hearkens back to the Davidic covenant and the divine promise of kingship granted to the dynasty of David (Isa 11:1; cf. 2 Sam 7:4-17). Second, the prophet Jeremiah equated the "Branch" with a Davidic king who would rule with wisdom and righteousness (Jer 23:5, cf. NLT mg).

According to Luke 1:78, Jesus is the predicted *anatolē* [TG395, ZG424]. This word goes back to the LXX, which translates the Hebrew word *tsemakh* [TH6780, ZH7542] (branch, sprout) with the Greek word *anatolē* (which usually means "sun rising" but may also mean "sprout" or "shoot"; cf. BAGD 62) in 3:8; 6:12; and in Jer 23:5. This is the only direct lexical connection between the NT and the use of this messianic title in the OT prophets. Some hold that Matthew refers to the Hebrew word "branch" (*netser*) in associating Jesus with the town of Nazareth in fulfillment of OT prophecy (although the exact words of Matthew's citation are not found in the OT; cf. Nicoll 1974:1.77-78). The emphasis on the geographical context of Galilee and Nazareth in Matt 2:19-23 makes the identification unlikely.

3:9 single stone. The abrupt shift from the symbol of the Branch to a stone is puzzling. The stone may anticipate the "final stone" in the Temple laid by Zerubbabel (4:7) or even refer to the foundation stone of Isaiah's prophecy (Isa 28:16). The stone may allude to the ephod of the high priest, which was decorated with precious stones (Exod 25:7; 35:9). The engraving of an inscription on the stone recalls the engraved golden rosette set in the priest's turban, the engraved onyx stones fastened to the shoulder pieces of the ephod (Exod 28:9, 36-39), and the engraved gemstones of the chestpiece (Exod 39:14). In any case, the stone signifies authority and represents another messianic metaphor or symbol.

seven facets. The number seven is the number of perfection and completeness. The seven facets of the stone may be related to the seven lamps of the golden lampstand (4:2). The facets (lit., "eyes") of the stone probably symbolize knowledge and wisdom and may allude to the "sevenfold Spirit" of God (Rev 1:4).

I will remove the sins of this land in a single day. The removal of the sin of Israel in a single day alludes to the Day of Atonement (Lev 16). Understood prophetically, the phrase may be a reference to the day of the crucifixion of Jesus Christ as "the Lamb of God who takes away the sin of the world" (John 1:29).

3:10 that day. This phrase is shorthand in the OT prophets for "the day of the LORD" (cf. 2:11; Isa 2:11; Joel 2:1; Zeph 1:14). This eschatological "day" of divine intervention in history brings both judgment of the wicked and deliverance of the righteous (cf. 12:8; 14:3). The Day of the Lord is an indefinite period of time of divine activity, but always impending (note the word "soon" [3:8] in reference to the coming of "the Branch," fulfilled some five centuries after Zechariah's vision with the incarnation of Jesus Christ!).

COMMENTARY

Jeshua (a later form of the name Joshua) was high priest during Zechariah's ministry. He was among the returnees to postexilic Judah from exile in Babylonia (Ezra 2:2). He and Zerubbabel represented the religious and civil leadership of the restoration community, and they were partners in the rebuilding of the Jerusalem Temple (Ezra 5:2; Hag 2:1-5).

In Zechariah's vision, Jeshua stands before the Lord as the representative of Israel, especially of those in exile. The twelve stones of the high priest's ephod and the two inscribed stones on the shoulder piece were perpetual reminders that the representation of Israel before the Lord was a function of the high priest (Exod 28:9-12). Like a "burning stick that has been snatched from the fire" (3:2), Jeshua and the Hebrew exiles were plucked by God from near destruction in Babylonia. Singed and soot covered, the Jewish nation now stood before the Lord in the person of Jeshua, facing the charges of the Accuser, Satan (3:1-2). Jeshua's "filthy clothes" (3:4) are symbols of the guilt and pollution of sin that prompted the divine judgment of exile. No doubt the Accuser contended that any priest clad in such fashion was unfit for Temple service (thus implying that the Hebrews were unfit to be the chosen people of God).

As the vision unfolds, the angel of the Lord orders other angels to remove the filthy clothes—a symbol of the removal of the sins and guilt of Jeshua and the Hebrew people (3:3-4). The placing of the priestly turban on Jeshua's head along with the new vestments was emblematic of the restoration to their former position accomplished in the divine cleansing (i.e., Jeshua to his service as high priest and Israel as the people of God, 3:5). This restoration to priestly service and access to the divine presence, however, was conditional—it had to be according to the pattern of the Mosaic covenant (cf. Deut 30:19-20). Jeshua's privilege and position were contingent upon obedience to God (3:6-7).

Zechariah's fourth vision serves as a reminder of several important theological principles that continue from the first Testament into the second Testament. The first is the principle of priestly mediation. Even as the tribe of Levi and the family of Aaron were chosen to represent the Israelites before God, so Jesus Christ is the only mediator who can reconcile God and people as High Priest (1 Tim 2:5; Heb 8:1). Second, redemption belongs to the Lord God of Israel; he alone is mighty to save (Zeph 3:17; Matt 1:21; Heb 7:25). This means the work of atoning for sins, cleansing from guilt, and restoration to position and service as the people of God are the exclusive prerogative of the triune God (Isa 64:6; Acts 4:12; Rom 10:13; Rev 7:10). Finally, the vision of the restoration of Jeshua speaks to the very nature and character of God—the one who is gracious and rich in unfailing love, who is righteous, and who takes delight in showing mercy and forgiving every kind of sin (Exod 34:6-7; Mic 7:18).

At this time in the historical development of Hebrew theology, the expression "the Accuser, Satan" should probably be understood as a title or description of function, rather than a personal name. (See the discussion on "Satan" in Hill and Walton 2000:335.) The "Accuser" has a role similar to the *rabisu* official of Mesopotamia in the Old Babylonian court. This officer was the most important court personage next to the judge; he was responsible for the preliminary examination of the accused at trials (see "Rabisu" in van der Toorn 2001:682-683). The word "satan" simply means "adversary," and the function of the adversary may be performed either by human or divine beings (cf. 1 Sam 29:4; 1 Chr 21:1). The role of the adversary (or the "satan") is not always an evil one, as evidenced by Balaam's encounter with the angel of the Lord (Num 22:22).

The context of Zechariah indicates that the function of the adversary in 3:1 was evil in its intent in that it sought to discredit Jeshua the high priest. The strong rebuke of the Accuser by the Lord supports this understanding (3:2). The Accuser (the "satan") appears to be a divine being or angel and a member of the divine council of Yahweh, having the formal function of "prosecuting attorney" (cf. Job 1:6; see the discussion in Meyers and Meyers 1987:183-186 on the divine council). By the time of the New Testament, "Satan" was being used as a personal name belonging to an evil angel considered to be the prince of the demons (Matt 4:10; 12:26). Satan is equated with "the serpent" and "the devil," and he is identified as both the deceiver of humanity and the adversary of God and all that is good (2 Cor 4:4; Eph 6:11; Rev 20:2).

The second half of the angel's speech to Jeshua is clearly messianic in nature (3:8-10). Jeshua himself is not identified as the Branch; rather, he and the other priests are "symbols" or prophetic signs pointing to a great priestly servant of God (3:8). Two distinctive figures of speech further underscore the messianic intent of the angel's message. The Branch (3:8) is associated with the Davidic covenant elsewhere in the Old Testament (Jer 23:5 mg); he is described both as a righteous king and a shepherd (Jer 33:15-17; Ezek 34:23; 37:24). The image of the Israelites sitting peacefully under vines (3:10) is a picture of security and prosperity under messianic rule, according to the Old Testament prophets (e.g., Mic 4:4), reminiscent of the ideals achieved during the reign of King Solomon (1 Kgs 4:25).

The preterist interpretation of this vision seeks to identify the Branch as Jeshua or Zerubbabel, the religious and civil leaders of the postexilic community during the period of Temple reconstruction (cf. Mason 1977:52). The futurist interpretation of the vision finds at least partial fulfillment of the messianic projections in the First Advent of Jesus Christ. Jesus is identified as the son of David and bears the title of king (Matt 1:1; 2:2).

Even as Jeshua was cleansed for his ministry as high priest, Jesus Christ, as the ultimate high priest, was sinless (Heb 7:26-27). Despite the fact that Jesus was the stone the builders rejected (1 Pet 2:7), in his own death he offered the one sacrifice necessary to atone for the sins of many people (Heb 9:28). As a result, Jesus Christ has implemented a spiritual kingdom of peace with God and prosperity in the form of righteousness (Rom 14:17). Some futurist interpreters suggest that the picture of the faithful people of God sitting peacefully under their vines will be fully and literally realized in the Second Advent of Jesus Christ and the establishment of his millennial kingdom (Rev 20).

◆   F. A Lampstand and Two Olive Trees (4:1-14)

Then the angel who had been talking with me returned and woke me, as though I had been asleep. ²"What do you see now?" he asked.

I answered, "I see a solid gold lampstand with a bowl of oil on top of it. Around the bowl are seven lamps, each having seven spouts with wicks. ³And I see two olive trees, one on each side of the bowl." ⁴Then I asked the angel, "What are these, my lord? What do they mean?"

⁵"Don't you know?" the angel asked.

"No, my lord," I replied.

⁶Then he said to me, "This is what the LORD says to Zerubbabel: It is not by force nor by strength, but by my Spirit, says the LORD of Heaven's Armies. ⁷Nothing, not even a mighty mountain, will stand in Zerubbabel's way; it will become a level plain before him! And when Zerubbabel sets the final stone of the Temple in place, the people will shout: 'May God bless it! May God bless it!'*"

⁸Then another message came to me

from the LORD: ⁹"Zerubbabel is the one who laid the foundation of this Temple, and he will complete it. Then you will know that the LORD of Heaven's Armies has sent me. ¹⁰Do not despise these small beginnings, for the LORD rejoices to see the work begin, to see the plumb line in Zerubbabel's hand."

(The seven lamps* represent the eyes of the LORD that search all around the world.)

¹¹Then I asked the angel, "What are these two olive trees on each side of the lampstand, ¹²and what are the two olive branches that pour out golden oil through two gold tubes?"

¹³"Don't you know?" he asked.

"No, my lord," I replied.

¹⁴Then he said to me, "They represent the two heavenly beings who stand in the court of the Lord of all the earth."

4:7 Hebrew *'Grace, grace to it.'*   4:10 Or *The seven facets* (see 3:9); Hebrew reads *These seven.*

NOTES

4:1 *woke me.* The series of visions came to Zechariah in a single night. The return (4:1) of the interpreting angel to awaken him suggests that the prophet had slept briefly before the fifth vision appeared to him.

4:2 *gold lampstand.* This is a reference to the golden menorah of the Mosaic Tabernacle replicated as the lamp for the second Temple in contrast to the ten lampstands of Solomon's Temple (Exod 25:31; 1 Kgs 7:49; cf. 1 Macc 1:21-23). (See the images of lamps and lampstands in Meyers and Meyers 1987: Illustrations 12, 13, 14.)

4:6-10a Many biblical commentators understand 4:6-10a as an intrusive oracle interrupting the explanation of the vision (which resumes in 4:10b). Yet, according to Ryken (1984:170), visionary literature reverses ordinary reality and instead of expecting a smooth flow of narrative, the reader should "be prepared for a disjointed series of diverse, self-contained units." The insertion of the oracle promising success to Zerubbabel in the rebuilding of the Jerusalem Temple is an emphatic device intended to place the focus of attention where it belongs—not on Zerubbabel as God's agent but on the God who empowers Zerubbabel.

4:7 *mighty mountain . . . will become a level plain.* This is a figure of speech in both the OT (cf. Isa 40:4; 49:11) and NT (cf. Matt 17:20; 1 Cor 13:2), signifying that faith in God enables his servants to overcome seemingly impossible obstacles.

final stone. This is the capstone or "headstone" (*ha'eben haro'shah* [TH68/7222, ZH74/8036]) that completes a stone wall or building once it is set in place (cf. Ps 118:22).

May God bless it! Lit., "Grace, grace to it!" Here the statement should be understood as a prayer seeking God's favor and blessing for the new Temple.

4:10 *plumb line.* A plumb line is a cord with a tin or lead weight attached to one end that is used to determine verticality in construction. The exact meaning of the Hebrew expression *ha'eben habbedil* [TH68/913, ZH74/974] is uncertain . The idea of a tin plumb on a line reflects the influence of the LXX (*ton lithon ton kassiterinon*, "stone of tin," hence, "plummet of tin"). Meyers and Meyers (1987:253) translate it "tin-stone," perhaps a ceremonial stone used to commemorate the completion of a building project similar to the "final stone" mentioned above (4:7; cf. NJB, "chosen stone"). Petersen (1984:243) suggests "tin-tablet," a building deposit of some sort acknowledging the completion of the Temple (perhaps including a ceremony in which a stone from the ruins of the old Temple was transferred to the new Temple; cf. Redditt 1995:69).

seven lamps. The seven lamps are equated with the eyes of the Lord that scan the earth. The number seven signifies completeness or perfection. God sees all that takes place on the earth, implying that he both knows and controls the peoples and nations as the "Lord of all the earth" (4:14; see also the note on 3:9 concerning the "seven facets" of the stone set before Jeshua).

4:14 *two heavenly beings.* Lit., "the two sons of (olive) oil" (*bene-hayyitsehar* [TH1121/3323, ZH1201/3658]), a phrase that may also be understood to refer to "the two anointed ones" or "the two branches of the olive tree" (cf. 4:12). Both Haggai and Zechariah singled out Jeshua and Zerubbabel, the religious and civic leaders of postexilic Jerusalem, for special messages from the Lord (3:1; 4:6; Hag 1:14; 2:2). The context of the sequence of night visions suggests the two beings in view here are the high priest Jeshua and the governor Zerubbabel (especially chs 3 and 4). It was under their leadership that the Temple of the Lord would be rebuilt and worship restored in Jerusalem. Jeshua was given a place standing in the presence of God with the rest of the divine council contingent upon his obedience to the Lord's requirements (3:7). Presumably this was the situation for Zerubbabel, as well. The NLT identifies the two as "heavenly" beings on the basis of Rev 11:4 (although the adjective "heavenly" is not found in the MT). It should also be noted that in the vision of Rev 11:4, there are two lampstands and two olive trees standing before the Lord, whereas Zechariah's vision reports a single lampstand (4:2).

COMMENTARY

The images in Zechariah's vision represent both unseen spiritual realities and tangible earthly offices and persons. The solid gold lampstand probably functions as a symbol for God, expressing his purity, holiness, and revelatory light (4:2). The two olive trees may represent the offices of priest and king in Israel, and the two branches of the olive trees are emblems for Jeshua and Zerubbabel (4:3, 12). The golden oil may be a symbol of God's Holy Spirit (4:12).

   The gist of the vision of the lampstand and the two olive trees is that God would enable Zerubbabel (and Jeshua) to rebuild his holy Temple, an important message of encouragement to postexilic Judah. The fifth vision reinforces three basic spiritual truths: First, with God everything is possible (cf. Matt 19:26); second, God accomplishes his purposes in the world through human servants empowered by the Holy Spirit (4:6; cf. 7:12; Hag 2:5; John 16:5-15); and third, God delights in "small beginnings" (4:10; cf. Hag 2:3). Such small beginnings are exemplified in the "small" lunch multiplied by Jesus to feed thousands (Matt 15:34), the "small" mustard seed that becomes a great tree (Matt 17:20), and the faithful management of "small" things yielding great reward (Matt 25:21-23).

   The preterist view of the fifth vision equates the two olive trees flanking the lampstand with Jeshua and Zerubbabel of postexilic Judah, and it considers the vision fulfilled in the completion of the second Temple. The futurist understanding of the fifth vision regards the two olive trees as symbols of the two offices of Messiah (priest and king) fulfilled in Jesus Christ. Most futurists would grant that the historical figures of Jeshua and Zerubbabel represent these two functions of Messiah in some sort of type/antitype relationship. On the basis of Revelation 11:4 (equating the two witnesses of the "tribulation" period with the two olive trees of 4:2-3), another futurist approach to the vision understands Israel as the light of the millennial earth under the Messiah as the priest-king (cf. Unger 1963:104-105). The reference to the completion of the Temple is variously interpreted as the millennial Temple (cf. 14:20-21) or as a metaphor for the Kingdom of God (Rev 11:15).

◆ G. A Flying Scroll (5:1-4)

I looked up again and saw a scroll flying through the air.

²"What do you see?" the angel asked.

"I see a flying scroll," I replied. "It appears to be about 30 feet long and 15 feet wide.*"

³Then he said to me, "This scroll contains the curse that is going out over the entire land. One side of the scroll says that those who steal will be banished from the land; the other side says that those who swear falsely will be banished from the land. ⁴And this is what the LORD of Heaven's Armies says: I am sending this curse into the house of every thief and into the house of everyone who swears falsely using my name. And my curse will remain in that house and completely destroy it—even its timbers and stones."

5:2 Hebrew *20 cubits* [9 meters] *long and 10 cubits* [4.5 meters] *wide.*

NOTES

5:1 *I looked up again.* The sixth of eight successive visions that Zechariah experienced in the same night.

scroll flying. A scroll (*megillah* [TH4039, ZH4479]) was the equivalent of a book in biblical times. It was most often made of rolled parchment (or leather), but sometimes papyrus or metal (like tin or copper) might be used as the writing material. Here the scroll is unfurled like a banner for all to see, much like a banner flown as an advertising trailer behind a small airplane (or perhaps a sort of precursor of the modern "billboard").

5:3 *the curse.* The term *'alah* [TH423, ZH460] may be understood as an "oath" (e.g., Deut 29:12, NIV) or a "curse" (Deut 29:19). The close relationship between the two meanings of the word stems from the fact that the act of oath-taking in a covenant ceremony binds the parties to the attendant curses threatened for any violation of the agreement. Here the word alludes to the curses invoked against those who violate the stipulations of the Mosaic covenant (Deut 29:20). By means of the literary device of personification, "the curse" is set loose like a law officer to do God's bidding in the punishment of covenant violations (5:4; cf. Ps 147:15; Isa 55:11).

COMMENTARY

Zechariah's vision of the flying scroll was a reminder to the leaders and the people of postexilic Judah that they were still obligated to obey the commandments of the Mosaic covenant. Beyond this, the Hebrew community needed to understand that the conditional curses of the Sinai treaty were still operative. This vision hearkens back to the charge to Jeshua, the high priest, to follow God's ways and serve him carefully by obeying the priestly prescriptions of the Torah (3:7). It also looks forward to the removal of sin from the community portrayed in the seventh vision (5:5-11) and to Zechariah's sermons calling for social justice (7:9-10; 8:16-17).

The preterist view understands the vision of the flying scroll as a call to postexilic Judah to return to God in covenant renewal and as a charge to the Levitical priesthood to instruct the people in obedience to the law of Moses (cf. Deut 33:9-10). The futurist view regards the vision as a projection of the righteous rule of Jesus Christ as the "Word of God" in the millennial kingdom when the Messiah will impose the law of God upon the nations (Rev 19-20). Some even suggest that the flying scroll declaring the message of the Mosaic covenant is the foreshadowing of the proclamation of the gospel of Christ via telecommunication satellites.

◆ H. A Woman in a Basket (5:5-11)

⁵Then the angel who was talking with me came forward and said, "Look up and see what's coming."

⁶"What is it?" I asked.

He replied, "It is a basket for measuring grain,* and it's filled with the sins* of everyone throughout the land."

⁷Then the heavy lead cover was lifted off the basket, and there was a woman sitting inside it. ⁸The angel said, "The woman's name is Wickedness," and he pushed her back into the basket and closed the heavy lid again.

⁹Then I looked up and saw two women flying toward us, gliding on the wind. They had wings like a stork, and they picked up the basket and flew into the sky.

¹⁰"Where are they taking the basket?" I asked the angel.

¹¹He replied, "To the land of Babylonia,* where they will build a temple for the basket. And when the temple is ready, they will set the basket there on its pedestal."

5:6a Hebrew *an ephah* [20 quarts or 22 liters]; also in 5:7, 8, 9, 10, 11.   5:6b As in Greek version; Hebrew reads *the appearance.*   5:11 Hebrew *the land of Shinar.*

NOTES

5:6 *basket for measuring grain.* This "basket" (*'epah* [TH374, ZH406], transliterated "ephah"; cf. NLT mg) was a standardized unit of dry measure equivalent to approximately one-half bushel. Typically the baskets of OT times were woven of willow or palm branches, reeds, or cane. The condemnation of an "unjust ephah" by the OT prophets makes the association between the ephah basket and evil a familiar one (cf. Ezek 45:10; Mic 6:10).

sins. The NLT agrees with most English versions (e.g., NIV, NRSV), which follow the reading in the LXX and Syriac "their iniquity" (reflecting *'awonam* [TH5771/3963.1, ZH6411/4392]) instead of the difficult MT "their eyes" (*'enam* [TH5869/3963.1, ZH6524/4392]). Meyers and Meyers (1987:296), however, prefer the MT and translate "this is its appearance [i.e., the ephah basket] in all the land" (rendering "their eyes" with the figurative meaning "appearance" or "shining").

5:7 *heavy lead cover.* The heavy metal lid is not a natural cover for the ephah basket (which might also refer to a clay barrel of an ephah). That the "cover" (*kikkar* [TH3603, ZH3971]) is made of a talent (60 or more pounds) of "lead" (*'opereth* [TH5777, ZH6769]) emphasizes "the fact that an extraordinary device is being used to enclose forcefully and unalterably the ephah's strange contents" (Meyers and Meyers 1987:299).

5:8 *Wickedness.* The term (*rish'ah* [TH7564, ZH8402]) refers to evil generally, whether moral or ceremonial. The word is sometimes used in word-pairs as the polar opposite of "righteousness" (e.g., Prov 13:6; Ezek 33:12; see commentary below). Since the word for "Wickedness" is a feminine noun, evil is personified as a woman (see further the discussion in Redditt 1995:73-74).

5:9 *two women.* The depiction of the two-winged creatures as "women" is unusual in the OT. Typically such divine or angelic beings are male figures. It is unclear whether these female divine beings are attendants of Yahweh or of the wicked woman enclosed in the ephah basket. If the two women are attendants of Yahweh, then they represent a unique class of angelic beings in the heavenly realm. If they are the angelic retainers of "Wickedness" (representing a foreign goddess), then their submission to the command of God demonstrates his power over false gods (see Meyers and Meyers 1987:305-306). Either way, the role of these female attendants who carry off "Wickedness" is significant in its contrast to the "evil woman" in the basket.

wind. The word (*ruakh* [TH7307, ZH8120]) may suggest the double entendre since it can mean either "wind" or "spirit" (i.e., "gliding on the Spirit").

stork. The stork is a migratory bird of the Mediterranean basin. Baldwin (1972:129) has suggested a wordplay with "stork" (*khasidah* [TH2624, ZH2884]) and "faithful one" (*khasid* [TH2623A, ZH2883]): "the removal of 'wickedness,' like the removal of Joshua's filthy garments (3:4), was an act of free grace on the part of the covenant-keeping (*khasid*) God."

5:11 Babylonia. Babylonia was the land of Hebrew captivity (Mic 4:10). The prophets condemned Babylon as a place of idolatry and wickedness (Isa 46–47; Jer 50–51). In the NT, Babylon is a metaphor for the evil of Rome and the Roman Empire (Rev 17:5; 18:2; cf. 1 Pet 5:13).

temple . . . pedestal. The reference to building a "house" or "temple" (*bayit* [TH1004, ZH1074]) for the woman in the ephah basket and then setting the basket upon a base or pedestal of some sort suggests that this woman named "Wickedness" is a goddess of the Babylonian pantheon.

COMMENTARY

There is general agreement that the seventh vision continues the theme of cleansing begun in the fourth vision with the investiture of the newly clad high priest, Jeshua (3:1-10). Most commentators also acknowledge that the symbolism of the evil woman in the basket represents a seductive and dangerous force that is difficult to contain (to the point of being "pushed" back into the basket that is closed with a "heavy lid"; 5:8). In fact, this evil is so potent and so aggressive that it cannot be confined but instead must be shipped back to its source (the land of Babylon) by divine decree. Beyond this broad understanding, however, interpreters tend to part ways when it comes to identifying the evil woman named "Wickedness" sitting in the ephah basket.

Several explanations have been put forth in an attempt to identify the woman in the basket named "Wickedness" (5:7-8). Most often, the woman is understood to represent a system of evil generally speaking, the moral and socials ills, the ceremonial impurities and religious apostasy, and the injustices of the political and legal institutions of Israel (regularly condemned by the Hebrew prophets). For some, the woman in the basket symbolizes the "pagan women" brought into the Hebrew community through wrongful intermarriage (an issue for the prophet Malachi in Mal 2:10-16, and one of the reform initiatives of Ezra and Nehemiah—see Ezra 9–10). Finally, the woman may be a figure for "spiritual adultery" or idolatry since the evil of ritual prostitution is usually associated with idol worship in the OT (e.g., Jer 23:10; Ezek 16:15; Hos 2:2; see the discussion in Harrington 2002:495-496). Whatever the case, God himself will both contain and remove "Wickedness" from his people and the land of Israel. Although cleansing from sin is the gracious work of God (Ps 51:2, 7), those guilty of sin and rebellion against God must turn to God and seek his cleansing for the forgiveness of sins and a restored relationship with him (cf. Ezek 24:13).

The Old Testament associates wickedness with idolatry, and it is this "wickedness of the other nations" that caused God to displace them from the land with Israel (Deut 9:4-5). It seems likely that the woman named "Wickedness" sitting in the basket represents one of the fertility goddesses of the ancient Near East (see the discussion in Meyers and Meyers 1987:302-303). The Queen of Heaven (cf. Jer 44:17-25) and Asherah (cf. Deut 7:5; 16:21) are likely candidates, especially since the word "wickedness" (rish'ah [TH7564, ZH8402]) is an anagram of the name "Asherah." The issue is not so much the identification of the woman seated in the ephah basket as the sin of idolatry itself. The people of the kingdoms of Israel and Judah were exiled to Mesopotamia for this same "wickedness," provoking God to anger with their idolatry (2 Kgs 17:16-18; 2 Chr 36:14).

The divine judgment of exile purged the Hebrews of idolatry—one sin that the postexilic prophets do not mention in their indictments of the restoration community. The land of Israel, however, was still contaminated by the spirit of idolatry. In the context of covenant relationship, the land is personified; it too had been defiled by Israel's idolatry. Hence, Zechariah's vision shows God removing the residue of pollution from idolatry from the Promised Land (Lev 18:24-25). The symbolism of the vision would suggest that this spirit of idolatry had been confined but still threatened the restoration community. For this reason God sends it (the woman in the basket) back to Babylonia. The destination of the woman in the basket may be a piece of dramatic irony since the Hebrew people had just returned from exile there. It may also be a metaphor for the removal of sin as far as the east is from the west so that it is remembered no more, as in the Psalms (Ps 103:12; cf. Isa 43:25). It may even be that the "Wickedness" in the basket is simply returning to its source to do its destructive work there, since the earlier visions of Zechariah make it clear that God intended to punish those nations who scattered and humbled Judah (1:21).

◆   I. Four Chariots (6:1-8)

Then I looked up again and saw four chariots coming from between two bronze mountains. ²The first chariot was pulled by red horses, the second by black horses, ³the third by white horses, and the fourth by powerful dappled-gray horses. ⁴"And what are these, my lord?" I asked the angel who was talking with me.

⁵The angel replied, "These are the four spirits* of heaven who stand before the Lord of all the earth. They are going out to do his work. ⁶The chariot with black horses is going north, the chariot with white horses is going west,* and the chariot with dappled-gray horses is going south."

⁷The powerful horses were eager to set out to patrol the earth. And the LORD said, "Go and patrol the earth!" So they left at once on their patrol.

⁸Then the LORD summoned me and said, "Look, those who went north have vented the anger of my Spirit* there in the land of the north."

6:5 Or the four winds.   6:6 Hebrew is going after them.   6:8 Hebrew have given my Spirit rest.

NOTES
6:1 four chariots. The chariots pulled by teams of horses in Zechariah's last vision stand in contrast to the horses in the first vision by virtue of their differing military role (1:7-18). According to Baldwin (1972:131) chariots were the "storm troops" of the ancient world. They symbolize both the swiftness and the decisive power of God in his intervention in human affairs.

two bronze mountains. Numerous explanations have been offered for the significance of the two bronze mountains of Zechariah's vision. Less likely are the suggestions that the bronze color simply represents the rising sun tinting the mountains with early morning amber light or that the prophet has borrowed the imagery of Babylonian mythology depicting the sun-god rising between two mountains. More likely are the ideas that the two bronze mountains are enhanced images of the two bronze pillars that once flanked the entrance to Solomon's Temple (1 Kgs 7:13-22), with bronze symbolizing the impregnable strength of God's abode (see the discussion in Baldwin 1972:130-131).

6:2 red . . . black . . . white . . . dappled-gray horses. Like the two bronze mountains, the search for the meaning behind the colors of the teams of chariot-horses has provoked considerable scholarly discussion. Most often, the colors of the four teams of horses are associated with the riders on horses in the seal vision of Revelation (with white representing victory, red for war and slaughter, black for famine, and dappled-gray for death; Rev 6:1-8). If this is a correct understanding of the symbolism, then divine judgment in the form of famine and pestilence is directed to the north (Mesopotamia), while divine judgment in the form of plague and death is headed south (Egypt)—the two directions marking the perennial enemies of Israel. The westerly direction (lit., "after them" [NLT mg], reflecting the directional orientation of the inhabitants of the biblical world to the east) of the white horses would then signify the victory of God in the form of the return of the Hebrews from exile in Mesopotamia (see Mason 1977:60 on the importance of this bilateral north–south movement in the vision).

6:5 four spirits. The four chariots (6:1) are identified as the "four spirits of heaven" by the interpreting angel (6:5). The four "spirits" or "winds" of heaven (*ruakh* [TH7307, ZH8120]) are generally understood to represent the four primary compass points (see note on 2:6 concerning the "four winds"). Here the "four spirits of heaven" represented by the teams of chariot-horses are personified as members of the divine council who report their reconnaissance missions to God. This suggests that each of the teams of chariot-horses may transport an angelic being of some sort, even as the NLT assumes the horses carried angelic riders in Zechariah's first vision (1:7-17; see notes on 1:8). The fact that the teams of chariot-horses have the capacity to serve as agents of God's judgment lends support to this idea (6:8). According to Mason (1977:60), the number four signifies "God's world-wide dominion."

6:7 patrol. See the discussion of "patrol the earth" in the note on 1:10. The teams of (chariot) horses are portrayed as both "powerful" and "eager" (6:7) to go out and do the Lord's work (6:5). It is important to note, however, that they only move on the Lord's command (6:7).

6:8 the LORD summoned me. It seems significant that the series of visions witnessed by Zechariah close with a word from the Lord directly to the prophet. It is unclear whether or not the interpreting angel continues to speak in vv. 7-8 (so Petersen 1984:270-272) or if the Lord himself now engages in the discourse (so NLT; cf. Meyers and Meyers 1987:329 who identify the speaker in vv. 7-8 as Yahweh on the basis of the possessive pronoun "my Spirit"). In bypassing the interpreting angel in the discourse at the very end of the sequence of night visions, God may be emphasizing the sure and effective implementation of his word to Israel through the prophet.

vented the anger of my Spirit. Lit., "given my Spirit rest" (NLT mg; cf. NRSV, "have set my spirit at rest"). The word "spirit" (*ruakh* [TH7307, ZH8120]) may indicate anger in certain contexts, as understood here by the NLT (cf. Judg 8:3; Isa 33:11). In Ezek 5:13 the combination of *nwh* ("rest") with *khemah* ("wrath") connotes the idea of God causing his wrath to rest in the sense of venting his anger (cf. McComiskey 1998:1110). Unlike Ezek 5:13, Zech 6:8 makes no reference to God's wrath suggesting that God's spirit has settled in the north country among the Hebrew exiles. Meyers and Meyers (1987:331) conclude that the pres-

ence of God's spirit in the northland legitimizes the restoration efforts of the Jews because
"no matter how powerful the Persian imperial domination may seem, the cosmic power of
Yahweh. . . . lies behind Persian political decisions."

COMMENTARY

Although the details of the two visions vary, the messages of Zechariah's first and
last visions are essentially the same. The horses and riders of the first vision (1:7-17)
patrol the earth as a divine scouting party. The addition of the chariots in the final
vision suggests that God was sending off these angelic agents on a military campaign. The basic message of the two visions, however, is expressed in the phrase
"the Lord of all the earth" (6:5). God's control of the "four spirits of heaven" (6:5)
stresses his universal sovereignty over the nations. The fact that this message
encloses the night vision section of Zechariah like a pair of bookends tells us that
this spiritual reality was vital to the prophet's message of comfort and encouragement to postexilic Judah.

According to Craigie (1984:186), the departure of the teams of chariot-horses on
a worldwide mission of military intervention establishes part of the core meaning
for all the visions. God's revelation to Zechariah indicated that beyond the rebuilt
Temple and a rejuvenated government, Israel could be assured that God would follow through on his promise to "shake the heavens and the earth . . . [and] overthrow
royal thrones," and then establish his kingdom in the world (cf. Hag 2:21-22).
"Only when foreign nations were overthrown could the chosen people be truly free
once again" (Craigie 1984:186).

Zechariah's final vision highlights two enduring theological truths that are
repeated themes in Zechariah and the Bible as a whole. First, God is indeed Lord of
human history (Isa 46:9-10; Jude 1:25; Rev 15:3). Second, God's word is absolutely
sure and true (Matt 5:17-20; John 10:34-35). These two messages are always relevant during troubled times, times when people, whether ancient or modern, need
anchors or moorings for lives adrift.

As to this vision's fulfillment, the preterist view considers the venting of God's
anger against the "land of the north" (6:8) as having been fulfilled in the Persian
conquest of Babylonia and the subsequent overthrow of Persia by Alexander the
Great and the Greeks. The futurist approach to the vision equates the judgment
against the "land of the north" (6:8) with the overthrow of the nations by the Messiah prior to the establishment of his millennial rule upon earth (cf. Rev 19-20).

◆   J. The Crowning of Jeshua (6:9-15)

⁹Then I received another message from the LORD: ¹⁰"Heldai, Tobijah, and Jedaiah will bring gifts of silver and gold from the Jews exiled in Babylon. As soon as they arrive, meet them at the home of Josiah son of Zephaniah. ¹¹Accept their gifts, and make a crown* from the silver and gold. Then put the crown on the head of Jeshua* son of Jehozadak, the high priest. ¹²Tell him, 'This is what the LORD of Heaven's Armies says: Here is the man called the Branch. He will branch out from where

he is and build the Temple of the LORD. ¹³Yes, he will build the Temple of the LORD. Then he will receive royal honor and will rule as king from his throne. He will also serve as priest from his throne,* and there will be perfect harmony between his two roles.'

¹⁴"The crown will be a memorial in the Temple of the LORD to honor those who gave it—Heldai,* Tobijah, Jedaiah, and Josiah* son of Zephaniah."

¹⁵People will come from distant lands to rebuild the Temple of the LORD. And when this happens, you will know that my messages have been from the LORD of Heaven's Armies. All this will happen if you carefully obey what the LORD your God says.

6:11a As in Greek and Syriac versions; Hebrew reads *crowns*.   6:11b Hebrew *Joshua*, a variant spelling of Jeshua.   6:13 Or *There will be a priest by his throne*.   6:14a As in Syriac version (compare 6:10); Hebrew reads *Helem*.   6:14b As in Syriac version (compare 6:10); Hebrew reads *Hen*.

NOTES

6:9 *another message.* On the prophetic word formula, see the note on 1:1 for "the LORD gave this message."

6:10 *Heldai, Tobijah, and Jedaiah.* The three are unknown apart from the references in 6:10, 14. They were recent returnees to Jerusalem from exile in Babylonia and apparently were the couriers designated by Jews still in Babylonia for donations to the second Temple building fund.

silver and gold. The gifts for the tabernacle and the first Temple included these precious metals, the offerings of choice for gods and kings in the ancient world (Exod 25:3; 1 Chr 29:2).

6:11 *crown.* The word (*'atarah* [TH5850, ZH6498]) describes a crown or a wreath; it is plural in the MT. The plural form of the noun is probably intended to describe a "double crown" or a single crown comprised of two circles or bands of metal (one gold and one silver). It is unclear whether the bands of gold and silver were intertwined or layered, but each band represented one of the offices to which Jeshua was appointed (those of king and priest).

6:12 *the Branch.* This is a title for the Messiah (see note on 3:8, "my servant, the Branch").

6:13 *two roles.* This merges the offices of king (associated with David and the tribe of Judah, 2 Sam 7:12-16) and priest (associated with Aaron and the tribe of Levi, Exod 29:44). The combination of the roles of king and priest in a single individual was anticipated in the figure of the king-priest Melchizedek (Ps 110:4). According to the NT, this dual role of priest and king is ultimately fulfilled in Jesus the Messiah (Heb 5:5-6; 7:15-22).

6:14 *memorial.* The word (*zikkaron* [TH2146, ZH2355]) denotes an object that serves as a sign of remembrance, evoking memories of special events or persons. The symbolic crown uniting kingship and priesthood in the office of the high priest Jeshua was placed as a memorial in the second Temple to the donors of the gold and silver. It also served as a permanent reminder of Jeshua's divinely ordained coronation as "priest-king" and as a visual aid for the priests in their teaching of this new development in the tradition of the Levitical priesthood (see Baldwin 1972:137). The name changes for two of the four individuals mentioned by the prophet (cf. 6:10) may be due to their desire to have their formal names entered in the official Temple records (cf. Baldwin 1972:137).

Josiah. His name is included among those honored by the memorial crown placed in the Temple due to his role as contact person or "broker" for the meeting between Zechariah and the three former exiles bearing gifts (cf. 6:10).

6:15 *distant lands.* The remote regions Zechariah had in mind are unspecified. The purpose of the reference seems to be to recognize the contribution of Diaspora Jews in rebuilding the second Temple so that "all Israel" might identify with the structure.

COMMENTARY

Like the accompanying oracle (2:6-13) of the third vision (2:1-5), the eighth and last vision of Zechariah (6:1-8) includes an accompanying oracle (6:9-15). Some biblical commentators regard the oracle as a later addition to the night vision section of the book, since the visions aptly conclude with God "at rest" (see note on 6:8). Yet the symbolic-action message depicting the coronation of Jeshua as both king and priest brings closure to the issue of leadership presented in the fourth (ch 3) and fifth (ch 4) visions. In that sequence of visions, both Jeshua, the high priest, and Zerubbabel, the governor, are singled out as divinely appointed leaders for postexilic Judah. Yet Zerubbabel is conspicuous in his absence from this concluding vision addressing leadership in postexilic Judah. This has raised numerous questions for interpreters of Zechariah's final vision.

Central to the sermon attached to Zechariah's final vision are the understanding of the word "crown" (6:11) and its placement, and the relationship of the priest to "his throne" (6:13). Those scholars who downplay the messianic implications of this oracle suggest that the plural form of the word crown (reading the MT, see the note above) indicates there were two crowns, one for Zerubbabel as governor and one for Jeshua as the high priest. According to Redditt (1995:79), "editorializing" on the part of a clever scribe saw to the removal of Zerubbabel's name from the fourth vision (3:8) and the insertion of Jeshua's name in the message appended to the final vision (6:11). This is sheer conjecture since there is no manuscript evidence supporting the deletion or insertion of Zerubbabel's name into the texts under discussion. Granted, Zerubbabel's abrupt disappearance from the biblical narrative is puzzling. (See the discussion of Zerubbabel in Hill 1998:68-70.) Zechariah offered no rationale for his absence, nor did he mention a successor to the governorship of postexilic Judah. The narrative, however, unambiguously indicates that the "crowns" are to be placed on Jeshua's head only (6:11).

The reference to the high priest on a throne is also troubling to those scholars committed to an entirely historical reading of Zechariah's message reporting the crowning of Jeshua. For example, it is suggested that Zechariah alludes to the premonarchy ideal of the wilderness experience of Israel when Moses was the civil leader and Aaron was the high priest, or that Zechariah was dealing with arrangements for governance in Judah ordered by the Persian overlords (Meyers and Meyers 1987:362). Others see Zechariah as a precursor to later intertestamental literature portraying two messiahs for Israel, one from the tribe of Levi and one from the tribe of Judah (see *Testament of Levi* 18 and *Testament of Judah* 24.) Still others interpret the phrase "priest from his throne" as the role of a priestly "adviser" who stands "by" the throne of a civil ruler (so Redditt 1995:78-79; cf. NRSV).

What seems clear, when the dust from the "exegetical excavations" settles, is that Zerubbabel, as governor of postexilic Judah, is a non-factor in the message concluding Zechariah's visions. More than this, one cannot escape the meaning of the clause "serve as priest from his throne" (6:13) as just that—a priestly figure ruling from a throne (cf. Meyers and Meyers 1987:361). There is no record, biblical or extrabiblical, that Jeshua ever ruled from a throne as high priest (i.e., there appears to have been no literal fulfillment). Beyond this, only Jeshua the high priest is granted the privilege of a place in the divine council of God (3:7), and only he and the other priests are designated as a "symbol" of things to come—namely the Branch (3:8).

The symbolic-action oracle concluding the vision sequence explains this typological relationship between Jeshua and the Branch. Jeshua is presented as the "Branch" who will complete the building of the second Temple (6:12a), but he will also "branch out from where he is" (6:12b). The literal meaning of this expression may be rendered "from under him someone will sprout up" (cf. Meyers and Meyers 1987:355). This means the immediate antecedent of the pronoun "he" (6:13) is the one who sprouts out of Jeshua—the Branch previously identified in the fourth vision (3:8). This figure will wear two crowns (or one double crown)—the symbols of kingship and priesthood—"and there will be perfect harmony between his two roles" (6:13b). It should be noted that the logical referent to the "two roles" (lit., "the two of them"; *shenehem* [TH8147/1992.1, ZH9109/2157]) are the two thrones of the immediate context of 6:13. Such a declaration should not surprise us because this development was anticipated in the Psalms with the introduction of the king-priest who would rule after the manner of both David and Melchizedek (Ps 110:2, 4). The New Testament identifies Jesus Christ as this Branch who is both king and priest according to the order of Melchizedek (Heb 7:1, 15). It would seem that the "Temple" this Branch ultimately builds is the "true place of worship"—the "heavenly Tabernacle" built by Jesus the Messiah through his death and resurrection (John 2:19; Heb 8:2).

Each of the two accompanying oracles in the vision section of the book (2:6-13; 6:9-15) includes the validation formula ("you will know that my messages have been from the LORD," 2:9; 6:15). The prophets Haggai, Zechariah, and Malachi faced a crisis in the credibility of the prophetic word during their early postexilic period ministries. In the minds of the people, the word of God had seemingly failed because the promises of Jeremiah and Ezekiel for a new covenant and a Davidic ruler were still unfulfilled (cf. Jer 31:30; Ezek 34:23).

The validation formulas, however, were intended to do more than bolster flagging confidence in prophetic preaching. The validation formulas are tied to specific acts of God in history, whether for judgment (2:9) or restoration (6:15). The validation formulas served as an indirect reminder to the people to look about them and see God's hand at work in current events (even as Malachi asked postexilic Judah to consider the fate of Edom—Mal 1:4-5). This lesson is no less important today, given the summons by Jesus to "interpret the present times" (Luke 12:54-56). God's prophet, whether ancient or modern, reads with the Bible in one hand and the daily paper in the other.

In addition, the sermon attached to the last vision assured those Hebrews still living in the Diaspora that they too had a stake in this second Temple and the restoration planned for Jerusalem and the land of Israel (6:15a). Finally, the conditional nature of the fulfillment of these divine revelations to Zechariah connects the vision section of the book to the prologue. God will see that his plans for the restoration of Jerusalem and Judah are implemented, but the people must also participate in the work of God by obeying his word. The prophet's challenge to "obey what the LORD your God says" (6:15b) brings his message back full circle to the call to repentance in the prologue (1:1-6). The promise of God's word would surely be fulfilled. The only question was whether the realization of Zechariah's visions would eventuate in the perpetuation of the grim reality of their current circumstances or in the joyful reversal of divine restoration. The answer rested upon the people's decision to "return" to the Lord (1:3).

◆ III. Zechariah's Messages (7:1–8:23)
   A. A Call to Justice and Mercy (7:1-14)

On December 7* of the fourth year of King Darius's reign, another message came to Zechariah from the LORD. ²The people of Bethel had sent Sharezer and Regemmelech,* along with their attendants, to seek the LORD's favor. ³They were to ask this question of the prophets and the priests at the Temple of the LORD of Heaven's Armies: "Should we continue to mourn and fast each summer on the anniversary of the Temple's destruction,* as we have done for so many years?"

⁴The LORD of Heaven's Armies sent me this message in reply: ⁵"Say to all your people and your priests, 'During these seventy years of exile, when you fasted and mourned in the summer and in early autumn,* was it really for me that you were fasting? ⁶And even now in your holy festivals, aren't you eating and drinking just to please yourselves? ⁷Isn't this the same message the LORD proclaimed through the prophets in years past when Jerusalem and the towns of Judah were bustling with people, and the Negev and the foothills of Judah* were well populated?'"

⁸Then this message came to Zechariah from the LORD: ⁹"This is what the LORD of Heaven's Armies says: Judge fairly, and show mercy and kindness to one another. ¹⁰Do not oppress widows, orphans, foreigners, and the poor. And do not scheme against each other.

¹¹"Your ancestors refused to listen to this message. They stubbornly turned away and put their fingers in their ears to keep from hearing. ¹²They made their hearts as hard as stone, so they could not hear the instructions or the messages that the LORD of Heaven's Armies had sent them by his Spirit through the earlier prophets. That is why the LORD of Heaven's Armies was so angry with them.

¹³"Since they refused to listen when I called to them, I would not listen when they called to me, says the LORD of Heaven's Armies. ¹⁴As with a whirlwind, I scattered them among the distant nations, where they lived as strangers. Their land became so desolate that no one even traveled through it. They turned their pleasant land into a desert."

7:1 Hebrew *On the fourth day of the ninth month, the month of Kislev,* of the ancient Hebrew lunar calendar. This event occurred on December 7, 518 B.C.; also see note on 1:1.   7:2 Or *Bethel-sharezer had sent Regemmelech.*   7:3 Hebrew *mourn and fast in the fifth month.* The Temple had been destroyed in the fifth month of the ancient Hebrew lunar calendar (August 586 B.C.); see 2 Kgs 25:8.   7:5 Hebrew *fasted and mourned in the fifth and seventh months.* The fifth month of the ancient Hebrew lunar calendar usually occurs within the months of July and August. The seventh month usually occurs within the months of September and October; both the Day of Atonement and the Festival of Shelters were celebrated in the seventh month.   7:7 Hebrew *the Shephelah.*

NOTES

7:1 *December 7 of the fourth year of King Darius's reign.* This is the last date formula in the book of Zechariah. It places the two sermons (chs 7–8) almost two years after the vision section of the book (1:7–6:15). It is possible that the date formula refers primarily to the timing of the delegation seeking answers to questions on fasting (7:2-7), rather than the synopses of the prophet's messages.

7:2 *people of Bethel.* The exact meaning of the opening clause of 7:2 is uncertain due to the corruption of the MT (cf. NLT mg). Either the "people" of the town of Bethel sent a delegation to Jerusalem to seek a ruling on the continuation of the fast day now that a second Temple would soon be erected, or a delegation headed by a man name Bethel-Sharezer from some unknown place (perhaps on behalf of a constituency of Hebrews still in Babylonia) came to Jerusalem seeking a priestly ruling on the fast day (see discussion in Baldwin 1972:142-143).

to seek the LORD's favor. The idiom *lekhalloth 'eth-pene* [TH2470B/6440, ZH2704/7156] (to soften the face) refers to a ritual act that entailed asking God to grant a petition or make a ruling on a question (cf. 1 Kgs 13:6). It probably included some kind of sacrifice or offering (see the discussion in Meyers and Meyers 1987:384).

7:3 *the prophets and the priests at the Temple.* It appears that the priests and prophets had complementary roles during the early postexilic period, and the reference suggests both groups were centered at the second Temple. This explains why the delegation posing questions about the fast days of the Hebrew calendar were sent to Jerusalem for a ruling. No doubt Haggai and Zechariah were numbered among those identified as "prophets."

fast each summer. The fast day held on the ninth day of Ab (July/August), the fifth month of the ancient Hebrew lunar calendar, lamented the destruction of Jerusalem by the Babylonians in 586 BC (see 2 Kgs 25:8-10).

7:5 *seventy years of exile.* According to the prophet Jeremiah, the Babylonian exile would last for 70 years (Jer 25:11-12; 29:10). The 70-year exile is linked to the Sabbath-year rest for the land that apparently went unobserved for nearly 500 years (2 Chr 36:21). If the Babylonian exile is reckoned from the captivity of Daniel (605 BC) until the decree of King Cyrus of Persia, which permitted captive people groups to return to their homelands (539 BC), then the figure 70 rounds off an actual 66-year exile.

fasted . . . in the summer and in early autumn. The early autumn fast held during the seventh month of the ancient Hebrew lunar calendar (Tishri, or September/October) lamented the assassination of Gedaliah, the governor of Judah (2 Kgs 25:22-26; cf. Jer 41:1-3. See also the note on 7:3).

7:7 *Negev . . . foothills of Judah.* The Negev is a triangular shaped region south of Judah running from Gaza in the west to Beersheba in the east and down to Kadesh-Barnea in the south. Pastoral nomads herded flocks in the Negev during the rainy season. The western foothills (or *shephelah*) lay between the hill country of Judah and the Mediterranean coast. The land was productive agriculturally, especially for grain and groves of olive trees and sycamore fig trees. (Cf. Deut 1:6-8, which lists the geographical regions of Palestine.)

7:8 *this message came.* On the prophetic word formula, see note on 1:1.

7:10 *Do not oppress.* In contexts emphasizing social justice, the word "oppress" (*'ashaq* [TH6231, ZH6943]) means to mistreat or exploit those people on the margins of society (e.g., the widow, the orphan, the resident alien, slaves, and the poor), who often did not have access to the same legal protection afforded the average citizen (cf. Deut 24:14, 17-18). The issues of fasting (7:5-6) and social justice are linked in Isaiah's call for true fasting (Isa 58:6).

7:11 refused to listen. The word (*ma'an* [TH3985, ZH4412]) essentially means to ignore orders, whether verbal or written (as in Yahweh's covenant stipulations; cf. Jer 11:10).

stubbornly turned away. This idiom, lit., "to set a defiant shoulder" (*nathan* [TH5414, ZH5989] + *kathep sorareth* [TH3802/5637, ZH4190/6253]; cf. Meyers and Meyers 1987:402), signifies a haughtiness that belies an unabashed recalcitrance (cf. Neh 9:29).

put their fingers in their ears. The word here (*kabed* [TH3513, ZH3877], Hiphil stem) means to "make dull" or "be insensitive" and places full responsibility upon the people for their obstinacy (cf. Isa 6:10). The same expression is used of Pharaoh when he "hardened his heart" against God and refused to release the Hebrews (Exod 8:32, NIV).

7:12 hearts as hard as stone. To make the heart "stony" is to steel one's own will against the will of God. The word (*shamir* [TH8068A, ZH9032]) is rare in the OT and may be a word for diamond, the hardest substance known (cf. Jer 17:1; Ezek 3:9). Meyers and Meyers (1987:402) note that the first and third phrases in the series of four phrases ending here ("refused to listen . . . as stone"; 7:11-12) feature terms used to describe Israel's hearing, the second to its body ("turned away"), and the fourth to the heart or will. The four expressions taken together (7:11-12a) paint preexilic Israel and Judah as incorrigibly rebellious. The pattern of four statements characterizing the Hebrew defiance of God and his covenant may have a literary parallel in the four precepts characterizing God's ethical standards for Israelite social life given in 7:9-10.

instructions. This word (*torah* [TH8451, ZH9368]) refers to the laws and commandments of the Mosaic covenant as taught and interpreted by the prophets.

7:14 As with a whirlwind, I scattered them. This form of the verb *sa'ar* [TH5590, ZH6192] (Piel stem) occurs only here in the OT. The word calls to mind the word picture from Hosea of the Israelites being scattered like chaff in the whirlwind of exile (Hos 13:3). The scattering of the Hebrews among the nations was one of the curses associated with the violation of the Mosaic covenant (cf. Deut 28:36-37, 64).

pleasant land . . . desert. The "pleasant land" (*khemdah* [TH2532, ZH2775]) was the land of God's covenant promise (Ps 106:24; Jer 3:19). This reversal of fortune was divine judgment for covenant unfaithfulness in the form of idolatry (cf. Jer 12:10).

COMMENTARY

Craigie (1984:189) is probably correct in his understanding that chapters 7 and 8 represent excerpts from messages or sermons preached by Zechariah and, as such, they convey a "patchwork quilt" of his thought and theology. The first sermon condenses to two messages the questions concerning fasting (7:1-7) and the reflection upon Israel's failure to practice social justice in the preexilic period of Hebrew history (7:8-14). Craigie (ibid.) characterizes chapter 8 as "an anthology of the prophet's sayings from different places and varying times." The two chapters are united by questions related to the topic of fasting (posed in 7:2-7 and answered in 8:18-19) and the theme of social justice (7:8-10; 8:16-17). In this regard, Zechariah stands in the tradition of preexilic prophets like Isaiah and Amos who also championed social justice concerns (cf. Isa 1; Amos 5).

The question of whether to continue observing a day of fasting to mourn the destruction of Solomon's Temple was posed to the priests and prophets by the delegation from Bethel and was of practical concern (7:2-3). They asked if the near completion of the second Temple made the fast lamenting the destruction of the first Temple unnecessary. Zechariah's formal answer to the question was delayed (cf. 8:18-19); instead, the prophet responded with questions of his own (7:4-7). Each rhetorical question was intended to drive home the point that whether in their fasting or feasting the people were engaged in self-centered rather than God-centered activity (7:6). Craigie (1984:192) has rightly observed that the "prophet emphasizes the folly of remembering an event if that remembrance is divorced from an understanding of the event."

Zechariah calls us to rediscover the difference between the "holy day" and the "holiday." The holy day celebrates and commemorates in communal worship (whether festive or solemn and penitential) the mighty deeds of God in the history of his people. The focus of the holiday, by contrast, is essentially the suspension of work routines to enable individuals to enjoy the present moment—"having a good time now." The Christian celebration of a holy day is not determined by the presence of a red number on the calendar. Rather, it is a biblically informed posture toward God's involvement in time and history, toward divine mystery and divine revelation in space and time.

In addition to his rhetorical questions countering the query about fasting (7:4-7), the prophet offered a remedy to the self-pleasing worship and lifestyle that characterized the people (7:8-10). As an alternative to the ethos of self-interest, Zechariah outlined God's expectations for Israelite society with four precepts: two exhortations and two admonitions (7:9-10; cf. Jer 22:3). The directives to "judge fairly" and to "show mercy and kindness" (7:9) anticipate Paul's instruction to "take an interest in others" and not just one's own affairs (Phil 2:4).

To "judge fairly" meant legal officials were to refuse bribes and hear cases and settle disputes on their merits alone (cf. Deut 10:17; Amos 5:12). More broadly, it also meant society as a whole had responsibilities as peacemakers and as a collective social conscience (cf. Lev 19:15). To "show mercy" (khesed [TH2617, ZH2876]) "and kindness" (rakhamim [TH7356, ZH8171]) was to live in such a way that attitudes of love and loyalty prompted acts of kindness and generosity (cf. Deut 15:10-11; Ps 37:21). These words are covenant terms, rooted in the character of God and embedded in the treaty he established with Israel at Mount Sinai through Moses (cf. Deut 7:9; 30:16). It was there that God ordained the Hebrew people as his "kingdom of priests" to serve the Lord and each other (Exod 19:6).

The injunctions against exploiting the weak and plotting evil schemes against others (7:10) call to mind the second great commandment taught by Jesus—to love your neighbor as you love yourself (Matt 22:39; cf. Lev 19:18, 34; Deut 10:19). Treating others with respect both dignifies them as people made in God's image and honors God as the Creator of all (cf. Prov 17:5; 19:17; 22:2). These representative ethical standards extracted from the Mosaic law were the "legislative glue" that bonded the covenant community together as the people of God. The recitation of the failure of their Hebrew ancestors to heed similar prophetic calls to social justice served as a veiled threat to Zechariah's audience—history, even the catastrophe of Babylonian exile, was repeatable (7:11-14).

Like Micah, Zechariah affirmed the role of the Holy Spirit as the divine agent behind the messages of the Hebrew prophets (7:12; cf. Mic 3:8). Nehemiah also credited to the Spirit of God the sermons of instruction and warning preached by the prophets (Neh 9:30). This is why the messages that came to Zechariah are understood as words "from the LORD" (7:4, 8). Reflecting on the ministry of the Old Testament prophets, Peter stated: "no prophecy in Scripture ever came from the prophet's own understanding. . . . No, those prophets were moved by the Holy Spirit, and they spoke from God" (2 Pet 1:20-21). The Spirit of God and the Old Testament prophetic ministry were vitally linked because it is "through the Spirit prophets are called, inspired, transported, motivated . . . to accomplish their difficult tasks within the nation" (Hildebrandt 1995:27).

◆ B. Promised Blessing for Jerusalem (8:1-23)

Then another message came to me from the LORD of Heaven's Armies: 2"This is what the LORD of Heaven's Armies says: My love for Mount Zion is passionate and strong; I am consumed with passion for Jerusalem!

3"And now the LORD says: I am returning to Mount Zion, and I will live in Jerusalem. Then Jerusalem will be called the Faithful City; the mountain of the LORD of Heaven's Armies will be called the Holy Mountain.

4"This is what the LORD of Heaven's Armies says: Once again old men and women will walk Jerusalem's streets with their canes and will sit together in the city squares. 5And the streets of the city will be filled with boys and girls at play.

6"This is what the LORD of Heaven's Armies says: All this may seem impossible to you now, a small remnant of God's people. But is it impossible for me? says the LORD of Heaven's Armies.

7"This is what the LORD of Heaven's Armies says: You can be sure that I will rescue my people from the east and from the west. 8I will bring them home again to live safely in Jerusalem. They will be my people, and I will be faithful and just toward them as their God.

9"This is what the LORD of Heaven's Armies says: Be strong and finish the task! Ever since the laying of the foundation of the Temple of the LORD of Heaven's Armies, you have heard what the prophets have been saying about completing the building. 10Before the work on the Temple began, there were no jobs and no money to hire people or animals. No traveler was safe from the enemy, for there were enemies on all sides. I had turned everyone against each other.

11"But now I will not treat the remnant of my people as I treated them before, says the LORD of Heaven's Armies. 12For I am planting seeds of peace and prosperity among you. The grapevines will be heavy with fruit. The earth will produce its crops, and the heavens will release the dew. Once more I will cause the remnant in Judah and Israel to inherit these blessings. 13Among the other nations, Judah and Israel became symbols of a cursed nation. But no longer! Now I will rescue you and make you both a symbol and a source of blessing. So don't be afraid. Be strong, and get on with rebuilding the Temple!

14"For this is what the LORD of Heaven's Armies says: I was determined to punish you when your ancestors angered me, and I did not change my mind, says the LORD of Heaven's Armies. 15But now I am determined to bless Jerusalem and the people of Judah. So don't be afraid. 16But this is what you must do: Tell the truth to each other. Render verdicts in your courts that are just and that lead to peace. [17]Don't scheme against each other. Stop your love of telling lies that you swear are the truth. I hate all these things, says the LORD."

[18]Here is another message that came to me from the LORD of Heaven's Armies. [19]"This is what the LORD of Heaven's Armies says: The traditional fasts and times of mourning you have kept in early summer, midsummer, autumn, and winter* are now ended. They will become festivals of joy and celebration for the people of Judah. So love truth and peace.

[20]"This is what the LORD of Heaven's Armies says: People from nations and cities around the world will travel to Jerusalem. [21]The people of one city will say to the people of another, 'Come with us to Jerusalem to ask the LORD to bless us. Let's worship the LORD of Heaven's Armies. I'm determined to go.' [22]Many peoples and powerful nations will come to Jerusalem to seek the LORD of Heaven's Armies and to ask for his blessing.

[23]"This is what the LORD of Heaven's Armies says: In those days ten men from different nations and languages of the world will clutch at the sleeve of one Jew. And they will say, 'Please let us walk with you, for we have heard that God is with you.'"

8:19 Hebrew *in the fourth, fifth, seventh, and tenth months.* The fourth month of the ancient Hebrew lunar calendar usually occurs within the months of June and July. The fifth month usually occurs within the months of July and August. The seventh month usually occurs within the months of September and October. The tenth month usually occurs within the months of December and January.

NOTES

8:1 *another message.* On the prophetic word formula, see note on 1:1, "the LORD gave this message."

8:2 *This is what the LORD of Heaven's Armies says.* On the messenger formula, see note on 1:3. The same title appears eight more times in this chapter: 8:4, 6, 7, 9, 14, 19, 20, 23.

My love for Mount Zion . . . Jerusalem! This is an echo of God's sentiment for Jerusalem expressed in Zechariah's first vision (cf. 1:14).

passion. Or "jealousy" (*qin'ah* [TH7068, ZH7863], "jealousy, zeal"). This is one of the basic elements of the OT conception of God (cf. Eichrodt 1967:216-217). God's passion marks him as a personal deity, not an abstract natural force. God is passionate for the word of his covenant and the people of his covenant, and that passion may result in punishment for sin or restoration for repentance and the pursuit of righteousness (see discussion of God's "passion" in the commentary on 1:7-17).

8:3 *I am returning to Mount Zion.* The repetition of the citation of God's intention to once again set up residence in his Temple (1:17) further connects the message of the restoration of Jerusalem in chapter 8 with the earlier vision of the restoration of God's "hometown" (1:7-17). Mason (1977:69) has noted that God's return is a consequence not just of the Temple's being rebuilt but also of the Hebrew community's purification (ch 3).

Faithful City. The prophet Isaiah likened the demise of Jerusalem to a "faithful" woman turned "prostitute" (Isa 1:21). Zechariah shared Isaiah's vision for the reversal of Jerusalem's status to a "Faithful City" (or "City of Truth," so NKJV) once again (Isa 1:26). Meyers and Meyers (1987:413) have observed that the word "truth" (or "faithful") appears in the messages of Zechariah but not the visions (cf. 7:9; 8:3, 8, 16, 19) and that the repetition of the term "conveys the importance of the holy city for the process of establishing justice in society."

Holy Mountain. The reference may be an allusion to other prophetic teachings emphasizing the inviolability of God's "Holy Mountain" or dwelling place by "unclean and godless people" (Isa 52:1; cf. Joel 3:17).

8:4-5 *old men and women . . . boys and girls.* The images of the elderly walking the streets and children playing in the streets signal the repopulation and resumption of normal family life in the once decimated city of Jerusalem. The return of God's presence to his rebuilt Temple will also bring the return of peace and safety for the inhabitants of the city (as foreseen by Jeremiah; Jer 30:18-22).

8:6 *impossible.* The OT portrays the Lord as the God of the impossible or the miraculous (*pala'* [TH6381, ZH7098]). Whether giving Abraham and Sarah a child in their old age (Gen 18:14) or delivering his own holy city to the Babylonians for destruction (Jer 32:27), nothing is too hard for the God who made the heavens and the earth (Jer 32:17). Jesus likewise taught his followers that "with God everything is possible" (Matt 19:26).

8:7 *from the east and from the west.* This is an idiom for all the regions where the Hebrews had been dispersed (cf. Isa 43:5-6).

8:8 *They will be my people . . . I will be . . . their God.* The expression is sometimes understood as an "adoption formula," and it depicts the intimate bond between Israel and God in covenant relationship (cf. Exod 19:5; Jer 30:22; 31:33; Ezek 34:30-31; Hos 2:23).

faithful and just. This word pair occurs elsewhere in conjunction with King David (1 Kgs 3:6), suggesting Zechariah's theocratic emphasis is compatible with the current postexilic situation (cf. Meyers and Meyers 1987:419). The word "faithful" (*'emeth* [TH571, ZH622], "fidelity, truth") completes an *inclusio,* or envelope construction, with "Faithful City" in 8:3.

8:9 *laying of the foundation.* A reference to the initial work of Zerubbabel and Jeshua in the building of the second Temple begun in 536 BC (Ezra 3:8-13).

the prophets. The Temple reconstruction project was soon abandoned, however, and did not resume until the prompting of the prophets Haggai and Zechariah 16 years later (cf. Ezra 5:1-2; Hag 1:1-2).

8:10 *enemies.* This is possibly a reference to the coalition of neighboring peoples (including the Samaritans, the Ammonites, and Arab tribes) that opposed Nehemiah's efforts to rebuild the walls of Jerusalem 50 years later (cf. Neh 4:7).

8:12 *seeds of peace and prosperity.* This expression (lit., "seed of the peace," *zera' hashalom* [TH2233/7965, ZH2446/8934]) is unique to Zechariah in the OT. The word "peace" (*shalom*) occurs four times in chapter 8 and is an important sub-theme of the prophet's message (8:10, 12, 16, 19). In agricultural contexts *shalom* can connote prosperity. Zechariah established a relationship in the agricultural cycle between the opportunity for the Hebrews to once again sow their crops in peaceful times and reap abundant harvests and the people's work in rebuilding the Temple.

earth . . . crops . . . heavens . . . dew. This is a reversal of the drought conditions described by Haggai (Hag 1:10).

remnant. The designation (*she'erith* [TH7611, ZH8642]) is applied to the small community of Hebrews who returned to Judah from the Babylonian exile (cf. Hag 1:12, 14). Theologically, the "remnant" signifies a small number of people who escape destruction as a result of the saving action of God. They serve as a bridge that links the threat of divine punishment with the promise of divine restoration (cf. NIDOTTE 4.17).

8:13 *Be strong.* The repetition of the exhortation found earlier in 8:9 forms an *inclusio,* or envelope, for the section, highlighting the reversal of Jerusalem's fortunes (8:9-13). Zechariah's message has affinities to Azariah's word to King Asa concerning religious reform in Judah (cf. 2 Chr 15:3-7). The expression "be strong" (lit., "strengthen your hands," *khazaq* [TH2388, ZH2616] + *yad* [TH3027, ZH3338]) may echo David's charge to all Israel to "be strong and loyal subjects" after the death of King Saul (2 Sam 2:7).

8:14-15 determined. The repetition of the verb "determined" (zamam [TH2161, ZH2372], "to plan, act purposefully") accents God's sovereign intentions in both judging Israel's sin and reversing the fortunes of his people by blessing them.

8:16 courts. Lit., "gates" (sha'arim [TH8179, ZH9133]), the place for conducting legal proceedings in the cities and Temples of the biblical world (cf. Deut 21:19; 25:7).

8:17 I hate all these things. Zechariah's audience was guilty of the same sins that brought about the Babylonian exile. Such behavior put God's plans for the restoration of the postexilic Hebrew community in jeopardy (8:16; cf. 7:8-10). God's hatred (sane' [TH8130, ZH8533]) of evil deeds and the people who persist in them (Ps 5:5; Prov 6:16) stems from his absolute holiness (Pss 5:4; 15:1; 24:3).

8:19 traditional fasts. The fast in the early summer (the fourth month) lamented the breaching of the walls of Jerusalem by the Babylonian armies (2 Kgs 25:3-4; Jer 52:6-7). The fast in midsummer (the fifth month) lamented the burning of Solomon's Temple (2 Kgs 25:8-10; Jer 52:12-14). The fast in autumn (the seventh month) marked the anniversary of the assassination of Gedaliah, the governor of Jerusalem (2 Kgs 25:22-25; Jer 41:1-3). The fast in winter (the tenth month) lamented the beginning of the siege of Jerusalem by King Nebuchadnezzar of Babylonia (2 Kgs 25:1; Jer 52:4).

8:19 love truth and peace. The prophet called the people to love what God himself loves, truth and peace (cf. Pss 29:11; 31:5). The repetition of the word truth ('emeth [TH571, ZH622]) makes this ethical ideal a sub-theme in chapter 8 (8:3, 8, 16, 19). Paul's citation of 8:16 indicates God's expectations have not changed (Eph 4:25).

8:23 ten men. At times the number ten is used in the OT to express completeness (e.g., the "ten plagues" of the Exodus account or the "ten words" as shorthand for the Decalogue). It may also represent hyperbole for "ten times" the normal situation (e.g., Num 14:22 [NIV]; 1 Sam 1:8; Dan 1:20); in the present verse it is used symbolically for a large group of people.

God is with you. The goal of OT eschatology as expressed in Zechariah's third vision (2:5, 10) is God's presence with humanity in a restoration of the Genesis ideal for divine–human fellowship (cf. Gen 3:8; Exod 25:8; 2 Chr 7:2-3; Isa 7:14; 57:15; Jer 30:11; Ezek 43:7-9).

COMMENTARY

Like the previous chapter, this literary unit of Zechariah is an anthology of sayings from the prophet's sermons and messages. The highlights or "quotable quotes" in these collected works of Zechariah are joined by a series of messenger formulas ("this is what the LORD of Heaven's Armies says," 8:4, 6, 7, 9, 14, 19, 20, 23). This chapter is connected to the previous one by the topic of fasting (questions posed in 7:2-7 and answered in 8:18-19) and the ethical demands of covenant relationship with Yahweh (7:8-10; 8:16-17). The overall tone and message of the chapter, however, shifts from admonition and judgment to exhortation and restoration. The stylized sermons of chapters 7 and 8 set up the interplay of these two themes, judgment and restoration, in the two closing oracles of Zechariah (8:9-11, 12-14).

The reestablishment of the divine presence in the midst of the faithful was the great hope of the postexilic restoration community—the Lord returning and dwelling among his people again ("and I will live in Jerusalem," 8:3; cf. 1:16-17; Hag 2:4-5, 7). All this is in fulfillment of the promise of Ezekiel's Temple vision, renaming the city of Jerusalem "The LORD Is There" (Ezek 48:35).

The idea of the manifest presence of God in his creation is perhaps the great theme of the Bible, beginning with the intimate fellowship with God experienced by that first human pair (cf. Gen 3:8-9) and ending with paradise regained when God himself will live with his people (Rev 21:3). This divine presence was symbolized for Israel in the Mosaic Tabernacle (Exod 25:8) and later Solomon's Temple (2 Chr 7:2). The Ark of the Covenant was the tangible point of interface between God and the Hebrew people during Old Testament times because it was there that God met with his people (Exod 25:22).

More than this, we experience what the saints of former times could only anticipate through the word of the prophets as "Immanuel" in that the person of Jesus Christ has indeed come (John 1:14; cf. Isa 7:14). The deposit of the Holy Spirit has been given as the pledge that God will once again live among his people (Eph 1:13-14). During the interim, the indwelling Holy Spirit resides in Christians as his spiritual temple (1 Cor 3:16-17; 6:19).

Zechariah's declaration to the remnant of God's people that nothing is impossible for God (8:6)—even the reversal of Israel's fortunes—builds on his earlier admonition to postexilic Jerusalem to "not despise these small beginnings" (cf. 4:10). This message of encouragement to the oppressed is basic to the genre of apocalyptic literature. The prophet called his audience to see beyond the dismal present to the glorious future through the eyes of faith. Zechariah may have had Habakkuk's preaching in mind, "the righteous will live by their faithfulness to God" (Hab 2:4)—whether in feast or famine (Hab 3:16-17).

It is important to remember that each of Zechariah's visions should be read against the touchstone of the call to repentance in the prologue (1:1-6). God's reversal of the plight of the Hebrew people from the cursed "remnant in Judah" (8:12-13) to "a symbol and a source of blessing" (8:13) was as certain as his punishment of their sin (8:14). Such a dramatic restoration of the people of God, however, was not automatic. Indeed, God had determined to bless his people (8:15), but the demands of covenant relationship meant Israel was under obligation to live out the ethical demands of the Mosaic charter (8:16-17; cf. 7:8-10). Obedience to the revealed word of God, whether Old Testament or New, is never optional (cf. Deut 4:1-2; Col 2:6).

Zechariah's prediction that one day "people from nations and cities around the world" will come to Jerusalem and worship the Lord with the Hebrews brings the covenant promise made to Abraham full circle in Israelite history—"all the families on earth will be blessed through you" (8:20-23; cf. Gen 12:3). Mason views this segment of Zechariah's message as the nearest thing "to an active missionary concept of the mission of the Jews that occurs in the Old Testament, outside the book of Jonah" (1977:73). Yet, the difference between Jonah and Zechariah is striking in that Jonah was commissioned to proclaim repentance to the Assyrians (Jonah 1:2). Here it appears that the reality of God's transforming presence among his people prompts the nations to almost beg to join Israel in the worship of the Lord (8:23). (On Israel's call to be God's witness to the nations, see Kaiser 2000.)

◆ IV. Zechariah's Oracles (9:1–14:21)
   A. First Oracle (9:1–11:17)
      1. Judgment against Israel's enemies (9:1-8)

This is the message* from the LORD against the land of Aram* and the city of Damascus, for the eyes of humanity, including all the tribes of Israel, are on the LORD.

2 Doom is certain for Hamath,
   near Damascus,
and for the cities of Tyre and Sidon,
   though they are so clever.
3 Tyre has built a strong fortress
   and has made silver and gold
   as plentiful as dust in the streets!
4 But now the Lord will strip away Tyre's
      possessions
   and hurl its fortifications into the sea,
   and it will be burned to the ground.
5 The city of Ashkelon will see Tyre fall
   and will be filled with fear.
Gaza will shake with terror,
   as will Ekron, for their hopes will
      be dashed.

Gaza's king will be killed,
   and Ashkelon will be deserted.
6 Foreigners will occupy the city of
      Ashdod.
I will destroy the pride of the
      Philistines.
7 I will grab the bloody meat from
      their mouths
   and snatch the detestable sacrifices
      from their teeth.
Then the surviving Philistines will
      worship our God
   and become like a clan in Judah.*
The Philistines of Ekron will join my
      people,
   as the ancient Jebusites once did.
8 I will guard my Temple
   and protect it from invading armies.
I am watching closely to ensure
   that no more foreign oppressors
      overrun my people's land.

9:1a Hebrew *An Oracle: The message.* 9:1b Hebrew *land of Hadrach.* 9:7 Hebrew *and will become a leader in Judah.*

NOTES

9:1 *This is the message.* The superscription or title (9:1) for the larger passage (chs 9–11) combines two formulaic prophetic expressions: the technical term "oracle" (*massa'* [TH4853A, ZH5363]) and the prophetic word formula. The word "oracle" means "burden" in the sense of a pronouncement of prophetic judgment and invests the prophet's message with divine authority. The combination of the two expressions is also found in 12:1 and Mal 1:1; it is a distinctive feature of late biblical prophecy (cf. Meyers and Meyers 1993:91). On the prophetic word formula, see note on 1:1, "the LORD gave this message."

Aram. Lit., "the land of Hadrach," a city-state on the northern boundary of modern Syria. It was probably the ancient city of Hatarikka cited in Assyrian texts and is associated with the site of Tell Afis southwest of Aleppo.

Damascus. This capital city of the Aramean state flourished in Syria during the tenth to eighth centuries BC. The Aramean kingdom was sometimes an ally and at other times an enemy to the divided kingdoms of Israel and Judah. The city lay adjacent to the Abana River and was located on the caravan route connecting Mesopotamia to the Mediterranean coast. The border of Damascus was regarded as the northern boundary of the ideal Hebrew state (Ezek 47:16-18).

9:2 *Hamath.* A fortress city on the Orontes River (modern-day Hama in Syria) located on one of the southern trade routes from Asia Minor. Hamath was considered the northern boundary of Israel according to Num 13:21 and Josh 13:5.

Tyre and Sidon. The twin Phoenician port cities were independent kingdoms located on the Mediterranean coast north of Israel (modern-day Lebanon) and are often paired in biblical texts (e.g., Jer 25:22; Joel 3:4). The cities were legendary for their wealth as a result of maritime trade. The OT prophets, however, condemned the pride and oppressive policies of the two cities and predicted their ultimate destruction (cf. Isa 23; Ezek 26:3-14; Amos 1:9-10).

9:3 strong fortress. The word (*matsor* [TH4692A, ZH5190]) is a pun on the name for the city of Tyre (*tsor* [TH6865A, ZH7450]). The verse makes reference to the famed island fortress of ancient Tyre (Isa 23:4; Ezek 26:5), which was captured and destroyed by Alexander the Great in 332 BC.

9:5-6 *Ashkelon . . . . Gaza . . . Ekron . . . . Ashdod.* These Philistine cities were located on the coastal plain of Israel, south of the port city of Joppa. The city of Gath was also numbered among the five principal cities of the Philistines (cf. 1 Sam 6:17). The Philistines were defeated by David (2 Sam 5:17-25), but later regained some measure of autonomy. The prophets Amos and Zephaniah pronounce similar judgments against the same four Philistine cities (Amos 1:6-8; Zeph 2:4-7).

9:6 *Foreigners.* The word (*mamzer* [TH4464, ZH4927]) occurs elsewhere only in Deut 23:2 and refers to illegitimate children (cf. KJV, "bastard;" NEB, "half-breeds;" NRSV, "mongrel people"). The significance of the expression for Zechariah is the eventual loss of both political and social identity for the Philistines.

9:7 *bloody meat.* This is an allusion to the Philistine practice of eating animal meat that had not been drained of its blood—a violation of Hebrew purity laws (cf. Gen 9:4; Lev 3:17; Acts 15:20).

detestable sacrifices. The term *shiqquts* [TH8251, ZH9199] refers generally to the despicable practices associated with pagan idolatry. Here it suggests the eating of unclean foods as determined by the ritual requirements of the Mosaic food laws (cf. Lev 11:2-23).

the surviving Philistines will worship our God. The "conversion" of the nations to worshipers of Yahweh is a theme in both the visions and the oracles of Zechariah (2:11; 9:7, 10; 14:16). Baldwin (1972:161) has noted that Zechariah's prediction of the Philistines worshiping the God of Israel anticipates the evangelistic ministry of Philip in the cities of the Philistine coastal plain (since Azotus was the Roman name for Ashdod, Acts 8:40).

Jebusites. The ethnic name of a Canaanite people group living in and around Jerusalem. According to the biblical genealogies, they descended from the third son of Canaan (Gen 10:16; 1 Chr 1:14). The city of Jebus (or Jerusalem) was sacked and burned by the tribe of Judah during the days of the judges (Judg 1:8) and later recaptured by David who made it the capital city of his kingdom (2 Sam 5:6-10). The Jebusites were absorbed by the Israelites through intermarriage during David's reign (cf. 2 Sam 5:13) and presumably became worshipers of Yahweh.

COMMENTARY

Part two of the book of Zechariah is composed of two distinct literary units, chapters 9–11 and 12–14. The second half of Zechariah differs from the first in several ways. There is a gradual shift in the literary genre of Zechariah 9–14 to one that is more distinctively apocalyptic in character, combining cryptic historical allusions with futuristic visions. The tone of the prophet's message shifts from one of exhortation and encouragement to one of admonition and warning. The section contains no explicit references to the prophet, and the messages are presumed to date from a later period of Zechariah's ministry.

Like the book of Malachi, each of the two speeches is prefaced by the compound title: "this message . . . this message is from the LORD" (lit., "an oracle, the word of Yahweh"; cf. 9:1; 12:1; Mal 1:1). The word "oracle" (*massa'* [TH4853A, ZH5363]) is a technical term for a prophetic pronouncement often understood as a "burden" due to the emphasis on divine judgment in this type of oracular speech. The prophetic word formula (*debar-yhwh* [TH1697/3068, ZH1821/3378], "the word of Yahweh") typically introduces a report of prophetic revelation and invests that report with divine authority. The two closing oracles are composite in nature in that they represent an anthology of the prophet's later sermons. They serve as fitting conclusions to the book of Zechariah because as Craigie (1984:199) has noted, the prophet's "intimations of a future world are here taken up and elaborated in greater detail, and there is a similar concern which incorporates the Gentiles, along with the Jews."

The visions of Zechariah have generated a wide range of interpretive understandings among Jewish and Christian scholars alike. The summary statements below are in keeping with the major interpretive approaches to visionary literature commonly employed in Christian scholarship (see "Literary Style" in the Introduction). The preterist and historicist approaches generally regard Zechariah's "visions" largely as reflections upon the earlier Babylonian exile (with the possibility that the visions may represent a vague projection of the future as a message of warning to the prophet's audience). The amillennial futurist interpretation locates the fulfillment of Zechariah's visions entirely in the New Testament accounts of the First Advent of Jesus the Messiah. The premillennial futurist interpretation finds a partial fulfillment of Zechariah's visions in the First Advent of Jesus the Messiah, but locates ultimate fulfillment of many of the prophecies in the future Second Advent of Christ. Time does not permit, nor is it within the scope of this analysis, to deal with the various interpretive schemes of biblical eschatology. Suffice it to say that a face-value reading of the New Testament and subsequent church history indicates that the First Advent of Jesus the Messiah does not exhaust the meaning of Zechariah's visions in terms of either literal or spiritualized fulfillment of the prophet's oracles.

The opening portion of the first oracle (9:1-8) is similar to earlier prophetic oracles against foreign nations (e.g., Isa 13–23; Jer 46–50; Amos 1–2) and provides an appropriate thematic introduction to the second half of the book. The message of judgment against Israel's enemies combines the dual emphases of (third-person) threats (9:1-6a) and (first-person) promises (9:6b-8). The abrupt shifts from the prophet's report of Yahweh's words to direct speech by God himself is a shared literary feature of the two concluding oracles (chs 9–11, 12–14). Likewise, the emphasis of Zechariah's message alternates between the threat of judgment against the nations and the promise of deliverance for Israel throughout the second part of the book.

The catalog of cities (9:1-6) represents people groups that historically were enemies of Israel, including the Arameans to the northeast (Damascus and Hamath, 9:1-2a), the Phoenicians to the northwest (9:2b-5a), and the Philistines to the southwest (Gaza, Ekron, Ashkelon, Ashdod, 9:5b-6). Three themes emerge in the first message (9:1-8) of the first oracle (chs 9-11) that are repeated in the subsequent messages of the two closing oracles. These themes include divine judgment against the nations (9:1-6), the "conversion" of the nations to worshipers of Yahweh (9:7), and divine protection for the nation of Israel (9:8). Specifically, the first message is a sober reminder that human cleverness (9:2), military prowess (9:3a), and opulent wealth (9:3b) provide no advantage in the day of God's visitation for judgment (9:6). Zechariah stands in theological agreement with the psalmist who warned against trusting in military power (Ps 20:7), or wealth (Ps 49:6), or clever leaders (Ps 146:3) instead of trusting in the God of Jacob for help (Pss 20:7b; 49:15; 146:5). The prophet's rebuke of the nations' self-reliance served as an indirect reminder to Judah that God would accomplish his purposes among his people "not by force nor by strength" but by his Spirit (4:6).

The numerous historical allusions in this section of the oracle prove difficult to locate chronologically with any precision. For example, the destruction of Damascus and Hamath (9:1-2) may be a reference to a military campaign of the Assyrian king Sargon II (722-705 BC) who captured both cities. The threat levied against the Philistine cities of Ashkelon, Gaza, Ekron, and Ashdod (9:5-6) may have been realized when King Nebuchadnezzar of Babylonia conquered the Philistines in the late 600s BC. And later still, the Phoenician ports of Tyre and Sidon (9:3-4) were captured by the Persians, but they were not sacked and made desolate until Alexander the Great destroyed the cities on his campaign into Egypt (332 BC). Baldwin's (1972:158) understanding that the writer took no particular historical viewpoint has merit; the author utilized past events in the manner characteristic of apocalyptic literature to typify the ultimate victory of Yahweh. It is even possible that Zechariah's ambiguous recital of earlier history was a veiled allusion to Daniel's vision of the successive beasts (or nations) that would rule the Mediterranean world prior to the intervention of God's Kingdom in the world (cf. Dan 2). As such, the message of the prophet becomes one of encouragement and hope for his audience—because God's plan for establishing his righteous Kingdom was still intact and on course.

◆ 2. Zion's coming king (9:9-17)

9 Rejoice, O people of Zion!*
  Shout in triumph, O people
    of Jerusalem!
  Look, your king is coming to you.
    He is righteous and victorious,*
  yet he is humble, riding on a donkey—
    riding on a donkey's colt.
10 I will remove the battle chariots
      from Israel*
    and the warhorses from Jerusalem.
  I will destroy all the weapons used
      in battle,

  and your king will bring peace
    to the nations.
  His realm will stretch from sea to sea
    and from the Euphrates River* to
      the ends of the earth.*
11 Because of the covenant I made
    with you,
    sealed with blood,
  I will free your prisoners
    from death in a waterless
      dungeon.
12 Come back to the place of safety,

all you prisoners who still
have hope!
I promise this very day
that I will repay two blessings
for each of your troubles.
¹³ Judah is my bow,
and Israel is my arrow.
Jerusalem* is my sword,
and like a warrior, I will brandish
it against the Greeks.*

¹⁴ The LORD will appear above his people;
his arrows will fly like lightning!
The Sovereign LORD will sound the
ram's horn
and attack like a whirlwind from
the southern desert.
¹⁵ The LORD of Heaven's Armies will
protect his people,

and they will defeat their enemies
by hurling great stones.
They will shout in battle as though
drunk with wine.
They will be filled with blood like
a bowl,
drenched with blood like the corners
of the altar.
¹⁶ On that day the LORD their God will
rescue his people,
just as a shepherd rescues his sheep.
They will sparkle in his land
like jewels in a crown.
¹⁷ How wonderful and beautiful they
will be!
The young men will thrive on
abundant grain,
and the young women will flourish
on new wine.

9:9a Hebrew *O daughter of Zion!*   9:9b Hebrew *and is being vindicated.*   9:10a Hebrew *Ephraim,* referring
to the northern kingdom of Israel; also in 9:13.   9:10b Hebrew *the river.*   9:10c Or *the end of the land.*
9:13a Hebrew *Zion.*   9:13b Hebrew *the sons of Javan.*

NOTES

9:9 *your king.* This is a reference to a future Davidic king, presumably the Messiah figure
described earlier by Zechariah as the Branch (3:8; 6:12).

riding on a donkey. The donkey was a humble animal and a royal mount in the biblical
world (cf. Judg 10:4; 12:14). The act symbolized the rider's intentions to come in peace.
The Gospel writers cited the verse as predictive of the Triumphal Entry of Jesus into Jerusalem at the beginning of his Passion Week (Matt 21:5; John 12:15). Although the NT writers
understood the "Palm Sunday event" as a messianic fulfillment of Zechariah's prophecy
about the "coming king," they appropriately quoted only portions of 9:9 consonant with
the First Advent of Jesus Christ (see further Merrill 1994:256).

9:10 *battle chariots . . . warhorses . . . . weapons.* The kingdoms of Assyria, Babylonia,
Persia, and even the Israelite kingdom of David, were established by military conquest. By
contrast, the Kingdom of God will dismantle the machinery of war and eradicate arsenals
of stockpiled weapons. Other OT prophets predicted a similar era of disarmament (cf. Isa
2:4; 9:5; Mic 5:10-11).

Israel. Lit., "Ephraim"; this was a designation for the northern Hebrew tribes. The pairing
of Israel (or Ephraim) and Jerusalem (9:10) or Judah (9:13) signified a reunited Israel and
the land of covenant promise regained.

the Euphrates River to the ends of the earth. The expression connotes the universal
character of the peace established by the righteous king. The Euphrates River (*nahar*
[TH5104A, ZH5643], lit., "the river") was the northern boundary of the Promised Land
(Gen 15:18).

9:11 *covenant I made with you, sealed with blood.* This is probably a reference to the
sacrifice and the "blood" of the "covenant" that sealed the Mosaic covenant (Exod 24:8).

free your prisoners. This is a reference to those Hebrews still living in the Mesopotamian
Diaspora after the Babylonian exile and repatriation of the land of Israel. In one sense,

those Hebrews who remained in Persia were "exiles" spiritually because they lived outside
the Promised Land—the land of spiritual blessing and rest (cf. Deut 12:10). The freeing
of prisoners was one of the defining activities of Messiah (Isa 61:1; cf. Luke 4:17-22).

9:13 Greeks. The Hebrew is *yawan* [TH3120, ZH3430] (or "Javan"). The Persians and Greeks
were engaged in a titanic struggle for control of the east at the time of Zechariah's ministry
(see the Introduction). The prophet forecasted a future day when God would execute
divine judgment against the Greeks (or perhaps "the nations" if the "Greeks" were representative of all the Gentiles). It is possible that Zechariah alludes to Daniel's vision of the
"goat with the large horn" in anticipation of the rise to power of Alexander the Great and
its implications for the people of Israel (Dan 8:21-22).

9:14 appear above his people. It is possible that Zechariah had in mind the idea that
Yahweh would go before Israel like a military banner or battle standard guaranteeing victory for his people (cf. Merrill 1994:261). It seems more likely that the prophet envisions a
theophany of Yahweh over Israel, much like the image of the winged sun disk that hovered
over and protected the Persian king (see further Hill 1982:350, 362).

sound the ram's horn. This is either an allusion to the blowing of a ram's horn by an
angelic being (cf. Exod 19:19; 20:18; Isa 27:13) or a metaphor for thunder (cf. Isa 29:6;
Jer 25:30; Joel 3:16).

whirlwind. The whirlwind as a military image depicts God's devastating power and
unpredictable swiftness as a divine warrior (Ps 77:18; Isa 66:15). Zechariah's references
to the trumpet and lightning (9:14) call to mind Israel's experience at Mount Sinai
(Exod 19:16).

9:15 hurling great stones. Lit., "sling-stones" (*'abne-qela'* [TH68/7050, ZH74/7845]) hurled at
defenders on city walls and catapulted onto the inhabitants inside. David's victory over the
Philistine champion Goliath attests to the deadly efficiency of the sling as a weapon in the
biblical world (cf. 1 Sam 17:49). The Maccabean triumph over the Hellenistic Seleucids in
the second century BC may be a partial fulfillment of Zechariah's prophecy of Israel's defeat
of the Greeks (9:13-15; cf. 1 Macc 3:16-24; 4:6-16; 7:40-50).

filled with blood like a bowl. This is a reference to the ceremonial "sprinkling bowls" filled
with animal blood that were used in the rituals associated with animal sacrifice (cf. Exod
24:6; 27:3; Lev 1:5; 16:18; Num 4:7).

9:16 On that day. The phrase is prophetic "shorthand" for the Day of the Lord, the eschatological "day" of an unspecified duration in which God judges the wicked, delivers the
righteous, and restores all of creation.

shepherd. The OT prophets portrayed the Messiah not only as a king, but also as a faithful
shepherd (Ezek 34:12, 16, 23). Zechariah may have had Ezekiel's "shepherd-king" in mind
in his use of both messianic titles (cf. Ezek 37:24). Jesus identified himself as the Good
Shepherd in fulfillment of Ezekiel's messianic ideal (John 10:11), and the NT ascribes to
Jesus the titles of "great Shepherd" (Heb 13:20) and "chief Shepherd" (1 Pet 5:4, NASB).

sparkle . . . like jewels. The word "sparkle" (a participle based on the root *nasas* [TH5264,
ZH5824], "to raise a banner/standard") is a rare term in the OT, occurring only in 9:16 and
Ps 60:4 [6]. The translation "sparkle" or "shine" fits the context of jewels set in a crown
(so Merrill 1994:263-264), but see the discussion in Mason (1977:94-95), who suggests
that the restored people of Judah will "serve as a standard by which others may find their
way to seek God."

9:17 abundant grain . . . new wine. Agricultural prosperity is a sign of God's blessing and
a tangible indication of divine restoration in the OT prophets (e.g., Joel 2:19; Amos 9:13;
cf. Hag 1:11).

COMMENTARY

The second message (9:9-17) of Zechariah's first oracle (chs 9–11) confronts his audience with the "coincidence of opposites." The first of the "polar pairs" is the portrayal of Judah's coming deliverer as both a "king" who is "victorious" in battle, yet "righteous" and "humble" (9:9). This king will bring peace to the nations and enjoy a universal reign (9:10). The second of the "polar pairs" is the dual reality of warfare and peace that has defined the course of human history. Our concern is the theological implications of these "coincidences of opposites" in Zechariah.

The Messiah in Zechariah. Like Isaiah and Amos, Zechariah stands in the tradition of the Hebrew prophets who announced a rejuvenated Davidic kingship (cf. Isa 9:6-7; 11:1; Amos 9:11). Specifically, Zechariah's messianic expectations were probably colored by the messages of Jeremiah and Ezekiel who predicted the coming of a shepherd-king after the manner of David (Jer 23:5; 30:9; Ezek 34:23-24; 37:24). Oddly, Zechariah does not use the term "messiah" (*mashiakh* [TH4899, ZH5431], "anointed one") in his visions or oracles. Yet biblical scholars have labeled Zechariah the "little Isaiah" due to his extensive predictions about the Messiah, which the New Testament writers recognized as fulfilled in the life and ministry of Jesus of Nazareth. For example, Zechariah's predictions about the Messiah include

His priesthood (6:13; cf. Heb 5-7)

His kingship (6:13; 9:9-10; 14:9, 16; cf. Heb 2:8-9)

His coming in a low and humble position in life (9:9; 13:7; cf. Matt 21:5; 26:31, 56)

His restoration of Israel by the blood of his covenant (9:11; cf. Mark 14:24)

His service as a shepherd to a people scattered like sheep (10:2; cf. Matt 9:36)

His rejection and betrayal for 30 pieces of silver (11:12-13; cf. Matt 26:15; 27:6-10)

His being pierced and struck down (12:10; 13:7; cf. Matt 26:31, 56)

His return in glory to deliver Israel from her enemies (14:1-6; cf. Matt 24:30; 25:31)

His establishment of a new world order (14:6-19; cf. Rev 21:25; 22:1, 5)

No doubt, the dual portrayals of Messiah as both king and servant-shepherd in the Old Testament proved difficult for the Hebrew faithful to reconcile. How could Messiah defeat the nations and rule as king in righteousness and yet die as a rejected shepherd-priest? How could one Messiah represent the kingship and priesthood that historically belonged to two different Hebrew tribes? The seeming incongruity of a Messiah who would hold both the offices of king and priest and possibly even die was resolved by some of the sects of intertestamental Judaism by speculating there would be two Messiahs. The one from the tribe of Levi would serve as priest, and the other, from the tribe of Judah, would rule as king (cf. 2 Esdr 12:32; *Testament of Levi* 18; *Testament of Judah* 24; CD 12:22–13:1; 14:19).

Reacting to the Christian gospel, some religious Jews today have adopted a similar "two messiah" theology. They willingly admit that Jesus is the Messiah for the

Gentiles, but they contend that the Jews still await their Messiah. Given the perspective of New Testament teachings, we now know that there is but one Messiah, Jesus of Nazareth (Matt 1:16; 16:16). And further, we now know that there will be two advents of Messiah in human history. His first appearance was as suffering servant and slain shepherd, as recorded in the New Testament (John 1:29; 10:11, 28; 1 Cor 5:7). The church, the bride of Jesus the Messiah, still awaits his second appearance as ruling king and Lord of all, as promised in other New Testament texts (Acts 1:11; Rev 19:7-8).

Zechariah's dual understanding of Messiah as both ruling king and humble servant (9:9; as well as slain shepherd, cf. 12:10; 13:7) challenges us to develop a balanced Christology in our preaching and theological instruction. The portrayal of the Messiah as both humble servant and ruling king in Zechariah anticipates what we now know are the two advents or comings of Messiah. The first was fulfilled in the incarnation of Jesus of Nazareth, and the second promised by the risen Lord to his disciples. Naturally, Zechariah's foreshadowing of the Messiah has implications for understanding the Messiah as both the offspring of the woman (Gen 3:15) and Immanuel (or "God is with us," Isa 7:14). With the help and illumination of the Holy Spirit, we must somehow hold in tension the paradoxical truths of Jesus' full humanity and full deity (cf. Heb 1:1-3; 2:5-10).

One practical way to affirm the divinity and humanity of Jesus the Messiah is to return to the recitation of the historic creeds of the church. The purpose of a creed is to compress historical events into a summary statement. The recitation of the creeds is one type of enactment in worship that dramatizes the relationship the Christian has with God. (On the place of the historic Christian creeds in worship and their catechetical value, see Webber 1994:73-76.) The Creed of Chalcedon (AD 451), for example, addressed the very issue of the two natures (divine and human) in the one person of Jesus Christ and substantially completed the orthodox Christology of the ancient church. How else to combat the "peril of the pendulum" as the relativistic and pluralistic trends of popular culture are bent on shaping the theology of the Christian subculture?

In addition, Zechariah's predictions concerning Messiah should foster a spirit of charity in our assessment of Jewish interpretation of the Hebrew Bible at the time of Jesus. It seems Christian interpreters have been quick to indict the religious leaders of first-century Judaism (and even Jesus' own disciples at times) for their lack of theological perception. In our smugness, however, we have failed to appreciate our privileged position on the "AD side" of the First Advent of Jesus Christ on the continuum of salvation history. Those biblical scholars and theologians who bring an irenic spirit to their scholarship, preaching, and teaching are to be commended. Thankfully, recent trends do suggest a nascent spirit of Christian charity stirring afresh in evangelical scholarship, even to the point of entertaining the idea that one's view may be wrong—how novel! (See Webb 2001:236-244.)

Finally, the complexity of Zechariah's visions and the manifold interpretations of those visions by biblical scholars through the 20 centuries of church history should prompt an attitude of humility in our own understandings and expositions of biblical texts. The Dutch theologian Herman Ridderbos has remarked that "God speaks to us through the Scriptures not in order to make us scholars, but to make us Christians. . . . what Scripture does intend is to place us as humans in right position to God, even in our scientific studies and efforts" (1978:23-24). We would do well to bring such Christian humility to bear in our scholarship!

War and Peace in Zechariah. The patterns of social and political conflict that characterize the human experience, whether in the biblical world or our own, may be traced to the sin of the first human pair (Gen 3). Their rebellion against the Creator fractured theological, sociological, and ecological relationships that God had originally established as good and right (Gen 3:14-19). As a result, adversarial relationships subverted God's good creation and humanity was set at odds with God, itself, and the natural order. The first divine promise (Gen 3:15) and the "gospel" message of the rest of the Bible are aimed at overcoming the dislocation of humanity and restoring all creation to proper relationship with God.

The abrupt shifts in tone and theme in Zechariah 9 from a king who brings universal peace (9:9-10) to a God who brandishes a sword against the nations and attacks like the whirlwind (9:13-14) are a stark reminder that the dual reality of war and peace persists into the eschaton. Craigie has noted that Zechariah 9 may be the welding together of separate sermons on the themes of war and peace for the purpose of accenting the Sovereign God as the divine warrior whose victories would ultimately establish permanent and worldwide peace (1984:200). According to a Christian interpretation, Jesus is identified as the "king" depicted in Zechariah 9:9, and his arrival in Jerusalem is the advent of peace on earth (Luke 2:14; cf. Matt 21:5).

Craigie aptly points out the reversal of ancient principles in the Gospel narrative, in that war is the exercise of the political monopoly of force, while the heavenly kingdom of Jesus the Messiah was established by the Godhead's receipt of violence in the form of Roman crucifixion. Like ancient Israel, the Christian church admits the tragic reality of war in a fallen world. Unlike the kingdom of ancient Israel that served as God's "bow" and "arrow" and "sword" (9:13), in the Kingdom of God, "war on the battlefield is to be exchanged for the warfare of the spirit" (Craigie 1984:202). The eschatological hope remains the same, however: God intervening in history to rescue his people from their enemies, abolish warfare forever, and establish universal peace (9:10, 16).

The question Craigie posed (1984:200) as to what we are to make of Zechariah's dark visions of savage warfare punctuated with a vision of universal peace remains pertinent. The New Testament also confronts the reader with the dual reality of war and peace. At the individual level we learn from Jesus that "here on earth [we] will have many trials and sorrows," and yet we can take heart because Jesus has "overcome the world" (John 16:33). On a national level, we learn from Jesus that wars will break out near and far, but we are not to panic (Matt 24:6). Perhaps even more troubling are Jesus' words that he did not come to bring peace to the earth—but a sword to sever even the most fundamental familial relationships (Matt 10:34-39)! Zechariah is a disquieting reminder that the gospel of Jesus Christ is not always a panacea—there is a cross to bear, a cost to Christian discipleship.

Beyond this, Zechariah's message points us to Paul's exhortation to put on God's armor since we wage battle in a spiritual war against "the evil rulers and authorities of the unseen world" (Eph 6:11-12). Finally, Zechariah's visions of "war and peace" call the Christian to "work for peace" (Matt 5:9) and the Christian church to be Christ's ambassador—pleading with the world to "come back to God" (2 Cor 5:20). Happily (though mysteriously), by the power of the Holy Spirit the Christian has already received the gift of God's peace—the "peace of mind and heart" granted by Jesus to all who love him and obey his teachings (John 14:27).

◆   ## 3. The Lord will restore his people (10:1–11:3)

Ask the LORD for rain in the spring,
    for he makes the storm clouds.
And he will send showers of rain
    so every field becomes a lush
    pasture.
[2] Household gods give worthless advice,
    fortune-tellers predict only lies,
and interpreters of dreams pronounce
    falsehoods that give no comfort.
So my people are wandering like lost
    sheep;
    they are attacked because they have
    no shepherd.

[3] "My anger burns against your
    shepherds,
    and I will punish these leaders.*
For the LORD of Heaven's Armies
    has arrived
    to look after Judah, his flock.
He will make them strong and
    glorious,
    like a proud warhorse in battle.
[4] From Judah will come the cornerstone,
    the tent peg,
    the bow for battle,
    and all the rulers.
[5] They will be like mighty warriors
    in battle,
    trampling their enemies in the
    mud under their feet.
Since the LORD is with them as
    they fight,

they will overthrow even the
    enemy's horsemen.

[6] "I will strengthen Judah and save
    Israel*;
    I will restore them because of
    my compassion.
It will be as though I had never
    rejected them,
    for I am the LORD their God, who
    will hear their cries.
[7] The people of Israel* will become like
    mighty warriors,
    and their hearts will be made happy
    as if by wine.
Their children, too, will see it and
    be glad;
    their hearts will rejoice in the
    LORD.
[8] When I whistle to them, they will
    come running,
    for I have redeemed them.
From the few who are left,
    they will grow as numerous as
    they were before.
[9] Though I have scattered them like
    seeds among the nations,
    they will still remember me in
    distant lands.
They and their children will survive
    and return again to Israel.
[10] I will bring them back from Egypt
    and gather them from Assyria.

I will resettle them in Gilead and
    Lebanon
until there is no more room for
    them all.
¹¹ They will pass safely through the sea
    of distress,*
for the waves of the sea will be held
    back,
and the waters of the Nile will dry up.
The pride of Assyria will be crushed,
    and the rule of Egypt will end.
¹² By my power* I will make my people
    strong,
and by my authority they will go
    wherever they wish.
I, the LORD, have spoken!"

CHAPTER 11

¹ Open your doors, Lebanon,
    so that fire may devour your cedar
    forests.
² Weep, you cypress trees, for all the
    ruined cedars;
the most majestic ones have fallen.
Weep, you oaks of Bashan,
    for the thick forests have been cut
    down.
³ Listen to the wailing of the shepherds,
    for their rich pastures are
    destroyed.
Hear the young lions roaring,
    for their thickets in the Jordan
    Valley are ruined.

10:3 Or *these male goats.* 10:6 Hebrew *save the house of Joseph.* 10:7 Hebrew *of Ephraim.* 10:11 Or *the sea of Egypt,* referring to the Red Sea. 10:12 Hebrew *In the LORD.*

NOTES

10:1 *rain in the spring.* The rainy season in Israel begins in the fall (October) with the "early rain" and ends in the spring with the "latter rain" (March–May, cf. Deut 11:14). The early rain fostered new growth, and the latter rain brought the crops to maturity. The OT prophets viewed rain as a sign of divine blessing (cf. Joel 2:23).

10:2 *Household gods.* The word *terapim* [TH8655, ZH9572] may refer to cultic idols of some sort or even ancestor statues used in necromancy rituals, since consultation with the dead was a widespread practice in the biblical world. The association of the household gods with fortune-tellers and interpreters of dreams in the immediate context might suggest that Zechariah has "ancestor figures" in mind, rather than idols (see the discussion in Meyers and Meyers 1993:185-187). Necromancy or consulting the dead for advice was forbidden for the Hebrews according to the Mosaic law (Deut 18:10-11).

fortune-tellers. The term (based on the root *qasam* [TH7080, ZH7876]) refers in general to those who practice forms of divination or soothsaying. The means of fortune-telling are not specified (whether mechanical manipulation such as mixing oil and water or observation of natural events and signs), but according to Mosaic law all such practices were forbidden (cf. Lev 20:27; Deut 18:10-11).

10:3 *My anger burns.* The idiom (*kharah* [TH2734, ZH3013] + *'ap* [TH639, ZH678]) signifies an intense wrath that burns like a raging and uncontrolled fire (cf. Exod 22:22-24). The object of this divine wrath is most often Israel, incited by their disobedience to covenant stipulations or lapses into idolatry (cf. Deut 6:14-15; Josh 7:1; Judg 2:20). The NT still warns the faithful against breaking God's covenant because it is "a terrible thing to fall into the hands of the living God" (Heb 10:31). (Cf. the discussion of God's anger in the commentary on 1:1-6.)

leaders. Lit., "he-goats" (*'attudim* [TH6260, ZH6966]), a figure of speech for princes and leaders in prophetic literature since male goats typically lead the goat herds (cf. Isa 14:9; 34:6; Jer 51:40; Ezek 34:17).

10:4 *cornerstone.* The first-laid foundation stone upon which a building's superstructure rests (*pinnah* [TH6438, ZH7157]; cf. Exod 27:2; 1 Kgs 7:30). At times the word designates the cornerstone of a foundation, which sets the right angle for a wall or a building (cf. Job

38:6; Ps 118:22; Isa 28:16). The NT identifies Jesus Christ as the "cornerstone" of the house of God's family, the church (Eph 2:20). Cf. the note on 3:9, "single stone."

tent peg. The word *yathed* [TH3489, ZH3845] is a technical term for the wooden stake that fastens the tent ropes securely to the ground (cf. Exod 27:19; 35:18) or a peg driven into a wall on which a vessel or valuable object can be securely hung and displayed (cf. Ezra 9:8, "security"). Just as the tent peg anchors the tent to ground, so future leadership will come from Judah that will provide the mooring needed to stabilize the Hebrew nation. The tent peg had even served as a weapon at times, as Jael used a tent peg to kill the Canaanite general Sisera (Judg 4:21-22). Delilah used a *yathed* to braid the locks of Samson's hair (Judg 16:14,"loom shuttle"). Such a peg also symbolized the permanence of Eliakim's appointment as palace administrator in the court of King Hezekiah (Isa 22:20-23).

bow for battle. The battle bow (*qesheth milkhamah* [TH7198/4421, ZH8008/4878]) was mentioned previously among the implements of war that God would destroy in the day of his visitation (9:10, NLT "weapons"). The shift from architectural images to one of warfare extends the scope of the leadership provided by Judah from political stability to military power (cf. 9:13). Following the Aramaic Targum, some Christian interpreters understand the metaphors of cornerstone, tent peg, and battle bow as messianic titles and apply them to Jesus Christ (e.g., Unger 1963:177-179).

10:6 save. The same word (*yasha'* [TH3467, ZH3828], "to deliver, save") is applied to the Israelite Exodus from Egypt, the "salvation-event" of the OT (cf. Exod 14:15; 15:2). Salvation or "victory" belongs to the Lord (Ps 3:8); only the God of Israel "has the power to save" (Isa 63:1).

my compassion. God saves and restores his people Israel because of his "compassion" (*rakham* [TH7355, ZH8163]). According to Meyers and Meyers (1993:209), the word embodied female attributes of caring and nurturing and of maternal concern for one's children. Compassion is an attribute of God (Ps 111:4), but it is also a divine prerogative, as he will show compassion or "mercy" to anyone he chooses (Exod 33:19). God's compassion extends to all those who fear him (Ps 103:13) and is bounded only by the greatness of his unfailing love (Lam 3:32).

10:8 whistle. Typically the word has a negative, even derisive meaning in the OT (see Meyers and Meyers 1993:213). Here the term is used in a positive sense as a signal that God's intentions to restore Israel are under way. The expression continues the pastoral imagery of the passage because shepherds in biblical times herded their flocks by whistling or piping to them (cf. Judg 5:16).

redeemed. The word (*padah* [TH6299, ZH7009]) can also mean "to ransom" as a legal act of redemption (e.g., buying slaves out of their servitude or indentured status). The term has associations with the Exodus, when the Lord redeemed Israel from their slavery in Egypt (Deut 15:15; 24:18). God's gracious redemption extends to all those who serve him; "No one who takes refuge in him will be condemned" (Ps 34:22).

they will grow as numerous as they were before. This is probably an allusion to the rapid population growth of the Hebrews during their sojourn as slaves in Egypt (Exod 1:7, 20). The propagation of the Hebrew nation was one of the promises associated with the Abrahamic covenant (Gen 12:1-3; cf. Gen 22:17; 32:12).

10:9 remember me. Remember (*zakar* [TH2142, ZH2349]) is perhaps a wordplay on the prophet's name, Zechariah ("the Lord remembers"). God always remembers his covenant (Ps 111:5) and his covenant people (Ps 115:12). God will sustain his people's memory of him despite their dispersion among the nations. Remembering God transforms the believer and the believing community because "recalling God's past saving work becomes a bridge from a grim present to a blessed future" (NIDOTTE 1.1102).

10:10 Egypt . . . Assyria. According to Isaiah, the Lord would "whistle" for the armies of Egypt and Assyria to come against King Ahaz and Judah as punishment for his unbelief (Isa 7:18). The two nations were traditional enemies of Israel and represented all nations, east and west, who were opposed to God and his people. Specifically, Egypt and Assyria were symbolic of the slavery and exile endured by the dispersed Hebrew people.

Gilead and Lebanon. Gilead is the fertile region east of the Jordan River and south of the Sea of Galilee suitable for grain-growing and pasturing settled by the tribes of Manasseh and Gad. Lebanon, a mountainous region north of Israel, was famed for its cedar forests and sometimes defined the northern reaches of the Promised Land for the biblical writers (cf. Deut 11:24; Josh 1:4). God's restoration and resettlement of the Hebrews will be so complete that even the fringe areas of Israelite territory will teem with people.

10:11 sea of distress. An allusion to the Exodus and the crossing of the Red Sea (or Sea of Reeds; Exod 14:22). The Hebrews' return to the land of Israel from exile in Babylonia (and their necessary fording of the Euphrates River) is likened to a "second exodus" experience (cf. Isa 43:2-6, 16-17).

10:12 I will make my people strong. The verse repeats the earlier promise that God himself would strengthen his people (10:6) and alludes to Isaiah's declaration that God would strengthen and help his people after calling them back from the ends of the earth (Isa 41:8-10). The psalmist recognized that true strength is found only in the Lord (Pss 18:1; 22:19; 28:8; 29:11).

11:1-3 This brief poem is a taunt song that anticipates the lament raised over the once proud and powerful nations justly destroyed by the Sovereign Lord (10:5, 11). The poem may be understood in one of two ways: either as the conclusion to Zechariah's message of divine deliverance and restoration of Israel (10:1-12), or as the introduction to the following message (the good and evil shepherds, 11:4-17). One view from the latter perspective takes the taunt song as a reference to the destruction of the power and pride of the nations, represented by the various types of trees (11:2). Another view understands the passage more literally as the devastation of Syro-Palestine as a result of rejecting the Messiah and Good Shepherd, fulfilled in the Roman campaigns associated with the first Jewish war (AD 66–73; see Barker 1985:674). Petersen (1995:84) also reads the poem literally rather than allegorically, but concludes more generally that the point of the oracle is to encourage the restoration community to accept the status quo—since any destruction (symbolized in the hewn timber) will have far reaching effects for the people of God. The NLT paragraphing sets the poem as the conclusion to the message of God's deliverance and restoration of Israel (10:1-12).

11:1 Lebanon. The region north of Israel (excluding the Phoenician coastal plain) boasted snow-covered mountains and fertile valleys. The land of Lebanon was a symbol of strength and fertility in biblical times. Baldwin (1972:178) rightly observes that the stress in Zechariah's oracle is the "downfall of the arrogant."

11:2 Bashan. The "cedars" of Lebanon and the "oaks" of Bashan are paired in other prophetic oracles (e.g., Isa 2:13; Ezek 27:5-6). The region of biblical Bashan was located east and northeast of the Sea of Galilee and, like Lebanon, its defining feature was superb stands of timber. Jeremiah identified Lebanon and Bashan as treacherous allies of the kingdom of Judah (Jer 22:20, 22). Like Egypt and Assyria, Lebanon and Bashan are representative of those nations that will experience divine judgment when God re-gathers and restores the people of Israel (see note on 10:11).

11:3 shepherds . . . lions. Figurative language for the leaders of Lebanon and Bashan lamenting the destruction of their forested slopes—the pride and livelihood of each region (cf. 10:11).

COMMENTARY

The prophet revisits the themes of Israel's re-gathering and return to the ancestral homeland of Palestine, the land of covenant promise (cf. 9:11-17). The second unit of Zechariah's first oracle (chs 9–11) consists of three messages: a rebuke of false shepherds (10:1-3), the promise of a true shepherd (10:4-12), and a taunt song of divine judgment against the regions of Lebanon and Bashan for their betrayal of Judah during the Babylonian crisis (11:1-3; cf. Jer 22:20, 22). The key idea of the section is found in the repeated phrases declaring that God would strengthen his people by his power and restore them because of his compassion (10:6, 12). The passage anticipates the allegory about the good and evil shepherds that follows (11:4-17).

The story of the Hebrew monarchies is one of failed leadership, a result of the rejection of God's rule over the Israelites (cf. 1 Sam 8:7). King Solomon's avarice and idolatry fractured David's empire (1 Kgs 11:9-11). The divided monarchies of Israel and Judah created by the split of Solomon's kingdom were ruled by a combined total of 39 kings and one queen. Only eight of those kings (all from the southern kingdom of Judah) were deemed "good" in the theological reviews posted by the writer of the royal annals found in the book of Kings. In large measure, Zechariah echoed the laments of the prophets Jeremiah and Ezekiel who decried the plight of a people scattered like lost sheep without a shepherd—victims of shepherds who fed themselves instead of their flocks (Jer 50:6-7; Ezek 34:1-6; but see Ollenburger [1996:814], who identifies the shepherds of 10:3 as the rulers of the nations who rule Judah and keep Israel in dispersion).

The eventual restoration of Israel forecast by Zechariah will witness the accompanying restoration of righteous leadership to the nation—responsible shepherds who will care for the flock of God's people (11:4; cf. Jer 23:4). The futurist interpretation of Zechariah understands the prophet's message as a projection of the rule of Messiah fulfilled in the life and ministry of Jesus of Nazareth (see Kaiser 1995:218-220, 232). This true shepherd would arise from the tribe of Judah, and he is called the "cornerstone" (10:4). The New Testament traces Jesus' lineage to the tribe of Judah and the family of David (Matt 1:3, 6), and Paul identifies Jesus Christ as the "cornerstone" (Eph 2:20). Beyond this, the New Testament identifies the Hebrews or Jews as God's lost sheep (Matt 10:6), and Jesus announced that he was indeed the "good shepherd" (John 10:11, 14). By an everlasting covenant signed with his blood, Jesus earned the title "the great Shepherd of the sheep" (Heb 13:20). His throne endures forever, and his royal power is expressed in righteousness (Heb 1:8), a righteousness made available by the ongoing work of the Counselor—the Holy Spirit in the church of Jesus Christ (John 16:7, 10; 1 Cor 6:11).

Preterist views understand the passage referencing the shepherds of Israel (10:3-12) as the priests and lay leaders of the postexilic Jewish community generally (so Redditt 1995:119-120, 123) or alternately to Yahweh himself (so Petersen 1995:70-78).

◆   4. Good and evil shepherds (11:4-17)

[4]This is what the LORD my God says: "Go and care for the flock that is intended for slaughter. [5]The buyers slaughter their sheep without remorse. The sellers say, 'Praise the LORD! Now I'm rich!' Even the shepherds have no compassion for them. [6]Likewise, I will no longer have pity on the people of the land," says the LORD. "I will let them fall into each other's hands and into the hands of their king. They will turn the land into a wilderness, and I will not rescue them."

[7]So I cared for the flock intended for slaughter—the flock that was oppressed. Then I took two shepherd's staffs and named one Favor and the other Union. [8]I got rid of their three evil shepherds in a single month.

But I became impatient with these sheep, and they hated me, too. [9]So I told them, "I won't be your shepherd any longer. If you die, you die. If you are killed, you are killed. And let those who remain devour each other!"

[10]Then I took my staff called Favor and cut it in two, showing that I had revoked the covenant I had made with all the nations. [11]That was the end of my covenant with them. The suffering flock was watching me, and they knew that the LORD was speaking through my actions.

[12]And I said to them, "If you like, give me my wages, whatever I am worth; but only if you want to." So they counted out for my wages thirty pieces of silver.

[13]And the LORD said to me, "Throw it to the potter*"—this magnificent sum at which they valued me! So I took the thirty coins and threw them to the potter in the Temple of the LORD.

[14]Then I took my other staff, Union, and cut it in two, showing that the bond of unity between Judah and Israel was broken.

[15]Then the LORD said to me, "Go again and play the part of a worthless shepherd. [16]This illustrates how I will give this nation a shepherd who will not care for those who are dying, nor look after the young,* nor heal the injured, nor feed the healthy. Instead, this shepherd will eat the meat of the fattest sheep and tear off their hooves.

[17]"What sorrow awaits this worthless
    shepherd
 who abandons the flock!
The sword will cut his arm
    and pierce his right eye.
His arm will become useless,
    and his right eye completely
        blind."

11:13 Syriac version reads *into the treasury;* also in 11:13b. Compare Matt 27:6-10.   11:16 Or *the scattered.*

NOTES

11:4 *flock.* The OT prophets often refer to the people of Israel as God's flock (e.g., Isa 40:11; Ezek 34:8; Mic 5:4). The relative helplessness of sheep places a premium on careful shepherding of the animals, making leadership the main subject of Zechariah's shepherd allegory.

intended for slaughter. Like sheep fattened for butchering, the people are treated as a commodity—"disposable goods" in a corrupt and oppressive economic system.

11:5 *buyers.* The sheep (i.e., the Hebrew people) are sold as slaves to the occupying foreign powers, foreign allies, or domestic slave-traders (cf. Amos 2:6).

sellers. The sellers of the sheep appear to be the shepherds themselves, the leaders of the people!

11:7 *two shepherd's staffs.* The staff or crook was a symbol of leadership in the biblical world. In ancient Egypt the ornamental shepherd's crook held by the Pharaoh represented his just rule of the people. Unlike the prophet Ezekiel, who joined two sticks into one symbolizing the reunification of the two Hebrew kingdoms (Ezek 37:15-19), Zechariah dramatized the reversal of covenant relationship and unity by breaking the two staffs (see 11:10, 14).

Favor. This staff symbolized the election of Israel as the people of God, as stipulated in the covenant with Abraham (Gen 12:1-3), and the promise of leadership after the manner of King David, as stipulated in the Davidic covenant (2 Sam 7:12-16).

Union. The second staff symbolized the unity of the Hebrew tribes as a single nation, achieved during the reign of King David (cf. 2 Sam 5:1-3). The reference to the "Union" staff alludes to the two sticks joined together by the prophet Ezekiel, representing the reunification of the divided kingdoms of Judah and Israel (Ezek 37:16-17).

11:8 *three evil shepherds.* This enigmatic historical reference has prompted more than 40 different identifications for the three shepherds, whether the last three kings of Judah, certain high priests from the intertestamental era, or various leaders from the offices of king, priest, and prophet (see further the discussions in Baldwin 1972:181-183; Redditt 1995:98; cf. Meyers and Meyers 1993:265, who observe that the number three is symbolic of completeness and conclude that the passage is "deliberately vague and, thereby, inclusive").

11:9 *devour each other.* Taken literally, this may be a reference to the cannibalism that resulted due to famine during the siege of Jerusalem first by the Babylonians in 587 BC (cf. Lam 4:10) and later by the Romans in AD 70 (cf. Josephus *Wars* 7.4.4). The expression may also be understood metaphorically as various forms of exploitation and oppression of the poor by the rich (cf. Mic 3:3).

11:10 *cut it in two.* The OT prophets often resorted to symbolic actions to dramatize their message. The snapping of the two staffs named Favor and Union spoke figuratively to the breaking of the covenant bond between God and his people (11:11) and the bond of unity between the kingdoms of Judah and Israel (11:14).

revoked the covenant. A covenant between Yahweh and the nations is otherwise unattested to in the OT. The prophet may be referring to a "covenant of restraint" by which God had protected Israel from the nations (cf. Ezek 34:28) or even the Jewish colonies scattered among the foreign powers (so Baldwin 1972:184). In either case, the annulment of the covenant puts the people of God at risk of "the sheep merchants, freed to prey on the sheep" (Ollenburger 1996:822). Meyers and Meyers (1993:270) boldly suggest that Zechariah actually proclaimed the dissolution of the historical covenant binding Israel to Yahweh as the people of God. Such a prophetic declaration was not unprecedented, as the sin of Israel prompted Hosea to disavow the northern kingdom as the people of God (Hos 1:9). Later, Jeremiah terminated the Davidic covenant as a result of Jehoiachin's sin (Jer 22:28-30; the end of this curse was later signaled during Haggai's ministry; cf. Hag 2:23).

11:12 *thirty pieces of silver.* This was the price of a slave later in the biblical world (cf. Exod 21:32). The standard rate for the purchase of slaves in the early second millennium was 20 shekels (cf. Gen 37:28). Hosea paid a similar amount to redeem the adulteress Gomer out of slavery (half in silver and half in barley and wine, Hos 3:2). In the allegory in Zechariah, the silver constitutes "severance pay" given by the sellers or merchants to the shepherd since he had renounced his role as shepherd (11:9).

11:13 *Throw it to the potter.* The silver was to be given as a donation to "the potter in the Temple of the LORD" (11:13c). Baldwin (1972:185) speculates that a guild of potters may have been minor Temple officials due to the continual need for sacred vessels (cf. Lev 6:28). The word "potter" (*yotser* [TH3335A, ZH3450]) is similar in sound to the word for "treasury" (*'otsar* [TH214, ZH238]), prompting the suggested reading "throw it into the treasury" (so NRSV). It is noteworthy that the NT account of Judas throwing the betrayal money onto the floor of the Temple conflates 11:12-13 and Jer 32:6-9 and cites both the "treasury"

(Matt 27:6) and the "potter's field" (Matt 27:10). The LXX translates "throw it into the furnace," suggesting that the silver was melted down by a smelter or founder and recast into a silver vessel of some sort for use in the Temple rituals.

magnificent sum. Thirty pieces of silver was a considerable amount of money in the ancient world (more than two years' wages for the average laborer; cf. Baldwin 1972:184). Rather than being sarcastic, the expression contributes to the overall theme of reversal in the allegory (so Meyers and Meyers 1993:279).

11:15 *worthless shepherd.* Zechariah's description of the "worthless shepherd" has parallels to the shepherds portrayed by Ezekiel as the enemies of God (Ezek 34:7-10). These corrupt and greedy leaders are driven by self-interest, unlike the true shepherd who rescues the scattered sheep, feeds them, and tends to the injured and weak among the flock (Ezek 34:11-16).

11:16 *tear off their hooves.* This cryptic Hebrew idiom describes the wanton and ravenous search for the last morsel of edible meat on an animal carcass. The prophet Micah used similar language to describe the leaders of Judah whose unjust rule was akin to eating the flesh of the people (Mic 3:3).

11:17 *cut his arm . . . pierce his right eye.* The woe-oracle against the worthless shepherd takes the form of a poetic curse invoked for abandoning the flock. The maiming of the arm and the blinding of the right eye are figures of speech that represent the physical and mental abilities of the shepherd. The loss of the "arm" and the "eye" render the worthless shepherd powerless, thus ending his selfish and opportunistic rule (cf. the discussion in Meyers and Meyers 1993:291-292).

COMMENTARY

The metaphor of the shepherd for the leaders of the Hebrew people provides the theme that binds the last three messages of Zechariah's first oracle together (9:16; 10:2-3; 11:3, 5, 7-9, 15-17). This final message (11:4-17) of the first oracle (chs 9–11) combines the genre of allegory with a report of symbolic action. Craigie (1984:208) has suggested that the text be understood as "an enacted prophecy, akin to those many cases in the Book of Ezekiel, where the prophet was instructed to perform certain actions which symbolized their own meaning." It is possible, however, that the report of symbolic action is simply a literary device designed to carry the gist of the prophet's message from God to the people of postexilic Judah (11:11).

The allegory of the good and evil shepherds consists of three distinct units: the call to Zechariah to shepherd a doomed flock of sheep (11:4-6), the rejection of the good shepherd (11:7-14), and the installation of a worthless shepherd over the people (11:15-17). The passage is difficult to interpret due to the obscure nature of the language and the lack of an immediate historical context for the story (e.g., the reference to the ousting of "three shepherds" in one month, 11:8). Thus, it is unclear whether this is a reflection on the recent Babylonian exile or a warning about a future "slaughter and scattering" of the Hebrew people. Beyond all this, Zechariah's role in the allegory is puzzling because the prophet is first charged to care for God's flock first as a good shepherd (11:4-14) and then to play the part of a worthless shepherd (11:15-17). Quite apart from the ambiguity of the allegory, basic theological truths emerge from the story related to "shepherds" (or leaders) and "sheep" (or people).

Calvin Miller (1987:84) reminds us that leaders are prone to abuse their power, given the natural inclinations of fallen people in a fallen culture. The compassionless and evil shepherds portrayed in Zechariah's allegory serve to confirm this observation (11:5, 8). The condemnation of corrupt leaders, whether political or religious, is a recurrent theme in the Old Testament prophets (e.g., Isa 1:23; Jer 25:34; Ezek 22:6; Hos 5:1; Zeph 1:8). Even King David, the prototype for the ultimate shepherd-king (cf. Ezek 37:24), succumbed to the lure of his own absolute power, as the sordid account of his affair with Bathsheba reveals (2 Sam 11).

Zechariah implicitly preaches that the shepherd-leader must have compassion for the sheep under his or her oversight (cf. 11:5). God, as the Father of all mercy (or compassion, NIV; 2 Cor 1:3), is full of mercy (or compassion, NIV; Ps 116:5). Jesus, the self-proclaimed "good shepherd" (John 10:11) had compassion on people "because they were like sheep without a shepherd" (Mark 6:34). The story of Jonah in the Old Testament and the parable of the Good Samaritan in the New Testament (Luke 10:30-37) reveal that God expects his faithful servants to exhibit compassion for others regardless of the size of their sphere of influence as a leader. The second great commandment, to "love your neighbor as yourself" (Matt 22:39), is a divine imperative to show compassion to the widest possible spectrum of human beings (Stott 1975:16-17). As John Piper (1996:277) has observed, compassion is all about "God-esteem and grace esteem, not self-esteem."

A second important theological lesson from Zechariah's allegory of the good and evil shepherds concerns the sheep. Craigie stuns us with the insightful observation that "the shepherd metaphor runs more deeply than at first appeared; human perversity and ignorance are so profound that human beings will not even accept good leadership if God gives it to them" (1984:210; cf. 11:7-8). Our penchant since the sin of Adam and Eve and the fall of all humanity (Gen 3:6-7; Rom 5:12) is to destroy what God made good because we love the darkness more than the light and our actions are continually evil (John 3:19-20). Tragically, even when the Good Shepherd appeared in the person of Jesus of Nazareth, he was despised and rejected by his own people—the Jews (John 1:11). The Good Shepherd, the compassionate Shepherd, necessarily gave his life for the sheep who demanded his death (cf. John 10:11, 15). Craigie has encouraged us to consider, however, that "the good news emerging from this dark scene is that, beyond the death of the Good Shepherd, the staff called 'Grace' [or 'Favor,' 11:10] was restored; still the doors are open for human beings to recognize in God the true and eternal Shepherd" (1984:210).

◆ B. Second Oracle (12:1–14:21)
1. Future deliverance for Jerusalem (12:1–14)

This* message concerning the fate of Israel came from the LORD: "This message is from the LORD, who stretched out the heavens, laid the foundations of the earth, and formed the human spirit. ²I will make Jerusalem like an intoxicating drink that makes the nearby nations stagger when they send their armies to besiege Jerusalem and Judah. ³On that day I will make Jerusalem an immovable rock. All the nations will gather against it to try to move it, but they will only hurt themselves.

⁴"On that day," says the LORD, "I will cause every horse to panic and every rider to lose his nerve. I will watch over the people of Judah, but I will blind all the horses of their enemies. ⁵And the clans of Judah will say to themselves, 'The people of Jerusalem have found strength in the LORD of Heaven's Armies, their God.'

⁶"On that day I will make the clans of Judah like a flame that sets a woodpile ablaze or like a burning torch among sheaves of grain. They will burn up all the neighboring nations right and left, while the people living in Jerusalem remain secure.

⁷"The LORD will give victory to the rest of Judah first, before Jerusalem, so that the people of Jerusalem and the royal line of David will not have greater honor than the rest of Judah. ⁸On that day the LORD will defend the people of Jerusalem; the weakest among them will be as mighty as King David! And the royal descendants will be like God, like the angel of the LORD who goes before them! ⁹For on that day I will begin to destroy all the nations that come against Jerusalem.

¹⁰"Then I will pour out a spirit* of grace and prayer on the family of David and on the people of Jerusalem. They will look on me whom they have pierced and mourn for him as for an only son. They will grieve bitterly for him as for a firstborn son who has died. ¹¹The sorrow and mourning in Jerusalem on that day will be like the great mourning for Hadad-rimmon in the valley of Megiddo.

¹²"All Israel will mourn, each clan by itself, and with the husbands separate from their wives. The clan of David will mourn alone, as will the clan of Nathan, ¹³the clan of Levi, and the clan of Shimei. ¹⁴Each of the surviving clans from Judah will mourn separately, and with the husbands separate from their wives.

12:1 Hebrew *An Oracle: This.*   12:10 Or *the Spirit.*

NOTES

12:1 *This message.* The Hebrew superscription or title (12:1) for the passage (chs 12–14) combines two formulaic prophetic expressions: the technical term "oracle" (*massa'* [TH4853A, ZH5363]) and the prophetic word formula. The word "oracle" means "burden" in the sense of a pronouncement of prophetic judgment and invests the prophet's message with divine authority. The combination of the two expressions is also found in 9:1 and Mal 1:1 and is a distinctive feature of late biblical prophecy (cf. Meyers and Meyers 1993:91). On the prophetic word formula, see the note on 1:1, "the LORD gave this message."

This message is from the LORD. The divine utterance formula (*ne'um yhwh* [TH5002/3068, ZH5536/3378], lit., "oracle of Yahweh") is a nominal exclamation ascribing divine authority to prophetic speech. The phrase is often a closing formula in the prophetic literature (Waltke and O'Connor 1990:40.2.3a).

12:2 *Jerusalem.* The city of Jerusalem is a key theme in ch 12 (mentioned 11 times). Meyers and Meyers (1993:342-343) note that "the constant repetition . . . depicts the eschatological future of Jerusalem—representing Zion, Judah, and all Israel—in the context of the rest of the world, and the future of Jerusalem as the setting of the royal leadership that will be restored to power." (Cf. the discussion of Jerusalem in the commentary on 1:7-17.)

intoxicating drink. Lit., a "bowl of reeling" or "cup of staggering" (*sap-ra'al* [TH5592/7478, ZH6195/8303]), a unique expression for Jerusalem in the OT. The cup of wine or strong drink is a common metaphor for God's judgment in the OT prophets (e.g., Isa 51:17; Jer 25:15; Hab 2:16). Jesus understood the suffering of the cross as a "cup" of divine wrath (Matt 26:39, 42), and the Apocalypse portrays God's judgment as bowls of wrath poured out upon the earth (Rev 14:10; 16:1).

stagger. This is perhaps an allusion to Jeremiah's description of God's cup of anger that will make the nations "stagger, crazed by the warfare I will send against them" (Jer 25:16).

12:3 On that day. The phrase is repeated in 12:4, 6, 8, 9, 11 and is shorthand in the OT prophets for "the day of the LORD" (cf. 2:11; Isa 2:11; Joel 2:1; Zeph 1:14).

immovable rock. Like the expression "intoxicating drink" (12:2), this is another unique metaphor for Jerusalem in the OT. This "burdensome stone" (*'eben ma'amasah* [TH68/4614, ZH74/5098]) has links to the prophet's previous references to stones in that the imagery is associated with the Temple—"the physical and spiritual core of Jerusalem" (Meyers and Meyers 1993:317). Jerusalem will prove an immovable rock for those who attempt to conquer and control her because the city was founded by the Lord and he loves it more than any other city of Israel (Ps 87:1-2).

12:4 panic . . . lose his nerve . . . . blind. Madness, blindness, and panic were among the curses threatened against Israel for covenant disobedience (Deut 28:28). The day of the Lord will witness a reversal wherein these curses will be turned against Israel's enemies. The language calls to mind the story of the panic the Lord stirred in the camp of the Aramean army that had assembled against Israel so that they fled in confusion into the night (2 Kgs 7:6-7).

watch over. Lit., "I will open my eyes" (*paqakh* [TH6491, ZH7219], "to open"). Here, God's open eyes are symbolic of his concern and provision (cf. Isa 37:17). In other passages, God's open eyes indicate his omniscient justice (Job 14:3; Jer 32:19).

12:5 the LORD of Heaven's Armies. This compound name for God is prominent in OT prophetic literature and is variously translated "LORD of Hosts" (NRSV) or "LORD Almighty" (NIV). The title occurs more than 50 times in the Hebrew text of Zechariah (1:3 [3x], 4, 6, 12, 14, 16, 17; 2:12, 13, 15; 3:7, 9, 10; 4:6, 9; 5:4; 6:12, 15; 7:3, 4, 9, 12 [2x], 13; 8:1, 2, 3, 4, 6 [2x], 7, 9 [2x], 11, 14 [2x], 18, 19, 20, 21, 22, 23; 9:15; 10:3; 12:5; 13:2, 7; 14:16, 17, 21 [2x]). The expression *yhwh tseba'oth* [TH3068/6635, ZH3378/7372] is often understood as a construct genitive, as is the case here. More precisely the construction is one of absolute nouns in apposition, perhaps conveying a verbal force: "Yahweh creates armies"; (cf. TDOT 5.515). The term for "Heaven's armies" (*tseba'oth*) has military connotations; in this case it refers to the angelic armies at God's disposal. The epithet emphasizes "the invincible might behind the Lord's commands" (Baldwin 1972:39), and the repetition of the title in Zechariah's second oracle (chs 12–14) assures his audience that the fulfillment of the divine promises concerning Judah's victory is certain (12:7).

12:6 flame. Lit., a "firepan" or "brazier" (*kiyor 'esh* [TH3595/784, ZH3963/836]). Bronze or gold firepans were used to carry hot coals to or from the sacrificial altars of both the Tabernacle and the Temple (Exod 27:3; 1 Kgs 7:50). In the eschaton, God will set Israel like a firepan burning with hot coals among the nations to both destroy and purify with fire akin to that which consumed the ritual sacrifices of Hebrew worship.

burning torch. The burning torch may also allude to the "smoking firepot" and "flaming torch" as symbols of the Abrahamic covenant, as well as God's election and protection of Israel (cf. Gen 15:17; see Larkin 1994:157).

12:8 King David. This is a reference to the warrior-king who was celebrated in song as Israel's champion after killing the Philistine giant Goliath (1 Sam 18:7).

angel of the LORD. The title is a manifestation of God himself as a divine warrior in this context and recalls the deliverance and protection he provided for Israel upon their Exodus from Egypt (Exod 14:19; 15:3). As Merrill has noted (1994:317), the comparisons to David and the angel of the Lord only serve to magnify God's glorious deliverance of his people Israel. By means of divine enabling the weak will become strong and the strong will become as powerful as God. Cf. the notes on 1:11 and 3:1, "angel of the LORD."

12:10 pour out. Zechariah employs the same word used by Joel to describe the outpouring of God's spirit of prophecy upon all people (Joel 2:28; *shapak* [TH8210, ZH9161]). The word is used in the Minor Prophets to describe the eschatological outpouring of God's Spirit upon Israel (12:10; Joel 2:28-29; cf. Ezek 39:29) and the cascading judgment of God upon the wicked—Hebrews and the nations alike (Hos 5:10; Zeph 3:8). In either case, the term is a metaphor for an abundant outpouring of blessing or judgment from heaven, a torrent or flood of rain (Hos 5:10) or even fire (Lam 2:4).

spirit of grace and prayer. The bestowing of the "spirit of grace" is an act of divine favor that is both unmerited and apparently unsought by the people of Israel. It is this persuasive activity of God that causes the Hebrews to seek him with prayers of contrition and repentance. The word "prayer" (*takhanunim* [TH8469, ZH9384]) connotes an earnest plea for divine mercy (cf. Ps 28:2). Such prayers of supplication are implicit affirmations of God's gracious and merciful character because people have learned from experience that he hears and responds to their pleas (cf. Ps 86:15). McComiskey (1998:1214) cautions against identifying the "spirit of grace" with the Spirit of God since it is not marked by references to God, as is the case in 4:6; 6:8; and 7:12. Yet the sin of grieving the Spirit of God may result in the work of God's Spirit that convicts the human heart of sin and prompts repentance (Ps 51:3-4; Isa 63:10; John 16:8; Eph 4:30).

12:11 Hadad-rimmon. The name is unique in the OT. The compound name joins two Syrian deities, the storm-god (Hadad) and the thunder-god (Rimmon). The meaning of the expression is obscure. It may be a reference to an unknown place name, perhaps marking the spot where King Josiah was killed (so Merrill 1994:324; see the note on "Meggido" below) or it may refer to an Israelite day of mourning to commemorate that event (so Meyers and Meyers 1993:343-344; later rabbinic tradition connected the day of mourning to the death of King Ahab, cf. Cathcart and Gordon 1989:219). Still others equate the eschatological weeping of Israel with the pagans wailing for their fertility gods (so Smith 1984:279). Whatever the exact meaning of Hadad-rimmon, the day will be one of unprecedented mourning for the Hebrews.

Megiddo. This was a major Canaanite city on the southwest edge of the Jezreel Valley captured by Joshua (Josh 12:21) and allotted to the tribe of Manasseh (Josh 17:11). The city was a district capital during Solomon's reign (1 Kgs 4:12). King Josiah was mortally wounded in a battle against Pharaoh Neco and the Egyptians on the plain of Megiddo (2 Chr 35:22-23). McComiskey (1998:1215) suggests that Zechariah may have understood Josiah's "piercing" by an arrow as a foreshadowing of the "pierced" figure of 12:10. The mountain of Megiddo (Har-Meggido or Armageddon) is the site of the great eschatological battle depicted in Rev 16:16.

12:12-13 clan of David . . . clan of Nathan . . . clan of Levi . . . clan of Shimei. Two different understandings of the roster of "mourning families" are commonly espoused: (1) Zechariah may be referring to the families of two royal persons (i.e., David and his son Nathan, cf. 1 Chr 14:4) and two priestly persons (i.e., Levi and his grandson Shimei, cf. Num 3:16-18; 1 Chr 6:16-17). (2) Alternatively, the four families may represent the four principal classes of leadership in OT times: the king (David, 1 Sam 16:1-13); the prophet (Nathan, 2 Sam 7:2), the priest (Levi, Deut 33:8-11), and the sage (Shimei, 1 Kgs 1:8; 4:18). The former interpretation seems the more likely, given Zechariah's emphasis on the Branch who will serve both as king and priest (cf. 6:12-13). This list of mourners (12:12-14), emphasizing the separation of families by gender, depicts the depth and totality of Israel's mourning.

COMMENTARY

As noted previously, part two of the book of Zechariah is composed of two distinct literary units, chapters 9–11 and 12–14. The literary genre of Zechariah 9–14 is more distinctively apocalyptic in character, combining cryptic historical allusions with futuristic visions. The tone of the prophet's message shifts from one of exhortation and encouragement to one of admonition and warning. The section contains no explicit references to the prophet, and the messages are presumed to date from a later period of Zechariah's ministry. (See the commentary on Zechariah 9:1-8 on the title "this message," which prefaces the two oracles, chs 9-11 and 12-14.)

Zechariah's second oracle may be outlined in four sections: future deliverance for Jerusalem (12:1-14), a fountain of cleansing (13:1-6), the scattering of the sheep (13:7-9), and the Lord will rule the earth (14:1-21). The theme of opposition between Jerusalem and the nations binds the four messages of the oracle together, as the nations are gathered against Jerusalem at the beginning (12:1-9) and at the end of the prophet's last sermon (14:1-15). The apocalyptic tone of the oracle is set by the repetition of the phrase "on that day," prophetic shorthand for the eschatological Day of the Lord (12:3, 4, 6, 8, 11; 13:1, 2, 4; 14:4, 6, 8, 9, 13, 20, 21). The second oracle presents a mixed picture of judgment and blessing, with portents of both destruction and deliverance determined for Jerusalem. The focal point of the second oracle is the cleansing of the people of Israel from all their sins and impurity (13:1). The oracle (and the book of Zechariah) culminates with the establishment of the universal kingdom of God (14:16-21).

The first section of Zechariah's final oracle has two parts: the assault of the nations against Jerusalem (12:1-9) and the repentance of Israel (12:10-14). As Mason (1977:118) has noted, the outward victory of Israel over the nations is complemented by the inward spiritual renewal of the people—and both are accomplished by God. The deliverance of Jerusalem (12:9) bridges the opening section of the second oracle with the visions and earlier messages of Zechariah (esp. 2:1-5 and ch 8), and the outpouring of the spirit of grace (12:10) connects the unit with the call to repentance in the prelude (1:1-6). The prophet's return to the theme of spiritual renewal helps join the oracles portion of the book (chs 9-14) with the larger Haggai–Zechariah–Malachi corpus.

The opening verse of Zechariah's second oracle contains a hymn-like expansion of the prophetic word formula praising God as Creator (12:1). Three specific spheres or realms of God's creative activity are specified, including the heavens, the earth, and the human spirit. The use of a participial form of the Hebrew verb for each of these divine epithets signifies the ongoing or perpetual creative activity of God. In addition, the first two domains of God's creative power have parallels in Psalm 104 and the book of Isaiah, where we learn that God alone created the heavens "and stretched them out" (Isa 42:5; 44:24; cf. Ps 104:2) and "laid the foundations of the earth" (Isa 51:13; cf. Ps 104:5).

The reference to God as the one who "formed the human spirit" is unique to Zechariah 12:1 in the Old Testament. No doubt the prophet drew on the imagery of the Genesis account of the creation of humanity where we learn that "the LORD God formed the man from the dust of the ground" and "breathed the breath of life into the man's nostrils" (Gen 2:7). The statement has a close parallel in the psalmist's description of Yahweh as the one who "made their hearts, so he understands everything they do" (Ps 33:15). This explains the effectiveness of God's outpouring of a spirit of grace (12:10) upon the people of Israel that will prompt prayers of repentance in that eschatological day—since our Maker knows everything about us (Ps 139)! Likewise, this truth should rejuvenate our prayers because God knows our needs before we ask (Matt 6:8, 32). This means our prayers are confessions of agreement with God as much they are petitions to God—so we keep on asking and looking and knocking because our heavenly Father gives good gifts to those who ask him (Matt 7:7-11).

The ministry of the Old Testament prophets was essentially that of revealing God, making him known to Israel and the nations (Hos 6:3). Like Isaiah, Zechariah was concerned that the Israel of his day know God both as Creator and Redeemer (cf. Isa 44:24).

Zechariah 12:1 is an appropriate introduction to the prophet's final oracle because it anticipates the consummation of all things in the universal worship of Yahweh (14:6-9). More specifically, the three epithets contribute to a biblical theology of God's creative and redemptive work in human history. Merrill (1994:312) has cogently summarized: "He redeems because He is the omnipotent creator, and He creates new things in order to redeem. Here at the brink of a new age it is important to know that the same God who brought everything into existence in the first place is well able to usher in the new creation of a restored people in a renewed and universal kingdom."

The enigmatic reference to a "pierced" figure (12:10) has proven to be one of the more difficult passages to interpret in the latter chapters of Zechariah. First, there is the problem of establishing the proper reading of the passage, since many commentators emend the Hebrew text to "they will look on *him* whom they have pierced" (see the discussions in Mason 1977:118-119 and Smith 1984:276). The more difficult (and preferred) reading is the Masoretic Text's "they will look on *me* whom they have pierced" (supported by the notable ancient versions; so NLT).

A second question concerns the antecedent of the pronoun "me" in 12:10; that is, whom will Israel "look on"? In context both the subject and the object of Israel's attention is God himself. But how, then, has Israel "pierced" God? One possible understanding is that the Hebrews pierced God metaphorically by their rebellion and unbelief, leading to their exile (cf. the expansion of the LXX in 12:10: "and they shall look upon me, *because they have mocked me*"). Or they may have pierced God symbolically in the rejection of his representatives, the priests and prophets. Some scholars have even attempted to correlate this symbolic "piercing" of God with the martyrdom of some historical figure commissioned by God to speak to Israel (e.g., the "shepherd" of 11:4-17 or Onias III, a later high priest; cf. Redditt 1995:133). Given the larger context of Zechariah's message, his audience probably understood the statement as a reference to the rejection of God's prophets by their ancestors (cf. 1:4; 7:11-12).

The Christian interpretation of Zechariah's second oracle considers the "piercing" of God as a messianic reference fulfilled in the wounding and death of Jesus of Nazareth. John's Gospel cites Zechariah 12:10 in connection with the piercing of Jesus' side by a Roman solider while he hung on the cross (John 19:34-37), but it does so in the third person ("they will look on *the one* they pierced") rather than the first person ("me") of the Old Testament text. Baldwin (1972:191) has commented that the Gospel writer was simply intending to give the general sense of the Old Testament passage from the viewpoint of recent historical perspective (i.e., the Gospel account makes reference to the OT promise and the NT fulfillment of the events associated with Jesus' death in the immediate past; cf. John 19:35).

The vision of Jesus the Messiah in the Apocalypse also alludes to Zechariah 12:10 in a veiled reference to the Jews as the ones who pierced Jesus (Rev 1:7). But Craigie (1984:214-215) is probably correct in his observation that the Passion narrative of the Gospels does not fully exhaust the meaning of Zechariah's vision. Clearly the crucifixion of Jesus is central to the Good News of Christian theology, and it accounts for his title as the "Lamb that . . . had been slaughtered" (Rev 5:6). And it is true that many Jews were filled with remorse, repented, and believed in Jesus as the "pierced Messiah" as a result of the apostolic preaching at the day of Pentecost (Acts 2:36-41). Yet Paul envisioned a time (after the complete number of Gentiles comes to Christ) when "all Israel will be saved" (Rom 11:25-26). It seems likely that Paul had in mind Zechariah's outpouring of "a spirit of grace" (12:10) that will turn the Hebrew people back to God in repentance. This will occur at the Second Advent of Jesus the Messiah (Rev 1:7).

◆   ## 2. A fountain of cleansing (13:1-6)

"On that day a fountain will be opened for the dynasty of David and for the people of Jerusalem, a fountain to cleanse them from all their sins and impurity.

2"And on that day," says the LORD of Heaven's Armies, "I will erase idol worship throughout the land, so that even the names of the idols will be forgotten. I will remove from the land both the false prophets and the spirit of impurity that came with them. 3If anyone continues to prophesy, his own father and mother will tell him, 'You must die, for you have prophesied lies in the name of the LORD.' And as he prophesies, his own father and mother will stab him.

4"On that day people will be ashamed to claim the prophetic gift. No one will pretend to be a prophet by wearing prophet's clothes. 5He will say, 'I'm no prophet; I'm a farmer. I began working for a farmer as a boy.' 6And if someone asks, 'Then what about those wounds on your chest?*' he will say, 'I was wounded at my friends' house!'

13:6 Hebrew *wounds between your hands?*

NOTES

13:1 *fountain.* The noun *maqor* [TH4726, ZH5227] refers to a spring or fountain of flowing water. The metaphor signifies an "artesian well" that gushes forth pure water to provide ritual cleansing and purification (Merrill 1994:328). Later, Zechariah describes the continuous flow of this spring or fountain as "life-giving waters" (14:8). Jesus proclaimed himself to be the source of this life-giving water (John 4:14), and John's vision of the new heaven and the new earth describes a river flowing with the "water of life" coursing out of the throne of God and the Lamb (Rev 22:1-2).

will be opened. This Niphal participle of the verb "open" (*patakh* [TH6605, ZH7337]) in combination with the verb "to be" (*hayah* [TH1961, ZH2118]) "implies that the fountain is to be opened continuously" (Smith 1984:280).

dynasty of David . . . people of Jerusalem. God's cleansing of Israel will include both leadership (represented by the family of David) and all the people of Judah and Israel (signified by Jerusalem as the spiritual center of the nation; cf. Meyers and Meyers 1993:364, 398-399).

cleanse them from all their sins. This kind of thorough cleansing or purification (*khatta'* [TH2403, ZH2633], Piel stem) could only be symbolized in the ritual washings and sacrifices of OT worship practices (cf. Exod 30:17-21; Heb 10:1-2). Such cleansing was a provision of the new covenant promised by Jeremiah (Jer 31:33) and Ezekiel (Ezek 36:25). The ultimate cleansing of sin was accomplished by the "blood of Jesus" (Heb 10:19), which has been sprinkled on us and made us clean (Heb 10:22). The NLT inserts "sins" as the object of the act of cleansing implied by the context.

impurity. The word "impurity" (*niddah* [TH5079, ZH5614]) often describes sexual impurity and ritual impurity (especially idolatry in Ezekiel; cf. Ezek 36:17, 25). Taken together, the clause indicates that the Hebrews will experience a complete moral and spiritual cleansing as a result of their sorrow and mourning over their sin (12:10-14).

13:2 *erase idol worship.* God, the Holy One of Israel, jealously guards his place in the universe as the only true and living deity (cf. Isa 43:10-13; 44:6-8). The cleansing of Israel associated with the new covenant will wash away the former penchant for idol worship and result in a "new heart" that will enable the people to worship God alone (Jer 32:38-40; Ezek 36:25-27). Then the "adoption" of Israel as the people of God will be complete, as they will truly be his people and he will be their God (Jer 31:33; Ezek 36:28).

names of the idols will be forgotten. Lit., "I will cut off the names of the idols." In the biblical world, the name of a thing or a person embodied the reality of that named entity. Thus, the name of that thing or person and its existence is closely related. To "cut off the names of the idols" means that these false deities will cease to exist because God will see to it that their names are forgotten (cf. Ezek 14:6-11; Meyers and Meyers 1993:367-370).

false prophets. The false prophet or the lying prophet misrepresented God by fabricating divine revelations or by speaking in the name of other gods (Deut 13:5-11; 18:17-22). False prophets had led Israel astray in the past by encouraging the worship of idols (Jer 23:13, 25). The threat of heretical teaching by false prophets continued into the postexilic period (cf. Neh 6:12-14), and Jesus warned that false messiahs and false prophets will deceive people until the end of the age (Mark 13:22). According to 1 John 4:1-3, false prophets promote a common teaching that denies the incarnation of Jesus the Messiah—motivated by the spirit of the Antichrist.

13:3 *You must die.* According to the law of Moses, a false prophet was to be executed by stoning (Deut 13:5, 10; 18:20).

stab. The same verb is translated "pierce" in 12:10 (*daqar* [TH1856, ZH1991]), indicating a reversal in the people's response to prophetic revelation. Previously the Israelites had rejected (and in some cases killed) the prophets of God (cf. 1:6; 7:11-12), but now their anger and rejection will be directed against the false prophets.

13:4 *prophetic gift.* Lit., "be ashamed of his vision" (*bosh* [TH954, ZH1017] + *khizzayon* [TH2384, ZH2612]). The OT prophet was sometimes identified as a "visionary" (*khozeh* [TH2377, ZH2606]; cf. 2 Sam 24:11), given the fact that divine revelation often came to them in dreams or visions at night (as with Zechariah's series of night visions in 1:7–6:15).

prophet's clothes. The distinctive garb of a coarse cloak of camel or goat hair was associated with the Hebrew prophets in OT times (cf. 2 Kgs 1:8; Matt 3:4).

13:5 *I'm a farmer.* This is perhaps a parody on Amos's claim that he was not a professional prophet, but a shepherd and a pruner of fig trees (Amos 7:14).

13:6 *wounds.* Perhaps a reference to self-inflicted bruises that sometimes betrayed the ecstatic prophet, especially in Canaanite religious circles (cf. 1 Kgs 18:28). Meyers and Meyers (1993:383) speculate this may have been the case at times for the Hebrew prophets as well (cf. 1 Kgs 20:35).

COMMENTARY

The second message (13:1-6) of the second oracle (chs 12–14) has a single theme—cleansing from sin. This cleansing will be applied to the dynasty of David and the people of Jerusalem (13:1) and will result in the purification of Hebrew religion (13:2-6). The third message extends this cleansing to the people of the land (13:8). The first verse of the message (13:1) is understood by some as the conclusion of the first message of the second oracle and is included with 12:10-14 as a complete literary unity (e.g., Baldwin 1972:190). Others acknowledge that the phrase "on that day" indicates that a new literary unit begins with chapter 13 (cf. Smith 1984:280; so NLT).

The sequence of mourning for sin followed by God's cleansing repeats a pattern similar to that found in Ezekiel's vision of Israel's restoration in which the people remembered past sin (and hated themselves for it) and then were purged of their sins (Ezek 36:31-32). This eschatological cleansing of Israel's sins has theological connections with the new covenant promised to Israel by the prophet Jeremiah (Jer 31:31-34). In fact, Barker (1985:685) has identified four divine provisions contained in this new covenant, including enablement through God's Spirit to obey his covenant laws (Jer 31:33a), an intimate relationship with God (Jer 31:33b), a saving knowledge of God (Jer 31:34a), and the forgiveness of sins (Jer 31:34b). Each of these new covenant provisions is found in some form in Zechariah's second oracle, specifically in the enablement for repentance and spiritual renewal in the outpouring of the spirit of grace and prayer (12:10), intimate relationship implicit in the affirmation that the Hebrews are God's people (13:9), a saving knowledge of God in his deliverance of Jerusalem (12:10; 14:9), and the forgiveness of sins represented in the fountain of cleansing (13:1).

The term for "cleansing" (*khatta'th* [TH2403, ZH2633], Piel stem) signifies the act of purging or purification from some sort of uncleanness or sin (13:1; see the discussion in Meyers and Meyers 1993:364-366). The linking of this act of cleansing with a flowing spring or fountain of water and the word for ritual impurity (*niddah* [TH5079, ZH5614]) indicates this is a spiritual purification since Yahweh possesses the fountain of life and he himself is the fountain of living waters (Ps 36:9; Jer 2:13).

It is possible that the cleansing of the people of Israel was foreshadowed in the purging of the sins of Jeshua the high priest, symbolized in his change of clothing (3:4-5). Although Zechariah's cleansing fountain addresses all the sins of the Hebrew people, the promise of purification cannot be separated from the specific sin of "piercing" God's representative, mentioned in the immediate context (12:10). As McComiskey (1998:1218) has noted, "against the background of this metaphor of cleansing, the sorrow of 12:11-14 becomes repentance."

The image of the flowing spring or fountain (13:1) suggests that this source of divine cleansing from sins and impurity is both abundant and continual. Beyond this, the flowing water implies the "removal" of the effects of sin and impurity— even as David pleaded that God would "remove the stain" of his guilt (Ps 51:9). According to the psalmist, God in his mercy and grace removes our sins "as far from us as the east is from the west" (Ps 103:12). God's cleansing and removal of sin for the Hebrew community was symbolized in the "live goat" ceremony on the Day of Atonement, when this "scapegoat" was sent out from the camp into the desert figuratively carrying the sins of the people (Lev 16).

Ollenburger (1996:829) has pointed out additional connections between Zechariah's spring of cleansing and Mosaic legislation, notably the cleansing of the priests with water to remove the impurity of contact with a corpse (Num 19:11-20). Two key points emerge from the comparison. First, the cleansing and removal of sins is the work of God—even as David recognized in his prayer of penitence (Ps 51:1-2). Second, this ritual cleansing was required for the restoration of the priest to his duties of service and ministry in the sanctuary before the presence of the Holy One of Israel (cf. Num 19:13, 20). And this is the goal of Zechariah's visions: the restoration of God's presence in the midst of Israel (1:16; 2:5, 10-11; 8:3, 23). In terms of New Testament fulfillment, Jesus the Messiah has already gone through the curtain of heaven into God's inner sanctuary (Heb 6:19-20). Therefore, we can enter God's presence and boldly approach the throne of our gracious God in prayer because as our high priest, Jesus is holy and blameless, unstained by sin (Heb 7:26).

Zechariah's vision anticipates the cross of Jesus the Messiah because it is the "fountain" of his blood spilled in a violent death that "cleanses" the Christian from every sin (1 John 1:7). Even as Paul reminded the church at Corinth, "you were cleansed; you were made holy" (1 Cor 6:11). Jesus himself spoke figuratively of this "washing" when he dramatized its effect in the bathing of the disciples' feet (John 13:6-11). The New Testament ends where Zechariah begins, as John's apocalyptic vision packs these same images into the scene before the throne of the Lamb, including robes washed white in the blood of the Lamb, the Lamb who is also the Shepherd, and the life-giving springs of water (Rev 7:14-17).

Zechariah's message against idolatry and false prophets (13:2-6) is usually understood as the cleansing or purifying of Hebrew religion. Israel's history was a story of covenant relationship with Yahweh perpetually compromised by the worship of idols and the perverted teaching of false prophets. So Craigie has noted that the "elimination of idolatry and false prophets would be a restoration of the faith to its purest form" (1984:216). Mason's (1977:121) observation that Zechariah refers instead to the application of the promise of the new covenant seems more in keeping with the context of the prophet's message. Since God himself would again be present in the midst of his people, there would no longer be any need for prophetic figures who mediated his word to the people. The people would no longer need "to teach their neighbors, nor . . . their relatives" because God would write his "instructions deep within them, and . . . on their hearts" (Jer 31:33-34). Thus "to appear as a prophet would be to cast doubt on the finality and totality of God's final act of salvation" (Mason 1977:121). If this is the case, then Zechariah anticipates the fulfillment of Joel's vision of a time when, in one sense, *everyone* is a prophet because of the outpouring of God's Spirit (Joel 2:28-29; cf. Acts 2:16-21). It is this universal knowledge of God that will ultimately bring about the cessation of the prophetic gift (Jer 31:34; cf. 1 Cor 13:9-10).

◆   ## 3. The scattering of the sheep (13:7-9)

7 "Awake, O sword, against my
       shepherd,
    the man who is my partner,"
    says the LORD of Heaven's Armies.
  "Strike down the shepherd,
    and the sheep will be scattered,
    and I will turn against the lambs.
 8 Two-thirds of the people in the land
    will be cut off and die," says the
    LORD.

"But one-third will be left in the land.
 9 I will bring that group through the fire
    and make them pure.
  I will refine them like silver
    and purify them like gold.
  They will call on my name,
    and I will answer them.
  I will say, 'These are my people,'
    and they will say, 'The LORD is
    our God.'"

NOTES

13:7 O sword. The personification of the sword as a warrior being called into battle serves to heighten the terrifying image of the weapon as an instrument of death (cf. Isa 31:8; 34:6; 66:16).

my shepherd . . . my partner. The phrase "my shepherd" signifies a divinely appointed leader of Israel and has messianic connotations (cf. Ezek 34:23; 37:24). The phrase "my partner" (*geber 'amithi* [TH1397/5997, ZH1505/6660], "a man, my neighbor") is unique in the OT. The expression conveys the idea of an intimate relationship. Taken together, the two expressions indicate "a parity between God and shepherd" (Meyers and Meyers 1993:386). Jesus quoted 13:7 with reference to his own imminent death and the scattering of his disciples (Matt 26:31; Mark 14:27).

Strike down. The word strike (*nakah* [TH5221, ZH5782]) when used with "sword" (*khereb* [TH2719, ZH2995]) means "to inflict mortal wounds" or "slay" (cf. Meyers and Meyers 1993:387).

13:8 Two-thirds . . . one-third. The fractional portions may be an allusion to Ezekiel's sign of the coming judgment of God in the dividing of his shaven hair into three equal parts (Ezek 5:1-2, 12). The magnitude of this unspecified act of divine judgment is catastrophic, but God will preserve a remnant of his people whose sins he will forgive

(Jer 50:20; cf. Isa 65:9). According to Merrill (1994:338), Zechariah envisioned an eschatological repetition of the Babylonian exile for Israel. In John's apocalyptic vision, one-
third of the people on the earth are killed in a series of three plagues that are part of
God's judgment of sinful humanity at the end of the age (Rev 9:15, 18).

13:9 fire. The word "fire" (*'esh* [TH784, ZH836]) is often used as a metaphor for divine judgment by the OT prophets (e.g., Isa 66:15; Jer 4:4; Ezek 36:5; Amos 5:6). This divine judgment may take the form of a natural disaster like an earthquake or pestilence or the
outbreak of plague or even the horrors of war. The purpose of God's "fire" may be the
destruction of the wicked or the testing and purification of the righteous (as it is in this
context).

refine them like silver and purify them like gold. Zechariah borrowed the image of God
purifying his people in the smelter's furnace from Isaiah (1:25), Jeremiah (6:29), and Ezekiel (22:22). Malachi, a later contemporary of Zechariah, likened the day of God's visitation
to "a blazing fire that refines metal" (Mal 3:2), and God himself is portrayed as the divine
metallurgist crouching over the fire, "burning away the dross" (Mal 3:3).

call on my name. The expression (*qara'* [TH7121, ZH7924] + *be* + *shem* [TH8034, ZH9005]) is an
idiom for prayer, in this case confession of sin and a plea for help in the form of divine
intervention and deliverance (cf. NIDOTTE 3.972).

These are my people . . . The LORD is our God. The expressions are sometimes understood as elements of the "adoption formula" of covenant relationship, depicting the
intimate bond between God and his people Israel (cf. Exod 19:5; Jer 30:22; 31:33). Zechariah's language is reminiscent of Hosea's prediction that one day God "will plant a crop
of Israelites" and he will say "now you are my people," and the people will respond
"you are our God" (Hos 2:23). The declarations of loyalty by God and Israel restore the
covenant relationship symbolically portrayed in the breaking of two staffs in the earlier
shepherd allegory (11:10, 14).

COMMENTARY

The third message (13:7-9) of the second oracle (chs 12–14) describes a coming day
when God's shepherd (i.e., a divinely appointed leader of Israel) will be struck
down (or killed, 13:7). This will result in the scattering of "the sheep" (i.e., the people of Israel), with a portion of the nation being given over to divine judgment and
destruction (13:8). Another portion of the nation will experience spiritual renewal,
the outcome of God-ordained testing and suffering that refines the faith and puri-
fies the character of the godly remnant (13:9). The difficult process that combines
both God's judgment and refinement brings about covenant renewal, the restoration of a right relationship between God and his people (13:9). This fulfills Zechariah's vision of God once again living among his people and his glory resting in
Jerusalem (cf. 1:16; 2:5, 10-11; 8:3, 23).

This subunit of Zechariah's second oracle (13:7-9) is a poem that resumes the
shepherd theme of 9:16; 10:2-3; and 11:4-17 in the first oracle (chs 9–12). Baldwin
(1972:197) is in agreement with Frost who considered the poem "a self-contained
little gem" and regarded it as the climax of chapters 12–13. The identity of the shepherd who is struck down is a matter of scholarly debate. Some link this slain shepherd to the "worthless shepherd" who abandons the flock (11:17; cf. Smith
1984:283). Others connect the slain shepherd with Zechariah the prophet, whose

ministry had been rejected by the postexilic Jewish community (so Mason 1977:112). Quite apart from the historical setting of the oracle, Jesus interpreted it eschatologically, identifying himself as the shepherd struck down by God (Matt 26:31; Mark 14:27; cf. Smith 1984:283-284).

Surprisingly, this brief three-verse literary unit packs considerable "theological punch." For instance, the phrase "the man who is my partner" (13:7) is used elsewhere only in Leviticus and refers to a neighbor, friend, or close associate (e.g., Lev 6:2; 7:21; 19:15; cf. Boda 2004:512). The precise identification of the shepherd is difficult to ascertain, but the shepherd (or leader) is struck down for some unspecified offense and the sheep (or people of Israel) are scattered. Jesus applied the verse to his own impending death and to his disciples, who would disown him during the process of his mock trials before the Jews and Romans (Matt 26:31; see the discussion in Boda 2004:514-516). Kaiser (1995:226-227) identifies the phrase ("the man who is close to me") as a messianic epithet and states, "thus, this shepherd is the one who is side by side with Yahweh: That is, he is his equal." Elsewhere in the NT, Jesus boldly disclosed his "partnership" with God when he declared that he is one with the Father (John 10:30; 14:11).

A second theological truth found in this section of the prophet's message that spans both the old and the new covenants is the doctrine of what Scott (1971:145-146) calls "corrective affliction." Such divinely appointed trial, testing, and suffering effects humility, encourages faith in God, and produces godly character (cf. Jas 1:2-4, 9-12). Moses reminded Israel that God humbled them by letting the people go hungry and then providing manna for them so that they would realize "that people do not live by bread alone" (Deut 8:3). Job's counselors urged him to "consider the joy of those corrected by God" because by means of their suffering, God "rescues those who suffer. For he gets their attention through adversity" (Job 5:17; 36:15). The Old Testament and the New Testament distill the idea of corrective affliction in the declaration that "the LORD disciplines those he loves" (Heb 12:6; cf. Prov 3:12).

The paradox of human freedom and divine sovereignty intersect in the oracles of Zechariah as the prophet's message relates to the shepherd figure. On the one hand, the Hebrew people appear to be responsible for "piercing" the divinely appointed shepherd-leader of Israel (12:10). On the other hand, the prophet's address to the sword by means of an apostrophe (or the literary device of personification) suggests that the striking of the shepherd-leader of Israel was no accident but rather an act foreordained by God (13:7).

Zechariah's prophecies concerning the "shepherd" make an important contribution to current theological discussion taking place under the rubric of "open-theism" or "free-will theism."[1] The "open" view holds that the future exists only as a set of indefinite possibilities and hence cannot be known by God. God must then accommodate his plans to the contingencies of human decisions, adapting his own plans to fit the changing situation. Critics contend that such a theology makes Christians "children of a lesser God"—a God who is neither omniscient nor sovereign.[2]

The "open theism" debate cannot be solved here. Suffice it to say that the teaching of Zechariah supports the traditional understanding that God possesses detailed foreknowledge with respect to the future. This is evidenced, in part, by his choice of vocabulary in describing the striking down of God's shepherd with the verb "pierce" (12:10; cf. John 19:34), as well as the unique phrase designating the Messiah as the "partner" of God (13:7; cf. John 1:14, 18). In addition, the New Testament documents demonstrate the precision with which the life and ministry of Jesus of Nazareth fulfilled Old Testament prophecy, including his Triumphal Entry into Jerusalem on a donkey and his betrayal for 30 pieces of silver (cf. 9:9; 11:12). The New Testament appeal to the Old Testament serves to confirm the fact that Jesus is the Lamb who was slaughtered before the world was made (Rev 13:8)—according to God's unchanging plan (Eph 1:5). Zechariah would agree with Isaiah the prophet that God's intimate knowledge of the future makes the Holy One of Israel distinctive from all other would-be gods (cf. Isa 41:22; 45:21; 46:10).

ENDNOTES

1. See Clark H. Pinnock, *The Openness of God: A Biblical Challenge to the Traditional Understanding of God.* (Downers Grove: InterVarsity, 1994); Greg A. Boyd, *God of the Possible: A Biblical Introduction to the Open View of God.* (Grand Rapids: Baker, 2000).
2. See Bruce A. Ware, *God's Lesser Glory: The Diminished God of Open Theism.* (Wheaton: Crossway, 2000).

◆   ### 4. The Lord will rule the earth (14:1-21)

Watch, for the day of the LORD is coming when your possessions will be plundered right in front of you! 2I will gather all the nations to fight against Jerusalem. The city will be taken, the houses looted, and the women raped. Half the population will be taken into captivity, and the rest will be left among the ruins of the city.

3Then the LORD will go out to fight against those nations, as he has fought in times past. 4On that day his feet will stand on the Mount of Olives, east of Jerusalem. And the Mount of Olives will split apart, making a wide valley running from east to west. Half the mountain will move toward the north and half toward the south. 5You will flee through this valley, for it will reach across to Azal.* Yes, you will flee as you did from the earthquake in the days of King Uzziah of Judah. Then the LORD my God will come, and all his holy ones with him.*

6On that day the sources of light will no longer shine,* 7yet there will be continuous day! Only the LORD knows how this could happen. There will be no normal day and night, for at evening time it will still be light.

8On that day life-giving waters will flow out from Jerusalem, half toward the Dead Sea and half toward the Mediterranean,* flowing continuously in both summer and winter.

9And the LORD will be king over all the earth. On that day there will be one LORD—his name alone will be worshiped.

10All the land from Geba, north of Judah, to Rimmon, south of Jerusalem, will become one vast plain. But Jerusalem will be raised up in its original place and will be inhabited all the way from the Benjamin Gate over to the site of the old gate, then to the Corner Gate, and from the Tower of Hananel to the king's winepresses. 11And

Jerusalem will be filled, safe at last, never again to be cursed and destroyed.

¹²And the LORD will send a plague on all the nations that fought against Jerusalem. Their people will become like walking corpses, their flesh rotting away. Their eyes will rot in their sockets, and their tongues will rot in their mouths. ¹³On that day they will be terrified, stricken by the LORD with great panic. They will fight their neighbors hand to hand. ¹⁴Judah, too, will be fighting at Jerusalem. The wealth of all the neighboring nations will be captured—great quantities of gold and silver and fine clothing. ¹⁵This same plague will strike the horses, mules, camels, donkeys, and all the other animals in the enemy camps.

¹⁶In the end, the enemies of Jerusalem who survive the plague will go up to Jerusalem each year to worship the King, the LORD of Heaven's Armies, and to celebrate the Festival of Shelters. ¹⁷Any nation in the world that refuses to come to Jerusalem to worship the King, the LORD of Heaven's Armies, will have no rain. ¹⁸If the people of Egypt refuse to attend the festival, the LORD will punish them with the same plague that he sends on the other nations who refuse to go. ¹⁹Egypt and the other nations will all be punished if they don't go to celebrate the Festival of Shelters.

²⁰On that day even the harness bells of the horses will be inscribed with these words: HOLY TO THE LORD. And the cooking pots in the Temple of the LORD will be as sacred as the basins used beside the altar. ²¹In fact, every cooking pot in Jerusalem and Judah will be holy to the LORD of Heaven's Armies. All who come to worship will be free to use any of these pots to boil their sacrifices. And on that day there will no longer be traders* in the Temple of the LORD of Heaven's Armies.

14:5a The meaning of the Hebrew is uncertain.   14:5b As in Greek version; Hebrew reads *with you*.
14:6 Hebrew *there will be no light, no cold or frost*. The meaning of the Hebrew is uncertain.   14:8 Hebrew *half toward the eastern sea and half toward the western sea*.   14:21 Hebrew *Canaanites*.

NOTES

14:1 *the day of the LORD.* This eschatological day is one of both judgment and deliverance for Israel. It is also a day of "cosmic change" and "end-time reversal" (see Redditt 1995:141). Amos cursed those Hebrews who longed for the day of Yahweh because they assumed it was only a day of deliverance and blessing (cf. Amos 5:18; see note on Zech 3:10).

14:2 *the rest.* The remnant of Israel that survives the sack of Jerusalem are most likely the one-third of the people who are left in the land and brought through the refiner's fire according to 13:8 (see note).

14:3 *fought in times past.* Lit., "on a day of battle" (*beyom qerab* [TH3117/7128, ZH3427/7930]), an equivalent expression for the Day of the Lord, when God will wage war on behalf of Israel and judge the nations in righteousness (cf. Exod 15:3; Isa 42:13).

14:4 *Mount of Olives.* This is a hill east of Jerusalem. David crossed the mount in his flight from Absalom (2 Sam 15:30, 32), and Solomon built a shrine to the Moabite god Chemosh there (1 Kgs 11:7). Jesus taught his disciples about the signs of the end times from the slopes of the Mount of Olives (his so-called "Olivet Discourse," Matt 24). Jesus ascended into heaven from the Mount of Olives, and the message of the attending angels to the disciples implied he would return there in a similar fashion (Acts 1:11-12).

Although the term is not used, Zechariah envisions an earthquake that will crack open the Mount of Olives and create a valley running east and west through the fissure. This valley will become an escape route for the Hebrews fleeing Jerusalem in the face of the assault against the city by the nations (14:5). Earthquakes are also part of the eschatological imagery associated with the Day of the Lord in Amos (cf. Amos 6:11; 8:8; 9:1-5).

14:5 *Azal.* The meaning of the term is uncertain. Meyers and Meyers (1993:426) identify Azal (or Azel, so also NIV) as a district of Jerusalem on the northeast side of the city inhabited by Benjaminites who were descendants of Azel. The place name Beth-ezel or Beth-Azel establishes the validity of Azel as a toponym (cf. Mic 1:11). Other English versions emend the Hebrew word *'atsel* [TH682A, ZH728] to *'etsel,* meaning "alongside" or "the side of (it)" (cf. NAB "reaches its edge").

earthquake in the days of King Uzziah. King Uzziah ruled Judah from 792–740 BC. The date of the earthquake mentioned is unknown, although Amos dated the beginning of his prophetic ministry to two years before the devastating event (Amos 1:1). According to Denis Baly (1974:24-25), major earthquakes occur in Israel about every 50 years and lesser tremors more frequently.

holy ones. The identity of the "holy ones" is uncertain, but the phrase is probably a reference to the angelic host that worships God and serves as his "army" (cf. Job 5:1; Ps 89:5, 7).

14:6 *On that day the sources of light will no longer shine.* The final portion is obscure. According to Baldwin (1972:203), the last two words of the verse may mean "the splendid ones [stars] congeal" or lose their brightness. Many English versions follow the variant rendering of the ancient versions (e.g., LXX, Syriac Peshitta, Aramaic Targum, and Latin Vulgate) and read "cold or frost" (so NIV, NRSV, NLT mg). In any event, this depicts cosmic upheaval, another motif characteristic of apocalyptic literature in the Bible. The luminaries of the sky will cease to give light in the Day of the Lord.

14:7 *continuous day!* In Isaiah's vision of the future glory of Jerusalem, the sun and moon will no longer be necessary for light because the presence of God will be the everlasting light of the new order (Isa 60:19-22). According to Isaiah the sun and moon will not rise or set (Isa 60:20), implying continual day. It may be that the light of the sun and moon is simply "washed out" by the brilliant light of the glory of God. The NT portrays the new Jerusalem in a similar fashion, with continual daylight and no need for the sun or moon because the glory of the Lamb illuminates the city (Rev 21:22-25). Elsewhere the NT describes Jesus as the spiritual light of the world (John 1:9); he proclaimed himself as that light as well (John 8:12).

14:8 *life-giving waters.* Zechariah's oracle describing "life-giving waters" flowing out of Jerusalem recalls Ezekiel's vision of a stream flowing from the Temple of Jerusalem eastward to the Dead Sea (Ezek 47:1). The prophet Joel has a similar vision of a fountain that bursts forth from the Lord's Temple to water the arid environs of Jerusalem (Joel 3:18). The waters of this stream bring life and healing, and everything it touches becomes fresh and pure, even the Dead Sea (Ezek 47:8-9)! The waters are symbolic of the life-giving presence of God living once again in the midst of his people. Redditt (1995:141) has observed, however, that Zechariah's vision pushes Ezekiel's image of life-giving water further because the river flows both east and west suggesting that divine blessings would extend worldwide. Zechariah's vision of the river of life-giving waters flowing from Jerusalem foreshadows the pure "river with the water of life" that flows from the throne of God and the Lamb in the new Jerusalem (Rev 22:1). No doubt this is the OT passage Jesus had in mind when he declared himself to be the "living water" (John 7:38).

flowing continuously. Unlike the wadis of Palestine that flowed with water only sporadically (as a result of the seasonal rains), the continual flow of the life-giving waters from Jerusalem will not be dependent upon the seasonal rainfall (see Baldwin 1972:203). Redditt (1995:141) has noted that a weak point in Jerusalem's defense was the city's dependence upon an external water supply for part of the year. This continually flowing river will provide the new Jerusalem with an abundant and permanent water resource. Meyers and Meyers (1993:442) remark that climate, continuous light, water supply, and terrain are all part of the eschatological transformation that will bring "wonderful harvests" to the land of Israel (cf. Isa 30:23-26).

14:9 the LORD will be king over all the earth. Zechariah envisions the fulfillment of the enthronement psalms, which testify that Yahweh is king (Pss 93:1; 97:1), he subdues the nations (Ps 47:3), Jerusalem will be elevated above the whole earth (Ps 48:1-2), the idols and the kings of the nations will bow before Yahweh in worship (Pss 97:7; 99:3), the mountains will be leveled (Ps 97:5), and his righteousness and holiness will permeate the world (Pss 93:5; 98:9). All of these elements are present in Zechariah's message about the Lord who will rule the earth (ch 14; cf. the discussion in Mason 1977:128).

one LORD. The declaration that there will be "one LORD" in that day is both a reaffirmation of the Hebrew credo that "Yahweh is One" (Deut 6:4) and a renunciation of idolatry.

14:10 Geba . . . to Rimmon. Geba was a village belonging to the tribe of Benjamin just northeast of Jerusalem (Josh 18:24). It was resettled by the Hebrews after the Babylonian exile (Ezra 2:26). The location of Rimmon is uncertain. The accompanying expression, "south of Jerusalem," provides the general direction of the site and suggests the place may not have been well known in Zechariah's day. Taken together, the two toponyms describe the north–south extent of Jerusalem's outlying regions.

Jerusalem. The eschatological Jerusalem will sit atop a vast plain as Yahweh's "cosmic mountain." The city and the Temple will be the central focus and conduit of "Yahweh's involvement with humanity" (see Meyers and Meyers 1993:441, 444). The references to the city gates and other features that follow appear to reflect the preexilic configuration of Jerusalem.

Benjamin Gate. The exact location of the Benjamin Gate is unknown. It has been identified with the Sheep Gate (cf. Neh 3:1, 32) and the Upper Gate (see Bahat 1990:30). According to Meyers and Meyers (1993:445), the general location on the east wall just north of the Temple Mount seems certain (perhaps near the modern-day St. Stephen's Gate, also known as the Lion Gate).

old gate. This gate has been situated by some scholars on the western wall of Jerusalem, and it has been identified with the Old City Gate (Neh 3:6), also called the Mishneh Gate (cf. Bahat 1990:30). Meyers and Meyers (1993:446) prefer to situate the gate on the eastern wall of the city.

Corner Gate. The Corner Gate was located on the western wall of Jerusalem (cf. 2 Kgs 14:13; Jer 31:38), probably in the vicinity of the Jaffa Gate in today's Old City Jerusalem (cf. Bahat 1990:30).

Tower of Hananel. This tower is mentioned several times in the OT, but its location on the city wall of Jerusalem is unknown (cf. Neh 3:1; Jer 31:38). Meyers and Meyers (1993:446-447) place the tower near the Benjamin Gate.

king's winepresses. These presses are not mentioned elsewhere in the OT, and their location is unknown. It is assumed they were located just south of the City of David, near the King's Pool (Neh 2:14) and the king's garden (Neh 3:15; cf. Meyers and Meyers 1993:447).

14:12 plague. The same word (*maggepah* [TH4046, ZH4487]) is used to describe the divine judgments against the Egyptians at the Exodus (cf. Exod 9:14). The term refers to torment or plague generally, whether in the form of pestilence, disease, war, or natural calamity (cf. Jer 14:11-12). As divine judge, God strikes those who rebel against him with sudden and deadly plagues—whether the nations or his own people Israel (cf. Num 14:37; 2 Sam 24:21).

walking corpses . . . flesh rotting. The plague that Zechariah portends is a lethal disease of an unspecified nature. The term for "rotting away" (*maqaq* [TH4743, ZH5245]) signifies decay, putrefaction, or wasting away. Here the word describes an unnatural and accelerated festering of wounds or perhaps rampant cancerous growth of some sort. Meyers and Meyers (1993:452-453) rightly point out that the prophet's horrific language portrays "an agonizing death." Biblical interpreters given to a more sensational approach to biblical prophecy equate the plague of the "rotting flesh" with the effects of massive amounts of radiation on human flesh in the aftermath of nuclear war.

14:13 great panic. The word *mehumah* [TH4103, ZH4539] signifies "confusion" generally. In this context it refers to a "deadly panic" induced by Yahweh himself among the enemies of Israel. The prophet Isaiah used the same word in describing the Day of the Lord as a day of "confusion and terror" (Isa 22:5). See the discussion on "panic" (*timmahon* [TH8541, ZH9451]) in the note on 12:4.

14:14 wealth. The day of the Lord is characterized by reversal, as God will turn the tables and do to the nations as they have done to his people Israel. The capture of the wealth of the nations overturns the looting of Jerusalem by the nations announced by the prophet earlier (14:1). Zechariah's reference to the "great quantities of gold and silver" (14:14) recalls Haggai's prediction that one day the "treasures of all the nations" would come to Yahweh's Temple (Hag 2:7-8).

14:16 Festival of Shelters. This is an annual festival that marks the beginning of the fall harvest season; it was one of the three Israelite pilgrimage festivals (cf. Exod 23:14-19). Also known as the Feast of Tabernacles or Booths, the seven-day celebration commemorated the Hebrew wilderness experience after the Exodus from Egypt. The festival falls in the biblical month of Tishri (September/October of the Julian calendar). Mosaic legislation calls for the Israelites to construct some type of temporary shelter (a booth, tent, or lean-to), and presumably live in it for all or some portion of the week-long feast (cf. Lev 23:33-43; Num 29:12-40; Deut 16:13-17). The feast recalls the temporary homes of Israel's wilderness wanderings and afforded the worshiping community the opportunity to offer thanksgiving for God's provision—both then and now—for their pilgrimage. This pilgrimage festival was an appropriate one to retain in the restored order of the Kingdom of God because thanksgiving will characterize the worship of the messianic era (cf. Isa 51:3; Jer 33:11).

14:16 enemies . . . will . . . worship the King. Zechariah anticipated the realization of the covenant promise that Israel would be a blessing to the nations and a light to the Gentiles (Gen 12:1-3; cf. Isa 49:6). The worship of Yahweh in Jerusalem by nations that were once enemies to Israel and hostile to the Lord is another example of the reversal that will occur in that eschatological day. In the NT, Paul associates this universal worship of God with the exaltation of Jesus Christ, at whose name "every knee should bow" (Phil 2:10).

14:17 come to Jerusalem to worship. Jerusalem and the Temple of Yahweh as the cosmic center of God's universal kingdom is a repeated motif in the eschatological visions of the OT prophets (Isa 56:6-7; Mic 4:1; Hag 2:7). Zechariah's vision echoes his earlier predictions that the nations will travel to Jerusalem to seek the Lord (8:20-22), and it anticipates the new Jerusalem of John's Apocalypse (Rev 21:10-27). Cf. the note on 12:2 ("Jerusalem") and the commentary on 1:7-17.

no rain. The lack of rainfall was one of the curses God pronounced against Israel for covenant disobedience (cf. Deut 28:22-24). Here that curse is extended to the nations by virtue of God's rule over all peoples (see note on 10:1).

14:20 HOLY TO THE LORD. This was the logo inscribed on the gold medallion attached to the turban of the high priest of Israel (Exod 28:36). Even as the Levitical priesthood was set apart as "HOLY TO THE LORD," so the nation of Israel was set apart at Mount Sinai to serve Yahweh as a kingdom of priests and a holy nation (Exod 19:6). According to Zechariah, that destiny will be fulfilled in the messianic kingdom. The anthem "Holy, holy, holy is the

Lord God, the Almighty" forms the foundation of the angelic worship in heaven (Rev 4:8). It also explains the mandate to Israel to be holy even as God is holy (Lev 11:44). The reference to the "harness bells of the horses" (14:20) is an illustration emphasizing the pervasive nature of the holiness that will mark the messianic kingdom (cf. Meyers and Meyers 1993:487).

14:21 *cooking pot.* The bronze pots of the Temple were used to carry away ashes from the burnt offerings, as well as the remnants of the sacrificial animal; in some cases they served as cooking utensils for the meals prepared for the priestly families from those portions of the sacrifices designated as edible (cf. Exod 27:3; Lev 7:6, 15). The holiness of Yahweh's kingdom will transform even the mundane cooking utensils into "sacred vessels" like those used in the sacrificial ritual of the Temple. That is, "the distinction between the sacred and profane would be eliminated" (Redditt 1995:144).

traders. The NLT (and NAB, NJB, NRSV, ESV) interprets the MT "Canaanite" as "merchant" or "trader" on the basis of the commercial activity associated with the Canaanites in Hos 12:7-8 and Zeph 1:11. Boda (2004:529) comments that the verse indicates that "there will be no room for such merchants, who may have abused worshipers through exorbitant prices" for proper sacrificial utensils and/or sacrificial animals and offerings—calling to mind the NT report of Jesus' cleansing of the temple (Matt 21:12-17). According to Meyers and Meyers (1993:489-491), the expression may be a euphemism for the idolater (taken as "Canaanite" proper) or simply another way of saying that under the rule of God the traditional boundaries (e.g., ethnicity) will be dissolved.

COMMENTARY

The final message (ch 14) of the second oracle (chs 12–14) mixes visions of both judgment and salvation for Israel and the nations. Israel will be besieged by the nations, teetering on the verge of utter destruction when the Lord himself will intervene and deliver his people (14:3-4). As a result, the nations will be punished by a terrible plague, an awesome demonstration of divine judgment (14:12). The nation of Israel will be restored as the people of God, and Jerusalem will be exalted as the political and religious center of the world (14:16-17). God's rule will be established over all the earth (14:9), and a divinely ordained transformation of the created order will take place (14:6-8, 10). Fittingly, God's holiness will be the pervasive characteristic of his rule over all the earth (14:20-21).

This last installment of Zechariah's apocalyptic vision for Israel has parallels to the beginning of his second oracle to postexilic Judah (cf. 12:1-9). Specifically, the two prophetic sermons share the themes of the nations waging war against Israel and God defending his people and punishing the nations for their insurrection. The two passages exhibit differences, as well—notably God himself gathers the nations against Jerusalem (14:2), and great cosmic upheaval will accompany the events of that eschatological day (14:3-6, 10-11).

According to Redditt (1995:144), the overall message of Zechariah's two oracles (chs 9–14) transmits three basic hopes of the Hebrew community in postexilic Jerusalem: the reunification of the Davidic kingdom, the reestablishment of the Davidic monarchy, and the restoration of Jerusalem as the Davidic royal city. The New Testament understands these hopes as fulfilled (at least partially) in the First Advent and (eventually completely) in the Second Advent of Jesus the Messiah, who, as the Son of David (Matt 21:9, 15), came preaching the Kingdom of Heaven (Matt 4:23), refused earthly kingship to establish a greater kingdom (one "not of this world"; John 18:36), and promised to return to Jerusalem to "sit upon his glorious throne" (Matt 25:31; cf. Matt 24:30; Acts 1:11).

In my discussion of the literary style (see Introduction), I pointed out that Zechariah may be classified as a type of "proto-apocalyptic" literature. By "proto-apocalyptic" I mean that Zechariah possesses some, but not all, of the literary features characteristic of later Jewish apocalyptic literature. I also stated that apocalyptic literature is "crisis" literature, in that it typically conveys specific messages to particular groups of people caught up in a dire situation. Generally, three types of messages are associated with apocalyptic literature. The first is a word of encouragement to the oppressed; the second, a warning to the oppressor; and the third, a call to faith for those wavering between God's truth and human wisdom.

Peter Craigie (1984:222) aptly reminds us that "although the language of apocalypse addresses the future, it reveals also the present, and the present from which such language emerges is usually a dark and bleak one." For this reason, apocalyptic literature gives expression to hope for reversal in the future. But this hope is not placed in the ingenuity or perfectibility of humanity—but rather in the transforming power of God in individual lives, the nations, and the course of human history. Craigie calls attention to two important theological applications for the contemporary Christian church that may be drawn from Zechariah's visions.

First, it is easy to neglect God as the Almighty sovereign of the universe when "the world is in a shambles and the chosen people are a tattered remnant" (Craigie 1984:222). Yet, true apocalyptic thought "retains its faith in the full knowledge of God" (ibid.) and affirms with the prophet Zechariah that indeed "the LORD will be king over all the earth" (14:9). Second, there is a danger in becoming so obsessed with the apocalyptic passages of the Bible that we find ourselves in the role of spectator rather than participant in God's unfolding drama of redemption—the story of "salvation history" being written by the Lord of history. As Craigie (1984:223) has noted, "history is also in large part the outworking of our own actions, and we are responsible for them. Faith in the vision of the future must be balanced by commitment to action in the present." The apostle Peter put it this way after reflecting upon the coming Day of the Lord: "Since everything around us is going to be destroyed like this, what holy and godly lives you should live, looking forward to the day of God and hurrying it along. . . . And so, dear friends, while you are waiting for these things to happen, make every effort to be found living peaceful lives that are pure and blameless in his sight" (2 Pet 3:11-12, 14).

Naturally, Zechariah's visions prompt numerous other theological lessons for contemporary application. Perhaps chief among them, given the "hour" of growing persecution in which the global church now finds itself, is a reality that Paul understood very clearly: "We are not fighting against flesh-and-blood enemies, but against evil rulers and authorities of the unseen world" (Eph 6:12). Zechariah's visions of Jerusalem besieged by the nations in the "day of the LORD" (12:1-3; 14:1-2), and the intervention of the Lord himself who wages war for Israel (14:3-4) call to mind the apocalyptic visions of John. There we learn that the eschatological warfare is truly cosmic in nature—the "winner-take-all" conflict between God's Messiah and Satan (Rev 12:9; 13:5-8; 19:19-20; 20:7-10).

Implicit in the Good News of Jesus Christ and the building of his church in the world is spiritual warfare. Our "call to arms" in response to this spiritual warfare is the call to "pray in the Spirit at all times and on every occasion. Stay alert and be persistent in your prayers for all believers everywhere" (Eph 6:18). We must not forget God's purpose in all of this: He will prepare a "bride" for the Bridegroom (Rev 19:7-10; 21:2). The biblical message of endurance in the face of persecution still holds currency, as John's vision exhorts: We are "partner[s] in suffering and in God's Kingdom and in the patient endurance to which Jesus calls us" (Rev 1:9). Thus, Zechariah's closing word to his audience in postexilic Jerusalem remains salient for this generation, as we must also "watch, for the day of the LORD is coming" (14:1).

BIBLIOGRAPHY

Achtemeier, E.
1986 *Nahum—Malachi*. Interpretation. Atlanta: John Knox.

Bahat, D.
1990 *The Illustrated Atlas of Jerusalem*. Translator, S. Ketko. Jerusalem: CARTA.

Baldwin, J. G.
1972 *Haggai, Zechariah, Malachi*. Tyndale Old Testament Commentary. Downers Grove: InterVarsity.

Baly, D.
1974 *The Geography of the Bible*. Rev. ed. New York: Harper & Row.

Barker, K. L.
1985 Zechariah. Pp. 595-697 in the *Expositor's Bible Commentary*, vol. 7. Editor, F. E. Gaebelein. Grand Rapids: Zondervan.

Boda, Mark
2003 *Haggai—Zechariah Research: A Bibliographic Survey*. Leiden: Deo.

2004 *Haggai, Zechariah*. NIV Application Commentary. Grand Rapids: Zondervan.

Boda, Mark, and Michael Floyd
2003 Bringing Out the Treasure: Inner Biblical Allusion in Zechariah 9–14. *Journal of the Study of the Old Testament Supplement 370*. Sheffield: Sheffield Academic Press.

Briant, Pierre
2002 *From Cyrus to Alexander: A History of the Persian Empire*. Winona Lake, IN: Eisenbrauns.

Butterworth, M.
1992 Structure and the Book of Zechariah. *Journal of the Study of the Old Testament Supplement 130*. Sheffield: Journal of the Study of the Old Testament Press.

Cathcart, K. J. and R. P. Gordon
1989 *The Targum of the Minor Prophets*. The Aramaic Bible, vol. 14. Wilmington, DE: Michael Glazier.

Conrad, Edgar W.
1999 *Zechariah*. Sheffield: Sheffield Academic Press.

Craigie, P. C.
1984 *The Twelve Prophets*. Philadelphia: Westminster.

Dorsey, David A.
1999 *The Literary Structure of the Old Testament: A Commentary on Genesis–Malachi*. Grand Rapids: Baker.

Eichrodt, W.
1967 *Theology of the Old Testament*. Old Testament Library. Translator, J. A. Baker. Philadelphia: Westminster.

Gowan, D. E.
1986 *Eschatology in the Old Testament*. Philadelphia: Fortress.

Hanson, P. D.
1983 *The Dawn of Apocalyptic*. Rev. ed. Philadelphia: Fortress.

1987 *Old Testament Apocalyptic*. Nashville: Abingdon.

Harrington, H. K.
2002 Zechariah. Pp. 495-496 in *The IVP Women's Bible Commentary*. Editors, C. C. Kroeger and M. J. Evans. Downers Grove: InterVarsity.

Hildebrandt, W.
1995 *An Old Testament Theology of the Spirit of God*. Peabody, MA: Hendrickson.

Hill, A. E.
1982 Dating "Second Zechariah": A Linguistic Reexamination. *Hebrew Annual Review* 6:105-134.

1998 *Malachi: A New Translation with Introduction and Commentary*. Anchor Bible. New York: Doubleday.

Hill, A. E., and J. H. Walton
2000 *A Survey of the Old Testament*. 2nd ed. Grand Rapids: Zondervan.

Jones, B. A.
1995 *The Formation of the Book of the Twelve: A Study in Text and Canon.* SBL Dissertation Series 149. Atlanta: Scholars Press.

Kaiser, W. C.
1995 *The Messiah in the Old Testament.* Grand Rapids: Zondervan.

2000 *Mission in the Old Testament: Israel As a Light to the Nations.* Grand Rapids: Baker.

Klein, W. W., C. L. Blomberg, and R. L. Hubbard
1993 *Introduction to Biblical Interpretation.* Dallas: Word.

Kline, Meredith
1991 The Structure of the Book of Zechariah. *Journal of the Evangelical Theological Society* 34:179-193.

Koch, K.
1984 *The Prophets: The Babylonian and Persian Periods.* Translator, M. Kohl. Philadelphia: Fortress.

Larkin, Katrina
1994 *The Eschatology of Second Zechariah.* Kampen, Netherlands: Kok Pharos.

Mason, R.
1977 *The Books of Haggai, Zechariah, and Malachi.* Cambridge Bible Commentary. Cambridge: Cambridge University Press.

1990 *Preaching the Tradition: Homily and Hermeneutics after the Exile.* Cambridge: Cambridge University Press.

McComiskey, T. E.
1998 Zechariah. Pp. 1003-1244 in *The Minor Prophets,* vol. 3. Editor, T. E. McComiskey. Grand Rapids: Baker.

Merrill, E. H.
1994 *Haggai, Zechariah, Malachi: An Exegetical Commentary.* Chicago: Moody.

Meyers, C. L. and E. M. Meyers
1987 *Haggai and Zechariah 1–8.* Anchor Bible. Garden City, NY: Doubleday.

1993 *Zechariah 9–14.* Anchor Bible. New York: Doubleday.

Miller, C.
1987 *Leadership: Thirteen Studies for Individuals or Groups.* Colorado Springs: NavPress.

Nicoll, W. R., Editor
1974 *The Expositor's Greek Testament.* Reprint. Grand Rapids: Eerdmans. 5 vols.

O'Brien, Julia M.
2004 *Nahum, Habakkuk, Zephaniah, Haggai, Zechariah, Malachi.* Abingdon Old Testament Commentaries. Nashville: Abingdon.

Ollenburger, B. C.
1996 The Book of Zechariah. Pp. 735-840 in *The New Interpreter's Bible,* vol. 7. Editor, L. E. Keck. Nashville: Abingdon.

Petersen, D. L.
1977 *Late Israelite Prophecy: Studies in Deutero-Prophetic Literature and Chronicles.* SBL Monograph Series 23. Missoula: Scholars Press.

1984 *Haggai and Zechariah 1–8.* Philadelphia: Westminster.

1995 *Zechariah 9–14 and Malachi.* Louisville: Westminster/John Knox.

Pierce, R. W.
1984a Literary Connectors and a Haggai–Zechariah–Malachi Corpus. *Journal of the Evangelical Theological Society* 27:277-289.

1984b A Thematic Development of the Haggai–Zechariah–Malachi Corpus. *Journal of the Evangelical Theological Society* 27:401-411.

Piper, J.
1996 *Desiring God: Meditations of a Christian Hedonist.* 2nd ed. Sisters, OR: Multnomah.

Radday, Y. T., and D. Wickman
1975 The Unity of Zechariah Examined in Light of Statistical Linguistics. *Zeitschrift fur die Alttestamentliche Wissenschaft* 87:30-55.

Redditt, P. L.
1995 *Haggai, Zechariah, and Malachi: Based on the Revised Standard Version.* New Century Bible Commentary. London: Marshall Pickering.

Ridderbos, H.
1978 *Studies in Scripture and Its Authority.* Grand Rapids: Eerdmans.

Rose, W. H.
2000 Zemah and Zerubbabel: Messianic Expectations in the Early Postexilic Period. *Journal of the Study of the Old Testament Supplement 340.* Sheffield: Sheffield Academic Press.

Ryken, L.
1984 *How to Read the Bible As Literature.* Grand Rapids: Zondervan.

Scott, R. B. Y.
1971 *The Way of Wisdom in the Old Testament.* New York: Macmillan.

Smith, R. L.
1984 *Micah–Malachi.* Word Biblical Commentary. Waco: Word.

Stott, J.
1975 *Who Is My Neighbor? The Challenge of Christ's Compassion.* London: InterVarsity.

Tollington, J. E.
1993 Tradition and Innovation in Haggai and Zechariah 1–8. *Journal of the Study of the Old Testament Supplement 150.* Sheffield: Journal of the Study of the Old Testament Press.

Ulrich, E.
1997 *Qumran Cave 4: The Prophets.* Discoveries in the Judaean Desert (Vol. XV). Oxford: Clarendon.

Unger, Merrill F.
1963 *Zechariah: Prophet of Messiah's Glory.* Grand Rapids: Zondervan.

van der Toorn, K., Editor
2001 *The Dictionary of Deities and Demons in the Bible.* 2nd ed. Grand Rapids: Eerdmans.

VanGemeren, W. A.
1990 *Interpreting the Prophetic Word.* Grand Rapids: Zondervan.

Waltke, B., and M. O'Connor
1990 *An Introduction to Biblical Hebrew Syntax.* Winona Lake, IN: Eisenbrauns.

Webb, W. J.
2001 What If I Am Wrong? Pp. 236–244 in *Slaves, Women & Homosexuals: Exploring the Hermeneutics of Cultural Analysis.* Downers Grove: InterVarsity.

Webber, R. E.
1994 *Worship Old & New.* 2nd ed. Grand Rapids: Zondervan.

Malachi

ANDREW E. HILL

INTRODUCTION TO
Malachi

MALACHI'S SERMONS were directed to a tough audience. Among those in his congregation were the disillusioned, the cynical, the callous, the dishonest, the apathetic, the doubting, the skeptical, and the outright wicked. What does a preacher say to this kind of crowd? As a sensitive pastor, Malachi offered the "valentine" of God's love to a disheartened people. As a lofty theologian, he instructed the people in a basic doctrinal catechism—emphasizing the nature of God as universal King, faithful Suzerain, and righteous Judge. As Yahweh's stern prophet, Malachi rebuked corrupt priests and warned of the coming day of God's judgment. As a spiritual mentor, he called his audience to a more sincere life of worship and challenged the people to incarnate the ethical standards of the Mosaic covenant. But above all, Malachi was Yahweh's messenger and his vital word to Israel was profoundly simple— "'I have always loved you,' says the LORD" (1:2).

AUTHOR

The book of Malachi is silent on the issue of authorship, although it is assumed that the prophetic word formula ("This is the message that the Lord gave to Israel through the prophet Malachi," 1:1) signifies that Malachi penned his own oracles. Based on the translation of Malachi 1:1 in the Septuagint ("by the hand of *his messenger*") and the etymology of the name Malachi, some scholars have taken the word "Malachi" to be a title for an anonymous prophet, perhaps a play on words with 3:1, "my messenger" (*mal'aki* [TH4401, ZH4858]; see 1:1 NLT mg).

The fact that "Malachi" stands as a unique proper noun in the Old Testament should not disqualify its use as a personal name since both Habakkuk and Jonah are also exceptional among the names of the Hebrew prophets. The name "Malachi" may be translated "my messenger" or "my angel" and serves as a fitting name for a prophet of God. The name Malachi also fits a pattern of other Hebrew names ending in "i" like Beeri (Hos 1:1) and Zicri (Exod 6:21). The Bible records no biographic information for Malachi. His inclusion among the Old Testament prophets both identifies Malachi as spokesperson for God and verifies his commission as a divine messenger.

DATE AND OCCASION OF WRITING

Typically the book of Malachi is dated between 450 and 430 BC. It is often assumed that Malachi was a contemporary of Ezra and Nehemiah because he addressed the same religious concerns and social ills confronted by these two postexilic reformers.

For example, Malachi denounced mixed marriages and divorce, a lax and corrupt priesthood, liturgical decay (including neglect of the tithe), and social injustice—the same abuses corrected during the ministries of Ezra and Nehemiah. A careful typological study of the language of Malachi's oracles, however, reveals that the Hebrew text of the book has great affinity to the books of Haggai and Zechariah (see Hill 1998:395-400). On the basis of this evidence, it seems much more likely that Malachi was a slightly later contemporary of these two postexilic prophets of Yahweh's second Temple (who preached c. 520 BC). It is even possible that the battle between the Persians and Greeks at Marathon (c. 490 BC) was the occasion prompting Malachi's message. The prophet may have interpreted that titanic struggle between East and West as at least a partial fulfillment of Haggai's prediction that God was about "to shake the heavens and the earth" and "overthrow royal thrones" (Hag 2:21-22).

The following timeline should be helpful in placing the writing of Malachi:

DATE	EVENT
538? BC	Return of Hebrews from exile led by Sheshbazzar (Ezra 1:11)
522? BC	Return of Hebrews from exile led by Zerubbabel (Ezra 2:2)
520 BC	Haggai preaches (Hag 1:1, 15; 2:1, 20)
520–518 BC (and later?)	Zechariah preaches (Zech 1:1, 7; 7:1)
515 BC	Second Temple completed (Ezra 6:15)
490 BC	Battle of Marathon, Malachi preaches
483–472 BC	Esther in Persia (Esth 1:3; 2:16; 3:7)
458 BC	Ezra arrives in Jerusalem (Ezra 7:7-9)
445 BC	Nehemiah arrives in Jerusalem (Neh 2:1)
432 BC	Nehemiah recalled to Babylon (Neh 13:6)

To understand the occasion of writing we need to understand the historical background. A decree issued in 538 BC by Cyrus the Great, the first of the Persian kings, permitted conquered people groups who had been deported to Mesopotamia by the Babylonians to return to their homelands. The royal edict was issued on a clay barrel, the famous Cyrus Cylinder. This pronouncement naturally included the Jews, although they are not named on the cylinder. The first wave of emigrants to Jerusalem numbered 42,360, along with 7,337 servants (Ezra 2:64-65).

These emigrants were led back by Sheshbazzar, a prince of Judah and the first governor of the restoration community in postexilic Judah (Ezra 1:5-11). The foundation for a new Temple was laid during the early stages of his administration, sometime in 538 or 537 BC (Ezra 5:16). The meager project was soon abandoned, however, and the construction site lay neglected for two decades. Not until the preaching of the prophets Haggai and Zechariah (520–518 BC) did the initiative to rebuild the Jerusalem Temple resume (cf. Hag 1:14). The second Temple was completed in March of 515 BC (Ezra 6:15). It was erected under the auspices of the Persian King, Darius I, and the monies granted for the rebuilding probably took the form of "tax rebates" from the Persian royal treasury.

Malachi addressed Jews in the recently formed province of Yehud (or Judah) in the Persian satrapy of Eber-Nahara during the reign of King Darius I (522–486 BC). His audience included expatriates resettled in Judah and the descendants of those Hebrews who survived the Babylonian sack of Jerusalem but had not been deported to Mesopotamia.

Politically, Judah struggled for identity amid a sea of hostile neighboring satrapy provinces. The office of provincial governor was still in its infancy, and the provincial bureaucracy was in an embryonic stage of development. Any deference shown to Judah by the Persian overlords, religious or otherwise, was largely a matter of political pragmatism since the Persian army needed a base of operations for the conquest and control of Egypt. Religiously, the Second Temple had been completed, but it paled in comparison to its Solomonic predecessor. Temple worship was in a sorry state, as worshipers cheated God in their sacrifices and tithes. The priesthood was also in need of reform, as the ministry of the apathetic priests was actually leading people into sin—not out of it!

The hopes raised by Haggai and Zechariah for a revival of the Davidic dynasty rooted in the figure of Zerubbabel seem to have disappeared by the time of Malachi. The priests and the Levites were the "power-brokers" when he preached to Judah. Socially, Malachi confronted a population given to religious cynicism and political skepticism. The disillusionment of the postexilic Jewish community was prompted by several theological misunderstandings, including the expectations for wealth that Haggai had promised once the Second Temple was rebuilt (Hag 2:7, 18-19), the restoration of the Davidic covenant predicted by Ezekiel (Ezek 34:13, 23-24), and the implementation of Jeremiah's "new covenant" (Jer 31:23, 31-33). In the minds of many in Malachi's audience, God had failed his people.

AUDIENCE

Malachi's first oracle (1:1-5) was addressed generally to the Hebrew community living in postexilic Jerusalem and environs. The prophet's second oracle (1:6–2:9) is aimed specifically at the priests and Levites serving in the Second Temple. The final four oracles of Malachi's prophecy (including the call to repentance, 3:6-12) are once again directed broadly to the inhabitants of postexilic Judah (2:10-16; 2:17–3:5; 3:6-12; 3:13–4:3), although the Levites are specifically mentioned again in the fourth oracle or disputation (cf. 3:3-4). The righteous Hebrews within the restoration community are singled out and contrasted with the wicked in the final oracle (cf. 3:16-18).

CANONICITY AND TEXTUAL HISTORY

Malachi is the twelfth book in the collection known as the Minor Prophets (or Book of the Twelve in the Hebrew Bible). The Twelve Prophets are usually grouped with the Latter Prophets and without exception are found in the earliest delineations of the Old Testament canon. These twelve books were always copied on one scroll in the ancient Hebrew manuscript tradition. The order of the Twelve Prophets does vary in some canon traditions, but the sequence of books from Nahum through Malachi seems quite stable in the various canon lists (cf. Jones 1995:54). Examples of the variations in order can be seen in that Amos and Micah follow Hosea in the Septuagint and one Qumran scroll fragment (4Q76) places Jonah as the last book of the Twelve Prophets.

The books of Haggai, Zechariah, and Malachi form a distinct subcollection or literary corpus within the Book of the Twelve. All three prophets belong to the period of early postexilic Hebrew history and are unified by literary device (e.g., the rhetorical question) and theological theme (cf. Pierce 1984a:277-289). The Haggai-Zechariah-Malachi corpus is sometimes described as a narrative profile of postexilic Jerusalem recounting the spiritual history of the Hebrew restoration community (e.g., Pierce 1984b:401-411).

Pierce (1984b:411) understands the record of the postexilic prophets more negatively as one of covenant failure, since Malachi ends where Haggai begins—with a religious community in disarray. Conversely, others interpret the "spiritual history" of the restoration community as recorded in the Haggai–Zechariah–Malachi corpus more positively as the record of worship renewal prompting the return of the community to Yahweh (Schneider 1979).

The Hebrew Masoretic Text (MT) of Malachi is in a very good state of preservation. Generally, the Greek Old Testament or Septuagint (LXX) represents a faithful translation of the Masoretic Text. However, the tendency for interpretive expansion and loose paraphrasing characteristic of the Septuagint in the prophetic books continues in Malachi as well (for examples of the former see 1:7; 2:2, 4; 3:2; and for examples of the latter see 1:3, 9; 2:10, 11). Hellenistic influence and certain theological motivations prompting midrashic-type exegetical practice are also discernible in the text of the Septuagint (e.g., 1:1, 12; 2:13). Some versions of the Septuagint reorder the last three verses of Malachi so the book does not end with the threat of divine judgment (i.e., reading 4:5-6 before 4:4).

Portions of the book of Malachi are attested by fragments of the Dead Sea Scrolls or Qumran manuscripts, including Malachi 1:13-14 and parts of Malachi 2:10–4:6. Preliminary study of these fragments reveals that portions of these manuscripts (4Q76) agree with the Septuagint against the Masoretic Text (see Fuller 1991:47-57). Two verses in the Masoretic Text of Malachi are especially difficult to interpret (2:15, 16), due to textual corruption and grammatical anomaly. Baldwin (1972:240) has suggested that the text at this point has "suffered perhaps at the hands of scribes who took exception to its teaching."

According to Kruse-Blinkenberg and Gelston, it is impossible to reconstruct or improve the Masoretic Text of Malachi on the basis of the Syriac Peshitta. The Aramaic Targum of Malachi shows a tendency towards midrashic paraphrasing in terms of later Jewish piety and is largely considered insufficient for the reconstruction of the Masoretic Text. Generally, the Latin Vulgate represents a faithful witness to the Masoretic Text and in some cases lends support to the Masoretic Text against the other ancient versions (e.g., 1:7, 12, 13; see the discussion in Hill 1998:3-10).

The versification of the Masoretic Text differs from the versification of the English Bible at the close of the book of Malachi. The Hebrew Bible orders the last six verses of the book (4:1-6) as a continuation of chapter 3 (MT = 3:19-24). The versification of the English Bible is used throughout this commentary on Malachi.

LITERARY STYLE

Like Haggai and Zechariah, the speeches of Malachi are essentially prose statements delivered in the third person. The speeches of Malachi are formally classified as belonging to the genre of oracular prose. The messages are "oracular" in nature because they represent authoritative prophetic speech motivated or inspired by God himself. By "prose" we mean that the literary texture of Malachi is a blend of prosaic and rhetorical features approaching poetic discourse but distinctive of prophetic style. This kind of prophetic speech is often characterized by formulaic language. Examples of such stylized expressions in Malachi include the prophetic word formula ("the message that the LORD gave," 1:1), the messenger formula ("says the LORD of Heaven's Armies," e.g., 1:8, 14; 2:4), the self-introduction formula ("I am the LORD," 3:6), and the call to repentance formula ("return to me," 3:7).

The discourse units in Malachi may be broadly categorized as judgment speeches since they accuse, indict, and pronounce judgment on the audience. More precisely, the literary form of Malachi's oracles may be linked to Westermann's *legal-procedure* (or trial speech) and the *disputation* (Westermann 1991:169-176). The disputation speech pits the prophet of God against his audience in combative dialogue. Typically in Malachi, the disputation features these elements:

A truth claim declared by the prophet
A hypothetical refutation on the part of the audience in the form of a question
The prophet's answer to the audience's rebuttal by restating his initial premise
The presentation of additional supporting evidence

The desired outcome in both covenant lawsuit and disputation speeches "is to leave the opponent devoid of further argumentation and resigned to the divine decision" (Patterson 1993:303). The disputation developed as an alternative form of prophetic speech because the people were unresponsive to the more conventional oracular speech. This rhetorical-question-and-disputation format gave rise to the dialogical method of exposition peculiar to the later rabbinic schools of Judaism (cf. the teaching method of Jesus in Matt 5:21, 27: "You have heard . . . but I say . . .").

MAJOR THEMES

The message of Malachi is all about "getting things right." The thrust of Malachi's preaching may be placed under the umbrella theme of *covenant*, specifically the covenant of Jacob (i.e., the patriarchs; cf. Mal 1:2), the covenant of Levi (2:5), the covenant of marriage (2:14), and the covenant of Moses (4:4). The basic idea of a covenant is essentially that of a treaty or pact that establishes a relationship between parties with attendant obligations and responsibilities. It is not surprising, then, that three of the book's disputations deal with right relationships. We should also take note of the fact that God's messenger works on the premise that proper knowledge is essential to maintaining these right relationships (as seen in his first disputation).

First, the prophet called the people back to a *right understanding* of who God is— Israel's Father, Suzerain, and Covenant-maker (1:2-5). Next he admonished the priests and the people to return to the practice of *right worship* by participating in the Temple sacrifices with honesty and integrity (1:6-2:9). The prophet addressed the issue of *right relationships* in marriage by decrying divorce and encouraging loyalty on the part of spouses (2:10-16). *Right relationships* must extend to the community at large in attitudes and behavior that promote honesty because God is just (2:17-3:5). The honesty foundational to social justice must also motivate *right giving* to God because he is gracious and generous in his response to those who are faithful (3:6-12).

Finally, Malachi summons his audience to a *right relationship* with God because he is faithful to his word and he desires genuine worship (3:13-4:3). Interestingly, a pervasive sub-theme in the book is honesty, as three of the six disputations urge the people of postexilic Judah to embrace this virtue. (Select portions of the commentary on Malachi's disputations in this work have been adapted from my book, *Malachi*, Anchor Bible. New York: Doubleday, 1998.)

THEOLOGICAL CONCERNS

The book of Malachi is primarily a theology of Yahweh (VanGemeren 1990:204-208). The prophet reminded his audience that Yahweh is "father" of Israel (1:6), as well as "master" and "king" (1:6, 14). Wary of the extremes of familiarity and formality, Malachi was careful to present a balanced picture of the Lord Almighty. God is both sovereign over the nations (1:3-5, 11, 14) and over Israel as his elect nation or "special treasure" (1:2; 3:17). Yet his love for Israel (1:2) does not preclude divine testing and even judgment for the sake of purifying his people (3:2-3).

Malachi's knowledge of and identification with Israel's covenant tradition place his book in the mainstream of Old Testament theology. The prophet recognized God as both the maker and keeper of his covenant with Israel (1:2; 2:10), and he understood the status of Israel as an "adopted child" by virtue of that covenant relationship (1:6). The conditional nature of Yahweh's covenant placed a premium on Israel's obedience to the treaty stipulations and the necessity of repentance for a breach of the covenant relationship (3:7, 16-18). Finally, Malachi acknowledged that Israel's relationship with Yahweh demanded both "vertical" and "horizontal" responsibilities in the form of proper worship and social justice (1:10-14; 3:5).

Malachi preached a lofty doctrine of marriage as companionship with the spouse of one's youth (2:14) and parenting as a shared responsibility (2:15). The prophet called attention to the sacred nature of the husband-wife relationship by placing the covenant of marriage (2:14, "marriage vows," NLT) within the context of the covenant between God and Israel (2:10; cf. Hugenberger 1998:27-47). This explains his censure of easy divorce and the exhortation to remain loyal to one's marriage vows (2:16). In one way, Malachi's teaching anticipates the more rigid instruction of Jesus and Paul on divorce (cf. Matt 19:9-11; 1 Cor 7:1-16). In context, the prophet's prescriptive treatment of divorce may be a reaction against the "exclusivist" tendencies of postexilic Judaism to reestablish the ethnic purity of Israel diluted by intermarriage. Malachi's eschatology conforms to the conventional prophetic paradigm of threat and promise. Like Zechariah, Malachi pictures divine judgment as both punishment for sin and a call to repentance (3:7). The goal of God's judgment is purification and restoration of the faithful of Israel (3:3-4). The New Testament understands that the work of the "messenger," or forerunner, who prepares the way for the Lord's appearance at his Temple, was realized in the ministry of John the Baptist (3:1; 4:5-6; cf. Matt 11:14). Malachi also made an original contribution to Old Testament eschatology with his reference to the "scroll of remembrance" in which the names of the righteous are recorded (3:16; cf. Dan 12:1; Rev 20:12).

OUTLINE
Superscription: Malachi, Yahweh's Messenger (1:1)

   I. First Disputation: Yahweh's Love for Israel (1:2-5)
   II. Second Disputation: Indictment of the Corrupt Priesthood (1:6–2:9)
   III. Third Disputation: Indictment of Faithless People (2:10-16)
   IV. Fourth Disputation: Yahweh's Messenger of Justice and Judgment (2:17–3:5)
   V. Fifth Disputation: The Call to Serve Yahweh (3:6-12)
   VI. Sixth Disputation: The Coming Day of Judgment (3:13–4:3)
   VII. Appendix: Appeals to Ideal Old Testament Figures (4:4-6)

COMMENTARY ON
Malachi

◆ Superscription: Malachi, Yahweh's Messenger (1:1)

This is the message* that the LORD gave to
Israel through the prophet Malachi.*

1:1a Hebrew *An Oracle: The message.*   1:1b *Malachi* means "my messenger."

NOTES

1:1 *the message.* Lit., "An oracle: the word of the Lord." The word "oracle" (*massa'* [TH4853A, ZH5363]) impregnates Malachi's message with a certain urgency; the audience is expected to pay attention and respond.

the LORD gave. The phrase "the word of the LORD" (*debar-yhwh* [TH1697/3068, ZH1821/3378]) comprises one element of the prophetic word formula. The second element of the formula, the verb "to be" (*hayah* [TH1961, ZH2118]), is omitted here (but assumed in the NLT rendering "gave"). The formula commonly introduces a report of a prophetic revelation in the oracular speech of the OT. See further the notes for Hag 1:1.

through. The expression "by the hand of" (*beyad* [TH8712/3027, ZH928/3338]) can denote the act of writing or speaking, a so-called genitive of authorship (Waltke and O'Connor 1990:9.5.1c).

prophet. The word "prophet" is an expansion of the NLT; the MT simply says "by the hand of Malachi." Typically, the title designates an emissary, one who speaks with the authority of the commissioning agent—in this case, Malachi speaking for God.

COMMENTARY

The literary form of the opening verse is that of superscription. A superscription is a statement of classification prefixed to a literary work. It is unclear whether these superscriptions were added by the author or by later editors during the process of collecting and arranging the contents of the Old Testament canon. Here, Malachi is classified as a prophetic text and an "oracle" or "message" (NLT). Typically the superscriptions prefixed to the prophetic books identify author, audience, date, and sometimes the occasion prompting the prophet's sermons and visions, as well as the source of the prophetic revelation—God himself. In some cases the superscription may provide the title for a composition. The superscription is understood as distinct from an introduction in that it stands outside or independent of the body of literature it prefaces.

◆ **I. First Disputation: Yahweh's Love for Israel (1:2-5)**

²"I have always loved you," says the LORD. But you retort, "Really? How have you loved us?"

And the LORD replies, "This is how I showed my love for you: I loved your ancestor Jacob, ³but I rejected his brother, Esau, and devastated his hill country. I turned Esau's inheritance into a desert for jackals."

⁴Esau's descendants in Edom may say, "We have been shattered, but we will rebuild the ruins."

But the LORD of Heaven's Armies replies, "They may try to rebuild, but I will demolish them again. Their country will be known as 'The Land of Wickedness,' and their people will be called 'The People with Whom the LORD Is Forever Angry.' ⁵When you see the destruction for yourselves, you will say, 'Truly, the LORD's greatness reaches far beyond Israel's borders!' "

NOTES

1:2 loved. When describing the relationship between the Lord and Israel, the word "love" (*'ahab* [TH157, ZH170]) has covenant implications. The term may be equated with God's choice or election of Israel as his people. The message of Malachi indicates that the other dimensions of God's unconditional covenant love for Israel are still operative as well (e.g., his patient mercy, cf. 3:6, 17).

1:3 rejected. The word "rejected" (*sane'* [TH8130, ZH8533], "to hate") is the antonym of the verb "to love" noted above. The two terms are used as a polar word-pair in OT legal and prophetic texts (e.g., Deut 7:10; Amos 5:15). The expression describes "the hostility of a broken covenant relationship" (Andersen and Freedman 1980:525). Such is the case here as God has rejected Esau (and consequently his descendants the Edomites) because Esau despised and rejected the tokens of covenant relationship with Yahweh (cf. Gen 25:34; 26:34-35).

1:3 Esau's inheritance. Esau was the ancestor of the Edomite nation; the "inheritance" or territory of Edom was located on the southeastern rim of the Dead Sea and extended from the Brook Zered in the north to the Gulf of Aqaba in the south. The names Jacob and Esau are intended to call to mind the patriarchal traditions of Genesis concerning the rivalry of the twin brothers (Gen 25:23-26).

1:4 the LORD of Heaven's Armies. This compound name for God is prominent in OT prophetic literature and is variously translated "LORD of Hosts" (NRSV) or "LORD Almighty" (NIV). The title occurs 20 times in Malachi (1:6, 8, 9, 10, 11, 13, 14; 2:2, 4, 8, 16; 3:1, 5, 7, 10, 11, 12, 17; 4:1, 3). The Hebrew expression (*yhwh tseba'oth* [TH3068/6635, ZH3378/7372]) is often understood as a construct genitive, as is the case here. More precisely the construction is one of absolute nouns in apposition, perhaps conveying a verbal force: "Yahweh *creates* armies" (cf. TDOT 5.515). The term for "Heaven's armies" (*tseba'oth*) has military connotations and in this case refers to the angelic armies at God's disposal. In either case, the epithet emphasizes "the invincible might behind the Lord's commands" (Baldwin 1972:39).

1:4 The Land of Wickedness. The story of Esau is one of selfishness and contempt for the tokens of Yahweh's covenant (cf. Gen 25:34). The nation of Edom came to personify the pride of a self-centered existence (cf. Jer 49:16). The Edomites were allies of the Babylonians in the sack of Jerusalem (cf. Ps 137:7-9; Obad vv. 10, 12). They moved into the Negev after the area was wrested from Judah by the Babylonians (cf. 2 Kgs 24:8-17). The Edomites also occupied Judean villages well into the Persian period (cf. 1 Esdr 4:50). The exact date of Edom's collapse is still unknown, and the specific circumstances causing its demise are uncertain. By the time of Malachi's preaching (c. 500–450 BC), the Edomite kingdom was in ruins (Mal 1:2-4). Edom apparently remained largely independent of Babylonian influence until about 550 BC or so (cf. Jer 40:11). According to scholarly consensus, a coalition of Arab tribes gradually infiltrated, overpowered, and displaced the Edomites sometime during the fifth century BC. By 312 BC, inscriptional evidence indicates the Nabatean Arabs had overrun the region of Edom, making Petra their capital city. Surviving Edomites either moved to Idumea or were absorbed by the Nabateans.

COMMENTARY

The book of Malachi is essentially a theology of Yahweh, and more specifically a catechism on the topic of covenant relationship with Yahweh. The prophet's speeches are also dialectical in the sense that they represent a logical and systematic theological treatise. The instruction begins with the Lord's love for Israel, then moves to the priorities of worship and social justice as the appropriate responses to God's love, and concludes with the affirmation of Yahweh's covenant love for the believing remnant. The first speech act is directed to the postexilic community at large and is intended to persuade the audience of Yahweh's love for Israel. As with all of Malachi's disputations, the three-part formula of declaration (1:2a), refutation (1:2b), and rebuttal (1:2c-5) is readily discernible.

Malachi mentions four distinct covenants pertinent to his message to postexilic Jerusalem, including (1) the covenant of Abraham (1:2); (2) the covenant of Levi (2:5, 8); (3) the covenant of marriage (2:14); and (4) the Mosaic covenant (implicit in the numerous references to the instructions and commands of God's law—2:6, 8; 4:4). A covenant in the biblical world was a unilateral treaty or contract that established a relationship between two parties with attendant obligations and responsibilities. There are basically two types of covenants enacted in the Old Testament, the obligatory (binding one party to obey a specified set of decrees or laws) and the promissory (in which one party pledges to do something for the other, often as a reward for past obedience, and typically imposing stipulations for the ongoing maintenance of the relationship).

The promissory covenant God made with Abraham is foundational to all subsequent Old Testament covenants, joining Yahweh and Israel in an exclusive relationship (Gen 12:1-3). God's covenant love "is an act of election which makes Israel Yahweh's child" (Andersen and Freedman 1980:576-577). Naturally, divine election did not override Israel's responsibility to obey the stipulations of God's covenant(s) (cf. Gen 26:5). God's predisposition to choose one people group to bless all the nations is one of the great mysteries of biblical theology. God's election of Israel was certainly not because of any inherent merit in the Hebrews. Rather, it was just the opposite, as we learn from Moses's admonition to Israel after the Exodus; God chose Israel not because they were righteous, but in spite of their stubbornness (Deut 7:7-8; 9:4-6). God's design in choosing a small and stubborn people group as his special possession was to ensure his glory before the nations as the one who keeps his covenant promises and empowers Israel in their greatness (Deut 8:17-18; 9:5).

Malachi's first oracle makes reference to Jacob as the heir of the Abrahamic covenant with the declaration, "This is how I showed my love for you: I loved your ancestor Jacob" (1:2). Yahweh's love for and election of Israel as his "special treasure" (3:17) was his free and unconditional choice as the Sovereign of creation. By contrast, God rejected Esau (1:3) despite his privilege of primogeniture. It should be noted, however, that God's rejection of Esau as the heir of the covenant promises was not capricious or arbitrary. The story of Esau is clearly one of selfishness and disdain for the tokens of Yahweh's covenant (Gen 25:34; 26:34-35; 28:8-9; cf. Heb 12:16).

The goal of Yahweh's covenant relationship with the Hebrews and the essence of Malachi's message was reciprocity in the sense that Israel's duty was "to reciprocate God's love, not in the original sense of emotion, but in the form of genuine obedience and pure devotion" (TDOT 1.115). The prophet's rhetorical refutation of the claim that Yahweh had not loved Jacob reveals the depth of the crisis of faith in postexilic Judah (1:2). Much like the audience of Malachi's earlier contemporary, Haggai, the people were still "looking for much and finding little"—and blaming God for their plight (Hag 1:6, 9). Mallone (1981:28) has observed that faith in crisis often needs the support of external evidence, "a sure footing outside our own individual experience, an objective signpost on which we can hang our mental convictions." Malachi offered his audience two external "proofs" of God's enduring covenant love for Israel. The first is the word of divine revelation, God's declaration that he still loves Israel (1:2). The second piece of supporting evidence forwarded by the prophet was more tangible if the people would only observe the current events swirling around them: God destroyed the nation of Edom (1:3-5). The event was actually an answer to the psalmist's prayer requesting that God judge the Edomites for their part in the destruction of Jerusalem (cf. Ps 137:7). The psalmist reminds us that remembering God's work in history is still a potent antidote for those in a crisis of faith (e.g., Ps 73:2, 16-17).

◆ II. Second Disputation: Indictment of the Corrupt Priesthood (1:6-2:9)

⁶The LORD of Heaven's Armies says to the priests: "A son honors his father, and a servant respects his master. If I am your father and master, where are the honor and respect I deserve? You have shown contempt for my name!

"But you ask, 'How have we ever shown contempt for your name?'

⁷"You have shown contempt by offering defiled sacrifices on my altar.

"Then you ask, 'How have we defiled the sacrifices?'

"You defile them by saying the altar of the LORD deserves no respect. ⁸When you give blind animals as sacrifices, isn't that wrong? And isn't it wrong to offer animals that are crippled and diseased? Try giving gifts like that to your governor, and see how pleased he is!" says the LORD of Heaven's Armies.

⁹"Go ahead, beg God to be merciful to you! But when you bring that kind of offering, why should he show you any favor at all?" asks the LORD of Heaven's Armies.

¹⁰"How I wish one of you would shut the Temple doors so that these worthless sacrifices could not be offered! I am not pleased with you," says the LORD of Heaven's Armies, "and I will not accept your offerings. ¹¹But my name is honored* by people of other nations from morning till night. All around the world they offer* sweet incense and pure offerings in honor of my name. For my name is great among

the nations," says the LORD of Heaven's Armies.

¹²"But you dishonor my name with your actions. By bringing contemptible food, you are saying it's all right to defile the Lord's table. ¹³You say, 'It's too hard to serve the LORD,' and you turn up your noses at my commands," says the LORD of Heaven's Armies. "Think of it! Animals that are stolen and crippled and sick are being presented as offerings! Should I accept from you such offerings as these?" asks the LORD.

¹⁴"Cursed is the cheat who promises to give a fine ram from his flock but then sacrifices a defective one to the Lord. For I am a great king," says the LORD of Heaven's Armies, "and my name is feared among the nations!

CHAPTER 2

"Listen, you priests—this command is for you! ²Listen to me and make up your minds to honor my name," says the LORD of Heaven's Armies, "or I will bring a terrible curse against you. I will curse even the blessings you receive. Indeed, I have already cursed them, because you have not taken my warning to heart. ³I will punish your descendants and splatter your faces

with the manure from your festival sacrifices, and I will throw you on the manure pile. ⁴Then at last you will know it was I who sent you this warning so that my covenant with the Levites can continue," says the LORD of Heaven's Armies.

⁵"The purpose of my covenant with the Levites was to bring life and peace, and that is what I gave them. This required reverence from them, and they greatly revered me and stood in awe of my name. ⁶They passed on to the people the truth of the instructions they received from me. They did not lie or cheat; they walked with me, living good and righteous lives, and they turned many from lives of sin.

⁷"The words of a priest's lips should preserve knowledge of God, and people should go to him for instruction, for the priest is the messenger of the LORD of Heaven's Armies. ⁸But you priests have left God's paths. Your instructions have caused many to stumble into sin. You have corrupted the covenant I made with the Levites," says the LORD of Heaven's Armies. ⁹"So I have made you despised and humiliated in the eyes of all the people. For you have not obeyed me but have shown favoritism in the way you carry out my instructions."

1:7 As in Greek version; Hebrew reads *defiled you?*   1:11a Or *will be honored.*   1:11b Or *will offer.*

NOTES

1:6 have shown contempt. The repetition of the verb "show contempt, despise" (*bazah* [TH959, ZH1022]) in the prophet's second oracle (1:6, 7, 12; 2:9) sets the tone and the theme for the speech unit.

1:7 defiled. The word *ga'al* [TH1351, ZH1458] signifies ritual pollution or contamination that disqualifies or renders unfit in religious terms an object (or person) for service in the worship of Yahweh. This ritual pollution or contamination is the result of some violation of the holiness code specified in the law of Moses (in this case the laws concerning acceptable animal sacrifices, cf. Lev 22:17-25; Deut 15:21).

1:8 governor. The term (*pekhah* [TH6346, ZH7068]) is a rather vague title for a government official, in this case designating the Persian-appointed overseer or governor of the province of Judah. The juxtaposition of "my altar" (1:7) and "your governor" (1:8) insinuates a confusion of loyalties on the part of the Levitical priesthood.

1:12 dishonor. Lit., "you are desecrating it" (i.e., desecrating God's name). The (Piel) participle of *khalal* [TH2490, ZH2725] describes an ongoing state of affairs. Ironically, the guardians of Israel's covenant relationship with Yahweh were habitually profaning his Temple with impure sacrifices.

1:13 turn up your noses. Lit., "to sniff at" or "snort" (*napakh* [TH5301, ZH5870]) contemptuously.

1:14 cursed. To "bind with a curse" (*'arar* [TH779, ZH826]) is to deliver an individual over to misfortune as punishment for a serious crime committed against the community (cf. TDOT 1.411). Malachi resorts to the curse in much the same fashion as Deut 27:15-26 and Jer 48:10, in the sense that "since Yahweh is speaking, the [curse] should be taken as a pronouncement of doom rather than as a wish" (Brichto 1963:82).

2:2 make up your minds. This idiomatic expression (lit., "lay it to heart") indicates this is an issue of the will, not the emotions.

terrible curse. The "terrible curse" (*me'erah* [TH3994, ZH4423]) the prophet has in mind is the utter destruction threatened against those who violate the Mosaic covenant (cf. Deut 28:20).

2:7 knowledge of God. The priests had been entrusted with a sacred deposit, the knowledge of God as revealed in the Torah or law of Moses. They functioned as guardians of Yahweh's covenant with Israel by means of their role as teachers of God's law (Deut 33:9-10).

messenger. The title "messenger" (*mal'ak* [TH4397, ZH4855]) may be a play on words with the name Malachi. Usually this title is reserved for the Hebrew prophets in the OT. Here, Malachi seems to be ascribing "prophetic" duties related to the interpretation of God's word to the Levitical priesthood.

2:9 shown favoritism. The literal OT idiom "lift up the face" (*nos'im panim* [TH5375/6440, ZH5951/7156]) is traditionally understood to the unjust favoritism of the priests in their administration of the Mosaic law (cf. NJB, "being partial in applying the law"). Assuming, however, that *'enekem* is the implied (or gapped) subject of the participle *nosim*, then the meaning of both verse 9c and 9d must be parallel in the sense that both are negated clauses. Literally, the expression reads "and *you are not* lifting up faces [of the people] in Torah" (cf. Peterson 1995:176 n. o.). Not only have the Levitical priests failed to keep the ways of Yahweh's Torah, but they have also been derelict in "raising faces in Torah"; that is, they have neglected to demonstrate the grace of kindness and justice in their administration of the rules of Torah. The expression has a parallel in 1:9 ("Why should he show you any favor," NLT), and the two may form an envelope construction for the second oracle. Note the irony in the prophet's opening question to the priests ("Will [God] lift up your face?"—1:9) and the implied answer to that question in his assertion that the priests were not lifting up the face of the people. How ridiculous to suppose God would show favor to the priests when they had shown partiality in discharging the prescribed duties of their divinely ordained office!

COMMENTARY

The prophet's second disputation consists of two distinct speech acts, with Yahweh the subject of the first (1:6-14) and the Levitical priesthood the subject of the second (2:1-9). Malachi's first speech is designed to persuade his audience that Yahweh is truly Lord. His second speech both warns and threatens the priests for their "liturgical malpractice" in that they have failed to honor Yahweh as Lord. Fishbane (1985:334) has convincingly demonstrated that Malachi's second disputation is a postexilic example of haggadic exegesis of the Aaronic blessing (Num 6:23-27). Typically, Jewish haggadic exegesis reuses earlier biblical texts and draws forth latent meanings from these traditional or well-known passages that are appropriate to the later historical setting. In this case, Malachi recasts the priestly prayer of Aaron in Numbers 6:23-27 as an "anti-blessing" or a curse for the corrupt priests and Levites (1:14; 2:2). Finally, Wells (1987:49-51) has pointed out Malachi's clever use of irony in exposing the recurring, dual crises of commitment (1:6-9; 2:1-5) and responsibility (1:10-14; 2:6-9) in the second disputation. The concepts of commitment (promise) and responsibility (stipulation) lie at the heart of covenant relationship—the unifying theme of the book of Malachi. Malachi exploded the myth that the dutiful discharging of responsibilities by people and priests, with the corresponding commitment to obey the covenant stipulations, was sufficient for sustaining a relationship with Yahweh.

The point of contention in the second disputation is improper worship of Yahweh in the form of unworthy sacrifices offered by the people (1:7-8) and corrupt ministry on the part of the priests (2:8). The dual crises of commitment and responsibility may be seen in the first speech of the prophet's second disputation in the failure of the community to honor Yahweh with appropriate sacrificial ritual (2:6-8). Consequently, this lack of commitment to offer God the worship he deserved had an impact on the responsibility of Israel to provide the model for the universal worship of Yahweh (1:11) and promote his reputation among the nations as "a great king" (1:14).

The commitment to revere God with proper worship is rooted in the core values of honor and shame found across the biblical world. Honor may be ascribed in the sense of the social status or position into which one is born or inherits. Honor may also be acquired in the sense of the social status or position that is earned or achieved by means of personal initiative in risk taking. Shame is the disgrace or reproach incurred when one acts out of character with the cultural protocols required for recognizing ascribed and acquired honor within the society. (For the social values of "honor" and "shame," see Pilch 1991:49-70.)

Malachi emphasized the ascribed honor of Yahweh as Creator and Deliverer of Israel and thereby attempted to shame the people and the priests into offering him proper worship. Ironically, in so doing, the prophet reversed the argument of the first disputation in which he had acknowledged the ascribed honor of Israel by virtue of Yahweh's election (1:2-5). The proposition that God deserved the honor of proper worship is further stressed by comparative degree in the analogies of the ascribed honor due a father (1:6) and a human governor (1:8). Israel's destiny was entwined with the nations from the very beginnings of its covenant relationship with Yahweh, as all the families of the earth would be blessed through Abram and Sarai (Gen 12:1-3). The supremacy of Yahweh as a universal deity, God of all the nations, was later demonstrated in the spiritual contests against the Egyptian gods at the Exodus (Exod 12:12) and the Canaanite gods at Mount Carmel (1 Kgs 18:24, 36-39).

Malachi revisited this theological truth in a triad of verses in his first and second disputations (1:5, 11, 14). The climactic arrangement of the three declarations is often recognized: First, Yahweh's greatness reaches beyond the borders of Israel (1:5); then he is honored by the worship of other people groups—making his name great among the nations (1:11); and finally, Yahweh is a great king, feared among the nations (1:14).

This theme of Yahweh's worship by the nations is central to the second disputation, and it fits the pattern of universal worship of Yahweh projected in each of the postexilic prophets (cf. Hag 2:7; Zech 14:16-17). More than the worship of the Diaspora Jews or even Jewish proselytes, Malachi seems to have in mind the eschatological future when the Kingdom of God is established over all the earth and the nations recognize Yahweh as the true Sovereign. Malachi rightly understood that Israel's proper worship of Yahweh had global implications (cf. Ps 86:9; John 3:16; Rev 7:9-10).

The second speech act (2:1-9) of the second disputation (1:6–2:9) is a warning directed specifically to the priesthood servicing the Second Temple (2:1). The themes of commitment (i.e., a heart of loyalty to Yahweh's covenant) and responsibility (i.e., a pliant will obedient to the commands of Yahweh's covenant) join the two speech acts. Both units of the second speech act (2:1-3 and 2:4-9) are connected first by a pair of key words, "honor" (*kabod* [TH3519, ZH3883], "glory"; 2:2) and "reverence, revered" (*yare'* [TH3372, ZH3707], "fear"; 2:5). Thus, the second speech act is structured as a response to the rhetorical questions posed in the first speech act: "Where are the *honor* (*kabod*) and *respect* (*mora'* [TH4172, ZH4616]) I deserve?" (1:6).

Even as kingship was the heritage of the tribe of Judah (Gen 49:9-10), so the priesthood was the heritage of the tribe of Levi. According to the farewell blessing of Moses, the Levites were charged to "watch over" the word of God and "guard" Yahweh's covenant (Deut 33:9). In addition, they were authorized to "teach" the law of God to Israel and "offer" sacrifices on Yahweh's altars (Deut 33:10). Right worship and right behavior on the part of the people of Israel (who were bound to God in covenant relationship) were dependent upon the virtuous priestly example in the ministry of worship and the sound priestly instruction of the Mosaic law. Sadly, the priests of Malachi's day failed on both counts.

What hope is there for sheep without a shepherd (Jer 50:6; Zech 10:2)? The very covenant of Levi was in jeopardy (2:4) because priests living unworthy lives were encouraging unworthy worship by God's people through unworthy and erroneous teaching. For this reason, the priests were shamed by God (2:2-3) and were despised and humiliated in the eyes of the people (2:9). The prophet ultimately attributed the corruption of the covenant of Levi to the sin of the priests, the sin of disobedience to the laws of God—the same laws they were to teach the Hebrew people (2:8-9.) Malachi's implicit cure for the malady threatening the covenant of Levi was a return to a posture of obedience to God's commandments by the Second Temple priesthood. The prophet's explicit remedy, for the ailing priesthood and people alike, was correct "instruction" in the knowledge of God (2:7). Such instruction would promote proper worship and righteous lives (2:5-6).

In his classic essay on worship, Tozer has forwarded the thesis that worship is the missing gem in the crown of the evangelical church. Tozer (1992:11-14) proposed to restore that missing jewel of worship, in part, through the teaching of sound doctrine—the knowledge of God. Granted, the biblically based knowledge of God's character and redemptive work in history is vital to restoring the element of mystery essential to Christian worship. Further, I would concur with Tozer (1992:22-24) that "admiration, fascination," and "adoration" are the spiritually prompted responses of the worshiping heart to the work of God in creation and redemption. I would suggest, however, that there is still something "missing" in Tozer's plan for restoring worship in the evangelical church. The missing component of which I speak is worship education itself, formal instruction in the history, theology, and practice of Christian worship.

This is hardly a revolutionary idea. For more than two decades Robert Webber has been calling for formal worship education as a part of the Christian education initiative in the church. In fact, worship education heads the lists of Webber's "nine proposals" for worship renewal among evangelical worshipers (1982:193-196). I can echo his appeal to make the study of the biblical, historical, and theological sources of Christian worship at all age levels a matter of priority in the Christian church. Worship education is essential because the heart of worship renewal is a recovery of the power of the Holy Spirit who enables the congregation to offer praise and thanksgiving to God. The value of studying the history and theology of worship is that it provides us with insights into the work of the Holy Spirit in the past and allows us to be open to his work in the present. In this way the Holy Spirit may lead us into the ways of worship (Webber 1982:193). Perhaps this is the legacy of the prophet Malachi, a ministry of worship education that prompts worship renewal among both "priests" and "people."

◆ III. Third Disputation: Indictment of Faithless People (2:10–16)

[10]Are we not all children of the same Father? Are we not all created by the same God? Then why do we betray each other, violating the covenant of our ancestors?

[11]Judah has been unfaithful, and a detestable thing has been done in Israel and in Jerusalem. The men of Judah have defiled the LORD's beloved sanctuary by marrying women who worship idols. [12]May the LORD cut off from the nation of Israel* every last man who has done this and yet brings an offering to the LORD of Heaven's Armies.

[13]Here is another thing you do. You cover the LORD's altar with tears, weeping and groaning because he pays no attention to your offerings and doesn't accept them with pleasure. [14]You cry out, "Why doesn't the LORD accept my worship?" I'll tell you why! Because the LORD witnessed the vows you and your wife made when you were young. But you have been unfaithful to her, though she remained your faithful partner, the wife of your marriage vows.

[15]Didn't the LORD make you one with your wife? In body and spirit you are his.* And what does he want? Godly children from your union. So guard your heart; remain loyal to the wife of your youth. [16]"For I hate divorce!" says the LORD, the God of Israel. "To divorce your wife is to overwhelm her with cruelty,*" says the LORD of Heaven's Armies. "So guard your heart; do not be unfaithful to your wife."

2:12 Hebrew *from the tents of Jacob.* The names "Jacob" and "Israel" are often interchanged throughout the Old Testament, referring sometimes to the individual patriarch and sometimes to the nation. 2:15 Or *Didn't the one LORD make us and preserve our life and breath?* or *Didn't the one LORD make her, both flesh and spirit?* The meaning of the Hebrew is uncertain. 2:16 Hebrew *to cover one's garment with violence.*

NOTES

2:10 same God. The phrase translates "one God" (*'el 'ekhad* [TH410A/259, ZH446/285]), a divine title unique to Malachi in the OT. The expression is parallel to the earlier phrase "the same Father" (*'ab 'ekhad* [TH1/259, ZH3/285] or "one Father," 2:10a) and serves to underscore the uniqueness of Yahweh as Creator and his exclusivity as Israel's Father. The reference to "one God" may be an allusion to the creedal statement of Deut 6:4-5.

betray. The word *bagad* [TH898, ZH953] means to "act faithlessly, deal treacherously with." The idea of "faithlessness" is the central thesis of the third disputation (note the repetition of *bagad* in 2:10, 11, 14, 15, 16).

2:11 a detestable thing has been done. This renders *to'ebah ne'estah* [TH8441/6213, ZH9359/ 6913]; the statement supports the prophet's denunciation of divorce for the purpose of intermarriage with "women who worship idols" and helps explain why God "hates" divorce (2:16).

the LORD's beloved sanctuary. Lit., "holiness of Yahweh" (*qodesh yhwh* [TH6944/3068, ZH7731/ 3378]). This phrase is difficult; it may refer to the Second Temple in Jerusalem as the symbol of the Lord's holiness in postexilic Judah.

2:12 cut off. The intent of the verb here (*karath* [TH3772, ZH4162]), though harsh, is to blot out or destroy the evildoers (cf. NJPS, "leave no descendants") in contrast to social banishment or religious excommunication (cf. NEB, "banish").

2:14 faithful partner. The word for "partner" (*khabereth* [TH2278, ZH2500]) is unique to Malachi in the OT. The expression identifies a "marriage companion." The connotation of the LXX translation "joint partner" (Gr., *koinōnos* [TG2844, ZG3128]) captures the idea of the term. The verbal root *khabar* II [TH2266, ZH2489] is used to signify a seam or joint in the context of building and construction, suggesting more or less a permanent bonding (cf. Exod 26:6, 9, 11).

wife of your marriage vows. Lit., "the wife of your covenant" (*'esheth beritheka* [TH802/1285, ZH851/1382]). According to Hugenberger (1998:27-30), the Hebrew marriage contract is a solemn covenant to which God is witness (cf. Prov 2:17).

2:16 I hate. The word "hate" (*sane'* [TH8130, ZH8533]) is typically used to register God's hostility in response to a broken covenant (cf. 1:3; Hos 9:15).

divorce. The verb "send away" (*shalakh* [TH7971, ZH8938]) connotes expulsion or divorce in marital contexts. Malachi attempted to correct abuses resulting from liberties taken in the application of the Mosaic divorce laws (cf. Deut 24:1-4).

cruelty. The word *khamas* [TH2555, ZH2805] describes acts of "violence" or "wrongdoing." The estrangement of divorce was violence or cruelty in the sense that it was a social crime. It fractured the divinely ordained marriage covenant and deprived the woman of the dignity and protection afforded by the spousal agreement.

COMMENTARY

The shift in style from an adversarial second-person accusation (2:8-9) in the second disputation to an inclusive first-person plea (2:10) in the third disputation is striking. Malachi "the prophet" now speaks to his audience as Malachi "the fellow citizen." Clearly the disjunction in form indicates that the topic of marriage and divorce is crucial to Malachi's argument. In fact, this discussion of faithlessness in marriage is a prelude to the treatment of faithlessness to God in the fifth oracle. But the grammatical shift to the inclusive first person also provides an important lesson for those engaged in ministry, whether ancient Israel or the contemporary Christian church.

The prophet, as God's servant, never disassociated himself from the audience he addressed. Part of the prophetic pathos was the tension in the divine commission to both "uproot and tear down" as well as "build and plant" (Jer 1:10). As Heschel (1962:12) has noted, "the words of the prophet are stern, sour, stinging. But behind his austerity is love and compassion for mankind." As divinely appointed "shepherds," the prophets were to "strengthen those who have tired hands, and encourage those who have weak knees" (Isa 35:3; cf. Heb 12:12). One cannot help but project to the ministry of Jesus who "had compassion on" the crowds because "they were confused and helpless, like sheep without a shepherd" (Matt 9:36).

The image of God as Father is rather rare in the Old Testament (2:10). Malachi earlier appealed metaphorically to God as "father" in the second oracle when he addressed the issue of unworthy animal sacrifices (1:6). The Song of Moses also identifies God as the Father who created and established Israel (Deut 32:6). The point of the figure of speech is that "Yahweh cares for the people and is responsible for their existence" (TDOT 1.17).

The prophet recognized that Yahweh held claim over the Israelites both as Creator and as Father in that he made them and "adopted" them through the covenant of the Israelite ancestors (2:10). Thus Malachi helped lay the theological foundation for understanding God as Father, which is developed more fully in the New Testament as a result of the incarnation of Jesus Christ. The Christian is invited to share the Son's relationship to God the Father by virtue of "adoption" into God's family through Jesus Christ (Eph 1:5). Jesus demonstrated this practically to his followers in the Lord's Prayer, which begins with the words "Our Father" (Matt 6:9). Paul extended the understanding of that familial relationship when he encouraged the children of God to address God as "Abba" (or "dear Father," or even "Daddy," Rom 8:15).

Malachi's lofty view of marriage deserves careful consideration in a society where pre- and post-nuptial agreements and "no-fault" divorce have made a mockery of the traditional wedding "vows." The prophet's use of the expression "faithful partner" (2:14) calls attention to the essential characteristic of the marriage relationship—faithfulness. The root word used here for the marriage "partner" has associations with a "seam" or a "joint" in architectural and building contexts and conveys the idea of a permanent bonding (cf. Paul's use of kollaomai [TG2853, ZG3140] [lit., "to glue, cement"] in his commentary on the biblical concept of "one flesh," 1 Cor 6:16-17). Beyond this, Garland (1987:420) has commented that the term suggests that the wife is not a piece of property to be discarded at will but that she holds the status of an "equal . . . as a covenant partner."

The prophet's understanding of marriage as a covenant ("wife of your marriage vows," 2:14 [lit., "wife of your covenant"]) further underscores the sanctity of the husband–wife relationship (cf. Hugenberger 1998:27-47). The subsequent stress placed on the "oneness" created by the marriage relationship suggests that Malachi offers a commentary of sorts on the Genesis ideal: "a man leaves his father and mother and is joined to his wife, and the two are united into one" (Gen 2:24). Since

God himself serves as a witness both to the pledge of marriage and the betrayal of divorce (2:14), the institution of marriage is a solemn and sacred covenant under his sovereign purview. Here the message of Malachi "shows an acute awareness that the terms of the covenant [of marriage] bound them in loyalty to each other as well as to God" (Mason 1977:149).

This explains why God hates divorce and why the prophet has such harsh words for those who "overwhelm" a spouse with the cruelty of divorce (2:16). The verb "hate" appropriately describes Yahweh's hostility to a broken covenant relationship because God's relationship with his people was to be characterized by faithfulness—and he expected no less from Israel (Exod 34:6; Deut 7:9; cf. Ps 101:3; Jer 3:6-10).

What does Malachi have to say to the Christian church about marriage and divorce? First, the prophet calls us to return to "first things" by reminding us of the Genesis ideal—the man and the woman united as one before God (Gen 2:23-24). Second, Malachi exhorts us to teach that marriage is a covenant bond for life, not a contract of convenience for short-term mutual benefit. Third, the prophet challenges us to censure easy divorce. Lastly, and most important, Malachi encourages us to model faithfulness and loyalty in our marriages by guarding our hearts and always remaining loyal to our spouses (2:16). Perhaps you have seen the billboard message: "I loved the wedding, how about inviting me to the marriage? —God." I think Malachi would approve of this "billboard theology" because the best theology is practical theology. What could be more practical than inviting God our Father to partner with us in our marriage relationships?

◆ IV. Fourth Disputation: Yahweh's Messenger of Justice and Judgment (2:17–3:5)

[17]You have wearied the LORD with your words.

"How have we wearied him?" you ask.

You have wearied him by saying that all who do evil are good in the LORD's sight, and he is pleased with them. You have wearied him by asking, "Where is the God of justice?"

CHAPTER 3

"Look! I am sending my messenger, and he will prepare the way before me. Then the Lord you are seeking will suddenly come to his Temple. The messenger of the covenant, whom you look for so eagerly, is surely coming," says the LORD of Heaven's Armies.

[2]"But who will be able to endure it when he comes? Who will be able to stand and face him when he appears? For he will be like a blazing fire that refines metal, or like a strong soap that bleaches clothes. [3]He will sit like a refiner of silver, burning away the dross. He will purify the Levites, refining them like gold and silver, so that they may once again offer acceptable sacrifices to the LORD. [4]Then once more the LORD will accept the offerings brought to him by the people of Judah and Jerusalem, as he did in the past.

[5]"At that time I will put you on trial. I am eager to witness against all sorcerers and adulterers and liars. I will speak against those who cheat employees of their wages, who oppress widows and orphans, or who deprive the foreigners living among you of justice, for these people do not fear me," says the LORD of Heaven's Armies.

NOTES

2:17 *wearied.* The Hiphil form of this verb (*yaga'* [TH3021, ZH3333]) occurs only here and in Isa 43:23-24. Malachi's audience has wearied God with insincere prayer and mechanical worship. Calvin's translation ("saddened his spirit") aptly conveys the effect that religious words and ritual acts devoid of any conviction, loyalty, or devotion have had upon God.

3:1 *my messenger.* The expression (*mal'aki* [TH4397/2967.1, ZH4855/3276]) plays on the prophet's name Malachi. "Messenger" (*mal'ak*) may indicate either an angel or a human being functioning as a divine courier.

messenger of the covenant. Malachi's audience probably would have understood this messenger as a divine being (like an angel) on the basis of the parallel with the angel of Yahweh in Exod 23:20-23.

3:2 *blazing fire.* Malachi borrowed the image of God purifying his people in the smelter's furnace from Isaiah (1:25), Jeremiah (6:29), and Ezekiel (22:22). The dross of the people's wickedness must be burned away by the fires of divine testing and chastisement.

strong soap. The word (*borith* [TH1287, ZH1383]) refers to a laundry detergent or lye in the form of alkali soda made from certain plants or herbs (cf. Jer 2:22).

3:5 *eager to witness.* The phrase *'ed memaher* [TH5707/4116, ZH6332/4554] is a legal expression and suggests a legal proceeding in which God is both prosecuting attorney (as accuser) and star witness (as a provider of evidence). The phrase not only connotes God's readiness or eagerness to testify against postexilic Judah but also that he takes the stand as an "expert witness" (Baldwin 1972:244).

sorcerers. The word *mekashepim* [TH3784A, ZH4175] denotes one who practices witchcraft and black magic. The activity Malachi refers to is probably "fortune-telling," predicting the future for personal gain.

COMMENTARY

The rhetorical question "where is the God of justice?" (2:17; reported as part of the "talk" that has wearied Yahweh) marks the beginning of the fourth disputation (note the paragraph marker between 2:16 and 2:17 in the MT). The oracle consists of two speech acts: an assertive speech intended to assure the audience that God is just (2:17–3:1) and an expressive speech (3:2-5) posed in the form of a threat that they will soon experience God's justice. According to VanGemeren (1990:204), the message of the third oracle (faithlessness in marriage, 2:10-16) and the message of the fifth oracle (faithlessness to God, 3:6-12) turn upon the hinge of divine judgment threatened in the fourth disputation (2:17–3:5).

The fourth disputation is addressed to the "righteous skeptics" in postexilic Jerusalem at large, including the priests (3:3). This is deduced from the emphasis placed on the order of purification (3:3-4) before judgment (3:5). The later reference to "those who feared the Lord" (3:16) also suggests Malachi's target audience was the "doubting Thomas"–type person among the faithful in the restoration community. The prophet confronted all those who had interpreted God's apparent non-involvement in the current crisis of faith within the community as the failure of divine justice (2:17). Thus, Wells (1987:45) has correctly isolated the crisis in Malachi to the meaning and value of covenant relationship with Yahweh for postexilic Judah.

Like Job and his "spiritual mentors," postexilic Judah had to learn that external acts of religious piety do not guarantee divine blessing (cf. Job 21:7; 41:11). At issue in the fourth disputation is the disparity (real or imagined) between divine justice and human justice. The problem of theodicy (or God's relationship to evil in the world) led to false ideas about God's application of the Mosaic covenant blessings and curses in postexilic Judah. The "righteous skeptics" assumed that the principle of divine retribution had been revoked or even inverted because it appeared that evildoers were thriving while God's faithful languished under the "corporate curse" of the law of Moses (Deut 28). Malachi's audience, expecting the exact opposite, presumed they had an "exemption" from divine judgment because of their participation in the Temple rituals (cf. 3:14). As they cried "foul" to God, they were implicitly clamoring for the "new covenant" paradigm that executes divine justice on an individual rather than a corporate basis (cf. Jer 31:29-30; Ezek 18:3-4).

The question "Where is the God of justice?" remains apropos as news reported today by the print and visual media often seems to reflect the situation of Malachi's day—evildoers thrive while the faithful of God suffer persecution at the hands of godless secularists and militant "religious" extremists. The Christian church must learn from Malachi's message that the biblical solution to theodicy is not found in what Baldwin (1972:242) describes as the faulty logic of "practical atheism." When we charge God with injustice, as did Malachi's audience, we impeach the divinity of the Godhead and challenge the very existence of God himself.

Ultimately, the issue of theodicy may be reduced to a crisis of lifestyle not a crisis of faith. The substance of the matter for postexilic Judah was not the fairness of God's judgment as meted out in the retribution principle of the covenant relationship, but Israel's purity as Yahweh's vassal. This is no less true today, as divine justice is always linked to God's ethical demands in the realm of human justice. Malachi recognized that spiritual decline may be reversed by a renewal movement that includes moral reform—hence, in the threat of divine judgment is an implicit call for the practice of social justice (3:5; cf. Jesus' rebuke of those who "shamelessly cheat widows," Mark 12:40). Jesus Christ seeks a pure "bride"—a cleansed and holy church wearing the "finest of pure white linen," which "represents the good deeds of God's holy people" (Rev 19:8). James was but a sounding board for the Old Testament prophetic voice when he equated "pure and genuine religion" with "caring for orphans and widows in their distress" (Jas 1:27; cf. Isa 1:17). The God of justice is seen through the just deeds of his people!

The ambiguities surrounding the number and identity of the divine "messengers" (3:1) who have roles in the coming day of Yahweh's judgment continue to invite scholarly discussion. Malachi appears to mention three distinct figures in his eschatological projection to the time of God's visitation: "my messenger," "the Lord," and "the messenger of the covenant" (3:1). In the context of formal entrance to temples in the ancient world, it is possible that Malachi envisioned Yahweh in a processional flanked by two angelic retainers. The question still remains whether these two "messengers" are distinct divine beings or some sort of dual representation of "the Angel of Yahweh" (see the discussion in Hill 1998:289).

Traditional Christian interpretation has identified the "messenger" figure as

John the Baptist on the basis of New Testament fulfillment as declared by Jesus himself (Matt 11:3, 10, 14). The "messenger [or angel] of the covenant" has been understood Christologically as a reference to Jesus Christ and hence equated with "the Lord" since patristic times. This has fixed a two-character understanding of Malachi 3:1 in Christian biblical interpretation—John the Baptist as the "messenger" and Jesus Christ equated with "the Lord" and "the messenger of the covenant."

Beyond these identifications, it is important to note that the messengers will enact a thorough purification for God's people. The eschaton will witness the transformation of God's people into a holy community by a spirit of burning, washing, and cleansing (3:2-3; cf. Isa 4:3-4; Zeph 3:11-13, 17). The "blazing fire" and "strong soap" mentioned in 3:2 (see note) signify a two-stage procedure in Israel's restoration to covenant faithfulness to Yahweh: testing (symbolized in the smelting process) and cleansing (symbolized in the laundering process). The desired outcome of this difficult and painful process of "refining" is genuine worship offered to Yahweh by his faithful people—now spiritually renewed.

◆ V. Fifth Disputation: The Call to Serve Yahweh (3:6-12)

⁶"I am the LORD, and I do not change. That is why you descendants of Jacob are not already destroyed. ⁷Ever since the days of your ancestors, you have scorned my decrees and failed to obey them. Now return to me, and I will return to you," says the LORD of Heaven's Armies.

"But you ask, 'How can we return when we have never gone away?'

⁸"Should people cheat God? Yet you have cheated me!

"But you ask, 'What do you mean? When did we ever cheat you?'

"You have cheated me of the tithes and offerings due to me. ⁹You are under a curse, for your whole nation has been cheating me. ¹⁰Bring all the tithes into the storehouse so there will be enough food in my Temple. If you do," says the LORD of Heaven's Armies, "I will open the windows of heaven for you. I will pour out a blessing so great you won't have enough room to take it in! Try it! Put me to the test! ¹¹Your crops will be abundant, for I will guard them from insects and disease.* Your grapes will not fall from the vine before they are ripe," says the LORD of Heaven's Armies. ¹²"Then all nations will call you blessed, for your land will be such a delight," says the LORD of Heaven's Armies.

3:11 Hebrew *from the devourer.*

NOTES

3:7 *return.* In contexts expressing covenant relationship, the word "return" (*shub* [TH7725, ZH8740]) expresses a change of loyalty on the part of Israel or God. Typically the term is understood as "repentance," a complete change of direction back to God, a total reorientation toward Yahweh. The imperative form of the verb conveys a sense of urgency and places a demand for immediate response on the audience.

3:8 *cheat.* The repetition of the word "cheat" (*qaba'* [TH6906, ZH7693]) in 3:8-9 underscores the seriousness of the offense in robbing God of the tithes and offerings due him. The term is rather rare in the OT, but it is well established in later Talmudic literature to mean "to take forcibly" (cf. Baldwin 1972:245).

tithes and offerings. The "tithe" or "tenth part" (*ma'aser* [TH4643, ZH5130]) refers to the general tithe of the produce of the land prescribed by Mosaic law (cf. Deut 12:6, 11, 17). The "offering" (*terumah* [TH8641, ZH9556]) may be a gift or contribution made to Yahweh or his sanctuary (so NIV, NJB, NRSV). The offering may include gifts of produce from the land along with material goods (e.g., construction materials and garments) or personal valuables (e.g., gold, silver, precious stones). The pairing of the two terms ("tithes and offerings") suggests that the prophet called for payment of both the "tithe" (*ma'aser*) and the "tithe tax" (*terumah*), thus appealing for the comprehensive renewal of the practices by the postexilic community. The tithe tax was the "tithe of the tithe" prescribed in Num 18:26 for the general provision of the central sanctuary (cf. Petersen 1995:216).

3:9 curse. The prophet seems to be equating the experience of postexilic Judah with "the curse" (*me'erah* [TH3994, ZH4423]) of the Mosaic covenant (cf. Deut 28:20, 27). This would explain the sense of urgency attached to Malachi's call to repentance and covenant renewal with Yahweh.

3:10 *Put me to the test!* The prophetic challenge is not in violation of the prohibition against "testing God" (Deut 6:16). The word for testing in that context (*nasah* [TH5254, ZH5814]) means to try or prove (or even tempt) from a posture of arrogance and cynical unbelief. The term employed here (*bakhan* [TH974, ZH1043]) signifies testing from a posture of honest doubt with the intent to encourage and approve faith in God. The divine invitation to "test God" offers the restoration community an opportunity to "prove" the faithfulness of Yahweh as it relates to his covenant promises with Israel.

COMMENTARY

Malachi's fifth oracle is a disputation (concerning the tithe, 3:8-10) embedded within another disputation (the need for repentance, 3:6-7). Analyzed as a series of "speech acts," this penultimate disputation consists of three elements: a divine assertion ("I do not change," 3:6), intended to assure the audience of God's constancy; a divine summons to repentance ("return to me," 3:7), meant to persuade the audience to shift their loyalty back to Yahweh; and a divine challenge ("put me to the test," 3:10), aimed at convincing the audience of Yahweh's commitment to restore his people (cf. Watts 1987:376-377).

Adapting Achtemeier's (1986:172) approach to Malachi as a courtroom drama, the fourth disputation constitutes the formal indictment (2:17-3:5), the fifth disputation represents the judge's verdict (3:6-12), and the final disputation is the sentencing of the defendant (3:13-4:3). The apparent non-effect of the summons to repentance in the fifth disputation is all the more remarkable, in that the prophet's call to renew loyalty to Yahweh is sandwiched between two disputations emphasizing themes of judgment and purification!

Yahweh's declaration, "I am the Lord, and I do not change" (3:6), was a reminder to postexilic Judah of the constancy of his divine character that continually manifests itself in unimpeachable faithfulness to this covenant word. It seems likely that Malachi has in mind the prophecy of Balaam to Balak: "God is not a man, so he does not lie. He is not human, so he does not change his mind. Has he ever spoken and failed to act? Has he ever promised and not carried it through?" (Num 23:19).

Israel had failed to recognize that her destiny and God's affirmation of constancy were entwined. Yahweh's ancient covenant with Israel's ancestors was still valid due to the unchanging nature of his character and his unswerving loyalty to his promissory oath (Ps 111:5). The very fact that repentance and restoration remained a possibility for Israel was testimony to God's enduring love for his people (cf. 1:2, "I have always loved you").

Thankfully, the Christian may have equal confidence in God's new covenant because "God has given both his promise and his oath. These two things are unchangeable because it is impossible for God to lie" (Heb 6:18a). This means we "can have great confidence as we hold to the hope that lies before us" because "Jesus Christ is the same yesterday, today, and forever" (Heb 6:18b; 13:8).

The word "return" (3:7) is the Hebrew term for repentance and signifies an "about-face" or a complete turnabout on the part of the person repenting. The expression connotes a change or shift in loyalty away from sin and self toward God, a reorientation to Yahweh and his covenant demands. The imperative form of the verb conveys a sense of urgency and places a demand for immediate and specific action on the part of those so addressed. The liturgical formula in the prophetic summons to repentance ("return to me and I will return to you") may be rooted in the penitential prayers of the Psalms (e.g., Pss 80:3, 7, 14, 19; 85:4-8).

The prophet Jeremiah offers us a theology of repentance that calls the wayward child Judah "home," almost in anticipation of the story of the "prodigal son" told by Jesus (Jer 3:12; cf. Luke 15:11ff). First, Jeremiah called the faithless people of Judah to recognize that God alone is the source of mercy as the Lord of Israel (Jer 3:12). Next, he urged the people to acknowledge their guilt before God (Jer 3:13a) and admit the specific nature of their wrongdoing (Jer 3:13b, 23). Then the penitents were encouraged to take responsibility for their shame and formally offer confession to God (Jer 3:25). Finally, those who had wandered away from God were healed and restored after they declared their intentions to obey God's word and behave accordingly (Jer 4:1-2; cf. Jer 3:22).

The prophet Malachi accused his audience of "cheating" or even "robbing" God (3:8-9). The real issue was not reinstitution of the legalistic giving of the tithe to fulfill the formal obligations of the Mosaic law. Nor was the point of the message the abundant agricultural blessing promised as the outcome of testing God's faithfulness (3:10-11). Malachi recognized that the "robbery" of God in the failure to pay the tithe and the tithe-tax was merely a symptom of a more serious cancer. The stinginess of postexilic Judah was rooted in unbelief. Only by returning to a posture of faith and reverence could the people experience the wisdom of the sage: "Give freely and become more wealthy; be stingy and lose everything" (Prov 11:24). Malachi understood that turning to God in spiritual renewal must begin somewhere, and God himself decreed the practical act of obedience to the Mosaic laws regulating the tithe as an important first step in reasserting the community's fidelity in covenant relationship with Yahweh. As Baldwin (1972:247) points out, "good harvests alone . . . would not make a country *a land of delight* . . . there were spiritual counterparts to the fruits of the soil."

Malachi's invitation to postexilic Jerusalem to "put God to the test" (3:10) should not be viewed as a contradiction with the Mosaic prohibition against "testing" God (Deut 6:16). The Old Testament teaches that God may "try" (*nasah* [TH5254, ZH5814]) and "test" (*bakhan* [TH974, ZH1043]) human beings, but in turn human beings may not *nasah* ("test") God. Malachi, however, called the restoration community of Judah to *bakhan* ("test") God for the purpose of proving his faithfulness in keeping his covenant promises (3:10).

Frequently, the Old Testament speaks of the Israelites' testing God as *nasah* (assuming a posture of rebellion and unbelief on Israel's part—e.g., Exod 17:2, 7; Ps 78:18, 41). By contrast, divine testing for the purpose of corrective judgment, purification, and character formation is usually described as *bakhan* (e.g., Jer 6:27; 9:7). The Septuagint consistently renders *nasah* with a form of the Greek word *peirazō* [TG3985, ZG4279] (tempt, test, try), while *bakhan* is nearly always translated with some form of *dokimazō* [TG1381, ZG1507] (examine, prove, test). This would suggest that later Judaism discerned a subtle theological distinction between the two terms in studying the questions of God's testing of human beings.

The New Testament documents represent one completed stage of this developmental theology of divine testing (albeit an early Jewish Christian perspective). According to James, God does not "test" (*peirazō*) anyone (Jas 1:13); Paul says the faithful are not to put God to the "test" (*peirazō*, see 1 Cor 10:9). Elsewhere the New Testament suggests that human beings bring such trials or tests upon themselves by yielding to personal desires exploited by the Tempter (Matt 4:3; Jas 1:14-16). We do learn, however, that God does "test" or "examine" (*dokimazō*) the faith and deeds of the righteous for the purpose of approving and purifying the faithful (1 Cor 3:13). Beyond this, God is able to transform a given "trial" (*peirazō*) and its destructive potential for biblical faith into an experience that affirms biblical faith and builds godly character (*dokimos* [TG1384, ZG1511] and *dokimion* [TG1383, ZG1510], Jas 1:3, 12; cf. Heb 11:17). This New Testament distinction between the testing and provocation intended to ruin biblical faith (*peirazō*) and the testing designed to affirm and nurture biblical faith (*dokimazō*) preserves human freedom and personal responsibility while also confirming the goodness and sovereignty of God.

◆ VI. Sixth Disputation: The Coming Day of Judgment (3:13–4:3)

13"You have said terrible things about me," says the LORD.

"But you say, 'What do you mean? What have we said against you?'

14"You have said, 'What's the use of serving God? What have we gained by obeying his commands or by trying to show the LORD of Heaven's Armies that we are sorry for our sins? 15From now on we will call the arrogant blessed. For those who do evil get rich, and those who dare God to punish them suffer no harm.'"

16Then those who feared the LORD spoke with each other, and the LORD listened to what they said. In his presence, a scroll of remembrance was written to record the names of those who feared him and always thought about the honor of his name.

17"They will be my people," says the LORD of Heaven's Armies. "On the day when I act in judgment, they will be my own special treasure. I will spare them as a father spares an obedient child. ¹⁸Then you will again see the difference between the righteous and the wicked, between those who serve God and those who do not."

CHAPTER 4

¹*The LORD of Heaven's Armies says, "The day of judgment is coming, burning like a

furnace. On that day the arrogant and the wicked will be burned up like straw. They will be consumed—roots, branches, and all. ²"But for you who fear my name, the Sun of Righteousness will rise with healing in his wings.* And you will go free, leaping with joy like calves let out to pasture. ³On the day when I act, you will tread upon the wicked as if they were dust under your feet," says the LORD of Heaven's Armies.

4:1 Verses 4:1-6 are numbered 3:19-24 in Hebrew text.   4:2 Or *the sun of righteousness will rise with healing in its wings.*

NOTES

3:14 *what have we gained?* Lit., "what profit?" (*betsa'* [TH1215, ZH1299]). The word is a technical term associated with the carpet-making industry and means "to cut off" (a completed piece of woven material), hence "take one's cut" or "gain profit." The word has neutral connotations in this context, as the issue is not illegal gain but the assumption that acts or righteousness should result in material blessing according to the blessings-and-curses theology of the Mosaic legal tradition (Deut 28).

sorry for our sins. The idea of the idiom here (*halak* [TH1980, ZH2143] + *qedorannith* [TH6941, ZH7726]) is to "parade mournfully" or "walk in funeral garb" as a demonstration of penitence.

3:16 *listened.* The word is a verb of hearing (*qashab* [TH7181, ZH7992]) and means to "listen carefully" or "take note." The expression emphasizes the high level of Yahweh's interest in his people.

scroll of remembrance. This type of document, following Persian tradition, was both a catalog of names and a record of events associated with those individuals. The "scroll of remembrance" (*seper zikkaron* [TH5612/2146, ZH6219/2355]) has a parallel in the "historical records" mentioned in Esth 6:1 (*seper hazzikeronoth*).

feared him. The word "fear" (*yare'* [TH3373, ZH3710]) especially connotes loyalty to Yahweh as the covenant-making God. The term assumes the volitional response of obedience to God's commands, the moral response of proper conduct, and the ritual response of right worship.

3:17 *special treasure.* The expression (*segullah* [TH5459, ZH6035]) is a covenant term that describes the privileged status of Israel as the people of God—his "private property," so to speak.

4:1 [3:19] *furnace.* The imagery of a burning furnace (*ba'ar* [TH1197, ZH1277] + *tannur* [TH8574, ZH9486]) used as an incinerator for destroying wicked people in the day of Yahweh's judgment is both graphic and frightening (cf. Ps 21:9).

4:2 [3:20] *Sun of Righteousness.* Typically the phrase is understood as a solar epithet for Yahweh or as a Christological title. The phrase may simply be a figurative description of the eschatological day, the dawning of a new era of righteousness in which God will overturn the curse of sin. The source for this title may have been the winged sun disk that is ubiquitous in ancient Near Eastern iconography.

COMMENTARY

Watts (1987:376-377) has identified Malachi's final disputation as a blend of several types of speech acts, including an assertive speech of accusation designed to persuade the audience that there is value in obeying God (3:13-15), a report intended to elicit a response of reverence for Yahweh (3:16), an assertive speech declaring that Yahweh is righteous (3:17-18), and a warning speech about the coming day of God's judgment (4:1-3). The prophet's final sermon distills the teaching of the previous disputations, especially the contrast between the faithful and the faithless and the call for community-wide repentance. More specifically, Malachi has addressed (in reverse order) the hypothetical questions raised by his audience in disputations four and five: The first question, "Where is the God of justice?" (2:17), is answered directly in the bold statements about the judgment accompanying the Day of the Lord (4:1-3); and the second question, "Who will be able to stand and face him when he appears?" (3:2), is dealt with in the affirmation that those who "fear" and "love" Yahweh will be spared in the day of God's visitation (3:17-18). Like the previous oracle, this message is addressed to the postexilic community at large, leaders, priests, and people (both the righteous and the wicked).

Klein (1986:150) has identified the primary audience of Malachi's fifth and sixth disputations as "latter-day Jobs" whose fate does not befit their faith. Like Job, these "Yahweh-fearers" assumed their righteousness held some claim on God for divine blessing. Yet God does not tolerate human beings' discrediting his justice for the sake of proving themselves correct (Job 40:8). Sadly, the prophet's constituency experienced the blurring of theological truths and moral values. This incapacity to discern "good" from "evil" and "right" from "wrong" was not peculiar to postexilic Israel, since preexilic prophets like Isaiah (Isa 5:20) and Micah (Mic 3:2) encountered a similar transposition of values. And as Craigie (1984:246) has observed, "a society may decide to abandon the distinction between good and evil, but God never abandons it." One illustration of this crisis of biblical values among Malachi's audience was the degeneration of personal spirituality into a commercial venture ("What have we gained by obeying his commands?" 3:14). The prophet's "flock" apparently could recognize the work of God only in the "doing of good" for them—and sooner not later!

Thankfully, Malachi's message could not be more relevant to contemporary Christians. There are still "latter-day Jobs" among us, as Jesus himself indicated: "Here on earth you will have many trials and sorrows" (John 16:33). Spirituality is at times still reduced to a commercial venture in the Christian church, as the ceaseless publishing blitz of books "guaranteeing" God's blessing and the glitzy marketing of religious paraphernalia attest. But fortunately something else has not changed: The "secret" of healthy biblical spirituality remains absolutely rooted in God and his Word. Whether for Malachi or John the Apostle, the litmus test for spiritual vitality is the fear of the Lord (3:16; cf. Rev 14:7). Malachi connected this reverence for God that prompts true worship with always thinking about the honor of God's name (3:16)—an idea similar to the first great commandment: "You must love the Lord your God with all your heart, all your soul, and all your mind" (Matt 22:37).

Malachi essentially understood the Day of the Lord as one of justice and judgment: justice in the form of the vindication and restoration of the righteous and judgment in the form of the punishment and destruction of the wicked (4:1-3). In that sense, much like other Old Testament prophets, Malachi's eschatology was based on the retribution principle—ultimately, God will bless the righteous and curse the wicked. This two-pronged response of the prophet to postexilic Judah served as an answer to the question posed earlier, "What's the use of serving God?" (3:14), and in another way, it conveyed the substance of his reply to the initial question raised in the opening disputation ("How have you loved us?" [1:2]). First, it is not futile to serve God because the God-fearers will survive the day of Yahweh's judgment as his special possession (3:18; 4:2). Second, Yahweh's love for Israel is demonstrated in this deliverance and the reversal of fortunes for the righteous (4:3). Like Malachi's audience, we must learn that part of the answer to the question of theodicy lies in the truth of the prophet's indictment of the entire Hebrew community: The righteous are among the guilty as well. Crucial then, as it is now, is the fact that the emblems of God's presence and God's judgment are not mutually exclusive (cf. Achtemeier 1986:187).

The more important element of Malachi's message about the Day of the Lord is that God will act (3:17). The New Testament guarantees this in the declaration that Jesus Christ "will return" (Acts 1:11) but also notes that "the Lord's patience gives people time to be saved" (2 Pet 3:15). The assurance of this coming day of the Lord's visitation for justice and judgment is rooted in salvation-history as revealed in the Bible. For example, God has already acted in the Genesis flood (cf. 2 Pet 3:6), God has already given the Hebrews an Exodus from Egypt (Exod 12-13), God has already acted in the contest against Baal on Mount Carmel (1 Kgs 18), and God has already acted at the cross of Jesus Christ (1 Cor 15:1-4). The righteous have every reason to be confident that God will act again on their behalf. This brings us to the real purposes of biblical eschatology, purposes that include engendering hope within the Christian church (2 Cor 5:19), affording the righteous an opportunity for mutual comfort and encouragement (1 Thess 4:18), prompting expectant and godly living among the people of God (2 Pet 3:11-12), fostering a spirit of willing service in the name of Christ (Gal 5:13), and exhorting the persecuted Christian church to patient endurance (Rev 1:9).

The prophet Malachi promised a day when God would act to distinguish between the righteous and the wicked (3:17). The Christian church awaits that day when Jesus Christ will return to "repay all people according to their deeds" (Rev 22:12). The Spirit and the bride say, "Come . . . Amen! Come, Lord Jesus!" (Rev 22:17, 20).

◆ VII. Appendix: Appeals to Ideal Old Testament Figures (4:4-6)

4"Remember to obey the Law of Moses, my servant—all the decrees and regulations that I gave him on Mount Sinai* for all Israel.

5"Look, I am sending you the prophet Elijah before the great and dreadful day of the LORD arrives. 6His preaching will turn the hearts of fathers to their children, and the hearts of children to their fathers. Otherwise I will come and strike the land with a curse."

4:4 Hebrew Horeb, another name for Sinai.

NOTES

4:4 [3:22] *remember.* This imperative verb (*zakar* [TH2142, ZH2349]) denotes more than the intellectual activity of recalling Yahweh's deeds in history. Rather, it is an exhortation to act upon that knowledge by harnessing one's will in obedience to God's commandments.

4:6 [3:24] *His preaching.* The phrase is interpretive for the literal "he will turn" (see the discussion of *shub* [TH7725, ZH8740] in the note on 3:7).

COMMENTARY

The appendixes to Malachi are an editorial conclusion containing two postscripts. The first postscript references the ideal figure of Moses (4:4) and the second the ideal figure of Elijah (4:5-6). This epilogue serves double duty, concluding both the Book of the Twelve Prophets and the collection of Latter Prophets in the Hebrew Bible. The purpose of the epilogue appears to be that of uniting the Book of the Twelve Prophets with the Latter Prophets (Isaiah, Jeremiah, Ezekiel) and the Primary History (Torah and Former Prophets) by means of the two ideal figures representing these literary collections in the Hebrew Bible. Thus, the association of the ideal figure of Elijah with the ideal of Moses works to invest the Latter Prophets with the same divine authority accorded the Primary History.

The first postscript calls the people of God to "remember to obey the Law of Moses" (4:4). The verb "remember" (see note on 4:4) "serves primarily to express an intellectual activity that is relational and personal" (TDOT 4.65). It is this "intellectual activity" that both informs and enables the human will to submit to the truth of God's law. But remembering in the biblical world is more than mere cognition—it involves action. The posture of obedience to the word of God is the expected human response to divine revelation, whether as in the first Testament (1 Sam 15:22, "obedience is better than sacrifice") or the second Testament (1 John 2:5, "those who obey God's word truly show how completely they love him"). The vitality of the spiritual life of the community of faith depends, in part, on the ability to "re-identify" with the past (cf. Isbell 1980:77). That is, faith in God in the present tense and hope for divine restoration in the future tense is conditioned by the ability to remember the words and deeds of Yahweh in the past tense.

Ancient Israel's identity was rooted in the Exodus event (Exod 12-14), and her existence was inseparably joined to the law of Moses (Deut 30:15). For this reason, the Hebrews were commanded: "This is a day to remember . . . [i.e., Passover] for all time" (Exod 12:14). The same is no less true for the Christian church. Her identity is inextricably tied to the cross of Christ (1 Cor 5:7, "Christ, our Passover Lamb, has been sacrificed for us"). Likewise, her reason for being is defined by the two great commandments: "You must love the Lord your God with all your heart . . ." and "Love your neighbor as yourself" (Matt 22:37). For this reason, the church gathers regularly at the Lord's Table to partake of bread and wine "in remembrance" of the new covenant sealed by the death of Jesus Christ (1 Cor 11:23-26).

The second postscript highlights two key themes prominent in Malachi and the entire Old Testament prophetic corpus: the "turning" of hearts and the ministry of reconciliation (4:6). The word "turn" is the Old Testament term for repentance and indicates a complete reversal in loyalties or an "about-face" in one's direction. Implicit in this act of repentance is turning toward God, as Malachi exhorted his audience (3:7). The practical outcome of this repentance is the "turning" of children to parents and parents to children—or inter-generational reconciliation (4:6). The postscript refers not so much to "family discord" as it does to covenant renewal with Yahweh—the "resolution of opposites" in the sense of faithful ancestors versus faithless descendants or vice versa (cf. Petersen 1995:231).

The message of repentance is still applicable to the contemporary setting. As Scott (1953:218) so ably reminds us, "today as in every age the message of the evangelist must begin with a call to repentance." Although the reconciliation of family discord is not the focus of the postscript in context, that message is certainly relevant given the breakdown of the nuclear family unit in Western society. The dissolution of the family is manifest in the rampant dysfunction seen in parents and children alike in the form of abuse, addiction, and obsessive behavior patterns. What better word for a society disintegrating slowly due to its own self-absorption than "turn" to God and to each other?

The announcement of Elijah as a forerunner prior to the "day of the LORD" may help clarify the nature and the character of the ministry of Malachi's "messenger of the covenant" (3:1). Typologically, John the Baptist has been identified as the iconoclastic preacher of repentance fulfilling this prophecy (cf. Matt 11:14). The Gospel of Matthew hints that John was the Elijah figure in a limited way and that Elijah both "has come" and "is coming"—perhaps in the form of one of the witnesses prior to the end of the age (cf. Rev 11:3).

The epilogue of Malachi became a summons to the people of God for watchful waiting; it became a prelude to the coming of the Messiah as recorded in the New Testament. That clarion call to be alert for the intrusion of God into human history remains appropriate, as the Christian church awaits the second advent of Jesus Christ.

BIBLIOGRAPHY

Achtemeier, E.
1986 *Nahum—Malachi.* Interpretation. Atlanta: John Knox.

Andersen, F. I. and D. N. Freedman
1980 *Hosea.* Anchor Bible. New York: Doubleday.

Baldwin, J. G.
1972 *Haggai, Zechariah, Malachi.* Tyndale Old Testament Commentary. Downers Grove: InterVarsity.

Berquist, J. L.
1995 *Judaism in Persia's Shadow: A Social and Historical Approach.* Minneapolis: Fortress.

Brichto, F. C.
1963 *The Problem of Curse in the Hebrew Bible.* Journal of Biblical Literature Monograph Series 13.
    Philadelphia: Society of Biblical Literature.

Calvin, John
1979 *Commentaries on the Twelve Minor Prophets.* Translator, J. Owen. Reprint (1848). Grand Rapids: Baker.

Chisolm, Robert
2002 *Handbook on the Prophets.* Grand Rapids: Baker.

Craigie, P. C.
1984 *The Twelve Prophets.* Philadelphia: Westminster.

Fishbane, Michael
1985 *Biblical Interpretation in Ancient Israel.* Oxford: Clarendon.

Fuller, Russell E.
1991 Text-Critical Problems in Malachi 2:10-16. *Journal of Biblical Literature* 110:47-57.

Garland, D. E.
1987 A Biblical View of Divorce. *Review and Expositor* 84:419-432.

Glazier-McDonald, B.
1987 *Malachi: The Divine Messenger.* Society of Biblical Literature Dissertation Series 98.
    Atlanta: Scholars Press.

Heschel, Abraham J.
1962 *The Prophets* (2 vols.). New York: Harper & Row.

Hill, A. E.
1998 *Malachi.* Anchor Bible. New York: Doubleday.

Hugenberger, Gordon P.
1998 *Marriage As a Covenant.* Grand Rapids: Baker.

Isbell, C. D.
1980 *Malachi.* Grand Rapids: Zondervan.

Jones, B. A.
1995 *The Formation of the Book of the Twelve: A Study in Text and Canon.* Society of Biblical
    Literature Dissertation Series 149. Atlanta: Scholars Press.

Kaiser, W. C.
1984 *Malachi: God's Unchanging Love.* Grand Rapids: Baker.

Klein, R. W.
1986 A Valentine for Those Who Fear Yahweh: The Book of Malachi. *Currents in Theology and Mission*
    13:143-152.

Kruse-Blinkenberg, L.
1967 The Book of Malachi according to Codex Syro-Hexaplaris Ambrosianus. *Studia Theologica* 21:62-82.

Mallone, G.
1981 *Furnace of Renewal.* Downers Grove: InterVarsity.

Mason, R.
1977 *The Books of Haggai, Zechariah, and Malachi.* Cambridge Bible Commentary. Cambridge: Cambridge
    University Press.

McKenzie, S. L. and H. W. Wallace
1983 Covenant Themes in Malachi. *Catholic Biblical Quarterly* 45:549-563.

Merrill, Eugene
1994 *An Exegetical Commentary: Haggai, Zechariah, Malachi.* Chicago: Moody.

O'Brien, Julia M.
2004 *Nahum, Habakkuk, Zephaniah, Haggai, Zechariah, Malachi.* Abingdon Old Testament Commentaries. Nashville: Abingdon.

Patterson, Richard D.
1993 Old Testament Prophecy. Pp. 296-309 in *A Complete Literary Guide to the Bible.* Editors, L. Ryken and T. Longman. Grand Rapids: Baker.

Petersen, D. L.
1995 *Zechariah 9-14 and Malachi.* Old Testament Library. Louisville: Westminster/John Knox.

Pierce, R. W.
1984a Literary Connectors and a Haggai-Zechariah-Malachi Corpus. *Journal of Evangelical Theological Society* 27:277-289.

1984b A Thematic Development of the Haggai-Zechariah-Malachi Corpus. *Journal of Evangelical Theological Society* 28:401-411.

Pilch, J.
1991 Core Cultural Values. *Introducing the Cultural Context of the Old Testament.* New York: Paulist.

Redditt, P. L.
1995 *Haggai, Zechariah, and Malachi.* New Century Bible Commentary. London: Marshall Pickering.

Schneider, D. A.
1979 *The Unity of the Book of the Twelve.* Ph.D. diss., Yale University.

Schuller, Eileen M.
1996 The Book of Malachi. Pp. 843-877 in *The New Interpreter's Bible,* vol. 12. Editor, L. E. Keck. Nashville: Abingdon.

Scott, R. B. Y.
1953 *The Relevance of the Prophets.* New York: Macmillan.

Smith, R. L.
1984 *Micah–Malachi.* Word Biblical Commentary. Waco: Word.

Taylor, Richard A. and E. Ray Clendenen
2004 *Haggai, Malachi.* New American Commentary 21A. Nashville: Broadman & Holman.

Tozer, A. W.
1992 *Worship: The Missing Jewel.* Reprint. Camp Hill, PA: Christian Publications.

VanGemeren, Willem A.
1990 *Interpreting the Prophetic Word.* Grand Rapids: Zondervan.

Verhoef, P. A.
1987 *The Books of Haggai and Malachi.* New International Commentary on the Old Testament. Grand Rapids: Eerdmans.

Waltke, B. and M. O'Connor
1990 *An Introduction to Biblical Hebrew Syntax.* Winona Lake: Eisenbrauns.

Watts, J. D. W.
1987 Introduction to the Book of Malachi. *Review and Expositor* 84:373-381.

Webber, Robert E.
1982 *Worship Old & New.* Grand Rapids: Zondervan.

Wells, C. R.
1987 The Subtle Crisis of Secularism: Preaching the Burden of Israel. *Criswell Theological Review* 1987:39-61.

Westermann, C.
1991 *Basic Forms of Prophetic Speech.* Translator, H. C. White. Reprint. Louisville: Westminster/John Knox.

Wolf, H. M.
1976 *Haggai and Malachi.* Everyman's Bible Commentary. Chicago: Moody.